Third Edition

PROGRAMMING LANGUAGES:

A GRAND TOUR

COMPUTER SOFTWARE ENGINEERING SERIES

ISSN 0888-2088

Wayne Amsbury
Structured BASIC and Beyond

Jean-Loup Baer
Computer Systems Architecture

Peter Calingaert
Assemblers, Compilers, and Program Translation

M. S. Carberry, H.M. Khalil, J. F. Leathrum, J. S. Levy
Foundations of Computer Science

Shimon Even
Graph Algorithms

W. Findlay and D. A. Watt
Pascal: An Introduction to Methodical Programming, Second Edition

Ellis Horowitz and Sartaj Sahni
Fundamentals of Computer Algorithms

Ellis Horowitz and Sartaj Sahni
Fundamentals of Data Structures

Ellis Horowitz and Sartaj Sahni
Fundamentals of Data Structures in Pascal

Ellis Horowitz
Fundamentals of Programming Languages, Second Edition

Ellis Horowitz, Editor
Programming Languages: A Grand Tour, Third Edition

Tom Logsdon
Computers and Social Controversy

Vern McDermott and Diana Fisher
Learning BASIC Step by Step

Vern McDermott, Andrew Young, and Diana Fisher
Learning Pascal Step by Step

Vern McDermott and Diana Fisher
Advanced BASIC Step by Step

Ronald Perrott
Pascal for FORTRAN Programmers

Ira Pohl and Alan Shaw
The Nature of Computation: An Introduction to Computer Science

Arto Salomaa
Jewels of Formal Language Theory

Donald D. Spencer
Computers in Number Theory

Jeffrey D. Ullman
Principles of Database Systems, Second Edition

Derick Wood
Paradigms and Programming with Pascal

Third Edition

PROGRAMMING LANGUAGES:

A GRAND TOUR

ELLIS HOROWITZ, Editor
University of Southern California

COMPUTER SCIENCE PRESS

Copyright © 1983 Computer Science Press, Inc. First Edition

Copyright © 1985 Computer Science Press, Inc. Second Edition

Copyright © 1987 Computer Science Press, Inc. Third Edition

Printed in the United States of America.

Computer Science Press, Inc.
1803 Research Blvd.
Rockville, MD 20850

1 2 3 4 5 6   92 91 90 89 88 87

Library of Congress Cataloging-in-Publication Data

Programming languages, a grand tour.

  Bibliography: p.
  Includes index.
  1. Programming languages (Electronic computers)
I. Horowitz, Ellis.
QA76.7.P78   1987   005.13'3   86-17136

FOREWORD

The arena of programming languages is a marvelously rich and diverse field. The objective of this work is to present an organized collection of readable articles for the student of programming languages. Several seminal articles in the programming languages field are also reproduced here. My original purpose in creating this book was to use it for a university course on comparative programming languages. Professional computer scientists will also find it useful. The book is divided into seven major sections. Each section has a theme that is supported by the articles found there.

The book begins with a section on the history of programming languages. But the articles do more than just chronicle the dates of appearance of each new language. They emphasize the difficulty of successful language design, cite specific contributions of different languages, and at the same time they throw darts at many existing languages. This sort of reading can be fun, especially when the articles are written by talented people such as Wirth, Hoare, and Wegner.

Section 2 is devoted to the ALGOL family of languages including ALGOL60, ALGOL68, Pascal, and MODULA-2. This group has had a major influence on the development of programming languages over the last twenty-five years and no student of computer science should miss reading these works.

Section 3 is an exposure to a very different world of computing. If we judge applicative languages by the number of people who write programs using them, then we would have to delete these articles entirely. But instead we must marvel at how these languages have survived and how they continue to please groups of people who make exceptionally strong demands on their computing languages. For any individual to be really knowledgeable in this field, he or she must have an understanding of the functional model of computation and languages based upon this model. The classic paper in this section is the one by John McCarthy in which he first introduced the notions of LISP. Second, I decided to reprint the first (and major) section of the LISP 1.5 manual, as it is rarely found in bookstores and yet it still represents the clearest and simplest introduction to the language. The articles by Falkoff-Iverson and Backus give a cogent presentation of APL and FP, two other relevant languages in this category.

Then in Section 4 we see a relatively new trend in programming languages, the abstract data type. The languages CLU, MODULA-2, and Ada were designed (in part) to incorporate this concept of good software design into a programming language. CLU was developed at MIT and has served as a model for language designers studying abstract data type facilities. MODULA-2 is Wirth's successor to Pascal. Its basic structuring unit is the *module*. The module plays the dual role of an abstract data type and a process. Ada is a language sponsored by the Department of Defense. It has a wealth of features including *packages* and *tasks* (modules and processes) which form its main program structuring units.

Another major trend in programming languages today is the notion of concurrent execution. This is the subject of Section 5. Advances in hardware have made the need to express concurrency a necessity. Now we are beginning to see how programming languages are adapting to this desire. Concurrent-Pascal is one such language which takes Pascal as its base and uses the monitor for process synchronization. MODULA-2 is another attempt to add concurrency to an imperative language, in this instance by extending the module's semantics so it can be used as a process. The article entitled "Communicating Sequential Processes" by C.A.R. Hoare represents an important intellectual step forward in the quest to find appropriate language primitives for concurrency. Hoare's CSP has stimulated a great deal of research on the subject of message passing as appropriate semantics for process synchronization. The last two articles are extremely valuable in that they survey the various mechanisms that have been proposed. They contain many good examples of concurrent execution from languages such as CSP, Ada, MODULA-2, and PL/1.

Section 6 is entitled *Old Languages with New Faces*. Many of us have grown up with BASIC, FORTRAN, or COBOL, and it may come as a surprise the extent to which they are often derided. But these languages continue to be entrenched in the programming community. Why? The articles in this section help to answer this question as they show the major directions these languages have taken in recent years. In the case of FORTRAN, there is an article on the current '77 standard. This standard inserted many new features into FORTRAN including a character string data type and several structured statements for control of execution. The standards committee meets every decade or so, and a new standard is expected near the end of the '80s. The next group of papers are on BASIC. With the phenomenal growth of microcomputers, BASIC has become the first language of instruction for many thousands of people. Moreover, the language has evolved in interesting ways as it has had to meet the user interface demands of microcomputer software developers. Features for manipulating graphics, color, and sound are just three such areas. The papers describe three species of BASIC: True BASIC, BetterBASIC, and Macintosh BASIC. The final paper in this section is on COBOL. Informal surveys continue to reaffirm the fact that more people program in COBOL than in any other single language. This article attempts to place the contributions of COBOL in perspective.

In the 1980s no anthology would be complete without some material on Ada. Ada is well represented here including an excellent survey paper by Barnes and articles in the sections on data abstraction and concurrency. The next article is a seminal one by the developers of the operating system called UNIX[1] and the language called C. The growing use of UNIX on 16- and 32-bit microprocessors has given a great impetus to the number of C programmers, making this article more important than ever. The final articles in this section are on Prolog and Logic Programming. The imperative model and the functional model were represented in earlier sections. The logic model attempts to place programming on a sound foundation of mathematical logic. The Japanese Fifth Generation computer project has chosen Prolog as its major development language. Thus I have included two papers on this subject. The first is an early paper by Kowalski where he presents the fundamental basis for Logic Programming. The second paper is a tutorial on the use of Prolog.

Even on "A Grand Tour" one cannot afford to visit all of the interesting places. So too with an anthology on programming languages, I could not afford to include all of the interesting articles. There are some seminal papers such as McCarthy's LISP article, Backus' FP paper, Ritchie et al. on C, Kowalski on Prolog. There are some important language reference manuals such as the ALGOL60 report, the FORTRAN77 report, and the LISP 1.5 manual. There are tutorials on Ada, MODULA-2, and Prolog. There are papers that deal in depth with abstract data types and concurrency. My hope is that I have provided a sufficiently broad spectrum of articles which are clearly focused on the topic of programming languages, so that this book is suitable both for a comparative programming languages course and as a reference work.

I would like to especially thank all of the authors and societies who have graciously permitted me to reprint their work. I had helpful discussions with Dean Jacobs, Jean Sammet, and Peter Wegner. Finally, thanks go to the University of Southern California for providing a stimulating environment.

Ellis Horowitz
Los Angeles, 1986

---

[1]UNIX is a trademark of AT&T.

ACKNOWLEDGMENTS

No anthology can be a success without the help and cooperation of many people and organizations. I would especially like to thank all of the authors, professional societies, and publishers who gave me permission to reprint these articles. The following list gives the full citation for all of the articles contained here plus an acknowledgment to the organization for allowing me to reproduce their copyrighted material.

1. **Programming Languages: History and Good Design**
   "Programming Languages—the First 25 Years" by P. Wegner, *IEEE Transactions on Computers*, Dec. 1976, 1207-1225, copyright 1976, reprinted by permission.
   "On the Design of Programming Languages" by N. Wirth, *Proc. IFIP Congress 74*, 386-393, North-Holland, Amsterdam, copyright 1974, North-Holland Publishing Company, reprinted by permission.
   "Hints on Programming Language Design" by C. A. R. Hoare, *Sigact/Sigplan Symposium on Principles of Programming Languages*, October 1973, no copyright.

2. **The ALGOL Family**
   "Revised Report on the Algorithmic Language ALGOL60" by P. Naur et al., *Comm ACM*, 6, 1, 1963, 1-17, copyright 1963, Association for Computing Machinery Inc., reprinted by permission.
   "The Remaining Troublespots in ALGOL60" by D. E. Knuth, *Comm ACM* 10, 10, 1967, 611-617, copyright 1967, Association for Computing Machinery Inc., reprinted by permission.
   "A Tutorial on ALGOL68, by A. S. Tanenbaum, *Computing Surveys*, 8, 2, June 1976, copyright 1976. Association for Computing Machinery Inc., reprinted by permission.
   "Ambiguities and Insecurities in Pascal" by J. Welsh, W. J. Sneeringer, and C. A. R. Hoare, *Software Practice and Experience*, 7, 1977, 685-696, copyright 1977, reprinted by permission.
   "An Assessment of the Programming Language Pascal" by N. Wirth, *IEEE Transactions on Software Engineering*, June 1975, 192-198, copyright 1975, reprinted by permission.
   "Some Improvements of ISO-Pascal" by J. F. H. Winkler, *ACM Sigplan Notices*, vol. 19, no. 9, September 1984, 49-62, reprinted by permission.

"An Introduction to MODULA-2" by R. J. Paul, *Byte*, August 1984, 195-210, reprinted by permission.
"Ambiguities and Insecurities in MODULA-2" by D. Spector, *ACM Sigplan Notices*, 43-51, reprinted by permission.

3. **Applicative Languages**
   "Can Programming Be Liberated from the von Neumann Style? A Functional Style and its Algebra of Programs" by J. Backus, *Comm ACM* 21, 8, August 1978, 613-641, copyright 1978, Association for Computing Machinery Inc., reprinted by permission.
   "Recursive Functions of Symbolic Expressions" by J. McCarthy, *Comm ACM*, 3, 4, April 1960, 184-195, copyright 1960, Association for Computing Machinery Inc., reprinted by permission.
   "LISP 1.5 Programmers Manual" by J. McCarthy and M. Levin, MIT Press, Cambridge, Mass. 1965, reprinted by permission of the MIT Press and John McCarthy.
   "The Design of APL" by A. D. Falkoff and K. E. Iverson, *IBM Journal of Research and Development*, July 1973, 324-334, copyright 1973, IBM Corp., reprinted by permission.

4. **Programming Languages and Data Abstraction**
   "Abstraction Mechanisms in CLU" by B. Liskov, A. Snyder, R. Atkinson, and C. Schaffert, *Comm ACM*, 20, 8, August 1977, 564-576, copyright 1977, Association for Computing Machinery Inc., reprinted by permission.
   "Exception Handling in CLU" by B. Liskov and A. Snyder, *IEEE Transactions on Software Engineering*, Nov. 1979, 546-558, reprinted by permission.
   "Tutorial on MODULA-2" by J. Gutknecht, *Byte*, August 1984, 157-176, reprinted by permission.
   "Pascal, Ada, and MODULA-2" by D. Coar, *Byte*, August 1984, 215-232, reprinted by permission.

5. **Programming Languages and Concurrency**
   "The Programming Lanaguage Concurrent-Pascal" by P. Brinch-Hansen, *IEEE Transactions on Software Engineering*, June 1975, 199-207 reprinted by permission.
   "Communicating Sequential Processes" by C. A. R.

Hoare, *Comm ACM*, 21, 8, August 1978, 666-677, copyright 1978, Association for Computing Machinery Inc., reprinted by permission.

"Concepts and Notations for Concurrent Programming" by G. R. Andrews and F. B. Schneider, *Computing Surveys*, vol. 15, no. 1, March 1983, 3–43, Copyright 1983, Association for Computing Machinery, Inc., reprinted by permission.

"Processes, Tasks and Monitors: A Comparative Study of Concurrent Programming Primitives" by P. Wegner and S. A. Smolka, *IEEE Trans. on Software Engineering*, vol. SE-9, no. 4, July 1983, 446-462, reprinted by permission.

6. Old Languages With New Faces

"FORTRAN77" by W. Brainerd, *C. ACM*, vol. 21, no. 10, October 1978, 806-820, copyright 1978, Association for Computing Machinery, Inc., reprinted by permission.

"True BASIC" by G. Stewart, *Popular Computing*, November 1984, 95-107, reprinted by permission.

"BetterBASIC" by G. M. Vose, *Byte*, April 1984, 302-314, reprinted by permission.

"Macintosh BASIC" by S. Kamins, *Byte*, April 1984, 318-330, reprinted by permission.

"The Relationship Between COBOL and Computer Science" by B. Shneiderman, *Annals of the History of Computing*, vol. 7, no. 4, October 1985, reprinted by permission.

7. More Languages for the 1980s

"An Overview of Ada" by J. G. P. Barnes, *Software Practice and Experience*, vol. 10, 851-887, 1980, copyright 1980, reprinted by permission.

"The C Programming Language" by D. M. Ritchie, S. C. Johnson, M. E. Lesk, B. W. Kernighan, *Bell System Technical Journal*, July-August 1978, 179-219, copyright 1978, American Telephone and Telegraph Company, reprinted by permission.

"Algorithm = Logic + Control" by R. Kowalski *Comm. ACM*, vol. 22, no. 7, July 1979, 424-436, copyright 1979, Association for Computing Machinery, Inc., reprinted by permission.

"Logic Programming and Prolog: A Tutorial" by R. E. Davis, *IEEE Software*, September 1985, 53-62, reprinted by permission.

TABLE OF CONTENTS

SECTION 1

PROGRAMMING LANGUAGES:
HISTORY AND GOOD DESIGN

PROGRAMMING LANGUAGES—THE FIRST
25 YEARS BY P. WEGNER

ON THE DESIGN OF PROGRAMMING
LANGUAGES BY N. WIRTH

HINTS ON PROGRAMMING LANGUAGE
DESIGN BY C. A. R. HOARE

INTRODUCTION

PROGRAMMING LANGUAGES: HISTORY AND GOOD DESIGN

The first paper, which is by P. Wegner, is a retrospection on computer languages which surveys the developments which have been made over the past three decades. It presents and evaluates the major trends both in programming language features and in programming language theory. For those people who are new to computer science this article is an excellent starting place.

One of the nice aspects of Wegner's paper is that he divides the past into thirty milestones. Each milestone represents a significant contribution to the field of programming languages. To help the reader see his organization, the milestones are listed here.

M1: EDVAC Report

M2: Book by Wilkes, Wheeler, Gill

M3: Development of assemblers

M4: Macro Assemblers '55-'65

M5: FORTRAN '54-'58

M6: ALGOL60 '57-'60

M7: COBOL61 '59-'61

M8: PL/1 '64-'69

M9: ALGOL68 '63-'69

M10: SIMULA 67

M11: IPL-V '54-'58

M12: LISP '59-'60

M13: SNOBOL '62-'67

M14: Language Theory

M15: Compiler Technology

M16: Compiler-Compilers

M17: Models of Implementation

M18: Language Definition

M19: Program Correctness

M20: Verification and Testing

M21: Verification and Synthesis

M22: Semantic Models

M23: Abstraction

M24: Pascal

M25: APL

M26: Structured Programming

M27: Structured Model Building

M28: Life-Cycle Concepts

M29: Modularity

M30: Data-Oriented Languages

From this list one observes that 11 programming languages are listed as milestones: FORTRAN, ALGOL60, COBOL, LISP, SNOBOL, APL, PL/1, ALGOL68, Pascal, SIMULA, and IPL-V. All of these languages are around today except IPL-V. FORTRAN and COBOL remain as two of the most widely used languages. Thus we see again the inability of the programming community to get rid of outmoded tools and replace them by better ones. As you read this paper, take note of why Wegner feels that these events were milestones.

The next two papers in this section all have at least one thing in common, the word *design* in their title. The subject of these papers is the design of programming languages, a difficult and challenging task for which only very few have been successful. The first author, Niklaus

Wirth is best known as the designer of the popular language Pascal. However, he is also the designer of several other languages including Euler, ALGOL-W, PL/360, and more recently MODULA. The author of the third paper, C.A.R. Hoare, is also a programming language designer, but is probably better known for his contribution to programming language theory (Hoare axiomatics), or for his sorting algorithm called QUICKSORT.

The third paper in this section is fascinating as it gives us a glimpse into the intellectual development of Niklaus Wirth as a programming language designer. We also see why simplicity has become a major design goal for him and for others. In his case it was the desire to see the programming language used as a tool to tame the baroque and complex technology that he encountered as a student. I observe in passing that not all programming language designers have pursued simplicity as a major goal, and the Ada programming language in Section 7 attests to this.

Many of the issues that Wirth discusses in his paper have been reconciled in Pascal. It will be useful to keep Pascal in mind as you read his discussion of simplicity versus generality, or the use of abstraction. His criticism of the pointer data type will be echoed in several papers in this anthology, but the concept is too important to eliminate it entirely. It must be tamed. The issue of aliasing is considered harmful by Wirth, but Pascal allows it. Many

of the issues concerning how to provide for the extension of data types are no longer considered issues at all. The solutions offered by Wirth are now normally included in new language designs. I am thinking in particular of enumerated data types, records, and sets.

The third paper in this section, by C.A.R. Hoare is primarily a lambasting of many of our existing languages. Every anthology on programming languages should have at least one such article. But in reading this paper you should not overlook the main outline that the author has used to guide his criticism. Topics such as program design, program debugging, simplicity, readability, fast translation, efficient object code, comment convention, syntax, arithmetic expressions, program structures, variables, block structure, types, procedures and parameters are the overall criteria under which his discussion is guided.

After you have read all of these papers you may wish to go back over them and list all the *advice to language designers* that they have offered. As Wirth has pointed out, many of these criteria will be contradictory. The challenge of the language designer is to concentrate on a few of these goals and use them to create a robust language. Though most of us will never design our own language, it is very helpful to know and understand the criteria by which a language is judged.

PROGRAMMING LANGUAGES—THE FIRST 25 YEARS*

P. WEGNER

Abstract—The programming language field is certainly one of the most important subfields of computer science. It is rich in concepts, theories, and practical developments. The present paper attempts to trace the 25 year development of programming languages by means of a sequence of 30 milestones (languages and concepts) listed in more or less historical order. The first 13 milestones (M1–M13) are largely concerned with specific programming languages of the 1950's and 1960's such as Fortran, Algol 60, Cobol, Lisp, and Snobol 4. The next ten milestones (M14–M23) relate to concepts and theories in the programming language field such as formal language theory, language definition, program verification, semantics and abstraction. The remaining milestones (M24–M30) relate to the software engineering methodology of the 1970's and include a discussion of structured programming and the life cycle concept. This discussion of programming language development is far from complete and there are both practical developments such as special purpose languages and theoretical topics such as the lambda calculus which are not adequately covered. However, it is hoped that the discussion covers the principal concepts and languages in a reasonably nontrivial way and that it captures the sense of excitement and the enormous variety of activity that was characteristic of the programming language field during its first 25 years.

Index Terms—Abstraction, assemblers, Algol, axioms, Cobol, compilers, Fortran, Lisp, modularity, programming languages, semantics, structures programming, syntax, verification.

I. THREE PHASES OF PROGRAMMING LANGUAGE DEVELOPMENT

THE 25 year development of programming languages may be characterized by three phases corresponding roughly to the 1950's, 1960's, and 1970's. The 1950's were concerned primarily with the *discovery* and *description* of programming language concepts. The 1960's were concerned primarily with the *elaboration* and *analysis* of concepts developed in the 1950's. The 1970's were concerned with the development of an effective software *technology*. As pointed out in [96], the 1950's emphasized the *empirical* approach to the study of programming language concepts, the 1960's emphasized a *mathematical* approach in its attempts to develop theories and generalizations of concepts developed in the 1950's, and the 1970's emphasized an *engineering* approach in its attempt to harness concepts and theories for the development of software technology.

Reprinted from IEEE Transactions on Computers, Dec. 1976, 1207–1225.

The author is with the Division of Applied Mathematics, Brown University, Providence, RI 02912.

Manuscript received September 3, 1976; revised August 23, 1976. This work was supported in part by the AFOST, the ARO, and the ONR under Contract N00014-76-C-0160.

1950–1960 Discovery and Description

A remarkably large number of the basic concepts of programming languages had been discovered and implemented by 1960. This period includes the development of symbolic assembly languages, macro-assembly languages, Fortran, Algol 60, Cobol, IPL V, Lisp, and Comit [72]. It includes the discovery of many of the basic implementation techniques such as symbol table construction and look-up techniques for assemblers and macro-assemblers, the stack algorithm for evaluating arithmetic expressions, the activation record stack with display technique for keeping track of accessible identifiers during execution of block structure languages, and marking algorithms for garbage collection in languages such as IPL V and Lisp.

This period was one of discovery and description of programming languages and implementation techniques. Programming languages were regarded solely as tools for facilitating the specification of programs rather than as interesting objects of study in their own right. The development of models, abstractions, and theories concerning programming languages was largely a phenomenon of the 1960's.

1961–1969 Elaboration and Analysis

The 1960's were a period of elaboration of programming languages developed in the 1950's and of analysis for the purpose of constructing models and theories of programming languages.

The languages developed in the 1960's include Jovial, PL/I, Simula 67, Algol 68, and Snobol 4. These languages are, each in a different way, elaborations of languages developed in the 1950's. For example, PL/I is an attempt to combine the "good" features of Fortran, Algol, Cobol, and Lisp into a single language. Algol 68 is an attempt to generalize, as systematically and clearly as possible, the language features of Algol 60. Both the attempt to achieve greater richness by synthesis of existing features and the attempt to achieve greater richness by generalization have led to excessively elaborate languages. We have learned that in order to achieve flexibility and power of expression in programming languages we must pay the price of greater complexity. In the 1970's there is a tendency to retrench towards simpler languages like Pascal, even at the price of restricting flexibility and power of expression.

Theoretical work in the 1960's includes many of the basic results of formal languages and automata theory with applications to parsing and compiling [1]. It includes the development of theories of operational and mathematical semantics, of language definition techniques, and of several frameworks for modeling the compilation and execution process [26]. It includes the development of the basic ideas of program correctness and program verification [54].

Although much of the theoretical work started in the 1960's continued into the 1970's, the emphasis on theoretical research as an end in itself is essentially a phenomenon of the 1960's. In the 1970's theoretical research in areas such as program verification is increasingly motivated by practical technological considerations rather than by the "pure research" objective of advancing our understanding independently of any practical payoff.

In the programming language field the pure research of the 1960's tended to emphasize the study of abstract structures such as the lambda calculus or complex structures such as Algol 68. In the 1970's this emphasis on abstraction and elaboration is gradually being replaced by an emphasis on methodologies aimed at improving the technology of programming.

1970–? Technology

During the 1970's emphasis shifted away from "pure research" towards practical management of the environment, not only in computer science but also in other scientific areas. Decreasing hardware costs and increasingly complex software projects created a "complexity barrier" in software development which caused the management of software-hardware complexity to become the primary practical problem in computer science. Research was directed away from the development of powerful new programming languages and general theories of programming language structure towards the development of tools and methodologies for controlling the complexity, cost, and reliability of large programs.

Research emphasized methodologies such as structured programming, module design and specification, and program verification [41]. Attempts to design verifiable languages which support structured programming and modularity are currently being made. Pascal, Clu, Alphard, Modula, and Euclid are examples of such "methodology-oriented languages."

The technological, methodology-oriented approach to language design results in a very different view of what is important in programming language research. Whereas work in the 1960's was aimed at increasing expressive power, work in the 1970's is aimed at constraining expressive power so as to allow better management of the process of constructing large programs from their components. It remains to be seen whether the management of software complexity can be substantially improved by imposing structure, modularity, and verifiability constraints on program construction.

II. Milestones, Languages, and Concepts

The body of this paper outlines in greater detail some of the principal milestones of programming language development. The milestones include the development of specific programming languages, and the development of implementation techniques, concepts and theories.

The four most important milestones are probably the following ones.

Fortran, which provided an existence proof for higher level languages, and is still one of the most widely used programming languages.

Algol 60, whose clean design and specification served as an inspiration for the development of a discipline of programming languages.

Cobol, which pioneered the development of data description facilities, was adopted as a required language on department of defense computers and has become the most widely used language of the 1970's.

Lisp, whose unique blend of simplicity and power have caused it to become both the most widely used language in artificial intelligence and the starting point for the development of a mathematical theory of computation.

We shall consider about 30 milestones, and use this section as a vehicle for presenting a brief history of the programming language field. The milestones can be split into three groups. Milestones M1–M13 are concerned largely with specific programming languages developed during the 1950's and 1960's. Milestones M14–M23 consider certain conceptual and theoretical programming language notions. Milestones M24–M30 are concerned with programming languages and methodology of the 1970's.

M1—The EDVAC report, 1944 [81]: This report, written by Von Neumann in September 1944, contains the first description of the stored program computers, subsequently called Von Neumann machines. It develops a (one address) machine language for such computers and some examples of programs in this machine language.

M2—Book by Wilkes, Wheeler, and Gill, 1951 [83]: This is the first book on both application software and system software. It discusses subroutines and subroutine linkage, and develops subroutines for a number of applications. It contains a set of "initial orders" which act like a sophisticated loader, performing decimal to binary conversion for operation codes and addresses, and having relative addressing facilities. Thus, the basic idea of using the computer to translate user specified instructions into a considerably different internal representation was already firmly established by 1951.

M3—The development of assemblers, 1950–1960: The term "assembler" was introduced by Wilkes, Wheeler, and Gill [83] to denote a program which assembles a master program with several subroutines into a single run-time program. The meaning of the term was subsequently narrowed to denote a program which translates from symbolic machine language (with symbolic instruction codes and addresses) into an internal machine representation. Early assemblers include Soap, developed for the IBM 650 in the mid 1950's and Sap developed for the IBM 704 in the late 1950's.

The principal phases of the assembly process are as follows:
1) scanning of input text;
2) construction of symbolic address symbol table;

3) transliteration of symbolic instruction and address codes;

4) code generation.

The first assemblers were among the most complex and ingeneous programs of their day. However, during the 1960's the writing of assemblers was transformed from an art into a science, so that an assembler may now be regarded as a "simple" program. The development of an implementation technology for assemblers was an essential prerequisite to the development of an implementation technology for compilers.

M4—Macro assemblers, 1955-1965: Macro-assemblers allow the user to define "macro-instructions" by means of macro-definitions and to call them by means of macro-calls. A macro-facility is effectively a language extension mechanism which allows the user to introduce new language forms (macro-calls) and to define the "meaning" of each new language form by a macro-definition.

A macro-assembler may be implemented by generalizing phases 2 and 3 of the previously discussed assembly process. Phase 2 is generalized by construction of an additional symbol table for macro-definitions. Phase 3 is generalized by requiring table look-up not only for symbolic instruction and address codes but also for macro-calls. The table look-up process for macro-calls is no longer simple transliteration, since the determination of a macro-value may involve parameter substitution and nested macro-calls. However, the implementation technology for macro-assemblers may be regarded as an extension and generalization of the implementation technology for assemblers. The seminal paper on macro-assemblers is the paper by McIlroy [54]. A discussion of implementation technology for macro-assemblers is given in [84].

Macro-systems may be generalized by relaxing restrictions on the form of the text generated as a result of a macro-call. Macro-systems which allow the "value" of a macro-call to be an arbitrary string (as opposed to a sequence of machine language instructions) are called macro-generators. Trac [55] is an interesting example of a macro-generator.

Macro-systems may be generalized even further by generalizing the permitted syntax of macro-calls. Waite's Limp system [85] and Leavenworth's syntax macros [52] are early examples of such generalized macro-systems. Macro-systems of this kind are useful for implementing language preprocessors which translate statement forms and abbreviations of an "extended language" into a "strict language" which generally has a smaller vocabulary but is more verbose.

Generalized macro-systems may be implemented by macro-definition tables which are constructed and used in precisely the same way as for macro-assemblers. Generalized macro "values" require more general macro-body specifications in the macro-definition table while more general syntax for macro-calls requires a more sophisticated scanner for recognizing macro-calls in the source language text.

Assembly and macro-languages have been discussed in some detail because they illustrate how a simple language idea (the idea of transliteration) backed up by a simple implementation mechanism (the symbol table) leads to a class of simple languages (symbolic assembly languages) and how progressive generalization of the language idea together with a corresponding generalization of the implementation technology leads to progressively more complex classes of languages. This example is useful also because it illustrates how the language and implementation mechanism for assemblers are related to the language and implementation mechanisms for compilers.

M5—Fortran, 1954-1958 [27]: Fortran is perhaps the single most important milestone in the development of programming languages. It was developed at a time of considerable scepticism concerning the compile-time and run-time efficiency of higher level languages, and its successful implementation provided an existence proof for both the feasibility and the viability of higher level languages. Important language concepts introduced by Fortran include:

variables, expressions and statements (arithmetic and Boolean);

arrays whose maximum size is known at compile-time;

iterative and conditional branching control structures;

independently compiled (nonrecursive) subroutines;

COMMON and EQUIVALENCE statements for data sharing;

FORMAT directed input-output.

Advances of implementation technology developed in connection with Fortran include the stack model of arithmetic expression evaluation.

Fortran was designed around a model of implementation in which run-time storage requirements for programs, data and working storage was known at compile-time so that relative addresses of entities in all subroutines and COMMON data blocks could be assigned at compile-time and converted to absolute addresses at load time.

This model of implementation required the exclusion from the language of arrays with dynamic bounds and recursive subroutines. Thus, Fortran illustrates the principle that the model of implementation in the mind of the language designers may strongly affect the design of the language. Although Fortran is machine independent in the sense that it is independent of the assembly level instruction set of a specific computer, it is machine dependent in the sense that its design is dependent on a virtual machine that constitutes the model of implementation in the mind of the programming language designer.

M6—Algol 60, 1957-1960: Whereas Fortran is the most important practical milestone in programming language development, Algol 60 is perhaps the most important conceptual milestone. Its defining document, known as the Algol report [62], presents a method of language definition which is an enormous advance over previous definition techniques and allows us for the first time to think of a language as an object of study rather than as a tool in problem solution. Language syntax is defined by a variant of the notation of context-free grammars known as Backus–Naur Form (BNF). The semantics of each syntactic language construct is characterized by an English language description of the execution time effect of the construct.

The Algol report generated a great deal of sometimes heated debate concerning obscurities, ambiguities and trouble spots in the language specification. The revised report [63] corrected many of the less controversial anomalies of the original report. Knuth's 1967 paper on "The remaining trouble spots of Algol 60" [44] illustrates the nature of this great programming language debate. The participants in the debate were at first called Algol lawyers and later called Algol theologians.

Important language constructs introduced by Algol 60 include:

block structure;

explicit type declaration for variables;

scope rules for local variables;

dynamic as opposed to static lifetimes for variables;

nested if-then-else expressions and statements;

call by value and call by name for procedure parameters;

recursive subroutines;

arrays with dynamic bounds.

Algol 60 is carefully designed around a model of implementation in which storage allocation for expression evaluation, block entry and exit and procedure entry and exit can be performed in a single run-time stack. Dijkstra developed an implementation of Algol 60 as early as the fall of 1960 based on this simple model of implementation [23]. However, this semantic model of implementation was implicit rather than explicit in the Algol report. Failure to understand the model led to a widespread view that Algol 60 required a high price in run-time overhead, and to an exaggerated view of the difficulty of implementing Algol 60. An explicit account of the model of implementation is given in [69].

Algol 60 is a good example of a language which becomes semantically very simple if we have the right model of implementation but appears to be semantically complex if we have the wrong model of implementation. The model of implementation is more permissive than Fortran with regard to run-time storage allocation, and can handle arrays with dynamic bounds and recursive procedures. However, it cannot handle certain other language features such as assignment of pointers to pointer valued variables and procedures which return procedures as their result. These language features are accordingly excluded from Algol 60, illustrating again the influence of the model of implementation on the source language.

The Algol 60 notion of block structure quickly became the accepted canonical programming language design folklore and, in spite of its merits, excercised an inhibiting influence on programming language designers during the 1960's. Viewed from the vantage point of the 1970's it appears that nested scope rules for accessibility of identifiers and nested lifetime rules for existence of data structures may be too restrictive a basis for specifying modules and module interconnections in programming languages of the future. Alternatives to block structures are discussed in the sections on Simula 67, Snobol 4, and APL.

M7—Cobol 61, 1959–1961 [12]: Cobol represents the culmination and synthesis of several different projects for the development of business data processing languages, the first of which (flowmatic) was started in the early 1950's by Hopper. See [72] for an account of this development. Important language constructs introduced by Cobol include:

explicit distinction between identification division, environment division, data division, and procedure division;

natural language style of programming;

record data structures;

file description and manipulation facilities.

The two principal contributions of Cobol are its natural language programming style and its greater emphasis on data description. Natural language programming style makes programs more readable (by executives) but does not enhance writability or the ability to find errors. It constitutes a cosmetic change of syntax, sometimes referred to as "syntactic sugaring." It has not been widely adopted in subsequent programming languages but may possibly come into its own if and when the use of computers becomes commonplace in the home and in other nontechnical environments.

The contribution of Cobol to programming language development is probably greater in the area of data description than in the area of natural language programming. By introducing an explicit data division for data description to parallel a procedure division for procedure description Cobol factors out the data description problem as being of equal importance and visibility as the procedure description problem.

The significance of Cobol was greatly enhanced when it was chosen as a required language on DOD computers. Cobol was one of the earliest languages to be standardized, and has provided valuable experience (both positive and negative) concerning the creation and maintenance of programming language standards. It is currently used by more programmers than any other programming language.

Why is it that Cobol, in spite of certain defects in its procedure division, has become the most widely used language among commercial, industrial and government programmers? One reason is perhaps that standardization carries with it advantages that make the use of an imperfect standard more desirable than a more perfect but possibly more volatile alternative. Another perhaps more important reason may be that the advantages of Cobol's powerful facilities in its data division outweigh its imperfections in the procedure division, making it more suitable than languages like Fortran in the large number of medium and large scale data processing applications in business, industry and government. Cobol was behind the state of the art in its procedure division facilities but ahead of the state of the art in its data division facilities. The attractiveness of a language for data processing problems does not appear to depend as critically on its procedure description facilities as on its data description facilities.

M8—PL/I, 1964–1969 [67]: Fortran, Algol 60, and Cobol 61 may be regarded as the three principal first generation higher level languages, while PL/I and Algol 68 may be regarded as the two principal second generation higher level languages. PL/I was developed as a synthesis of Fortran, Algol 60, and Cobol, taking over its expression and statement syntax from Fortran, block structure and type declaration from Algol 60, and data description facilities from Cobol. Additional language features include the following:

programmer defined exception conditions (the ON statement);

based variables (pointers and list processing);

static, automatic and controlled storage;

external (independently compiled) procedures;

multitasking.

PL/I illustrates both the advantages and the problems of developing a rich general purpose language by synthesis of features of existing languages. One of the lessons learned was that greater richness and power of expression led to greater complexity both in language definition and in language use. PL/I is a language in which programming is relatively easy once the language has been mastered, but in which verifiability and subsequent readability of programs may present a problem. Any language definition of PL/I is so complex that its use for the informal or formal verification of correctness for specific programs is intractable.

M9—Algol 68, 1963–1969 [82]: Whereas PL/I was developed by synthesis of the features of a number of existing languages, Algol 68 was developed by systematic generalization of the features of a single language, namely Algol 60. The language contains a relatively small number of "orthogonal" language concepts. The power of the language is obtained by minimizing the restrictions on how features of the language may be combined. Interesting language features of Algol 68 include:

a powerful mechanism for building up composite modes from the five primitive modes *int, real, bool, char, format*;

identity declarations;

pointer values, structures, etc;

carefully designed coercion from one mode to another;

a parallel programming facility.

The generality of the language can be illustrated by considering the mode (type) mechanism. Composite modes can be built up from modes *m,n* by the mode construction operators [ ] *m* (multiples), *struct (m,n)* (structures), *proc (m)n* (procedures), *ref m* (references) and *union (m,n)* (unions). Any mode constructed in this way may itself be the "operand" of a further mode construction operator as in *struct ([ ] ref m, proc (ref ref m) ref n)*. Thus, an infinite number of different modes can be constructed from the primitive ones. Each definable mode has a set of values which must be manipulatable by the assignment operator and other applicable operators. Procedures may have any definable mode as a parameter, so that there must be provision for passing of parameters in any definable mode. The above discussion illustrates how generality in Algol 68 is obtained by starting from a small set of orthogonal concepts (the primitive modes and mode construction operators) and generating a very rich class of objects

(modes and mode values) by simply removing all restrictions on the manner of composition.

The defining document for Algol 68 (Algol 68 report) [80], is an important example of a high quality language definition, using a powerful syntactic notation for expressing syntax and semiformal English for expressing semantics. However, the report introduces its own syntactic and semantic terminology and can be read only after a considerable investment of time and effort. The reader must become familiar with syntactic terms such as "notion," "metanotion," and "protonotion," and with semantic terms such as "elaboration," "unit," "closed clause," and "identity declaration."

Algol 68 has not been widely accepted by the programming language community in part because of the lack of adequate implementation and user manuals. However, an ultimately more important reason appears to be that the language constructs of Algol 68 are too general and flexible to be readily assimilated and used by the applications programmer.

M10—Simula 67 1965–1967 [17]: Simula 67 is a milestone in the development of programming languages because it contains an important generalization of the notion of a block, which is called a *class*. A Simula class, just like an Algol block, consists of a set of procedure and data declarations followed by a sequence of executable statements enclosed in begin-end parentheses. However, Simula has a "class" data type and allows the assignment of instances of classes to class-valued variables. Whereas local procedures and data structures of a block are created on entry to the block and disappear on exit from a block, local objects of a class (declared in its outer block) remain in existence independently of whether the class body is being executed as long as the variable to which the instance of the class has been assigned as a value remains in existence.

Classes may function as *coroutines* with interleaved execution of executable instructions of two or more class bodies. Execution of a command "resume C_2" in class C_1 causes the current state of execution of C_1 to be saved followed by transfer of control to the current point of execution of C_2.

The separation between class creation and class execution allows data structures in a class to endure between instances of execution and makes the class more useful than the block as a modeling tool for inventory control systems, operating system modules, data types and other entities which may be characterized by a data structure representing the "current state" and a set of operations for querying and updating the current state.

The usefulness of classes in modeling is enhanced even further by Simula conventions concerning the accessibility of local procedure and data declarations in a class.

If an instance of the class C has been assigned to the variable X, then the local identifier I of this instance of the class C can be accessed as $X \cdot I$. The ability to access local identifiers of a class in this way has both advantages (direct access to class attributes) and disadvantages (not enough control over restricting communication between system modules).

The *subclass* mechanism of Simula 67 allows the procedure and data declarations of a class C to become part of the environment of the class B by means of the declaration "C *class* B." If we think of the procedure and data declarations of a class as its set of attributes, then "C *class* B" causes B to have all the attributes of C plus any additional attributes local to B. B is called a subclass of C since it is the subset of C which has the attributes of B in addition to those of C.

The subclass mechanism is a very effective language extension mechanism. It has been used by the Simula 67 designers to design hierarchies of environments for Simula 67 users. Perhaps the best known of these environments is the simulation environment, which is created by first creating a list processing class containing a set of useful list processing procedures, and then defining a subclass simulation which uses list processing procedures to implement simulation primitives. Thus, Simula is not inherently a simulation language but merely a language which may easily be adapted to simulation by language extension.

A Simula class is a better primitive module for modeling objects or concepts than the Algol procedure because of its ability to remember its data state between instances of execution. It has been used as a starting point for the development of a notion of modularity appropriate to modular programming languages of the 1970's.

M11—IPL V, 1954–1958 [65]: IPL V is a list processing language developed specifically for the solutions of problems in artificial intelligence. It was widely used in the 1950's and 1960's for the programming artificial intelligence applications in areas such as chess, automatic theorem proving and general problem solving.

IPL V has primitive instructions for creating and manipulating list data structures. It is an assembly level list processing language with a $1 + 1$ address code (the first address names an operand and the second address names the next instruction). Both programs and data are represented by lists. There are a number of system cells with reserved names, such as a communication cell for communicating system parameters, a subroutine call stack and a free storage list cell. A large number (over 100) of system defined subroutines (processes) are available to aid the user. The semantics of IPL V instructions is specified by defining an instruction interpreter for IPL V instructions.

IPL V was an important milestone both because it was widely used for a period of over ten years by an important segment of the artificial intelligence community and because it pioneered many of the basic concepts of list processing. For example, the notion of a free storage list serving as a source for storage allocation and as a sink to which cells no longer needed are returned was pioneered in IPL V. IPL V may well have been the first language to define its instructions by a software specified instruction execution cycle (virtual machine).

M12—Lisp, 1959–1960 [56]: Lisp, like IPL V, was developed for the solution of problems in artificial intelligence. However, Lisp may be thought of as a higher level (as opposed to machine level) programming language.

Lisp has two primitive data types referred to as lists and atoms. It has the following simple but powerful set of primitive operations.

A *constructor cons*[x;y] for constructing a composite list from components x and y.

Two *selectors car*[x], *cdr*[x] for, respectively, selecting the first component and remainder of the list.

Two predicates atom[x], eq[x;y] which, respectively, test whether x is an atom and whether two atoms x and y are identical.

A compound conditional of the form [$p_1 \rightarrow a_1; p_2 \rightarrow a_2; \cdots; p_n \rightarrow a_n$] which may be read as "*if* p_1 *then* a_1 *else if* p_2 *then* $a_2 \cdots$ *else if* p_n *then* a_n" and results in execution of the action a_i corresponding to the first true predicate p_i. Binding operators *lambda*[x;f] and *label*[x;f] which bind free instances of x in f so that they, respectively, denote function arguments and recursive function calls.

The set of primitive Lisp operations have been enumerated explicitly because they exhibit in the simplest terms the essential operators in a nonnumerical processing language. Every nonnumerical processing language must contain constructors for constructing composite structures from their components, selectors for selecting components of composite structures and predicates which permit conditional branching determined by the "value" of the arguments. The compound conditional is a very attractive control structure which was first developed for Lisp and later incorporated into Algol 60. The Lisp binding operators (lambda and label) provide a mechanism for handling functions which have functions as arguments as in the lambda calculus.

Lisp is sufficiently simple to permit the development of a relatively tractable mathematical model. McCarthy used this model as a starting point for the development of a mathematical theory of computation [57]. He considered many of the basic theoretical programming language issues such as mathematical semantics, proofs of program correctness (including compiler correctness) and proofs of program equivalence (by recursion induction) several years before they were considered by anyone else.

McCarthy also developed a definition of Lisp by means of a Lisp interpreter (the APPLY function) which, given an arbitrary Lisp program P with its data D executes the program P with data D. The Lisp APPLY function demonstrated as early as 1960 the technique of defining a programming language L by an interpreter written either in L or in some language definition language. It became the starting point for the subsequent development of theories of operational semantics [95], and for the development of interpreter based language definition languages such as VDL [49].

Lisp contributed a great deal to our understanding of programming language theory. It is also the most influential and widely used artificial intelligence language, its popularity being due in no small measure to its unique blend of simplicity and power. Lisp is certainly among the most important milestones in the development of programming languages.

M13—Snobol 4 1962–1967 [32]: During the 1950's it was felt that mechanical translation and other glamorous language understanding tasks could be greatly facilitated by the development of string manipulation languages with special purpose linguistic transformation aids. The Comit language [99] was developed for this purpose during the period 1957–1961. Comit was a good linguists language with many special purpose linguistic transformation features, but is not a clean programming language because it does not have string-valued variables to which strings may be assigned as values. The deficiencies of Comit led to the development of Snobol 4 during 1962–1967.

Snobol 4 has data values of the type—integer, real, string and pattern, as well as programmer defined data types. However, Snobol 4 has no block structure or declarations. A given variable, say X, may take on string values, numerical values or pattern values at different points of execution. The data type is carried along as part of the Snobol 4 data value and is checked dynamically at execution time to determine whether it is compatible with the operation that is to be applied to it. Dynamic type checking runs counter to the philosophy of static type checking in conventional block structure languages. It introduces additional run-time overhead and increases the proportion of programming errors that will not be discovered until execution time. However, introduction of block structure and explicit type declarations into Snobol 4 would totally change its character, and it is not clear that such a change would be for the better.

The most important programming language contribution of Snobol 4 is the pattern data type. A pattern is an ordered (finite or infinite) set of strings (and string attributes). Snobol 4 has pattern construction operators for constructing composite patterns from their constituents, pattern valued functions, and pattern matching operations which determine if a string S is an instance of the pattern P. The pattern matching process may be extremely complex involving the matching of a sequence of subpatterns, back-tracking if a partial match of subpatterns cannot be completed into a complete match, and possible side effects during pattern matching caused by assignments triggered by subpattern matching. The development of Snobol 4 has considerably advanced both our theoretical understanding of the nature of one dimensional (string) patterns and our ability to manipulate such patterns. A good theoretical discussion of Snobol 4 patterns is given by Gimpel [33].

Another nice feature of Snobol 4 is its programmer defined data types facility which allows selector names for each field of a structured data type to be easily defined. The mechanisms for defining, creating and manipulating data types are greatly simplified because no explicit type information need be specified in the program.

The use of the Snobol 4 data definition mechanism in defining and using Lisp data structures will be briefly illustrated. The data type definition "DATA('CONS-(CAR,CDR)')" defines a new data type called CONS with two subfields called CAR and CDR. The assignment statement "X = CONS('A', 'NIL')" constructs an initialized instance of this data structure and assigns it to X. The expression "CAR(X)" selects the first subfield "A" of the data structure assigned to X. The naturalness of Snobol 4 for specifying nested construction and selection for programmer defined

data structures is illustrated by the assignment statement "Y = CONS('B', CONS('A', 'NIL'))" and the expression "CAR(CDR(Y))" which retrieves the CAR subfield of the CDR subfield of Y (which happens again to be the element "A").

Although Snobol 4 is a relatively rich and complex language its implementation appears to be an order of magnitude simpler than PL/I or Algol 68. In order to increase portability of the language, it has been defined in terms of a relatively machine-independent macro-language, and can be implemented on a new machine simply by implementing the macro-language. An efficient compiler—the Spitbol compiler [18]—makes Snobol 4 competitive for a wide range of nonnumerical programming problems.

M14—Language theory, 1948–1962: Whereas milestones M1–M13 were concerned largely with the development of programming languages, milestones M14–M23 will be concerned with concepts and theories in the programming language field. The topics to be considered include language theory, models of implementation, language definition, program verification, semantics and abstraction. The starting point both historically and conceptually, is the development of language theory.

Both natural languages and programming languages are mechanisms for the communication of messages from a "sender" or "generator" to a "receiver" or "recognizer."

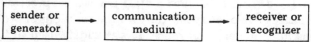

This model of communication was used by Shannon in the late 1940's in developing a mathematical theory of communication [73]. It was used in the late 1950's by linguists and psychologists, such as Chomsky and Miller [16], in the development of a theory of natural languages. In the field of computer science, the great success of the generative (context-free grammar) definition of Algol 60 [63] led to the generative specification of language syntax for all subsequent programming languages, and to the systematic use of recognizers (finite automata and pushdown automata) in implementing translators and interpreters.

The study of natural languages concerns itself with the study of *mental* mechanisms that allow *human* senders and receivers to generate and comprehend a potentially infinite class of sentences after having encountered and learned only a small finite subset of the set of all possible sentences in a language. The study of computer languages is similarly concerned with finite structures that allow languages with an infinite number of sentences to be defined. However, in the case of computer languages, we are not restricted to the study of preexisting human mental mechanisms, but can create language generating and recognition mechanisms with nice mathematical and computational properties. The language generating mechanisms are called *grammars* while the language recognition mechanisms are called *automata*.

One of the most important results in language theory is due to Chomsky, who defined a hierarchy of grammars (type 0, 1, 2, 3 grammars) and a hierarchy of automata (Turing machines, linear bounded automata, pushdown automata, finite automata) and proved the following remarkable four-part result concerning the equivalence of language generating power of grammars and language recognition power of automata.

1) A language L can be generated by a type 0 (unrestricted) grammar iff it can be recognized by a Turing machine.

2) A language L can be generated by a type 1 (context-sensitive) grammar if it can be recognized by a linear bounded automaton.

3) A language L can be generated by a type 2 (context-free) grammar iff it can be recognized by a pushdown automaton.

4) A language L can be generated by a type 3 (finite-state) grammar iff it can be recognized by a finite automaton.

Proof of the above result provides a number of interesting insights concerning the relation between the processes of language generation and language recognition. Moreover, the four part hierarchy allows us to distinguish between type 0 and type 1 grammars and automata, which are primarily of theoretical interest, and type 2 and type 3 grammars and automata, which are occasionally useful in compiler construction. Much of the practical work in language theory is concerned with the characterization and study of subclasses of type 2 and type 3 grammars and automata.

M15—Compiler technology and theory 1960–1970: The notion of a compiler was developed in the early and mid 1950's by Hopper, the developers of Fortran and many others. By the early 1960's the notion that compiling was a three phase process consisting of lexical analysis, parsing and code generation had been firmly established. During the 1960's there was a great deal of both practical and theoretical work on the mechanization of lexical analysis and parsing [28]. Lexical analysis was modeled by finite automata while parsing was modeled by various subclasses of context-free grammars, such as precedence grammars, $LR(k)$ grammars and $LL(k)$ grammars. The mechanization of code generation proved to be more difficult because it was target language dependent but there was some progress in this area also. The cost of building compilers of given complexity decreased considerably in the 1960's as our understanding of compiler structure increased. In the late 1960's and 1970's there was considerable work on program optimization using techniques such as interval analysis for analyzing the flowchart of a program. The state of the art in compiler technology and theory is ably summarized in [1].

M16—Compiler Compilers: Since there is a lot of similarity between compilers for different languages, the notion was developed of a program which, when primed with the syntatic and semantic specification of a given programming language L, would create a compiler for the programming language L. This concept led to interesting work on specifying the compiler-oriented semantics of programming languages by rules for translating source language constituents into the target language. However, the creation of a working compiler compiler which could actually be used in the production of compilers for new languages or new target machines proved to be too ambitious, because the complexity and diversity of languages and machines is simply too great to permit automation. The purely syntactic task of creating an efficient automatic parser from a BNF syntax specification of a language is possible for certain restricted classes of grammars such as precedence grammars, but becomes unmanageable for more ambitious classes of grammars such as $LR(k)$ grammars because of the difficulty of automatically constructing the tables required for automatic parsing. The automation of compiler semantics is even more difficult than the automation of parsing. The best documented example of a compiler compiler (compiler generator) is probably [58].

M17—Models of implementation, interpreters, 1965–1971: Programming languages such as Fortran and Algol 60 have a lot of "surface complexity" but derive their "integrity" from a simple underlying model of implementation, which specifies how programs are to be executed. A model of implementation is a programming language interpreter rather than a compiler. In the early 1960's compiler models of programming languages were emphasized because compiler construction was a pressing technological problem. By the late 1960's it was realized that interpreter models captured the important characteristics of programming languages much more directly than compiler models, so that serious students of programming language structure discarded compiler models in favor of interpreter models.

Fortran is based on a model in which subroutines and COMMON storage areas occupy fixed size blocks, each object is characterized by a relative address relative to the beginning of its block, and no storage allocation is performed during execution. This model gives rise to language restrictions against arrays with dynamic bounds and recursive subroutines.

Algol 60 is based on an activation record stack model of implementation [84] which can handle recursive procedures and arrays with dynamic bounds but cannot handle pointer-valued variables or procedures which return procedures as their values. Algol 68 can be clearly modeled by a run-time environment with two stacks and one heap [86]. Simula 67 requires each created instance of a class to be modeled by a stack. PL/I has no clean model of implementation, and its lack of integrity may be due precisely to the fact that the language designers were more concerned with the synthesis of source language features than with the development of an underlying model of implementation.

The notion of a model of implementation is important because it pinpoints the simple starting point from which the apparent complexity of a programming language is derived. Man is inherently incapable of handling or manipulating great complexity so it stands to reason that there is some simple internalized model that is used as a starting point for designing complex structures such as programming languages. It is argued here that the simple starting point for developing a complex programming language may well be a model of implementation in the mind of the designer.

The 1971 conference on data structures in programming languages [26] contained several papers on models of implementation including a paper on the contour model by Johnston [42], a paper on the B 6700 by Organick and Cleary [66], and a paper on data structure models in programming languages by Wegner [87].

Wegner [86] proposed a class of models called information structure models for characterizing models of implementation by their execution time states and state transitions. An information structure model is a triple $M = (I, I^0, F)$ where I is a set of states $I^0 \subseteq I$ is a set of initial states and F is a state transition function which specifies how a state S can be transformed into a new state S' by the execution of an instruction. A computation in an information structure model is a sequence $S_0 \to S_1 \to S_2 \to \cdots$ where $S_0 \in I^0$ and S_{i+1} is otained from S_i by the execution of an instruction (state transition).

The Lisp APPLY function and the Vienna definition language, discussed in the next section, can be characterized very naturally by information structure models.

Specific assumptions about the structure of the state I and the state transition function F give rise to specific models of implementation. For example states of a Turing machine may be described in terms of three components (t, q, i) where t is the current tape content, q is the current state, and i is the position of the input head. Finite automata are distinguished from Turing machines by the fact that the state transition function F cannot modify the tape component. Pushdown automata have an additional state component called a pushdown tape with characteristic transformation properties.

Programming languages have more complex states and state transitions than automata but may generally be characterized by states with three components (P, C, D) where P is a program component, C is a control component, and D is a data component. Programming languages may be classified in terms of attributes of the P, C, D, components associated with models of implementation. For example the model of implementation of Algol 60 assumes an invariant (reentrant) program component P, a control component C consisting of an instruction pointer ip and an environment pointer ep, and a data component D which is an activation record stack. Fortran does not require P to be reentrant, but requires the size of P, C, and D to be fixed prior to execution.

Information structure models provide a very natural framework for describing programming languages and systems operationally in terms of a specific, possibly abstract, model of implementation. This approach goes against the conventional view that higher level languages should be defined in an implementation-independent way. However, implementation-dependent models reflect the fact that programming-language designers and system programmers think in implementation-dependent ways about programming languages. Implementation-depen-

dent models are therefore valid and important for language designers and system programmers, while implementation independent models are important in other contexts such as program verification.

M18—Language definition, 1960–1970: It is convenient to distinguish between interpreter-oriented language definitions which define the meaning of programs and program constituents in terms of their execution-time effect and compiler-oriented language definitions which define the meaning of source programs in terms of compiled target programs of a target language.

The Algol report is an example of an early (1960) interpreter-oriented language definition with verbal definitions of the meaning of source program constituents. The Lisp APPLY function is an interpreter-oriented language definition in which the execution time effect of source language constructs is rigorously specified by a program.

During the 1960's the interest in compiler technology gave rise to a number of compiler-oriented definitions such as the definition of Euler [89]. Feldman and Gries [28] includes a good review of compiler-oriented language definitions. Knuth [43] proposed an interesting compiler-oriented method of defining the semantics of context-free grammars by associating inherited and synthesized attributes with each vertex of the parse tree of language strings.

During the late 1960's interpreter-oriented definitions of programming languages came back into fashion. The Algol 68 report [80] uses a powerful syntactic notation (VWF notation) to define syntax and semiformal English to define interpreter-oriented semantics. The Vienna definition language [48], [86] is an extension of the Lisp APPLY function definition technique which allows complex languages like PL/I to be defined in terms of an execution-time interpreter.

The Vienna definition language is probably the most practical of the above-mentioned language definition mechanisms. However, it requires approximately 400 pages of "programs" to define PL/I and about 50 pages to define Algol 60. The work on language definition suggests that languages like PL/I are inherently complex in the sense that there simply is no simple way of defining them.

Programming language definitions are intended to serve at least the following two purposes.

1) As a specification of "correctness" for the language implementer.

2) As a specification of "correctness" for the user who wishes to determine whether a program performs its intended task.

The language definition of Algol 60 served as an important frame of reference for a spirited discussion of ambiguities and trouble spots [44]. It was sufficiently precise to serve as an informal tool in checking implementation correctness and program correctness, but was of little help in developing formal methods of program verification. Tools for specifying formal (axiomatic) models of programming languages were developed in the late 1960's and led to an intensive effort in the 1970's to develop tractable formal language definition models [37], [71].

It is important that programming languages of the future have tractable formal language definitions so that program correctness can be formally determined. One of the objectives of programming language design in the 1970's is "simplicity" where simplicity is increasingly defined in terms of ease of developing a formal definition.

M19—Program correctness, 1963–1969: A program is said to be correct if it correctly performs a designated task (computes a designated function). A program may be thought of as a "how" specification and the designated task or function as an associated "what" specification. A correctness demonstration is a demonstration that the how specification determined by the program is a realization (implementation) of the independently given what specification.

Program correctness was considered by McCarthy (1962) [57], Naur (1965) [64], Dijkstra (1966) [19], Floyd (1967) [29] and Hoare (1969) [36]. Floyd developed the axiomatic approach to program correctness which specifies axioms for primitive program statements and a rule of inference for statement composition. Input-output relations of composite programs may be derived as theorems from input-output relations for primitive statements using the rule of inference for statement composition.

Hoare [36] developed a linear notation for the Floyd formalism. Both axioms and theorems have the form $\{P\}S\{Q\}$ where S is a program statement, P is a precondition, and Q is a post condition. Hoare stated axioms for assignment statements, if-then-else statements and while statements, thus producing a formal system sufficient to prove theorems for programs written in a strict structured programming style. Subsequently, Hoare, together with Wirth, developed a formal definition of Pascal [37] which has been widely used as a starting point for correctness proofs by research workers in program verification.

The axiomatic approach has been widely used for proving the correctness of "small" programs [50], but there are some unresolved problems which prevent its being used as a standard tool for program verification in a production environment. One of the principal limitations of correctness proof techniques is that such techniques are applicable only when the what specification of a program can be given in a simple functional form. The majority of large problems have intractable what specifications (requirements specifications) which may be several hundred pages long, and constantly changing. Thus, it may turn out that formal correctness proofs are simply not applicable to "real" problems, being applicable only to "toy" problems with simple functional what specifications.

M20—Verification, testing and symbolic execution: Program verification may be regarded as an ambitious attempt to prove the correctness of program execution for *all* elements of an infinite input domain and may be contrasted with program testing which is concerned with establishing correctness for individual elements of the input domain. Program correctness for subsets of the input domain may be established by a technique called symbolic

execution which is intermediate in generality between program verification and program testing.

The concept of symbolic execution arrived on the scene relatively late and was first publicly presented in 1975 at the international conference on reliable software [41] in papers by King [47] and Boyer, Elspas, and Levitt [6]. It involves the tracing of execution paths of a program with symbolic values of program variables. The set of all execution paths of a program may be thought of as a (possibly infinite) execution tree. Terminal nodes of the tree represent completed execution paths. When a terminal node is reached during symbolic execution then symbolic relations between input and output values for that terminal node are available and program correctness (or incorrectness) can be determined for the subset of values of the input domain which cause the particular execution path to be executed.

Symbolic execution is marginally easier than complete program verification because it is unnecessary to determine loop invariants of program loops. However, other problems which arise in program verification such as the algebraic simplification of algebraic expressions along an execution path are, if anything, more acute because "unfolding" of loops in symbolic execution requires longer sequences of algebraic transformations to be handled. The problem of keeping track of the input domain associated with an execution path is also very difficult. The difficulty of this problem is illustrated by the fact that the "emptiness problem" for execution paths is undecidable. That is, we cannot in general determine whether the input domain associated with a given execution path is empty.

Program testing for a particular value of the input domain is clearly easier than symbolic execution or complete verification since it only involves running the program for the particular input value. However, the key problem in testing is to determine "good" test cases by means of a test data selection criterion.

We may think of a "good" test case as a representative of an equivalence class of "similar" data values with the property that correct execution of the test case increases our confidence in the correctness of the program for all data elements in the equivalence class. If we can partition the input domain into a finite, relatively small, number of such equivalence classes then testing of the program for one element of each equivalence class should increase our level of confidence in the correctness of the complete program.

A number of alternative criteria may be used for determining such equivalence classes. For example the set of all data values associated with a given control path is an example of such an equivalence class. Alternatively, we may directly partition the input domain into input equivalence classes (such as large, medium, and small). Equivalence classes based on the internal program structure which systematically select test cases to exercise all control paths are on the whole more effective than arbitrary equivalence classes imposed on the input domain.

Test data selection criteria can be developed by *program*

structure analysis (control path analysis) *operational profile analysis* (classification of inputs by expected frequency of use) and *error analysis* (testing for specific kinds of errors). The papers by Goodenough and Gerhardt [35], Brown and Lipow [7], and Schneiderwind [74], all presented at the International Conference on Reliable Software [41], illustrate these three approaches to test data selection.

M21—Program verification, program synthesis and semantic definition [98]: Program verification is the process of verifying that a given program Prog correctly performs the task specified by a predicate P. If we are given axioms of the form $\{Q\}S\{P\}$ for a set of primitive statement types and an axiom for statement composition then verification that a program Prog correctly performs the task P requires us to prove the theorem $\{true\}\text{Prog}\{P\}$. That is, the postcondition P for the program Prog implies the precondition *true*.

In the case of program synthesis, we are given a specification of a task P and are required to find a program Prog that correctly performs the task. Program synthesis clearly involves program verification of the synthesized program P as a subtask. However, verification need be performed only for the class of programs which can be synthesized and not for all possible programs of a programming language. Systematic (or automatic) program synthesis avoids unnecessary complexity resulting from bad programming and might actually turn out to be easier than the development of a general purpose verifier for both good and bad programs.

The object of program synthesis is to convert a static description P of what is to be computed into a dynamic description Prog of how it is computed. This can be done in a structured way by the stepwise introduction of dynamic features into the static description. At each step one or more statically defined components is expanded into a structure composed of dynamically defined components which may have inner statically defined components as parameters. A structured development of a program Prog from a specification P consists of a sequence $P_0, P_1, \cdots, P_n$ of successively more dynamic descriptions of P where $P_0 = P, P_n = \text{Prog}$ and P_{i+1} is obtained from P_i by "expanding" a component of P_i into a more dynamic form. A formal system such as Hoare [36] may be used to prove that P_{i+1} realizes P if P_i realizes P. Examples of this approach are given by Manna [59], Wirth [90] and Mills [60].

A semantic definition of a programming language L is a mechanism which, given an arbitrary program Prog $\in L$, defines the "meaning" of the program. If the task specification P for a program Prog is taken to be the meaning of Prog, then the semantic definition supplies P given Prog and may be regarded as an inverse process to program synthesis (which supplies Prog given P).

It is very reasonable to think of the input-output predicate P as the meaning of program Prog whenever Prog determines a well defined input-output relation. Unfortunately, there are programs (with an undecidable halting problem) which have no associated input-output predicate

P and therefore would have no "meaning" using this notion semantics. Since a semantic definition of a programming language L should associate a meaning with *all* programs of the programming language, this method of assigning meaning is not altogether satisfactory. The set of meanings expressible by input-output predicates P is restricted to the set of recursive functions while the set of meanings expressible by programs is the richer set of recursively enumerable functions.

Floyd [29] called his seminal paper or program verification "Assigning Meaning to Programs," implying that a formal system for program verification also provides a framework for program semantics. It is often convenient for practical purposes to think of the meaning of a program Prog as its input-output predicate. However, input-output semantics determined by axiomatic models is incomplete because the domain of meanings is not sufficiently rich to express the meaning of all programs. In order to achieve completeness, mathematically more sophisticated semantic theories such as those of Scott [71], [80] must be used which map programs into partial recursive functions rather than total recursive functions.

M22—Semantic models: In order to clarify the notion of semantics, it is convenient to introduce the notion of a semantic model as a triple $M = (E, D, \phi)$ where E is a syntactic domain (of programs) D is a semantic domain of denotations and ϕ is a semantic mapping function which maps elements $e \in E$ of the syntactic domain into their denotations $\phi(e) \in D$.

Semantic models for programming languages may be classified in terms of the nature of the domain D of denotations. In particular it is convenient to distinguish between compiler models in which the semantic domain D is a set of programs in a target language, interpreter models in which the meaning of a program is defined in terms of the computations to which it gives rise, and mathematical models in which the meaning of a program is defined in terms of the mathematical function it denotes. Mathematical models may in turn be subdivided into axiomatic models which restrict the semantic domain to total functions and specify functions by a relation between a precondition (inputs) and a post condition (outputs), and functional models (such as those of Scott [71]) in which the meaning of a program is given by an abstract (partial recursive) function. The relation among these models is given by the following figure:

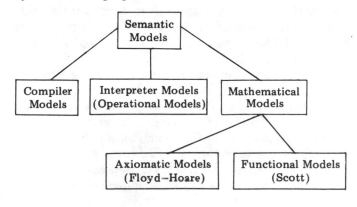

The above discussion makes it clear that the semantics (meaning) of a program is not an absolute (platonic) notion but rather a relative notion which depends on the context of discourse. When we are concerned with compiling, it is natural to think in terms of a compiler oriented semantics for programs. When we are concerned with the process of execution, it is natural to make use of an interpreter oriented semantics. When we are concerned with program verification, then axiomatic semantics is appropriate. When programs are regarded as abstract mathematical objects then the functional semantics of Scott is appropriate.

Each group of semantic models has given rise to a subculture of computer science with its own group of researchers. The subcultures associated with compiler models, interpreter models and axiomatic models have already been discussed (in the sections on compiler methodology, models of implementation and program verification). The Scott approach is the most abstract and Scott's notion of "meaning" has perhaps a greater claim than any other to be considered *the* (platonic) meaning of a program. However, one difficulty with Scott's notion of meaning is that the difference between the how specification of a program and the what specification as an abstract function is so great that the mapping from programs to functions cannot be effectively performed. If it could be effectively performed, then we could decide whether two programs realize the same function by mapping them onto their abstract functions and checking for identity. However, we know that the problem of determining whether two programs realize the same function is undecidable (not even partially decidable) and therefore conclude that the semantic mapping function from programs to abstract functions cannot be constructive.

M23—Abstraction [91]: An abstraction of an object (program) is a characterization of the object by a subset of its attributes. The attribute subset determines an equivalence class objects containing the original object as an element. The objects in the equivalence class are called refinements, realizations or implementations of the abstraction. If the attribute subset captures the "essential" attributes of the object then the user need not be concerned with the object itself but only with the abstract attributes. Moreover, if the attribute subset defining the abstraction is substantially simpler than its realizations then use of the abstraction in place of a realization simplifies the problem addressed by the user.

The input-output relation realized by a program is an example of a program abstraction. It determines an equivalence class of programs (the set of all programs realizing the given input-output relation). Any program in the equivalence class is a realization (refinement) of the abstraction. The input-output relation captures the essential behavior of the program. When the input-output behavior is a simple or well known mathematical function then use of the abstraction in place of a realization serves a useful purpose.

The input-output relation determined by a program may be thought of as a *what* specification (of what the program does) while the program itself is a *how* specification (of how the program is realized). We may, in general, think of an abstraction as a what specification and of its realizations as associated how specifications. The process of abstraction is useful if the what specification characterizing the essential attributes of an object is substantially simpler than the how specification.

Unfortunately, the what specification for programs is not always simpler than the how specification. A program is a relatively compact specification of a functional correspondence between arbitrarily large input and output domains and there is no reason why an explicit description of the input-output relation in a mathematical notation should be simpler than the implicit description by the program. In fact, programs are a more powerful notation for describing functional correspondences than input-output relations because programs can describe recursively enumerable functions (including functions with an undecidable halting problem) while input-output relations can describe only recursive functions (for which the halting problem is decidable).

The equivalence class of all programs (algorithms) associated with a given functional abstraction is studied in the analysis of algorithms. Such equivalence classes can be extraordinarily rich. For example, Knuth in [45] develops an enormous number of different programs for the problem of sorting. It can be shown that the problem of determining whether two programs realize the same abstraction is undecidable (not even partially decidable). The study of the structure of equivalences of how specifications realizing a given what specification is of interest both for programs and other kinds of abstraction.

The notion of abstraction is important in the study of program modularity. All forms of modular programming are concerned with breaking a complex task into modular components where each component has a what specification (abstraction) specifying what the module accomplishes and a how specification (refinement) which specifies how the what specification is realized. If the how specification is specified in terms of a collection of modules which are what specifications to lower level how specifications, then we are led to stepwise abstraction and stepwise refinement. The process of stepwise refinement is illustrated in [88].

The notion of abstraction arises in many different disciplines and may always be characterized in terms of a relation between an equivalence class specification and elements of the equivalence class. The problem of specifying abstractions (equivalence classes) as well as the problem of characterizing the structure of the space of realization (elements) is of interest in many domains of discourse. However, the tools for studying the specification problem and the equivalence problem is determined by the nature of the elements in the domain of discourse. We have already discussed the nature of the specification and equivalence problems when our elements are programs. In the section on "modularity" we will consider the specification and equivalence problems for a class of modules called *data abstractions* which cannot be completely specified by an input-output relation because they have an internal state.

M24—Pascal [92]: Although Pascal was developed in the late 1960's, its structure and design objectives make it a language of the 1970's. Its designer, Wirth, participated in the early stages of design of Algol 68 as a member of the IFIP working group 2.1, but felt that the generality and attendant complexity of the emerging language was a step in the wrong direction. Pascal, like Algol 68, was designed as a successor to Algol 60. However, whereas Algol 68 aimed at generality, Pascal was concerned with simplicity at the conceptual level, the user level and the implementation level. Conceptual simplicity allows simple axiomatization which facilitates verifiability. User simplicity gives the programmer a better understanding of what he is doing and results in more readable, better structured programs with fewer errors. Simplicity of implementation enhances efficiency and portability and ensures simplicity of the associated operational semantic model.

Pascal provides richer data structures than Algol 60, including records, files, sets and programmer defined type specifications but is otherwise as simple as possible. For example, it excludes arrays with dynamic bounds so as to enhance compile time type checking, and excludes pointers and parameters called by name in the interests of conceptual and user simplicity. The notion of compile time checkable data types is central to the structure of Pascal and provides a degree of program redundancy that enhances program reliability. Control structures are designed so as to encourage good programming style such as that advocated in structured programming.

Because Pascal is conceptually simple, it has been possible to develop a fairly complete formal definition for the language [37]. The existence of this formal definition has in turn led to the widespread use of Pascal as a base language for program verification research [50]. The availability of an axiomatized language has removed one of the obstacles to the development of automatic program verification systems, thus allowing researchers to focus more explicitly on other more formidable obstacles such as the handling of tasks with complex or intractable what specifications.

Pascal and Algol 68 represent two very different approaches to the development of a successor to Algol 60. Although the verdict is not yet in, it may turn out that the Pascal approach will turn out to be more relevant to the development of future programming languages than the Algol 68 approach. However, the discussion of "the APL phenomenon" below indicates that the demands of interactive programming may require us to discard notions such as block structure and explicit type declarations which are fundamental to both Pascal and Algol 68.

M25—The APL phenomenon: The idea of time sharing caught the imagination of the computing community as early as 1960, and led to the development of a number of on-line languages in the early 1960's. Quiktran [60] was developed in 1961–1963 by IBM as an on-line dialect of Fortran but never caught on, perhaps because it could not be adequately supported by existing technology. Joss [75] was developed in 1963–1964 by Shaw and others at the Rand Corporation. Basic (beginners all purpose symbolic instruction code) [48] was developed in 1965–1966 at Dartmouth and has had great success in high schools, two year colleges, and other environments concerned with teaching elementary programming.

APL was developed by Iverson in the early 1960's [40], was implemented as an interactive language in 1967 [30], and has proved to be enormously popular in the 1970's among engineers and mathematicians who need a versatile "desk calculator" to aid them in their work.

APL has a richer set of operators than conventional languages like PL/I or Pascal, including ingeneous extensions of scalar operations to vector and matrix operations which allow loop control structures of conventional programming languages to be implicitly specified in APL. Its emphasis on expressive power at the level of expressions is appropriate to on-line languages, since use of on-line languages in the desk calculator mode is largely concerned with the evaluation of expressions. The richness of APL operators and expressions permits a far greater number of essentially different ways of accomplishing a given computation than in conventional languages. The greater scope for programmer ingenuity leads to greater programmer satisfaction but may lead to programs that are more difficult to read, debug, or maintain.

APL has an explicit mechanism for specifying scopes of identifiers, but has a mechanism for specifying local variables of subroutines. Workspaces are a very effective APL mechanism for defining "modules" containing named subroutines and data sets. There are APL extensions such as APL*PLUS and APL SV [34] specifically designed to allow use of APL for large data processing applications.

APL has no explicitly typed variables or block structure and has the *go to* statement as its only form of transfer control. There is not even an "if-then-else" statement, and conditional branching is performed by an implementation trick (branch to a label 0 is interpreted as exit from a subroutine and branch to an ill-formed label is interpreted as a "continue" statement with no effect). In these respects the structure of APL differs markedly from the current conventional wisdom of the software engineering community. However, it nevertheless strikes a strong responsive chord among practical programmers, indicating that explicit type declarations, block structure and control structure might possibly be discarded in future on-line languages, perhaps because the potential gains in program efficiency and reliability are insufficient to offset the extra program complexity resulting from redundant constituents and additional interrelations among program-constituents.

Arguments *against* block structure, explicit types and explicit control structures may be formulated as follows.

Argument against block structure: One of the original reasons for block structure was the savings in storage resulting from overlays of variables in disjoint blocks. The price paid for this rather trivial saving is an inflexible set of interrelations among program identifiers which adds greatly to the program complexity. APL has scoping mechanisms at the subroutine and workspace level, but none at the block structure level. This looser scoping mechanism appears to be very appealing to practical programmers. Prior to 1970, we might have dismissed the tendency towards looser scoping as being due to a lack of education. However, now that we have become complexity conscious, we can see that block structure imposes additional complexity on a program and that the desire to ruthlessly prune such complexity by eliminating block structure may be justified by the canons of software engineering.

Argument against explicit type declarations: APL is designed so that types of variables may be determined implicitly by context, and there are in fact many syntactic checks on type compatibility between operators and operands in an APL system. Implicit type definitions may well correspond much more closely to the programmers intuitive thought processes than explicit type definitions. Moreover, explicit type declarations greatly increase the number of interactions among program constituents, and therefore increase the complexity of the program. If the programmer needs explicit information about types, APL has query facilities for providing such information to the programmer.

Argument against explicit control structures: The rich operator structure of APL often allows explicit loops and other explicit control specifications to be avoided. Since control structures are probably the single most significant cause of program complexity, languages which allow control structures to be specified implicitly rather than explicitly clearly give rise to textually simpler programs.

Since language usage in the future is likely to become increasingly interactive, and APL is probably the most widely used interactive language, language designers should analyze very carefully the reasons for the popularity of APL. It is not at present clear how much the popularity of APL is due to the quality of its programming system and how much it is due to the quality of the language design. However, it may well turn out that programming languages of the future will be more APL-like than Pascal-like.

M26—Structured programming: The term "structured programming" was introduced by Dijkstra in 1969 in a seminal paper entitled "Notes on structured programming" [24]. These notes are the culmination of several years of personal development, documented by his 1965 paper entitled "Programming Considered as a Human Activity" [20] which emphasizes the importance of programming style and program verification and contains the observation that "the quality of programmers is inversely proportional to the density of go-to statements in their programs," and by his 1968 letter entitled "Go-to Statement Considered Harmful" [21] which sparked a debate concerning the role of the go-to statements in programming that is ably summarized by Knuth [46]. Dijkstra's

recent book entitled *A Discipline of Programming* [22] reflects his current thinking on the subject.

Structured programming in its purest (narrow) form is concerned with the development of programs from assignment statements, conditional branching (if-then-else) statements and iteration (while-do) statements by statement composition. These statement forms can be nicely axiomatized [36] and correspond to "natural" forms of mathematical reasoning (the if-then-else statement corresponds to enumerative (case analysis) reasoning and the while-do statement corresponds to inductive reasoning). It was shown by Bohm and Jacopini [4] that these statement forms are sufficient for expressing any computable function. Moreover, it turns out that these statement forms are appropriate for many practical problems although they must be supplemented by other statement forms in certain cases such as unusual exit from a loop.

Structured programming in its more general meaning is concerned with the better organization of the program development process to achieve objectives such as simplicity, understandability, verifiability, modifiability, maintainability, etc. In order to achieve these objectives it is important to develop a methodology for the modular decomposition of programs into components suitable both for bottom-up and top-down program development. In this connection, it is convenient to distinguish between "programming in the small" concerned with modularity and program structuring at the primitive statement level and "programming in the large" concerned with modularity at a higher (subprogram and data structure) level. The if-then-else and while-do constructs are appropriate module building constructs for programming in the small. The Algol procedure, Simula class and APL workspace are examples of module building constructs for programming in the large. Current research on modularity will be discussed in a separate section.

Structured programming has affected programming language usage in placing greater emphasis on if-then-else and while-do constructs and deemphasizing the go-to statement. It is likely to affect the design of future programming languages by introducing new kinds of program modules for programming in the large, and by placing greater emphasis on verifiability as a programming language design objective. The availability of appropriate concepts of modularity should help the user in systematic modular program development for complex problems. However, there are important areas of program development, such as choice of an appropriate modular data structure where available tools are of little help to the programmer. The influence of the choice of data structure on program structure is discussed in a paper on "top-down program development" by Wirth [90]. The duality between program structure and data structure is discussed in a provocative way by Hoare [38], [39].

The techniques of structured programming have had an impact not only on academic computer science but also on production programming [8]. The chief programmer team approach developed by Mills and Baker [61] is an example of a management structure which makes use of structured programming. The New York Times project [9] is perhaps the most widely advertised success story for the chief programmer team approach, claiming a productivity of 10 000 instructions per man year with only one error per man year. However, the reported success of this project was subsequently challenged, on the basis that maintenance and modifiability of the completed program was unsatisfactory. It appears that the chief programmer team approach is designed to optimize program development but pays insufficient attention to the operations and maintenance part of the life cycle (see the section on life cycle).

M27—Structured model building: Specifications of programming languages are effectively complex programs in some specification language. The notions of abstraction structuring, and stepwise refinement are just as applicable to the construction of semantic models (definitions) of programming languages as they are to the construction of applications programs. Thus, the abstract notion of a semantic model (for a specific language) can be realized by a compiler model, interpreter model, axiomatic model, or functional model (see M22). Once the desired class of models has been chosen, there is enormous scope for "structuring" the language definition by first making "high-level" decisions concerning the overall structure of the model and then filling in lower level details by a process of stepwise refinement. The term "partial model" may be used to describe an intermediate partial language specification in this process of stepwise refinement.

The above structured model building approach will be briefly illustrated by showing how stepwise refinement may be used to build an information structure model (interpreter model) of Algol 60 [97]. In the case of information structure models $(I,I°,F)$ the partial models of the stepwise refinement process will have partial (successively more complete) specifications of the state components $I,I°$, and the state transition function F. The initial model M_0 would be an arbitrary model with no restriction on $I,I°,F$. A "first-order" model M, might require states I to be of the form (P,C,D) where P is an invariant (read only) program component, C has the form (ip,ep) where ip is an instruction pointer into P and ep is an environment pointer into D, and D is a stack of activation records. A "second-order" model M_2 might then be introduced which defines the state transitions (instructions) for block entry and exit and procedure call and return. Eventually, a final model M_n would completely define the state structure I and state transitions F for every Algol statement.

The partial models which arise in the above stepwise refinement process specify partial (operational) semantics for partial syntax specifications and may be thought of as defining language classes which are abstractions of the language that is being defined. For example, the abstraction "Algol-like languages" may in principle be defined by a partial information structure model which fixes those semantic and syntactic features that are essential if the language is to be Algol-like and leaves open optional language features of Algol-like languages.

The use of structured techniques of model specification is likely to lead to more understandable definitions of a number of existing programming languages. However, an even more potent way of developing programming languages with simple specifications is to use simplicity of specification as one of the criteria of programming language design, as was done in the case of the programming language Pascal.

M28—The life cycle concept: The software life cycle as formalized by department of defense agencies consists of a *concept formulation* and *requirements specification* stage, a *software development* stage, and an *operations* and *maintenance* stage. These stages may in turn be refined so that the software development stage might consist of a requirements analysis stage, a program design stage, an implementation and debugging stage and a testing and evaluation stage. In analyzing three large military software projects, it was estimated that such systems typically have a life cycle of 16 years, consisting of a concept formulation and requirements stage of 6 years, a software development stage of 2 years, and an operations and maintenance stage of 8 years [70]. Thus, the software development stage comprises only one eighth of the total life cycle of a typical large military software project.

The life cycle concept provides a basis for a more complete analysis of software systems than was previously possible. In the 1960's and early 1970's programming projects were organized to minimize software development costs rather than total life cycle costs. This led to a disproportionate emphasis on program design and implementation and a comparative neglect of both the initial determination of what it is that we really want to accomplish and the long years of program usage in an environment which may involve frequent program modification.

Emphasis on the life cycle as opposed to the software development phase affects both programming language design and programming language usage. For example emphasis on software development requires programming languages to be designed for rapid and correct program development while emphasis on the life cycle requires programs to be readable and modifiable during the long operations and maintenance period, providing a strong argument for simplicity of language design. Language usage should be modular, so that modifications of one part of the program do not have unexpected side effects in another part of the program. Clever tricks which make the program less readable should be avoided like the plague.

The life cycle approach allows the systematic study of cost and effort in all stages of existence of a software system [69]. Bottlenecks can be uncovered in the manner of critical path analysis and tools and techniques may be developed for eliminating such bottlenecks. Studies of software systems have in fact uncovered some quite unexpected facts about system behavior such as the fact that 64 percent of errors are system design errors while only 36 percent are system implementation errors. This suggests that design, rather than implementation, is the bottleneck in software system development and has implications concerning the allocation of funds for research in software engineering.

M29—Modularity: The subroutine mechanism for realizing program modularity was developed as early as 1951 [83]. It was a fundamental feature of Fortran, whose design provided an enormous impetus towards modular programming. Algol 60 was in some ways a backward step from the viewpoint of modularity because its nested module structure discouraged independent module development and because procedure modules could not adequately handle data which remained in existence between instances of execution of a procedure.

The Simula class is a very flexible generalization of the Algol 60 procedure module. It separates creation and deletion of instances of a class from entry and exit for purposes of execution. Coroutine control allows the program and data state at arbitrary points of execution to be preserved and subsequently restored. Access to objects declared in the outermost block of a class provides a more flexible (too flexible) mechanism for module intercommunication. The subclass facility is an ingenious syntactic mechanism for providing the advantages of hierarchical (nested) modular environments while avoiding the need for physical textual nesting of the associated modules. The class concept has served as an inspiration to designers of modular programming languages but is probably too rich in properties to serve as a prototype for modular design.

The collection of declarations in the outer block of a module may be regarded as a set of attributes or resources. One of the purposes of a module is to erect a "fence" around this set of attributes which allows systematic *information hiding* [68] of internal (hidden) attributes of a module and selective specification of a subset of externally known (*exportable*) attributes. Recent research on Clu [51] and Alphard [94] has been concerned with mechanisms for hiding and exporting module attributes.

The experimental language Clu [51] requires its program modules to consist of a collection of exportable procedures operating on a hidden (internal) data structure, and refers to such modules as *clusters*. Clusters are convenient for defining data types (such as stacks) by means of operations (such as push, pop, top, create, testempty) independently of the internal data structure (linear list or array) used to realize the cluster. The user sees an abstraction (the stack abstraction) which is defined by hiding the internal data structure and exporting only the operations. Such an abstraction is called a *data abstraction* because it abstracts from a specific data representation. The effect of the operators is defined by axioms such as "top(push(x,stack)) = x" which defines the effect of the "top" operation in terms of previously executed "push" operations without making any commitment to data representation. Any data structure which causes the defining axioms for the operations to be satisfied is an adequate realization of the data abstraction. Of course, the development of complete and sound sets of axioms for characterizing the set of cluster operations in a data independent way may, in general, be difficult. However, in most practical cases, we can characterize the behavior of "output" operations of a data abstraction reasonably simply in terms of the effect of previous input operations, and a complete set of axioms can be developed by systematically using our knowledge of what the operations are supposed to accomplish.

The experimental modular programming language Alphard [94] calls its modules *forms*. Recent research on Alphard has emphasized verifiability as an objective of the language. Forms have a *representation* component which defines the representation of hidden data structures, an *implementation* component which defines the implementation of external attributes (operators) of the form and a *specification* component which specifies the "abstract" properties of attributes so that the correctness of their implementation can be verified.

Other work on modular programming languages includes Brinch Hansen's development of *monitors* in concurrent Pascal [9] and Wirth's introduction of *modules* in a Pascal-like language for modular multiprogramming called Modula [97]. Both monitors and modules are motivated by the need to provide the user with machine independent abstractions of machine resources such as disks, user consoles, synchronization primitives, etc. In [9] the relation between the implementation and user abstraction for monitors is described by considering how monitors are implemented. In [97] the relation between abstraction and implementation of modules is described at the language level by introducing notions such as *define list* of objects defined in the module for use outside the module and a *use list* of objects declared outside the module and used inside the module.

Among the problems which must be addressed in any modular programming language are the problems of module interface definition and module interconnection. These problems had already been identified in the 1950's in connection with the development of Fortran (the transfer vector mechanism). One recent example of work in this area is the thesis by Thomas [79] who develops a module interconnection language (MIL) for specifying module interfaces in terms of inherited attributes (use lists), synthesized attributes (define lists), and locally generated attributes using a model similar to Knuth's attribute grammars [43].

Although recent research on modularity and abstraction has greatly increased our understanding of how modules may be designed, it is not yet clear how effectively these notions can be incorporated in future programming languages. The explicit support of clusters or Simula classes introduces extra complexity into a language both at the level of verifiability and at the level of implementation, determining complete and consistent specifications for clusters to serve as a starting point for formal verification. Simula 67 has not become a widely used application language in spite of its superior modularity facilities. The modular programming facilities of a language are clearly among its most important design features, and it is quite likely that future programming languages will contain new kinds of primitives for defining both program and data abstractions. But the precise nature of these primitives has not yet been determined.

M30—Data oriented programming languages: We may distinguish between the program-centered and data-centered views of programming. The program-centered view emphasizes program development and considers data only piecemeal as and when it becomes the object of program transformation. This view is appropriate to numerical problems involving complex functional transformations on simple data structures. The data-centered point of view considers the data structure (data base) as the central part of a problem specification and views programs as "bugs" which crawl around the data base and occasionally query, update or augment the portion of the data base at which they currently reside. This view is appropriate for airline reservation systems, management information systems, information retrieval systems or any other systems whose state description requires a complex data structure and whose operations (transactions) are local queries or perturbations of that data structure.

Bachman in his Turing lecture [11] compares the shift from the program-centered to the data-centered point of view with the shift from an earth-centered to a sun-centered model of the universe brought about by the Copernican revolution. There is no doubt that the increasing importance of the data-centered view of programming will affect the design of future programming languages.

Since programming was initially motivated by numerical problems early programming languages and programming methodology emphasized the programming centered point of view. Algol 60 blocks and procedures are examples of program-centered constructs since internal data structures are forced to disappear between instances of execution. Simula classes generalize block structure so that it becomes appropriate for data-centered programming.

Cobol is an example of an early programming language which allows program and data to be handled in a symmetrical fashion. Programming systems for data-centered programming developed during the 1960's include IDS (integrated data store) [5], and IMS (information management system) [25]. The data-centered view of programming led in the 1970's to the development of database languages and systems [14], [25].

Data-base systems may be classified [25] into *network systems* which require the user to view the data base as a network (spagghetti bowl); *hierarchical systems* which require the data base to be tree structured, and *relational data-base systems* which permit the user to view the data base as a set of abstract relations. Network and hierarchical systems give rise to "low level" data base languages since they require the user to be explicitly aware of the data structure implementation. Relational systems give rise to high level data base languages which allow programs to specify transactions independently of the internal data structure representation, but lead to formidable implementation problems.

Network systems are a direct outgrowth of the work of the Codasyl data-base task group (DBTG) [14] and were heavily influenced by Bachman's work on IDS [5]. Hierarchical systems are the simplest class of data-base management systems, and most of the practical systems of the 1960's such as IMS were hierarchical. The relational approach to data-base management systems was pioneered by Codd in 1970 [13]. A good recent survey of the state of the art may be found in [77].

There is a great deal of current work on the design and implementation of data-base language. Recently developed relational data-base languages include Sequel [14], Quel [2], and query by example [100].

CONCLUSIONS

The above collection of concepts and milestones is by no means complete, but illustrates the great variety of programming language concepts and products developed during the last 25 years. One of the more interesting facts that emerges from a study of programming language development is the remarkable stability of early programming languages like Fortran and Cobol, and the comparative lack of success of subsequently developed languages like PL/I, Algol 68, Simula 67, and Pascal in capturing significant numbers of adherents in a nonuniversity environment. The exception is perhaps APL which has captured the hearts of a new class of user (the desk calculator user).

All the programming languages described in this paper were developed and implemented in the 1950's and 1960's. Although there have been a number of proposals for general purpose languages in the 1970's such as CS 4 [15] and the Tinman requirements specification for a new DOD-sponsored common higher order language [31], no new general purpose languages comparable to PL/I, Algol 68, or Pascal have been launched during this period. The 1970's have been a period of retrenchment in the development of general purpose languages. A number of new insights have been developed such as the importance of simplicity, readability, verifiability, and maintainability in program design and language design. A better appreciation of the concept of modularity has been developed and we have made some gains in our understanding of program verification. But these insights have led to changes in the mode of use of existing programming languages rather than in the design of a new class of programming languages which are so clearly superior that they are automatically accepted as a replacement for existing programming languages.

The demonstrated reluctance of the programming community to accept a new language is due partly to the costs of a changeover, and partly to the natural resistance to changes in technology. It is due partly to the fact that programming language designers have not been able to come up with an acceptable compromise between simplicity and versatility that is a substantial improvement over Fortran or Cobol. However, a further reason may be that programmer productivity is not as sensitive to language changes as programming language professionals would like to think. Fortran-like languages provided a significant increment of productivity over assembly language but it may well be that further language refinements cause only marginal or even negative increments in programmer productivity. Programming style, structured programming and other methodologies are largely language independent and are probably far more important in increasing programmer productivity than the development of new languages. Ultimately, it is the quality of programming rather than the programming language that determines the cost and reliability of production programs.

The field of programming languages was central to the development of computer science in the 1950's and 1960's, leading to important practical products and to important theoretical advances in our understanding of the nature of computer sciences. It may well be that programming language professionals did their work so well in the 1950's and 1960's that most of the important concepts have already been developed. The programming language field may play a less central (though still important) role in computer science in the 1970's and 1980's than it did in the 1950's and 1960's.

REFERENCES

Note: OSIPL refers to [25]. ICRS refers to [40].

[1] A. V. Aho and J. R. Ullman, *The Theory of Parsing, Translation and Compiling.* Englewood Cliffs, NJ: Prentice-Hall, vol. I, 1972; vol. II, 1973.
[2] E. Allman, M. Stonebraker, and G. Held, "Embedding a relational sublanguage in a general purpose programming language'" *SIGPLAN Notices,* Mar. 1976.
[3] M. M. Astrahan and D. Chamberlin, "Implementation of a structured English query language," *Commun. Ass. Comput. Mach.,* Oct. 1975.
[4] C. Bohm and G. Jacopini, "Flow diagrams, turing machines, and languages with only two formation rules," *Commun. Ass. Comput. Mach.,* May 1966.
[5] C. W. Bachman, "A general purpose system for random access, memories," in *FJCC Proc.,* 1964.
[6] R. S. Boyer, B. Elspas, and K. N. Levitt, "A formal system for testing and debugging programs by symbolic execution," *ICRS,* Apr. 1975.
[7] J. R. Brown and M. Lipow, "Testing for software reliability," *ICRS,* Apr. 1975.
[8] F. T. Baker, "Structured programming in a production programming environment," *ICRS,* Apr. 1975.
[9] P. Brinch Hansen, "The purpose of concurrent PASCAL," *ICRS,* Apr. 1975.
[10] F. T. Baker and H. D. Mills, "Chief programmer teams," *Datamation,* 1973.
[11] C. W. Bachman, "The programmer as navigator," (1973 Turing lecture), *Commun. Ass. Comput. Mach.,* Nov. 1973.
[12] *COBOL 1961: Revised Specifications for a Common Business Oriented Programming Language,* U. S. Govt. Printing Office, 1961.
[13] E. F. Codd, "A relational submodel for large shared data banks," *Commun. Ass. Comput. Mach.,* June 1970.
[14] "CODASYL," Data Base Task Group Rep., Apr. 1971.
[15] *CS-4 Language Reference Manual and Operating System Interface,* Intermetrics Publ., Oct. 1975.
[16] N. Chomsky and G. A. Miller, *Introduction to the Formal Analysis of Natural Languages, Handbook of Mathematical Psychology,* vol. II. New York: Wiley, 1963.
[17] D. Dahl and C. A. R. Hoare, *Hierarchical Program Structures, in Dahl, Dijkstra and Hoare, Structured Programming.* New York: Academic, 1972.
[18] R. Dewar, "SPITBOL 2.0," Illinois Inst. Technol. Rep., 1971.
[19] E. W. Dijkstra, "A constructive approach to the problem of program correctness, *BIT,* Aug. 1968.
[20] ——, "Programming as a human activity," *Proc. IFIP Congress,* 1965.
[21] ——, "Go to statement considered harmful," *Commun. Ass. Comput. Mach.* (Lett.), Mar. 1968.
[22] ——, *A Discipline of Programming.* Englewood Cliffs, NJ: Prentice-Hall, 1976.
[23] ——, "Making a translator for ALGOL 60," *APIC Bull.,* vol. 7, 1961.
[24] ——, *Notes on Structured Programming, in Dahl, Dijkstra and Hoare, Structured Programming.* New York: Academic, 1972.
[25] C. J. Date, *An Introduction to Data Base Systems.* New York: Addison-Wesley, 1975.
[26] *Data Structures in Programming Languages, Proc. of Symp., SIGPLAN Notices,* Feb. 1971.
[27] "FORTRAN vs. basic FORTRAN," *Commun. Ass. Comput. Mach.,* Oct. 1964.
[28] J. Feldman and D. Gries, "Translator writing systems," *Commun. Ass. Comput. Mach.,* Nov. 1968.
[29] R. W. Floyd, *Assigning Meanings to Programs, Proc. Symp. App. Math.* vol XIX, AMS, 1967.
[30] A. D. Falkoff and K. E. Iverson, *The APL Terminal System, in Klerer and Reinfelds, Interactive Systems for Experimental Applied Mathematics.* New York: Academic, 1968.
[31] D. A. Fischer, "A common programming language for the department of defense, background and technical requirements," IDA Sci. Technol. Division, paper P-1191, June 1976.
[32] R. Griswold, J. Poage, and I. Polonsky, *The SNOBOL 4 Programming Language.* Englewood Cliffs, NJ: Prentice-Hall, 1971.
[33] J. Gimpel, "A theory of discrete patterns and their implementation in SNOBOL 4," *Commun. Ass. Comput. Mach.,* Feb. 1973.
[34] L. Gilman and A. J. Rose, *APL, an Interactive Approach,* 2nd Ed. New York: Wiley, 1974.
[35] J. B. Goodenough and S. L. Gerhard, "Towards a theory of test data selection," *ICRS,* Apr. 1975.
[36] C. A. R. Hoare, "An axiomatic basis for computer programming," *Commun. Ass. Comput. Mach.,* Oct. 1969.
[37] C. A. R. Hoare and N. Wirth, "An axiomatic definition of the programming language PASCAL," *Acta Inform.,* vol. 2, no. 4, 1973.
[38] ——, *Notes on Data Structuring, In Dahl, Dijkstra and Hoare, Structured Programming.* New York: Academic, 1972.
[39] ——, "Data reliability," *ICRS,* Apr. 1975.
[40] K. E. Iverson, *A Programming Language.* New York: Wiley, 1962.
[41] *Proc. Int. Conf. Reliable Software,* Apr. 1975; also *SIGPLAN Notices,* June 1975.
[42] J. Johnston, "The contour model of block structured processes," *DSIPL,* Feb. 1971.
[43] D. E. Knuth, "The Semantics of Context Free Languages," in *Mathematical Systems Theory,* vol. II, no. 2, 1968.
[44] ——, "The remaining trouble spots in ALGOL 60," *Commun. Ass. Comput. Mach.,* Oct. 1967.
[45] ——, *The Art of Computer Programming Volume III, Sorting and Searching,* 1973.
[46] ——, "Structured programming with go to statements," *Comput. Surveys,* Dec. 1974.
[47] J. C. King, "Symbolic execution and program testing," *Commun. Ass. Comput. Mach.,* July 1976.
[48] J. G. Kemeny and T. E. Kurtz, *Basic Programming.* New York: Wiley, 1967.
[49] P. Lucas and K. Walk, "On the formal description of PL/I," *Annu. Rev. Automatic Programming,* vol. 6, pt 3. New York: Pergamon, 1969.
[50] R. L. London, "A view of program verification," *ICRS,* Apr. 1975.
[51] B. H. Liskov, "A note on CLU," Computation Structures Group Memo 112, Nov. 1974.
[52] B. M. Leavenworth, "Syntax macros and extended translation," *Commun. Ass. Comput. Mach.,* Nov. 1966.
[53] B. H. Liskov and S. N. Zillies, "Specification techniques for data abstractions," *ICRS,* Apr. 1975.
[54] M. D. McIlroy, "Macro instruction extensions to compiler languages," *Commun. Ass. Comput. Mach.,* Apr. 1960.
[55] C. N. Mooers, "TRAC-A procedure-describing language for a reactive typewriter," *Commun. Ass. Comput. Mach.,* Mar. 1976.

[56] J. McCarthy et al., *LISP 1.5 Programmers Manual*. Cambridge, MA: MIT Press, 1965.

[57] J. McCarthy, "Towards a mathematical science of computation," in *Proc. IFIP Congr.*, 1962.

[58] W. M. McKeeman, J. H. Horning, and D. B. Wortman, *A Compiler Generator*. Englewood Cliffs, NJ: Prentice-Hall, 1970.

[59] Z. Manna, *Mathematical Theory of Computation*. New York: McGraw-Hill, 1974.

[60] H. D. Mills, "Mathematical foundations for structured programming," IBM Corp., Gaithersburg, MD, FSC 72-6012, 1972.

[61] J. H. Morissey, "The QUIKTRAN system," *Datamation*, Feb. 1964.

[62] P. Naur, Ed., "Report on the algorithmic language ALGOL 60," *Commun. Ass. Comput. Mach.*, May 1960.

[63] ——, "Revised report on the algorithmic language ALGOL 60," *Commun. Ass. Comput. Mach.*, Jan. 1963.

[64] ——, Proofs of Algorithms by General Snapshots, BIT 6, 1966.

[65] Newell et al., *Information Processing Language V Manual*, 2nd Ed. Englewood Cliffs, NJ: Prentice-Hall, 1965.

[66] E. I. Organick and J. G. Cleary, "A data structure model of the B6500 computer system," *DSIPL*, Feb. 1971.

[67] *PL/I, Current IBM System 360 Reference Manual*, (or Bates and Douglas), 2nd Ed. Englewood Cliffs, NJ: Prentice-Hall, 1975.

[68] D. I. Parnas, "A technique for software module specification with examples," *Commun. Ass. Comput. Mach.*, May 1972.

[69] B. Randell and L. J. Russell, *ALGOL 60 Implementation*. New York: Academic, 1964.

[70] D. J. Reifer, "Automated aids for reliable software," *ICRS*, Apr. 1975.

[71] D. Scott and S. Strachey, "Towards a mathematical semantics for computer languages," PRG 6, Oxford Univ. Comput. Lab., 1971.

[72] J. Sammet, *Programming Languages, History and Fundamentals*. Englewood Cliffs, NJ: Prentice-Hall, 1969.

[73] C. E. Shannon and W. Weaver, *The Mathematical Theory of Communications*. Urbana, IL: Univ. Illinois Press, 1962.

[74] N. F. Schneiderwind, "Analysis of error processes in computer software," *ICRS*, 1975.

[75] C. J. Shaw, "JOSS, a designers view of an experimental on-line system," in *Proc. FJCC*, 1964.

[76] ——, "A specification of JOVIAL," *Commun. Ass. Comput. Mach.*, Dec. 1963.

[77] E. H. Sibley, Ed., "Special issue: Data base management systems," *Comput. Surveys*, Mar. 1976.

[78] A. M. Turing, "On computable numbers with an application to the entscheidungsproblem," in *Proc. London Math. Soc.*, 1936.

[79] J. Thomas, "Module interconnection in programming systems supporting abstractions," Ph.D. dissertation, Brown Univ., Providence, RI, May 1976.

[80] R. D. Tennent, "The denotational semantics of programming languages," *Commun. Ass. Comput. Mach.*, Aug. 1976.

[81] J. Von Neumann, "The EDVAC report," in *Computer from PASCAL to Von Neumann*, H. Goldstein, Ed. Princeton, NJ: Princeton Univ. Press, 1972, Ch. 7, discussion.

[82] V. Wingaarden et al., "Report on the algorithmic language ALGOL 68," *Numer. Math.*, Feb. 1969; also revised report, *Numer. Math.*, Feb. 1975.

[83] M. V. Wilkes, D. J. Wheeler, and S. Gill, *The Preparation of Programs for a Digital Computer*. New York: Addison-Wesley, 1951 (revised Ed., 1957).

[84] P. Wegner, *Programming Languages, Information Structures and Machine Organization*. New York: McGraw-Hill, 1968.

[85] W. Waite, "A language independent macro processor," *Commun. Ass. Comput. Mach.*, July 1967.

[86] P. Wegner, "Three computer cultures, computer technology, computer mathematics and computer science," in *Advances in Computers*, vol. 10. New York: Academic, 1972.

[87] ——, "Data structure models in programming languages," *DSIPL*, Feb. 1971.

[88] ——, "The Vienna definition language," *Comput. Surveys*, Mar. 1972.

[89] N. Wirth and H. Weber, "Euler—A generalization of ALGOL and its formal definition," *Commun. Ass. Comput. Mach.*, Jan. and Feb. 1966.

[90] N. Wirth, "Program development by stepwise refinement," *Commun. Ass. Comput. Mach.*, Apr. 1971.

[91] P. Wegner, "Abstraction—A tool in the management of complexity," in *Proc. 4th Texas Symp. Comput.*, Nov. 1975.

[92] N. Wirth, "The programming language PASCAL," *Acta Inform.*, 1971.

[93] P. Wegner, "Structured model building," Brown Univ., Providence, RI, Rep., 1974.

[94] W. Wulf, R. L. London, and M. Shaw, "Abstraction and verification in ALPHARD, introduction to language and methodology," Carnegie-Mellon Univ., Dep. Comput. Sci. Rep., June 1976.

[95] P. Wegner, "Operational semantics of programming languages," in *Proc. Symp. Proving Assertions about Programs*, Jan. 1972.

[96] ——, "Research paradigms in computer science," in *Proc. 2nd Int. Conf. Reliable Software*, Nov. 1976.

[97] N. Wirth, "Modula: A language for modular multiprogramming," ETH Institute for Informatics, TR18, Mar. 1976.

[98] P. Wegner, "Structured programming, program synthesis and semantic definition," Brown Univ. Rep., Providence, RI, 1972.

[99] V. Yngve, "COMIT as an IR language," *Commun. Ass. Comput. Mach.*, Jan. 1962.

[100] M. Zloof, "Query by example," in *Proc. Nat. Comput. Conf.*, 1975.

Peter Wegner received the B.Sc. degree in mathematics from the Imperial College, London, England, the Diploma in numerical analysis and automatic computing from Cambridge University, Cambridge, England, the M.A. degree in economics from Penn State University, and the Ph.D. degree in computer science from London University, London, England.

He has taught at the London School of Economics, Penn State, Cornell University, and Brown University and has been on the staff of the Computation Center at the Massachusetts Institute of Technology, and Harvard University. He is currently with the Division of Applied Mathematics, Brown University, Providence, RI. His publications are primarily in the programming language area but include papers in operations research and statistics.

Dr. Wegner has been consultant to the ACM Curriculum Committee (1965–1968), SIGPLAN Chairman (1969–1971) and is presently a member of the ACM Council.

ON THE DESIGN OF PROGRAMMING LANGUAGES*

N. WIRTH

This paper reports on some past experiments in the design of programming languages. It presents the view that a language should be simple, and that simplicity must be achieved by transparence and clarity of its features and by a regular structure, rather than by utmost conciseness and unwanted generality. The paper contains an overview of the language designer's problems and dilemmas, and ends with some hints drawn from past experience.

In order to prevent misunderstanding or even disappointment, I should like to warn the reader not to interpret this title as an announcement of a general critique of commonly used languages. Although this might be a very entertaining subject, probably all that can be said about it has been said and heard by those willing to listen. There is no reason to repeat it now. Neither do I intend to present an objective assessment of the general situation in the development of programming languages, the technical trends, the commercial influences, and the psychology of their users. The activities in this field were enormous over the past years, and it would be presumptuous to believe that a single person could present a comprehensive, objective picture. Moreover, many aspects have been aptly reviewed and commented elsewhere (1-3).

Instead, I should like to convey a view of the development of design attitudes, of the shift of emphasis in design goals over the past decade. Also, I will try to provide some insight into the multitude of problems aspects, and demands that the designer of a language is facing, and to woo gently for recognition of the difficulties of this profession. Let me start by recalling some of my own reminiscences of incidents that caused me to end up in this role of language designer.

AN EXCURSION INTO "HISTORY"

My interest in computers had been awakened when I was an engineering student in the late 1950s; I was fascinated on the one hand by simplicity and inherent reliability of the basic building blocks, the digital circuits, and on the other hand by the astounding variety of effects that could be obtained by combining many of them in different ways. Moreover, these combinations could be varied not by extensive and cumbersome use of the soldering iron, but by merely composing ingenious sequences of hexadecimal digits placed on a magnetic drum. As the general task of an engineer is the improvement of his technical gadgets, I perceived that computers were an ideal ground for

engineering activities, and felt that there was ample room for further improvement. This assessment turned out to be correct up to the present day. But how was progress to be achieved? One way was by enhancing the reliability and effectiveness of their electronic components. The other – hazily defined path – seemed to be to make computers more conveniently usable, to make them less of an exclusive domain of the highly trained specialist.

This was the situation when I entered graduate school at Berkeley: In one room there stood a huge prototype of a computer with a bewildering number of wires and tubes. In a much smaller room nearby there were a few such specialists, talking about a "language" and a "translator". Luckily for me, a student helping to bring the big monster of a computer into operation didn't report too enthusiastically about that project, and I perceived the feeling that the future of computer hardware design did not lie in a university department anyway. Hence, I decided to explore the other alley, although that group was surrounded by skepticism, as word passed that some of these people did neither know Ohm's law nor Maxwell's equations.

The new and fascinating project under the direction of H.D. Huskey consisted in adding facilities to the programming language NELIAC by extending the translator program. This program was, remarkably, coded in the very language that it was compiling and, in retrospect, quite advanced for its time (4). Indeed, the fascination of the project originated much more from the sense of adventurousness than from the satisfaction of achieved perfection. For, although programming in NELIAC proved to be considerably more convenient than exercises in the cryptology of hexadecimal codes, the room for still further improvements continued to appear unlimited. Looking at it from the distance, that compiler was a horror; the excitement came precisely from having insight into a machinery that nobody understood fully. There was the distinct air of sorcery.

Then Algol 60 appeared in the literature and – after the difficulties of learning the new syntactic formalism were mastered – began to provide some relief from the oppressive feeling that there was no way to bring order into large languages and compilers. Yet even then, the task of constructing an Algol

*Reprinted from *Proc. IFIP Congress 74*, 386–393, North-Holland, Amsterdam, North-Holland Publishing Company.

The author is with the Institut für Informatik, Eidg. Technische Hochschule, Zurich, Switzerland.

compiler generating acceptably good code appeared enormous. The more the Algol compiler project neared completion, the more vanished order and clarity of purpose. It was then that I clearly felt the distinct yearning for simplicity for the first time. I became convinced that we should learn to master simpler tasks before tackling big ones, and that we need to be equipped with much better linguistic and mental tools. But apparently "useful" languages had to be big.

SIMPLICITY IN GENERALITY

In this situation, A. van Wijngaarden appeared like a prophet with his idea of Generalised Algol (5). His point was that languages were not only too complex, but due to this very complexity also too restrictive. "In order that a language be powerful and elegant it should not contain many concepts and it should not be defined with many words." The new trend was to discover the fundamental concepts of algorithms, to extract them from their various incarnations in different language features, and to present them in a pure, distilled form, free from arbitrary and restrictive rules of applicability.

The following short example may illustrate the principle. In Algol 60, the concept of a subprogram appears in two features: as declared procedure, and as name parameter to procedures. The passing of a parameter is realised as an assignment of an object (the actual parameter) to a variable (the formal parameter). A simplification and concurrent increase in power and flexibility of Algol can therefore be obtained by unifying the notions of procedure and parameter, by letting them become objects that can be assigned to variables like numbers or logical values. Let such an object be denoted by the program text enclosed by quote marks; the correspondence between constructs of Algol 60 and the generalised notation are shown by the following table:

Algol 60	Generalisation
procedure P; <statement>	P := '<statement>'
Q(<expression>)	Q('<expression>')

The gain in simplicity of language is obvious and the resulting gain in flexibility is striking. For example, it is now possible to assign different subroutines to a variable at different times, or even to replace a function subroutine by a constant! We are suddenly offered the power so far reserved to the assembly language coder letting his program modify some of its own instructions.

Implementation of such far reaching generalisations were on open challenge. I decided to investigate, whether these concepts could be condensed into a minimal language and compiler, as a language without compiler seemed to be of marginal value to me. This effort resulted in my first programming language, called Euler (5). It was a success in several ways, certainly if measured by the number of subsequent implementations on a wide variety of computers. The language was accepted as an intellectual challenge, a

flexible and powerful vehicle. Its simplicity and compactness made it an ideal implementation exercise for many prospective compiler engineers. Its greatest value, however, lay in revealing how simplicity should not be understood and achieved.

The premise that a language should not be burdened by (syntactical) rules that define meaningful texts (5) led to a language where it was difficult and almost impossible to detect a flaw in the logic of a program. It led to what I like to call a high-level Turing machine. Making mistakes is human (particularly in programming), and we need all the help possible to avoid committing them. But how can one expect a language to aid in avoiding mistakes, if it is even incapable of assisting in their detection.

The lesson is, then, that if we try to achieve simplicity through generality of language we may end up with programs that through their very conciseness and lack of redundancy elude our limited intellectual grasp. It is a mistake to consider the prime characteristic of high-level languages to be that they allow to express programs merely in their shortest possible form and in terms of letters, words, and mathematical symbols instead of coded numbers. Instead, the language is to provide a framework of abstractions and structures that are appropriately adapted to our mental habits, capabilities, and limitations. The "distance" of these abstractions from the actual realisation in terms of a computer is an established measure for the "height" of a language's level.

The key, then, lies not so much in minimising the number of basic features of a language, but rather in keeping the included facilities simple to understand in all their consequences of usage and free from unexpected interactions when they are combined. A form must be found for these facilities which is convenient to remember and intuitively clear to a programmer, and which acts as a natural guidance in the formulation of his ideas. The language should not be burdened with syntactical rules, it must be supported by them. They must therefore be purposeful, and prohibit the construction of ambiguities. It is a good idea to employ adequate, concise key words, and to forbid that they can be used in any other way. Prolixity is to be avoided, as it introduces a wrong kind of redundancy.

LEVELS OF ABSTRACTIONS

One of the most crucial steps in the design of a language is the choice of the abstraction upon which programs are to base. They can be selected only if the designer has a clear picture of the purpose of his language, of the area of its intended application. But all too often that purpose is not neatly specified and includes so many diverse aspects that a designer is given only inadequate guidance from prospective users. But at least he should restrict his selection to abstractions from the same level which are in some sense compatible with each other. I should like to offer three examples to this topic.

Algol 60 has chosen a well-defined set of abstract objects of computation: numbers and logical values, replacing bits and words as used on a lower level. The operations that are applicable to them are governed by mathematical laws and axioms which can be understood without referring to the number's representation in terms of bits and words. In the realm of control structures, the language introduces the operations of selective execution and repetition in the form of neatly structured statements. But their form was not sufficiently flexible - e.g. repetition is intimately coupled with a variable progressing through an arithmetic series of values, and selection is only provided among two alternatives. To provide the user with a facility for cases not covered by these control structures, the designers of Algol resorted to borrowing the universally applicable jump order from the lower level of machine coding. The <u>goto</u> statement is but a polished form of the jump.

This may not seem too serious in itself. But consider that now the programmer is able to use these facilities combined. The following example - which an honest Algol programmer will refrain from using, or otherwise will at least get a bad conscience - shows the point.

<u>for</u> i := 1 <u>step</u> 1 <u>until</u> 100 <u>do</u>
<u>begin</u> S; <u>if</u> p <u>then</u> <u>goto</u> L <u>end</u>

The whole purpose of the for clause is to proclamate to the reader: "the qualified statement is going to be executed once for every i = 1,2,3,...,100". The jump, however, may sneakily cause this promise to be broken! Whereas jumping out of a substructure may be considered to be a matter of morale only, jumping back into a structure even raises technical problems. They require the establishment of protective rules and restrictions which are afflicted by the stigma of improvisation and afterthought. They complicate the language by burdening its definition, its comprehension, and its compiler.

The second example concerns the notion of <u>pointers</u> or <u>references</u> in high-level languages. When programming in assembly code, probably the most powerful pitfall is the possibility to compute the address of a storage cell that is to be changed. The effective address may range over the entire store (and even be that of the instruction itself). A very essential feature of high-level languages is that they permit a conceptual dissection of the store into disjoint parts by declaring distinct variables. The programmer may then rely on the assertion that every assignment affects only that variable which explicitly appears to the left of the assignment operator in his program. He may then focus his attention to the change of that single variable, whereas in machine coding he always has - in principle - to consider the entire store as the state of the computation. The necessary prerequisite for being able to think in terms of safely independent variables is of course the condition that no part of the store may assume more than a single name. Whereas this highly desirable property is sacrificed in Fortran by the use of the "equivalence" statement,

Algol loses it through its generality of parameter mechanism and rule of scope. Even if the sensible rule is observed that a procedure's parameters must denote disjoint variables, one and the same variable may be referred to under more than one name, as shown by the following example.

<u>begin</u> <u>integer</u> a;
    <u>procedure</u> S(x); <u>integer</u> x;
    <u>begin</u> a := a+1; x := x↑2
    <u>end</u>;
    a := 1; S(a); write(a)
<u>end</u>

This design partly stems from the failure to separate the roles of textual abbreviation and of parametric program decomposition, both projected onto the same facility of the procedure. For mere textual abbreviations, one might be more willing to refrain from the use of parameters; in the case of program decomposition, communication with the environment might advantageously be restricted to explicit parameters. Hence, the notion of simplicity and frugality was rather counterproductive when viewed from the point of programming security.

We note that a parameter substitution represents an assignment of the storage address of the actual variable (a) to the formal parameter (x). In the spirit of generalisation it appeared as highly logical to admit the address into the society of computable objects. The address of a variable a - now called a reference - was thus introduced in the language Euler and denoted by @ a . It can be assigned to any other variable, say x . The variable a is then openly available under two names, a and x., and there is no limit to the number of further names that can be given to a . This experiment of reopening Pandora's box of storage addresses in Euler provided a clear warning of their undesirability, but didn't prevent the introduction of references into Algol 68 in their fullest flexibility.

The concept of <u>data type</u> provides added security insofar as a compiler may check against inadvertant use of incompatible variables in, for instance, assignments. This is, in itself, introducing another restriction unknown at the level of machine code, where every cell can be loaded with a copy of every other cell's content. The idea of simplicity through generality again led to the elimination of restrictive type rules, and of the data type in general. It was adopted by a family of languages designed to fill the apparent gap between high-level languages and assembly code, which are now known as machine oriented higher order languages (Mohols). They permit the construction of expressions with "untyped" operands and the application of both arithmetic and logical operations on the same variables. The result of programs written in such languages can only be understood through knowledge of the particular storage representation of data in terms of bits and words. Although effects may be produced that turn out to be the desired ones, they force the programmer to leave the realm of abstraction that a language is pretending to offer him.

So much for the third example of transgression of levels of abstraction in languages.

THE THREE EXAMPLES REVISITED

I do not deny that there are situations in programming which call for facilities not present in Algol-like languages. But they should not be met by compromising on the level of abstraction. The sneaky reintroduction of patently pernicious facilities from the era of machine coding is not an acceptable solution. In order to establish remedies, we must discover the true reasons for the programmers wish of such facilities. The language designer must not ask "what do you want?", but rather "how does your problem arise?" For, the answer to the first question will inevitably be "jumps, type-less operands, and addresses".

To convey an idea of the spirit in which a designer ought to approach such problems, I will sketch possible solutions to the three mentioned cases. The presented features do <u>not</u> provide the full flexibility inherent in jumps, type-less operands, and free address manipulation. But this is precisely their virtue; they still impose certain sensible restrictions of usage, and help maintain a programming discipline. In particular, they do not compromise the language's high level of abstraction; they do not introduce notions which can be explained only in terms of an underlying machine.

In the case of the for statement, what the programmer really needs is not necessarily a jump order, but merely a more flexible way to express termination of a repetition. The solution consists in providing a simpler form of repetitive statement whose termination does not necessarily depend on a variable moving through an arithmetic progression. Widely accepted forms are the while- and repeat statements, for example

> <u>while</u> B <u>do</u> S
> <u>repeat</u> S <u>until</u> B

The important point is that now the total effect of the composite statement can be deduced solely from the properties of the repeated component. The pertinent deduction rule can be formally expressed, for instance in Hoare's formalism (7). If P and Q denote any assertions on the state of the computation, then $P\{S\}Q$ means: if P holds before the execution of S, and this execution terminates, then Q holds after termination. The two deduction rules governing the above statement forms are (8):

$$\frac{P \wedge B \ \{S\} \ P}{P\{\underline{while} \ B \ \underline{do} \ S\} \ P \wedge \neg B}$$

$$\frac{P\{S\}Q \ , \ \neg B \wedge Q\{S\}Q}{P\{\underline{repeat} \ S \ \underline{until} \ B\} \ Q \wedge B}$$

Another situation requiring the use of a jump in Algol arises when one statement has to be selected among many. A feature invented by Hoare in exactly the same spirit, that not only replaces a jump and a switch declaration, but expresses the selection of one case among many in a structured, orderly way, is the case statement (9).

As for the second example, one may ask why addresses or pointers are needed anyway. I do not intend to pursue this argument here, but claim that if one consents to their necessity, they should be admitted only in a considerably tamed form. Security in pointer handling can be improved drastically by the following measures:

1. Every pointer variable is allowed to point to objects of a single type only (or to none); it is said to be <u>bound</u> to that type. This rule allows to maintain a compiler's capability of full type checking.

2. Pointers may only refer to variables that have no explicit name declared in the program, that is, they point exclusively to anonymous variables allocated when needed during execution. This rule protects the programmer from the dangers arising when variables are accessible under different names.

3. The programmer must explicitly specify whether he refers to a pointer itself or to the object to which the pointer refers (no automatic "coercion"). This rule helps to avoid ambiguous constructs and complicated default conventions liable to misunderstanding.

The reasons why programmers sometimes wish to deal with type-less variables are more difficult to pinpoint. The most frequent one is probably the necessity to pack different kinds of data densely into a single word, which the available language always regards as an indivisible entity. For instance, we might have to pack a triple r - say a file descriptor - consisting of a name x of 6 characters, a 5-bit status information s, and a 2-digit length count n. (The 5 status bits may, for example, indicate a tape's loadpoint, end of tape, and end of record positions, its density mode and parity check status.) A pictorial representation might be

	x	s	n
r	A B C D E F	10001	89
	36	5	7

and a common way to denote the value of such a triple is as an octal (or hexadecimal) number, because the word is available in the language under the misnomer "integer". In order to determine this number, the programmer must forget his original abstractions and perform the binary encoding "by hand". If he is lucky, he obtains

$r = 0102030405064331_8$ or $r = 0420C41468C9_{16}$

Part of the true information is arithmetic in its nature (n), another is logical (s), and a third alphabetic (x). Hence, all kinds

of orders must be applicable. But this is
only possible, if the operand is not restricted by its characterisation through an associated type. What the programmer really
needs in this case is a data structuring
facility relieving him from the tedious and
errorprone labor of data encoding and
packing.

As an illustration, in the programming
language Pascal the triple r can be directly
declared as a structured variable, yielding
the dense packing indicated by the picture
above (10). The first component of r is
declared to be an array of 6 characters, the
second to be a set of status indicators, and
the third a number in the range of 0 to 99.

```
type string = packed array[0..5] of char;
   indicator = (loadpoint,eof,eor,pchk,
                highdensity);
var r: packed record
        x: string;
        s: set of indicator;
        n: 0 .. 99
     end
```

Assignments, instead of involving obscure
arithmetic operations expressing shifts etc.,
are simply written as

```
   r.x := 'ABCDEF';
   r.s := [loadpoint,highdensity];
   r.n := 89
```

Each of the three components has a distinct
name and a distinct type. Its proper usage
can be completely checked by compiler and
program reader alike. Naturally, such a
structuring facility complicates a compiler
considerably, much depending on the quality
of the underlying hardware architecture. It
even increases the "volume" of a language;
but significantly, it does not reduce its
conceptual simplicity.

The proposed solutions to the three mentioned
problem areas lie in introducing restrictive
rules, and are contrary to the spirit of
"power through simplicity" and "simplicity
through generality". But they have already
proven to be wisely chosen precautions and
have aided tremendously in practical programming. The additional burden of type
checking by the compiler has been much more
than compensated by the amount of confidence
gained in the final programs. And this is
what good language design should mainly aim
for.

COMBINING FEATURES INTO A LANGUAGE

A characteristic of a well-designed feature
is that is does not imply any unexpected,
hidden inefficiencies of implementation. The
packed record structure shown above displays
this property: a compiler has full knowledge
of the address of each such variable and of
the position of the components within a word.
It can therefore generate appropriate and
efficient instructions for access, packing
and unpacking. The whole advantage of this
scheme, however, immediately vanishes, if,
for example, we introduce so-called dynamic
arrays, that is, if we allow information
about the actual dimensions of an array to

be withheld from the compiler. The textual
scan of the program does not reveal the
amount of storage needed; as a consequence
dynamic allocation must be used involving
indirect addressing. This not only impairs
the efficiency of the code, but - more
importantly - destroys the whole scheme of
storage economy.

This is but one example for many that could
be listed to show how the combination of two
seemingly harmless and well-understood
features may suddenly have disastrous effects.
A capable language designer must not only be
able to select appropriate features, but must
also be able to foresee all effects of their
being used in combination.

Naturally, one might suggest that a compiler
be designed that generates efficient and
dense code when the component sizes are known,
and less effective code otherwise. But this
attitude leads to the optimising monster
compilers so well known for their bulkiness
and unreliability. Even more significant is
the consideration that a good language should
not only aid the programmer in avoiding
mistakes, but that it must also give him an
idea of the complexity and effectiveness of
the features it offers. However, if the use
of the same feature under only slightly
different circumstances yields widely
different factors of economy, then the
language clearly lacks this highly desirable
property. It is very important that the
basic method of implementation of each
feature can be explained independently from
all other features in a manner sufficiently
precise to give the programmer a good
estimate of the computational effort involved.
Some modern languages fail miserably when
measured on this criterion.

Transparence is particularly vital with
respect to storage allocation and access
technique, since storage access is such a
frequent operation that any unanticipated,
hidden complexity can have disastrous effects
of the performance on a whole program. In
fact, I found that a large number of programs
perform poorly because of the language's
tendency to hide "what is going on" with the
misguided intention of "not bothering the
programmer with details". Transparence of
access mechanism can be achieved by neatly
categorising data structuring facilities
with respect to applicable access technique.
This rule was taken as a guiding principle
in the design of the language Pascal, which
offers the following structuring facilities:

1. Arrays. Components are selected by
   computable index. Their offset calculation
   must in general be deferred until execution time (using index registers if
   available).

2. Records. Components are selected by a
   fixed selector name. Their address can
   therefore be evaluated entirely at compile
   time. As the compiler may retain their
   offsets individually in a table, the
   components are not restricted to be of the
   same size and type, as in the case of
   arrays.

3. Sets. Components are not individually selectable at all. Instead, the membership operator in allows to test for their presence or absence. If the size of sets is sufficiently small, they can be represented by their characteristic function fitting into a single word.

4. Files (sequences). Since the length of a sequence may vary during program execution, a dynamic allocation mechanism is required. But it is considerably simplified, because only sequential access is permitted through a "window" displaying the component at the current position.

Variables of these fundamental structures can either be declared explicitly, or they may be invoked dynamically. In the first case they are known by their identifier, in the latter they must be accessed via pointer.

Knowledge of these access characteristics is vital for the programmer, as it is indispensible for the selection of data representation suitable for the algorithm. Regrettably, the current trend in language design seems to move in the opposite direction, namely to obscure these differences. The common excuse is that through the development of more suitable and more efficient hardware these differences would gradually disappear. The fact remains, however, that supposedly more suitable hardware becomes phenomenally complex. It is no longer economical to realise it directly in terms of electronic circuitry, and a new technique has therefore been invented – microprogramming. The essence of this development is that complicated features become the standard with their weird complexity well disguised, and that the programmer is denied the possibility to solve his tasks by simpler means. He doesn't even have a possibility to measure the built-in inefficiencies through quantitative comparisons!

LANGUAGE DESIGN IS DECISION MAKING

From the foregoing it may appear that the secret of good language design lies in a few rules and a sound attitude. In pracitce, of course, the designer is confronted with a bewildering variety of demands from various agents ranging from theoreticians to practitioners, from novices to experts, from revolutionaries crying for innovations to conservatives emphasising compatibility. Let me list a few of the most frequently encountered demands.

- The language must be easy to learn and easy to use.

- It must be safe from misinterpretation and misuse.

- It must be extensible without change of existing features.

- There must be a rigorous, mathematical definition, based on axioms and withstanding the scrutiny of logicians.

- The notation must be convenient and compatible with widely used (and sometimes not so logical) standards.

- The definition must be machine independent, that is without reference to a particular mechanism.

- The language must allow to make efficient use of the facilities of the available computer.

- The compiler must be able to generate efficient code and economise storage.

- The compiler must be fast and compact; it should be void of complex optimisation routines that are rarely used.

- The definition must be self-contained and complete. A reader must easily be able to identify the facilities needed for his purpose.

- The implementation must provide ready access to other facilities available on the system, such as program libraries and (therefore) subprograms written in different languages.

- The language and its compiler must be easily adaptable to different environments with different character sets and different operating system facilities.

- The compiler must be easily portable to other computers. Almost all of it should be conceived without specific reliance on a given order code and storage organisation.

- Time and cost for developing compiler and documentation must be minimal.

It is plain that several of these points are contradictory, but certainly not all of them. The designer must decide where he wishes to place emphasis. It is his task to find a carefully balanced compromise. In fact, the reconciliation of conflicting demands by well chosen compromises is an essential part of every engineering profession; language design should therefore be regarded as a typical engineering discipline. It can be mastered only by experience, and experience is usually gained only after a few failures! The designer's task is even aggravated by the fact that the conflicting demands come from different people whom he is supposed to serve. Whatever he decides, he should never expect unanimous approval.

However, I do not wish to convey the impression that sytisfying one criterion must necessarily mean sacrificing another. True progress appears through the invention of facilities that cater to several seemingly contradictory aims. The three examples mentioned before demonstrate that such progress is indeed feasible.

LANGUAGE DESIGN IS COMPILER CONSTRUCTION

In practice, a programming language is as good as its compiler(s). The believe that it should first be designed entirely in the abstract realm of, say, a set of axioms or an official document, is equally mistaken as the opinion that it must grow out of a practical experiment of implementation before being neatly documented. A successful language must grow out of clear ideas of design goals and of simultaneous attempts to define it in terms of abstract structures, and to implement it on a computer, or preferrably even on several computers. It follows that experience in compiler construction is a prerequisite to successful language design. Compiler design courses have indeed appeared in the curricula of many computer science department, and seem to be regarded as the epitome of the software craft. Unfortunately they are often strongly biased toward the aspect of syntax analysis, since much theoretical work has been done in this subject. However, the deep penetration of this branch of theory has been of rather small benefit to language design and sometimes was even detrimental. I am afraid that it has misled many language designers to believe that the complexity of a language's syntax was of no concern, since an appropriate parsing algorithm, if not already available, could readily be found for any construction introduced. But it is evident that a language that is simple to parse for the compiler, is also simple to parse for the human programmer, and that can only be an asset. Moreover, the real challenge in compiling is not the detection of correct sentential forms, but coping with ill-formed, erroneous programs, in diagnosing the mistakes and in being able to proceed in a sensible way.

The really essential prerequisite for successful compiler construction is experience in the development of large, complex programs. This includes mastery of techniques in structuring programs and data in general, and in selecting methods for various tasks in particular, such as for scanning of text, construction and search of symbol tables, and composition of code sequences.

One is inclined to wonder where the training of so many compiler and language designers will lead, and whether it is justified. Here I should like to point out that a general appreciation of compiler principles will help the understanding of computer operations and promote the state of the art of programming at large. But there is no reason to believe that the growth rate of the population of programming languages is thereby going to decrease. The emphasis in new developments, however, is gradually shifting from general purpose toward application oriented languages. It is precisely toward this trend that design courses should be directed: exposition of features and presentation of techniques that are common to most areas amenable to algorithmic solution. Such features are, for instance, the fundamental control concepts of sequencing, conditioning, selection, repetition, and recursion. They form a well established basis from which a designer can proceed to fill the given framework with specific facilities oriented toward his particular task and area of application (11).

CONCLUSIONS

I have tried to convey a picture of the problems, challenges, and ordeals facing a language designer, and to draw some lessons from experience gained in the design of a series of languages and compilers. To conclude, let me summarise these lessons learned.

- If you wish to develop a language, you must have a clear idea of how it is intended to be used.

- Keep in mind that a programming language is of no use without an efficient, reliable compiler and a clear, readable documentation. This should provide sufficient incentive to keep the language as simple as ever possible.

- Do not equate simplicity with lack of structure or limitless generality, but rather with transparence, clarity of purpose, and integrity of concepts.

- Adhere to a syntactic structure that can be analysed by simple techniques such as recursive descent with one-symbol lookahead. This not only aids a compiler, but also the programmer, and is vital for successful diagnosis of errors.

- Identify the basic abstractions on which the language is to be based. Try to define the language in terms of a mathematical formalism. This may help to detect hidden inconsistencies and to eliminate notions that cannot be understood in terms of the given abstractions.

- Do not consider the establishment of a formal definition as an end in itself. In particular, the formal definition cannot be a substitute for an informal presentation and for tutorial material. It is mostly an aid to the designer but not a user's document, in which mathematical rigor will contribute to volume but seldom serves the programmer's needs.

- Choose the basic features from the same level of abstraction. Obtain a clear idea on how to represent them in terms of a computer's order code and store. Be aware of the consequences arising from the coexistence of all the various features. They can sometimes be surprising and disastrous.

- Do not hesitate to exclude certain features that prove to be incompatible and too costly in terms of implementation. The fact that other languages include them is no guarantee for their indispensability.

- Obtain a sketch of the complete language before starting work on the compiler. Refrain from adopting highly controversial features; language changes are usually costly in time and effort even during development, and are virtually impossible after a compiler's release, if the language is successful.

- Design the language such that most checking operations can be performed at compile time and need not be deferred until execution. The concept of static data types of variables is essential in this respect, and enhances both programming security and system efficiency.

- Keep the responsability for the design of the language (and possible changes) confined to a single person. If implementation work is delegated, keep closely in touch with it, and make sure to obtain adequate feedback. Beware of programmers who will quietly find solutions no matter what they cost.

And finally, when the project is at its end, carefully reassess it, recognise that many aspects could be improved, and do it all over again.

REFERENCES

[1] T.E. Cheatham, Jr., The recent evolution of programming languages, <u>Information Processing 71</u> (ed. C.V. Freimann), North-Holland Publ. Co., Amsterdam, 1972, 298-313.

[2] J. Sammet, Programming languages: history and fundamentals, Prentice-Hall, Englewood-Cliffs, 1969.

[3] P. Naur, Programming languages - Status and trends, <u>Proc. NordDATA 72</u>, Helsinki 1972, 36-38.

[4] H.D. Huskey, R. Love, N. Wirth, A syntactic description of BC NELIAC, <u>Comm. ACM</u> vol. <u>6</u>, no. 7, 367-375 (July 1963).

[5] A. van Wijngaarden, Generalised ALGOL, Ann. Rev. in <u>Autom. Programming 3</u>, (1963) 17-26.

[6] N. Wirth, H. Weber, EULER, A generalization of ALGOL, and its formal description, <u>Comm. ACM</u> vol. <u>9</u>, no. 1 and 2, 13-23, 89-99, and no. 12, 878 (Jan., Feb., Dec. 1966).

[7] C.A.R. Hoare, An axiomatic basis for computer programming, <u>Comm. ACM</u> vol. <u>12</u>, no. 10, (Oct. 1969) 576-581.

[8] C.A.R. Hoare, N. Wirth, An axiomatic definition of the programming language Pascal, <u>Acta Informatica</u> vol. <u>2</u>, (1973) 335-355.

[9] C.A.R. Hoare, Hints on programming language design, SIGACT/SIGPLAN Symposium on priciples of programming languages, Boston, Oct. 1973.

[10] N. Wirth, The programming language Pascal, <u>Acta Informatica</u> vol. <u>1</u>, (1971) 35-63.

[11] M.V. Wilkes, The outer and inner syntax of a programming language, <u>Comp. J.</u> vol. <u>11</u>, no. 3, (Nov. 1968) 260-263.

HINTS ON PROGRAMMING LANGUAGE DESIGN*†

C. A. R. HOARE

Introduction

I would like in this paper to present a philosophy of the design and evaluation of programming languages which I have adopted and developed over a number of years, namely that the primary purpose of a programming language is to help the programmer in the practice of his art. I do not wish to deny that there are many other desirable properties of a programming language—for example, machine independence, stability of specification, use of familiar notations, a large and useful library, existing popularity, or sponsorship by a rich and powerful organization. These aspects are often dominant in the choice of a programming language by its users, but I wish to argue that they ought not to be. I shall therefore express myself strongly. I fear that each reader will find some of my points wildly controversial; I expect he will find other points that are obvious and even boring; I hope that he will find a few points which are new and worth pursuing.

My approach is first to isolate the most difficult aspects of the programmer's task, and state in general terms how a programming language design can assist in meeting these difficulties. I discuss a number of goals which have been followed in the past by language designers, and which I regard as comparatively irrelevant or even illusory. I then turn to particular aspects of familiar high-level programming languages and explain why they are in some respects much better than machine code programming, and in certain cases worse. Finally, I draw a distinction between language feature design and the design of complete languages. The appendix contains an annotated reading list; I recommend it as a general educational background for language designers of the future.

Principles

If a programming language is regarded as a tool to aid the programmer, it should give him the greatest assistance in the most difficult aspects of his art, namely program design, documentation, and debugging.

†Reprinted from *Sigact/Sigplan Symposium on Principles of Programming Languages*, October 1973.

The author is with the Oxford University Computing Laboratory.
*First published as Stanford University Computer Science Department Technical Report No. CS-73-403, Dec. 1973.

Program design. The first and very difficult aspect of design is deciding what the program is to do, and formulating this as a clear, precise, and acceptable specification. Often just as difficult is deciding how to do it—how to divide a complex task into simpler subtasks, specify the purpose of each part, and define clear, precise, and efficient interfaces between them. A good programming language should give assistance in expressing not only how the program is to run, but what it is intended to accomplish; and it should enable this to be expressed at various levels, from the overall strategy to the details of coding and data representation. It should assist in establishing and enforcing the programming conventions and disciplines which will ensure harmonious cooperation of the parts of a large program when they are developed separately and finally assembled together.

Programming documentation. The purpose of program documentation is to explain to a human reader the way in which a program works, so that it can be successfully adapted after it goes into service, either to meet the changing requirements of its users, to improve it in the light of increased knowledge, or just to remove latent errors and oversights. The view that documentation is something that is added to a program after it has been commissioned seems to be wrong in principle and counterproductive in practice. Instead, documentation must be regarded as an integral part of the process of design and coding. A good programming language will encourage and assist the programmer to write clear self-documenting code, and even perhaps to develop and display a pleasant style of writing. The readability of programs is immeasurably more important than their writeability.

Program debugging. Program debugging can often be the most tiresome, expensive, and unpredictable phase of program development, particularly at the stage of assembling subprograms written by many programmers over a long period. The best way to reduce these problems is by successful initial design of the program and by careful documentation during the construction of code. But even the best designed and documented programs will contain errors and inadequacies which the computer itself can help to eliminate. A good programming language will give maximum assistance in this. First, the notations should be designed to reduce as far as possible the scope for coding error; or at least to guarantee that such errors can be detected by a compiler, before the program even begins to run. Certain programming errors cannot always be detected in this way, and must be cheaply detectable at run time; in no case can they be allowed to give rise to machine or implementation dependent effects, which are inexplicable in terms of the language itself. This is a criterion to which I give the name "security." Of course, the compiler itself must be utterly reliable, so that its user has complete confidence that any unexpected effect was obtained by his own program. And the compiler must be compact and fast, so that there is no appreciable delay or cost involved in correcting a program in source code and resubmitting for another run; and the object code too should be fast and efficient, so that extra instructions can be inserted even in large and time-consuming programs in order to help detect their errors or inefficiencies.

A necessary condition for the achievement of any of these objectives is the utmost simplicity in the design of the language. Without simplicity, even the language designer himself cannot evaluate the consequences of his design decisions. Without simplicity, the compiler writer cannot achieve even reliability, and certainly cannot construct compact, fast, and efficient compilers. But the main beneficiary of simplicity is the user of the language. In all spheres of human intellectual and practical activity, from carpentry to golf, from sculpture to space travel, the true craftsman is the one who thoroughly understands his tools. And this applies to programmers too. A programmer who fully understands his language can tackle more complex tasks, and complete them more quickly and more satisfactorily than if he did not. In fact, a programmer's need for an understanding of his language is so great that it is almost impossible to persuade him to change to a new one. No matter what the deficiencies of his current language, he has learned to live with them; he has learned how to mitigate their effects by discipline and documentation, and even to take advantage of them in ways which would be impossible in a new and cleaner language which avoided the deficiency.

It therefore seems especially necessary in the design of a new programming language, intended to attract programmers away from their current high-level language, to pursue the goal of simplicity to an extreme, so that a programmer can readily learn and remember all its features, can select the best facility for each of his purposes, can fully understand the effects and consequences of each decision, and can then concentrate the major part of his intellectual effort on understanding his problem and his programs rather than his tool.

A high standard of simplicity is set by the machine or assembly code programming for a small computer. Such a machine has an extremely uniform structure—for example, a main store consisting of 2^m words numbered consecutively from zero up, a few registers, and a simple synchronous standard interface for communication and control of peripheral equipment. There is a small range of instructions, each of which has a uniform format; and the effect of each instruction is simple, affecting at most one register and one location of store or one peripheral. Even more important, this effect can be described and understood quite independently of every other instruction in the repertoire. And finally, the programmer has an immediate feedback on the compactness and efficiency of his code. Enthusiasts for high-level languages are often surprised at the complexity of the problems which have been tackled with such simple tools.

On larger modern computers, with complex instruction repertoires and even more complex operating systems, it is especially desirable that a high-level language design should aim at the simplicity and clear modular description of the best hardware designs. But the only widely used languages which approach this ideal are Fortran, LISP, and Algol 60, and a few languages developed from them. I fear that most more modern programming languages are getting even more complicated; and it is particularly irritating when their proponents claim that future hardware designs should be oriented toward the implementation of this complexity.

Discussion

The previous two sections have argued that the objective criteria for good language design may be summarized in five catch phrases: simplicity, security, fast translation, efficient object code, and readability. However desirable these may seem, many language designers have adopted alternative principles which belittle the importance of some or all of these criteria, perhaps those which their own languages have failed to achieve.

Simplicity. Some language designers have replaced the objective of simplicity by that of modularity, by which they mean that a programmer who cannot understand the whole of his language can get by with a limited understanding of only part of it. For programs that work as the programmer intended this may be feasible; but if his program does not work, and accidentally invokes some feature of the language which he does not know, he will get into serious trouble. If he is lucky, the implementation will detect his mistake, but he will not be able to understand the diagnostic message. Otherwise, he is even more helpless. If to the complexity of his language is added the complexity of its implementation, the complexity of its operating environment, and even the complexity of institutional standards for the use of the language, it is not surprising that when faced with a complex programming task, so many programmers are overwhelmed.

Another replacement of simplicity as an objective has been orthogonality of design. An example of orthogonality is the provision of complex integers, on the argument that we need reals and integers and complex reals, so why not complex integers? In the early days of hardware design, some very ingenious but arbitrary features turned up in order codes as a result of orthogonal combinations of the function bits of an instruction, on the grounds that some clever programmer would find a use for them—and some clever programmer always did. Hardware designers have now learned more sense; but language designers are clever programmers and have not.

The principles of modularity, or orthogonality, insofar as they contribute to overall simplicity, are an excellent means to an end; but as a substitute for simplicity they are very questionable. Since in practice they have proved to be a technically more difficult achievement than simplicity, it is foolish to adopt them as primary objectives.

Security. The objective of security has also been widely ignored; it is believed instead that coding errors should be removed by the programmer with the assistance of a so-called "checkout" compiler. But this approach has several practical disadvantages. For example, the debugging compiler and the standard compiler are often not equally reliable. Even if they are, it is impossible to guarantee that they will give the same results, especially on a subtly incorrect program; and when they do not, there is nothing to help the programmer find the mistake. For a large and complex program, the extra inefficiency of the debugging runs may be serious; and even on small programs, the cost of loading a large debugging system can be high. You should always pity the fate of the programmer whose task is so difficult that his program will not fit into the computer together with your sophisticated debugging package. Finally, it is absurd to make elaborate security checks on debugging runs, when no trust is put in the results, and then remove them in production runs, when an erroneous result could be expensive or disastrous. What would we think of a sailing enthusiast who wears his lifejacket when training on dry land, but takes it off as soon as he goes to sea? Fortunately, with a secure language the security is equally tight for production and for debugging.

Fast translation. In the early days of high-level languages, it was openly stated that speed of compilation was of minor importance, because programs would be compiled only once and then executed many times. After a while it was realized that the reverse was often true, that a program would be compiled frequently while it was being debugged. But instead of constructing a fast translator, language designers turned to independent compilation, which permits a programmer to avoid recompiling parts of his program which he has not changed since the last time. But this is a poor substitute for fast compilation, and has many practical disadvantages. Often it encourages or even forces a programmer to split a large program into modules which are too small to express properly the structure of his problem. It entails the use of wide interfaces and cumbersome and expensive parameter lists at inappropriate places. And even worse, it prevents the compiler from adequately checking the validity of these interfaces. It requires additional file space to store bulky intermediate code, in addition to source code which must, of course, never be thrown away. It discourages the programmer from making changes in his data structure or representation, since this would involve a heavy burden of recompilation. And, finally, the linkage editor is often cumbersome to invoke and expensive to execute. And it is all so unnecessary, if the compiler for a good language can work faster than the linkage editor anyway.

If you want to make a fast compiler even faster still, I can suggest three techniques which have all the benefits of independent compilation and none of the disadvantages.

(1) Prescan. The slowest part of a modern fast compiler is the lexical scan which inputs individual characters, assembles them into words or numbers, identifies basic symbols, removes spaces and separates the comments. If the source text of the program can be stored in a compact form in which this character handling does not have to be repeated, compilation time may be halved, with the added advantage that the original source program may still be listed (with suitably elegant indentation); and so the amount of file storage is reduced by a factor considerably greater than two. A similar technique was used by the PACT I assembler for the IBM 701.

(2) Precompile. This is a directive which can be given to the compiler after submitting *any* initial segment of a large program. It causes the compiler to make a complete dump of its workspace, including dictionary and object code, in a specified user file. When the user wishes to add to his program and run it, he directs the compiler to recover the dump and proceed. When his additions are adequately tested, a further precompile instruction can be given. If the programmer needs to modify a precompiled procedure, he can just redeclare it in the block containing his main program, and normal Algol-like scope rules will do the rest. An occasional complete recompilation will consolidate the changes after they have been fully tested. The technique of precompilation is effective only on single-pass compilers; it was successfully incorporated in the Elliott Algol programming system.

(3) Dump. This is an instruction which can be called by the user program during execution, and causes a complete binary dump of its code and workspace into a named user file. The dump can be restored and restarted at the instruction following the dump by an instruction to the operating system. If all necessary data input and initialization is carried out before the dump, the time spent on this as well as recompilation time can be saved. This provides a simple and effective way of achieving the Fortran effect of block data, and was successfully incorporated in the implementation of Elliott Algol.

The one remaining use of independent compilation is to link a high-level language with machine code. But even here independent compilation is the wrong technique, involving all the inefficiency of procedure call and all the complexity of parameter access at just the point where it hurts most. A far better solution is to allow machine code instructions to be inserted in-line within a high-level language program, as was done in Elliott Algol; or better, provide a macro facility for machine code, as in PL/360.

Independent compilation is a solution to yesterday's problems; today it has grown into a problem in its own right. The wise designer will prefer to avoid rather than solve such problems.

Efficient object code. There is another argument which is all too prevalent among enthusiastic language designers—that efficiency of object code is no longer important, that the speed and capacity of computers is increasing and their price is coming down, and the programming language designer might as well take advantage of this. This is an argument that would be quite acceptable if used to justify an efficiency loss of 10 or 20 percent, or even 30 and 40 percent. But all too frequently it is used to justify an efficiency loss of a factor of two, or 10, or even more; and worse, the overhead is not only in time taken but in space occupied by the running program. In no other engineering discipline would such avoidable overhead be tolerated, and it should not be in programming language design, for the following reasons:

- The magnitude of the tasks we wish computers to perform is growing faster than the cost-effectiveness of the hardware.
- However cheap and fast a computer is, it will be cheaper and faster to use it more efficiently.
- In the future we must hope that hardware designers will pay increasing attention to reliability rather than to speed and cost.
- The speed, cost, and reliability of peripheral equipment is not improving at the same rate as those of processors.

- If anyone is to be allowed to introduce inefficiency, it should be the user programmer, not the language designer. The user programmer can take advantage of this freedom to write better structured and clearer programs, and should not have to expend extra effort to obscure the structure and write less clear programs just to regain the efficiency which has been so arrogantly preempted by the language designer.

There is a widespread myth that a language designer can afford to ignore machine efficiency, because it can be regained, when required, by the use of a sophisticated optimizing compiler. This is false; there is nothing that the good engineer can afford to ignore. The only language which has been optimized with general success is Fortran, which was very specifically designed for that very purpose. But even in Fortran, optimization has grave disadvantages:

- An optimizing compiler is usually large, slow, unreliable, and late.
- Even with a reliable compiler, there is no guarantee that an optimized program will have the same results as a normally compiled one.
- A small change in an optimized program may switch off optimization with an unpredictable and unacceptable loss of efficiency.
- The most subtle danger is that optimization tends to remove from the programmer his fundamental control over and responsibility for the quality of his programs.

The solution to these problems is to produce a language for which a simple straightforward "non-pessimising" compiler will produce straightforward object programs of acceptable compactness and efficiency—similar to those produced by a resolutely non-clever (but also non-stupid) machine code programmer. Make sure that the language is sufficiently expressive that most other optimizations can be made in the language itself; and, finally, make the language so simple, clear, regular, and free from side effects that a general machine-independent optimizer can simply translate an inefficient program into a more efficient one with guaranteed identical effects, expressed in the same source language. The fact that the user can inspect the results of optimization in his own language mitigates many of the defects listed above.

Readability. The objective of readability by human beings has sometimes been denied in favor of readability by a machine; and sometimes it has even been denied in favor of abbreviation of writing, achieved by a wealth of default conventions and implicit assumptions. It is, of course, possible for a compiler or service program to expand the abbreviations, fill in the defaults, and make explicit the assumptions. But in practice, experience shows that it is very unlikely that the output of a computer will ever be more readable than its input, except in such trivial but important aspects as improved indentation. Since, in principle, programs should be read by others, or reread by their authors, *before* being submitted to the computer, it would be wise for the programming language designer to concentrate on the easier task of designing a readable language to begin with.

Comment conventions

If the purpose of a programming language is to assist in the documentation of programs, the design of a superb comment convention is obviously our most important concern. In low-level programming, the greater part of the space on each line is devoted to comment. A comment is always terminated by an end of line, and starts either in a fixed column, or with a special symbol allocated for this purpose:

LDA X [THIS IS A COMMENT

The introduction of free format into high-level languages prevents the use of the former method; but it is surprising that few languages have adopted the latter.

Algol 60 has two comment conventions. One is to enclose the text of a comment between the basic word *comment* and a semicolon:

comment this is a comment;

This has several disadvantages over the low-level comment convention:

(1) The basic word *comment* is too long. It occupies space which would be better occupied by the text of the comment and is particularly discouraging to short comments.

(2) The comment can appear only after a *begin* or a semicolon, although it would sometimes be more relevant elsewhere.

(3) If the semicolon at the end is accidentally omitted, the compiler will without warning ignore the next following statement.

(4) One cannot put program text within a comment, since a comment must not contain a semicolon.

The second comment convention of Algol 60 permits a comment between an *end* and the next following semicolon, *end* or *else*. This has proved most unfortunate, since omission of a semicolon has frequently led to ignoring the next following statement:

... *end* this is a mistake A[i] : = x;

The Fortran comment convention defines as comment the whole of a line containing a C in the first column:

C   THIS IS A COMMENT

Its main disadvantages are that it does not permit comments on the same line as the code to which they refer, and that it discourages the use of short comments. An unfortunate consequence is that a well-annotated Fortran program occupies many pages, even though the greater part of each page is blank. This in itself makes the program unnecessarily difficult to read and understand.

The comment convention of Cobol suffers from the same disadvantages as Fortran, since it insists that commentary should be a separate paragraph.

More recently designed languages have introduced special bracketing symbols (e.g., /* and */) to enclose comments, which can therefore be placed anywhere in the program text where they are relevant:

/*THIS IS A COMMENT */ .

But there still remains the awkward problem of omitting or mispunching one of the comment brackets. In some languages, this will cause omission of statements between two comments; in others it may cause the whole of the rest of the program to be ignored. Neither of these disasters are likely to occur in low-level programs, where the end of line terminates a comment.

Syntax

Another aspect of programming language design which is often considered trivial or arbitrary is its syntax. But this is also a mistake; the designer should select and observe the best possible syntactic framework for his language, for two important practical reasons:

(1) In a modern fast compiler, a significant time can be taken in assembling characters into meaningful symbols —identifiers, numbers, and basic words—and in checking the context-free structure of the program.

(2) When a program contains a syntactic error, it is important that the compiler should be able to pinpoint the error accurately, to diagnose its cause, recover from it, and continue checking the rest of the program. Recall the first American space probe to Venus, reportedly lost because Fortran cannot recognize a missing comma in a DO statement. In Fortran the statement

DO 17 I = 1 10

looks to the compiler like an assignment to a (probably undeclared) variable DO17I:

DO17I = 110

In low-level programming, the use of fixed field format neatly solves both problems. The position and length of each meaningful symbol is known, and it can be copied and compared as a whole without even examining the individual characters; and if one field contains an error, it can be immediately pinpointed, and checking can be resumed at the very next field.

Fortunately, free format techniques have been discovered which solve the problems nearly as neatly as fixed format. The use of a finite state machine to define the assembly of characters into symbols, and one of the more restrictive forms of context-free grammars (e.g., precedence or top-down or both) to define the structure of a program—these must be recommended to every language designer. It is certainly possible for a machine to analyze more complex grammars, but there is every indication that the human programmer will find greater difficulty, particularly if an error is present or even only suspected. If a compiler cannot diagnose the syntax of an individual statement until it reaches the end of the program, what hope has a poor human?

As an example of what happens when a language departs from the best known technology, that of context-free syntax, consider the case of the labeled END. This is a convention in PL/I whereby any identifier between an END and its semicolon automatically signals the end of the procedure with that name, and of any enclosed program structure, even if it has no END of its own. At first sight this is a harmless notational convenience which Peter Landin might call "syntactic sugar"; but in practice the consequences are disastrous. If the programmer accidentally omits an END anywhere in his program, it will automatically and without warning be inserted just before the next following labeled END, which is very unlikely to be where it was wanted. Landin's phrase for this would be "syntactic rat poison." Wise programmers have therefore learned to avoid the labeled END, which is a great pity, since if the labeled END was used merely to *check* the correctness of the nesting of statements, it would have been very useful, and permitted earlier and cleaner error recovery, as well as remaining within the disciplines of context-free languages. Here is a classic example of a language feature which combines danger to the programmer with difficulty for the implementor. It is all too easy to reconcile criteria of demerit.

Arithmetic expressions

A major feature of Fortran, which gives it the name FORmula TRANslator, is the introduction of the arithmetic expression. Algol 60 extends this idea by the introduction of a conditional expression. Why is this such an advance over assembly code? The traditional answer is that it appeals to the programmer's familiarity with mathematical notation. But this only leads to the more fundamental question, why is the notation of arithmetic expressions of such benefit to the mathematician? The reason seems to be quite subtle and fundamental. It embodies the principles of structuring, which underlie all our attempts to master a complex problem or control a complex situation by analyzing it into simpler subproblems with clean and narrow interfaces between them.

Consider an arithmetic expression of the form

$$E + F,$$

where E and F may themselves be simple or complex arithmetic expressions. (1) The meaning of this whole expression can be understood wholly in terms of an understanding of the meanings of E and F; (2) the purpose of each part consists solely in its contribution to the purpose of the whole; (3) the meaning of the two parts can be understood wholly independently of each other; (4) if E or F is itself an arithmetic expression, the same structuring principle can be applied to the analysis of the parts as is applied to the understanding of the whole; (5) the interface between the parts is clear, narrow, and well controlled—in this case just a single number. And, finally, (6) the separation of the parts and their relation to the whole is clearly apparent from their written form.

These seem to be six fundamental principles of structuring—transparency of meaning and purpose, independence of parts, recursive application, narrow interfaces, and manifestness of structure. In the case of arithmetic expressions, these six principles are reconciled and achieved together with very high efficiency of implementation. But the applicability of the arithmetic expression is seriously limited by the extreme narrowness of the interface. Often the programmer wishes to deal with much larger data structures—for example, vectors or matrices or lists; and languages such as APL and LISP have permitted the use of expressions with these structures as operands and results. This seems to be an excellent direction of advance in programming language design, particularly for special-purpose languages. But the advance is not purchased without some penalty in efficiency and programmer control. The very reason why arithmetic expressions can be evaluated with such efficiency is that the operands and results of each subexpression are sufficiently small to be held in a high-speed register, or stored and recovered from a mainstore location in a single instruction. When the operands are too large, and especially when they may be partially or wholly stored on backing store, it becomes much more efficient to use updating operations, since then the space occupied by one of the operands can be used to hold the result. It would therefore seem advisable to introduce special notations into a language to denote such operations as adding one matrix to another, appending one list to another, or making a new entry in a file. For example,

$$A. + B \quad \text{instead of } A := A + B \text{ if } A \text{ and } B \text{ are matrices}$$
$$L1.\text{append}(L2) \quad \text{if } L1 \text{ and } L2 \text{ are lists.}$$

Another efficiency problem which arises from the attempt of a language to provide large data structures and built-in operations on them is that the implementation must select a particular machine representation for the data, and use it uniformly, even in cases where other representations might be considerably more efficient. For example, the APL representation is fine for small matrices, but is very inappropriate or even impossible for large and sparse ones. The LISP representation of lists is very efficient for data held wholly in main store, but becomes inefficient when the lists are so long that they must be held on backing store, particularly disks and tapes. Often the efficiency of a representation depends on the relative frequency of various forms of operation, and therefore should be different in different programs, or even be changed from one phase of a program to another.

A solution to this problem is to design a general-purpose language which provides the programmer with the tools to design and implement his own representation for data and code the operations upon it. This is the main justification for the design of "extensible" languages, which so many designers have aimed at, with rather great lack of success. In order to succeed, it will be necessary to recognize the following:

(1) The need for an exceptionally efficient base language in order to define the extensions.

(2) The avoidance of any form of syntactic extension to the language. All that is needed is to extend the meaning of the existing operators of the language, an idea which was called "overloading" by McCarthy.

(3) The complete avoidance of any form of automatic type transfer, coercion, or default convention, other than those implemented as an extension by the programmer himself.

I fear that most designers of extensible languages have spurned the technical simplifications which make them feasible.

Program structures

However far the use of expressions and functional notations may be extended, a programmer will eventually require the capability of updating his environment. Sometimes this will be because he wants to perform input and output, sometimes because it is more efficient to store the results of a computation so that the stored value can be used rather than recomputed at a later time, and sometimes because it is a natural way of representing his problem—for example, in the case of discrete event simulation or the monitoring and control of some real world process.

Thus it is necessary to depart from the welcome simplicity of the mathematical expression, but to attempt to preserve as far as possible the structuring principles which it embodies. Fortunately, Algol 60 (in its compound, conditional, for, and procedure statements) has shown the way in which this can be done. The advantages of the use of these program structures is becoming apparent even to program-

mers using languages which do not provide the notations to express them.

The introduction of program structures into a language not only helps the programmer, but does not injure the efficiency of an implementation. Indeed, the avoidance of wild jumping will be of positive benefit on machines with slave stores or paging hardware; and if a compiler makes any attempt at optimization, the clear indication of the control structure of a program can only simplify this task.

There is one case where Algol 60 does not provide an appropriate structure, and that is when a selection must be made from more than two alternatives in accordance with some integer value. In this case, the programmer must declare a switch, specifying a list of labels, and then jump to the ith label in this list.

$$switch \quad SS = L1, L2, L3;$$
$$\ldots$$
$$go\ to\ SS[i];$$
$$L1: \quad Q_1; go\ to\ L;$$
$$L2: \quad Q_2; go\ to\ L;$$
$$L3: \quad Q_3;$$
$$L:$$

Unfortunately, introduction of the switch as a nameable entity is not only an extra complexity in the language and implementation, but gives plenty of scope for tricky programming and even trickier errors, particularly when jumping to some common continuation point on completion of the alternative action.

The first language designers to deal with the problem of the switch proposed to generalize it by providing the concept of the label array, into which the programmer could store label values. This has some peculiarly unpleasant consequences in addition to the disadvantages of the switch. First, it obscures the program, so that its control structure is not apparent from the form of the program, but can be determined only by a run-time trace. And second, the programmer is given the power to jump back into the middle of a block he has already exited, with unpredictable consequences unless a run-time check is inserted. In Algol 60 the scope rules make this error detectable at compile time.

The way to avoid all these problems is a very simple extension to the Algol 60 conditional notation, a construction which I have called the case construction. In this notation, the example of the switch shown above would take the form

$$case\ i\ of$$
$$\{Q_1,$$
$$Q_2,$$
$$Q_3\};$$

This was my first programming language invention, of which I am still most proud, since it appears to bear no trace of compensating disadvantage.

Variables

One of the most powerful and most dangerous aspects of machine code programming is that each individual instruction of the code can change the content of any register, any location of store, and alter the condition of any peripheral; it can even change its neighboring instructions or itself. Worse still, the identity of the location changed is not always apparent from the written form of the instruction; it cannot be determined until run time, when the values of base registers, index registers, and indirect addresses are known. This does not matter if the program is correct, but if there is the slightest error, even only in a single bit, there is no limit to the damage which may be done, and no limit to the difficulty of tracing the cause of the damage. In summary, the interface between every two consecutive instructions in a machine code program consists of the state of the entire machine— registers, mainstore, backing stores and all peripheral equipment.

In a high-level language, the programmer is deprived of the dangerous power to update his own program while it is running. Even more valuable, he has the power to split his machine into a number of separate variables, arrays, files, etc. When he wishes to update any of these, he must quote its name explicitly on the left of the assignment so that the identity of the part of the machine subject to change is immediately apparent. And, finally, a high-level language can guarantee that all variables are disjoint, and that updating any one of them cannot possibly have any effect on any other.

Unfortunately, many of these advantages are not maintained in the design of procedures and parameters in Algol 60 and other languages. But instead of mending these minor faults, many language designers have preferred to extend them throughout the whole language by introducing the concept of reference, pointer, or indirect address into the language as an assignable item of data. This immediately gives rise in a high-level language to one of the most notorious confusions of machine code, namely that between an address and its contents. Some languages attempt to solve this by even more confusing automatic coercion rules. Worse still, an indirect assignment through a pointer, just as in machine code, can update any store location whatsoever, and the damage is no longer confined to the variable explicitly named as the target of assignment. For example, in Algol 68, the assignment

$$x := y;$$

always changes x, but the assignment

$$x := y + 1;$$

if x is a reference variable, may change any other variable (of appropriate type) in the whole machine. One variable it can *never* change is x!. Unlike all other values (integers, strings, arrays, files, etc.) references have no meaning independent of a particular run of a program. They cannot be input as data, and they cannot be output as results. If either data or references to data have to be stored on files or backing stores, the problems are immense. And on many machines they have a surprising overhead on performance; for example, they will clog up instruction pipelines, data lookahead, slave stores, and even paging systems. References are like jumps, leading wildly from one part of a data structure to another. Their introduction into high-level languages has been a step backward from which we may never recover.

Block structure

In addition to the advantages of disjoint named variables, high-level languages provide the programmer with a powerful tool for achieving even greater security, namely the scope and locality associated with block structure. In Fortran or Algol 60, if the programmer needs a variable for the purposes of a particular part of his program, he can declare it locally to that part of the program. This enables the programmer to make manifest in the structure of his program the close association between the variable and the code which uses it; and he can be absolutely confident that no other part of the program, whether written by himself or another, can ever interfere with, or even look at, the variable without his written permission, i.e., unless he passes it as a parameter to a particular named procedure. The use of locality also greatly reduces the width of the interfaces between parts of the program; the fact that programmers no longer need to tell each other the names of their working variables is only one of the beneficial consequences.

Like all the best programming language features, the locality and scope rules of Algol 60 are not only of great assistance to the programmer in the decomposition of his task and the implementation of its subtasks; they also permit economy in the use of machine resources, for example main store. The fact that a group of variables is required for purposes local only to part of a program means that their values will usually be relevant only while that part of the program is being executed. It is therefore possible to reallocate to other purposes the storage assigned to these variables as soon as they are no longer required. Since the blocks of a program in Algol 60 are always completed in the exact reverse of the order in which they were entered, the dynamic reallocation of storage can be accomplished by stack techniques, with small overhead of time and space, or none at all in the case of blocks which are not procedure bodies, for which the administration can be done at compile time. Finally, the programmer is encouraged to declare at the same time those variables which will be used together, and these will be allocated in contiguous locations, which will increase the efficiency of slave storage and paging techniques.

It is worthy of note that the economy of dynamic reallocation is achieved without any risk that the programmer will accidentally refer to a variable that has been reallocated, and this is guaranteed by a compile-time and not a run-time check. All these advantages are achieved in Algol 60 by the close correspondence between the statically visible scope of a variable in a source program and the dynamic lifetime of its storage when the program is run. A language designer should therefore be extremely reluctant to break this correspondence, which can easily be done, for example, by the introduction of references which may point to variables of an exited block. The rules of Algol 68, designed to detect such so-called "dangling references" at compile time, are both complicated and ineffective; and PL/I does not bother at all.

Procedures and parameters

According to current theories of structured programming, every large-scale programming project involves the design, use, and implementation of a special-purpose programming language, with its own data concepts and primitive operations, specifically oriented to that particular project. The procedure and parameter are the major tool provided for this purpose by high-level languages since Fortran. In itself, this affords all the major advantages claimed for extensible languages. Furthermore, in its implementation as a closed subroutine, the procedure can achieve very great economies of storage at run time. For these reasons, the language designer should give the greatest attention to this feature of his language. Procedure calls and parameter passing should produce very compact code. Lengthy preludes and postludes must be avoided. The effect of the procedure on its parameters should be clearly manifest from its syntactic form, and should be simple to understand and resistant to error. And, finally, since the procedure interface is so often the interface between major parts of a program, the correctness of its use should be subjected to the most rigorous compile-time check.

The chief defects of the Fortran parameter mechanism are:

(1) It fails to give a notational distinction at the call side between parameters that convey values into a procedure, that convey values out of a procedure, and that do both. This negates many of the advantages which the assignment statement has over machine code programming.

(2) The shibboleth of independent compilation prohibits compile-time checks on parameter passing, just where interface errors are most likely and most disastrous and most difficult to debug.

(3) The ability to define side effects of function calls negates many of the advantages of arithmetic expressions.

At least Fortran permits efficient implementation, unless a misguided but all too frequent attempt is made to permit a mixture of languages across the procedure interface. A subroutine that does not know whether it is being called from Algol or from Fortran has a hard life.

Algol 60 perpetuates all these disadvantages, but not the advantage. The difficulty of compile-time parameter checking is due to the absence of parameter specifications. Even if an implementation insists on full specification (and most do), the programmer has no way of specifying the parameters of a formal procedure parameter. This is one of the excuses for the inefficiency of many Algol implementations. The one great advance of Algol 60 is the value parameter, which is immeasurably superior to the dummy parameter of Fortran and PL/I. What a shame that the name parameter is the default!

But perhaps the most subtle defect of the Algol 60 parameter is that the user is permitted to pass the same variable twice as an actual parameter corresponding to two distinct formal parameters. This immediately violates the principle of disjointness and can lead to many curious, unexpected effects. For example, if a procedure

$$\text{matrix multiply } (A, B, C)$$

is intended to have the effect

$$A := B \times C,$$

it would seem reasonable to square A by

$$\text{matrix multiply } (A, A, A).$$

This error is prohibited in standard Fortran, but few programmers realize it, and it is rarely enforced by compile-time or run-time check. No wonder the procedure interface is the one on which run-time debugging aids have to concentrate.

Types

Among the most trivial but tiresome errors of low-level programming are type errors—for example, using a fixed-point operation to add floating-point numbers, using an address as an integer or vice versa, or forgetting the position of a field in a data structure. The effects of such errors, although fully explicable in terms of bit patterns and machine operations, are so totally unrelated to the concepts in terms of which the programmer is thinking that the detection and correction of such errors can be exceptionally tedious. The trouble is that the hardware of the computer is far too tolerant and forgiving. It is willing to accept almost any sequence of instructions and make sense of them at its own level. That is the secret of the power, flexibility, simplicity, and even reliability of computer hardware, and should therefore be cherished.

But it is also one of the main reasons why we turn to high-level languages, which can eliminate the risk of such error by a compile-time check. The programmer declares the type of each variable, and the compiler can work out the type of each result; it therefore always knows what type of machine code instruction to generate. In cases where there is no meaningful operation (for example, the addition of an integer and a Boolean), the compiler can inform the programmer of his mistake, which is far better than having to chase its curious consequences after the program has run.

However, not all language designers would agree. Some languages, by complex rules of automatic type transfers and coercions, prefer the dangerous tolerance of machine code, but with the following added disadvantages:

(1) The result will often be "nearly" right, so that the programmer has less warning of his error.

(2) The inefficiency of the conversion is often a shock.

(3) The language is much complicated by the rules.

(4) The introduction of genuine language extensibility is made much more difficult.

Apart from the elimination of risk of error, the concept of type is of vital assistance in the design and documentation phases of program development. The design of abstract and concrete data structures is one of the first tools for refining our understanding of problems, and for defining the common interfaces between the parts of a large program. The declaration of the name and structure or range of values of each variable is a most important aspect of clear programming, and the formal description of the relationship of each variable to other program variables is a most important part of its annotation. Finally, an informal description of the purpose of each variable and its manner of use is a most important part of program documentation. In fact, I believe a language should enable the programmer to declare the units in which his numbers are expressed, so that a compiler can check that he is not confusing radians and degrees, adding heights to weights, or comparing meters with yards.

Again not all language designers would agree. Many languages do not require the programmer to declare his variables at all. Instead they define complex default rules which the compiler must apply to undeclared variables. But this can only encourage sloppy program design and documentation, and nullify many of the advantages of block structure and type checking; the default rules soon get so complex that they are very likely to give results not expected by the programmer, and as ludicrously or subtly inappropriate to his intentions as a machine code program which contains a type error.

Of course, wise programmers have learned that it is worthwhile to expend the effort to avoid these dangers. They eagerly scan the compiler listings to ensure that every variable has been declared, and that all the characteristics assigned to it by default are acceptable. What a pity that the designers of these languages take such trouble to give such trouble to their users and themselves.

Language feature design

This paper has given many practical hints on how *not* to design a programming language. It has even suggested that many recent languages have followed these hints. But there are very few positive hints on what to put into your next language design. Nearly everything I have ever published is full of positive and practical suggestions for programming language features, notations, and implementation methods; furthermore, for the last 10 years, I have tried to pursue the same objectives in language design that I have expounded here, and I have tried to make my proposals as convincing as I could. And yet I have never designed a programming language—only programming language features. It is my belief that these two design activities should be more clearly separated in the future.

(1) The designer of a new feature should concentrate on one feature at a time. If necessary, he should design it in the context of some well known programming language which he likes. He should make sure that his feature mitigates some disadvantage or remedies some incompleteness of the language, without compromising any of its existing merits. He should show how the feature can be simply and efficiently implemented. He should write a section of a user manual, explaining clearly with examples how the feature is intended to be used. He should check carefully that there are not traps lurking for the unwary user, which cannot be checked at compile time. He should write a number of example programs, evaluating all the consequences of using the feature, in comparison with its many alternatives. And, finally, if a simple proof rule can be given for the feature, this would be the final accolade.

(2) The language designer should be familiar with many alternative features designed by others, and should have excellent judgment in choosing the best and rejecting any that are mutually inconsistent. He must be capable of reconciling, by good engineering design, any remaining minor inconsistencies or overlaps between separately designed features. He must have a clear idea of the scope and purpose and range of application of his new language, and how far it should go in size and complexity. He should have the resources to implement the language on one or more machines, to write user manuals, introductory texts, advanced texts; he should construct auxiliary programming aids and library programs and procedures; and, finally, he should have the political will and resources to sell and distribute the language to its intended range of customers. One thing he should not do is to include untried ideas of his own. His task is consolidation, not innovation.

Conclusion

A final hint: listen carefully to what language users *say* they want, until you have an understanding of what they *really* want. Then find some way of achieving the latter at a small fraction of the cost of the former. This is the test of success in language design, and of progress in programming methodology. Perhaps these two are the same subject anyway. ∎

Appendix: Annotated reading list

"Report on the Algorithmic Language ALGOL 60," ed. P. Naur, *Comm. ACM*, Vol. 3, 1960, pp. 299-314. The more I ponder the principles of language design and the techniques which put them into practice, the more is my amazement and admiration of Algol 60. Here is a language so far ahead of its time, that it was not only an improvement on its predecessors, but also on nearly all its successors.

Of particular interest are its introduction of all the main program structuring concepts, the simplicity and clarity of its description, rarely equalled and never surpassed. Consider especially the avoidance of abbreviation in the syntax names and equations, and the inclusion of examples in every section.

D. E. Knuth, "The Remaining Troublespots in ALGOL 60," *Comm. ACM*, Vol. 10, No. 10, Oct. 1967, pp. 611-618. Most of these troublespots have been eliminated in the widely used subsets of the language. When you can design a language with so few troublespots, you can be proud. The real remaining troublespot is the declining quality of implementations.

N. Wirth and C. A. R. Hoare, "A Contribution to the Development of ALGOL," *Comm. ACM*, Vol. 9, No. 6, June 1966, pp. 413-432. This language is widely known as Algol W. It remedies many of the defects of Algol 60 and includes many of the good features of Fortran IV and LISP. Its introduction of references avoids most of the defects described above under "Block structure." It has been extremely well implemented on the IBM 360 and has a small and scattered band of devoted followers.

N. Wirth, "PL/360," *J. ACM*, Vol. 15, No. 1, Jan. 1968. This introduces the benefits of program structures to low-level programming for the IBM/360. It was hastily designed and implemented as a tool for implementing Algol W; it excited more interest than Algol W and has been widely imitated on other machines.

N. Wirth, "The Programming Language PASCAL," *Acta Informatica*, Vol. 1, No. 1, 1971, pp. 35-63. Designed to combine the machine-independence of Algol W with the efficiency and control of PL/360. New features are the simple but powerful and efficient type-definition capabilities, including sets and a very clean treatment of files. When used to write its own translator, it achieves a remarkable combination of clarity of structure and detail together with high efficiency in producing good object code.

O-J. Dahl, E. W. Dijkstra, and C. A. R. Hoare, *Structured Programming*, Academic Press, New York, 1972. Expounds a systematic approach to the design and development and documentation of computer programs. The last section is an excellent introduction to SIMULA 67 and the ideas which underlie it.

J. McCarthy, "Recursive Functions of Symbolic Expressions and Their Computation by Machine, Part 1," *Comm. ACM*, Vol. 3, No. 4, Apr. 1960. Describes a beautifully simple and powerful, fully functional language for symbol manipulation. Introduces the scan-mark garbage collection technique, which makes such languages feasible. LISP has some good interactive implementations, widely used in artificial intelligence projects. It has also been extended in many ways, some good and some bad, some local and some short-lived.

"ASA Standard FORTRAN," *Comm. ACM*, Vol. 7, No. 10, Oct. 1964. This language had the right objectives. It introduces the array, the arithmetic expression, and the procedure. The parameter mechanism is very efficient and potentially secure. It has some very efficient implementations for numerical applications. When used outside this field, it is little more helpful or machine-independent than assembly code, and can be remarkably inefficient. Its input/output is cumbersome, prone to error, and surprisingly inefficient. The standardizers have maintained the horrors of early implementations (the equivalence algorithm, second-level definition), and have resolutely set their face against the advance of language design technology, thereby saving it from many later horrors.

"ASA Standard COBOL," *Codasyl COBOL J. Development*, 1968 (National Bureau of Standards Handbook 106). Describes a language suitable for simple applications in business data processing. It contains good data structuring capability, but poor facilities for abstraction. It aimed at readability, but unfortunately achieved only prolixity; it aimed to provide a complete programming tool, in a way few languages have since. It is poor for variable format processing. The primacy of the character data item makes it rather inefficient on modern machines; and the methods provided to regain efficiency (e.g., SYNCHRONIZED) often introduce machine-dependency and insecurity.

Acknowledgments

The form of this paper owes much to the kind suggestions of Don Knuth.

The work on this paper was supported in part by the National Science Foundation under grant number GJ 36473X and by ARPA Research Contract DAHC 15-73-C-0435.

SECTION 2

THE ALGOL FAMILY

REPORT ON THE ALGORITHMIC
LANGUAGE ALGOL 60 BY P. NAUR ET AL.

THE REMAINING TROUBLESPOTS IN
ALGOL 60 BY D. E. KNUTH

A TUTORIAL ON ALGOL 68 BY
A. S. TANENBAUM

AMBIGUITIES AND INSECURITIES IN
PASCAL BY J. WELSH, W. SNEERINGER, AND
C. A. R. HOARE

AN ASSESSMENT OF THE PROGRAMMING
LANGUAGE PASCAL BY N. WIRTH

SOME IMPROVEMENTS OF ISO-PASCAL
BY J. F. H. WINKLER

AN INTRODUCTION TO MODULA-2
BY R. J. PAUL

AMBIGUITIES AND INSECURITIES IN
MODULA-2 BY D. SPECTOR

INTRODUCTION

THE ALGOL FAMILY

The first paper in this chapter is a *classic* paper in the field of programming languages and it should be read by all computer professionals who regard programming languages as their field of specialization. Why, you ask, is it so important if ALGOL60 is rarely used by the computing community? First of all, this statement is not true as ALGOL60 was used extensively throughout western Europe. But reading the document is also important for many other reasons. First of all, this paper has become a model for the way a programming language should be presented. Secondly, it was the paper which introduced Backus-Naur Form (BNF) to the world. Also, ALGOL60 introduced many concepts in programming languages for the first time. And many of those concepts are still in use today. For example if one reads the *Rationale for the Design of Ada*, (ACM Sigplan Notices, July 1979), one sees credit given to ALGOL60 for several of its major features.

As you read the ALGOL60 report take note of the difference between the reference language and the publication language. Note the description of the BNF formalism as it appears for the first time. As one reads the report, it is useful to keep in mind a language similar to ALGOL60 which you know well, such as Pascal. Think about what data types are included and which ones are missing. Note the introduction of the **if-then-else** and the statements for loop control such as the **for**-statement. Notice the complete definition of the **for**-statement and compare it to definitions of the same construct in other languages.

On the other hand, notice those things in ALGOL60 which are no longer included in modern programming languages such as **own** variables and switches. Why are they no longer there? Also remember that ALGOL60 included recursive procedures. Can you find where that is mentioned in the report? After reading this article we can still marvel at the step forward that this committee made in language development so early in the history of computers.

But no language definition is entirely free of errors. The second paper in this chapter, by Donald E. Knuth, was written to help identify the *last* remaining trouble spots in ALGOL60. One major problem was the question of side-effects in the order of evaluation of expressions. Knuth points out that if side-effects are to be disallowed then several areas of expression evaluation must be made more precise. Later language definitions have eliminated side-effects in expressions, in part to avoid this need for excessive definition and for the resulting clarity in the semantics of the language. Another area worth studying is the call-by-name parameter mechanism which was introduced for the first time in ALGOL60. Knuth points out a simple program which cannot be implemented because this mechanism is used. Call-by-name has not been incorporated in modern programming languages and we conclude that the criticisms of this method are sufficient to outweigh its advantages. Finally, as so many subsequent language designs followed the ALGOL60 tradition (i.e. they were called ALGOL-like), they had to answer the ambiguities which Knuth points out. Thus it is good to keep them in mind as you read the reports of other languages in this section.

The next paper in this chapter is entitled "A Tutorial on ALGOL68." ALGOL68 is the *official* successor language to ALGOL60. After its introduction it quickly acquired a reputation as being obscure and unintelligible. This was largely due to the fact that the developers introduced a great deal of new terminology. Their purpose was to avoid terms which had vague or conflicting meanings and instead to introduce new terms which were clearly defined. Unfortunately this well-meaning objective subverted their attempt to get the rest of us to read and admire the product of their creation. Nevertheless the language developed a set of adherents and in 1975 a Revised Report was published. This was followed by more readable introductions to the language. The paper included here discusses ALGOL68 as it is defined in its revised version. More importantly it makes a special effort to avoid the use of the new terminology wherever it can be avoided. But before beginning to read this paper one must make a commitment to oneself to remain dedicated to the task at hand. I personally have found that several casual readings have helped, culminated by a complete reading later on.

ALGOL68 has introduced many new and interesting features. Moreover it gives us a chance to see where the design goals of generality and orthogonality can lead. There are some features which ALGOL68 has in common with its predecessors. It is block structured and uses static scoping. The procedure is the major form of abstraction. Its built-in data types, called modes, include the usual integer, real, boolean and char, but also included are string, complex, bits, bytes, semaphores, formats and files. In fact, ALGOL68 does a lot with modes which even Pascal does not do.

In reading through the paper notice the way arrays can be handled and the form of the control and conditional statements. Coercions or the conversion of one type into another is an area where ALGOL68 has a carefully worked out solution. Another is the determination of type equivalence (it is done structurally). It has been pointed out that the Pascal report did not specify the method for determining type equivalence, but left it to the compiler writers. Finally, one should note that the language has provided for concurrent execution of processes and provides a mechanism for their synchronization. In conclusion, ALGOL68 remains an interesting and worthwhile object of study.

The next three papers in this chapter are concerned with Pascal. Most of my readers will be familiar with Pascal as it has become the standard language for introductory computer science courses. For those readers who are unfamiliar with Pascal there are many primers which are more than adequate for learning the language. The first paper on Pascal was written by three people who are strong advocates of the language. But in part because of their fondness for the language, they have been motivated, like Knuth was for ALGOL60, to write about the language's weaknesses. Though several other papers critical of Pascal

have appeared, this one provides a balanced and reasonable presentation. One major point in their discussion is the lack of definition of type equivalence. The authors give two possible solutions, termed *name* and *structural equivalence*. Other points include the difficulty of one pass compilation and problems with variant records and procedure parameters. Many of these objections have been cleared up in the new ISO standard version of Pascal, and the paper appearing here was an inspiration to the members of that committee. The second paper on Pascal deserves to be included here because it is by the language's designer, Niklaus Wirth. Here he surveys from his own point of view the strengths and weaknesses, the strong points, and the mistakes of the language as he sees them. The two points he raises are the inappropriate definition of files and the trap-door to strong typing using variant records. In the case of file structures, Wirth provides a revised definition. Perhaps the author of the language has not covered the major deficiencies? The third paper on Pascal discusses the ISO-Pascal standard. Many fine examples are shown that point to inconsistencies/inadequacies in the original drafts that have since been corrected.

The last two articles are on Wirth's successor to Pascal, Modula-2. The first article surveys the language and compares it to Pascal. Be sure to note how Wirth has dealt with the problems mentioned earlier. The second article follows a tradition, namely a paper whose goal is to isolate problems in a language. Will Modula-2 become Pascal's successor?

REPORT ON THE ALGORITHMIC LANGUAGE ALGOL 60*

P. NAUER, EDITOR

Dedicated to the Memory of WILLIAM TURANSKI

SUMMARY

The report gives a complete defining description of the international algorithmic language ALGOL 60. This is a language suitable for expressing a large class of numerical processes in a form sufficiently concise for direct automatic translation into the language of programmed automatic computers.

The introduction contains an account of the preparatory work leading up to the final conference, where the language was defined. In addition, the notions, reference language, publication language and hardware representations are explained.

In the first chapter, a survey of the basic constituents and features of the language is given, and the formal notation, by which the syntactic structure is defined, is explained.

The second chapter lists all the basic symbols, and the syntactic units known as identifiers, numbers and strings are defined. Further, some important notions such as quantity and value are defined.

The third chapter explains the rules for forming expressions and the meaning of these expressions. Three different types of expressions exist: arithmetic, Boolean (logical) and designational.

The fourth chapter describes the operational units of the language, known as statements. The basic statements are: assignment statements (evaluation of a formula), go to statements (explicit break of the sequence of execution of statements), dummy statements, and procedure statements (call for execution of a closed process, defined by a procedure declaration). The formation of more complex structures, having statement character, is explained. These include: conditional statements, for statements, compound statements, and blocks.

In the fifth chapter, the units known as declarations, serving for defining permanent properties of the units entering into a process described in the language, are defined.

The report ends with two detailed examples of the use of the language and an alphabetic index of definitions.

CONTENTS

*Reprinted from *Comm ACM*, 6, 1, 1963, 1–17, copyright 1963.

INTRODUCTION

Background

After the publication of a preliminary report on the algorithmic language ALGOL,[1,2] as prepared at a conference in Zürich in 1958, much interest in the ALGOL language developed.

As a result of an informal meeting held at Mainz in November 1958, about forty interested persons from several European countries held an ALGOL implementation conference in Copenhagen in February 1959. A "hardware group" was formed for working cooperatively right down to the level of the paper tape code. This conference also led to the publication by Regnecentralen, Copenhagen, of an *ALGOL Bulletin*, edited by Peter Naur, which served as a forum for further discussion. During the June 1959 ICIP Conference in Paris several meetings, both formal and informal ones, were held. These meetings revealed some misunderstandings as to the intent of the group which was primarily responsible for the formulation of the language, but at the same time made it clear that there exists a wide appreciation of the effort involved. As a result of the discussions it was decided to hold an international meeting in January 1960 for improving the ALGOL language and preparing a final report. At a European ALGOL Conference in Paris in November 1959 which was attended by about fifty people, seven European representatives were selected to attend the January 1960 Conference, and they represent the following organizations: Association Française de Calcul, British Computer Society, Gesellschaft für Angewandte Mathematik und Mechanik, and Nederlands Rekenmachine Genootschap. The seven representatives held a final preparatory meeting at Mainz in December 1959.

Meanwhile, in the United States, anyone who wished to suggest changes or corrections to ALGOL was requested to send his comments to the *Communications of the ACM*, where they were published. These comments then became the basis of consideration for changes in the ALGOL language. Both the SHARE and USE organizations established ALGOL working groups, and both organizations were represented on the ACM Committee on Programming Languages. The ACM Committee met in Washington in November 1959 and considered all comments on ALGOL that had been sent to the ACM *Communications*. Also, seven representatives were selected to attend the January 1960 international conference. These seven representatives held a final preparatory meeting in Boston in December 1959.

January 1960 Conference

The thirteen representatives,[3] from Denmark, England, France, Germany, Holland, Switzerland, and the United States, conferred in Paris from January 11 to 16, 1960.

Prior to this meeting a completely new draft report was worked out from the preliminary report and the recommendations of the preparatory meetings by Peter Naur and the conference adopted this new form as the basis for its report. The Conference then proceeded to work for agreement on each item of the report. The present report represents the union of the Committee's concepts and the intersection of its agreements.

April 1962 Conference [Edited by M. Woodger]

A meeting of some of the authors of ALGOL 60 was held on April 2–3, 1962 in Rome, Italy, through the facilities and courtesy of the International Computation Centre. The following were present:

Authors	Advisers	Observer
F. L. Bauer	M. Paul	W. L. van der Poel
J. Green	R. Franciotti	(Chairman, IFIP
C. Katz	P. Z. Ingerman	TC 2.1 Working
R. Kogon		Group ALGOL)
(representing J. W. Backus)		
P. Naur		
K. Samelson	G. Seegmüller	
J. H. Wegstein	R. E. Utman	
A. van Wijngaarden		
M. Woodger	P. Landin	

The purpose of the meeting was to correct known errors in, attempt to eliminate apparent ambiguities in, and otherwise clarify the ALGOL 60 Report. Extensions to the language were not considered at the meeting. Various proposals for correction and clarification that were submitted by interested parties in response to the Questionnaire in *ALGOL Bulletin* No. 14 were used as a guide.

This report* constitutes a supplement to the ALGOL 60 Report which should resolve a number of difficulties therein. Not all of the questions raised concerning the original report could be resolved. Rather than risk hastily drawn conclusions on a number of subtle points, which might create new ambiguities, the committee decided to report only those points which they unanimously felt could be stated in clear and unambiguous fashion.

Questions concerned with the following areas are left for further consideration by Working Group 2.1 of IFIP, in the expectation that current work on advanced pro-

---

* [EDITOR'S NOTE. The present edition follows the text which was approved by the Council of IFIP. Although it is not clear from the Introduction, the present version is the original report of the January 1960 conference modified according to the agreements reached during the April 1962 conference. Thus the report mentioned here is incorporated in the present version. The modifications touch the original report in the following sections: Changes of text: 1 with footnote; 2.1 footnote; 2.3; 2.7; 3.3.3; 3.3.4.2; 4.1.3; 4.2.3; 4.2.4; 4.3.4; 4.7.3; 4.7.3.1; 4.7.3.3; 4.7.5.1; 4.7.5.4; 4.7.6; 5; 5.3.3; 5.3.5; 5.4.3; 5.4.4; 5.4.5. Changes of syntax: 3.4.1; 4.1.1; 4.2.1; 4.5.1.]

[1] Preliminary report—International Algebraic Language. *Comm. ACM* 1, 12 (1958), 8.

[2] Report on the Algorithmic Language ALGOL by the ACM Committee on Programming Languages and the GAMM Committee on Programming, edited by A. J. Perlis and K. Samelson. *Num. Math. 1* (1959), 41–60.

[3] William Turanski of the American group was killed by an automobile just prior to the January 1960 Conference.

gramming languages will lead to better resolution:
1. Side effects of functions
2. The call by name concept
3. **own:** static or dynamic
4. For statement: static or dynamic
5. Conflict between specification and declaration

The authors of the ALGOL 60 Report present at the Rome Conference, being aware of the formation of a Working Group on ALGOL by IFIP, accepted that any collective responsibility which they might have with respect to the development, specification and refinement of the ALGOL language will from now on be transferred to that body.

This report has been reviewed by IFIP TC 2 on Programming Languages in August 1962 and has been approved by the Council of the International Federation for Information Processing.

As with the preliminary ALGOL report, three different levels of language are recognized, namely a Reference Language, a Publication Language and several Hardware Representations.

REFERENCE LANGUAGE

1. It is the working language of the committee.
2. It is the defining language.
3. The characters are determined by ease of mutual understanding and not by any computer limitations, coders notation, or pure mathematical notation.
4. It is the basic reference and guide for compiler builders.
5. It is the guide for all hardware representations.
6. It is the guide for transliterating from publication language to any locally appropriate hardware representations.

7. The main publications of the ALGOL language itself will use the reference representation.

PUBLICATION LANGUAGE

1. The publication language admits variations of the reference language according to usage of printing and handwriting (e.g., subscripts, spaces, exponents, Greek letters).
2. It is used for stating and communicating processes.
3. The characters to be used may be different in different countries, but univocal correspondence with reference representation must be secured.

HARDWARE REPRESENTATIONS

1. Each one of these is a condensation of the reference language enforced by the limited number of characters on standard input equipment.
2. Each one of these uses the character set of a particular computer and is the language accepted by a translator for that computer.
3. Each one of these must be accompanied by a special set of rules for transliterating from Publication or Reference language.

For transliteration between the reference language and a language suitable for publications, among others, the following rules are recommended.

Reference Language	Publication Language
Subscript bracket [ ]	Lowering of the line between the brackets and removal of the brackets
Exponentiation ↑	Raising of the exponent
Parentheses ( )	Any form of parentheses, brackets, braces
Basis of ten $_{10}$	Raising of the ten and of the following integral number, inserting of the intended multiplication sign

DESCRIPTION OF THE REFERENCE LANGUAGE

> Was sich überhaupt sagen lässt, lässt
> sich klar sagen; und wovon man nicht
> reden kann, darüber muss man schweigen.
> LUDWIG WITTGENSTEIN.

1. Structure of the Language

As stated in the introduction, the algorithmic language has three different kinds of representations—reference, hardware, and publication—and the development described in the sequel is in terms of the reference representation. This means that all objects defined within the language are represented by a given set of symbols—and it is only in the choice of symbols that the other two representations may differ. Structure and content must be the same for all representations.

The purpose of the algorithmic language is to describe computational processes. The basic concept used for the description of calculating rules is the well-known arithmetic expression containing as constituents numbers, variables, and functions. From such expressions are compounded, by applying rules of arithmetic composition, self-contained units of the language—explicit formulae—called assignment statements.

To show the flow of computational processes, certain nonarithmetic statements and statement clauses are added which may describe, e.g., alternatives, or iterative repetitions of computing statements. Since it is necessary for the function of these statements that one statement refer to another, statements may be provided with labels. A sequence of statements may be enclosed between the statement brackets **begin** and **end** to form a compound statement.

Statements are supported by declarations which are not themselves computing instructions but inform the translator of the existence and certain properties of objects appearing in statements, such as the class of numbers taken on as values by a variable, the dimension of an array of numbers, or even the set of rules defining a function. A sequence of declarations followed by a sequence of statements and enclosed between **begin** and **end** constitutes a block. Every declaration appears in a block in this way and is valid only for that block.

A program is a block or compound statement which is not contained within another statement and which makes no use of other statements not contained within it.

In the sequel the syntax and semantics of the language will be given.[4]

1.1. FORMALISM FOR SYNTACTIC DESCRIPTION

The syntax will be described with the aid of metalinguistic formulae.[5] Their interpretation is best explained by an example

$$\langle ab \rangle ::= (\mid [\mid \langle ab \rangle (\mid \langle ab \rangle \langle d \rangle$$

Sequences of characters enclosed in the brackets ⟨ ⟩ represent metalinguistic variables whose values are sequences of symbols. The marks ::= and | (the latter with the meaning of **or**) are metalinguistic connectives. Any mark in a formula, which is not a variable or a connective, denotes itself (or the class of marks which are similar to it). Juxtaposition of marks and/or variables in a formula signifies juxtaposition of the sequences denoted. Thus the formula above gives a recursive rule for the formation of values of the variable ⟨ab⟩. It indicates that ⟨ab⟩ may have the value (or [or that given some legitimate value of ⟨ab⟩, another may be formed by following it with the character (or by following it with some value of the variable ⟨d⟩. If the values of ⟨d⟩ are the decimal digits, some values of ⟨ab⟩ are:

$$[((((1(37(
$$(12345(
$$(((
$$[86$$

In order to facilitate the study, the symbols used for distinguishing the metalinguistic variables (i.e. the sequences of characters appearing within the brackets ⟨ ⟩ as ab in the above example) have been chosen to be words describing approximately the nature of the corresponding variable. Where words which have appeared in this manner are used elsewhere in the text they will refer to the corresponding syntactic definition. In addition some formulae have been given in more than one place.

Definition:

$$\langle empty \rangle ::=$$
(i.e. the null string of symbols).

---

[4] Whenever the precision of arithmetic is stated as being in general not specified, or the outcome of a certain process is left undefined or said to be undefined, this is to be interpreted in the sense that a program only fully defines a computational process if the accompanying information specifies the precision assumed, the kind of arithmetic assumed, and the course of action to be taken in all such cases as may occur during the execution of the computation.

[5] Cf. J. W. Backus, The syntax and semantics of the proposed international algebraic language of the Zürich ACM-GAMM conference. Proc. Internat. Conf. Inf. Proc., UNESCO, Paris, June 1959.

2. Basic Symbols, Identifiers, Numbers, and Strings. Basic Concepts.

The reference language is built up from the following basic symbols:

$$\langle basic\ symbol \rangle ::= \langle letter \rangle \mid \langle digit \rangle \mid \langle logical\ value \rangle \mid \langle delimiter \rangle$$

2.1. LETTERS

$$\langle letter \rangle ::= a \mid b \mid c \mid d \mid e \mid f \mid g \mid h \mid i \mid j \mid k \mid l \mid m \mid n \mid o \mid p \mid q \mid r \mid s \mid t \mid u \mid v \mid w \mid x \mid y \mid z \mid$$
$$A \mid B \mid C \mid D \mid E \mid F \mid G \mid H \mid I \mid J \mid K \mid L \mid M \mid N \mid O \mid P \mid Q \mid R \mid S \mid T \mid U \mid V \mid W \mid X \mid Y \mid Z$$

This alphabet may arbitrarily be restricted, or extended with any other distinctive character (i.e. character not coinciding with any digit, logical value or delimiter).

Letters do not have individual meaning. They are used for forming identifiers and strings[6] (cf. sections 2.4. Identifiers, 2.6. Strings).

2.2.1. DIGITS

$$\langle digit \rangle ::= 0 \mid 1 \mid 2 \mid 3 \mid 4 \mid 5 \mid 6 \mid 7 \mid 8 \mid 9$$

Digits are used for forming numbers, identifiers, and strings.

2.2.2. LOGICAL VALUES

$$\langle logical\ value \rangle ::= \textbf{true} \mid \textbf{false}$$

The logical values have a fixed obvious meaning.

2.3. DELIMITERS

$$\langle delimiter \rangle ::= \langle operator \rangle \mid \langle separator \rangle \mid \langle bracket \rangle \mid \langle declarator \rangle \mid \langle specificator \rangle$$
$$\langle operator \rangle ::= \langle arithmetic\ operator \rangle \mid \langle relational\ operator \rangle \mid \langle logical\ operator \rangle \mid \langle sequential\ operator \rangle$$
$$\langle arithmetic\ operator \rangle ::= + \mid - \mid \times \mid / \mid \div \mid \uparrow$$
$$\langle relational\ operator \rangle ::= < \mid \leq \mid = \mid \geq \mid > \mid \neq$$
$$\langle logical\ operator \rangle ::= \equiv \mid \supset \mid \vee \mid \wedge \mid \neg$$
$$\langle sequential\ operator \rangle ::= \textbf{go to} \mid \textbf{if} \mid \textbf{then} \mid \textbf{else} \mid \textbf{for} \mid \textbf{do}^{7}$$
$$\langle separator \rangle ::= , \mid . \mid _{10} \mid : \mid ; \mid := \mid \sqcup \mid \textbf{step} \mid \textbf{until} \mid \textbf{while} \mid \textbf{comment}$$
$$\langle bracket \rangle ::= (\mid) \mid [\mid] \mid ` \mid ' \mid \textbf{begin} \mid \textbf{end}$$
$$\langle declarator \rangle ::= \textbf{own} \mid \textbf{Boolean} \mid \textbf{integer} \mid \textbf{real} \mid \textbf{array} \mid \textbf{switch} \mid \textbf{procedure}$$
$$\langle specificator \rangle ::= \textbf{string} \mid \textbf{label} \mid \textbf{value}$$

Delimiters have a fixed meaning which for the most part is obvious or else will be given at the appropriate place in the sequel.

Typographical features such as blank space or change to a new line have no significance in the reference language. They may, however, be used freely for facilitating reading.

For the purpose of including text among the symbols of

---

[6] It should be particularly noted that throughout the reference language underlining [in typewritten copy; boldface type in printed copy—Ed.] is used for defining independent basic symbols (see sections 2.2.2 and 2.3). These are understood to have no relation to the individual letters of which they are composed. Within the present report [not including headings—Ed.], boldface will be used for no other purpose.

[7] **do** is used in for statements. It has no relation whatsoever to the *do* of the preliminary report, which is not included in ALGOL 60.

a program the following "comment" conventions hold:

The sequence of basic symbols:	*is equivalent to*
; **comment** ⟨any sequence not containing ;⟩;	;
begin comment ⟨any sequence not containing ;⟩;	**begin**
end ⟨any sequence not containing **end** or ; or **else**⟩	**end**

By equivalence is here meant that any of the three structures shown in the left-hand column may be replaced, in any occurrence outside of strings, by the symbol shown on the same line in the right-hand column without any effect on the action of the program. It is further understood that the comment structure encountered first in the text when reading from left to right has precedence in being replaced over later structures contained in the sequence.

2.4. IDENTIFIERS
2.4.1. Syntax

⟨identifier⟩ ::= ⟨letter⟩|⟨identifier⟩⟨letter⟩|⟨identifier⟩⟨digit⟩

2.4.2. Examples

q
Soup
V17a
a34kTMNs
MARILYN

2.4.3. Semantics

Identifiers have no inherent meaning, but serve for the identification of simple variables, arrays, labels, switches, and procedures. They may be chosen freely (cf., however, section 3.2.4. Standard Functions).

The same identifier cannot be used to denote two different quantities except when these quantities have disjoint scopes as defined by the declarations of the program (cf. section 2.7. Quantities, Kinds and Scopes, and section 5. Declarations).

2.5. NUMBERS
2.5.1. Syntax

⟨unsigned integer⟩ ::= ⟨digit⟩|⟨unsigned integer⟩⟨digit⟩
⟨integer⟩ ::= ⟨unsigned integer⟩|+⟨unsigned integer⟩|
   −⟨unsigned integer⟩
⟨decimal fraction⟩ ::= .⟨unsigned integer⟩
⟨exponent part⟩ ::= ₁₀⟨integer⟩
⟨decimal number⟩ ::= ⟨unsigned integer⟩|⟨decimal fraction⟩|
   ⟨unsigned integer⟩⟨decimal fraction⟩
⟨unsigned number⟩ ::= ⟨decimal number⟩|⟨exponent part⟩|
   ⟨decimal number⟩⟨exponent part⟩
⟨number⟩ ::= ⟨unsigned number⟩|+⟨unsigned number⟩|
   −⟨unsigned number⟩

2.5.2. Examples

0	−200.084	−.083₁₀−02
177	+07.43₁₀8	−₁₀7
.5384	9.34₁₀+10	₁₀−4
+0.7300	2−₁₀4	+₁₀+5

2.5.3. Semantics

Decimal numbers have their conventional meaning. The exponent part is a scale factor expressed as an integral power of 10.

2.5.4. Types

Integers are of type **integer**. All other numbers are of type **real** (cf. section 5.1. Type Declarations).

2.6. STRINGS
2.6.1. Syntax

⟨proper string⟩ ::= ⟨any sequence of basic symbols not containing ' or '⟩|⟨empty⟩
⟨open string⟩ ::= ⟨proper string⟩|'⟨open string⟩'|
   ⟨open string⟩⟨open string⟩
⟨string⟩ ::= '⟨open string⟩'

2.6.2. Examples

'5k,,−'[[['∧=/:'Tt''
'.. This ⊔ is ⊔ a ⊔ 'string''

2.6.3. Semantics

In order to enable the language to handle arbitrary sequences of basic symbols the string quotes ' and ' are introduced. The symbol ⊔ denotes a space. It has no significance outside strings.

Strings are used as actual parameters of procedures (cf. sections 3.2. Function Designators and 4.7. Procedure Statements).

2.7. QUANTITIES, KINDS AND SCOPES

The following kinds of quantities are distinguished: simple variables, arrays, labels, switches, and procedures.

The scope of a quantity is the set of statements and expressions in which the declaration of the identifier associated with that quantity is valid. For labels see section 4.1.3.

2.8. VALUES AND TYPES

A value is an ordered set of numbers (special case: a single number), an ordered set of logical values (special case: a single logical value), or a label.

Certain of the syntactic units are said to possess values. These values will in general change during the execution of the program. The values of expressions and their constituents are defined in section 3. The value of an array identifier is the ordered set of values of the corresponding array of subscripted variables (cf. section 3.1.4.1).

The various "types" (**integer, real, Boolean**) basically denote properties of values. The types associated with syntactic units refer to the values of these units.

3. Expressions

In the language the primary constituents of the programs describing algorithmic processes are arithmetic, Boolean, and designational expressions. Constituents of these expressions, except for certain delimiters, are logical values, numbers, variables, function designators, and elementary arithmetic, relational, logical, and sequential operators. Since the syntactic definition of both variables and function designators contains expressions, the definition of expressions, and their constituents, is necessarily recursive.

⟨expression⟩ ::= ⟨arithmetic expression⟩|⟨Boolean expression⟩|
   ⟨designational expression⟩

3.1. Variables
3.1.1. Syntax

⟨variable identifier⟩ ::= ⟨identifier⟩
⟨simple variable⟩ ::= ⟨variable identifier⟩
⟨subscript expression⟩ ::= ⟨arithmetic expression⟩
⟨subscript list⟩ ::= ⟨subscript expression⟩|⟨subscript list⟩,
    ⟨subscript expression⟩
⟨array identifier⟩ ::= ⟨identifier⟩
⟨subscripted variable⟩ ::= ⟨array identifier⟩[⟨subscript list⟩]
⟨variable⟩ ::= ⟨simple variable⟩|⟨subscripted variable⟩

3.1.2. Examples

epsilon
detA
a17
Q[7,2]
x[*sin*(*n*×*pi*/2),*Q*[3,*n*,4]]

3.1.3. Semantics

A variable is a designation given to a single value. This value may be used in expressions for forming other values and may be changed at will by means of assignment statements (section 4.2). The type of the value of a particular variable is defined in the declaration for the variable itself (cf. section 5.1. Type Declarations) or for the corresponding array identifier (cf. section 5.2. Array Declarations).

3.1.4. Subscripts

3.1.4.1. Subscripted variables designate values which are components of multidimensional arrays (cf. section 5.2. Array Declarations). Each arithmetic expression of the subscript list occupies one subscript position of the subscripted variable, and is called a subscript. The complete list of subscripts is enclosed in the subscript brackets [ ]. The array component referred to by a subscripted variable is specified by the actual numerical value of its subscripts (cf. section 3.3. Arithmetic Expressions).

3.1.4.2. Each subscript position acts like a variable of type **integer** and the evaluation of the subscript is understood to be equivalent to an assignment to this fictitious variable (cf. section 4.2.4). The value of the subscripted variable is defined only if the value of the subscript expression is within the subscript bounds of the array (cf. section 5.2. Array Declarations).

3.2. Function Designators
3.2.1. Syntax

⟨procedure identifier⟩ ::= ⟨identifier⟩
⟨actual parameter⟩ ::= ⟨string⟩|⟨expression⟩|⟨array identifier⟩|
    ⟨switch identifier⟩|⟨procedure identifier⟩
⟨letter string⟩ ::= ⟨letter⟩|⟨letter string⟩⟨letter⟩
⟨parameter delimiter⟩ ::= ,|)⟨letter string⟩:(
⟨actual parameter list⟩ ::= ⟨actual parameter⟩|
    ⟨actual parameter list⟩⟨parameter delimiter⟩
    ⟨actual parameter⟩
⟨actual parameter part⟩ ::= ⟨empty⟩|(⟨actual parameter list⟩)
⟨function designator⟩ ::= ⟨procedure identifier⟩
    ⟨actual parameter part⟩

3.2.2. Examples

sin(*a*−*b*)
J(*v*+*s*,*n*)
R
S(*s*−5)Temperature:(*T*)Pressure:(*P*)
Compile(' := ')Stack:(*Q*)

3.2.3. Semantics

Function designators define single numerical or logical values, which result through the application of given sets of rules defined by a procedure declaration (cf. section 5.4. Procedure Declarations) to fixed sets of actual parameters. The rules governing specification of actual parameters are given in section 4.7. Procedure Statements. Not every procedure declaration defines the value of a function designator.

3.2.4. Standard functions

Certain identifiers should be reserved for the standard functions of analysis, which will be expressed as procedures. It is recommended that this reserved list should contain:

abs(E)   for the modulus (absolute value) of the value of the expression E
sign(E)   for the sign of the value of E(+1 for E>0, 0 for E=0, −1 for E<0)
sqrt(E)   for the square root of the value of E
sin(E)   for the sine of the value of E
cos(E)   for the cosine of the value of E
arctan(E) for the principal value of the arctangent of the value of E
ln(E)   for the natural logarithm of the value of E
exp(E)   for the exponential function of the value of E (e^E).

These functions are all understood to operate indifferently on arguments both of type **real** and **integer**. They will all yield values of type **real**, except for *sign*(E) which will have values of type **integer**. In a particular representation these functions may be available without explicit declarations (cf. section 5. Declarations).

3.2.5. Transfer functions

It is understood that transfer functions between any pair of quantities and expressions may be defined. Among the standard functions it is recommended that there be one, namely,

$$entier(E),$$

which "transfers" an expression of real type to one of integer type, and assigns to it the value which is the largest integer not greater than the value of E.

3.3. Arithmetic Expressions
3.3.1. Syntax

⟨adding operator⟩ ::= +|−
⟨multiplying operator⟩ ::= ×|/|÷
⟨primary⟩ ::= ⟨unsigned number⟩|⟨variable⟩|
    ⟨function designator⟩|(⟨arithmetic expression⟩)
⟨factor⟩ ::= ⟨primary⟩|⟨factor⟩↑⟨primary⟩
⟨term⟩ ::= ⟨factor⟩|⟨term⟩⟨multiplying operator⟩⟨factor⟩
⟨simple arithmetic expression⟩ ::= ⟨term⟩|
    ⟨adding operator⟩⟨term⟩|⟨simple arithmetic expression⟩
    ⟨adding operator⟩⟨term⟩
⟨if clause⟩ ::= **if** ⟨Boolean expression⟩**then**
⟨arithmetic expression⟩ ::= ⟨simple arithmetic expression⟩|
    ⟨if clause⟩⟨simple arithmetic expression⟩**else**
    ⟨arithmetic expression⟩

3.3.2. Examples

Primaries:

$$7.394_{10}-8$$
$$sum$$
$$w[i+2,8]$$
$$cos(y+z\times3)$$
$$(a-3/y+vu\uparrow8)$$

Factors:

$$omega$$
$$sum\uparrow cos(y+z\times3)$$
$$7.394_{10}-8\uparrow w[i+2,8]\uparrow(a-3/y+vu\uparrow8)$$

Terms:

$$U$$
$$omega\times sum\uparrow cos(y+z\times3)/7.394_{10}-8\uparrow w[i+2,8]\uparrow$$
$$(a-3/y+vu\uparrow8)$$

Simple arithmetic expression:

$$U-Yu+omega\times sum\uparrow cos(y+z\times3)/7.394_{10}-8\uparrow w[i+2,8]\uparrow$$
$$(a-3/y+vu\uparrow8)$$

Arithmetic expressions:

$$w\times u-Q(S+Cu)\uparrow2$$
if $q>0$ then $S+3\times Q/A$ else $2\times S+3\times q$
if $a<0$ then $U+V$ else if $a\times b>17$ then U/V else if
$\quad k\neq y$ then V/U else 0
$a\times sin(omega\times t)$
$0.57_{10}12\times a[N\times(N-1)/2, 0]$
$(A\times arctan(y)+Z)\uparrow(7+Q)$
if q then $n-1$ else n
if $a<0$ then A/B else if $b=0$ then B/A else z

3.3.3. Semantics

An arithmetic expression is a rule for computing a numerical value. In case of simple arithmetic expressions this value is obtained by executing the indicated arithmetic operations on the actual numerical values of the primaries of the expression, as explained in detail in section 3.3.4 below. The actual numerical value of a primary is obvious in the case of numbers. For variables it is the current value (assigned last in the dynamic sense), and for function designators it is the value arising from the computing rules defining the procedure (cf. section 5.4.4. Values of Function Designators) when applied to the current values of the procedure parameters given in the expression. Finally, for arithmetic expressions enclosed in parentheses the value must through a recursive analysis be expressed in terms of the values of primaries of the other three kinds.

In the more general arithmetic expressions, which include if clauses, one out of several simple arithmetic expressions is selected on the basis of the actual values of the Boolean expressions (cf. section 3.4. Boolean Expressions). This selection is made as follows: The Boolean expressions of the if clauses are evaluated one by one in sequence from left to right until one having the value **true** is found. The value of the arithmetic expression is then the value of the first arithmetic expression following this Boolean (the largest arithmetic expression found in this position

is understood). The construction:

$$\textbf{else}\ \langle\text{simple arithmetic expression}\rangle$$

is equivalent to the construction:

$$\textbf{else if true then}\ \langle\text{simple arithmetic expression}\rangle$$

3.3.4. Operators and types

Apart from the Boolean expressions of if clauses, the constituents of simple arithmetic expressions must be of types **real** or **integer** (cf. section 5.1. Type Declarations). The meaning of the basic operators and the types of the expressions to which they lead are given by the following rules:

3.3.4.1. The operators $+$, $-$, and $\times$ have the conventional meaning (addition, subtraction, and multiplication). The type of the expression will be **integer** if both of the operands are of **integer** type, otherwise **real**.

3.3.4.2. The operations $\langle\text{term}\rangle/\langle\text{factor}\rangle$ and $\langle\text{term}\rangle\div\langle\text{factor}\rangle$ both denote division, to be understood as a multiplication of the term by the reciprocal of the factor with due regard to the rules of precedence (cf. section 3.3.5). Thus for example

$$a/b\times7/(p-q)\times v/s$$

means

$$((((a\times(b^{-1}))\times7)\times((p-q)^{-1}))\times v)\times(s^{-1})$$

The operator $/$ is defined for all four combinations of types **real** and **integer** and will yield results of **real** type in any case. The operator $\div$ is defined only for two operands both of type **integer** and will yield a result of type **integer**, mathematically defined as follows:

$$a\div b=\ sign\ (a/b)\times entier(abs(a/b))$$

(cf. sections 3.2.4 and 3.2.5).

3.3.4.3. The operation $\langle\text{factor}\rangle\uparrow\langle\text{primary}\rangle$ denotes exponentiation, where the factor is the base and the primary is the exponent. Thus, for example,

$$2\uparrow n\uparrow k \qquad \text{means} \qquad (2^n)^k$$

while

$$2\uparrow(n\uparrow m) \qquad \text{means} \qquad 2^{(n^m)}$$

Writing i for a number of **integer** type, r for a number of **real** type, and a for a number of either **integer** or **real** type, the result is given by the following rules:

$a\uparrow i$ If $i>0$, $a\times a\times\ldots\times a$ (i times), of the same type as a.
       If $i=0$, if $a\neq0$, 1, of the same type as a.
         if $a=0$, undefined.
       If $i<0$, if $a\neq0$, $1/(a\times a\times\ldots\times a)$ (the denominator has
           $-i$ factors), of type **real**.
         if $a=0$, undefined.
$a\uparrow r$ If $a>0$, $exp(r\times ln(a))$, of type **real**.
       If $a=0$, if $r>0$, 0.0, of type **real**.
         if $r\leq0$, undefined.
       If $a<0$, always undefined.

3.3.5. Precedence of operators

The sequence of operations within one expression is

generally from left to right, with the following additional rules:

3.3.5.1. According to the syntax given in section 3.3.1 the following rules of precedence hold:

$$\text{first:} \quad \uparrow$$
$$\text{second:} \times / \div$$
$$\text{third:} \quad + -$$

3.3.5.2. The expression between a left parenthesis and the matching right parenthesis is evaluated by itself and this value is used in subsequent calculations. Consequently the desired order of execution of operations within an expression can always be arranged by appropriate positioning of parentheses.

3.3.6. Arithmetics of **real** quantities

Numbers and variables of type **real** must be interpreted in the sense of numerical analysis, i.e. as entities defined inherently with only a finite accuracy. Similarly, the possibility of the occurrence of a finite deviation from the mathematically defined result in any arithmetic expression is explicitly understood. No exact arithmetic will be specified, however, and it is indeed understood that different hardware representations may evaluate arithmetic expressions differently. The control of the possible consequences of such differences must be carried out by the methods of numerical analysis. This control must be considered a part of the process to be described, and will therefore be expressed in terms of the language itself.

3.4. BOOLEAN EXPRESSIONS

3.4.1. Syntax

⟨relational operator⟩ ::= $<|\leqq|=|\geqq|>|\neq$
⟨relation⟩ ::= ⟨simple arithmetic expression⟩
⟨relational operator⟩⟨simple arithmetic expression⟩
⟨Boolean primary⟩ ::= ⟨logical value⟩|⟨variable⟩|
⟨function designator⟩|⟨relation⟩|(⟨Boolean expression⟩)
⟨Boolean secondary⟩ ::= ⟨Boolean primary⟩|¬⟨Boolean primary⟩
⟨Boolean factor⟩ ::= ⟨Boolean secondary⟩|
⟨Boolean factor⟩∧⟨Boolean secondary⟩
⟨Boolean term⟩ ::= ⟨Boolean factor⟩|⟨Boolean term⟩
∨⟨Boolean factor⟩
⟨implication⟩ ::= ⟨Boolean term⟩|⟨implication⟩⊃⟨Boolean term⟩
⟨simple Boolean⟩ ::= ⟨implication⟩|
⟨simple Boolean⟩≡⟨implication⟩
⟨Boolean expression⟩ ::= ⟨simple Boolean⟩|
⟨if clause⟩⟨simple Boolean⟩ **else** ⟨Boolean expression⟩

3.4.2. Examples

$$x = -2$$
$$Y > V \lor z < q$$
$$a+b > -5 \land z-d > q\uparrow 2$$
$$p \land q \lor x \neq y$$
$$g \equiv \neg a \land b \land \neg c \lor d \lor e \supset \neg f$$
if $k < 1$ **then** $s > w$ **else** $h \leqq c$
if if if a **then** b **else** c **then** d **else** f **then** g **else** $h < k$

3.4.3. Semantics

A Boolean expression is a rule for computing a logical value. The principles of evaluation are entirely analogous to those given for arithmetic expressions in section 3.3.3.

3.4.4. Types

Variables and function designators entered as Boolean primaries must be declared **Boolean** (cf. section 5.1. Type Declarations and section 5.4.4. Values of Function Designators).

3.4.5. The operators

Relations take on the value **true** whenever the corresponding relation is satisfied for the expressions involved, otherwise **false**.

The meaning of the logical operators ¬ (not), ∧ (and), ∨ (or), ⊃ (implies), and ≡ (equivalent), is given by the following function table.

b1	false	false	true	true
b2	false	true	false	true
¬b1	true	true	false	false
b1∧b2	false	false	false	true
b1∨b2	false	true	true	true
b1⊃b2	true	true	false	true
b1≡b2	true	false	false	true

3.4.6. Precedence of operators

The sequence of operations within one expression is generally from left to right, with the following additional rules:

3.4.6.1. According to the syntax given in section 3.4.1 the following rules of precedence hold:

first: arithmetic expressions according to section 3.3.5.
second: $< \leqq = \geqq > \neq$
third: ¬
fourth: ∧
fifth: ∨
sixth: ⊃
seventh: ≡

3.4.6.2. The use of parentheses will be interpreted in the sense given in section 3.3.5.2.

3.5. DESIGNATIONAL EXPRESSIONS

3.5.1. Syntax

⟨label⟩ ::= ⟨identifier⟩|⟨unsigned integer⟩
⟨switch identifier⟩ ::= ⟨identifier⟩
⟨switch designator⟩ ::= ⟨switch identifier⟩[⟨subscript expression⟩]
⟨simple designational expression⟩ ::= ⟨label⟩|⟨switch designator⟩|
(⟨designational expression⟩)
⟨designational expression⟩ ::= ⟨simple designational expression⟩|
⟨if clause⟩⟨simple designational expression⟩ **else**
⟨designational expression⟩

3.5.2. Examples

17
$p9$
$Choose[n-1]$
$Town[$**if** $y < 0$ **then** N **else** $N+1]$
if $Ab < c$ **then** 17 **else** $q[$**if** $w \leqq 0$ **then** 2 **else** $n]$

3.5.3. Semantics

A designational expression is a rule for obtaining a label of a statement (cf. section 4. Statements). Again the principle of the evaluation is entirely analogous to that of arithmetic expressions (section 3.3.3). In the general case the Boolean expressions of the if clauses will select a simple designational expression. If this is a label the desired result is already found. A switch designator refers to the corresponding switch declaration (cf. section 5.3.

Switch Declarations) and by the actual numerical value of its subscript expression selects one of the designational expressions listed in the switch declaration by counting these from left to right. Since the designational expression thus selected may again be a switch designator this evaluation is obviously a recursive process.

3.5.4. The subscript expression

The evaluation of the subscript expression is analogous to that of subscripted variables (cf. section 3.1.4.2). The value of a switch designator is defined only if the subscript expression assumes one of the positive values $1, 2, 3, \ldots, n$, where n is the number of entries in the switch list.

3.5.5. Unsigned integers as labels

Unsigned integers used as labels have the property that leading zeros do not affect their meaning, e.g. 00217 denotes the same label as 217.

4. Statements

The units of operation within the language are called statements. They will normally be executed consecutively as written. However, this sequence of operations may be broken by go to statements, which define their successor explicitly, and shortened by conditional statements, which may cause certain statements to be skipped.

In order to make it possible to define a specific dynamic succession, statements may be provided with labels.

Since sequences of statements may be grouped together into compound statements and blocks the definition of statement must necessarily be recursive. Also since declarations, described in section 5, enter fundamentally into the syntactic structure, the syntactic definition of statements must suppose declarations to be already defined.

4.1. COMPOUND STATEMENTS AND BLOCKS

4.1.1. Syntax

⟨unlabelled basic statement⟩ ::= ⟨assignment statement⟩|
    ⟨go to statement⟩|⟨dummy statement⟩|⟨procedure statement⟩
⟨basic statement⟩ ::= ⟨unlabelled basic statement⟩|⟨label⟩:
    ⟨basic statement⟩
⟨unconditional statement⟩ ::= ⟨basic statement⟩|
    ⟨compound statement⟩|⟨block⟩
⟨statement⟩ ::= ⟨unconditional statement⟩|
    ⟨conditional statement⟩|⟨for statement⟩
⟨compound tail⟩ ::= ⟨statement⟩ **end** |⟨statement⟩ ;
    ⟨compound tail⟩
⟨block head⟩ ::= **begin** ⟨declaration⟩|⟨block head⟩ ;
    ⟨declaration⟩
⟨unlabelled compound⟩ ::= **begin** ⟨compound tail⟩
⟨unlabelled block⟩ ::= ⟨block head⟩ ; ⟨compound tail⟩
⟨compound statement⟩ ::= ⟨unlabelled compound⟩|
    ⟨label⟩:⟨compound statement⟩
⟨block⟩ ::= ⟨unlabelled block⟩|⟨label⟩:⟨block⟩
⟨program⟩ ::= ⟨block⟩|⟨compound statement⟩

This syntax may be illustrated as follows: Denoting arbitrary statements, declarations, and labels, by the letters S, D, and L, respectively, the basic syntactic units take the forms:

Compound statement:

L: L: ... **begin** S ; S ; ... S ; S **end**

Block:

L: L: ... **begin** D ; D ; .. D ; S ; S ; ...S ;
    S **end**

It should be kept in mind that each of the statements S may again be a complete compound statement or block.

4.1.2. Examples

Basic statements:

> $a := p+q$
> **go to** *Naples*
> *START*: *CONTINUE*: *W* := 7.993

Compound statement:

> **begin** $x := 0$; **for** $y := 1$ **step** 1 **until** n **do**
> $x := x+A[y]$;
>   **if** $x>q$ **then go to** *STOP* **else if** $x>w-2$ **then**
>   **go to** *S* ;
>   Aw: St: $W := x+bob$ **end**

Block:

> Q: **begin integer** i, k ; **real** w ;
>   **for** $i := 1$ **step** 1 **until** m **do**
>   **for** $k := i+1$ **step** 1 **until** m **do**
>   **begin** $w := A[i, k]$;
> $A[i, k] := A[k, i]$;
> $A[k, i] := w$ **end for** i **and** k
> **end block** Q

4.1.3. Semantics

Every block automatically introduces a new level of nomenclature. This is realized as follows: Any identifier occurring within the block may through a suitable declaration (cf. section 5. Declarations) be specified to be local to the block in question. This means (a) that the entity represented by this identifier inside the block has no existence outside it, and (b) that any entity represented by this identifier outside the block is completely inaccessible inside the block.

Identifiers (except those representing labels) occurring within a block and not being declared to this block will be nonlocal to it, i.e. will represent the same entity inside the block and in the level immediately outside it. A label separated by a colon from a statement, i.e. labelling that statement, behaves as though declared in the head of the smallest embracing block, i.e. the smallest block whose brackets **begin** and **end** enclose that statement. In this context a procedure body must be considered as if it were enclosed by **begin** and **end** and treated as a block.

Since a statement of a block may again itself be a block the concepts local and nonlocal to a block must be understood recursively. Thus an identifier, which is nonlocal to a block A, may or may not be nonlocal to the block B in which A is one statement.

4.2. ASSIGNMENT STATEMENTS

4.2.1. Syntax

⟨left part⟩ ::= ⟨variable⟩ := |⟨procedure identifier⟩ :=
⟨left part list⟩ ::= ⟨left part⟩|⟨left part list⟩⟨left part⟩
⟨assignment statement⟩ ::= ⟨left part list⟩⟨arithmetic expression⟩|
    ⟨left part list⟩⟨Boolean expression⟩

4.2.2. Examples

$$s := p[0] := n := n+1+s$$
$$n := n+1$$
$$A := B/C-v-q \times S$$
$$S[v,k+2] := 3-arctan(s \times zeta)$$
$$V := Q>Y \wedge Z$$

4.2.3. Semantics

Assignment statements serve for assigning the value of an expression to one or several variables or procedure identifiers. Assignment to a procedure identifier may only occur within the body of a procedure defining the value of a function designator (cf. section 5.4.4). The process will in the general case be understood to take place in three steps as follows:

4.2.3.1. Any subscript expressions occurring in the left part variables are evaluated in sequence from left to right.

4.2.3.2. The expression of the statement is evaluated.

4.2.3.3. The value of the expression is assigned to all the left part variables, with any subscript expressions having values as evaluated in step 4.2.3.1.

4.2.4. Types

The type associated with all variables and procedure identifiers of a left part list must be the same. If this type is **Boolean**, the expression must likewise be **Boolean.** If the type is **real** or **integer,** the expression must be arithmetic. If the type of the arithmetic expression differs from that associated with the variables and procedure identifiers, appropriate transfer functions are understood to be automatically invoked. For transfer from **real** to **integer** type, the transfer function is understood to yield a result equivalent to

$$entier(E+0.5)$$

where E is the value of the expression. The type associated with a procedure identifier is given by the declarator which appears as the first symbol of the corresponding procedure declaration (cf. section 5.4.4).

4.3. Go To Statements

4.3.1. Syntax

⟨go to statement⟩ ::= **go to** ⟨designational expression⟩

4.3.2. Examples

```
go to 8
go to exit [n+1]
go to Town[if y<0 then N else N+1]
go to if Ab<c then 17 else q[if w<0 then 2 else n]
```

4.3.3. Semantics

A go to statement interrupts the normal sequence of operations, defined by the write-up of statements, by defining its successor explicitly by the value of a designational expression. Thus the next statement to be executed will be the one having this value as its label.

4.3.4. Restriction

Since labels are inherently local, no go to statement can lead from outside into a block. A go to statement may, however, lead from outside into a compound statement.

4.3.5. Go to an undefined switch designator

A go to statement is equivalent to a dummy statement if the designational expression is a switch designator whose value is undefined.

4.4. Dummy Statements

4.4.1. Syntax

⟨dummy statement⟩ ::= ⟨empty⟩

4.4.2. Examples

```
L:
begin ...  ;  John: end
```

4.4.3. Semantics

A dummy statement executes no operation. It may serve to place a label.

4.5. Conditional Statements

4.5.1. Syntax

⟨if clause⟩ ::= **if** ⟨Boolean expression⟩ **then**
⟨unconditional statement⟩ ::= ⟨basic statement⟩|
    ⟨compound statement⟩|⟨block⟩
⟨if statement⟩ ::= ⟨if clause⟩ ⟨unconditional statement⟩
⟨conditional statement⟩ ::= ⟨if statement⟩|⟨if statement⟩ **else**
    ⟨statement⟩|⟨if clause⟩⟨for statement⟩|
    ⟨label⟩ : ⟨conditional statement⟩

4.5.2. Examples

```
if x>0 then n := n+1
if v>u then V: q := n+m else go to R
if s<0∨P≤Q then AA: begin if q<v then a := v/s
            else y := 2×a end
        else if v>s then a := v-q else if v>s-1
            then go to S
```

4.5.3. Semantics

Conditional statements cause certain statements to be executed or skipped depending on the running values of specified Boolean expressions.

4.5.3.1. If statement. The unconditional statement of an if statement will be executed if the Boolean expression of the if clause is true. Otherwise it will be skipped and the operation will be continued with the next statement.

4.5.3.2. Conditional statement. According to the syntax two different forms of conditional statements are possible. These may be illustrated as follows:

if B1 then S1 else if B2 then S2 else S3   ;   S4

and

if B1 then S1 else if B2 then S2 else if B3 then S3   ;   S4

Here B1 to B3 are Boolean expressions, while S1 to S3 are unconditional statements. S4 is the statement following the complete conditional statement.

The execution of a conditional statement may be described as follows: The Boolean expression of the if clauses are evaluated one after the other in sequence from left to right until one yielding the value **true** is found. Then the unconditional statement following this Boolean is executed. Unless this statement defines its successor explicitly the next statement to be executed will be S4, i.e. the statement following the complete conditional statement. Thus the effect of the delimiter **else** may be described by saying that it defines the successor of the statement it follows to be the statement following the complete conditional statement.

The construction

else ⟨unconditional statement⟩

is equivalent to

else if true then ⟨unconditional statement⟩

If none of the Boolean expressions of the if clauses is true, the effect of the whole conditional statement will be equivalent to that of a dummy statement.

For further explanation the following picture may be useful:

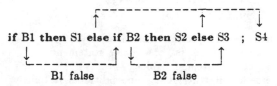

if B1 **then** S1 **else if** B2 **then** S2 **else** S3   ;   S4

B1 false   B2 false

4.5.4. Go to into a conditional statement

The effect of a go to statement leading into a conditional statement follows directly from the above explanation of the effect of **else**.

4.6. FOR STATEMENTS

4.6.1. Syntax

⟨for list element⟩ ::= ⟨arithmetic expression⟩|
  ⟨arithmetic expression⟩ **step** ⟨arithmetic expression⟩ **until**
  ⟨arithmetic expression⟩|⟨arithmetic expression⟩ **while**
  ⟨Boolean expression⟩
⟨for list⟩ ::= ⟨for list element⟩|⟨for list⟩ , ⟨for list element⟩
⟨for clause⟩ ::= **for** ⟨variable⟩ := ⟨for list⟩ **do**
⟨for statement⟩ ::= ⟨for clause⟩⟨statement⟩|
  ⟨label⟩: ⟨for statement⟩

4.6.2. Examples

> **for** q := 1 **step** s **until** n **do** $A[q] := B[q]$
> **for** k := 1, $V1 \times 2$ **while** $V1 < N$ **do**
>   **for** j := $I + G$, L, 1 **step** 1 **until** N, $C + D$ **do**
> $A[k,j] := B[k,j]$

4.6.3. Semantics

A for clause causes the statement S which it precedes to be repeatedly executed zero or more times. In addition it performs a sequence of assignments to its controlled variable. The process may be visualized by means of the following picture:

Initialize ; test ; statement S ; advance ; successor

for list exhausted

In this picture the word initialize means: perform the first assignment of the for clause. Advance means: perform the next assignment of the for clause. Test determines if the last assignment has been done. If so, the execution con-

tinues with the successor of the for statement. If not, the statement following the for clause is executed.

4.6.4. The for list elements

The for list gives a rule for obtaining the values which are consecutively assigned to the controlled variable. This sequence of values is obtained from the for list elements by taking these one by one in the order in which they are written. The sequence of values generated by each of the three species of for list elements and the corresponding execution of the statement S are given by the following rules:

4.6.4.1. Arithmetic expression. This element gives rise to one value, namely the value of the given arithmetic expression as calculated immediately before the corresponding execution of the statement S.

4.6.4.2. Step-until-element. An element of the form A **step** B **until** C, where A, B, and C, are arithmetic expressions, gives rise to an execution which may be described most concisely in terms of additional ALGOL statements as follows:

> V := A ;
> L1: **if** (V−C)× $sign$(B) >0 **then go to** *element exhausted*;
>   statement S ;
>   V := V+B ;
>   **go to** L1 ;

where V is the controlled variable of the for clause and *element exhausted* points to the evaluation according to the next element in the for list, or if the step-until-element is the last of the list, to the next statement in the program.

4.6.4.3. While-element. The execution governed by a for list element of the form E **while** F, where E is an arithmetic and F a Boolean expression, is most concisely described in terms of additional ALGOL statements as follows:

> L3: V := E ;
>   **if** −F **then go to** *element exhausted* ;
>   Statement S ;
>   **go to** L3 ;

where the notation is the same as in 4.6.4.2 above.

4.6.5. The value of the controlled variable upon exit

Upon exit out of the statement S (supposed to be compound) through a go to statement the value of the controlled variable will be the same as it was immediately preceding the execution of the go to statement.

If the exit is due to exhaustion of the for list, on the other hand, the value of the controlled variable is undefined after the exit.

4.6.6. Go to leading into a for statement

The effect of a go to statement, outside a for statement, which refers to a label within the for statement, is undefined.

4.7. PROCEDURE STATEMENTS

4.7.1. Syntax

⟨actual parameter⟩ ::= ⟨string⟩|⟨expression⟩|⟨array identifier⟩|
  ⟨switch identifier⟩|⟨procedure identifier⟩
⟨letter string⟩ ::= ⟨letter⟩|⟨letter string⟩⟨letter⟩

⟨parameter delimiter⟩ ::= ,|) ⟨letter string⟩:(
⟨actual parameter list⟩ ::= ⟨actual parameter⟩|
    ⟨actual parameter list⟩⟨parameter delimiter⟩
    ⟨actual parameter⟩
⟨actual parameter part⟩ ::= ⟨empty⟩|
    (⟨actual parameter list⟩)
⟨procedure statement⟩ ::= ⟨procedure identifier⟩
    ⟨actual parameter part⟩

4.7.2. Examples

Spur (*A*)Order: (7)Result to: (*V*)
Transpose (*W*,*v*+1)
Absmax(*A*,*N*,*M*,*Yy*,*I*,*K*)
Innerproduct(*A*[*t*,*P*,*u*],*B*[*P*],10,*P*,*Y*)

These examples correspond to examples given in section 5.4.2.

4.7.3. Semantics

A procedure statement serves to invoke (call for) the execution of a procedure body (cf. section 5.4. Procedure Declarations). Where the procedure body is a statement written in ALGOL the effect of this execution will be equivalent to the effect of performing the following operations on the program at the time of execution of the procedure statement:

4.7.3.1. Value assignment (call by value)

All formal parameters quoted in the value part of the procedure declaration heading are assigned the values (cf. section 2.8. Values and Types) of the corresponding actual parameters, these assignments being considered as being performed explicitly before entering the procedure body. The effect is as though an additional block embracing the procedure body were created in which these assignments were made to variables local to this fictitious block with types as given in the corresponding specifications (cf. section 5.4.5). As a consequence, variables called by value are to be considered as nonlocal to the body of the procedure, but local to the fictitious block (cf. section 5.4.3).

4.7.3.2. Name replacement (call by name)

Any formal parameter not quoted in the value list is replaced, throughout the procedure body, by the corresponding actual parameter, after enclosing this latter in parentheses wherever syntactically possible. Possible conflicts between identifiers inserted through this process and other identifiers already present within the procedure body will be avoided by suitable systematic changes of the formal or local identifiers involved.

4.7.3.3. Body replacement and execution

Finally the procedure body, modified as above, is inserted in place of the procedure statement and executed. If the procedure is called from a place outside the scope of any nonlocal quantity of the procedure body the conflicts between the identifiers inserted through this process of body replacement and the identifiers whose declarations are valid at the place of the procedure statement or function designator will be avoided through suitable systematic changes of the latter identifiers.

4.7.4. Actual-formal correspondence

The correspondence between the actual parameters of the procedure statement and the formal parameters of the procedure heading is established as follows: The actual parameter list of the procedure statement must have the same number of entries as the formal parameter list of the procedure declaration heading. The correspondence is obtained by taking the entries of these two lists in the same order.

4.7.5. Restrictions

For a procedure statement to be defined it is evidently necessary that the operations on the procedure body defined in sections 4.7.3.1 and 4.7.3.2 lead to a correct ALGOL statement.

This imposes the restriction on any procedure statement that the kind and type of each actual parameter be compatible with the kind and type of the corresponding formal parameter. Some important particular cases of this general rule are the following:

4.7.5.1. If a string is supplied as an actual parameter in a procedure statement or function designator, whose defining procedure body is an ALGOL 60 statement (as opposed to non-ALGOL code, cf. section 4.7.8), then this string can only be used within the procedure body as an actual parameter in further procedure calls. Ultimately it can only be used by a procedure body expressed in non-ALGOL code.

4.7.5.2. A formal parameter which occurs as a left part variable in an assignment statement within the procedure body and which is not called by value can only correspond to an actual parameter which is a variable (special case of expression).

4.7.5.3. A formal parameter which is used within the procedure body as an array identifier can only correspond to an actual parameter which is an array identifier of an array of the same dimensions. In addition if the formal parameter is called by value the local array created during the call will have the same subscript bounds as the actual array.

4.7.5.4. A formal parameter which is called by value cannot in general correspond to a switch identifier or a procedure identifier or a string, because these latter do not possess values (the exception is the procedure identifier of a procedure declaration which has an empty formal parameter part (cf. section 5.4.1) and which defines the value of a function designator (cf. section 5.4.4). This procedure identifier is in itself a complete expression).

4.7.5.5. Any formal parameter may have restrictions on the type of the corresponding actual parameter associated with it (these restrictions may, or may not, be given through specifications in the procedure heading). In the procedure statement such restrictions must evidently be observed.

4.7.6. Deleted.

4.7.7. Parameter delimiters

All parameter delimiters are understood to be equivalent. No correspondence between the parameter delimiters used in a procedure statement and those used in the procedure heading is expected beyond their number being the same. Thus the information conveyed by using the elaborate ones is entirely optional.

4.7.8. Procedure body expressed in code

The restrictions imposed on a procedure statement calling a procedure having its body expressed in non-ALGOL code evidently can only be derived from the characteristics of the code used and the intent of the user and thus fall outside the scope of the reference language.

5. Declarations

Declarations serve to define certain properties of the quantities used in the program, and to associate them with identifiers. A declaration of an identifier is valid for one block. Outside this block the particular identifier may be used for other purposes (cf. section 4.1.3).

Dynamically this implies the following: at the time of an entry into a block (through the **begin**, since the labels inside are local and therefore inaccessible from outside) all identifiers declared for the block assume the significance implied by the nature of the declarations given. If these identifiers had already been defined by other declarations outside they are for the time being given a new significance. Identifiers which are not declared for the block, on the other hand, retain their old meaning.

At the time of an exit from a block (through **end**, or by a go to statement) all identifiers which are declared for the block lose their local significance.

A declaration may be marked with the additional declarator **own**. This has the following effect: upon a re-entry into the block, the values of own quantities will be unchanged from their values at the last exit, while the values of declared variables which are not marked as own are undefined. Apart from labels and formal parameters of procedure declarations and with the possible exception of those for standard functions (cf. sections 3.2.4 and 3.2.5), all identifiers of a program must be declared. No identifier may be declared more than once in any one block head.

Syntax.

⟨declaration⟩ ::= ⟨type declaration⟩|⟨array declaration⟩|
    ⟨switch declaration⟩|⟨procedure declaration⟩

5.1. TYPE DECLARATIONS

5.1.1. Syntax

⟨type list⟩ ::= ⟨simple variable⟩|
    ⟨simple variable⟩ , ⟨type list⟩
⟨type⟩ ::= **real** | **integer** | **Boolean**
⟨local or own type⟩ ::= ⟨type⟩|**own** ⟨type⟩
⟨type declaration⟩ ::= ⟨local or own type⟩⟨type list⟩

5.1.2. Examples

integer p,q,s
own Boolean $Acryl,n$

5.1.3. Semantics

Type declarations serve to declare certain identifiers to represent simple variables of a given type. Real declared variables may only assume positive or negative values

including zero. Integer declared variables may only assume positive and negative integral values including zero. Boolean declared variables may only assume the values **true** and **false**.

In arithmetic expressions any position which can be occupied by a real declared variable may be occupied by an integer declared variable.

For the semantics of **own**, see the fourth paragraph of section 5 above.

5.2. ARRAY DECLARATIONS

5.2.1. Syntax

⟨lower bound⟩ ::= ⟨arithmetic expression⟩
⟨upper bound⟩ ::= ⟨arithmetic expression⟩
⟨bound pair⟩ ::= ⟨lower bound⟩:⟨upper bound⟩
⟨bound pair list⟩ ::= ⟨bound pair⟩|⟨bound pair list⟩,⟨bound pair⟩
⟨array segment⟩ ::= ⟨array identifier⟩[⟨bound pair list⟩]|
    ⟨array identifier⟩,⟨array segment⟩
⟨array list⟩ ::= ⟨array segment⟩|⟨array list⟩,⟨array segment⟩
⟨array declaration⟩ ::= **array** ⟨array list⟩|⟨local or own type⟩
    array ⟨array list⟩

5.2.2. Examples

array a, b, $c[7:n,2:m]$, $s[-2:10]$
own integer array A[**if** $c<0$ **then** 2 **else** 1:20]
real array $q[-7:-1]$

5.2.3. Semantics

An array declaration declares one or several identifiers to represent multidimensional arrays of subscripted variables and gives the dimensions of the arrays, the bounds of the subscripts and the types of the variables.

5.2.3.1. Subscript bounds. The subscript bounds for any array are given in the first subscript bracket following the identifier of this array in the form of a bound pair list. Each item of this list gives the lower and upper bound of a subscript in the form of two arithmetic expressions separated by the delimiter : The bound pair list gives the bounds of all subscripts taken in order from left to right.

5.2.3.2. Dimensions. The dimensions are given as the number of entries in the bound pair lists.

5.2.3.3. Types. All arrays declared in one declaration are of the same quoted type. If no type declarator is given the type **real** is understood.

5.2.4. Lower upper bound expressions

5.2.4.1 The expressions will be evaluated in the same way as subscript expressions (cf. section 3.1.4.2).

5.2.4.2. The expressions can only depend on variables and procedures which are nonlocal to the block for which the array declaration is valid. Consequently in the outermost block of a program only array declarations with constant bounds may be declared.

5.2.4.3. An array is defined only when the values of all upper subscript bounds are not smaller than those of the corresponding lower bounds.

5.2.4.4. The expressions will be evaluated once at each entrance into the block.

5.2.5. The identity of subscripted variables

The identity of a subscripted variable is not related to the subscript bounds given in the array declaration. However, even if an array is declared **own** the values of the corresponding subscripted variables will, at any time, be defined only for those of these variables which have subscripts within the most recently calculated subscript bounds.

5.3. Switch Declarations

5.3.1. Syntax

⟨switch list⟩ ::= ⟨designational expression⟩|
   ⟨switch list⟩,⟨designational expression⟩
⟨switch declaration⟩ ::= **switch** ⟨switch identifier⟩:= ⟨switch list⟩

5.3.2. Examples

   switch S := $S1,S2,Q[m]$, **if** $v > -5$ **then** $S3$ **else** $S4$
   switch Q := $p1,w$

5.3.3. Semantics

A switch declaration defines the set of values of the corresponding switch designators. These values are given one by one as the values of the designational expressions entered in the switch list. With each of these designational expressions there is associated a positive integer, 1, 2, ... , obtained by counting the items in the list from left to right. The value of the switch designator corresponding to a given value of the subscript expression (cf. section 3.5. Designational Expressions) is the value of the designational expression in the switch list having this given value as its associated integer.

5.3.4. Evaluation of expressions in the switch list

An expression in the switch list will be evaluated every time the item of the list in which the expression occurs is referred to, using the current values of all variables involved.

5.3.5. Influence of scopes

If a switch designator occurs outside the scope of a quantity entering into a designational expression in the switch list, and an evaluation of this switch designator selects this designational expression, then the conflicts between the identifiers for the quantities in this expression and the identifiers whose declarations are valid at the place of the switch designator will be avoided through suitable systematic changes of the latter identifiers.

5.4. Procedure Declarations

5.4.1. Syntax

⟨formal parameter⟩ ::= ⟨identifier⟩
⟨formal parameter list⟩ ::= ⟨formal parameter⟩|
   ⟨formal parameter list⟩⟨parameter delimiter⟩
   ⟨formal parameter⟩
⟨formal parameter part⟩ ::= ⟨empty⟩|(⟨formal parameter list⟩)
⟨identifier list⟩ ::= ⟨identifier⟩|⟨identifier list⟩,⟨identifier⟩
⟨value part⟩ ::= **value**⟨identifier list⟩ ; |⟨empty⟩
⟨specifier⟩ ::= **string**|⟨type⟩|**array**|⟨type⟩**array**|**label**|**switch**|
   procedure|⟨type⟩**procedure**
⟨specification part⟩ ::= ⟨empty⟩|⟨specifier⟩⟨identifier list⟩ ; |
   ⟨specification part⟩⟨specifier⟩⟨identifier list⟩ ;
⟨procedure heading⟩ ::= ⟨procedure identifier⟩
   ⟨formal parameter part⟩ ; ⟨value part⟩⟨specification part⟩
⟨procedure body⟩ ::= ⟨statement⟩|⟨code⟩
⟨procedure declaration⟩ ::=
   procedure ⟨procedure heading⟩⟨procedure body⟩|
   ⟨type⟩ **procedure** ⟨procedure heading⟩⟨procedure body⟩

5.4.2. Examples (see also the examples at the end of the report)

```
procedure Spur(a)Order:(n)Result:(s) ; value n ;
array a ; integer n ; real s ;
begin integer k ;
s := 0 ;
for k := 1 step 1 until n do s := s+a[k,k]
end
```

```
procedure Transpose(a)Order:(n) ; value n ;
array a ; integer n ;
begin real w ; integer i, k ;
for i := 1 step 1 until n do
    for k := 1+i step 1 until n do
    begin w := a[i,k] ;
        a[i,k] := a[k,i] ;
        a[k,i] := w
    end
end Transpose
```

```
integer procedure Step (u) ; real u ;
Step := if 0≤u∧u≤1 then 1 else 0
```

```
procedure Absmax(a)size:(n,m)Result:(y)Subscripts:(i,k);
comment The absolute greatest element of the matrix a,
    of size n by m is transferred to y, and the subscripts of this
    element to i and k ;
array a ; integer n, m, i, k ; real y ;
begin integer p, q ;
y := 0 ;
for p := 1 step 1 until n do for q := 1 step 1 until m do
if abs(a[p,q])>y then begin y := abs(a[p,q]) ; i := p ;
    k := q
end end Absmax
```

```
procedure Innerproduct(a,b)Order:(k,p)Result:(y) ; value k ;
integer k,p ; real y,a,b ;
begin real s ;
s := 0 ;
for p := 1 step 1 until k do s := s+a×b ;
y := s
end Innerproduct
```

5.4.3. Semantics

A procedure declaration serves to define the procedure associated with a procedure identifier. The principal constituent of a procedure declaration is a statement or a piece of code, the procedure body, which through the use of procedure statements and/or function designators may be activated from other parts of the block in the head of which the procedure declaration appears. Associated with the body is a heading, which specifies certain identifiers occurring within the body to represent formal parameters. Formal parameters in the procedure body will, whenever the procedure is activated (cf. section 3.2. Function Designators and section 4.7. Procedure Statements) be assigned the values of or replaced by actual parameters. Identifiers in the procedure body which are not formal will be either local or nonlocal to the body depending on whether they are declared within the body or not. Those of them which are nonlocal to the body may well be local to the block in the head of which the procedure declaration appears. The procedure body always acts like a block, whether it has the form of one or not. Consequently the scope of any label labelling a statement within the body or the body itself can never extend beyond the procedure body. In addition, if the identifier of a formal parameter is declared anew within the procedure body (including the case of its use as a label as in section 4.1.3), it is thereby given a local significance and actual parameters which correspond to it are inaccessible throughout the scope of this inner local quantity.

5.4.4. Values of function designators

For a procedure declaration to define the value of a function designator there must, within the procedure body, occur one or more explicit assignment statements with the procedure identifier in a left part; at least one of these must be executed, and the type associated with the procedure identifier must be declared through the appearance of a type declarator as the very first symbol of the procedure declaration. The last value so assigned is used to continue the evaluation of the expression in which the function designator occurs. Any occurrence of the procedure identifier within the body of the procedure other than in a left part in an assignment statement denotes activation of the procedure.

5.4.5. Specifications

In the heading a specification part, giving information about the kinds and types of the formal parameters by means of an obvious notation, may be included. In this part no formal parameter may occur more than once. Specifications of formal parameters called by value (cf. section 4.7.3.1) must be supplied and specifications of formal parameters called by name (cf. section 4.7.3.2) may be omitted.

5.4.6. Code as procedure body

It is understood that the procedure body may be expressed in non-ALGOL language. Since it is intended that the use of this feature should be entirely a question of hardware representation, no further rules concerning this code language can be given within the reference language

Examples of Procedure Declarations:

EXAMPLE 1.

```
procedure euler (fct, sum, eps, tim) ; value eps, tim ;
integer tim ; real procedure fct ; real sum, eps ;
comment euler computes the sum of fct(i) for i from zero up to
infinity by means of a suitabley refined euler transformation. The
summation is stopped as soon as tim times in succession the abso-
lute value of the terms of the transformed series are found to be
less than eps. Hence, one should provide a function fct with one
integer argument, an upper bound eps, and an integer tim. The
output is the sum sum. euler is particularly efficient in the case
of a slowly convergent or divergent alternating series  ;
begin integer i, k, n, t ; array m[0:15] ; real mn, mp, ds  ;
i := n := t := 0  ;  m[0] := fct(0)  ;  sum := m[0]/2  ;
nextterm: i := i+1  ;  mn := fct(i)  ;
        for k := 0 step 1 until n do
            begin mp := (mn+m[k])/2  ;  m[k] := mn  ;
            mn := mp end means  ;
```

```
        if (abs(mn)<abs(m[n]))∧(n<15) then
            begin ds := mn/2  ;  n := n+1  ;  m[n] :=
            mn end accept
    else ds := mn ;
    sum := sum + ds  ;
    if abs(ds)<eps then t := t+1 else t := 0  ;
    if t<tim then go to nextterm
end euler
```

EXAMPLE 2.[8]

```
procedure RK(x,y,n,FKT,eps,eta,xE,yE,fi)  ;  value x,y  ;
integer n  ;  Boolean fi  ;  real x,eps,eta,xE  ;  array
y,yE  ;  procedure FKT  ;
comment: RK integrates the system yk'=fk(x,y₁ ,y₂ , ... , yₙ)
```

comment: RK integrates the system $y_k'=f_k(x,y_1 ,y_2 , ... , y_n)$ ($k=1,2, ... ,n$) of differential equations with the method of Runge-Kutta with automatic search for appropriate length of integration step. Parameters are: The initial values x and $y[k]$ for x and the unknown functions $y_k(x)$. The order n of the system. The procedure $FKT(x,y,n,z)$ which represents the system to be integrated, i.e. the set of functions f_k . The tolerance values eps and eta which govern the accuracy of the numerical integration. The end of the integration interval xE. The output parameter yE which represents the solution at $x=xE$. The Boolean variable fi, which must always be given the value **true** for an isolated or first entry into RK. If however the functions y must be available at several meshpoints $x_0 , x_1 , ... , x_n$, then the procedure must be called repeatedly (with $x=x_k$, $xE=x_{k+1}$, for $k=0, 1, ... , n-1$) and then the later calls may occur with $fi=$**false** which saves computing time. The input parameters of FKT must be x,y,n, the output parameter z represents the set of derivatives $z[k]=f_k(x,y[1], y[2], ... , y[n])$ for x and the actual y's. A procedure $comp$ enters as a nonlocal identifier ;

```
begin
    array z,y1,y2,y3[1:n]  ;  real x1,x2,x3,H  ;  Boolean out  ;
    integer k,j  ;  own real s,Hs  ;
    procedure  RK1ST(x,y,h,xe,ye)  ;  real  x,h,xe  ;  array
            y,ye  ;
        comment: RK1ST integrates one single RUNGE-KUTTA
            with initial values x,y[k] which yields the output
            parameters xe=x+h and ye[k], the latter being the
            solution at xe. Important: the parameters n, FKT, z
            enter RK1ST as nonlocal entities  ;
    begin
        array w[1:n], a[1:5]  ;  integer k,j  ;
        a[1] := a[2] := a[5] := h/2  ;  a[3] := a[4] := h  :
        xe := x  ;
        for k := 1 step 1 until n do ye[k] := w[k] := y[k]  ;
        for j := 1 step 1 until 4 do
        begin
            FKT(xe,w,n,z)  ;
            xe := x+a[j]  ;
            for k := 1 step 1 until n do
            begin
                w[k] := y[k]+a[j]×z[k]  ;
                ye[k] := ye[k] + a[j+1]×z[k]/3
```

---

[8] This RK-program contains some new ideas which are related to ideas of S. GILL, A process for the step-by-step integration of differential equations in an automatic computing machine, [Proc. Camb. Phil. Soc. 47 (1951), 96]; and E. FRÖBERG, On the solution of ordinary differential equations with digital computing machines, [Fysiograf. Sällsk. Lund, Förhd. 20, 11 (1950), 136–152]. It must be clear, however, that with respect to computing time and round-off errors it may not be optimal, nor has it actually been tested on a computer.

```
        end k
      end j
    end RK1ST  ;
Begin of program:
    if fi then begin H := xE−x  ;  s := 0 end else H := Hs  ;
    out := false  ;
AA: if (x+2.01×H−xE>0)≡(H>0) then
      begin Hs := H  ;  out := true  ;  H := (xE−x)/2
      end if  ;
    RK1ST (x,y,2×H,x1,y1)  ;
BB: RK1ST (x,y,H,x2,y2)  ;  RK1ST (x2,y2,H,x3,y3)  ;
    for k := 1 step 1 until n do
      if comp(y1[k],y3[k],eta)>eps then go to CC  ;
```

comment: comp(a,bc,) is a function designator, the value of which is the absolute value of the difference of the mantissae of a and b, after the exponents of these quantities have been made equal to the largest of the exponents of the originally given parameters a,b,c :

```
    x := x3  ;  if out then go to DD  ;
    for k := 1 step 1 until n do y[k] := y3[k]  ;
    if s=5 then begin s := 0  ;  H := 2×H end if  ;
    s := s+1  ;  go to AA  ;
CC: H := 0.5×H  ;  out := false  ;  x1 := x2  ;
    for k := 1 step 1 until n do y1[k] := y2[k]  ;
    go to BB  ;
DD: for k := 1 step 1 until n do yE[k] := y3[k]
end RK
```

ALPHABETIC INDEX OF DEFINITIONS OF CONCEPTS AND SYNTACTIC UNITS

⟨factor⟩, def 3.3.1
false, synt 2.2.2
for, synt 2.3, 4.6.1
⟨for clause⟩, def 4.6.1 text 4.6.3
⟨for list⟩, def 4.6.1 text 4.6.4
⟨for list element⟩, def 4.6.1 text 4.6.4.1, 4.6.4.2, 4.6.4.3
⟨formal parameter⟩, def 5.4.1 text 5.4.3
⟨formal parameter list⟩, def 5.4.1
⟨formal parameter part⟩, def 5.4.1
⟨for statement⟩, def 4.6.1 synt 4.1.1, 4.5.1 text 4.6 (complete section)
⟨function designator⟩, def 3.2.1 synt 3.3.1, 3.4.1 text 3.2.3, 5.4.4

go to, synt 2.3, 4.3.1
⟨go to statement⟩, def 4.3.1 synt 4.1.1 text 4.3.3

⟨identifier⟩, def 2.4.1 synt 3.1.1, 3.2.1, 3.5.1, 5.4.1 text 2.4.3
⟨identifier list⟩, def 5.4.1
if, synt 2.3, 3.3.1, 4.5.1
⟨if clause⟩, def 3.3.1, 4.5.1 synt 3.4.1, 3.5.1 text 3.3.3, 4.5.3.2
⟨if statement⟩, def 4.5.1 text 4.5.3.1
⟨implication⟩, def 3.4.1
integer, synt 2.3, 5.1.1 text 5.1.3
⟨integer⟩, def 2.5.1 text 2.5.4

label, synt 2.3, 5.4.1
⟨label⟩, def 3.5.1 synt 4.1.1, 4.5.1, 4.6.1 text 1, 4.1.3
⟨left part⟩, def 4.2.1
⟨left part list⟩, def 4.2.1
⟨letter⟩, def 2.1 synt 2, 2.4.1, 3.2.1, 4.7.1
⟨letter string⟩, def 3.2.1, 4.7.1
local, text 4.1.3
⟨local or own type⟩, def 5.1.1 synt 5.2.1
⟨logical operator⟩, def 2.3 synt 3.4.1 text 3.4.5
⟨logical value⟩, def 2.2.2 synt 2, 3.4.1
⟨lower bound⟩, def 5.2.1 text 5.2.4

minus −, synt 2.3, 2.5.1, 3.3.1 text 3.3.4.1
multiply ×, synt 2.3, 3.3.1 text 3.3.4.1
⟨multiplying operator⟩, def 3.3.1

nonlocal, text 4.1.3
⟨number⟩, def 2.5.1 text 2.5.3, 2.5.4

⟨open string⟩, def 2.6.1
⟨operator⟩, def 2.3
own, synt 2.3, 5.1.1 text 5, 5.2.5

⟨parameter delimiter⟩, def 3.2.1, 4.7.1 synt 5.4.1 text 4.7.7
parentheses ( ), synt 2.3, 3.2.1, 3.3.1, 3.4.1, 3.5.1, 4.7.1, 5.4.1 text 3.3.5.2
plus +, synt 2.3, 2.5.1, 3.3.1 text 3.3.4.1
⟨primary⟩, def 3.3.1
procedure, synt 2.3, 5.4.1
⟨procedure body⟩, def 5.4.1
⟨procedure declaration⟩, def 5.4.1 synt 5 text 5.4.3
⟨procedure heading⟩, def 5.4.1 text 5.4.3
⟨procedure identifier⟩ def 3.2.1 synt 3.2.1, 4.7.1, 5.4.1 text 4.7.5.4
⟨procedure statement⟩, def 4.7.1 synt 4.1.1 text 4.7.3
⟨program⟩, def 4.1.1 text 1
⟨proper string⟩, def 2.6.1

quantity, text 2.7

real, synt 2.3, 5.1.1 text 5.1.3
⟨relation⟩, def 3.4.1 text 3.4.5
⟨relational operator⟩, def 2.3, 3.4.1

scope, text 2.7
semicolon ;, synt 2.3, 4.1.1, 5.4.1
⟨separator⟩, def 2.3
⟨sequential operator⟩, def 2.3
⟨simple arithmetic expression⟩, def 3.3.1 text 3.3.3
⟨simple Boolean⟩, def 3.4.1
⟨simple designational expression⟩, def 3.5.1
⟨simple variable⟩, def 3.1.1 synt 5.1.1 text 2.4.3
space ⊔, synt 2.3 text 2.3, 2.6.3
⟨specification part⟩, def 5.4.1 text 5.4.5
⟨specificator⟩, def 2.3
⟨specifier⟩, def 5.4.1
standard function, text 3.2.4, 3.2.5
⟨statement⟩, def 4.1.1, synt 4.5.1, 4.6.1, 5.4.1 text 4 (complete section)
statement bracket, see: **begin end**
step, synt 2.3, 4.6.1 text 4.6.4.2
string, synt 2.3, 5.4.1
⟨string⟩, def 2.6.1 synt 3.2.1, 4.7.1 text 2.6.3
string quotes ' ', synt 2.3, 2.6.1, text 2.6.3
subscript, text 3.1.4.1
subscript bound, text 5.2.3.1
subscript brackets [ ], synt 2.3, 3.1.1, 3.5.1, 5.2.1
⟨subscripted variable⟩, def 3.1.1 text 3.1.4.1
⟨subscript expression⟩, def 3.1.1 synt 3.5.1
⟨subscript list⟩, def 3.1.1
successor, text 4
switch, synt 2.3, 5.3.1, 5.4.1
⟨switch declaration⟩, def 5.3.1 synt 5 text 5.3.3
⟨switch designator⟩, def 3.5.1 text 3.5.3
⟨switch identifier⟩, def 3.5.1 synt 3.2.1, 4.7.1, 5.3.1
⟨switch list⟩, def 5.3.1

⟨term⟩, def 3.3.1
ten 10, synt 2.3, 2.5.1
then, synt 2.3, 3.3.1, 4.5.1
transfer function, text 3.2.5
true, synt 2.2.2
⟨type⟩, def 5.1.1 synt 5.4.1 text 2.8
⟨type declaration⟩, def 5.1.1 synt 5 text 5.1.3
⟨type list⟩, def 5.1.1

⟨unconditional statement⟩, def 4.1 .1, 4.5.1
⟨unlabelled basic statement⟩, def 4.1.1
⟨unlabelled block⟩, def 4.1.1
⟨unlabelled compound⟩, def 4.1.1
⟨unsigned integer⟩, def 2.5.1, 3.5.1
⟨unsigned number⟩, def 2.5.1 synt 3.3.1
until, synt 2.3, 4.6.1 text 4.6.4.2
⟨upper bound⟩, def 5 2.1 text 5.2.4

value, synt 2.3, 5.4.1
value, text 2.8, 3.3.3
⟨value part⟩, def 5.4.1 text 4.7.3.1
⟨variable⟩, def 3.1.1 synt 3.3.1, 3.4.1, 4.2.1, 4.6.1 text 3.1.3
⟨variable identifier⟩, def 3.1.1

while, synt 2.3, 4.6.1 text 4.6.4.3

END OF THE REPORT

THE REMAINING TROUBLESPOTS IN ALGOL 60*

D. E. KNUTH

This paper lists the ambiguities remaining in the language ALGOL 60, which have been noticed since the publication of the Revised ALGOL 60 Report in 1963.

There is little doubt that the programming language ALGOL 60 has had a great impact on many areas of computer science, and it seems fair to state that this language has been more carefully studied than any other programming language.

When ALGOL 60 was first published in 1960 [1], many new features were introduced into programming languages, primarily with respect to the generality of "procedures." It was quite difficult at first for anyone to grasp the full significance of each of the linguistic features with respect to other aspects of the language, and therefore people commonly would discover ALGOL 60 constructions they had never before realized were possible, each time they reread the Report. Such constructions often provided counterexamples to many of the usual techniques of compiler implementation, and in many cases it was possible to construct programs that could be interpreted in more than one way.

The most notable feature of the first ALGOL 60 Report was the new standard it set for language definition, based on an almost completely systematic use of syntactic rules that prescribed the structure of programs; this innovation made it possible to know exactly what the language ALGOL 60 was, to a much greater degree than had ever been achieved previously. Of course it was inevitable that a complex document such as the ALGOL 60 Report (roughly 75 typewritten pages, prepared by an international committee) would contain some ambiguities and contradictions, since it involves a very large number of highly interdependent elements. As time passed, and especially as ALGOL 60 translators were written, these problems were noticed by many people, and in 1962 a meeting of the international committee was called to help resolve these

*Reprinted from *Comm ACM* 10, 10, 1967, 611–617.

The preparation of this paper has been supported in part by the National Science Foundation and in part by the Burroughs Corporation.

issues. The result was the Revised ALGOL 60 Report [2], which cleaned up many of the unclear points.

Now that several more years have gone by, it is reasonable to expect that ALGOL 60 is pretty well understood. A few points of ambiguity and contradiction still remain in the Revised ALGOL 60 Report, some of which were left unresolved at the 1962 meeting (primarily because of high feelings between people who had already implemented conflicting interpretations of ambiguous aspects), and some of which have come to light more recently.

In view of the widespread interest in ALGOL 60 it seems appropriate to have a list of all its remaining problem areas, or at least of those which are now known. This list will be useful as a guide to users of ALGOL 60, who may find it illuminating to explore some of the comparatively obscure parts of this language and who will want to know what ambiguous constructions should be avoided; and useful also to designers of programming languages, who will want to avoid making similar mistakes.

The following sections of this paper therefore enumerate the blemishes which remain. A preliminary list of all the known trouble spots was compiled by the author for use by the ALGOL subcommittee of the ACM Programming Languages committee in November 1963; and after receiving extensive assistance from the committee members, the author prepared a revised document which appeared in mimeographed form in *ALGOL Bulletin 19, AB19.3.7* (Mathematisch Centrum, Amsterdam, January 1965). The present paper is a fairly extensive modification of the *ALGOL Bulletin* article; it has been prepared at the request of several people who do not have ready access to the *ALGOL Bulletin* and who have pointed out the desirability of wider circulation.

The following list is actually more remarkable for its shortness than its length. A complete critique which goes to the same level of detail would be almost out of the question for other languages comparable to ALGOL 60, since the list would probably be a full order of magnitude longer.

This paper is divided into two parts, one which lists *ambiguities* and one which lists *corrections* which seem to be necessary to the Revised Report. The word "ambiguous" is itself quite ambiguous, and it is used here in the following sense: An aspect of ALGOL 60 is said to be ambiguous if, on the basis of the Revised ALGOL 60 Report, it is possible to write an ALGOL 60 program for which this feature can be interpreted in two ways leading to different computations in the program, and if it is impossible to prove conclusively from the Revised Report that either of these conflicting interpretations is incorrect. So-called "syntactic ambiguities" are not necessarily ambiguities of the language in this sense, although the original ALGOL 60 Report contained some syntactic ambiguities that did lead to discrepancies. (See [3] and [4] for a discussion of the former ambiguities; and see correction 7 below and the discussion at the end of Section 3 in [5] for comments on syntactic ambiguities remaining in the Revised Report.)

The distinction between an "ambiguity" in ALGOL 60 and a "correction" that is necessary to the Report is not clear cut; for when the Report contains an error or contradictory statement, this might lead to ambiguous interpretations, and conversely any ambiguity might be considered an error in the Report. The difference is mainly a matter of degree; the true meanings of the points that merely need to be corrected are almost universally agreed upon by people who have studied the Report carefully, because of the overall spirit of the language in spite of the fact that some of the rules are incorrectly stated.

Frequent references are made in the discussions below to the numbered sections of the Revised Report [2], and the reader is advised to have this document available for comparison if he is going to understand the significance of the comments which follow.

People who have studied the ALGOL Report carefully have often been called "ALGOL theologians," because of the analogy between the Bible and the Revised Report (which is the ultimate source of wisdom about ALGOL 60). Using the same analogy, it is possible to view the following sections as a more or less objective discussion of the conflicting doctrines that have been based on these Scriptures.

1. Ambiguities

AMBIGUITY 1: SIDE EFFECTS

A "side effect" is conventionally regarded as a change (invoked by a function designator) in the state of some quantities which are **own** variables or which are not local to the function designator. In other words, when a procedure is being called in the midst of some expression, it has side effects if in addition to computing a value it does input or output or changes the value of some variable that is not internal to the procedure.

For example, let us consider the following program:

```
begin integer a;
  integer procedure f(x,y);  value y,x;  integer y,x;
    a := f := x + 1;
  integer procedure g(x);  integer x;  x := g := a + 2;
    a := 0;  outreal (1, a + f(a, g(a))/g(a)) end.
```

Here both f and g have as a side effect the alteration of an external variable.

It is clear that the value output by this program depends heavily upon the order of computation. Many compilers find more efficient object programs are obtained if the denominator of a complicated fraction is evaluated before the numerator; if we first compute $g(a)$, then $f(a, g(a))$, then $a + f(a, g(a))/g(a)$, and if the evaluation of the **value** parameters in $f(a, g(a))$ is done in the order $a, g(a)$, then we get the answer $4\frac{1}{2}$. Other possible answers are $\frac{1}{3}$, $\frac{3}{5}$, $\frac{3}{2}$, $\frac{5}{2}$, $\frac{4}{3}$, $3\frac{3}{5}$, $3\frac{1}{3}$, $5\frac{3}{5}$, $3\frac{1}{2}$, and $7\frac{1}{2}$.

The major point left unresolved in the Revised Report was the ambiguity about side effects: Are they allowed in ALGOL 60 programs, and if so what do the programs mean? If side effects are allowable, then the order of computation must be specified in the following places: evaluating the primaries of an expression; evaluating the subscripts of a variable; evaluating bound pairs in a block head; evaluating **value** parameters; and (perhaps) the step-until element of a for clause. Note, for example, that **value** parameters (which are to be evaluated just after entry to a procedure, Section 4.7.3.1.) might conceivably be evaluated in the order of their appearance in the parameter list or in the value part.

An argument may actually be made for the opinion that side effects are implicitly outlawed by the fifth paragraph in Section 4.5.3.2; or at least that paragraph says that all side effects occurring during the evaluation of an if clause of a conditional statement must be cancelled if the Boolean expression comes out false! A similar situation occurs in Section 4.3.5 where side effects, occurring during the evaluation of a designational expression which is ultimately undefined, must presumably be nullified. (On the other hand, the wording of these sections is probably just an oversight, and the implication about side effects was probably not intended.)

How close does the Report come to prescribing the order of computation? Section 3.3.5 says "the sequence of operations within one expression is generally from left to right," but the context here refers to the order of carrying out arithmetic operations; and it does not say whether the value of the first term "a" in the above example should be calculated before or after the second term "$f(a, g(a))/g(a)$" since no "operation" in the sense of the Report is involved here. Section 4.2.3.1 says subscript expressions in the left part variables of an assignment statement are evaluated "in sequence from left to right." (So in the assignment statement

$$A[a + B[f(a)] + g(a)] := C[a] := 0$$

we are perhaps to evaluate "$a + B[f(a)] + g(a)$" first, then "$f(a)$" again, then "a"?)

Section 1, footnote 4, says "Whenever ... the outcome of a certain process is left undefined ... a program only fully defines a computational process if accompanying information specifies ... the course of action to be taken in all such cases as may occur during the execution of the computation." In Section 3.3.6 we read, "It is indeed understood that different hardware representations may evaluate arithmetic expressions differently." The latter remark was made with reference to arithmetic on **real** quantities (i.e., floating-point arithmetic), but it is remarkable when viewed also from the standpoint of side effects! Footnote 4 says essentially that ALGOL 60 is not intended to be free of ambiguity, and much can be said for the desirability of incompletely specified formalisms; indeed, this incompleteness is the basis of the axiomatic method in mathematics and it is also the basis of many good jokes. But it is doubtful whether the ambiguity of side effects is a desirable one; for further remarks in this vein see Ambiguity 9.

In view of the ambiguities of side effects, which many people do not realize because they know only the interpretations given by the ALGOL compiler they use, the author has founded SPASEPA, the Society for the Prevention of the Appearance of Side Effects in Published Algorithms. Members and/or donations are earnestly solicited.

It may be of value to digress for a moment here and to ask whether side effects are desirable or not; should ALGOL or comparable languages allow side effects? Do side effects serve any useful purpose or are they just peculiar constructions for programmers who like to be tricky? Objections to side effects have often been voiced, and the most succinct formulation is perhaps that due to Samelson and Bauer in *ALGOL Bulletin 12*, pp. 7–8. The principal points raised are that (i) an explanation of the "use" of side effects tends to waste inordinate amounts of classroom time when explaining ALGOL, giving an erroneous impression of the spirit of the language; (ii) familiar identities such as $f(x) + x = x + f(x)$ are no longer valid, and this is an unnatural deviation from mathematical conventions; (iii) many "applications" of side effects are merely programming tricks making puzzles of programs; other uses can almost always be reprogrammed easily by changing a function designator to a procedure call statement. Essentially the same objections have been voiced with respect to the concept of parameters "called by name," which was the chief new feature of ALGOL 60.

Another objection to side effects is that they may cause apparently needless computation. For example, consider

"**if** $g(a) = 2 \lor g(a) = 3$ **then** 1 **else** 0"

in connection with the procedure $g(x)$ above; according to the rules of the Revised Report it is necessary to evaluate $g(a)$ twice, thereby increasing a by 4 even if the first relation involving $g(a)$ is found to be true.

We might also mention the fact that ALGOL's call-by-name feature is deficient in the following respect: It is impossible to write an ALGOL 60 procedure "*increment* (x)" which increases the value of the variable x by unity. In particular the procedure statement "*increment* $(A[i])$" should increase the current value of $A[i]$ by unity, where i is a function designator which may produce different values when it is invoked twice.

On the other hand, consider the following procedure:

real procedure $SIGMA$ (i, l, u, x);   **value** l, u;   **integer** i, l, u;
   real x;
  begin real s; $s := 0$;   **for** $i := l$ **step** 1 **until** u **do** $s := s + x$;
   $SIGMA := s$ **end**.

This procedure computes $\sum_{i=l}^{u} x$ and has the additional side effect of changing variable i. It is quite natural to be able to write

$$SIGMA\ (i, 1, m, SIGMA\ (j, 1, n, A[i, j]))\ \text{for}\ \sum_{i=1}^{m} \sum_{j=1}^{n} A_{ij}$$

without adding special summation conventions to the language itself; this is a tame and unambiguous use of side effects which also is the principal example that has been put forward to point out the usefulness of parameters called by name. (See [6] for further discussion.)

If we alter the above procedure by inserting "**integer** $i0$; $i0 := i$;" after "**real** s;" and "; $i := i0$" before "**end**", we would find that no side effect is introduced as a consequence of the total execution of the function $SIGMA$ (i, l, u, x), provided the actual parameter x does not involve side effects. So the above example does not constitute an inherent use of side effects; in fact, a study of this particular case indicates that it might be better to have some sort of facility for defining dummy variables (like i and j) which have existence only during the evaluation of a function but which may appear within the arguments to that function.

We should remark also that the principal objection to allowing parameters called by name, even in natural situations like the above example, is that the machine language implementation of these constructions is necessarily much slower than we would expect a simple summation operation to be; the inner loop (incrementation of i, testing against u, adding x to s) involves a great deal of more or less irrelevant bookkeeping because i and x are called by name, even on machines like the Burroughs B5500 [12] whose hardware was specifically designed to facilitate ALGOL's call by name. The use of "macro" definition facilities to extend languages, instead of relying solely on procedures for this purpose, results in a more satisfactory running program.

Other situations for which function designators with side effects can be useful are not uncommon, e.g., in connection with a procedure for input or for random number generation. Side effects also arise naturally in connection with the manipulation of data structures, when a function changes the structure while it computes a value; for example, it is often useful to have a function "$pop(S)$" which deletes the top value from a "stack" S and which retains the deleted value as its result. See also [7] for examples of Boolean function designators with side effects that are specifically intended for use in constructions like $p \lor q$, where q is *never* to be evaluated when p is true and where p is to be evaluated first in any case.

The objection above that $x + f(x)$ should be equal to $f(x) + x$, because of age old mathematical conventions, is not very strong; there are simple and natural rules for sequencing operations of an expression so that a programmer knows what he is doing when he is using side effects. The people who complain about "$x + f(x)$" are generally compiler writers who don't want to generate extra code to save x in temporary storage before computing $f(x)$, since this is almost always unnecessary. Such inefficiency is the real reason for the objections to side effects. These same people would *not* like to see "$x = 0 \lor f(x) = 0$" be treated the same as "$f(x) = 0 \lor x = 0$" since the former relation can be used to suppress the computation of "$f(x) = 0$" when it is known that "$x = 0$"; in fact one naturally likes to write "$x = 0 \lor f(x) = 0$" in situations where $f(0)$ is undefined.

AMBIGUITY 2: INCOMPLETE FUNCTIONS

The question of exit from a function designator via a **go to** statement is another lively issue. This might be regarded as a special case of point 1, since such an exit is a "side effect," and indeed the discussion under point 1 does apply here. Some further points are relevant to this case, however.

Some people feel this is an important feature because of "error exits." However, the same effect can be achieved by using a procedure call statement and adding an output parameter.

Two rather convincing arguments can be put forward to contend that this type of exit is not really allowed by ALGOL, so the matter is not really an ambiguity at all.

(a) In Section 3.2.3 we read, "Function designators define single numerical or logical values." An incomplete function would not. Or, if it would, there would be mysterious, ambiguous consequences such as this:

```
begin real x, y;  real procedure F;  begin F := 1;
   go to L end;
  x := F + 1;  y := 1;  L:  end.
```

We question whether x is replaced by 2, and if so, whether y is replaced by 1 (thus incorporating simultaneity into the language?). After all, F rigorously defines the value 1 and "the value so assigned is used to continue the evaluation of the expression in which the function designator occurs." (Cf. Section 5.4.4.)

(b) The discussion of the control of the program in Section 5.4.3.2 is based entirely on the values of the Boolean expressions, and the language used there implicitly excludes such a possibility. In many places the Report speaks of expressions as if they have a value, and no mention is ever made of expressions that are left unevaluated due to exits from function designators.

A further point about incomplete functions (though not really part of the ambiguity) concerns the implementation problems caused when such an exit occurs during the evaluation of the bound expressions while array declarations are being processed. Since the control words for a storage allocation scheme are not entirely set up at this time, such exits have caused bugs in more than one ALGOL compiler!

AMBIGUITY 3: STEP-UNTIL

The exact sequence occurring during the evaluation of the "step-until" element of a for clause has been the subject of much (rather heated) debate. The construction

$$\text{for } V := A \text{ step } B \text{ until } C \text{ do } S$$

(where V is a variable, A, B, C are expressions, and S is a procedure) can be replaced by a procedure call

$$\text{for } (V, A, B, C, S)$$

with suitable procedure called "*for*." The debate centers, more or less, on which of these parameters are to be thought of as called by value, and which as called by name.

Conservative ALGOL theologians follow the sequence given in Section 4.6.4.2 very literally, so that if statement S is executed n times, the value of A is computed once, B is computed $2 \times n + 1$ times, C is computed $n + 1$ times, and (if V is subscripted) the subscripts of V are evaluated $3 \times n + 2$ times. Liberal theologians take the expansion more figuratively, evaluating these things just once. There are many points of view between these two "extremist" positions. As a result, the following program will probably give at least four or five different output values when run on different present-day ALGOL implementations:

```
begin array V, A, C[1:1];  integer k;
  integer procedure i;  begin i := 1;  k := k + 1 end;
  k := 0;  A[1] := 1;  C[1] := 3;
  for V[i] := A[i] step A[i] until C[i] do;
  outreal (1, k) end;
```

The liberal interpretation gives an output of 4, the conservative interpretation gives something like 23, and intermediate interpretations give intermediate values; for example the compromise suggested in [9] gives the value 16.

The conservative argument is, "Read Section 4.6.4.2." The liberal arguments are: (a) "If Section 4.6.4.2 is to be taken literally, it gives a perfectly well defined value for the controlled variable upon exit. Since Section 4.6.5 says the value is undefined, however, it must mean Section 4.6.4.2 is not to be taken literally." (b) "The repeated phase '*the* controlled variable' is always used in the singular, implying that the subscript(s) of the variable need be evaluated only once during the entire for clause. Other interpretations make Section 4.6.5 meaningless."

Examination of published algorithms shows that in well over 99 % of the uses of for statements, the value of the "step" B is $+1$, and in the vast majority of the exceptions the step is a constant. It is clear that programmers seldom feel the need to make use of any ambiguous cases. The liberal interpretation is clearly more efficient and it would be recommended for future programming languages; a programmer who really feels the need for some of the woollier uses of a for statement can be told to write the statements out by adding a tiny bit of program instead of using a for statement. Even though uses can be contrived for examples like

$$\text{for } x := .1 \text{ step } x \text{ until } 10^6$$

or

$$\text{for } y := 1 \text{ step } 1 \text{ until } y + 1$$

these are rewritten easily using the "while" element.

AMBIGUITY 4: SPECIFICATIONS

The wording of Section 5.4.5 can be interpreted as saying that parameters called by value must be specified only if the specification part is given at all! Furthermore, it is not stated to what extent, *if any*, the actual parameters must agree with a given specification, and to what extent the specifications which do appear will affect the meaning of the program. For example, is the following program legitimate?

```
begin integer array A, B, C[0:10];   array D[0:10];
  procedure P(A, B, C);   array A, B, C;
    begin integer i;
      for i := 0 step 1 until 10 do
        C[i] := A[i]/B[i]
    end;
  integer i;
  for i := 0 step 1 until 10 do
    begin A[i] := 1;   B[i] := 2 end;
  P(A, B, C);   P(A, B, D)
end.
```

If so, the assignment statement inside the procedure will have to *round* the result or not depending on the actual parameter used. Consider also the same procedure with the formal parameters specified to be *integer* arrays. For further discussion see [9].

AMBIGUITY 5:   REPEATED PARAMETERS

Several published algorithms have a procedure heading like

$$\textbf{procedure } invert \ (A) \ order\colon (n) \ output\colon (A)$$

where two of the formal parameters have the same name. The Report does not specifically exclude this, and it does not say what interpretation is to be taken.

AMBIGUITY 6:   VALUE LABELS

It has not been clear whether or not a designational expression can be called by value, and if so, whether its value may be "undefined" as used in Section 4.3.5. This may or may not be allowed by the language of Section 4.7.3.1 (which talks about "assignment" of values to the formal parameters in a "fictitious block"). Cf. Section 4.7.5.4; if a designational expression could be called by value, a switch identifier with a single component could be also, in the same way as an array identifier can be called by value. The first paragraph of Section 2.8 is relevant here also.

AMBIGUITY 7:   OWN

This has so many interpretations it will take too much space to repeat the arguments here. See [8, 9] for a discussion of the two principal interpretations, "dynamic" and "static," each of which can be useful. The additional complications of own arrays with dynamically varying subscript bounds combined with recursion, adds further ambiguities; for one apparently reasonable way to define this, see [11].

AMBIGUITY 8:   NUMERIC LABELS AND "QUANTITIES"

Most ALGOL compilers exclude implementation of numeric labels, primarily because a correct implementation requires an unsigned integer constant parameter to be denoted, in machine language, both as a number and a label. Consider for example

$$\textbf{procedure } P1(q, r); \quad \textbf{if } q < 5 \textbf{ then go to } r;$$
$$\textbf{procedure } P2(q, r); \quad \textbf{if } r < 5 \textbf{ then go to } q;$$
$$\textbf{procedure } W(Z); \quad \textbf{procedure } Z; \quad Z(2, 2);$$
$$\cdots W(P1); \quad x := 0; \quad W(P2); \quad 2: \ \cdots$$

There is no ambiguity here in the sense we are considering, just a difficulty of implementation in view of the double meaning of a parameter "2."

The author has shown the following procedure to several authoritative people, however, and a 50% split developed between those saying it was or was not valid ALGOL:

$$\textbf{procedure } P(q); \quad \textbf{if } q < 5 \textbf{ then go to } q;$$

The idea of course is that we might later call $P(2)$ where 2 is a numeric label. Actually this seems to be specifically outlawed by Section 2.4.3 (the identifier q cannot refer to two different quantities). But consider

$$\textbf{procedure } P(q); \quad \textbf{if } B(q) \textbf{ then } G(q);$$
$$\textbf{procedure } G(q); \quad \textbf{go to } q;$$
$$\textbf{Boolean procedure } B(q); \quad B := q < 5;$$

Is this now valid?

Consider also

```
begin integer I;   array A[0:0];
procedure P1(X);   array X;   X[0] := 0;
procedure P2(X);   integer X;   X := 0;
procedure call (X, Y);   X(Y);
call (P1, A);   call (P2, I) end
```

The identifier Y is used to denote two different quantities (an array and a simple variable) which have the same scope, yet this program seems to be valid in spite of the wording of Section 2.4.3.

The latter procedure is believed to be admissible because the expansion of procedure bodies should be considered from a dynamic (not static) point of view. For example consider

$$\textbf{integer procedure } factorial \ (n); \quad \textbf{integer } n;$$
$$factorial := \textbf{if } n > 0 \textbf{ then } n \times factorial \ (n - 1) \textbf{ else } 1;$$

In this procedure body the call of *factorial* $(n - 1)$ should not be expanded unless $n > 0$, or else the expansion will never terminate. From the dynamic viewpoint the identifier Y in *call* (X, Y) never does in fact denote two different quantities at the same time.

Another strong argument can be put forward that even our earlier example "**if** $q < 5$ **then go to** q" is allowable. Notice that Section 2.4.3 does *not* say that an identifier may denote a string; but in fact a formal parameter *may* denote a string. Therefore we conclude that Section 2.4.3 does not apply specifically to formal parameters; this is consistent with the entire spirit of the Report, which does not speak of formal parameters except where it tells how they are to be replaced by actual parameters. The syntax equations in particular reflect this philosophy. Consider for example

$$\textbf{procedure } P(Q, S); \quad \textbf{procedure } Q; \quad \textbf{string } S; \quad Q(S);$$

there is no way to use the syntax of ALGOL to show that "$Q(S)$" is a procedure statement and at the same time to reflect the fact that S is a string. We show S is an ⟨identifier⟩, but to show it is an ⟨actual parameter⟩ we must show it is either an ⟨expression⟩, an ⟨array identifier⟩, a ⟨switch identifier⟩, or a ⟨procedure identifier⟩, and it really is not any of these. So the only way to account for this is to first replace Q and S by their actual parameters, in any invocation of P, and *then* to apply the syntax equations to the result.

The distinction between what is valid and what is not according to Section 3.4.3 is unclear.

AMBIGUITY 9:   REAL ARITHMETIC

The precision of arithmetic on **real** quantities has intentionally been left ambiguous (see Section 3.3.6). In an interesting discussion van Wijngaarden [13] gives arguments to show among other things that because of this ambiguity it is not necessarily true that the relation "3.14 = 3.14" is the same as "**true**" in all implementations of ALGOL. As we have mentioned above, ambiguities as such are not necessarily undesirable; but is clear that ambiguities 1–8 are of a different nature than this one, since it can be quite useful to describe fixed ALGOL programs with varying arithmetic substituted.

So a language need not be unambiguous, but of course when intentionally ambiguous elements are introduced it is far better to state specifically what the ambiguities are, not merely to leave them undefined, lest too many people think they are writing unambiguous programs when they are not.

2.   Corrections

CORRECTION 1:   OMITTED else

In Section 3.3.3 it is stated that "the construction

$$\textbf{else } \langle \text{simple arithmetic expression} \rangle$$

is equivalent to the construction

$$\textbf{else if true then } \langle \text{simple arithmetic expression} \rangle$$

But the latter construction is erroneous since if fails to meet the syntax; we cannot write $A := \textbf{if } B \textbf{ then } C \textbf{ else if true then } D$. The original incorrect sentence adds nothing to the Report and means little or nothing to non-LISP programmers.

CORRECTION 2:   CONDITIONAL STATEMENT SEQUENCE

In Section 4.5.3.2, the paragraph "If none . . . dummy statement" should be deleted or at least accompanied by a qualification that it applies only to the second form of a conditional statement. This well-known error and also Correction 11 would have been fixed in the Revised Report except for the fact that these proposals were tied to other ones involving side effects; in the heated discussion which took place, the less controversial issues were overlooked.

The Revised Report changed the syntax of conditional statements and this makes Section 4.5.3.2. even more erroneous. And the explanation is incorrect in yet another respect, since control of the program should not pass to the statement called "$S4$" when the conditional statement is a procedure body or is preceded by a for clause.

Therefore Section 4.5.3.2 should be completely rewritten, perhaps as follows:

4.5.3.2.   Conditional statement. According to the syntax, three forms of unlabelled conditional statements are possible. These may be illustrated as follows (with Section 4.5.4 eliminated):

$$\textbf{if } B \textbf{ then } S_u$$
$$\textbf{if } B \textbf{ then } S_u \textbf{ else } S$$
$$\textbf{if } B \textbf{ then } S_{for}$$

Here B is a Boolean expression, S_u is an unconditional statement, S is a statement, and S_{for} is a for statement.

The execution of a conditional statement may be described as follows: The Boolean expression B is evaluated. If its value is **true**, the statement S_u or S_{for} following "**then**" is executed. If its value is **false** and if the conditional statement has the second form, the statement S following "**else**" is executed. (This statement S may of course be another conditional statement, which is to be interpreted according to the same rule.)

If a go to statement refers to a label within S_u or S_{for}, the effect is the same as if the remainder of the conditional statement (namely "**if** B **then**," and in the second case also "**else** S") were not present.

CORRECTION 3:   FOR EXAMPLE

The second example in Section 4.6.2 is not very good since (precluding side effects) it nearly always gets into an unending loop. Therefore, change "$V1$" to "k" in both places.

CORRECTION 4:   FUNCTION VALUES

Two sentences of Section 5.4.4 should say " . . . as a left part . . . " rather than " . . . in a left part . . . " since a function designator may appear in a subscript. A clarification, stating that the value is lost if a **real**, **integer**, or **Boolean** procedure is called in a procedure statement, might also be added here.

Change sentence 2, Section 4.2.3 " . . . a function designator of the same name . . . ". This makes an implied rule explicit. Or else, consider

real procedure A; $A := B := 0$;
integer procedure $B(k)$;   **if** $k > 0$ **then** A **else** $B := 2$;

which appears to conform to all of the present rules.

CORRECTION 5:   EXPRESSIONS

In the second sentence of Section 3, insert "labels, switch designators," after "function designators." This describes the constituents of expressions much more accurately.

CORRECTION 6:   DIVISION BY ZERO

Insert after the second sentence of 3.3.4.2: "The operation is undefined if the factor has the value zero. In other cases," The present wording of this section seems to imply $1/0$ is defined somehow.

CORRECTION 7:   STRING SYNTAX

The advent of syntax-oriented compilers and the fact that the syntax of ALGOL is (in large measure) formally unambiguous, make it desirable to change the most flagrantly ambiguous syntax rule in the Report. Therefore it is suggested that in Section 2.6.1 the definition of open string be replaced by

$\langle \text{open string} \rangle ::= \langle \text{proper string} \rangle \ |$

$\qquad\qquad \langle \text{open string} \rangle \langle \text{string} \rangle \langle \text{proper string} \rangle$

Correction 8: Library Procedures

Section 2.4.3 says "[Identifiers] may be chosen freely (cf. however, Section 3.2.4, Standard Functions)." Section 3.2.4 says "Certain identifiers should be reserved for the standard functions of analysis, which will be expressed as procedures." If the quotation from 2.4.3 is not self-contradictory it seems to be saying that an identifier like "*abs*" may not be used by a programmer. But this would be disastrous since the list of reserved identifiers is not defined. A programmer using the name "*gamma*" for a variable may find out next year that this identifier is reserved for the gamma function. It should be made clear that any identifier may be redeclared (although this can of course lead to some difficulties when a procedure is copied from the literature into the middle of a program).

Moreover, the fourth paragraph of Section 5 specifically disallows the use of any procedures assumed to exist without declaration, except function designators denoting "standard functions of analysis." Thus, procedures such as "*inreal*," etc. for accomplishing input would have to be declared in any program which uses them! A suggested change (which I think most people would say was no change from the original intention) would be to drop the sentence "Apart from labels . . . must be declared" from the paragraph mentioned, and to add the following paragraph to Section 5:

"It is understood that certain identifiers may have meaning without explicit declaration, as if they were declared in a block external to the entire program (cf. Section 3.2.4). Such identifiers might include, for example, names of standard input and output procedures. Apart from labels, formal parameters of procedure declarations, and these standard identifiers, each identifier appearing in a program must be declared."

This paragraph makes available other types of identifiers if there is a need for them, e.g., an identifier denoting a real-time clock, or a label denoting a particular part of a control program, etc.

Correction 9: Outer Bounds

The statement of Section 5.2.4.2: "Consequently in the outermost block of a program only array declarations with constant bounds may be declared," should be amended to allow for the possibility of calls on standard functions (or other standard identifiers as noted in correction 8). The declaration

$$\textbf{array } A\,[0: abs(-2)]$$

is allowable in the outermost block, or the word "consequently" does not apply.

Correction 10: Labelled Programs

The syntax for ⟨program⟩ allows a program to be labelled but the remainder of the Report always talks about labels being local to some block. To rectify this, insert three words into Section 4.1.3:

" . . . a procedure body or a program must be considered . . . "

This is in fact the way a compiler should probably do the implementation (see [10]). As an example, consider the following:

$$A: \quad \textbf{begin array } B[1: read]; \quad outarray\ (B); \quad \textbf{go to } A \textbf{ end};$$

Correction 11: Undefined go to

The use of the word "undefined" in Section 4.3.5 is highly ambiguous, and under some interpretations it leads to undecidable questions which would make ALGOL 60 truly impossible to implement. Under what conditions is a switch designator "undefined"? For example we could say it is undefined if its evaluation procedure makes use of real arithmetic, or if its evaluation procedure never terminates. By a suitable construction, the latter condition can be made equivalent to the problem of deciding whether or not a Turing Machine will ever stop.

The following procedure is an amusing (although unambiguous) example of the application of an undefined go to statement, which points out how difficult it can be for an optimizing ALGOL 60 translator to detect the fact that a procedure is being called recursively:

```
begin integer nn;
  switch A := B[1], B[2];
  switch B := A[G], A[2];
  integer procedure F(n, S);  value n;  integer n;  switch S;
    begin nn := n;  go to S[1];  F := nn end F;
  integer procedure G;
    begin integer n;
    n := nn; G := 0;
    nn := if n ≤ 1 then n else F(n−1, A) + F(n−2, A)
    end S;
  outreal (1, F(20, A)) end.
```

The output of this program should be 6765 (the twentieth Fibonacci number).

Correction 12: Call by Name

Instead of "Some important particular cases of this general rule" at the end of Section 4.7.5, it should be e.g., "Some important particular cases of this general rule, and some additional restrictions." The restrictions of Subsection 4.7.5.2 are not always special cases of the general rule, as shown in the following amusing example:

```
begin procedure S(x);  x := 0;
  real procedure r;  S(r);
  real x;  x := 1;
  S (if x = 1 then r else x);  outreal (1, x) end.
```

This program seems to have a historical claim of being the last "surprise" noticed by ALGOL punsters; it contains two unexpected twists, the first of which was suggested by P. Ingerman:

(a) Procedure r uses $S(r)$ to set the value of r to zero.

(b) The expansion of the procedure statement on the last line, according to the rules of "call by name," leads to a valid ALGOL program which has a completely different structure than the body of S:

$$\textbf{if } x = 1 \textbf{ then } r \textbf{ else } x := 0$$

Here an unconditional statement plus a conditional expression has become a conditional statement.

Fortunately both of these situations have been ruled out by Section 4.7.5.2.

Conclusion

For centuries astronomers have given the name ALGOL to a star which is also called Medusa's head. The author has tried to indicate every known blemish in [2]; and he hopes that nobody will ever scrutinize any of his own writings as meticulously as he and others have examined the ALGOL Report.

RECEIVED JANUARY 1967; REVISED JULY 1967

REFERENCES

1. NAUR, P. (Ed.) Report on the algorithmic language ALGOL 60. *Comm. ACM 3* (1960), 299–314.
2. NAUR, P., AND WOODGER, M. (Eds.) Revised report on the algorithmic language ALGOL 60. *Comm. ACM 6* (1963), 1–20.
3. ABRAHAMS, P. W. A final solution to the dangling **else** of ALGOL 60 and related languages. *Comm. ACM 9* (1966), 679–682.
4. MERNER, J. N. Discussion question. *Comm. ACM 5* (1964), 71.
5. KNUTH, D. E. On the translation of languages from left to right. *Inf. Contr. 8* (1965), 607–639.
6. DIJKSTRA, E. W. Letter to the editor. *Comm. ACM 4* (1961), 502–503.
7. LEAVENWORTH, B. M. FORTRAN IV as a syntax language. *Comm. ACM 7* (1964), 72–80.
8. KNUTH, D. E., AND MERNER, J. N. ALGOL 60 confidential. *Comm. ACM 4* (1961), 268–272.
9. INGERMAN P. Z., AND MERNER, J. N. Suggestions on ALGOL 60 (Rome) issues. *Comm. ACM 6* (1963), 20–23.
10. RANDELL, B., AND RUSSELL, L. J. *ALGOL 60 Implementation.* Academic Press, London, 1964.
11. NAUR, P. Questionnaire. *ALGOL Bulletin 14*, Regnecentralen, Copenhagen, Denmark, 1962.
12. B5500 Information processing systems reference manual. Burroughs Corp., 1964.
13. VAN WIJNGAARDEN, A. Switching and programming. In H. Aiken and W. F. Main (EDS.), *Switching Theory in Space Technology*, Stanford U. Press, Stanford, 1963, pp. 275–283.

A TUTORIAL ON ALGOL 68*

A. S. TANENBAUM

This paper is an introduction to the main features of ALGOL 68, emphasizing the novel features not found in many other programming languages. The topics, data types (modes), type conversion (coercion), generalized expressions (units), procedures, operators, the standard prelude, and input/output, form the basis of the paper. The approach is informal, relying heavily on many short examples. The paper applies to the Revised Report, published in 1975, rather than to the original report, published in 1969.

Keywords and Phrases: ALGOL 68, ALGOrithmic Language, expression languages, general programming languages, high-level languages, problem-oriented languages.

CR Categories: 4.20, 4.22.

INTRODUCTION

This paper is an introduction to ALGOL 68—in plain English—for the nonspecialist. In its short lifetime, ALGOL 68 has acquired something of an international reputation for being obscure. An early description of the language [8] was entitled "ALGOL 68 with Fewer Tears." The feeling has persisted. One recent author [11] has written, "The ALGOL 68 Report is one of the most unreadable documents which has ever been printed." It is our intention to demonstrate that ALGOL 68 is neither inscrutable nor difficult, but rather is an extremely powerful programming language which is easily learned and which is applicable to a wide variety of problems.

One reason ALGOL 68 has been slow to be accepted is not hard to discover. The defining report used a completely new kind of grammar to define the language, instead of the now familiar and comfortable Backus-Naur grammar (BNF). This new grammar, often called a vW-grammar (in honor of its inventor, A. van Wijngaarden), is context sensitive rather than context free. Like many new ideas, it takes some getting used to, just as BNF grammars did. The new grammar was introduced for some very good reasons. In particular, it allows not only the syntax, but also that part of the semantics having to do with declarations to be defined by the grammar. For example, the nonterminal <program> simply does not generate any program in which variables are undefined, multiply defined, or defined inconsistently with their usage. No English prose is needed to say that variables must not be defined twice, etc. Consequently, W-grammars provide a more complete and accurate definition than do BNF grammars.

During several years of experience with the language, several trouble spots came to light, particularly features of the language

*Reprinted from *Computing Surveys*, 8, 2, June 1976.

CONTENTS

that were tricky to implement efficiently. A Revised Report [13] was published in 1975, describing a slightly modified language that does not have these problems. Furthermore, the original report itself was completely rewritten, in order to make it easier to understand. It is the revised language and the Revised Report that are described in this article. References to sections in the Revised Report are indicated by the letters RR preceding the section number.

Rather than attempting to explore every nook and cranny of ALGOL 68, we concentrate on the major features, illustrating them with many examples. Readers wishing a book length introduction to ALGOL 68 are referred to the books listed in Section 11, Where To From Here?

The ALGOL 68 Report introduced a veritable cornucopia of new terminology to the computing community, all of which are precisely defined in the Revised Report (RR 2.1). This was done to force the reader to rely on the Report's definitions, rather than to rely on his previous experience with similar concepts that nonetheless may differ from the Report's definitions in subtle, but crucial, ways.

Nevertheless, to avoid inundating the reader, we try to shun when possible the bus tokens (RR 1.3.3e) invisible production trees (RR 1.1.3.2h), primal environs (RR 2.2.2a), incestuous unions (RR 4.7), notions (RR 1.1.3.1c), protonotions (RR 1.1.3.1b), metanotions (RR 1.1.3.1d), hypernotions (RR 1.1.3.1e), paranotions (RR 1.1.4.2), and their ilk, for more familiar nomenclature. As a starter, we refrain from using "assignation" when "assignment" does just as nicely, and we use "integer" rather than "integral" as an adjective.

Before plunging into the description of the language itself, it is perhaps worthwhile to say something about the principles of its design. One of the key ideas is that of orthogonality. An orthogonal language has a small number of basic constructions, and rules for combining them in regular and systematic ways. A very deliberate attempt is made to eliminate arbitrary restrictions.

The concept of orthogonal design may be made clearer by an example of nonorthogonal design. Many programming languages (for example, FORTRAN, ALGOL 60, and PL/I) have a concept of data types that includes arrays. They also have a concept of functions as rules for mapping parameters onto results. Logically one might expect to be able to combine the "orthogonal" (that is, independent) concepts of data types and functions to construct functions that take an array as parameter and yield an array as the result. An arbitrary restriction that allows arrays to be used as parameters but prohibits them to be used as results is an example of nonorthogonal design. A fundamental principle of ALGOL 68 is that arbitrary rules like this restriction are only used to resolve situations which might otherwise be syntactically or semantically ambiguous.

Another principle, related to that of orthogonality, is the principle of extensibility. ALGOL 68 provides a small number of primitive data types, or modes, as well as mechanisms for the user to extend these in a systematic way. For example, the programmer may create his own data types and his own operators to manipulate them. This philosophy may be contrasted with, say APL, which provides a very large number of standard operators, rather than a very small number and the machinery for programmers to define new ones. Together, orthogonality and extensibility tend to produce a "compact" yet powerful language.

1. BIRD'S-EYE VIEW OF ALGOL 68

In the following subsections we briefly mention some basic features of ALGOL 68 that are common to many programming languages in order to be able to use them in subsequent examples.

1.1 Program Structure

An ALGOL 68 program consists of a sequence of symbols enclosed by **begin** and **end,** or by parentheses. Some symbols are written in boldface type to distinguish them as keywords. Other symbols are variable identifiers (written in the same general font that is used in programs) and special characters such as ⟨ ⟩, =, ( ), +, −, etc.

Spaces and carriage returns (change to a new card) may be used freely to improve readability. Spaces are explicitly allowed "inside" identifiers. Thus *the three little pigs* and *thethreelittlepigs* are the same identifier. Identifiers (for example, variable names) may be arbitrarily long.

Comments are enclosed between comment symbols, of which four representations are allowed: ¢, #, **co,** and **comment.** The comment must begin and end with the same comment symbol. A comment may be inserted between any two symbols.

ALGOL 68 is a block structured language, like PL/I and ALGOL 60. Blocks and procedures may be nested arbitrarily deep. Declarations may appear in any block. Semicolons are used to separate statements, similar to ALGOL 60 (and in contrast to PL/I, which uses them to terminate statements).

1.2 Data and Declarations

One of the most basic features of a programming language is the kind of data that it can manipulate. ALGOL 68 provides a rich collection of data types (described in Section 2, Modes). The ALGOL 68 Report uses the term mode instead of type, and we do too. Four of the simplest modes are integer, real (floating point), Boolean, and character. As one might expect, there are integer, real, Boolean, and character variables. All variables must be declared. Any variable used but not declared will be flagged by the compiler as an error. The declaration of a variable consists of a mode, followed by one or more identifiers. The following program illustrates variable declarations. An ALGOL 68 program must contain at least one statement; **skip** is a dummy statement that can be used to turn a collection of declarations into a syntactically valid program.

```
begin
real e,x,y,z; ¢ 4 real variables ¢
bool maybe; ¢ 1 boolean variable ¢
char first initial, middle initial,
    grade desired; ¢ 3 character variables ¢
int i,j,girlfriends; ¢ 3 integer variables ¢
skip ¢ dummy statement ¢
end
```

Note that the declarations are separated by semicolons. The symbols **int, real, bool,** and **char** are not abbreviations; **integer, boolean,** and **character** are not allowed (although one can explicitly define them as modes if so desired).

1.3 Statements

ALGOL 68 is an expression language. This means that every construction in the language yields a value and in principle can appear on the right-hand side of an assignment. Nevertheless, certain constructions can also be used as statements. Among these constructions are assignment statements, **if** statements, procedure calls, **for** statements, **while** statements, **case** statements, and **goto** statements. Since these are all quite familiar from other programming languages, a few examples, shown in the next column, should suffice.

A few explanatory notes may be in order. Observe that **if** statements are closed by **fi** (**if** backwards). This solves the dangling else problem. Suppose **fi** were not used. Then the statement

```
if i<0 then if j<0
then print ("hello") else print ("goodbye")
```

would be ambiguous, possibly meaning

```
if i<0
   then if j<0 then print ("hello") fi
   else print ("goodbye")
fi
```

or perhaps meaning

```
if i<0
   then if j<0 then print ("hello")
                else print ("goodbye")
        fi
fi
```

With the **fi** there is no ambiguity. Furthermore, since both **then** and **else** parts must be explicitly closed, either may contain an arbitrary number of statements without the need for **begin end** as delimiters.

```
begin
¢ mentally insert the above declarations here ¢
¢ assignment statements ¢
girlfriends := girlfriends-1;
middle initial := "x";
e := 2.78;

¢ if statements ¢
if maybe
   then grade desired := "d"
   else grade desired := "f"
fi; ¢ fi delimits if—see note below ¢
if x<0 then x := −x fi;
if i = j+2
   then x := pi;
        y := 2*e;
        z := 3*e
fi;

¢ procedure calls ¢
¢ sum & initialize must be defined elsewhere ¢
initialize; ¢ no parameters ¢
sum(x,y,z);
print(grade desired);

¢ for − while statements ¢
¢ the following 5 statements are all equivalent ¢
for k from 1 by 1 to j+3 while true
   do print (new line) od;

for k from 1 by 1 to j+3
   do print (new line) od;

for k from 1 to j+3
   do print (new line) od;

for k to j+3
   do print (new line) od;

to j+3
   do print (new line) od;

while i<j ∨ i<0
   do i := i+1;
      j := j+2;
      print ((i,j))
   od;

¢ case statements ¢
case i+4 in
   j := 0, j := 3, i := i−5, print(i)
esac;
case i in
   j := j+3,
   if j = 0 then j := i fi,
   print (i)
out j := 4
esac;

¢ goto statement ¢
bed: goto bed

end
```

To simplify nested **if** statements, **else if** may be contracted to **elif,** providing the **fi** matching the contracted **if** is deleted. For example,

```
if word = "oui"
   then print ("french")
   else if word = "yes"
           then print ("english")
           else if word = "ja"
                   then print ("dutch")
                   else print ("minor language")
                fi
        fi
fi
```

can be written as

```
if word = "oui"
   then print ("french")
   elif word = "yes"
      then print ("english")
      elif word = "ja"
         then print ("dutch")
         else print ("minor language")
fi
```

Even with **elif, begin** and **end** are never needed as delimiters.

The **for** and **while** statements shown on page 158 are all special cases of a general **for** statement including both counting parts (**from ... by ... to**) and **while** parts. The **from, by,** and **to** parts are each optional, with default values of 1, 1, and infinity, respectively. Each part may occur only once. The "controled variable" following **for** is automatically an integer; it can neither be declared nor assigned. If the same identifier occurs outside the statement, it is a different variable. This makes the controled variable inaccessible outside the loop (to give the compiler writer more freedom, and to make correctness proofs easier). Furthermore, the **from, by,** and **to** parts are evaluated once and for all before the loop begins. Subsequent changes to any of their variables have no effect on the step size or loop termination condition.

The **case** statement has an integer expression which selects the first, second, third, etc., clause if the expression is 1,2,3, etc., respectively. A clause is a statement (or a group of statements separated by semicolons and enclosed by **begin end** or parentheses). The clauses are separated by commas. If an **out** clause is present, it will be selected when the expression exceeds the number of clauses or is less than 1. If the **out** clause is omitted and the expression is out of range, the **case** statement is skipped. **esac** is **case** backwards.

Input/output in ALGOL 68 is performed by calling certain input/output procedures, rather than by executing special statements. Procedures are provided for unformatted, formatted, and binary input/output. Files and input/output devices can be handled in a consistent and machine-independent way. We examine these input/output procedures in a later section; for now, $read(x)$ is used for input and $print(x)$ is used for output. Each of these procedures may be passed a parenthesized list of variables as parameter, for example, $read((x,y,z))$ and $print((i,j,x+z))$. (The reason for the extra parentheses is explained later on.) The calls $print(new\ line)$ and $print(new\ page)$ cause subsequent output to begin at the beginning of the next line or next page, respectively.

A sample ALGOL 68 program is shown on page 160.

2. MODES

One of the most powerful features of ALGOL 68 is its rich collection of data types (modes), and the facilities it provides programmers to define their own modes. Programmer-defined modes are constructed from primitive modes, using a few simple rules for creating new modes from old modes. In the following subsections we examine primitive modes, methods for constructing new modes, and finally the mode definition facility in its full glory.

An object is an entity stored in memory during the execution of a program. Integers and reals are typical objects. Each object has a unique mode, for example, **int, real, bool,** or **char.** Each object also has a value. It is objects that are assigned to variables. For example, an integer with value 3 (some bit pattern in memory) can be assigned to an integer variable. A variable should be

```
begin
¢This program reads two numbers: the price of
an item, and the amount the customer gave to
the cashier. It then calculates how much change
he should get, and prints out the correct number
of quarters, dimes, nickels, and pennies, mini-
mizing the number of coins returned. The pro-
gram only handles change up to 99 cents. ¢

begin
int price, amount paid, change, quarters, dimes,
    nickels, pennies;

read ((price, amount paid)); ¢ read input data ¢
change := amount paid − price;
if change > 99 ∨ change < 0
   then print ("input data incorrect")
   else
   if change = 0 ¢ was the payment exact?¢
      then print ("no change")
      else ¢ compute how many of each coin ¢
        quarters := 0;
        dimes := 0;
        nickels := 0;
        while change ≥ 25
          do quarters := quarters + 1;
             change := change − 25
          od;
        while change ≥ 10
          do dimes := dimes + 1;
             change := change − 10
          od;
        while change ≥ 5
          do nickels := nickels + 1;
             change := change − 5
          od;
        pennies := change
        ¢ print results ¢
        print ((new page, "the change is",
                new line, quarters, " quarters",
                new line, dimes, " dimes",
                new line, nickels, " nickels",
                new line, pennies, " pennies",
                new line
              ))
   fi ¢ this matches if change = 0 . . . ¢
fi ¢ this matches if change > 99 . . . ¢
end
```

thought of as a container (memory location) into which a certain class of objects can be put. Be aware that the container and the containee are distinct kinds of entities.

2.1 Primitive Modes

We have already seen how to declare **int, real, bool,** and **char** variables. These are not the only possibilities, however. A list of the predefined modes with a brief description of each follows:

int	integer;
real	real number;
char	character;
bool	boolean;
string	string of characters;
compl	complex number (2 reals);
bits	machine word full of bits;
bytes	machine word full of characters;
sema	Dijkstra semaphore [4];
format	mode used with formatted I/O;
file	mode used for input/output.

For some applications, the number of bits in an integer or real is insufficient. To accommodate these situations, ALGOL 68 allows primitive modes of **long int, long long int,** etc., and **long real, long long real, long long long real,** etc. Furthermore, to accommodate applications where very many integers or reals are needed, but where fewer than the standard number of bits will suffice, there are modes of **short int, short short int** and **short real, short short real,** etc.

The number of different lengths and the number of bits in each is up to each ALGOL 68 compiler writer. However, the number of available lengths and the size of each is available to programs at run time to facilitate transfer of programs from one machine to another. For a computer with an 8-bit byte and a 32-bit word, a typical implementation might have: **short short int** (8 bits), **short int** (16 bits), **int** (32 bits), **long int** (64 bits), **long long int** (96 bits), and **long long long int** (128 bits).

The mode **string** defines a string of zero or more characters. Strings may be arbitrarily long, and strings of any length may be assigned to any string variable. In PL/I terms, all strings are of maximum length equal to infinity and VARYING. The following is a valid ALGOL 68 program:

```
begin
  string s;
  s := " "; ¢ an empty string ¢
  s := "little"; ¢ a 6 character string ¢
  s := "hello there, mommies and daddies"
end
```

The modes **bits** and **bytes** are intended to give the programmer the ability to pack information into machine words to save space. The number of bits in an object of mode **bits** is not determined by the programmer, but by the ALGOL 68 compiler writer. It is to be expected that in most implementations an object of mode **bits** will occupy a full machine word. Operations are provided, among others, to insert, extract, and test the individual bits. The mode **bytes** is similar, providing a way to pack characters into machine words to save storage. How many characters to pack into a machine word is a decision left to the implementer. Like **int** and **real, bits** and **bytes** have **long** and **short** versions.

The modes **sema, format,** and **file** have specialized uses and are covered later on.

ALGOL 68 allows more complex modes to be constructed from simpler modes in a variety of ways. Roughly speaking, these ways involve arrays, structures, procedures, sets, and pointers. We examine each of these in turn.

2.2 Array Modes

Many problems involve data which are organized into vectors or matrices. A vector is a one-dimensional sequence of objects, all of which have the same mode. A matrix is a two-dimensional ordering of objects of the same mode. Likewise, three, four, and higher dimensional arrays also consist of collections of objects of the same mode. The elements of an array may be of a primitive mode, such as **int**, or they may be of a constructed mode.

The official ALGOL 68 term for array is multiple value (RR 2.1.3.4); however, we continue to use the more familiar word "array." An array is a run-time object and therefore has a value and a mode. Array variables exist and may be declared and assigned values, just as variables of any other mode are. A one-dimensional array of integers has mode [ ] **int**, pronounced "row of integer"; a two-dimensional array of reals has mode [,] **real**, pronounced "row row of real"; a three-dimensional array of characters has mode [,,] **char**, pronounced "row row row of character." In general, the mode of an n-dimensional array is an opening square bracket followed by $n-1$ commas, a closing square bracket, and then the mode of the elements. Objects of different dimensions have different modes.

When array variables are declared, the bounds must be specified in order to allow sufficient space to be reserved. To declare a one-dimensional integer array variable named "month" which is to contain an array whose elements are numbered 1 to 12, one writes

[1:12] **int** *month*

The lower and upper bounds are integer expressions; they are separated by a colon. Much as you would expect,

[0:$n-1$,0:$n-1$] **real** *physicist, chemist*

declares *physicist* and *chemist* to be $n \times n$ real matrices. Note that *physicist* is a [,] **real** variable; the bounds are not part of the mode (unlike PASCAL). Thus if

[1:100,3: 9] **real** *geologist*

declares a nonsquare matrix, *physicist* and *geologist* have the same mode, albeit different sizes. The following program declares several variables:

```
begin int n,m;
read((m,n)); ¢ read 2 integers ¢
¢ unlabeled statements may be followed by
  more declarations, i.e., it is not necessary to
  put all declarations first ¢
[−n:n] int hamlet; ¢ size depends on n ¢
[1:m,1:n] real macbeth;
[1:10,1:10,1:10] bool othello;
[−100:−80] char richard 3;
[0:9∗m + 6∗m∗n] string henry 8;

¢ array elements may themselves be arrays ¢
[1:10] [1:5,1:5] int king lear;

skip ¢ dummy statement ¢
end
```

Elements of arrays may be extracted by subscripting and trimming (see Section 3.4, Slices).

In the preceding program, *king lear* is a 10-element vector, each of whose elements is a 5×5 square matrix. A vector whose elements are matrices might be a more natural representation for, say, the successive digitized frames of television broadcasting, than a three-dimensional array. Note that *king lear*[n] can be used anywhere an object of mode [,] **int** is needed, for example, as an actual parameter. It can also be subscripted, as in *king lear*[n] [2,3], but not as in *king lear*[n,2,3].

An array variable may be declared to be flexible, in which case arrays of different sizes may be successively assigned to it, provided they are of the proper mode. A string variable is actually a flexible one-dimensional character array variable.

2.3 Structured Modes

Arrays are used to group together objects of the same mode. Structures (RR 2.1.3.3) are used to group together objects whose modes need not be identical. A structure is composed of one or more fields, each having a name, or more properly, a field selector (RR 4.8.1f). Structures themselves are objects and have modes. The mode of a structure depends upon the modes of its fields, their order, and the field selectors. Two structured modes are the same if and only if the corresponding fields have the same modes and field selectors. Structured variables exist, and may be assigned to one field at a time or "all at once." Structures are called "records" in some programming languages. An example of a structured variable declaration is:

struct (**string** *species*,
        int *number of feet*,
        bool *makes good pet*) *beastie*

This declares *beastie* to be a variable with three fields whose field selectors are: *species*, *number of feet*, and *makes good pet*. To use any of the fields of *beastie*, one writes the field selector, followed by the word **of**, followed by the name of the structured variable, for example:

species **of** *beastie*   := "brontosaurus";
number of feet **of** *beastie* := 4;
makes good pet **of** *beastie* := **false**

The extraction of one field of a structure is called selecting. Alternatively, it is possible to assign all three fields at once by using a structure display (RR 3.3.1h) on the right-hand side of the assignment statement, for example:

beastie := ("guinea pig", 4, **true**)

Some examples of structured variables follow:

```
begin int n; read(n);
struct (real value, string color,
        bool leaks, has fireplace) house;
struct ([1:3] char aircraft type,
        int wheels, max speed) plane;
struct ([1:3] char area code,
        [1:7] char phone number) telephone;
¢ farm has 3 fields: crop, farmer and dairy ¢
struct ([1:n] struct (string variety,
                      real acres) crop,
        string farmer, bool dairy) farm;
skip
end
```

2.4 Procedure Modes

In contrast to most programming languages, ALGOL 68 considers procedures to be objects, complete with values and modes. Furthermore, there are procedure variables, to which procedures can be assigned. The mode of a procedure is uniquely determined by the mode of its parameters (if there are any) and the mode of the value it returns. A procedure that takes an integer as a parameter and returns a real as a value has mode **proc (int) real.** A procedure that takes a character and a Boolean matrix as parameters and returns a real vector as a value has mode **proc (char, [,] bool) [ ] real.**

A procedure that is not used as a function, that is, does not return any explicit value, is said to return **void.** For example, a procedure that accepts an **int** as parameter and cancels the corresponding flight (in an airline reservation system) has mode **proc (int) void.** A procedure which has no parameters, but which returns a **real,** such as random, has mode **proc real.** A procedure which has no parameters and which delivers no explicit value has mode **proc void.**

Both parameters and results may have any mode. Unlike FORTRAN, ALGOL 60, and PL/I, in ALGOL 68, procedures may yield strings, arrays, structures, pointers, or any other mode. Furthermore, there is no reason procedure modes cannot be used as parameters or results. For example, a procedure used to perform a numerical integration of a real function (that is, a **proc (real) real**) between two real limits might have mode

proc (proc (real) real, real, real) real.

The order of the parameters is significant; **proc (real, int) void** and **proc (int, real) void** are different modes. Because there are an infinite number of combinations of parameters and results, there are an infinite number of procedure modes, just as there are an infinite number of procedure modes.

As mentioned earlier, procedure variables exist, and can be assigned values. The following program illustrates this feature:

```
begin real x;
¢ f is a proc (real) real variable ¢
proc (real) real f;
x := 3.14;
¢ sin, cos, and tan are standard ¢
f := sin; ¢ assign sin to f ¢
print (f(x)); ¢ print sin(3.14) ¢
f := cos; ¢ now assign cos to f ¢
print (f(x)); ¢ print cos(3.14) ¢
f := tan; ¢ now assign tan to f ¢
print (f(x)) ¢ three guesses ¢
end
```

When an integer variable acquires a new value, as in $i := 3$, the bit pattern for the integer 3 is put into location i. Obviously, assigning *sin* to *f* is not going to cause a copy of the procedure's machine code to be stuffed into the variable *f*. The ALGOL 68 compiler writer must determine how to implement this, but presumably he will assign pointers to the procedure's code and environment (or the equivalent) to *f*. Some examples of procedure variable declarations follow:

```
begin
  proc (real) real cotangent;
  proc (int, int) int integer divide;
  proc (int, int) bool coprime;
  proc (char, char) bool char compare;
  proc ([,] real, [,] real) [,] real matrix add;
  proc (string, string) string concatenate;
  proc (int) void page eject;
  proc (int) struct (string name, int age) find;
  proc (int) proc (int) int pick function;
  proc (proc (real) real, real, real) real simpson;
  skip ¢ dummy statement ¢
end
```

2.5 United Modes

As we discuss later on, actual parameters in procedure calls must be of the mode expected, for example, a **proc (int) real** requires an **int** as a parameter and will not accept a **real**. Sometimes it is convenient to have a procedure with a formal parameter that can be any one of several modes. For example, we might want to write a procedure that accepts a vector parameter of mode [ ] **int**, [ ] **real**, or [ ] **compl** and checks to see if any elements are zero.

To permit this sort of flexibility, ALGOL 68 permits programmers to create a special kind of mode called a **united mode**. A variable united from **int** and **real** can be assigned either an **int** value or a **real** value. Similarly, a variable united from [ ] **int**, [ ] **real**, and [ ] **compl** can accept a vector of integers, reals, or complex numbers as a value (but not a vector of Booleans). United mode variables are declared as indicated here:

```
begin
  union (int, real) ir;
  union ([ ] int, [ ] real, [ ] compl) irc;
  union (proc (int) real, proc (real) real) u;
  skip ¢ dummy statement ¢
end
```

It is possible at run time to determine the mode of the value currently occupying a variable of united mode. This is done by using a variation on the **case** statement (RR 3.4.1h) with clauses for the various possible modes. Each clause is headed by a mode and (optionally) by an identifier, fol-lowed by a colon. The clause corresponding to the current mode of the united variable is executed. Unlike the normal **case** statement, the order of the clauses is irrelevant.

```
begin
union (int, real, bool, char, bits,
          bytes, [ ] int, [ ] real) kitchen sink;
¢ here are 4 valid assignments ¢
kitchen sink := 3;
kitchen sink := 3.14;
kitchen sink := true;
kitchen sink := "a";
¢ random is a standard proc real ¢
if random < .5
  then kitchen sink := 1
    else kitchen sink := 2.78
fi;
¢ now figure out whether random was < .5 ¢
case kitchen sink in
  (int i): print (("integer", i)),
  (real r): print (("real", r))
esac
end
```

In this example we determined the mode of the union by using the case clause, and used the value in *kitchen sink* once its mode was known. Observe the (**int** *i*) and (**real** *r*) in the case clause. To compute with the value in *kitchen sink* in the **int** part (first clause) we can use the identifier *i*, now known to be an **int**. The value of *i* is the value of *kitchen sink*. Likewise the identifier *r* can be used in the second clause in any context where a real number is allowed. If *j* had been declared as an integer variable in the preceding program, *j* := *kitchen sink* would have been forbidden (by the grammar) and would have been flagged by the compiler. The reason is obvious: At the time of the assignment the compiler cannot guarantee that *kitchen sink* contains an integer, and we would be in trouble if it contained a [ ] **real**. However, inside the first case clause it is guaranteed that *kitchen sink* contains an integer. To make life easier for the compiler writer, the new name *i* is introduced; there is no doubt about the mode of *i*. Although *j*:= *kitchen sink* would be forbidden, even inside the first clause, the assignment *j* := *i* would be allowed (only) in the first clause.

You may be wondering how unions are implemented. Presumably the compiler will have to reserve enough space in a united variable for the largest of the alternatives (or if that is too painful, perhaps only a pointer will be stored). Also, there must be some information stored that tells which mode is the "current" one. Note that there are no objects or values of united modes, just variables.

2.6 Reference-to Modes

Most programming languages are somewhat lax about making a distinction between the address of a variable and the contents of that variable. The nature of the difficulty can be most easily seen by means of an example from FORTRAN:

```
SUBROUTINE SUM(I,J,K)
INTEGER I, J, K
I = J+K
RETURN
END
```

Now consider the result of the following call:

```
CALL SUM(1,2,3)
```

Although the subroutine declaration is grammatically correct, and the call is also grammatically correct, something is obviously wrong.

The problem is not that the actual parameters are of the wrong type. *I* is declared an integer, and the number 1 is certainly an integer. The trouble occurs because the left-hand side of an integer assignment must evaluate to the address of a variable, not to an integer value. Few compilers will even

give a precise error message at run time, let alone at compile time. Typically an address pointing into the run-time constant table is passed as a parameter, and the value of the constant 1 is changed to 5 so that subsequent $N = 1+1$ statements set N equal to 10 (decimal, not binary). In ALGOL 68 integer variables and integer values have different modes; so the error we are considering will be detected at compile time as a parameter mismatch.

An integer variable in ALGOL 68 has mode **ref int**, (**ref** is a shortened form of reference to); a real variable has mode **ref real**, etc. Consider the ALGOL 68 program

begin int *i; i* := 3 **end**

In this program, *i* is an integer variable and has mode **ref int**. The constant 3, on the other hand, has mode **int**. A **ref int** corresponds to the address of a memory location into which an integer can be put, whereas an **int** is a value, not an address.

This distinction is very important and bears repeating. An integer constant and an integer variable are different kinds of objects and have different modes. The mode of the former is **int** and the mode of the latter is **ref int**. The value of an integer variable is its memory address. Of course, given an integer variable one can ask about both its value and the value of the integer it contains, but these are clearly different objects.

The ALGOL 68 rule for an integer assignment is that the left-hand side must be, or be convertible to, an object of mode **ref int**, while the right-hand side must be, or be convertible to, an object of mode **int**. Precisely the same considerations hold for other modes, of course. Although procedure definitions are discussed later, the ALGOL 68 version of SUM is presented here for contrast with the FORTRAN version.

proc *sum* = (**ref int** *i*, **int** *j,k*) **void:** *i* := *j+k*

Here *i* is clearly a different mode from *j* and *k*. Furthermore, the call *sum*(1,2,3) is invalid because the modes of the actual parameters (**int, int, int**) do not match the modes of the formal parameters (**ref int, int, int**). If *i* had been specified as mode **int** instead of

ref int, then the assignment $i := j+k$ would have been detected as an error because the left-hand side of an integer assignment must evaluate to something of mode **ref int**. Either way the error would have been detected by the compiler, which is obviously better than its subsequent appearance as an obscure program bug.

We have consistently said that the right-hand side must be, or be convertible to, to an object of mode **int**, rather than having said that the right-hand side must be an object of mode **int**. This choice of words was deliberate.

Consider the following program:

   begin int i,j; $i := 3$; $j := i$ **end**

In this program, i and j are both of mode **ref int**. In the first assignment the right-hand side has mode **int** as it should, but in the second assignment the right-hand side has mode **ref int**. Thus it would appear that $j := i$ is forbidden. Fortunately, there exists an automatic conversion between mode **ref int** and **int**, which is called dereferencing. Conversions between data types are familiar from other programming languages; for example, nearly all programming languages allow an integer to be written in a position where a real number is required, with automatic conversion implied.

In exactly the same way, ALGOL 68 often allows an object of mode **ref m** to be written when an object of mode **m** (some arbitrary mode) is expected, with automatic conversion implied. Such automatic mode conversions are called coercions. There are six kinds, of which dereferencing is one. Integer to real coercion, called widening, is another. Chapter 6 of the Revised Report gives the exact rules about which coercions are allowed in what situations.

It should be pointed out that although widening from **int** to **real** is typically an actual operation performed on integers at run time, dereferencing need not be performed at run time. If the computer has an instruction to move the contents of location i to location j, the compiler writer is obviously allowed to use it. No one is going to compel him to first put the address of i in a register and then explicitly dereference it using in-

direct addressing before storing the contents of i in j.

Dereferencing is more than simply a syntactic trick to allow variables on the right-hand side of assignments. Since **ref int** is a valid mode, the curious reader may wonder if reference-to-integer variables exist. The answer is yes. Just as an integer variable is a location in memory intended to hold an integer, a reference-to-integer variable is a location in memory intended to hold an object of mode **ref int**, that is, the address of an integer variable. In other words, a reference-to-integer variable can contain a pointer to an integer variable. It cannot contain a pointer to a real variable or to any other kind of variable, however. Likewise, a reference-to-complex variable may contain only a pointer to a complex variable.

Consider the following program:

```
begin
ref int pt;
int i,j;
i := 0; j := 4;
if random < 0.5
   then pt := i
   else pt := j
fi
end
```

If pt is dereferenced once, it yields either the address of i or the address of j. If it is dereferenced twice, it yields either 0 or 4. Barring some unusual hardware, dereferencing a pointer twice is going to involve some run-time action. Note that pt itself has mode **ref ref int**.

Finally we get back to the subject of mode construction. The rule for creating pointer modes is simple. If **m** is some arbitrary mode, then **ref m** is also a mode of pointers to **m**. Applied repeatedly we discover that, **m ref m**, **ref ref m**, **ref ref ref m**, etc., are all distinct modes. The program at the top of page 167 shows how to declare some modes involving pointers:

Variables involving **ref** "something" are typically used in list processing applications. The distinction between the mode of a variable and the mode of the objects that can be assigned to it is crucial, but often initially confusing to people accustomed to other programming languages. Variables have

```
begin
[ ] ref int a; ¢ a row of pointers ¢
ref [ ] real b; ¢ a pointer to a vector ¢
ref [ ] ref char c; ¢ a pointer to a pointer vector ¢
struct (ref int p, ref real q) d; ¢ 2 pointers ¢
proc ref bool e; ¢ proc yielding a pointer ¢
ref proc bool f; ¢ pointer to a proc bool ¢
union (ref int, ref bool) g; ¢ either of 2 pointers ¢
skip ¢ dummy statement ¢
end
```

mode **ref** "something," and can contain objects of mode "something." In addition, a variable is itself an object, with a mode and a value. The mode of an integer variable is **ref int**, and its value is the address where its integer is stored. Thus an integer variable can be regarded as an object of mode **ref int**, and it can be assigned to a pointer variable whose mode is **ref ref int**.

In some programming languages (for example, PL/I), a pointer can point to an object of any mode. This is a frequent source of errors. Often a pointer somehow ends up pointing to a variable of the wrong mode, or worse yet, points into the program itself or to unused memory. By strictly categorizing pointers according to what they may point to, ALGOL 68 greatly reduces the opportunities for making errors.

2.7 Mode Declarations

We have now seen how ALGOL 68 programmers can construct new modes from primitive modes through the use of arrays, structures, procedures, unions, and references. ALGOL 68 provides a mechanism for programmers to give names to newly created modes, so they can be used in the same way that built-in modes are used. New modes are declared by means of a mode declaration (RR 4.2) as illustrated in the next column.

Mode declarations are used to create new data types. It is possible for user-defined modes to be used to create still more complex modes, as in **family**, which uses **person**. ALGOL 68 provides the ability for the programmer to build up an entire library of mode definitions tailored to his particular application.

```
begin int n, size; read ((n, size));
mode vector = [1:n] real;
mode matrix = [1:n, 1 :n] real;
mode rational = struct (int num, denom);
mode functionset = [1:n] proc (real) real;
mode book = struct (string title, author,
        publisher, int pages, year,
        bool paperback);
mode magazine = struct (string title,
        int subscribers, publ frequency);
        publisher,
mode library = [1: size] union (book,
        magazine);
mode person = struct (string initials,
                ref person ma, pa,
                int age,
                bool too fat);
mode family = struct (person mommy, daddy,
                [1:2] person child);
mode bridgehand = [1:13] struct (char rank,
        suit);
mode word = [0:15] bool;
mode memory = [0:4095] words;
mode instruction1 = struct (int opcode,
        address1,address2,address3);
mode instruction2 = [1:4] int;
mode flight = struct (string plane, pilot,
        movie, bool nonstop, [1:size] struct
        (string name, [1:10] char phone)
        passenger);
mode multireal = union (real, long real,
                long long real);
mode tree = struct (int value,
                ref tree right, left);
mode integer = int;
mode interger = int; ¢ for bad spellors ¢
skip ¢ dummy statement ¢
end
```

A few comments about mode declarations may be helpful. The modes **instruction1** and **instruction2** each consist of four integers. If *add* is declared to be **instruction1** and *sub* is declared to be **instruction2**, then the fields of *add* are accessed via the field selections:

opcode **of** *add*, *address1* **of** *add*,
address2 **of** *add*, *address3* **of** *add*,

whereas the components of *sub* are accessed by subscripting:

sub[1], *sub*[2], *sub*[3], *sub*[4].

Which choice is made depends upon the application.

The mode **tree** is interesting. It has three fields, an integer and two pointers. In terms of allocating space for **tree** variables, it hardly matters that the pointers point to objects of mode **tree**. Binary trees and graphs are widely used in computer science, so modes like this are valuable. A mode that is defined in terms of itself, like **tree**, is called a recursive mode. Note that although the nonrecursive mode declarations are used merely for convenience, the recursive modes really require the mode definition facility (try declaring a variable with the same mode as **tree** just using a **struct (ref . . .)**).

One must exercise some care when defining recursive modes. For example:

mode bush = **struct** (**int** *v*, **bush** *h,t*)

is incorrect. Suppose that an **int** requires one word of memory, and a **bush** requires k words of memory. Then a declaration like

bush *blueberry*

would require that the variable *blueberry* be allocated enough memory to store one object of mode **int** (one word) and two objects of mode **bush** ($2k$ words) for a total of $2k+1$ words. This contradicts our statement that a **bush** requires only k words. The mode declaration is impossible. A **bush** can hardly contain two **bush**es and then some. In contrast, the mode **tree** presents no such problem since it only claims space for an **int** and two addresses (pointers), not two objects of mode **tree**. As you might expect, ALGOL 68 allows all the modes that are intuitively reasonable and prohibits those that are not (RR 7.4).

Same modes can be "spelled" in more than one way. For example, in

mode m1 = **union** (**int, real**);
mode m2 = **union** (**real, int**)

m1 and **m2** represent the same mode. On the other hand,

mode m3 = **struct** (**int** *i*, **real** *r*);
mode m4 = **struct** (**int** *j*, **real** *r*);
mode m5 = **struct** (**real** *r*, **int** *i*)

are three different modes because the field selectors are part of the mode. Mode equivalence is dealt with in RR 7.3.

At least one aspect of the orthogonal design of ALGOL 68 may now be clearer. From the 11 primitive modes listed in Section 2.1 and the five simple mode construction rules listed in Sections 2.2 through 2.6, one has the ability to create a large and powerful collection of new data types.

In contrast, PL/I is not orthogonally designed; there are no simple rules telling which combinations of attributes are allowed and which are not. A complete specification of the allowed "modes" in PL/I can only be encoded by giving a large table of compatible and incompatible attributes. This difference is characteristic of other aspects of ALGOL 68 and PL/I as well.

2.8 Using New Modes

Variables of user-created modes are defined in the same way that variables of the primitive modes are: first the mode, then a list of one or more identifiers. Declarations are commands to the compiler to reserve storage for variables. Keep in mind that the compiler needs to know how much storage to reserve. When declaring an array variable, one must specify the actual bounds (evaluated at run time) in order for the compiler to reserve enough space. On the other hand, when declaring a pointer to an array (for example, **ref [ ] int**), the bounds are not needed, since the only storage reserved is that required for the pointer, not the array; a pointer to a big array takes up the same space as a pointer to a small array. However, to be used, the pointer must appear on the left-hand side of an assignment, with some array (itself declared with bounds) on the right-hand side.

The rules for when bounds are and are not needed are given in RR 4.6.

When a mode declaration contains a variable or an expression in an array bound, for example, *n* in mode **vector** above, the question arises whether the value of *n* at mode declaration time or at variable declaration time is the one that is used. Consider this program:

```
begin
int n;
n := 3;
mode vector = [1:n] int;
n := 25;
vector x;
n := 75;
vector y;
skip ¢ dummy statement ¢
end
```

It is the value of *n* at variable declaration time that matters; *x* has 25 elements and *y* has 75 elements. The value of *n* at mode declaration time is irrelevant. In a certain sense, variable declarations are "carried

out" at run time, providing more flexibility than most languages allow. (Of course, a clever compiler writer will try to do as much as possible at compile time.)

Variables may be declared with initial values by following the identifier with a "becomes" symbol (:=) and the initial value. Structures and arrays may also be initialized, with parenthesized lists of values. It is also possible to partially initialize structures or arrays by using **skip** for some of the fields or elements. The value of **skip** is undefined; these elements or fields must be initialized by explicit assignment before being used.

Some sample variable declarations are shown below.

3. UNITS

Like other programming languages, ALGOL 68 requires that expressions be placed in certain contexts, for example, on the right-hand side of assignments, as actual parameters in procedure calls, and as subscripts. Expressions are called units in ALGOL 68 and are much more general than in many other pro-

```
begin ¢ mentally insert the mode
          declarations of section 2.7 here ¢
int n := 3, size := 2;
char c := "q";
real length := 2.503;
vector v := (14.2,−9.1,3.5678);
matrix a := ((1.0,2.0,3.0), (0.6,−0.9,100.0),
             (1.1,2.1,3.4));
rational rat :− (1,2), tar :− (3,4);
functionset f := (sin,cos,tan);
book censored := (skip,skip,skip,skip,skip,false);
magazine cs := ("computing surveys", "acm",22000,4);
library mini := (censored,cs);
person tom := ("trj", skip,skip,40,true);
person mary := ("mej", skip,skip,41,false);
family jones := (mary, tom, (skip,skip));
bridgehand south := (
   ("A", "S"), ("K", "S"), ("Q", "S"), ("J", "S"),
   ("A", "H"), ("Q", "H"), ("9", "H"), ("7", "H"),
   ("K", "D"), ("Q", "D"), ("T", "D"),
   ("Q", "C"), ("J", "C"));
word w; memory mem;
flight twa 156:=
   ("747", "bill", "frankenstein", true, skip);
skip ¢ dummy statement ¢
end
```

gramming languages. In the following subsections we discuss 15 kinds of units. The complete list is given in RR 5.1A.

3.1 Denotations

The simplest form of a unit is a denotation (usually called a constant in other programming languages). Typical denotations of mode **int, real, bool, char,** and **string** are: 4, 3.6, **true,** "x", and "hi". "Constants" of array and structured modes are also allowed. They are called row displays and structure displays, respectively, and consist of parenthesized lists of values. For example,

[1:2,1:3] **int** $x2$:= ((1,2,4),(8,16,32))

illustrates the use of a row display. Denotations are described in Chapter 8 of the Revised Report.

3.2 Variables

The next simplest unit is the variable. In this statement,

begin int i,j; i := 3; j := i **end**

i, a variable, is used as a unit in the second assignment. (Remember that it is dereferenced to an integer unit.)

3.3 Formulas

A formula (RR 5.4.2) is an operator and its operand or operands. A monadic formula has one operand, for example, **abs** i, $-x$, and **sign** y. Dyadic formulas have two operands, for example, $i-j$, $x<y$, and "abc" + "xyz".

ALGOL 68 has well over 100 "built-in" operators (listed in RR 10.2) and provides a mechanism that allows programmers to define new ones, just as it provides a mechanism to define new modes. Operators are akin to procedures. Each operator expects to have one or two operands of specific modes, and delivers a result of a specific mode. The same symbol may represent two different operators (cf. GENERIC in PL/I).

In the following program:

```
begin
int i := 1, j := 2, k;
real x:= 0.1, y := 0.3, z;
k := i+j;
z := x+y
end
```

the first + represents an operator with integer operands and an integer result, whereas the second + represents a different operator with real operands and a real result. Very likely they will require different hardware instructions.

A formula may be used as an operand. For example, the formula $i+j$ could be used as an operand of $<$, as in $i+j<k$, which is a formula yielding a Boolean result (assuming + has higher precedence than $<$, which it has).

3.4 Slices

Arrays may be subscripted as in other languages. When an object of mode [ ] **m** is subscripted, an object of mode **m** is yielded. ALGOL 68 also permits a generalization of subscripting called trimming, yielding some cross section of the original array. If z has been declared by [1:10] **int** z, then $z[1:7]$, $z[1:10]$, and $z[2:5]$ are examples of units (slices) and can be used in assignments, actual parameters, etc. For example:

```
begin
[1:10] int a,b;
[1:20] real x; [1:20,1:20] real xx;
read((a,b,x,xx));
b[1:4] := a[1:4]; ¢ assigns 4 elements ¢
b[3:9] := a[1:7]; ¢ assigns 7 elements ¢
b[1:10] := a[1:10]; ¢ assigns a to b ¢
b := a; ¢ same as above ¢
xx[4,1:20] := x; ¢ assign to row 4 of xx ¢
xx[8:9,7] := x[1:2] ¢ xx[8,7] := x[1];
                      xx[9,7] := x[2] ¢
end
```

A trimmer, such as 1:4 in the first assignment does not affect the dimensionality of the array, whereas a subscript (just one bound, with no colon) reduces it by one, as in $xx[4,1:20]$.

All combinations of trimming and subscripting are valid. For example, if s is a three-dimensional array, $s[i,j,k],s[i,j,k1:k2]$, $s[i,j1:j2,k1:k2]$, and $s[i1:i2,j1:j2,k1:k2]$ can be used as a variable, and one-, two-, and three-dimensional arrays, respectively. Furthermore, $s[i,j1:j2,k]$, $s[i1:i2,j,k1:k2]$ and other combinations are also allowed. In an assignment, the bounds must "match," as described in RR 5.3.2. Subscripting and trimming are collectively called slicing.

3.5 Selections

A selection consists of a field selector, the symbol **of**, and a structure to be selected from. The field selector must be an identifier and cannot be computed (because it is not an object). The structure being selected from may, however, be the result of evaluating an expression.

If a mode involves both structures and rows, a unit derived from an object of that mode may involve slicing (subscripting or trimming) and selecting. Slicing binds more tightly than selecting; so *tail* **of** *dog* $[k]$ means *tail* **of** $(dog[k])$ and not $(tail$ **of** $dog)[k]$. If *tail* **of** *dog* yields an array, then $(tail$ **of** $dog)[k]$ is the correct way to extract the kth element of that array. When combining selecting and slicing, keep in mind that any array can be sliced and that any structure can be selected from. Here are some examples:

```
begin int m := 25, n := 40, k := 2;
mode person = struct (string initials,
                      int age);
mode course = struct (person prof,
                      [1:n]person student);
mode dept = [1:m] course;
person smith, jones, brown, davis;
course painting, drawing, etching;
dept art;
¢ begin assigning values ¢
  initials of smith := "rbs";
age of smith := 47;
jones := ("tmj", 32);
prof of painting := ("jed", 47);
prof of drawing := smith;
prof of etching := prof of painting;
art[1:3] := (painting, drawing, etching);
prof of art[2] := jones; ¢ smith quit ¢
age of prof of art[2] := 39;
(student of art[2]) [1] := davis;
age of (student of art[2]) [1] := 18;
(student of art[k+1]) [k−1] := ("tns", 19)
end
```

This may look imposing at first, but it is really quite logical. The key is to keep track of the mode of the objects. When faced with an array, like (*student* **of** *art*[2]), one slices. When confronted with a structure, like *prof* **of** *art*[2], one selects a field from it. If you still think ALGOL 68 is unnecessarily complicated, try to rewrite the preceding program in FORTRAN.

3.6 Procedure Calls

The mode of a procedure is uniquely determined by the modes of its parameters and its result. If a procedure returns mode **m**, then a call of that procedure is a unit of mode **m** and may be used anywhere a unit of mode **m** is needed. If a procedure *p1* has mode **proc (real, bool) int**, then $a[p1(3.14,\textbf{true})]$ shows a call of *p1* used as a subscript. Similarly, if a procedure *p2* has mode **proc (int) bool**, then **if** $p2(6)$ **then** $print(k)$ **fi** is legitimate.

A procedure call has two parts: the procedure to be called, and the parameter list. The first part may be the result of a computation, for example,

```
begin int i; real x,y;
[1:3] proc (real) real f := (sin,cos,tan);
to 100 ¢ repeat 100 times ¢
  do read ((i,x));
       ¢ i selects sin, cos, or tan to call ¢
       y := f[i](x);
       print(y)
  od
end
```

A function with no parameters (that is, of mode **proc m**) is not "called". Instead the procedure name is written with no parameter list. For technical reasons this is not regarded as a procedure call, but as a type conversion (coercion) from mode **proc m** to mode **m**. It is called deproceduring (RR 6.3) and is completely analogous to the widening coercion from **int** to **real** in **real** $x := 3$ or the dereferencing coercion in (**int** $i := 1, j; j := i$). If deproceduring did not exist, then **real** $x := random$ would have to be prohibited, since *random* has mode **proc real** and on the right-hand side in the preceding example a **real** is needed.

3.7 Assignments

An assignment (called an assignation in the Revised Report) consists of a destination (the left-hand side), a "becomes" symbol (:=), and a source (the right-hand side). A **ref m** assignment has a **ref m** unit as the destination and an **m** unit, or something coerceable to an **m** unit, as the source (RR 5.2.1.1).

Having detected a **ref m** destination, the compiler will coerce the source by all possible means to **m**. We emphasize that after all coercion the destination is mode **ref m** and the source is mode **m**.

An assignment can stand by itself as a statement, or be used itself as a unit. It may, for example, be used as a source in another assignment (but not as a destination to avoid certain ambiguities). For example, $j := k$ is an assignment and as such may be used as the source in $i := source$, yielding $i := j := k$. Because ALGOL 68 allows assignments as sources, it also gets multiple assignments, as an extra added attraction, for free. Furthermore, $a[i := i+1]$ is a perfectly valid way of subscripting the array a: first the assignment is carried out, and then the newly assigned value of i is used as a subscript.

3.8 Generators

ALGOL 68 provides two storage management strategies: local and heap. Local storage consists of a last-in, first-out stack. Whenever a procedure is called (and perhaps when a **begin end** block is entered, depending on the implementation) a new stack frame is created for all local variables needed in it. When it is exited, the storage is released by resetting the stack pointer to the value it had prior to entry. This leads to a simple and efficient method for allocating storage.

All variables declared in the usual way use the local storage discipline. In addition, the programmer may explicitly request more stack storage to be reserved by using a local generator, **loc**, followed by a specification of the mode desired (the mode is needed because **loc [1:n] compl** may take much more space than **loc bool**). The value of the generator **loc m** is the address of the new object, that is, a pointer to it, and as such has mode **ref m**.

An example may make the use of local generators clearer.

```
begin ¢ calculate something ¢
  begin ¢ demonstrate triangular arrays ¢
  int n; read(n);
  [1:n] ref [ ] real triangle;
  for k from 1 to n
    do triangle[k] := loc[1:k] real;
       ¢ fill in some values ¢
       for j from 1 to k
       do triangle[k][j] := k+j od
    od
  end
  ¢ storage used by triangle is now
  released ¢
end
```

Numerical analysts often deal with symmetric $n \times n$ matrices. Using a representation of n columns of n elements each is wasteful of storage. The preceding program declares *triangle* to be a row of pointers, each pointing to a different real vector. The vectors pointed to are created during execution of the program, each newly created vector being one element larger than its predecessor. When the preceding block is exited, all the storage reserved can be released. That is why these generators are called *local* generators: the effect is local to the block they occur in.

The array *hamlet* in the example at the end of Section 2.2 is allocated by essentially the same mechanism as the array triangle just given. That is why unlabeled statements can be allowed before declarations.

Incidently, the declaration of *triangle* should be carefully noted. Actual bounds are needed in the first brackets, but not in the second because *triangle* is a vector of pointers. The compiler has to know how large the vector is in order to reserve space for it, but for the purposes of allocating space to *triangle*, it does not matter what is being pointed to. In fact, bounds are never needed in a mode following a **ref**.

The other storage management scheme is the heap. The heap is a single homogeneous section of memory from which storage can be acquired by heap generators, of the form **heap m**, where **m** is the specification of the mode of the object needed. Because heap objects are not dependent on the stack discipline, they do not vanish when the block in which they were created is exited. When the heap is exhausted, a run-time garbage collector has to come in and recycle the garbage. For example,

```
begin ref [ ] real ptr;
to 1 000 000 ¢ repeat a million times ¢
    do ptr := heap[1:1000] real od
end
```

is a lovely little test to see whether your garbage collector is working properly. Passing through the loop the first time, a piece of the heap is allocated for a 1000-element real array and the address of the array is assigned to *ptr*. Passing through the loop the next time, the same thing happens, overwriting the address of the first array, which now becomes garbage because there is no way to access it. On some subsequent pass, all the free space on the heap will be gone, and garbage collection will be automatically invoked to recover unused storage.

Note that if a local instead of a heap generator had been used in the preceding example, the stack frame would have kept growing and growing until all of memory was full. Since stack storage is only released at procedure (or possibly block) exit, the program eventually would have been aborted with a "stack overflow" message.

3.9 Nil

In list processing applications, it is necessary to have some marker to indicate the end of a list. When programming in Assembly Language, zero is often used. In ALGOL 68 a special symbol, **nil** (RR 5.2.4), is provided to end lists.

3.10 Identity Relations

When performing list processing, it is sometimes necessary to compare two pointers to see if they point to the same object. This can be done using identity relations.

Identity relations are also used to compare pointers to **nil**. In practice, it is usually necessary that the programmer specify the mode required using a cast (see next Section 3.11). For example, consider a variable, *ptr*, declared by: **ref person** *ptr*, that is, *ptr* can point to an object of mode **person**. To see if *ptr* points to **nil**, one uses the construction

$$ptr := : \textbf{ref person (nil)}.$$

The identity relators $:=:$ and $:\neq:$ are not operators (because they act on an infinite number of modes), but they may be regarded roughly as operators of infinitely low precedence. Thus, for example,

$$\textbf{if } i < j \wedge ptr := : \textbf{nil then } \ldots$$

means

$$\textbf{if}(i < j \wedge ptr) := : \textbf{nil then } \ldots$$

which is probably not what was intended.

To illustrate heap generators, **nil**, and identity relations, we give a simple program that reads in people's bowling scores and stores the information as a singly linked list. In phase two, names are looked up and the scores are retrieved.

```
begin
mode person = struct(string name,
        int score, ref person next);
ref person first := nil, ptr,
string bowler; int bowled;
bool still looking;
    make term (stand in, " ");
while read((bowled,bowler)); bowled > 0
do first := heap person
        := (bowler,bowled,first)
od;

¢ phase 2. look up the scores ¢
while read ((newline,bowler)); bowler ≠ " "
do ptr := first; still looking := true;
    while (ptr :≠: ref person(nil)) ∧
            still looking
    do if name of ptr = bowler
        then print((bowler,score of ptr,
                    newline));
                still looking := false
        else ptr := next of ptr
        fi
    od;
    if still looking
        then print((bowler, "not in our league",
                    new line))
    fi
od
end
```

Some comments may be helpful. The condition in a **while** statement consists of zero or more statements followed by a unit. In the first **while** statement in the preceding program, two variables are first read, and then the condition (bowled > 0) is evaluated. The data are arranged in such a way that there is one person per card, first a score, and then a name. It is necessary to specify the string delimiter for the name, and this is done by the call to the procedure *make term*, defining space as the string delimiter for the standard input file, *stand in* (see Section 9, Input/Output).

Let us imagine that the first two people are named Adam and Eve, with bowling scores of 105 and 107, respectively. Prior to execution of the initial **while** loop, *first* points to **nil**. After the loop has been executed once, an object of mode **person** has been created, with its three fields initialized to ("Adam", 105, **nil**). The variable *first* then points to this object. Passing through the loop the next time, a second object of mode **person** is created, with its fields initialized to ("Eve", 107, pointer to first object). Now *first* points to Eve, which points to Adam, which points to **nil**.

3.11 Casts

Most of the time it is not necessary to specify the mode of a source, destination, operand, etc., explicitly. It is usually obvious from context. However, to handle those situations that are inherently ambiguous, the required mode may be specified explicitly using a construction called a cast (RR 5.5.1), one form of which consists of a mode followed by a parenthesized unit, as in **ref int**(i).

To understand why casts are needed, examine this program:

```
begin int i := 0, k := 1;
ref int ptr := i;
ptr := k;
print (i)
end
```

Consider what $ptr := k$ does. On one hand, it looks like an innocuous assignment of the address of k to a pointer variable (ptr has mode **ref ref int**, and k has mode **ref int**).

But on the other hand, suppose both *ptr* and k were dereferenced, yielding a **ref int** object as destination and an **int** object as source. If that happened, i would be assigned the value 1, quite different from assigning k to *ptr*. To avoid the occurrence of this ambiguity, the ALGOL 68 grammar was constructed in such a way as to prevent dereferencing destinations. This means that the preceding program prints 0, not 1.

Now comes the 64 dollar question: suppose you actually intended the second interpretation; how can that be achieved? Answer: use a cast; that is, replace the assignment by **ref int** (*ptr*) := k. The cast explicitly forces *ptr* to be converted to mode **ref int**. Since k cannot be assigned to a **ref int**, k is dereferenced. (Dereferencing is allowed for sources.)

When a cast is used, two modes are involved: the starting mode (the mode of the object inside the parentheses), and the goal mode (the mode listed before the open parenthesis). If there is no coercion path between the starting and the goal modes, the cast is invalid. For example, if *ptr* has mode **ref proc ref int**, then **real**(*ptr*) is a valid cast because *ptr* can be dereferenced, deprocedured, dereferenced, again, and widened. However, **bits** (3.14) is invalid because there is no coercion path from **real** to **bits**. Coercion is discussed in more detail in Section 4, Coercions.

3.12 Choice Clauses

ALGOL 68 allows **if** "statements" and **case** "statements" to be used as units if they produce the proper mode. This is illustrated by the following program:

```
begin ¢ examples of choice clauses ¢
int i,j,k;
real x := 0.1, y := 0.2, z := 3.1;
read ((i,j,k));
[1:10] bool a, b;
x := if i<0 then .3/x else z+4.0 fi;
for n from i to if j = 2 then 1 else k fi
    do b[n] := true od;
b[case i in 6,3 out 4 esac] := false;
if i = 0 then j else k fi :=
        if j>0 then j+1 else k−1 fi;
[if i>0 then 1 else k−1 fi : 10] int c;
z := if i>3 then sin else cos fi (3.14);
end
```

Three kinds of choice clauses exist: Boolean, integer, and united.

- The Boolean choice clause is the familiar **if ... then ... else ... fi** construction. If the **else** part is absent and the condition is false, the result is undefined.
- The second choice clause has the form **case ... in** clause1, clause2, clause3, ..., clause n **out ... esac**. The integer expression between **case** and **in** selects one of the clauses by indexing into the clause list. Thus the order of the clauses is critical. If there is no **out** part, and the expression is out of range, the result is undefined.
- The third choice clause takes a united variable (such as *kitchen sink* used in Section 2.5) and, selects one of the clauses based upon its current mode. The order of the clauses for this type of choice clause is irrelevant.

Variables may be declared in the condition, or integer parts, initialized, and then used in the succeeding parts; that is, their scope encompasses the entire choice clause. For example:

```
begin ¢ print smaller of 2 numbers ¢
if int i,j; read ((i,j)); i<j
   then print (i)
   else print (j)
fi
end
```

ALGOL 68 (and common sense) requires that all the possible choices in a unit be of the same mode, or be coerceable to the same mode. The unit **if** $i<0$ **then** 4 **else** j **fi** can be used anywhere an integer unit is expected, because the **then** part is already an integer and the **else** part can be converted to one by dereferencing it. The unit cannot be used as a destination, however, because the **then** part cannot be converted to a **ref int**; there is no "referencing" coercion.

Now consider the assignment in:

```
begin int i,k; read (k);
   i:= if k<0 then 6 else true fi
end
```

This assignment is incorrect because an integer unit is needed as the source, and it is not possible to coerce all choices to mode **int**; namely, **true** cannot be turned into an integer. The problem of making sure all choices can be converted to the proper mode is called **balancing** (RR 3.2.1e). Since an assignment may have long **case** units, both as source and destination, just determining the proper mode of the assignment may itself be a substantial task for the compiler. However, the grammar was constructed in such a way as to insure that there is only one possibility.

ALGOL 68 allows **if, then, else,** and **fi** to be written as (, |, |, and), respectively. Thus **if** $k<0$ **then** i **else** j **fi** can be written $(k<0 \mid i \mid j)$. This is often convenient in constructions like:

$$x := (i<0 \mid y \mid z) + (j<0 \mid 4.0 \mid z+5)$$

3.13 Closed Clauses

ALGOL 68 is an expression language. This means that every executable statement or group of statements can (at least potentially) deliver a value. A serial clause (RR 3.2) is a series of zero or more declarations and/or "statements" followed by a unit. The mode and value of the serial clause consist of the mode and value of the final unit. A closed clause is a serial clause enclosed by **begin end** or by parentheses. A closed clause has the mode and value of the serial clause, that is, of the last unit in the clause.

Some examples of closed clauses follow:

```
begin ¢ closed clauses ¢
begin int i; read(i); i end
begin real x; read(x); sin(x) end;
begin int i,j; read((i,j)); i+j end;
begin [1:10] int a;
   for i from 1 to 10 do a[i] := i*i od; a
end;
(int i; i := 20);
("horse");
((10,20,30,40));
((((((0))))));
(int i; (i := 3))
end
```

Since closed clauses are units, they may be used in the same way any other units are used, even if this seems peculiar at first.

Closed clauses may be used as sources; subscripts; **from**, **by**, or **to** parts in **for** statements; etc. For example, the following statement is perfectly valid:

$$k := (\textbf{int } i; read(i); i+1)$$

3.14 Skip

There is a special unit, **skip**, which is explicitly undefined. It takes on whatever mode is needed. As we have seen earlier, it can be used to omit the initialization of an element or field of a row or structure display, or to serve as a dummy statement. Do not confuse **skip** with **nil**; **nil** is a specific value that can be tested for; **skip** is just "filler" to make a construction syntactically correct, vaguely analogous to CONTINUE statements in FORTRAN.

3.15 Routine Texts

Since ALGOL 68 allows procedure variables, it is only natural that it also allow procedure units, so that there is something to assign to these procedure variables. A routine text is a procedure body, headed by the formal parameter list, if there is one. We discuss routine texts in the context of procedures and operators later. As a preview, we give a few examples of routine texts as sources:

```
begin proc (real) real f;
proc int p; proc void q;
f := (real r) real: 3.14/r;
f := (real s) real: s+4.0;
f := (real t) real: sin(cos(t));
p := int: 3;
p := int: (int k; read(k); k);
q := void: print ("hello")
¢ note: no procedures have been called ¢
end
```

Note that the formal parameters can be used in the body of the routine text, following the colon.

3.16 Other Units

For the sake of completeness, we note that loop clauses (**for** loops), jumps (**goto** statements), formats, parallel clauses, and collateral clauses (for example, row displays) are also units in the technical sense (RR 5.1A).

4. COERCIONS

Coercion is the ALGOL 68 term for automatic mode conversion. Unlike some languages (notably PL/I) that allow practically anything to be converted into practically anything else, ALGOL 68 has very few automatic conversions. Automatic conversions often lead to unexpected and unwanted results, so ALGOL 68 was specifically designed to keep them well in hand.

There are exactly six kinds of coercions, each converting some class of modes into another. The six kinds of coercions are:

coercion	input mode	output mode
dereferencing	**ref m**	**m**
deproceduring	**proc m**	**m**
widening	**int**	**real**
widening	**real**	**compl**
widening	**bits**	**[ ] bool**
widening	**bytes**	**[ ] char**
rowing	**m**	**[ ] m, [,] m** etc.
uniting	**m**	**union (m,m1, ...)**
voiding	**m**	(no mode at all)

We have already discussed dereferencing (Section 2.6, Reference-to Modes), widening (Section 2.6), and deproceduring (Section 3.6, Procedure Calls). Widening also applies to the **long** and **short** forms of **int, real, bits,** and **bytes.**

Rowing can convert a unit into a one-element array where required by the context, such as in [1:1] **int** $a := 3$. Uniting turns a unit into a union where required by the syntax, as in **union(int, real)** $u := 4$. Rowing and uniting happen when needed and are of little interest to the average garden variety programmer.

As is probably apparent by now, constructions called statements (for example, assignments, procedure calls) in most languages are called units in ALGOL 68 and can be used as sources, parameters, etc. Sometimes, however, the value of a unit is not needed. Consider what happens to the value of $i := j$ in the closed clause:

$$(\textbf{int } i,j := 3; i := j; i+j)$$

it is discarded after the assignment is performed. Technically this is called voiding (RR 6.7). ALGOL 68 "statements" are properly called void units. Chapter 6 of the

Revised Report describes the coercions in full.

Note that there is no coercion from **real** to **int**. However, the monadic operators **round** and **entier** operate on reals and deliver integers, rounding and truncating, respectively.

5. CONTEXTS

Not every coercion is allowed in every context (for example, in source, destination, subscript, actual parameter). In Section 3.11 Casts, we saw that ambiguities could result if dereferencing of destinations was allowed. Each context has an intrinsic strength. The strength specifies which coercions are allowed. There are five strengths: strong, firm, meek, weak, and soft. In some contexts no coercions at all are allowed.

Strong contexts are those in which the mode of the unit is uniquely determined by the context. For example, in

  (**real** x; x := big hairy mess)

the destination is known to be of mode **ref real**. Any and all coercions may be used (repeatedly) to turn the source into an object of mode **real**. If the source is an **int**, it can be widened; if it is a **ref real**, it can be dereferenced; if it is a **proc real**, it can be deprocedured; if it is a **ref proc ref int**, it can be dereferenced to **proc ref int**, deprocedured to **ref int**, dereferenced again to **int**, and finally widened to **real**. Some examples of strong contexts are: sources in assignments, initial values in declarations, actual parameters, and procedure bodies.

In other contexts some coercions must be prohibited to avoid ambiguities. For example, consider:

  begin int i := 2, j;
  real x := 3.0, y;
  j := $i+i$;
  y := $x+x$
  end

The $+$ in $i+i$ is an operator that operates on integers and yields an integer. The $+$ in $x+x$ is a different operator acting on reals. The two operators correspond to different hardware instructions. The compiler tells which operator is to be used by looking at the modes of the operands. If operands could be widened, the operands of the first $+$ could be dereferenced and then widened, yielding reals. Then the compiler could not tell which operator was meant. Operands are always in firm context.

If every kind of unit were allowed in every context, certain ambiguities would arise, as can be easily seen by means of an example. Consider what would happen to the integer assignment i := $j+2$ if j, which is an operand of $+$, were replaced by the assignment k := 3. We would have i := k := $3+2$, which is perfectly legal, but not what was intended. It adds $3+2$ and then assigns the result, 5, to k and i. If we wrote the operand k := 3 as a closed clause (k := 3), we would get i := (k := 3)$+2$, which first assigns 3 to k, and then 5 to i. This is quite a different result than in the first case! To avoid ambiguities, ALGOL 68 only allows constructions in positions where no confusion can arise.

6. PROCEDURES

In ALGOL 68 procedures are objects and have values, just as any other objects. Procedure variables exist and may be declared, just as other variables. They may also be initialized to some value of the appropriate mode; for example, by using a routine text:

  proc real $p1$:= **real**: 1.0/(1.0 | *random*);
  proc int $p2$:= **int**: (**int** k; *read*(k);k);
  proc (**int** k) **int** $p3$:= (**int**) **int**:($k+1$) **div** 2

Procedures (and all other modes) may also be declared in a slightly different way, by use of what is technically called an identity declaration (RR 4.4.1a). This form consists of **proc**, the identifier, an equals sign, and a routine text. In this form the identifier is no longer a variable and cannot be assigned a new procedure. Some examples of this form are:

  begin ¢ proc declarations ¢
  proc *next* = (**int** k) **int**: $k+1$;
  proc *bump* = (**ref int** k) **void**: k := $k+1$;
  proc *less* = (**int** j,k) **bool**: $j<k$;
  proc *readin* = **int**: (**int** k; *read*(k);k);
  proc *eject* = **void**: *print*(*new page*);

```
proc dot product = (int n,[ ] real a,b) real:
begin real sum := 0;
  for k from 1 to n do sum := sum+a[k]*b[k]
  od;
  sum
end;
  skip ¢ dummy statement ¢
end
```

Note that the procedure body (the part following the colon) is a unit. In the dot product example, the unit is a closed clause.

6.1 Parameter Mechanism

A procedure may be declared with an arbitrary number of formal parameters, but calls to the procedure must supply precisely the proper number of actual parameters, no more and no less. The nth actual parameter is accessed by using the identifier of the nth formal parameter, just as in FORTRAN, PL/I, ALGOL 60, etc. Thus the order of the formal parameters is very important.

Unlike these other languages, however, the modes of the parameters are specified directly in the formal parameter list. The mode specified before the identifier of each formal parameter is the mode of that parameter. In the declaration:

```
proc recip = (real x) real: 1.0/x
```

the mode of x is **real**, It is not **ref real**. By way of contrast, in the variable declaration **real** x, x is of mode **ref real**. This difference is crucial to the understanding of the ALGOL 68 parameter mechanism.

The parameter passing works as follows. The actual parameters are first coerced to the modes specified by the formal parameters (if necessary). Then each actual parameter is evaluated. (An actual parameter is a unit, and might be a closed clause 10 pages long.) Copies of the values yielded are then passed to the procedure. This may be regarded as a generalization of the call by value used in ALGOL 60, except that in ALGOL 68 a parameter may be of any mode, including **ref** "something," in which case an address is passed.

To shed more light on the parameter mechanism, let us begin with a syntactically incorrect program:

```
begin int n := 4; ¢ incorrect program ¢
proc wrong = (int k) void: k := k+1;
wrong(n);
print(n)
end
```

The problem here is that k has mode **int** and not **ref int**. The destination of an assignment must be of mode **ref** "something;" the assignment $k := k+1$ will be flagged by the compiler as incorrect. Now let us try again.

```
begin int n := 4; ¢ correct program ¢
proc right = (ref int k) void: k := k+1;
right(n);
print(n)
end
```

This program will print 5. When a formal parameter is declared **int** rather than **ref int**, the corresponding actual parameter is protected from being changed. This often helps catch bugs.

To illuminate the more subtle aspects of the parameter mechanism, consider these two programs:

```
begin int i := 0;
proc jekyll = (int a) void:
  (i := i+1; print (a));
jekyll(i)
end
```

```
begin int i := 0;
proc hyde = (ref int a) void:
  (i := i+1; print (a));
hyde (i)
end
```

The call $jekyll(i)$ is executed in the following steps. Since the formal parameter is of mode **int**, the actual parameter, i, is dereferenced to yield an integer. A copy of this integer value is then passed to $jekyll$ (on the stack, in a register, or some other way). Then $jekyll$ increments i. Finally, $jekyll$ accesses the actual parameter passed to it and prints it. The number 0 is printed.

The call $hyde(i)$ is executed differently. The formal parameter in program 2 is of mode **ref int**; so i is not dereferenced, because it is already in the proper mode. A copy of the address of i is made and put on the stack, in a register, or elsewhere. After incrementing i, $hyde$ picks up the actual parameter, the address of i, dereferences it, getting 1, and then prints the number 1.

An object of mode **int** is passed to *jekyll*, but an object of mode **ref int** is passed to *hyde*. In a sense, *jekyll* uses the ALGOL 60 call-by-value parameter mechanism, whereas *hyde* uses something similar to a call-by-reference mechanism. ALGOL 68 effectively gives the programmer some control over how parameters are passed via the modes of the formal parameters.

In summary, the parameter mechanism has three key features:

1) A formal parameter is written as a mode followed by an identifier. A formal parameter written as **int** k really has mode **int**, not mode **ref int**.

2) An actual parameter may be any unit, and any coercion may be used on it, but the result after coercion must match the mode of the formal parameter. If a formal parameter has mode **ref real**, the actual parameter must yield a real variable; the value 3.14 will not suffice. The calling, and not the called, procedure performs the coercions.

3) A copy is made of the actual parameter (after coercion). This copy is what is passed (conceptually). All references to the formal parameter use this copy. Thus the parameter is only evaluated once (as opposed to the call-by-name mechanism used in ALGOL 60, where the parameter is reevaluated on every access).

6.2 More About Procedures

Unlike PL/I, parameters and results in ALGOL 68 may have any mode; pointers, arrays, structures, unions, and even procedures are all allowed. As an example of using a procedure as a parameter, consider the following procedure for computing the sum:

$$f(1) + f(2) + f(3) + \cdots + f(n).$$

proc *sum* = (**int** n, **proc** (**real**) **real** f) **real**:
begin real *sum* := 0;
for i **to** n **do** sum := sum+f(i) **od**;
sum
end

In this example, i is allowed as a parameter to a **proc**(**real**) **real** because parameters are strong units and therefore can be widened. A typical call to *sum* might be *sum*(100,*cos*), which would yield $cos(1) + cos(2) + \cdots + cos(100)$.

In ALGOL 68 a routine text is a unit and as such can be used as an actual parameter. In the previous examples, routine texts were used to the right of the equals sign. Some examples of routine texts as actual parameters of *sum* are:

sum(100, (**real** x) **real**: $1/x$)
sum(50, (**real** x) **real**: $sin(x)$)
sum(k+1, (**real** x) **real**: *random*)

ALGOL 60 fanciers will notice that using a routine text as an actual parameter is essentially equivalent to Jensen's device [5], but a lot less sneaky.

It is sometimes useful to be able to write procedures that accept a variable number of parameters. Although strictly speaking this is not possible in ALGOL 68, something very close is possible. A procedure with one formal parameter, an array, must have one actual parameter, also an array. However, this array may have an arbitrary number of elements, provided it is of the proper mode. Remember that a one-dimensional integer array has mode [ ] **int** no matter how large it is; the bounds are not part of the mode.

When it is expected that a procedure be called with different sized arrays as parameters, there must be some way of determining the bounds of its actual parameters. Two operators are provided for this purpose: **lwb** and **upb**. If *vec* is a one-dimensional array of any mode, **lwb** *vec* and **upb** *vec* have the values of the lower and upper bounds, respectively. For a higher dimensional array, q, n **lwb** q and n **upb** q return the lower and upper bounds of the nth subscript, respectively. The lower bound of a row display is 1.

The following program declares a procedure, *outp*, that accepts an integer array as parameter and prints each of its elements on a new line. Note that calls to *outp* (and also to *read*) have two sets of parentheses. One set is needed to enclose the parameter list and one set is needed to construct the row display;

```
begin int i,j,k;
proc outp = ([ ] int a) void:
   begin for i to upb a
         do print ((new line, a[i])) od
   end;
read ((i,j,k));
outp ((1,2,3,4));
outp ((i,j,7,k,j+1,k−4));
outp ((if i<j then 1 else k fi,
       if j>0 then 4 else 2 fi,
       10,k+6,j,−k,−6,+7,0))
end
```

that is, (1,2,3,4) is a unit, but 1,2,3,4 is nothing. This is why $print((x,y))$ and not $print(x,y)$ has been used to print two variables.

It is possible to write procedures that accept any one of a prespecified list of modes as a parameter by making the formal parameter a union. The following example is a program that accepts parameters of mode **int**, **real**, or **bool** and returns the mode as a string:

```
begin int k := 0; union(real,bool) u := 4.0;
proc mohd = (union(int,real,bool) a) string:
   case a in
      (int): "int",
      (real): "real",
      (bool): "bool"
   esac;
print((mohd(k), " ", mohd(u)))
end
```

The output of this program consists of
   int **real**.

7. OPERATORS

The following program defines a new mode, **vector**, and a procedure, *vecadd*, to add two vectors:

```
begin int n; read(n);
mode vector = [1:n] real;
vector v1,v2,v3,v4,v5;
proc vecadd = (vector x,y) vector:
   begin vector sum;
      for i to upb x
         do sum[i] := x[i] + y[i] od;
      sum
   end;
```

```
¢ read in 4 vectors ¢
read ((v1,v2,v3,v4));
v5 := vecadd(vecadd(vecadd(v1,v2),v3),v4);
print(v5)
end
```

The statement $v5 := vecadd(vecadd(vecadd(v1,v2),v3),v4)$, although ghastly to look at, is quite correct. Because $vecadd(v1,v2)$ is a call, and hence a unit, it may be used as an actual parameter to another call of *vecadd*.

The difficulty with the preceding expression is that although it is perfectly acceptable to the ALGOL 68 compiler, for many applications, infix operators (that is, operators placed between the operands) are much more natural than nested procedure calls. ALGOL 68 solves this problem by allowing programmers to define new infix operators, just as they can define new modes.

Operators are defined very much as procedures are. First comes **op**, followed by the operator symbol (which may also be a **boldface** word), then an equals sign, and a routine text. An operator must have either one or two parameters, no more and no fewer. Like those of a procedure, the parameters and the result of an operator may be of any mode. Let us try the vector addition program again, using an operator this time.

```
begin int n; read(n);
mode vector = [1:n] real;
vector v1,v2,v3,v4,v5;
op + = (vector x,y) vector:
   begin vector sum;
      for i to upb x
         do sum[i] := x[i] + y[i] od;
      sum
   end;
```

```
¢ read in 4 vectors ¢
read ((v1,v2,v3,v4));
v5 := v1 + v2 + v3 + v4;
print (v5)
end
```

Just to prove that any mode can be used as an operand or as a result of an operator, we present an operator that takes an **int** and a **proc void** as operands, does something useful, and delivers nothing.

```
begin
op * = (int n,proc void p) void:
   to n do p od; ¢ deprocedure p n times ¢
proc eject = void: print(new page);
proc skip = void: print(new line);
2 * eject; ¢ skip 2 pages ¢
3 * skip ¢ skip 3 lines ¢
end
```

7.1 Operator Identification

Operators have one complication which procedures lack: the same symbol can be used to represent different routine texts. This property is called GENERIC in PL/I. The + in 1+2 is a completely different + than the + in 8.711+8.72. When the ALGOL 68 compiler sees an operator symbol, it determines which operator definition to use by looking at the modes of the operands. If they have modes **m1** and **m2**, it looks to see if an operator with that symbol and those modes has been defined. If so, it uses it. If not, it begins coercing the operands to see if they can be converted into some other modes for which an operator exists.

The process of determining which operator a symbol corresponds to is called **operator identification** (RR 7.2). It is one of the great achievements of the ALGOL 68 Revised Report that this entire process has been described completely in the grammar; that is, the nonterminal <program> simply does not generate any ambiguous programs. No English text is needed to describe what is and what is not permitted.

After an operator has been identified, the evaluation of its formula is the same as that for procedure calls, including the parameter mechanism. Even Jensen's device will work if you provide a routine text as an operand.

To illustrate how operator identification works, consider the following program:

```
begin
op ? = (int i,j) real: i+j;
op ? = (int i,real x) real: i−x;
op ? = (real x,int i) real: i+x+19;
op ? = (real x,y) real: (x<y | x | y);
print ((2?9, 6?2.0, 3.14?8, 9.2?9.9))
end
```

This program yields: 11.0, 4.0, 30.14, 9.2. Each of the four occurrences of ? in the print procedure invokes a different routine text.

Not only can one define new operators on existing modes (for example, "?" on **ints**) and existing operators on new modes (for example, + on **vectors**) and new operators on new modes (for example, **invert** on **matrix**), but one can even redefine the existing operators on the existing modes. If you really want to redefine + on integers to mean subtract, that is your business; the compiler will not complain.

More realistically, someone writing a simulator for a two's complement computer on a one's complement computer (for example, a PDP-11 simulator running on a CDC Cyber) might be very concerned about the specific bit patterns used to represent integers, rather than just their numerical values. In particular, he might want to redefine integer arithmetic to prevent −0 from ever occurring.

Or a numerical analyst might want to redefine real arithmetic to handle rounding differently, or to print a warning message when too much significance has been lost.

7.2 Operator Priorities

When someone writes $print(6+3*5)$ he expects to get 21, because multiplication has higher precedence (priority) than addition. In ALGOL 68 the priority of an operator symbol can be set by the programmer. For example,

```
begin
   prio + = 3, * = 2;
   print (6+3*5)
end
```

will print 45, that is, $(6+3) * 5$. Monadic operators all have priority 10 and cannot be changed. Dyadic operators may have priorities 1 to 9. This means that $-1 \uparrow 2$ is + 1, not −1 because it is equivalent to $(-1)^2$.

8. STANDARD PRELUDE

Section 10.2 of the Revised Report consists of several hundred definitions of modes, operators, procedures, and values. Collectively they are called the **standard prelude**. Every ALGOL 68 program is presumed to be declared within the scope of these declarations. The modes, operators, etc., declared in the standard prelude may be used in any ALGOL 68 program. In fact, that is precisely why they are there. The standard prelude is written (almost entirely) in ALGOL 68.

It can now be pointed out that the basic nucleus of ALGOL 68 (the part defined by the grammar) is really much smaller than one might expect. For example, some of the "primitive" modes are not really primitive at all, but are defined in the standard prelude; for example,

mode compl = **struct**(**real** *re,im*)

appears in RR 10.2.2f. Furthermore, none of the operators, trigonometric functions, or input/output procedures are part of the language proper. An implementor who was not concerned at all about compilation or execution efficiency, either in time or in space, could have nearly the whole standard prelude textually substituted in front of every ALGOL 68 program, saving himself a great deal of work.

8.1 Environment Enquiries

The standard prelude begins with the environment enquiries (RR 10.2.1). These enquiries allow a program to learn properties of the implementation it is running under without having to deduce them by experiment. The largest integer is called *max int*, the largest real is called *max real*, the smallest positive real is called *small real*, the number of bits in an object of mode **bits** is called *bits width*, etc. For example, here is a program to determine the largest integer in an implementation: (*print(max int)*).

Since each implementor has the freedom to decide how many long and short integers he wants to provide, environment enquiries are provided to allow the program to find out how many there are. These include *int*

lengths, *real lengths*, *bits lengths*, and *bytes lengths* among others. The purpose of these and the other environment enquiries is to ease the task of exchanging programs between computers. For example, a program needing integers of at least 47 bits could first check the value of *max int*; finding it less than $2^{47}-1$, it could use **long int**s instead of **int**s.

8.2 Standard Prelude Operators

10.2.2 of the Revised Report lists the standard modes. Section 10.2.3.0a of the Revised Report lists the priorities of all the standard operators, followed by the definitions of the standard operators. For example, the operators on Boolean operands are as follows:

op ∨ = (**bool** *a,b*) **bool**: (*a* | **true** | *b*);
op ∧ = (**bool** *a,b*) **bool**: (*a* | *b* | **false**);
op ⌐ = (**bool** *a*) **bool**: (*a* | **false** | **true**);
op = = (**bool** *a,b*) **bool**: (*a*∧*b*)∨(⌐*a*∧⌐*b*);
op ≠ = (**bool** *a,b*) **bool**: ⌐(*a*=*b*);
op abs = (**bool** *a*) **int**: (*a* | 1 | 0)

From the standard prelude one can see precisely which operators are defined on which operands, and what they do. For example, to determine if **abs true** has a value of 0 or 1, a glance at the standard prelude will show that it has a value of 1. Few languages offer such precise definitions of their operators as ALGOL 68.

Subsequent sections of the standard prelude define the operators for comparison, arithmetic, string handling, etc. If one wants to see exactly what + on strings (concatenation) means, one can consult RR 10.2.3.10i. A very small number of operators are defined in English, such as − on reals. To provide a full definition one would have in fact had to define how floating point arithmetic works. This would have wreaked havoc with implementations on computers whose floating point hardware worked differently. The implementor would either have had to ignore the standard prelude, or simulate floating point operations in software.

ALGOL 68 allows mixed mode arithmetic. The formula 3.14+6 yields the real 9.14. The mechanism by which this happens can now be safely revealed: The operator + is defined for parameters of modes (**int, int**), (**int, real**), (**real, int**), and (**real, real**). Four definitions are necessary because operands are firm and because widening is forbidden in firm positions (to avoid ambiguities in operator identification).

An interesting new idea in operators is that of combining arithmetic and assignment. For example, RR 10.2.3.11d states:

op +:= = (**ref int** a, **int** b) **ref int**: $a := a+b$

This enables one to write: n +:= 1 rather than $n := n+1$. The "plus and becomes" operator, +:=, may also ease the task of optimizing the object code, especially on computers which can add directly to memory. Similar operators exist for real numbers and the other operations; for example, −:= means "subtract and becomes."

A number of standard mathematical functions are provided in RR 10.2.3.12 including *sqrt, exp, ln, cos, arccos, sin, arcsin, tan,* and *arctan.* Anyone who prefers sines as operators rather than as procedure calls need only write:

op sin = (**real** x) **real**: $sin(x)$.

If you don't care what values your functions return, you may enjoy *random* (RR 10.5.1b). And finally, *pi* is defined as a real value close to you-know-what (RR 10.2.3.12a). Standard prelude declarations may be overridden simply by supplying other declarations.

9. INPUT/OUTPUT

ALGOL 60 was widely criticized for not discussing such mundane matters as input/output. That is one problem from which ALGOL 68 will not suffer. An extremely powerful and flexible set of input/output procedures is defined in the standard prelude. A variety of input/output styles is provided, ranging from the lowly *print* procedure to formatted input/output on files with user control over conversion codes, error handling, and the like. The ALGOL 68 term for input/output is transput.

9.1 Books, Channels, and Files

A **book** is a collection of information in the form of a three-dimensional character array (RR 10.3.1.1a). Books are comparable to what some other languages call data sets. A book consists of a certain number of pages, each page consisting of a certain number of lines, each line consisting of a certain number of characters.

For example, line printer output may consist of many pages of 60 lines, each line having 132 characters. Each position in the output can be described by a triple (page, line, char). Likewise, a multifile magnetic tape can be modeled with page = file number, line = record number, and character = position within a record. A book on a card reader might have only 1 page with many 80-character lines. Books may not be read or written by being subscripted; instead special procedures are provided for reading and writing. We have already seen two of these: *read* and *print*.

A **channel** (RR 10.3.1.2) corresponds to an input/output device type, for example, a disk, card reader, plotter, holographic store, or on-line experimental rat. A **file** (RR 10.3.1.3) provides the machinery to use a particular channel.

An object of mode **file** is actually a structure specifying a book, a channel, the current position on the file (page, line, char), the conversion code to use, and a number of procedures of mode **proc(ref file) bool**, as well as a few other details. A typical procedure is: *page mended*. When the program has filled up a page, *page mended* is automatically called. Programmers may supply their own versions of *page mended*: for example, eject to a new page, print a heading, and return **true**, indicating that the difficulty has been corrected. A new version of *page mended*, p, can only be associated with a file, f, by the call

on page end(f,p)

and not by directly referencing the field selector *page mended*. The other procedures handle end of file, end of line, end of format, and invalid data detected.

To access an existing book via a particular channel, declare a **file** and call the procedure *open* to associate the book and channel with it. *Open* has three parameters: the file, an identification string, and the channel. The identification string and channel are installation dependent. To close a file, call *close* with the file as parameter. To create a new book, call *create*, specifying the file and channel.

Three files are declared and opened in the standard prelude (RR 10.5.1c): *stand in*, *stand out*, and *stand back*. These files correspond to the normal input and output files, and the binary scratch files. At some installations the files may be card reader, printer, and magnetic tape; at others they may be an on-line terminal, an on-line terminal and a disk. These files need (must) not be declared by the programmer.

Here is a simple program to copy 1000 lines from file1 to file2:

```
begin file in, out;
string s;
open (in,("file1", stand in channel);
open(out,"file2", stand out channel);
for i from 1 to 1000
  do get(in,(s, new line));
     put(out,(s, new line))
  od;
close(in);
close(out)
end
```

The procedure *open* defines a correspondence between an ALGOL 68 file name and a preexisting operating system file name. The procedures *get* and *put* are the analogs of *read* and *print*. In fact, *read(x)* is declared (RR 10.5.1e) as *get(stand in,x)* and *print* is declared (RR 10.5.1d) as *put(stand out,x)*. The inclusion of *new line* in the calls to *get* and *put* is needed to advance the current position to the start of the next line.

ALGOL 68 supports random access books as well as sequential books. Each installation must decide which channels are random access, and which are not. Typically, disks and drums will be random access, whereas card readers and paper tape punches will not be. If a book is randomly accessible via a file *f*, the procedure call *set possible(f)* will yield **true**, if not, it will yield **false**. To set the current position of file *f* to (p,l,c) call *set(f,p,l,c)*.

A list of some (but not all) of the file handling procedures declared in the standard prelude follows; *f* represents a file; *p* represents a **proc(ref file) bool**; *c* represents a character, and *x* represents a variable, a constant, or a row display.

get possible (*f*)	**true** if *f* is readable
put possible (*f*)	**true** if *f* is writeable
bin possible (*f*)	**true** if binary transput ok
set possible (*f*)	**true** if *f* is random access
reset possible (*f*)	**true** if *f* is rewindable
chan (*f*)	yields *f*'s channel
page number (*f*)	yields the current page
line number (*f*)	yields the current line
char number (*f*)	yields the current char
lock (*f*)	protects *f* from further access
scratch (*f*)	detach and burn the book
get (*f,x*)	read *x* from file *f*
put (*f,x*)	write *x* to file *f*
new page (*f*)	advance to a new page
new line (*f*)	advance to a new line
space (*f*)	advance one character
backspace (*f*)	go back one character
set (*f,pg,l,c*)	current pos := (pg,l,c)
reset (*f*)	rewind to (1,1,1)
on logical file end(*f,p*)	make *p* the procedure
on page end (*f,p*)	to be called when the
on line end (*f,p*)	corresponding event
on format end (*f,p*)	occurs on file *f*
make term (*f,"c"*)	make *c* string terminator on *f*

It is also possible to perform transput directly to a three-dimensional character array in memory rather than to an external book (cf. ENCODE/DECODE in CDC 6000 FORTRAN). To make an array *buffer* the pseudobook of file *f*, call *associate(f,buffer)*.

9.2 Formatless Transput

The simplest form of transput is formatless transput, of which *read*, *print*, *get*, and *put* are the most important examples. Since *get* works precisely like *read*, except on arbitrary files instead of on *stand in*, and *put* is analogous to *print*, we concentrate on *read* and *print*.

Read and *print* have modes that ordinary programmers cannot construct. Roughly speaking, the mode of *print* is **proc**([ ] **union**(**int**,**real**,**bool**,**char**,[ ]**int**,[,,]**int**, and everything else that can be printed, and **proc**(**file**)**void**))**void**. *Read* has a similar mode.

The procedure *get* is given in its entirety in RR 10.3.3.2a. For the beginner, the following rules will be enough to get started. The input book is regarded as a continuous stream of values separated by delimiters.

Integers, reals, and complex numbers may be signed. Reals and complex numbers may contain a decimal point and an exponent part, indicated by the letter "*e*". When a character variable is to be read, the next character is taken (even space), except at the end of a line or page, when the line or page will be advanced first. Strings are delimited by end of line or by a special termination character associated with the file.

When reading vectors and matrices, the order in which the elements are read is important. The question of how an array (or structure) is turned into a linear sequence of elements is called **straightening** (RR 10.3.2.3). In short, vectors are read from lowest element to highest element. Matrices are read in row order, beginning with the first row, then the second row, etc.

The procedures *new line*, *new page*, *space*, and *backspace* may be passed as parameters to *read*. The first three advance the current position before reading. The last one moves it backwards before reading, but not beyond the beginning of the current line. Using backspace, input data can be reread.

Print works as follows. For each mode of data there is a standard format that is used. The widths of the fields are implementation dependent, depending on *max int* and *max real*. *Print* refrains from splitting numbers across lines or pages; if the number will not fit, the line or page is advanced before printing. The procedures new line, new page, space, and backspace may be included as parameters to print, and both *read* and *print* expect a single parameter. If this is a row display, an extra set of parentheses is required, for example,

print((*new page*, "title",*new line*,*x*,*y*,*z*))

For people who are slightly discriminating about what their output looks like, but who are nevertheless too lazy to use formatted output, the procedures *whole*, *fixed*, and *float* may be helpful (RR 10.3.2.1). The calls

print(*whole*(*i*,*size*)); ¢ e.g. +3 ¢
print(*fixed*(*x*,*size*,*d*)); ¢ e.g. 6.02 ¢
print(*float*(*x*,*size*,*d*,*e*); ¢ e.g. 1.234e−07 ¢

output the integer *i* or real *x* in a field of width **abs** *size*. If *size* is positive, an explicit sign is printed; if *size* is negative, plus signs are suppressed. The integer *d* specifies the number of places to the right of the decimal point. The integer *e* specifies the number of digits in the exponent field.

9.3 Formatted Transput

The standard prelude declares four procedures for formatted transput: *readf*, *printf*, *getf*, and *putf*. Inasmuch as *readf* and *printf* are merely calls to *getf* and *putf* with *stand in* and *stand out*, respectively, used as files, it is not necessary to examine all four of them. For simplicity we discuss only *readf* and *printf*. Note that *readf*, *printf*, *getf*, and *putf* are the formatted analogs of *read*, *print*, *get*, and *put*.

There is a mode **format** whose values describe how values are to be laid out on the output or are expected to appear on the input. A simple format text (that is, "denotation") and its meaning on output is

$$ p \text{ "m=" } 5d, \text{ "n=" } 5d \$$$

This first advances to a new page, then prints the string m=, then the value of a variable as five digits, then the string n=, and finally another value as five more digits. We discuss the construction of format texts in a subsequent paragraph. For now, it is sufficient to say that **format** is a mode (declared in the standard prelude in RR 10.3.4.1.1a) and may be manipulated like any other mode; that is, [ ]**format**, **proc**(**int**)**format**, and **ref format** are all perfectly valid modes. Variables of mode **format** exist and may be assigned values, namely, format texts.

Associated with each file is a format that applies to that file. The format may be changed whenever a new one is needed, but a format remains in effect until explicitly changed. The four formatted input/output procedures each process their parameters sequentially. If a parameter is a unit, it is transmitted according to the format currently associated with the file. However, if the parameter is a format, it supersedes the current format and is used for transmitting units until it itself is explicitly superseded. Note that a format can remain associated with a file over a time spanning many input/output calls. (Contrast this with FORTRAN, PL/I, and other languages which require exactly one explicit format on each input/output call.)

The procedure *printf* expects a single parameter, roughly [ ]**union**(all transputtable modes, **format**). Here are some examples of calls to the formatted transput procedures:

```
begin real x,y,z;
file f; open (f,"a",disk 1);
readf($ 1 5d, 7d $); ¢ new format for
    stand in ¢
printf($ 1 10x 6d $); ¢ new format for
    stand out ¢
putf(f, $ p "heading", 9d $); ¢ new format
    for f ¢
printf((x,y,z)); ¢ use existing format ¢
printf(($ 1 9d $,x,y,z)); ¢ use this format ¢
close (f)
end
```

A format text can be used directly in a call to one of the formatted transput procedures, as a source in an assignment to a format variable, as the result of a procedure yielding **format**, etc. Format texts are delimited by $ as we have seen. Between the dollar signs are a series of pictures, separated by commas. Each value input or output is controled by some picture, although a picture need not input or output a value; for example, it may merely eject to a new page. Pictures may be replicated as in 2(5d 4x, 7d 2x), which means 5d 4x, 7d 2x, 5d 4x, 7d 2x. Replicators need not be constants; the letter "*n*" followed by a closed clause is also acceptable (among other possibilities).

Pictures can be subdivided into literal strings, alignments, and patterns. Literal strings, such as "x =" or "page heading" are output as is, or are expected to be exactly so on input. Literal strings may be repeated by putting an integer in front; for example, 7"x" is the same as "xxxxxxx".

Alignments describe changes in the current position of the book, such as "go to the next line before reading or printing." There are six alignments (RR 10.3.4.1.1f):

code	meaning
p	advance to new page
l	advance to new line
x	advance one character
y	backspace one character
q	output/expect one blank
k	move to specific character position

The alignments may also be replicated; for example, p 21 5q on output means go to the next page, skip 2 lines and 5 spaces. The difference between x and q is this: on input x just skips, whereas q expects blanks; on output after backspace, x skips and q overwrites with blanks. The alignments p,l,x,y, and k cause the procedures *new page*, *new line*, *space*, *backspace*, and *set char number* to be called, respectively.

Patterns are used for converting values, for example, integers, reals, Booleans, or strings. They are described in detail in RR 10.3.4. The following is a rough summary of some patterns. Each pattern consists of one or more frames. A frame allows a certain class of character, for example, sign, digit, exponent symbol, or any character. A list of frames and the allowed characters in each follows:

code	meaning
−	blank or minus sign
+	plus or minus sign
z	blank or digit
d	digit
e	letter e (exponent)
.	decimal point
b	Boolean (namely, 0 or 1)
i	letter i (for complex numbers)
a	any character

Rather than attempting to give the precise rules for combining frames into patterns, we give some examples of how the integer 12345 would appear with various patterns. (The letter B is used to indicate a blank space in the output.) Note that z suppresses leading zeros.

pattern	result of printing 12345
8d	00012345
6d	012345
7zd	BBB12345
+7zd	+BBB12345
−7zd	BBBB12345
7z+d	BBB+12345
7z−d	BBBB12345

The following examples show how the real number 123.45 would appear with various patterns:

pattern	result of printing 123.45
5d.2d	00123.45
4d.3d	0123.450
3zd.2d	B123.45
3z+d.2d	B+123.45
+d.4dezd	+1.2345eB2
−d.4dezd	B1.2345eB2

To understand how patterns work, first remove the replicators by writing out the pattern in full. For example, +4zd.2d means +zzzzd.dd. This pattern contains nine frames: one plus, four z's, one d, one point, and two more d's. A number output using this pattern will therefore occupy nine positions. The leftmost position will be a + or − sign. The next four positions will be digits, except that leading zeros will be converted to blanks. The four positions following this will be: one digit (even zero), one point, and two more digits (even 00). For example, 123.45 will be output as +BB123.45.

To allow leading signs to "float rightword" to the immediate left of the first nonzero digit, two special combinations are provided: Nz+d and Nz−d (N is some integer). This does not cause ambiguities, because putting the sign in the middle of the digits is clearly something special. The field width for Nz+d or Nz−d is N+2; for example, 6z+d means zzzzzz+d and gives an eight-position field.

A picture may consist solely of a literal string, an alignment, or a pattern, or a sequence of these. Thus $p 1 8d$ is a format text with one picture, and $p,l,8d$ is an equivalent format text with three pictures.

As a final example of outputting numbers, consider this program:

```
begin int i := 2;
  printf (( $ p "hi" 21 3d, 2z+d, 3q5zd.d,
        z−d.2d $, i, −i, i+999, pi))
end
```

The output begins with "hi" on top of a new page, then a blank line, then

002BB-2BBBBB1001.0BB3.14

Characters and strings are read and written using "a" frames. Booleans are transput using "b" frames, with implementation defined characters flip and flop (as in, T and F), corresponding to **true** and **false**, respectively. Values of modes **bits** can be handled in binary, quaternary, octal, or hexadecimal, using 2r, 4r, 8r, or 16r, respectively, as illustrated in the following program:

```
begin bits n;
  ¢ print the first 100 integers in decimal, binary,
    octal; and hexadecimal, each in an 8 position
    field with 2 spaces between fields. ¢
  for i to 100
  do ¢ assign bit pattern of i to n (because only
       objects of mode bits can be output in non-
       decimal radices) ¢
    n := bin i;
    printf(( $ 1 7zd,2q2r7zd, 2q8r7zd, 2q16r7zd $,
        i, n, n, n))
  od
end
```

Pictures may be replicated (as in 71 or 3d), and replicators may be **proc ints**. Furthermore, there is a facility that chooses dynamically among several formats during transput, and a number of other sophisticated techniques.

The procedures *readbin*, *writebin*, *getbin*, and *putbin* are the analogs of *readf*, *printf*, *getf*, and *putf* for binary transput (cf. PL/I record input/output).

10. SERIAL COLLATERAL, AND PARALLEL PROCESSING

In general, ALGOL 68 statements are executed one after another, in the order written. The semicolon can be regarded as a go-on operator that causes execution to continue.

The void units in a serial clause are executed sequentially, for example. In some situations, however, there is no inherent sequencing. For example, there is no reason for the first unit of a row display to be evaluated before the last one. Nor is there any reason for the left operand of a dyadic operator to be evaluated before the right operand. In some other programming languages operands are evaluated strictly from left to right, but nothing in classical mathematics suggests any precedent for this. Actions that have no specific ordering in time are said to be carried out collaterally.

In formulating ALGOL 68, the designers intentionally specified that the order of evaluating certain things, such as the left and right operands of a dyadic operator, be undefined. This was done to help compilers produce an optimized object code and to take advantage of multiprocessor systems.

By not fixing the order of evaluation of operands and certain other constructions, ALGOL 68 provides the compiler writer with the freedom to do the evaluations in the most efficient order. In some situations, evaluating the right operand before the left operand may be more efficient. For example, consider:

```
begin real x,y,z;
proc f = (real x)real: (random < .5 | x | −x);
read(x);
y := (pi+x)/8;
z := f(x) + f(y);
print(z)
end
```

On a computer with a single accumulator used for arithmetic, after evaluating $(pi+x)/8$, y is very likely to be in the accumulator. It is also likely that better object code can be generated if $f(y)$ is evaluated before $f(x)$, because y is already in the accumulator, and x is not. If the ALGOL 68 specifications had required that left operands be evaluated before right operands, the compiler would have no choice but to do the call of $f(x)$ first, even though it is less efficient in that order.

The second reason for having the order of evaluation of certain constructions be explicitly undefined is that some computers have more than one processor and are capable of performing several computations in parallel. As the price of CPU's continues to fall, both in absolute terms and relative to total system cost, multi-CPU systems will become more and more common. Consider the following block, where f is assumed to be a horrendously complicated function declared in an outer block:

```
begin [1:4] real x;
int a,b,c,d;
read((a,b,c,d));
x := (f(a),f(b),f(c),f(d))
end
```

On a computer with four (or more) CPUs, the ALGOL 68 compiler might decide to have $f(a)$, $f(b)$, $f(c)$, and $f(d)$ all evaluated simultaneously, each on its own CPU. If the language required $f(a)$ to be evaluated before $f(b)$, this would be impossible.

Some of the constructions that are evaluated collaterally are: Source and destination in assignments; operands of a dyadic operator; elements of a row display; fields of a structure display; actual parameters in a call; **from, to,** and **by** parts of a **for** statement; subscripts and bounds in a slice; upper and lower bounds in an array declarations; array to be sliced and its subscripts; procedure to be called and its parameters; declarations separated by commas; and units of a collateral clause.

10.1 Collateral Clauses

A collateral clause is a list of units separated by commas and enclosed by **begin** and **end**, or by parentheses. The order in which the units of a collateral clause are evaluated is expressly undefined. An important kind of collateral clause is one composed of statements (technically **void** units). Whereas the statements of a serial clause are executed sequentially, the execution order of the statements in a collateral clause is explicitly undefined. An example of a **void** collateral clause is:

begin $k := 3$, $x := 3.14$, $s :=$ "a" **end**

Consider the following two programs; the first contains a closed clause, and the second contains a collateral clause:

```
begin ¢ program 1 ¢
int k := 0;
(k:=k+1; k := k+1);
print(k)
end

begin ¢ program 2 ¢
int k := 0;
(k := k+1, k := k+1);
print(k)
end
```

The only difference between the two programs is the use of a semicolon versus the use of a comma between the assignments. There is only one tiny spot of ink in typography, but a world of difference in meaning, as we shall see.

The first program prints 2, as you would expect; the second program requires closer scrutiny. Since the order of evaluation of the units in a collateral clause is undefined, the first one might be completed before the second one was started, giving 2 as an answer. However, on a computer with two CPUs the compiler might arrange to give each CPU one unit to process with the following sequence of actions occurring.

1) CPU 1 fetches k into its accumulator;
2) CPU 2 fetches k into its accumulator;
3) CPU 1 adds 1 to its accumulator;
4) CPU 2 adds 1 to its accumulator;
5) CPU 1 stores 1 into k;
6) CPU 2 stores 1 into k.

The result is that k becomes 1 instead of 2. Depending upon the order of evaluation, the second program may print 1 or 2. Random numbers are very useful in computer science, but this is not a recommended technique for producing them. On the other hand,

```
begin int m := 0, n := 0;
(m := m+1, n := n+1);
print((m,n))
end
```

operates correctly no matter what the order of evaluation is. The moral of this story is: Collateral clauses are an important programming technique for exploiting parallel processing, but some care is required in their use.

It should be noted, however, that race conditions of this kind are not unique to ALGOL 68; any language or system permitting parallel processes unrestricted access to a common data base can produce the same peculiar effects. To be safe, one should avoid using collateral clauses which have an execution order that matters, or which modify each other's variables.

Collateral clauses may be nested, of course, allowing more complicated mixtures of collateral-serial execution to be described. For example,

$$(a; \quad (b, (c; d), ((e,f); g)); \quad h)$$

describes the following situation (the letters are assumed to be **void** units, for example, procedure calls or closed clauses). First a is executed. When a is finished, three actions proceed collaterally:

1) b
2) $(c;d)$
3) $((e,f); g)$

If enough CPUs are available, b, c, e, and f may all begin at once. When c finishes, d may start. When e and f are both finished, g may start. If e finishes before f, then g must be held up until f is also done. When b, c, d, e, f, and g are all completed, h begins.

10.2 Synchronized Parallel Processing

Collateral clauses are primarily useful for allowing independent, noncommunicating processes to run in parallel. For some applications however, the processes must communicate with each other. Typical examples are producer-consumer problems, where one process fills a shared buffer and the other one empties it. The two processes need to be synchronized to ensure that the producer stops when the buffer is full and that the consumer restarts the producer when it has (partially) emptied it again.

Dijkstra [4] has described a general synchronization method for parallel processing based on semaphores, and operators that increment and decrement them. An attempt to decrement a semaphore which has value 0 causes the decrementing process to be stopped. ALGOL 68 provides a mode **sema** (for semaphore) and two operators, **up** and **down**, to increment and decrement variables of mode **sema**. These are given in RR 10.2.4.

When semaphores are used in a collateral

clause, the symbol **par** must appear directly before the opening **begin** or parenthesis. This is to warn the compiler. Such clauses are then called parallel clauses (RR 3.3.1c).

As a simple example of parallel processing using semaphores, consider the problem of two processes running in parallel, each of which needs exclusive access to a certain data base during part of its computation cycle. (Readers unfamiliar with this type of synchronization problem should see Brinch Hansen [2]. A semaphore, mutex, initialized to 1 (using the **level** operator) is used here to achieve mutual exclusion.

```
begin sema mutex := level 1;
bool not finished := true;
¢ declare the data base here ¢
proc producer = void:
  while not finished
    do down mutex;
        ¢ insert item into data base here ¢
        up mutex
    od;
proc consumer = void:
  while not finished
    do down mutex;
        ¢ remove item from data base here ¢
        up mutex
    od;
    ¢ here is the parallel processing ¢
    par (producer, consumer)
end
```

11. Where To From Here?

Readers who want to continue their study of ALGOL 68 may wish to read Lindsey [8], Woodward and Bond [15], Woodward [14], Valentine [11], Branquart *et al.* [1], Cleaveland and Uzgalis [3], Peck [10], and the Revised Report, in roughly that order. For those readers who want a book length exposition, Learner and Powell [6], Peck [9], and Lindsey and van der Meulen [7] are recommended. For those who read German, van der Meulen and Kühling [12] is a good introductory text. In these references, beware of minor differences between the Revised Report, which is described in this article, and the original report, which is described in most of the references.

An even better way to learn ALGOL 68 is to write programs in this language. Compilers for various computers exist, including the IBM 370, CDC Cyber, Burroughs B6700, and ICL 1900. A fairly large subset of the language is even being implemented on a minicomputer (PDP-11).

ACKNOWLEDGMENTS

I wish to express my appreciation to the numerous people who have read and criticized this article, especially Jack Alanen, Willem Paul de Roever, Dick Grune, Ad König, Kees Koster, Efrem Mallach, John Peck, Mitchell Tanenbaum, Robert Uzgalis, Reind van de Riet, A. van Wijngaarden and P. M. Woodward.

REFERENCES

[1] BRANQUART, P.; LEWI, J.; SINTZOFF, M.; AND WODON, P. L. "The composition of semantics in ALGOL 68," *Comm. ACM* **14**, 11 (Nov. 1971), 697–707.

[2] BRINCH HANSEN, PER. "Concurrent programming concepts," *Computing Surveys* **5**, 4 (Dec. 1973), 223–245.

[3] CLEAVELAND, J. C.; AND UZGALIS, R. C. *Grammars for programming languages: What every programmer should know about grammar*, American Elsevier Publ. Co., New York, 1976.

[4] DIJKSTRA, E. W. "Cooperating sequential processes," In *Programming language*, F. Genuys (Ed.), Academic Press, New York, 1968.

[5] JENSEN, J.; AND NAUR, P. "Call by name: An implementation of ALGOL 60 procedures," *BIT* **1**, (1961), 38.

[6] LEARNER, A.; AND POWELL, A. J. *An introduction to ALGOL 68 through problems*, MacMillan, New York, 1974.

[7] LINDSEY, C. H.; AND VAN DER MEULEN, S. G. *An informal introduction to ALGOL 68.* North Holland Publ. Co., Amsterdam, The Netherlands, 1971.

[8] LINDSEY, C. H. "ALGOL 68 with fewer tears," *Computer J.* **15**, (1972), 176–188.

[9] PECK, J. E. L. *An ALGOL 68 companion*, Univ. of British Columbia, 1972.

[10] PECK, J. E. L. "Two-level grammars in action," in *Proc. IFIP Congress 74*, North-Holland Publ. Co., Amsterdam, The Netherlands, 1974, 317–321.

[11] VALENTINE, S. H. "Comparative notes on ALGOL 68 and PL/I," *Computer J.* **17**, (1974), 325–331.

[12] VAN DER MEULEN, S. G.; AND KÜHLING, P. *Programmieren in ALGOL 68.* Walter de Guyter & Co., New York, 1974 (in German).

[13] VAN WIJNGAARDEN, A.; MAILLOUX, B. J.; PECK J. E. L.; KOSTER, C. H. A.; SINTZOFF, M.; LINDSEY, C. H.; MEERTENS, L. G. L. T.; AND FISKER, R. G. "Revised report on the Algorithmic Language Algol 68," *Acta Informatica* **5**, (1975), 1–236.

[14] WOODWARD, P. M. "Practical experience with ALGOL 68" *Software—Practice and Experience*, **2**, (1972), pp. 7–9.

[15] WOODWARD, P. M.; AND BOND, S. G. *ALGOL 68-R users guide*, 2nd Ed. Her Majesty's Stationery Office, London, England, 1974.

[16] PAGAN, F. G., *A practical guide to Algol 68*, John Wiley Inc., New York, 1976.

AMBIGUITIES AND INSECURITIES IN PASCAL*

J. WELSH, W. SNEERINGER AND C. A. R. HOARE

SUMMARY

Ambiguities and insecurities in the programming language Pascal are discussed.

KEY WORDS   Pascal   Language design   Language definition   Security

INTRODUCTION

On rare occasions in programming language development there appears a programming language which is widely recognized as superior, and which propagates itself among discerning implementors and users solely by its merits, and without any political or commercial backing. ALGOL 60[1] was such a language. Pascal[2] is another.

One characteristic of such superior languages is that they rapidly give rise to a host of suggested extensions, improvements and imitations. From ALGOL 60 came ALGOL D,[3] ALGOL W,[4] ALGOL 68,[5] PL/I,[6] Simula 67[7] and Pascal itself. Pascal has been followed by the critique by Habermann,[8] Concurrent Pascal,[9] Pasqual,[10] Modula[11] and Euclid.[12] It is one of the symptoms of the superiority of these languages that their original design remains superior to many of their successors, and even the authors themselves can find little to improve in formulating a revised version.[13-15] Thus the very superiority of the language may inhibit for a while the further progress of the art of language design.

One reason for this is that there is no immediate recognition of exactly what constitute the merits of the language. Indeed, the merits of ALGOL 60 have only recently been appreciated under the new name of *structured programming*. Similarly, most criticism of the language is rather superficial, concentrating on critics' favourite 'features' and 'facilities' which have been left out.

If future language designs, and indeed future users, are to benefit fully from the significant advances made by Pascal, it is essential that its defects, as well as its virtues, should be carefully identified and catalogued. The detailed, almost pettifogging nature of the criticisms in this paper may be taken as a testimony to a belief that Pascal is at the present time the best language in the public domain for purposes of systems programming and software implementation. Nevertheless, these criticisms may lead to a better understanding of the definitional problems created in Pascal, and to a better treatment of these problems in the languages which must inevitably follow it.

No consideration is given to changes to Pascal other than those necessary to overcome the ambiguities and insecurities identified.

*Reprinted from *Software Practice and Experience*, 7, 1977, 685–696.

---

* Present address: IBM Corporation, 11400 Burnet Road, Austin, Texas 78759, U.S.A.
† Address from October 1977: Programming Research Group, Oxford University, 45 Banbury Road, Oxford.

Received 27 May 1977

Throughout this paper, the abbreviations *User Manual* and *Report* are used to stand for the first and second parts, respectively, of the *Pascal User Manual and Report*.[15] There are several earlier versions of the *Report*.[14] The abbreviation *Axiomatic Definition* is also used for the formal definition of Pascal's semantics given by Hoare and Wirth.[17]

AMBIGUITIES

Ambiguities and omissions in the *Report* or *User Manual* are not mentioned in what follows if they can be easily resolved. The objective is to criticize the language, not the *Report* or the *User Manual*; but insofar as the language's features (or apparent intentions) create problems of definition, the *Report* must be considered as well.

Equivalence of types

Section 9.1.1 of the *Report* states that the two sides of an assignment statement 'must be of identical type', with certain exceptions involving reals and subranges. The phrase *identical type* is not defined and its meaning is not obvious. Much of Habermann's criticism of Pascal hinged on the omission from the *Report* of similar exception rules for other contexts in which subrange or real variables might or might not appear. As the Axiomatic Definition shows, the subrange problem can be resolved by the systematic introduction of implicit subrange–range transfers as context requires. However, the notion of type equivalence creates problems for other Pascal types too.

In the declarations,

```
type T    = array [1..10] of INTEGER;
var A, B:   array [1..10] of INTEGER;
    C:      array [1..10] of INTEGER;
    D:      T;
    E:      T;
```

consider the following two possible definitions of equivalence of types.

Name equivalence

Two variables are considered to be of the same type only if they are declared together (as A and B) or if they are declared using the same type identifier (as D and E). Any type specification other than a type identifier creates a new type which is not equivalent to any other type. Thus A, C and D all have different types. Notice that primitive types are specified using type identifiers, so two variables will have the same type if they are both declared INTEGER. This is called *name equivalence* because two variables that are not declared together can have the same type only if they are declared using the same type name.

Structural equivalence

Two variables are considered to be of the same type whenever they have components of the same type structured in the same way. Using this definition, all of the variables in the example above have the same type.

Name equivalence is quite a nuisance to the programmer, since he or she must often make up extra type names. On the other hand, name equivalence provides extra protection against type errors. Furthermore, structural equivalence causes a logical problem. Consider this example using structural equivalence.

```
var K: (MALE, FEMALE);
    L: (MALE, FEMALE);
```

Clearly the types of K and L are equivalent, since they have the same structure. However,
var M: (MALE, FEMALE);
       N: (FEMALE, MALE);
is illegal because the identifiers MALE and FEMALE are not unique. Distinguishing between these two cases will be difficult for the compiler. It cannot simply consider the construct (MALE, FEMALE) to be a declaration of the identifiers MALE and FEMALE as it could in the case of name equivalence. If it did, it would reject the legal declaration of identifier L.

Even worse, suppose that the type (MALE, FEMALE) is created and then the identifier MALE is used for an unrelated purpose in an inner block. Then, in a block inside both of these, the construct (MALE, FEMALE) is used again. Is it a reference to the first type? A new type? An error? There seems to be no good answer.

The use of structural equivalence also creates a problem with record types, which is illustrated by the following:
var F: **record** T, U: REAL **end**;
      G: **record** V, W: REAL **end**;
Do F and G have the same type? Either answer seems reasonable and consistent.

Structural equivalence creates a further dilemma for the implementor in relation to the **packed** prefix for structured types. Section 6.2 of the *Report* states that the prefix 'has no effect on the meaning of the program but is a hint to the compiler that storage should be economized even at the price of some loss in efficiency of access'. Presumably therefore a packed type is equivalent to an otherwise structurally equivalent unpacked one, and the compiler must permit, and generate code for, assignment or, worse still, actual-formal parameter correspondence between them. This problem does not arise with name equivalence since the syntax of ⟨type⟩ excludes the form **packed** ⟨*type identifier*⟩.

Name equivalence is not, however, without its problems. It precludes, for example, the assignment of a string constant to a variable of a corresponding string type. Section 4 of the *Report* states that a string constant of *n* characters has an implicit type
packed array [1..*n*] **of** *char*
With name equivalence, however, this implied type cannot be equivalent to any other so the string may only appear in certain limited contexts such as calls on the built-in procedure *write*. A similar problem arises with constructed sets, whose type is also implicitly specified; this problem is considered further in a later section of this paper.

Name equivalence also creates a potential confusion for the user of the type definition
type T1 = T2;
where T2 is the name of a type defined elsewhere. With name equivalence this will not produce a convenient local synonym for type T2 as might be expected, but a new type T1 which is not equivalent to type T2 in any context.

Clearly the current features of Pascal do not permit a simple choice between name or structural equivalence as defined. Some alternative or compromise equivalence definition must be adopted. In practice of course each implementation of Pascal has already made some choice. The ETH compiler (the compiler described by the *User Manual*) uses structural equivalence in most cases.[16] However, a scalar type declaration such as (MALE, FEMALE) is taken to be a declaration of the identifiers MALE and FEMALE, and therefore causes a message about a duplicate declaration if repeated in the same block. (It will create a new type equivalent to the first if used in an inner block.) Record types are equivalent if the corresponding field types are the same, but packed structured types are not equivalent to corresponding unpacked ones.

It is unsatisfactory that implementors should be left to make such decisions, since any divergence in their choice imperils the portability of Pascal programs. The authors of Euclid, Pascal's most recent derivative, were clearly conscious of Pascal's deficiencies in this area. Although the definition of Euclid has been modelled on the Pascal *Report*, it incorporates an explicit definition of type equivalence based on the repeated replacement of type identifiers by the sequence of symbols appearing in their definition. Two types are equivalent if, in the sequences of symbols which they produce,

(a) corresponding occurrences of free constant identifiers (i.e. those not declared by these types) denote the same value;

(b) corresponding symbols are otherwise identical.

The resultant definition of type equivalence is close to the structural equivalence suggested above. Whether this particular definition is the best for the language remains an open question, but the provision of *some* such explicit definition is an important requirement, both for Pascal and for any language which imitates its repertoire of data types.

Scope rules and one-pass compilation

One of the design objectives stated for Pascal was to enable efficient compilation of its programs. Although the *Report* does not say so explicitly, the language features appear to favour one-pass compilation as a means to this end, and implementors have assumed this to be the designer's intent. However, this implicit one-pass compilation capability creates some traps for the unwary, into which implementors have duly fallen.

In general, one-pass compilation requires that the declaration of an identifier precede all other references to that identifier. The Pascal *Report* does not specify at any point that an identifier's declaration must precede its use. It does, however, impose a rigid order on the different classes of declaration which are made within a block, thus:

⟨*block*⟩ ::= ⟨*label declaration part*⟩
⟨*constant definition part*⟩
⟨*type definition part*⟩
⟨*variable declaration part*⟩
⟨*procedure and function declaration part*⟩
⟨*statement part*⟩

This has the effect of ensuring that constant identifiers are defined before they can be used in type definitions, that type identifiers are defined before they can be used in variable declarations and that variable identifiers are declared before they can be used in the statement part or as non-locals in nested procedures and function. However, it does not guarantee declaration before use *within* the type definition or procedure declaration parts. For example, the following program segment is unacceptable to a one-pass compiler because the use of the identifier COMPLEX to declare type MATRIX precedes the declaration of COMPLEX.

type MATRIX = **array** [1..10, 1..10] **of** COMPLEX;
COMPLEX = **record** REALPART, IMAGPART: REAL **end**;
var M: MATRIX;
⋮
WRITE(M[2, 2].REALPART);

Now consider the same program segment and assume that this declaration is in the containing block:

type COMPLEX = **record** RE, IM: REAL **end**;

There are at least two possible interpretations of this program by a one-pass system:

(1) The elements of M each have two real components with names RE and IM, since the outer declaration of COMPLEX was current when the declaration of MATRIX was scanned. (2) The program is in error because the inner declaration of COMPLEX is the one that should apply, and it follows the declaration of MATRIX.

This program is incorrect in either case. Under interpretation (1), the call to WRITE is incorrect because the REALPART is not a valid field name for variable M. We are not just haggling over which statement gets the error message, however. If the field name REAL-PART in the call to WRITE were replaced by RE, the resulting program would be correct according to interpretation (1) and incorrect according to (2).

Notice that (1) is the easier interpretation to implement. Each reference to an identifier is simply bound to the most recent declaration of that identifier. One way to implement (2) might be to bind the element type of MATRIX to the outer definition of COMPLEX, but record this binding so that an error can be declared when the inner definition of COMPLEX is scanned. The recorded binding has to be applied not only in the current scope but also in any enclosing scopes between it and the outer definition.

Unfortunately, interpretation (1) has some problems involving pointer types, and (2) is the better interpretation. Consider the following example:

```
type FLIGHT =
       record
           NUMBER: 0..999;
           FIRSTPAS: ↑PASSENGER;
           ...
       end;
     PASSENGER =
       record
           FLIGHTBOOKED; ↑FLIGHT;
           NEXTPAS: ↑PASSENGER
           ...
       end;
```

Each of the two types in the example refers to the other, so whichever type is declared second in the program will have its identifier referenced before it is declared. This is a case where the rule that identifiers must be declared before they are used is too restrictive to be practical, and Pascal implementations make an exception to accommodate this case. Pointer declarations, such as ↑PASSENGER, are allowed to precede the declaration of the identifier used. Fortunately, the compiler can allocate storage for a pointer without knowing what type of thing it will reference, since the size of a pointer does not depend on what it points at.

The problem with interpretation (1) is illustrated by the example above if there happens to be a type PASSENGER declared in an outer block. In that case, interpretation (1) demands that the name PASSENGER in field FIRSTPAS be bound to the outer definition of type PASSENGER. This is very bad, because the meaning of a valid block can be changed by declaring an identifier in an outer block.

In fact the *Report* does exclude interpretation (1) since Section 4 states that the 'association (of identifiers) must be unique within their scope of validity, i.e. within the procedure or function in which they are declared'. (No explicit definition of scope for main program identifiers is given.) However, the significance of Section 4 is clearly not apparent to its implementors, since the ETH compiler itself follows interpretation (1), even to the extent of binding the pointer type ↑ PASSENGER to a non-local instance of PASSENGER if one exists.

A similar difficulty arises with mutually recursive procedures and functions. To retain one-pass compilation with checking of parameters the ETH compiler requires a FORWARD declaration, which is not described in the *Report* or included in the syntax diagrams or BNF. It is described only in Section 11.C of the *User Manual*, from which we take the following example.

```
procedure Q(X:T); FORWARD;
procedure P(Y:T);
begin
    Q(A)
end;
procedure Q; (* PARAMETERS NOT REPEATED *)
    begin
        P(B)
    end;
begin
    P(A);
    Q(B)
end.
```

The line

```
procedure Q(X:T); FORWARD;
```

which must precede the procedure P, provides enough information so that the call to Q from within P can be compiled.

These problems arise because the *Report* does not define any precise rules for the relative positions of the declaration and use of identifiers. Implementors of one-pass compilers must impose additional restrictions on the language definition, or create the unsatisfactory implementation effects outlined above. If one-pass compilation is to be a language objective it should be made explicit in the language definition and an explicit declaration-before-use rule should be adopted, with whatever exceptions the language features may require.

With such a rule the rigid order which Pascal imposes on the constant, type, variable and procedure declaration parts could be relaxed, allowing natural groupings of the types, variables and procedures which manipulate them. The inability to make such groupings in structuring large programs is one of Pascal's most frustrating limitations.

Given such groupings, or modules, of course the additional controls on their mutual interaction such as those which Modula and Euclid provide are clearly desirable. The control over the use of identifiers which these languages offer is a clear indication that the current needs of programming have moved well beyond the implicit scope rules of simple block structure, and Pascal.

Set constructors

As was indicated earlier, the implicit types of string constants and constructed sets create problems in defining type equivalence. However, the implicit type definition creates additional problems in the representation of sets.

According to Section 8 of the *Report*, 'Expressions which are members of a set must all be of the same type, which is the base type of the set.' This leads to the conclusion that the type of the set constructor [1, 5, 10..19, 23] is **set of** INTEGER, since Section 4 makes it clear that the types of 1, 5, 10, 19 and 23 are INTEGER. However, Section 14 states that 'The implementer may set a limit to the size of a base type over which a set can be defined.

(Consequently, a bit pattern representation may reasonably be used for sets).' Since the apparent base type in the example is INTEGER and the size of type INTEGER is larger than any reasonable limit, one might conclude that the example is illegal in at least some implementations. The example comes from Section 8 of the *Report*, so it seems fair to say that the *Report* is confusing, if not ambiguous.

In practice the conflict is yet another which is resolved by an implicit range to subrange transfer. Given that a limit on the size of base types exists, the compiler may assume that the intended base type of [1, 5, 10..19, 23] is some subrange of the integers, and apply an implicit range to subrange transfer to its member values. The problem is that the intended subrange is not apparent, which in turn has consequences for the representation of the set.

Using a bit pattern representation for sets, the type

set of 20..29

is represented by a bit pattern very much like the type

packed array [20..29] **of** BOOLEAN

where element N of the array is TRUE if and only if N is in the set. The trouble is that the base type of [1, 5, 10..19, 23] has not been specified, so the compiler does not know what the bounds of its Boolean array should be.

Implementations overcome this problem by imposing an additional limit on the base types of sets. For example, in the ETH compiler the limit on the size of a base type is 59, so the compiler knows that the Boolean array can be no larger than 59. However, the compiler also needs its upper and lower bounds. The ETH compiler therefore adds the restriction that each element of any set of integers must be between 0 and 58. This rule allows any set of integers to be represented by an array with bounds 0 and 58. A similar rule applies to sets of non-integers. In that case, no element E is allowed unless $ORD(E) \leqslant 58$. This solution has the consequence that apparently representable set types such as

DATES = **set of** 1939..1945

are excluded by current implementations.

For implementations which choose, or are forced by short word lengths or byte orientation, to use multilength representations of sets the implicit type of the set constructor presents an additional problem. Either all sets over subranges of a given type must use the same length of representation, or the required length of a constructed set must be deduced from context. The extreme case occurs when the empty set [ ] (which has no implicit base type at all) occurs as an actual parameter of a formal procedure or function (which provides no contextual indication of the representation required).

All these problems can be avoided by requiring an explicit specification of the base type of every set constructor. For example, given a set type

DIGITS = **set of** 0..9

the constructor notation used might be

DIGITS (1, 3, 5)

This makes the programmer write a bit more, but allows the base type of a set to be any scalar type that does not have too many elements. Not only are the restrictions simpler and less constraining, but the language is cleaner because every set constructor has a type which can be determined during compilation without any use of context. A version of Pascal using such a constructor, and a multiword representation of sets, has been implemented[18] and shown to provide a more flexible, and more efficient, set manipulation facility. A similar notation has now been adopted in Euclid.

This notation also reconciles the set constructor with the name equivalence convention for types discussed earlier. A similar solution for string constants might be considered. Given a string type

MESSAGE = **packed array** [1..16] **of** *char*

a constant of the type might be written thus

MESSAGE('ILLEGAL OPERANDS')

In this case the additional burden on the programmer may be unacceptable in contexts where named type specification is unecessary, e.g. in calls to the built-in procedure *write*, and some default for omitting the type name and parentheses may be appropriate.

INSECURITIES

For the purposes of this discussion, an insecurity is a feature that cannot be implemented without either (1) a risk that violations of the language rules will go undetected, or (2) run-time checking that is comparable in cost to the operation being performed.

Pascal has fewer insecurities than most comparable languages. For example, it is not possible to use a pointer to access a dynamic variable of the wrong type. This error is caught during compilation because each pointer can only point at variable or a single type. The remarkable thing about Pascal is that the number of insecurities is small enough to make it worthwhile to prepare a list in the hope that future research will lead to languages with even fewer or perhaps no insecurities.

Variant records

Pascal allows variant records with and without tag fields. An example of a variant record with a tag field is

```
V: record AREA:REAL;
     case S:SHAPE of
       TRIANGLE: (SIDE:REAL;
                  INCLINATION, ANGLE1, ANGLE2:REAL);
       CIRCLE:   (DIAMETER:REAL)
   end
```

The field *AREA* always exists, but whether *DIAMETER* exists or not depends on whether the value of the tag field, *S*, is *CIRCLE* or not. A version of this record without a tag field can be created by omitting 'S' after the symbol *case*.

If there is no tag field, then the variant record is inevitably insecure. Either ANGLE1 or ANGLE2 could be referenced when it is not present, and there is no way to catch the error, even at run-time. This is bad, because such an error is likely to be difficult to find.

The compiler could insert a tag field even when the programmer does not request it, but it would be misleading and pointless to allow the programmer to omit the tag field if the compiler included it anyway. The introduction to Pascal of variant records without tag fields must be regarded as a retrograde step, to be regretted by Pascal users, and avoided by the designers of future languages.

Given that a tag field is present in all variant records, a run-time check is still required to achieve security. However, the run-time check can be avoided when code like the following is used to reference the variant part

case V.S **of**
　　TRIANGLE: **begin** (references to V.SIDE, etc.) **end**;
　　CIRCLE:　　**begin** (references to V.DIAMETER) **end**
end

since the value of the tag field when the references occur is known when the program is compiled. This is done in Simula 67 with an **inspect when** statement, which is similar to the **case** statement above. A similar modification to Pascal has been investigated,[19] which showed that direct violations from within the **case** construct were easily detected, but that detection of indirect changes of the variant by reassignment of the entire record variable, possibly during procedure calls from within the case, was impractical. The *Report* does outlaw such changes with a **with** statement (Section 9.2.4) but this restriction is equally impractical to enforce by compile-time or run-time checking.

Euclid incorporates an explicit construct which enables direct variant violations to be detected at compile-time. For more general reasons of program verification Euclid's definition also goes to considerable lengths to enable variable overlaps, such as might cause an implicit change of variant, to be detected. Whether the added complexity of the rules required, and the added restrictions which they impose on the programmer, are an acceptable price to pay for variable access security, may be shown by experience of implementing and using Euclid. The rules and restrictions involved cannot be readily added to current framework of Pascal.

Functions and procedures as parameters

When a Pascal formal parameter is a function or a procedure, the language does not require or even permit the programmer to specify the number and types of any parameters. The following example, which is due to Lecarme and Desjardins,[20] illustrates a program which contains an error that cannot reasonably be detected at compile-time:

procedure P(**procedure** Q);
　　begin Q(2, 'A') **end**;
procedure R(X:BOOLEAN);
　　begin WRITE(X) **end**;
begin P(R) **end**.

The apparent solution is to allow full specification of parameters in this case, as is done in ALGOL 68. The normal syntax for parameter specification is excessive for this purpose since it includes specification of names of the formal parameters, and these names are not required. Lecarme and Desjardins proposed a syntax for specifying the types without giving names. With their syntax, the first line of the example above is written

procedure P(**procedure** Q(INTEGER, CHAR));
　　begin Q(2, 'A') **end**;

which gives enough information for the error to be detected during compilation.

To enable the correct parameter passing code to be generated for their calls, Pascal currently allows procedures and functions passed as parameters to take value parameters only. Given an adequate notation for expressing the parameter requirements of formal procedures or functions, this restriction can in principle be relaxed. The notation required is more complicated than that of Lecarme and Desjardins, however, since it must distinguish between variable and value parameters. If procedure parameters which themselves

45

take procedure parameters are allowed the notation must also provide a nested, and potentially recursive, specification of parameter requirements.

The Pascal compiler for UNIVAC 1100 computers, developed at DIKU in Copenhagen, incorporates an extension which meets these requirements.[21] Formal parameter lists can be defined and named in a separate parameter declaration part of each block. The parameter requirements of actual procedures may then be specified by reference to a named parameter list, and those of formal procedures must be specified in this way. In the DIKU system formal parameter names are always included in the parameter list specification, so that procedures sharing a parameter specification must use the same formal parameter names as well.

Range violations

As in most compiled languages, accessing an element of a Pascal array is insecure if an index is out of bounds. Since almost all languages have this problem, it is appropriate to try to solve it with hardware. The extra hardware cost is quite small. The descriptor mechanism of the ICL 2900 series computers provides an implicit bound check during array access but, while it works well for the arrays allowed in languages such as FORTRAN or ALGOL 60, it is inadequate for some of the array structures permitted in Pascal.[22]

Array access is just one of a number of contexts in which a value outside a permitted range can arise in Pascal. Others are assignment to a subrange variable, case selection, set membership creation and testing, and indeed overflow in integer and real arithmetic. While it is unreasonable to hope to exclude by language design the possibility of all such violations, designers must aim to reduce the cost of their run-time detection. It should be noted that Pascal's provision of enumerated and subrange types is a significant step in this direction. Each use of a variable of an enumerated type removes a potential insecurity by ensuring that the finite set of values which the variable may take is verified at compile-time. For a subrange variable run-time verification of the values taken may be necessary but, assuming these checks are made, other more frequent and hence more expensive checks may be avoided at each point where the variable value is used. A Pascal compiler which exploits this technique has been constructed[23] for ICL 1900 computers, and has shown that for simple array manipulations run-time subscript checking can be eliminated, or reduced to insignificance.

Uninitialized variables

Uninitialized variables are also difficult to detect, and all hardware detection mechanisms known to us are quite expensive. Possible solutions are to require that every variable be initialized when it is declared or that every variable be assigned in such a way that the compiler can easily verify that there are no references to uninitialized variables. The latter might work very well in a language without jumps, and deserves further investigation.

Dangling references

Accessing of dynamic variables (those found via pointers) is not secure because the storage for the dynamic variable may have been released. This is a very common insecurity for which Pascal allows no obvious solution.

It can be argued that Pascal's pointer is a low-level facility provided for use in those situations for which the high-level data constructs are inadequate, and that it is unreasonable to expect security from a low-level facility. Whatever the philosophical validity of this argument it is little consolation to a programmer whose pointers go wrong!

Euclid offers an optional security against such errors by enabling reference counts to be maintained for collections of dynamically allocated variables. Storage release is then an implicit operation occurring when a reference count reaches zero, rather than an explicit programmable action. Maintaining reference counts is, of course, a considerable overhead if applied to every pointer variable assignment. The success of the Euclid proposal depends on the degree to which the compiler can detect those program segments which use local pointer variables to trace a dynamically allocated structure without altering the non-local reference pattern in any way. Reference counting code can then be avoided for the pointer manipulation within the segment.

CONCLUSION

At the time that Pascal was first designed and developed, the most fashionable languages in the learned and practical world were ALGOL 68 and PL/I. The discovery that the advantages of a high-level language could be combined with high efficiency in such a simple and elegant manner as in Pascal was a revelation that deserves the title of breakthrough. Because of the very success of Pascal, which greatly exceeded the expectations of its author, the standards by which we judge such languages have also risen. It is grossly unfair to judge an engineering project by standards which have been proved attainable only by the success of the project itself, but in the interests of progress, such criticism must be made.

Of the criticisms made in this paper, some identify shortcomings of Pascal which can readily be made good by minor changes to the language or its definition. Others indicate problems for which there is no easy solution within the current framework. As a language which attempts to overcome most of the problems listed, Euclid deserves special mention, though it should also be pointed out that no implementation of Euclid has yet been reported. Unfortunately, Euclid achieves its goals at the expense of a significant loss of simplicity and elegance in the language definition. Whether this trade-off is inevitable or whether some future breakthrough can restore elegance and simplicity without loss of security is a question which language designers must ponder for some time to come.

ACKNOWLEDGEMENTS

The research on this paper was supported in part by a grant from the Science Research Council of Great Britain.

REFERENCES

1. P. Naur (Ed.), 'Report on the algorithmic language ALGOL 60', *Comm. ACM*, **3**, 299–314 (1960).
2. N. Wirth, 'The programming language Pascal', *Acta Informatica*, **1**, 35–63 (1971).
3. B. A. Galler and A. J. Perlis, 'A proposal for definitions in ALGOL', *Comm. ACM*, **10**, 204–219 (1967).
4. N. Wirth and C. A. R Hoare, 'A contribution to the development of ALGOL', *Comm. ACM*, **9**, 413–432 (1966).
5. A. van Winjngaarden (Ed.), 'Report on the algorithmic language ALGOL 68', *Numerische Mathematik*, **14**, 79–218 (1969).
6. IBM, *PL/I(F) Language Reference Manual, Order Number C28–8201*, IBM, 1969.
7. G. Birtwistle *et al.*, *Simula Begin*, Auerbach, 1975.
8. A. N. Habermann, 'Critical comments on the programming language Pascal', *Acta Informatica*, **3**, 47–57 (1973).

9. P. Brinch Hansen, 'The programming language Concurrent Pascal', *IEEE Trans. Software Engng*, **1**, 2 (1975).

10. R. D. Tennent, 'Pasqual: a proposed generalisation of Pascal', *Technical Report No. 75–32*, Department of Computing and Information Science, Queen's University, Kingston, Ontario, Canada.

11. N. Wirth, 'Modula: a language for modular multiprogramming', *Software—Practice and Experience*, **7**, 3–35 (1977).

12. B. W. Lampson *et al.*, 'Report on the programming language Euclid', *ACM Sigplan Notices*, **12**, 2 (1977).

13. P. Naur, 'Revised report on the algorithmic language ALGOL 60', *Comm. ACM*, **6**, 1 (1963).

14. N. Wirth, 'The programming language Pascal (Revised Report)', *Berichte der Fachgruppe Computer-Wissenschaften Nr. 5*, ETH Zurich (1973).

15. K. Jensen and N. Wirth, 'Pascal—User Manual and Report', *Lecture Notes in Computer Science*, **18**, Springer Verlag, 1974.

16. U. Ammann, 'The Zurich implementation', *Proc. Symp. on Pascal—the language and its implementation*, *Southampton* (1977).

17. C. A. R. Hoare and N. Wirth, 'An axiomatic definition of the programming language Pascal', *Acta Informatica*, **2**, 335–355 (1973).

18. C. J. Copeland, 'Extensions to Pascal', *MSc. dissertation*, Queen's University, Belfast (1975).

19. P. W. C. Sinte, 'Recursive data structures in Pascal', *MSc. dissertation*, Queen's University, Belfast (1975).

20. O. Lecarme and P. Desjardins, 'More comments on the programming language Pascal', *Acta Informatica*, **4**, 231–243 (1975).

21. J. Steensgaard-Madsen, *Procedures as Monitors in Sequential Programming*, DIKU, Copenhagen, Denmark, 1977.

22. M. Rees, 'Pascal on an advanced architecture', *Proc. Symp. on Pascal—the language and its implementation*, *Southampton* (1977).

23. J. Welsh, 'Two ICL 1900 Pascal compilers', *Proc. Symp. on Pascal—the language and its implementation*, *Southampton* (1977).

AN ASSESSMENT OF THE PROGRAMMING LANGUAGE PASCAL*

N. WIRTH

Abstract—The programming language Pascal is assessed in the light of "reliable programming" and with the background of five years of experience with the language. Some features are selected to point out remaining problems, either inherent or specific, from which some guidelines for the design or choice of languages for reliable programming are derived. Among the discussed features are the concept of data type, the sequential file structure, and the type union.

Index Terms—Data types, files and sequences, language evaluation, language and reliable programming, parametrized types, Pascal, program correctness versus reliability, type union.

WHAT IS RELIABLE SOFTWARE?

RELIABLE is the attribute for a person, an organization, or a mechanism that you can trust, that you can depend on, that is worthy of your confidence. For example, a reliable clock is one that indicates accurate time even during an earthquake, a reliable railway system is one where trains run punctually even during a snowstorm, a reliable bridge is a bridge that does not crack even under heavy load, and a reliable transistor is one that operates for years, possibly under extreme temperature and radiation. The common enemy of reliability in these examples are adverse circumstances and influences that may cause a deterioration of the physical properties of material. The accumulation of these influences is called aging. Reliability is achieved by dimensioning the mechanisms properly, taking such adverse conditions into consideration. In a railway system the schedule is arranged such that it leaves room for catching up on lost time, and an ample supply of spare engines is kept on the alert for emergencies. A bridge is built stronger than actually needed most of the time—and a transistor is equipped with cooling devices and radiation shields.

What does this all have to do with software? Well, we all have experienced failures of computer systems; and we all would like them to be reliable too. When a computer fails, the first question among its intimates is usually: is the hardware or the software the culprit? Most customers of a computation center show signs of relief when the latter is announced, for the disruption of service is then quickly ended by a so-called dead start, and life goes on as if (almost) nothing had occurred. Indeed there had been neither an earthquake, nor a snowstorm, nor a weighty load, nor heat or radiation. Instead, merely unpredictable circumstances had led to a state of computa-

tion for which the logical structure of the program had not been designed, which the system's designers did not anticipate. And when pressing the dead start button, the computer operator is reasonably confident that these circumstances would not reoccur too soon.

What must we conclude? We understand by the term software the collection of programs that deterministically prescribe a system's detailed behavior and transitions of state. These programs are constants and are independent of any "adverse conditions" of an environment. Hence, software cannot fail because of unpredictable happenings and age, but only due to defects in its logical design. This leads us to a replacement of the attribute "reliable" by "correct."

We may be accused of nitpicking with words. To this I can only reply that the choice of words often reveals a speaker's *attitude* more profoundly than is dear to him. The attitude through which we content ourselves at producing "reliable" software instead of correct software, bears the danger that we may also consider various *degrees* of reliability. Software may then be termed reliable and "more reliable"; we may also call it correct, but certainly not "more correct."

The difference in these words is also manifested in the techniques to be employed in producing reliability in software versus in clocks, bridges, and transistors. In most technical phenomena, reliability is achieved by over dimensioning the components, by using high-quality material, or by supplying standby equipment that automatically goes into action when a failure occurs. In programs, merely repeating a logical test 18 times instead of performing it once does not help, if the logical structure is correct and the underlying hardware is reliable. In fact, the degree to which a program is unreliable is exactly the probability with which its incorrect parts are executed. But this measure is *not* a property of the program itself.

Reconciling ourselves with the word correct in place of reliable has the advantage that we more readily identify the causes of failures of our products to meet their goal. They are not to be sought in external, unforeseeable, adverse circumstances, but solely in our own inadequate minds, and in our failure to communicate, if several people participate in a program's design. The advantage of this recognition is that we know where to concentrate our efforts; its unpleasant part is the fact that it will be a never-ending crusade, because committing mistakes is a truly human characteristic.

The most sensible targets in our drive at producing correct software are evidently *the programmers themselves*. Nothing whatsoever can replace a sound, systematic

*Reprinted from *IEEE Transactions on Software Engineering*, June 1975, 192–198.

Manuscript received February 1, 1975.
The author is with the Federal Institute of Technology (ETH), Zürich, Switzerland.

FACILITIES AND CONVENTIONS THAT HAMPER THE CLARITY OF PROGRAMS

1) Operator Precedence: In the interest of simplicity and efficient translatability, Pascal aimed at a reasonably small number of operator precedence levels. Algol 60's hierarchy of 9 levels seemed clearly too baroque. An additional incentive for change was the replacement of the equivalence operator for Boolean expressions by the equality operator. Since these two operators reside on different priority levels in Algol 60, some departure from the old rules were mandatory. In retrospect, however, the decision to break with a widely used tradition seems ill-advised, particularly with the growing significance of complicated Boolean expressions in connection with program verification.

Algol 60	Pascal
$\uparrow$	$\neg$
$* \ / \div$	$* \ / $ div mod $\qquad \wedge$
$+ \ -$	$+ \ - \qquad\qquad \vee$
$= \neq < \leq \geq >$	$= \neq < \leq \geq >$
$\neg$	
$\wedge$	
$\vee$	
$\supset$	
$\equiv$	

Examples of expressions in Algol 60 and Pascal:

$$\neg x < y \qquad\qquad \neg (x < y)$$

$$x < y \wedge y < z \qquad (x < y) \wedge (y < z)$$

$$x < y \equiv y < z \qquad (x < y) = (y < z)$$

2) The GOTO *Statement:* There is hardly any doubt that the use of GOTO statements which disassociate the control structure of a process with the textual structure of its program is a frequent source of mistakes and impairs the verifiability of programs. This was perfectly clear even when the decision to include the GOTO statement in Pascal was taken [2]. Yet even now there is no general agreement on an adequate replacement. Placing further restrictions upon the GOTO statement—for instance, allowing only forward jumps—may be one solution. But clearly, allowing integers only instead of identifiers as labels is no sufficient deterrent to programmers who have previously worked with Fortran! In teaching programming, the use of a subset Pascal system *without* GOTO statement is strongly recommended.

THE EXPLICIT DISTINCTION BETWEEN "TYPES" AND "VARIABLES"

The most widely used technique of program verification is based on the explicit statement of assertions about the state of the computation at different points in the program. Recently, it has been recognized that it would be even more useful to attach assertions to specific variables rather than program points.

Declarations are essentially a statement of invariant properties of the respective variables. In Pascal, every variable is said to be of a certain *type*, and a data type can be defined explicitly by the programmer. It implies essential invariants needed for the verification of programs, and it moreover supplies a compiler with sufficient information to decide on a suitable storage representation. In essence, a compiler translates a type definition into a storage template to be used upon allocation of each variable of this type.

Moreover, the type definition determines the set of operators that are applicable to variables (sometimes called "instances") of that type.

It follows that a type definition should combine all attributes of a variable that are constant and known at the time of compilation (static). In fact, Pascal goes so far as to exclude *all* information from a type definition that cannot be determined from a simple textual scan. This rule has its important merits, but also bears some inconveniences, as shall be explained below. Our experience shows that the advantages of explicit type definitions are enormous and indispensible, if program transparence and efficiency of compiled code are both an issue.

Unfortunately, the Pascal concept of type has also stirred some controversy [3]. It seems to be largely originating from a too strict interpretation of the word *type* based on its use in the world of mathematics. There, the concept of types distinguishes between numbers and truth values, between numbers and sets of numbers, or between sets and sets of sets, but not between integers and natural numbers (a subrange of the former) or between small sets and larger sets. In the world of programming it is both natural and necessary to extend this concept of type, because objects can become different (types) because of far more (detailed) reasons than in abstract mathematics, where problems of representation are immaterial.

Which were, then, the negative consequences of adhering to the rule of strictly static type definitions? They became manifest in the form of two restrictions in the use of arrays, as compared to Algol 60. The first is the exclusion of so-called *dynamic arrays*, because the array type definition includes the specification of its size. There are good reasons for wanting dynamic arrays, but also convincing arguments against them [9]. The fact remains that dynamic arrays in the sense of Algol 60 are sort of a hermaphroditic (hybrid) species: their size can neither be determined at compile time, nor can it be changed during program execution. Instead, it is fixed upon block entry.

The second drawback is in practice much more severe. It originates from the essential requirement that formal procedure parameters specify their types. But in the case of *array parameters*, this once again includes their size. As a consequence, a given procedure can only be applied to arrays of one fixed size. This rule hardly contributes to program security and transparence, but seriously impairs the highly desirable flexibility of procedures.

Both problems can be overcome by allowing type definitions—in particular array types—to be parametrized. The following example shows the use of such a *parametrized type*.

```
type table(m,n) = array[m. . .n] of integer;
var t1: table(1,100);
    t2: table(0,999);
function sum (t: table; u,v: integer): integer;
  var i,s: integer;
begin s := 0;
  for i := u to v do s := t[ i ] + s;
  sum := s
end;
begin . . .
  s1 := sum(t1,1,100);
  s2 := sum(t2,0,999);
  . . .
end.
```

From this example we can see both the utility and the dangers of such a generalization, and possibly also the consequences upon a compiler. A most sensible decision is to restrict parametrization to the index bounds of array types, and to allow for constants only as actual parameters (in variable declarations). This already solves the dilemma of array parameters. If dynamic arrays are to be allowed, the latter rule may be relaxed. I would caution, however, against any further generalization: allowing the component type of an array to be a parameter too, for example, would destroy many advantages of the Pascal type concept at once.

AN IMPORTANT CONCEPT AND A PERSISTENT SOURCE OF PROBLEMS: FILES

In Pascal, files are understood to be strictly sequential files, and are defined in terms of the mathematical notion of a *sequence*. Like the array, they are homogeneous structures, but in contrast to the array, their size changes (truly) dynamically. Naturally, we not only aimed at a simple and consistent mathematical definition of files and their operators, but also kept in mind their efficient realization, particularly with a view towards the involvement of secondary storage media. As it turned out, the original file concept was right in terms of implementation, but not in terms of mathematical axiomatization which seemed highly desirable for a tool to construct reliable software. Therefore, the file scheme was slightly modified in a revision of the language made in 1973 that is summarized in [6]. Although the revised file facility proved to be a definite improvement, some inherent difficulties became evident only after extended usage. This may be the reason that the file concept had never been mentioned in any critical commentary about Pascal.

What are these deficiencies, and where do they have their roots? I presume that the main culprit is the attempt to hide from the programmer and the verifier the fact that files must be allocatable on secondary storage media. In this case, an efficient buffering mechanism is involved. Indeed, such technicalities may well be withheld from the programmer who is concerned with correctness only, if the scheme presented to him is rigorously defined and faultless, and if the consequences on efficiency are fully understood and accepted.

Originally, a file f was viewed as a sequence in which at any time only a single element was accessible, if there existed one. Conceptually, one could think of a *window*, through which that element, denoted by $f\uparrow$, could be seen (the arrow denotes the "window position"). But that description is not honest, of course, if $f\uparrow$ actually represents a buffer variable in primary store, via which data are transferred to and from secondary stores (tapes, disks). Therefore the appealing fiction of a sliding window was dropped in favor of a distinct *buffer variable*. But of course, also this is not quite honest, if the true buffer comprises several logical file elements, such that the operation *put* (f) will actually be effectuated by a mere pointer updating until the buffer is full. For then it is difficult to explain why $f\uparrow$ suddenly changes its value during the operation *put* (f). In reality we now have a buffer of which a single component is visible through a sliding window; and this situation is slightly too complicated to be neatly expressed by a simple scheme of axioms.

I wish to suggest two possible solutions to this dilemma. Characteristically, the choice depends on the intended application of the language. If Pascal is to serve for system construction purposes, then the file facility might be dropped entirely, because the very purpose would be the description of possible file mechanisms in terms of more primitive concepts. If, however, Pascal is viewed as a general purpose language in which files are an indispensible concept, then the basic operators *get* and *put* might be replaced by *read* and *write* statements defined in terms of the former as follows:

$$read\ (f,x) \equiv x := f\uparrow\ ; get\ (f)$$
$$write\ (f,x) \equiv f\uparrow\ := x; put\ (f)$$

This makes it possible to hide the chosen buffering mechanism entirely, and to ignore the existence of a window or of a buffer variable. (Incidentally, Pascal states exactly these abbreviations, but allows them only for textfiles. The relaxation of this restriction is an obvious step.)

A premise of the axiomatic scheme was that the predicate $eof(f)$ be always defined (true, if the part of the file to the right of the reading position is empty, false otherwise). This implies that a file access must be made before the program actually specifies any reading. The solution lies in combining the rewinding of the file with the initial loading of the buffer. Emptiness can be recognized during this operation. The unpleasant consequence is that a program can never leave a file in a properly rewound state. This may itself not be of any concern, as long as we remain strictly in the world of the Pascal program; but if this program is considered as one action upon a more permanent environment, it must be considered as a deficiency. Indeed, the appropriateness of the primitive *rewrite*(f) appears at least questionable. It is, from a theoretical point of view, indispensible, because it is the only operation by which a file variable can be given an initial value, namely the empty sequence (see [6]). In practice, however, rewinding (a tape) is considered as the basic operation, and rewinding does *not* cause the tape to be erased. An obvious "solution" consists in splitting *reset*(f) and *rewrite*(f) into the "more primitive" operations as follows:

$$reset(f) \equiv rewind(f); openread(f)$$
$$rewrite(f) \equiv rewind(f); openwrite(f)$$

The drawbacks are that the state of the predicate *eof*(f) and the buffer $f\uparrow$ are undetermined in between, and that a programmer is liable to forget to specify the openread or openwrite operation.

The most unsatisfactory consequences of the Pascal file concept lie in the area of substructures, and in particular textfiles. Originally, the idea of substructures could well be ignored. Texts were considered as sequences of characters, separated into lines by control characters. This concept is also embodied by the ISO (and ASCII) conventions, and proved to be most conveniently implementable. On a CDC 6000 computer with 6-bit characters and a set of 63 printing characters, the obvious choice was to introduce a 64th control character **eol** to signal the end of a line.

A program reading a textfile f, performing an operation L at the beginning of each line and an operation P after reading each character, is easily expressed by the following schema:

```
while ¬eof(f) do
   begin L; read(f,ch);
      while ch ≠ eol do
         begin P(ch); read (f,ch)
         end
   end                                          (1)
```

But then, alas, a new operating system came along with a set of 64 characters. It supposedly incorporates a true miracle: the coding of 64 characters *and* a line separation within 6 bits only! How can reliable software be constructed at all on the basis of such premises?

The new situation left no escape from providing textfiles with an explicit substructure: a textfile was to be considered as a sequence of lines, each line being itself a sequence of characters. In analogy to the predicate *eof*(f), a predicate *eoln*(f) was introduced to indicate the end of a line. Evidently, also a pair of new operators became necessary, *writeln*(f) to terminate the generation of a line, and *readln*(f) to initiate the reading of a next line.

Another problem arose simultaneously. At the end of a line, the predicate *eoln*(f) becomes true. Should at the end of the last line the predicate *eof*(f) also become true simultaneously? Probably so, because evidently the end of the last line is also the end of the text. Once again, we are faced with a dilemma: when reading the end of a line, we either find out whether there exists a next line, and we therefore read on (which may not be the intent of the programmer), or we refrain from looking ahead, and must leave the definition of *eof*(f) up to a further explicit *readln* instruction. Neither solution is fully satisfactory.

In the latter case (as in rev. Pascal), the program corresponding to schema (1) is

```
while ¬eof(f) do
begin L;
   while ¬eoln(f) do
      begin read(f,ch); P(ch)
      end;
   readln(f)
end                                             (2)
```

In the former case, the resulting program is slightly but significantly different:

```
while ¬eof(f) do
   begin readln(f); L;
      while ¬eoln(f) do
         begin read(f,ch); P(ch)
         end
   end                                          (3)
```

The difference may appear to be minimal, even negligible. It lies not so much in the form of the program but in the underlying concepts. And frequently such details decide ultimately about the acceptability—the healthiness—of a language. The issue of files is a typical case of the devil persistently and successfully hiding in the details.

SECURITY VERSUS FLEXIBILITY: TYPE UNIONS

It is sometimes desirable that a variable may assume values of different types. Its type is then said to be the *union* of these types. There appear to be three different motivations behind the desire for union types.

1) The need for *heterogeneous structures*. For example, in an interpreter a stack may have to consist of integer, real, and Boolean components. If the stack is represented by an array, its homogeneity is a hindrance. Although each "stack" element assumes only one fixed type during its lifetime, the underlying (static) array element appears to have a varying type.

2) *Storage sharing* (overlays). This implies the use of the same storage area—expressed in the language as "the same actual variable"—for different purposes, i.e., for representing different abstract variables whose lifetimes are disjoint.

3) Realization of implicit *type transfer functions*. For instance, a variable of type real is interpreted as being of type integer for the purpose of printing the internal representation in, say, octal form.

The dangers of the type union facility lie in the possibility to err about the current type of a variable and in the difficulty to identify the mistake. If it occurs in an assignment, the consequences may be disastrous. Efforts must be made to provide automatic checking facilities. We therefore distinguish between *discriminated* and *free unions* [5]. In the former case, the variable carries along a tag which indicates the currently valid type (which is one among the types specified in the definition of the union type). In the latter case, no such direct information is stored. Clearly, the latter provides greater freedom in programming, the former increased security through automatic consistency checks.

In Pascal, the concept of type union is embodied in the form of *variants of record structures*. The discriminated union inherently dictates a record structure, because every value consists of (at least) two components: the actual value and the tag value identifying its current type.

Example:

```
type stackelement =
  record
    case tag: (A,B,C) of
      A: (i: integer);
      B: (r: real);
      C: (b: Boolean)
  end;

var s: array[1..100] of stackelement
```

In a program with these declarations, the occurrence of a variable designator $s[i].r$ is only valid if at this point that variable is of type real. It is so, if and only if $s[i].tag = B$. A compiler may generate this test automatically, provided that it also ensures an appropriate setting of the tag upon assignment. This, however, implies an appreciable, although worthwhile overhead. Suggestions have been made to provide syntactic structures which let the compiler determine the current tag value from context. One such feature is the *inspect when* statement of Simula [1]. But these constructs sometimes turn out to leave insufficient freedom to express a given situation in a natural way.

No such facility was included in Pascal; to the contrary, in its revised version (1973) the tagfield of a variant record definition was declared to be optional. If it is omitted, we obtain the equivalent of a free type union, and a compiler has *no* chance of checking consistency in its application. One may rightly criticize this development which clearly opens the door for a very dangerous sort of programming errors, but there seem to exist applications where the discriminated union is insufficiently flexible. (Even so, my advice is to refrain from using variants without tagfield.)

The issue of type unions is a clear example of a case where a language may offer added security only at the expense of flexibility, or vice versa. The programmer must make his own choice. Yet, we have the impression that a more satisfactory solution must be found. It will not necessarily be found in new language facilities, but may lie in a different approach to data organization.

The truly disconcerting fact is that facilities such as the record variant, provided for a genuine need for flexibility (motivation 1 above), can be (and are!) easily misused. The example for the third motivation (see above) is characteristic for programmers who (habitually) think in terms of machine facilities and assembly code, and (love to) show that their techniques can also be expressed in a higher level language. It is probably the most disheartening experience for a language designer to discover how features provided with honest intentions are "ingeniously" misused to betray the language's very principles.

SUMMARY AND CONCLUSIONS

We have argued that the concept of a *degree of program reliability* is ill conceived and helps to foster a mistaken attitude in software engineering. Instead, a program can be called *correct*, if and only if its operations are fully consistent with static specifications of the expected results of the dynamic process. As programs used in practice are enormously complex and have a tendency to become even more complex in future applications, programming errors will always be with us. Instead of relying too much on either antiquated "debugging tools" or on futuristic automatic program verifiers, we should give more emphasis to the systematic construction of programs with languages that facilitate transparent formulation and automatic consistency checks.

The language Pascal was designed with exactly these aims. Five years of experience in its use have proven its significant merits with respect to ease of programming, suitability for formal program verification [7], [10], efficient implementability, and practical portability. They have also revealed some weaknesses and some remaining difficulties. After analyzing the roots of these problems, we are tempted to list a few conclusions about the design and the choice of languages for "reliable programming."

The language must rest on a foundation of simple, flexible, and neatly axiomatized features, comprising the basic structuring techniques of data and program.

Language rules must not deviate from widely accepted traditions of formal notations, even if these traditions are sometimes inconsistent or inconvenient. More importantly, *new* features must be designed with utmost care to notational regularity and consistency.

The urge to gain flexibility and "power" through generalizations must be restrained. A generalization may easily be carried too far and have revolutionary consequences on implementation (e.g., full parametrization of types).

Every basic feature is to be governed by a consistent set of "obvious" rules (axioms). The rules must be such that efficient implementability does not depend on particular (or even peculiar) properties of a specific computer system (e.g., on the existence of a line-end-character).

In many cases, security and flexibility are antagonistic

properties. Security is obtained through redundancy which is used by the system to perform consistency checks. Often, redundancy is cumbersome to provide, and the programmer must decide whether to choose a straightjacket providing relative security, or a free language where the responsibility is entirely his own (e.g., discriminated versus free type unions).

Every rule of the language must be enforceable by the system. It follows that rules should preferably be checkable by a mere textual scan, but also run-time checks should become widely used.

A rich language may be welcome to the professional program *writer* who's principle delight is his familiarization with all its intricate facets. But the interests of the program *reader* dictate a reasonably frugal language. People who want to understand a program (including their own), compilers, and automatic verification aids all belong to the class of readers.

In the interest of increased quality of software products, we may be well advised to get rid of many facilities of modern, baroque programming languages that are widely advertised in the name of "user-orientation," "scientific sophistication," and "progress."

ACKNOWLEDGMENT

The author wishes to acknowledge the criticism and suggestions of members of the International Federation of Information Processing Working Group 2.3 which helped to clarify this presentation.

REFERENCES

[1] Birtwistle, Dahl, Myhrhaug, Nygaard, "SIMULA Begin," *Studentlitteratur*, Univ. Lund, Lund, Sweden, 1974.
[2] E. W. Dijkstra, "GOTO statements considered harmful," *Commun. Ass. Comput. Mach.*, vol. 11, pp. 147–148, Mar. 1968.
[3] A. N. Habermann, "Critical comments on the programming language PASCAL," *Acta Informatica*, vol. 3, pp. 47–58, 1973.
[4] C. A. R. Hoare, "Set manipulation," *Algol Bulletin*, vol. 27, pp. 29–37, Dec. 1967.
[5] O.-J. Dahl, E. W. Dijkstra, and C. A. R. Hoare, "Notes on data structuring," in *Structured Programming*. New York: Academic, 1972.
[6] C. A. R. Hoare and N. Wirth, "An axiomatic definition of the programming language PASCAL," *Acta Informatica*, vol. 2, pp. 335–355, 1973.
[7] S. Igarashi, R. L. London, and D. C. Luckham, "Automatic program verification: a logical basis and its implementation," Dep. Comput. Sci., Stanford Univ., Stanford, Calif., Comput. Sci. Rep. 73-365, May 1973.
[8] K. Jensen and N. Wirth, "PASCAL—User Manual and Report," in *Lecture Notes in Computer Science*, vol. 18, New York: Springer-Verlag, 1974.
[9] O. Lecarme and P. Desjardins, "Reply to a paper by A. N Habermann on the programming language PASCAL," *SIGPLAN Notices*, vol. 9, pp. 21–27, Oct. 1974.
[10] E. Marmier, "A program verifier for Pascal," in *Proc. Int. Fed. Inform. Processing Congr.*, Inform. Processing 74. Amsterdam, The Netherlands: North-Holland, 1974.
[11] J. Welsh and C. Quinn, "A PASCAL compiler for ICL 1900 series computers," *Software—Practice and Experience*, vol. 2, pp. 73–77, 1972.
[12] N. Wirth, "The design of a Pascal compiler," *Software—Practice and Experience*, vol. 1, pp. 309–333, 1971.
[13] ——, "The programming language PASCAL," *Acta Informatica*, vol. 1, pp. 35–63, 1971.

SOME IMPROVEMENTS OF ISO PASCAL*

J. F. H. WINKLER

1 INTRODUCTION

The programming language Pascal [Wi 71a; JW 75] was a significant contribution to the evolution of programming languages. It is a simple but powerful language in the tradition of Algol 60 [Nau 63]. Compared with Algol 60 it contains more mechanisms for the definition of data structures: enumeration types, records, pointers, and I/O. Algol 60 contains only the array schema which is also included in Pascal. These data structuring facilities are the main reason for the usefulness of Pascal as a language for formulating general algorithms. Some more complicated mechanisms of Algol 60 were left out of Pascal : call by name, switch, dynamic arrays, and the general for-loop.

The proliferation of Pascal was also facilitated by the highly portable Pascal compiler developed at the ETH Zürich. This compiler system consisted of two parts : a compiler from Pascal to P-code (an instruction code for a simple stack computer) written in Pascal and the same compiler written in P-code. To implement Pascal on a new computer it was only necessary to make a P-code interpreter or code generator for the new machine.

Originally Pascal was a language intended for teaching and learning programming. But since it was a very useful language and easy to implement it was and is also used in the commercial field for writing system and application software. For this use the scarce set of mechanisms (which was quite right for teaching and learning) was not sufficient. This led to the situation that different implementors implemented different extensions (e.g. dynamic arrays, random access files, data bases, independent compilation, etc.). Furthermore this compromised portability which was traditionally good for pure Pascal since most compilers were derived from the Zürich compiler. To overcome this situation a group of BCS started work on standardization of Pascal in 1976 [Add 80]. Through numerous drafts and discussions this led to the Draft ISO Standard 7185 [ISO 82].

This draft standard describes essentially the language as it was defined by Wirth [JW 75; Wi 71a]. From the beginning of the standardization effort it was a goal not to revise the language [Add 80] but only to establish a more precise definition of it since the report in [JW 75] was felt inadequate and vague [Add

Author's Address: Siemens AG ZTI SOF 213, Otto-Hahn-Ring 6, D-8000 München 83 West Germany

*Reprinted from ACM *SIGPLAN Notices*, 19, 9, 1984. Copyright © J.F.H. Winkler.

80; BF 80; Rav 79]. This guideline was followed in the work
which led finally to [ISO 82].This document contains one
extension and some restrictions of the language but is much more
precise and explicit than the report in [JW 75]. The extension
consists of a sort of dynamic array called conformant array
schema. It can be used as parameters of subprograms.

The decision to standardize Pascal "as it is" retains
deficiencies of the language which were seen already by Wirth
[Wir 75a]. Furthermore new problems are introduced by the
extension and restrictions mentioned above and by the attempt to
define some concepts more precisely.

The following paper discusses only features contained in [ISO
82]. We do not look at Pascal with the eyes of someone requiring
a language with much more concepts [Pos 79].

Since the future goal of the standardization committee is the
standardization of an enriched Pascal the paper may be useful
for this undertaking.

The body of the paper contains a number of programs resp.
program fragments. They should not be misunderstood in a way
that they express a recommended style of programming. Their main
purpose is to show the difficulties a processor (processor in
the general sense used in [ISO 82]) has while checking a program
for conformity with the rules laid down in [ISO 82].

2   SCOPE RULE

The scope rule in [ISO 82] is the same as in [JW 75] (see e.g.
[Sal 79]). This rule can be characterized by the following three
properties :

    s1) declaration precedes application

    s2) scope = block

    s3) inner blocks with redeclarations are <u>totally</u> excluded
        from the scope of an outer declaration.

At first glance these three properties seem to characterize a
sound scope rule. But unfortunately property s2 has consequences
which indicate that it should be modified. The problem comes
from the fact that the scope of a declared entity extends from
the beginning of the block the declaration is immediately
contained in until the end of this block, and may thus encompass
a piece of program text preceding the declaration itself.

A very popular example for a program which violates this scope
rule is depicted in (2-1).

```
(1)    const A = 10;
               . . .
(2)    procedure P;
(3)        const B = A;                                    (2-1)
               . . .
(4)              A = 15;
               . . .
(5)    end { P } ;
```

According to s3 the A in line 3 cannot refer to the outer A declared in 1 because the whole block of P is excluded from the scope of this outer A. This is a consequence of the redeclaration in line 4. Since the applied occurence in line 3 precedes the defining occurence in line 4 the program is illegal (s1).

In order to indicate this violation of the Pascal scope rule all declarations from outer blocks used in the declaration part of an inner block must be marked or imported in the inner block [BF 80a]. This results in a complication of the compiler.

A more complicated example of the scope rule is depicted in (2-2).

```
function F;
        . . .
    function F;
        . . .
    end { F } ;                                            (2-2)
        . . .
begin   { body of the outer F }
.   F := 10;   { illegal !! }
```

It is impossible to define the value of the outer function because its block is excluded from the scope of its declaration. Apart from the scope problems this may be an indication that the assignment form is not well suited for the definition of the result of a function. The return-clause as used in PL/I [ECM 76], Ada[1][Ref 83] and Modula-2 [Wir 78, 80, Mul 84] or the result-clause and return-clause of CHILL [ITU 81] are preferable solutions.

A further complication is shown in (2-3) [BF 80].

```
procedure P0;
        . . .
end { P0 };
procedure P1;
        . . .
    procedure P2;
    begin
```

---

[1]   Ada is a trademark of the United States Department of Defense (AJPO).

                                                                  (2-3)
```
                        . . .
                   PO;
                     . . .
              end { P2 };
                   . . .
              procedure PO;  { illegal !! }
                   . . .
              end { PO };
                  . . .
         end { P1 };
```

The example (2-3) shows that an outer declaration which is used
in an inner block must also be imported in all   blocks
hierarchically between these two blocks.

The general problem with the scope rule of [ISO 82] can best be
seen in the following example, where a procedure-declaration P,
which contains a global reference G, is inserted at the point S
into a procedure Q (2-4). Since Pascal has a monolithic program
concept such an insertion of "building blocks" will often be
necessary during the development of large programs.

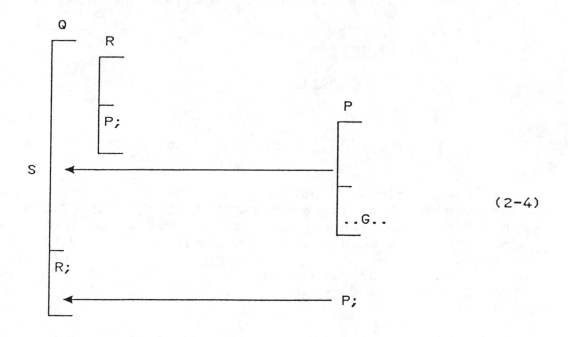

                                                                  (2-4)

A sound condition that P may be inserted at point S would be :

   a) there is no immediate name clash within Q, i.e. no
      declaration for P is already immediately contained
      in Q.

   b) the global references of P can be associated with
      corresponding declarations in Q (before the point
      S) or in the program part before Q.

If we assume that these two conditions hold in (2-4) and that R
does not contain a local declaration for P the rule "scope =

block" has the consequence to invalidate Q by the insertion of P. This follows from the fact that the applied occurrence of P inside of R precedes the new defining occurence of P inside of Q, after the insertion of P has been carried out. This situation is not easy to understand, and should not be part of a language intended text model" of Ada [Ref 83] is preferable. In this model property s2 is replaced by "the scope begins with the declaration and ends with the end of the immediately embracing block" and s3 by "parts of inner blocks with a redeclaration are excluded corresponding to property s2)".

The best solution for these scope problems seems to be to forbid the global view [SW 73] and to use explicit import clauses for global entities.

A further complication arises if the declarations of two (or more) entities are mutually dependent as in the case of mutual recursive subprograms or self-referencing data types. The problem of mutually dependent subprograms is resolved in [ISO 82] by the compiler directive FORWARD. The solution of the problem of self-referencing data types is achieved by an exception of rule s1 : "namely that an identifier may have an applied occurrence in the type-identifier of the domain-type of any new-pointer-types contained by the type-definition-part that contains the defining-point of the type-identifier" [ISO 82: 6.2.2.9].

Therefore the following program fragment (2-5) conforms to the requirements of the Draft Standard.

```
(1)     type A = 1 .. 10;
              . . .
(2)     procedure P;
(3)         type B = ↑A;
              . . .                                      (2-5)
(4)         A = record
(5)             K1 : CHAR;
(6)             K2 : B;
(7)         end;
```

In this situation the applied occurrence of A in line 3 must be associated with the declaration starting in line 4.

In order to avoid the above mentioned exception of rule s1 the same mechanism as for subprograms could be used. This would simplify the language and is shown in (2-6).

```
    type A = 1 .. 10;
          . . .
    procedure P;
        type A = forward;                                (2-6)
            B = ↑A;
          . . .
            A = record
                K1 : CHAR;
                K2 : B;
            end;
```

(2-6) shows quite instructively that the forward-declaration separates the problem of mutually dependent entities from the scope problem since in (2-6) there is no potential reference to the outer A as in (2-5).

With this solution rule s1 holds without any exception for all conformant programs. The compiler could give a warning or a hint if a type is unnecessarily declared as forward. The forward-declaration is only necessary for a situation as depicted in (2-6); the situation in (2-1) can easily resolved by a simple renaming. But this is not sufficient for (2-5). For the solution (2-6) to work in every case it is necessary that forward is a word-symbol. This is preferable to the solution in [ISO 82] were FORWARD is a so called compiler directive. If forward is a word-symbol the concept of a directive is no longer necessary for the definition of the language since the only required directive in [ISO 82] is FORWARD. Thus the language becomes simpler and easier to learn.

In general rule s1 can only be fulfilled by using some sort of forward construct or by forbidding the declaration of entities refering to each other.

3   LOOP VARIABLE

The Draft Standard [ISO 82] states that

    l1) the loop variable of a for-loop must be declared in the immediately surrounding block;

    l2) no assignment to the loop variable is allowed during the execution of the body of the loop.

    l3) neither a loop-body nor the declaration-part, which contains the declaration of a loop variable I immediately, shall contain a statement which may assign a value to I. There are four kinds of statements S which may assign a value to I:

        • S is an assignment statement with I as left hand side;

        • S contains I as an actual var-parameter;

        • S contains I as a parameter to one of the required procedures READ or READLN;

        • S is a for-statement and the control-variable of S denotes I.

Rule l3, which is quite restrictive and complicated, is

necessary to make the enforcing of rule L2 by the compiler feasible. The language could be made simpler if a loop construct were chosen such that the first occurrence of the loop variable in the for-list acts as the declaration of a constant local to the loop as in Algol 68 [FKL 76; HM 80] and Ada [Ref 83] . The loop would then form a scope by itself. Such a solution is also suggested by the results reported in [PS 79a].

4   ARRAY TYPES AND PARAMETERS

4.1   THE ACTUAL SITUATION

The introduction of a new sort of formal parameter, the conformant array parameter (CAP), is the main extension of [ISO 82] in comparison to [JW 75]. It was also the main problem which delayed acceptance of a final standard by the ISO [Min 80]. This extension was only included in the Proposed Standard after "two critical pressures were applied to the Committee by N.Wirth and C.A.R. Hoare (independently)" [Sal 80a: 54].

An example for a CAP is :

P : array [u .. v : IT] of ET

The part after the colon is called a conformant array schema (CAS).

IT is an identifier of an ordinal type. It indicates the index type of actual parameters admissible for the formal parameter P. The identifiers u and v denote the smallest resp. largest value of the actual parameter's index type. These values must always be values of IT.

ET is a type identifier or another CAS and indicates the element type of actual parameters admissible for the formal parameter P.

The CAP removes a significant technical deficiency of Pascal which had already pointed out by Wirth [Wir 75a: 26]. This deficiency was also a subject of critical papers on Pascal [Hab 73 :48; Con 76 : 15]. The reason for this criticism is that it was e.g. impossible to write library procedures for matrix handling in Pascal [BJ 81: 215; DL 75; EH 82]. As a consequence of the extremely static view of data types and objects a Pascal subprogram could only accept arrays of a fixed size as actual parameters.

The description of the new kind of parameter - the conformant array parameter- in [ISO 82] is quite complicated and it is questionable if this is adequate in a language "suitable for teaching programming".

The essential program properties related to the CAP are :

c1) every conformant array schema (CAS) defines a new type different from all other types in the program.

c2) a CAP cannot be used as an actual value-parameter in a subprogram call.

c3) a CAP is not assignment compatible to a local array variable with the same bounds and the same element type.

c4) assignment statements involving arrays need no dynamic checks on index ranges since assignment compatible array types have always the same number of elements. This does also hold for CAP.

c5) the length of an activation record for any subprogram activation may be determined at compile time.

There is one main reason in favor of property c2 given in [ISO 82] : the length of the activation record for any subprogram call can be determined at compile time (property c5). Property c5 does not seem to be very important since the heap storage of a Pascal program can generally not be determined at compile time. There are arbitrary sequences of allocations and deallocations possible. Compared with this highly dynamic structure of the heap it seems not important that the length of the stack frames can be computed in advance. It must also be noted that the number of stack frames cannot be computed at compile time. It seems more natural to look at the whole data storage of a Pascal program as a segmented memory like the heap [Mar 79].

It is also possible to retain the property of fixed length of stack frames if the stack contains only anonymous pointers to the dynamic arrays which are located on the heap [EH 82].

4.2   TOWARDS A NEW SOLUTION

A practically useful array feature sould have the following properties :

    a1) dynamic array parameters can be used as actual parameters;

    a2) there are dynamic array objects;

    a3) the declaration of objects assignment compatible to a dynamic array parameter is possible.

Ad a1:
    the reason for this property is given in 4.1. If value parameters are allowed property c5 may compromised. This dependes on the implementation strategy.

Ad a2:
    the CAS does not allow to write a program, which reads a number N and then declares an array with the index range 1 .. N. This is typical for programs solving problems with varying problem sizes e.g. the solution of systems of linear equations where the number of equations and/or unknowns may vary. Using the CAS concept has the consequence that there must always be a static array which may then be used as an argument for a dynamic array parameter. This is essentially the same situation as in Fortran [FOR 78]. Thus it is not possible to write programs which may adapt themselves to varying problems sizes. Introducing dynamic arrays in this more general sense is not very expensive if a feature like CAS is already in the language since the CAS concept requires descriptors for arrays and the mechanisms for the addressing of such arrays. Thus there are no additional mechanisms necessary to realize this more general array feature. Only property c5 does no longer hold.

Ad a3:
    this property is essential for algorithms involving sequences of arrays e.g. iterative solution of systems of linear equations or iterative computation of eigenvalues [SS 76]. After one iteration usually an assignment statement of the form "Old_Array := New_Array;" will be executed. The size of these arrays could be given by a dynamic array parameter. If the CAS concept is used such an assignment is only possible if Old_Array and New_Array are both declared in the same CAS. This means that an internal auxiliary variable must be supplied from outside as an actual parameter. This would lead to an unacceptable programming style. If an internal auxiliary variable is used the above assignment can only be realized by a loop statement. This would lead to inefficient code on most machine architectures.

The main problem now is how the properties a3 and c4 can both

be fulfilled. If we use a similar scheme for dynamic array
parameters as in [ISO 82] the type of these parameters will
be an anonymous type. There will be no type identifier to
indicate the type of the local object which should be
assignment compatible (in the sense of c4) to the dynamic
array parameter. The following proposal uses the Like clause
to indicate that the properties of a new object are to be the
same as those of an already declared object.

The proposal consists of three parts : the introduction of
dynamic array types, dynamic array parameters, and the Like
clause[1].

4.3   DYNAMIC ARRAY TYPES

```
array-type = "array" "["index-range ("," index-range)"]"
             "of" component-type.
index-range = ordinal-type-identifier |
              ordinal-expression ".." ordinal-expression.
ordinal-expression = expression.
```

The new feature in this proposal is the production

index-range = ordinal-expression ".." ordinal-expression. (4-2)

which allows arbitrary ordinal-expressions for the bounds of
index-ranges. Both expressions in one index-range must be of the
same type. The expressions of an index-range are evaluated in an
arbitrary order. Their values are the lower resp. the upper
bound of the index-range. If the uppper bound is a predecessor
of the lower bound the index-range is empty. The index-ranges of
an array-type are elaborated in an arbitrary order.

If at least one of the two ordinal-expressions in (4-2) cannot
be determined at compile time the corresponding index-range
constitutes a dynamic index-range. An array-type which contains
at least one dynamic index-range is a dynamic array-type.

The rules for assignment compatibility are the same as in [ISO
82]. As a consequence of this property c4 does also hold in our
proposal.

The production (4-2) is only necessary because we do not assume
the existence of dynamic ordinal-types. If there were dynamic
ordinal-types in the language the production

———————————

[1]   A Like clause is contained in the earlier version of PL/1 [IBM
       72: 345]. But this clause was not incorporated into the PL/I
       standard [ECM 76].
       Independent of our paper here, a Like clause was just recently
       proposed in [Wha 83].

```
            index-range = ordinal-type-identifier
```

alone would be sufficient.

There are a lot of proposals for dynamic arrays in the
literature [EH 82; Kit 77; Mac 75; Mof 81; Pok 76; Ste 76; Ten
83; Wir 76a]. The solution in this proposal is similar to the
scheme already used in Algol 60 [Nau 63] and was also proposed
by Wirth [Wir 76a].

4.4 DYNAMIC ARRAY PARAMETERS

```
    formal-parameter-section >
        dynamic-array-parameter-specification.

    dynamic-array-parameter-specification =
        ["var"] identifier-list ":" "dyn" ["packed"]
        static-array-type-identifier.
    static-array-type-identifier = type-identifier.
```

A formal dynamic-array-parameter-specification has essentially
the same structure as other data parameter specifications [Ten
80: 11] :

```
        ["var"] id-list ":" type-indication .
```

This means that the language becomes simpler and easier to learn
by this proposal. Instead of

$$\underline{var} \; PAR : \underline{array} \; [L \; .. \; U] \; \underline{of} \; ET$$

we simply write

$$\underline{var} \; PAR : \underline{dyn} \; AT$$

AT would be a one dimensional array type with element type ET.
In general AT can denote any (static) array-type which has been
declared previously and is visible at this point.

In a dynamic-array-parameter-specification a new (anonymous)
array-type is introduced whose properties are derived from an
already declared (static) array-type.

Conformability is defined as in [ISO 82: 6.6.3.8].

The definition of parameter compatibility is much more simpler
than in [ISO 82] :

    pc) an array A may be an argument for a formal
         dynamic array parameter D iff the type of A
         conforms to the type of D.

Intuitively this means that an actual array is "not greater"
than the formal, and the element types of both are the same.

The rule above allows also the use of a dynamic array parameter as an argument for another dynamic array parameter (even for itself in the case of a recursive subprogram).

In contrast to [EH 82; Pok 76] we have introduced a new sort of parameter which is simply indicated by "dyn". This tells the reader of the program directly what the properties of the corresponding parameter are and seems to be much more simpler than the concept of parametric types [EH 82].

Inside a subprogram containing a dynamic array parameter in its heading it is necessary to know the index bounds of the corresponding actual-parameter. In this proposal two families of required functions are introduced for this : LBound and HBound. They are defined for any array type and array object. Let t denote an array type or an array object. LBound(t) (HBound(t)) yields the lower (upper) bound of the first index-range of t. Let n be a static integer expression yielding a number greater than zero. LBound(t,n) (HBound(t,n)) yields the lower (upper) bound of the n-th index-range of t. It is an error if the value of n exceeds the number of index-ranges of t.

An example for this proposal is given in figure 4-1.

```
type AT1 = array [1..10] of INTEGER;
     AT2 = array [1..100] of AT1;

var  AV1 : array [1..100] of AT1;
     AV2 : array [50..60] of array [1..5] of INTEGER;

procedure P (var  A : dyn AT2);
   var I : LBound(AT2,1) .. HBound(AT2,1);
               {since AT2 must be a static array type
                  the type of I is also static }
       J : LBound(AT2,2) .. HBound(AT2,2);
begin
   for I := LBound(A,1) to HBound(A,1)
               { the iteration clause comprises exactly the
                  index values of the actual parameter }
   do begin
      for J := LBound (A,2) to HBound(A,2)
      do A[I,J] := A[I,J]  + 7;
      end;
end;
   . . .
P(AV1);
P(AV2);
```

Figure 4-1. The use of dynamic array parameters

This approach to the problem of adjustable array parameters also avoids the main problems pointed out in [Min 80: 79..83]. The main reason for this are the two newly introduced (families of) required functions "LBound" and "HBound" which are used instead of the "bound-identifiers" in [ISO 82]. These functions lead to a better semantic coherence of the program, in that a semantic dependency between several items (the object A and its index bounds) is used to compute the dependent value from the independent one.

The example in figure 4-1 contains one remaining insecurity: LBound(A,1)..HBound(A,1) may be a proper subset of LBound(AT2,1)..HBound(AT2,1). This insecurity can be removed by using the proposal for the implicit declaration of the loop variable (conf. sect. 3). This leads to the program fragment (4-3) where the set of admissible values for I and J are (automatically) constrained as far as possible.

```
    type AT1  .....
        {as in figure 4-1}
    procedure P (var A: dyn AT2);
        { no declaration for I and J }
    begin                                            (4-3)
        for I := LBound(A,1) to HBound(A,1)
        do begin
            for J := LBound(A,2) to HBound(A,2)
            do A[I,J] := A[I,J] + 7;
            end;
    end { P } ;
```

The restriction of the type of a dyn-parameter to a static-array-type is only necessary because we do not assume the existence of dynamic ordinal-types. If there were dynamic ordinal-types in the language the procedure P in figure 4-1 could simply be written as in (4-4). In (4-4) the type AT2 could then also be a dynamic array-type.

```
    procedure P (var A : dyn AT2);
        var I : LBound(A,1) .. HBound(A,1);
            { now I has the proper value range }
            J : LBound(A,2) .. HBound(A,2);           (4-4)
    begin
        { as in figure 4.1 }
```

4.5   THE LIKE-CLAUSE

The declaration of local array variables which are assignment compatible with a formal dynamic array parameter is not possible using the elements defined so far. If the dynamic parameter is defined by "var P: dyn AT;" then "dyn AT" defines a new type different to all other types in the program. A variable V declared locally by the declaration "var V: AT;" is therefore not assignment compatible with P.

Assignment compatibility can be achieved by deriving the properties of the local variable V directly from the parameter itself by the Like-clause :

```
        var V: Like P;
```

This means that V has the same type as the <u>actual</u> parameter corresponding to the formal parameter P. As a consequence the assignment

$$V := P;$$

is perfectly legal and does not need dynamic checks on the index bounds since V and P have by definition the same number of components.

An example for the use of the <u>Like</u>-clause is given in figure 4-5.

```
    type VECTOR = array [INTEGER] of REAL;
              . . .
    procedure P(var OldVector : dyn VECTOR);
       var NewVector : Like OldVector;
    begin
       repeat                                          (4-5)
          OldVector := NewVector;
          {computation of
           NewVector := F(OldVector)  }
       until  Cond(NewVector, OldVector);
    end  { P };
```

It is not necessary to restrict the use of the <u>Like</u>-clause to dynamic array parameters. Any variable already declared could be used in the <u>Like</u>-clause. This could avoid the introduction of type names, when it is not really necessary [Ker 81: 6], and may thus reduce the conceptual load for the writer and the reader of the program [Bak 80]. It does furthermore enhance the semantic coherence of the program because the relationship between two (or more) variables is expressed more directly than by using a type. The <u>Like</u>-clause is not intended to replace the type definition facility. It is an alternative which may be better suited for certain situations. In which cases the use of the <u>Like</u>-clause is to be preferred to the use of a type can only be decided by practical experience. One situation in favour of the <u>Like</u>-clause has been discussed above.

5   INPUT-OUTPUT

In the input-output area the problem is the input for interactive programs [FG 82: 88; Kay 80]. Before we describe the problems we will briefly mention the main charcteristics of input-output in Pascal.

Input-output is realized via variables of type "<u>file</u> <u>of</u> ElementType" where ElementType can be any type which does not contain (directly or indirectly) a file type. A file (value) is a linear sequence of values of the ElementType. With each file variable f a so called buffer variable f↑ of ElementType is associated. The buffer variable contains one element of the associated file variable. Only this component can be accessed and manipulated directly. Other elements can only be accessed by scanning the file variable sequentially. In this framework input-output consits of the manipulation of file variables and/or buffer variables. The following predefined procedures and functions may be used for this : RESET, REWRITE, GET, PUT, READ, WRITE, READLN, WRITELN, EOF, EOLN, and PAGE.

For human readable I/O Pascal has a predefined file type called TEXT. A value of type TEXT is a sequence of lines where each line is a sequence of characters containing exactly one end of line marker as the last component. Together with the file type TEXT two procedures READ and READLN for formatted input are defined. Furthermore a required TEXT variable INPUT is defined which may occur in the parameterlist of the program and is intended to be associated with the standard input device. In case of an interactive program the standard input device will usually be the input part of a CRT-terminal.

Most of the above mentioned subprograms for doing I/O embody a prefetch discipline which causes one more component to be transferred as is actually needed. "RESET(FileVar)" puts the FileVar in input mode and places the first element (if it exists) into the associated buffer variable FileVar↑.

        READ(FileVar,ElemVar);

is defined as

        begin ElemVar:=FileVar↑; GET(FileVar); end .

The actual element in the file buffer is assigned to the second parameter of READ and the next element of FileVar is assigned to the buffer variable FileVar↑ by executing the procedure GET.

READLN also embodies this prefetch discipline. It places "the current file position just past the end of the current line in the textfile" [ISO 82: 62]. The naive user would rather expect that READLN (= read line ??) reads just a line from INPUT. Pugh and Simpson also report difficulties of novices caused by READLN [PS 79a].

For the required textfiles INPUT and OUTPUT [JW 75] defined that an implicit RESET(INPUT) resp. REWRITE(OUTPUT) is automatically performed by the system. Neither the user manual nor the report define exactly when this RESET(INPUT) is to be executed. Therefore lazy input [HS 78b] has always been allowed in Pascal. Unfortunately the report left many questions open. The real definition was the compiler distributed from Zurich. This compiler implemented the rule about the implicit RESET(INPUT) in such a way that it occurred before the execution of the first statement of the program.

With this implementation the realization of sound interactive programs is impossible because the program requires some input from the terminal (as a consequence of the prefetch discipline

in RESET) before it can give any prompting message to the user
[HS 78b: 93]. A sound interactive program works the other way
round: it gives first some message to the user, e.g. that it is
running at all and is expecting some input, and then reads this
input from the user.

To avoid this unsatisfactory situation [ISO 61a: 67] suggests
Lazy I/O for the program parameters INPUT and OUTPUT. The
post-assertions of RESET resp. REWRITE shall hold "prior to the
first access to the textfile or its associated buffer-variable".

The main drawback of this deferred input is the complication of
the translator and the object program [Per 81: 87]. Each
reference to INPUT↑ must check if RESET(INPUT) has already been
executed. The program fragment (5-1) shows an example for this.

```
        (1)    program PROG(INPUT);
        (2)      { Declarations }
        (3)    begin
        (4)      if Condition                              (5-1)
        (5)      then CharVar := INPUT↑;
        (6)      { arbitrary statements
        (6)         not referencing INPUT or INPUT↑ }
        (7)      CharVar2 := INPUT↑;
```

When the statement in line 7 is executed it must be known wether
RESET(INPUT) has already been executed or not. This means that
generally each reference to INPUT↑ must check the status of
INPUT.

The situation is even worse if the file buffer (INPUT↑) is used
as an actual var-parameter. Even the paper [HS 78b], which deals
with the problems of Lazy I/O, does not offer a solution for
this problem. The complete implementation of Lazy I/O seems to
involve a certain runtime overhead since, a var-parameter must
carry with it the information wether it is a file buffer or not,
and each reference to this parameter must interpret this
information.

Using a discipline without prefetch RESET(INPUT) could be
executed without any harm before the first executable statement
of the program body and no checks at the referencing points were
necessary.

Summarizing this discussion gives the result that the real
culprit is the prefetch discipline and not the implicit
RESET(INPUT).

6   SPECIFICATION OF FORMAL SUBPROGRAMS

In [JW 75] the exact nature of formal subprograms need and can
not be indicated in the corresponding parameter specification.

As a consequence the actual parameters belonging to calls of formal subprograms have to be checked dynamically. This can be seen in the program fragment (6-1).

```
program PROG61(INPUT,OUTPUT);
    procedure P1(Par1: BOOLEAN; procedure Par2);
    begin
        if Par1
        then Par2(10)
        else Par2(10,10);
    end { P1 };

    procedure P2(Par1: INTEGER);                    (6-1)
    begin
        WRITELN("P2; Par1 = ", Par1);
    end { P2 };

    procedure P3(Par1, Par2 : INTEGER);
    begin
        WRITELN("P3; Par1 = ",Par1,"Par2 = ",Par2);
    end { P3 };

begin { of program }
    P1(TRUE, P2);
    P1(FALSE,P3);
end.
```

It is interesting to note that in Algol 60, which has similar facilities for the specification of parameters and does also not allow to describe the types of parameters of formal subprograms, a program analogous to (6-1) would be illegal. The reason for this is that the semantics of the procedure call is there defined by the replacement of the call statement by the (modified) body of the called procedure (copy rule). The modification of the body consists essentially of the replacement of the formal parameters by the actual ones. This modification must "lead to a correct ALGOL statement" [Nau 63: 4.7.5]. This additional condition is not fulfilled in (6-1).

In [ISO 82] a parameter which is a subprogram must be fully specified with all its own parameters and in the case of a function additionally with its result type.

As a consequence programs as (6-1) are no longer possible and no dynamic type checking in the calls of formal subprograms is necessary. This is a real deviation from [JW 75]. Unfortunately this has been done in a somewhat unsatisfactory manner in that the specification of the formal subprogram contains parameter identifiers which are superfluous and disturbing. This is exemplified in (6-2) and (6-3).

```
program PROG62(INPUT,OUTPUT);
    procedure P1(Par11 : BOOLEAN;
                    procedure Par12(Par : BOOLEAN));
    begin
        Par12(Par11);
    end { P1 };
```

```
      procedure P2(Par21 : BOOLEAN);
      begin
         WRITELN("P2; Par21 = ",Par21);                    (6-2)
      end  { P2 };
      procedure P3(Par31, Par32 : BOOLEAN);
      begin
         WRITELN("P3; Par31 = ",Par31," ; Par32 = ",Par32);
      end  { P3 };
   begin   { of program }
      P1(TRUE, P2);
      P1(FALSE,P3);    { this is now illegal }
   end.
```

Inside the procedure P1 the identifier "Par" cannot be used for any purpose and the programmer may be disturbed by the fact that in the heading of P2 the corresponding parameter is named by "Par21". In Pascal the form depicted in (6-3) would be sufficient.

```
   procedure P1 (Par11 : BOOLEAN;                          (6-3)
            procedure Par12 (BOOLEAN) );
```

If the keyword notation for actual parameters [Fra 77; Har 76; Par 78] were allowed in Pascal, as it is e.g. in Ada [Ref 83], the identifier "Par" of this second order formal parameter could be useful. This is shown in (6-4).

```
   procedure P1 (Par11 : BOOLEAN;
            procedure Par12(Par : BOOLEAN) );
   begin                                                    (6-4)
      Par12 (Par => Par11);
   end  { P1 };
```

But for third and higher order formal parameters there is even with key word notation no need for identifiers (6-5).

```
   procedure P1 (Par11 : BOOLEAN;
            procedure Par12(
               procedure Par21(Par31 : BOOLEAN)));
   begin                                                    (6-5)
      Par12 (Par21 => P2 {as defined in (6-1)});
   end  { P1 };
```

There are only a few new syntax rules necessary to specify second and higher order formal parameters without identifiers [Win 76b: 11; DL 74: 25].

7   ORDER OF DECLARATIONS

The rule for the ordering of declarations in [ISO 82] is essentially the same as in [JW 75] and [Wir 71]. This rule states that the declarations of the different kinds of entities must be arranged in each declaration-part in the following order : labels, constants, types, variables, subprograms. There seems to be no sound technical reason for this rule. This rule is especially not necessary for the existence of a one pass compiler. A one pass compiler only requires that any declared entity is declared before its first use ("linear text model", property s2 in section 2).

On the other hand the declaration rule of [ISO 82] has negative effects on the software engineering properties of Pascal [HSW 77]. It hinders the programmer to put together what belongs together.

Despite the fact that Pascal does not incorporate the concept of program module one could "simulate" it within the monolithic Pascal program if there were not this rule for the declaration order. An example for this is given in (7-1). A similar approach for modular programming in Pascal is contained in [ADD (4].

```
program P (INPUT,OUTPUT);
    { package PACK1 }
        const   .....
        type    .....
        var     .....
        { subprograms }
    { end  PACK1 }                           (7-1)

    { package  PACK2 }
        . . .
    { end  PACK2 }
        .
        .
        .
    begin
        { main program }
    end.
```

By removing this artificial restriction on the order of declarations a program structure similar to Ada or Modula-2 [Wir 80] could be achieved. The essential difference to Ada would be that a Pascal program is one compilation unit whereas in Ada each package can be a compilation unit.

A programming style like that depicted in (7-1) was already possible in Algol 60. In this respect Pascal seems to be overly restrictive in its current form.

8   STRUCTURED STATEMENTS

Pascal uses the "open" form for most of its structured statements, e.g. the if-statement :

```
if-statement = if condition
                 then statement                          (8-1)
               [ else statement ]
```

This forces the user to use a compound statement if the then-part or the else-part of the if-statement consists of more than one statement :

```
if A < 10
then begin
        C := A + 5;                                       (8-2)
        D := 0;
        end ;
```

The "closed" form of the structured statements, which is incorporated in most languages developed during the seventies, has several advantages. A first advantage is that it leads to a less clumsy formulation. The statement (8-2) would be written as :

```
if A < 10
then C := A + 5;                                          (8-3)
     D := 0;
end if    ( or fi  )
```

There has been and is a controversary discussion about the form of closing key words for the closed form of structured statements [Bro 76; Ham 80; Hun 81; Knu 74a: 266; Kov 78; Mar 81]. From a purely technical point of view any unequivocal symbol would do it. In comparison to the usual usage of brackets in mathematical formulae the use of symmetric key words (e.g. fi, od etc.) seems to be quite natural. To a certain degree this can be a matter of taste and other solutions (end if, end loop, etc.) may also work well. An additional requirement which belongs to the area of human engineering would be that all word-symbols sould be easily pronounceable. In the following example we use symmetric and pronouncable key words.

A second advantage is the fact that the endings of several structured statements, which are nested, can be clearly discriminated, if different structured statements have different closing symbols. (8-4) shows a nesting using Pascal as it is and (8-5) shows the same nesting using symmetric closing symbols.

```
else
    begin
        if I > DIGMAX then begin
            ERROR(203);
            VAL.IVAL := 0
            end
        else
            with VAL do begin
                IVAL := 0;
                for K := 1 to I do begin            (8-4)
                    J := ORD(DIGIT[K]) - ORD('0');
                    if IVAL <= (MAXINT - J) DIV 10 then
                        IVAL := IVAL * 10 + J
```

```
                         else begin
                            ERROR(203);
                            IVAL := 0
                            end
                      end;
                   SY := INTCONST
                   end
            end


      else
         if I > DIGMAX
         then ERROR(203);
            VAL.IVAL := 0;
         else
            fix VAL
            in IVAL := 0;
               for K := 1 to I                        (8-5)
               do J := ORD(DIGIT[K]) - ORD('0');
                  if IVAL <= (MAXINT - J) DIV 10
                  then IVAL := IVAL * 10 + J;
                  else ERROR(203);
                        IVAL := 0;
                  fi
               rof
               SY := INTCONST;
            xif
      fi
```

Note the use of the word-symbol fix instead of with in the
example (8-5) in order to get a pronounceable inverse (xif). fix
.. in seems to reflect the semantics of this language construct
quite well.

9   INITIALIZATION OF CONSTANTS AND VARIABLES

9.1   INITIALIZATION OF CONSTANTS

Like [JW 75] the ISO standard allows only signed constants in
the initialization part of a constant-definition. Therefore it
is not possible to express dependencies between different
constants in the program in order to enhance the semantic
coherence and thus the maintainability of the program.

A simple and popular example is :

Solution according to [ISO 82] :

```
const  Pi =     3.1415926536;
       TwoPi = 6.2831853072;
```

Better solution :

```
const  Pi =     3.1415926536;
       TwoPi = 2.0 * Pi;
```

If the program is modified in such a way that the number of digits in the initialization of Pi is eg changed from eleven to sixteen (3.141592653589793) the second solution needs less effort.

A similar example is the following:

```
[ISO 82] :    const  CharsPerLine = 72;
                     LinesPerPage = 21;
                     CharsPerPage = 1512;
```

```
better   :    const  CharsPerLine = 72;
                     LinesPerPage = 21;
                     CharsPerPage = CharsPerLine * LinesPerPage;
```

9.2   INITIALIZATION OF VARIABLES

Pascal does not allow the initialization of variables immediateley in the variable-declaration. This leads to two problems :

- a variable may be used without having a defined value. This will usually neither be detected by the compiler nor by the machine which executes the object program.

- If the variable is initialized in the statement part of the body, which contains the declaration immediately, the distance between the point of declaration and the point of initialization will often be quite large.
  Often programmers append a comment to a variable-declaration indicating the initial value. During the maintenance phase this can easily lead to confusion if the initialization is modified but the corresponding comment is not.

Thus, initialization of (at least scalar) variables should be allowed.

10   CASE STATEMENT

10.1   ELSE CLAUSE

The language as defined in [ISO 82] could be enhanced by introducing an "otherwise" clause into the case-statement. This would remove one error situation from the language and would result in better and safer programs. If the keyword else is used to indicate this case-list-element no new keyword would be necessary.

An example for this enhanced form of the case statement is :

```
    case Digit  of
        '0','1'   : Process(Digit);
        else      : Error;
    end;
```

10.2   RANGE IN CASE-LABEL-LIST

The case-statement could be further enhanced by allowing ranges as an element of a case-constant-list. An example for the application of this construct is:

```
    case NextChar of
        'A'..'Z', 'a'..'z'  : Identifier;
        '0'..'9'            : Number;
        else                : OtherSymbol;
    end;
```

A solution using [ISO 82] results in long case-label-lists enumerating explicitly all letters resp. digits.

11   COMPATIBILITY WITH THE STANDARD

In this section we discuss to what degree the new features proposed in this paper are compatible with the Draft Standard. The crucial point is how many of the already existing conforming programs had to be modified.

SCOPE RULE

The scope rule of [ISO 82] is more restricted than the linear text model. The examples in (2-1), (2-3) and (2-4) are not conformant with [ISO 82] but are conformant with the linear text model. Thus no modifications of conformant programs were necessary.

The introduction of the forward-declaration for mutually dependent data types would make the modification of programs containing such entities necessary. This can be seen in the examples (2-5) and (2-6). Also programs which use "forward" as an identifier would be affected. But this should not happen very frequently because "forward" was already a compiler directive in [JW 75].

LOOP VARIABLE

Only those programs had to be modified in which a for loop is terminated by a goto statement and the actual value of the loop variable is used after this termination. The reason for this is that in [ISO 82] a loop variable can only get a defined value if a loop with this loop variable is executed.

ARRAY TYPES AND PARAMETERS

No program which conforms to [JW 75] or which conforms to [ISO 82] and does not use the conformant-array-schema would be affected by the new concepts proposed in section 4. If a program contains one of the identifiers HBound and LBound a renaming could be necessary in order to use the proposed required functions HBound and LBound. The lexical unit "like" should not be used as an identifier since it would be a new word-symbol.

INPUT/OUTPUT

If RESET were defined similar to OPEN, which is contained in most command languages of operating systems, and if READ read just the next component into its actual parameter, then an interactive program, which uses only RESET and READ should not be affected.
The postcondition of READ should imply that the component read is the last component of the left part of the file. This condition holds already in [ISO 82]. The definition of EOLN could remain the same as in [ISO 82]. Note that READLN should not be used in its current form for interactive input.

SPECIFICATION OF FORMAL SUBPROGRAMS

Only programs which use formal, parameterized subprograms would be affected by this proposal. Note that the formal subprogram is a concept used quite rarely.

STRUCTURED STATEMENTS

Almost every program would be affected, but an automatic conversion tool could be realized easily.

ORDER OF DECLARATIONS

No program would be affected since the property "declaration precedes application" holds already in [ISO 82].

INITIALIZATION OF CONSTANTS AND VARIABLES

No existing program would be affected by the introduction of the initializations proposed in this paper, since the proposal is a pure extension.

IMPROVEMENT OF THE CASE-STATEMENT

No existing program would be affected by the improvements proposed, since the proposals are pure extensions.

12   CONCLUSION

The outcome of the standardization effort for Pascal is a very enhanced form of the original language [JW 75]. But there are still some trouble spots in the language, which should be resolved in a future revision of the standard.

The main problems are :

- the scope rules as defined in [ISO 81] are difficult to understand, to learn, and to use. Scope rules oriented towards the "linear text model" are better suited.

- the solution for adaptable arrays as parameters is a little bit clumsy and quite difficult to understand and learn. In this paper a simpler solution with a better functionality is proposed.

- the concept of I/O as defined in the original Pascal is not adequate for expressing interactive programs. It is very regrettable that this flaw of Pascal was not removed during the standardization process. It may be a little disadvantageous if a novice is introduced to I/O by means of this I/O-discipline.

- the specification of formal subprograms has been enhanced but it could have easily done better by using some additional syntax rules.

The main problem with this standardization effort still is the fact that the thing which is being standardized nearly doesn't exist because most of the implementations intended for serious programming (e.g. [Sie 82, 82a; Tex 79; UCS 80]) implement a superset of Pascal. Some often added features are :

- a mechanism for independent compilation

- dynamic arrays

- string handling

- random access files

It cannot be expected that such useful features will not be used in the future. Since they are not in the language portability is still compromised.

ACKNOWLEDGMENTS

The author thanks M.Sommer and C.Stoffel for a critical review of an earlier draft and valuable suggestions.

13   REFERENCES

ADD 84   Ancona, M.; De Floriani, L.; Dodero, G.; Mancosu, S.
          Integrating Library Modules into Pascal Programs
          Software - Pratice + Experience 14,5(1984)401..412.

Add 80   Addyman, Anthony M.
          Pascal
          = [HM 80: 81..91].

AH 80   Austermühl, Burkhard; Henhapl, Wolfgang
          A critical review of PASCAL based on a formal storage
          model
          = [Hof 80: 57..69].

Bak 80   Baker, Henry G. Jr.
          A Source of redundant Identifiers in PASCAL Programs
          SIGPLAN Notices 15,2(1980)14..16.

BF 80   Baker, T.P.; Fleck, A.C.
          Does Scope = Block in Pascal ?
          Pascal News #17 (March,1980)60..61.

BJ 81   Boute, R.T.; Jackson, M.I.
          A Joint Evaluation of the Programming Languages Ada and
          CHILL
          = [IEE 81: 214..220].

Bro 76   Brown, Robert E.
          Toward a Better Language for Structured Programming
          SIGPLAN Notices 11,7(1976)41..54.

BWW 76   Wettstein, H.; Becker-Weimann, K.; Winkler, J.F.H.;
          Wosnitza, H.
          Ein modernes, modulares Betriebssystem für Prozeßrechner
          und seine Generierung
          PDV-E71, Gesellschaft für Kernforschung, Karlsruhe Juni
          1976.

Cai 82   Cailliau, R.

How to Avoid Getting Schlonked by Pascal
SIGPLAN Notices 17,12(1982)31..40.

Con 76   Conradi, Reidar
         Further critical comments on Pascal, particulary as a
         systems programming language
         SIGPLAN Notices 11,11(1976)8..25.

DL 74   Lecarme, Olivier; Desjardins, Pierre
         Reply to a paper by A.N. Habermann on the programming
         language Pascal
         SIGPLAN Notices 9,10(1974)21..27.

DL 75   Desjardins, P.; Lecarme, O.
         More Comments on the Programming Language Pascal
         Acta Informatica 4(1975)231..243.

ECM 76   ECMA - European Computer Manufacturers Association
         Standard ECMA-50. Programming Language PL/I
         Geneva, December 1976.

EH 82   Hennessy, John; Elmquist, Hilding
         The Design and Implementation of Parametric Types in
         Pascal
         Software - Practice & Experience 12,2(1982)169..184.

FG 82   Feuer, Alan R.; Gehani, Narain, H.
         A Comparison of the Programming Languages C and PASCAL
         Computing Surveys 14,1(1982)73..92.

FKL 76   van Wijngaarden, A.; Mailloux, B.J.; Peck, J.E.L.;
         Koster, C.H.A.; Sintzoff, M.; Lindsay, C.H.; Meertens,
         L.G.L.T.; Fisker, R.G. (eds.)
         Revised Report on the Algorithmic Language Algol 68
         Springer, Berlin usw. 1976.

FL 82   Leblanc, Richard J.; Fischer, Charles N.
         A Case Study of Run-Time Errors in Pascal Programs
         Software - Practice Experience 12,9(1982)825..834.

FOR 78   ANSI - American National Standards Institute
         ANSI X3.9 - 1978. Programming Language FORTRAN

Fra 77   Francez, Nissim
         Another Advantage of Keyword Notation for Parameter
         Communication with Subprograms
         CACM 20,8(1977)604..605.

Hab 73   Habermann, A.N.
         Critical Comments on the Programming Language Pascal
         Acta Informatica 3(1973)47..57.

Ham 80   Hamlet, Richard
         A Further Note on Symmetric Keyword Pairs
         SIGPLAN Notices 15,5(1980)7.

Har 76   Hardgrave, W.T.

Positional versus Keyword Parameter Communication in
Programming Languages
SIGPLAN Notices 11,5(1976)52..58.

HM 80   Hill, I.D.; Meek, B.L.
Programming Language Standardisation
Ellis Horwood Ltd. + Halstead Press, Chichester, New
York etc. 1980.

Hof 80   Hoffmann, H.-J. (Hrsg)
Programmiersprachen und Programmentwicklung
Springer, Berlin usw. 1980.

HS 78b   Hisgen, A.; Saxe, J.B.
Lazy evaluation of the file buffer for interactive I/O
Pascal News #13 (1978)93..94.

Hun 81   Hunt, J.G.
Bracketing Programme Constructs
SIGPLAN Notices 16,4(1981)64..67.

IBM 72   International Business Machines Corp.
IBM System/360 Operating System
PL/1 (F) Language Reference Manual
Order No. GC28-8201-4, 5.ed. Dec. 1972.

IEE 81   IEE - Institute of Electrical Engineers
Fourth International Conference on Software Engineering
for Telecommunication Switching Systems.
IEE, 1981.

ISO 82   ISO - International Organization for Standardization
Programming Languages - PASCAL, ISO/DIS 7185,
1982-08-12.

ITU 81   ITU - International Telecommunication Union
CCITT High Level Language (CHILL) - Recommendation Z.200
Geneva, 1981.

JW 75   Jensen, Kathleen; Wirth, Niklaus
PASCAL. User Manual and Report
Springer, Berlin usw. 1975.

Kay 80   Kaye, Douglas R.
Interactive Pascal Input
SIGPLAN Notices 15,1(1980)66..68.

Ker 81   Kernighan, Brian W.
Why Pascal is Not My Favorite Programming Language
CS-TR No.100, Bell Laboratories, Murray Hill
July 18, 1981.

Kit 77   Kittlitz, Edward N.
Another Proposal for Variable Size Arrays in PASCAL
SIGPLAN Notices 12,1(1977)82..86.

Knu 74a Knuth, Donald E.

Structured Programming with goto Statements
Computing Surveys 6,4(1974)261..301.

Kov 78   Kovats, T.A.
Program Readability, Closing Keywords and Prefix-Style
Intermediate Keywords
SIGPLAN Notices 13,11(1978)30..42.

Mac 75   MacLennan, B.J.
A Note on Dynamic Arrays in PASCAL
SIGPLAN Notices 10,9(1975)39..40.

Mar 79   Marlin, C.D.
A Heap-based Implementation of the Programming Language
Pascal
Software - Practice & Experience 9(1979)101..119.

Mar 81   Marca, David
Some Pascal Style Guidelines
SIGPLAN Notices 16,4(1981)70..80.

Min 80   Miner, Jim
Pascal Standard : Progress Report
Pascal News #19 (Sept 1980)74..84.

Mof 81   Moffat, David V.
Conformant Arrays and Strong Typing
ACM Annual Conference 1981, 161..163.

Mul 84   Muller, Hausi A.
Differences between Modula-2 and Pascal
SIGPLAN Notices 19,10(1984)32..39.

Nau 63   Naur, Peter (ed.)
Revised Report on the Algorithmic Language Algol 60
CACM 6,1(1963)1..17.

Par 78   Parkin, Rodney
On the Use of Keywords for Passing Procedure Parameters
SIGPLAN Notices 13,7(1978)41..42.

Per 81   Perkins, Hal
Lazy I/O is not the answer
SIGPLAN Notices 16,4(1981)81..88.

Pok 76   Pokrovsky, Sergei
Formal Types and Their Application to Dynamic Arrays in
Pascal
SIGPLAN Notices 11,10(1976)36..42.

Pos 79   Posa, John G.
Pascal people unhappy over standard
Electronics (Feb 15, 1979)96.

PS 79a   Pugh, J.; Simpson, D.
Pascal errors - empirical evidence
Computer Bulletin 2,19(1979)26..28.

Rav 79   Ravenel, Bruce W.
          Toward a Pascal Standard
          Computer 12,4(1979)68..82.

Ref 83   Reference Manual for the Ada Programming Language.
          ANSI/MIL-STD 1815A.
          United States Department of Defense, January 1983.

Sal 79   Sale, Arthur
          Scope and Pascal
          SIGPLAN Notices 14,9(1979)61..63.

Sal 80a   Sale, A.H.J.
          Conformant Arrays in Pascal
          Pascal News #17 (March 1980)54..56.

Sie 82   Siemens AG
          Programmiersystem PASCAL. Benutzerhandbuch   Teil   1,
          Sprachbeschreibung.
          Best. Nr. U685-J-Z55-1, January 1982.

Sie 82a   Siemens AG
          Programmiersystem PASCAL. Benutzerhandbuch   Teil   2,
          Bedienungsanleitung
          Best. Nr. U964-J-Z55-1, July 1982.

SS 76   Schmeißer, Gerhard; Schirmeier, Horst
          Praktische Mathematik
          Walter de Gruyter, Berlin usw. 1976.

Ste 76   Steensgaard-Madsen, J.
          More on dynamic arrays in PASCAL
          SIGPLAN Notices 11,5(1976)63..64.

SW 73   Wulf, W.; Shaw, Mary
          Global Variable Considered Harmful
          SIGPLAN Notices 8,2(1973)28..34.

Ten 83   Tennent, R.D.
          An Alternative to Conformant-Array Parameters in Pascal
          SIGPLAN Notices 18,10(1983)38..43.

Tex 79   Texas Instruments Inc.
          Model 990 Computer. TI Pascal User's Manual
          Part. No. 946290-9701 *A, 1 July 1979.

UCS 80   UCSD Pascal - Version II.0. USER'S MANUAL
          SOFTECH, Microsystems, San Diego, California.
          Third printing Feb. 1980.

Wha 83   Wharton, Michael R.
          A Note on Types and Prototypes.
          SIGPLAN Notices 18,12 (1983) 122..126.

Win 76b   Winkler, J.F.H.
          A Program Generation Language
          = [BWW 76: 5..18] (in german).

Wir 71   Wirth, Niklaus
          The Programming Language PASCAL
          Acta Informatica 1(1971)35..63.

Wir 75a   Wirth, Niklaus
          An Assessment of the Programming Language Pascal
          SIGPLAN Notices 10,6(1975)23..30.

Wir 76a   Wirth, N.
          Comment on A Note on Dynamic Arrays in PASCAL
          SIGPLAN Notices 11,1(1976)37..38.

Wir 78   Wirth, Niklaus
          MODULA-2
          Eidgenössische Technische Hochschule Zürich,   Institut
          für Informatik. Bericht Nr. 27, Dezember 1978.

Wir 80   Wirth, Niklaus
          MODULA-2
          Eidgenössische Technische Hochschule Zürich,   Institut
          für Informatik. Bericht Nr. 36, March 1980.

AN INTRODUCTION TO MODULA-2*

ROBERT J. PAUL

*This new language is
a superset of Pascal*

IN THIS ARTICLE we'll take a look at the differences in control structure, expressions, and general syntax between Pascal and Modula-2. First, however, I should mention three fundamental philosophical differences between the two languages.

First, the introduction of the module concept in Modula-2 extends the "separate compilation" features that various Pascal implementations have often added. You can build a library of modules that provide standard routines to perform common operations. You can also use the modules to create hidden data structures and to isolate a program from the specific data structures used.

Second, Modula-2 replaces the Pascal I/O (input/output) routines **read** and **write** with the standard module TTIO, a logical change considering the module concept. This module provides the primitive routines **Read** and **Write**, which function one character at a time. Another module, **InOut**, provides more sophisticated routines, including **ReadInt**, to read an integer in character form; **WriteInt** and **WriteCard**, to write integers and cardinals (unsigned integers) in decimal notation; **WriteOct** and

WriteHex, to write integers or cardinals in octal and hexadecimal notation, respectively; and **WriteString**, to write character strings.

The third major change from Pascal is the addition of concurrency primitives to Modula-2, which lets you write concurrent (multitasking) programs in a standard and portable way. Concurrency can make certain programming tasks easier, and some applications require it. Concurrent variations of many languages (including Pascal) have been developed, but Modula-2 is a standard language in which to write concurrent programs.

COMPARISON TO PASCAL

You can use several criteria to distinguish one programming language from another: program structure, control structure, expressions, and data typing facilities. One language is clearly superior to another, for example, if it ranks higher in all four areas; mixed results, on the other hand, highlight the

....

Robert J. Paul is a senior software engineer with Turning Point Software (11A Main St., Watertown, MA 02172). He has a B.S. in computer science from Rensselaer Polytechnic Institute.

relative strengths and weaknesses of each one.

Of course, these criteria refer to the language definition alone. Its implementation on a specific machine determines the time required to compile and execute a program. In general, competent implementations of either Pascal or Modula-2 should result in almost identical compile and run times.

PROGRAM STRUCTURE AND PROCEDURES

The main routine in a Modula-2 program is called the "main module." It contains all the sections of a Pascal program as well as features that provide for external subroutines (in other modules). Listing 1 shows a schematic of the main module.

The bulk of any Pascal or Modula-2 program is a collection of procedures or subprograms that perform specific functions. Pascal distinguishes between a function, which returns a value, and a procedure, which does not. Modula-2 offers the same facilities, although the distinction between procedures and functions blurs because the keyword PROCEDURE introduces both of them.

(continued)

Listing 1: *A schematic representation of the main module. The programmer provides the names in lowercase; the words in uppercase are Modula-2 keywords.*

```
MODULE modulename;
FROM librarymodule IMPORT libraryroutine1, libraryroutine2;
FROM librarymodule2 IMPORT libraryroutine3;
CONST                                    (* constant declarations go here *)
  charcount = 80 * 24;                          (* sample constant *)
TYPE                                     (* type declarations go here *)
  type1 = (apple, pear, orange);              (* enumeration type *)
  type2 = | 1960 .. 1990 |;                      (* subrange type *)
  returntype = CARDINAL;                       (* unsigned integer *)
VAR                                      (* variable declarations go here *)
  foo: returntype;                              (* declare 1 variable *)

PROCEDURE procedure1(parm1, parm2: type1; VAR parm3: type2);
VAR                                      (* local variables declared here *)
BEGIN                                    (* body of procedure goes here *)
  END procedure1;

PROCEDURE function1(parm1: type1) : returntype;
VAR                                      (* local variables declared here *)
BEGIN                                    (* body of function goes here *)
                              (* to exit with value use the return statement... *)

  RETURN integerexpression;
END function1;
BEGIN                                    (* beginning of main procedure *)
                                         (* body of main program goes here *)
  procedure1(apple,orange,1967);
  foo := function1(pear);
END modulename.
```

Listing 2: *Variable-size array as a procedure parameter of the function Count-Them. This example also illustrates the output routines required to write text strings and cardinals and to terminate an output line.*

```
MODULE sample1;
FROM WriteStrings IMPORT WriteString, WriteLn;
FROM TTIO IMPORT WriteCardinal;
CONST
  smallsize = 20;                               (* small sized array *)
  largesize = 35;                               (* large sized array *)
VAR
  i: CARDINAL;
  smallarray: ARRAY [0 .. smallsize] OF CARDINAL;
  largearray: ARRAY [0 .. largesize] OF CARDINAL;
(*
Procedure: CountThem
Parameters: one variable size array of CARDINALs (unsigned integers)
Returns: CARDINAL, sum of the elements in the array
*)
PROCEDURE CountThem( vector: ARRAY OF CARDINAL ) : CARDINAL;
VAR
  i, sum: CARDINAL;
BEGIN
  sum := 0;                                      (* initialize sum *)
  FOR i := 0 TO HIGH(vector) DO                  (* for all elements *)
    sum := sum + vector[ i ];                    (* add to sum *)
  END;                                           (* end of FOR *)
  RETURN sum;                                    (* and return value *)
END CountThem;
(*
Main Program starts here
Initialize two arrays and call the function CountThem
once with each of the two arrays.
*)
  BEGIN (* main program *)
    FOR i := 0 TO smallsize DO                   (* initialize small array *)
      smallarray[i] := i;
```

(continued)

The syntax of a procedure definition is

```
PROCEDURE
  name (<fp>|;<fp>|)
  |: return-type|;
|CONST (* optional constant
  declarations *)|
|TYPE (* optional type
  declarations *)|
|VAR (* optional variable
  declarations *)|
BEGIN
  statement-sequence
END name;
```

Above, <fp> is shorthand notation for a formal parameter section (an identifier list followed by a colon and a type name).

The two methods of passing parameters in Pascal are the same in Modula-2. "Call by value" means that a copy of the parameter value is sent to the subprogram. This makes it impossible for the subprogram to modify the calling program's copy of the parameter. In the alternative method, "call by reference," the subprogram receives the parameter's address, meaning that changes made to its value by the subprogram also affect its value in the calling program. You can request "call by reference" in Modula-2 by placing the keyword VAR (the same as in Pascal) before the formal parameter section. The default is "call by value."

Modula-2 can also pass variable-size arrays to procedures; Pascal cannot. If you substitute ARRAY OF **typename** for the type name in the formal parameter section, you can pass an array of the specified type to the procedure. The special function HIGH(**arrayname**) returns the upper bound of the array passed (see listing 2).

STATEMENTS AND CONTROL STRUCTURES

The heart of any language is how you control the program-execution flow. Modula-2 provides all the familiar Pascal control structures and a few more to make special programming circumstances easier to handle.

One important change from Pascal is that every control structure in Modula-2 has an explicit termination, usually an END statement. This prevents the ambiguity possible in the following Pascal program sequence:

(continued)

```
    END;                                              (* end of FOR *)
    FOR i := 0 TO largesize DO               (* initialize large array *)
      largearray[i] := i;
    END;                                              (* end of FOR *)
    WriteString('The sum of the numbers 0 to  ');
    WriteCardinal( smallsize, 5 );
    WriteString(' is ');
    WriteCardinal( CountThem(smallarray), 5 );
    WriteLn;
    WriteString('The sum of the numbers 0 to ');
    WriteCardinal( largesize, 5 );
    WriteString(' is ');
    WriteCardinal( CountThem(largearray), 5 );
    WriteLn;
  END sample1.
```

```
IF (oregano IN recipe[1])
  THEN
    IF (thyme IN recipe[1])
      THEN writeln('Use oregano
              and thyme')
  ELSE
      writeln('No oregano');
```

Although the indentation implies that the first message should print if the recipe specifies both oregano and thyme and the second message if it does not specify oregano, this is not how the program executes. In fact, the program matches the ELSE clause with the most recent IF statement, so the second message prints if the recipe does have oregano but does not have thyme.

Modula-2 smooths out this Pascal problem and a few other rough edges. The basic control structure needed to provide conditional execution, the IF-THEN-ELSE statement, is the best example of this improvement.

```
IF expression
  THEN statement sequence
  |ELSIF expression
    THEN statement sequence|
    |ELSE statement sequence|
END
```

You can repeat the ELSIF clause as many times as you wish, providing for a number of mutually exclusive cases. When the program encounters the expression, it can execute only one of the statement sequences; if none of the expressions is true, then the program executes the ELSE clause. You can write the Pascal oregano example in Modula-2 as

```
IF (oregano IN recipe[1])
  THEN
```

```
IF (thyme IN recipe[1])
  THEN
    WriteString('Use oregano
      and thyme')
END
ELSE WriteString('No oregano');
END
```

The placement of the END statements tells the compiler which IF statement goes with the ELSE clause.

The CASE statement provides a way to select between mutually exclusive conditions.

```
CASE expression OF
  label1 [,label2, . . .]
    : statement sequence
  | label3 [,label4. . . .]
    : statement sequence
  |ELSE statement sequence|
END
```

The expression is evaluated and compared to the labels; if the program finds a match, it executes the corresponding statement sequence. If it does not find a match, the program executes the ELSE clause. You can place as many labels as you wish before each statement sequence, and you can specify as many statement sequences as you need. The type of the case expression must be INTEGER, CARDINAL, CHAR, BOOLEAN, or an enumeration or subrange type, and you cannot repeat labels. For example, the following program fragment determines what type of character the variable **ch** contains.

```
CASE ch OF
  '0' . . '9'
    : WriteString("Digit")
| 'a' . . 'z'
    : WriteString("Lowercase
      letter")
```

```
| 'A' . . 'Z'
    : WriteString("Uppercase
      letter")
| '+', '-', '*', '/'
    : WriteString("Operator")
ELSE WriteString("Other
      punctuation or symbols")
END
```

The next basic type of control flow is the loop. Modula-2 provides three loop-control statements like Pascal's and one new statement that provides a more general form of loop control.

The FOR statement sets a control variable to some initial value and then executes a statement sequence, varying the control variable through the progression of values specified in the FOR statement.

```
FOR var := expr1 TO expr2
  | BY expr3 |
  DO statement sequence
END
```

This initializes the simple variable **var** to the value of the expression **expr1**. If the variable is not greater than the second expression, **expr2**, the program executes the statement sequence and increments the variable by the value of the third expression, **expr3**. This process repeats itself until **var** exceeds the limit in **expr2**. If you omit **expr3**, the default increment is one. If the increment is negative, the repetition continues until **var** is less than **expr2**. Thus, Modula-2 offers greater flexibility through the use of **expr3** while Pascal requires the increment to be either 1 or -1.

In Modula-2 as in Pascal, the WHILE and REPEAT statements provide indefinite looping. These statements have the following forms:

```
WHILE expression
  DO statement sequence
END
```

and

```
REPEAT
  statement sequence
UNTIL expression
```

The WHILE statement evaluates **expression**, and, if it is logically true, executes the statement sequence. The program repeats this process until **expression** is logically false. The REPEAT

(continued)

A new looping statement, appropriately called LOOP, provides an infinite iteration.

Listing 3: Examples of the LOOP construct. The first example shows proper use of the LOOP statement; the second, poor use; and the third, the appropriate corrections to the second.

```
(*
The following procedure processes keystrokes until it reads the character 'X'. If it reads the com-
mand 'A', 'B', or 'C', the procedure calls the function function1, function2, or function3, respectively. These
functions return a positive integer return code. This routine also demonstrates the proper use of
the LOOP and CASE constructs. Note that this logic is virtually impossible to duplicate in Pascal
without the use of a GOTO statement.
*)
   PROCEDURE ProcessCommand( VAR cmd: CHAR ) : CARDINAL;
   VAR
     rc: CARDINAL;
   BEGIN
     LOOP
       Read(cmd);                              (* read one character *)
       CASE cmd OF
       'X' : EXIT;                             (* get out of LOOP stmt *)
       'A' : rc := function1();
       'B' : rc := function2();
       'C' : rc := function3();
       ELSE rc := 0;
       END;                                    (* end of CASE *)
       IF (rc # 0) THEN RETURN rc;             (* end of IF *)
       END.                                    (* end of LOOP *)
     END;
(*
If you are here, you must have executed the EXIT statement above
*)
     WriteString('Normal termination');
     RETURN 0;
   END ProcessCommand;
(*
The following procedure illustrates a questionable use of the LOOP construct. It is improper because
the WHILE statement is a more informative way of expressing the logic. This procedure reads an
input file and looks for a match with an already initialized global array, MasterArray. The search
continues until either a match or an end-of-data character, '@', is found. If it finds a match, the
procedure returns the position in the array. If no match is found, it returns a zero.
*)
   PROCEDURE SearchList ( VAR token: CHAR ) : CARDINAL;
   VAR
     index: CARDINAL;
   BEGIN
     LOOP
       Read(token);
       index := 1;
       IF (token = MasterArray[ index ])
         THEN RETURN index;
       END;                                    (* end of IF *)
       index := index + 1;
       IF (index > MaxIndex)
         THEN
           Read(token);
           index := 1;
           IF (token = '@')
             THEN RETURN 0;
           END;                                (* end of nested IF *)
         END;                                  (* end of outer IF *)
       END;                                    (* end of LOOP *)
   END SearchList;
(*
The better procedure to handle this is . . .
*)
   PROCEDURE SearchList( VAR token: CHAR ) : CARDINAL;
   VAR
     index: CARDINAL;
   BEGIN
     index := 1;
     Read(token);
     WHILE (token # '@') DO
```
(continued)

statement, on the other hand, executes the statement sequence first and then evaluates expression. If expression is logically false, the process repeats until it is true. The major difference between the two loops is that a WHILE statement executes its statement sequence *zero* or more times, while the REPEAT statement executes its statement sequence at least *once*. Note that the REPEAT statement does not end with the END clause but rather with the UNTIL clause.

The new looping statement is called, strangely enough, LOOP. The syntax is simply

LOOP statement sequence END

and provides for an infinite loop. There are two statements that can terminate this endless loop, EXIT and RETURN. The EXIT statement can appear only within the statement sequence of a LOOP statement; program execution continues at the first statement after the LOOP statement. The RETURN statement, on the other hand, terminates the current procedure and returns control to the calling procedure. If you use this statement in a function, an expression follows the RETURN statement, indicating the value to return. If RETURN appears in a main procedure, it terminates the program. For both good and bad examples of the LOOP statement, see listing 3.

DATA TYPES

The data types available in Modula-2 are almost identical to those of Pascal. The basic data types BOOLEAN, INTEGER, REAL, and CHAR from Pascal are all available, along with the data type CARDINAL, which represents an unsigned (positive) integer. Enumeration types, which permit the programmer to name the acceptable values for the type, and subrange types are also available. Array types, which create a collection of identical data items, and record types, which create a collection

(continued)

```
        IF (token = MasterArray| index |)
          THEN RETURN index:
        END:                                          (* end of IF *)
        index := index + 1:
        IF (index > MaxIndex)
          THEN
            Read(token):
              index := 1:
        END:                                          (* end of IF *)
      END:                                            (* end of WHILE *)
    RETURN 0:
  END SearchList:
```

Listing 4: *Examples of type and variable declarations and their uses. The three sections give several type definitions, variable declarations using the type definitions, and some program fragments that manipulate the variables.*

```
    MODULE sample2:                                   (* sample module header *)
    TYPE
(*
Declare an enumeration type Color with 5 possible values.
*)
    Color = (yellow, red, green, blue, purple):
(*
Declare a subrange type Index that can take on values between 1 and 80, inclusively.
*)
    Index = | 1 .. 80 |:
(*
Declare an array type CardImage to be an array of 80 characters, identified by indexes of 1 to 80.
*)
    CardImage = ARRAY Index OF CHAR:
(*
Declare a record type Name to be a last name, a first name, and a middle initial.
*)
    NameType = RECORD
      last: ARRAY |1 .. 20| OF CHAR:
      first: ARRAY |1 .. 10| OF CHAR:
      middle: CHAR:
    END:
(*
Declare a record type Person to be a collection of a name, city, state, zipcode, and age. Note that
you must store the zip code as characters, not as integers or cardinals, because a 16-bit computer
only allows integers up to 32767 and cardinals to 65535.
*)
    Person = RECORD
      name: NameType:
      city: ARRAY |1 .. 30| OF CHAR:
      state: ARRAY |1 .. 2| OF CHAR:
      zipcode: ARRAY |1 .. 5| OF CHAR: .
      age: CARDINAL:
    END:
(*
Now, declare some variables using the above types
*)
    VAR
      yes, no: BOOLEAN:                               (* logical true/false *)
      foo, bar: INTEGER:                              (* signed integers *)
      temperature, height: REAL:                      (* floating-point numbers *)
      ch, nextchar: CHAR:                             (* single characters *)
      distance, age: CARDINAL:                        (* unsigned integers *)
      myrose, herdaisy: Color:                        (* can be any of 5 colors *)
      i, j, k: Index:                                 (* indexes into a CardImage *)
      card1, card2: CardImage:                        (* arrays of 1 .. 80 chars *)
      me, you: NameType:                              (* records for names *)
      somebodyelse: Person:                           (* record for name and addr *)
(*
This declaration creates an array with room for 50 people
*)
```

(continued)

```
        friends: ARRAY [0 .. 49] OF Person;
    BEGIN                                      (* begin main program of module sample2 *)
        yes := TRUE;                                      (* set yes to logical TRUE *)
        no := (NOT yes);                               (* set no to the opposite of yes *)
        foo := -32768;                           (* signed integers have range -32768 *)
        bar := 32767;                                    (*to 32767 on a 16-bit machine *)
        temperature := 96.8;                         (* floating point numbers have *)
        height := 6.125;                         (* several decimal places of precision *)
        Read(ch);                                      (* read a single character *)
        IF (ch = 'Y')                                       (* do a comparison *)
            THEN nextchar := 'N';                        (* and some assignments *)
            ELSE nextchar := 'Y';
        END;
        distance := 65535;                        (* unsigned integers have range 0 *)
        age := 0;                                     (*to 65535 on a 16-bit machine *)
        myrose := red;                                (* the color names are constants *)
        herdaisy := purple;
        IF (myrose = herdaisy)
            THEN WriteString('We Match!');
        END;
        FOR i := 1 TO 80 DO                               (* can't exceed this range *)
            j := 81 - i;
            card1[ i ] := card2[ j ];
        END;
        me.last := 'Paul';                            (* note that string assignments *)
        me.first := 'Robert';                           (* pad with nulls if necessary *)
        me.middle := 'J';
        somebodyelse.name := me;                     (* record assignments allowable *)
        somebodyelse.city := 'Watertown';
        somebodyelse.state := 'MA';
        somebodyelse.zipcode := '02172';
        somebodyelse.age := 23;
    (*
    Because Modula-2 allows record assignments, you can copy the entire structure above into another
    structure using one statement. In this case, it would appear that I am my own best friend.
    *)
        friends[ 0 ] := somebodyelse;
    END sample2.                                 (* don't forget to end the module definition *)
```

of nonidentical data items, also follow the Pascal precedent (see listing 4).

Modula-2 inherits another data type, sets, from Pascal in a restricted form. The set type reflects the mathematical concept of a set: a collection of items that is not ordered—either an element is a set member or it's not. Pascal permits sets with many elements (the exact number depends on the implementation); Modula-2 restricts the set size to the number of bits in a word, the basic unit of storage. On most microcomputers and minicomputers, the word size is 16 bits, so sets can have only 16 elements on these systems. Listing 5 shows the declaration and use of a set type.

Modula-2 pointers provide a means of dynamically allocating storage. They are identical to the pointers available in Pascal. The compiler translates the standard Modula-2 procedures NEW and DISPOSE into calls to routines called ALLOCATE and DEALLOCATE—an interesting feature. You must either import these procedures from the standard library module *Storage* providing the standard functionality, or provide your own version. Thus, you can tailor storage allocation and deallocation routines to your particular application, if that is appropriate. Listing 6 illustrates the declaration and use of pointers in Modula-2.

One new data type added to Modula-2, the procedure type, is used to declare a formal parameter as a procedure. This allows you to pass the name of a function or procedure as a parameter to another procedure. (Note that you cannot declare the passed procedure local to any other procedures and that it cannot be a standard procedure.) Listing 7 illustrates the declaration and use of this facility.

EXPRESSIONS

Expressions in Modula-2 are virtually identical to those in Pascal. Operands, the items you manipulate, can be sim-

(continued)

Listing 5: *This example of set type and variable declarations uses sets to represent a collection of spices in recipes. It's a reasonable use of sets, because you don't care about the order of the spices, and you wouldn't list the same spice twice for one recipe.*

```
    MODULE sample3;
    TYPE
(*
Declare an enumeration type that represents the spices that can go into a recipe
*)
        Spices = (basil, ginger, oregano, paprika, parsley, thyme);
(*
Declare a data type to indicate that none, some, or all of the individual spices have been selected
*)
        SetOfSpices = SET OF Spices;
    VAR                                              (* Declare an array of recipes *)
        recipes: ARRAY [1 . . 20] OF SetOfSpices;
    BEGIN                                                    (* main program *)
(*
Mark the first recipe as using oregano and thyme, but no other spices
*)
        recipes[1] := { oregano, thyme };
(*
Mark the second recipe as using no spices; the third recipe as using ginger, parsley, and thyme;
and the fourth recipe as using those spices used in recipes 1, 2, and 3 (that is, ginger, oregano,
parsley, and thyme). Note that you can't list thyme twice, as the set merely records whether the
item appears in the list or not.
*)
        recipes[2] := {};
        recipes[3] := { ginger, parsley, thyme };
        recipes[4] := recipes[1] + recipes[2] + recipes[3];
    END sample3.
```

Listing 6: *An example of pointer types and usage. Pointers are one of the most difficult features of Modula-2 (and Pascal, for that matter) to use properly. This example reads characters from the input file until a control character (value less than ASCII space) is found. If a space is read, the list assembled so far is printed; otherwise, the character is added to the list. The list is singly linked, with each entry pointing to the next one using the "next" field of the record. The list is stored in ascending alphabetical order, so you must search the list to look for an appropriate place to insert.*

```
    MODULE sample4;
(*
Note: the usage of the standard procedures NEW and DISPOSE requires, in turn, the definition
of procedures ALLOCATE and DEALLOCATE. Usually, these are the standard routines.
*)
    FROM Storage IMPORT ALLOCATE, DEALLOCATE;
    FROM TTIO IMPORT Read, Write, WriteLn;
    TYPE
        link = POINTER TO element;                   (* declaration of pointer type *)
        element = RECORD                             (* type that we're pointing to *)
          symbol: CHAR;                                    (* data in element *)
          next: link;                                 (* pointer to next element *)
          END;
    VAR
        list: link;                                  (* the list is merely a pointer *)
(*
Procedure: Insert
Parameters: sym, CHAR, element to insert
Purpose: inserts the element sym into the linked list
Local variables:
    p = pointer to new element created for sym
    ptr = pointer into list, points to element just AFTER the element to be inserted
    last = pointer into list, points to element just BEFORE the element to be inserted
*)
```

(continued)

```
PROCEDURE Insert(sym: CHAR);
VAR
  p, ptr, last: link;                                           (* local pointers *)
BEGIN
  NEW(p);                                                (* create a new element *)
  p^.symbol := sym;                                          (* and initialize it *)
  ptr := list;                                        (* make copy of pointer to list *)
  last := NIL;                                  (* pointer to element pointing to ptr *)
  WHILE (ptr # NIL) AND (ptr^.symbol < sym) DO
    last := ptr;                                            (* track parent of ptr *)
    ptr := ptr^.next;                                    (* and get next element *)
  END;                                                        (* end of WHILE *)
  IF (last = NIL)
    THEN                                                  (* insert at top of list *)
      p^.next := ptr;                                      (* point to rest of list *)
      list := p;                                         (* make new first element *)
    ELSE                                                (* insert in middle of list *)
      last^.next := p;                                 (* point to p instead of ptr *)
      p^.next := ptr;                                 (* new element points to rest *)
  END;                                                            (* end of IF *)
END Insert;
(*

Procedure: PrintList
Parameters: t, link, list to print
Purpose: write the characters in the list to the terminal
*)
PROCEDURE PrintList(t: link);
BEGIN
  WHILE (t # NIL) DO                                            (* for entire list *)
    Write(t^.sym);                                             (* print characters *)
    t := t^.next;                                             (* go to next entry *)
  END;                                                        (* end of WHILE *)
  WriteLn;                                                   (* go to next line *)
END PrintList;
BEGIN                                                          (* main program *)
  list := NIL;                                          (* initialize to empty list *)
  LOOP
    Read(ch);                                          (* get character command *)
    IF (ch > ' ')
      THEN Insert(ch);                                      (* insert the character *)
    ELSIF (ch = ' ')
      THEN PrintList(list);                                      (* print the list *)
    ELSE
      EXIT;                                                  (* exit the program *)
    END;                                                         (* end of IF *)
  END;                                                        (* end of LOOP *)
END sample4
```

```
Listing 7: Example of the PROCEDURE data type. This facility lets you construct
general-purpose routines that require an (otherwise unspecified) auxiliary function to
perform some calculation. For example, many FORTRAN libraries provide plotting,
graphing, or statistical functions that require a user-specified function to work.


MODULE sample5;
(*
This module sets up a statistical function, Average, which computes the average value of a function fx.
*)
TYPE
  fcn = PROCEDURE ( REAL ) : REAL;
VAR
  avg1, avg2: REAL;
PROCEDURE Average( fx: fcn; low, high, step: REAL) : REAL;
VAR
  sum: REAL;
BEGIN
  sum := 0;
```

(continued)

```
        WHILE ( low < high ) DO                                      (* until entire range done *)
          sum := sum + fx(low);                                      (* find value and sum *)
          low := low + step;                                         (* bump index *)
        END;
        RETURN (sum / (high - low));                                 (* return average value *)
      END Average;
      (*                              Sample function : f(x) = x                    *)
      PROCEDURE Linear(x: REAL) : REAL;
      BEGIN
        RETURN x;
      END Linear;
      (*                              Sample function : f(x) = x*x                  *)
      PROCEDURE Quadratic(x: REAL) : REAL;
      BEGIN
        RETURN x*x;
      END Quadratic;
      (*                              Begin main procedure                          *)
      BEGIN
        avg1 := Average(Linear,     - 1.0, 1.0, 0.01);
        avg2 := Average(Quadratic, - 1.0, 1.0, 0.01);
      END sample5.
```

ple variables (foo, count), array references (recipe[4] refers to the fourth element of array recipe; priceindex [april, 1967] refers to the 1967th element of the aprilth array of priceindex), record field references (bob.name.middle refers to the middle field of record name, in the name field of record bob), and pointer dereferences (ptr^ refers to the item referenced by pointer ptr).

The standard operators from Pascal are also available in Modula-2. Arithmetic operators that work on both signed integers (INTEGER) and unsigned integers (CARDINAL) are addition (+), subtraction (−), multiplication (*), integer division (DIV), and modulus (MOD). Integer division (x DIV y) produces the integer part of the result of real division (x / y); the modulus function produces the remainder after an in-

teger division. Real arithmetic includes addition (+), subtraction (−), multiplication (*), and real division (/).

Set operators include set union (+), yielding all elements that appear in either set; set difference (−), yielding all elements in the first set and not in the second set; set intersection (*), yielding those elements appearing in both sets; and symmetric set difference (/), yielding all elements in one set and not in the other (that is, a/b is equivalent to $(a-b)+(b-a)$ if a and b are sets).

Relational operators produce Boolean (TRUE or FALSE) results, and you can use them to compare the basic types—INTEGER, CARDINAL, REAL, and CHAR—as well as enumeration and subrange types. These operators include equal to (=), not equal to (#), less than (<), less than or equal to (≤),

greater than (>), and greater than or equal to (≥). You can use the relational operators set membership (IN) and improper set inclusion (≤ and ≥) to operate on sets. However, you can compare only pointer variables with the equality and inequality operators.

CONCLUSION

Modula-2 clearly surpasses Pascal in terms of its program-structuring facilities. It contains all the procedures and functions of Pascal and adds a standard way to separately compile portions of a program.

The control structures of the two languages are very close. Modula-2 has the edge over Pascal with the new LOOP statement and the consistent use of the END clause to terminate control statements.

Data typing in the two languages is also very close, but this time Pascal has a slight edge—Modula-2's restriction of sets to 16 elements (on a 16-bit computer) is unnecessary and too often inconvenient.

Both Modula-2 and Pascal provide powerful and flexible expressions, and neither language has an advantage over the other in this respect.

In many ways, Modula-2 is really a superset of Pascal. It takes the good points of the language and strengthens them with some logical and important extensions. When high-quality compilers become available on many machines, Modula-2 may replace Pascal as a language of choice. You can use Modula-2 everywhere you can use Pascal, and in many places where you can't. ∎

AMBIGUITIES AND INSECURITIES IN MODULA-2*

DAVID SPECTOR

Introduction

Modula-2 is a recent programming language designed by combining some of the best features of Pascal, Modula, and Mesa. It is explicitly meant to be a systems programming language.

This paper briefly reviews the advantages offered by Modula-2 for systems programming and other applications, then presents a critique of [Wirt80], the Modula-2 language manual, with the most important issues flagged as such. A number of problem areas have been omitted due to lack of space.

Detailed familiarity with the Modula-2 language is assumed in the critique sections; no tutorial material is included.

Advantages

While it is not yet clear whether Ada [Ichb80], BLISS [Wulf71], Mary/2 [Rain81], Modula-2 [Wirt80], Mesa [Mitc78], C [Kern78], CLU [Lisk79], Edison [BHan81], Concurrent Euclid [Cord81], Icon [Gris80], Newton [Rapi81], PLAIN [Wass81], PLUS [Stod80], Praxis [Gree80], Smalltalk [Xero81], SQURL [Jone81], Y [Han81a], or some other language is "best" for systems programming, each language represents an advance towards the goal of supporting an understandable and efficient organization of the many details and relationships inherent in systems programming. Unfortunately, no one language has yet achieved the delicate balance between simplicity and power that would distinguish it as ideal, but it appears that Modula-2 comes quite close. Modula-2 represents a step forward in language design, both because it incorporates existing features instead of inventing its own, and because of its evident concern for simplicity.

Modula-2 offers the following valuable language features:

o **Simplicity**. Few primitive datatypes are defined, few control constructs are supported (there is no "go to" [Dijk68]), and input-output operations are not provided as part of the language (they can be provided via extensions written in Modula-2). This simplicity allows for easier standardization and better portability than can be achieved with most other languages.

The author is with Prime Computer, Inc., 500 Old Connecticut Path, Framingham, Massachusetts 01701.

*Reprinted from ACM *SIGPLAN Notices*, 17, 8, 1982. Copyright © D. Spector.

o   <u>Modules</u>. A module is a named collection of variables and
procedures, similar to an Ada <u>package</u>. It controls the
interfacing and encapsulation of the conceptual parts
making up large software systems [Lisk77] [Robs81].
Modules provide a more flexible solution to the problem of
partitioning the name space of a large program than does
the more familiar hierarchical nesting of procedures
[Clar80] [Han81b]. They are so valuable they are even
being force-fitted onto existing languages [Chin80]
[Stro82].

o   <u>Separate Compilation</u>. Modules may be compiled separately,
providing good management for large programs, and
<u>definition modules</u> allow for specifying interfaces without
giving implementation details [Parn72].

o   <u>Flexible Datatypes</u>. Strong datatypes are enforced, but
this can be relaxed when necessary in systems programming
to just declaring a parameter to be a word, an address, or
an array of words.

o   <u>Machine Access</u>. Access to specific memory addresses and
other characteristics of the underlying machine is
supported.

o   <u>Tasking</u>. Flexible and efficient tasking is provided by
coroutine management routines.

<u>Language Problem Areas</u>

This section begins the critique by listing specific problems found in
the Modula-2 language itself.

1.   (<u>Important</u>) Only one precision (N bits, where N is usually 16) is
supported for INTEGER and CARDINAL arithmetic, and machine
addresses are assumed to be of this same size and in this same
format.   These assumptions are incorrect for many machines,
although they do work well for the PDP-11 and Lilith computers
targeted by Prof. Wirth's group at ETH.

2.   (<u>Important</u>) Bit strings, signed and unsigned integers, and
enumerations cannot be referenced in or assigned to fields within a
machine word.   Records and portions of records cannot be specified
as "packed" or "unaligned". These are serious deficiencies for
systems programming.

3.   There is no way to include both apostrophes and quotes in a
character string literal.   This is an unfortunate limitation in a
systems programming language, since some systems applications need
strings containing large subsets of the underlying character set.

4.   There appears to be no way to specify a character string literal
containing one character, since a lexeme such as "M" is interpreted

as being of type CHAR. Note also that CHAR is not type-compatible with ARRAY OF CHAR (a character string).

5. It is not clear whether a function may return a record or an array (including a character string).

6. Comments require four bracket characters, "(**)". In addition, many programmers will add a two more (spaces) to improve the visibility of comments. Compare with Ada's visually clear "--" and with the use of single characters in many languages.

7. The unary operators + and - are restricted to occurring at most once adjacently. This unnecessarily contradicts their intuitive semantics and is inconsistent with the behavior of NOT.

8. The use of string variables is not well defined and is clearly a weak area of the language. Only two definitions are given: that a string is the same as an array, and that assignment of a shorter string to a longer causes padding by NULs. Note that padding by NULs is supported by far fewer machines than padding by spaces, and that both are inefficient on many machines compared to no padding at all. Nothing is said about the case of assigning a longer string to a shorter. Worst of all, there is no support for either variable-length or varying (in the sense of PL/I) strings.

9. WITH is a block rather than an attribute of a block, causing unnecessary ENDs and complicating program editing.

10. EXIT statements are limited to transferring control past the end of the innermost enclosing loop. This unnecessarily complicates some algorithms and is not consistent with the fact that a RETURN statement can be used to exit any number of nested loops when they happen to be enclosed by a procedure declaration. Compare with Ada, where loop labels make exits clear.

11. No opposite of the ODD function is defined. This is probably an example of an unnecessary simplification, since EVEN is clearer than NOT ODD.

12. The number of bits per word and other essential implementation constants are not provided as predefined variables or functions or defined in a standard "implementation" module.

13. When exporting a variable, it is not possible to make it read-only. This significantly limits the usefulness of exporting variables as opposed to procedures.

14. Module priority is unnecessarily limited to being a constant expression rather than a variable expression. It also applies to an entire module rather than to a small region of code, or to a procedure; this limitation makes the LISTEN procedure ([Wirt80], p. 29) necessary.

Language Manual Problem Areas

This section lists specific problems found in the Modula-2 language manual [Wirt80].

1. It is unclear whether the expression "+x" is legal for all types; clearly, "-x" is not.

2. The DIV and MOD operators are not well defined for negative arguments; see Ada for appropriate definitions.

3. The final value of FOR control variables is not specified, nor is the execution behavior when the BY expression is negative. Compare with FORTRAN X3.9-1978, page 11-7. Also, the behavior when FOR control variables are of type REAL is not discussed.

4. The execution of a failing CASE statement having no ELSE part is undefined (it causes a run-time error).

5. The situation where multiple WITH blocks create a conflict in two or more field names is not discussed.

6. Direct recursion is mentioned as being signalled by a reference or an invocation of a procedure from inside itself, but indirect recursion is not discussed (it is also allowed).

7. The behavior of CAP when applied to entities other than alphabetic letters is undefined. Also, no corresponding lower-case function is provided (this would be used far less often but might be nice for symmetry).

8. The behavior of INC and DEC at enumeration and character extremes is not discussed.

9. The concept of process workspace is required but never defined. It is particularly puzzling why its size must be specified by the programmer rather than by the compiler and/or operating system. Assuming that the process workspace is the size of its stack, The compiler and/or operating system could assign the process stack size as the sum of the contained procedure stack sizes, if the procedures are nonrecursive (and other constraints are met, such as nonuse of procedure variables), and it could allocate stack frames from a heap otherwise. Specifying a fixed maximum stack size risks producing unreliable software (what will happen when a recursive procedure needs more stack space than was provided?) in the pursuit of efficiency.

10. The definitions of OR and AND do not clearly state that they have "short-circuit" evaluation semantics (they do).

Personal Opinions

This section lists specific debatable criticisms of the Modula-2 language as personal opinions of the author.

1. The comment brackets (* and *) must be paired, as in Pascal [Jens79]. This gives rise to the common problem of missing right comment brackets; note that Ada avoids this problem, but at the expense of disallowing small comments embedded in a line. Very few languages seem to adopt the simple solution of having comments start from a comment character and extend to the next comment character or end of line, whichever comes first.

2. Identifiers may not contain underscores (or, indeed, any non-alphanumeric characters). This forces reliance on capital letters to make multi-word identifiers readable. The trend of thinking today seems to be that underscores improve readability; that "select_next_item" is more readable than "SelectNextItem".

3. Character strings are zero-indexed, conflicting with the de facto world standards for column numbering and substring specification.

4. Keywords must be capitalized, and case is significant in user identifiers. These limitations appear to offer little reward in return for the bother they cause.

5. There is no syntax to express a record or array literal, except in the case of character strings.

6. Since there is no ambiguity among variable reference, array reference, and function call, programmers must know exactly how an entity has been declared, even when it has been imported from another module. Compare with CLU, where references can look like procedure calls even when they are implemented as variable references, and Ada, where some amount of ambiguity has been provided among these forms.

7. A reference to a record field through a pointer requires something like "p^.f" instead of the shorter and clearer "p.f". This relates also to the previous point. Compare with Ada access types.

8. Proper set inclusion ("<" and ">") is not supported directly, although the corresponding improper operations are supported. Is efficiency more important than clarity?

9. Most structured constructions end with "END" rather than with a keyword appropriate to the construction being ended. This will be particularly hard to read in those places where many constructions are being terminated together. Compare "END; END;" with "ENDIF; ENDFOR;" (or "END IF; END FOR;").

10. EXIT statements are limited to occurring inside LOOP statements rather than inside any of the repetitive statements. If this limitation is felt to be good, it deserves some explicit

justification. Note that RETURN statements are permitted in such contexts.

11. The use of VAR to distinguish variable formal arguments (call-by-reference) from value formal arguments (call-by-value) is clear but may be quite error prone, since this distinction is sometimes made for efficiency reasons and sometimes for algorithmic ones, and since changes in the calling sites (particularly in using expressions where variables were used before) must be accompanied by changes in the called procedures. Note that the more appropriate designation is read/write or read-only (compare with Ada and Mary/2).

12. It is not possible to specify 'import all of module x' or (more importantly) 'export all entities'. Again, if this felt to be good it deserves some explicit justification.

13. Certain predefined operators and procedures are generic (overloaded), but users cannot define their own generic procedures. Note that the module containing the predefined functions, SYSTEM, is actually called a "pseudo-module" for this reason! This inconsistency does not appear to be in keeping with the Modula-2 philosophy of extensibility and completeness.

14. The rationale for putting implementation-dependent constructs such as WORD in the predefined module SYSTEM is so that implementation-dependent modules will be marked "FROM SYSTEM"; this is inconsistent with including NEWPROCESS and TRANSFER in SYSTEM, as these ought to be implementation-independent.

15. IOTRANSFER is unnecessarily oriented towards the PDP-11; a more general mechanism would have been better.

16. No _exception_ or other non-local transfer mechanism is defined. Lack of such a mechanism can sometimes force extra arguments and conditional _return_s throughout a large set of subroutines. Compare with CLU and Ada.

17. The semicolon is used as a statement separator rather than as a statement terminator, repeating the mistake made by Pascal. [Kern81], page 10, has an explanation of how programs are harder to edit using separator syntax. In addition, the need for empty statements and for the nonfunctional DO keyword arises largely because of this unfortunate choice.

18. The character "|" acts as a separator rather than as a terminator, making programs harder to edit.

19. The predefined name FLOAT is inconsistent with the name REAL. There is also some general confusion over type conversion versus renaming.

20. There is a predefined function HIGH but no predefined function LOW.

21. Opaque (<u>obscure</u> as opposed to <u>transparent</u>) export is not available for all user-defined types. This would appear to be a strong limitation on data abstraction, as opaque user-defined types are thus limited to being pointers (leading to allocation/deallocation inefficiency) or other single-word (sic) entities.

22. QUALIFIED is error-prone because the conflicts it intends to resolve are created outside of the module in which it is specified. It is not clear that using QUALIFIED is any improvement over simply requiring module qualification for ambiguous names, as is done in Ada.

23. Procedure and function arguments are passed by position only, rather than by keyword or other such syntax (compare with Ada and Mary/2). Note that a case can also be made for avoiding such syntax, due to the complexity involved.

24. The results of division by zero, arithmetic overflow, and other erroneous operations are not discussed. Modula-2 ignores many such important run-time issues.

SECTION 3

APPLICATIVE LANGUAGES

CAN PROGRAMMING BE LIBERATED FROM THE
VON NEUMANN STYLE? A FUNCTIONAL STYLE
AND ITS ALGEBRA OF PROGRAMS
BY J. BACKUS

RECURSIVE FUNCTIONS OF SYMBOLIC
EXPRESSIONS BY J. MCCARTHY

LISP 1.5 PROGRAMMER'S MANUAL BY
J. MCCARTHY, PAUL W. ABRAHAMS,
DANIEL J. EDWARDS, TIMOTHY P. HART,
AND M. LEVIN

THE DESIGN OF APL BY A. D. FALKOFF
AND K. E. IVERSON

INTRODUCTION

APPLICATIVE LANGUAGES

What are applicative languages? The domination of FORTRAN, COBOL, and even Pascal on the computing community have made applicative programming languages an esoteric subject. They are something that is studied in advanced courses of computer science or encountered in the form of the language called LISP. Is the applicative language doomed to remain in this subjugated position? I do not know, but I do know that it is an idea, or rather a model of computation which has merit and therefore it should be studied. But if this were the only reason, then perhaps one paper would be enough. There are other reasons.

The best statement about the weaknesses of existing languages and about the strengths of applicative languages is given in the paper by John Backus, the first in this chapter. It is only right and proper that Backus is making these criticisms, having been a principal developer of both FORTRAN and ALGOL60. In his paper he cogently and eloquently describes the weaknesses of today's languages. They are *both fat and weak in a global sense*. For those people who have gone from FORTRAN to PL/1 to Pascal and now to Ada this thought must seem peculiar if not outright heresy. So read Backus' article and see if you agree or at least if you understand his point of view. If you read through Section 10 of Backus' paper and you are still open minded, the remaining sections will present his attempt to define a programming language which is semantically clean, simple, and yet fully powerful. Then in Section 12, he shows how one can derive theorems about program forms, such that proofs of correctness of programs can be accomplished in a manner similar to the way we prove things in group theory.

The second paper in this chapter is a classic in the programming language field, essentially on a par with the ALGOL60 report. *"Recursive functions of Symbolic Expressions and Their Computation by Machine, Part One"* by John McCarthy is the paper in which the seminal ideas underlying the language LISP were presented. Part II has yet to appear. LISP is a language which has been highly favored by researchers in artificial intelligence since its introduction. Despite the fact that it has not had the backing of a major computer manufacturer, it has continued to survive these past twenty-five or so years. The people who

favor it are a community of scholars who make high demands on their computing equipment because they build large prototype systems. With the growth of interest in artificial intelligence, the LISP community is increasing rapidly.

This section has two papers on LISP. The first one presents the theoretical basis of the language coupled with many examples and elaborations on the formalism. The second paper is an excerpt from the LISP 1.5 Programmer's Manual. This original manual by McCarthy and Levin embodies a clear and concise description of (pure)-LISP and may still be the best introduction to the language.

One of the most impressive facts about LISP is that its semantics are sufficiently simple that it permits a mathematical model which is relatively tractable. McCarthy used this model as a starting point to develop a theory of computation. He considered many important theoretical issues including proofs of program correctness, proofs of compiler correctness, and proofs of program equivalence long before these topics became fashionable. Another important consequence of the simple semantics is the definition of LISP by an interpreter. This interpreter can be found reprinted here in the LISP 1.5 Manual. The interpreter was an early demonstration of the technique of defining a programming language by an interpreter written in the same language. This became the start of the field of operational semantics. In addition to all of the theoretical benefits of LISP, the language has many practical aspects as well. The reliance on the notion of function without side-effects greatly aids modularity. The technique of garbage collection is an important step in freeing the programmer of the responsibility of storage management. This in turn leads to more reliable programs. As prototyping continues to be an important element of large-scale software development, the LISP language and its derivatives continue to offer important advantages not found in the ALGOL-like variety of programming language.

Another important applicative language is APL. A creation of Iverson, the language was used primarily to describe algorithms until its first implementation appeared about ten years after its initial development. There are many good primers describing how to use APL. Thus I have included here a paper which concentrates on the design of the language. But before one can appreciate this paper, one needs to have some experience with the language. APL has a devoted body of followers, most of whom are in industry and are using APL to write complicated applications. As with LISP, APL eschews the notion of strong typing and static scoping. It is an interpreted rather than a compiled language. These features appear to make it a better language to use for many applications than the compiled, statically scoped languages. The reader should be aware of these issues in this section.

CAN PROGRAMMING BE LIBERATED FROM THE VON NEUMANN STYLE? A FUNCTIONAL STYLE AND ITS ALGEBRA OF PROGRAMS*

J. BACKUS

Author's address: 91 Saint Germain Ave., San Francisco, CA 94114.

*Reprinted from *Comm ACM* 21, 8, August 1978, 613–641, copyright 1978.

grams, and no conventional language even begins to meet that need. In fact, conventional languages create unnecessary confusion in the way we think about programs.

For twenty years programming languages have been steadily progressing toward their present condition of obesity; as a result, the study and invention of programming languages has lost much of its excitement. Instead, it is now the province of those who prefer to work with thick compendia of details rather than wrestle with new ideas. Discussions about programming languages often resemble medieval debates about the number of angels that can dance on the head of a pin instead of exciting contests between fundamentally differing concepts.

Many creative computer scientists have retreated from inventing languages to inventing tools for describing them. Unfortunately, they have been largely content to apply their elegant new tools to studying the warts and moles of existing languages. After examining the appalling type structure of conventional languages, using the elegant tools developed by Dana Scott, it is surprising that so many of us remain passively content with that structure instead of energetically searching for new ones.

The purpose of this article is twofold; first, to suggest that basic defects in the framework of conventional languages make their expressive weakness and their cancerous growth inevitable, and second, to suggest some alternate avenues of exploration toward the design of new kinds of languages.

Introduction

I deeply appreciate the honor of the ACM invitation to give the 1977 Turing Lecture and to publish this account of it with the details promised in the lecture. Readers wishing to see a summary of this paper should turn to Section 16, the last section.

1. Conventional Programming Languages: Fat and Flabby

Programming languages appear to be in trouble. Each successive language incorporates, with a little cleaning up, all the features of its predecessors plus a few more. Some languages have manuals exceeding 500 pages; others cram a complex description into shorter manuals by using dense formalisms. The Department of Defense has current plans for a committee-designed language standard that could require a manual as long as 1,000 pages. Each new language claims new and fashionable features, such as strong typing or structured control statements, but the plain fact is that few languages make programming sufficiently cheaper or more reliable to justify the cost of producing and learning to use them.

Since large increases in size bring only small increases in power, smaller, more elegant languages such as Pascal continue to be popular. But there is a desperate need for a powerful methodology to help us think about pro-

2. Models of Computing Systems

Underlying every programming language is a model of a computing system that its programs control. Some models are pure abstractions, some are represented by hardware, and others by compiling or interpretive programs. Before we examine conventional languages more closely, it is useful to make a brief survey of existing models as an introduction to the current universe of alternatives. Existing models may be crudely classified by the criteria outlined below.

2.1 Criteria for Models
2.1.1 Foundations. Is there an elegant and concise mathematical description of the model? Is it useful in proving helpful facts about the behavior of the model? Or is the model so complex that its description is bulky and of little mathematical use?

2.1.2 History sensitivity. Does the model include a notion of storage, so that one program can save information that can affect the behavior of a later program? That is, is the model history sensitive?

2.1.3 Type of semantics. Does a program successively transform states (which are not programs) until a terminal state is reached (state-transition semantics)? Are states simple or complex? Or can a "program" be successively reduced to simpler "programs" to yield a final "normal form program," which is the result (reduction semantics)?

2.1.4 Clarity and conceptual usefulness of programs. Are programs of the model clear expressions of a process or computation? Do they embody concepts that help us to formulate and reason about processes?

2.2 Classification of Models

Using the above criteria we can crudely characterize three classes of models for computing systems—simple operational models, applicative models, and von Neumann models.

2.2.1 Simple operational models. Examples: Turing machines, various automata. *Foundations*: concise and useful. *History sensitivity*: have storage, are history sensitive. *Semantics*: state transition with very simple states. *Program clarity*: programs unclear and conceptually not helpful.

2.2.2 Applicative models. Examples: Church's lambda calculus [5], Curry's system of combinators [6], pure Lisp [17], functional programming systems described in this paper. *Foundations*: concise and useful. *History sensitivity*: no storage, not history sensitive. *Semantics*: reduction semantics, no states. *Program clarity*: programs can be clear and conceptually useful.

2.2.3 Von Neumann models. Examples: von Neumann computers, conventional programming languages. *Foundations*: complex, bulky, not useful. *History sensitivity*: have storage, are history sensitive. *Semantics*: state transition with complex states. *Program clarity*: programs can be moderately clear, are not very useful conceptually.

The above classification is admittedly crude and debatable. Some recent models may not fit easily into any of these categories. For example, the data-flow languages developed by Arvind and Gostelow [1], Dennis [7], Kosinski [13], and others partly fit the class of simple operational models, but their programs are clearer than those of earlier models in the class and it is perhaps possible to argue that some have reduction semantics. In any event, this classification will serve as a crude map of the territory to be discussed. We shall be concerned only with applicative and von Neumann models.

3. Von Neumann Computers

In order to understand the problems of conventional programming languages, we must first examine their intellectual parent, the von Neumann computer. What is a von Neumann computer? When von Neumann and others conceived it over thirty years ago, it was an elegant, practical, and unifying idea that simplified a number of engineering and programming problems that existed then. Although the conditions that produced its architecture have changed radically, we nevertheless still identify the notion of "computer" with this thirty year old concept.

In its simplest form a von Neumann computer has three parts: a central processing unit (or CPU), a store, and a connecting tube that can transmit a single word between the CPU and the store (and send an address to the store). I propose to call this tube the *von Neumann bottleneck*. The task of a program is to change the contents of the store in some major way; when one considers that this task must be accomplished entirely by pumping single words back and forth through the von Neumann bottleneck, the reason for its name becomes clear.

Ironically, a large part of the traffic in the bottleneck is not useful data but merely names of data, as well as operations and data used only to compute such names. Before a word can be sent through the tube its address must be in the CPU; hence it must either be sent through the tube from the store or be generated by some CPU operation. If the address is sent from the store, then *its* address must either have been sent from the store or generated in the CPU, and so on. If, on the other hand, the address is generated in the CPU, it must be generated either by a fixed rule (e.g., "add 1 to the program counter") or by an instruction that was sent through the tube, in which case *its* address must have been sent . . . and so on.

Surely there must be a less primitive way of making big changes in the store than by pushing vast numbers of words back and forth through the von Neumann bottleneck. Not only is this tube a literal bottleneck for the data traffic of a problem, but, more importantly, it is an intellectual bottleneck that has kept us tied to word-at-a-time thinking instead of encouraging us to think in terms of the larger conceptual units of the task at hand. Thus programming is basically planning and detailing the enormous traffic of words through the von Neumann bottleneck, and much of that traffic concerns not significant data itself but where to find it.

4. Von Neumann Languages

Conventional programming languages are basically high level, complex versions of the von Neumann computer. Our thirty year old belief that there is only one kind of computer is the basis of our belief that there is only one kind of programming language, the conventional—von Neumann—language. The differences between Fortran and Algol 68, although considerable, are less significant than the fact that both are based on the programming style of the von Neumann computer. Although I refer to conventional languages as "von Neumann languages" to take note of their origin and style, I do not, of course, blame the great mathematician for their complexity. In fact, some might say that I bear some responsibility for that problem.

Von Neumann programming languages use variables to imitate the computer's storage cells; control statements elaborate its jump and test instructions; and assignment statements imitate its fetching, storing, and arithmetic.

The assignment statement is the von Neumann bottleneck of programming languages and keeps us thinking in word-at-a-time terms in much the same way the computer's bottleneck does.

Consider a typical program; at its center are a number of assignment statements containing some subscripted variables. Each assignment statement produces a one-word result. The program must cause these statements to be executed many times, while altering subscript values, in order to make the desired overall change in the store, since it must be done one word at a time. The programmer is thus concerned with the flow of words through the assignment bottleneck as he designs the nest of control statements to cause the necessary repetitions.

Moreover, the assignment statement splits programming into two worlds. The first world comprises the right sides of assignment statements. This is an orderly world of expressions, a world that has useful algebraic properties (except that those properties are often destroyed by side effects). It is the world in which most useful computation takes place.

The second world of conventional programming languages is the world of statements. The primary statement in that world is the assignment statement itself. All the other statements of the language exist in order to make it possible to perform a computation that must be based on this primitive construct: the assignment statement.

This world of statements is a disorderly one, with few useful mathematical properties. Structured programming can be seen as a modest effort to introduce some order into this chaotic world, but it accomplishes little in attacking the fundamental problems created by the word-at-a-time von Neumann style of programming, with its primitive use of loops, subscripts, and branching flow of control.

Our fixation on von Neumann languages has continued the primacy of the von Neumann computer, and our dependency on *it* has made non-von Neumann languages uneconomical and has limited their development. The absence of full scale, effective programming styles founded on non-von Neumann principles has deprived designers of an intellectual foundation for new computer architectures. (For a brief discussion of that topic, see Section 15.)

Applicative computing systems' lack of storage and history sensitivity is the basic reason they have not provided a foundation for computer design. Moreover, most applicative systems employ the substitution operation of the lambda calculus as their basic operation. This operation is one of virtually unlimited power, but its complete and efficient realization presents great difficulties to the machine designer. Furthermore, in an effort to introduce storage and to improve their efficiency on von Neumann computers, applicative systems have tended to become engulfed in a large von Neumann system. For example, pure Lisp is often buried in large extensions with many von Neumann features. The resulting complex systems offer little guidance to the machine designer.

5. Comparison of von Neumann and Functional Programs

To get a more detailed picture of some of the defects of von Neumann languages, let us compare a conventional program for inner product with a functional one written in a simple language to be detailed further on.

5.1 A von Neumann Program for Inner Product

```
c := 0
for i := 1 step 1 until n do
    c := c + a[i]×b[i]
```

Several properties of this program are worth noting:

a) Its statements operate on an invisible "state" according to complex rules.

b) It is not hierarchical. Except for the right side of the assignment statement, it does not construct complex entities from simpler ones. (Larger programs, however, often do.)

c) It is dynamic and repetitive. One must mentally execute it to understand it.

d) It computes word-at-a-time by repetition (of the assignment) and by modification (of variable i).

e) Part of the data, n, is in the program; thus it lacks generality and works only for vectors of length n.

f) It names its arguments; it can only be used for vectors a and b. To become general, it requires a procedure declaration. These involve complex issues (e.g., call-by-name versus call-by-value).

g) Its "housekeeping" operations are represented by symbols in scattered places (in the **for** statement and the subscripts in the assignment). This makes it impossible to consolidate housekeeping operations, the most common of all, into single, powerful, widely useful operators. Thus in programming those operations one must always start again at square one, writing "**for** i := ..." and "**for** j := ..." followed by assignment statements sprinkled with i's and j's.

5.2 A Functional Program for Inner Product

Def Innerproduct
$$\equiv (\text{Insert} +)\circ(\text{ApplyToAll} \times)\circ\text{Transpose}$$

Or, in abbreviated form:

Def IP $\equiv (/+)\circ(\alpha\times)\circ$Trans.

Composition ($\circ$), Insert ($/$), and ApplyToAll (α) are *functional forms* that combine existing functions to form new ones. Thus $f\circ g$ is the function obtained by applying first g and then f, and αf is the function obtained by applying f to every *member* of the argument. If we write $f:x$ for the result of applying f to the object x, then we can explain each step in evaluating Innerproduct applied to the pair of vectors $<<1, 2, 3>, <6, 5, 4>>$ as follows:

```
IP:<<1,2,3>, <6,5,4>> =
Definition of IP        ⇒ (/+)∘(α×)∘Trans: <<1,2,3>, <6,5,4>>
Effect of composition, ∘  ⇒ (/+):((α×):(Trans:
                                            <<1,2,3>, <6,5,4>>))
```

Applying Transpose	$\Rightarrow (/+):((\alpha\times):\ <<1,6>,\ <2,5>,\ <3,4>>)$
Effect of ApplyToAll, α	$\Rightarrow (/+):\ <\times:\ <1,6>,\ \times:\ <2,5>,\ \times:\ <3,4>>$
Applying $\times$	$\Rightarrow (/+):\ <6,10,12>$
Effect of Insert, /	$\Rightarrow +:\ <6,\ +:\ <10,12>>$
Applying +	$\Rightarrow +:\ <6,22>$
Applying + again	$\Rightarrow 28$

Let us compare the properties of this program with those of the von Neumann program.

a) It operates only on its arguments. There are no hidden states or complex transition rules. There are only two kinds of rules, one for applying a function to its argument, the other for obtaining the function denoted by a functional form such as composition, $f\circ g$, or ApplyToAll, αf, when one knows the functions f and g, the *parameters* of the forms.

b) It is hierarchical, being built from three simpler functions ($+$, $\times$, Trans) and three functional forms $f\circ g$, αf, and $/f$.

c) It is static and nonrepetitive, in the sense that its structure is helpful in understanding it without mentally executing it. For example, if one understands the action of the forms $f\circ g$ and αf, and of the functions $\times$ and Trans, then one understands the action of $\alpha\times$ and of $(\alpha\times)\circ$Trans, and so on.

d) It operates on whole conceptual units, not words; it has three steps; no step is repeated.

e) It incorporates no data; it is completely general; it works for any pair of conformable vectors.

f) It does not name its arguments; it can be applied to any pair of vectors without any procedure declaration or complex substitution rules.

g) It employs housekeeping forms and functions that are generally useful in many other programs; in fact, only $+$ and $\times$ are not concerned with housekeeping. These forms and functions can combine with others to create higher level housekeeping operators.

Section 14 sketches a kind of system designed to make the above functional style of programming available in a history-sensitive system with a simple framework, but much work remains to be done before the above applicative style can become the basis for elegant and practical programming languages. For the present, the above comparison exhibits a number of serious flaws in von Neumann programming languages and can serve as a starting point in an effort to account for their present fat and flabby condition.

6. Language Frameworks versus Changeable Parts

Let us distinguish two parts of a programming language. First, its *framework* which gives the overall rules of the system, and second, its *changeable parts,* whose existence is anticipated by the framework but whose particular behavior is not specified by it. For example, the **for** statement, and almost all other statements, are part of Algol's framework but library functions and user-defined procedures are changeable parts. Thus the framework of a language describes its fixed features and provides a general environment for its changeable features.

Now suppose a language had a small framework which could accommodate a great variety of powerful features entirely as changeable parts. Then such a framework could support many different features and styles without being changed itself. In contrast to this pleasant possibility, von Neumann languages always seem to have an immense framework and very limited changeable parts. What causes this to happen? The answer concerns two problems of von Neumann languages.

The first problem results from the von Neumann style of word-at-a-time programming, which requires that words flow back and forth to the state, just like the flow through the von Neumann bottleneck. Thus a von Neumann language must have a semantics closely coupled to the state, in which every detail of a computation changes the state. The consequence of this semantics closely coupled to states is that every detail of every feature must be built into the state and its transition rules.

Thus every feature of a von Neumann language must be spelled out in stupefying detail in its framework. Furthermore, many complex features are needed to prop up the basically weak word-at-a-time style. The result is the inevitable rigid and enormous framework of a von Neumann language.

7. Changeable Parts and Combining Forms

The second problem of von Neumann languages is that their changeable parts have so little expressive power. Their gargantuan size is eloquent proof of this; after all, if the designer knew that all those complicated features, which he now builds into the framework, could be added later on as changeable parts, he would not be so eager to build them into the framework.

Perhaps the most important element in providing powerful changeable parts in a language is the availability of combining forms that can be generally used to build new procedures from old ones. Von Neumann languages provide only primitive combining forms, and the von Neumann framework presents obstacles to their full use.

One obstacle to the use of combining forms is the split between the expression world and the statement world in von Neumann languages. Functional forms naturally belong to the world of expressions; but no matter how powerful they are they can only build expressions that produce a one-word result. And it is in the statement world that these one-word results must be combined into the overall result. Combining single words is not what we really should be thinking about, but it is a large part of programming any task in von Neumann languages. To help assemble the overall result from single words these languages provide some primitive combining forms in the statement world—the **for, while,** and **if-then-else** statements—but the split between the two worlds prevents the combining forms in either world from attaining the full power they can achieve in an undivided world.

A second obstacle to the use of combining forms in von Neumann languages is their use of elaborate naming conventions, which are further complicated by the substitution rules required in calling procedures. Each of these requires a complex mechanism to be built into the framework so that variables, subscripted variables, pointers, file names, procedure names, call-by-value formal parameters, call-by-name formal parameters, and so on, can all be properly interpreted. All these names, conventions, and rules interfere with the use of simple combining forms.

8. APL versus Word-at-a-Time Programming

Since I have said so much about word-at-a-time programming, I must now say something about APL [12]. We owe a great debt to Kenneth Iverson for showing us that there are programs that are neither word-at-a-time nor dependent on lambda expressions, and for introducing us to the use of new functional forms. And since APL assignment statements can store arrays, the effect of its functional forms is extended beyond a single assignment.

Unfortunately, however, APL still splits programming into a world of expressions and a world of statements. Thus the effort to write one-line programs is partly motivated by the desire to stay in the more orderly world of expressions. APL has exactly three functional forms, called inner product, outer product, and reduction. These are sometimes difficult to use, there are not enough of them, and their use is confined to the world of expressions.

Finally, APL semantics is still too closely coupled to states. Consequently, despite the greater simplicity and power of the language, its framework has the complexity and rigidity characteristic of von Neumann languages.

9. Von Neumann Languages Lack Useful Mathematical Properties

So far we have discussed the gross size and inflexibility of von Neumann languages; another important defect is their lack of useful mathematical properties and the obstacles they present to reasoning about programs. Although a great amount of excellent work has been published on proving facts about programs, von Neumann languages have almost no properties that are helpful in this direction and have many properties that are obstacles (e.g., side effects, aliasing).

Denotational semantics [23] and its foundations [20, 21] provide an extremely helpful mathematical understanding of the domain and function spaces implicit in programs. When applied to an applicative language (such as that of the "recursive programs" of [16]), its foundations provide powerful tools for describing the language and for proving properties of programs. When applied to a von Neumann language, on the other hand, it provides a precise semantic description and is helpful in identifying trouble spots in the language. But the complexity of the language is mirrored in the complexity of the description, which is a bewildering collection of productions, domains, functions, and equations that is only slightly more helpful in proving facts about programs than the reference manual of the language, since it is less ambiguous.

Axiomatic semantics [11] precisely restates the inelegant properties of von Neumann programs (i.e., transformations on states) as transformations on predicates. The word-at-a-time, repetitive game is not thereby changed, merely the playing field. The complexity of this axiomatic game of proving facts about von Neumann programs makes the successes of its practitioners all the more admirable. Their success rests on two factors in addition to their ingenuity: First, the game is restricted to small, weak subsets of full von Neumann languages that have states vastly simpler than real ones. Second, the new playing field (predicates and their transformations) is richer, more orderly and effective than the old (states and their transformations). But restricting the game and transferring it to a more effective domain does not enable it to handle real programs (with the necessary complexities of procedure calls and aliasing), nor does it eliminate the clumsy properties of the basic von Neumann style. As axiomatic semantics is extended to cover more of a typical von Neumann language, it begins to lose its effectiveness with the increasing complexity that is required.

Thus denotational and axiomatic semantics are descriptive formalisms whose foundations embody elegant and powerful concepts; but using them to describe a von Neumann language can not produce an elegant and powerful language any more than the use of elegant and modern machines to build an Edsel can produce an elegant and modern car.

In any case, proofs about programs use the language of logic, not the language of programming. Proofs talk *about* programs but cannot involve them directly since the axioms of von Neumann languages are so unusable. In contrast, many ordinary proofs are derived by algebraic methods. These methods require a language that has certain algebraic properties. Algebraic laws can then be used in a rather mechanical way to transform a problem into its solution. For example, to solve the equation

$$ax + bx = a + b$$

for x (given that $a+b \neq 0$), we mechanically apply the distributive, identity, and cancellation laws, in succession, to obtain

$$(a + b)x = a + b$$
$$(a + b)x = (a + b)1$$
$$x = 1.$$

Thus we have proved that x = 1 without leaving the "language" of algebra. Von Neumann languages, with their grotesque syntax, offer few such possibilities for transforming programs.

As we shall see later, programs can be expressed in a language that has an associated algebra. This algebra can be used to transform programs and to solve some equations whose "unknowns" are programs, in much the same way one solves equations in high school algebra. Algebraic transformations and proofs use the language of the programs themselves, rather than the language of logic, which talks about programs.

10. What Are the Alternatives to von Neumann Languages?

Before discussing alternatives to von Neumann languages, let me remark that I regret the need for the above negative and not very precise discussion of these languages. But the complacent acceptance most of us give to these enormous, weak languages has puzzled and disturbed me for a long time. I am disturbed because that acceptance has consumed a vast effort toward making von Neumann languages fatter that might have been better spent in looking for new structures. For this reason I have tried to analyze some of the basic defects of conventional languages and show that those defects cannot be resolved unless we discover a new kind of language framework.

In seeking an alternative to conventional languages we must first recognize that a system cannot be history sensitive (permit execution of one program to affect the behavior of a subsequent one) unless the system has some kind of state (which the first program can change and the second can access). Thus a history-sensitive model of a computing system must have a state-transition semantics, at least in this weak sense. But this does *not* mean that every computation must depend heavily on a complex state, with many state changes required for each small part of the computation (as in von Neumann languages).

To illustrate some alternatives to von Neumann languages, I propose to sketch a class of history-sensitive computing systems, where each system: a) has a loosely coupled state-transition semantics in which a state transition occurs only once in a major computation; b) has a simply structured state and simple transition rules; c) depends heavily on an underlying applicative system both to provide the basic programming language of the system and to describe its state transitions.

These systems, which I call applicative state transition (or AST) systems, are described in Section 14. These simple systems avoid many of the complexities and weaknesses of von Neumann languages and provide for a powerful and extensive set of changeable parts. However, they are sketched only as crude examples of a vast area of non-von Neumann systems with various attractive properties. I have been studying this area for the past three or four years and have not yet found a satisfying solution to the many conflicting requirements that a good language must resolve. But I believe this search has indicated a useful approach to designing non-von Neumann languages.

This approach involves four elements, which can be summarized as follows.

a) *A functional style of programming without variables.* A simple, informal functional programming (FP) system is described. It is based on the use of combining forms for building programs. Several programs are given to illustrate functional programming.

b) *An algebra of functional programs.* An algebra is described whose variables denote FP functional programs and whose "operations" are FP functional forms, the combining forms of FP programs. Some laws of the algebra are given. Theorems and examples are given that show how certain function expressions may be transformed into equivalent infinite expansions that explain the behavior of the function. The FP algebra is compared with algebras associated with the classical applicative systems of Church and Curry.

c) *A formal functional programming system.* A formal (FFP) system is described that extends the capabilities of the above informal FP systems. An FFP system is thus a precisely defined system that provides the ability to use the functional programming style of FP systems and their algebra of programs. FFP systems can be used as the basis for applicative state transition systems.

d) *Applicative state transition systems.* As discussed above. The rest of the paper describes these four elements, gives some brief remarks on computer design, and ends with a summary of the paper.

11. Functional Programming Systems (FP Systems)

11.1 Introduction

In this section we give an informal description of a class of simple applicative programming systems called functional programming (FP) systems, in which "programs" are simply functions without variables. The description is followed by some examples and by a discussion of various properties of FP systems.

An FP system is founded on the use of a fixed set of combining forms called functional forms. These, plus simple definitions, are the only means of building new functions from existing ones; they use no variables or substitution rules, and they become the operations of an associated algebra of programs. All the functions of an FP system are of one type: they map objects into objects and always take a single argument.

In contrast, a lambda-calculus based system is founded on the use of the lambda expression, with an associated set of substitution rules for variables, for building new functions. The lambda expression (with its substitution rules) is capable of defining all possible computable functions of all possible types and of any number of arguments. This freedom and power has its disadvantages as well as its obvious advantages. It is analogous to the power of unrestricted control statements in conventional languages: with unrestricted freedom comes chaos. If one constantly invents new combining forms to suit the occasion, as one can in the lambda calculus, one will not become familiar with the style or useful properties of the few combining forms that are adequate for all purposes. Just as structured programming eschews many control statements to obtain programs with simpler structure, better properties, and uniform methods for understanding their behavior, so functional programming eschews the lambda expression, substitution, and multiple function types. It thereby achieves programs built with familiar functional forms with known useful properties. These programs are so structured that their behavior can often be understood and proven by mechanical use of algebraic techniques similar to those used in solving high school algebra problems.

Functional forms, unlike most programming constructs, need not be chosen on an ad hoc basis. Since they are the operations of an associated algebra, one chooses only those functional forms that not only provide powerful programming constructs, but that also have attractive algebraic properties: one chooses them to maximize the strength and utility of the algebraic laws that relate them to other functional forms of the system.

In the following description we shall be imprecise in not distinguishing between (a) a function symbol or expression and (b) the function it denotes. We shall indicate the symbols and expressions used to denote functions by example and usage. Section 13 describes a formal extension of FP systems (FFP systems); they can serve to clarify any ambiguities about FP systems.

11.2 Description

An FP system comprises the following:
1) a set O of *objects*;
2) a set F of *functions* f that map objects into objects;
3) an operation, *application*;
4) a set F of *functional forms*; these are used to combine existing functions, or objects, to form new functions in F;
5) a set D of *definitions* that define some functions in F and assign a name to each.

What follows is an informal description of each of the above entities with examples.

11.2.1 Objects, O. An *object* x is either an *atom*, a sequence $<x_1, \ldots, x_n>$ whose *elements* x_i are objects, or $\perp$ ("bottom" or "undefined"). Thus the choice of a set A of atoms determines the set of objects. We shall take A to be the set of nonnull strings of capital letters, digits, and special symbols not used by the notation of the FP system. Some of these strings belong to the class of atoms called "numbers." The atom ϕ is used to denote the empty sequence and is the only object which is both an atom and a sequence. The atoms T and F are used to denote "true" and "false."

There is one important constraint in the construction of objects: if x is a sequence with $\perp$ as an element, then $x = \perp$. That is, the "sequence constructor" is "$\perp$-preserving." Thus no proper sequence has $\perp$ as an element.

Examples of objects

$\perp$ 1.5 ϕ $AB3$ $<AB, 1, 2.3>$
$<A, <<B>, C>, D>$ $<A, \perp> = \perp$

11.2.2 Application. An FP system has a single operation, application. If f is a function and x is an object, then $f:x$ is an *application* and denotes the object which is the result of applying f to x. f is the *operator* of the application and x is the *operand*.

Examples of applications

$+:<1,2> = 3$ $tl:<A,B,C> = <B,C>$
$1:<A,B,C> = A$ $2:<A,B,C> = B$

11.2.3 Functions, F. All functions f in F map objects into objects and are *bottom-preserving*: $f:\perp = \perp$, for all f in F. Every function in F is either *primitive*, that is, supplied with the system, or it is *defined* (see below), or it is a *functional form* (see below).

It is sometimes useful to distinguish between two cases in which $f:x=\perp$. If the computation for $f:x$ terminates and yields the object $\perp$, we say f is *undefined* at x, that is, f terminates but has no meaningful value at x. Otherwise we say f is *nonterminating* at x.

Examples of primitive functions

Our intention is to provide FP systems with widely useful and powerful primitive functions rather than weak ones that could then be used to define useful ones. The following examples define some typical primitive functions, many of which are used in later examples of programs. In the following definitions we use a variant of McCarthy's conditional expressions [17]; thus we write

$$p_1 \rightarrow e_1; \ldots ; p_n \rightarrow e_n; e_{n+1}$$

instead of McCarthy's expression

$$(p_1 \rightarrow e_1, \ldots , p_n \rightarrow e_n, T \rightarrow e_{n+1}).$$

The following definitions are to hold for all objects x, x_i, y, y_i, z, z_i:

Selector functions

$1:x \equiv x=<x_1, \ldots , x_n> \rightarrow x_1; \perp$

and for any positive integer s

$s:x \equiv x = <x_1, \ldots , x_n> \& n \geq s \rightarrow x_s; \perp$

Thus, for example, $3:<A,B,C> = C$ and $2:<A> = \perp$. Note that the function symbols 1, 2, etc. are distinct from the atoms *1, 2*, etc.

Tail

$tl:x \equiv x=<x_1> \rightarrow \phi;$
$\qquad x=<x_1, \ldots , x_n> \& n \geq 2 \rightarrow <x_2, \ldots , x_n>; \perp$

Identity

$id:x \equiv x$

Atom
atom:$x \equiv x$ is an atom $\rightarrow T$; $x{\neq}\bot \rightarrow F$; $\bot$

Equals
eq:$x \equiv x{=}{<}y,z{>}$ & $y{=}z \rightarrow T$; $x{=}{<}y,z{>}$ & $y{\neq}z \rightarrow F$; $\bot$

Null
null:$x \equiv x{=}\phi \rightarrow T$; $x{\neq}\bot \rightarrow F$; $\bot$

Reverse
reverse:$x \equiv x{=}\phi \rightarrow \phi$;
$$x{=}{<}x_1, \dots , x_n{>} \rightarrow {<}x_n, \dots , x_1{>}; \bot$$

Distribute from left; distribute from right
distl:$x \equiv x{=}{<}y,\phi{>} \rightarrow \phi$;
$$x{=}{<}y,{<}z_1, \dots , z_n{>>} \rightarrow {<<}y,z_1{>}, \dots , {<}y,z_n{>>}; \bot$$
distr:$x \equiv x{=}{<}\phi,y{>} \rightarrow \phi$;
$$x{=}{<<}y_1, \dots , y_n{>},z{>} \rightarrow {<<}y_1,z{>}, \dots , {<}y_n,z{>>}; \bot$$

Length
length:$x \equiv x{=}{<}x_1, \dots , x_n{>} \rightarrow$ n; $x{=}\phi \rightarrow 0$; $\bot$

Add, subtract, multiply, and divide
$+$:$x \equiv x{=}{<}y,z{>}$ & y,z are numbers $\rightarrow y{+}z$; $\bot$
$-$:$x \equiv x{=}{<}y,z{>}$ & y,z are numbers $\rightarrow y{-}z$; $\bot$
$\times$:$x \equiv x{=}{<}y,z{>}$ & y,z are numbers $\rightarrow y{\times}z$; $\bot$
$\div$:$x \equiv x{=}{<}y,z{>}$ & y,z are numbers $\rightarrow y{\div}z$; $\bot$
$$\text{(where } y{\div}0 = \bot)$$

Transpose
trans:$x \equiv x{=}{<}\phi, \dots , \phi{>} \rightarrow \phi$;
$$x{=}{<}x_1, \dots , x_n{>} \rightarrow {<}y_1, \dots , y_m{>}; \bot$$
where
$x_i{=}{<}x_{i1}, \dots , x_{im}{>}$ and
$$y_j{=}{<}x_{1j}, \dots , x_{nj}{>}, 1{\leq}i{\leq}n, 1{\leq}j{\leq}m.$$

And, or, not
and:$x \equiv x{=}{<}T,T{>} \rightarrow T$;
$$x{=}{<}T,F{>} \vee x{=}{<}F,T{>} \vee x{=}{<}F,F{>} \rightarrow F; \bot$$
etc.

Append left; append right
apndl:$x \equiv x{=}{<}y,\phi{>} \rightarrow {<}y{>}$;
$$x{=}{<}y,{<}z_1, \dots , z_n{>>} \rightarrow {<}y,z_1, \dots , z_n{>}; \bot$$
apndr:$x \equiv x{=}{<}\phi,z{>} \rightarrow {<}z{>}$;
$$x{=}{<<}y_1, \dots , y_n{>},z{>} \rightarrow {<}y_1, \dots , y_n,z{>}; \bot$$

Right selectors; Right tail
1r:$x \equiv x{=}{<}x_1, \dots , x_n{>} \rightarrow x_n$; $\bot$
2r:$x \equiv x{=}{<}x_1, \dots , x_n{>}$ & $n{\geq}2 \rightarrow x_{n-1}$; $\bot$
etc.
tlr:$x \equiv x{=}{<}x_1{>} \rightarrow \phi$;
$$x{=}{<}x_1, \dots , x_n{>} \text{ & } n{\geq}2 \rightarrow {<}x_1, \dots , x_{n-1}{>}; \bot$$

Rotate left; rotate right
rotl:$x \equiv x{=}\phi \rightarrow \phi$; $x{=}{<}x_1{>} \rightarrow {<}x_1{>}$;
$$x{=}{<}x_1, \dots , x_n{>} \text{ & } n{\geq}2 \rightarrow {<}x_2, \dots , x_n,x_1{>}; \bot$$
etc.

11.2.4 Functional forms, F. A functional form is an expression denoting a function; that function depends on the functions or objects which are the *parameters* of the expression. Thus, for example, if f and g are any functions, then $f{\circ}g$ is a functional form, the *composition* of f

and g, f and g are its parameters, and it denotes the function such that, for any object x,

$$(f{\circ}g){:}x = f{:}(g{:}x).$$

Some functional forms may have objects as parameters. For example, for any object x, $\bar{x}$ is a functional form, the *constant* function of x, so that for any object y

$$\bar{x}{:}y \equiv y{=}\bot \rightarrow \bot; x.$$

In particular, $\bot$ is the everywhere-$\bot$ function.

Below we give some functional forms, many of which are used later in this paper. We use p, f, and g with and without subscripts to denote arbitrary functions; and x, $x_1, \dots , x_n$, y as arbitrary objects. Square brackets [...] are used to indicate the functional form for *construction*, which denotes a function, whereas pointed brackets ${<}...{>}$ denote sequences, which are objects. Parentheses are used both in particular functional forms (e.g., in *condition*) and generally to indicate grouping.

Composition
$(f{\circ}g){:}x \equiv f{:}(g{:}x)$

Construction
$[f_1, \dots , f_n]{:}x \equiv {<}f_1{:}x, \dots , f_n{:}x{>}$ (Recall that since ${<}\dots , \bot, \dots{>} = \bot$ and all functions are $\bot$-preserving, so is $[f_1, \dots , f_n]$.)

Condition
$(p \rightarrow f; g){:}x \equiv (p{:}x){=}T \rightarrow f{:}x$; $(p{:}x){=}F \rightarrow g{:}x$; $\bot$

Conditional *expressions* (used outside of FP systems to describe their functions) and the *functional form* condition are both identified by "$\rightarrow$". They are quite different although closely related, as shown in the above definitions. But no confusion should arise, since the elements of a conditional expression all denote values, whereas the elements of the functional form condition all denote functions, never values. When no ambiguity arises we omit right-associated parentheses; we write, for example, $p_1 \rightarrow f_1$; $p_2 \rightarrow f_2$; g for $(p_1 \rightarrow f_1; (p_2 \rightarrow f_2; g))$.

Constant (Here x is an object parameter.)
$\bar{x}{:}y \equiv y{=}\bot \rightarrow \bot$; x

Insert
$/f{:}x \equiv x{=}{<}x_1{>} \rightarrow x_1$; $x{=}{<}x_1, \dots , x_n{>}$ & $n{\geq}2$
$$\rightarrow f{:}{<}x_1, /f{:}{<}x_2, \dots , x_n{>>}; \bot$$

If f has a unique right unit $u_f \neq \bot$, where $f{:}{<}x,u_f{>} \in \{x, \bot\}$ for all objects x, then the above definition is extended: $/f{:}\phi = u_f$. Thus

$/+{:}{<}4,5,6{>} = +{:}{<}4, +{:}{<}5, /+{:}{<}6{>>>}$
$$= +{:}{<}4, +{:}{<}5,6{>>} = 15$$
$/+{:}\phi{=}0$

Apply to all
$\alpha f{:}x \equiv x{=}\phi \rightarrow \phi$;
$$x{=}{<}x_1, \dots , x_n{>} \rightarrow {<}f{:}x_1, \dots , f{:}x_n{>}; \bot$$

Binary to unary (*x* is an object parameter)

(bu *f* *x*):*y* ≡ *f*:<*x,y*>

Thus

(bu + *1*):*x* = *1+x*

While

(while *p* *f*):*x* ≡ *p*:*x*=T → (while *p* *f*):(*f*:*x*);

$$p:x=F \to x; \perp$$

The above functional forms provide an effective method for computing the values of the functions they denote (if they terminate) provided one can effectively apply their function parameters.

11.2.5 Definitions. A *definition* in an FP system is an expression of the form

Def *l* ≡ *r*

where the left side *l* is an unused function symbol and the right side *r* is a functional form (which may depend on *l*). It expresses the fact that the symbol *l* is to denote the function given by *r*. Thus the definition **Def** last1 ≡ 1∘reverse defines the function last1 that produces the last element of a sequence (or ⊥). Similarly,

Def last ≡ null∘tl → 1; last∘tl

defines the function last, which is the same as last1. Here in detail is how the definition would be used to compute last:<*1,2*>:

last:<*1,2*> =
definition of last   ⇒ (null∘tl → 1; last∘tl):<*1,2*>
action of the form (*p*→*f*; *g*) ⇒ last∘tl:<*1,2*>
            since null∘tl:<*1,2*> = null:<*2*>
            = F
action of the form *f*∘*g* ⇒ last:(tl:<*1,2*>)
definition of primitive tail → last:<*2*>
definition of last ⇒ (null∘tl → 1; last∘tl):<*2*>
action of the form (*p*→*f*; *g*) ⇒ 1·<*2*>
            since null∘tl:<*2*> = null:ϕ − T
definition of selector 1 ⇒ *2*

The above illustrates the simple rule: to apply a defined symbol, replace it by the right side of its definition. Of course, some definitions may define nonterminating functions. A set D of definitions is *well formed* if no two left sides are the same.

11.2.6 Semantics. It can be seen from the above that an FP system is determined by choice of the following sets: (a) The set of atoms A (which determines the set of objects). (b) The set of primitive functions P. (c) The set of functional forms F. (d) A well formed set of definitions D. To understand the semantics of such a system one needs to know how to compute *f*:*x* for any function *f* and any object *x* of the system. There are exactly four possibilities for *f*:

(1) *f* is a primitive function;
(2) *f* is a functional form;
(3) there is one definition in D, **Def** *f* ≡ *r*; and
(4) none of the above.

If *f* is a primitive function, then one has its description

and knows how to apply it. If *f* is a functional form, then the description of the form tells how to compute *f*:*x* in terms of the parameters of the form, which can be done by further use of these rules. If *f* is defined, **Def** *f* ≡ *r*, as in (3), then to find *f*:*x* one computes *r*:*x*, which can be done by further use of these rules. If none of these, then *f*:*x* ≡ ⊥. Of course, the use of these rules may not terminate for some *f* and some *x*, in which case we assign the value *f*:*x* ≡ ⊥.

11.3 Examples of Functional Programs

The following examples illustrate the functional programming style. Since this style is unfamiliar to most readers, it may cause confusion at first; the important point to remember is that no part of a function definition is a result itself. Instead, each part is a *function* that must be applied to an argument to obtain a result.

11.3.1 Factorial.

Def ! ≡ eq0 → 1̄; ×∘[id, !∘sub1]

where

Def eq0 ≡ eq∘[id, 0̄]
Def sub1 ≡ −∘[id, 1̄]

Here are some of the intermediate expressions an FP system would obtain in evaluating !·*2*:

!:*2* ⇒ (eq0 → 1̄; ×∘[id, !∘sub1]):*2*
         ⇒ ×∘[id, !∘sub1]:*2*
    ⇒ ×:<id:*2*, !∘sub1:*2*> ⇒ ×:<*2*, !:*1*>
           ⇒ ×:<*2*, ×:<*1*, !:*0*>>
   ⇒ ×:<*2*, ×:<*1*,1̄:*0*>> ⇒ ×:<*2*, ×:<*1*,*1*>>
            ⇒ ×:<*2,1*> ⇒ *2*.

In Section 12 we shall see how theorems of the algebra of FP programs can be used to prove that ! is the factorial function.

11.3.2 Inner product. We have seen earlier how this definition works.

Def   IP ≡ (/+)∘(α×)∘trans

11.3.3 Matrix multiply. This matrix multiplication program yields the product of any pair <*m,n*> of conformable matrices, where each matrix *m* is represented as the sequence of its rows:

m = <*m*₁, ... , *m*ᵣ>
         where m_i = <m_{i1}, ... , m_{is}> for i = 1, ... , r.
Def MM ≡ (ααIP)∘(αdistl)∘distr∘[1, trans∘2]

The program MM has four steps, reading from right to left; each is applied in turn, beginning with [1, trans∘2], to the result of its predecessor. If the argument is <*m,n*>, then the first step yields <*m,n′*> where *n′* = trans:*n*. The second step yields <<*m*₁,*n′*>, ... , <*m*ᵣ,*n′*>>, where the m_i are the rows of *m*. The third step, αdistl, yields

<distl:<*m*₁,*n′*>, ... , distl:<*m*ᵣ,*n′*>> = <*p*₁, ... , *p*ᵣ>

where

$p_i = $ distl: $<m_i,n'> = <<m_i,n_1'>, ... , <m_i,n_s'>>$

for i = 1, ... , r

and n_j' is the jth column of n (the jth row of n'). Thus p_i, a sequence of row and column pairs, corresponds to the i-th product row. The operator $\alpha\alpha$IP, or $\alpha(\alpha$IP), causes αIP to be applied to each p_i, which in turn causes IP to be applied to each row and column pair in each p_i. The result of the last step is therefore the sequence of rows comprising the product matrix. If either matrix is not rectangular, or if the length of a row of m differs from that of a column of n, or if any element of m or n is not a number, the result is $\perp$.

This program MM does not name its arguments or any intermediate results; contains no variables, no loops, no control statements nor procedure declarations; has no initialization instructions; is not word-at-a-time in nature; is hierarchically constructed from simpler components; uses generally applicable housekeeping forms and operators (e.g., αf, distl, distr, trans); is perfectly general; yields $\perp$ whenever its argument is inappropriate in any way; does not constrain the order of evaluation unnecessarily (all applications of IP to row and column pairs can be done in parallel or in any order); and, using algebraic laws (see below), can be transformed into more "efficient" or into more "explanatory" programs (e.g., one that is recursively defined). None of these properties hold for the typical von Neumann matrix multiplication program.

Although it has an unfamiliar and hence puzzling form, the program MM describes the essential operations of matrix multiplication without overdetermining the process or obscuring parts of it, as most programs do; hence many straightforward programs for the operation can be obtained from it by formal transformations. It is an inherently inefficient program for von Neumann computers (with regard to the use of space), but efficient ones can be derived from it and realizations of FP systems can be imagined that could execute MM without the prodigal use of space it implies. Efficiency questions are beyond the scope of this paper; let me suggest only that since the language is so simple and does not dictate any binding of lambda-type variables to data, there may be better opportunities for the system to do some kind of "lazy" evaluation [9, 10] and to control data management more efficiently than is possible in lambda-calculus based systems.

11.4 Remarks About FP Systems

11.4.1 FP systems as programming languages. FP systems are so minimal that some readers may find it difficult to view them as programming languages. Viewed as such, a function f is a program, an object x is the contents of the store, and $f:x$ is the contents of the store after program f is activated with x in the store. The set of definitions is the program library. The primitive functions and the functional forms provided by the system are the basic statements of a particular programming language. Thus, depending on the choice of prim-

itive functions and functional forms, the FP framework provides for a large class of languages with various styles and capabilities. The algebra of programs associated with each of these depends on its particular set of functional forms. The primitive functions, functional forms, and programs given in this paper comprise an effort to develop just one of these possible styles.

11.4.2 Limitations of FP systems. FP systems have a number of limitations. For example, a given FP system is a fixed language; it is not history sensitive: no program can alter the library of programs. It can treat input and output only in the sense that x is an input and $f:x$ is the output. If the set of primitive functions and functional forms is weak, it may not be able to express every computable function.

An FP system cannot compute a program since function expressions are not objects. Nor can one define new functional forms within an FP system. (Both of these limitations are removed in formal functional programming (FFP) systems in which objects "represent" functions.) Thus no FP system can have a function, apply, such that

apply: $<x,y> \equiv x:y$

because, on the left, x is an object, and, on the right, x is a function. (Note that we have been careful to keep the set of function symbols and the set of objects distinct: thus 1 is a function symbol, and I is an object.)

The primary limitation of FP systems is that they are not history sensitive. Therefore they must be extended somehow before they can become practically useful. For discussion of such extensions, see the sections on FFP and AST systems (Sections 13 and 14).

11.4.3 Expressive power of FP systems. Suppose two FP systems, FP_1 and FP_2, both have the same set of objects and the same set of primitive functions, but the set of functional forms of FP_1 properly includes that of FP_2. Suppose also that both systems can express all computable functions on objects. Nevertheless, we can say that FP_1 is more expressive than FP_2, since every function expression in FP_2 can be duplicated in FP_1, but by using a functional form not belonging to FP_2, FP_1 can express some functions more directly and easily than FP_2.

I believe the above observation could be developed into a theory of the expressive power of languages in which a language A would be *more expressive* than language B under the following roughly stated conditions. First, form all possible functions of all types in A by applying all existing functions to objects and to each other in all possible ways until no new function of any type can be formed. (The set of objects is a type; the set of continuous functions [T→U] from type T to type U is a type. If $f\in$[T→U] and $t\in$T, then ft in U can be formed by applying f to t.) Do the same in language B. Next, compare each type in A to the corresponding type in B. If, for every type, A's type includes B's corresponding type, then A is more expressive than B (or equally expressive). If some type of A's functions is incomparable to B's, then A and B are not comparable in expressive power.

11.4.4 Advantages of FP systems. The main reason FP systems are considerably simpler than either conventional languages or lambda-calculus-based languages is that they use only the most elementary fixed naming system (naming a function in a definition) with a simple fixed rule of substituting a function for its name. Thus they avoid the complexities both of the naming systems of conventional languages and of the substitution rules of the lambda calculus. FP systems permit the definition of different naming systems (see Sections 13.3.4 and 14.7) for various purposes. These need not be complex, since many programs can do without them completely. Most importantly, they treat names as functions that can be combined with other functions without special treatment.

FP systems offer an escape from conventional word-at-a-time programming to a degree greater even than APL [12] (the most successful attack on the problem to date within the von Neumann framework) because they provide a more powerful set of functional forms within a unified world of expressions. They offer the opportunity to develop higher level techniques for thinking about, manipulating, and writing programs.

12. The Algebra of Programs for FP Systems

12.1 Introduction

The algebra of the programs described below is the work of an amateur in algebra, and I want to show that it is a game amateurs can profitably play and enjoy, a game that does not require a deep understanding of logic and mathematics. In spite of its simplicity, it can help one to understand and prove things about programs in a systematic, rather mechanical way.

So far, proving a program correct requires knowledge of some moderately heavy topics in mathematics and logic: properties of complete partially ordered sets, continuous functions, least fixed points of functionals, the first-order predicate calculus, predicate transformers, weakest preconditions, to mention a few topics in a few approaches to proving programs correct. These topics have been very useful for professionals who make it their business to devise proof techniques; they have published a lot of beautiful work on this subject, starting with the work of McCarthy and Floyd, and, more recently, that of Burstall, Dijkstra, Manna and his associates, Milner, Morris, Reynolds, and many others. Much of this work is based on the foundations laid down by Dana Scott (denotational semantics) and C. A. R. Hoare (axiomatic semantics). But its theoretical level places it beyond the scope of most amateurs who work outside of this specialized field.

If the average programmer is to prove his programs

correct, he will need much simpler techniques than those the professionals have so far put forward. The algebra of programs below may be one starting point for such a proof discipline and, coupled with current work on algebraic manipulation, it may also help provide a basis for automating some of that discipline.

One advantage of this algebra over other proof techniques is that the programmer can use his programming language as the language for deriving proofs, rather than having to state proofs in a separate logical system that merely talks *about* his programs.

At the heart of the algebra of programs are laws and theorems that state that one function expression is the same as another. Thus the law $[f,g] \circ h \equiv [f \circ h, g \circ h]$ says that the construction of f and g (composed with h) is the same function as the construction of (f composed with h) and (g composed with h) no matter what the functions f, g, and h are. Such laws are easy to understand, easy to justify, and easy and powerful to use. However, we also wish to use such laws to solve equations in which an "unknown" function appears on both sides of the equation. The problem is that if f satisfies some such equation, it will often happen that some extension f' of f will also satisfy the same equation. Thus, to give a unique meaning to solutions of such equations, we shall require a foundation for the algebra of programs (which uses Scott's notion of least fixed points of continuous functionals) to assure us that solutions obtained by algebraic manipulation are indeed least, and hence unique, solutions.

Our goal is to develop a foundation for the algebra of programs that disposes of the theoretical issues, so that a programmer can use simple algebraic laws and one or two theorems from the foundations to solve problems and create proofs in the same mechanical style we use to solve high-school algebra problems, and so that he can do so without knowing anything about least fixed points or predicate transformers.

One particular foundational problem arises: given equations of the form

$$f \equiv p_0 \rightarrow q_0; \dots; p_i \rightarrow q_i; E_i(f), \qquad (1)$$

where the p_i's and q_i's are functions not involving f and $E_i(f)$ is a function expression involving f, the laws of the algebra will often permit the formal "extension" of this equation by one more "clause" by deriving

$$E_i(f) \equiv p_{i+1} \rightarrow q_{i+1}; E_{i+1}(f) \qquad (2)$$

which, by replacing $E_i(f)$ in (1) by the right side of (2), yields

$$f \equiv p_0 \rightarrow q_0; \dots; p_{i+1} \rightarrow q_{i+1}; E_{i+1}(f). \qquad (3)$$

This formal extension may go on without limit. One question the foundations must then answer is: when can the least f satisfying (1) be represented by the infinite expansion

$$f \equiv p_0 \rightarrow q_0; \dots; p_n \rightarrow q_n; \dots \qquad (4)$$

in which the final clause involving f has been dropped,

so that we now have a solution whose right side is free of f's? Such solutions are helpful in two ways: first, they give proofs of "termination" in the sense that (4) means that $f:x$ is defined if and only if there is an n such that, for every i less than n, $p_i:x = F$ and $p_n:x = T$ and $q_n:x$ is defined. Second, (4) gives a case-by-case description of f that can often clarify its behavior.

The foundations for the algebra given in a subsequent section are a modest start toward the goal stated above. For a limited class of equations its "linear expansion theorem" gives a useful answer as to when one can go from indefinitely extendable equations like (1) to infinite expansions like (4). For a larger class of equations, a more general "expansion theorem" gives a less helpful answer to similar questions. Hopefully, more powerful theorems covering additional classes of equations can be found. But for the present, one need only know the conclusions of these two simple foundational theorems in order to follow the theorems and examples appearing in this section.

The results of the foundations subsection are summarized in a separate, earlier subsection titled "expansion theorems," without reference to fixed point concepts. The foundations subsection itself is placed later where it can be skipped by readers who do not want to go into that subject.

12.2 Some Laws of the Algebra of Programs

In the algebra of programs for an FP system variables range over the set of functions of the system. The "operations" of the algebra are the functional forms of the system. Thus, for example, $[f,g] \circ h$ is an expression of the algebra for the FP system described above, in which f, g, and h are variables denoting arbitrary functions of that system. And

$$[f,g] \circ h \equiv [f \circ h, g \circ h]$$

is a law of the algebra which says that, whatever functions one chooses for f, g, and h, the function on the left is the same as that on the right. Thus this algebraic law is merely a restatement of the following proposition about any FP system that includes the functional forms $[f,g]$ and $f \circ g$:

PROPOSITION: For all functions f, g, and h and all objects x, $([f,g] \circ h):x \equiv [f \circ h, g \circ h]:x$.
PROOF:
$([f,g] \circ h):x = [f,g]:(h:x)$
$\qquad\qquad$ by definition of composition
$= <f:(h:x), g:(h:x)>$
$\qquad\qquad$ by definition of construction
$= <(f \circ h):x, (g \circ h):x>$
$\qquad\qquad$ by definition of composition
$= [f \circ h, g \circ h]:x$
$\qquad\qquad$ by definition of construction $\quad\square$

Some laws have a domain smaller than the domain of all objects. Thus $1 \circ [f,g] \equiv f$ does not hold for objects x such that $g:x = \bot$. We write

$defined \circ g \longrightarrow 1 \circ [f,g] \equiv f$

to indicate that the law (or theorem) on the right holds within the domain of objects x for which $defined \circ g:x = T$. Where

Def $defined \equiv \bar{T}$

i.e. $defined:x \equiv x = \bot \rightarrow \bot; T$. In general we shall write a *qualified functional equation*:

$$p \longrightarrow f \equiv g$$

to mean that, for any object x, whenever $p:x = T$, then $f:x = g:x$.

Ordinary algebra concerns itself with two operations, addition and multiplication; it needs few laws. The algebra of programs is concerned with more operations (functional forms) and therefore needs more laws.

Each of the following laws requires a corresponding proposition to validate it. The interested reader will find most proofs of such propositions easy (two are given below). We first define the usual ordering on functions and equivalence in terms of this ordering:

DEFINITION $f \leq g$ iff for all objects x, either $f:x = \bot$, or $f:x = g:x$.
DEFINITION $f \equiv g$ iff $f \leq g$ and $g \leq f$.

It is easy to verify that $\leq$ is a partial ordering, that $f \leq g$ means g is an extension of f, and that $f \equiv g$ iff $f:x = g:x$ for all objects x. We now give a list of algebraic laws organized by the two principal functional forms involved.

I   Composition and construction
I.1 $[f_1, \ldots , f_n] \circ g \equiv [f_1 \circ g, \ldots , f_n \circ g]$
I.2 $\alpha f \circ [g_1, \ldots , g_n] \equiv [f \circ g_1, \ldots , f \circ g_n]$
I.3 $/f \circ [g_1, \ldots , g_n]$
$\qquad \equiv f \circ [g_1, /f \circ [g_2, \ldots , g_n]]$ when $n \geq 2$
$\qquad \equiv f \circ [g_1, f \circ [g_2, \ldots , f \circ [g_{n-1}, g_n] \ldots]]$
$\qquad /f \circ [g] \equiv g$
I.4 $f \circ [\bar{x},g] \equiv (bu\ f\ x) \circ g$
I.5 $1 \circ [f_1, \ldots , f_n] \leq f_1$
$\qquad s \circ [f_1, \ldots , f_s, \ldots , f_n] \leq f_s$ for any selector s, s$\leq$n
$\qquad defined \circ f_i$ (for all i$\neq$s, 1$\leq$i$\leq$n) $\longrightarrow$
$\qquad\qquad\qquad\qquad\qquad s \circ [f_1, \ldots , f_n] \equiv f_s$
I.5.1 $[f_1 \circ 1, \ldots , f_n \circ n] \circ [g_1, \ldots , g_n] \equiv [f_1 \circ g_1, \ldots , f_n \circ g_n]$
I.6 $tl \circ [f_1] \leq \bar{\phi}$ and
$\qquad\qquad tl \circ [f_1, \ldots , f_n] \leq [f_2, \ldots , f_n]$ for n$\geq$2
$\qquad defined \circ f_1 \longrightarrow tl \circ [f_1] \equiv \bar{\phi}$
$\qquad$ and $tl \circ [f_1, \ldots , f_n] \equiv [f_2, \ldots , f_n]$ for n$\geq$2
I.7 $distl \circ [f, [g_1, \ldots , g_n]] \equiv [[f,g_1], \ldots , [f,g_n]]$
$\qquad defined \circ f \longrightarrow distl \circ [f,\bar{\phi}] \equiv \bar{\phi}$
$\qquad$ The analogous law holds for distr.
I.8 $apndl \circ [f, [g_1, \ldots , g_n]] \equiv [f,g_1, \ldots , g_n]$
$\qquad null \circ g \longrightarrow apndl \circ [f,g] \equiv [f]$
And so on for apndr, reverse, rotl, etc.
I.9 $[\ldots , \bot, \ldots] \equiv \bot$
I.10 $apndl \circ [f \circ g, \alpha f \circ h] \equiv \alpha f \circ apndl \circ [g,h]$
I.11 $pair\ \&\ not \circ null \circ 1 \longrightarrow$
$\qquad\qquad apndl \circ [[1 \circ 1,2], distr \circ [tl \circ 1,2]] \equiv distr$

Where $f \& g \equiv and \circ [f,g]$;
$$pair \equiv atom \to \bar{F}; eq \circ [length, \bar{2}]$$

II Composition and condition (right associated parentheses omitted) (Law II.2 is noted in Manna et al. [16], p. 493.)

II.1 $(p \to f; g) \circ h \equiv p \circ h \to f \circ h; g \circ h$

II.2 $h \circ (p \to f; g) \equiv p \to h \circ f; h \circ g$

II.3 $or \circ [q, not \circ q] \to\to and \circ [p,q] \to f;$
     $and \circ [p, not \circ q] \to g; h \equiv p \to (q \to f; g); h$

II.3.1 $p \to (p \to f; g); h \equiv p \to f; h$

III Composition and miscellaneous

III.1 $\bar{x} \circ f \leq \bar{x}$
     $defined \circ f \to\to \bar{x} \circ f \equiv \bar{x}$

III.1.1 $\bar{\perp} \circ f \equiv f \circ \bar{\perp} \equiv \bar{\perp}$

III.2 $f \circ id \equiv id \circ f \equiv f$

III.3 $pair \to\to 1 \circ distr \equiv [1 \circ 1, 2]$ also:
              $pair \to\to 1 \circ tl \equiv 2$ etc.

III.4 $\alpha(f \circ g) \equiv \alpha f \circ \alpha g$

III.5 $null \circ g \to\to \alpha f \circ g \equiv \bar{\phi}$

IV Condition and construction

IV.1 $[f_1, \ldots, (p \to g; h), \ldots, f_n]$
     $\equiv p \to [f_1, \ldots, g, \ldots, f_n]; [f_1, \ldots, h, \ldots, f_n]$

IV.1.1 $[f_1, \ldots, (p_1 \to g_1; \ldots; p_n \to g_n; h), \ldots, f_m]$
     $\equiv p_1 \to [f_1, \ldots, g_1, \ldots, f_m];$
     $\ldots; p_n \to [f_1, \ldots, g_n, \ldots, f_m]; [f_1, \ldots, h, \ldots, f_m]$

This concludes the present list of algebraic laws; it is by no means exhaustive, there are many others.

Proof of two laws

We give the proofs of validating propositions for laws I.10 and I.11, which are slightly more involved than most of the others.

PROPOSITION 1

$apndl \circ [f \circ g, \alpha f \circ h] \equiv \alpha f \circ apndl \circ [g, h]$

PROOF. We show that, for every object x, both of the above functions yield the same result.

CASE 1. $h{:}x$ is neither a sequence nor ϕ.
Then both sides yield $\perp$ when applied to x.

CASE 2. $h{:}x = \phi$. Then
$apndl \circ [f \circ g, \alpha f \circ h]{:} x$
   $= apndl{:} <f \circ g{:}x, \phi> = <f{:}(g{:}x)>$
$\alpha f \circ apndl \circ [g,h]{:} x$
   $= \alpha f \circ apndl{:} <g{:}x, \phi> = \alpha f{:}<g{:}x>$
   $= <f{:}(g{:}x)>$

CASE 3. $h{:}x = <y_1, \ldots, y_n>$. Then
$apndl \circ [f \circ g, \alpha f \circ h]{:} x$
   $= apndl{:} <f \circ g{:}x, \alpha f{:} <y_1, \ldots, y_n>>$
   $= <f{:}(g{:}x), f{:}y_1, \ldots, f{:}y_n>$
$\alpha f \circ apndl \circ [g,h]{:} x$
   $= \alpha f \circ apndl{:} <g{:}x, <y_1, \ldots, y_n>>$
            $= \alpha f{:} <g{:}x, y_1, \ldots, y_n>$
   $= <f{:}(g{:}x), f{:}y_1, \ldots, f{:}y_n>$ $\square$

PROPOSITION 2

$Pair \& not \circ null \circ 1 \to\to$
           $apndl \circ [[1^2, 2], distr \circ [tl \circ 1, 2]] \equiv distr$

where $f \& g$ is the function: $and \circ [f, g]$, and $f^2 \equiv f \circ f$.
PROOF. We show that both sides produce the same result when applied to any pair $<x,y>$, where $x \neq \phi$, as per the stated qualification.

CASE 1. x is an atom or $\perp$. Then distr: $<x,y> = \perp$, since $x \neq \phi$. The left side also yields $\perp$ when applied to $<x,y>$, since $tl \circ 1{:}<x,y> = \perp$ and all functions are $\perp$-preserving.

CASE 2. $x = <x_1, \ldots, x_n>$. Then

   $apndl \circ [[1^2, 2], distr \circ [tl \circ 1, 2]]{:}<x, y>$
     $= apndl{:} <<1{:}x, y>, distr{:} <tl{:}x, y>>$
     $= apndl{:} <<x_1,y>, \phi> = <<x_1,y>>$ if $tl{:}x = \phi$
     $= apndl{:} <<x_1,y>, <<x_2,y>, \ldots, <x_n,y>>>$
                       if $tl{:}x \neq \phi$

       $= <<x_1,y>, \ldots, <x_n,y>>$
   $= distr{:} <x,y>$ $\square$

12.3 Example: Equivalence of Two Matrix Multiplication Programs

We have seen earlier the matrix multiplication program:

Def $MM \equiv \alpha\alpha IP \circ \alpha distl \circ distr \circ [1, trans \circ 2]$.

We shall now show that its initial segment, MM′, where

Def $MM' \equiv \alpha\alpha IP \circ \alpha distl \circ distr$,

can be defined recursively. (MM′ "multiplies" a pair of matrices after the second matrix has been transposed. Note that MM′, unlike MM, gives $\perp$ for all arguments that are not pairs.) That is, we shall show that MM′ satisfies the following equation which recursively defines the same function (on pairs):

$f \equiv null \circ 1 \to \bar{\phi}; apndl \circ [\alpha IP \circ distl \circ [1 \circ 1, 2], f \circ [tl \circ 1, 2]]$.

Our proof will take the form of showing that the following function, R,

Def $R \equiv null \circ 1 \to \bar{\phi};$
           $apndl \circ [\alpha IP \circ distl \circ [1 \circ 1, 2], MM' \circ [tl \circ 1, 2]]$

is, for all pairs $<x,y>$, the same function as MM′. R "multiplies" two matrices, when the first has more than zero rows, by computing the first row of the "product" (with $\alpha IP \circ distl \circ [1 \circ 1, 2]$) and adjoining it to the "product" of the tail of the first matrix and the second matrix. Thus the theorem we want is

$pair \to\to MM' \equiv R$,

from which the following is immediate:

$MM \equiv MM' \circ [1, trans \circ 2] \equiv R \circ [1, trans \circ 2]$;

where

Def $pair \equiv atom \to \bar{F}; eq \circ [length, \bar{2}]$.

THEOREM: $pair \to\to MM' \equiv R$
where

Def $MM' \equiv \alpha\alpha IP \circ \alpha distl \circ distr$
Def $R \equiv null \circ 1 \rightarrow \bar{\phi};$
$$apndl \circ [\alpha IP \circ distl \circ [1^2, 2], MM' \circ [tl \circ 1, 2]]$$

PROOF.

CASE 1. $pair \& null \circ 1 \longrightarrow MM' \equiv R.$

$pair \& null \circ 1 \longrightarrow R \equiv \bar{\phi}$ by def of R
$pair \& null \circ 1 \longrightarrow MM' \equiv \bar{\phi}$
   since $distr: <\phi,x> = \phi$ by def of $distr$
and $\alpha f{:}\phi = \phi$ by def of Apply to all.
And so: $\alpha\alpha IP \circ \alpha distl \circ distr: <\phi,x> = \phi.$
Thus $pair \& null \circ 1 \longrightarrow MM' \equiv R.$

CASE 2. $pair \& not \circ null \circ 1 \longrightarrow MM' \equiv R.$

$$pair \& not \circ null \circ 1 \longrightarrow R \equiv R', \tag{1}$$

by def of R and R', where

Def $R' \equiv apndl \circ [\alpha IP \circ distl \circ [1^2, 2], MM' \circ [tl \circ 1, 2]].$

We note that

$$R' \equiv apndl \circ [f \circ g, \alpha f \circ h]$$

where

$f \equiv \alpha IP \circ distl$
$g \equiv [1^2, 2]$
$h \equiv distr \circ [tl \circ 1, 2]$
$$\alpha f \equiv \alpha(\alpha IP \circ distl) \equiv \alpha\alpha IP \circ \alpha distl \quad \text{(by III.4)}. \tag{2}$$

Thus, by I.10,

$$R' \equiv \alpha f \circ apndl \circ [g,h]. \tag{3}$$

Now $apndl \circ [g,h] \equiv apndl \circ [[1^2, 2], distr \circ [tl \circ 1, 2]],$
thus, by I.11,

$$pair \& not \circ null \circ 1 \longrightarrow apndl \circ [g,h] \equiv distr. \tag{4}$$

And so we have, by (1), (2), (3) and (4),

$pair \& not \circ null \circ 1 \longrightarrow R \equiv R'$
$$\equiv \alpha f \circ distr \equiv \alpha\alpha IP \circ \alpha distl \circ distr \equiv MM'.$$

Case 1 and Case 2 together prove the theorem.   □

12.4 Expansion Theorems

In the following subsections we shall be "solving" some simple equations (where by a "solution" we shall mean the "least" function which satisfies an equation). To do so we shall need the following notions and results drawn from the later subsection on foundations of the algebra, where their proofs appear.

12.4.1 Expansion. Suppose we have an equation of the form

$$f \equiv E(f) \tag{E1}$$

where $E(f)$ is an expression involving f. Suppose further that there is an infinite sequence of functions f_i for $i = 0, 1, 2, \ldots$, each having the following form:

$f_0 \equiv \bar{\perp}$
$$f_{i+1} \equiv p_0 \rightarrow q_0; \ldots; p_i \rightarrow q_i; \bar{\perp} \tag{E2}$$

where the p_i's and q_i's are particular functions, so that E has the property:

$$E(f_i) \equiv f_{i+1} \text{ for } i = 0, 1, 2, \ldots \tag{E3}$$

Then we say that E is *expansive* and has the f_i's as *approximating functions*.

If E is expansive and has approximating functions as in (E2), and if f is the solution of (E1), then f can be written as the infinite expansion

$$f \equiv p_0 \rightarrow q_0; \ldots; p_n \rightarrow q_n; \ldots \tag{E4}$$

meaning that, for any x, $f{:}x \neq \perp$ iff there is an $n \geq 0$ such that (a) $p_i{:}x = F$ for all $i < n$, and (b) $p_n{:}x = T$, and (c) $q_n{:}x \neq \perp$. When $f{:}x \neq \perp$, then $f{:}x = q_n{:}x$ for this n. (The foregoing is a consequence of the "expansion theorem".)

12.4.2 Linear expansion. A more helpful tool for solving some equations applies when, for any function h,

$$E(h) \equiv p_0 \rightarrow q_0; E_1(h) \tag{LE1}$$

and there exist p_i and q_i such that

$$E_1(p_i \rightarrow q_i; h) \equiv p_{i+1} \rightarrow q_{i+1}; E_1(h)$$
$$\text{for } i = 0, 1, 2, \ldots \tag{LE2}$$

and

$$E_1(\bar{\perp}) \equiv \bar{\perp}. \tag{LE3}$$

Under the above conditions E is said to be *linearly expansive*. If so, and f is the solution of

$$f \equiv E(f) \tag{LE4}$$

then E is expansive and f can again be written as the infinite expansion

$$f \equiv p_0 \rightarrow q_0; \ldots; p_n \rightarrow q_n; \ldots \tag{LE5}$$

using the p_i's and q_i's generated by (LE1) and (LE2).

Although the p_i's and q_i's of (E4) or (LE5) are not unique for a given function, it may be possible to find additional constraints which would make them so, in which case the expansion (LE5) would comprise a canonical form for a function. Even without uniqueness these expansions often permit one to prove the equivalence of two different function expressions, and they often clarify a function's behavior.

12.5 A Recursion Theorem

Using three of the above laws and linear expansion, one can prove the following theorem of moderate generality that gives a clarifying expansion for many recursively defined functions.

RECURSION THEOREM: Let f be a solution of

$$f \equiv p \rightarrow g; Q(f) \tag{1}$$

where

$$Q(k) \equiv h \circ [i, k \circ j] \text{ for any function } k \tag{2}$$

and p, g, h, i, j are any given functions, then

$f \equiv p \rightarrow g; \, p \circ j \rightarrow Q(g); \, \dots \, ; \, p \circ j^n \rightarrow Q^n(g); \, \dots$ (3)

(where $Q^n(g)$ is $h \circ [i, \, Q^{n-1}(g) \circ j]$, and j^n is $j \circ j^{n-1}$ for $n \geq 2$) and

$Q^n(g) \equiv /h \circ [i, \, i \circ j, \, \dots \, , \, i \circ j^{n-1}, \, g \circ j^n].$ (4)

PROOF. We verify that $p \rightarrow g; Q(f)$ is linearly expansive. Let p_n, q_n and k be any functions. Then

$Q(p_n \rightarrow q_n; k)$
$\quad \equiv h \circ [i, \, (p_n \rightarrow q_n; k) \circ j] \quad$ by (2)
$\quad \equiv h \circ [i, \, (p_n \circ j \rightarrow q_n \circ j; k \circ j)] \quad$ by II.1
$\quad \equiv h \circ (p_n \circ j \rightarrow [i, q_n \circ j]; [i, k \circ j]) \quad$ by IV.1
$\quad \equiv p_n \circ j \rightarrow h \circ [i, q_n \circ j]; h \circ [i, k \circ j] \quad$ by II.2
$\quad \equiv p_n \circ j \rightarrow Q(q_n); Q(k) \quad$ by (2)   (5)

Thus if $p_0 \equiv p$ and $q_0 \equiv g$, then (5) gives $p_1 \equiv p \circ j$ and $q_1 \equiv Q(g)$ and in general gives the following functions satisfying (LE2)

$p_n \equiv p \circ j^n \quad$ and $\quad q_n \equiv Q^n(g).$ (6)

Finally,

$Q(\bar{\bot}) \equiv h \circ [i, \, \bar{\bot} \circ j]$
$\quad \equiv h \circ [i, \, \bar{\bot}] \quad$ by III.1.1
$\quad \equiv h \circ \bar{\bot} \quad$ by I.9
$\quad \equiv \bar{\bot} \quad$ by III.1.1.   (7)

Thus (5) and (6) verify (LE2) and (7) verifies (LE3), with $E_1 \equiv Q$. If we let $E(f) \equiv p \rightarrow g; Q(f)$, then we have (LE1); thus E is linearly expansive. Since f is a solution of $f \equiv E(f)$, conclusion (3) follows from (6) and (LE5). Now

$Q^n(g) \equiv h \circ [i, \, Q^{n-1}(g) \circ j]$
$\quad = h \circ [i, \, h \circ [i \circ j, \, \dots \, , \, h \circ [i \circ j^{n-1}, \, g \circ j^n] \, \dots \,]]$
               by I.1, repeatedly
$\quad \equiv /h \circ [i, \, i \circ j, \, \dots \, , \, i \circ j^{n-1}, \, g \circ j^n] \quad$ by I.3   (8)

Result (8) is the second conclusion (4). □

12.5.1 Example: correctness proof of a recursive factorial function. Let f be a solution of

$f \equiv eq0 \rightarrow \bar{1}; \times \circ [id, f \circ s]$

where

Def $s \equiv - \circ [id, \bar{1}] \quad$ (subtract 1).

Then f satisfies the hypothesis of the recursion theorem with $p \equiv eq0$, $g \equiv \bar{1}$, $h \equiv \times$, $i \equiv id$, and $j \equiv s$. Therefore

$f \equiv eq0 \rightarrow \bar{1}; \, \dots \, ; \, eq0 \circ s^n \rightarrow Q^n(\bar{1}); \, \dots$

and

$Q^n(\bar{1}) \equiv / \times \circ [id, \, id \circ s, \, \dots \, , \, id \circ s^{n-1}, \, \bar{1} \circ s^n].$

Now $id \circ s^k \equiv s^k$ by III.2 and $eq0 \circ s^n \rightarrow\!\!\!\rightarrow \bar{1} \circ s^n \equiv \bar{1}$ by III.1, since $eq0 \circ s^n : x$ implies defined $\circ s^n : x$; and also $eq0 \circ s^n : x \equiv eq0: (x - n) \equiv x = n$. Thus if $eq0 \circ s^n : x = T$, then $x = n$ and

$Q^n(\bar{1}): n = n \times (n - 1) \times \dots \times (n - (n - 1))$
                     $\times (\bar{1}: (n - n)) = n!.$

Using these results for $\bar{1} \circ s^n$, $eq0 \circ s^n$, and $Q^n(\bar{1})$ in the previous expansion for f, we obtain

$f : x \equiv x = 0 \rightarrow 1; \, \dots \, ; \, x = n$
                    $\rightarrow n \times (n - 1) \times \dots \times 1 \times 1; \, \dots$

Thus we have proved that f terminates on precisely the set of nonnegative integers and that it is the factorial function thereon.

12.6 An Iteration Theorem
    This is really a corollary of the recursion theorem. It gives a simple expansion for many iterative programs.

ITERATION THEOREM: Let f be the solution (i.e., the least solution) of

$f \equiv p \rightarrow g; \, h \circ f \circ k$

then

$f \equiv p \rightarrow g; \, p \circ k \rightarrow h \circ g \circ k; \, \dots \, ; \, p \circ k^n \rightarrow h^n \circ g \circ k^n; \, \dots$

PROOF. Let $h' \equiv h \circ 2$, $i' \equiv id$, $j' \equiv k$, then

$f \equiv p \rightarrow g; \, h' \circ [i', \, f \circ j']$

since $h \circ 2 \circ [id, f \circ k] \equiv h \circ f \circ k \quad$ by I.5 (id is defined except for $\bot$, and the equation holds for $\bot$). Thus the recursion theorem gives

$f = p \rightarrow g; \, \dots \, , \, p \circ k^n \rightarrow Q^n(g); \, \dots$

where

$Q^n(g) \equiv h \circ 2 \circ [id, \, Q^{n-1}(g) \circ k]$
$\quad \equiv h \circ Q^{n-1}(g) \circ k \equiv h^n \circ g \circ k^n$

by I.5 □

12.6.1 Example: Correctness proof for an iterative factorial function. Let f be the solution of

$f \equiv eq0 \circ 1 \rightarrow 2; f \circ [s \circ 1, \times]$

where **Def** $s \equiv - \circ [id, \bar{1}]$ (subtract 1). We want to prove that $f : <x, 1> = x!$ iff x is a nonnegative integer. Let $p \equiv eq0 \circ 1$, $g \equiv 2$, $h \equiv id$, $k \equiv [s \circ 1, \times]$. Then

$f \equiv p \rightarrow g; \, h \circ f \circ k$

and so

$f \equiv p \rightarrow g; \, \dots \, ; \, p \circ k^n \rightarrow g \circ k^n; \, \dots$ (1)

by the iteration theorem, since $h^n \equiv id$. We want to show that

$pair \rightarrow\!\!\!\rightarrow k^n \equiv [a_n, b_n]$ (2)

holds for every $n \geq 1$, where

$a_n \equiv s^n \circ 1$ (3)
$b_n \equiv / \times \circ [s^{n-1} \circ 1, \, \dots \, , \, s \circ 1, 1, 2]$ (4)

Now (2) holds for $n = 1$ by definition of k. We assume it holds for some $n \geq 1$ and prove it then holds for $n + 1$. Now

$pair \rightarrow\!\!\!\rightarrow k^{n+1} \equiv k \circ k^n \equiv [s \circ 1, \times] \circ [a_n, b_n]$ (5)

since (2) holds for n. And so

pair $\longrightarrow k^{n+1} \equiv [s\circ a_n, \times\circ[a_n, b_n]]$ by I.1 and I.5   (6)

To pass from (5) to (6) we must check that whenever a_n or b_n yield $\perp$ in (5), so will the right side of (6). Now

$$s\circ a_n \equiv s^{n+1}\circ 1 \equiv a_{n+1} \tag{7}$$
$$\times\circ[a_n, b_n] \equiv /\times \circ [s^n\circ 1, s^{n-1}\circ 1, ... , s\circ 1, 1, 2]$$
$$\equiv b_{n+1} \text{ by I.3.} \tag{8}$$

Combining (6), (7), and (8) gives

$$\text{pair} \longrightarrow k^{n+1} \equiv [a_{n+1}, b_{n+1}]. \tag{9}$$

Thus (2) holds for n = 1 and holds for n + 1 whenever it holds for n, therefore, by induction, it holds for every $n \geq 1$. Now (2) gives, for pairs:

$$\text{defined}\circ k^n \longrightarrow p\circ k^n \equiv \text{eq}0\circ 1\circ[a_n, b_n]$$
$$\equiv \text{eq}0\circ a_n \equiv \text{eq}0\circ s^n\circ 1 \tag{10}$$
$$\text{defined}\circ k^n \longrightarrow g\circ k^n$$
$$\equiv 2\circ[a_n, b_n] \equiv /\times \circ [s^{n-1}\circ 1, ... , s\circ 1, 1, 2] \tag{11}$$

(both use I.5). Now (1) tells us that $f{:}{<}x,1{>}$ is defined iff there is an n such that $p\circ k^i{:}{<}x,1{>} = F$ for all i < n, and $p\circ k^n{:}{<}x,1{>} = T$, that is, by (10), $\text{eq}0\circ s^n{:}x = T$, i.e., x=n; and $g\circ k^n{:}{<}x,1{>}$ is defined, in which case, by (11),

$$f{:}{<}x,1{>} = /\times{:}{<}1, 2, ... , x{-}1, x, 1{>} = \text{n!},$$

which is what we set out to prove.

12.6.2 Example: proof of equivalence of two iterative programs. In this example we want to prove that two iteratively defined programs, f and g, are the same function. Let f be the solution of

$$f \equiv p\circ 1 \rightarrow 2; h\circ f\circ[k\circ 1, 2]. \tag{1}$$

Let g be the solution of

$$g \equiv p\circ 1 \rightarrow 2; g\circ[k\circ 1, h\circ 2]. \tag{2}$$

Then, by the iteration theorem:

$$f \equiv p_0 \rightarrow q_0; ... ; p_n \rightarrow q_n; ... \tag{3}$$
$$g \equiv p'_0 \rightarrow q'_0; ... ; p'_n \rightarrow q'_n; ... \tag{4}$$

where (letting $r^0 \equiv \text{id}$ for any r), for n = 0, 1, ...

$$p_n \equiv p\circ 1\circ[k\circ 1, 2]^n \equiv p\circ 1\circ[k^n\circ 1, 2] \quad \text{by I.5.1} \tag{5}$$
$$q_n \equiv h^n\circ 2\circ[k\circ 1, 2]^n \equiv h^n\circ 2\circ[k^n\circ 1, 2] \quad \text{by I.5.1} \tag{6}$$
$$p'_n \equiv p\circ 1\circ[k\circ 1, h\circ 2]^n \equiv p\circ 1\circ[k^n\circ 1, h^n\circ 2] \quad \text{by I.5.1} \tag{7}$$
$$q'_n \equiv 2\circ[k\circ 1, h\circ 2]^n \equiv 2\circ[k^n\circ 1, h^n\circ 2] \quad \text{by I.5.1.} \tag{8}$$

Now, from the above, using I.5,

$$\text{defined}\circ 2 \longrightarrow p_n \equiv p\circ k^n\circ 1 \tag{9}$$
$$\text{defined}\circ h^n\circ 2 \longrightarrow p'_n \equiv p\circ k^n\circ 1 \tag{10}$$
$$\text{defined}\circ k^n\circ 1 \longrightarrow q_n \equiv q'_n \equiv h^n\circ 2 \tag{11}$$

Thus

$$\text{defined}\circ h^n\circ 2 \longrightarrow \text{defined}\circ 2 \equiv \bar{T} \tag{12}$$
$$\text{defined}\circ h^n\circ 2, \longrightarrow p_n \equiv p'_n \tag{13}$$

and

$$f \equiv p_0 \rightarrow q_0; ... ; p_n \rightarrow h^n\circ 2; ... \tag{14}$$
$$g \equiv p'_0 \rightarrow q'_0; ... ; p'_n \rightarrow h^n\circ 2; ... \tag{15}$$

since p_n and p'_n provide the qualification needed for $q_n \equiv q'_n \equiv h^n\circ 2$.

Now suppose there is an x such that $f{:}x \neq g{:}x$. Then there is an n such that $p_i{:}x = p'_i{:}x = F$ for i < n, and $p_n{:}x \neq p'_n{:}x$. From (12) and (13) this can only happen when $h^n\circ 2{:}x = \perp$. But since h is $\perp$-preserving, $h^m\circ 2{:}x = \perp$ for all m $\geq$ n. Hence $f{:}x = g{:}x = \perp$ by (14) and (15). This contradicts the assumption that there is an x for which $f{:}x \neq g{:}x$. Hence $f \equiv g$.

This example (by J. H. Morris, Jr.) is treated more elegantly in [16] on p. 498. However, some may find that the above treatment is more constructive, leads one more mechanically to the key questions, and provides more insight into the behavior of the two functions.

12.7 Nonlinear Equations

The preceding examples have concerned "linear" equations (in which the "unknown" function does not have an argument involving itself). The question of the existence of simple expansions that "solve" "quadratic" and higher order equations remains open.

The earlier examples concerned solutions of $f \equiv \text{E}(f)$, where E is linearly expansive. The following example involves an E(f) that is quadratic and expansive (but not linearly expansive).

12.7.1 Example: proof of idempotency ([16] p. 497). Let f be the solution of

$$f \equiv \text{E}(f) \equiv p \rightarrow \text{id}; f^2\circ h. \tag{1}$$

We wish to prove that $f \equiv f^2$. We verify that E is expansive (Section 12.4.1) with the following approximating functions:

$$f_0 \equiv \bar{\perp} \tag{2a}$$
$$f_n \equiv p \rightarrow \text{id}; ... ; p\circ h^{n-1} \rightarrow h^{n-1}; \bar{\perp} \quad \text{for n > 0} \tag{2b}$$

First we note that $p \longrightarrow f_n \equiv \text{id}$ and so

$$p\circ h^i \longrightarrow f_n\circ h^i \equiv h^i. \tag{3}$$

Now $\text{E}(f_0) \equiv p \rightarrow \text{id}; \bar{\perp}^2\circ h \equiv f_1,$ (4)

and

E(f_n)
$$\equiv p \rightarrow \text{id}; f_n\circ(p \rightarrow \text{id}; ... ; p\circ h^{n-1} \rightarrow h^{n-1}; \bar{\perp})\circ h$$
$$\equiv p \rightarrow \text{id}; f_n\circ(p\circ h \rightarrow h; ... ; p\circ h^n \rightarrow h^n; \bar{\perp}\circ h)$$
$$\equiv p \rightarrow \text{id}; p\circ h \rightarrow f_n\circ h; ... ; p\circ h^n \rightarrow f_n\circ h^n; f_n\circ\bar{\perp}$$
$$\equiv p \rightarrow \text{id}; p\circ h \rightarrow h; ... ; p\circ h^n \rightarrow h^n; \bar{\perp} \quad \text{by (3)}$$
$$\equiv f_{n+1}. \tag{5}$$

Thus E is expansive by (4) and (5); so by (2) and Section 12.4.1 (E4)

$$f \equiv p \rightarrow \text{id}; ... ; p\circ h^n \rightarrow h^n; ... . \tag{6}$$

But (6), by the iteration theorem, gives

$$f \equiv p \rightarrow \text{id}; f\circ h. \tag{7}$$

Now, if $p{:}x = T$, then $f{:}x = x = f^2{:}x$, by (1). If $p{:}x = F$, then

$$f{:}x = f^2\circ h{:}x \quad \text{by (1)}$$

$= f{:}(f{\circ}h{:}x) = f{:}(f{:}x)$ by (7)

$= f^2{:}x.$

If $p{:}x$ is neither T nor F, then $f{:}x = \bot = f^2{:}x$. Thus $f \equiv f^2$.

12.8 Foundations for the Algebra of Programs

Our purpose in this section is to establish the validity of the results stated in Section 12.4. Subsequent sections do not depend on this one, hence it can be skipped by readers who wish to do so. We use the standard concepts and results from [16], but the notation used for objects and functions, etc., will be that of this paper.

We take as the domain (and range) for all functions the set O of objects (which includes $\bot$) of a given FP system. We take F to be the set of functions, and **F** to be the set of functional forms of that FP system. We write $E(f)$ for any function expression involving functional forms, primitive and defined functions, and the function symbol f; and we regard E as a functional that maps a function f into the corresponding function $E(f)$. We assume that all $f \in$ F are $\bot$-preserving and that all functional forms in **F** correspond to continuous functionals in every variable (e.g., $[f, g]$ is continuous in both f and g). (All primitive functions of the FP system given earlier are $\bot$-preserving, and all its functional forms are continuous.)

DEFINITIONS. Let $E(f)$ be a function expression. Let

$f_0 \equiv \bot$

$f_{i+1} \equiv p_0 \to q_0; \dots ; p_i \to q_i; \bot$ for $i = 0, 1, \dots$

where $p_i, q_i \in$ F. Let E have the property that

$E(f_i) \equiv f_{i+1}$ for $i = 0, 1, \dots$.

Then E is said to be *expansive* with the *approximating functions* f_i. We write

$f \equiv p_0 \to q_0; \dots ; p_n \to q_n; \dots$

to mean that $f \equiv \lim_i\{f_i\}$, where the f_i have the form above. We call the right side an *infinite expansion* of f. We take $f{:}x$ to be defined iff there is an $n \geq 0$ such that (a) $p_i{:}x = F$ for all $i < n$, and (b) $p_n{:}x = T$, and (c) $q_n{:}x$ is defined, in which case $f{:}x = q_n{:}x$.

EXPANSION THEOREM: Let $E(f)$ be expansive with approximating functions as above. Let f be the least function satisfying

$f \equiv E(f).$

Then

$f \equiv p_0 \to q_0; \dots ; p_n \to q_n; \dots$

PROOF. Since E is the composition of continuous functionals (from **F**) involving only monotonic functions ($\bot$-preserving functions from F) as constant terms, E is continuous ([16] p. 493). Therefore its least fixed point f is $\lim_i\{E^i(\bot)\} \equiv \lim_i\{f_i\}$ ([16] p. 494), which by definition is the above infinite expansion for f.   □

DEFINITION. Let $E(f)$ be a function expression satisfying the following:

$E(h) \equiv p_0 \to q_0; E_1(h)$ for all $h \in$ F   (LE1)

where $p_i \in$ F and $q_i \in$ F exist such that

$E_1(p_i \to q_i; h) \equiv p_{i+1} \to q_{i+1}; E_1(h)$
for all $h \in$ F and i = 0, 1, ...   (LE2)

and

$E_1(\bot) \equiv \bot.$ (LE3)

Then E is said to be *linearly expansive* with respect to these p_i's and q_i's.

LINEAR EXPANSION THEOREM: Let E be linearly expansive with respect to p_i and q_i, i = 0, 1, ... Then E is expansive with approximating functions

$f_0 \equiv \bot$ (1)

$f_{i+1} \equiv p_0 \to q_0; \dots ; p_i \to q_i; \bot.$ (2)

PROOF. We want to show that $E(f_i) \equiv f_{i+1}$ for any $i \geq 0$. Now

$E(f_0) \equiv p_0 \to q_0; E_1(\bot) \equiv p_0 \to q_0; \bot \equiv f_1$ (3)
by (LE1) (LE3) (1).

Let i > 0 be fixed and let

$f_i \equiv p_0 \to q_0; w_1$ (4a)

$w_1 \equiv p_1 \to q_1; w_2$ (4b)

etc.

$w_{i-1} \equiv p_{i-1} \to q_{i-1}; \bot.$ (4-)

Then, for this i > 0

$E(f_i) \equiv p_0 \to q_0; E_1(f_i)$ by (LE1)

$E_1(f_i) \equiv p_1 \to q_1; E_1(w_1)$ by (LE2) and (4a)

$E_1(w_1) \equiv p_2 \to q_2; E_1(w_2)$ by (LE2) and (4b)

etc.

$E_1(w_{i-1}) \equiv p_i \to q_i; E_1(\bot)$ by (LE2) and (4-)
$\equiv p_i \to q_i; \bot$ by (LE3)

Combining the above gives

$E(f_i) \equiv f_{i+1}$ for arbitrary i > 0, by (2).   (5)

By (3), (5) also holds for i = 0; thus it holds for all $i \geq 0$. Therefore E is expansive and has the required approximating functions.   □

COROLLARY. If E is linearly expansive with respect to p_i and q_i, i = 0, 1, ... , and f is the least function satisfying

$f \equiv E(f)$ (LE4)

then

$f \equiv p_0 \to q_0; \dots ; p_n \to q_n; \dots .$ (LE5)

12.9 The Algebra of Programs for the Lambda Calculus and for Combinators

Because Church's lambda calculus [5] and the system of combinators developed by Schönfinkel and Curry [6] are the primary mathematical systems for representing the notion of application of functions, and because they are more powerful than FP systems, it is natural to enquire what an algebra of programs based on those systems would look like.

The lambda calculus and combinator equivalents of FP composition, $f \circ g$, are

$$\lambda fgx.(f(gx)) \equiv B$$

where B is a simple combinator defined by Curry. There is no direct equivalent for the FP object $<x,y>$ in the Church or Curry systems proper; however, following Landin [14] and Burge [4], one can use the primitive functions prefix, head, tail, null, and atomic to introduce the notion of list structures that correspond to FP sequences. Then, using FP notation for lists, the lambda calculus equivalent for construction is $\lambda fgx.<fx,gx>$. A combinatory equivalent is an expression involving prefix, the null list, and two or more basic combinators. It is so complex that I shall not attempt to give it.

If one uses the lambda calculus or combinatory expressions for the functional forms $f \circ g$ and $[f,g]$ to express the law I.1 in the FP algebra, $[f,g] \circ h \equiv [f \circ h, g \circ h]$, the result is an expression so complex that the sense of the law is obscured. The only way to make that sense clear in either system is to name the two functionals: composition $\equiv B$, and construction $\equiv A$, so that $Bfg \equiv f \circ g$, and $Afg \equiv [f,g]$. Then I.1 becomes

$$B(Afg)h \equiv A(Bfh)(Bgh),$$

which is still not as perspicuous as the FP law.

The point of the above is that if one wishes to state clear laws like those of the FP algebra in either Church's or Curry's system, one finds it necessary to select certain functionals (e.g., composition and construction) as the basic operations of the algebra and to either give them short names or, preferably, represent them by some special notation as in FP. If one does this and provides primitives, objects, lists, etc., the result is an FP-like system in which the usual lambda expressions or combinators do not appear. Even then these Church or Curry versions of FP systems, being less restricted, have some problems that FP systems do not have:

a) The Church and Curry versions accommodate functions of many types and can define functions that do not exist in FP systems. Thus, Bf is a function that has no counterpart in FP systems. This added power carries with it problems of type compatibility. For example, in $f \circ g$, is the range of g included in the domain of f? In FP systems all functions have the same domain and range.

b) The semantics of Church's lambda calculus depends on substitution rules that are simply stated but whose implications are very difficult to fully comprehend. The true complexity of these rules is not widely recognized but is evidenced by the succession of able logicians who have published "proofs" of the Church-Rosser theorem that failed to account for one or another of these complexities. (The Church-Rosser theorem, or Scott's proof of the existence of a model [22], is required to show that the lambda calculus has a consistent semantics.) The definition of pure Lisp contained a related error for a considerable period (the "funarg" problem). Analogous problems attach to Curry's system as well.

In contrast, the formal (FFP) version of FP systems (described in the next section) has no variables and only an elementary substitution rule (a function for its name), and it can be shown to have a consistent semantics by a relatively simple fixed-point argument along the lines developed by Dana Scott and by Manna et al [16]. For such a proof see McJones [18].

12.10 Remarks

The algebra of programs outlined above needs much work to provide expansions for larger classes of equations and to extend its laws and theorems beyond the elementary ones given here. It would be interesting to explore the algebra for an FP-like system whose sequence constructor is not $\perp$-preserving (law I.5 is strengthened, but IV.1 is lost). Other interesting problems are: (a) Find rules that make expansions unique, giving canonical forms for functions; (b) find algorithms for expanding and analyzing the behavior of functions for various classes of arguments; and (c) explore ways of using the laws and theorems of the algebra as the basic rules either of a formal, preexecution "lazy evaluation" scheme [9, 10], or of one which operates during execution. Such schemes would, for example, make use of the law $1 \circ [f,g] \leq f$ to avoid evaluating $g:x$.

13. Formal Systems for Functional Programming (FFP Systems)

13.1 Introduction

As we have seen, an FP system has a set of functions that depends on its set of primitive functions, its set of functional forms, and its set of definitions. In particular, its set of functional forms is fixed once and for all, and this set determines the power of the system in a major way. For example, if its set of functional forms is empty, then its entire set of functions is just the set of primitive functions. In FFP systems one can create new functional forms. Functional forms are represented by object sequences; the first element of a sequence determines which form it represents, while the remaining elements are the parameters of the form.

The ability to define new functional forms in FFP systems is one consequence of the principal difference between them and FP systems: in FFP systems objects are used to "represent" functions in a systematic way. Otherwise FFP systems mirror FP systems closely. They are similar to, but simpler than, the Reduction (Red) languages of an earlier paper [2].

We shall first give the simple syntax of FFP systems, then discuss their semantics informally, giving examples, and finally give their formal semantics.

13.2 Syntax

We describe the set O of objects and the set E of expressions of an FFP system. These depend on the choice of some set A of *atoms*, which we take as given. We assume that T (true), F (false), ϕ (the empty sequence), and # (default) belong to A, as well as "numbers" of various kinds, etc.

1) Bottom, $\perp$, is an *object* but not an atom.

2) Every atom is an *object*.

3) Every object is an *expression*.

4) If $x_1, \ldots, x_n$ are objects [expressions], then $<x_1, \ldots, x_n>$ is an *object* [resp., *expression*] called a *sequence* (of *length* n) for $n \geq 1$. The object [expression] x_i for $1 \leq i \leq n$, is the ith *element* of the sequence $<x_1, \ldots, x_i, \ldots, x_n>$. ($\phi$ is both a sequence and an atom; its length is 0.)

5) If x and y are expressions, then $(x{:}y)$ is an *expression* called an *application*. x is its *operator* and y is its *operand*. Both are *elements* of the expression.

6) If $x = <x_1, \ldots, x_n>$ and if one of the elements of x is $\perp$, then $x = \perp$. That is, $<\ldots, \perp, \ldots> = \perp$.

7) All objects and expressions are formed by finite use of the above rules.

A *subexpression* of an expression x is either x itself or a subexpression of an element of x. An FFP object is an expression that has no application as a subexpression. Given the same set of atoms, FFP and FP objects are the same.

13.3 Informal Remarks About FFP Semantics

13.3.1 The meaning of expressions; the semantic function μ.
Every FFP expression e has a *meaning*, μe, which is always an object; μe is found by repeatedly replacing each innermost application in e by its meaning. If this process is nonterminating, the meaning of e is $\perp$. The meaning of an innermost application $(x{:}y)$ (since it is innermost, x and y must be objects) is the result of applying the function *represented* by x to y, just as in FP systems, except that in FFP systems functions are represented by objects, rather than by function expressions, with atoms (instead of function symbols) representing primitive and defined functions, and with sequences representing the FP functions denoted by functional forms.

The association between objects and the functions they represent is given by the *representation function*, ρ, of the FFP system. (Both ρ and μ belong to the description of the system, not the system itself.) Thus if the atom $NULL$ represents the FP function null, then $\rho NULL =$ null and the meaning of $(NULL{:}A)$ is $\mu(NULL{:}A) = (\rho NULL){:}A =$ null$:A = F$.

From here on, as above, we use the colon in two senses. When it is between two objects, as in $(NULL{:}A)$, it identifies an FFP application that denotes only itself; when it comes between a *function* and an object, as in $(\rho NULL){:}A$ or null$:A$, it identifies an FP-like application that denotes the *result* of applying the function to the object.

The fact that FFP operators are objects makes possible a function, apply, which is meaningless in FP systems:

$$\text{apply:}<x,y> = (x{:}y).$$

The result of apply:$<x,y>$, namely $(x{:}y)$, is meaningless in FP systems on two levels. First, $(x{:}y)$ is not itself an object; it illustrates another difference between FP and FFP systems: some FFP functions, like apply, map objects into expressions, not directly into objects as FP functions do. However, the *meaning* of apply:$<x,y>$ *is* an object (see below). Second, $(x{:}y)$ could not be even an intermediate result in an FP system; it is meaningless in FP systems since x is an object, not a function and FP systems do not associate functions with objects. Now if $APPLY$ represents apply, then the meaning of $(APPLY{:}<NULL,A>)$ is

$$
\begin{aligned}
\mu(APPLY{:}&<NULL,A>) \\
&= \mu((\rho APPLY){:}<NULL,A>) \\
&= \mu(\text{apply:}<NULL,A>) \\
&= \mu(NULL{:}A) = \mu((\rho NULL){:}A) \\
&= \mu(\text{null:}A) = \mu F = F.
\end{aligned}
$$

The last step follows from the fact that every object is its own meaning. Since the meaning function μ eventually evaluates all applications, one can think of apply:$<NULL,A>$ as yielding F even though the actual result is $(NULL{:}A)$.

13.3.2 How objects represent functions; the representation function ρ.
As we have seen, some atoms (*primitive* atoms) will represent the primitive functions of the system. Other atoms can represent defined functions just as symbols can in FP systems. If an atom is neither primitive nor defined, it represents $\perp$, the function which is $\perp$ everywhere.

Sequences also represent functions and are analogous to the functional forms of FP. The function represented by a sequence is given (recursively) by the following rule.

Metacomposition rule

$$(\rho<x_1, \ldots, x_n>){:}y = (\rho x_1){:}<<x_1, \ldots, x_n>, y>,$$

where the x_i's and y are objects. Here ρx_1 determines what functional form $<x_1, \ldots, x_n>$ represents, and $x_2, \ldots, x_n$ are the parameters of the form (in FFP, x_1 itself can also serve as a parameter). Thus, for example, let **Def** $\rho CONST \equiv 2 \circ 1$; then $<CONST,x>$ in FFP represents the FP functional form $\bar{x}$, since, by the metacomposition rule, if $y \neq \perp$,

$$
\begin{aligned}
(\rho<CONST,x>){:}y &= (\rho CONST){:}<<CONST,x>,y> \\
&= 2 \circ 1{:}<<CONST,x>,y> = x.
\end{aligned}
$$

Here we can see that the first, controlling, operator of a sequence or form, $CONST$ in this case, always has as its operand, after metacomposition, a pair whose first element is the sequence itself and whose second element is the original operand of the sequence, y in this case. The controlling operator can then rearrange and reapply the elements of the sequence and original operand in a great variety of ways. The significant point about metacomposition is that it permits the definition of new functional forms, in effect, merely by defining new functions. It also permits one to write recursive functions without a definition.

We give one more example of a controlling function for a functional form: **Def** $\rho CONS \equiv \alpha apply \circ tl \circ distr$. This definition results in $<CONS, f_1, \ldots, f_n>$—where the f_i are objects—representing the same function as $[\rho f_1, \ldots, \rho f_n]$. The following shows this.

$(\rho<CONS, f_1, \ldots, f_n>):x$

$$= (\rho CONS):<<CONS, f_1, \ldots, f_n >, x>$$

by metacomposition

$$= \alpha apply \circ tl \circ distr:<<CONS, f_1, \ldots, f_n>, x>$$

by def of $\rho CONS$

$$= \alpha apply:<<f_1, x>, \ldots, <f_n, x>>$$

by def of tl and distr and $\circ$

$$= <apply:<f_1, x>, \ldots, apply:<f_n, x>>$$

by def of α

$$= <(f_1:x), \ldots, (f_n:x)> \quad \text{by def of apply.}$$

In evaluating the last expression, the meaning function μ will produce the meaning of each application, giving $\rho f_i:x$ as the ith element.

Usually, in describing the function represented by a sequence, we shall give its overall effect rather than show how its controlling operator achieves that effect. Thus we would simply write

$$(\rho<CONS, f_1, \ldots, f_n>):x = <(f_1:x), \ldots, (f_n:x)>$$

instead of the more detailed account above.

We need a controlling operator, *COMP*, to give us sequences representing the functional form composition. We take $\rho COMP$ to be a primitive function such that, for all objects x,

$(\rho<COMP, f_1, \ldots, f_n>):x$

$$= (f_1:(f_2:(\ldots :(f_n:x)\ldots))) \quad \text{for n} \geq 1.$$

(I am indebted to Paul McJones for his observation that ordinary composition could be achieved by this primitive function rather than by using two composition rules in the basic semantics, as was done in an earlier paper [2].)

Although FFP systems permit the definition and investigation of new functional forms, it is to be expected that most programming would use a fixed set of forms (whose controlling operators are primitives), as in FP, so that the algebraic laws for those forms could be employed, and so that a structured programming style could be used based on those forms.

In addition to its use in defining functional forms, metacomposition can be used to create recursive functions directly without the use of recursive definitions of the form **Def** $f \equiv E(f)$. For example, if $\rho MLAST \equiv$ null$\circ$tl$\circ$2 $\rightarrow$ 1$\circ$2; apply$\circ$[1, tl$\circ$2], then $\rho<MLAST> \equiv$ last, where last$:x \equiv x = <x_1, \ldots, x_n> \rightarrow x_n; \perp$. Thus the operator $<MLAST>$ works as follows:

$$\mu(<MLAST>:<A,B>)$$

$$= \mu(\rho MLAST:<<MLAST>,<A,B>>)$$

by metacomposition

$$= \mu(apply \circ [1, tl \circ 2]:<<MLAST>,<A,B>>)$$

$$= \mu(apply:<<MLAST>,<B>>)$$

$$= \mu(<MLAST>:<B>)$$

$$= \mu(\rho MLAST:<<MLAST>,<B>>)$$

$$= \mu(1 \circ 2:<<MLAST>,<B>>)$$

$$= B.$$

13.3.3 Summary of the properties of ρ and μ. So far we have shown how ρ maps atoms and sequences into functions and how those functions map objects into expressions. Actually, ρ and all FFP functions can be extended so that they are defined for all expressions. With such extensions the properties of ρ and μ can be summarized as follows:

1) $\mu \in$ [expressions $\rightarrow$ objects].
2) If x is an object, $\mu x = x$.
3) If e is an expression and $e = <e_1, \ldots, e_n>$, then $\mu e = <\mu e_1, \ldots, \mu e_n>$.
4) $\rho \in$ [expressions $\rightarrow$ [expressions $\rightarrow$ expressions]].
5) For any expression e, $\rho e = \rho(\mu e)$.
6) If x is an object and e an expression, then $\rho x:e = \rho x:(\mu e)$.
7) If x and y are objects, then $\mu(x:y) = \mu(\rho x:y)$. In words: the meaning of an FFP application $(x:y)$ is found by applying ρx, the function represented by x, to y and then finding the meaning of the resulting expression (which is *usually* an object and is then its own meaning).

13.3.4 Cells, fetching, and storing. For a number of reasons it is convenient to create functions which serve as names. In particular, we shall need this facility in describing the semantics of definitions in FFP systems. To introduce naming functions, that is, the ability to *fetch* the contents of a cell with a given name from a store (a sequence of cells) and to *store* a cell with given name and contents in such a sequence, we introduce objects called *cells* and two new functional forms, *fetch* and *store*.

Cells

A *cell* is a triple $<CELL,name,contents>$. We use this form instead of the pair $<name,contents>$ so that cells can be distinguished from ordinary pairs.

Fetch

The functional form *fetch* takes an object n as its parameter (n is customarily an atom serving as a name); it is written $\uparrow n$ (read "fetch n"). Its definition for objects n and x is

$$\uparrow n:x \equiv x = \phi \rightarrow \#; \text{atom}:x \rightarrow \perp;$$
$$(1:x) = <CELL,n,c> \rightarrow c; \uparrow n \circ tl:x,$$

where # is the atom "default." Thus $\uparrow n$ (fetch n) applied to a sequence gives the contents of the first cell in the sequence whose name is n; If there is no cell named n, the result is default, #. Thus $\uparrow n$ is the name function for the name n. (We assume that $\rho FETCH$ is the primitive function such that $\rho<FETCH,n> \equiv \uparrow n$. Note that $\uparrow n$ simply passes over elements in its operand that are not cells.)

Store and push, pop, purge

Like fetch, *store* takes an object n as its parameter; it is written $\downarrow n$ ("store n"). When applied to a pair $<x,y>$, where y is a sequence, $\downarrow n$ removes the first cell named n from y, if any, then creates a new cell named n with contents x and appends it to y. Before defining $\downarrow n$ (store n) we shall specify four auxiliary functional forms. (These can be used in combination with fetch n and store n to obtain multiple, named, LIFO stacks within a storage sequence.) Two of these auxiliary forms are specified by recursive functional equations; each takes an object n as its parameter.

(cellname n) $\equiv$ atom $\to \bar{F}$;
   eq$\circ$[length, $\bar{3}$] $\to$ eq$\circ$[[$\overline{CELL}$, $\bar{n}$], [1, 2]]; $\bar{F}$
(push n) $\equiv$ pair $\to$ apndl$\circ$[[$\overline{CELL}$, $\bar{n}$, 1], 2]; $\perp$
(pop n) $\equiv$ null $\to \bar{\phi}$;
   (cellname n)$\circ$1 $\to$ tl; apndl$\circ$[1, (pop n)$\circ$tl]
(purge n) $\equiv$ null $\to \bar{\phi}$; (cellname n)$\circ$1 $\to$ (purge n)$\circ$tl;
   apndl$\circ$[1, (purge n)$\circ$tl]
$\downarrow n \equiv$ pair $\to$ (push n)$\circ$[1, (pop n)$\circ$2]; $\perp$

The above functional forms work as follows. For $x \neq \perp$, (cellname n):x is T if x is a cell named n, otherwise it is F. (pop n):y removes the first cell named n from a sequence y; (purge n):y removes all cells named n from y. (push n):$<x,y>$ puts a cell named n with contents x at the head of sequence y; $\downarrow n$:$<x,y>$ is (push n):$<x,$ (pop n):$y>$.

(Thus (push n):$<x,y> = y'$ pushes x onto the top of a "stack" named n in y'; x can be read by $\uparrow n$:$y' = x$ and can be removed by (pop n):y'; thus $\uparrow n\circ$(pop n):y' is the element below x in the stack n, provided there is more than one cell named n in y'.)

13.3.5 Definitions in FFP systems. The semantics of an FFP system depends on a fixed set of definitions D (a sequence of cells), just as an FP system depends on its informally given set of definitions. Thus the semantic function μ depends on D; altering D gives a new μ' that reflects the altered definitions. We have represented D as an *object* because in AST systems (Section 14) we shall want to transform D by applying functions to it and to fetch data from it—in addition to using it as the source of function definitions in FFP semantics.

If $<CELL,n,c>$ is the first cell named n in the sequence D (and n is an atom) then it has the same effect as the FP definition **Def** $n \equiv \rho c$, that is, the meaning of $(n$:$x)$ will be the same as that of ρc:x. Thus for example, if $<CELL,CONST,<COMP,2,1>>$ is the first cell in D named $CONST$, then it has the same effect as **Def** $CONST \equiv 2\circ1$, and the FFP system with that D would find

$\mu(CONST$:$<<x,y>,z>) = y$

and consequently

$\mu(<CONST,A>$:$B) = A$.

In general, in an FFP system with definitions D, the meaning of an application of the form $(atom$:$x)$ is de-pendent on D; if $\uparrow atom$:D $\neq$ # (that is, $atom$ is defined in D) then its meaning is $\mu(c$:$x)$, where $c = \uparrow atom$:D, the contents of the first cell in D named $atom$. If $\uparrow atom$:D = #, then $atom$ is not defined in D and either $atom$ is primitive, i.e. the system knows how to compute $\rho atom$:x, and $\mu(atom$:$x) = \mu(\rho atom$:$x)$, otherwise $\mu(atom$:$x) = \perp$.

13.4 Formal Semantics for FFP Systems

We assume that a set A of atoms, a set D of defini-tions, a set P $\subset$ A of primitive atoms and the primitive functions they represent have all been chosen. We as-sume that ρa is the primitive function represented by a if a belongs to P, and that $\rho a = \perp$ if a belongs to Q, the set of atoms in A-P that are not defined in D. Although ρ is defined for all expressions (see 13.3.3), the formal semantics uses its definition only on P and Q. The functions that ρ assigns to other expressions x are im-plicitly determined and applied in the following semantic rules for evaluating $\mu(x$:$y)$. The above choices of A and D, and of P and the associated primitive functions de-termine the objects, expressions, and the semantic func-tion μ_D for an FFP system. (We regard D as fixed and write μ for μ_D.) We assume D is a sequence and that $\uparrow y$:D can be computed (by the function $\uparrow y$ as given in Section 13.3.4) for any atom y. With these assumptions we define μ as the least fixed point of the functional τ, where the function $\tau\mu$ is defined as follows for any function μ (for all expressions x, x_i, y, y_i, z, and w):

$(\tau\mu)x \equiv x \in A \to x$;
   $x = <x_1, \ldots, x_n> \to <\mu x_1, \ldots, \mu x_n>$;
   $x = (y$:$z) \to$
      $(y \in A \& (\uparrow y$:D$) = \# \to \mu((\rho y)(\mu z)))$;
      $y \in A \& (\uparrow y$:D$) = w \to \mu(w$:$z)$;
      $y = <y_1, \ldots, y_n> \to \mu(y_1$:$<y,z>)$; $\mu(\mu y$:$z))$; $\perp$

The above description of μ expands the operator of an application by definitions and by metacomposition be-fore evaluating the operand. It is assumed that predicates like "$x \in A$" in the above definition of $\tau\mu$ are $\perp$-preserving (e.g., "$\perp \in A$" has the value $\perp$) and that the conditional expression itself is also $\perp$-preserving. Thus $(\tau\mu)\perp \equiv \perp$ and $(\tau\mu)(\perp$:$z) \equiv \perp$. This concludes the seman-tics of FFP systems.

14. Applicative State Transition Systems (AST Systems)

14.1 Introduction

This section sketches a class of systems mentioned earlier as alternatives to von Neumann systems. It must be emphasized again that these applicative state transi-tion systems are put forward not as practical program-ming systems in their present form, but as examples of a class in which applicative style programming is made available in a history sensitive, but non-von Neumann system. These systems are loosely coupled to states and depend on an underlying applicative system for both their programming language and the description of their state transitions. The underlying applicative system of the AST system described below is an FFP system, but other applicative systems could also be used.

To understand the reasons for the structure of AST systems, it is helpful first to review the basic structure of a von Neumann system, Algol, observe its limitations, and compare it with the structure of AST systems. After that review a minimal AST system is described; a small, top-down, self-protecting system program for file maintenance and running user programs is given, with directions for installing it in the AST system and for running an example user program. The system program uses "name functions" instead of conventional names and the user may do so too. The section concludes with subsections discussing variants of AST systems, their general properties, and naming systems.

14.2 The Structure of Algol Compared to That of AST Systems

An Algol program is a sequence of statements, each representing a transformation of the Algol state, which is a complex repository of information about the status of various stacks, pointers, and variable mappings of identifiers onto values, etc. Each statement communicates with this constantly changing state by means of complicated protocols peculiar to itself and even to its different parts (e.g., the protocol associated with the variable x depends on its occurrence on the left or right of an assignment, in a declaration, as a parameter, etc.).

It is as if the Algol state were a complex "store" that communicates with the Algol program through an enormous "cable" of many specialized wires. The complex communications protocols of this cable are fixed and include those for every statement type. The "meaning" of an Algol program must be given in terms of the total effect of a vast number of communications with the state via the cable and its protocols (plus a means for identifying the output and inserting the input into the state). By comparison with this massive cable to the Algol state/store, the cable that is the von Neumann bottleneck of a computer is a simple, elegant concept.

Thus Algol statements are not expressions representing state-to-state functions that are built up by the use of orderly combining forms from simpler state-to-state functions. Instead they are complex *messages* with context-dependent parts that nibble away at the state. Each part transmits information to and from the state over the cable by its own protocols. There is no provision for applying general functions to the *whole* state and thereby making large changes in it. The possibility of large, powerful transformations of the state S by function application, $S \rightarrow f{:}S$, is in fact inconceivable in the von Neumann—cable and protocol—context: there could be no assurance that the new state $f{:}S$ would match the cable and its fixed protocols unless f is restricted to the tiny changes allowed by the cable in the first place.

We want a computing system whose semantics does not depend on a host of baroque protocols for communicating with the state, and we want to be able to make large transformations in the state by the application of general functions. AST systems provide one way of achieving these goals. Their semantics has two protocols for getting information from the state: (1) get from it the definition of a function to be applied, and (2) get the whole state itself. There is one protocol for changing the state: compute the new state by function application. Besides these communications with the state, AST semantics is applicative (i.e. FFP). It does not depend on state changes because the state does not change at all during a computation. Instead, the result of a computation is output *and* a new state. The structure of an AST state is slightly restricted by one of its protocols: It must be possible to identify a definition (i.e. cell) in it. Its structure—it is a sequence—is far simpler than that of the Algol state.

Thus the structure of AST systems avoids the complexity and restrictions of the von Neumann state (with its communications protocols) while achieving greater power and freedom in a radically different and simpler framework.

14.3 Structure of an AST System

An AST system is made up of three elements:

1) An *applicative subsystem* (such as an FFP system).

2) A *state* D that is the set of definitions of the applicative subsystem.

3) A set of *transition rules* that describe how inputs are transformed into outputs and how the state D is changed.

The programming language of an AST system is just that of its applicative subsystem. (From here on we shall assume that the latter is an FFP system.) Thus AST systems can use the FP programming style we have discussed. The applicative subsystem cannot change the state D and it does not change during the evaluation of an expression. A new state is computed along with output and replaces the old state when output is issued. (Recall that a set of definitions D is a sequence of cells; a cell name is the name of a defined function and its contents is the defining expression. Here, however, some cells may name data rather than functions; a data name n will be used in $\uparrow n$ (fetch n) whereas a function name will be used as an operator itself.)

We give below the transition rules for the elementary AST system we shall use for examples of programs. These are perhaps the simplest of many possible transition rules that could determine the behavior of a great variety of AST systems.

14.3.1 Transition rules for an elementary AST system. When the system receives an input x, it forms the application $(SYSTEM{:}x)$ and then proceeds to obtain its meaning in the FFP subsystem, using the current state D as the set of definitions. *SYSTEM* is the distinguished name of a function defined in D (i.e. it is the "system program"). Normally the result is a pair

$\mu(SYSTEM{:}x) = <o,d>$

where o is the system output that results from input x and d becomes the new state D for the system's next input. Usually d will be a copy or partly changed copy of the old state. If $\mu(SYSTEM{:}x)$ is not a pair, the output is an error message and the state remains unchanged.

14.3.2 Transition rules: exception conditions and startup. Once an input has been accepted, our system will not accept another (except $<RESET,x>$, see below) until an output has been issued and the new state, if any, installed. The system will accept the input $<RESET,x>$ at any time. There are two cases: (a) If $SYSTEM$ is defined in the current state D, then the system aborts its current computation without altering D and treats x as a new normal input; (b) if $SYSTEM$ is not defined in D, then x is appended to D as its first element. (This ends the complete description of the transition rules for our elementary AST system.)

If $SYSTEM$ is defined in D it can always prevent any change in its own definition. If it is not defined, an ordinary input x will produce $\mu(SYSTEM{:}x) = \bot$ and the transition rules yield an error message and an unchanged state; on the other hand, the input $<RESET, <CELL,SYSTEM,s>>$ will define $SYSTEM$ to be s.

14.3.3 Program access to the state; the function $\rho\,DEFS$. Our FFP subsystem is required to have one new primitive function, defs, named $DEFS$ such that for any object $x \neq \bot$,

$\text{defs}{:}x = \rho DEFS{:}x = D$

where D is the current state and set of definitions of the AST system. This function allows programs access to the whole state for any purpose, including the essential one of computing the successor state.

14.4 An Example of a System Program

The above description of our elementary AST system, plus the FFP subsystem and the FP primitives and functional forms of earlier sections, specify a complete history-sensitive computing system. Its input and output behavior is limited by its simple transition rules, but otherwise it is a powerful system once it is equipped with a suitable set of definitions. As an example of its use we shall describe a small system program, its installation, and operation.

Our example system program will handle queries and updates for a file it maintains, evaluate FFP expressions, run general user programs that do not damage the file or the state, and allow authorized users to change the set of definitions and the system program itself. All inputs it accepts will be of the form $<key,input>$ where key is a code that determines both the input class (*system-change*, *expression*, *program*, *query*, *update*) and also the identity of the user and his authority to use the system for the given input class. We shall not specify a format for key. *Input* is the input itself, of the class given by key.

14.4.1 General plan of the system program. The state

D of our AST system will contain the definitions of all nonprimitive functions needed for the system program and for users' programs. (Each definition is in a cell of the sequence D.) In addition, there will be a cell in D named $FILE$ with contents $file$, which the system maintains. We shall give FP definitions of functions and later show how to get them into the system in their FFP form. The transition rules make the input the operand of $SYSTEM$, but our plan is to use name-functions to refer to data, so the first thing we shall do with the input is to create two cells named KEY and $INPUT$ with contents key and $input$ and append these to D. This sequence of cells has one each for key, $input$, and $file$; it will be the operand of our main function called subsystem. Subsystem can then obtain key by applying $\uparrow KEY$ to its operand, etc. Thus the definition

Def system $\equiv$ pair $\to$ subsystem$\circ f$; $[\overline{NONPAIR}, \text{defs}]$

where

$f \equiv \downarrow INPUT\circ[2, \downarrow KEY\circ[1, \text{defs}]]$

causes the system to output $NONPAIR$ and leave the state unchanged if the input is not a pair. Otherwise, if it is $<key,input>$, then

$f{:}<key,input> = <<CELL,INPUT,input>,$
$\qquad\qquad\qquad <CELL,KEY,key>, d_1, \quad , d_n>$

where $D = <d_1, \dots , d_n>$. (We might have constructed a different operand than the one above, one with just three cells, for key, $input$, and $file$. We did not do so because real programs, unlike subsystem, would contain many name functions referring to data in the state, and this "standard" construction of the operand would suffice then as well.)

14.4.2 The "subsystem" function. We now give the FP definition of the function subsystem, followed by brief explanations of its six cases and auxiliary functions.

Def subsystem $\equiv$
 is-system-change$\circ\uparrow KEY \to$ [report-change, apply]$\circ[\uparrow INPUT, \text{defs}]$;
 is-expression$\circ\uparrow KEY \to [\uparrow INPUT, \text{defs}]$;
 is-program$\circ\uparrow KEY \to$ system-check$\circ$apply$\circ[\uparrow INPUT, \text{defs}]$;
 is-query$\circ\uparrow KEY \to$ [query-response$\circ[\uparrow INPUT, \uparrow FILE], \text{defs}]$;
 is-update$\circ\uparrow KEY \to$
   [report-update, $\downarrow FILE\circ$[update, defs]]
       $\circ[\uparrow INPUT, \uparrow FILE]$;
     [report-error$\circ[\uparrow KEY,\uparrow INPUT], \text{defs}]$.

This subsystem has five "$p \to f$;" clauses and a final default function, for a total of six classes of inputs; the treatment of each class is given below. Recall that the *operand* of subsystem is a sequence of cells containing key, $input$, and $file$ as well as all the defined functions of D, and that subsystem:*operand* $= <output,newstate>$.

Default inputs. In this case the result is given by the last (default) function of the definition when key does not satisfy any of the preceding clauses. The output is report-error: $<key,input>$. The state is unchanged since it is given by defs:*operand* $= D$. (We leave to the reader's imagination what the function report-error will generate from its operand.)

System-change inputs. When

is-system-change∘↑*KEY:operand* =

is-system-change:*key* = *T*,

key specifies that the user is authorized to make a system change and that *input* = ↑*INPUT:operand* represents a function *f* that is to be applied to D to produce the new state *f*:D. (Of course *f*:D can be a useless new state; no constraints are placed on it.) The output is a report, namely report-change:<*input*,D>.

Expression inputs. When is-expression:*key* = *T*, the system understands that the output is to be the meaning of the FFP expression *input*; ↑*INPUT:operand* produces it and it is evaluated, as are all expressions. The state is unchanged.

Program inputs and system self-protection. When is-program:*key* = *T*, both the output and new state are given by (ρinput):D = <*output,newstate*>. If *newstate* contains *file* in suitable condition and the definitions of system and other protected functions, then
system-check: <*output,newstate*> = <*output,newstate*>. Otherwise, system-check:<*output,newstate*>

= <*error-report*,D>.

Although *program* inputs can make major, possibly disastrous changes in the state when it produces *newstate*, system-check can use any criteria to either allow it to become the actual new state or to keep the old. A more sophisticated system-check might correct only prohibited changes in the state. Functions of this sort are possible because they can always access the old state for comparison with the new state-to-be and control what state transition will finally be allowed.

File query inputs. If is-query:*key* = *T*, the function query-response is designed to produce the output = answer to the query *input* from its operand <*input,file*>.

File update inputs. If is-update:*key* = *T, input* specifies a file transaction understood by the function update, which computes *updated-file* = update:<*input,file*>. Thus ↓*FILE* has <*updated-file*,D> as its operand and thus stores the updated file in the cell *FILE* in the new state. The rest of the state is unchanged. The function report-update generates the output from its operand <*input,file*>.

14.4.3 Installing the system program. We have described the function called system by some FP definitions (using auxiliary functions whose behavior is only indicated). Let us suppose that we have FP definitions for all the nonprimitive functions required. Then each definition can be converted to give the name and contents of a cell in D (of course this conversion itself would be done by a better system). The conversion is accomplished by changing each FP function name to its equivalent atom (e.g., update becomes *UPDATE*) and by replacing functional forms by sequences whose first member is the controlling function for the particular form. Thus ↓*FILE*∘[update, defs] is converted to

<*COMP*,<*STORE,FILE*>,

<*CONS,UPDATE,DEFS*>>,

and the FP function is the same as that represented by the FFP object, provided that update ≡ ρ*UPDATE* and *COMP, STORE*, and *CONS* represent the controlling functions for composition, store, and construction.

All FP definitions needed for our system can be converted to cells as indicated above, giving a sequence D_0. We assume that the AST system has an empty state to start with, hence *SYSTEM* is not defined. We want to define *SYSTEM* initially so that it will install its next input as the state; having done so we can then input D_0 and all our definitions will be installed, including our program—system—itself. To accomplish this we enter our first input

<*RESET*, <*CELL,SYSTEM,loader*>>

where *loader* ≡ <*CONS*, <*CONST,DONE*>,*ID*>.
Then, by the transition rule for *RESET* when *SYSTEM* is undefined in D, the cell in our input is put at the head of D = ϕ, thus defining ρ*SYSTEM* ≡ ρ*loader* ≡ [$\overline{DONE}$, id]. Our second input is D_0, the set of definitions we wish to become the state. The regular transition rule causes the AST system to evaluate

μ(*SYSTEM*:D_0) = [$\overline{DONE}$, id]:D_0 = <*DONE*,D_0>. Thus the output from our second input is *DONE*, the new state is D_0, and ρ*SYSTEM* is now our system program (which only accepts inputs of the form <*key,input*>).

Our next task is to load the file (we are given an initial value *file*). To load it we input a *program* into the newly installed system that contains *file* as a constant and stores it in the state; the input is
<*program-key*, [$\overline{DONE}$,store-file]> where

ρstore-file ≡ ↓*FILE*∘[$\overline{file}$, id].

Program-key identifies [$\overline{DONE}$, store-file] as a program to be applied to the state D_0 to give the output and new state D_1, which is:

ρstore-file:D_0 = ↓*FILE*∘[$\overline{file}$, id]:D_0,

or D_0 with a cell containing *file* at its head. The output is $\overline{DONE}$:D_0 = *DONE*. We assume that system-check will pass <*DONE*,D_1> unchanged. FP expressions have been used in the above in place of the FFP objects they denote, e.g. $\overline{DONE}$ for <*CONST,DONE*>.

14.4.4 Using the system. We have not said how the system's file, queries or updates are structured, so we cannot give a detailed example of file operations. However, the structure of subsystem shows clearly how the system's response to queries and updates depends on the functions query-response, update, and report-update.

Let us suppose that matrices *m, n* named *M*, and *N* are stored in D and that the function MM described earlier is defined in D. Then the input

<*expression-key*, (*MM*∘[↑*M*, ↑*N*]∘*DEFS:#*)>

would give the product of the two matrices as output and an unchanged state. *Expression-key* identifies the application as an expression to be evaluated and since defs:*#* = D and [↑*M*, ↑*N*]:D = <*m,n*>, the value of the expression is the result MM:<*m,n*>, which is the output.

Our miniature system program has no provision for giving control to a user's program to process many inputs, but it would not be difficult to give it that capability while still monitoring the user's program with the option of taking control back.

14.5 Variants of AST Systems

A major extension of the AST systems suggested above would provide combining forms, "system forms," for building a new AST system from simpler, component AST systems. That is, a system form would take AST systems as parameters and generate a new AST system, just as a functional form takes functions as parameters and generates new functions. These system forms would have properties like those of functional forms and would become the "operations" of a useful "algebra of systems" in much the same way that functional forms are the "operations" of the algebra of programs. However, the problem of finding useful system forms is much more difficult, since they must handle *RESETS*, match inputs and outputs, and combine history-sensitive systems rather than fixed functions.

Moreover, the usefulness or need for system forms is less clear than that for functional forms. The latter are essential for building a great variety of functions from an initial primitive set, whereas, even without system forms, the facilities for building AST systems are already so rich that one could build virtually any system (with the general input and output properties allowed by the given AST scheme). Perhaps system forms would be useful for building systems with complex input and output arrangements.

14.6 Remarks About AST Systems

As I have tried to indicate above, there can be innumerable variations in the ingredients of an AST system—how it operates, how it deals with input and output, how and when it produces new states, and so on. In any case, a number of remarks apply to any reasonable AST system:

a) A state transition occurs once per major computation and can have useful mathematical properties. State transitions are not involved in the tiniest details of a computation as in conventional languages; thus the linguistic von Neumann bottleneck has been eliminated. No complex "cable" or protocols are needed to communicate with the state.

b) Programs are written in an applicative language that can accommodate a great range of changeable parts, parts whose power and flexibility exceed that of any von Neumann language so far. The word-at-a-time style is replaced by an applicative style; there is no division of programming into a world of expressions and a world of statements. Programs can be analyzed and optimized by an algebra of programs.

c) Since the state cannot change during the computation of system:*x*, there are no side effects. Thus independent applications can be evaluated in parallel.

d) By defining appropriate functions one can, I believe, introduce major new features at any time, using the same framework. Such features must be built into the framework of a von Neumann language. I have in mind such features as: "stores" with a great variety of naming systems, types and type checking, communicating parallel processes, nondeterminacy and Dijkstra's "guarded command" constructs [8], and improved methods for structured programming.

e) The framework of an AST system comprises the syntax and semantics of the underlying applicative system plus the system framework sketched above. By current standards, this is a tiny framework for a language and is the only fixed part of the system.

14.7 Naming Systems in AST and von Neumann Models

In an AST system, naming is accomplished by functions as indicated in Section 13.3.3. Many useful functions for altering and accessing a store can be defined (e.g. push, pop, purge, typed fetch, etc.). All these definitions and their associated naming systems can be introduced without altering the AST framework. Different kinds of "stores" (e.g., with "typed cells") with individual naming systems can be used in one program. A cell in one store may contain another entire store.

The important point about AST naming systems is that they utilize the functional nature of names (Reynolds' GEDANKEN [19] also does so to some extent within a von Neumann framework). Thus name functions can be composed and combined with other functions by functional forms. In contrast, functions and names in von Neumann languages are usually disjoint concepts and the function-like nature of names is almost totally concealed and useless, because a) names cannot be applied as functions; b) there are no general means to combine names with other names and functions; c) the objects to which name functions apply (stores) are not accessible as objects.

The failure of von Neumann languages to treat names as functions may be one of their more important weaknesses. In any case, the ability to use names as functions and stores as objects may turn out to be a useful and important programming concept, one which should be thoroughly explored.

15. Remarks About Computer Design

The dominance of von Neumann languages has left designers with few intellectual models for practical computer designs beyond variations of the von Neumann computer. Data flow models [1] [7] [13] are one alternative class of history-sensitive models. The substitution rules of lambda-calculus based languages present serious problems for the machine designer. Berkling [3] has developed a modified lambda calculus that has three kinds of applications and that makes renaming of variables unnecessary. He has developed a machine to evaluate expressions of this language. Further experience is needed to show how sound a basis this language is for an effective programming style and how efficient his machine can be.

Magó [15] has developed a novel applicative machine built from identical components (of two kinds). It evaluates, directly, FP-like and other applicative expressions from the bottom up. It has no von Neumann store and no address register, hence no bottleneck; it is capable of evaluating many applications in parallel; its built-in operations resemble FP operators more than von Neumann computer operations. It is the farthest departure from the von Neumann computer that I have seen.

There are numerous indications that the applicative style of programming can become more powerful than the von Neumann style. Therefore it is important for programmers to develop a new class of history-sensitive models of computing systems that embody such a style and avoid the inherent efficiency problems that seem to attach to lambda-calculus based systems. Only when these models and their applicative languages have proved their superiority over conventional languages will we have the economic basis to develop the new kind of computer that can best implement them. Only then, perhaps, will we be able to fully utilize large-scale integrated circuits in a computer design not limited by the von Neumann bottleneck.

16. Summary

The fifteen preceding sections of this paper can be summarized as follows.

Section 1. Conventional programming languages are large, complex, and inflexible. Their limited expressive power is inadequate to justify their size and cost.

Section 2. The models of computing systems that underlie programming languages fall roughly into three classes: (a) simple operational models (e.g., Turing machines), (b) applicative models (e.g., the lambda calculus), and (c) von Neumann models (e.g., conventional computers and programming languages). Each class of models has an important difficulty: The programs of class (a) are inscrutable; class (b) models cannot save information from one program to the next; class (c) models have unusable foundations and programs that are conceptually unhelpful.

Section 3. Von Neumann computers are built around a bottleneck: the word-at-a-time tube connecting the CPU and the store. Since a program must make its overall change in the store by pumping vast numbers of words back and forth through the von Neumann bottleneck, we have grown up with a style of programming that concerns itself with this word-at-a-time traffic through the bottleneck rather than with the larger conceptual units of our problems.

Section 4. Conventional languages are based on the programming style of the von Neumann computer. Thus variables = storage cells; assignment statements = fetching, storing, and arithmetic; control statements = jump and test instructions. The symbol ":=" is the linguistic von Neumann bottleneck. Programming in a conventional—von Neumann—language still concerns itself with the word-at-a-time traffic through this slightly more sophisticated bottleneck. Von Neumann languages also split programming into a world of expressions and a world of statements; the first of these is an orderly world, the second is a disorderly one, a world that structured programming has simplified somewhat, but without attacking the basic problems of the split itself and of the word-at-a-time style of conventional languages.

Section 5. This section compares a von Neumann program and a functional program for inner product. It illustrates a number of problems of the former and advantages of the latter: e.g., the von Neumann program is repetitive and word-at-a-time, works only for two vectors named a and b of a given length n, and can only be made general by use of a procedure declaration, which has complex semantics. The functional program is nonrepetitive, deals with vectors as units, is more hierarchically constructed, is completely general, and creates "housekeeping" operations by composing high-level housekeeping operators. It does not name its arguments, hence it requires no procedure declaration.

Section 6. A programming language comprises a framework plus some changeable parts. The framework of a von Neumann language requires that most features must be built into it; it can accommodate only limited changeable parts (e.g., user-defined procedures) because there must be detailed provisions in the "state" and its transition rules for all the needs of the changeable parts, as well as for all the features built into the framework. The reason the von Neumann framework is so inflexible is that its semantics is too closely coupled to the state: every detail of a computation changes the state.

Section 7. The changeable parts of von Neumann languages have little expressive power; this is why most of the language must be built into the framework. The lack of expressive power results from the inability of von Neumann languages to effectively use combining forms for building programs, which in turn results from the split between expressions and statements. Combining forms are at their best in expressions, but in von Neumann languages an expression can only produce a single word; hence expressive power in the world of expressions is mostly lost. A further obstacle to the use of combining forms is the elaborate use of naming conventions.

Section 8. APL is the first language not based on the lambda calculus that is not word-at-a-time and uses functional combining forms. But it still retains many of the problems of von Neumann languages.

Section 9. Von Neumann languages do not have useful properties for reasoning about programs. Axiomatic and denotational semantics are precise tools for describing and understanding conventional programs, but they only talk about them and cannot alter their ungainly properties. Unlike von Neumann languages, the language of ordinary algebra is suitable both for stating its laws and for transforming an equation into its solution, all within the "language."

Section 10. In a history-sensitive language, a program can affect the behavior of a subsequent one by changing some store which is saved by the system. Any such language requires some kind of state transition semantics. But it does not need semantics closely coupled to states in which the state changes with every detail of the computation. "Applicative state transition" (AST) systems are proposed as history-sensitive alternatives to von Neumann systems. These have: (a) loosely coupled state-transition semantics in which a transition occurs once per major computation; (b) simple states and transition rules; (c) an underlying applicative system with simple "reduction" semantics; and (d) a programming language and state transition rules both based on the underlying applicative system and its semantics. The next four sections describe the elements of this approach to non-von Neumann language and system design.

Section 11. A class of informal functional programming (FP) systems is described which use no variables. Each system is built from objects, functions, functional forms, and definitions. Functions map objects into objects. Functional forms combine existing functions to form new ones. This section lists examples of primitive functions and functional forms and gives sample programs. It discusses the limitations and advantages of FP systems.

Section 12. An "algebra of programs" is described whose variables range over the functions of an FP system and whose "operations" are the functional forms of the system. A list of some twenty-four laws of the algebra is followed by an example proving the equivalence of a nonrepetitive matrix multiplication program and a recursive one. The next subsection states the results of two "expansion theorems" that "solve" two classes of equations. These solutions express the "unknown" function in such equations as an infinite conditional expansion that constitutes a case-by-case description of its behavior and immediately gives the necessary and sufficient conditions for termination. These results are used to derive a "recursion theorem" and an "iteration theorem," which provide ready-made expansions for some moderately general and useful classes of "linear" equations. Examples of the use of these theorems treat: (a) correctness proofs for recursive and iterative factorial functions, and (b) a proof of equivalence of two iterative programs. A final example deals with a "quadratic" equation and proves that its solution is an idempotent function. The next subsection gives the proofs of the two expansion theorems.

The algebra associated with FP systems is compared with the corresponding algebras for the lambda calculus and other applicative systems. The comparison shows some advantages to be drawn from the severely restricted FP systems, as compared with the much more powerful classical systems. Questions are suggested about algorithmic reduction of functions to infinite expansions and about the use of the algebra in various "lazy evaluation" schemes.

Section 13. This section describes formal functional programming (FFP) systems that extend and make precise the behavior of FP systems. Their semantics are simpler than that of classical systems and can be shown to be consistent by a simple fixed-point argument.

Section 14. This section compares the structure of Algol with that of applicative state transition (AST) systems. It describes an AST system using an FFP system as its applicative subsystem. It describes the simple state and the transition rules for the system. A small self-protecting system program for the AST system is described, and how it can be installed and used for file maintenance and for running user programs. The section briefly discusses variants of AST systems and functional naming systems that can be defined and used within an AST system.

Section 15. This section briefly discusses work on applicative computer designs and the need to develop and test more practical models of applicative systems as the future basis for such designs.

Acknowledgments. In earlier work relating to this paper I have received much valuable help and many suggestions from Paul R. McJones and Barry K. Rosen. I have had a great deal of valuable help and feedback in preparing this paper. James N. Gray was exceedingly generous with his time and knowledge in reviewing the first draft. Stephen N. Zilles also gave it a careful reading. Both made many valuable suggestions and criticisms at this difficult stage. It is a pleasure to acknowledge my debt to them. I also had helpful discussions about the first draft with Ronald Fagin, Paul R. McJones, and James H. Morris, Jr. Fagin suggested a number of improvements in the proofs of theorems.

Since a large portion of the paper contains technical material, I asked two distinguished computer scientists to referee the third draft. David J. Gries and John C. Reynolds were kind enough to accept this burdensome task. Both gave me large, detailed sets of corrections and overall comments that resulted in many improvements, large and small, in this final version (which they have not had an opportunity to review). I am truly grateful for the generous time and care they devoted to reviewing this paper.

Finally, I also sent copies of the third draft to Gyula A. Magó, Peter Naur, and John H. Williams. They were kind enough to respond with a number of extremely helpful comments and corrections. Geoffrey A. Frank and Dave Tolle at the University of North Carolina reviewed Magó's copy and pointed out an important error in the definition of the semantic function of FFP systems. My grateful thanks go to all these kind people for their help.

References

1. Arvind, and Gostelow, K.P. A new interpreter for data flow schemas and its implications for computer architecture. Tech. Rep. No. 72, Dept. Comptr. Sci., U. of California, Irvine, Oct. 1975.

2. Backus, J. Programming language semantics and closed applicative languages. Conf. Record ACM Symp. on Principles of Programming Languages, Boston, Oct. 1973, 71–86.

3. Berkling, K.J. Reduction languages for reduction machines. Interner Bericht ISF-76-8, Gesellschaft für Mathematik und Datenverarbeitung MBH, Bonn, Sept. 1976.

4. Burge, W.H. *Recursive Programming Techniques*. Addison-Wesley, Reading, Mass., 1975.

5. Church, A. *The Calculi of Lambda-Conversion*. Princeton U. Press, Princeton, N.J., 1941.

6. Curry, H.B., and Feys, R. *Combinatory Logic, Vol. 1*. North-Holland Pub. Co., Amsterdam, 1958.

7. Dennis, J.B. First version of a data flow procedure language. Tech. Mem. No. 61, Lab. for Comptr. Sci., M.I.T., Cambridge, Mass., May 1973.

8. Dijkstra, E.W. *A Discipline of Programming*. Prentice-Hall, Englewood Cliffs, N.J., 1976.

9. Friedman, D.P., and Wise, D.S. CONS should not evaluate its arguments. In *Automata, Languages and Programming*, S. Michaelson and R. Milner, Eds., Edinburgh U. Press, Edinburgh, 1976, pp. 257–284.

10. Henderson, P., and Morris, J.H. Jr. A lazy evaluator. Conf. Record Third ACM Symp. on Principles of Programming Languages, Atlanta, Ga., Jan. 1976, pp. 95–103.

11. Hoare, C.A.R. An axiomatic basis for computer programming. *Comm. ACM 12*, 10 (Oct. 1969), 576–583.

12. Iverson, K. *A Programming Language*. Wiley, New York, 1962.

13. Kosinski, P. A data flow programming language. Rep. RC 4264, IBM T.J. Watson Research Ctr., Yorktown Heights, N.Y., March 1973.

14. Landin, P.J. The mechanical evaluation of expressions. *Computer J. 6*, 4 (1964), 308–320.

15. Magó, G.A. A network of microprocessors to execute reduction languages. To appear in *Int. J. Comptr. and Inform. Sci.*

16. Manna, Z., Ness, S., and Vuillemin, J. Inductive methods for proving properties of programs. *Comm. ACM 16*, 8 (Aug. 1973) 491–502.

17. McCarthy, J. Recursive functions of symbolic expressions and their computation by machine, Pt. 1. *Comm. ACM 3*, 4 (April 1960), 184–195.

18. McJones, P. A Church-Rosser property of closed applicative languages. Rep. RJ 1589, IBM Res. Lab., San Jose, Calif., May 1975.

19. Reynolds, J.C. GEDANKEN—a simple typeless language based on the principle of completeness and the reference concept. *Comm. ACM 13*, 5 (May 1970), 308–318.

20. Reynolds, J.C. Notes on a lattice-theoretic approach to the theory of computation. Dept. Syst. and Inform. Sci., Syracuse U., Syracuse, N.Y., 1972.

21. Scott, D. Outline of a mathematical theory of computation. Proc. 4th Princeton Conf. on Inform. Sci. and Syst., 1970.

22. Scott, D. Lattice-theoretic models for various type-free calculi. Proc. Fourth Int. Congress for Logic, Methodology, and the Philosophy of Science, Bucharest, 1972.

23. Scott, D., and Strachey, C. Towards a mathematical semantics for computer languages. Proc. Symp. on Comptrs. and Automata, Polytechnic Inst. of Brooklyn, 1971.

RECURSIVE FUNCTIONS OF SYMBOLIC EXPRESSIONS*

J. McCARTHY

JOHN McCARTHY, *Massachusetts Institute of Technology, Cambridge, Mass.*

1. Introduction

A programming system called LISP (for LISt Processor) has been developed for the IBM 704 computer by the Artificial Intelligence group at M.I.T. The system was designed to facilitate experiments with a proposed system called the Advice Taker, whereby a machine could be instructed to handle declarative as well as imperative sentences and could exhibit "common sense" in carrying out its instructions. The original proposal [1] for the Advice Taker was made in November 1958. The main requirement was a programming system for manipulating expressions representing formalized declarative and imperative sentences so that the Advice Taker system could make deductions.

In the course of its development the LISP system went through several stages of simplification and eventually came to be based on a scheme for representing the partial recursive functions of a certain class of symbolic expressions. This representation is independent of the IBM 704 computer, or of any other electronic computer, and it now seems expedient to expound the system by starting with the class of expressions called S-expressions and the functions called S-functions.

In this article, we first describe a formalism for defining functions recursively. We believe this formalism has advantages both as a programming language and as vehicle for developing a theory of computation. Next, we describe S-expressions and S-functions, give some examples, and then describe the universal S-function *apply* which plays the theoretical role of a universal Turing machine and the practical role of an interpreter. Then we describe the representation of S-expressions in the memory of the IBM 704 by list structures similar to those used by Newell, Shaw and Simon [2], and the representation of S-functions by program. Then we mention the main features of the LISP programming system for the IBM 704. Next comes another way of describing computations with symbolic expressions, and finally we give a recursive function interpretation of flow charts.

We hope to describe some of the symbolic computations for which LISP has been used in another paper, and also to give elsewhere some applications of our recursive function formalism to mathematical logic and to the problem of mechanical theorem proving.

*Reprinted from *COMM ACM*, 3, 4, April 1960, 184–195, copyright 1960.

2. Functions and Function Definitions

We shall need a number of mathematical ideas and notations concerning functions in general. Most of the ideas are well known, but the notion of *conditional expression* is believed to be new, and the use of conditional expressions permits functions to be defined recursively in a new and convenient way.

a. *Partial Functions.* A partial function is a function that is defined only on part of its domain. Partial functions necessarily arise when functions are defined by computations because for some values of the arguments the computation defining the value of the function may not terminate. However, some of our elementary functions will be defined as partial functions.

b. *Propositional Expressions and Predicates.* A propositional expression is an expression whose possible values are T (for truth) and F (for falsity). We shall assume that the reader is familiar with the propositional connectives $\wedge$ ("and"), $\vee$ ("or"), and $\sim$ ("not"). Typical propositional expressions are:

$$x < y$$

$$(x < y) \wedge (b = c)$$

$$x \text{ is prime}$$

A predicate is a function whose range consists of the truth values T and F.

c. *Conditional Expressions.* The dependence of truth values on the values of quantities of other kinds is expressed in mathematics by predicates, and the dependence of truth values on other truth values by logical connectives. However, the notations for expressing symbolically the dependence of quantities of other kinds on truth values is inadequate, so that English words and phrases are generally used for expressing these dependences in texts that describe other dependences symbolically. For example, the function $|x|$ is usually defined in words.

Conditional expressions are a device for expressing the dependence of quantities on propositional quantities. A conditional expression has the form

$$(p_1 \rightarrow e_1 , \cdots , p_n \rightarrow e_n)$$

where the p's are propositional expressions and the e's are expressions of any kind. It may be read, "If p_1 then e_1 , otherwise if p_2 then e_2, $\cdots$, otherwise if p_n then e_n," or "p_1 yields e_1, $\cdots$, p_n yields e_n."

We now give the rules for determining whether the value of $(p_1 \to e_1, \cdots, p_n \to e_n)$ is defined, and if so what its value is. Examine the p's from left to right. If a p whose value is T is encountered before any p whose value is undefined is encountered, then the value of the conditional expression is the value of the corresponding e (if this is defined). If any undefined p is encountered before a true p, or if all p's are false, or if the e corresponding to the first true p is undefined, then the value of the conditional expression is undefined. We now give examples.

$$(1 < 2 \to 4, 1 \geqq 2 \to 3) = 4$$

$$(2 < 1 \to 4, 2 > 1 \to 3, 2 > 1 \to 2) = 3$$

$$(2 < 1 \to 4, T \to 3) = 3$$

$$\left(2 < 1 \to \frac{0}{0}, T \to 3\right) = 3$$

$$\left(2 < 1 \to 3, T \to \frac{0}{0}\right) \text{ is undefined}$$

$$(2 < 1 \to 3, 4 < 1 \to 4) \text{ is undefined}$$

Some of the simplest applications of conditional expressions are in giving such definitions as

$$|x| = (x < 0 \to -x, T \to x)$$

$$\delta_{ij} = (i = j \to 1, T \to 0)$$

$$\text{sgn}(x) = (x < 0 \to -1, x = 0 \to 0, T \to 1)$$

d. *Recursive Function Definitions.* By using conditional expressions we can, without circularity, define functions by formulas in which the defined function occurs. For example, we write

$$n! = (n = 0 \to 1, T \to n \cdot (n - 1)!)$$

When we use this formula to evaluate 0! we get the answer 1; because of the way in which the value of a conditional expression was defined, the meaningless expression $0 \cdot (0 - 1)!$ does not arise. The evaluation of 2! according to this definition proceeds as follows:

$$2! = (2 = 0 \to 1, T \to 2 \cdot (2 - 1)!)$$

$$= 2 \cdot 1!$$

$$= 2 \cdot (1 = 0 \to 1, T \to 1 \cdot (1 - 1)!)$$

$$= 2 \cdot 1 \cdot 0!$$

$$= 2 \cdot 1 \cdot (0 = 0 \to 1, T \to 0 \cdot (0 - 1)!)$$

$$= 2 \cdot 1 \cdot 1$$

$$= 2$$

We now give two other applications of recursive function definitions. The greatest common divisor, gcd(m,n), of two positive integers m and n is computed by means of the Euclidean algorithm. This algorithm is expressed by the recursive function definition:

$$\gcd(m,n) = (m > n \to \gcd(n,m), \text{rem}(n,m)$$

$$= 0 \to m, T \to \gcd(\text{rem}(n,m),m))$$

where rem(n, m) denotes the remainder left when n is divided by m.

The Newtonian algorithm for obtaining an approximate square root of a number a, starting with an initial approximation x and requiring that an acceptable approximation y satisfy $|y^2 - a| < \epsilon$, may be written as

$$\text{sqrt}(a, x, \epsilon)$$

$$= (|x^2 - a| < \epsilon \to x, T \to \text{sqrt}\left(a, \frac{1}{2}\left(x + \frac{a}{x}\right), \epsilon\right))$$

The simultaneous recursive definition of several functions is also possible, and we shall use such definitions if they are required.

There is no guarantee that the computation determined by a recursive definition will ever terminate and, for example, an attempt to compute n! from our definition will only succeed if n is a non-negative integer. If the computation does not terminate, the function must be regarded as undefined for the given arguments.

The propositional connectives themselves can be defined by conditional expressions. We write

$$p \wedge q = (p \to q, T \to F)$$

$$p \vee q = (p \to T, T \to q)$$

$$\sim p = (p \to F, T \to T)$$

$$p \supset q = (p \to q, T \to T)$$

It is readily seen that the right-hand sides of the equations have the correct truth tables. If we consider situations in which p or q may be undefined, the connectives $\wedge$ and $\vee$ are seen to be noncommutative. For example if p is false and q is undefined, we see that according to the definitions given above p $\wedge$ q is false, but q $\wedge$ p is undefined. For our applications this noncommutativity is desirable, since p $\wedge$ q is computed by first computing p, and if p is false q is not computed. If the computation for p does not terminate, we never get around to computing q. We shall use propositional connectives in this sense hereafter.

e. *Functions and Forms.* It is usual in mathematics—outside of mathematical logic—to use the word "function" imprecisely and to apply it to forms such as $y^2 + x$. Because we shall later compute with expressions for functions, we need a distinction between functions and forms and a notation for expressing this distinction. This distinction and a notation for describing it, from which we deviate trivially, is given by Church [3].

Let f be an expression that stands for a function of two integer variables. It should make sense to write $f(3, 4)$ and the value of this expression should be determined. The expression $y^2 + x$ does not meet this requirement;

$y^2 + x(3, 4)$ is not a conventional notation, and if we attempted to define it we would be uncertain whether its value would turn out to be 13 or 19. Church calls an expression like $y^2 + x$ a form. A form can be converted into a function if we can determine the correspondence between the variables occurring in the form and the ordered list of arguments of the desired function. This is accomplished by Church's λ-notation.

If $\mathcal{E}$ is a form in variables $x_1, \cdots, x_n$, then $\lambda((x_1, \cdots, x_n), \mathcal{E})$ will be taken to be the function of n variables whose value is determined by substituting the arguments for the variables $x_1, \cdots, x_n$ in that order in $\mathcal{E}$ and evaluating the resulting expression. For example, $\lambda((x,y),y^2+x)$ is a function of two variables, and $\lambda((x, y), y^2+x)(3,4) = 19$.

The variables occurring in the list of variables of a λ-expression are dummy or bound, like variables of integration in a definite integral. That is, we may change the names of the bound variables in a function expression without changing the value of the expression, provided that we make the same change for each occurrence of the variable and do not make two variables the same that previously were different. Thus $\lambda((x,y),y^2+x), \lambda((u,v),\ v^2+u)$ and $\lambda((y, x), x^2+y)$ denote the same function.

We shall frequently use expressions in which some of the variables are bound by λ's and others are not. Such an expression may be regarded as defining a function with parameters. The unbound variables are called free variables.

An adequate notation that distinguishes functions from forms allows an unambiguous treatment of functions of functions. It would involve too much of a digression to give examples here, but we shall use functions with functions as arguments later in this report.

Difficulties arise in combining functions described by λ-expressions, or by any other notation involving variables, because different bound variables may be represented by the same symbol. This is called collision of bound variables. There is a notation involving operators that are called combinators for combining functions without the use of variables. Unfortunately, the combinatory expressions for interesting combinations of functions tend to be lengthy and unreadable.

f. *Expressions for Recursive Functions.* The λ-notation is inadequate for naming functions defined recursively. For example, using λ's, we can convert the definition

$$\text{sqrt}(a, x, \epsilon)$$

$$= (\,|\,x^2 - a\,| < \epsilon \to x, T \to \text{sqrt}(a, \tfrac{1}{2}(x + \tfrac{a}{x}), \epsilon))$$

into

$$\text{sqrt} = \lambda((a, x, \epsilon), (\,|\,x^2 - a\,| < \epsilon \to x, T \to$$

$$\text{sqrt}\,(a, \tfrac{1}{2}(x + \tfrac{a}{x})\,, \epsilon)))$$

but the right-hand side cannot serve as an expression for the function because there would be nothing to indicate that the reference to sqrt within the expression stood for the expression as a whole.

In order to be able to write expressions for recursive functions, we introduce another notation label$(a,\mathcal{E})$ denotes the expression $\mathcal{E}$, provided that occurrences of a within $\mathcal{E}$ are to be interpreted as referring to the expression as a whole. Thus we can write

$$\text{label}(\text{sqrt}, \lambda((a, x, \epsilon), (\,|\,x^2 - a\,|$$

$$< \epsilon \to x, T \to \text{sqrt}\,(a, \tfrac{1}{2}(x + \tfrac{a}{x}), \epsilon))))$$

as a name for our sqrt function.

The symbol a in label$(a,\mathcal{E})$ is also bound, that is, it may be altered systematically without changing the meaning of the expression. It behaves differently from a variable bound by a λ, however.

3. Recursive Functions of Symbolic Expressions

We shall first define a class of symbolic expressions in terms of ordered pairs and lists. Then we shall define five elementary functions and predicates, and build from them by composition, conditional expressions, and recursive definitions an extensive class of functions of which we shall give a number of examples. We shall then show how these functions themselves can be expressed as symbolic expressions, and we shall define a universal function *apply* that allows us to compute from the expression for a given function its value for given arguments. Finally, we shall define some functions with functions as arguments and give some useful examples.

a. *A Class of Symbolic Expressions.* We shall now define the S-expressions (S stands for symbolic). They are formed by using the special characters

$$.$$
$$)$$
$$($$

and an infinite set of distinguishable atomic symbols. For atomic symbols, we shall use strings of capital Latin letters and digits with single imbedded blanks. Examples of atomic symbols are

A

ABA

APPLE PIE NUMBER 3

There is a twofold reason for departing from the usual mathematical practice of using single letters for atomic symbols. First, computer programs frequently require hundreds of distinguishable symbols that must be formed from the 47 characters that are printable by the IBM 704 computer. Second, it is convenient to allow English words and phrases to stand for atomic entities for mnemonic reasons. The symbols are atomic in the sense that any substructure they may have as sequences of characters is ignored. We assume only that different symbols can be distinguished.

S-expressions are then defined as follows:
1. Atomic symbols are S-expressions.
2. If e_1 and e_2 are S-expressions, so is $(e_1 \cdot e_2)$.
Examples of S-expressions are

$$AB$$
$$(A \cdot B)$$
$$((AB \cdot C) \cdot D)$$

An S-expression is then simply an ordered pair, the terms of which may be atomic symbols or simpler S-expressions. We can represent a list of arbitrary length in terms of S-expressions as follows. The list

$$(m_1, m_2, \cdots, m_n)$$

is represented by the S-expression

$$(m_1 \cdot (m_2 \cdot (\cdots (m_n \cdot NIL) \cdots)))$$

Here NIL is an atomic symbol used to terminate lists.

Since many of the symbolic expressions with which we deal are conveniently expressed as lists, we shall introduce a list notation to abbreviate certain S-expressions. We have

1. (m) stands for $(m \cdot NIL)$.
2. $(m_1, \cdots, m_n)$ stands for $(m_1 \cdot (\cdots (m_n \cdot NIL) \cdots))$.
3. $(m_1, \cdots, m_n \cdot x)$ stands for $(m_1 \cdot (\cdots (m_n \cdot x) \cdots))$.

Subexpressions can be similarly abbreviated. Some examples of these abbreviations are

$$((AB, C), D) \text{ for } ((AB \cdot (C \cdot NIL)) \cdot (D \cdot NIL))$$
$$((A, B), C, D \cdot E) \text{ for } ((A \cdot (B \cdot NIL)) \cdot (C \cdot (D \cdot E)))$$

Since we regard the expressions with commas as abbreviations for those not involving commas, we shall refer to them all as S-expressions.

b. *Functions of S-expressions and the Expressions That Represent Them.* We now define a class of functions of S-expressions. The expressions representing these functions are written in a conventional functional notation. However, in order to clearly distinguish the expressions representing functions from S-expressions, we shall use sequences of lower-case letters for function names and variables ranging over the set of S-expressions. We also use brackets and semicolons, instead of parentheses and commas, for denoting the application of functions to their arguments. Thus we write

$$car [x]$$
$$car [cons [(A \cdot B); x]]$$

In these M-expressions (meta-expressions) any S-expressions that occur stand for themselves.

c. *The Elementary S-functions and Predicates.* We introduce the following functions and predicates:
1. atom.   atom [x] has the value of T or F, accordingly as x is an atomic symbol or not. Thus

$$atom [X] = T$$
$$atom [(X \cdot A)] = F$$

2. eq.   eq [x; y] is defined if and only if both x and y are atomic. eq [x; y] = T if x and y are the same symbol, and eq [x; y] = F otherwise. Thus

$$eq [X; X] = T$$
$$eq [X; A] = F$$
$$eq [X; (X \cdot A)] \text{ is undefined.}$$

3. car.   car [x] is defined if and only if x is not atomic. car $[(e_1 \cdot e_2)] = e_1$. Thus car [X] is undefined.

$$car [(X \cdot A)] = X$$
$$car [((X \cdot A) \cdot Y)] = (X \cdot A)$$

4. cdr.   cdr [x] is also defined when x is not atomic. We have cdr $[(e_1 \cdot e_2)] = e_2$. Thus cdr [X] is undefined.

$$cdr [(X \cdot A)] = A$$
$$cdr [((X \cdot A) \cdot Y)] = Y$$

5. cons.   cons [x; y] is defined for any x and y. We have cons $[e_1; e_2] = (e_1 \cdot e_2)$. Thus

$$cons [X; A] = (X \cdot A)$$
$$cons [(X \cdot A); Y] = ((X \cdot A) \cdot Y)$$

car, cdr, and cons are easily seen to satisfy the relations

$$car [cons [x; y]] = x$$
$$cdr [cons [x; y]] = y$$
$$cons [car [x]; cdr [x]] = x, \quad \text{provided that x is not atomic.}$$

The names "car" and "cons" will come to have mnemonic significance only when we discuss the representation of the system in the computer. Compositions of car and cdr give the subexpressions of a given expression in a given position. Compositions of cons form expressions of a given structure out of parts. The class of functions which can be formed in this way is quite limited and not very interesting.

d. *Recursive S-functions.* We get a much larger class of functions (in fact, all computable functions) when we allow ourselves to form new functions of S-expressions by conditional expressions and recursive definition.

We now give some examples of functions that are definable in this way.
1. ff [x].   The value of ff [x] is the first atomic symbol of the S-expression x with the parentheses ignored. Thus

$$ff [((A \cdot B) \cdot C)] = A$$

We have

$$ff [x] = [atom [x] \to x; T \to ff [car [x]]]$$

We now trace in detail the steps in the evaluation of ff $[((A \cdot B) \cdot C)]$:

ff $[((A \cdot B) \cdot C)]$

$$= [atom [((A \cdot B) \cdot C)] \to ((A \cdot B) \cdot C);$$
$$T \to ff [car [((A \cdot B) \cdot C)]]]$$
$$= [F \to ((A \cdot B) \cdot C); T \to ff [car [((A \cdot B) \cdot C)]]]$$
$$= [T \to ff [car [((A \cdot B) \cdot C)]]]$$

$= \text{ff} [\text{car} [((A \cdot B) \cdot C)]]$

$= \text{ff} [(A \cdot B)]$

$= [\text{atom} [(A \cdot B)] \rightarrow (A \cdot B); T \rightarrow \text{ff} [\text{car} [(A \cdot B)]]]$

$= [F \rightarrow (A \cdot B); T \rightarrow \text{ff} [\text{car} [(A \cdot B)]]]$

$= [T \rightarrow \text{ff} [\text{car} [(A \cdot B)]]]$

$= \text{ff} [\text{car} [(A \cdot B)]]$

$= \text{ff} [A]$

$= [\text{atom} [A] \rightarrow A; T \rightarrow \text{ff} [\text{car} [A]]]$

$= [T \rightarrow A; T \rightarrow \text{ff} [\text{car} [A]]]$

$= A$

2. subst [x; y; z].   This function gives the result of substituting the S-expression x for all occurrences of the atomic symbol y in the S-expression z. It is defined by

$\text{subst} [x; y; z] = [\text{atom} [z] \rightarrow [\text{eq} [z; y] \rightarrow x; T \rightarrow z];$

$T \rightarrow \text{cons} [\text{subst} [x; y; \text{car} [z]]; \text{subst} [x; y; \text{cdr} [z]]]]$

As an example, we have

$\text{subst} [(X \cdot A); B; ((A \cdot B) \cdot C)] = ((A \cdot (X \cdot A)) \cdot C)$

3. equal [x; y].   This is a predicate that has the value T if x and y are the same S-expression, and has the value F otherwise. We have

$\text{equal} [x; y] = [\text{atom} [x] \wedge \text{atom} [y] \wedge \text{eq} [x; y]]$

$\vee [\sim\text{atom} [x] \wedge \sim\text{atom} [y] \wedge \text{equal} [\text{car} [x]; \text{car} [y]]$

$\wedge \text{equal} [\text{cdr} [x]; \text{cdr} [y]]]$

It is convenient to see how the elementary functions look in the abbreviated list notation. The reader will easily verify that

(i) $\text{car} [(m_1, m_2, \cdots, m_n)] = m_1$

(ii) $\text{cdr} [(m_1, m_2, \cdots, m_n)] = (m_2, \cdots, m_n)$

(iii) $\text{cdr} [(m)] = \text{NIL}$

(iv) $\text{cons} [m_1; (m_2, \cdots, m_n)] = (m_1, m_2, \cdots, m_n)$

(v) $\text{cons} [m; \text{NIL}] = (m)$

We define

$\text{null} [x] = \text{atom} [x] \wedge \text{eq} [x; \text{NIL}]$

This predicate is useful in dealing with lists.

Compositions of car and cdr arise so frequently that many expressions can be written more concisely if we abbreviate

cadr [x]   for   car [cdr [x]],

caddr [x]   for   car [cdr [cdr [x]]], etc.

Another useful abbreviation is to write list $[e_1; e_2; \cdots; e_n]$ for cons $[e_1; \text{cons} [e_2; \cdots; \text{cons} [e_n; \text{NIL}] \cdots]]$. This function gives the list, $(e_1, \cdots, e_n)$, as a function of its elements.

The following functions are useful when S-expressions are regarded as lists.

1. append [x; y].

$\text{append} [x; y] = [\text{null} [x] \rightarrow y; T \rightarrow \text{cons} [\text{car} [x];$

$\text{append} [\text{cdr} [x]; y]]]$

An example is

$\text{append} [(A, B); (C, D, E)] = (A, B, C, D, E)$

2. among [x; y].   This predicate is true if the S-expression x occurs among the elements of the list y. We have

$\text{among} [x; y] = \sim\text{null} [y] \wedge [\text{equal} [x; \text{car} [y]]$

$\vee \text{among} [x; \text{cdr} [y]]]$

3. pair [x; y].   This function gives the list of pairs of corresponding elements of the lists x and y. We have

$\text{pair} [x; y] = [\text{null} [x] \wedge \text{null} [y] \rightarrow \text{NIL}; \sim\text{atom} [x]$

$\wedge \sim\text{atom} [y] \rightarrow \text{cons} [\text{list} [\text{car} [x]; \text{car} [y]];$

$\text{pair} [\text{cdr} [x]; \text{cdr} [y]]]]$

An example is

$\text{pair} [(A, B, C); (X, (Y, Z), U)] = ((A, X),$

$(B, (Y, Z)), (C, U))$

4. assoc [x; y].   If y is a list of the form $((u_1, v_1), \cdots, (u_n, v_n))$ and x is one of the u's, then assoc [x; y] is the corresponding v. We have

$\text{assoc} [x; y] = \text{eq}[\text{caar} [y]; x] \rightarrow \text{cadar} [y];$

$T \rightarrow \text{assoc} [x; \text{cdr} [y]]]$

An example is

$\text{assoc} [X; ((W, (A, B)), (X, (C, D)),$

$(Y, (E, F)))] = (C, D)$

5. sublis [x; y].   Here x is assumed to have the form of a list of pairs $((u_1, v_1), \cdots, (u_n, v_n))$, where the u's are atomic, and y may be any S-expression. The value of sublis [x; y] is the result of substituting each v for the corresponding u in y. In order to define sublis, we first define an auxiliary function. We have

$\text{sub2} [x; z] = [\text{null} [x] \rightarrow z; \text{eq} [\text{caar} [x]; z] \rightarrow \text{cadar} [x];$

$T \rightarrow \text{sub2} [\text{cdr} [x]; z]]$

and

$\text{sublis} [x; y] = [\text{atom} [y] \rightarrow \text{sub2} [x; y];$

$T \rightarrow \text{cons} [\text{sublis} [x; \text{car} [y]]; \text{sublis} [x; \text{cdr} [y]]]]$

We have

$\text{sublis} [((X, (A, B)), (Y, (B, C))); (A, X \cdot Y)]$

$= (A, (A, B), B, C)$

e. *Representation of S-Functions by S-Expressions.* S-functions have been described by M-expressions. We now give a rule for translating M-expressions into S-expressions, in order to be able to use S-functions for making certain computations with S-functions and for answering certain questions about S-functions.

The translation is determined by the following rules in which we denote the translation of an M-expression ε by ε*.

1. If ε is an S-expression E* is (QUOTE, ε).

2. Variables and function names that were represented by strings of lower-case letters are translated to the corresponding strings of the corresponding upper-case letters. Thus car* is CAR, and subst* is SUBST.

3. A form f[e_1 ; $\cdots$; e_n] is translated to (f*, e_1*, $\cdots$, e_n*). Thus {cons [car [x]; cdr [x]]}* is (CONS, (CAR, X), (CDR, X)).

4. {[$p_1 \rightarrow e_1$; $\cdots$; $p_n \rightarrow e_n$]}* is (COND, (p_1*, e_1*), $\cdots$, (p_n*. e_n*)).

5. {λ[[x_1 ; $\cdots$; x_n]; ε]}* is (LAMBDA, (x_1*, $\cdots$, x_n*), ε*).

6. {label [a; ε]}* is (LABEL, a*, ε*).

With these conventions the substitution function whose M-expression is label [subst; λ[[x; y; z]; [atom [z] $\rightarrow$ [eq [y; z] $\rightarrow$ x; T $\rightarrow$ z]; T $\rightarrow$ cons [subst [x; y; car [z]]; subst [x; y; cdr [z]]]]]]] has the S-expression

(LABEL, SUEST, (LAMBDA, (X, Y, Z), (COND

((ATOM, Z), (COND, (EQ, Y, Z), X), ((QUOTE,

T), Z))), ((QUOTE, T), (CONS, (SUBST, X, Y,

(CAR Z)), (SUBST, X, Y, (CDR, Z)))))))))

This notation is writable and somewhat readable. It can be made easier to read and write at the cost of making its structure less regular. If more characters were available on the computer, it could be improved considerably.

f. *The Universal S-Function* apply. There is an S-function *apply* with the property that if f is an S-expression for an S-function f' and args is a list of arguments of the form (argl, $\cdots$, argn), where argl, $\cdots$, argn are arbitrary S-expressions, then apply[f; args] and f'[argl; $\cdots$; argn] are defined for the same values of argl, $\cdots$, argn, and are equal when defined. For example,

λ[[x; y]; cons [car [x]; y]] [(A, B); (C, D)]

= apply [(LAMBDA, (X, Y), (CONS, (CAR, X),

Y)); ((A, B), (C, D))] = (A, C, D)

The S-function *apply* is defined by

apply [f; args] = eval [cons [f; appq [args]]; NIL]

where

appq [m] = [null [m] $\rightarrow$ NIL;

T $\rightarrow$ cons [list [QUOTE; car [m]]; appq [cdr [m]]]]

and

eval [e; a] = [

atom [e] $\rightarrow$ assoc [e; a];

atom [car [e]] $\rightarrow$ [

eq [car [e]; QUOTE] $\rightarrow$ cadr [e];

eq [car [e]; ATOM] $\rightarrow$ atom [eval [cadr [e]; a]];

eq [car [e]; EQ] $\rightarrow$ [eval [cadr [e]; a] = eval [caddr [e]; a]];

eq [car [e]; COND] $\rightarrow$ evcon [cdr [e]; a];

eq [car [e]; CAR] $\rightarrow$ car [eval [cadr [e]; a]];

eq [car [e]; CDR] $\rightarrow$ cdr [eval [cadr [e]; a]];

eq [car [e]; CONS] $\rightarrow$ cons [eval [cadr [e]; a]; eval [caddr [e]; a]]; T $\rightarrow$ eval [cons [assoc [car [e]; a];

evlis [cdr [e]; a]]; a]];

eq [caar [e]; LABEL] $\rightarrow$ eval [cons [caddar [e]; cdr [e]];

cons [list [cadar [e]; car [e]; a]];

eq [caar [e]; LAMBDA] $\rightarrow$ eval [caddar [e];

append [pair [cadar [e]; evlis [cdr [e]; a]; a]]]

and

evcon [c; a] = [eval [caar [c]; a] $\rightarrow$ eval [cadar [c]; a];

T $\rightarrow$ evcon [cdr [c]; a]]

and

evlis [m; a] = [null [m] $\rightarrow$ NIL;

T $\rightarrow$ cons [eval [car [m]; a]; evlis [cdr [m]; a]]]

We now explain a number of points about these definitions.

1. *apply* itself forms an expression representing the value of the function applied to the arguments, and puts the work of evaluating this expression onto a function eval. It uses appq to put quotes around each of the arguments, so that eval will regard them as standing for themselves.

2. eval [e; a] has two arguments, an expression e to be evaluated, and a list of pairs a. The first item of each pair is an atomic symbol, and the second is the expression for which the symbol stands.

3. If the expression to be evaluated is atomic, eval evaluates whatever is paired with it first on the list a.

4. If e is not atomic but car [e] is atomic, then the expression has one of the forms (QUOTE, e) or (ATOM, e) or (EQ, e_1, e_2) or (COND, (p_1, e_1), $\cdots$, (p_n, e_n)), or (CAR, e) or (CDR, e) or (CONS, e_1, e_2) or (f, e_1, $\cdots$, e_n) where f is an atomic symbol.

In the case (QUOTE; e) the expression e, itself, is taken. In the case of (ATOM, e) or (CAR, e) or (CDR, e) the expression e is evaluated and the appropriate function taken. In the case of (EQ, e_1, e_2) or (CONS, e_1, e_2) two expressions have to be evaluated. In the case of (COND,

$(p_1, e_1), \cdots, (p_n, e_n))$ the p's have to be evaluated in order until a true p is found, and then the corresponding e must be evaluated. This is accomplished by evcon. Finally, in the case of $(f, e_1, \cdots, e_n)$ we evaluate the expression that results from replacing f in this expression by whatever it is paired with in the list a.

5. The evaluation of $((\text{LABEL}, f, \mathcal{E}), e_1, \cdots, e_n)$ is accomplished by evaluating $(\mathcal{E}, e_1, \cdots, e_n)$ with the pairing $(f, (\text{LABEL}, f, \mathcal{E}))$ put on the front of the previous list a of pairs.

6. Finally, the evaluation of $((\text{LAMBDA}, (x_1, \cdots, x_n), \mathcal{E}), e_1, \cdots, e_n)$ is accomplished by evaluating $\mathcal{E}$ with the list of pairs $((x_1, e_1), \cdots, ((x_n, e_n))$ put on the front of the previous list a.

The list a could be eliminated, and LAMBDA and LABEL expressions evaluated by substituting the arguments for the variables in the expressions $\mathcal{E}$. Unfortunately, difficulties involving collisions of bound variables arise, but they are avoided by using the list a.

Calculating the values of functions by using *apply* is an activity better suited to electronic computers than to people. As an illustration, however, we now give some of the steps for calculating

apply [(LABEL, FF, (LAMBDA, (X), (COND,

((ATOM, X), X), ((QUOTE, T),

(FF, (CAR, X)))))); ((A·B))] = A

The first argument is the S-expression that represents the function ff defined in section 3d. We shall abbreviate it by using the letter ϕ. We have

apply $[\phi; ((A \cdot B))]$

= eval [((LABEL, FF, ψ), (QUOTE, (A·B))); NIL]

where ψ is the part of ϕ beginning (LAMBDA

= eval [((LAMBDA, (X), ω), (QUOTE, (A·B))); ((FF, ϕ))]

where ω is the part of ψ beginning (COND

= eval [(COND, (π_1, ϵ_1), (π_2, ϵ_2)); ((X, (QUOTE, (A·B))), (FF, ϕ))]

Denoting ((X, (QUOTE, (A·B))), (FF, ϕ)) by α, we obtain

= evcon [(((π_1, ϵ_1), (π_2, ϵ_2)); α]

This involves eval [π_1 ; α]

= eval [(ATOM, X); α]

= atom [eval [X; α]]

= atom [eval [assoc [X; ((X, (QUOTE, (A·B))), (FF, ϕ))]; α]]

= atom [eval [(QUOTE, (A·B)); α]]

= atom [(A·B)]

= F

Our main calculation continues with

apply $[\phi; ((A \cdot B))]$

= evcon [((π_2, ϵ_2)); α],

which involves eval [π_2 ; α] = eval [(QUOTE, T); α] = T.

Our main calculation again continues with

apply $[\phi; ((A \cdot B))]$

= eval [ϵ_2 ; α]

= eval [(FF, (CAR, X)); α]

= eval [cons [ϕ; evlis [((CAR, X)); α]]; α]

Evaluating evlis [((CAR, X)); α] involves

eval [(CAR, X); α]

= car [eval [X; α]]

= car [(A·B)], where we took steps from the earlier computation of atom [eval [X; α]] = A,

and so evlis [((CAR, X)); α] then becomes

list [list [QUOTE; A]] = ((QUOTE, A)),

and our main quantity becomes

= eval [(ϕ, (QUOTE, A)); α]

The subsequent steps are made as in the beginning of the calculation. The LABEL and LAMBDA cause new pairs to be added to α, which gives a new list of pairs α_1. The π_1 term of the conditional eval [(ATOM, X); α_1] has the value T because X is paired with (QUOTE, A) first in α_1, rather than with (QUOTE, (A·B)) as in α.

Therefore we end up with eval [X; α_1] from the *evcon*, and this is just A.

g. *Functions with Functions as Arguments.* There are a number of useful functions some of whose arguments are functions. They are especially useful in defining other functions. One such function is maplist [x; f] with an S-expression argument x and an argument f that is a function from S-expressions to S-expressions. We define

maplist [x; f] = [null [x] → NIL;

T → cons [f[x]; maplist [cdr [x]; f]]]

The usefulness of *maplist* is illustrated by formulas for the partial derivative with respect to x of expressions involving sums and products of x and other variables. The S-expressions that we shall differentiate are formed as follows.

1. An atomic symbol is an allowed expression.

2. If $e_1, e_2, \cdots, e_n$ are allowed expressions, (PLUS, e_1, $\cdots$, e_n) and (TIMES, e_1, $\cdots$, e_n) are also, and represent the sum and product, respectively, of $e_1, \cdots, e_n$.

This is, essentially, the Polish notation for functions, except that the inclusion of parentheses and commas allows functions of variable numbers of arguments. An example of an allowed expression is (TIMES, X, (PLUS, X, A), Y), the conventional algebraic notation for which is $X(X + A)Y$.

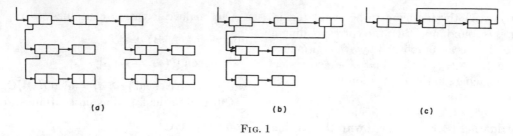

(a)   (b)   (c)

Fig. 1

Our differentiation formula, which gives the derivative of y with respect to x, is

diff [y; x] = [atom [y] → [eq [y; x] → ONE; T → ZERO];
eq [car [y]; PLUS] → cons [PLUS; maplist [cdr [y]; λ[[z];
diff[car [z]; x]]]]; eq[car [y]; TIMES] → cons[PLUS;
maplist[cdr[y]; λ[[z]; cons [TIMES; maplist[cdr [y];
λ[[w]; ~eq [z; w] → car [w]; T → diff [car [[w]; x]]]]]]]]]

The derivative of the allowed expression, as computed by this formula, is

(PLUS, (TIMES, ONE, (PLUS, X, A), Y),

(TIMES, X, (PLUS, ONE, ZERO), Y),

(TIMES, X, (PLUS, X, A), ZERO))

Besides *maplist*, another useful function with functional arguments is *search*, which is defined as

search [x; p; f; u] = [null [x] → u; p[x] → f[x];

T → search [cdr [x]; p; f; u]

The function *search* is used to search a list for an element that has the property p, and if such an element is found, f of that element is taken. If there is no such element, the function u of no argument is computed.

4. The LISP Programming System

The LISP programming system is a system for using the IBM 704 computer to compute with symbolic information in the form of S-expressions. It has been or will be used for the following purposes:

1. Writing a compiler to compile LISP programs into machine language.

2. Writing a program to check proofs in a class of formal logical systems.

3. Writing programs for formal differentiation and integration.

4. Writing programs to realize various algorithms for generating proofs in predicate calculus.

5. Making certain engineering calculations whose results are formulas rather than numbers.

6. Programming the Advice Taker system.

The basis of the system is a way of writing computer programs to evaluate S-functions. This will be described in the following sections.

In addition to the facilities for describing S-functions, there are facilities for using S-functions in programs written as sequences of statements along the lines of FORTRAN (4) or ALGOL (5). These features will not be described in this article.

a. Representation of S-Expressions by List Structure. A list structure is a collection of computer words arranged as in figure 1a or 1b. Each word of the list structure is represented by one of the subdivided rectangles in the figure. The *left* box of a rectangle represents the *address* field of the word and the *right* box represents the *decrement* field. An arrow from a box to another rectangle means that the field corresponding to the box contains the location of the word corresponding to the other rectangle.

It is permitted for a substructure to occur in more than one place in a list structure, as in figure 1b, but it is not permitted for a structure to have cycles, as in figure 1c.

An atomic symbol is represented in the computer by a list structure of special form called the *association list* of the symbol. The address field of the first word contains a special constant which enables the program to tell that this word represents an atomic symbol. We shall describe association lists in section 4b.

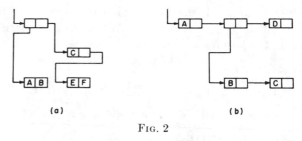

(a)   (b)

Fig. 2

An S-expression x that is not atomic is represented by a word, the address and decrement parts of which contain the locations of the subexpressions car[x] and cdr[x], respectively. If we use the symbols A, B, etc. to denote the locations of the association list of these symbols, then the S-expression ((A·B)·(C·(E·F))) is represented by the list structure *a* of figure 2. Turning to the list form of S-expressions, we see that the S-expression (A, (B, C), D), which is an abbreviation for (A·((B·(C·NIL))·(D·NIL))), is represented by the list structure of figure 2b. When a list structure is regarded as representing a list, we see that each term of the list occupies the address part of a word, the decrement part of which *points* to the word containing the next term, while the last word has NIL in its decrement.

An expression that has a given subexpression occurring more than once can be represented in more than one way. Whether the list structure for the subexpression is or is not repeated depends upon the history of the program. Whether or not a subexpression is repeated will make no difference in the results of a program as they appear outside the machine, although it will affect the time and storage requirements. For example, the S-expression $((A \cdot B) \cdot (A \cdot B))$ can be represented by either the list structure of figure 3a or 3b.

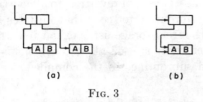

(a)   (b)

FIG. 3

The prohibition against circular list structures is essentially a prohibition against an expression being a subexpression of itself. Such an expression could not exist on paper in a world with our topology. Circular list structures would have some advantages in the machine, for example, for representing recursive functions, but difficulties in printing them, and in certain other operations, make it seem advisable not to use them for the present.

The advantages of list structures for the storage of symbolic expressions are:

1. The size and even the number of expressions with which the program will have to deal cannot be predicted in advance. Therefore, it is difficult to arrange blocks of storage of fixed length to contain them.

2. Registers can be put back on the free storage list when they are no longer needed. Even one register returned to the list is of value, but if expressions are stored linearly, it is difficult to make use of blocks of registers of odd sizes that may become available.

3. An expression that occurs as a subexpression of several expressions need be represented in storage only once.

b. *Association Lists.* In the LISP programming system we put more in the association list of a symbol than is required by the mathematical system described in the previous sections. In fact, any information that we desire to associate with the symbol may be put on the association list. This information may include: the *print name*, that is, the string of letters and digits which represents the symbol outside the machine; a numerical value if the symbol represents a number; another S-expression if the symbol, in some way, serves as a name for it; or the location of a routine if the symbol represents a function for which there is a machine-language subroutine. All this implies that in the machine system there are more primitive entities than have been described in the sections on the mathematical system.

For the present, we shall only describe how *print names* are represented on association lists so that in reading or printing the program can establish a correspondence between information on punched cards, magnetic tape or printed page and the list structure inside the machine. The association list of the symbol DIFFERENTIATE has a segment of the form shown in figure 4. Here *pname* is a symbol that indicates that the structure for the print

name of the symbol whose association list this is hangs from the next word on the association list. In the second row of the figure we have a list of three words. The address part of each of these words points to a word containing six 6-bit characters. The last word is filled out with a 6-bit combination that does not represent a character printable by the computer. (Recall that the IBM 704 has a 36-bit word and that printable characters are each represented by 6 bits.) The presence of the words with character information means that the association lists do not themselves represent S-expressions, and that only some of the functions for dealing with S-expressions make sense within as association list.

c. *Free-Storage List.* At any given time only a part of the memory reserved for list structures will actually be in use for storing S-expressions. The remaining registers (in our system the number, initially, is approximately 15,000) are arranged in a single list called the *free-storage list*. A certain register, FREE, in the program contains the location of the first register in this list. When a word is required to form some additional list structure, the first word on the *free-storage list* is taken and the number in register FREE is changed to become the location of the second word on the free-storage list. No provision need be made for the user to program the return of registers to the free-storage list.

This return takes place automatically, approximately as follows (it is necessary to give a simplified description of this process in this report): There is a fixed set of base registers in the program which contains the locations of list structures that are accessible to the program. Of course, because list structures branch, an arbitrary number of registers may be involved. Each register that is accessible to the program is accessible because it can be reached from one or more of the base registers by a chain of car and cdr operations. When the contents of a base register are changed, it may happen that the register to which the base register formerly pointed cannot be reached by a car-cdr chain from any base register. Such a register may be considered abandoned by the program because its contents can no longer be found by any possible program; hence its contents are no longer of interest, and so we would like to have it back on the free-storage list. This comes about in the following way.

Nothing happens until the program runs out of free storage. When a free register is wanted, and there is none left on the free-storage list, a reclamation cycle starts.

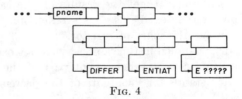

FIG. 4

First, the program finds all registers accessible from the base registers and makes their signs negative. This is accomplished by starting from each of the base registers and changing the sign of every register that can be reached from it by a car-cdr chain. If the program encounters a register in this process which already has a negative sign, it assumes that this register has already been reached.

After all of the accessible registers have had their signs changed, the program goes through the area of memory reserved for the storage of list structures and puts all the registers whose signs were not changed in the previous step back on the free-storage list, and makes the signs of the accessible registers positive again.

This process, because it is entirely automatic, is more convenient for the programmer than a system in which he has to keep track of and erase unwanted lists. Its efficiency depends upon not coming close to exhausting the available memory with accessible lists. This is because the reclamation process requires several seconds to execute, and therefore must result in the addition of at least several thousand registers to the free-storage list if the program is not to spend most of its time in reclamation.

d. *Elementary S-Functions in the Computer.* We shall now describe the computer representations of atom, =, car, cdr, and cons. An S-expression is communicated to the program that represents a function as the location of the word representing it, and the programs give S-expression answers in the same form.

atom. As stated above, a word representing an atomic symbol has a special constant in its address part: atom is programmed as an open subroutine that tests this part. Unless the M-expression atom[e] occurs as a condition in a conditional expression, the symbol T or F is generated as the result of the test. In case of a conditional expression, a conditional transfer is used and the symbol T or F is not generated.

eq. The program for eq[e; f] involves testing for the numerical equality of the locations of the words. This works because each atomic symbol has only one association list. As with *atom*, the result is either a conditional transfer or one of the symbols T or F.

car. Computing car[x] involves getting the contents of the address part of register x. This is essentially accomplished by the single instruction CLA 0, i, where the argument is in index register i, and the result appears in the address part of the accumulator. (We take the view that the places from which a function takes its arguments and into which it puts its results are prescribed in the definition of the function, and it is the responsibility of the programmer or the compiler to insert the required data-moving instructions to get the results of one calculation in position for the next.) ("car" is a mnemonic for "contents of the address part of register.")

cdr. cdr is handled in the same way as car, except that the result appears in the decrement part of the accumulator. ("cdr" stands for "contents of the decrement part of register.")

cons. The value of cons[x; y] must be the location of a register that has x and y in its address and decrement parts, respectively. There may not be such a register in the computer and, even if there were, it would be time-consuming to find it. Actually, what we do is to take the first available register from the *free-storage list*, put x and y in the address and decrement parts, respectively, and make the value of the function the location of the register taken. ("cons" is an abbreviation for "construct.")

It is the subroutine for cons that initiates the reclamation when the free-storage list is exhausted. In the version of the system that is used at present cons is represented by a closed subroutine. In the compiled version, cons is open.

e. *Representation of S-Functions by Programs.* The compilation of functions that are compositions of car, cdr, and cons, either by hand or by a compiler program, is straightforward. Conditional expressions give no trouble except that they must be so compiled that only the p's and e's that are required are computed. However, problems arise in the compilation of recursive functions.

In general (we shall discuss an exception), the routine for a recursive function uses itself as a subroutine. For example, the program for subst[x;y;z] uses itself as a subroutine to evaluate the result into the subexpressions car[z] and cdr[z]. While subst[x;y:cdr[z]] is being evaluated, the result of the previous evaluation of subst[x; y; car[z]] must be saved in a temporary storage register. However, subst may need the same register for evaluating subst[x;y;cdr[z]]. This possible conflict is resolved by the SAVE and UNSAVE routines that use the *public push-down list*. The SAVE routine is entered at the beginning of the routine for the recursive function with a request to save a given set of consecutive registers. A block of registers called the *public push-down list* is reserved for this purpose. The SAVE routine has an index that tells it how many registers in the push-down list are already in use. It moves the contents of the registers which are to be saved to the first unused registers in the push-down list, advances the index of the list, and returns to the program from which control came. This program may then freely use these registers for temporary storage. Before the routine exits it uses UNSAVE, which restores the contents of the temporary registers from the push-down list and moves back the index of this list. The result of these conventions is described, in programming terminology, by saying that the recursive subroutine is transparent to the temporary storage registers.

f. *Status of the LISP Programming System* (February 1960). A variant of the function *apply* described in section 5f has been translated into a program APPLY for the IBM 704. Since this routine can compute values of S-functions given their descriptions as S-expressions and their arguments, it serves as an interpreter for the LISP programming language which describes computation processes in this way.

The program APPLY has been imbedded in the LISP programming system which has the following features:

1. The programmer may define any number of S-func-

tions by S-expressions. These functions may refer to each other or to certain S-functions represented by machine language program.

2. The values of defined functions may be computed.

3. S-expressions may be read and printed (directly or via magnetic tape).

4. Some error diagnostic and selective tracing facilities are included.

5. The programmer may have selected S-functions compiled into machine language programs put into the core memory. Values of compiled functions are computed about 60 times as fast as they would if interpreted. Compilation is fast enough so that it is not necessary to punch compiled program for future use.

6. A "program feature" allows programs containing assignment and **go to** statements in the style of ALGOL.

7. Computation with floating point numbers is possible in the system but this is inefficient.

8. A programmer's manual is being prepared.

The LISP programming system is appropriate for computations where the data can conveniently be represented as symbolic expressions allowing expressions of the same kind as subexpressions. A version of the system for the IBM 709 is being prepared.

5. Another Formalism for Functions of Symbolic Expressions

There are a number of ways of defining functions of symbolic expressions which are quite similar to the system we have adopted. Each of them involves three basic functions, conditional expressions, and recursive function definitions, but the class of expressions corresponding to S-expressions is different, and so are the precise definitions of the functions. We shall describe one of these variants called linear LISP.

The L-expressions are defined as follows:

1. A finite list of characters is admitted.

2. Any string of admitted characters is an L-expression. This includes the null string denoted by Λ.

There are three functions of strings:

1. first[x] is the first character of the string x.
   first[Λ] is undefined.
For example: first[ABC] = A

2. rest[x] is the string of characters which remains when the first character of the string is deleted.
   rest[Λ] is undefined.
For example: rest[ABC] = BC

3. combine[x; y] is the string formed by prefixing the character x to the string y.
For example: combine[A; BC] = ABC

There are three predicates on strings:

1. char[x],   x is a single character.

2. null[x],   x is the null string.

3. x = y, defined for x and y characters.

The advantage of linear LISP is that no characters are given special roles, as are parentheses, dots, and commas in LISP. This permits computations with all expressions that can be written linearly. The disadvantage of linear LISP is that the extraction of subexpressions is a fairly involved, rather than an elementary, operation. It is not hard to write, in linear LISP, functions that correspond to the basic functions of LISP, so that, mathematically, linear LISP includes LISP. This turns out to be the most convenient way of programming, in linear LISP, the more complicated manipulations. However, if the functions are to be represented by computer routines, LISP is essentially faster.

6. Flowcharts and Recursion

Since both the usual form of computer program and recursive function definitions are universal computationally, it is interesting to display the relation between them. The translation of recursive symbolic functions into computer programs was the subject of the rest of this report. In this section we show how to go the other way, at least in principle.

The state of the machine at any time during a computation is given by the values of a number of variables. Let these variables be combined into a vector ξ. Consider a program block with one entrance and one exit. It defines and is essentially defined by a certain function f that takes one machine configuration into another, that is, f has the form $\xi' = f(\xi)$. Let us call f the associated function of the program block. Now let a number of such blocks be combined into a program by decision elements π that decide after each block is completed which block will be entered next. Nevertheless, let the whole program still have one entrance and one exit.

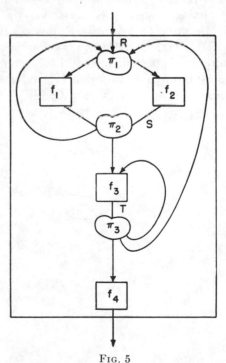

FIG. 5

We give as an example the flowchart of figure 5. Let us describe the function r[ξ] that gives the transformation of the vector ξ between entrance and exit of the whole block.

We shall define it in conjunction with the functions $s[\xi]$ and $t[\xi]$, which give the transformations that ξ undergoes between the points S and T, respectively, and the exit. We have

$$r[\xi] = [\pi_{11}[\xi] \rightarrow s[f_1[\xi]]; T \rightarrow s[f_2[\xi]]]$$

$$s[\xi] = [\pi_{21}[\xi] \rightarrow r[\xi]; T \rightarrow t[f_3[\xi]]]$$

$$t[\xi] = [\pi_{31}[\xi] \rightarrow f_4[\xi]; \pi_{32}[\xi] \rightarrow r[\xi]; T \rightarrow t[f_3[\xi]]]$$

Given a flowchart with a single entrance and a single exit, it is easy to write down the recursive function that gives the transformation of the state vector from entrance to exit in terms of the corresponding functions for the computation blocks and the predicates of the branch points. In general, we proceed as follows.

In figure 6, let β be an n-way branch point, and let $f_1, \cdots, f_n$ be the computations leading to branch points $\beta_1, \beta_2, \cdots, \beta_n$. Let ϕ be the function that transforms ξ between β and the exit of the chart, and let $\phi_1, \cdots, \phi_n$ be the corresponding functions for $\beta_1, \cdots, \beta_n$. We then write

$$\phi[\xi] = [p_1[\xi] \rightarrow \phi_1[f_1[\xi]]; \cdots ; p_n[\xi] \rightarrow \phi_n[f_n[\xi]]]$$

Acknowledgments

The inadequacy of the λ-notation for naming recursive functions was noticed by N. Rochester, and he discovered an alternative to the solution involving *label* which has been used here. The form of subroutine for *cons* which permits its composition with other functions was invented, in connection with another programming system, by C. Gerberick and H. L. Gelernter, of IBM Corporation. The LISP programming system was developed by a group including R. Brayton, D. Edwards, P. Fox, L. Hodes, D. Luckham, K. Maling, J. McCarthy, D. Park, S. Russell.

The group was supported by the M.I.T. Computation Center, and by the M.I.T. Research Laboratory of Electronics (which is supported in part by the U.S. Army (Signal Corps), the U.S. Air Force (Office of Scientific Research, Air Research and Development Command), and the U.S. Navy (Office of Naval Research)). The author also wishes to acknowledge the personal financial support of the Alfred P. Sloan Foundation.

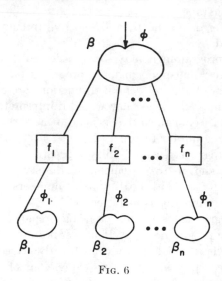

FIG. 6

REFERENCES

1. J. McCarthy, Programs with common sense, Paper presented at the Symposium on the Mechanization of Thought Processes, National Physical Laboratory, Teddington, England, Nov. 24–27, 1958. (Published in Proceedings of the Symposium by H. M. Stationery Office).
2. A. Newell and J. C. Shaw, Programming the logic theory machine, Proc. Western Joint Computer Conference, Feb. 1957.
3. A. Church, *The Calculi of Lambda-Conversion* (Princeton University Press, Princeton, N. J., 1941).
4. FORTRAN Programmer's Reference Manual, IBM Corporation, New York, Oct. 15, 1956.
5. A. J. Perlis and K. Samelson, International algebraic language, Preliminary Report, *Comm. Assoc. Comp. Mach.*, Dec. 1958.

LISP 1.5 PROGRAMMER'S MANUAL*

J. McCARTHY, P. W. ABRAHAMS, D. J. EDWARDS, T. P. HART, AND M. LEVIN

I. THE LISP LANGUAGE

The LISP language is designed primarily for symbolic data processing. It has been used for symbolic calculations in differential and integral calculus, electrical circuit theory, mathematical logic, game playing, and other fields of artificial intelligence.

LISP is a formal mathematical language. It is therefore possible to give a concise yet complete description of it. Such is the purpose of this first section of the manual. Other sections will describe ways of using LISP to advantage and will explain extensions of the language which make it a convenient programming system.

LISP differs from most programming languages in three important ways. The first way is in the nature of the data. In the LISP language, all data are in the form of symbolic expressions usually referred to as S-expressions. S-expressions are of indefinite length and have a branching tree type of structure, so that significant subexpressions can be readily isolated. In the LISP programming system, the bulk of available memory is used for storing S-expressions in the form of list structures. This type of memory organization frees the programmer from the necessity of allocating storage for the different sections of his program.

The second important part of the LISP language is the source language itself which specifies in what way the S-expressions are to be processed. This consists of recursive functions of S-expressions. Since the notation for the writing of recursive functions of S-expressions is itself outside the S-expression notation, it will be called the meta language. These expressions will therefore be called M-expressions.

Third, LISP can interpret and execute programs written in the form of S-expressions. Thus, like machine language, and unlike most other higher level languages, it can be used to generate programs for further execution.

1.1 Symbolic Expressions

The most elementary type of S-expression is the atomic symbol.

Definition: An atomic symbol is a string of no more than thirty numerals and capital letters; the first character must be a letter.

Examples

```
A
APPLE
PART2
EXTRALONGSTRINGOFLETTERS
A4B66XYZ2
```

These symbols are called atomic because they are taken as a whole and are not capable of being split within LISP into individual characters. Thus A, B, and AB have no relation to each other except in so far as they are three distinct atomic symbols.

All S-expressions are built out of atomic symbols and the punctuation marks "(", ")", and " . ". The basic operation for forming S-expressions is to combine two

*Reprinted from MIT Press, Cambridge, Mass. 1965.

of them to produce a larger one. From the two atomic symbols A1 and A2, one can form the S-expression (A1 . A2).

<u>Definition</u>: An S-expression is either an atomic symbol or it is composed of these elements in the following order: a left parenthesis, an S-expression, a dot, an S-expression, and a right parenthesis.

Notice that this definition is recursive.

<u>Examples</u>

ATOM
(A . B)
(A . (B . C))
((A1 . A2) . B)
((U . V) . (X . Y))
((U . V) . (X . (Y . Z)))

1.2 Elementary Functions

We shall introduce some elementary functions of S-expressions. To distinguish the functions from the S-expressions themselves, we shall write function names in lower case letters, since atomic symbols consist of only upper case letters. Furthermore, the arguments of functions will be grouped in square brackets rather than parentheses. As a separator or punctuation mark we shall use the semicolon.

The first function that we shall introduce is the function <u>cons</u>. It has two arguments and is in fact the function that is used to build S-expressions from smaller S-expressions.

<u>Examples</u>

cons[A;B]=(A . B)
cons[(A . B);C]=((A . B) . C)
cons[cons[A;B];C]=((A . B) . C)

The last example is an instance of composition of functions. It is possible to build any S-expression from its atomic components by compositions of the function <u>cons</u>.

The next pair of functions do just the opposite of <u>cons</u>. They produce the subexpressions of a given expression.

The function <u>car</u> has one argument. Its value is the first part of its composite argument. <u>car</u> of an atomic symbol is undefined.

<u>Examples</u>

car[(A . B)]=A
car[(A . (B1 . B2))]=A
car[((A1 . A2) . B)]=(A1 . A2)
car[A] is undefined

The function <u>cdr</u> has one argument. Its value is the second part of its composite argument. <u>cdr</u> is also undefined if its argument is atomic.

<u>Examples</u>

cdr[(A . B)]=B
cdr[(A . (B1 . B2))]=(B1 . B2)
cdr[((A1 . A2) . B)]=B
cdr[A] is undefined
car[cdr[(A . (B1 . B2))]]=B1
car[cdr[(A . B)]] is undefined
car[cons[A;B]]=A

Given any S-expression, it is possible to produce any subexpression of it by a suitable composition of car's and cdr's. If $\underline{x}$ and $\underline{y}$ represent any two S-expressions, the following identities are true:

$$car[cons[x;y]]=x$$
$$cdr[cons[x;y]]=y$$

The following identity is also true for any S-expression x such that x is composite (non-atomic):

$$cons[car[x];cdr[x]]=x$$

The symbols $\underline{x}$ and $\underline{y}$ used in these identities are called variables. In LISP, variables are used to represent S-expressions. In choosing names for variables and functions, we shall use the same type of character strings that are used in forming atomic symbols, except that we shall use lower case letters.

A function whose value is either true or false is called a predicate. In LISP, the values true and false are represented by the atomic symbols T and F, respectively. A LISP predicate is therefore a function whose value is either T or F.

The predicate eq is a test for equality on atomic symbols. It is undefined for non-atomic arguments.

Examples

$$eq[A;A]=T$$
$$eq[A;B]=F$$
eq[A;(A . B)] is undefined
eq[(A . B);(A . B)] is undefined

The predicate atom is true if its argument is an atomic symbol, and false if its argument is composite.

Examples

$$atom[EXTRALONGSTRINGOFLETTERS]=T$$
$$atom[(U . V)]=F$$
$$atom[car[(U . V)]]=T$$

1.3 List Notation

The S-expressions that have been used heretofore have been written in dot notation. It is usually more convenient to be able to write lists of expressions of indefinite length, such as (A B C D E).

Any S-expression can be expressed in terms of the dot notation. However, LISP has an alternative form of S-expression called the list notation. The list $(m_1\ m_2\ \ldots\ m_n)$ can be defined in terms of dot notation. It is identical to $(m_1 . (m_2 . (\ldots . (m_n . NIL) \ldots)))$.

The atomic symbol NIL serves as a terminator for lists. The null list ( ) is identical to NIL. Lists may have sublists. The dot notation and the list notation may be used in the same S-expression.

Historically, the separator for elements of lists was the comma (,); however, the blank is now generally used. The two are entirely equivalent in LISP. (A, B, C) is identical to (A B C).

Examples

$$(A \ B \ C)=(A \ . \ (B \ . \ (C \ . \ NIL)))$$
$$((A \ B) \ C)=((A \ . \ (B \ . \ NIL)) \ . \ (C \ . \ NIL))$$
$$(A \ B \ (C \ D))=(A \ . \ (B \ . \ ((C \ . \ (D \ . \ NIL)) \ . \ NIL)))$$
$$(A)=(A \ . \ NIL)$$
$$((A))=((A \ . \ NIL) \ . \ NIL)$$
$$(A \ (B \ . \ C))=(A \ . \ ((B \ . \ C) \ . \ NIL))$$

It is important to become familiar with the results of elementary functions on S-expressions written in list notation. These can always be determined by translating into dot notation.

Examples

$$car[(A \ B \ C)]=A$$
$$cdr[(A \ B \ C)]=(B \ C)$$
$$cons[A; \ (B \ C)]=(A \ B \ C)$$
$$car[((A \ B) \ C)]=(A \ B)$$
$$cdr[(A)]=NIL$$
$$car[cdr[(A \ B \ C)]]=B$$

It is convenient to abbreviate multiple car's and cdr's. This is done by forming function names that begin with c, end with r, and have several a's and d's between them.

Examples

$$cadr[(A \ B \ C)]=car[cdr[(A \ B \ C)]]=B$$
$$caddr[(A \ B \ C)]=C$$
$$cadadr[(A \ (B \ C) \ D)]=C$$

The last a or d in the name actually signifies the first operation in order to be performed, since it is nearest to the argument.

1.4 The LISP Meta-language

We have introduced a type of data called S-expressions, and five elementary functions of S-expressions. We have also discussed the following features of the meta-language.

1. Function names and variable names are like atomic symbols except that they use lower case letters.

2. The arguments of a function are bound by square brackets and separated from each other by semicolons.

3. Compositions of functions may be written by using nested sets of brackets.

These rules allow one to write function definitions such as

$$third[x]=car[cdr[cdr[x]]].$$

This function selects the third item on a list. For example,

$$third[(A \ B \ C \ D)]=C$$

third is actually the same function as caddr.

The class of functions that can be formed in this way is quite limited and not very interesting. A much larger class of functions can be defined by means of the conditional expression, a device for providing branches in function definitions.

A conditional expression has the following form:

$$[p_1 \to e_1; \; p_2 \to e_2; \; \ldots; \; p_n \to e_n],$$

where each p_i is an expression whose value may be truth or falsity, and each e_i is any expression. The meaning of a conditional expression is: if p_1 is true, then the value of e_1 is the value of the entire expression. If p_1 is false, then if p_2 is true the value of e_2 is the value of the entire expression. The p_i are searched from left to right until the first true one is found. Then the corresponding e_i is selected. If none of the p_i are true, then the value of the entire expression is undefined.

Each p_i or e_i can itself be either an S-expression, a function, a composition of functions or may itself be another conditional expression.

Example

$$[eq[car[x];A] \to cons[B;cdr[x]]; \; T \to x]$$

The atomic symbol T represents truth. The value of this expression is obtained if one replaces <u>car</u> of x by B if it happens to be A, but leaving x unchanged if <u>car</u> of it is not A.

The main application of conditional expressions is in defining functions recursively.

Example

$$ff[x] = [atom[x] \to x; \; T \to ff[car[x]]]$$

This example defines the function <u>ff</u> which selects the first atomic symbol of any given expression. This expression can be read: If x is an atomic symbol, then x itself is the answer. Otherwise the function <u>ff</u> is to be applied to <u>car</u> of x.

If x is atomic, then the first branch which is "x" will be selected. Otherwise, the second branch "ff[car[x]]" will be selected, since T is always true.

The definition of <u>ff</u> is recursive in that <u>ff</u> is actually defined in terms of itself. If one keeps taking <u>car</u> of any S-expression, one will eventually produce an atomic symbol; therefore the process is always well defined.

Some recursive functions may be well defined for certain arguments only, but infinitely recursive for certain other arguments. When such a function is interpreted in the LISP programming system, it will either use up all of the available memory, or loop until the program is halted artificially.

We shall now work out the evaluation of ff[((A . B) . C)]. First, we substitute the arguments in place of the variable x in the definition and obtain

$$ff[((A . B) . C)] = [atom[((A . B) . C)] \to ((A . B) . C); \; T \to ff[car[((A . B) . C)]]]$$

but ((A . B) . C) is not atomic, and so we have

$$= [T \to ff[car[((A . B) . C)]]]$$
$$= ff[car[((A . B) . C)]]$$
$$= ff[(A . B)]$$

At this point, the definition of ff must be used recursively. Substituting (A . B) for x gives

$$= [atom[(A . B)] \rightarrow (A . B); T \rightarrow ff[car[(A . B)]]]$$
$$= [T \rightarrow ff[car[(A . B)]]]$$
$$= ff[car[(A . B)]]$$
$$= ff[A]$$
$$= [atom[A] \rightarrow A; T \rightarrow ff[car[A]]]$$
$$= A$$

The conditional expression is useful for defining numerical computations, as well as computations with S-expressions. The absolute value of a number can be defined by

$$|x| = [x < 0 \rightarrow -x; T \rightarrow x].$$

The factorial of a non-negative integer can be defined by

$$n! = [n = 0 \rightarrow 1; T \rightarrow n \cdot [n-1]!]$$

This recursive definition does not terminate for negative arguments. A function that is defined only for certain arguments is called a partial function.

The Euclidean algorithm for finding the greatest common divisor of two positive integers can be defined by using conditional expressions as follows:

$$gcd[x;y] = [x > y \rightarrow gcd[y;x];$$
$$rem[y;x] = 0 \rightarrow x;$$
$$T \rightarrow gcd[rem[y;x];x]]$$

$rem[u;v]$ is the remainder when $\underline{u}$ is divided by $\underline{v}$.

A detailed discussion of the theory of functions defined recursively by conditional expressions is found in "A Basis for a Mathematical Theory of Computation" by J. McCarthy, Proceedings of the Western Joint Computer Conference, May 1961 (published by the Institute of Radio Engineers).

It is usual for most mathematicians—exclusive of those devoted to logic—to use the word "function" imprecisely, and to apply it to forms such as $y^2 + x$. Because we shall later compute with expressions that stand for functions, we need a notation that expresses the distinction between functions and forms. The notation that we shall use is the lambda notation of Alonzo Church.[1]

Let $\underline{f}$ be an expression that stands for a function of two integer variables. It should make sense to write $f[3;4]$ and to be able to determine the value of this expression. For example, $\underline{sum[3;4]} = 7$. The expression $\underline{y^2 + x}$ does not meet this requirement. It is not at all clear whether the value of $y^2 + x[3;4]$ is 13 or 19. An expression such as $\underline{y^2 + x}$ will be called a form rather than a function. A form can be converted to a function by specifying the correspondence between the variables in the form and the arguments of the desired function.

If ϵ is a form in the variables $x_1; \ldots; x_n$, then the expression $\lambda[[x_1; \ldots; x_n]; \epsilon]$ represents the function of n variables obtained by substituting the n arguments in order for the variables $x_1; \ldots; x_n$, respectively. For example, the function $\lambda[[x;y]; y^2 + x]$ is a function of two variables, and $\lambda[[x;y]; y^2 + x][3;4] = 4^2 + 3 = 19$. $\lambda[[y;x]; y^2 + x][3;4] = 3^2 + 4 = 13$.

---

1. A. Church, <u>The Calculi of Lambda-Conversion</u> (Princeton University Press, Princeton, New Jersey, 1941).

The variables in a lambda expression are dummy or bound variables because systematically changing them does not alter the meaning of the expression. Thus $\lambda[[u;v];v^2+u]$ means the same thing as $\lambda[[x;y];y^2+x]$.

We shall sometimes use expressions in which a variable is not bound by a lambda. For example, in the function of two variables $\lambda[[x;y];x^n+y^n]$ the variable n is not bound. This is called a free variable. It may be regarded as a parameter. Unless n has been given a value before trying to compute with this function, the value of the function must be undefined.

The lambda notation alone is inadequate for naming recursive functions. Not only must the variables be bound, but the name of the function must be bound, since it is used inside an expression to stand for the entire expression. The function __ff__ was previously defined by the identity

$$ff[x]=[atom[x]\rightarrow x;\ T\rightarrow ff[car[x]]].$$

Using the lambda notation, we can write

$$ff=\lambda[[x];[atom[x]\rightarrow x;\ T\rightarrow ff[car[x]]]]$$

The equality sign in these identities is actually not part of the LISP meta language and is only a crutch until we develop the correct notation. The right side of the last equation cannot serve as an expression for the function __ff__ because there is nothing to indicate that the occurrence of __ff__ inside it stands for the function that is being defined.

In order to be able to write expressions that bear their own name, we introduce the __label__ notation. If ϵ is an expression, and a is its name, we write $label[a;\epsilon]$. The function __ff__ can now be written without an equal sign:

$$label[ff;\lambda[[x];[atom[x]\rightarrow x;\ T\rightarrow ff[car[x]]]]]$$

In this expression, __x__ is a bound variable, and __ff__ is a bound function name.

1.5 Syntactic Summary[1]

All parts of the LISP language have now been explained. That which follows is a complete syntactic definition of the LISP language, together with semantic comments. The definition is given in Backus notation[2] with the addition of three dots( ) to avoid naming unnecessary syntactic types.

In Backus notation the symbols " ::= ", " < ", " > ", and " | " are used. The rule <S-expression>::=<atomic symbol>|(<S-expression> . <S-expression>) means that an S-expression is either an atomic symbol, or it is a left parenthesis followed by an S-expression followed by a dot followed by an S-expression followed by a right parenthesis. The vertical bar means " or ", and the angular brackets always enclose elements of the syntax that is being defined.

The Data Language

```
<LETTER>::=A|B|C|...|Z
<number>::=0|1|2|...|9
<atomic-symbol>::=<LETTER><atom part>
<atom part>::=<empty>|<LETTER><atom part>|<number><atom part>
```

Atomic symbols are the smallest entities in LISP. Their decomposition into characters has no significance.

---

1. This section is for completeness and may be skipped upon first reading.

2. J. W. Backus, The Syntax and Semantics of the Proposed International Algebraic Language of the Zurich ACM-Gamm Conference. ICIP Paris, June 1959.

$$<S\text{-expression}>::=<atomic\ symbol>\ |$$
$$(<S\text{-expression}>.<S\text{-expression}>)\ |$$
$$(<S\text{-expression}>...<S\text{-expression}>)$$

When three dots are used in this manner, they mean that any number of the given type of symbol may occur, including none at all. According to this rule, ( ) is a valid S-expression. (It is equivalent to NIL.)

The dot notation is the fundamental notation of S-expressions, although the list notation is often more convenient. Any S-expression can be written in dot notation.

The Meta-Language

$$<letter>::=a\ |\ b\ |\ c\ |\ ...\ |\ z$$
$$<identifier>::=<letter><id\ part>$$
$$<id\ part>::=<empty>\ |\ <letter><id\ part>\ |\ <number><id\ part>$$

The names of functions and variables are formed in the same manner as atomic symbols but with lower-case letters.

$$<form>::=<constant>\ |$$
$$<variable>\ |$$
$$<function>[<argument>;\ ...\ ;<argument>]\ |$$
$$[<form>\rightarrow<form>;\ ...\ ;<form>\rightarrow<form>]$$
$$<constant>::=<S\text{-expression}>$$
$$<variable>::=<identifier>$$
$$<argument>::=<form>$$

A form is an expression that can be evaluated. A form that is merely a constant has that constant as its value. If a form is a variable, then the value of the form is the S-expression that is bound to that variable at the time when we evaluate the form.

The third part of this rule states that we may write a function followed by a list of arguments separated by semicolons and enclosed in square brackets. The expressions for the arguments are themselves forms; this indicates that compositions of functions are permitted.

The last part of this rule gives the format of the conditional expression. This is evaluated by evaluating the forms in the propositional position in order until one is found whose value is T. Then the form after the arrow is evaluated and gives the value of the entire expression.

$$<function>::=<identifier>\ |$$
$$\lambda[<var\ list>;<form>]\ |$$
$$label[<identifier>;<function>]$$
$$<var\ list>::=[<variable>;\ ...\ ;<variable>]$$

A function can be simply a name. In this case its meaning must be previously understood. A function may be defined by using the lambda notation and establishing a correspondence between the arguments and the variables used in a form. If the function is recursive, it must be given a name by using a label.

1.6 A Universal LISP Function

An interpreter or universal function is one that can compute the value of any given function applied to its arguments when given a description of that function. (Of course, if the function that is being interpreted has infinite recursion, the interpreter will recur infinitely also.)

We are now in a position to define the universal LISP function evalquote[fn;args]. When evalquote is given a function and a list of arguments for that function, it computes the value of the function applied to the arguments.

LISP functions have S-expressions as arguments. In particular, the argument "fn" of the function evalquote must be an S-expression. Since we have been writing functions as M-expressions, it is necessary to translate them into S-expressions.

The following rules define a method of translating functions written in the meta-language into S-expressions.

1. If the function is represented by its name, it is translated by changing all of the letters to upper case, making it an atomic symbol. Thus car is translated to CAR.

2. If the function uses the lambda notation, then the expression $\lambda[[x_1;...;x_n];\epsilon]$ is translated into (LAMBDA (X1 ... XN) ϵ*), where ϵ* is the translation of ϵ.

3. If the function begins with label, then the translation of label$[a;\epsilon]$ is (LABEL a* ϵ*).

Forms are translated as follows:

1. A variable, like a function name, is translated by using uppercase letters. Thus the translation of var1 is VAR1.

2. The obvious translation of letting a constant translate into itself will not work. Since the translation of x is X, the translation of X must be something else to avoid ambiguity. The solution is to quote it. Thus X is translated into (QUOTE X).

3. The form fn$[arg_1;...;arg_n]$ is translated into (fn* arg_1* ... arg_n*)

4. The conditional expression $[p_1 \rightarrow e_1;...;p_n \rightarrow e_n]$ is translated into (COND (p_1* e_1*) ... (p_n* e_n*)).

Examples

M-expressions	S-expressions
x	X
car	CAR
car[x]	(CAR X)
T	(QUOTE T)
ff[car[x]]	(FF (CAR X))
[atom[x]→x; T→ff[car[x]]]	(COND ((ATOM X) X) ((QUOTE T) (FF (CAR X))))
label[ff;λ[[x];[atom[x]→x; T→ff[car[x]]]]]	(LABEL FF (LAMBDA (X) (COND ((ATOM X) X) ((QUOTE T) (FF (CAR X)))))))

Some useful functions for handling S-expressions are given below. Some of them are needed as auxiliary functions for evalquote.

equal[x;y]

This is a predicate that is true if its two arguments are identical S-expressions, and is false if they are different. (The elementary predicate eq is defined only for atomic arguments.) The definition of equal is an example of a conditional expression inside a conditional expression.

equal[x;y]=[atom[x]→[atom[y]→eq[x;y]; T→F];
            equal[car[x];car[y]]→equal[cdr[x];cdr[y]];
            T→F]

This can be translated into the following S-expression:

(LABEL EQUAL (LAMBDA (X Y) (COND
    ((ATOM X) (COND ((ATOM Y) (EQ X Y)) ((QUOTE T) (QUOTE F))))
    ((EQUAL (CAR X) (CAR Y)) (EQUAL (CDR X) (CDR Y)))
    ((QUOTE T) (QUOTE F))   )))

subst[x;y;z]

This function gives the result of substituting the S-expression x for all occurrences of the atomic symbol y in the S-expression z. It is defined by

$$subst[x;y;z] = [equal[y;z] \rightarrow x;atom[z] \rightarrow z;T \rightarrow cons[subst$$
$$[x;y;car[z]];subst[x;y;cdr[z]]]]]$$

As an example, we have

$$subst[(X . A);B;((A . B) . C)] = ((A . (X . A)) . C)$$

<u>null[x]</u>

This predicate is useful for deciding when a list is exhausted. It is true if and only if its argument is NIL.

The following functions are useful when S-expressions are regarded as lists.

1. <u>append[x;y]</u>

$$append[x;y] = [null[x] \rightarrow y;T \rightarrow cons[car[x];append[cdr[x];y]]]$$

An example is

$$append[(A \ B);(C \ D \ E)] = (A \ B \ C \ D \ E)$$

2. <u>member[x;y]</u>

This predicate is true if the S-expression x occurs among the elements of the list y. We have

$$member[x;y] = [null[y] \rightarrow F;$$
$$equal[x;car[y]] \rightarrow T;$$
$$T \rightarrow member[x;cdr[y]]]$$

3. <u>pairlis[x;y;a]</u>

This function gives the list of pairs of corresponding elements of the lists x and y, and appends this to the list a. The resultant list of pairs, which is like a table with two columns, is called an association list. We have

$$pairlis[x;y;a] = [null[x] \rightarrow a;T \rightarrow cons[cons[car[x];car[y]];$$
$$pairlis[cdr[x];cdr[y];a]]]$$

An example is

$$pairlis[(A \ B \ C);(U \ V \ W);((D . X) (E . Y))] =$$
$$((A . U) (B . V) (C . W) (D . X) (E . Y))$$

4. <u>assoc[x;a]</u>

If a is an association list such as the one formed by pairlis in the above example, then assoc will produce the first pair whose first term is x. Thus it is a table searching function. We have

$$assoc[x;a] = [equal[caar[a];x] \rightarrow car[a];T \rightarrow assoc[x;cdr[a]]]$$

An example is

$$assoc[B;((A . (M \ N)), (B . (CAR \ X)), (C . (QUOTE \ M)), (C . (CDR \ X)))]$$
$$= (B . (CAR \ X))$$

5. <u>sublis[a;y]</u>

Here a is assumed to be an association list of the form $((u_1 . v_1) ... (u_n . v_n))$, where the u's are atomic, and y is any S-expression. What sublis does, is to treat the u's as variables when they occur in y, and to substitute the corresponding v's from the pair list. In order to define sublis, we first define an auxiliary function.

We have

$$\text{sub2}[a;z] = [\text{null}[a]\rightarrow z;\text{eq}[\text{caar}[a];z]\rightarrow \text{cdar}[a];T\rightarrow$$
$$\text{sub2}[\text{cdr}[a];z]]$$

and

$$\text{sublis}[a;y] = [\text{atom}[y]\rightarrow \text{sub2}[a;y];T\rightarrow \text{cons}[\text{sublis}[a;\text{car}[y]];$$
$$\text{sublis}[a;\text{cdr}[y]]]]$$

An example is

$$\text{sublis}[((X \ . \ \text{SHAKESPEARE}) \ (Y \ . \ (\text{THE TEMPEST})));(X \ \text{WROTE} \ Y)] =$$
$$(\text{SHAKESPEARE WROTE (THE TEMPEST)})$$

The universal function evalquote that is about to be defined obeys the following identity. Let f be a function written as an M-expression, and let fn be its translation. (fn is an S-expression.) Let f be a function of n arguments and let args=$(\text{arg}_1 \ldots \text{arg}_n)$, a list of the n S-expressions being used as arguments. Then

$$\text{evalquote}[\text{fn};\text{args}]=\text{f}[\text{arg}_1;\ldots;\text{arg}_n]$$

if either side of the equation is defined at all.

Example

f: $\lambda[[x;y];\text{cons}[\text{car}[x];y]]$
fn: (LAMBDA (X Y) (CONS (CAR X) Y))
arg_1:   (A B)
arg_2:   (C D)
args: ((A B) (C D))

$$\text{evalquote}[(\text{LAMBDA (X Y) (CONS (CAR X) Y)}); ((A \ B) (C \ D))] =$$
$$\lambda[[x;y];\text{cons}[\text{car}[x];y]][(A \ B);(C \ D)]=$$
$$(A \ C \ D)$$

evalquote is defined by using two main functions, called eval and apply. apply handles a function and its arguments, while eval handles forms. Each of these functions also has another argument that is used as an association list for storing the values of bound variables and function names.

$$\text{evalquote}[\text{fn};x] = \text{apply}[\text{fn};x;\text{NIL}]$$

where

$$apply[fn;x;a] =$$
$$[atom[fn] \rightarrow [eq[fn;CAR] \rightarrow caar[x];$$
$$eq[fn;CDR] \rightarrow cdar[x];$$
$$eq[fn;CONS] \rightarrow cons[car[x];cadr[x]];$$
$$eq[fn;ATOM] \rightarrow atom[car[x]];$$
$$eq[fn;EQ] \rightarrow eq[car[x];cadr[x]];$$
$$T \rightarrow apply[eval[fn;a];x;a]];$$
$$eq[car[fn];LAMBDA] \rightarrow eval[caddr[fn];pairlis[cadr[fn];x;a]];$$
$$eq[car[fn];LABEL] \rightarrow apply[caddr[fn];x;cons[cons[cadr[fn];$$
$$caddr[fn]];a]]]$$

$$eval[e;a] = [atom[e] \rightarrow cdr[assoc[e;a]];$$
$$atom[car[e]] \rightarrow$$
$$[eq[car[e],QUOTE] \rightarrow cadr[e];$$
$$eq[car[e];COND] \rightarrow evcon[cdr[e];a];$$
$$T \rightarrow apply[car[e];evlis[cdr[e];a];a]];$$
$$T \rightarrow apply[car[e];evlis[cdr[e];a];a]]$$

pairlis and assoc have been previously defined.

$$evcon[c;a] = [eval[caar[c];a] \rightarrow eval[cadar[c];a];$$
$$T \rightarrow evcon[cdr[c];a]]$$

and

$$evlis[m;a] = [null[m] \rightarrow NIL;$$
$$T \rightarrow cons[eval[car[m];a];evlis[cdr[m];a]]]$$

We shall explain a number of points about these definitions.

The first argument for apply is a function. If it is an atomic symbol, then there are two possibilities. One is that it is an elementary function: car, cdr, cons, eq, or atom. In each case, the appropriate function is applied to the argument(s). If it is not one of these, then its meaning has to be looked up in the association list.

If it begins with LAMBDA, then the arguments are paired with the bound variables, and the form is given to eval to evaluate.

If it begins with LABEL, then the function name and definition are added to the association list, and the inside function is evaluated by apply.

The first argument of eval is a form. If it is atomic, then it must be a variable, and its value is looked up on the association list.

If car of the form is QUOTE, then it is a constant, and the value is cadr of the form itself.

If car of the form is COND, then it is a conditional expression, and evcon evaluates the propositional terms in order, and choses the form following the first true predicate.

In all other cases, the form must be a function followed by its arguments. The arguments are then evaluated, and the function is given to apply.

The LISP Programming System has many added features that have not been described thus far. These will be treated hereafter. At this point, it is worth noting the following points.

1. In the pure theory of LISP, all functions other than the five basic ones need to be defined each time they are to be used. This is unworkable in a practical sense. The LISP programming system has a larger stock of built-in functions known to the interpreter, and provision for adding as many more as the programmer cares to define.

2. The basic functions car, and cdr were said to be undefined for atomic arguments.

In the system, they always have a value, although it may not always be meaningful. Similarly, the basic predicate eq always has a value. The effects of these functions in unusual cases will be understood after reading the chapter on list structures in the computer.

3. Except for very unusual cases, one never writes (QUOTE T) or (QUOTE F), but T, and F respectively.

4. There is provision in LISP for computing with fixed and floating point numbers. These are introduced as psuedo-atomic symbols.

The reader is warned that the definitions of apply and eval given above are pedagogical devices and are not the same functions as those built into the LISP programming system. Appendix B contains the computer implemented version of these functions and should be used to decide questions about how things really work.

II. THE LISP INTERPRETER SYSTEM

The following example is a LISP program that defines three functions union, intersection, and member, and then applies these functions to some test cases. The functions union and intersection are to be applied to "sets," each set being represented by a list of atomic symbols. The functions are defined as follows. Note that they are all recursive, and both union and intersection make use of member.

$$member[a;x] = [null[x] \rightarrow F; eq[a; car[x]] \rightarrow T; T \rightarrow$$
$$member[a; cdr[x]]]$$

$$union[x;y] = [null[x] \rightarrow y; member[car[x]; y] \rightarrow union$$
$$[cdr[x]; y]; T \rightarrow cons[car[x]; union[cdr[x]; y]]]$$

$$intersection[x;y] = [null[x] \rightarrow NIL; member[car[x]; y]$$
$$\rightarrow cons[car[x]; intersection[cdr[x]; y]]; T \rightarrow$$
$$intersection[cdr[x]; y]]$$

To define these functions, we use the pseudo-function define. The program looks like this:

```
DEFINE ((
(MEMBER (LAMBDA (A X) (COND ((NULL X) F)
     ( (EQ A (CAR X) ) T) (T (MEMBER A (CDR X))) )))
(UNION (LAMBDA (X Y) (COND ((NULL X) Y) ((MEMBER
     (CAR X) Y) (UNION (CDR X) Y)) (T (CONS (CAR X)
     (UNION (CDR X) Y))) )))
(INTERSECTION (LAMBDA (X Y) (COND ((NULL X) NIL)
     ( (MEMBER (CAR X) Y) (CONS (CAR X) (INTERSECTION
     (CDR X) Y))) (T (INTERSECTION (CDR X) Y)) )))
))
INTERSECTION ((A1 A2 A3) (A1 A3 A5))
UNION ((X Y Z) (U V W X))
```

This program contains three distinct functions for the LISP interpreter. The first function is the pseudo-function define. A pseudo-function is a function that is executed for its effect on the system in core memory, as well as for its value. define causes these functions to be defined and available within the system. Its value is a list of the functions defined, in this case (MEMBER UNION INTERSECTION).

The value of the second function is (A1 A3). The value of the third function is

(Y Z U V W X). An inspection of the way in which the recursion is carried out will show why the "elements" of the "set" appear in just this order.

Following are some elementary rules for writing LISP 1.5 programs.

1. A program for execution in LISP consists of a sequence of doublets. The first list or atomic symbol of each doublet is interpreted as a function. The second is a list of arguments for the function. They are evaluated by <u>evalquote</u>, and the value is printed.

2. There is no particular card format for writing LISP. Columns 1-72 of any number of cards may be used. Card boundaries are ignored. The format of this program, including indentation, was chosen merely for ease of reading.

3. A comma is the equivalent of a blank. Any number of blanks and/or commas can occur at any point in a program except in the middle of an atomic symbol.

4. Do not use the forms (QUOTE T), (QUOTE F), and (QUOTE NIL). Use T, F, and NIL instead.

5. Atomic symbols should begin with alphabetical characters to distinguish them from numbers.

6. Dot notation may be used in LISP 1.5. Any number of blanks before or after the dot will be ignored.

7. Dotted pairs may occur as elements of a list, and lists may occur as elements of dotted pairs. For example,

((A . B) X (C . (E F G)))

is a valid S-expression. It could also be written

((A . B) . (X . ((C . (E . (F . (G . NIL)))) . NIL))) or
((A . B) X (C E F G))

8. A form of the type (A B C . D) is an abbreviation for (A . (B . (C . D))). Any other mixing of commas (spaces) and dots on the same level is an error, e.g. (A . B C).

9. A selection of basic functions is provided with the LISP system. Other functions may be introduced by the programmer. The order in which functions are introduced is not significant. Any function may make use of any other function.

2.1 Variables

A variable is a symbol that is used to represent an argument of a function. Thus one might write "a + b, where a = 341 and b = 216." In this situation no confusion can result and all will agree that the answer is 557. In order to arrive at this result, it is necessary to substitute the actual numbers for the variables, and then add the two number (on an adding machine for instance).

One reason why there is no ambiguity in this case is that "a" and "b" are not acceptable inputs for an adding machine, and it is therefore obvious that they merely represent the actual arguments. In LISP, the situation can be much more complicated. An atomic symbol may be either a variable or an actual argument. To further complicate the situation, a part of an argument may be a variable when a function inside another function is evaluated. The intuitive approach is no longer adequate. An understanding of the formalism in use is necessary to do any effective LISP programming.

Lest the prospective LISP user be discouraged at this point, it should be pointed out that nothing new is going to be introduced here. This section is intended to reinforce the discussion of Section I. Everything in this section can be derived from the rule for translating M-expressions into S-expressions, or alternatively everything in this section can be inferred from the universal function <u>evalquote</u> of Section I.

The formalism for variables in LISP is the Church lambda notation. The part of the interpreter that binds variables is called <u>apply</u>. When <u>apply</u> encounters a function beginning with LAMBDA, the list of variables is paired with the list of arguments and added to the front of the a-list. During the evaluation of the function, variables may be encountered. They are evaluated by looking them up on the a-list. If a variable has been bound several times, the last or most recent value is used. The part of the interpreter that does this is called eval. The following example will illustrate this discussion. Suppose the interpreter is given the following doublet:

>   fn: (LAMBDA (X Y) (CONS X Y))

>   args: (A B)

evalquote will give these arguments to apply. (Look at the universal function of Section I.)

>   apply[(LAMBDA (X Y) (CONS X Y)); (A B);NIL]

apply will bind the variables and give the function and a-list to eval.

>   eval[(CONS X Y); ((X . A) (Y . B))]

eval will evaluate the variables and give it to cons.

>   cons[A;B] = (A . B)

The actual interpreter skips one step required by the universal function, namely, apply[CONS;(A B);((X . A) (Y . B))].

2.2 Constants

It is sometimes assumed that a constant stands for itself as opposed to a variable which stands for something else. This is not a very workable concept, since the student who is learning calculus is taught to represent constants by a, b, c . . . and variables by x, y, z . . . . It seems more reasonable to say that one variable is more nearly constant than another if it is bound at a higher level and changes value less frequently.

In LISP, a variable remains bound within the scope of the LAMBDA that binds it. When a variable always has a certain value regardless of the current a-list, it will be called a constant. This is accomplished by means of the property list[1] (p-list) of the variable symbol. Every atomic symbol has a p-list. When the p-list contains the indicator APVAL, then the symbol is a constant and the next item on the list is the value. eval searches p-lists before a-lists when evaluating variables, thus making it possible to set constants.

Constants can be made by the programmer. To make the variable X always stand for (A B C D), use the pseudo-function cset.

---

1. Property lists are discussed in Section VII.

>   cset[X;(A B C D)]

An interesting type of constant is one that stands for itself. NIL is an example of this. It can be evaluated repeatedly and will still be NIL. T, F, NIL, and other constants cannot be used as variables.

2.3 Functions

When a symbol stands for a function, the situation is similar to that in which a symbol stands for an argument. When a function is recursive, it must be given a name. This is done by means of the form LABEL, which pairs the name with the function definition on the a-list. The name is then bound to the function definition, just as a variable is bound to its value.

In actual practice, LABEL is seldom used. It is usually more convenient to attach the name to the definition in a uniform manner.   This is done by putting on the property list of the name, the symbol EXPR followed by the function definition. The pseudo-function define used at the beginning of this section accomplishes this.   When apply interprets a function represented by an atomic symbol, it searches the p-list of the atomic symbol before searching the current a-list.   Thus a define will override a LABEL.

The fact that most functions are constants defined by the programmer, and not variables that are modified by the program, is not due to any weakness of the system. On the contrary, it indicates a richness of the system which we do not know how to exploit very well.

2.4 Machine Language Functions

Some functions instead of being defined by S-expressions are coded as closed machine language subroutines. Such a function will have the indicator SUBR on its property list followed by a pointer that allows the interpreter to link with the subroutine.   There are three ways in which a subroutine can be present in the system.

1. The subroutine is coded into the LISP system.

2. The function is hand-coded by the user in the assembly type language, LAP.

3. The function is first defined by an S-expression, and then compiled by the LISP compiler. Compiled functions run from 10 to 100 times as fast as they do when they are interpreted.

2.5 Special Forms

Normally, eval evaluates the arguments of a function before applying the function itself. Thus if eval is given (CONS X Y), it will evaluate X and Y, and then cons them. But if eval is given (QUOTE X), X should not be evaluated. QUOTE is a special form that prevents its argument from being evaluated.

A special form differs from a function in two ways. Its arguments are not evaluated before the special form sees them. COND, for example, has a very special way of evaluating its arguments by using evcon. The second way which special forms differ from functions is that they may have an indefinite number of arguments. Special forms have indicators on their property lists called FEXPR and FSUBR for LISP-defined forms and machine language coded forms, respectively.

2.6 Programming for the Interpreter

The purpose of this section is to help the programmer avoid certain common errors.

Example 1

    fn: CAR
    args: ((A B))

The value is A. Note that the interpreter expects a list of arguments. The one argument for car is (A B). The extra pair of parentheses is necessary.

One could write (LAMBDA (X) (CAR X)) instead of just CAR. This is correct but unnecessary.

Example 2

    fn: CONS
    args: (A (B . C))

The value is cons[A;(B . C)] = (A . (B . C)).
The print program will write this as (A B . C).

Example 3

    fn: CONS

    args: ((CAR (QUOTE (A . B))) (CDR (QUOTE (C . D))))

The value of this computation will be ((CAR (QUOTE (A . B))) . (CDR (QUOTE (C . D)))). This is not what the programmer expected. He expected (CAR (QUOTE (A . B))) to evaluate to A, and expected (A . D) as the value of cons.

The interpreter expects a list of arguments. It does not expect a list of expressions that will evaluate to the arguments. Two correct ways of writing this function are listed below. The first one makes the car and cdr part of a function specified by a LAMBDA. The second one uses quoted arguments and gets them evaluated by eval with a null a-list.

    fn: (LAMBDA (X Y) (CONS (CAR X) (CDR Y)))

    args: ((A . B) (C . D))

    fn: EVAL

    args: ((CONS (CAR (QUOTE (A . B))) (CDR (QUOTE (C . D)))) NIL)

The value of both of these is (A . D).

III. EXTENSION OF THE LISP LANGUAGE

Section I of this manual presented a purely formal mathematical system that we shall call pure LISP. The elements of this formal system are the following.

1. A set of symbols called S-expressions.

2. A functional notation called M-expressions.

3. A formal mapping of M-expressions into S-expressions.

4. A universal function (written as an M-expression) for interpreting the application of any function written as an S-expression to its arguments.

Section II introduced the LISP Programming System. The basis of the LISP Programming System is the interpreter, or evalquote and its components. A LISP program in fact consists of pairs of arguments for evalquote which are interpreted in sequence.

In this section we shall introduce a number of extensions of elementary LISP. These extensions of elementary LISP are of two sorts. The first includes propositional connectives and functions with functions as arguments, and they are also of a mathematical nature; the second is peculiar to the LISP Programming System on the IBM 7090 computer.

In all cases, additions to the LISP Programming System are made to conform to the functional syntax of LISP even though they are not functions. For example, the command to print an S-expression on the output tape is called print. Syntactically, print is a function of one argument. It may be used in composition with other functions, and will be evaluated in the usual manner, with the inside of the composition being evaluated first. Its effect is to print its argument on the output tape (or on-line). It is a function only in the trivial sense that its value happens to be its argument, thus making it an identity function.

Commands to effect an action such as the operation of input-output, or the defining functions define and cset discussed in Chapter II, will be called pseudo-functions. It is characteristic of the LISP system that all functions including psuedo-functions must have values. In some cases the value is trivial and may be ignored.

This Chapter is concerned with several extensions of the LISP language that are in the system.

3.1 Functional Arguments

Mathematically, it is possible to have functions as arguments of other functions. For example, in arithmetic one could define a function <u>operate</u> [op;a;b], where op is a functional argument that specifies which arithmetic operation is to be performed on a and b. Thus

operate[+;3;4]=7   and
operate[x;3;4]=12

In LISP, functional arguments are extremely useful. A very important function w a functional argument is <u>maplist</u>. Its M-expression definition is

maplist[x;fn]=[null[x]→NIL;
$\qquad\qquad$ T→cons[fn[x];maplist[cdr[x];fn]]]

An examination of the universal function <u>evalquote</u> will show that the interpreter can handle <u>maplist</u> and other functions written in this manner without any further addition. The functional argument is, of course, a function translated into an S-expression. It is bound to the variable <u>fn</u> and is then used whenever <u>fn</u> is mentioned as a function. The S-expression for <u>maplist</u> itself is as follows:

```
(MAPLIST (LAMBDA (X FN) (COND ((NULL X) NIL)
      (T (CONS (FN X) (MAPLIST (CDR X) FN))) )))
```

Now suppose we wish to define a function that takes a list and changes it by <u>cons</u>-ing an X onto every item of the list so that, for example,

change[(A B (C D))]=((A . X) (B . X) ((C . D) . X))

Using <u>maplist</u>, we define <u>change</u> by

change[a]=maplist[a;λ[[j];cons[car[j];X]]]

This is not a valid M-expression as defined syntactically in section 1.5 because a function appears where a form is expected. This can be corrected by modifying the rule defining an argument so as to include functional arguments:

<argument>:: = <form>|<function>

We also need a special rule to translate functional arguments into S-expression. If <u>fn</u> is a function used as an argument, then it is translated into (FUNCTION fn*).

Example

```
(CHANGE (LAMBDA (A) (MAPLIST A (FUNCTION
      (LAMBDA (J) (CONS (CAR J) (QUOTE X))) )))
```

An examination of evalquote shows that QUOTE will work instead of FUNCTION, <u>provided</u> that there are no free variables present. An explanation of how the interpreter processes the atomic symbol FUNCTION is given in the Appendix B.

3.2 Logical Connectives

The logical or Boolian connectives are usually considered as primitive operators. However, in LISP, they can be defined by using conditional expressions:

p∧q=[p→q;T→F]
p∨q=[p→T;T→q]
$\quad$~q=[q→F;T→T]

In the System, <u>not</u> is a predicate of one argument. However, <u>and</u> and <u>or</u> are predicates of an indefinite number of arguments, and therefore are special forms. In writing M-expressions it is often convenient to use infix notation and write expressions such as a∨b∨c for or[a;b;c]. In S-expressions, one must, of course, use prefix notation and write (OR A B C).

The order in which the arguments of <u>and</u> and <u>or</u> are given may be of some significance in the case in which some of the arguments may not be well defined. The definitions of these predicated given above show that the value may be defined even if all of the arguments are not.

<u>and</u> evaluates its arguments from left to right. If one of them is found that is false, then the value of the <u>and</u> is false and no further arguments are evaluated. If the arguments are all evaluated and found to be true, then the value is true.

<u>or</u> evaluates its arguments from left to right. If one of them is true, then the value of the <u>or</u> is true and no further arguments are evaluated. If the arguments are all evaluated and found to be false, then the value is false.

3.3 Predicates and Truth in LISP

Although the rule for translating M-expressions into S-expressions states that T is (QUOTE T), it was stated that in the system one must always write T instead. Similarly, one must write F rather than (QUOTE F). The programmer may either accept this rule blindly or understand the following Humpty-Dumpty semantics.

In the LISP programming system there are two atomic symbols that represent truth and falsity respectively. These two atomic symbols are *T* and NIL. It is these symbols rather than T and F that are the actual value of all predicates in the system. This is mainly a coding convenience.

The atomic symbols T and F have APVAL's whose values are *T* and NIL, respectively. The symbols T and F for constant predicates will work because:

eval[T;NIL]=*T*
eval[F;NIL]=NIL

The forms (QUOTE *T*) and (QUOTE NIL) will also work because

eval[(QUOTE *T*);NIL]=*T*
eval[(QUOTE NIL);NIL]=NIL

T and NIL both have APVAL's that point to themselves. Thus *T* and NIL are also acceptable because

eval[*T*;NIL]=*T*
eval[NIL;NIL]=NIL

But

eval[(QUOTE F);NIL]=F

which is wrong and this is why (QUOTE F) will not work. Note that

eval[(QUOTE T);alist]=T

which is wrong but will work for a different reason that will be explained in the paragraph after next.

There is no formal distinction between a function and a predicate in LISP. A predicate can be defined as a function whose value is either *T* or NIL. This is true of all predicates in the System.

One may use a form that is not a predicate in a location in which a predicate is called for, such as in the p position of a conditional expression, or as an argument of a logical predicate. Semantically, any S-expression that is not NIL will be regarded as truth in such a case. One consequence of this is that the predicates null and not are identical. Another consequence is that (QUOTE T) or (QUOTE X) is equivalent to T as a constant predicate.

The predicate eq has the following behavior.

1. If its arguments are different, the value of eq is NIL.

2. If its arguments are both the same atomic symbol, its value is *T*.

3. If its arguments are both the same, but are not atomic, then the value is *T* or NIL depending upon whether the arguments are identical in their representation in core memory.

4. The value of eq is always *T* or NIL. It is never undefined even if its arguments are bad.

IV. ARITHMETIC IN LISP

Lisp 1.5 has provision for handling fixed-point and floating-point numbers and log-ical words. There are functions and predicates in the system for performing arithmetic and logical operations and making basic tests.

4.1 Reading and Printing Numbers

Numbers are stored in the computer as though they were a special type of atomic symbol. This is discussed more thoroughly in section 7.3. The following points should be noted :

1. Numbers may occur in S-expressions as though they were atomic symbols.

2. Numbers are constants that evaluate to themselves. They do not need to be quoted.

3. Numbers should not be used as variables or function names.

a. Floating-Point Numbers

The rules for punching these for the read program are:

1. A decimal point must be included but not as the first or last character.

2. A plus sign or minus sign may precede the number. The plus sign is not required.

3. Exponent indication is optional. The letter E followed by the exponent to the base 10 is written directly after the number. The exponent consists of one or two digits that may be preceded by a plus or minus sign.

4. Absolute values must lie between 2^{128} and 2^{-128} (10^{38} and 10^{-38}).

5. Significance is limited to 8 decimal digits.

6. Any possible ambiguity between the decimal point and the point used in dot no-tation may be eliminated by putting spaces before and after the LISP dot. This is not required when there is no ambiguity.

Following are examples of correct floating-point numbers. These are all different forms for the same number, and will have the same effect when read in.

$$60.0$$
$$6.E1$$
$$600.00E-1$$
$$0.6E+2$$

The forms .6E+2 and 60. are incorrect because the decimal point is the first or last character respectively.

b. Fixed-Point Numbers

These are written as integers with an optional sign.

Examples

        −17
        32719

c. Octal Numbers or Logical Words

The correct form consists of
1. A sign (optional).
2. Up to 12 digits (0 through 7).
3. The letter Q.
4. An optional scale factor. The scale factor is a decimal integer, no sign allowed.

Example

        a. 777Q
        b. 777Q4
        c. −3Q11
        d. −7Q11
        e. +7Q11

The effect of the read program on octal numbers is as follows.

1. The number is placed in the accumulator three bits per octal digit with zeros added to the left-hand side to make twelve digits. The rightmost digit is placed in bits 33-35; the twelfth digit is placed in bits P, 1, and 2.

2. The accumulator is shifted left three bits (one octal digit) times the scale factor. Thus the scale factor is an exponent to the base 8.

3. If there is a negative sign, it is OR-ed into the P bit. The number is then stored as a logical word.

The examples a through e above will be converted to the following octal words. Note that because the sign is OR-ed with the 36th numerical bit c, d, and e are equivalent.

        a. 000000000777
        b. 000007770000
        c. 700000000000
        d. 700000000000
        e. 700000000000

4.2 Arithmetic Functions and Predicates

We shall now list all of the arithmetic functions in the System. They must be given numbers as arguments; otherwise an error condition will result. The arguments may be any type of number. A function may be given some fixed-point arguments and some floating-point arguments at the same time.

If all of the arguments for a function are fixed-point numbers, then the value will be a fixed-point number. If at least one argument is a floating-point number, then the value of the function will be a floating-point number.

plus[x_1;...;x_n] is a function of any number of arguments whose value is the algebraic sum of the arguments.

difference[x;y] has for its value the algebraic difference of its arguments.

minus[x] has for its value −x.

times[x_1;...;x_n] is a function of any number of arguments, whose value is the product (with correct sign) of its arguments.

add1[x] has x+1 for its value. The value is fixed-point or floating-point, depending on the argument.

sub1[x] has x−1 for its value. The value is fixed-point or floating-point, depending on the argument.

max[x_1;...;x_n] chooses the largest of its arguments for its value .   Note that max[3;2.0] = 3.0.

min[x_1;...;x_n] chooses the smallest of its arguments for its value.

recip[x] computes 1/x. The reciprocal of any fixed point number is defined as zero.

quotient[x;y] computes the quotient of its arguments. For fixed-point arguments, the value is the number theoretic quotient. A divide check or floating-point trap will result in a LISP error.

remainder[x;y] computes the number theoretic remainder for fixed-point numbers, and the floating-point residue for floating-point arguments.

divide[x;y] = cons[quotient[x;y]; cons[remainder[x;y];NIL]]

expt[x;y] = x^y. If both x and y are fixed-point numbers, this is computed by iterative multiplication. Otherwise the power is computed by using logarithms. The first argument cannot be negative.

We shall now list all of the arithmetic predicates in the System.   They may have fixed-point and floating-point arguments mixed freely. The value of a predicate is *T* or NIL.

lessp[x;y] is true if x < y, and false otherwise.

greaterp[x;y] is true if x > y.

zerop[x] is true if x=0, or if $|x| \leq 3 \times 10^{-6}$.

onep[x] is true if $|x-1| \leq 3 \times 10^{-6}$.

minusp[x] is true if x is negative.

   "−0" is negative.

numberp[x] is true if x is a number (fixed-point or floating-point).

fixp[x] is true only if x is a fixed-point number. If x is not a number at all, an error will result.

floatp[x] is similar to fixp[x] but for floating-point numbers.

equal[x;y] works on any arguments including S-expressions incorporating numbers inside them. Its value is true if the arguments are identical. Floating-point numbers must satisfy $|x-y| < 3 \times 10^{-6}$.

The logical functions operate on 36-bit words. The only acceptable arguments are fixed-point numbers. These may be read in as octal or decimal integers, or they may be the result of a previous computation.

logor[x_1;...;x_n] performs a logical OR on its arguments.

logand[x_1;...;x_n] performs a logical AND on its arguments.

logxor[x_1;...;x_n] performs an exclusive OR
   $(0 \veebar 0 = 0, \ 1 \veebar 0 = 0 \veebar 1 = 1, \ 1 \veebar 1 = 0)$.

leftshift[x;n] = $x \times 2^n$. The first argument is shifted left by the number of bits specified by the second argument. If the second argument is negative, the first argument will be shifted right.

4.3 Programming with Arithmetic

The arithmetic functions may be used recursively, just as other functions available to the interpreter. As an example, we define factorial as it was given in Section I.

$$n! = [\ n = 0 \rightarrow 1;\ T \rightarrow n.(n-1)\ !\ ]$$

```
DEFINE ((
(FACTORIAL (LAMBDA (N) (COND
    ((ZEROP N) 1)
    (T (TIMES N (FACTORIAL (SUB1 N)))) )))
))
```

4.4 The Array Feature

Provision is made in LISP 1.5 for allocating blocks of storage for data. The data may consist of numbers, atomic symbols or other S-expressions.

The pseudo-function <u>array</u> reserves space for arrays, and turns the name of an array into a function that can be used to fill the array or locate any element of it.

Arrays may have up to three indices. Each element (uniquely specified by its co-ordinates) contains a pointer to an S-expression (see Section VII).

<u>array</u> is a function of one argument which is a list of arrays to be declared. Each item is a list containing the name of an array, its dimensions, and the word LIST. (Non-list arrays are reserved for future developments of the LISP system.)

For example, to make an array called <u>alpha</u> of size 7×10, and one called <u>beta</u> of size $3 \times 4 \times 5$ one should execute:

$$\text{array}[((\text{ALPHA (7 10) LIST}) (\text{BETA (3 4 5) LIST}))]$$

After this has been executed, both arrays exist and their elements are all set to NIL. Indices range from 0 to n-1.

<u>alpha</u> and <u>beta</u> are now functions that can be used to set or locate elements of these respective arrays.

To set $\text{alpha}_{i,j}$ to x, execute —

$$\text{alpha}[\text{SET};x;i;j]$$

To set $\text{alpha}_{3,4}$ to (A B C) execute —

$$\text{alpha}[\text{SET};(\text{A B C});3;4]$$

Inside a function or program X might be bound to (A B C), I bound to 3, and J bound to 4, in which case the setting can be done by evaluating —

(ALPHA (QUOTE SET) X I J)

To locate an element of an array, use the array name as a function with the coordinates as axes. Thus any time after executing the previous example —

$$\text{alpha}[3;4] = (\text{A B C})$$

Arrays use marginal indexing for maximum speed. For most efficient results, specify dimensions in increasing order. Beta$[3;4;5]$ is better than beta$[5;3;4]$.

Storage for arrays is located in an area of memory called binary program space.

V. THE PROGRAM FEATURE

The LISP 1.5 program feature allows the user to write an Algol-like program containing LISP statements to be executed.

An example of the program feature is the function <u>length</u>, which examines a list and decides how many elements there are in the top level of the list. The value of <u>length</u> is an integer.

Length is a function of one argument ℓ. The program uses two program variables u and v, which can be regarded as storage locations whose contents are to be changed by the program. In English the program is written:

  This is a function of one argument ℓ.

    It is a program with two program variables u and v.

  Store 0 in v.

  Store the argument ℓ in u.

A If u contains NIL, then the program is finished,

    and the value is whatever is now in v.

  Store in u, cdr of what is now in u.

  Store in v, one more than what is now in v.

  Go to A.

We now write this program as an M-expression, with a few new notations. This corresponds line for line with the program written above.

   length[ℓ] = prog[[u;v];

     v:= 0;

     u:= ℓ;

  A [null[u]→return[v]];

     u:= cdr[u];

     v:= v+1;

     go [A]]

Rewriting this as an S-expression, we get the following program.

```
DEFINE ((
(LENGTH (LAMBDA (L)
(PROG (U V)
        (SETQ V 0)
        (SETQ U L)
A       (COND ((NULL U) (RETURN V)))
        (SETQ U (CDR U))
        (SETQ V (ADD1 V))
        (GO A) )))        ))
LENGTH ((A  B  C  D))

        LENGTH (((X · Y) A CAR (N B) (X Y Z)))
```

The last two lines are test cases. Their values are four and five, respectively.

The program form has the structure —

(PROG, list of program variables, sequence of statements and atomic symbols...)

An atomic symbol in the list is the location marker for the statement that follows. In the above example, A is a location marker for the statement beginning with COND.

The first list after the symbol PROG is a list of program variables. If there are none, then this should be written NIL or (). Program variables are treated much like bound variables, but they are not bound by LAMBDA. The value of each program variable is NIL until it has been set to something else.

To set a program variable, use the form SET. To set variable PI to 3.14 write (SET (QUOTE PI) 3.14). SETQ is like SET except that it quotes its first argument. Thus (SETQ PI 3.14). SETQ is usually more convenient. SET and SETQ can change variables that are on the a-list from higher level functions. The value of SET or SETQ is the value of its second argument.

Statements are normally executed in sequence. Executing a statement means evaluating it with the current a-list and ignoring its value. Program statements are often executed for their effect rather than their value.

GO is a form used to cause a transfer. (GO A) will cause the program to continue at statement A. The form GO can be used only as a statement on the top level of a PROG or immediately inside a COND which is on the top level of a PROG.

Conditional expressions as program statements have a useful peculiarity. If none of the propositions are true, instead of an error indication which would otherwise occur, the program continues with the next statement. This is true only for conditional expressions that are on the top level of a PROG.

RETURN is the normal end of a program. The argument of RETURN is evaluated, and this is the value of the program. No further statements are executed.

If a program runs out of statements, it returns with the value NIL.

The program feature, like other LISP functions, can be used recursively. The function rev, which reverses a list and all its sublists is an example of this.

$$rev[x] = prog[[y;z];$$
$$A \quad [null[x] \rightarrow return[y]];$$
$$z := car[x];$$
$$[atom[z] \rightarrow go[B]];$$
$$z := rev[z];$$
$$B \quad y := cons[z;y];$$
$$x := cdr[x];$$
$$go[A]]$$

The function rev will reverse a list on all levels so that

$$rev[(A ((B C) D))] = ((D (C B)) A)$$

THE DESIGN OF APL*

A. D. FALKOFF AND K. E. IVERSON

Abstract: This paper discusses the development of APL, emphasizing and illustrating the principles underlying its design. The principle of simplicity appears most strongly in the minimization of rules governing the behavior of APL objects, while the principle of practicality is served by the design process itself, which relies heavily on experimentation. The paper gives the rationale for many specific design choices, including the necessary adjuncts for system management.

Introduction

This paper attempts to identify the general principles that guided the development of APL and its computer realizations, and to show the role these principles played in the evolution of the language. The reader will be assumed to be familiar with the current definition of APL [1]. A brief chronology of the development of APL is presented in an appendix.

Different people claiming to follow the same broad principles may well arrive at radically different designs; an appreciation of the actual role of the principles in design can therefore be communicated only by illustrating their application in a variety of specific instances. It must be remembered, of course, that in the heat of battle principles are not applied as consciously or systematically as may appear in the telling. Some notion of the evolution of the ideas may be gained from consulting earlier discussions, particularly Refs. 2–4.

The actual operative principles guiding the design of any complex system must be few and broad. In the present instance we believe these principles to be simplicity and practicality. Simplicity enters in four guises: *uniformity* (rules are few and simple), *generality* (a small number of general functions provide as special cases a host of more specialized functions), *familiarity* (familiar symbols and usages are adopted whenever possible), and *brevity* (economy of expression is sought). Practicality is manifested in two respects: concern with actual application of the language, and concern with the practical limitations imposed by existing equipment.

We believe that the design of APL was also affected in important respects by a number of procedures and circumstances. Firstly, from its inception APL has been developed by *using* it in a succession of areas. This emphasis on application clearly favors practicality and simplicity. The treatment of many different areas fostered generalization; for example, the general inner product was developed in attempting to obtain the advantages of ordinary matrix algebra in the treatment of symbolic logic.

Secondly, the lack of any machine realization of the language during the first seven or eight years of its development allowed the designers the freedom to make radical changes, a freedom not normally enjoyed by designers who must observe the needs of a large working population dependent on the language for their daily computing needs. This circumstance was due more to the dearth of interest in the language than to foresight.

Thirdly, at every stage the design of the language was controlled by a small group of not more than five people. In particular, the men who designed (and coded) the implementation were part of the language design group, and all members of the design group were involved in broad decisions affecting the implementation. On the other hand, many ideas were received and accepted from people outside the design group, particularly from active users of some implementation of APL.

Finally, design decisions were made by Quaker consensus; controversial innovations were deferred until they could be revised or reevaluated so as to obtain unanimous agreement. Unanimity was not achieved without cost in time and effort, and many divergent paths were explored and assessed. For example, many different notations for the circular and hyperbolic functions were entertained over a period of more than a year

*Reprinted from *IBM Journal of Research and Development*, July 1973, 324–334, copyright 1973.

before the present scheme was proposed, whereupon it was quickly adopted. As the language grows, more effort is needed to explore the ramifications of any major innovation. Moreover, greater care is needed in introducing new facilities, to avoid the possibility of later retraction that would inconvenience thousands of users. An example of the degree of preliminary exploration that may be involved is furnished by the depth and diversity of the investigations reported in the papers by Ghandour and Mezei [5] and by More [6].

The character set

The typography of a language to be entered at a simple keyboard is subject to two major practical restrictions: it must be linear, rather than two-dimensional, and it must be printable by a limited number of distinct symbols.

When one is not concerned with an immediate machine realization of a language, there is no strong reason to so limit the typography and for this reason the language may develop in a freer *publication form*. Before the design of a machine realization of APL, the restrictions appropriate to a keyboard form were not observed. In particular, different fonts were used to indicate the rank of a variable. In the keyboard form, such distinctions can be made, if desired, by adopting classes of names for certain classes of things.

The practical objective of linearizing the typography also led to increased uniformity and generality. It led to the present bracketed form of indexing, which removes the rank limitation on arrays imposed by use of superscripts and subscripts. It also led to the regularization of the form of dyadic functions such as $N\alpha J$ and $N\omega J$ (later eliminated from the language). Finally, it led to writing inner and outer products in the linear form $+.\times$ and $\circ.\times$ and eventually to the recognition of such expressions as instances of the use of *operators*.

The use of arrays and of operators greatly reduced the demand for distinct characters in APL, but the limitations imposed by the normal 88-symbol typewriter keyboard fostered two innovations which greatly increased the utility of the 88 symbols: the systematic use of most function symbols to represent both a dyadic and a monadic function, as suggested in conventional notation by the double use of the minus sign to represent both subtraction (a *dyadic* function) and negation (a *monadic* function); and the use of composite characters formed by typing one symbol over another (through the use of a backspace), as in ϕ and ! and $\circledast$.

It was necessary to restrict the alphabetic characters to a single font and capitals were chosen for readability. Italics were initially favored because of their common use for denoting variables in mathematics, but were finally chosen primarily because they distinguished the letter O from the digit 0 and letters like L and T from the graphic symbols $\llcorner$ and $\top$.

To allow the possibility of adding complete alphabetic fonts by overstriking, the underscore (_), diaeresis (¨), overbar (‾), and quad (□) were provided. In the APL\360 realization, only the underscore is used in this way. The inclusion of the overbar on the typeball fortunately filled a need we had not anticipated—a symbol for negative constants, distinct from the symbol for the negation function. The quad proved a useful symbol alone and in combination (as in ⊟), and the diaeresis still remains unassigned.

The SELECTRIC® typewriter imposed certain practical limitations on the placement of symbols on the keyboard, e.g., only narrow characters can appear in the upper row of the typing element. Within these limitations we attempted to make the keyboard easy to learn by grouping related symbols (such as the relations) in a rational order and by making mnemonic associations between letters and the functions associated with them in the shifted case (such as the *magnitude* function | with M, and the membership symbol ϵ with E).

Valence and order of execution

The *valence* of a function is the number of arguments it takes; APL primitives have valences of 1 (monadic functions) and 2 (dyadic functions), and user-defined functions may have a valence of 0 as well. The form for all APL primitives follows the familiar model of arithmetic, that is, the symbol for a dyadic function occurs between its arguments (as in 3+4) and the symbol for a monadic function occurs before its argument (as in ⁻4).

A function f of valence greater than two is conventionally written in the form $f(a,b,c,d)$. This can be construed as a monadic function F applied to the vector argument a,b,c,d, and this interpretation is used in APL. In the APL\360 realization, the arguments a,b,c, and d must share a common structure. The definition and implementation of generalized arrays, whose elements include *enclosed* arrays, will, of course, remove this restriction.

The result of any primitive APL function depends only on its immediate arguments, and the interpretation of each part of an APL statement is therefore localized. Likewise, the interpretation of each statement is independent of other statements in a program. This independence of context contributes significantly to the readability and ease of implementation of the language.

The order of execution of an APL expression is controlled by parentheses in the familiar way, and parentheses are used for no other purpose. The order is otherwise determined by one simple rule: the right argument of any function is the value of the entire expression following it. In particular, there is no precedence among functions; all functions, user-defined as well as primitive, are treated alike.

This simple rule has several consequences of practical advantage to the user:

a) An unparenthesized expression is easy to read from left to right because the first function encountered is the major function, the next is the major function in its right argument, etc.

b) An unparenthesized expression is also easy to read from right to left because this is the order in which it is executed.

c) If T is any vector of numerical terms, then the present rule makes the expressions $-/T$ and $\div/T$ very useful: the former is the alternating sum of T and the latter is the alternating product. Moreover, a continued fraction may be written without parentheses in the form $3+\div4+\div5+\div6$, and the efficient evaluation of a polynomial can be written without parentheses in the form $3+X\times4+X\times5+X\times6$.

The rule that multiplication is executed before addition and that the power function is executed before multiplication has been long accepted in mathematics. In discarding any established rule it is wise to speculate on the reasons for its adoption and on whether they still apply. This rule makes parentheses unnecessary in the writing of polynomials, and this alone appears to be a sufficient reason for its original adoption. However, in APL a polynomial can be written more perspicuously in the form $+/C\times X\star E$, which also requires no parentheses. The question of the order of execution has been discussed in several places: Falkoff et al. [2,3], Berry [7], and Appendix A of Iverson [8].

The order in which isolated parts of a statement, such as the parts $(X+4)$ and $(Y-2)$ in the statement $(Y+4)\times(Y-2)$, are executed is normally immaterial, but does matter when repeated specifications are permitted in a statement as in $(A\leftarrow2)+A$. Although the use of such expressions is poor practice, it is desirable to make the interpretation unequivocal: the rule adopted (as given in Lathwell and Mezei [9]) is that the rightmost function or specification which can be performed is performed first.

It is interesting to note that the use of embedded assignment was first suggested during the course of the implementation when it was realized that special steps were needed to prevent it. The order of executing isolated parts of a statement was at first left unspecified (as stated in Falkoff and Iverson [1]) to allow freedom in implementation, since isolated parts could then be executed in parallel on any machine offering parallel processing. However, embedded assignment found such wide use that an unambiguous definition became essential to fix the behavior of programs moving from system to system.

Another aspect of the order of execution is the order among statements, which is normally taken as the order of appearance, except as modified by explicit *branches*. In the publication form of the language branches were denoted by arrows drawn from a branch point to the set of possible destinations, and the drawing of branch arrows is still to be recommended as an adjunct for clarifying the structure of a program (Iverson [10], page 3).

In formalizing branching it was necessary to introduce only one new concept (denoted by $\rightarrow$) and three simple conventions: 1) continuing with the statement indicated by the first element of a vector argument of $\rightarrow$, or with the next statement in sequence if the argument is an empty vector, 2) terminating the function if the indicated continuation is not the index of a statement in the program, and 3) the use of *labels*, local names defined by the indices of juxtaposed statements. At first labels were treated as local variables, but it was found to be more convenient in both use and implementation to treat them as local constants.

Since the branch arrow can be followed by any valid expression it provides convenient multi-way conditional branches. For example, if L is a Boolean vector and S is a corresponding set of statement numbers (often formed as the catenation of a set of labels), then $\rightarrow L/S$ provides a $(1+\rho L)$-way branch (to one of the elements of S or falling through if every element of L is zero); if I is an empty vector or an index to the vector S, then $\rightarrow S[I]$ provides a similar $(1+\rho L)$-way branch.

Programming languages commonly incorporate special forms of sequence control, typified by the DO statement of FORTRAN. These forms are excluded from APL because their cost in complication of the language outweighs their utility. The array operations in APL obviate many instances of iteration, and those which remain can be represented in a variety of ways. For example, grouping the initialization, modification, and testing of the control variable at the head of the iterated segment provides a particularly perspicuous arrangement. Moreover, specialized sequence control statements are usually context dependent and necessarily introduce new rules.

Conditional statements of the IF THEN ELSE type are not only context dependent, but their inherent limitation to a sequence of binary choices often leads to awkward constructions. These, and other, special sequence control forms can usually be modeled readily in APL and provided as application packages if desired.

Scalar functions

The emphasis on generality is illustrated in the definitions of many of the scalar functions. For example, the definition of the factorial is not limited to non-negative integers but is extended in the manner of the gamma function. Similarly, the residue is extended to all numbers in a simple and useful way: $M|N$ is defined as the smallest (in magnitude) among the quantities $N-M\times I$ (where I is an integer) which lie in the range from 0 to M. If no such quantity exists (as in the case where M is zero) then the restriction to the range 0 to M is discarded, that is, $0|X$ is X. As another example, $0*0$ is defined as 1 because that is the limiting value of $X*Y$ when the point 0 0 is approached along any path other than the X axis, and because this definition is needed to make the common general form of writing a polynomial (in which the constant term C is written as $C\times X*0$) applicable when the value of the argument X is zero.

The urge to generality must be tempered to avoid setting traps for the unwary, and compromise is sometimes necessary. For example, $X\div 0$ could be defined as infinity (i.e., the largest representable number in an implementation) so as to obviate special treatment of the case $Y=0$ when computing the arc tangent of $X\div Y$, but is instead defined to yield a domain error. Nevertheless, $0\div 0$ is given the value 1, in spite of the fact that the mathematical argument for it is much weaker than that for $0*0$, because it was deemed desirable to avoid an error stop in this case.

Eventually it will be desirable to be able to set separate limits on domains to suit various classes of users. For example, an implementation that incorporates complex numbers must yield a result for the expression $^-1*.5$ but should admit of being set to yield a domain error for a user studying elementary arithmetic. The experienced user should be permitted to use an implementation in a mode that gives him complete control of domain and other errors, i.e., an error should not stop execution but should give necessary information about the error in a form which can be used by the program in which it occurs. Such a facility has not yet been incorporated in APL implementations.

A very general and useful set of functions was introduced by adopting the relation symbols $< \leq = \geq > \neq$ to represent functions (i.e., propositions) rather than assertions. The result of any proposition was defined to be 0 or 1 (rather than, say, *true* or *false*) so that it would lie in the domain of other arithmetic functions. Thus $X=Y$ and $X\neq Y$ represent general comparisons, but if X and Y are integers then $X=Y$ is the Kronecker delta and $X\neq Y$ is its inverse; if X and Y are Boolean variables, then $X\neq Y$ is the *exclusive-or* and $X\leq Y$ is material implication. This definition also allows expressions that incorporate both relational and arithmetic functions (such as $(2=+/[1]0=S\circ.|S)/S\leftarrow\iota N$, which yields the primes up to integer N). Moreover, identities among Boolean functions are more evident when expressed in these terms than when expressed in more conventional symbols.

The adoption of the relation symbols as functions does not preclude their use as *assertions* in informal sentences. For example, although one might feel compelled to substitute "$X\leq Y$ is true" for "$X\leq Y$" in the sentence "If $X\leq Y$ then $(X<Y)\vee(X=Y)$", there is no more reason to do so than to substitute "Bob is there is true" for "Bob is there" in the sentence which begins "If Bob is there then . . ."

Although we strove to adopt familiar symbols and usage, any clash with the principle of uniformity was invariably resolved in favor of uniformity. For example, familiar symbols (such as $+ - \times \div$) are used where possible, but anomalies such as $|X|$ for magnitude and $N!$ for factorial are regularized to $|X$ and $!N$. Notation such as X^N for power and $\binom{M}{N}$ for the binomial coefficient are replaced by regular dyadic forms $X*N$ and $M!N$. Elision of the times sign is not permitted; this allows the use of multiple-character names and avoids confusion between multiplication, as in $X(X+3)$, and the application of a function, as in $F(X+3)$.

Moreover, each of the primitive scalar functions in APL is extended to arrays in exactly the same way. In particular, if V and W are vectors the expressions $V\times W$ and $3+V$ are permitted as well as the expressions $V+W$ and $3\times V$, although only the latter pair would be permitted (in the sense used in APL) in conventional vector algebra.

One view of simplicity might exclude as redundant those functions which are easily expressed in terms of others. For example, $\lceil X$ may be written as $-\lfloor -X$, and $\lceil /X$ may be written as $-\lfloor /-X$, and $\wedge /L$ may be written as $\sim\vee/\sim L$. From another viewpoint it is simpler to use a more complete or symmetric set of primitives, since one need not remember which of a pair is provided and how to express the other in terms of it. In APL, completeness has been favored. For example, symbols are provided for all of the nontrivial logical functions although all are easily expressed in terms of a small subset of them.

The use of the circle to denote the whole family of functions related to the circular functions is a practical technique for conserving symbols as well as a useful generalization. It leads to many convenient expressions involving reduction and inner and outer products (such as $1\ 2\ 3\circ.\circ X$ for a table of sines, cosines and tangents). Moreover, anyone wishing to use the symbol SIN for the sine function can define the function SIN as either $1\circ X$ (for radian arguments) or $1\circ X\times 180\div\circ 1$ (for degree arguments). The notational scheme employed for the circular functions must clearly be used with discretion; it could be used to replace all monadic functions by a single dyadic function with an integer left argument to encode each monadic function.

Operators

The dot in the expression $M+.\times N$ is an example of an *operator*; it takes functions (in this case $+$ and $\times$) as arguments and produces a new function called an *inner product*. (In elementary mathematics the term *operator* is also used as a synonym for *function*, but in APL we eschew this usage.) The evolution of operators in APL furnishes an example of growing generality which has as yet been neither fully exploited nor fully regularized.

The operators now in APL were introduced one by one (reduction, then inner product, then outer product, then axis operators such as $\phi[I]$) without being recognized as members of a class. When this class property was recognized it was apparent that the operators had not been given a consistent syntax and that the notation should eventually be regularized to give operators the same syntax as functions, i.e., an operator taking two arguments occurs between its (function) arguments (as in $+.\times$) and an operator taking one argument appears in front of it. It also became evident that our treatment of operators had introduced a useful heirarchy into the order of execution, operators being executed before functions.

The recognition of operators as such has also made clear the much broader role they might be expected to play — derivative and integral operators are only two of many useful operators that must be added to the language.

The use of the outer product operator furnishes a clear example of a significant process in the evolution of the language: when a new facility is introduced it takes considerable time to recognize the many ways in which it can be used and therefore to appreciate its role in the further development of the language. The notation $\alpha^j(n)$ (later regularized to $N\alpha J$) had been introduced early to represent a *prefix* vector, i.e., a Boolean vector of N elements with J leading 1's. Some thought had been given to extending the definition to a *vector* J (perhaps to yield an N=column matrix whose rows were prefix vectors determined by the elements of J) but no decision had been taken. When considering such an extension we normally communicate by defining any proposed notation in terms of existing primitives. After the outer product was introduced the proposed extension was written simply as $J\circ.\geq\iota N$, and it became clear that the function α was now redundant.

One should not conclude from this example that every function or set of functions easily expressed in terms of another is discarded as redundant; judgment must be exercised. In the present instance the α was discarded partly because it was too restrictive, i.e., the outer product form could be applied to yield a host of related functions (such as $J\circ.<\iota N$ and $J\circ.<\phi\iota N$) not all of which were expressible in terms of the prefix and suffix functions α and ω. As mentioned in the discussion of scalar functions, the completeness of an obvious family of functions is also a factor to be considered.

Operators are attractive from several points of view. Because they provide a scheme for denoting whole classes of related functions, they offer uniformity of expression and great economy of symbols. The conciseness of expression that they allow can also be directly related to efficiency of implementation. Moreover, they introduce a new level of generality which plays an important role in the formal manipulability of the language.

Formal manipulation

APL is rich in identities and is therefore amenable to a great deal of fruitful formal manipulation. For example, many of the familiar identities of ordinary matrix algebra extend to inner products other than $+.\times$, and de Morgan's law and other dualities extend to inner and outer products on arrays. The emphasis on generality, uniformity, and simplicity is likely to lead to a language rich in identities, but our emphasis on identities has been such that it should perhaps be enunciated as a separate and important guiding principle. Indeed, the preface to Iverson [10] cites one chapter (on the logical calculus) as illustration of "the formal manipulability of the language and its utility in theoretical work". A variety of identities is treated in [10] and [11], and a schema for proofs in APL is presented in [12].

Two examples will be used to illustrate the role of identities in the development of the language. The identity

$$(+/X)=(+/U/X)++/(\sim U)/X$$

applies for any numerical vector X and logical vector U. Maintaining this identity for the case where U is a vector of zeros forces one to define the sum over an empty vector as zero. A similar identity holds for reduction by any associative and commutative function and leads one to define the reduction of an empty array by any function as the identity element of that function.

The dyadic transpose $I\phi A$ performs a general permutation on the coordinates of A as specified by the argument I. The monadic transpose is a special case which, in order to yield ordinary matrix transpose for an array of rank two, was initially defined to interchange the last two coordinates. It was later realized that the identity

$$\wedge/,(M+.\times N)=\phi(\phi N)+.\times\phi M$$

expected to hold for matrices would not hold for higher rank arrays. To make the identity true in general, the monadic transpose was defined to reverse the order of the coordinates as follows:

$$\wedge/,(\phi A)=(\phi\iota\rho\rho A)\phi A.$$

Moreover, the form chosen for the left argument of the dyadic transpose led to the following important identity:

$$\wedge/,(I\phi J\phi A)=I[J]\phi A.$$

Execute and format

In designing an executable language there is a fundamental choice to be made: Is the statement of an expression to be taken as an order to evaluate it, or must the evaluation be indicated by an explicit function in the language? This decision was made very early in the development of APL, albeit with little deliberation. Nevertheless, once the choice became manifest, early in the development of the implementation, it was applied uniformly in all situations.

There were some arguments against this, of course, particularly in the application of a function to its arguments, where it is often useful to be able to "call by name," which requires that the evaluation of the argument be deferred. But if implemented literally (i.e., if functions could be defined with this as an option) then names per se would have to be known to the language and would constitute an additional object type with its own rules of behavior and specialized primitive functions. A deliberate effort had been made to eliminate unnecessary type distinctions, as in the uniform language treatment of numbers regardless of their internal representation, and this point of view prevailed. In the interest of keeping the semantic rules simple, the idea of "call by name" was rejected as a primitive concept in APL.

Nevertheless, there are important cases where the formal argument of a function should not be evaluated at the time of invocation—as in the application of a generalized root finder to an arbitrary function. There are also situations where it is useful to inhibit evaluation of an expression, as in certain conditional forms, and the need for some treatment of the problem was clear. The basis for a solution was at hand in the form of character arrays, which were already objects of the language. Effectively, putting quotes around a statement inhibits its execution by making it a data item, a character array subject to the normal language functions. To get the effect of working with names, or with expressions to be conditionally evaluated, it was only necessary to introduce the notion of "unquote," or more properly "execute," as a function that would cause a character array to be evaluated as if it were the same expression without the inhibition.

The actual introduction of the execute function did not come for some time after its recognition as the likely solution. The development that preceded its final acceptance into APL illustrates several design principles.

The concept of an execute function is a very powerful one. In a sense, it makes the language "self-conscious," and introduces endless possibilities for obscurity in programs. This might have been a reason for not allowing it, but we had long since realized that a general-purpose language cannot be made foolproof and remain effective. Furthermore, APL is easily partitioned, and beginning users, or users of application packages, need not know about more sophisticated aspects of the language. The real issues were whether the function was of sufficiently broad utility, whether it could be defined simply, and whether it was perhaps a special case of a more general capability that should be implemented instead. There was also the need to establish a symbol for it.

The case for general utility was easily made. The execute function does allow names to be used as arguments to functions without the need for a new data type; it provides the means for generating variables under program control, which can be useful, for example, in managing data that do not conveniently fit into rectangular arrays; it allows the construction and execution of statements under program control; and in interpretive implementations it provides conversion from characters to numbers at machine speeds.

The behavior of the execute function is simply described: it treats a character array argument as a representation of an APL statement and attempts to evaluate or execute the statement so represented. System commands and attempts to enter function definition mode are not valid APL statements and are excluded from the domain of execute. It can be said that, except for these exclusions, execute acts upon a character array as if the elements of the array were entered at a terminal in the immediate execution mode.

Incidentally, there was pressure to arbitrarily include system commands in the domain of execute as a means of providing access to other workspaces under program control in order to facilitate work with large collections of data. This was resisted on the basis that the execute function should not allow by subterfuge what was otherwise disallowed. Indeed, consideration of this aspect of the behavior of execute led to the removal of certain anomalies in function definition and a clarification of the role of the escape characters) and ∇.

The question of generality has not been finally settled. Certainly, the execute function could be considered a member of a class that includes constructs like those of the lambda calculus. But it is not necessary to have the ultimate answer in order to proceed, and the simplicity of the definition adopted gives some assurance that generalizations are not being foreclosed.

For some time during its experimental implementation the symbol for execute was the epsilon. This was chosen for obvious mnemonic reasons and because no other monadic use was made of this symbol. As thought was being given to another new function—format—it was observed that over some part of each of their domains format and execute were inverses. Furthermore, over these parts of their domains they were strongly related to the functions encode and decode, and we therefore adopted their symbols overstruck by the symbol ∘.

The format function furnishes another example of a primitive whose behavior was first defined and long experimented with by means of APL defined functions. These defined functions were the *DFT* (Decimal Format) and *EFT* (Exponential Format) familiar to most users of the APL system. The main advantage of the primitive format function over these definitions is its much more efficient use of computer time.

The format function has both a dyadic and a monadic definition, but the execute function is monadic only. This leaves the way open for a related dyadic function, for which there has been no dearth of suggestions, but none will be adopted until more experience has been gained in the use of what we already have.

System commands and other environmental facilities

The definition of APL is purely abstract: the objects of the language, arrays of numbers and characters, are acted upon by the primitive functions in a manner independent of their representation and independent of any practical interpretation placed upon them. The advantages of such an abstract definition are that it makes the language truly machine independent, and avoids bias in favor of particular application areas. But not everything in a computing system is abstract, and provision must be made to manage system resources and otherwise communicate with the environment in which the language functions operate.

Maintaining the abstract nature of the language in a real computing system therefore seemed to imply a need for language-like facilities in some sense outside of APL. The need was first met by the use of system commands, which are syntactically not part of APL, and are also excluded from dynamic use within APL programs. They provided a simple and, in some ways, convenient answer to the problem of system management, but proved insufficient because the actions and information provided by them are often required dynamically.

The exclusion of system commands from programs was based more strongly on engineering considerations than on a theoretic compulsion, since the syntactic distinction alone sets them apart from the language, but there remained a reluctance to allow such syntactic anomalies in a program. The real issue, which was whether the functions provided by the system commands were properly the province of APL, was tabled for the time being, and defined functions that mimic the actions of certain of them were introduced to allow dynamic execution. The functions so provided were those affecting only the environment within a workspace, such as width and origin, while those that would have affected major physical resources of the system were still excluded for engineering reasons.

These environmental defined functions were based on the use of still another class of functions—called "I-beams" because of the shape of the symbol used for them—which provide a more general facility for communication between APL programs and the less abstract parts of the system. The I-beam functions were first introduced by the system programmers to allow them to execute System/360 instructions from within APL programs, and thus use APL as a direct aid in their programming activity. The obvious convenience of functions of this kind, which appeared to be part of the language, led to the introduction of the monadic I-beam function for direct use by anyone. Various arguments to this function yielded information about the environment such as available space and time of day.

Though clearly an ad hoc facility, the I-beam functions appear to be part of the language because they obey APL syntax and can be executed from within an APL program. They were too useful to do without in the absence of a more rational solution to the problem, and so were graced with the designation "system-dependent functions," while we continued to use the system and think about the general problem of communication among the subsystems composing it.

Shared variables

The logical basis for a generalized communication facility in APL\360 was laid in 1964 with the publication of the formal description of System/360 [2]. It was then observed that the interaction between concurrent "asynchronous" processes (programs) could be completely comprehended by an interface comprising variables that were shared by the cooperating processes. (Another facility was also used, where one program forced a branch in another, but this can be regarded as a derivative representation based on variables shared between one program and a processor that drives the other.) It was not until six or seven years later, however, that the full force of this observation was brought to bear on the practical problem of controlling in an organic way the environment in which APL programs run.

Three processors can be identified during the execution of an APL program: APL, or the processor that actually executes the program; the *system*, or host that manages libraries and other environmental factors, which in APL\360 is the System/360 processor; and the user, who may be observing and processing output or providing input to the program. The link between APL and system is the set of I-beam functions, that between user and system is the set of system commands, and between user and APL, the quad and quote-quad. With the exception of the quote-quad, which is a true variable, all these links are constructs on the interfaces rather than the interfaces themselves.

It can be seen that the quote-quad is shared by the user and APL. Characteristically, a value assigned to it in a program is presented to the user at the terminal, who utilizes this information as he sees fit. If later read by the program, the value of the quote-quad then has no fixed relationship to what was earlier specified by the program. The values written and read by the program are *a fortiori* APL objects — abstract arrays — but they may have practical significance to the user-processor, suggesting, for example, that an experimental observation be made and the results entered at the keyboard.

Using the quote-quad as the paradigm for their behavior, a general facility for shared variables was designed and implemented starting in late 1969 (see Lathwell [13]). The underlying concept was to provide communication across the boundary between independent processors by explicitly establishing certain variables as being shared between them. A shared variable is syntactically indistinguishable from others and may be used normally either on the right or left of an assignment arrow.

Although motivated most strongly at the time by a need to provide a "file and I/O" capability for APL\360, the shared variable facility satisfied other needs as well, a significant criterion for the inclusion of a new feature in the language. It provides for general communication, not only between APL and the host system, but also between APL programs running concurrently at different terminals, which is in a sense a more fundamental use of the idea.

Perhaps as important as the practical use of the facility is the potency that an implementation lends to the concept of shared variables as a basis for understanding communication in any system. With respect to APL\360, for example, we had long used the term "distinguished variable" in discussing the interface between APL and system, meaning thereby variables, like trace and stop vectors, which hold control or state information. It is now clear that "distinguished variables" are shared variables, distinguished from ordinary variables by the fact of their being shared, and further qualified by their membership in a particular interface. In principle, the environment and resources of APL\360 could be completely controlled through the use of an appropriate set of such distinguished variables.

System functions

In a given application area it is usually easier to work with APL augmented by defined functions, designed to embody the significant concepts of the area, than with the primitive functions of the language alone. Such defined functions, together with the relevant variables or data objects, constitute an application language, or application extension. Managing the resources or environment of an APL computing system is a particular application, in which the data objects are the distinguished variables that define the interface between APL and system.

For convenience, the defined functions constituting an application extension for system management should behave differently from other defined functions, at least to the extent of being available at all times, like the primitives, without having to be copied from workspace to workspace. Such ubiquity requires that the names of these functions be distinguished from those a user might invent. This distinction can only be made, if APL is to remain essentially context independent, by the establishment of a class of reserved names. This class has been defined as names starting with the quad character, and functions having such names are called *system functions*. A similar naming convention applies to distinguished variables, or *system variables*, as they are now called.

In principle, system functions work with system variables that are independently identifiable. In practice, the system variables in a particular situation may not be available explicitly, and the system functions may be locked. This can come about because direct access to the interface by the user is deemed undesirable for technical reasons, or because of economic considerations such as efficiency or protection of proprietary rights. In such situations system functions are superficially distinguishable from primitive functions only by virtue of the naming convention.

The present I-beam functions behave like system functions. Fortunately, there are only two of them: the monadic function that is familiar to all users of APL, and the dyadic function that is still known mostly to system programmers. Despite their usefulness, these functions are hardly to be taken as examples of good application language design, depending as they do on arbitrary numerical arguments to give them meaning, and having no meaningful relationships with each other. The monadic I-beams are more like read-only variables — changeable constants, as it were — than functions. Indeed, except for their syntax, they behave precisely like shared variables where the processor on the other side replaces the value between each reference on the APL side.

The shared variable facility itself requires communication between APL and system in order to establish a desired interface between APL and cooperating processors. The prospect of inventing new system commands for this, or otherwise providing an ad hoc facility, was most distasteful, and consideration of this problem was a major factor in leading toward the system function concept. It was taken as an indication of the validity of the shared variable approach to communication when the solution to the problem it engendered was found within the conceptual framework it provided, and this solution also proved to be a basis for clarifying the role of facilities already present.

In due course a set of system functions must be designed to parallel the facilities now provided by system commands and go beyond them. Aside from the obvious advantage of being dynamically executable, such a set of system functions will have other advantages and some disadvantages. The major operational advantage is that the system functions will be able to use the full power of APL to generate their arguments and exploit their results. Countering this, there is the fact that this power has a price: the automatic name isolation provided by the extralingual system commands will not be available to the system functions. Names used as arguments will have to be presented as character arrays, which is not a disadvantage in programs, although it is less convenient for casual keyboard entry than is the use of unadorned names in system commands.

A more profound advantage of system functions over system commands lies in the possibility of designing the former to work together constructively. System commands are foreclosed from this by the rudimentary nature of their syntax; they do constitute a language, but one having no constructive potential.

Workspaces, files, and input-output

The workspace organization of APL\360 libraries serves to group together functions and variables intended to work together, and to render them active or inactive as a group, preserving the state of the computation during periods of inactivity. Workspaces also implicitly qualify the names of objects within them, so that the same name may be used independently in a multiplicity of workspaces in a given system. These are useful attributes; the grouping feature, for example, contributes strongly to the convenience of using APL by obviating the linkage problems found in other library systems.

On the other hand, engineering decisions made early in the development of APL\360 determined that the workspaces be of fixed size. This limits the size of objects that can be managed within them and often becomes an inconvenience. Consequently, as usage of APL\360 developed, a demand arose for a "file" facility, at first to work with large volumes of data under program control, and later to utilize data generated by other systems. There was also a demand to make use of high-speed input and output equipment. As noted in an earlier section, these demands led in time to the development of the shared variable facility. Three considerations were paramount in arriving at this solution.

One consideration was the determination to maintain the abstract nature of APL. In particular, the use of primitive functions whose definitions depend on the representation of their arguments was to be avoided. This alone was sufficient to rule out the notion of a file as a

formal concept in the language. APL has primitive array structures that either encompass the logical structure of files or can be extended to do so by relatively simple functions defined on them. The user of APL may regard any array or collection of arrays as a file, and in principle should be able to use the data so organized without regard to the medium on which these arrays may be stored.

The second consideration was the not uncommon observation that files are used in two ways, as a medium for exchange of information and as a dynamic extension of working storage during computation (see Falkoff [14]). In keeping with the principle just noted, the proper solution to the second problem must ultimately be the removal of workspace size limitations, and this will probably be achieved in the course of general developments in the industry. We saw no prospect of a satisfactory direct solution being achieved locally in a reasonable time, so attention was concentrated on the first problem in the expectation that, with a good general communication facility, on-line storage devices could be used for workspace extension at least as effectively as they are so used in other systems.

The third consideration was one of generality. One possible approach to the communication problem would have been to increase the roster of system commands and make them dynamically executable, or add variations to the I-beam functions to manage specific storage media and I/O equipment or access methods. But in addition to being unpleasant because of its ad hoc nature, this approach did not promise to be general enough. In working interactively with large collections of data, for example, the possible functional variations are almost limitless. Various classes of users may be allowed access for different purposes under a variety of controls, and unless it is intended to impose restrictive constraints ahead of time, it is futile to try to anticipate the solutions to particular problems. Thus, to provide a communication facility by accretion appeared to be an endless task.

The shared variable approach is general enough because, by making the interface explicitly available with primitive controls on the behavior of the shared variable, it provides only the basic communication mechanism. It then remains for the specific problem to be managed by bringing to bear on it the full power of APL on one side, and that of the host system on the other. The only remaining question is one of performance: does the shared variable concept provide the basis for an effective implementation? This question has been answered affirmatively as a result of direct experimentation.

The net effect of this approach has been to provide for APL an application extension comprising the few system functions necessary to manage shared variables. Actual file or I/O applications are managed, as required, by user-defined functions. The system functions are used only to establish sharing, and the shared variables are then used for the actual transfer of information between APL workspaces and file or I/O processors.

Appendix. Chronology of APL development

The development of APL was begun in 1957 as a necessary tool for writing clearly about various topics of interest in data processing. The early development is described in the preface of Iverson [10] and Brooks and Iverson [15]. Falkoff became interested in the work shortly after Iverson joined IBM in 1960, and used the language in his work on parallel search memories [16]. In early 1963 Falkoff began work on a formal description of System/360 in APL and was later joined in this work by Iverson and Sussenguth [2].

Throughout this early period the language was used by both Falkoff and Iverson in the teaching of various topics at various universities and at the IBM Systems Research Institute. Early in 1964 Iverson began using it in a course in elementary functions at the Fox Lane High School in Bedford, New York, and in 1966 published a text that grew out of this work [8]. John L. Lawrence (who, as editor of the *IBM Systems Journal*, procured and assisted in the publication of the formal description of System/360) became interested in the use of APL at high school and college level and invited the authors to consult with him in the development of curriculum material based on the use of computers. This work led to the preparation of curriculum material in a number of areas and to the publication of an APL\360 Reference Manual by Sandra Pakin [17].

Although our work through 1964 had been focused on the language as a tool for communication among *people*, we never doubted that the same characteristics which make the language good for this purpose would make it good for communication with a machine. In 1963 Herbert Hellerman implemented a portion of the language on an IBM/1620 as reported in [18]. Hellerman's system was used by students in the high school course with encouraging results. This, together with our earlier work in education, heightened our interest in a full-scale implementation.

When the work on the formal description of System/360 was finished in 1964 we turned our attention to the problem of implementation. This work was brought to rapid fruition in 1965 when Lawrence M. Breed joined the project and, together with Philip S. Abrams, produced an implementation on the 7090 by the end of 1965. Influenced by Hellerman's interest in time-sharing we had already developed an APL typing element for the IBM 1050 computer terminal. This was used in early 1966 when Breed adapted the 7090 system to an experimental time-sharing system developed under Andrew Kinslow, allowing us the first use of APL in the manner familiar today. By November 1966, the system had been reprogrammed for System/360 and APL service has been available within IBM since that date. The system became available outside IBM in 1968.

A paper by Falkoff and Iverson [3] provided the first published description of the APL\360 system, and a companion paper by Breed and Lathwell [19] treated the implementation. R. H. Lathwell joined the design group in 1966 and has since been concerned primarily with the implementations of APL and with the use of APL itself in the design process. In 1971 he published, together with Jorge Mezei, a formal definition of APL in APL [9].

The APL\360 System benefited from the contributions of many outside of the central design group. The preface to the User's Manual [1] acknowledges many of these contributions.

References

1. A. D. Falkoff and K. E. Iverson, *APL\360 User's Manual*, IBM Corporation, (GH20-0683-1) 1970.
2. A. D. Falkoff, K. E. Iverson, and E. H. Sussenguth, "A Formal Description of System/360," *IBM Systems Journal*, 3, 198 (1964).
3. A. D. Falkoff and K. E. Iverson, "The APL\360 Terminal System", *Symposium on Interactive Systems for Experimental Applied Mathematics*, eds., M. Klerer and J. Reinfelds, Academic Press, New York, 1968.
4. A. D. Falkoff, "Criteria for a System Design Language," *Report on NATO Science Committee Conference on Software Engineering Techniques*, April 1970.
5. Z. Ghandour and J. Mezei, "General Arrays, Operators and Functions," *IBM J. Res. Develop.* 17, 335 (1973, this issue).
6. T. More, "Axioms and Theorems for a Theory of Arrays—Part I," *IBM J. Res. Develop.* 17, 135 (1973).
7. P. C. Berry, *APL\360 Primer*, IBM Corporation, (GH-20-0689-2) 1971.
8. K. E. Iverson, *Elementary Functions: An Algorithmic Treatment*, Science Research Associates, Chicago, 1966.
9. R. H. Lathwell and J. E. Mezei, "A Formal Description of APL," *Colloque APL*, Institut de Recherche d'Informatique et d'Automatique, Rocquencourt, France, 1971.
10. K. E. Iverson, *A Programming Language*, Wiley, New York, 1962.
11. K. E. Iverson, "Formalism in Programming Languages," *Communications of the ACM*, 7, 80 (February, 1964).
12. K. E. Iverson, *Algebra: an algorithmic treatment*, Addison-Wesley Publishing Co., Reading, Mass., 1972.
13. R. H. Lathwell, "System Formulation and APL Shared Variables," *IBM J. Res. Develop.* 17, 353 (1973, this issue).
14. A. D. Falkoff, "A Survey of Experimental APL File and I/O Systems in IBM", *Colloque APL*, Institut de Recherche d'Informatique et D'Automatique, Rocquencourt, France, 1971.
15. F. P. Brooks and K. E. Iverson, *Automatic Data Processing*, Wiley, New York, 1963.
16. A. D. Falkoff, "Algorithms for Parallel Search Memories," *Journal of the ACM*, 488 (1962).
17. S., Pakin, *APL\360 Reference Manual*, Science Research Associates, Inc., Chicago, 1968.

18. H. Hellerman, "Experimental Personalized Array Translator System," *Communications of the ACM* 7, 433 (July, 1964).

19. L. M. Breed and R. H. Lathwell, "Implementation of APL/360," *Symposium on Interactive Systems for Experimental Applied Mathematics*, eds., M. Klerer and J. Reinfelds, Academic Press, New York, 1968.

Received May 16, 1972

The authors are located at the IBM Data Processing Division Scientific Center, 3401 Market Street, Philadelphia, Pennsylvania 19104.

SECTION 4

PROGRAMMING LANGUAGES AND DATA ABSTRACTION

ABSTRACTION MECHANISMS IN CLU BY B. LISKOV, A. SNYDER, R. ATKINSON, AND C. SCHAFFERT

EXCEPTION HANDLING IN CLU BY B. LISKOV AND A. SNYDER

TUTORIAL ON MODULA-2 BY J. GUTKNECHT

PASCAL, ADA, AND MODULA-2 BY D. COAR

INTRODUCTION

PROGRAMMING LANGUAGES AND DATA ABSTRACTION

All of us who have programmed computers appreciate the importance of the procedure as a mechanism for structuring programs. In fact, the procedure was the main structuring feature provided by all of the early higher level programming languages such as FORTRAN, ALGOL60, PL/1, and ALGOL68. The 1970s saw an important step forward in language design in the form of another basic structuring mechanism, the so-called *abstract data type*. A data type is a set of objects and an associated set of operations. The operations are designed to create instances of the data type, to build up and take apart these instances. For example, a stack is a last-in-first-out list (these are the objects) which has the operations: *push, pop*, and *isempty*. Or, the integers are a data type with the operations being the usual *addition, subtraction, multiplication*, and *division*.

So what is new about abstract data types? As we see above some data types are already built into the language, like the integers, while others must be created by the programmer. The notion of abstract data types in a programming language is concerned with those types that are created by the programmer. But languages such as Pascal introduced the idea of user defined data types and provided the enumerated data type feature, the array and the record to form new types of data from the basic set. This concept is not what we mean by the term abstract data type.

The idea of an abstract data type in a programming language is to provide a mechanism whereby a new type definition is *isolated* and *protected* from the rest of the program. Access to the data type may be made only in a very restricted manner, thus guaranteeing greater program reliability. The representation of the data type will be hidden from the rest of the program so that outside the definition of the type the programmer cannot rely on its representation. These ideas of good program structuring were espoused by many including David Parnas in his concept called *information hiding*. Therefore we conclude that an abstract data type as seen in a modern programming language is a means whereby the programmer defines and protects new data types he creates. Thus its scoping elements are one of its most important characteristics.

The first two papers in this section present the language CLU which was developed at MIT by B. Liskov and her team. The language is now flourishing there and is being distributed around the world. Though CLU has many interesting aspects, the one we are most concerned with here is the manner in which abstract data types are implemented and the way exceptions are handled. In CLU an abstract data type is referred to as a *cluster*. As one reads this paper one should keep in mind how the design is done incorporating the idea of an abstract data type. This concept is used at the design stage, but then one should have a language which offers support for abstract data types. The authors show how CLU supports such a design with special language features.

As an example of a cluster in CLU, consider from their paper the abstract data type *tree*. First we observe that the cluster is parameterized and has one argument called T. T is a type which permits the operations: *equal* and *lt*. The data items contained in the tree will be of type T. The operations on the tree include: *create, insert*, and *increasing*. Following the heading there appears the definition of the structure in terms of a record called *node*. The keyword **rep** stands for representation and it encloses the representation of trees. This representation will be shielded from outside use. Following the representation is the implementation of the three operations on this data type. The CLU cluster is similar in form to several other abstract data type facilities found in modern programming languages. It will be instructive to compare the cluster in CLU with the package in Ada.

It should be noted that CLU provides not only a means for data abstraction, but means for procedural and control abstraction as well. These three concepts are described in the paper. Together they imply that CLU supports a software development methodology which is based upon these three concepts.

The next paper addresses itself to the exception handling facility in CLU. A regular mechanism for treating this common situation in programming has been lacking, even in more recent languages such as Pascal. The facility as offered in PL/1 gives us a glimpse as to how useful the feature is and also into the problems of defining the feature adequately. The paper by Liskov and Snyder discusses the problem of exception handling design in a general way. Then they discuss the implementation in CLU. The CLU solution was well thought out and became the basis for exception handling in Ada.

While you are reading this paper consider the following points which are important for assessing the quality of exception handling:

- ☐ Can the normal system interrupt action be overridden?
- ☐ Are user defined exceptions possible and how are they raised?
- ☐ What are the scope rules for an enabled exception?
- ☐ Can exceptions be attached to statements, blocks, procedures, or expressions?
- ☐ What are the scope rules of the exception handler?
- ☐ Is the procedure where an exception arose resumed after the handler is executed or not?
- ☐ Can signaled exceptions have parameters?

- ☐ Is there a mechanism for catching unexpected exceptions?
- ☐ Can exceptions be raised within an exception handler?

By keeping these points in mind one will see that the CLU solution works fairly well, and adequately addresses many of these points.

The tutorial on Modula-2 differs from the earlier papers in that it focuses on the *module*. It has been claimed that the use of abstract data types helps in the structuring of programs. By using several examples, this paper shows how modules are best used, and possibly misused. A set of guidelines for how to make best use of modules is provided near the end of the paper.

The final paper in this section offers a comparison of Pascal, Ada, and Modula-2. Major points that are discussed include: typing, storage allocation, control structures, exception handling, task management, and modularity.

ABSTRACTION MECHANISMS IN CLU*

B. LISKOV, A. SNYDER, R. ATKINSON AND C. SCHAFFERT

CLU is a new programming language designed to support the use of abstractions in program construction. Work in programming methodology has led to the realization that three kinds of abstractions — procedural, control, and especially data abstractions — are useful in the programming process. Of these, only the procedural abstraction is supported well by conventional languages, through the procedure or subroutine. CLU provides, in addition to procedures, novel linguistic mechanisms that support the use of data and control abstractions. This paper provides an introduction to the abstraction mechanisms in CLU. By means of programming examples, the utility of the three kinds of abstractions in program construction is illustrated, and it is shown how CLU programs may be written to use and implement abstractions. The CLU library, which permits incremental program development with complete type checking performed at compile time, is also discussed.

Key Words and Phrases: programming languages, data types, data abstractions, control abstractions, programming methodology, separate compilation

CR Categories: 4.0, 4.12, 4.20, 4.22

*Reprinted from Comm ACM, 20, 8, August 1977, 564–576, copyright 1977.

1. Introduction

The motivation for the design of the CLU programming language was to provide programmers with a tool that would enhance their effectiveness in constructing programs of high quality—programs that are reliable and reasonably easy to understand, modify, and maintain. CLU aids programmers by providing constructs that support the use of abstractions in program design and implementation.

The quality of software depends primarily on the programming methodology in use. The choice of programming language, however, can have a major impact on the effectiveness of a methodology. A methodology can be easy or difficult to apply in a given language, depending on how well the language constructs match the structures that the methodology deems desirable. The presence of constructs that give a concrete form for the desired structures makes the methodology more understandable. In addition, a programming language influences the way that its users think about programming; matching a language to a methodology increases the likelihood that the methodology will be used.

CLU has been designed to support a methodology (similar to [6, 22]) in which programs are developed by means of problem decomposition based on the recognition of abstractions. A program is constructed in many stages. At each stage, the problem to be solved is how to implement some abstraction (the initial problem is to implement the abstract behavior required of the entire program). The implementation is developed by envisioning a number of subsidiary abstractions (abstract objects and operations) that are useful in the problem domain. Once the behavior of the abstract objects and operations has been defined, a program can be written to solve the original problem; in this program, the abstract objects and operations are used as primitives. Now the original problem has been solved, but new problems have arisen, namely, how to implement the subsidiary abstractions. Each of these abstractions is considered in turn as a new problem; its implementation may introduce further abstractions. This process terminates when all the abstractions introduced at various stages have been implemented or are present in the programming language in use.

In this methodology, programs are developed incrementally, one abstraction at a time. Further, a distinction is made between an abstraction, which is a kind of behavior, and a program, or *module*, which implements that behavior. An abstraction isolates use from implementation: an abstraction can be used without knowledge of its implementation and implemented without knowledge of its use. These aspects of the methodology are supported by the CLU *library*, which maintains information about abstractions and the CLU modules that implement them. The library permits separate compilation of modules with complete type checking at compile time.

To make effective use of the methodology, it is necessary to understand the kinds of abstractions that are useful in constructing programs. In studying this question, we identified an important kind of abstraction, the data abstraction, that had been largely neglected in discussions of programming methodology.

A data abstraction [8, 12, 20] is used to introduce a new type of data object that is deemed useful in the domain of the problem being solved. At the level of use, the programmer is concerned with the *behavior* of these data objects, what kinds of information can be stored in them and obtained from them. The programmer is *not* concerned with how the data objects are represented in storage nor with the algorithms used to store and access information in them. In fact, a data abstraction is often introduced to delay such implementation decisions until a later stage of design.

The behavior of the data objects is expressed most naturally in terms of a set of operations that are meaningful for those objects. This set includes operations to create objects, to obtain information from them, and possibly to modify them. For example, push and pop are among the meaningful operations for stacks, while meaningful operations for integers include the usual arithmetic operations. Thus a data abstraction consists of a set of objects and a set of operations characterizing the behavior of the objects.

If a data abstraction is to be understandable at an abstract level, the behavior of the data objects must be *completely* characterized by the set of operations. This property is ensured by making the operations the *only direct means* of creating and manipulating the objects. One effect of this restriction is that, when defining an abstraction, the programmer must be careful to include a sufficient set of operations, since every action he wishes to perform on the objects must be realized in terms of this set.

We have identified the following requirements that must be satisfied by a language supporting data abstractions:

1. A linguistic construct is needed that permits a data abstraction to be implemented as a unit. The implementation involves selecting a representation for the data objects and defining an algorithm for each operation in terms of that representation.

2. The language must limit access to the representation to just the operations. This limitation is necessary to ensure that the operations completely characterize the behavior of the objects.

CLU satisfies these requirements by providing a linguistic construct called a *cluster* for implementing data abstractions. Data abstractions are integrated into the language through the data type mechanism. Access to the representation is controlled by type checking, which is done at compile time.

In addition to data abstractions, CLU supports two other kinds of abstractions: procedural abstractions and control abstractions. A procedural abstraction performs a computation on a set of input objects and produces a set of output objects; examples of procedural abstractions are sorting an array and computing a square root. CLU supports procedural abstractions by means of procedures, which are similar to procedures in other programming languages.

A control abstraction defines a method for sequencing arbitrary actions. All languages provide built-in control abstractions; examples are the **if** statement and the **while** statement. In addition, however, CLU allows user definitions of a simple kind of control abstraction. The method provided is a generalization of the repetition methods available in many programming languages. Frequently the programmer desires to perform the same action for all the objects in a collection, such as all characters in a string or all items in a set. CLU provides a linguistic construct called an *iterator* for defining how the objects in the collection are obtained. The iterator is used in conjunction with the **for** statement; the body of the **for** statement describes the action to be taken.

The purpose of this paper is to illustrate the utility of the three kinds of abstractions in program construction and to provide an informal introduction to CLU. We do not attempt a complete description of the language; rather, we concentrate on the constructs that support abstractions. The presence of these constructs constitutes the most important way in which CLU differs from other languages. The language closest to CLU is Alphard [24], which represents a concurrent design effort with goals similar to our own. The design of CLU has been influenced by Simula 67 [4] and to a lesser extent by Pascal [23] and Lisp [15].

In the next section we introduce CLU and, by means of a programming example, illustrate the use and implementation of data abstractions. Section 3 describes the basic semantics of CLU. In Section 4, we discuss control abstractions and more powerful kinds of data abstractions. We present the CLU library in Section 5. Section 6 briefly describes the current implementation of CLU and discusses efficiency considerations. Finally, we conclude by discussing the quality of CLU programs.

2. An Example of Data Abstraction

This section introduces the basic data abstraction mechanism of CLU, the cluster. By means of an example, we intend to show how abstractions occur naturally in program design and how they are used and implemented in CLU. In particular, we show how a data abstraction can be used as structured intermediate storage.

Consider the following problem: given some document, we wish to compute, for each distinct word in the document, the number of times the word occurs and its frequency of occurrence as a percentage of the total

number of words. The document will be represented as a sequence of characters. A word is any nonempty sequence of alphabetic characters. Adjacent words are separated by one or more nonalphabetic characters such as spaces, punctuation, or newline characters. In recognizing distinct words, the difference between upper and lower case letters should be ignored.

The output is also to be a sequence of characters, divided into lines. Successive lines should contain an alphabetical list of all the distinct words in the document, one word per line. Accompanying each word should be the total number of occurrences and the frequency of occurrence. For example:

a	2	3.509%
access	1	1.754%
and	2	3.509%

Specifically, we are required to write the procedure *count_words*, which takes two arguments: an *instream* and an *outstream*. The former is the source of the document to be processed, and the latter is the destination of the required output. The form of this procedure will be

count_words = **proc** (i: instream, o: outstream);

    . . .

    end count_words;

Note that *count_words* does not return any results; its only effects are modifications of *i* (reading the entire document) and of *o* (printing the required statistics).

Instream and *outstream* are data abstractions. An *instream i* contains a sequence of characters. Of the primitive operations on *instreams*, only two will be of interest to us. *Empty* (*i*) returns **true** if there are no characters available in *i* and returns **false** otherwise. *Next* (*i*) removes the first character from the sequence and returns it. Invoking the *next* operation on an empty *instream* is an error.[1] An *outstream* also contains a sequence of characters. The interesting operation on *outstreams* is *put_string* (*s*, *o*), which appends the string *s* to the existing sequence of characters in *o*.

Now consider how we might implement *count_words*. We begin by deciding how to handle words. We could define a new abstract data type *word*. However, we choose instead to use strings (a primitive CLU type), with the restriction that only strings of lower case alphabetic characters will be used.[2]

Next we investigate how to scan the document. Reading a word requires knowledge of the exact way in which words occur in the input stream. We choose to isolate this information in a procedural abstraction, called *next_word*, which takes in the *instream i* and returns the next word (converted to lower case charac-

---

[1] The CLU error handling mechanism is discussed in [10].

[2] Sometimes it is difficult to decide whether to introduce a new data abstraction or to use an existing abstraction. Our decision to use strings to represent words was made partly to shorten the presentation.

ters) in the document. If there are no more words, *next_word* must communicate this fact to *count_words*. A simple way to indicate that there are no more words is by returning an "end of document" word, one that is distinct from any other word. A reasonable choice for the "end of document" word is the empty string.

It is clear that in *count_words* we must scan the entire document before we can print our results, and therefore we need some receptacle to retain information about words between these two actions (scanning and printing). Recording the information gained in the scan and organizing it for easy printing will probably be fairly complex. Therefore we defer such considerations until later by introducing a data abstraction *wordbag* with the appropriate properties. In particular, *wordbag* provides three operations: *create*, which creates an empty *wordbag*; *insert*, which adds a word to the *wordbag*; and *print*, which prints the desired statistical information about the words in the *wordbag*.[3]

The implementation of *count_words* is shown in Figure 1. The "%" character starts a comment, which continues to the end of the line. The "~" character stands for boolean negation. The notation *variable: type* is used in formal argument lists and declarations to specify the types of variables; a declaration may be combined with an assignment specifying the initial value of the variable. Boldface is used for reserved words, including the names of primitive CLU types.

The *count_words* procedure declares four variables: *i*, *o*, *wb*, and *w*. The first two denote the *instream* and *outstream* that are passed as arguments to *count_words*. The third, *wb*, denotes the *wordbag* used to hold the words read so far, and the fourth, *w*, the word currently being processed.

Operations of a data abstraction are named by a compound form that specifies both the type and the operation name. Three examples of operation calls appear in *count_words*: *wordbag$create( )*, *wordbag$insert (wb, w)* and *wordbag$print (wb, o)*. The CLU system provides a mechanism that avoids conflicts between names of abstractions; this mechanism is discussed in Section 5. However, operations of two different data abstractions may have the same name; the compound form serves to resolve this ambiguity. Although the ambiguity could in most cases be resolved by context, we have found in using CLU that the compound form enhances the readability of programs.

The implementation of *next_word* is shown in Figure 2. The *string$append* operation creates a new string by appending a character to the characters in the string argument (it does *not* modify the string argument). Note the use of the *instream* operations *next* and *empty*. Note also that two additional procedures have been used: *alpha (c)*, which tests whether a character is alphabetic or not, and *lower_case (c)*, which returns the lower case version of a character. The implementations

---

[3] The *print* operation is not the ideal choice, but a better solution requires the use of control abstractions. This solution is presented in Section 4.

Fig. 1. The *count_words* procedure.

```
count_words = proc (i: instream, o: outstream);
  % create an empty wordbag
  wb: wordbag := wordbag$create ( );
  % scan document, adding each word found to wb
  w: string := next_word (i);
  while w ~= " " do
    wordbag$insert (wb, w);
    w := next_word (i);
    end;
  % print the wordbag
  wordbag$print (wb, o);
  end count_words;
```

Fig. 2. The *next_word* procedure.

```
next_word = proc (i: instream) returns (string);
  c: char := '';
  % scan for first alphabetic character
  while ~alpha (c) do
    if instream$empty (i)
      then return " ";
      end;
    c := instream$next (i);
    end;
  % accumulate characters in word
  w: string := " ";
  while alpha (c) do
    w := string$append (w, c);
    if instream$empty (i)
      then return (w);
      end;
    c := instream$next (i);
    end;
  return (w);     % the nonalphabetic character c is lost
  end next_word;
```

of these procedures are not shown in the paper.

Now we must implement the type *wordbag*. The cluster will have the form

```
wordbag = cluster is create, insert, print;
  . . .
  end wordbag;
```

This form expresses the idea that the data abstraction is a set of operations as well as a set of objects. The cluster must provide a representation for objects of the type *wordbag* and an implementation for each of the operations. We are free to choose from the possible representations the one best suited to our use of the *wordbag* cluster.

The representation that we choose should allow reasonably efficient storage of words and easy printing, in alphabetic order, of the words and associated statistics. For efficiency in computing the statistics, maintaining a count of the total number of words in the document would be helpful. Since the total number of words in the document is probably much larger than the number of distinct words, the representation of a *wordbag* should contain only one "item" for each distinct word (along with a multiplicity count), rather than one "item" for each occurrence. This choice of representation requires that, at each insertion, we check whether the new word is already present in the *wordbag*. We would like a representation that allows the search for a matching "item" and the insertion of a not previously present "item" to be efficient. A binary tree representation [9] fits our requirements nicely.

Thus the main part of the *wordbag* representation consists of a binary tree. The binary tree is another data abstraction, *wordtree*. The data abstraction *wordtree* provides operations very similar to those of *wordbag*: *create* ( ) returns an empty *wordtree*; *insert* (*tr*, *w*) returns a *wordtree* containing all the words in the *wordtree tr* plus the additional word *w* (the *wordtree tr* may be modified in the process); and *print* (*tr*, *n*, *o*) prints the contents of the *wordtree tr* in alphabetic order on *outstream o* along with the number of occurrences and the frequency (based on a total of *n* words).

The implementation of *wordbag* is given in Figure 3. Following the header, we find the definition of the representation selected for *wordbag* objects:

rep = **record** [contents: wordtree, total: **int**];

The reserved type identifier **rep** indicates that the type specification to the right of the equal sign is the representing type for the cluster. We have defined the representation of a *wordbag* object to consist of two pieces: a *wordtree*, as explained above, and an integer, which records the total number of words in the *wordbag*.

A CLU record is an object with one or more named components. For each component name, there is an operation to select and an operation to set the corresponding component. The operation *get_n* (*r*) returns the *n* component of the record *r* (this operation is usually abbreviated *r.n*). The operation *put_n* (*r*, *x*) makes *x* the *n* component of the record *r* (this operation is usually abbreviated *r.n* := *x*, by analogy with the assignment statement). A new record is created by an expression of the form type${name₁: value₁, . . .}.

There are two different types associated with any cluster: the abstract type being defined (*wordbag* in this case) and the representation type (the record). Outside of the cluster, type checking ensures that a *wordbag* object will always be treated as such. In particular, the ability to convert a *wordbag* object into its representation is not provided (unless one of the *wordbag* operations does so explicitly).

Inside the cluster, however, it is necessary to view a *wordbag* object as being of the representation type, because the implementations of the operations are defined in terms of the representation. This change of viewpoint is signalled by having the reserved word **cvt** appear as the type of an argument (as in the *insert* and *print* operations). **Cvt** may also appear as a return type (as in the *create* operation); here it indicates that a returned object will be changed into an object of abstract type. Whether **cvt** appears as the type of an argument or as a return type, it stipulates a "conversion" of viewpoint between the external abstract type

Fig. 3. The *wordbag* cluster.

```
wordbag = cluster is
  create,      % create an empty bag
  insert,      % insert an element
  print;       % print contents of bag
  rep = record [contents: wordtree, total: int];
create = proc ( ) returns (cvt);
         return (rep${contents: wordtree$create ( ), total: 0});
         end create;
insert = proc (x: cvt, v: string);
         x.contents := wordtree$insert (x.contents, v);
         x.total := x.total + 1;
         end insert;
print = proc (x: cvt, o: outstream);
        wordtree$print (x.contents, x.total, o);
        end print;
end wordbag;
```

and the internal representation type. **Cvt** can be used only within a cluster, and conversion can be done only between the single abstract type being defined and the (single) representation type.[4]

The procedures in *wordbag* are very simple. *Create* builds a new instance of the **rep** by use of the record constructor

rep${contents: wordtree$create ( ), total: 0}

Here *total* is initialized to 0 and *contents* to the empty *wordtree* (by calling the *create* operation of *wordtree*). This **rep** object is converted into a *wordbag* object as it is being returned. *Insert* and *print* are implemented directly in terms of *wordtree* operations.

The implementation of *wordtree* is shown in Figure 4. In the *wordtree* representation, each node contains a word and the number of times that word has been inserted into the *wordbag*, as well as two subtrees. For any particular node, the words in the "lesser" subtree must alphabetically precede the word in the node, and the words in the "greater" subtree must follow the word in the node. This information is described by

node = **record** [value: **string**, count: **int**,
                 lesser: wordtree, greater: wordtree];

which defines "node" to be an abbreviation for the information following the equal sign. (The reserved word **rep** is used similarly as an abbreviation for the representation type.)

Now consider the representation of *wordtrees*. A nonempty *wordtree* can be represented by its top node. An empty *wordtree*, however, contains no information. The ideal type to represent an empty *wordtree* is the CLU type **null**, which has a single data object **nil**. So the representation of a *wordtree* should be either a node or **nil**. This representation is expressed by

rep = **oneof** [empty: **null**, non_empty: node];

Just as the record is the basic CLU mechanism to

---

[4] **Cvt** corresponds to Morris' seal and unseal [16] except that **cvt** represents a change in viewpoint only; no computation is required.

form an object that is a collection of other objects, the oneof is the basic CLU mechanism to form an object that is "one of" a set of alternatives. Oneof is CLU's method of forming a discriminated union, and is somewhat similar to a variant component of a record in Pascal [23].

An object of the type **oneof** [s_1: T_1 . . . s_n: T_n] can be thought of as a pair. The "tag" component is an identifier from the set {s_1 . . . s_n}.[5] The "value" component is an object of the type corresponding to the tag. That is, if the tag component is s_i, then the value is some object of type T_i.

Objects of type **oneof** [s_1: T_1 . . . s_n: T_n] are created by the operations $make\_s_i(x)$, each of which takes an object x of type T_i and returns the pair $\langle s_i, x \rangle$. Because the type of the value component of a oneof object is not known at compile time, allowing direct access to the value component could result in a run-time type error (e.g. assigning an object to a variable of the wrong type). To eliminate this possibility, we require the use of a special **tagcase** statement to decompose a oneof object:

```
tagcase e
    tag s₁ (id₁: T₁):    statements . . .
         . . .
    tag sₙ (idₙ: Tₙ):    statements . . .
    end;
```

This statement evaluates the expression *e* to obtain an object of type **oneof** [s_1: T_1 . . . s_n: T_n]. If the tag is s_i, then the value is assigned to the new variable id_i and the statements following the ith alternative are executed. The variable id_i is local to those statements. If, for some reason, we do not need the value, we can omit the parenthesized variable declaration.

The reader should now know enough to understand Figure 4. Note, in the *create* operation, the use of the construction operation *make_empty* of the representation type of *wordtree* (the discriminated union **oneof** [empty: **null**, nonempty: node]) to create the empty *wordtree*. The **tagcase** statement is used in both *insert* and *print*. Note that if *insert* is given an empty *wordtree*, it creates a new top node for the returned value, but if *insert* is given a nonempty *wordtree*, it modifies the given *wordtree* and returns it.[5] The *insert* operation depends on the dynamic allocation of space for newly created records (see Section 3).

The *print* operation uses the obvious recursive descent. It makes use of procedure *print_word* (w, c, t, o), which generates a single line of output on *o* consisting of the word w, the count c, and the frequency of occurrence derived from c and t. The implementation of *print_word* has been omitted.

We have now completed our first discussion of the

---

[5] It is necessary for *insert* to return a value in addition having a side effect because in the case of an empty *wordtree* argument side effects are not possible. Side effects are not possible because of the representation chosen for the empty *wordtree* and because of the CLU parameter passing mechanism (see Section 3).

Fig. 4. The *wordtree* cluster.

```
wordtree = cluster is
    create,     % create empty contents
    insert,     % add item to contents
    print;      % print contents
    node = record [value: string, count: int,
                   lesser: wordtree, greater: wordtree];
    rep = oneof [empty: null, non_empty: node];
create = proc ( ) returns (cvt);
    return (rep$make_empty (nil));
    end create;
insert = proc (x: cvt, v: string) returns (cvt);
    tagcase x
        tag empty:
            n: node := node${value: v, count: 1,
                             lesser: wordtree$create ( ),
                             greater: wordtree$create ( )};
            return (rep$make_non_empty (n));
        tag non_empty (n: node):
            if v = n.value
                  then n.count := n.count + 1;
              elseif v < n.value
                  then n.lesser := wordtree$insert (n.lesser, v);
              else n.greater := wordtree$insert (n.greater, v);
              end;
            return (x);
        end;
    end insert;
print = proc (x: cvt, total: int, o: outstream);
    tagcase x
        tag empty: ;
        tag non_empty (n: node):
            wordtree$print (n.lesser, total, o);
            print_word (n.value, n. count, total, o);
            wordtree$print (n.greater, total, o);
        end;
    end print;
end wordtree;
```

court_words procedure. We return to this problem in Section 4, where we present a superior solution.

3. Semantics

All languages present their users with some model of computation. This section describes those aspects of CLU semantics that differ from the common Algol-like model. In particular, we discuss CLU's notions of objects and variables and the definitions of assignment and argument passing that follow from these notions. We also discuss type correctness.

3.1 Objects and Variables

The basic elements of CLU semantics are *objects* and *variables*. Objects are the data entities that are created and manipulated by CLU programs. Variables are just the names used in a program to refer to objects.

In CLU, each object has a particular *type*, which characterizes its behavior. A type defines a set of operations that create and manipulate objects of that type. An object may be created and manipulated only via the operations of its type.

An object may *refer* to objects. For example, a

record object refers to the objects that are the components of the record. This notion is one of logical, not physical, containment. In particular, it is possible for two distinct record objects to refer to (or *share*) the same component object. In the case of a cyclic structure, it is even possible for an object to "contain" itself. Thus it is possible to have recursive data structure definitions and shared data objects without explicit reference types. The *wordtree* type described in the previous section is an example of a recursively defined data structure. (This notion of object is similar to that in Lisp.)

CLU objects exist independently of procedure activations. Space for objects is allocated from a dynamic storage area as the result of invoking constructor operations of certain primitive CLU types. For example, the record constructor is used in the implementation of *wordbag* (Figure 3) to acquire space for new *wordbag* objects. In theory, all objects continue to exist forever. In practice, the space used by an object may be reclaimed when the object is no longer accessible to any CLU program.[6]

An object may exhibit time-varying behavior. Such an object, called a *mutable* object, has a state which may be modified by certain operations without changing the identity of the object. Records are examples of mutable objects. The record update operations (*put_s* (r, v), written as $r.s := v$ in the examples), change the state of record objects and therefore affect the behavior of subsequent applications of the select operations (*get_s* (r), written as $r.s$). The *wordbag* and *wordtree* types are additional examples of types with mutable objects.

If a mutable object m is shared by two other objects x and y, then a modification to m made via x will be visible when m is examined via y. Communication through shared mutable objects is most beneficial in the context of procedure invocation, described below.

Objects that do not exhibit time-varying behavior are called *immutable* objects, or *constants*. Examples of constants are integers, booleans, characters, and strings. The value of a constant object can not be modified. For example, new strings may be computed from old ones, but existing strings do not change. Similarly, none of the integer operations modify the integers passed to them as arguments.

Variables are names used in CLU programs to *denote* particular objects at execution time. Unlike variables in many common programming languages, which *are* objects that *contain* values, CLU variables are simply names that the programmer uses to refer to objects. As such, it is possible for two variables to denote (or *share*) the same object. CLU variables are much like those in Lisp and are similar to pointer variables in other languages. However, CLU variables are *not* objects; they cannot be denoted by other variables or

referred to by objects. Thus variables are completely private to the procedure in which they are declared and cannot be accessed or modified by any other procedure.

3.2 Assignment and Procedure Invocation

The basic actions in CLU are *assignment* and *procedure invocation*. The assignment primitive $x := E$, where x is a variable and E is an expression, causes x to denote the object resulting from the evaluation of E. For example, if E is a simple variable y, then the assignment $x := y$ causes x to denote the object denoted by y. The object is *not* copied; after the assignment is performed, it will be *shared* by x and y. Assignment does not affect the state of any object. (Recall that $r.s := v$ is not a true assignment, but an abbreviation for *put_s* (r, v).)

Procedure invocation involves passing argument objects from the caller to the called procedure and returning result objects from the procedure to the caller. The formal arguments of a procedure are considered to be local variables of the procedure and are initialized, by assignment, to the objects resulting from the evaluation of the argument expressions. Thus argument objects are shared between the caller and the called procedure. A procedure may modify mutable argument objects (e.g. records), but of course it cannot modify immutable ones (e.g. integers). A procedure has no access to the variables of its caller.

Procedure invocations may be used directly as statements; those that return objects may also be used as expressions. Arbitrary recursive procedures are permitted.

3.3 Type Correctness

Every variable in a CLU module must be declared; the declaration specifies the type of object that the variable may denote. All assignments to a variable must satisfy the variable's declaration. Because argument passing is defined in terms of assignment, the types of actual argument objects must be consistent with the declarations of the corresponding formal arguments.

These restrictions, plus the restriction that only the code in a cluster may use **cvt** to convert between the abstract and representation types, ensure that the behavior of an object is indeed characterized completely by the operations of its type. For example, the type restrictions ensure that the only modification possible to a record object that represents a *wordbag* (Figure 3) is the modification performed by the *insert* operation.

Type checking is performed on a module by module basis at compile time (it could also be done at run time). This checking can catch all type errors—even those involving intermodule references—because the CLU library maintains the necessary type information for all modules (see Section 5).

---

[6] An object is accessible if it is denoted by a variable of an active procedure or is a component of an accessible object.

4. More Abstraction Mechanisms

In this section we continue our discussion of abstraction mechanisms in CLU. A generalization of the *wordbag* abstraction, called *sorted_bag*, is presented as an illustration of parameterized clusters, which are a means for implementing more generally applicable data abstractions. The presentation of *sorted_bag* is also used to motivate the introduction of a control abstraction called an *iterator*, which is a mechanism for incrementally generating the elements of a collection of objects. Finally, we show an implementation of the *sorted_bag* abstraction and illustrate how *sorted_bag* can be used in implementing *count_words*.

4.1 Properties of the Sorted_bag Abstraction

In the *count_words* procedure given earlier, a data abstraction called *wordbag* was used. A *wordbag* object is a collection of strings, each with an associated count. Strings are inserted into a *wordbag* object one at a time. Strings in a *wordbag* object may be printed in alphabetical order, each with a count of the number of times it was inserted.

Although *wordbag* has properties that are specific to the usage in *count_words*, it also has properties in common with a more general abstraction, *sorted_bag*. A bag is similar to a set (it is sometimes called a multiset) except that an item can appear in a bag many times. For example, if the integer 1 is inserted in the set {1, 2}, the result is the set {1, 2}, but if 1 is inserted in the bag {1, 2}, the result is the bag {1, 1, 2}. A *sorted_bag* is a bag that affords access to the items it contains according to an ordering relation on the items.

The concept of a *sorted_bag* is meaningful not only for strings but for many types of items. Therefore we would like to parameterize the *sorted_bag* abstraction, the parameter being the type of item to be collected in the *sorted_bag* objects.

Most programming languages provide built-in parameterized data abstractions. For example, the concept of an array is a parameterized data abstraction. An example of a use of arrays in Pascal is

array 1..n **of integer**

These arrays have two parameters, one specifying the array bounds (1..n) and one specifying the type of element in the array (integer). In CLU we provide mechanisms allowing user-defined data abstractions (like *sorted_bag*) to be parameterized.

In the *sorted_bag* abstraction, not all types of items make sense. Only types that define a total ordering on their objects are meaningful since the *sorted_bag* abstraction depends on the presence of this ordering. In addition, information about the ordering must be expressed in a way that is useful for programming. A natural way to express this information is by means of operations of the item type. Therefore we require that the item type provide less than and equal operations

(called *lt* and *equal*). This constraint is expressed in the header for *sorted_bag*:

sorted_bag = **cluster** [t: **type**] **is** create, insert, . . .
    where t **has**
        lt, equal: **proctype** (t, t) **returns** (**bool**);

The item type *t* is a *formal parameter* of the *sorted_bag* cluster; whenever the *sorted_bag* abstraction is used, the item type must be specified as an *actual parameter*, e.g.

sorted_bag[**string**]

The information about required operations informs the programmer about legitimate uses of *sorted_bag*. The compiler will check each use of *sorted_bag* to ensure that the item type provides the required operations. The **where** clause specifies exactly the information that the compiler can check. Of course, more is assumed about the item type *t* than the presence of operations with appropriate names and functionalities: these operations must also define a total ordering on the items. Although we expect formal and complete specifications for data abstractions to be included in the CLU library eventually, we do not include in the CLU language declarations that the compiler cannot check. This point is discussed further in Section 7.

Now that we have decided to define a *sorted_bag* abstraction that works for many item types, we must decide what operations this abstraction provides. When an abstraction (like *wordbag*) is written for a very specific purpose, it is reasonable to have some specialized operations. For a more general abstraction, the operations should be more generally useful.

The *print* operation is a case in point. Printing is only one possible use of the information contained in a *sorted_bag*. It was the only use in the case of *wordbag*, so it was reasonable to have a *print* operation. However, if *sorted_bags* are to be generally useful, there should be some way for the user to obtain the elements of the *sorted_bag*; the user can then perform some action on the elements (for example, print them).

What we would like is an operation on *sorted_bags* that makes all of the elements available to the caller in increasing order. One possible approach is to map the elements of a *sorted_bag* into a sequence object, a solution potentially requiring a large amount of space. A more efficient method is provided by CLU and is discussed below. This solution computes the sequence one element at a time, thus saving space. If only part of the sequence is used (as in a search for some element), then execution time can be saved as well.

4.2 Control Abstractions

The purpose of many loops is to perform an action on some or all of the objects in a collection. For such loops, it is often useful to separate the selection of the next object from the action performed on that object.

Fig. 5. Use and definition of a simple iterator.

```
count_numeric = proc (s: string) returns (int);
  count: int := 0;
  for c: char in string_chars (s) do
    if char_is_numeric (c)
      then count := count + 1;
      end;
    end;
  return (count);
  end count_numeric;
string_chars = iter (s: string) yields (char);
  index: int := 1;
  limit: int := string$size (s);
  while index < = limit do
    yield (string$fetch (s, index));
    index := index + 1;
    end;
  end string_chars;
```

CLU provides a control abstraction that permits a complete decomposition of the two activities. The **for** statement available in many programming languages provides a limited ability in this direction: it iterates over ranges of integers. The CLU **for** statement can iterate over collections of any type of object. The selection of the next object in the collection is done by a user-defined *iterator*. The iterator produces the objects in the collection one at a time (the entire collection need not physically exist); each object is consumed by the **for** statement in turn.

Figure 5 gives an example of a simple iterator called *string_chars*, which produces the characters in a string in the order in which they appear. This iterator uses string operations *size(s)*, which tells how many characters are in the string *s*, and *fetch (s, n)*, which returns the *n*th character in the string *s* (provided the integer *n* is greater than zero and does not exceed the size of the string).[7]

The general form of the CLU **for** statement is

for declarations **in** iterator_invocation **do**
  body
  end;

An example of the use of the **for** statement occurs in the *count_numeric* procedure (see Figure 5), which contains a loop that counts the number of numeric characters in a string. Note that the details of how the characters are obtained from the string are entirely contained in the definition of the iterator.

Iterators work as follows: A **for** statement initially invokes an iterator, passing it some arguments. Each time a **yield** statement is executed in the iterator, the objects yielded[8] are assigned to the variables declared in the **for** statement (following the reserved word **for**)

---

[7] A **while** loop is used in the implementation of *string_chars* so that the example will be based on familiar concepts. In actual practice, such a loop would be written by using a **for** statement invoking a primitive iterator.

[8] Zero or more objects may be yielded, but the number and types of objects yielded each time by an iterator must agree with the number and types of variables in a **for** statement using the iterator.

in corresponding order, and the body of the **for** statement is executed. Then the iterator is resumed at the statement following the **yield** statement, in the same environment as when the objects were yielded. When the iterator terminates, by either an implicit or explicit **return**, the invoking **for** statement terminates. The iteration may also be prematurely terminated by a **return** in the body of the **for** statement.

For example, suppose that *string_chars* is invoked with the string "a3". The first character yielded is 'a'. At this point, within *string_chars*, *index* = 1 and *limit* = 2. Next the body of the **for** statement is performed. Since the character 'a' is not numeric, *count* remains at 0. Next *string_chars* is resumed at the statement after the **yield** statement, and when resumed, *index* = 1 and *limit* = 2. Then *index* is assigned 2, and the character '3' is selected from the string and yielded. Since '3' is numeric, *count* becomes 1. Then *string_chars* is resumed, with *index* = 2 and *limit* = 2, and *index* is incremented, which causes the **while** loop to terminate. The implicit **return** terminates both the iterator and the **for** statement, with control resuming at the statement after the **for** statement, and *count* = 1.

While iterators are useful in general, they are especially valuable in conjunction with data abstractions that are collections of objects (such as sets, arrays, and *sorted_bags*). Iterators afford users of such abstractions access to all objects in the collection without exposing irrelevant details. Several iterators may be included in a data abstraction. When the order of obtaining the objects is important, different iterators may provide different orders.

4.3 Implementation and Use of Sorted_bag

Now we can describe a minimal set of operations for *sorted_bag*. The operations are *create*, *insert*, *size*, and *increasing*. *Create*, *insert*, and *size* are procedural abstractions that, respectively, create a *sorted_bag*, insert an item into a *sorted_bag*, and give the number of items in a *sorted_bag*. *Increasing* is a control abstraction that produces the items in a *sorted_bag* in increasing order; each item produced is accompanied by an integer representing the number of times the item appears in the *sorted_bag*. Note that other operations might also be useful for *sorted_bag*, for example, an iterator yielding the items in decreasing order. In general, the definer of a data abstraction can provide as many operations as seems reasonable.

In Figure 6, we give an implementation of the *sorted_bag* abstraction. It is implemented by using a sorted binary tree, just as *wordbag* was implemented. Thus a subsidiary abstraction is necessary. This abstraction, called *tree*, is a generalization of the *wordtree* abstraction (used in Section 2), which has been parameterized to work for all ordered types. An implementation of *tree* is given in Figure 7. Notice that both the *tree* abstraction and the *sorted_bag* abstraction place the same constraints on their type parameters.

Fig. 6. The *sorted_bag* cluster.

```
sorted_bag = cluster [t: type] is create, insert, size, increasing
    where t has equal, lt: proctype (t, t) returns (bool);
    rep = record [contents: tree[t], total: int];
create = proc ( ) returns (cvt);
    return (rep${contents: tree[t]$create ( ), total: 0});
    end create;
insert = proc (sb: cvt, v: t);
    sb.contents := tree[t]$insert (sb.contents, v);
    sb.total := sb.total + 1;
    end insert;
size = proc (sb: cvt) returns (int);
    return (sb.total);
    end size;
increasing = iter (sb: cvt) yields (t, int);
    for item: t, count: int
        in tree[t]$increasing (sb.contents) do
            yield (item, count);
            end;
        end increasing;
    end sorted_bag;
```

Fig. 7. The *tree* cluster.

```
tree = cluster [t: type] is create, insert, increasing
    where t has equal, lt: proctype (t, t) returns (bool);
    node = record [value: t, count: int,
                        lesser: tree[t], greater: tree[t]];
    rep = oneof [empty: null, non_empty: node];
create = proc ( ) returns (cvt);
    return (rep$make_empty (nil));
    end create;
insert = proc (x: cvt, v: t) returns (cvt);
    tagcase x
        tag empty:
            n: node := node${value: v, count: 1,
                                lesser: tree[t]$create ( ),
                                greater: tree[t]$create ( )};
            return (rep$make_non_empty (n));
        tag non_empty (n: node):
            if t$equal (v, n.value)
                    then n.count := n.count + 1;
                elseif t$lt (v, n.value)
                    then n.lesser := tree[t]$insert (n.lesser, v);
                else n.greater := tree[t]$insert (n.greater, v);
                end;
            return (x);
        end;
    end insert;
increasing = iter (x: cvt) yields (t, int);
    tagcase x
        tag empty: ;
        tag non_empty (n: node):
            for item: t, count: int
                in tree[t]$increasing (n.lesser) do
                    yield (item, count);
                    end;
            yield (n.value, n.count);
            for item: t, count: int
                in tree[t]$increasing (n.greater) do
                    yield (item, count);
                    end;
        end;
    end increasing;
end tree;
```

An important feature of the *sorted_bag* and *tree* clusters is the way that the cluster parameter is used in places where the type **string** was used in *wordbag* and *wordtree*. This usage is especially evident in the implementation of *tree*. For example, *tree* has a representation that stores values of type t: the *value* component of a *node* must be an object of type t.

In the *insert* operation of *tree*, the *lt* and *equal* operations of type t are used. We have used the compound form, e.g. $t\$equal$ $(v, n.value)$, to emphasize that the *equal* operation of t is being used. The short form, $v = n.value$, could have been used instead.

The *increasing* iterator of *tree* works as follows: first it yields all items in the current tree that are less than the item at the top node; the items are obtained by a recursive use of itself, passing the *lesser* subtree as an argument. Next it yields the contents of the top node, and then it yields all items in the current tree that are greater than the item at the top node (again by a recursive use of itself). In this way it performs a complete walk over the tree, yielding the values at all nodes, in increasing order.

Finally, we show in Figure 8 how the original procedure *count_words* can be implemented in terms of *sorted_bag*. Note that the *count_words* procedure now uses *sorted_bag* [**string**] instead of *wordbag*. *Sorted_bag* [**string**] is legitimate since the type **string** provides both *lt* and *equal* operations. Note that two **for** statements are used in *count_words*. The second **for** statement prints the words in alphabetic order, using the *increasing* iterator of *sorted_bag*. The first **for** statement inserts the words into the *sorted_bag*; it uses an iterator

```
words = iter (i: instream) yields (string);
            . . .
        end words;
```

The definition of *words* is left as an exercise for the reader.

5. The CLU Library

So far, we have shown CLU modules as separate pieces of text, without explaining how they are bound together to form a program. This section describes the CLU library, which plays a central role in supporting intermodule references.

The CLU library contains information about abstractions. The library supports incremental program development, one abstraction at a time, and, in addition, makes abstractions that are defined during the construction of one program available as a basis for subsequent program development. The information in the library permits the separate compilation of single modules with complete type checking of all external references (such as procedure invocations).

The structure of the library derives from the fundamental distinction between abstractions and implementations. For each abstraction, there is a *description unit* which contains all system-maintained information about that abstraction. Included in the description unit are zero or more modules that implement the abstraction.[9]

The most important information contained in a description unit is the abstraction's *interface specification*, which is that information needed to type-check uses of the abstraction. For procedural and control abstractions, this information consists of the number and types of parameters, arguments, and output values, plus any constraints on type parameters (i.e. required operations, as described in Section 4). For data abstractions, it includes the number and types of parameters, constraints on type parameters, and the name and interface specification of each operation.

An abstraction is entered in the library by submitting the interface specification; no implementations are required. In fact, a module can be compiled before any implementations have been provided for the abstractions that it uses; it is necessary only that interface specifications have been given for those abstractions. Ultimately, there can be many implementations of an abstraction; each implementation is required to satisfy the interface specification of the abstraction. Because all uses and implementations of an abstraction are checked against the interface specification, the actual selection of an implementation can be delayed until just before (or perhaps during) execution. We imagine a process of binding together modules into programs, prior to execution, at which time this selection would be made.

An important detail of the CLU system is the method by which CLU modules refer to abstractions. To avoid problems of name conflicts that can arise in large systems, the names used by a module to refer to abstractions can be chosen to suit the programmer's convenience. When a module is submitted for compilation, its external references must be bound to description units so that type checking can be performed. The binding is accomplished by constructing an *association list*, mapping names to description units, which is passed to the compiler along with the source code when compiling the module. The mapping in the association list is stored by the compiler in the library as part of the module. A similar process is involved in entering interface specifications of abstractions, as these will include references to other (data) abstractions.

When the compiler type-checks a module, it uses the association list to map the external names in the module to description units and then uses the interface specifications in those description units to check that the abstractions are used correctly. The type correctness of the module thus depends upon the binding of

---

[9] Other information that may be stored in the library includes information about relationships among abstractions, as might be expressed in a module interconnection language [5, 21].

Fig. 8. The *count_words* procedure using iterators.

```
count_words = proc (i: instream, o: outstream);
  wordbag = sorted_bag[string];
  % create an empty wordbag
  wb: wordbag := wordbag$create ( );
  % scan document, adding each word found to wb
  for word: string in words (i) do
    wordbag$insert (wb, word);
    end;
  % print the wordbag
  total: int := wordbag$size (wb);
  for w: string, count: int in wordbag$increasing (wb) do
    print_word (w, count, total, o);
    end;
  end count_words;
```

names to description units and the interface specifications in those description units, and could be invalidated if changes to the binding or the interface specifications were subsequently made. For this reason, the process of compilation permanently binds a module to the abstractions it uses, and the interface description of an abstraction, once defined, is not allowed to change. (Of course, a new description unit can be created to describe a modified abstraction.)

6. Implementation

This section briefly describes the current implementation of CLU and discusses its efficiency.

The implementation is based on a decision to represent all CLU objects by *object descriptors*, which are fixed-size values containing a type code and some type-dependent information.[10] In the case of mutable types, the type-dependent information is a pointer to a separately allocated area containing the state information. For constant types, the information either directly contains the value (if the value can be encoded in the information field, as for integers, characters, and booleans) or contains a pointer to separately allocated space (as for strings). The type codes are used by the garbage collector to determine the physical representation of objects so that the accessible objects can be traced; they are also useful for supporting program debugging.

The use of fixed-size object descriptors allows variables to be fixed-size cells. Assignment is efficient: the object descriptor resulting from the evaluation of the expression is simply copied into the variable. In addition, a single size for variables facilitates the separate compilation of modules and allows most of the code of a parameterized module to be shared among all instantiations of the module. The actual parameters are made available to this code by means of a small parameter-dependent section, which is initialized prior to execution.

---

[10] Object descriptors are similar to capabilities [11].

Procedure invocation is relatively efficient. A single program stack is used, and argument passing is as efficient as assignment. Iterators are a form of coroutine; however, their use is sufficiently constrained that they are implemented using just the program stack. Using an iterator is therefore only slightly more expensive than using a procedure.

The data abstraction mechanism is not inherently expensive. No execution-time type checking is necessary. Furthermore, the type conversion implied by **cvt** is merely a change in the view taken of an object's type and does not require any computation.

A number of optimization techniques can be applied to a collection of modules if one is willing to give up the flexibility of separate compilation. The most effective such optimization is the inline substitution of procedure (and iterator) bodies for invocations [18]. The use of data abstractions tends to introduce extra levels of procedure invocations that perform little or no computation. As an example, consider the *word-bag$insert* operation (Figure 3), which merely invokes the *wordtree$insert* operation and increments a counter. If data abstractions had not been used, these actions would most likely have been performed directly by the *count_words* procedure. The *wordbag$insert* operation is thus a good candidate for being compiled inline. Once inline substitution has been performed, the increase in context will enhance the effectiveness of conventional optimization techniques [1–3].

7. Discussion

Our intent in this paper has been to provide an informal introduction to the abstraction mechanisms in CLU. By means of programming examples, we have illustrated the use of data, procedural, and control abstractions and have shown how CLU modules are used to implement these abstractions. We have not attempted to provide a complete description of CLU, but, in the course of explaining the examples, most features of the language have appeared. One important omission is the CLU exception handling mechanism (which does support abstractions); this mechanism is described in [10].

In addition to describing constructs that support abstraction, previous sections have covered a number of other topics. We have discussed the semantics of CLU. We have described the organization of the CLU library and discussed how it supports incremental program development and separate compilation and type checking of modules. Also we have described our current implementation and discussed its efficiency.

In designing CLU, our goal was to simplify the task of constructing reliable software that is reasonably easy to understand, modify, and maintain. It seems appropriate, therefore, to conclude this paper with a discussion of how CLU contributes to this goal.

The quality of any program depends upon the skill of the designer. In CLU programs, this skill is reflected in the choice of abstractions. In a good design, abstractions will be used to simplify the connections between modules and to encapsulate decisions that are likely to change [17]. Data abstractions are particularly valuable for these purposes. For example, through the use of a data abstraction, modules that share a system database rely only on its abstract behavior as defined by the database operations. The connections among these modules are much simpler than would be possible if they shared knowledge of the format of the database and the relationship among its parts. In addition, the database abstraction can be reimplemented without affecting the code of the modules that use it. CLU encourages the use of data abstractions and thus aids the programmer during program design.

The benefits arising from the use of data abstractions are based on the constraint, inherent in CLU and enforced by the CLU compiler, that only the operations of the abstraction may access the representations of the objects. This constraint ensures that the distinction made in CLU between abstractions and implementations applies to data abstractions as well as to procedural and control abstractions.

The distinction between abstractions and implementations eases program modification and maintenance. Once it has been determined that an abstraction must be reimplemented, CLU guarantees that the code of all modules using that abstraction will be unaffected by the change. The modules need not be reprogrammed or even recompiled; only the process of selecting the implementation of the abstraction must be redone. The problem of determining what modules must be changed is also simplified because each module has a well-defined purpose—to implement an abstraction—and no other module can interfere with that purpose.

Understanding and verification of CLU programs is made easier because the distinction between abstractions and implementations permits this task to be decomposed. One module at a time is studied to determine that it implements its abstraction. This study requires understanding the behavior of the abstractions it uses, but it is not necessary to understand the modules implementing those abstractions. Those modules can be studied separately.

A promising way to establish the correctness of a program is by means of a mathematical proof. For practical reasons, proofs should be performed (or at least checked) by a verification system, since the process of constructing a proof is tedious and error-prone. Decomposition of the proof is essential for program proving, which is practical only for small programs (like CLU modules). Note that when the CLU compiler does type checking, it is, in addition to enforcing the constraint that permits the proof to be decomposed, also performing a small part of the actual proof.

We have included as declarations in CLU just the information that the compiler can check with reasonable efficiency. We believe that the other information required for proofs (specifications and assertions) should be expressed in a separate "specification" language. The properties of such a language are being studied [7, 13, 14, 19]. We intend eventually to add formal specifications to the CLU system; the library is already organized to accommodate this addition. At that time various specification language processors could be added to the system.

We believe that the constraints imposed by CLU are essential for practical as well as theoretical reasons. It is true that data abstractions can be used in any language by establishing programming conventions to protect the representations of objects. However, conventions are no substitute for enforced constraints. It is inevitable that the conventions will be violated—and are likely to be violated just when they are needed most, in implementing, maintaining, and modifying large programs. It is precisely at this time, when the programming task becomes very difficult, that a language like CLU will be most valuable and appreciated.

Acknowledgments. The authors gratefully acknowledge the contributions made by members of the CLU design group over the last three years. Several people have made helpful comments about this paper, including Toby Bloom, Dorothy Curtis, Mike Hammer, Eliot Moss, Jerry Saltzer, Bob Scheifler, and the referees.

References

1. Allen, F.E., and Cocke, J. A catalogue of optimizing transformations. Rep. RC 3548. IBM Thomas J. Watson Res. Ctr., Yorktown Heights, N.Y., 1971.
2. Allen, F.E. A program data flow analysis procedure. Rep. RC 5278, IBM Thomas J. Watson Res. Ctr., Yorktown Heights, N.Y., 1975.
3. Atkinson, R.R. Optimization techniques for a structured programming language. S.M. Th., Dept. of Electr. Eng. and Comptr. Sci., M.I.T., Cambridge, Mass., June 1976.
4. Dahl, O.J., Myhrhaug, B., and Nygaard, K. The SIMULA 67 common base language. Pub. S-22, Norwegian Comptng. Ctr., Oslo, 1970.
5. DeRemer, F., and Kron, H. Programming-in-the-large versus programming-in-the-small. Proc. Int. Conf. on Reliable Software, SIGPLAN Notices 10, 6 (June 1975), 114–121.
6. Dijkstra, E.W. Notes on structured programming. *Structured Programming, A.P.I.C. Studies in Data Processing No. 8*, Academic Press, New York, 1972, pp. 1–81.
7. Guttag, J.V., Horowitz, E., and Musser, D.R. Abstract data types and software validation. Rep ISI/RR-76-48, Inform. Sci. Inst., U. of Southern California, Marina del Rey, Calif., Aug. 1976.
8. Hoare, C.A.R. Proof of correctness of data representations. *Acta Informatica 4* (1972), 271–281.
9. Knuth, D. *The Art of Computer Programming*, Vol. 3: *Sorting and Searching*. Addison Wesley, Reading, Mass., 1973.
10. Laboratory for Computer Science Progress Report 1974–1975. Comput. Structures Group. Rep. PR-XII, Lab. for Comptr. Sci., M.I.T. To be published.
11. Lampson, B.W. Protection. Proc. Fifth Annual Princeton Conf. on Inform. Sci. and Syst., Princeton U., Princeton, N.J., 1971, pp. 437–443.
12. Liskov, B.H., and Zilles, S.N. Programming with abstract data types. Proc. ACM SIGPLAN Conf. on Very High Level Languages, SIGPLAN Notices 9, 4 (April 1974), 50–59.
13. Liskov, B.H., and Zilles, S.N. Specification techniques for data abstractions. *IEEE Trans. Software Eng., SE-1* (1975), 7–19.
14. Liskov, B.H., and Berzins, V. An appraisal of program specifications. Comput. Structures Group Memo 141, Lab. for Comptr. Sci., M.I.T., Cambridge, Mass., July 1976.
15. McCarthy, J., et al. *LISP 1.5 Programmer's Manual*. M.I.T. Press, Cambridge, Mass., 1962.
16. Morris, J.H. Protection in programming languages. *Comm. ACM 16*, 1 (Jan. 1973), 15–21.
17. Parnas, D.L. Information distribution aspects of design methodology. Information Processing 71, Vol. 1, North-Holland Pub. Co., Amsterdam, 1972, pp. 339–344.
18. Scheifler, R.W. An analysis of inline substitution for the CLU programming language. Comput. Structures Group Memo 139, Lab. for Comptr. Sci., M.I.T., Cambridge, Mass., June 1976.
19. Spitzen, J., and Wegbreit, B. The verification and synthesis of data structures. *Acta Informatica 4* (1975), 127–144.
20. Standish, T.A. Data structures: an axiomatic approach. Rep. 2639, Bolt, Beranek and Newman, Cambridge, Mass., 1973.
21. Thomas, J.W. Module interconnection in programming systems supporting abstraction. Rep. CS-16, Comptr. Sci. Prog., Brown U., Providence, R.I., 1976.
22. Wirth, N. Program development by stepwise refinement. *Comm. ACM 14*, 4 (1971), 221–227.
23. Wirth, N. The programming language PASCAL. *Acta Informatica 1* (1971), 35–63.
24. Wulf, W.A., London, R., and Shaw, M. An introduction to the construction and verification of Alphard programs. *IEEE Trans. Software Eng. SE-2* (1976), 253–264.

EXCEPTION HANDLING IN CLU*

B. LISKOV AND A. SNYDER

Abstract—For programs to be reliable and fault tolerant, each program module must be defined to behave reasonably under a wide variety of circumstances. An exception handling mechanism supports the construction of such modules. This paper describes an exception handling mechanism developed as part of the CLU programming language. The CLU mechanism is based on a simple model of exception handling that leads to well-structured programs. It is engineered for ease of use and enhanced program readability. This paper discusses the various models of exception handling, the syntax and semantics of the CLU mechanism, and methods of implementing the mechanism and integrating it in debugging and production environments.

Index Terms—Exception handling, exit mechanisms, procedural abstractions, programming languages, structured programming.

I. INTRODUCTION

RECENTLY, there has been considerable emphasis on the development of programming language features that enhance the verifiability of programs [5]. While it is desirable that the task of developing correct programs be simplified as much as possible, another important goal of program construction is that programs behave "reasonably" under a wide range of circumstances. Such programs have been variously termed as reliable, robust, or fault tolerant.

In a reliable program, each procedure must be designed to behave as generally as possible. Its specifications should require a well-defined response to all possible combinations of legal inputs (inputs satisfying the type constraints), even when lower level modules on which this procedure is depending fail. Of course, different responses will be appropriate in the different cases. Note that even if the software has been verified, the possibility of hardware failure implies that software modules may fail, as does the presence of resource constraints.

This paper describes a linguistic mechanism that supports the construction of reliable software. The mechanism, called an *exception handling mechanism*, facilitates communication of certain information among procedures at different levels. The mechanism supports the view that different responses are appropriate in different situations. We assume that for each procedure there is a set of circumstances in which it will terminate "normally"; in general, this happens when the input arguments satisfy certain constraints and the lower level modules (implemented in both hardware and software) on which the procedure depends are all working properly. In other circumstances, the procedure is unable to perform any action that would lead to normal termination, but instead must notify some other procedure (for example, the invoking

Manuscript received March 8, 1979; revised June 25, 1979. This work was supported in part by the Advance Research Projects Agency of the Department of Defense, monitored by the Office of Naval Research under Contract N00014-75-C-0661, and in part by the National Science Foundation under Grants DCR74-21892 and MCS 74-21892.

B. H. Liskov is with the Laboratory for Computer Science, Massachusetts Institute of Technology, Cambridge, MA 02139.

A. Snyder is with the Hewlett-Packard Corporation, Palo Alto, CA 94304.

*Reprinted from *IEEE Transactions on Software Engineering*, Nov. 1979, 546–558.

procedure) that an *exceptional condition* (or *exception*) has occurred.

For example, suppose *search* is a procedure that retrieves information associated with a given identifier in a symbol table. *Search* can return this information only if the identifier is present in the symbol table. The absence of the identifier constitutes an exceptional condition. Other exceptional conditions might also occur, for example, if the symbol table is implemented using a stack and the module implementing stacks is not working properly.

In referring to the condition as exceptions rather than errors we are following Goodenough [2]. The term "exception" is chosen because, unlike the term "error," it does not imply that anything is wrong; this connotation is appropriate because an event that is viewed as an error by one procedure may not be viewed that way by another. In fact, the term "exception" indicates that something unusual has occurred, and even this may be misleading: if the exception handling mechanism were efficient enough, exceptions might be used to convey information about normal and usual situations. For example, the *search* procedure might terminate normally only if the identifier were a local variable of the current block and use the exception handling mechanism to convey extra information about nonlocal variables.

Exception handling mechanisms have been largely ignored in programming languages. For a discussion of existing mechanisms, the reader is referred to [2] and [3]. In our opinion, the existing mechanisms are overly powerful and ill-structured. For example, in the on-condition mechanism of PL/I, on-units are associated with invocations dynamically rather than statically, and global variables must be used to communicate data between the procedure performing the **signal** and the on-unit. Goodenough [2] proposes a new mechanism that is more constrained and better structured. The mechanism presented in this paper is still more constrained. We also believe it to be more conducive to the development of well-structured programs.

The mechanism we describe facilitates communication of information that can be used to recover from faults such as erroneous data and failures of lower level modules. We do not discuss the methods, e.g., redundancy, that are used for fault detection and recovery. Mechanisms that are designed to facilitate fault detection and recovery, e.g., recovery blocks [8], are complementary to ours, as was noted in [7].

The mechanism we describe has been defined as part of the CLU programming language [4]. The mechanism is of general interest because it is constrained and simple. Its design was based on a tradeoff between simplicity and expressive power; major design goals were ease of use and program readability. The mechanism was designed for a sequential language (without coroutines or parallel processes). Otherwise, however, the mechanism is not dependent on CLU semantics, and could be incorporated in any procedure oriented language.

In the next section we discuss the main decisions that must be made in designing an exception handling mechanism and the exception handling models that result from these decisions; we also discuss our decisions and our reasons for making them. In Section III we describe the syntax and semantics of the

CLU exception handling mechanism. In Section IV we discuss some methods of implementing the mechanism and also how the mechanism can enhance programmer effectiveness in a debugging and a production environment. In Section V, we discuss the expressive power of our mechanism and compare it with some other mechanisms of greater power. Finally, in Section VI we summarize and evaluate what we have done.

II. THE MODEL

To discuss exception handling we must first introduce some terminology about programs. The term *procedure* will be used to mean program text, either in a higher level language or in machine language. A procedure implements a *procedural abstraction*, which is a mapping from a set of argument objects to a set of result objects, possibly modifying some of the argument objects. A procedure may be *invoked* (or called) by an *invocation*, which is textually part of some procedure; that procedure is referred to as the *caller*. Invocation results in *activation* of the invoked procedure. An activation may *signal* an exception; the invocation that caused the activation *raises* that exception. The program text intended to be executed when an exception is raised is called the *handler*.

Our model of exception handling involves the communication of information from the procedure activation that detects an exceptional condition (the *signaler*) to some other procedure activation that is prepared to handle an occurrence of that condition (the *catcher*). In designing this model, we faced two major questions: 1) which procedure activations may catch an exception signaled by a procedure activation and 2) does the signaler continue to exist after signaling. These two questions are independent and may be addressed separately.

A. Single Versus Multilevel Mechanisms

The obvious candidates[1] for handling an exception signaled by some procedure activation are the activations in existence at the time the signal occurs. We can rule out the signaler itself, as exceptions are, by definition, conditions that the signaling procedure is unable to handle. The remaining question is whether to allow activations other than the immediate caller of the signaler to handle the exception.

Our answer to this question is based on the hierarchical program design methodology that CLU is intended to support [4]. As was explained above, each procedure implements a mapping. The caller of a procedure invokes the procedure to have the mapping performed; the caller need know only what the mapping is, and not how the procedure implements the mapping. Thus, while it is appropriate for the caller to know about the exceptions signaled by the procedure (and these are part of the abstraction implemented by that procedure), the caller should know nothing about the exceptions signaled by procedures used in the implementation of the invoked procedure.

The above considerations lead us to allow only the immediate caller of a procedure to handle exceptions signaled

---

[1]Levin [3] proposes an additional set of candidates. We will discuss Levin's work in Section V.

by that procedure. Of course, the handler in the caller can it-self signal an exception, but that exception will then be part of the caller's abstraction.

We believe that the decision to limit handling of exceptions to the immediate caller is necessary for any well-structured exception handling mechanism. To maintain intellectual manage-ability of software, program structures that support under-standing and verification through local code examination are needed. In particular, to understand how a procedure is im-plemented, one should not have to examine implementations of any other procedures. An understanding of the mappings performed by invoked procedures is needed, but this under-standing should be obtained by reading specifications of those procedures and not their code. This requirement implies that specifications must describe all exceptions arising from invok-ing a procedure, including information about exceptions arising from procedures called at a lower level if the mechanism does not limit the handling of these exceptions. The point is that all exceptions that may be raised by a procedure, whether explicitly or implicitly, must be considered part of that pro-cedural abstraction. Limiting the handling of exceptions to just the caller simply ensures that the linguistic constructs match the proper conceptual view. Note, however, that this constraint does *not* prevent the language designer from pro-viding simplified ways of passing exceptions from one level to the next where appropriate.

The exception handling mechanism proposed by Good-enough [2] does impose our constraint on handling excep-tions. The PL/I mechanism does not, nor does the mechanism in Mesa [6].

B. Resumption Versus Termination Model

The second question, whether the signaler should continue to exist after the exception is signaled, involves a tradeoff be-tween expressive power and the complexity of the semantics. If the signaler can continue to exist after signaling, then it is possible that a catcher may fix up the exceptional condition so that processing of the signaler may be resumed. For this reason, we refer to this model as the *resumption model*. The model in which the signaling activation ceases to exist we refer to as the *termination model*. In this section we assume that the decision to support a one-level mechanism has been made, and we therefore limit our analysis to this case.

A one-level resumption model works as follows. Suppose that there are three procedures P, Q, and R, and that P in-vokes Q and Q invokes R. If R signals an exception r, then Q must handle it. Let H_r denote the statements in Q that handle r (H_r is the handler for r). In the course of handling r, H_r may signal an exception q, which must be handled by P (since P is the caller of Q).[2] Let H_q denote the statements in P that handle q (H_q is the handler for q). When H_q terminates, then

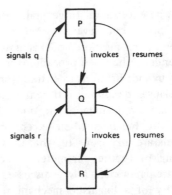

Fig. 1. Flow of control in the resumption model.

Q is resumed in the middle of H_r; only when H_r terminates is the execution of R continued. This situation is illustrated in Fig. 1. Note that information about signals flows upward one level at a time, while resumption flows downward one level at a time; multilevel flow is not permitted in either direction.

The resumption model is most easily understood by viewing the handler as an implicit procedure parameter of the signaler. The handler is called by the signaler when the exception it handles is signaled. The handler procedure is declared in the calling procedure, and its free variables get their meaning in the caller's environment, as do any exceptions it signals.[3]

In the termination model, occurrence of an exception causes the signaler to terminate. However, different kinds of be-havior are expected of the called procedure under different conditions. The view taken is that a procedure may terminate in one of a number of conditions. One of these is the *normal condition*, while others are *exception conditions*. In each con-dition, it may be convenient to return a number of result ob-jects; these will differ in number and type in the different conditions.

The resumption model is more complex than the termina-tion model. This can be appreciated by considering how re-sumption affects the interrelationships among procedures, specifications of procedures, and linguistic mechanisms for exception handling.

The ordinary view of procedures is that, in the absence of recursion, the calling procedure is dependent on the called procedure but not vice versa. This view is upheld in the termination model. However, in the resumption model, the signaler and caller are mutually dependent: the caller invokes the signaler to perform some mapping, or satisfy some input/output relation, but the signaler depends on (the handler in) the caller to satisfy a similar relation when an exception is signaled.

Specifications of procedural abstractions in the termination model consist of a number of clauses, one specifying the be-havior for the normal case and one for each exception case. Such clauses also exist in the resumption model, since it is still possible that the signaler is unable to terminate normally, for example, because a handler is unable to clear up the prob-

---

[2] If dynamic binding for exception names is used (as in PL/I), then R would be required to handle q. Making this assumption leads to a model at least as complex as the one we are considering. Furthermore, it is impossible under this assumption for H_r to raise exception in P without resorting to a multilevel mechanism.

[3] That is, exception names have static scope.

lem that led to the exception. In general, specifications have a termination model form (several termination states are defined) even when the resumption model is in use.

The interdependence between procedures in the resumption model show up in specifications as extra information. In addition to the clauses describing different termination states, it is also necessary to include descriptions of the behavior expected from the handlers when exceptions are signaled. Such descriptions are analogous to what must be given for a procedure taking procedure parameters, since handlers are implicit procedure parameters, as was discussed earlier.

The complexity of a linguistic mechanism supporting resumption is illustrated by Goodenough's proposal [2], which is a carefully considered design of a complete mechanism. Goodenough's design recognizes that to be really useful, termination must be supported as well as resumption. Three types of signals are recognized, corresponding to cases where the signaler may not be resumed, must be resumed, or where resumption is optional. In case the caller does not resume a signaler that must or could be resumed, a special ability is provided to permit the signaler to clean up (i.e., restore some nonlocal variables to a consistent state) before its activation is terminated. In addition, a default mechanism is provided to permit the signaler to handle its own exception in case the caller does not.

The termination model requires a simpler linguistic mechanism for its support than does the resumption model. Since a signal terminates the signaler, there is no need for multiple kinds of signals. Also, special mechanisms for cleaning up are not needed (the signaler must always clean up before signaling).

Since the termination model is simpler, it is preferable to the resumption model, provided it supplies adequate expressive power. We conjecture that the expressive power is adequate: that situations handled awkwardly by the termination model and simply by the resumption model are not frequent. We will discuss this conjecture further in Section V. In the next section we discuss the design of an exception handling mechanism based on the termination model.

III. SYNTAX AND SEMANTICS OF THE CLU EXCEPTION MECHANISM

In Section II we explained the rationale for our major decisions.

1) The exceptions signaled by a procedure must be caught by the immediate caller.

2) Signaling an exception terminates the signaling procedure.

These two decisions lead to a single-level termination model of computation in which a procedure may terminate in one of a number of conditions. Thus, instead of a single return path, each procedure has several return paths. One of these is considered the normal path, while others are considered exceptional. In each case, result objects may be returned; the result objects may differ in number and type in the different cases.

An exception handling semantics that terminates execution of the signaling procedure could be incorporated in a programming language with no additional mechanism. The signaling procedure could simply return, passing back in addition to the real result objects a tag that identifies the reason for termination. Indeed, such a convention is often adopted as a way of dealing with exceptions in a language that has no exception handling mechanism. However, this approach has a major defect: every invocation must be followed by a conditional test to determine what the outcome was. This requirement leads to programs that are difficult to read, and probably inefficient as well, thus discouraging programmers from signaling and handling exceptions.

To aid programmers in building reliable software, an exception handling mechanism must be devised that can be implemented efficiently and that enhances program readability. In the remainder of this section we describe the CLU exception handling mechanism, which was developed to satisfy these goals. The discussion identifies some problems that arise in designing any such mechanism; the CLU mechanism provides a possible set of solutions to these problems.

A. Signaling

To provide a convenient method of signaling information about exceptions, we included directly in CLU the model of a procedure having many kinds of returns. A CLU procedure, therefore, can terminate in the normal way by returning and can terminate in an exceptional condition by signaling. In each case, result objects, differing in number and type, can be returned.

The information about the ways in which a procedure may terminate must be included in its heading. For example, the procedure performing integer division has the following heading:

div = **proc** (x, y: int) **returns** (int) **signals** (zero_divide)

which indicates that *div* may terminate by returning a single integer (the quotient of the two input arguments) or by signaling *zero_divide* (which indicates that the second argument was zero) and returning no results.

A CLU procedure terminates its execution by performing a *return statement* or a *signal statement*. The return statement terminates execution normally, while the signal statement terminates execution in the named exceptional condition. For example, the following (fairly useless) procedure determines the sign of an integer:

```
sign = proc(x: int) returns (int) signals (zero, neg (int))
        if x < 0 then signal neg (x)
          elseif x = 0 then signal zero
          else return (x)
        end
      end sign
```

The information in the procedure heading is used to check that the exception names actually signaled are the correct ones and that the correct number and types of result objects are returned in both the normal and exceptional cases. This information is also used to determine that the exceptions handled by a calling procedure are named in the heading of the called procedure, and that, again, the number and types of result objects are correct in both the normal and exceptional cases.

B. Handling Exceptions

In CLU, exceptions arise only from invocations.[4] In particular, all uses of infix and prefix operators in CLU are considered to be "syntactic sugar" for invocations. For example, the expression

$x + y$

is syntactic sugar for the invocation

t$add (x, y)

where t is the type of x. Thus, if x is an integer, $x + y$ is an invocation of the integer addition operation. This viewpoint permits exceptions arising from built-in operations and user-defined procedures to be treated uniformly.[5]

In this section we discuss how handlers are associated with invocations. For usability and program readability, it is necessary to permit considerable flexibility in the placement of handlers. For example, requiring that the text of a handler be attached to the invocation that raises the exception would lead to unreadable programs in which expressions were broken up with handlers. Furthermore, the control flow of a program is often affected by the occurrence of an exception (for example, an *end_of_file* exception will terminate a loop). Therefore, our mechanism was designed to permit placement of a handler where the programmer deemed convenient, out of the main flow when possible to enhance readability, and altering the control flow when this was desired.

Two major decisions determined the form of CLU exception handling statements.

1) Handlers are statically associated with invocations.

2) Handlers may be attached only to statements, not to expressions.

Static association means that the handler associated with a particular exception condition that may be raised by a particular invocation can be determined by static analysis of the program text. This decision not only enhances program readability, but makes possible a more efficient implementation of the exception handling mechanism.

The decision to attach handlers only to statements and not expressions was made to simplify the mechanism. When a handler attached to an expression terminates, unless an explicit return, signal, or exit (see Section III-C) is performed, it must provide a value to be used as the value of the expression. By allowing handlers to be attached only to statements, we avoid providing a mechanism for substituting new values for expressions. We believe that the need to substitute a value for an expression is not great. In any case, the effect of attaching handlers to expressions can be obtained by breaking up complex expressions into sequences of assignment statements.

Handlers are placed in CLU programs by means of the *except statement*, which has the form

statement **except** *handler list* **end**

This statement has the following interpretation: the *statement* raises all the exceptions raised by the invocations it textually contains, excluding those handled by embedded except statements. The *handler list* will handle some subset (possibly all) of these exceptions. The except statement as a whole raises all the exceptions of the *statement* that are not handled by the *handler list* plus any exceptions raised by the *handler list*. Thus, when an exception is raised by an invocation, control goes to the innermost handler that handles that exception and is part of an except statement containing the invocation in its *statement* part.

Each handler in the *handler list* names one or more exceptions to be handled, followed by a list of statements (called the *handler body*) describing what to do. Permitting several exceptions to be named in the same handler avoids code duplication when the exceptions are all handled in the same way.

Several different forms are available for handlers depending on whether the named exceptions have associated result objects and whether those objects are used in the handler body. To handle one or more exceptions with no associated objects, the exception names are simply listed. For example,

when underflow, zero_divide: *body*

will handle exceptions named *underflow* and *zero_divide*, neither of which has any associated result objects.

To handle exceptions with result objects that are to be used in the handler body, names must be associated with the objects. Again a list of exception names is given, but it is followed by declarations of local variables to name the result objects, for example,

when e1, e2 (s: string, i: int): *body*

The scope of the declarations is the handler body. All of the named exceptions must return objects of the types listed in the declaration, in the order stated. When the handler is executed, these objects are bound to the declared variables and the body is executed. (This binding is similar to the binding of actual arguments to formal arguments that occurs when procedures are invoked. However, a return or signal in the handler body, rather than terminating just the handler, will instead terminate the entire enclosing procedure.)

To handle exceptions with result objects when the objects are not used in the handler body, the list of exception names is followed by (*) as shown below:

when neg, underflow (*): *body*

There need be no agreement between the number and types of result objects associated with the exceptions in this form; for example, the *neg* exception had a single argument, while *underflow* had none. This form encourages a programming style in which a procedure returns all possibly useful information when signaling; if this information is not needed in the calling procedure, it can easily be ignored.

If the programmer wishes to handle all remaining exceptions without listing their names, one of the following two forms

---

[4]Except for the special exception *failure* (described in Section III-D), which may be signaled at any point by the underlying implementation of CLU.

[5]The viewpoint does *not* require that a built-in operation be implemented by a closed routine; in-line code is perfectly permissible and consistent.

can be used as the last handler in an except statement. The form

>   **others**: *body*

is used when information about exception names and result objects is not important. If information about the exception name is desired, the form

>   **others** (e_ name: string): *body*

may be used. Here the name of the exception is given to the handler body as a string.

The handler body may contain any legal CLU statement. If the handler body returns or signals, then the containing procedure will be terminated as discussed in Section III-A. The handler body may also be terminated by an exit (see next section) or because an invocation within it raises an exception that is not handled within the handler body. Otherwise, when the handler body is finished, the next statement following the except statement in the normal flow will be executed.

The example below illustrates the association of handlers with exceptions:

```
begin % start of inner block
    S1 except
        when zero: S2
        end
    . . .
    end % end of inner block
    except
        when zero: S3
        others: S4
        end
```

If *zero* is raised by an invocation in *S1*, it will be handled by *S2*, not *S3*. However, if *zero* is raised by an invocation in *S2*, it will be handled by *S3*. All other exceptions raised in *S1* and *S2* will be handled by *S4*.

C. Exits and the Placement of Handlers

Our intention in defining the except statement is to permit the programmer to position handlers as is convenient. There are two constraints on the placement of handlers.

1) The handler must be placed on the statement whose execution is to be terminated if the handler body terminates without returning or signaling.

2) Suppose that an exception named *e* is raised by two invocations, and we wish to handle the occurrences of *e* differently. We do not permit multiple handlers to be provided for *e* in a single except statement. (This rule holds even if the invocations raising *e* provide different numbers or types of result objects; we do not allow such information to be used in selecting a handler.) Therefore, the two handlers must be in two except statements, each situated such that only one of the invocations raising *e* is in its scope.

These two constraints may conflict. For example, suppose that within a statement, *S*, the procedure *sign*, mentioned earlier, is invoked at two different points. Suppose also that the programmer wishes to handle the *neg* exception signaled

```
begin  % beginning of S
    a := sign(x)
        except when neg(i: int):
                    S1
                    exit done
        end
    b := sign(y)
        except when neg(i: int):
                    S2
                    exit done
        end
    ...
    end  % end of S
        except when done:
            ...
        end
```

Fig. 2. Example illustrating use of the exit mechanism.

by *sign* in a different manner for each of the two invocations, but in each case wishes execution to then continue with the statement following *S*. The first constraint would require that both handlers be placed on *S*, so that the execution of *S* would be terminated when the exceptions are raised. However, the second constraint requires that at least one handler be placed within *S* to resolve the ambiguous association between the invocations and the handlers.

We resolve this conflict in CLU by the addition of an exit mechanism, similar to those proposed by Zahn [9] and Bochmann [1]. The handlers are placed near the invocations. They terminate by exiting to a handler attached to the statement *S*. For example, one could handle the *neg* exceptions as shown in Fig. 2.

The exit statement can be used anywhere within a CLU procedure; its use is not restricted to handler bodies. The exit statement is similar to the signal statement, except that while the signal statement signals the condition to the calling procedure activation, the exit statement directly raises the condition so that it can be handled in the same procedure activation. The exit statement can specify a number of result objects to be passed to the handler.

We chose to have separate mechanisms for exits and exceptions (rather than using the signal statement for both exits and exceptions) because the two mechanisms capture different programmer intentions and thus naturally have different restrictions on their use. The intent of an exit is a local transfer of control. Thus, we require that exits be handled in the same procedure activation where they are raised. Furthermore, we require that exits be handled by a when arm (not an others arm), and if there are result objects, these must be accepted as arguments by the handler. The justification for these requirements is that exit names and result objects (unlike exception names and result objects) are under the control of the programmer of the procedure, and therefore should be chosen to mean something within that procedure.

The exit mechanism meshes nicely with the exception handling mechanism. In fact, the signal statement can be viewed simply as terminating a procedure invocation and exiting to the appropriate handler in the caller.

D. Uncaught Exceptions

Now we address the question of what happens if a procedure provides no handler for an exception raised by some contained invocation. One possibility is to consider the procedure to be illegal; checking for unhandled exceptions can be performed at compile-time. This approach is taken by Goodenough [2].

We have taken another approach. We felt it was unrealistic to require the programmer to provide handlers in situations where no meaningful action can be taken. Such situations will occur when a used abstraction is not working properly. For example, consider the statement

```
if ~ stack$empty(s) then
        . . .
    x := stack$pop(s)
        . . .
    end
```

Here the programmer invokes the *pop* operation for stacks only when the stack is nonempty. Now suppose that nevertheless stack underflow occurs. This situation is unlikely to arise in a debugged or verified program (but see Section IV). If it does arise, it indicates that the stack abstraction is not behaving correctly. Often there is no appropriate action for this procedure to take other than to report the fact to its caller. Since almost every abstraction can potentially behave incorrectly or in a way not expected by its caller, procedures must always be prepared to handle such cases. However, the action taken is almost always the same, and to require explicit handling of such cases would load every procedure with uninteresting code.

To facilitate reporting of failures and to relieve the programmer of the burden of handling such errors, CLU has one language-defined exception, named *failure*. *Failure* has one associated result object, a string that may contain some information about the cause of the failure. Every procedure can potentially signal *failure*; therefore *failure* is implicitly an exception of every procedure and may not be listed in the procedure heading explicitly. *Failure* may be signaled explicitly, however, in the usual way:

signal failure ("reason is . . . ")

The most common way that *failure* is signaled, however, is by an uncaught exception being automatically turned into a *failure* exception. For example, procedure *nonzero*

```
nonzero = proc (x: int) returns (int)
        return (sign (x))
            except
                when neg(y: int): return (y)
                end
        end nonzero
```

does not catch exception *zero* signaled by *sign*. If this exception is signaled, the invocation of *nonzero* will be terminated with the exception

failure ("unhandled exception: zero")

The effect is equivalent to attaching a handler to the proce-

dure body, e.g.,

```
nonzero = · · ·
        · · ·
            except
                others(s: string): signal failure (
                    "unhandled exception: "|| s)
                end
        end nonzero
```

Here the symbol || is string concatenation.

A common case in which an exception will not be handled is when the unhandled exception is *failure*. Note that in this case it is the string argument of *failure* (rather than the string "failure") that is of interest. Therefore, this string is retained when *failure* is passed up to the next level. This effect is equivalent to attaching to the procedure body the handler

```
except
        when failure (s:  string): signal failure (s)
        end
```

Sometimes before signaling *failure* some cleaning up is needed. In this case, the others or when form is used explicitly, and after cleaning up, *failure* is signaled explicitly.

E. Example

We now present an example demonstrating the use of exception handlers. We will write a procedure, *sum_stream*, which reads in a sequence of signed decimal integers from a character stream and returns the sum of those integers. The input stream is viewed as containing a sequence of fields separated by spaces and newlines; each field must consist of a nonempty sequence of digits, optionally preceded by a single minus sign. *Sum_stream* has the form

```
sum_stream = proc (s: stream) returns (int)
                signals (overflow,
                            unrepresentable_integer (string),
                            bad_format (string))
        · · ·
            end sum_stream
```

Sum_stream will signal *overflow* if the sum of the numbers or an intermediate sum is outside the implemented range of integers. *Unrepresentable_integer* will be signaled if the stream contains an individual number that is outside the implemented range of integers. *Bad_format* will be signaled if the stream contains a field that is not an integer.

An implementation of *sum_stream* is presented in Fig. 3. It consists of a simple loop that accumulates the sum, using a procedure *get_number* to remove the next integer from the stream. *Get_number* will signal *end_of_file* if the stream contains no more fields, in which case *sum_stream* will return the accumulated sum. *Get_number* will also signal *bad_format* or *unrepresentable_integer* if an invalid field is encountered; these exceptions are passed upward by *sum_stream*. The *overflow* handler in *sum_stream* catches exceptions signaled by the *int$add* procedure, which is invoked using the infix + notation. We have placed the exception handlers on

```
sum_stream = proc (s: stream) returns (int)
                  signals (overflow,
                           unrepresentable_integer (string),
                           bad_format (string))
       sum: int := 0
       while true do
              sum := sum + get_number (s)
              end
       except
          when end_of_file:
              return (sum)
          when unrepresentable_integer (f: string):
              signal unrepresentable_integer (f)
          when bad_format (f: string):
              signal bad_format (f)
          when overflow:
              signal overflow
          end
       end sum_stream
```

Fig. 3. The sum_stream procedure.

```
get_number = proc (s: stream) returns (int)
                  signals (end_of_file,
                           unrepresentable_integer (string),
                           bad_format (string))
       field: string := get_field (s)
          except when end_of_file:
              signal end_of_file
              end
       return (s2i (field))
          except
             when unrepresentable_integer:
                 signal unrepresentable_integer (field)
             when bad_format, invalid_character (*):
                 signal bad_format (field)
             end
       end get_number
```

Fig. 4. The get_number procedure.

the while statement for readability; they could also have been placed directly on the assignment statement.

The procedure *get_number* is presented in Fig. 4. It calls a procedure *get_field* to obtain the next field in the stream and then uses *s2i* to convert the returned string to an integer. *S2i* has the following form:

```
s2i = proc (s: string) returns (int)
         signals (invalid_character (char),
                  bad_format,
                  unrepresentable_integer)
       ...
       end s2i
```

S2i will signal *invalid_character* if the string *s* contains a character other than a digit or a minus sign. *Bad_format* will be signaled if *s* contains a minus sign following a digit, more than one minus sign, or no digits. *Unrepresentable_integer* will be signaled if *s* represents an integer that is outside the implemented range of integers. *Get_number* handles the excep-

tions signaled by *get_field* and *s2i* and signals them upward in terms that are meaningful to its callers. Although some of the names may be unchanged, the meanings of the exceptions (and even the number of arguments) are different in the two levels. Note the use of the (*) form in the handler for the *bad_format* and *invalid_character* exceptions since the signal arguments are not used.

The *get_field* procedure is presented in Fig. 5. It uses the following operation of the *stream* data type:

```
getc = proc (s: stream) returns (char) signals (end_of_file)
       ...
       end getc
```

The *stream$getc* operation returns the next character from the stream and signals *end_of_file* if the stream is empty. Note that if *end_of_file* is signaled when a field is being accumulated, then that field is returned. Otherwise, *get_field* signals *end_of_file*.

Programming of the procedures in Figs. 3-5 would be

```
get_field = proc (s: stream) returns (string) signals (end_of_file)
     field: string := ""
     begin   % delimits scope of outermost end_of_file handler
             c: char := stream$getc (s)
             % search for field
             while c = ' ' cor c = '\n' do
                     c := stream$getc (s)
                     end
             % accumulate field
             while c ~= ' ' cand c ~= '\n' do
                     field := string$append (field, c)
                     c := stream$getc (s)
                         except when end_of_file:
                                 return (field)
                                 end
                     end
             end
                 except when end_of_file:
                         signal end_of_file
                         end
     return (field)
     end get_field
```

Fig. 5. The get_field procedure.

simplified if the mechanism permitted implicit upward propagation of exceptions. This would permit arms of the form

```
when unrepresentable_integer (f: string):
     signal unrepresentable_integer (f)
```

to be omitted from the program text. As we gain experience in using the mechanism, we will learn how to modify it to enhance its convenience.

F. On Disabling Exceptions

One question that naturally arises about an exception handling mechanism is whether exceptions can be disabled. By disabling exceptions two kinds of savings can (potentially) be realized: the time spent detecting the occurrence of the exception can be saved, and the space used for the handlers and the information used to find the handlers can be saved. However, it is unacceptable if the result of disabling exceptions is that errors still occur, but are simply not recognized. Therefore, we do not believe that providing a means for programmer disabling of exceptions is consistent with encouraging good programming practice, and no such mechanism has been provided in CLU.

The situation still arises, however, in which it is possible to *guarantee* that the exception cannot occur, and it is desirable to take advantage of that guarantee to generate more efficient code. Looked at in this way, disabling of exceptions is seen as a kind of program optimization technique, since program optimization makes use of properties detected from program analysis to control the generation of code. There are two ways in which such properties can be detected. First, the combination of in-line substitution followed by analysis across module boundaries can result in more efficient code. For example, consider

```
if ~stack$empty(s) then x := stack$pop(s) · · ·
```

where *s* is a *stack*. If both *empty* and *pop* are expanded in-line, the result will be code roughly like

```
if s.size > 0 % body of empty
   then % body of pop
       if s.size > 0 then · · ·
```

Conventional techniques like redundant expression elimination and dead code removal can then be used to improve the code.

Alternatively, it would be fruitful to integrate the activities of a program verification system with the compiler. Then, for example, a verifier might prove of the user of *s* that *pop* is never called if *s* is empty. This assertion could then be used later to control the compilation of both the program using *s*, and the program implementing the *stack* module.

IV. Implementation, Debugging, and Diagnostics

In this section we discuss some implementation issues. First we sketch some methods for implementing the exception handling mechanism. Then we discuss how the mechanism can be incorporated in a debugging environment and in a production environment.

A. Implementation

There are several possible methods of implementing the exception handling mechanism. As usual, tradeoffs must be made between efficiency of space and time. We believe the following are appropriate criteria for an implementation:

1) normal case execution efficiency should not be impaired at all;
2) exceptions should be handled reasonably quickly, but not necessarily as fast as possible;
3) use of space should be reasonably efficient.

The tradeoff to be made is the speed with which exceptions are handled versus the space required for code or data used to locate handlers.

The implementation of signaling an exception involves the following actions:

1) discarding the activation record of the signaling activation (but saving the result objects associated with the exception),
2) locating the appropriate handler in the calling procedure,
3) adjusting the caller's activation record to reflect the possible termination of execution of expressions and statements,
4) copying the result objects into the caller's activation record,
5) transferring control to the handler.

Actions 3) and 5) are equivalent to a **goto** from the invocation to the handler. Actions 1) and 4) are similar to those occurring in normal procedure returns. Because the association between invocations and handlers is static, the compiler can provide the information needed to perform actions 2) and 3). Below we sketch two methods of providing this information; these methods differ considerably in their performance characteristics.

The first method, called the *branch table method*, is to follow each invocation with a branch table containing one entry for each exception that can be raised by the invocation. The

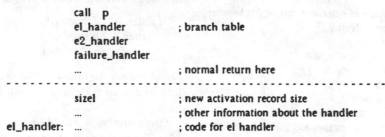

Fig. 6. Sketch of code generated by the branch table method.

invocation of a procedure whose heading lists *n* exceptions will have a branch table of *n* + 1 entries; the first *n* entries correspond to the exceptions listed in the heading, while the last entry is for *failure*. Each entry contains the location of a handler for the corresponding exception.

Using this method, return and signal are easy to implement: return transfers control to the location following the branch table, while signal transfers control to the location stored in the branch table entry for the exception being signaled. The information needed to adjust the caller's activation record could be stored with the handler, as could information about whether to discard the returned objects and whether this is an others handler; for example, this information could be stored in a table placed just before the first instruction of the handler. An example is given in Fig. 6 of the code generated by this method.

The branch table method provides for efficient signaling of exceptions, but at a considerable cost in space, since every invocation must be followed by a branch table (all invocations may at least signal *failure*). A second method, the *handler table method*, is the one used by the current CLU implementation. This method trades off some speed for space, and was designed under the assumption that there are many fewer handlers than invocations, which is consistent with our experience in using the mechanism.

The handler table method works as follows. Rather than build a branch table per invocation, the compiler builds a single table for each procedure. This table contains an entry for each handler in the procedure. An entry contains the following information: 1) a list of the exceptions handled by the handler (a null list can be used to indicate an **others** handler), 2) a pair of values defining the scope of the handler, that is, the object code corresponding to the statement to which the handler is attached, 3) the location of the code of the handler, 4) the new activation record size, and 5) an indicator of whether the returned objects are used in the handler. The scope and exceptions list together permit candidate handlers to be located: only an invocation occurring within the scope and raising an exception named in the exception list can possibly be handled by the handler (for an others handler, only the scope matters).

In this method, a return statement is implemented just as it would be in a language without exception handling. A signal statement requires searching the handler table to find entries for candidate handlers; if several candidates exist,

the one with the smallest scope is selected. Placing the entries in the table in the (linear) order in which the corresponding handlers appear in the source text guarantees that the first candidate found is the handler to use. Unhandled exceptions can be recognized either by the absence of candidates or by storing one additional entry at the end of the handler table for this case.

B. Debugging and Diagnostics

Our exception handling mechanism is designed explicitly to provide information that programs, not programmers, can use to recover from exceptional conditions. However, the mechanism can also mesh smoothly with mechanisms intended to collect information of interest to programmers. The kind of behavior desired will differ, however, from a debugging environment to a production environment.

In an interactive debugging environment it is likely that a programmer would wish to be informed about the occurrence of some or all exceptions as they are signaled and be given a chance to handle them himself or take some other corrective action. Two possible modes might be useful here. The programmer may be interested only in signals of *failure* (especially those resulting from unhandled exceptions), or he may in addition name some particular exceptions of interest.

An exception handling mechanism running in such an environment, before locating a handler, would consult some debugging system information to determine if the current exception is one that the programmer wishes to know about. If the exception is of interest to the programmer, then system routines can be invoked to initiate a dialogue with the programmer. This dialogue may result in the program being continued or terminated.

It is worth noting that one argument in favor of the resumption model has been that it integrates debugging with program execution. The programmer (or actually the system as his representative) is thought of as the highest level activation, which will handle all exceptions not otherwise handled and which may later resume execution of some lower level activation. Note that this viewpoint allows the programmer to examine only unhandled exceptions. At any rate, we believe that it is not productive to try to merge debugging with ordinary processing, since the requirements in the two cases are quite different.

In a production environment, there is no programmer

available to interact with the program. Of course, there may be an operator present, and a program may attempt to recover by requesting some operator action (e.g., mounting a tape). This action can be accomplished by ordinary program structures (e.g., invoking a procedure to print a message on the operator's console).

When *failure* occurs in a production environment, there is still a good chance that program error is responsible. Therefore, it would be helpful if information about the failing program were collected for later examination by a programmer. This capability can easily be provided. Whenever *failure* is signaled, the exception handling mechanism can output information about each activation before terminating it. In the case of the first implicit signal of the "unhandled exception" failure, the mechanism should also provide information about the activation that signaled the unhandled exception. The information collected as *failure* propagates upwards will provide a trace of the failing program, which should be helpful for the programmer who determines later what the problem was. Debugging in a batch environment can be facilitated similarly, except that information about more exceptions than just *failure* may be of interest. Note that in either case the information being collected is *not* useful to programs (since it describes the states of implementations of other procedures) and therefore need not be made available to them.

V. Expressive Power

As we stated earlier, the decision to choose a termination model instead of a resumption model involves a tradeoff between the expressive power of the exception handling mechanism and its complexity. In our opinion, a more complex mechanism can be justified only if the additional expressive power it provides is frequently needed. In this section we explore this issue by considering examples of problems often put forth as justifying a resumption model.

The first problem concerns exceptions such as *underflow* that are generated by numeric operations. Often when an operation like *multiply* signals *underflow*, the desired action is to substitute a particular value (e.g., zero) for the result of the operation and continue the computation. In a resumption model, this behavior can be obtained by resuming the operation and passing it the value to be returned.

This behavior is equally easily obtained using a termination model. Because the *multiply* operation is not performing any computation after being resumed (it is merely returning the value provided), it is acceptable to terminate its activation. The only problem is for the handler to somehow substitute the new value for the result of the operation. For simple examples like

z := x * y

"substituting" for the result of the invocation of *multiply* can be done simply by assigning to z. For more complicated examples, e.g.,

z := x * y + z

using our mechanism it is necessary to introduce additional statements and temporary variables. However, such awkward-

ness is not a defect of the termination model but rather a result of our decision not to allow handlers to be attached to expressions. If such examples turned out to be frequent, our mechanism could be changed to accommodate them.

In fact, resumption is truly useful only in the following situation: when the exception is signaled, the signaler is in the middle of a computation that can be completed by performing additional computation upon receipt of a value from the handler. Resumption permits completion of the computation in this situation without redoing work already performed.

We can imagine that such a situation could arise during a numeric computation. If it did, and resumption were not available, then a default value (or, in the most general case, a procedure to compute a default value) could be passed as an extra input of the numeric routine.

This method is clearly not as convenient as using resumption; it becomes unacceptable if there are many default values or if there is deep nesting of procedures within the numeric routine, so that even a single default value must be passed down through many invocations. In our experience, neither of these characteristics hold for the routines in numeric libraries; on the contrary, default values are almost never of use, and the nesting is shallow.

The other example often used to support the choice of a resumption model is that of a storage pool that performs storage allocation for a number of objects in a program. If the amount of free storage in the storage pool becomes too low to satisfy a particular allocation request, it may still be possible to satisfy the request if some of the objects stored in the pool can be reorganized to use less storage. Many objects can be implemented in a number of ways, some that permit fast execution but use a lot of space and others that are slower but use less space. The idea would be to start out using fast representations but switch to more compact representations if free storage became too low. Note that this example is an instance of the general situation, described above, in which resumption is truly useful.

Levin [3] has designed an exception handling mechanism that directly supports the desired behavior. In Levin's mechanism, an exception can be associated with an object (the mechanisms discussed previously associate exceptions only with invocations). Thus, if the storage pool were unable to satisfy a request, it could signal an exception associated with the storage pool object. The mechanism would then allow all users of the object (in this case, modules that have objects allocated in the storage pool) to handle the exception. The handlers would attempt to free storage by reorganizing their associated objects.

Note that Levin's mechanism is strictly more powerful (in terms of expressive power) than the resumption models we discussed in Section II, since the users of the storage pool do not necessarily have any outstanding procedure activations at the time the exception is signaled. Furthermore, those objects that are in the middle of being operated upon are likely to be in an inconsistent state and thus not prepared for reorganization. Levin's mechanism makes it easy to inhibit the handling of an exception for objects in an inconsistent state.

In CLU, this recovery algorithm could be programmed by

having the storage pool explicitly maintain a collection of handler procedures to be invoked whenever free storage became too low.[6] The storage pool abstraction provides operations *alloc*, to add an object to a pool, and *delete*, to remove an object from a pool. *Alloc* would have an additional argument: the handler procedure to invoke if it becomes necessary to shrink the object being added to the pool. *Alloc* would add this procedure to the collection, while *delete* would remove from the collection the handler procedure associated with the object being deleted from the pool.

There is no doubt that the method sketched above is more complicated and more error prone than what could be done using Levin's mechanism. However, we believe that the storage pool example is both unusual and a special case. We doubt the existence of a large number of cases where the amount of storage freed would make the difference between successful and unsuccessful execution of a program.

In selecting examples for discussion, we examined those presented in papers favoring the resumption model [2], [3], and chose the ones that made the strongest case for resumption. In both examples, the solutions achieved using resumption were more natural than those possible without resumption. However, unless it is shown that such cases arise frequently, they do not justify the more complex mechanism.

VI. Discussion

In this paper we have discussed exception handling and described an exception handling mechanism. An exception handling mechanism is a tool for enhancing program reliability and fault tolerance. To enhance reliability procedures should be defined as generally as possible, that is, they should respond "reasonably" in as many situations as possible. An exception handling mechanism simplifies the writing of such procedures; it is primarily a mechanism for generalizing the behavior of procedures.

In Section II we discussed major decisions that must be made in designing an exception handling mechanism and the exception handling models that result from these decisions. We argued that any well-structured mechanism should be one-level: only the caller should handle exceptions raised by the invoked procedure. We further argued that the termination model, in which the signaling activation terminates, is better than the resumption model, in which the signaling activation continues to exist. The termination model is clearly simpler than the resumption model; we also believe that it has sufficient expressive power. Note that in our termination model, a procedure may terminate in one of a number of conditions (one of which is the so-called "normal" condition) and may return result objects differing in number and type for each condition. The ability to return objects provides a kind of expressive power not found in most other exception handling mechanisms.

Section III described the syntax and semantics of the CLU exception handling mechanism, which supports the termina-

tion model. While in Section II we were concerned primarily with interprocedure control and data flow, in Section III, we were concerned primarily with intraprocedure control and data flow. Our goal was to permit the programmer to place handlers where they are needed, without constraints due to conflict of exception names. This goal led to the introduction of an exit mechanism similar to those described by Zahn [9] and Bochmann [1]. Our design also acknowledged that many exceptions cannot be handled. These exceptions may not occur often, but they can potentially occur almost anywhere. The special exception named *failure*, which is signaled implicitly for all uncaught exceptions, was introduced to accommodate this situation. We also discussed why disabling exceptions is not a good idea, and suggested that research in program optimization techniques may be fruitful in avoiding the cost of checking for errors that are known not to occur.

In Section IV, we discussed two methods of implementing the exception handling mechanism, the branch table method and the handler table method. Both methods process normal returns as fast as possible; the branch table method also processes exceptions as fast as possible, while the handler table method is somewhat slower, but more space efficient. We also discussed the integration of the mechanism in debugging and production environments. The mechanism is defined to communicate information that can be used by *programs*, but this does not preclude an implementation that produces additional information for use by *programmers*.

In Section V, we discussed the expressive power of our exception handling model. We described two examples commonly put forward to justify the resumption model and discussed how they could be programmed in the termination model. The termination model solutions were inferior to the resumption model solutions. However, we believe that the examples under discussion occur very rarely, so a mechanism like the resumption model, which eases their programming at the cost of extra complexity, is not justified.

The CLU exception handling mechanism has been implemented by the handler table method. We have used the mechanism in writing many CLU programs (for example, most of the CLU compiler is written in CLU). We are convinced that our programs are better structured than they would be in the absence of the mechanism. Furthermore, we have not encountered any situations where a more powerful exception handling mechanism (e.g., resumption) was desired. Thus, our experience so far supports our belief that the mechanism is a good compromise between expressive power and simplicity. However, we have not written programs that attempt to handle the problem of resource constraints, a situation where resumption is most likely to be needed. Further experimentation is needed to reach a final conclusion on the wisdom of our choices.

Acknowledgment

The design of our exception handling mechanism was the work of the CLU design team, including R. Atkinson, T. Bloom, E. Moss, C. Schaffert, and R. Scheifler. This paper was improved by the comments of the referees and many others.

---

[6]Each procedure would have to be bound to the environment in which reorganization should be done. Since CLU procedures do not have free variables, the storage pool would have to maintain these environment objects also.

REFERENCES

[1] G. V. Bochmann, "Multiple exits from a loop without the GOTO," *Commun. Ass. Comput. Mach.*, vol. 16, pp. 443–444, July 1973.

[2] J. B. Goodenough, "Exception handling: Issues and a proposed notation," *Commun. Ass. Comput. Mach.*, vol. 18, pp. 683–696, Dec. 1975.

[3] R. Levin, "Program structures for exceptional condition handling," Ph.D. dissertation, Dep. Comput. Sci., Carnegie-Mellon Univ., Pittsburgh, PA, June 1977.

[4] B. Liskov, A. Snyder, R. Atkinson, and C. Schaffert, "Abstraction mechanisms in CLU," *Commun. Ass. Comput. Mach.*, vol. 20, pp. 564–576, Aug. 1977.

[5] *Proc. ACM Conf. on Language Design for Reliable Software, SIGPLAN Notices*, vol. 12, Mar. 1977.

[6] J. G. Mitchell, W. Maybury, and R. Sweet, "Mesa language manual," Xerox Res. Cent., Palo Alto, CA, Rep. CSL-78-1, Feb. 1978.

[7] P. M. Melliar-Smith and B. Randell, "Software reliability: The role of programmed exception handling," in *Proc. ACM Conf. on Language Design for Reliable Software, SIGPLAN Notices*, vol. 12, pp. 95–100, Mar. 1977.

[8] B. Randell, "System structure for software fault tolerance," *IEEE Trans. Software Eng.*, vol. SE-1, pp. 220–232, June 1975.

[9] C. T. Zahn, Jr., "A control statement for natural top-down structured programming," *Programming Symposium, Lecture Notes in Computer Science*, vol. 19, B. Robinet, Ed. New York: Springer-Verlag, 1974, pp. 170–180.

From 1968 to 1972, she was associated with the Mitre Corporation, Bedford, MA, where she participated in the design and implementation of the Venus Machine and the Venus Operating System. She is presently Associate Professor of Electrical Engineering and Computer Science at the Massachusetts Institute of Technology, Cambridge. Her research interests include programming methodology, distributed systems, and the design of languages and systems to support structured programming.

Barbara H. Liskov received the B.A. degree in mathematics from the University of California, Berkeley, and the M.S. and Ph.D. degrees in computer science from Stanford University, Stanford, CA.

Alan Snyder received the S.B., S.M., and Ph.D. degrees in computer science from the Massachusetts Institute of Technology, Cambridge.

He is currently a member of the Technical Staff in the Computer Research Laboratory at Hewlett-Packard Laboratories, Palo Alto, CA, working primarily in the area of integrated circuit design automation. His other interests include programming languages and machine architecture.

Dr. Snyder is a member of the Association for Computing Machinery.

TUTORIAL ON MODULA-2*

JURG GUTKNECHT

A *structured programming language*
based upon the concept of autonomous modules

MODULA-2 INTRODUCES the module into the world of systems engineering. It is a basic constituent of Modula-2 programs, appears in a variety of formats, and is comparable to that of procedures brought in by ALGOL and Pascal for structuring programs.

One module may combine a set of logically connected procedures; a second module may hide a complex data structure and provide operations to influence this structure; a third module may define the fundamental data types in a large program. Modules are either autonomous or embedded, as submodules, into larger modules. The autonomous are said to be embedded into the universe.

The module is essentially a separate program part, with an infrastructure that is similar to the infrastructure of a Pascal program. Types, constants, variables, and procedures declared within the module are generally not visible outside the module, and objects defined outside the module are not accessible from within.

The module technique has turned out to be surprisingly difficult to master. We have been involved with Modula-2 at the Institut für Informatik and our experience shows that it is easier to misuse the module than to use it profitably. Nevertheless, we find it to be indispensable. This tutorial may help you in developing a good eye for appropriate program modularization.

Let us define some integral concepts. The nature of permanency is common to all types of modules. The lifetime of the module and its objects equals that of the whole program. This is in contrast to the temporary character of procedures. In fact, the notion of a module is more closely related to the notion of *record* than to that of *procedure*.

We define a module as active at a given moment if statements of the module are executed. The first time a module becomes active is when it has been loaded. The module body (also called initialization part) is then executed as a subroutine of the program loader. The last module loaded is the main module and its initialization part is the main program. A module is reactivated whenever one of its exported procedures has been called.

AN EXAMPLE

To get firm ground under our feet, we will develop a Modula-2 sample program—a text formatter. For this example, assume that the text must be printed on sheets of paper in adjusted

....

Dr. Jurg Gutknecht (Institut für Informatik, ETH—Zentrum (Clausiusstrasse), CH-8092, Zürich, Switzerland) is actively involved in the use of Modula-2.

and multicolumn form. Assume further that this text is available in an ordinary text file that consists of lines of text (see figure 1a). Let us define a paragraph as a sequence of lines that is terminated by an empty line. Thus, from our text formatter's point of view, line terminators (hereafter referred to as EOL characters) are equivalent to space characters, except when they terminate an empty line, which concludes a nonempty sequence of lines.

The crucial thing for our formatter to do is to convert the text from "straight text" representation into "columnar text" representation. We shall organize our program so that it creates a new text file, which contains the text in its new format. A standard utility program may later produce the desired printout.

The overall dynamic structure of our program now suggests itself: read text lines from the input file in sequence, and build up the text pagewise in its new format. Completed pages should be written immediately into the output file to make way for the next page in the memory. Clearly, the events of reading lines and writing pages are asynchronous.

An appropriate program structure should certainly reflect the described situation. We could regard the input handler as the main, and therefore con-

(continued)

trolling part of the program. Alternately, we might structure the output formatter as the translation controller that periodically demands a new text portion from the input routine. From our experience, the former point of view is superior to the latter, particularly if the input stream includes control information.

Further, we propose to encapsulate the formatter into a submodule. Let us now develop the interface to this submodule that we shall call *Layout*. Essentially, communications will consist of a single operation: formatting an appropriate piece of text. We shall therefore call this procedure Format. Format accepts and formats a paragraph. The paragraph is handed over in the form of a pointer *lim* (end of text) into a

(continued)

1a

```
Lara is a document processing program consisting of an interactive editor (lara)
and a printer companion (laraprint) producing hardcopies of Lara documents on
the laser printer.
Lara introduces several new concepts.
We shall roughly outline the most important of them in this memo.
The memo also includes basic rules and guidelines for working with Lara.
We shall expect the reader to be familiar with the program editor and the
text editor Andra.

Concepts of Lara:
Self-Consistency:
Each Lara document completely describes itself, i.e. it does not refer to any
other information such as styles and user profiles.
Thus, the values of all formatting attributes occuring within the document
are included in the (header of the) document file.

Hierarchical document structure:
A Lara document is structured as a sequence of so called chapters.
Each chapter starts on a new page and is made up of a sequence of paragraphs.
Each paragraph starts on a new line and consists of a sequence of characters.  A
chapter, resp. paragraph, is created by typing a form-feed (CTRL L), resp.
line-feed (CTRL J).
In the case of adjusted paragraphs, RETURN is equivalent to line-feed.

Document, Chapter, Paragraph, Character
are the structural units of which a Lara document consists.
Each structural unit is connected with a set of formatting attributes
(applicable to instances of that structure, see table below).
A structural unit of higher level is selected by a multiple click of the
select button pointing at the same location.
Each clicking increases the selection menu by one.
For a selection to be successful, the beginning and end of the respective
structural unit must be displayed.
An unsuccessful level may be skipped by simply clicking again.
```

1b

```
Lara is a document processing
program consisting of an
interactive editor (lara) and
a printer companion
(laraprint) producing
hardcopies of Lara documents
on the laser printer. Lara
introduces several new
concepts. We shall roughly
outline the most important of
them in this memo. The memo
also includes basic rules and
guidelines for working with
Lara. We shall expect the
reader to be familiar with the
program editor and the text
editor Andra.
Concepts of Lara:
Self-Consistency: Each Lara
document completely describes
itself, i.e. it does not refer
to any other information such
```
```
as styles and user profiles.
Thus, the values of all
formatting attributes occuring
within the document are
included in the (header of
the) document file.
Hierarchical document
structure: A Lara document is
structured as a sequence of so
called chapters. Each chapter
starts on a new page and is
made up of a sequence of
paragraphs. Each paragraph
starts on a new line and
consists of a sequence of
characters. A chapter, resp.
paragraph, is created by
typing a form-feed (CTRL L),
resp. line-feed (CTRL J). In
the case of adjusted
paragraphs, RETURN is
equivalent to line-feed.
```
```
Document, Chapter, Paragraph,
Character are the structural
units of which a Lara document
consists. Each structural
unit is connected with a set
of formatting attributes
(applicable to instances of
that structure, see table
below). A structural unit of
higher level is selected by a
multiple click of the select
button pointing at the same
location. Each clicking
increases the selection menu
by one. For a selection to be
successful, the beginning and
end of the respective
structural unit must be
displayed. An unsuccessful
level may be skipped by simply
clicking again.
```

Figure 1: *The test file (1a) prior to being converted into 3-column format (1b).*

character buffer *buf* (see listing 1).

A few explanations on this program fragment are in order. Although similar to Pascal, some conspicuous differences can be detected:

Import lists: these refer to separate standard modules, namely *FileSystem* and *InOut*, members of the basic module library. We shall discuss the library concept later. The entries in the import lists designate objects declared in and exported from the library modules. Apart from *File*, which is a type, all listed objects are procedures. Note that *File* is a record type, as can be seen from the statement **WHILE NOT IN.EOF DO** .... Fields of imported records (such as *eof*) are implicitly imported together. In Modula-2's syntax, **WHILE** and **IF** statements are never initiated with a **BEGIN** but are always terminated by a keyword (UNTIL or END). This rule lets nested statements appear more elegant than their counterparts in Pascal. Also, the ambiguities that arise in Pascal with nested

IF...THEN...ELSE statements have been eliminated.

Type *Cardinal*: this is a new standard type describing natural numbers. Repetition of names: the module name has to be repeated at the end of the module. (This repetition convention also applies to procedures.) Character constants: *nC* designates the character with octal ordinal number *n*. Abbreviations: # is equivalent to < > and & is an abbreviation for *AND*.

In our program fragment, we could have used the standard Modula-2 procedure *INC* for incrementing *lim* (i.e., *INC(lim)* is equivalent to *lim:= lim + 1*).

Let us now examine the imported procedures ReadString and WriteString. They accept as their parameter an array of characters of arbitrary length. The corresponding formal parameter is a so-called *dynamic* or *open* array:

```
PROCEDURE ReadString(VAR s:
  ARRAY OF CHAR);
```

Dynamic arrays are of major importance in Modula-2. The index type of dynamic arrays is always CARDINAL, and the low boundary is 0. The boundary of the actual array parameter can be obtained by *HIGH(s)* using the standard function *HIGH*. Dynamic arrays can only be used as formal parameters.

Next, let us look at strings (i.e., sequences of characters). Assume that a function procedure had to be developed that returns the actual length of a string. A string within an array of characters is terminated by *OC* or by the upper array boundary, whichever comes first. Consider the procedure declaration in listing 2.

In Modula-2, functions differ from ordinary procedures solely by the supplement of a result type. The result is returned by the RETURN statement. We point out the amazing simplicity of this algorithm. It has its roots in the conditional evaluation of the test in the **WHILE** statement. If $l <= HIGH(s)$ is false, then the second part of the expression is ignored rather than evaluated. Thus, an index out-of-range error cannot occur.

LAYING OUT LAYOUT

Let our attention now turn to the submodule *Layout*. We know that *Layout* exports the procedure Format, which formats a paragraph that is stored in the global buffer *buf*. Therefore, the wall around *Layout* has to be transparent for this variable: *buf* must be imported. But how should Format record its results? An obvious solution is to introduce the two-dimensional array *form* that represents a text page. By successively calling the formatting procedure, a map of the current text page will be built up. The variables *row* and *col* indicate the current status of the formatting process. Of course, these variables have to survive the procedure Format. On the other hand, the significance of the variables *form*, *row*, and *col* is strictly related to the specific implementation of Format. They have no meaning outside the submodule. They are, in fact, invisible outside the module as they are not exported. We shall say that these variables constitute the private data structure of the (sub)module.

We have seen that the procedure Format operates on the status variables *row*

Listing 1: *A program fragment written in Modula-2 designed to format text into columns.*

```
MODULE Formatter;
  FROM FileSystem IMPORT File, Lookup, Close, ReadChar, WriteChar;
  FROM InOut IMPORT ReadString, WriteString, Write;
  CONST EOL = 36C;
  VAR in, out: File;
    name: ARRAY [0..31] OF CHAR;
    ch: CHAR;
    buf: ARRAY [0..1000] OF CHAR;
    lim: CARDINAL;
BEGIN
  WriteString("in > "); ReadString(name); Write(EOL);
  Lookup(in, name, FALSE);
  WriteString("out> "); ReadString(name); Write(EOL);
  Lookup(out, name, TRUE);
  lim := 0; ReadChar(in, ch);
  WHILE NOT in.eof DO
    WHILE ch # EOL DO
      lim := lim + 1; buf[lim] := ch; ReadChar(in, ch)
    END;
    lim := lim + 1; buf[lim] := " "; ReadChar(in, ch);
    IF ch = EOL THEN Format; lim := 0; ReadChar(in, ch) END
  END;
  Close(in); Close(out)
END Formatter.
```

Listing 2: *A procedure used to return the length of a given string within an array of characters.*

```
PROCEDURE Len(VAR s: ARRAY OF CHAR): CARDINAL;
  VAR l: CARDINAL;
BEGIN l := 0;
  WHILE (l <= HIGH(s)) & (s[l] # OC) DO l := l + 1 END;
  RETURN l
END Len;
```

(continued)

and *col*. How are these variables initialized? Remember the initialization part mentioned above. The Modula-2 linking loader guarantees that the statement sequence in the module body has been executed whenever an exported procedure is called from the outside. So introducing the initialization statements in the module body solves our problem.

So far we have disregarded the output. Clearly, a page should be written line by line into the output text file each time the page is completed. Format calls procedure OutPage when *row* and *col* have reached their maximum. Is this the only situation in which a page has to be written? It is likely that the last page of the text is only partially filled, so that the variables *row* and *col* won't reach their maximum values. So OutPage should also be called from the main program as termination procedure immediately before closing the files. We therefore generalize OutPage to include the handling of a partially filled *form* and include it in the export list.

Our submodule, *Layout*, appears in listing 3. Its text has to be included in the declaration part of the main module.

Notice the presence of a new repetitive LOOP statement. The loop statement is used whenever a repetition with more than one exit, or no exit at all, has to be programmed. The LOOP is left whenever an EXIT statement has been encountered within the loop brackets LOOP and END. It is noteworthy that the loop statement makes a jump statement (like GOTO) unnecessary. In our example, the loop is left when either the paragraph is terminated ("emergency exit") or when the current word has no room on the current line ("regular exit").

Constant expressions are another innovation of Modula-2 over Pascal. They are particularly useful for the specification of array bounds such as in |0 . . . *maxRow*-1| and can also be used for the declaration of dependent constants (e.g., *bndRow* = *maxRow* − *len*).

Until now, we have underexploited the possibilities of our submodule *Layout*. In fact, we have fixed the number of columns and the column widths as constants, although the module works correctly for arbitrary (appropriate) values of these quantities. Let us extend the format of input files with an optional header line that is initiated by a *CTLF(6C)*. *CTLF* has to be followed by a digit from 1 to 4 indicating the desired number of text columns.

A second modification concerns the overall program flow. It is not a good idea to terminate the program after having processed a single text file. Instead, the program should be ready to process

(continued)

Listing 3: *The submodule* Layout, *the output formatter, must appear within the main module.*

```
MODULE Layout;
  IMPORT buf, lim, out, WriteChar, EOL;
  EXPORT Format, OutPage;
  CONST len = 30; wid = 33; maxRow = 70;
        maxCol = 3•len; bndCol = maxCol-len;
        FF = 14C; (•form feed•)
  VAR form: ARRAY |0..maxRow-1|, |0..maxCol-1| OF CHAR;
      row, col: CARDINAL; (•current coordinates•)

  PROCEDURE OutPage;
    VAR c, r, p: CARDINAL;
  BEGIN r := 0;
    WHILE r # maxRow DO c := 0;
      WHILE c # col DO p := 0;
        WHILE p # len DO WriteChar(out, form[r, c + p]); p := p + 1 END;
        WHILE p # wid DO WriteChar(out, " "); p := p + 1 END;
        c := c + len
      END;
      IF r < row THEN p := 0;
        WHILE p # len DO WriteChar(out, form[r, c + p]); p := p + 1 END
      END;
      WriteChar(out, EOL);
      r := r + 1
    END;
    WriteChar(out, FF)
  END OutPage;

  PROCEDURE Format;
    VAR beg, cur, end, pos, wds, spc, rem: CARDINAL;
  BEGIN
    beg := 0; cur := 0;
    REPEAT cur := cur + 1 UNTIL buf[cur] = " ";
    REPEAT wds := 0; beg := beg + 1;
      LOOP
        wds := wds + 1; end := cur;
        IF end = lim THEN spc := 0; rem := 0; EXIT END;
        REPEAT cur := cur + 1 UNTIL buf[cur] = " ";
        IF cur - beg > len THEN
          IF wds > 1 THEN
            spc := (len + beg - end) DIV (wds - 1);
            rem := (len + beg - end) MOD (wds - 1)
          END;
          EXIT
        END
      END;
      pos := 0;
      WHILE pos # len DO form[row, col + pos] := " "; pos := pos + 1 END;
      pos := 0;
      WHILE beg # end DO
        form[row, col + pos] := buf[beg];
        IF buf[beg] = " " THEN pos := pos + spc;
          IF rem > 0 THEN pos := pos + 1; rem := rem - 1 END
        END;
        pos := pos + 1; beg := beg + 1
      END;
      row := row + 1;
      IF row = maxRow THEN
        IF col = bndCol THEN OutPage; col := 0 ELSE col := col + len END;
        row := 0
      END;
    UNTIL end = lim
  END Format;

BEGIN col := 0; row := 0
END Layout;
```

Structuring elements allow and invite software designers to group declarations and procedures into distinct modules.

another file. Hence, we embed our previous main program into a WHILE statement. We shall specify that entering *ESC(33C)* instead of a filename will bring the process to an end. Module *In-Out* exports a variable *termCH* containing the termination character of the string read by *ReadString*. Of course, this variable is exported for inspection only. See listing 4 for our extended main program.

In listing 4 we find yet another new Modula-2 statement. The IF statement from Pascal has been extended by the *ELSIF* clause. The meaning and possible application of this clause should be obvious from our example.

In contrast to our earlier solution, the submodule *Layout* may need to be initialized several times (i.e., each time new text is to be processed). The way to master this problem is to introduce

an explicit initialization procedure; in our case, this procedure is called Init-Form, which replaces (and extends) the previous submodule body. The body of the new submodule is empty.

With that, however, the responsibility for the correct sequence of module initialization has passed over from the Modula-2 loader to the programmer.

DIVIDE AND CONQUER

Since the late 1960s serious programmers have based their software development on structured programming. This means that they have structured the dynamic flow of their programs such that a procedure call corresponds to each action in the formulation of the respective algorithm. Thereby, the question of where to program all these procedures has not been raised or answered "in the declaration section of the program." This is the point where Modula-2 intervenes. As we have already seen in the previous section, Modula-2's structuring elements allow and even invite the software designer to divide and logically group the set of declarations and procedures into distinct units called modules.

The consequences of this division reach further than expected. Separate

compilation is one new aspect. It is a small step from encapsulating a program part within a main module to completely removing this part from its environment and defining it as autonomous. In fact, the Modula-2 compiler accepts autonomous modules as compilation units and performs full compatibility checking across module boundaries.

But Modula-2 goes one step further: separate modules can be split up into a definition and an implementation part. The definition part defines the module from a functional point of view, while its implementation companion lays down the methods used to realize these functions or to represent data. The definition part can be regarded as a separately stated (and compiled), extended export list.

This concept clearly opens a new door for software engineers. They may define centrally the components of large software systems in a concise and unified way and leave the implementation to a team of programmers.

It is crucial to separate compilation that imports must always refer to definition (parts of) modules. An important consequence of this is that recompilation of an implementation (part of a) module does not influence the module's clients. However, the recompilation of a (modified) definition part can trigger a chain reaction of which the extent is determined by the number of importations in dependent definition modules. It is therefore a good idea to minimize imports in definition modules.

Let us illustrate all that by two examples: a compiler and an editor. Think of the compiler as being designed according to the method of recursive descent. The different parts in recursive-descent compilers are known to be closely interwoven. On the other hand, we have seen that modularization essentially amounts to a textual splitting of the program. Hence, modularizing a compiler has to be a difficult undertaking. Nevertheless, some functional units can be extracted: lexical analysis (scanner), syntactical analysis (parser), generating of the symbol table, and type checking and code generation. We shall assign each of these functional units to a separate module.

These modules are obviously tightly

(continued)

Listing 4: *The main program that has been extended to a) use variables for the number of columns and column widths, and b) request a new text file to process after completing file output.*

```
  BEGIN
    WriteString("in > "): ReadString(name); Write(EOL):
    WHILE termCH # ESC DO
      Lookup(in, name, FALSE);
      WriteString("out > "): ReadString(name); Write(EOL):
      Lookup(out, name, TRUE);
    lim := 0; ReadChar(in, ch):
    IF ch = CTLF THEN ReadChar(in, ch):
      IF ch = "1" THEN InitForm(96, 96, 70, 0)
        ELSIF ch = "2" THEN InitForm(46, 49, 70, 1)
        ELSIF ch = "3" THEN InitForm(30, 33, 70, 2)
        ELSIF ch = "4" THEN InitForm(22, 24, 70, 3)
        ELSE InitForm(96, 96, 70, 0)
      END:
      REPEAT ReadChar(in, ch) UNTIL ch = EOL:
      ReadChar(in, ch)
    ELSE InitForm(96, 96, 70, 0)
    END:
    WHILE NOT in.eof DO
      WHILE ch # EOL DO lim := lim + 1; buf[lim] := ch; ReadChar(in, ch) END:
      lim := lim + 1; buf[lim] := " "; ReadChar(in, ch):
      IF ch = EOL THEN Format; lim := 0; ReadChar(in, ch) END
    END:
    OutPage:
    Close(in); Close(out):
    WriteString("in > "): ReadString(name); Write(EOL)
    END
  END Formatter.
```

coupled. They all rely on a central and dynamic data structure: the symbol table. How can this common data structure (i.e., the respective data types) be presented to the different modules? The solution is to place the description of the data structure itself into a module, a so-called data-type module. This data module constitutes a common base that must be imported by any module that participates in the handling of the symbol table. Notice the contrast to our first example: there, a public procedure operated on a private and hidden data structure. Here, private and public procedures operate on a common and public data structure.

What can be hidden at all in our compiler modules? Methods is the answer. Consider, for example, the symbol-table generator. Listing 5 is an excerpt from its definition module.

ObjPtr, ObjClass, StrPtr, and *StrForm* are data types which are imported from the data module. *NewScope* and *CloseScope* open and close scopes, and *NewObj* and *NewStr* are procedures to create new entries in the symbol table. *Find* and *Find-Field* search for objects with a given name. *InitTableHandler* initializes explicitly the table handler, and *EndTableHandler* is the termination procedure for this module. We emphasize that no information is given about methods. It is left open, for example, which strategy is applied and whether a certain object is searched with a linear or a binary search.

Only the implementation module in listing 6 lifts the veil of secrecy.

Listing 5: TableHandler, *the definition module from a symbol-table generator.*

```
DEFINITION MODULE TableHandler;
  FROM DataTypes IMPORT ObjPtr, ObjClass, StrPtr, StrForm;
  EXPORT QUALIFIED Scope.
    NewScope, CloseScope, NewObj, NewStr, Find, FindField,
  InitTableHandler, EndTableHandler;

  VAR Scope: ObjPtr; (*header of scope located by Find*)

  PROCEDURE NewScope(kind: ObjClass): ObjPtr;
  PROCEDURE CloseScope;
  PROCEDURE NewObj(id: CARDINAL; class: ObjClass): ObjPtr;
  PROCEDURE NewStr(form: StrForm): StrPtr;
  PROCEDURE Find(id: CARDINAL): ObjPtr;
  PROCEDURE FindField(id: CARDINAL; rec: StrPtr): ObjPtr;
  PROCEDURE InitTableHandler;
  PROCEDURE EndTableHandler;
END TableHandler.
```

Listing 6: TableHandler, *the implementation module that contains the logic (see also listing 5).*

```
IMPLEMENTATION MODULE TableHandler;
  FROM Data IMPORT ObjPtr, Object, ObjClass, StrPtr, Structure, StrForm;
    ...

  PROCEDURE Find(id: CARDINAL): ObjPtr;
  VAR objx: ObjPtr;
  BEGIN Scope := topScope;
      LOOP objx := FindInScope(id, Scope);
      IF objx # NIL THEN EXIT
      ELSIF Scope↑.kind = Module THEN
        objx := FindImport(id, Scope);
        IF objx = NIL THEN objx := FindInScope(id, universe) END ;
        EXIT
      ELSE Scope := Scope↑.base
      END
    END;
    RETURN objx
  END Find;

  ...
END TableHandler.
```

Figure 2 shows the modular structure of our compiler in graphical representation. An arrow from module "M" to module "N" indicates that "N" imports "M" (i.e., "N" depends on the definition module of "M").

It is noteworthy that most multipass compilers show, from the point of view of time, a similar structure—first pass, lexical and syntactical analysis; second pass, table generating; third pass, type checking; and fourth pass, code generating. However, the spatial and temporal structures must not be mixed up (see figure 3).

Our second example of separate compilation is a text editor. In contrast to compilers, editors are interactive programs. Their dynamic flow is typically action oriented. Actions influence the text document's contents and, therefore, its representation on the display. This knowledge may result in the attempt of a modularization seen in figure 4.

But the display handler has to rely on the document handler. In fact, the document handler can be regarded as an abstract file system delivering a stream of characters and formatting information to the display. So we have mutual imports between the document and display handler.

Although this situation does not lead to a conflict as long as mutual import doesn't occur between definition modules, it indicates that the coupling of the two modules is too tight. A fundamental rule states that the "thinner" the interface between modules, the better the modularization.

In our example, we shall remedy the situation by eliminating the arrow from the display to the document handler and replacing it with an arrow from the display to the command interpreter (see figure 5).

This modification has some desirable consequences. First, the command interpreter can directly pass over display-oriented commands—such as scrolling the text—to the display handler without primarily involving the document handler. The second consequence is of even greater importance: the document handler is now freed from its dependence on the display. Therefore, it can also be imported by modules that process the text in a different way, say, by

(continued)

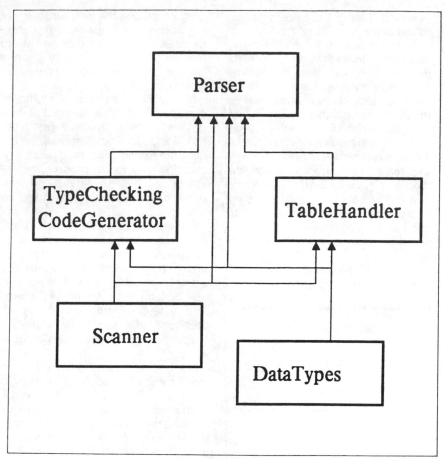

Figure 2: *A representation of the modular structure of the compiler example. The arrows from one module to another indicate that the latter imports the former.*

3a

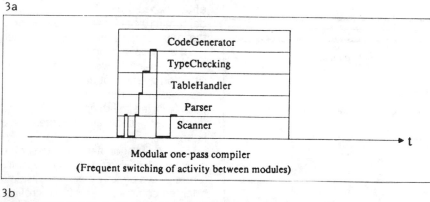

3b

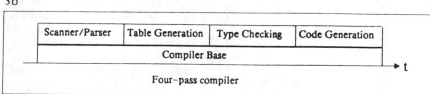

Figure 3: *A one-pass compiler (3a) as contrasted to a four-pass compiler (3b) over t time.*

a printing program or by an off-line statistics program.

FROM PROGRAM COMPONENTS TO LIBRARY MODULES

We have seen that a specific module can be used by different programs. This thought naturally leads to the notion of a module library. The fact that the word *library* stands for a collection of books tempts me to create the word *modulary* for a collection of modules. Actually, in a Modula-2 environment even the operating system is simply a collection of basic and usable modules. The sharp boundary that separates system and application software thus becomes even less distinct.

Most of the features that do not belong directly to the programming language but are indispensable for real programming, such as I/O (input/output) string handling and process scheduling, are transferred to modules in Modula-2. On one hand this relieves, and also generalizes, the language and, on the other hand, increases its flexibility. Figure 6 shows an example of a hierarchy of Modula-2 library modules.

When designing a library module, the question of which facilities should be made available is paramount. If the set of offered procedures is too complicated, then most users will create their own modules; if the procedures are too simplistic, they are again dissatisfied. Our goal is to find the "golden mean."

We can summarize our experience relating to this quest in the following guidelines. We recommend that the library-module designer obey these rules.

GUIDELINE 1

Do not export complex procedures from your library module (i.e., procedures with a large number of explicit or—even worse—implicit parameters and assumptions). Instead, export the atoms of complex operations as individua. This gives the user of your module the chance to "tailor" the operation as a whole to his requests.

For example, assume that a mouse-handling module offers a procedure TrackMouse to track the mouse until a mouse button has been pressed or a character typed. This procedure would

(continued)

satisfy all users *N* who agree to use this termination condition and to give away program control during the tracking loop.

But what about user *A* who wants the loop to stop when the left mouse button has been pressed, or user *B* who wishes to keep the cursor on a grid, or user *C* who wants to make the shape of the cursor depend on its location on the display? (See listing 7 for the general and specific cases of "mouse tracking.")

They would prefer two exported procedures, GetMouse and DrawCursor.

GUIDELINE 2

If complex objects are to be handled by your module, divide it up into several physical modules or groups of modules, each of them operating on the objects at a different level of abstraction ("distributed processing"). This enables your module's client not only to import a suitably restricted set of operations, but also to select the entry level to the module set, i.e., the level of abstraction on which he wants to have the objects handled.

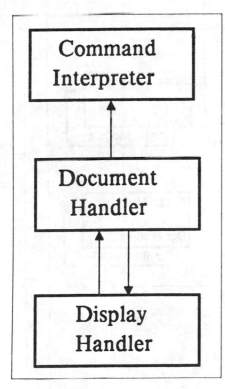

Figure 4: *Our first effort to modularize the text editor leads to mutual imports between the document and display handler modules.*

Moreover, later modifications in the definition can be restricted to individual modules in the set, thus reducing the number of user modules that have to be recompiled.

For example, the window handler base *Windows* (see figure 6) handles windows as a whole. It merely operates on the graph of their global overlapping hierarchy and completely disregards contents. By contrast, module *TextWindows* exports procedures to write text into the windows.

GUIDELINE 3

Assume again that your library module handles complex objects. If the maximum number of objects to be simultaneously handled is sufficiently small, identify each object by a number; for instance, define a subrange as object type. Thus, each user may store that information about the objects that is relevant for his sphere of activity in a private table that is indexed by the data type (distributed data).

Alternatively, a pointer type could have been chosen as object type. In such a case, each object points to its descriptor record. As the object descriptors are public, they cannot be effectively protected. This somehow contradicts the module concept. In fact, Modula-2 offers the possibility of hiding a type. A hidden (or abstract) type is defined in the definition module without structure indication and declared in the corresponding implementation module

(normally as a pointer). But hidden object types restrict the handling of the objects strictly to the module.

In the case under discussion, the subrange is preferable to a pointer type (be it hidden or not) as the latter demands fixing the descriptor record once and for all (see listing 8).

GUIDELINE 4

If you design a library module that handles objects of a certain category, you may decide to include a merely restricted set of (universal) operations. If so, make use of the Modula-2 procedure-type parameter mechanism to enable the user to install his own procedures. Thereby, the range of potential users of your module can radically be enlarged without its size and complexity being increased. Procedure-type parameters make it possible to keep away details from a module. Keeping away details is somehow dual to hiding details in the module.

If a default procedure is provided for a certain operation, this procedure should be exported to enable the user to reassign the default whenever required. For example, the procedure OpenWindow in module *Windows* expects as parameter a procedure which, upon calling, restores the contents of the window. The window handler calls this procedure whenever restoration of this window becomes necessary (see listing 9).

(continued)

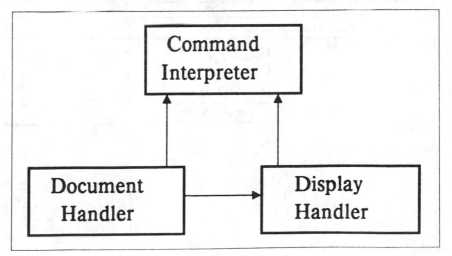

Figure 5: *Our second effort to modularize the text editor frees the document handler from dependence on the display handler.*

CONCURRENCY

Concurrent processes have a particular attraction for software engineers. The aspect of *parallelism* opens up the purely sequential world of ordinary programming. We shall distinguish between *genuine* and *logical* concurrency. "Genuine concurrency" implies that several *processors* are available to execute a program; this is not usually the case these days. "Logical concurrency" is of much greater importance. In Modula-2, an autonomously running process is called a *coroutine*.

You can create coroutines in your Modula-2 program using the standard procedure NewProcess. Each coroutine is controlled by a procedure. In a way, a coroutine is an "instantiation" of its

(continued)

Listing 7: *Four types of users and their respective use of the procedures GetMouse and DrawCursor.*

```
User N: REPEAT GetMouse(buttons, x, y);
        DrawCursor(x, y); BusyRead(ch)
        UNTIL (buttons # {}) OR (ch # 0C);

User A: REPEAT GetMouse(buttons, x, y);
        DrawCursor(x, y); BusyRead(ch)
        UNTIL (left IN buttons) OR (ch # 0C);

User B: REPEAT GetMouse(buttons, x, y);
        DrawCursor(x DIV unit•unit, y DIV unit•unit); BusyRead(ch)
        UNTIL (buttons # {}) OR (ch # 0C);

User C:REPEAT GetMouse(buttons, x, y);
       IF x < wid THEN SetPattern(private) ELSE ResetPattern END;
       DrawCursor(x, y); BusyRead(ch)
       UNTIL (buttons # {}) OR (ch # 0C);
```

Listing 8: *An example of a hidden (or abstract) type.*

```
TYPE Window = |0..7|; (•subrange type•)
TYPE Window; (•hidden type•)
```

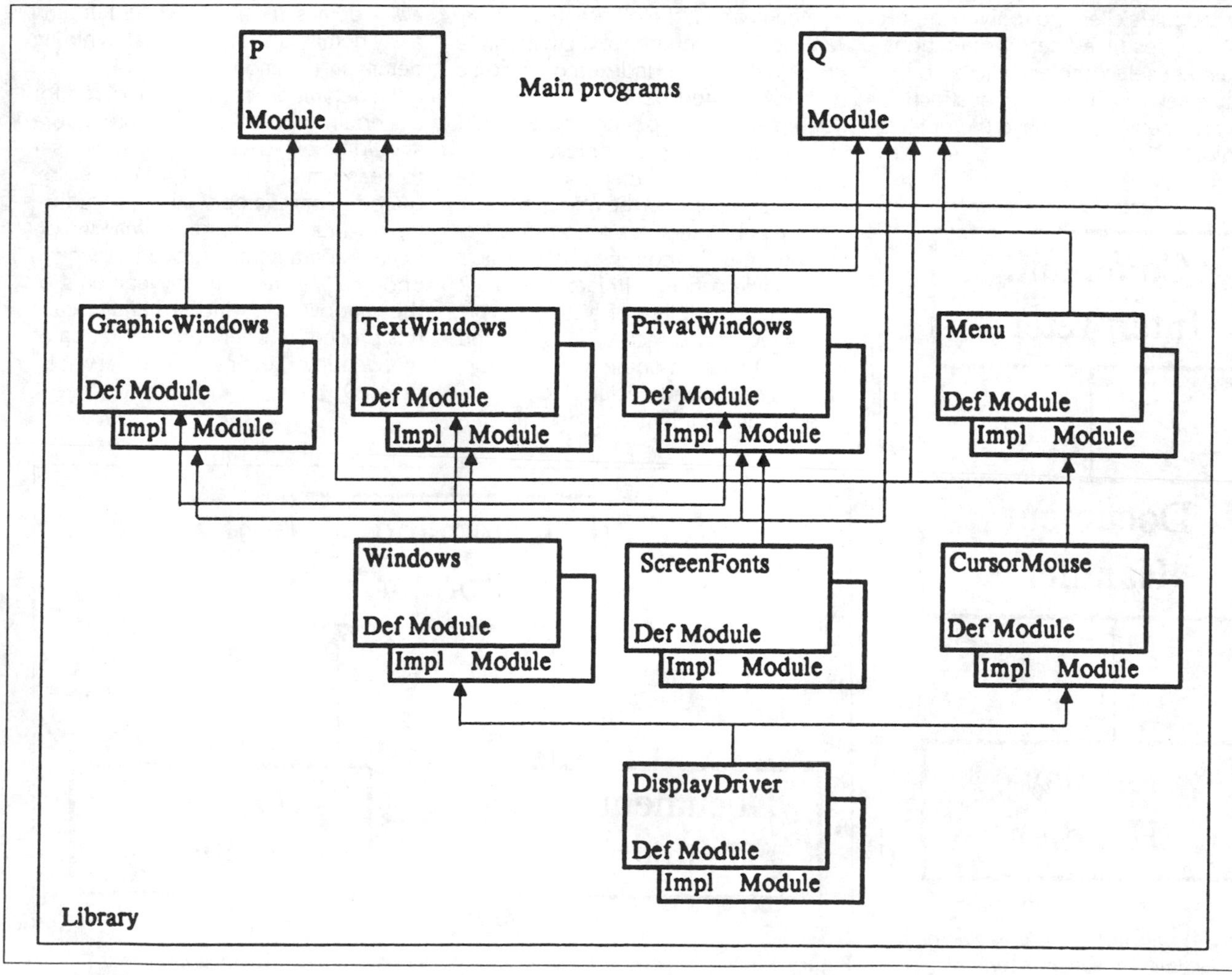

Figure 6: *The structure of Modula-2 programs that use the display software library modules.*

procedure. The essence of the coroutine concept is that control can be transferred between the different coroutines. When your program calls the standard procedure TRANSFER with parameters p and q (both of type *PROCESS*), control is passed from p to q. Thereby, the current state of the coroutine p is saved and coroutine q is reactivated in the state of its previous interruption.

Whenever a coroutine of a program terminates, i.e., its procedure terminates, then the program itself terminates. Therefore, procedures of auxiliary coroutines are typically embedded into an (infinite) *LOOP. . . END* loop, such that program termination is controlled by the main process, i.e., the coroutine created by the program loader.

Let us elucidate the coroutine with a program that creates reservation lists.

Assume that different courses in informatics with restricted attendance were announced. Students are accepted according to the sequence of their registration.

We shall design the program so that it accepts chronologically ordered reservations stored on a text file *in*. A reservation is a pair of the desired course (0–9) and the student's name. As long as the number of applicants for a course has not yet reached the limit, the name of each new student is alphabetically inserted into the main list of that course. Additionally, our program maintains a standby list for each course containing the names of surplus applicants. Obviously, the standby lists have to be chronologically ordered.

Of course, the process of generating (and printing) the two lists is exactly the same for each course. We shall formulate it as a procedure GenList. Notice that *name* is in fact an index into a name buffer *buf* and that *name* = 0 signals termination. See listing 10.

Let us emphasize again that this procedure describes the whole process of generating and printing the two lists of an individual course in a very coherent way. Hence, we should try to find a formulation that does not force us to split up the procedure—for technical reasons—into smaller portions.

In fact, assigning a coroutine to each course—with GenList as controlling procedure—is an elegant way of formulating our program. The main process shall activate the respective coroutine whenever it has read a new reservation item from the input file. The coroutine will transfer control back to the main process when it is ready to accept a new registration.

You can obtain the final form of GenList by simply embedding the procedure body into a *LOOP. . . END* loop and replacing *GetRegistration* (marked with a >) by TRANSFER (*handler[cur]*, *main*).

The crucial thing for the main process to do is reading reservations from the input file, one after the other, and passing control to the appropriate course handler (see listing 11).

Notice that all process-oriented types and procedures stem from a standard module *SYSTEM*. This module can be regarded as the interface between

(continued)

Listing 9: *The default procedure OpenWindow will restore the contents of the window when needed.*

```
TYPE RestoreProc = PROCEDURE(Window);
PROCEDURE OpenWindow(VAR wdw: Window; x,y,w,h: CARDINAL; Repaint: RestoreProc);
```

Listing 10: *Procedure GenList, which creates reservation lists, demonstrates the use of coroutines in Modula-2.*

```
PROCEDURE GenList;
  CONST lim = 20;
  VAR i, j, k, entry: CARDINAL;
      list: ARRAY [0..50] OF RECORD name, next: CARDINAL END;
  BEGIN
    list[0].name = 0; list[0].next := 1; (*sentinel*)
    list[1].name := 1; list[1].next := 0; (*sentinel*)
    entry := 2; (*create alphabetic list*)
    LOOP
      IF entry = lim THEN EXIT END;
>     GetRegistration;
      IF name = 0 THEN EXIT END;
      list[entry].name := name;
      k := 0; (*insert item*)
      LOOP
        i := list[list[k].next].name; j := name;
        WHILE (buf[i] = buf[j]) & ((buf[i] # 0C) OR (buf[j] # 0C)) DO
          i := i + 1; j := j + 1
        END;
        IF buf[i] > buf[j] THEN EXIT END;
        k := list[k].next
      END;
      list[entry].next := list[k].next; list[k].next := entry;
      entry := entry + 1
    END;
    IF entry = lim THEN (*create chronological list*)
      LOOP
>       GetRegistration;
        IF name = 0 THEN EXIT END;
        list [entry].name := name;
        entry := entry + 1
      END
    END;
    (*print list*)
    k := list[0].next;
    WHILE list[k].next # 0 DO i := list[k].name;
      WHILE buf[i] # 0C DO WriteChar(out, buf[i]); i := i + 1 END;
      WriteChar(out, EOL);
      k := list[k].next
    END;
    WriteChar(out, EOL);
    k := lim;
    WHILE k < entry DO i := list[k].name;
      WHILE buf[i] # 0C DO WriteChar(out, buf[i]); i := i + 1 END;
      WriteChar(out, EOL);
      k := k + 1
    END;
    WriteChar(out, FF)
  END GenList;
```

Modula-2 and the system. *SYSTEM* also exports a type *ADDRESS*. An object of type *ADDRESS* is a pointer to a memory-word. (The type *WORD* is also exported from *SYSTEM*.)

Each coroutine is connected with a memory section where its variables are allocated. Beginning and size of this sec-

tion have to be specified as parameters of *NEWPROCESS* at the time of creating the coroutine. In our example, we have called procedure AllocateHeap of another low-level module *Program* to reserve the desired amount of storage (400 bytes).

Notice finally that the standard function *CAP* returns the uppercase variant of its character argument.

SUMMARY

Modula-2 is a modern programming language invented for the development of large software systems. The module is a new structuring tool, comparable in its relevance with the procedure and locality introduced by ALGOL and Pascal. Although conceptually simple, the module has proven to be surprisingly difficult to master. On the other hand, the modular way of thinking has far-reaching and unexpected consequences, even for the design of operating systems and for computer architecture.

The coroutine concept of Modula-2 allows processes to be coherently formulated as procedures. Coroutines are a kind of dynamic counterpart to modules. In contrast to modules, procedures can be instantiated. Thus, thanks to a mechanism to transfer control between coroutines, different instances of the same procedure may simultaneously be alive. ∎

Listing II: *Module* Lists *reads a reservation item from the input file and then invokes the respective coroutine* handler.

```
MODULE Lists;
    FROM SYSTEM IMPORT ADDRESS, PROCESS, NEWPROCESS, TRANSFER;
    FROM Program IMPORT AllocateHeap;
    FROM FileSystem IMPORT File, Lookup, Close, ReadChar, WriteChar;
    FROM InOut IMPORT ReadString, Write, WriteString;

    CONST EOL = 36C; FF = 14C; (*form-feed*)
    VAR buf: ARRAY [0..10000] OF CHAR;
        name, i, cur: CARDINAL; ch: CHAR; A: ADDRESS;
        main: PROCESS; handler: ARRAY [0..9] OF PROCESS;
        in, out: File; fname: ARRAY [0..31] OF CHAR;
BEGIN
    buf[0] := 0C; buf[1] := 255C; buf[2] := 0C; i := 3;
    FOR cur := 0 TO 9 DO
        A := AllocateHeap(400); NEWPROCESS(GenList, A, 400, handler[cur])
    END;
    WriteString("in> "); ReadString(fname); Write(EOL);
    Lookup(in, fname, FALSE);
    WriteString("out> "); ReadString(fname); Write(EOL);
    Lookup(out, fname, TRUE);
    ReadChar(in, ch);
    WHILE (ch >= "0") & (ch <= "9") DO
        cur := ORD(ch) − ORD("0"); name := i;
        ReadChar(in, ch); ReadChar(in, ch);
        WHILE (CAP(ch) >= "A") & (CAP(ch) <= "Z") DO
            buf[i] := ch; i := i + 1; ReadChar(in, ch)
        END;
        buf[i] := 0C; i := i + 1;
        TRANSFER(main, handler[cur]);
        ReadChar(in, ch)
    END;
    name := 0;
    FOR cur := 0 TO 9 DO TRANSFER(main, handler[cur]) END;
    Close(in); Close(out)
END Lists.
```

PASCAL, ADA, AND MODULA-2*

DAVID COAR

WHEN FACED WITH a reasonably large software project, many factors can influence the choice of an implementation language. Some are technical and some are not. In comparing Pascal, Ada, and Modula-2, I will deal with the major technical factors by using basic properties that these languages possess as measuring tools. In each case, I will describe the relevant programming issues briefly and then discuss the three languages within that context, pointing out differences, commenting on the relative merits of certain features, and offering opinions concerning possible improvements. Since I'm focusing on the capabilities provided by the language features rather than the specific syntax used to invoke them, this article complements detailed descriptions published elsewhere (see references).

Why did I choose these particular languages? Over the years, Pascal has achieved popularity as an implementation language. Nevertheless, its creator, Niklaus Wirth, apparently never thought of Pascal as a true systems-implementation language. Modula-2, on the other hand, represents a conscious effort on his part to define such a language. Modula-2 has facilities for hardware interfacing and allows many programmers to work together on the same project. Of course, these are the same goals that were established by the Department of

Defense for the new programming language, Ada. Thus, Pascal and Modula-2 are different attempts by the same person to design a programming language, while Ada and Modula-2 have different origins but the same stated goals.

STRONG TYPING

In most modern programming languages you must declare each data element and routine before using it. First, you choose an alphanumeric identifier to serve as its name. Then, specify its type. You know certain primitive types, such as integer, real, Boolean, and character in advance (see table 1). You must declare the others explicitly before using them. You may create new types either by making certain minor modifications to previous types or by combining one or more previous types into composite structures such as arrays and records. In any case, the type of an element completely determines its storage requirements and the uses to which it may be put. This is what is meant by strong typing. Typing plays a major role in all three languages by restricting the

....

David Coar (POB 23489, Portland, OR 97223) is a member of the technical product staff of Floating Point Systems Inc. He received his bachelor's and master's degrees in mathematics from the University of California at Berkeley. His hobbies include skiing and classical guitar.

way you can allocate and use data elements.

STORAGE ALLOCATION

In order to generate code for your program, the compiler must know the size and location of each data element you declare. The data element's type completely determines its size. Its location normally is offset from the beginning of a multiple-element memory area. The compiler assigns an offset of zero to the first element in the area, the second gets offset more than the first, and so on. The details of this algorithm completely determine the resulting memory area's size. Each memory area location and the way it gets allocated depend on the kind of memory area it is. There are three possibilities: *stack*, *heap*, and *main*.

Stack areas are contained within a large memory area called an execution stack. A special *top-of-stack* pointer keeps track of the execution stack's current end. When you call a function or procedure, you change the top-of-stack pointer and the program uses the area between the old and new top-of-stack for your newly called routine's data elements. When the call completes, the program restores the top-of-stack pointer to its previous value and returns control to the calling procedure or function.

(continued)

Heap-memory areas contain a single data element, usually an array or a record. To use this data element, you must have a pointer to the heap-memory area containing it. A pointer is a special kind of data element that always contains the address of a data element in the heap. Your program must explicitly allocate each heap area that it needs, using special syntax provided for this purpose. The address of each new area is stored in a pointer. Pascal and Modula-2 also have syntax for explicit release of heap areas, but not Ada.

Main memory is allocated once when you load your program. A Pascal program has only one main-memory area, which contains all the data elements declared in the main part of your program and all the executable code. In Modula-2, each *library module* your program uses has a separate main-memory area that contains its data elements and the executable code for all its procedures and functions. Similarly, each *library unit* of an Ada program has its own main-memory area for data elements and executable code.

Ada is the only one of these three languages that gives you explicit control over the size and relative location of data elements. In Pascal and Modula-2, an element's size, as well as location within each enclosing memory area, is controlled completely by the compiler. For most applications this is not a prob-

lem. However, if you must generate or use data that has a predefined, external format, then you must have control over a data element's size and relative location within a record.

Both Ada and Modula-2 let you specify an absolute address for a data element or routine. This facility, which does not exist in Pascal, is essential for implementing interrupt handlers and memory-mapped I/O (input/output). It would be nice if there were a related facility in any of the three languages that would allow you to specify a data element or routine's symbolic address for linking it with an external system.

It's a little surprising that Modula-2 has no mechanism for creating variable-length arrays. Instead, when you declare an array you must specify its type fully, including the range of acceptable index values. Because the upper and lower bounds for such a range must be constant, the number of elements in the array will also be constant. Modula-2 inherited this unfortunate feature from Pascal with only one minor improvement. When you specify the type of an array parameter to a procedure or function in Modula-2, you need not include its size. This allows you to use a parameter to pass different size arrays to a procedure or function. However, Modula-2 doesn't let you create an array whose size is determined at run time, which makes the language unnec-

essarily restrictive. It should at least give you pointers to such arrays.

TYPE CONFLICTS

Each expression in your program belongs to two potentially different data types. One type comes from the way it's used, because that tells you the type of data value it must produce. The second comes from the expression's structure. Given inputs of a specific type, each operator in the expression produces outputs of a specific type. So the expression's data elements and the operators that are used to combine them tell you what type of data value it will produce.

If these two types are different, the compiler must decide how to resolve the conflict. In a strongly typed language, conflicts are generally treated as programming errors. This has one unfortunate consequence: an element's data type is not determined by its intrinsic properties but by your need to combine it with other data elements. In Modula-2, for instance, I learned to avoid cardinal (unsigned integer) data elements quickly because they could not be mixed with integers in expressions.

Pascal provides almost no relief from the regimen of strict typing. There are few implicit type conversions, and functions for explicit type conversion are limited to ORD, CHR, TRUNC, and ROUND. With the function ORD you can convert an enumerated value into an unsigned integer. With the function CHR you can convert an unsigned integer into a character. The functions TRUNC and ROUND convert values of type real into values of type integer. The program has to handle other type conversions by using case statements, explicitly initialized arrays, or untagged variant records. In particular, there is no safe and easy way to recover an enumerated value from an unsigned integer. All too often conversions that are perfectly natural from a conceptual standpoint, and which should be programmatically simple, lead to the use of untagged variant records—probably the least safe construct in the language.

Modula-2 provides a little more relief from strict typing. In certain situations, it provides implicit type conversion when a value is assigned to a different-

Table 1: *The data types available in each of the three languages are shown in the table. Enumerated types, records, and arrays are not primitive types; the others are. Strictly speaking, characters are a special enumerated type and strings are a particular class of character arrays.*

Language	Integer Types	Real Types	Structured Types	Special Types
Pascal	enumerated character integer	real	record array string	pointer Boolean set (bit mask)
Modula-2	enumerated character integer	real	record array	word address Boolean set (bit mask) procedure
Ada	enumerated character integer short long integer	real short real long real	record array string	pointer Boolean exception task

(continued)

ly typed data element. For example, you may store a cardinal value in an integer data element and a positive integer in a cardinal element. However, neither an integer nor a cardinal may be stored in a real element. There is a slightly richer set of functions for making explicit type conversions. In particular, the function VAL allows you to recover enumerated values from unsigned integers. Additionally, certain types have a built-in function that shares the type name and converts input values of that type. The drawback of this feature is that it appears to be system dependent because no computation can be performed in making the conversion. Consequently, use it with care if you intend to move your software from one system to another.

Ada is similar to Modula-2 in its enforcement of strict typing. For certain well-defined types, there is a built-in function that shares the type name and converts input values into the particular values of that type. This means that many type conversions are reasonably easy. Moreover, the collection of type names that can be used for sharing and converting is well defined, and the results are independent of any implementation. All of this is a definite improvement over Modula-2.

Ada's implicit type conversion is based on the notion of a *subtype*. When a type is created by placing restrictions on another one, it is called a subtype (see listing 1). Its values may be mixed with expressions of the original type and values of either type may be stored

in data elements on the other, as long as the constraints of the subtype are not violated. While subtypes (called subranges) exist in both Pascal and Modula-2, Ada tries to make their meaning more precise.

Derived Types and Overloading

Ada further refines strong typing by introducing the notion of a *derived type*: an exact copy of another logically distinct type (see listing 1). Derived types allow you to have look-alike data types whose corresponding data elements cannot be confused with one another. In order to make the derived type an exact copy of the original, Ada gives it logically distinct copies of each original operation. While this feature seems reasonable at first, it has some undesirable side effects. To understand them, however, we must first discuss another distinctive Ada feature, overloading.

Two elements of your program are *overloaded* if both are visible and have the same name. In a strongly typed language, overloaded elements normally cannot be confused with one another as long as they have different types. In spite of this, both Pascal and Modula-2 prohibit overloading. Ada allows it, but only for procedures and functions. An Ada procedure or function call may refer to any one of several routines with the same name. The compiler then chooses the correct one according to the number of its parameters, the type of each parameter, and the type, if any, of its return value.

Overloading is closely associated with another distinctive Ada feature, the ability to redefine basic operators such as addition, subtraction, and multiplication. To do this, you simply declare a function that has the right number of parameters and use the appropriate symbol for its name. If you have defined a collection of operators, you can use them in an expression with values of the correct type exactly as you would use any ordinary operator. One desirable consequence of all this is that it lets you create versions of the basic operators that mix types in a more or less arbitrary way.

Another less desirable consequence of overloading comes from the rules governing types in general and derived types in particular. There is a set of operations for each type in your Ada program. Each set of operations is a procedure or function with at least one type-oriented parameter or return value. The operations belong to the type either because they were inherited by the type or because both the type and the operations set were declared in the visible part of the same package.

Now consider the following situation. Types $x1$ and $x2$ are declared in package x along with a procedure q whose parameters are of type $x1$ and $x2$. In package y, type $y1$ is derived from $x1$, and type $y2$ is derived from $x2$. As mentioned earlier, a derived type inherits a copy of each operation belonging to the original type. Inside y there are now two procedures named q: one with parameters of type $y1$ and $x2$ belonging to $y1$, and one with parameters of type $x1$ and $y2$ belonging to $y2$ (see figure 1). Of course, you probably wanted a procedure with parameters of type $y1$ and $y2$, but to get it you'd have to explicitly declare it. And that would not be the end of your problems. The literal values for types $x1$ and $y1$ are indistinguishable, as are those for $x2$ and $y2$. So a call on q that substitutes a literal value for one of its parameters will be ambiguous inside y, unless the literal value is appropriately qualified. What makes this ambiguity especially frustrating is that there is really only one procedure q. The copies are merely pseudonyms. Ambiguity regarding a literal value's type is probably unavoidable. Nevertheless, the automatic proliferation of overloaded procedures and functions that occurs in the Ada language seems unreasonable.

INITIALIZATION

The problem of initialization is related to strong typing and storage allocation. When you declare a data element, you often might want to give it an initial value. Occasionally, you might even want to specify an initial value for all data elements of a given type. This would let you document important properties of such data elements. For stack and heap elements, convenience, documentation, and control centralization are the major advantages provided by initial values. For main-memory data elements, however, the initial value's primary virtue is efficiency, since the loader generates them from a map at run time. If you don't generate them at that time, you wind up with two copies of each initial value in main memory. The list of hardware instructions that must be executed to initialize the data element will contain one copy, while the data element itself will hold the other once the hardware instructions are executed. In addition, there will be hardware instructions to write the value into the correct memory location. For a large table of error messages, this could lead to a significant increase in memory requirements.

Beyond some reasonably simple syntax extensions for declarations, a strongly typed language must have facilities for creating structured constants if you want to implement initial values. Otherwise you can't describe the initial values for compound data structures such as records and arrays. Ada is the only one of the three languages that supports either declarations or structured constants. The decision not to include these features in Pascal and Modula-2 presumably was motivated by a desire to keep the language as simple as possible. Most Pascal implementations have extensions in this area, but they differ substantially and will cause problems if you want software that is easy to move from one system to another.

STRUCTURED CONTROL

The data elements in your program control its behavior. Depending on their contents, you may decide to examine an input value, compute a new value for one of them, or produce an output value. Statement lists in the body of the program specify these actions in detail. Program execution is basically sequential in nature. At any given instant, only one statement controls your program. Certain kinds of statements let you transfer control to either a different statement list or to another statement within the same list. In the absence of such explicit transfers, however, the program executes the statement list in order, starting with the first one. All three languages provide essentially the same facilities for dealing with this type of deliberate, sequential control. Ada provides two additional control mechanisms, the rendezvous and the exception, but both have serious flaws, and the rendezvous is not an appropriate construct for a low-level systems implementation language.

SEQUENTIAL CONTROL

All languages let you explicitly transfer control from one part of your program to another. The GOTO statement is the most primitive example of such a feature. It lets you jump to a more or less arbitrary location within the same list of statements. Often, a particular relationship between two or more data elements, such as $x + y = z$, is consciously preserved for a number of consecutive statements. Because you run the risk of destroying such relations whenever you jump into the middle of a list of statements, you should use GOTO statements sparingly. Good programming languages discourage explicit transfers by providing more structured methods for altering the flow of control, e.g., procedures, functions, conditional statements, and looping constructs. Ada and Modula-2 transfer control similarly and both are a substantial improvement over Pascal.

In both Ada and Modula-2, a procedure's or function's return statement lets you cut off its execution and transfer control to the place where it was called. However, when you invoke the return statement to get you out of a function, you must always supply an appropriate return value. Unlike Pascal, neither Ada nor Modula-2 have a special data element that contains the

(continued)

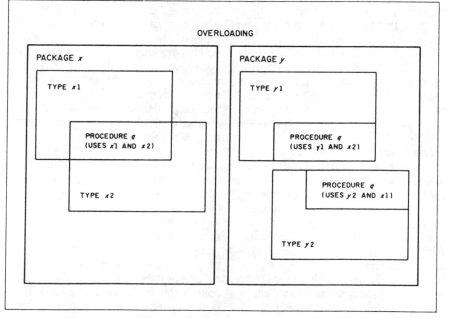

Figure 1: *Procedure* q *in package* x *has parameters of type* x1 *and* x2. *Type* y1 *in package* y *is derived from type* x1. *Type* y2 *is derived from type* x2. *As a result, package* y *contains two procedures named* q. *One has parameters of type* y1 *and* x2. *The other has parameters of type* y2 *and* x1. *If you want a procedure that does the same thing for* y1 *and* y2 *that the original* q *does for* x1 *and* x2, *you will have to declare it yourself. If you call it* q, *it will be overloaded with these two other procedures named* q *that you got for free.*

result of the function. Consequently, the function cannot return an uninitialized data value. If you reach the end of a function before executing a return statement, the program generates a run-time error. This makes it much easier to guarantee that the generated value is appropriate.

In both Ada and Modula-2, an exit statement within a program loop allows you to cut off its execution and transfer control to the next statement beyond it. In Ada you can label a loop, and you can exit from any one of several nested loops by supplying the correct label. In Modula-2, however, you cannot label loops, and there is no easy way to curtail an outer loop. The exit statement always terminates the innermost loop, as it does in Ada when the program doesn't supply a label.

Of the three languages, only Modula-2 has no GOTO statement. The availability of exit and return statements makes them unnecessary. However, Ada has retained them. The Modula-2 exit statement, on the other hand, is too restrictive, and the Ada construct seems more appropriate. In fact, it might be better if an exit statement always required a label. This would prevent problems from arising when one loop is inserted within another after it's written.

A final difference between the three languages has to do with the handling of statement lists. When you write a loop in Ada or Modula-2, the body of the loop is assumed to contain a list of statements. The same is true for each branch of a conditional or case statement. In Pascal, on the other hand, most of these constructs require a single statement, which can, if necessary, be a list of statements enclosed within a begin-end pair. The absence of explicit begin-end bracketing in Ada and Modula-2 creates the need for a way to terminate the corresponding statement list. Ada has introduced three new tokens, **end if**, **end case**, and **end loop**, while Modula-2 has simply reused the reserved word **end** for all three. The Ada solution is often helpful in pinpointing the cause of syntax errors.

EXCEPTION HANDLING

Exceptions are conditions you wish to exclude from normal processing considerations. They are normally the result of an unlikely set of circumstances that may or may not represent an error.

Many times a particular exception can arise at almost any point during the execution of your program, and you would like to be able to deal with it without continually testing for it. A hardware interrupt, especially one caused by an arithmetic error such as dividing by zero, is a perfect example of this type of exception. Since the hardware must check for it, additional software tests may be wasteful. A mechanism for handling exceptions should probably be rated by its ability to deal with this kind of hardware interrupt.

Of the three languages, only Ada has attempted to solve the problem of exception handling. At the end of each function or procedure, and at certain other points in your program, you can define an exception handler. It is essentially a case statement containing one branch for each exception you are willing to handle. Exceptions must be declared and you may activate one at any point in your program by executing a raise statement that references it. When an exception is raised during the execution of a procedure or function, by the routine itself, by another routine that it called, or by the hardware, the appropriate branch of its exception handler is invoked.

Once a routine has dealt with an exception, it must return control to the list of statements that called it. You can prevent the exception from propagating, but you can't fix things up and return to the place where the exception occurred. For this reason, Ada exceptions have only marginal value. They will be adequate for many situations, but they aren't useful enough to justify an expensive implementation.

TASK MANAGEMENT

As mentioned earlier, most program execution is sequential. If you wish to simultaneously execute more than one statement sequence you need to create a separate task or process. You also need to control it once you create it. At any given moment, there is a potentially different statement in control of each task in your program. If your program contains more than one active task, a collection of statements (rather than just one) determine its behavior. A task may or may not be active, and an active task may or may not be executing on a processor. Active tasks must share the available processors. If there are several pro-

cessors, then several tasks may be executing at once. Otherwise there will be only one.

Pascal has no task-management facilities. Modula-2 allows you to create them by calling the procedure NEW-PROCESS and to control them by calling the procedure TRANSFER, which suspends the execution of one task and resumes the execution of another at the point where you last left it. Both of these routines as well as the type PROCESS, are contained in the special module called SYSTEM, and little is said about their implementation. Ada, on the other hand, has defined an elaborate set of tasking facilities.

An Ada task is activated along with the part of your program that contains its declaration, and it must be terminated before that part of your program can be deactivated. If it's declared within a procedure or function, a copy of the task will be activated each time the routine is called, and this copy must terminate before the call can complete. If you don't want the task to run to completion, you can terminate it explicitly with an ABORT statement.

To communicate with an Ada task you must declare one or more *entries* for it. When you declare an entry you specify only its name and parameter structure. An **accept** statement within the body of your task associates a list of statements with the entry and thus defines its meaning. If there is an outstanding call on the entry, it will be executed and the caller will be activated. Otherwise the task suspends execution until the entry is called. If an entry is called before the accept statement is executed, the call is queued along with any others that are pending for that entry and the caller is suspended. The pairing of a **call** and an **accept** statement is called a **rendezvous**. Special syntax allows you to accept one of several possible entries and to make conditional calls on an entry.

The Ada tasking model is complex and cumbersome. It has lots of features and not much flexibility. As a result, it will be costly to implement and not very useful. And to top it off, the problems associated with updating shared data elements are dealt with only as an afterthought. The moral of this story is that elaborate tasking models have no place in a systems-implementation language. A few simple mechanisms are needed, not a complicated structure.

MODULARITY

You can partition almost any large software system into reasonably small, self-contained units, or modules—each with a number of related data elements and the procedures and functions needed to manipulate them. If you have carefully defined and suitably restricted the module interfaces, you will be able to code and debug them independently. As a general rule, focusing on individual modules reduces the number of variables you have to contend with at any given moment and makes the system as a whole easier to design, debug, and maintain. Moreover, to the extent that you can overlap work on several parts of the system, less time will be required to implement it.

Pascal discourages modular design by preventing you from breaking up your implementation. In the first place, you must group your declarations as follows: label declarations, followed by type declarations, then variable declarations, and finally, procedure and function declarations. This makes it virtually impossible to group functionally related elements. In the second place, there are no mechanisms for splitting your program into smaller pieces for separate encoding. Everything you do is part of a single program, and data files are the only mechanism for communicating between separate programs.

As its name implies, modularity is a strong point of Modula-2. A Modula-2 module contains data elements, procedures, and functions, all of which are declared within its scope. You must explicitly export any elements you need somewhere else, and you must explicitly import any external elements you need inside. A module that is not contained within another is called a library module. You may declare a library module all at once, in which case it is called a program module. Alternatively, you may declare it in two stages. The first stage is called a definition module. In it you declare only those portions of the module that are visible from the outside. Procedures and functions may be introduced but not fully declared. The second stage is called an implementation module. You use it to complete your declaration of the elements you introduced in the corresponding definition module. Additionally, you declare any other elements that may be required. A definition module and its implementation module need not import the same external elements (see listing 2). This lets library modules serve each other without creating circular de-

Listing 2: *This listing shows a pair of library modules that depend on each other. The implementation of module a makes use of procedure q in module b, while the implementation of module b makes use of procedure p in module a. In Pascal and Modula-2 everything between the symbols ''(*'' and ''*)'' is ignored by the compiler.*

```
DEFINITION MODULE a;
  EXPORT QUALIFIED p;
  PROCEDURE p(x: INTEGER);
END a.
DEFINITION MODULE b;
  EXPORT QUALIFIED q;
  PROCEDURE q(x,y: INTEGER);
END b.
IMPLEMENTATION MODULE a;
  FROM b IMPORT q;
  PROCEDURE p(x: INTEGER);
  BEGIN
    (* statements defining the behavior of p *)
  END p;
  PROCEDURE r(x: INTEGER);
  BEGIN
    (* statements defining the behavior of r *)
    q(x,4); (* a call on the procefure q from module b *)
    (* more statements defining the rest of r *)
  END r;
BEGIN
  (* statements for initializing a *)
END a.
IMPLEMENTATION MODULE b;
  FROM a IMPORT p;
  PROCEDURE q(x,y: INTEGER);
  BEGIN
    (* statements defining the behavior of p *)
  END q;
  PROCEDURE r(x: INTEGER);
  BEGIN
    (* statements defining the behavior of r *)
    p(2); (* a call on the procedure p from module a *)
    (* more statements defining the rest of r *)
  END r;
BEGIN
  (* statements for initializing a *)
END b.
```

pendencies in their definition modules.

All of the Modula-2 compilers I know implement the following mechanism to allow one library module to use the exported element of another. When a definition module is compiled, a file is created that contains a summary of its declarations and a timestamp that was generated by the compiler. This summary file is used to establish correct typing information for any elements that are imported by other library modules

(see listing 3). It is also used when the implementation module is compiled. In both cases, the timestamp contained in it is copied to the resulting code file, and run-time checks guarantee that all code referring to the definition module was compiled using the same summary file. Since the functionality provided by this mechanism is a requirement of the language, Modula-2 is excellent for modular decomposition of large systems.

An Ada package equates to a Modula-2

module, except for the way you make elements visible externally. All elements declared in a package specification (the Ada equivalent of a definition module) are assumed to be visible outside the package unless they are declared in its private part. In Ada you must explicitly hide an element, while in Modula-2 you must explicitly make it public.

In Modula-2 a compilation unit must be a library module. In Ada it may be a procedure, a function, or a package, and it may or may not be declared within another compilation unit. Ada's generality adds little to the overall capabilities of the language but does increase the compiler's cost by making it more difficult to implement. The facilities provided by Modula-2 seem adequate for most applications, and anything less would certainly be unacceptable.

One final point on modularity. In Ada you may demand in-line expansion for selected procedures and functions. You can thus implement new arithmetic operators and have the compiler generate the code for them in line, exactly as it would for normal arithmetic operators. Since this code can make use of any resource within the package that declared the operator, it can create external dependencies on routines and data elements of the package that are supposed to be hidden. If you change the implementation of such a package in any way, you must recompile every compilation unit that uses one of its inline routines. It would be better if Ada required you to supply a complete definition for any such routine in the public part of its package. However, this is not only not required, it's not allowed.

ABSTRACT TYPING

When combined with modules or packages, strong typing provides a fine tool for creating data structures that have specific, well-defined properties. However, strong typing is representation-oriented by its very nature. It is inevitably tied to the production of types and data structures rather than to their consumption. Another form of typing, which I shall call abstract typing, has to do with consumption rather than production. It comes into play when you wish to write a program dealing with data structures having certain properties but whose exact representation is

(continued)

Listing 3: *When a definition module is compiled, a summary file is produced that contains a timestamp. When a module imports anything from another module, the compiler uses information from the appropriate summary file to insure correct usage. When an implemenation module is compiled, the timestamp from its definition module is included in the resulting code file, along with timestamps for any imported modules. At load time, all copies of the timestamp for a particular module must agree.*

```
DEFINITION MODULE a;
    EXPORT QUALIFIED p;
    PROCEDURE p(x,y: INTEGER);
END a.
```

The summary file resulting from this definition module contains a timestamp whose value, for instance, is v1.

```
MODULE b;
    FROM a IMPORT p;
    (* declarations for b *)
BEGIN
    (* statements initializing b *)
    p(32,2); (* calls the procedure p from module a *)
    (* other statements defining the behavior of b *)
END b.
```

The code file for module b contains a copy of the timestamp value v1. The compiler obtained this value from the summary file for module a because of the import statement at the beginning of b.

```
IMPLEMENTATION MODULE a;
    PROCEDURE p(x,y: INTEGER);
    BEGIN
        (* statements defining the behavior of p *)
    END p;
BEGIN
    (* statements initializing the module a *)
END a.
```

The code file for this implementation module contains the timestamp value v1. The compiler obtained this value from the summary file for module a. The implementation module may be changed and recompiled. As long as it agrees with the description contained in the summary file, there will be no need to recompile module b.

```
DEFINITION MODULE a;
    EXPORT QUALIFIED p;
    PROCEDURE p(x: INTEGER);
END a.
```

The summary file resulting from this definition module contains a timestamp whose value v2 is not equal to v1.

```
IMPLEMENTATION MODULE a;
    PROCEDURE p(x: INTEGER);
    BEGIN
        (* statements defining the behavior of p *)
    END p;
BEGIN
    (* statements initializing the module a *)
END a.
```

The code file for this implementation module contains the timestamp value v2. The compiler obtained this value from the summary file for the second definition module. The module b must now be changed and recompiled before it can be used with this new version of module a.

unimportant to the algorithm.

The traditional way of doing this is to require that each external data structure be represented internally by a tag or address, and that all necessary operations on them be passed as explicit parameters to the algorithm. You can do this in Pascal and Modula-2 but not in Ada. The first two languages allow you to pass procedures and functions as parameters, while the latter does not. In Pascal, you would probably use integers for the data structure tags. In Modula-2, you could use pointers passed in as parameters of type "word." Of course, this solution forces you to bypass all type checking by the compiler. It would be nice if you could declare a routine with some parameters that are pointers to a data structure of type x and others that are routines to manipulate such pointers where x is left unspecified. Then the compiler could verify that all appropriate types matched.

At first glance, this is what an Ada

generic declaration appears to do. You specify a collection of parameters, some of which may be types, and then you declare a routine or package using these parameters wherever necessary. However, what you get is not a simple routine or package. Instead, you get a routine or package that will generate a second one when supplied with the correct parameters. You may use it to declare any number of nongeneric instances, and each time you execute a part of your program that contains such a nongeneric routine, a new version of the underlying routine or package will be generated. By using generics you end up with more routines and packages, not fewer. While the algorithm is shared the code and data are not, and each copy of the generic routine or package will require its own memory. However, since Ada doesn't allow you to pass procedures and functions as parameters, generics are all you've got.

With procedure types, Modula-2 has

provided a consistent way of dealing with functions and procedures as data values in an arbitrary data structure, and not just as parameters to a routine. With this feature, which has no counterpart in either Pascal or Ada, you can declare a type that defines the parameter structure for a procedure or function. A data element of that type behaves like a procedure or function, but it may be located anywhere in memory, including the heap (see listing 4). Any routine that belongs to a library module and has the right parameter structure may be assigned to it. Procedure types may be used in high-level structures, such as files, that include both data and control, and in low-level structures such as interrupt handlers. They allow you to simplify the structure of your application without obscuring its intent.

CONCLUSIONS

As a systems-implementation language, Modula-2 is a major improvement over Pascal. In fact, it is substantially better than most currently available languages. From what I have said so far, you might be tempted to call it the "poor man's Ada," but this is certainly wrong. While there are many extra features in Ada, most of them are marginal improvements. The only one that seems really necessary is the feature that allows you to control the size and relative location of data elements within a data structure.

With all its shortcomings, Modula-2 is a good implementation language and a technical success. It has no surprises and no overlapping functionality. Ada, on the other hand, is a questionable experiment at best. It contains several costly features that are of little value, and the implications of certain other features, such as derived types, seem to lack forethought. Of course it's easier to criticize than to create, but it seems that without the support of the Department of Defense the many "gotchas" and funny features of Ada would have caused its demise. ∎

Listing 4: Modula-2 procedure variables can be used to provide handlers for a data structure within the data structure itself.

```
DEFINITION MODULE structure;
  EXPORT QUALIFIED reference, node, handler, create;
  TYPE reference = POINTER TO node;
  TYPE handler = PROCEDURE(REAL,INTEGER,reference);
  TYPE node =
    RECORD
      link: reference;
      x,y: INTEGER;
      h: handler;
    END;
  PROCEDURE create(h: handler): reference;
END structure.
IMPLEMENTATION MODULE structure;
  FROM Storage IMPORT ALLOCATE;
  PROCEDURE create(h: handler): reference;
    VAR r: reference;
  BEGIN
    NEW(r); (* calls ALLOCATE *)
    r↑.h := h;
    RETURN(r);
  END create;
BEGIN
  (* statements initializing the module structure *)
END structure.
MODULE manager;
  FROM structure IMPORT reference, node, handler, create;
  PROCEDURE transition(x: REAL; y: INTEGER; r: reference);
  BEGIN
    (* statements defining the behavior of transition *)
  END transition;
  VAR ref: reference;
BEGIN
  ref := create(transition);
END manager.
```

REFERENCES

The Ada Programming Language. ANSI/MIL-STD-1815A: American National Standards Institute, 1983.

Jensen, K., and N. Wirth. Pascal User Manual and Report. New York, Heidelberg, Berlin: Springer-Verlag, 1975.

Wirth, N. Programming in Modula-2. New York, Heidelberg, Berlin: Springer-Verlag, 1982.

SECTION 5

PROGRAMMING LANGUAGES AND CONCURRENCY

THE PROGRAMMING LANGUAGE
CONCURRENT PASCAL BY P. BRINCH-HANSEN

COMMUNICATING SEQUENTIAL PROCESSES
BY C. A. R. HOARE

CONCEPTS AND NOTATIONS FOR CONCURRENT
PROGRAMMING BY G. R. ANDREWS AND
F. B. SCHNEIDER

PROCESSES, TASKS, AND MONITORS: A
COMPARATIVE STUDY OF CONCURRENT
PROGRAMMING PRIMITIVES
BY P. WEGNER AND S. A. SMOLKA

INTRODUCTION

PROGRAMMING LANGUAGES AND CONCURRENCY

Concurrent execution of processes is a problem that has been with us for as long as people have been writing operating systems. It also appears naturally with applications such as process control or discrete event simulation. But despite these rather important applications not many languages have provided explicitly for describing concurrent execution. Perhaps PL/1 was one of the earliest with multitasking, followed by ALGOL 68's parallel and collateral clauses. This chapter is devoted to newer languages which have been designed with concurrency in mind.

Concurrent Pascal is an effort to adjoin to an already successful language the features necessary to achieve the description of concurrency. Three new kinds of entities, processes, monitors, and classes, have been added to the language. Classes are a form of data abstraction first introduced in SIMULA and subsequently used in Concurrent Pascal. The essential contribution of Concurrent Pascal is that it shows how to exploit the monitor concept for the description of parallel programs. A *monitor* defines a shared data structure and all the operations that can be performed on it. These operations are synchronized by the monitor, so that only one person has access at any given time. If this person requests a resource which is busy, the request is suspended and another person is granted access rights. For example in this paper a disk buffer is defined as a monitor type. There are two operations called *send* and *receive* and an initialization segment which sets the disk to empty.

The next paper does not actually present an implemented language, but instead concentrates on some language features for describing concurrency. In contrast to the previous languages, the concurrency in Communicating Sequential Processes (CSP), is based upon the concept of message passing. Message passing as a paradigm for concurrency makes sense in the context of a distributed computer system where many processors are connected via communication links. Hoare introduces a generalized form of input and output as a means for communicating between concurrent processes. He also adapts the so-called guarded commands, first introduced by E. Dijkstra, for determining which of several alternatives will be executed. This mechanism is a means for controlling nondeterminancy in the language. A guarded command is

executed if and only if the execution of the guard condition is true. If more than one guard is simultaneously true, then the decision as to which one is selected is made at random. As an example of a CSP program consider the following rather simple routine:

$$[n : integer; \ X \ ? \ insert(n) \rightarrow INSERT/$$

$$n:integer: \ X \ ? \ has(n) \rightarrow SEARCH; \ X \ ! \ (i < size)]$$

We see this program is enclosed in square barckets and the left bracket is preceded by an asterisk. The brackets are scope delimiters and the asterisk stands for repetition. It means that the program contained within will be successively repeated until no conditions (or guards) are true. There are two alternatives contained within the brackets, separated by the vertical bar. Consider the first alternative. The variable n is declared. The question mark denotes that an input operation is expected from the process named X. If the input message is *insert(n)* then the first alternative can be chosen, whereas if the message is *has(n)* the second can be selected. If *insert* is selected then the program segment *INSERT* is invoked, which is not visible here but is contained within the article. If the request is *has*, then a call to *SEARCH* is made. *SEARCH* will look for an i such that $A(i) = n$. If i is less than size then the answer is true and this is output to X by virtue of the exclamation point. Otherwise the result of the comparison is false and that is output.

This paper is a carefully developed tutorial on the use of these primitives to express concurrency. Note that in this paper the author discusses the famous *dining philosophers* problem. This problem has become a standard one for testing the expressibility of any concurrency primitives.

The next paper, by Andrews and Schneider, surveys a decade of experimentation on concepts for expressing concurrency. The authors begin with coroutines, followed by fork-join statements, and then **cobegin-coend**. The notion of a process and its specification is given. Then they discuss synchronization of processes based upon two techniques: shared variables and message passing. Techniques using shared variables include busy waiting, semaphores, conditional critical regions, monitors, and path expressions. Message passing is viewed axiomatically.

The final paper, by Wegner, is also a survey of concurrency notations. The focus here is on comparing Ada with CSP and monitors. It appears that message passing is a better model for a concurrent, distributed system while monitors work well in the case of shared memory. This paper is full of good examples showing the benefits of each.

THE PROGRAMMING LANGUAGE CONCURRENT PASCAL*

P. BRINCH-HANSEN

Abstract—The paper describes a new programming language for structured programming of computer operating systems. It extends the sequential programming language Pascal with concurrent programming tools called processes and monitors. Section I explains these concepts informally by means of pictures illustrating a hierarchical design of a simple spooling system. Section II uses the same example to introduce the language notation. The main contribution of Concurrent Pascal is to extend the monitor concept with an explicit hierarchy of access rights to shared data structures that can be stated in the program text and checked by a compiler.

Index Terms—Abstract data types, access rights, classes, concurrent processes, concurrent programming languages, hierarchical operating systems, monitors, scheduling, structured multiprogramming.

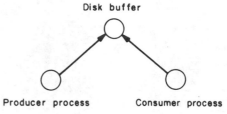

Fig. 1. Process communication.

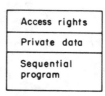

Fig. 2. Process.

I. THE PURPOSE OF CONCURRENT PASCAL

A. Background

SINCE 1972 I have been working on a new programming language for structured programming of computer operating systems. This language is called Concurrent Pascal. It extends the sequential programming language Pascal with concurrent programming tools called processes and monitors [1]–[3].

This is an informal description of Concurrent Pascal. It uses examples, pictures, and words to bring out the creative aspects of new programming concepts without getting into their finer details. I plan to define these concepts precisely and introduce a notation for them in later papers. This form of presentation may be imprecise from a formal point of view, but is perhaps more effective from a human point of view.

B. Processes

We will study concurrent processes inside an operating system and look at one small problem only: how can large amounts of data be transmitted from one process to another by means of a buffer stored on a disk?

Fig. 1 shows this little system and its three components: a process that produces data, a process that consumes data, and a disk buffer that connects them.

The circles are *system components* and the arrows are the *access rights* of these components. They show that both processes can use the buffer (but they do not show that data flows from the producer to the consumer). This kind of picture is an *access graph*.

The next picture shows a process component in more detail (Fig. 2).

A *process* consists of a *private data* structure and a *sequential program* that can operate on the data. One process cannot operate on the private data of another process. But concurrent processes can share certain data structures (such as a disk buffer). The *access rights* of a process mention the shared data it can operate on.

C. Monitors

A disk buffer is a data structure shared by two concurrent processes. The details of how such a buffer is constructed are irrelevant to its users. All the processes need to know is that they can *send* and *receive* data through it. If they try to operate on the buffer in any other way it is probably either a programming mistake or an example of tricky programming. In both cases, one would like a compiler to detect such misuse of a shared data structure.

To make this possible, we must introduce a language construct that will enable a programmer to tell a compiler how a shared data structure can be used by processes. This kind of system component is called a monitor. A monitor can synchronize concurrent processes and transmit data between them. It can also control the order in which competing processes use shared, physical resources. Fig. 3 shows a monitor in detail.

A *monitor* defines a *shared data* structure and all the operations processes can perform on it. These synchronizing operations are called *monitor procedures*. A monitor also defines an *initial operation* that will be executed when its data structure is created.

Manuscript received February 1, 1975. This project is supported by the National Science Foundation under Grant DCR74-17331.

The author is with the Department of Information Science, California Institute of Technology, Pasadena, Calif. 91125.

*Reprinted from *IEEE Transactions on Software Engineering*, June 1975, 199–207.

Fig. 3.   Monitor.

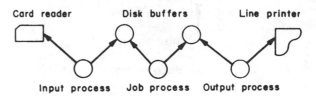

Fig. 4.   Spooling system.

We can define a *disk buffer* as a monitor. Within this monitor there will be shared variables that define the location and length of the buffer on the disk. There will also be two monitor procedures, *send* and *receive*. The initial operation will make sure that the buffer starts as an empty one.

Processes cannot operate directly on shared data. They can only call monitor procedures that have access to shared data. A monitor procedure is executed as part of a calling process (just like any other procedure).

If concurrent processes simultaneously call monitor procedures that operate on the same shared data these procedures must be executed strictly one at a time. Otherwise, the results of monitor calls will be unpredictable. This means that the machine must be able to delay processes for short periods of time until it is their turn to execute monitor procedures. We will not be concerned about how this is done, but will just notice that a monitor procedure has *exclusive access* to shared data while it is being executed.

So the (virtual) machine on which concurrent programs run will handle *short-term scheduling* of simultaneous monitor calls. But the programmer must also be able to delay processes for longer periods of time if their requests for data and other resources cannot be satisfied immediately. If, for example, a process tries to receive data from an empty disk buffer it must be delayed until another process sends more data.

Concurrent Pascal includes a simple data type, called a *queue*, that can be used by monitor procedures to control *medium-term scheduling* of processes. A monitor can either *delay* a calling process in a queue or *continue* another process that is waiting in a queue. It is not important here to understand how these queues work except for the following essential rule: a process only has exclusive access to shared data as long as it continues to execute statements within a monitor procedure. As soon as a process is delayed in a queue it loses its exclusive access until another process calls the same monitor and wakes it up again. (Without this rule, it would be impossible for other processes to enter a monitor and let waiting processes continue their execution.)

Although the disk buffer example does not show this yet, monitor procedures should also be able to call procedures defined within other monitors. Otherwise, the language will not be very useful for hierarchical design. In the case of a disk buffer, one of these other monitors could perhaps define simple input/output operations on the disk. So a monitor can also have *access rights* to other system components (see Fig. 3).

D. System Design

A process executes a sequential program—it is an active component. A monitor is just a collection of procedures that do nothing until they are called by processes—it is a passive component. But there are strong similarities between a process and a monitor: both define a data structure (private or shared) and the meaningful operations on it. The main difference between processes and monitors is the way they are scheduled for execution.

It seems natural therefore to regard processes and monitors as *abstract data types* defined in terms of the operations one can perform on them. If a compiler can check that these operations are the only ones carried out on the data structures, then we may be able to build very reliable, concurrent programs in which *controlled access* to data and physical resources is guaranteed before these programs are put into operation. We have then to some extent solved the *resource protection* problem in the cheapest possible manner (without hardware mechanisms and run time overhead).

So we will define processes and monitors as data types and make it possible to use several instances of the same component type in a system. We can, for example, use two disk buffers to build a *spooling system* with an input process, a job process, and an output process (Fig. 4). I will distinguish between definitions and instances of components by calling them *system types* and *system components*. Access graphs (such as Fig. 4) will always show system components (not system types).

Peripheral devices are considered to be monitors implemented in hardware. They can only be accessed by a single procedure *io* that delays the calling process until an input/output operation is completed. Interrupts are handled by the virtual machine on which processes run.

To make the programming language useful for stepwise system design it should permit the division of a system type, such as a disk buffer, into smaller system types. One of these other system types should give a disk buffer access to the disk. We will call this system type a *virtual disk*. It gives a disk buffer the illusion that it has its own private disk. A virtual disk hides the details of disk input/output from the rest of the system and makes the disk look like a data structure (an array of disk pages). The only operations on this data structure are *read* and *write* a page.

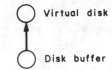

Virtual disk

Disk buffer

Fig. 5.   Buffer refinement.

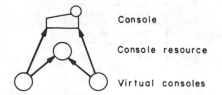

Console

Console resource

Virtual consoles

Fig. 7.   Decomposition of virtual consoles.

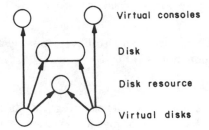

Virtual consoles

Disk

Disk resource

Virtual disks

Fig. 6.   Decomposition of virtual disks.

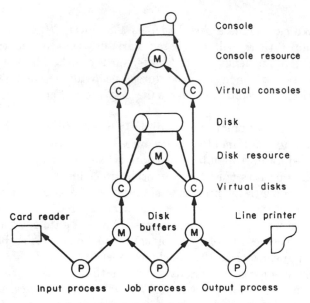

Console

Console resource

Virtual consoles

Disk

Disk resource

Virtual disks

Card reader   Disk   Line printer
                     buffers

Input process   Job process   Output process

Fig. 8.   Hierarchical system structure.

Each virtual disk is only used by a single disk buffer (Fig. 5). A system component that cannot be called simultaneously by several other components will be called a *class*. A class defines a data structure and the possible operations on it (just like a monitor). The exclusive access of class procedures to class variables can be guaranteed completely at compile time. The virtual machine does not have to schedule simultaneous calls of class procedures at run time, because such calls cannot occur. This makes class calls considerably faster than monitor calls.

The spooling system includes two virtual disks but only one real disk. So we need a single *disk resource* monitor to control the order in which competing processes use the disk (Fig. 6). This monitor defines two procedures, *request* and *release* access, to be called by a virtual disk before and after each disk transfer.

It would seem simpler to replace the virtual disks and the disk resource by a single monitor that has exclusive access to the disk and does the input/output. This would certainly guarantee that processes use the disk one at a time. But this would be done according to the built-in short-term scheduling policy of monitor calls.

Now to make a virtual machine efficient, one must use a very simple short-term scheduling rule (such as first come, first served) [2]. If the disk has a moving access head this is about the worst possible algorithm one can use for disk transfers. It is vital that the language make it possible for the programmer to write a medium-term scheduling algorithm that will minimize disk head movements [3]. The data type *queue* mentioned earlier makes it possible to implement arbitrary scheduling rules within a monitor.

The difficulty is that while a monitor is performing an input/output operation it is impossible for other processes to enter the same monitor and join the disk queue. They will automatically be delayed by the short-term scheduler and only allowed to enter the monitor one at a time after each disk transfer. This will, of course, make the attempt

to control disk scheduling within the monitor illusory. To give the programmer complete control of disk scheduling, processes should be able to enter the disk queue during disk transfers. Since *arrival* and *service* in the disk queueing system potentially are simultaneous operations they must be handled by different system components, as shown in Fig. 6.

If the disk fails persistently during input/output this should be reported on an operator's console. Fig. 6 shows two instances of a class type, called a *virtual console*. They give the virtual disks the illusion that they have their own private consoles.

The virtual consoles get exclusive access to a single, real console by calling a *console resource* monitor (Fig. 7). Notice that we now have a standard technique for dealing with virtual devices.

If we put all these system components together, we get a complete picture of a simple spooling system (Fig. 8). Classes, monitors, and processes are marked C, M, and P.

E. Scope Rules

Some years ago I was part of a team that built a multiprogramming system in which processes can appear and disappear dynamically [4]. In practice, this system was used mostly to set up a fixed configuration of processes. Dynamic process deletion will certainly complicate the semantics and implementation of a programming language considerably. And since it appears to be unnecessary for a large class of real-time applications, it seems wise to exclude it altogether. So an operating system written in Concurrent Pascal will consist of a fixed number of processes, monitors, and classes. These components and their data structures will exist forever after system initialization. An operating system can, however, be extended by recompilation. It remains to be seen whether this restriction will simplify or complicate operating system design. But the poor quality of most existing operating systems clearly demonstrates an urgent need for simpler approaches.

In existing programming languages the data structures of processes, monitors, and classes would be called "global data." This term would be misleading in Concurrent Pascal where each data structure can be accessed by a single component only. It seems more appropriate to call them *permanent data structures*.

I have argued elsewhere that the most dangerous aspect of concurrent programming is the possibility of *time-dependent programming errors* that are impossible to locate by program testing ("lurking bugs") [2], [5], [6]. If we are going to depend on real-time programming systems in our daily lives, we must be able to find such obscure errors before the systems are put into operation.

Fortunately, a compiler can detect many of these errors if processes and monitors are represented by a structured notation in a high-level programming language. In addition, we must exclude low-level machine features (registers, addresses, and interrupts) from the language and let a virtual machine control them. If we want real-time systems to be highly reliable, we must stop programming them in assembly language. (The use of hardware protection mechanisms is merely an expensive, inadequate way of making arbitrary machine language programs behave almost as predictably as compiled programs.)

A Concurrent Pascal compiler will check that the private data of a process only are accessed by that process. It will also check that the data structure of a class or monitor only is accessed by its procedures.

Fig. 8 shows that *access rights* within an operating system normally are not tree structured. Instead they form a directed graph. This partly explains why the traditional scope rules of block-structured languages are inconvenient for concurrent programming (and for sequential programming as well). In Concurrent Pascal one can state the access rights of components in the program text and have them checked by a compiler.

Since the execution of a monitor procedure will delay the execution of further calls of the same monitor, we must prevent a monitor from calling itself recursively. Otherwise, processes can become *deadlocked*. So the compiler will check that the access rights of system components are hierarchically ordered (or, if you like, that there are no cycles in the access graph).

The *hierarchical ordering* of system components has vital consequences for system design and testing [7].

A hierarchical operating system will be tested component by component, bottom up (but could, of course, be conceived top down or by iteration). When an incomplete operating system has been shown to work correctly (by proof or testing), a compiler can ensure that this part of the system will continue to work correctly when new untested program components are added on top of it. Programming errors within new components cannot cause old components to fail because old components do not call new components, and new components only call old components through well-defined procedures that have already been tested.

(Strictly speaking, a compiler can only check that single monitor calls are made correctly; it cannot check sequences of monitor calls, for example whether a resource is always reserved before it is released. So one can only hope for compile time assurance of *partial correctness*.)

Several other reasons besides program correctness make a hierarchical structure attractive:

1) a hierarchical operating system can be studied in a stepwise manner as a sequence of *abstract machines* simulated by programs [8];

2) a partial ordering of process interactions permits one to use *mathematical induction* to prove certain overall properties of the system (such as the absence of deadlocks) [2];

3) *efficient resource utilization* can be achieved by ordering the program components according to the speed of the physical resources they control (with the fastest resources being controlled at the bottom of the system) [8];

4) a hierarchical system designed according to the previous criteria is often *nearly decomposable* from an analytical point of view. This means that one can develop stochastic models of its dynamic behavior in a stepwise manner [9].

F. Final Remarks

It seems most natural to represent a hierarchical system structure, such as Fig. 8, by a two-dimensional picture. But when we write a concurrent program we must somehow represent these access rules by linear text. This limitation of written language tends to obscure the simplicity of the original structure. That is why I have tried to explain the purpose of Concurrent Pascal by means of pictures instead of language notation.

The class concept is a restricted form of the class concept of Simula 67 [10]. Dijkstra suggested the idea of monitors [8]. The first structured language notation for monitors was proposed in [2], and illustrated by examples in [3]. The queue variables needed by monitors for process scheduling were suggested in [5] and modified in [3].

The main contribution of Concurrent Pascal is to extend monitors with explicit access rights that can be checked at compile time. Concurrent Pascal has been implemented at Caltech for the PDP 11/45 computer. Our system uses sequential Pascal as a job control and user programming language.

II. THE USE OF CONCURRENT PASCAL

A. Introduction

In Section I the concepts of Concurrent Pascal were explained informally by means of pictures of a hierarchical spooling system. I will now use the same example to introduce the language notation of Concurrent Pascal. The presentation is still informal. I am neither trying to define the language precisely nor to develop a working system. This will be done in other papers. I am just trying to show the flavor of the language.

B. Processes

We will now program the system components in Fig. 8 one at a time from top to bottom (but we could just as well do it bottom up).

Although we only need one *input process*, we may as well define it as a general system type of which several copies may exist:

```
type inputprocess =
process(buffer: diskbuffer);
var block: page;
cycle
   readcards(block);
   buffer.send(block);
end
```

An input process has access to a *buffer* of type diskbuffer (to be defined later). The process has a private variable *block* of type page. The data type page is declared elsewhere as an array of characters:

$$\text{type page} = \text{array } (.1..512.) \text{ of char}$$

A process type defines a *sequential program*—in this case, an endless cycle that inputs a block from a card reader and sends it through the buffer to another process. We will ignore the details of card reader input.

The *send* operation on the buffer is called as follows (using the block as a parameter):

$$\text{buffer.send(block)}$$

The next component type we will define is a *job process*:

```
type jobprocess =
process(input, output: diskbuffer);
var block: page;
cycle
   input.receive(block);
   update(block);
   output.send(block);
end
```

A job process has access to two disk buffers called *input* and *output*. It receives blocks from one buffer, updates them, and sends them through the other buffer. The details of updating can be ignored here.

Finally, we need an *output process* that can receive data from a disk buffer and output them on a line printer:

```
type outputprocess =
process(buffer: diskbuffer);
var block: page;
cycle
   buffer.receive(block);
   printlines(block);
end
```

The following shows a declaration of the main system components:

```
var buffer1, buffer2: diskbuffer;
   reader: inputprocess;
   master: jobprocess;
   writer: outputprocess;
```

There is an input process, called the *reader*, a job process, called the *master*, and an output process, called the *writer*. Then there are two disk buffers, *buffer1* and *buffer2*, that connect them.

Later I will explain how a disk buffer is defined and initialized. If we assume that the disk buffers already have been initialized, we can initialize the input process as follows:

$$\text{init reader(buffer1)}$$

The *init* statement allocates space for the *private variables* of the reader process and starts its execution as a sequential process with access to buffer1.

The *access rights* of a process to other system components, such as buffer1, are also called its *parameters*. A process can only be initialized once. After initialization, the parameters and private variables of a process exist forever. They are called *permanent variables*.

The init statement can be used to start concurrent execution of several processes and define their access rights. As an example, the statement

```
init reader(buffer1), master(buffer1, buffer2),
   writer(buffer2)
```

starts concurrent execution of the reader process (with access to buffer1), the master process (with access to both buffers), and the writer process (with access to buffer2).

A process can only access its own parameters and private variables. The latter are not accessible to other system components. Compare this with the more liberal scope rules of block-structured languages in which a program block can access not only its own parameters and local variables, but also those declared in outer blocks. In Concurrent Pascal, all variables accessible to a system component are declared within its type definition. This access rule and the init statement make it possible for a programmer to state access rights explicitly and have them checked by a compiler. They also make it possible to study a system type as a self-contained program unit.

Although the programming examples do not show this, one can also define constants, data types, and procedures within a process. These objects can only be used within the process type.

C. Monitors

The *disk buffer* is a monitor type:

```
type diskbuffer =
monitor(consoleaccess, diskaccess: resource;
  base, limit: integer);

var disk: virtualdisk; sender, receiver: queue;
  head, tail, length: integer;

procedure entry send(block: page);
begin
  if length = limit then delay(sender);
  disk.write(base + tail, block);
  tail:= (tail + 1) mod limit;
  length:= length + 1;
  continue(receiver);
end;

procedure entry receive(var block: page);
begin
  if length = 0 then delay(receiver);
  disk.read(base + head, block);
  head:= (head + 1) mod limit;
  length:= length - 1;
  continue(sender);
end;

begin "initial statement"
  init disk(consoleaccess, diskaccess);
  head:= 0; tail:= 0; length:= 0;
end
```

A disk buffer has access to two other components, *consoleaccess* and *diskaccess*, of type resource (to be defined later). It also has access to two integer constants defining the *base* address and *limit* of the buffer on the disk.

The monitor declares a set of *shared variables:* the *disk* is declared as a variable of type virtualdisk. Two variables of type queue are used to delay the *sender* and *receiver* processes until the buffer becomes nonfull and nonempty. Three integers define the relative addresses of the *head* and *tail* elements of the buffer and its current *length*.

The monitor defines two *monitor procedures*, send and receive. They are marked with the word *entry* to distinguish them from local procedures used within the monitor (there are none of these in this example).

Receive returns a page to the calling process. If the buffer is empty, the calling process is *delayed* in the receiver queue until another process sends a page through the buffer. The receive procedure will then read and remove a page from the head of the disk buffer by calling a *read* operation defined within the virtual disk type:

$$disk.read(base + head, block)$$

Finally, the receive procedure will *continue* the execution of a sending process (if the latter is waiting in the sender queue).

Send is similar to receive.

The queuing mechanism will be explained in detail in the next section.

The *initial statement* of a disk buffer initializes its virtual disk with access to the console and disk resources. It also sets the buffer length to zero. (Notice, that a disk buffer does not use its access rights to the console and disk, but only passes them on to a virtual disk declared within it.)

The following shows a declaration of two system components of type resource and two integers defining the base and limit of a disk buffer:

```
var consoleaccess, diskaccess: resource;
  base, limit: integer;
  buffer: diskbuffer;
```

If we assume that these variables already have been initialized, we can initialize a disk buffer as follows:

```
init buffer(consoleaccess, diskaccess, base, limit)
```

The *init* statement allocates storage for the parameters and shared variables of the disk buffer and executes its initial statement.

A monitor can only be initialized once. After initialization, the parameters and shared variables of a monitor exist forever. They are called *permanent variables*. The parameters and local variables of a monitor procedure, however, exist only while it is being executed. They are called *temporary variables*.

A monitor procedure can only access its own temporary and permanent variables. These variables are not accessible to other system components. Other components can, however, call procedure entries within a monitor. While a monitor procedure is being executed, it has *exclusive access* to the permanent variables of the monitor. If concurrent processes try to call procedures within the same monitor simultaneously, these procedures will be executed strictly one at a time.

Only monitors and constants can be permanent parameters of processes and monitors. This rule ensures that processes only communicate by means of monitors.

It is possible to define constants, data types, and local procedures within monitors (and processes). The local procedures of a system type can only be called within the system type. To prevent *deadlock* of monitor calls and ensure that access rights are hierarchical the following rules are enforced: a procedure must be declared before it can be called; procedure definitions cannot be nested and cannot call themselves; a system type cannot call its own procedure entries.

The absence of recursion makes it possible for a compiler to determine the store requirements of all system components. This and the use of permanent components make it possible to use *fixed store allocation* on a computer that does not support paging.

Since system components are permanent they must be declared as permanent variables of other components.

D. Queues

A monitor procedure can delay a calling process for any length of time by executing a *delay* operation on a queue variable. Only one process at a time can wait in a queue. When a calling process is delayed by a monitor procedure it loses its exclusive access to the monitor variables until another process calls the same monitor and executes a continue operation on the queue in which the process is waiting.

The *continue* operation makes the calling process return from its monitor call. If any process is waiting in the selected queue, it will immediately resume the execution of the monitor procedure that delayed it. After being resumed, the process again has exclusive access to the permanent variables of the monitor.

Other variants of process queues (called "events" and "conditions") are proposed in [3], [5]. They are multi-process queues that use different (but fixed) scheduling rules. We do not yet know from experience which kind of queue will be the most convenient one for operating system design. A single-process queue is the simplest tool that gives the programmer complete control of the scheduling of individual processes. Later, I will show how multi-process queues can be built from single-process queues.

A queue must be declared as a permanent variable within a monitor type.

E. Classes

Every disk buffer has its own virtual disk. A virtual disk is defined as a class type:

```
type virtualdisk =
class(consoleaccess, diskaccess: resource);

var terminal: virtualconsole; peripheral: disk;

procedure entry read(pageno: integer; var block: page);
var error: boolean;
begin
  repeat
    diskaccess.request;
    peripheral.read(pageno, block, error);
    diskaccess.release;
    if error then terminal.write('disk failure');
  until not error;
end;

procedure entry write(pageno: integer; block: page);
begin "similar to read" end;

begin "initial statement"
  init terminal(consoleaccess), peripheral;
end
```

A virtual disk has access to a console resource and a disk resource. Its permanent variables define a virtual console and a disk. A process can access its virtual disk by means of *read* and *write* procedures. These procedure entries *request* and *release* exclusive access to the real disk before and after each block transfer. If the real disk fails, the virtual disk calls its virtual console to report the error.

The *initial statement* of a virtual disk initializes its virtual console and the real disk.

Section II-C shows an example of how a virtual disk is declared and initialized (within a disk buffer).

A class can only be initialized once. After initialization, its parameters and private variables exist forever. A class procedure can only access its own temporary and permanent variables. These cannot be accessed by other components.

A class is a system component that cannot be called simultaneously by several other components. This is guaranteed by the following rule: a class must be declared as a permanent variable within a system type; a class can be passed as a permanent parameter to another class (but not to a process or monitor). So a chain of nested class calls can only be started by a single process or monitor. Consequently, it is not necessary to schedule simultaneous class calls at run time—they cannot occur.

F. Input/Output

The real *disk* is controlled by a class

```
type disk = class
```

with two procedure entries

```
read(pageno, block, error)
write(pageno, block, error)
```

The class uses a standard procedure

```
io(block, param, device)
```

to transfer a block to or from the disk device. The io parameter is a record

```
var param: record
           operation: iooperation;
           result: ioresult;
           pageno: integer
         end
```

that defines an input/output operation, its result, and a page number on the disk. The calling process is delayed until an io operation has been completed.

A *virtual console* is also defined as a class

```
type virtualconsole =
class(access: resource);
var terminal: console;
```

It can be accessed by read and write operations that are similar to each other:

```
procedure entry read(var text: line);
begin
  access.request;
  terminal.read(text);
  access.release;
end
```

The real *console* is controlled by a class that is similar to the disk class.

G. Multiprocess Scheduling

Access to the console and disk is controlled by two monitors of type *resource*. To simplify the presentation, I will assume that competing processes are served in first-come, first-served order. (A much better disk scheduling algorithm is defined in [3]. It can be programmed in Concurrent Pascal as well, but involves more details than the present one.)

We will define a multiprocess queue as an array of single-process queues

```
type multiqueue = array (.0..qlength-1.) of queue
```

where $qlength$ is an upper bound on the number of concurrent processes in the system.

A first-come, first-served scheduler is now straightforward to program:

```
type resource =
monitor

var free: Boolean; q: multiqueue;
  head, tail, length: integer;

procedure entry request;
var arrival: integer;
begin
  if free then free:= false else
  begin
    arrival:= tail;
    tail:= (tail + 1) mod qlength;
    length:= length + 1;
    delay(q(.arrival.));
  end;
end;

procedure entry release;
var departure: integer;
begin
  if length = 0 then free:= true else
  begin
    departure:= head;
    head:= (head + 1) mod qlength;
    length:= length - 1;
    continue(q(.departure.));
  end;
end;

begin "initial statement"
  free:= true; length:= 0;
  head:= 0; tail:= 0;
end
```

H. Initial Process

Finally, we will put all these components together into a concurrent program. A Concurrent Pascal program consists of nested definitions of system types. The outermost system type is an anonymous process, called the initial process. An instance of this process is created during system loading. It initializes the other system components.

The initial process defines system types and instances of them. It executes statements that initialize these system components. In our example, the initial process can be sketched as follows (ignoring the problem of how base addresses and limits of disk buffers are defined):

```
type
  resource = monitor···end;
  console = class···end;
  virtualconsole =
    class(access: resource);···end;
  disk = class···end;
  virtualdisk =
    class(consoleaccess, diskaccess: resource);···end;
  diskbuffer =
    monitor(consoleaccess, diskaccess: resource;
      base, limit: integer);···end;
  inputprocess =
    process(buffer: diskbuffer);···end;
  jobprocess =
    process(input, output: diskbuffer);···end;
  outputprocess =
    process(buffer: diskbuffer);···end;
var
  consoleaccess, diskaccess: resource;
  buffer1, buffer2: diskbuffer;
  reader: inputprocess;
  master: jobprocess;
  writer: outputprocess;
begin
  init consoleaccess, diskaccess,
    buffer1(consoleaccess, diskaccess, base1, limit1),
    buffer2(consoleaccess, diskaccess, base2, limit2),
    reader(buffer1),
    master(buffer1, buffer2),
    writer(buffer2);
end.
```

When the execution of a process (such as the initial process) terminates, its private variables continue to exist. This is necessary because these variables may have been passed as permanent parameters to other system components.

ACKNOWLEDGMENT

It is a pleasure to acknowledge the immense value of a continuous exchange of ideas with C. A. R. Hoare on structured multiprogramming. I also thank my students L. Medina and R. Varela for their helpful comments on this paper.

REFERENCES

[1] N. Wirth, "The programming language Pascal," *Acta Informatica*, vol. 1, no. 1, pp. 35–63, 1971.
[2] P. Brinch Hansen, *Operation System Principles*. Englewood Cliffs, N. J.: Prentice-Hall, July 1973.
[3] C. A. R. Hoare, "Monitors: An operating system structuring concept," *Commun. Ass. Comput. Mach.*, vol. 17, pp. 549–557, Oct. 1974.
[4] P. Brinch Hansen, "The nucleus of a multiprogramming

system," *Commun. Ass. Comput. Mach.*, vol. 13, pp. 238–250, Apr. 1970.

[5] ——, "Structured multiprogramming," *Commun. Ass. Comput. Mach.*, vol. 15, pp. 574–578, July 1972.

[6] ——, "Concurrent programming concepts," *Ass. Comput. Mach. Comput. Rev.*, vol. 5, pp. 223–245, Dec. 1974.

[7] ——, "A programming methodology for operating system design," in *1974 Proc. IFIP Congr.* Stockholm, Sweden: North-Holland, Aug. 1974, pp. 394–397.

[8] E. W. Dijkstra, "Hierarchical ordering of sequential processes," *Acta Informatica*, vol. 1, no. 2, pp. 115–138, 1971.

[9] H. A. Simon, "The architecture of complexity," in *Proc. Amer. Philosophical Society*, vol. 106, no. 6, 1962, pp. 468–482.

[10] O.-J. Dahl and C. A. R. Hoare, "Hierarchical program structures," in *Structured Programming*, O.-J. Dahl, E. W. Dijkstra, and C. A. R. Hoare.   New York: Academic, 1972.

Per Brinch Hansen was born in Copenhagen, Denmark, on November 13, 1938. He received the M.S. degree in electronic engineering from the Technical University of Denmark, Copenhagen, in 1963.

Afterwards he joined the Danish computer manufacturer, Regnecentralen, as a systems programmer and designer. In 1967 he became head of the department at Regnecentralen which developed the architecture of the RC 4000 computer and its multiprogramming system. From 1970 to 1972 he visited Carnegie-Mellon University, Pittsburgh, Pa., where he wrote the book *Operating System Principles* (Englewood Cliffs, N. J., Prentice-Hall, July 1973). This book contains the first proposal of the *monitor concept* on which the programming language Concurrent Pascal is based. In 1972 he became Associate Professor of Computer Science at the California Institute of Technology, Pasadena. He has been a consultant to Burroughs Corporation, Control Data Corporation, Jet Propulsion Laboratory, Philips, and Varian Data Machines. His main research interests are computer architecture and programming methodology.

Dr. Brinch Hansen is a member of the Working Group 2.3 on Programming Methodology sponsored by the International Federation for Information Processing.

COMMUNICATING SEQUENTIAL PROCESSES*

C. A. R. HOARE

This paper suggests that input and output are basic primitives of programming and that parallel composition of communicating sequential processes is a fundamental program structuring method. When combined with a development of Dijkstra's guarded command, these concepts are surprisingly versatile. Their use is illustrated by sample solutions of a variety of familiar programming exercises.

Key Words and Phrases: programming, programming languages, programming primitives, program structures, parallel programming, concurrency, input, output, guarded commands, nondeterminacy, coroutines, procedures, multiple entries, multiple exits, classes, data representations, recursion, conditional critical regions, monitors, iterative arrays

CR Categories: 4.20, 4.22, 4.32

1. Introduction

Among the primitive concepts of computer programming, and of the high level languages in which programs are expressed, the action of assignment is familiar and well understood. In fact, any change of the internal state of a machine executing a program can be modeled as an assignment of a new value to some variable part of that machine. However, the operations of input and output, which affect the external environment of a machine, are not nearly so well understood. They are often added to a programming language only as an afterthought.

Among the structuring methods for computer pro-

This research was supported by a Senior Fellowship of the Science Research Council.

Author's present address: Programming Research Group, 45, Banbury Road, Oxford, England.

*Reprinted from Comm ACM, 21, 8, August 1978, 666–677, copyright 1978.

grams, three basic constructs have received widespread recognition and use: A repetitive construct (e.g. the **while** loop), an alternative construct (e.g. the conditional **if..then..else**), and normal sequential program composition (often denoted by a semicolon). Less agreement has been reached about the design of other important program structures, and many suggestions have been made: Subroutines (Fortran), procedures (Algol 60 [15]), entries (PL/I), coroutines (UNIX [17]), classes (SIMULA 67 [5]), processes and monitors (Concurrent Pascal [2]), clusters (CLU [13]), forms (ALPHARD [19]), actors (Hewitt [1]).

The traditional stored program digital computer has been designed primarily for deterministic execution of a single sequential program. Where the desire for greater speed has led to the introduction of parallelism, every attempt has been made to disguise this fact from the programmer, either by hardware itself (as in the multiple function units of the CDC 6600) or by the software (as in an I/O control package, or a multiprogrammed operating system). However, developments of processor technology suggest that a multiprocessor machine, constructed from a number of similar self-contained processors (each with its own store), may become more powerful, capacious, reliable, and economical than a machine which is disguised as a monoprocessor.

In order to use such a machine effectively on a single task, the component processors must be able to communicate and to synchronize with each other. Many methods of achieving this have been proposed. A widely adopted method of communication is by inspection and updating of a common store (as in Algol 68 [18], PL/I, and many machine codes). However, this can create severe problems in the construction of correct programs and it may lead to expense (e.g. crossbar switches) and unreliability (e.g. glitches) in some technologies of hardware implementation. A greater variety of methods has been proposed for synchronization: semaphores [6], events (PL/I), conditional critical regions [10], monitors and queues (Concurrent Pascal [2]), and path expressions [3]. Most of these are demonstrably adequate for their purpose, but there is no widely recognized criterion for choosing between them.

This paper makes an ambitious attempt to find a single simple solution to all these problems. The essential proposals are:

(1) Dijkstra's guarded commands [8] are adopted (with a slight change of notation) as sequential control structures, and as the sole means of introducing and controlling nondeterminism.

(2) A parallel command, based on Dijkstra's *parbegin* [6], specifies concurrent execution of its constituent sequential commands (processes). All the processes start simultaneously, and the parallel command ends only when they are all finished. They may not communicate with each other by updating global variables.

(3) Simple forms of input and output command are introduced. They are used for communication between concurrent processes.

(4) Such communication occurs when one process names another as destination for output *and* the second process names the first as source for input. In this case, the value to be output is copied from the first process to the second. There is *no* automatic buffering: In general, an input or output command is delayed until the other process is ready with the corresponding output or input. Such delay is invisible to the delayed process.

(5) Input commands may appear in guards. A guarded command with an input guard is selected for execution only if and when the source named in the input command is ready to execute the corresponding output command. If several input guards of a set of alternatives have ready destinations, only one is selected and the others have *no* effect; but the choice between them is arbitrary. In an efficient implementation, an output command which has been ready for a long time should be favored; but the definition of a language cannot specify this since the relative speed of execution of the processes is undefined.

(6) A repetitive command may have input guards. If all the sources named by them have terminated, then the repetitive command also terminates.

(7) A simple pattern-matching feature, similar to that of [16], is used to discriminate the structure of an input message, and to access its components in a secure fashion. This feature is used to inhibit input of messages that do not match the specified pattern.

The programs expressed in the proposed language are intended to be implementable both by a conventional machine with a single main store, and by a fixed network of processors connected by input/output channels (although very different optimizations are appropriate in the different cases). It is consequently a rather static language: The text of a program determines a fixed upper bound on the number of processes operating concurrently; there is no recursion and no facility for process-valued variables. In other respects also, the language has been stripped to the barest minimum necessary for explanation of its more novel features.

The concept of a communicating sequential process is shown in Sections 3–5 to provide a method of expressing solutions to many simple programming exercises which have previously been employed to illustrate the use of various proposed programming language features. This suggests that the process may constitute a synthesis of a number of familiar and new programming ideas. The reader is invited to skip the examples which do not interest him.

However, this paper also ignores many serious problems. The most serious is that it fails to suggest any proof method to assist in the development and verification of correct programs. Secondly, it pays no attention to the problems of efficient implementation, which may be particularly serious on a traditional sequential computer. It is probable that a solution to these problems will require (1) imposition of restrictions in the use of the proposed features; (2) reintroduction of distinctive no-

tations for the most common and useful special cases; (3) development of automatic optimization techniques; and (4) the design of appropriate hardware.

Thus the concepts and notations introduced in this paper (although described in the next section in the form of a programming language fragment) should not be regarded as suitable for use as a programming language, either for abstract or for concrete programming. They are at best only a partial solution to the problems tackled. Further discussion of these and other points will be found in Section 7.

2. Concepts and Notations

The style of the following description is borrowed from Algol 60 [15]. Types, declarations, and expressions have not been treated; in the examples, a Pascal-like notation [20] has usually been adopted. The curly braces { } have been introduced into BNF to denote none or more repetitions of the enclosed material. (Sentences in parentheses refer to an implementation: they are not strictly part of a language definition.)

```
<command> ::= <simple command>|<structured command>
<simple command> ::= <null command>|<assignment command>
    |<input command>|<output command>
<structured command> ::= <alternative command>
    |<repetitive command>|<parallel command>
<null command> ::= skip
<command list> ::= {<declaration>; |<command>;} <command>
```

A command specifies the behavior of a device executing the command. It may succeed or fail. Execution of a simple command, if successful, may have an effect on the internal state of the executing device (in the case of assignment), or on its external environment (in the case of output), or on both (in the case of input). Execution of a structured command involves execution of some or all of its constituent commands, and if any of these fail, so does the structured command. (In this case, whenever possible, an implementation should provide some kind of comprehensible error diagnostic message.)

A null command has no effect and never fails.

A command list specifies sequential execution of its constituent commands in the order written. Each declaration introduces a fresh variable with a scope which extends from its declaration to the end of the command list.

2.1 Parallel Commands

```
<parallel command> ::= [<process>{||<process>}]
<process> ::= <process label> <command list>
<process label> ::= <empty>|<identifier> ::
    |<identifier>(<label subscript>{,<label subscript>}) ::
<label subscript> ::= <integer constant>|<range>
<integer constant> ::= <numeral>|<bound variable>
<bound variable> ::= <identifier>
<range> ::= <bound variable>:<lower bound>..<upper bound>
<lower bound> ::= <integer constant>
<upper bound> ::= <integer constant>
```

Each process of a parallel command must be *disjoint* from every other process of the command, in the sense that it does not mention any variable which occurs as a target variable (see Sections 2.2 and 2.3) in any other process.

A process label without subscripts, or one whose label subscripts are all integer constants, serves as a name for the command list to which it is prefixed; its scope extends over the whole of the parallel command. A process whose label subscripts include one or more ranges stands for a series of processes, each with the same label and command list, except that each has a different combination of values substituted for the bound variables. These values range between the lower bound and the upper bound inclusive. For example, $X(i:1..n)$ :: CL stands for

$$X(1) :: CL_1 || X(2) :: CL_2 || ... || X(n) :: CL_n$$

where each CL_j is formed from CL by replacing every occurrence of the bound variable i by the numeral j. After all such expansions, each process label in a parallel command must occur only once and the processes must be well formed and disjoint.

A parallel command specifies concurrent execution of its constituent processes. They all start simultaneously and the parallel command terminates successfully only if and when they have all successfully terminated. The relative speed with which they are executed is arbitrary.
Examples:

(1) [cardreader?cardimage||lineprinter!lineimage]

Performs the two constituent commands in parallel, and terminates only when both operations are complete. The time taken may be as low as the longer of the times taken by each constituent process, i.e. the sum of its computing, waiting, and transfer times.

(2) [west :: DISASSEMBLE||X :: SQUASH||east :: ASSEMBLE]

The three processes have the names "west," "X," and "east." The capitalized words stand for command lists which will be defined in later examples.

(3) [room :: ROOM||fork(i:0..4) :: FORK||phil(i:0..4) :: PHIL]

There are eleven processes. The behavior of "room" is specified by the command list ROOM. The behavior of the five processes fork(0), fork(1), fork(2), fork(3), fork(4), is specified by the command list FORK, within which the bound variable i indicates the identity of the particular fork. Similar remarks apply to the five processes PHIL.

2.2 Assignment Commands

```
<assignment command> ::= <target variable> := <expression>
<expression> ::= <simple expression>|<structured expression>
<structured expression> ::= <constructor>(<expression list>)
<constructor> ::= <identifier>|<empty>
<expression list> ::= <empty>|<expression>{,<expression>}
<target variable> ::= <simple variable>|<structured target>
<structured target> ::= <constructor>(<target variable list>)
<target variable list> ::= <empty>|<target variable>
    {,<target variable>}
```

An expression denotes a value which is computed by an executing device by application of its constituent operators to the specified operands. The value of an expression is undefined if any of these operations are undefined. The value denoted by a simple expression may be simple or structured. The value denoted by a structured expression is structured; its constructor is that of the expression, and its components are the list of values denoted by the constituent expressions of the expression list.

An assignment command specifies evaluation of its expression, and assignment of the denoted value to the target variable. A simple target variable may have assigned to it a simple or a structured value. A structured target variable may have assigned to it a structured value, with the same constructor. The effect of such assignment is to assign to each constituent simpler variable of the structured target the value of the corresponding component of the structured value. Consequently, the value denoted by the target variable, if evaluated *after* a successful assignment, is the same as the value denoted by the expression, as evaluated *before* the assignment.

An assignment fails if the value of its expression is undefined, or if that value does not *match* the target variable, in the following sense: A *simple* target variable matches any value of its type. A *structured* target variable matches a structured value, provided that: (1) they have the same constructor, (2) the target variable list is the same length as the list of components of the value, (3) each target variable of the list matches the corresponding component of the value list. A structured value with no components is known as a "signal."

Examples:

(1) $x := x + 1$	the value of x after the assignment is the same as the value of $x + 1$ before.
(2) $(x, y) := (y, x)$	exchanges the values of x and y.
(3) $x := cons(left, right)$	constructs a structured value and assigns it to x.
(4) $cons(left, right) := x$	fails if x does not have the form $cons(y, z)$; but if it does, then y is assigned to left, and z is assigned to right.
(5) $insert(n) := insert(2*x + 1)$	equivalent to $n := 2*x + 1$.
(6) $c := P()$	assigns to c a "signal" with constructor P, and no components.
(7) $P() := c$	fails if the value of c is not $P()$; otherwise has no effect.
(8) $insert(n) := has(n)$	fails, due to mismatch.

Note: Successful execution of both (3) and (4) ensures the truth of the postcondition $x = cons(left, right)$; but (3) does so by changing x and (4) does so by changing left and right. Example (4) will fail if there is *no* value of left and right which satisfies the postcondition.

2.3 Input and Output Commands

```
<input command> ::= <source>?<target variable>
<output command> ::= <destination>!<expression>
<source> ::= <process name>
```

<destination> ::= <process name>
<process name> ::= <identifier>|<identifier>(<subscripts>)
<subscripts> ::= <integer expression>{,<integer expression>}

Input and output commands specify communication between two concurrently operating sequential processes. Such a process may be implemented in hardware as a special-purpose device (e.g. cardreader or lineprinter), or its behavior may be specified by one of the constituent processes of a parallel command. Communication occurs between two processes of a parallel command whenever (1) an input command in one process specifies as its source the process name of the other process; (2) an output command in the other process specifies as its destination the process name of the first process; and (3) the target variable of the input command matches the value denoted by the expression of the output command. On these conditions, the input and output commands are said to *correspond*. Commands which correspond are executed simultaneously, and their combined effect is to assign the value of the expression of the output command to the target variable of the input command.

An input command fails if its source is terminated. An output command fails if its destination is terminated or if its expression is undefined.

(The requirement of synchronization of input and output commands means that an implementation will have to delay whichever of the two commands happens to be ready first. The delay is ended when the corresponding command in the other process is also ready, or when the other process terminates. In the latter case the first command fails. It is also possible that the delay will never be ended, for example, if a group of processes are attempting communication but none of their input and output commands correspond with each other. This form of failure is known as a deadlock.)

Examples:

(1) cardreader?cardimage	from cardreader, read a card and assign its value (an array of characters) to the variable cardimage
(2) lineprinter!lineimage	to lineprinter, send the value of lineimage for printing
(3) $X?(x, y)$	from process named X, input a pair of values and assign them to x and y
(4) DIV!$(3*a + b, 13)$	to process DIV, output the two specified values.

Note: If a process named DIV issues command (3), and a process named X issues command (4), these are executed simultaneously, and have the same effect as the assignment: $(x, y) := (3*a + b, 13)$ ($\equiv x := 3*a + b; y := 13$).

(5) console(i)?c	from the ith element of an array of consoles, input a value and assign it to c
(6) console($j - 1$)!"A"	to the $(j - 1)$th console, output character "A"
(7) $X(i)?V( )$	from the ith of an array of processes X, input a signal V( ); refuse to input any other signal
(8) sem!P( )	to sem output a signal P( )

2.4 Alternative and Repetitive Commands

<repetitive command> ::=*<alternative command>
<alternative command> ::= [<guarded command>
      {⫿<guarded command>}]
<guarded command> ::= <guard> → <command list>
      |(<range>{,<range>})<guard> → <command list>
<guard> ::= <guard list>|<guard list>;<input command>
      |<input command>
      <guard list> ::= <guard element>{;<guard element>}
<guard element> ::= <boolean expression>|<declaration>

A guarded command with one or more ranges stands for a series of guarded commands, each with the same guard and command list, except that each has a different combination of values substituted for the bound variables. The values range between the lower bound and upper bound inclusive. For example, $(i:1..n)G \to CL$ stands for

$$G_1 \to CL_1 ⫿ G_2 \to CL_2 ⫿ ... ⫿ G_n \to CL_n$$

where each $G_j \to CL_j$ is formed from $G \to CL$ by replacing every occurrence of the bound variable i by the numeral j.

A guarded command is executed only if and when the execution of its guard does not fail. First its guard is executed and then its command list. A guard is executed by execution of its constituent elements from left to right. A Boolean expression is evaluated: If it denotes false, the guard fails; but an expression that denotes true has no effect. A declaration introduces a fresh variable with a scope that extends from the declaration to the end of the guarded command. An input command at the end of a guard is executed only if and when a corresponding output command is executed. (An implementation may test whether a guard fails simply by trying to execute it, and discontinuing execution if and when it fails. This is valid because such a discontinued execution has no effect on the state of the executing device.)

An alternative command specifies execution of exactly one of its constituent guarded commands. Consequently, if all guards fail, the alternative command fails. Otherwise an arbitrary one with successfully executable guard is selected and executed. (An implementation should take advantage of its freedom of selection to ensure efficient execution and good response. For example, when input commands appear as guards, the command which corresponds to the earliest ready and matching output command should in general be preferred; and certainly, no executable and ready output command should be passed over unreasonably often.)

A repetitive command specifies as many iterations as possible of its constituent alternative command. Consequently, when all guards fail, the repetitive command terminates with no effect. Otherwise, the alternative command is executed once and then the whole repetitive command is executed again. (Consider a repetitive command when all its true guard lists end in an input guard. Such a command may have to be delayed until either (1) an output command corresponding to one of the input guards becomes ready, or (2) all the sources named by the input guards have terminated. In case (2), the repetitive command terminates. If neither event ever occurs, the process fails (in deadlock.)

Examples:

(1) $[x \geq y \rightarrow m := x [\![y \geq x \rightarrow m := y]$

If $x \geq y$, assign x to m; if $y \geq x$ assign y to m; if both $x \geq y$ and $y \geq x$, either assignment can be executed.

(2) $i := 0; *[i < \text{size}; \text{content}(i) \neq n \rightarrow i := i + 1]$

The repetitive command scans the elements content(i), for $i = 0, 1, \ldots$, until either $i \geq$ size, or a value equal to n is found.

(3) $*[c\text{:character}; \text{west}?c \rightarrow \text{east}!c]$

This reads all the characters output by west, and outputs them one by one to east. The repetition terminates when the process west terminates.

(4) $*[(i:1..10)\text{continue}(i); \text{console}(i)?c \rightarrow X!(i, c); \text{console}(i)!\text{ack}();$
$\quad \text{continue}(i) := (c \neq \text{sign off})]$

This command inputs repeatedly from any of ten consoles, provided that the corresponding element of the Boolean array continue is true. The bound variable i identifies the originating console. Its value, together with the character just input, is output to X, and an acknowledgment signal is sent back to the originating console. If the character indicated "sign off," continue(i) is set false, to prevent further input from that console. The repetitive command terminates when all ten elements of continue are false. (An implementation should ensure that no console which is ready to provide input will be ignored unreasonably often.)

(5) $*[n\text{:integer}; X?\text{insert}(n) \rightarrow \text{INSERT}$
$\quad [\![n\text{:integer}; X?\text{has}(n) \rightarrow \text{SEARCH}; X!(i < \text{size})$
$\quad]$

(Here, and elsewhere, capitalized words INSERT and SEARCH stand as abbreviations for program text defined separately.)

On each iteration this command accepts from X *either* (a) a request to "insert(n)," (followed by INSERT) *or* (b) a question "has(n)," to which it outputs an answer back to X. The choice between (a) and (b) is made by the next output command in X. The repetitive command terminates when X does. If X sends a nonmatching message, deadlock will result.

(6) $*[X?V() \rightarrow \text{val} := \text{val} + 1$
$\quad [\![\text{val} > 0; Y?P() \rightarrow \text{val} := \text{val} - 1$
$\quad]$

On each iteration, accept *either* a V () signal from X and increment val, *or* a P() signal from Y, and decrement val. But the second alternative cannot be selected unless val is positive (after which val will remain invariantly nonnegative). (When val > 0, the choice depends on the relative speeds of X and Y, and is not determined.) The repetitive command will terminate when both X and Y are terminated, or when X is terminated and val ≤ 0.

3. Coroutines

In parallel programming coroutines appear as a more fundamental program structure than subroutines, which can be regarded as a special case (treated in the next section).

3.1 COPY

Problem: Write a process X to copy characters output by process west to process east.
Solution:

$X :: *[c\text{:character}; \text{west}?c \rightarrow \text{east}!c]$

Notes: (1) When west terminates, the input "west?c" will fail, causing termination of the repetitive command, and of process X. Any subsequent input command from east will fail. (2) Process X acts as a single-character buffer between west and east. It permits west to work on production of the next character, before east is ready to input the previous one.

3.2 SQUASH

Problem: Adapt the previous program to replace every pair of consecutive asterisks "**" by an upward arrow "↑". Assume that the final character input is not an asterisk.
Solution:

$X :: *[c\text{:character}; \text{west}?c \rightarrow$
$\quad [c \neq \text{asterisk} \rightarrow \text{east}!c$
$\quad [\![c = \text{asterisk} \rightarrow \text{west}?c;$
$\quad\quad [c \neq \text{asterisk} \rightarrow \text{east}!\text{asterisk}; \text{east}!c$
$\quad\quad [\![c = \text{asterisk} \rightarrow \text{east}!\text{upward arrow}$
$\quad]\!] \quad]$

Notes: (1) Since west does not end with asterisk, the second "west?c" will not fail. (2) As an exercise, adapt this process to deal sensibly with input which ends with an odd number of asterisks.

3.3 DISASSEMBLE

Problem: to read cards from a cardfile and output to process X the stream of characters they contain. An extra space should be inserted at the end of each card.
Solution:

$*[\text{cardimage}:(1..80)\text{character}; \text{cardfile}?\text{cardimage} \rightarrow$
$\quad i\text{:integer}; i := 1;$
$\quad *[i \leq 80 \rightarrow X!\text{cardimage}(i); i := i + 1]$
$\quad X!\text{space}$
$]$

Notes: (1) "$(1..80)$character" declares an array of 80 characters, with subscripts ranging between 1 and 80. (2) The repetitive command terminates when the cardfile process terminates.

3.4 ASSEMBLE

Problem: To read a stream of characters from process X and print them in lines of 125 characters on a lineprinter. The last line should be completed with spaces if necessary.

Solution:

```
lineimage:(1..125)character;
i:integer; i := 1;
*[c:character; X?c →
    lineimage(i) := c;
    [i ≤ 124 → i := i + 1
    []i = 125 → lineprinter!lineimage; i := 1
    ]    ];
[i = 1 → skip
[]i > 1 → *[i ≤ 125 → lineimage(i) := space; i := i + 1];
    lineprinter!lineimage
]
```

Note: (1) When X terminates, so will the first repetitive command of this process. The last line will then be printed, if it has any characters.

3.5 Reformat

Problem: Read a sequence of cards of 80 characters each, and print the characters on a lineprinter at 125 characters per line. Every card should be followed by an extra space, and the last line should be completed with spaces if necessary.
Solution:

[west::DISASSEMBLE||X::COPY||east::ASSEMBLE]

Notes: (1) The capitalized names stand for program text defined in previous sections. (2) The parallel command is designed to terminate after the cardfile has terminated. (3) This elementary problem is difficult to solve elegantly without coroutines.

3.6 Conway's Problem [4]

Problem: Adapt the above program to replace every pair of consecutive asterisks by an upward arrow.
Solution:

[west::DISASSEMBLE||X::SQUASH||east::ASSEMBLE]

4. Subroutines and Data Representations

A conventional nonrecursive subroutine can be readily implemented as a coroutine, provided that (1) its parameters are called "by value" and "by result," and (2) it is disjoint from its calling program. Like a Fortran subroutine, a coroutine may retain the values of local variables (*own* variables, in Algol terms) and it may use input commands to achieve the effect of "multiple entry points" in a safer way than PL/I. Thus a coroutine can be used like a SIMULA class instance as a concrete representation for abstract data.

A coroutine acting as a subroutine is a process operating concurrently with its user process in a parallel command: [subr::SUBROUTINE||X::USER]. The SUBROUTINE will contain (or consist of) a repetitive command: *[X?(value params) → ... ; X!(result params)], where ... computes the results from the values input. The subroutine will terminate when its user does. The USER will call the subroutine by a pair of commands: subr!(arguments);

... ; subr?(results). Any commands between these two will be executed concurrently with the subroutine.

A multiple-entry subroutine, acting as a representation for data [11], will also contain a repetitive command which represents each entry by an alternative input to a structured target with the entry name as constructor. For example,

```
*[X?entry1(value params) → ...
[]X?entry2(value params) → ...
]
```

The calling process X will determine which of the alternatives is activated on each repetition. When X terminates, so does this repetitive command. A similar technique in the user program can achieve the effect of multiple exits.

A recursive subroutine can be simulated by an array of processes, one for each level of recursion. The user process is level zero. Each activation communicates its parameters and results with its predecessor and calls its successor if necessary:

[recsub(0)::USER||recsub(i:1..reclimit)::RECSUB].

The user will call the first element of

recsub: recsub(1)!(arguments); ... ; recsub(1)?(results);.

The imposition of a fixed upper bound on recursion depth is necessitated by the "static" design of the language.

This clumsy simulation of recursion would be even more clumsy for a mutually recursive algorithm. It would not be recommended for conventional programming; it may be more suitable for an array of microprocessors for which the fixed upper bound is also realistic.

In this section, we assume each subroutine is used only by a *single* user process (which may, of course, itself contain parallel commands).

4.1 Function: Division With Remainder

Problem: Construct a process to represent a function-type subroutine, which accepts a positive dividend and divisor, and returns their integer quotient and remainder. Efficiency is of no concern.
Solution:

```
[DIV::*[x,y:integer; X?(x,y) →
    quot,rem:integer;quot := 0; rem := x;
    *[rem ≥ y → rem := rem − y; quot := quot + 1];
    X!(quot,rem)
    ]
||X::USER
]
```

4.2 Recursion: Factorial

Problem: Compute a factorial by the recursive method, to a given limit.
Solution:

```
[fac(i:1..limit)::
*[n:integer;fac(i − 1)?n →
    [n = 0 → fac(i − 1)!1
```

```
[]n > 0 → fac(i + 1)!n − 1;
    r:integer;fac(i + 1)?r;fac(i − 1)!(n ∗ r)
]]
]|fac(0)::USER
]
```

Note: This unrealistic example introduces the technique of the "iterative array" which will be used to a better effect in later examples.

4.3 Data Representation: Small Set of Integers [11]

Problem: To represent a set of not more than 100 integers as a process, S, which accepts two kinds of instruction from its calling process X: (1) S!insert(n), insert the integer n in the set, and (2) S!has(n); ... ; S?b, b is set true if n is in the set, and false otherwise. The initial value of the set is empty.

Solution:

```
S::
content:(0..99)integer; size:integer; size := 0;
*[n:integer;X?has(n) → SEARCH;X!(i < size)
[]n:integer; X?insert(n) → SEARCH;
    [i < size → skip
    []i = size; size < 100 →
        content (size) := n; size := size + 1
]    ]
```

where SEARCH is an abbreviation for:

```
i:integer; i := 0;
*[i < size; content(i) ≠ n → i := i + 1]
```

Notes: (1) The alternative command with guard "size < 100" will fail if an attempt is made to insert more than 100 elements. (2) The activity of insertion will in general take place concurrently with the calling process. However, any subsequent instruction to S will be delayed until the previous insertion is complete.

4.4 Scanning a Set

Problem: Extend the solution to 4.3 by providing a fast method for scanning all members of the set without changing the value of the set. The user program will contain a repetitive command of the form:

```
S!scan( ); more:boolean; more := true;
*[more;x:integer; S?next(x) → ... deal with x ....
[]more; S?noneleft( ) → more := false
]
```

where S!scan( ) sets the representation into a scanning mode. The repetitive command serves as a **for** statement, inputting the successive members of x from the set and inspecting them until finally the representation sends a signal that there are no members left. The body of the repetitive command is *not* permitted to communicate with S in any way.

Solution: Add a third guarded command to the outer repetitive command of S:

```
... []X?scan( ) → i:integer; i := 0;
        *[i < size → X!next(content(i)); i := i + 1];
        X!noneleft( )
```

4.5 Recursive Data Representation: Small Set of Integers

Problem: Same as above, but an array of processes is to be used to achieve a high degree of parallelism. Each process should contain at most one number. When it contains no number, it should answer "false" to all inquiries about membership. On the first insertion, it changes to a second phase of behavior, in which it deals with instructions from its predecessor, passing some of them on to its successor. The calling process will be named S(0). For efficiency, the set should be sorted, i.e. the ith process should contain the ith largest number.

Solution:

```
S(i:1..100)::
*[n:integer; S(i − 1)?has(n) → S(0)!false
[]n:integer; S(i − 1)?insert(n) →
    *[m:integer; S(i − 1)?has(m) →
        [m ≤ n → S(0)!(m = n)
        []m > n → S(i + 1)!has(m)
        ]
    []m:integer; S(i − 1)?insert(m) →
        [m < n → S(i + 1)!insert(n); n := m
        []m = n → skip
        []m > n → S(i + 1)!insert(m)
]    ]    ]
```

Notes: (1) The user process S(0) inquires whether n is a member by the commands S(1)!has(n); ... ; [(i:1..100)S(i)? b → skip]. The appropriate process will respond to the input command by the output command in line 2 or line 5. This trick avoids passing the answer back "up the chain." (2) Many insertion operations can proceed in parallel, yet any subsequent "has" operation will be performed correctly. (3) All repetitive commands and all processes of the array will terminate after the user process S(0) terminates.

4.6 Multiple Exits: Remove the Least Member

Exercise: Extend the above solution to respond to a command to yield the least member of the set and to remove it from the set. The user program will invoke the facility by a pair of commands:

```
S(1)!least( ); [x:integer;S(1)? x → ... deal with x ...
               []S(1)?noneleft( ) → ...
               ]
```

or, if he wishes to scan and empty the set, he may write:

```
S(1)!least( );more:boolean; more := true;
        *[more; x:integer; S(1)?x → ... deal with x ... ; S(1)!least( )
        []more; S(1)?noneleft( ) → more := false
        ]
```

Hint: Introduce a Boolean variable, b, initialized to true, and prefix this to all the guards of the inner loop. After responding to a !least( ) command from its predecessor, each process returns its contained value n, asks its successor for its least, and stores the response in n. But if the successor returns "noneleft( )," b is set false and the inner loop terminates. The process therefore returns to its initial state (solution due to David Gries).

5. Monitors and Scheduling

This section shows how a monitor can be regarded as a single process which communicates with more than one user process. However, each user process must have a different name (e.g. producer, consumer) or a different subscript (e.g. $X(i)$) and each communication with a user must identify its source or destination uniquely.

Consequently, when a monitor is prepared to communicate with *any* of its user processes (i.e. whichever of them calls first) it will use a guarded command with a range. For example: $*[(i:1..100)X(i)?($value parameters$) \rightarrow ... ; X(i)!($results$)]$. Here, the bound variable i is used to send the results back to the calling process. If the monitor is not prepared to accept input from some particular user (e.g. $X(j)$) on a given occasion, the input command may be preceded by a Boolean guard. For example, two successive inputs from the same process are inhibited by $j = 0$; $*[(i:1..100)i \neq j; X(i)?($values$) \rightarrow ... ; j := i]$. Any attempted output from $X(j)$ will be delayed until a subsequent iteration, after the output of some other process $X(i)$ has been accepted and dealt with.

Similarly, conditions can be used to delay acceptance of inputs which would violate scheduling constraints—postponing them until some later occasion when some other process has brought the monitor into a state in which the input can validly be accepted. This technique is similar to a conditional critical region [10] and it obviates the need for special synchronizing variables such as events, queues, or conditions. However, the absence of these special facilities certainly makes it more difficult or less efficient to solve problems involving priorities—for example, the scheduling of head movement on a disk.

5.1 Bounded Buffer

Problem: Construct a buffering process X to smooth variations in the speed of output of portions by a producer process and input by a consumer process. The consumer contains pairs of commands $X!$more$( )$; $X?p$, and the producer contains commands of the form $X!p$. The buffer should contain up to ten portions.
Solution:

```
X::
buffer:(0..9) portion;
in,out:integer; in := 0; out := 0;
comment 0 ≤ out ≤ in ≤ out + 10;
  *[in < out + 10; producer?buffer(in mod 10) → in := in + 1
  []out < in; consumer?more( ) → consumer!buffer(out mod 10);
    out := out + 1
  ]
```

Notes: (1) When out < in < out + 10, the selection of the alternative in the repetitive command will depend on whether the producer produces before the consumer consumes, or vice versa. (2) When out = in, the buffer is empty and the second alternative cannot be selected even if the consumer is ready with its command $X!$more$( )$.

However, after the producer has produced its next portion, the consumer's request can be granted on the next iteration. (3) Similar remarks apply to the producer, when in = out + 10. (4) X is designed to terminate when out = in and the producer has terminated.

5.2 Integer Semaphore

Problem: To implement an integer semaphore, S, shared among an array $X(i:1..100)$ of client processes. Each process may increment the semaphore by $S!V( )$ or decrement it by $S!P( )$, but the latter command must be delayed if the value of the semaphore is not positive.
Solution:

```
S::val:integer; val := 0;
  *[(i:1..100)X(i)?V( ) → val := val + 1
  [](i:1..100)val > 0; X(i)?P( ) → val := val - 1
  ]
```

Notes: (1) In this process, no use is made of knowledge of the subscript i of the calling process. (2) The semaphore terminates only when all hundred processes of the process array X have terminated.

5.3 Dining Philosophers (Problem due to E.W. Dijkstra)

Problem: Five philosophers spend their lives thinking and eating. The philosophers share a common dining room where there is a circular table surrounded by five chairs, each belonging to one philosopher. In the center of the table there is a large bowl of spaghetti, and the table is laid with five forks (see Figure 1). On feeling hungry, a philosopher enters the dining room, sits in his own chair, and picks up the fork on the left of his place. Unfortunately, the spaghetti is so tangled that he needs to pick up and use the fork on his right as well. When he has finished, he puts down both forks, and leaves the room. The room should keep a count of the number of philosophers in it.

Fig. 1.

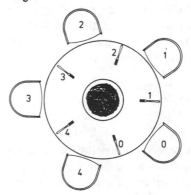

Solution: The behavior of the ith philosopher may be described as follows:

```
PHIL = *[... during ith lifetime ... →
    THINK;
    room!enter( );
    fork(i)!pickup( ); fork((i + 1) mod 5)!pickup( );
    EAT;
    fork(i)!putdown( ); fork((i + 1) mod 5)!putdown( );
    room!exit( )
    ]
```

The fate of the *i*th fork is to be picked up and put down by a philosopher sitting on either side of it

```
FORK =
  *[phil(i)?pickup( ) → phil(i)?putdown( )
  []phil((i − 1)mod 5)?pickup( ) → phil((i − 1) mod 5)?putdown( )
  ]
```

The story of the room may be simply told:

```
ROOM = occupancy:integer; occupancy := 0;
  *[(i:0..4)phil(i)?enter( ) → occupancy := occupancy + 1
  [](i:0..4)phil(i)?exit( ) → occupancy := occupancy − 1
  ]
```

All these components operate in parallel:

```
[room::ROOM||fork(i:0..4)::FORK||phil(i:0..4)::PHIL].
```

Notes: (1) The solution given above does not prevent all five philosophers from entering the room, each picking up his left fork, and starving to death because he cannot pick up his right fork. (2) Exercise: Adapt the above program to avert this sad possibility. Hint: Prevent more than four philosophers from entering the room. (Solution due to E. W. Dijkstra).

6. Miscellaneous

This section contains further examples of the use of communicating sequential processes for the solution of some less familiar problems; a parallel version of the sieve of Eratosthenes, and the design of an iterative array. The proposed solutions are even more speculative than those of the previous sections, and in the second example, even the question of termination is ignored.

6.1 Prime Numbers: The Sieve of Eratosthenes [14]

Problem: To print in ascending order all primes less than 10000. Use an array of processes, SIEVE, in which each process inputs a prime from its predecessor and prints it. The process then inputs an ascending stream of numbers from its predecessor and passes them on to its successor, suppressing any that are multiples of the original prime. Solution:

```
[SIEVE(i:1..100)::
  p,mp:integer;
  SIEVE(i − 1)?p;
  print!p;
  mp := p; comment mp is a multiple of p;
  *[m:integer; SIEVE(i − 1)?m →
    *[m > mp → mp := mp + p];
    [m = mp → skip
    []m < mp → SIEVE(i + 1)!m
  ] ]
||SIEVE(0)::print!2; n:integer; n := 3;
    *[n < 10000 → SIEVE(1)!n; n := n + 2]
||SIEVE(101)::*[n:integer;SIEVE(100)?n → print!n]
||print::*[(i:0..101) n:integer; SIEVE(i)?n → ...]
]
```

Note: (1) This beautiful solution was contributed by David Gries. (2) It is algorithmically similar to the program developed in [7, pp. 27–32].

6.2 An Iterative Array: Matrix Multiplication

Problem: A square matrix A of order 3 is given. Three streams are to be input, each stream representing a column of an array IN. Three streams are to be output, each representing a column of the product matrix IN $\times$ A. After an initial delay, the results are to be produced at the same rate as the input is consumed. Consequently, a high degree of parallelism is required. The solution should take the form shown in Figure 2. Each of the nine nonborder nodes inputs a vector component from the west and a partial sum from the north. Each node outputs the vector component to its east, and an updated partial sum to the south. The input data is produced by the west border nodes, and the desired results are consumed by south border nodes. The north border is a constant source of zeros and the east border is just a sink. No provision need be made for termination nor for changing the values of the array A.

Fig. 2.

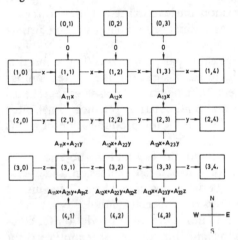

Solution: There are twenty-one nodes, in five groups, comprising the central square and the four borders:

```
[M(i:1..3,0)::WEST
||M(0,j:1..3)::NORTH
||M(i:1..3,4)::EAST
||M(4,j:1..3)::SOUTH
||M(i:1..3,j:1..3)::CENTER
]
```

The WEST and SOUTH borders are processes of the user program; the remaining processes are:

```
NORTH = *[true → M(1,j)!0]
EAST = *[x:real; M(i,3)?x → skip]
CENTER = *[x:real; M(i,j − 1)?x →
    M(i,j + 1)!x; sum:real;
    M(i − 1,j)?sum; M(i + 1,j)!(A(i,j)*x + sum)
  ]
```

7. Discussion

A design for a programming language must necessarily involve a number of decisions which seem to be fairly arbitrary. The discussion of this section is intended to explain some of the underlying motivation and to mention some unresolved questions.

7.1 Notations

I have chosen single-character notations (e.g. !,?) to express the primitive concepts, rather than the more traditional boldface or underlined English words. As a result, the examples have an APL-like brevity, which some readers find distasteful. My excuse is that (in contrast to APL) there are only a very few primitive concepts and that it is standard practice of mathematics (and also good coding practice) to denote common primitive concepts by brief notations (e.g. $+,\times$). When read aloud, these are replaced by words (e.g. plus, times).

Some readers have suggested the use of assignment notation for input and output:

<target variable> := <source>
<destination> := <expression>

I find this suggestion misleading: it is better to regard input and output as distinct primitives, justifying distinct notations.

I have used the same pair of brackets ([...]) to bracket all program structures, instead of the more familiar variety of brackets (if..fi, begin..end, case...esac, etc.). In this I follow normal mathematical practice, but I must also confess to a distaste for the pronunciation of words like fi, od, or esac.

I am dissatisfied with the fact that my notation gives the same syntax for a structured expression and a subscripted variable. Perhaps tags should be distinguished from other identifiers by a special symbol (say #).

I was tempted to introduce an abbreviation for combined declaration and input, e.g. $X?(n{:}integer)$ for $n{:}integer; X?n$.

7.2 Explicit Naming

My design insists that every input or output command must name its source or destination explicitly. This makes it inconvenient to write a library of processes which can be included in subsequent programs, independent of the process names used in that program. A partial solution to this problem is to allow one process (the *main* process) of a parallel command to have an empty label, and to allow the other processes in the command to use the empty process name as source or destination of input or output.

For construction of large programs, some more general technique will also be necessary. This should at least permit substitution of program text for names defined elsewhere—a technique which has been used informally throughout this paper. The Cobol COPY verb also permits a substitution for formal parameters within the copied text. But whatever facility is introduced, I would recommend the following principle: Every program, after assembly with its library routines, should be printable as a text expressed wholly in the language, and it is this printed text which should describe the execution of the program, independent of which parts were drawn from a library.

Since I did not intend to design a complete language, I have ignored the problem of libraries in order to concentrate on the essential semantic concepts of the program which is actually executed.

7.3 Port Names

An alternative to explicit naming of source and destination would be to name a *port* through which communication is to take place. The port names would be local to the processes, and the manner in which pairs of ports are to be connected by channels could be declared in the head of a parallel command.

This is an attractive alternative which could be designed to introduce a useful degree of syntactically checkable redundancy. But it is semantically equivalent to the present proposal, provided that each port is connected to exactly one other port in another process. In this case each channel can be identified with a tag, together with the name of the process at the other end. Since I wish to concentrate on semantics, I preferred in this paper to use the simplest and most direct notation, and to avoid raising questions about the possibility of connecting more than two ports by a single channel.

7.4 Automatic Buffering

As an alternative to synchronization of input and output, it is often proposed that an outputting process should be allowed to proceed even when the inputting process is not yet ready to accept the output. An implementation would be expected automatically to interpose a chain of buffers to hold output messages that have not yet been input.

I have deliberately rejected this alternative, for two reasons: (1) It is less realistic to implement in multiple disjoint processors, and (2) when buffering is required on a particular channel, it can readily be specified using the given primitives. Of course, it could be argued equally well that synchronization can be specified when required by using a pair of buffered input and output commands.

7.5 Unbounded Process Activation

The notation for an array of processes permits the same program text (like an Algol recursive procedure) to have many simultaneous "activations"; however, the exact number must be specified in advance. In a conventional single-processor implementation, this can lead to inconvenience and wastefulness, similar to the fixed-length array of Fortran. It would therefore be attractive to allow a process array with no a priori bound on the number of elements; and to specify that the exact number of elements required for a particular execution of the program should be determined dynamically, like the maximum depth of recursion of an Algol procedure or the number of iterations of a repetitive command.

However, it is a good principle that every actual run of a program with unbounded arrays should be identical to the run of some program with all its arrays bounded in advance. Thus the unbounded program should be defined as the "limit" (in some sense) of a series of bounded programs with increasing bounds. I have chosen to concentrate on the semantics of the bounded case—which is necessary anyway and which is more realistic for implementation on multiple microprocessors.

7.6 Fairness
Consider the parallel command:

```
[X:: Y!stop( )|| Y::continue:boolean; continue := true;
    *[continue; X?stop( ) → continue := false
    []continue → n := n + 1
    ]
].
```

If the implementation always prefers the second alternative in the repetitive command of Y, it is said to be *unfair*, because although the output command in X could have been executed on an infinite number of occasions, it is in fact always passed over.

The question arises: Should a programming language definition specify that an implementation must be *fair*? Here, I am fairly sure that the answer is NO. Otherwise, the implementation would be obliged to successfully complete the example program shown above, in spite of the fact that its nondeterminism is unbounded. I would therefore suggest that it is the programmer's responsibility to prove that his program terminates correctly—without relying on the assumption of fairness in the implementation. Thus the program shown above is incorrect, since its termination cannot be proved.

Nevertheless, I suggest that an efficient implementation should try to be reasonably fair and should ensure that an output command is not delayed unreasonably often after it first becomes executable. But a proof of correctness must not rely on this property of an efficient implementation. Consider the following analogy with a sequential program: An efficient implementation of an alternative command will tend to favor the alternative which can be most efficiently executed, but the programmer must ensure that the logical correctness of his program does not depend on this property of his implementation.

This method of avoiding the problem of fairness does not apply to programs such as operating systems which are intended to run forever because in this case termination proofs are not relevant. But I wonder whether it is ever advisable to write or to execute such programs. Even an operating system should be designed to bring itself to an orderly conclusion reasonably soon after it inputs a message instructing it to do so. Otherwise, the *only* way to stop it is to "crash" it.

7.7 Functional Coroutines
It is interesting to compare the processes described here with those proposed in [12]; the differences are most striking. There, coroutines are strictly deterministic: No choice is given between alternative sources of input. The output commands are automatically buffered to any required degree. The output of one process can be automatically fanned out to any number of processes (including itself!) which can consume it at differing rates. Finally, the processes there are designed to run forever, whereas my proposed parallel command is normally intended to terminate. The design in [12] is based on an elegant theory which permits proof of the properties of programs. These differences are not accidental—they seem to be natural consequences of the difference between the more abstract applicative (or functional) approach to programming and the more machine-oriented imperative (or procedural) approach, which is taken by communicating sequential processes.

7.8 Output Guards
Since input commands may appear in guards, it seems more symmetric to permit output commands as well. This would allow an obvious and useful simplification in some of the example programs, for example, in the bounded buffer (5.1). Perhaps a more convincing reason would be to ensure that the externally visible effect and behavior of every parallel command can be modeled by some sequential command. In order to model the parallel command

$$Z :: [X!2||Y!3]$$

we need to be able to write the sequential alternative command:

$$Z :: [X!2 → Y!3[]Y!3 → X!2]$$

Note that this *cannot* be done by the command

$$Z :: [true → X!2; Y!3[]true → Y!3; X!2]$$

which can fail if the process Z happens to choose the first alternative, but the processes Y and X are synchronized with each other in such a way that Y must input from Z before X does, e.g.

```
  Y :: Z?y; X!go( )
||X :: Y?go( ); Z?x
```

7.9 Restriction: Repetitive Command With Input Guard
In proposing an unfamiliar programming language feature, it seems wiser at first to specify a highly restrictive version rather than to propose extensions—especially when the language feature claims to be primitive. For example, it is clear that the multidimensional process array is not primitive, since it can readily be constructed in a language which permits only single-dimensional arrays. But I have a rather more serious misgiving about the repetitive command with input guards.

The automatic termination of a repetitive command on termination of the sources of all its input guards is an extremely powerful and convenient feature but it also involves some subtlety of specification to ensure that it is implementable; and it is certainly not primitive, since the required effect can be achieved (with considerable inconvenience) by explicit exchange of "end()" signals. For example, the subroutine DIV(4.1) could be rewritten:

```
[DIV :: continue:boolean; continue := true;
*[continue; X?end() → continue := false
[]continue; x,y:integer; X?(x,y) → ... ; X!(quot,rem)
||X :: USER PROG; DIV!end()
]
```

Other examples would be even more inconvenient.

But the dangers of convenient facilities are notorious. For example, the repetitive commands with input guards may tempt the programmer to write them without making adequate plans for their termination; and if it turns out that the automatic termination is unsatisfactory, reprogramming for explicit termination will involve severe changes, affecting even the interfaces between the processes.

8. Conclusion

This paper has suggested that input, output, and concurrency should be regarded as primitives of programming, which underlie many familiar and less familiar programming concepts. However, it would be unjustified to conclude that these primitives can wholly replace the other concepts in a programming language. Where a more elaborate construction (such as a procedure or a monitor) is frequently useful, has properties which are more simply provable, and can also be implemented more efficiently than the general case, there is a strong reason for including in a programming language a special notation for that construction. The fact that the construction can be defined in terms of simpler underlying primitives is a useful guarantee that its inclusion is logically consistent with the remainder of the language.

Acknowledgments. The research reported in this paper has been encouraged and supported by a Senior Fellowship of the Science Research Council of Great Britain. The technical inspiration was due to Edsger W. Dijkstra [9], and the paper has been improved in presentation and content by valuable and painstaking advice from D. Gries, D. Q. M. Fay, Edsger W. Dijkstra, N. Wirth, Robert Milne, M. K. Harper, and its referees. The role of IFIP W.G.2.3 as a forum for presentation and discussion is acknowledged with pleasure and gratitude.

Received March 1977; revised August 1977

References

1. Atkinson, R., and Hewitt, C. Synchronisation in actor systems. Working Paper 83, M.I.T., Cambridge, Mass., Nov. 1976.
2. Brinch Hansen, P. The programming language Concurrent Pascal. *IEEE Trans. Software Eng. 1*, 2 (June 1975), 199–207.
3. Campbell, R.H., and Habermann, A.N. The specification of process synchronisation by path expressions. *Lecture Notes in Computer Science 16*, Springer, 1974, pp. 89–102.
4. Conway, M.E. Design of a separable transition-diagram compiler. *Comm. ACM 6*, 7 (July 1963), 396–408.
5. Dahl, O-J., et al. SIMULA 67, common base language. Norwegian Computing Centre, Forskningveien, Oslo, 1967.
6. Dijkstra, E.W. Co-operating sequential processes. In *Programming Languages*, F. Genuys, Ed., Academic Press, New York, 1968, pp. 43–112.
7. Dijkstra, E.W. Notes on structured programming. In *Structured Programming*, Academic Press, New York 1972, pp. 1–82.
8. Dijkstra, E.W. Guarded commands, nondeterminacy, and formal derivation of programs. *Comm. ACM 18*, 8 (Aug. 1975), 453–457.
9. Dijkstra, E.W. Verbal communication, Marktoberdorf, Aug. 1975.
10. Hoare, C.A.R. Towards a theory of parallel programming. In *Operating Systems Techniques*, Academic Press, New York, 1972, pp. 61–71.
11. Hoare, C.A.R. Proof of correctness of data representations. *Acta Informatica 1*, 4 (1972), 271–281.
12. Kahn, G. The semantics of a simple language for parallel programming. In *Proc. IFIP Congress 74*, North Holland, 1974.
13. Liskov, B.H. A note on CLU. Computation Structures Group Memo. 112, M.I.T., Cambridge, Mass, 1974.
14. McIlroy, M.D. Coroutines. Bell Laboratories, Murray Hill, N.J., 1968.
15. Naur, P., Ed. Report on the algorithmic language ALGOL 60. *Comm. ACM 3*, 5 (May 1960), 299–314.
16. Reynolds, J.C. COGENT. ANL-7022, Argonne Nat. Lab., Argonne, Ill., 1965.
17. Thompson, K. The UNIX command language. In *Structured Programming*, Infotech, Nicholson House, Maidenhead, England, 1976, pp. 375–384.
18. van Wijngaarden, A. Ed. Report on the algorithmic language ALGOL 68. *Numer. Math. 14* (1969), 79–218.
19. Wulf, W.A., London, R.L., and Shaw, M. Abstraction and verification in ALPHARD. Dept. of Comptr. Sci., Carnegie-Mellon U., Pittsburgh, Pa., June 1976.
20. Wirth, N. The programming language PASCAL. *Acta Informatica 1*, 1 (1971), 35–63.

CONCEPTS AND NOTATIONS FOR CONCURRENT PROGRAMMING

GREGORY R. ANDREWS AND FRED B. SCHNEIDER

Much has been learned in the last decade about concurrent programming. This paper identifies the major concepts of concurrent programming and describes some of the more important language notations for writing concurrent programs. The roles of processes, communication, and synchronization are discussed. Language notations for expressing concurrent execution and for specifying process interaction are surveyed. Synchronization primitives based on shared variables and on message passing are described. Finally, three general classes of concurrent programming languages are identified and compared.

Categories and Subject Descriptors: D.1.3 [**Programming Techniques**]: Concurrent Programming; D.3.3 [**Programming Languages**]: Language Constructs—*concurrent programming structures, coroutines*; D.4.1 [**Operating Systems**]: Process Management; D.4.7 [**Operating Systems**]: Organization and Design

General Terms: Algorithms, Languages

INTRODUCTION

The complexion of concurrent programming has changed substantially in the past ten years. First, theoretical advances have prompted the definition of new programming notations that express concurrent computations simply, make synchronization requirements explicit, and facilitate formal correctness proofs. Second, the availability of inexpensive processors has made possible the construction of distributed systems and multiprocessors that were previously economically infeasible. Because of these two developments, concurrent programming no longer is the sole province of those who design and implement operating systems; it has become important to programmers of all kinds of applications, including database management systems, large-scale parallel scientific computations, and real-time, embedded control systems. In fact, the discipline has matured to the point that there are now undergraduate-level text books devoted solely to the topic [Holt et al., 1978; Ben-Ari, 1982]. In light of this growing range of applicability, it seems appropriate to survey the state of the art.

This paper describes the concepts central to the design and construction of concurrent programs and explores notations for describing concurrent computations. Although this description requires detailed discussions of some concurrent programming languages, we restrict attention to those whose designs we believe to be influential or conceptually innovative. Not all the languages we discuss enjoy widespread use. Many are experimental efforts that focus on understanding the interactions of a given collection of constructs. Some have not even been implemented; others have been, but with little concern for efficiency, access control, data types, and other important (though nonconcurrency) issues.

We proceed as follows. In Section 1 we

Gregory R. Andrews is with the Department of Computer Science, University of Arizona, Tucson, Arizona 85721

Fred B. Schneider is with the Department of Computer Science, Cornell University, Ithaca, New York 14853

CONTENTS

---

discuss the three issues that underlie all concurrent programming notations: how to express concurrent execution, how processes communicate, and how processes synchronize. These issues are treated in detail in the remainder of the paper. In Section 2 we take a closer look at various ways to specify concurrent execution: coroutines, **fork** and **cobegin** statements, and **process** declarations. In Section 3 we discuss synchronization primitives that are used when communication uses shared variables. Two general types of synchronization are considered—exclusion and condition synchronization—and a variety of ways to implement them are described: busy-waiting, semaphores, conditional critical regions, monitors, and path expressions. In Section 4 we discuss message-passing primitives. We describe methods for specifying channels of communication and for synchronization, and higher level constructs for performing remote procedure calls and atomic transactions. In Section 5 we identify and compare three general classes of concurrent programming languages. Finally, in Section 6, we summarize the major topics and identify directions in which the field is headed.

1. CONCURRENT PROGRAMS: PROCESSES AND PROCESS INTERACTION

1.1 Processes

A *sequential program* specifies sequential execution of a list of statements; its execution is called a *process*. A *concurrent program* specifies two or more sequential programs that may be executed concurrently as *parallel processes*. For example, an airline reservation system that involves processing transactions from many terminals has a natural specification as a concurrent program in which each terminal is controlled by its own sequential process. Even when processes are not executed simultaneously, it is often easier to structure a system as a collection of cooperating sequential processes rather than as a single sequential program. A simple batch operating system can be viewed as three processes: a *reader* process, an *executer* process, and a *printer* process. The *reader* process reads cards from a card reader and places card images in an input buffer. The *executer* process reads card images from the input buffer, performs the specified computation (perhaps generating line images), and stores the results in an output buffer. The *printer* process retrieves line images from the output buffer and writes them to a printer.

A concurrent program can be executed either by allowing processes to share one or more processors or by running each process on its own processor. The first approach is referred to as *multiprogramming*; it is supported by an operating system kernel [Dijkstra, 1968a] that multiplexes the processes on the processor(s). The second approach is referred to as *multiprocessing* if the processors share a common memory (as in a multiprocessor [Jones and Schwarz, 1980]), or as *distributed processing* if the processors are connected by a communications network.[1] Hybrid approaches also exist—for example, processors in a distributed system are often multiprogrammed.

The rate at which processes are executed depends on which approach is used. When each process is executed on its own processor, each is executed at a fixed, but perhaps unknown, rate; when processes share a processor, it is as if each is executed on a variable-speed processor. Because we would like to be able to understand a concurrent program in terms of its component

---

[1] A concurrent program that is executed in this way is often called a *distributed program*.

sequential processes and their interaction, without regard for how they are executed, we make no assumption about execution rates of concurrently executing processes, except that they all are positive. This is called the *finite progress assumption*. The correctness of a program for which only finite progress is assumed is thus independent of whether that program is executed on multiple processors or on a single multiprogrammed processor.

1.2 Process Interaction

In order to cooperate, concurrently executing processes must communicate and synchronize. Communication allows execution of one process to influence execution of another. Interprocess communication is based on the use of shared variables (variables that can be referenced by more than one process) or on message passing.

Synchronization is often necessary when processes communicate. Processes are executed with unpredictable speeds. Yet, to communicate, one process must perform some action that the other detects—an action such as setting the value of a variable or sending a message. This only works if the events "perform an action" and "detect an action" are constrained to happen in that order. Thus one can view synchronization as a set of constraints on the ordering of events. The programmer employs a *synchronization mechanism* to delay execution of a process in order to satisfy such constraints.

To make the concept of synchronization a bit more concrete, consider the batch operating system described above. A shared buffer is used for communication between the *reader* process and the *executer* process. These processes must be synchronized so that, for example, the *executer* process never attempts to read a card image from the input if the buffer is empty.

This view of synchronization follows from taking an *operational approach* to program semantics. An execution of a concurrent program can be viewed as a sequence of *atomic actions*, each resulting from the execution of an indivisible operation.[2] This sequence will comprise some interleaving of the sequences of atomic ac-

tions generated by the individual component processes. Rarely do all execution interleavings result in acceptable program behavior, as is illustrated in the following. Suppose initially that $x = 0$, that process $P1$ increments x by 1, and that process $P2$ increments x by 2:

$$P1: x := x + 1 \qquad P2: x := x + 2$$

It would seem reasonable to expect the final value of x, after $P1$ and $P2$ have executed concurrently, to be 3. Unfortunately, this will not always be the case, because assignment statements are not generally implemented as indivisible operations. For example, the above assignments might be implemented as a sequence of three indivisible operations: (i) load a register with the value of x; (ii) add 1 or 2 to it; and (iii) store the result in x. Thus, in the program above, the final value of x might be 1, 2, or 3. This anomalous behavior can be avoided by preventing interleaved execution of the two assignment statements—that is, by controlling the ordering of the events corresponding to the atomic actions. (If ordering were thus controlled, each assignment statement would be an indivisible operation.) In other words, execution of $P1$ and $P2$ must be synchronized by enforcing restrictions on possible interleavings.

The *axiomatic approach* [Floyd, 1967; Hoare, 1969; Dijkstra, 1976] provides a second framework in which to view the role of synchronization.[3] In this approach, the semantics of statements are defined by axioms and inference rules. This results in a formal logical system, called a "programming logic." Theorems in the logic have the form

$$\{P\}\, S\, \{Q\}$$

and specify a relation between statements (S) and two predicates, a *precondition* P and a *postcondition* Q. The axioms and inference rules are chosen so that theorems have the interpretation that if execution of S is started in any state that satisfies the precondition, and if execution terminates, then the postcondition will be true of the resulting state. This allows statements to be viewed as relations between predicates.

A *proof outline*[4] provides one way to present a program and its proof. It consists

---

[2] We assume that a single memory reference is indivisible; if two processes attempt to reference the same memory cell at the same time, the result is as if the references were made serially. This is a reasonable assumption in light of the way memory is constructed. See Lamport [1980b] for a discussion of some of the implications of relaxing this assumption.

---

[3] We include brief discussions of axiomatic semantics here and elsewhere in the paper because of its importance in helping to explain concepts. However, a full discussion of the semantics of concurrent computation is beyond the scope of this paper.

[4] This sometimes is called an asserted program.

of the program text interleaved with assertions so that for each statement S, the triple (formed from (1) the assertion that textually precedes S in the proof outline, (2) the statement S, and (3) the assertion that textually follows S in the proof outline) is a theorem in the programming logic. Thus the appearance of an assertion R in the proof outline signifies that R is true of the program state when control reaches that point.

When concurrent execution is possible, the proof of a sequential process is valid only if concurrent execution of other processes cannot invalidate assertions that appear in the proof [Ashcroft, 1975; Keller, 1976; Owicki and Gries, 1976a, 1976b; Lamport, 1977, 1980a; Lamport and Schneider, 1982]. One way to establish this is to assume that the code between any two assertions in a proof outline is executed atomically[5] and then to prove a series of theorems showing that no statement in one process invalidates any assertion in the proof of another. These additional theorems constitute a proof of *noninterference*. To illustrate this, consider the following excerpt from a proof outline of two concurrent processes $P1$ and $P2$:

$$P1: \quad \cdots \qquad\qquad P2: \quad \cdots$$
$$\{x > 0\} \qquad\qquad\qquad \{x < 0\}$$
$$S1: x := 16 \qquad\qquad\quad S2: x := -2$$
$$\{x = 16\} \qquad\qquad\qquad \cdots$$
$$\cdots$$

In order to prove that execution of $P2$ does not interfere with the proof of $P1$, part of what we must show is that execution of $S2$ does not invalidate assertions $\{x > 0\}$ and $\{x = 16\}$ in the proof of $P1$. This is done by proving

$$\{x < 0 \text{ and } x > 0\} \ x := -2 \ \{x > 0\}$$

and

$$\{x < 0 \text{ and } x > 0\} \ x := -2 \ \{x = 16\}$$

Both of these are theorems because the precondition of each, $\{x < 0 \text{ and } x > 0\}$, is false. What we have shown is that execution of $S2$ is not possible when either the precondition or postcondition of $S1$ holds (and thus $S1$ and $S2$ are mutually exclusive). Hence, $S2$ cannot invalidate either of these assertions.

Synchronization mechanisms control interference in two ways. First, they can delay

execution of a process until a given condition (assertion) is true. By so doing, they ensure that the precondition of the subsequent statement is guaranteed to be true (provided that the assertion is not interfered with). Second, a synchronization mechanism can be used to ensure that a block of statements is an indivisible operation. This eliminates the possibility of statements in other processes interfering with assertions appearing within the proof of that block of statements.

Both views of programs, operational and axiomatic, are useful. The operational approach—viewing synchronization as an ordering of events—is well suited to explaining how synchronization mechanisms work. For that reason, the operational approach is used rather extensively in this survey. It also constitutes the philosophical basis for a family of synchronization mechanisms called *path expressions* [Campbell and Habermann, 1974], which are described in Section 3.5.

Unfortunately, the operational approach does not really help one understand the behavior of a concurrent program or argue convincingly about its correctness. Although it has borne fruit for simple concurrent programs—such as transactions processed concurrently in a database system [Bernstein and Goodman, 1981]—the operational approach has only limited utility when applied to more complex concurrent programs [Akkoyunlu et al., 1978; Bernstein and Schneider, 1978]. This limitation exists because the number of interleavings that must be considered grows exponentially with the size of the component sequential processes. Human minds are not good at such extensive case analysis. The axiomatic approach usually does not have this difficulty. It is perhaps the most promising technique for understanding concurrent programs. Some familiarity with formal logic is required for is use, however, and this has slowed its acceptance.

To summarize, there are three main issues underlying the design of a notation for expressing a concurrent computation:

(i) how to indicate concurrent execution;
(ii) which mode of interprocess communication to use;
(iii) which synchronization mechanism to use.

Also, synchronization mechanisms can be viewed either as constraining the ordering of events or as controlling interference. We consider all these topics in depth in the remainder of the paper.

---

[5] This should be construed as specifying what assertions must be included in the proof rather than as a restriction on how statements are actually executed.

2. SPECIFYING CONCURRENT EXECUTION

Various notations have been proposed for specifying concurrent execution. Early proposals, such as the **fork** statement, are marred by a failure to separate process definition from process synchronization. Later proposals separate these distinct concepts and characteristically possess syntactic restrictions that impose some structure on a concurrent program. This structure allows easy identification of those program segments that can be executed concurrently. Consequently, such proposals are well suited for use with the axiomatic approach, because the structure of the program itself clarifies the proof obligations for establishing noninterference.

Below, we describe some representative constructs for expressing concurrent execution. Each can be used to specify computations having a *static* (fixed) number of processes, or can be used in combination with process-creation mechanisms to specify computations having a *dynamic* (variable) number of processes.

2.1 Coroutines

Coroutines are like subroutines, but allow transfer of control in a symmetric rather than strictly hierarchical way [Conway, 1963a]. Control is transferred between coroutines by means of the **resume** statement. Execution of **resume** is like execution of procedure **call**: it transfers control to the named routine, saving enough state information for control to return later to the instruction following the **resume**. (When a routine is first resumed, control is transferred to the beginning of that routine.) However, control is returned to the original routine by executing another **resume** rather than by executing a procedure **return**. Moreover, any other coroutine can potentially transfer control back to the original routine. (For example, coroutine *C1* could **resume** *C2*, which could **resume** *C3*, which could **resume** *C1*.) Thus **resume** serves as the only way to transfer control between coroutines, and one coroutine can transfer control to any other coroutine that it chooses.

A use of coroutines appears in Figure 1. Note that **resume** is used to transfer control between coroutines *A* and *B*, a **call** is used to initiate the coroutine computation, and **return** is used to transfer control back to the caller *P*. The arrows in Figure 1 indicate the transfers of control.

Each coroutine can be viewed as implementing a process. Execution of **resume** causes process sychronization. When used with care, coroutines are an acceptable way to organize concurrent programs that share a single processor. In fact, multiprogramming can also be implemented using coroutines. Coroutines are not adequate for true parallel processing, however, because their semantics allow for execution of only one routine at a time. In essence, coroutines are concurrent processes in which process switching has been completely specified, rather than left to the discretion of the implementation.

Statements to implement coroutines have been included in discrete event simulation languages such as SIMULA I [Nygaard and Dahl, 1978] and its successors; the string-processing language SL5 [Hanson and Griswold, 1978]; and systems implementation languages including BLISS [Wulf et al., 1971] and most recently Modula-2 [Wirth, 1982].

2.2 The fork and join Statements

The **fork** statement [Dennis and Van Horn, 1966; Conway, 1963b], like a **call** or **resume**, specifies that a designated routine should start executing. However, the invoking routine and the invoked routine proceed concurrently. To synchronize with completion of the invoked routine, the invoking routine can execute a **join** statement. Executing **join** delays the invoking routine until the designated invoked routine has terminated. (The latter routine is often designated by a value returned from execution

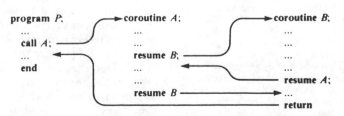

Figure 1. A use of coroutines.

of a prior **fork**.) A use of **fork** and **join** follows:

```
program P1;          program P2;
   ...                  ...
   fork P2;             ...
   ...                  ...
   join P2;             end
   ...
```

Execution of *P2* is initiated when the **fork** in *P1* is executed; *P1* and *P2* then execute concurrently until either *P1* executes the **join** statement or *P2* terminates. After *P1* reaches the **join** and *P2* terminates, *P1* executes the statements following the **join**.

Because **fork** and **join** can appear in conditionals and loops, a detailed understanding of program execution is necessary to understand which routines will be executed concurrently. Nevertheless, when used in a disciplined manner, the statements are practical and powerful. For example, **fork** provides a direct mechanism for dynamic process creation, including multiple activations of the same program text. The UNIX[6] operating system [Ritchie and Thompson, 1974] makes extensive use of variants of **fork** and **join**. Similar statements have also been included in PL/I and Mesa [Mitchell et al., 1979].

2.3 The cobegin Statement

The **cobegin** statement[7] is a structured way of denoting concurrent execution of a set of statements. Execution of

cobegin $S_1 \parallel S_2 \parallel \cdots \parallel S_n$ coend

causes concurrent execution of $S_1, S_2, \ldots, S_n$. Each of the S_i's may be any statement, including a **cobegin** or a block with local declarations. Execution of a **cobegin** statement terminates only when execution of all the S_i's have terminated.

Although **cobegin** is not as powerful as **fork/join**,[8] it is sufficient for specifying

---

[6] UNIX is a trademark of Bell Laboratories.
[7] This was first called **parbegin** by Dijkstra [1968b].
[8] Execution of a concurrent program can be represented by a *process flow graph*: an acyclic, directed graph having one node for each process and an arc from one node to another if the second cannot execute until the first has terminated [Shaw, 1974]. Without introducing extra processes or idle time, **cobegin** and sequencing can only represent series–parallel (properly nested) process flow graphs. Using **fork** and **join**, the computation represented by any process flow graph can be specified directly. Furthermore, **fork** can be used to create an arbitrary number of concurrent processes, whereas **cobegin** as defined in any existing language, can be used only to activate a fixed number of processes.

most concurrent computations. Furthermore, the syntax of the **cobegin** statement makes explicit which routines are executed concurrently, and provides a single-entry, single-exit control structure. This allows the state transformation implemented by a **cobegin** to be understood by itself, and then to be used to understand the program in which it appears.

Variants of **cobegin** have been included in ALGOL68 [van Wijngaarden et al., 1975], Communicating Sequential Processes [Hoare, 1978], Edison [Brinch Hansen, 1981], and Argus [Liskov and Scheifler, 1982].

2.4 Process Declarations

Large programs are often structured as a collection of sequential routines, which are executed concurrently. Although such routines could be declared as procedures and activated by means of **cobegin** or **fork**, the structure of a concurrent program is much clearer if the declaration of a routine states whether it will be executed concurrently. The *process declaration* provides such a facility.

Use of process declarations to structure a concurrent program is illustrated in Figure 2, which outlines the batch operating system described earlier. We shall use this notation for process declarations in the remainder of this paper to denote collections of routines that are executed concurrently.

In some concurrent programming languages (e.g., Distributed Processes [Brinch Hansen, 1978] and SR [Andrews, 1981]), a collection of process declarations is equivalent to a single **cobegin**, where each of the declared processes is a component of the **cobegin**. This means there is exactly one instance of each declared process. Alternatively, some languages provide an explicit mechanism—**fork** or something similar—for activating instances of process declarations. This explicit activation mechanism can only be used during program initialization in some languages (e.g., Concurrent PASCAL [Brinch Hansen, 1975] and Modula [Wirth, 1977a]). This leads to a fixed number of processes but allows multiple instances of each declared process to be created. By contrast, in other languages (e.g., PLITS [Feldman, 1979] and Ada [U. S. Department of Defense, 1981]) processes can be created at any time during execution, which makes possible computations having a variable number of processes.

```
program OPSYS;

    var input_buffer : array [0..N−1] of cardimage;
        output_buffer : array [0..N−1] of lineimage;

    process reader;
        var card : cardimage;
        loop
            read card from cardreader;
            deposit card in input_buffer
        end
    end;

    process executer;
        var card : cardimage;
            line : lineimage;
        loop
            fetch card from input_buffer;
            process card and generate line;
            deposit line in output_buffer
        end
    end;

    process printer;
        var line : lineimage;
        loop
            fetch line from output_buffer;
            print line on lineprinter
        end
    end

end.
```

Figure 2.   Outline of batch operating system.

3. SYNCHRONIZATION PRIMITIVES BASED ON SHARED VARIABLES

When shared variables are used for interprocess communication, two types of synchronization are useful: mutual exclusion and condition synchronization. *Mutual exclusion* ensures that a sequence of statements is treated as an indivisible operation. Consider, for example, a complex data structure manipulated by means of operations implemented as sequences of statements. If processes concurrently perform operations on the same shared data object, then unintended results might occur. (This was illustrated earlier where the statement $x := x + 1$ had to be executed indivisibly for a meaningful computation to result.) A sequence of statements that must appear to be executed as an indivisible operation is called a *critical section*. The term "mutual exclusion" refers to mutually exclusive execution of critical sections. Notice that the effects of execution interleavings are visible only if two computations access shared varibles. If such is the case, one computation can see intermediate results produced by incomplete execution of the other. If two routines have no variables in common, then their execution need not be mutually exclusive.

Another situation in which it is necessary to coordinate execution of concurrent processes occurs when a shared data object is in a state inappropriate for executing a particular operation. Any process attempting such an operation should be delayed until the state of the data object (i.e., the values of the variables that comprise the object) changes as a result of other processes executing operations. We shall call this type of synchronization *condition synchronization*.[9] Examples of condition synchronization appear in the simple batch operating system discussed above. A process attempting to execute a "deposit" operation on a buffer (the buffer being a shared data object) should be delayed if the buffer has no space. Similarly, a process attempting to "fetch" from a buffer should be delayed if there is nothing in the buffer to remove.

Below, we survey various mechanisms for implementing these two types of synchronization.

3.1 Busy-Waiting

One way to implement synchronization is to have processes set and test shared vari-

_____

[9] Unfortunately, there is no commonly agreed upon term for this.

ables. This approach works reasonably well for implementing condition synchronization, but not for implementing mutual exclusion, as will be seen. To signal a condition, a process sets the value of a shared variable; to wait for that condition, a process repeatedly tests the variable until it is found to have a desired value. Because a process waiting for a condition must repeatedly test the shared variable, this technique to delay a process is called *busy-waiting* and the process is said to be *spinning*. Variables that are used in this way are sometimes called *spin locks*.

To implement mutual exclusion using busy-waiting, statements that signal and wait for conditions are combined into carefully constructed protocols. Below, we present Peterson's solution to the two-process mutual exclusion problem [Peterson, 1981]. (This solution is simpler than the solution proposed by Dekker [Shaw, 1974].) The solution involves an *entry protocol*, which a process executes before entering its critical section, and an *exit protocol*, which a process executes after finishing its critical section:

```
process P1;
  loop
    Entry Protocol;
    Critical Section;
    Exit Protocol;
    Noncritical Section
  end
  end
process P2;
  loop
    Entry Protocol;
    Critical Section;
    Exit Protocol;
    Noncritical Section
  end
  end
```

Three shared variables are used as follows to realize the desired synchronization. Boolean variable *enteri* ($i = 1$ or 2) is true when process Pi is executing its entry protocol or its critical section. Variable *turn* records the name of the next process to be granted entry into its own critical section; *turn* is used when both processes execute their respective entry protocols at about the same time. The solution is

```
program Mutex_Example;
  var enter1, enter2 : Boolean initial (false,false);
    turn : integer initial ("P1");   { or "P2" }
  process P1;
    loop
      Entry_Protocol:
        enter1 := true;   { announce intent to enter }
        turn := "P2";   { set priority to other process }
        while enter2 and turn = "P2"
          do skip; { wait if other process is in and it is his turn }
      Critical Section;
      Exit_Protocol:
        enter1 := false;   { renounce intent to enter }
      Noncritical Section
    end
  end;
  process P2;
    loop
      Entry_Protocol:
        enter2 := true;   { announce intent to enter }
        turn := "P1";   { set priority to other process }
        while enter1 and turn = "P1"
          do skip; { wait if other process is in and it is his turn }
      Critical Section;
      Exit_Protocol:
        enter1 := false;   { renounce intent to enter }
      Noncritical Section
    end
  end
end.
```

In addition to implementing mutual exclusion, this solution has two other desirable properties. First, it is *deadlock free*. *Deadlock* is a state of affairs in which two or more processes are waiting for events that will never occur. Above, deadlock could occur if each process could spin forever in its entry protocol; using *turn* precludes deadlock. The second desirable property is *fairness*:[10] if a process is trying to enter its critical section, it will eventually be able to do so, provided that the other process exits its critical section. Fairness is a desirable property for a synchronization mechanism because its presence ensures that the finite progress assumption is not invalidated by delays due to synchronization. In general, a synchronization mechanism is *fair* if no process is delayed forever, waiting for a condition that occurs infinitely often; it is *bounded fair* if there exists an upper bound on how long a process will be delayed waiting for a condition that occurs infinitely often. The above protocol is bounded fair, since a process waiting to enter its critical section is delayed for at most one execution of the other process' critical section; the variable *turn* ensures this. Peterson [1981] gives operational proofs of mutual exclusion, deadlock free-

---

[10] A more complete discussion of fairness appears in Lehmann et al. [1981].

dom, and fairness; Dijkstra [1981a] gives axiomatic ones.

Synchronization protocols that use only busy-waiting are difficult to design, understand, and prove correct. First, although instructions that make two memory references part of a single indivisible operation (e.g., the TS (test-and-set) instruction on the IBM 360/370 processors) help, such instructions do not significantly simplify the task of designing synchronization protocols. Second, busy-waiting wastes processor cycles. A processor executing a spinning process could usually be employed more productively by running other processes until the awaited condition occurs. Last, the busy-waiting approach to synchronization burdens the programmer with deciding both what synchronization is required and how to provide it. In reading a program that uses busy-waiting, it may not be clear to the reader which program variables are used for implementing synchronization and which are used for, say, interprocess communication.

3.2 Semaphores

Dijkstra was one of the first to appreciate the difficulties of using low-level mechanisms for process synchronization, and this prompted his development of semaphores [Dijkstra, 1968a, 1968b]. A *semaphore* is a nonnegative integer-valued variable on which two operations are defined: P and V. Given a semaphore s, P(s) delays until $s > 0$ and then executes $s := s - 1$; the test and decrement are executed as an indivisible operation. V(s) executes $s := s + 1$ as an indivisible operation.[11] Most semaphore implementations are assumed to exhibit fairness: no process delayed while executing P(s) will remain delayed forever if V(s) operations are performed infinitely often. The need for fairness arises when a number of processes are simultaneously delayed, all attempting to execute a P operation on the same semaphore. Clearly, the implementation must choose which one will be allowed to proceed when a V is ultimately performed. A simple way to ensure fairness is to awaken processes in the order in which they were delayed.

Semaphores are a very general tool for solving synchronization problems. To implement a solution to the mutual exclusion problem, each critical section is preceded by a P operation and followed by a V operation on the same semaphore. All mutually exclusive critical sections use the same semaphore, which is initialized to one. Because such a semaphore only takes on the values zero and one, it is often called a *binary* semaphore.

To implement condition synchronization, shared variables are used to represent the condition, and a semaphore associated with the condition is used to accomplish the synchronization. After a process has made the condition true, it signals that it has done so by executing a V operation; a process delays until a condition is true by executing a P operation. A semaphore that can take any nonnegative value is called a *general* or *counting* semaphore. General semaphores are often used for condition synchronization when controlling resource allocation. Such a semaphore has as its initial value the initial number of units of the resource; a P is used to delay a process until a free resource unit is available; V is executed when a unit of the resource is returned. Binary semaphores are sufficient for some types of condition synchronization, notably those in which a resource has only one unit.

A few examples will illustrate uses of semaphores. We show a solution to the two-process mutual exclusion problem in terms of semaphores in the following:

```
program Mutex_Example;
  var mutex : semaphore initial (1);
  process P1;
    loop
      P(mutex);        { Entry Protocol }
      Critical Section;
      V(mutex);        { Exit Protocol }
      Noncritical Section
    end
  end;
  process P2;
    loop
      P(mutex);        { Entry Protocol }
      Critical Section;
      V(mutex);        { Exit Protocol }
      Noncritical Section
    end
  end
end.
```

[11] P is the first letter of the Dutch word "passeren," which means "to pass"; V is the first letter of "vrygeven," the Dutch word for "to release" [Dijkstra, 1981b]. Reflecting on the definitions of P and V, Dijkstra and his group observed the P might better stand for "prolagen" formed from the Dutch words "proberen" (meaning "to try") and "verlagen" (meaning "to decrease") and V for the Dutch word "verhogen" meaning "to increase." Some authors use **wait** for P and **signal** for V.

Notice how simple and symmetric the entry and exit protocols are in this solution to the mutual exclusion problem. In particular, this use of **P** and **V** ensures both mutual exclusion and absence of deadlock. Also, if the semaphore implementation is fair and both processes always exit their critical sections, each process eventually gets to enter its critical section.

Semaphores can also be used to solve *selective mutual exclusion* problems. In the latter, shared variables are partitioned into disjoint sets. A semaphore is associated with each set and used in the same way as *mutex* above to control access to the variables in that set. Critical sections that reference variables in the same set execute with mutual exclusion, but critical sections that reference variables in different sets execute concurrently. However, if two or more processes require simultaneous access to variables in two or more sets, the programmer must take care or deadlock could result. Suppose that two processes, *P1* and *P2*, each require simultaneous access to sets of shared variables *A* and *B*. Then, *P1* and *P2* will deadlock if, for example, *P1* acquires access to set *A*, *P2* acquires access to set *B*, and then both processes try to acquire access to the set that they do not yet have. Deadlock is avoided here (and in general) if processes first try to acquire access to the same set (e.g., *A*), and then try to acquire access to the other (e.g., *B*).

Figure 3 shows how semaphores can be used for selective mutual exclusion and condition synchronization in an implementation of our simple example operating system. Semaphore *in_mutex* is used to implement mutually exclusive access to *input_buffer* and *out_mutex* is used to implement mutually exclusive access to *output_buffer*.[12] Because the buffers are disjoint, it is possible for operations on *input_buffer* and *output_buffer* to proceed concurrently. Semaphores *num_cards*, *num_lines*, *free_cards*, and *free_lines* are used for condition synchronization: *num_cards* (*num_lines*) is the number of card images (line images) that have been deposited but not yet fetched from *input_buffer* (*output_buffer*); *free_cards* (*free_lines*) is the number of

free slots in *input_buffer* (*output_buffer*). Executing **P**(*num_cards*) delays a process until there is a card in *input_buffer*; **P**(*free_cards*) delays its invoker until there is space to insert a card in *input_buffer*. Semaphores *num_lines* and *free_lines* play corresponding roles with respect to *output_buffer*. Note that before accessing a buffer, each process first waits for the condition required for access and then acquires exclusive access to the buffer. If this were not the case, deadlock could result. (The order in which **V** operations are performed after the buffer is accessed is not critical.)

Semaphores can be implemented by using busy-waiting. More commonly, however, they are implemented by system calls to a kernel. A *kernel* (sometimes called a *supervisor* or *nucleus*) implements processes on a processor [Dijkstra, 1968a; Shaw,

```
program OPSYS;

    var in_mutex, out_mutex : semaphore initial (1,1);
        num_cards, num_lines : semaphore initial (0,0);
        free_cards, free_lines : semaphore initial (N,N);
        input_buffer : array [0..N−1] of cardimage;
        output_buffer : array [0..N−1] of lineimage;

    process reader;
      var card : cardimage;
      loop
        read card from cardreader;
        P(free_cards); P(in_mutex);
          deposit card in input_buffer;
        V(in_mutex); V(num_cards)
      end
    end;

    process executer;
      var card : cardimage;
          line : lineimage;
      loop
        P(num_cards); P(in_mutex);
          fetch card from input_buffer;
        V(in_mutex); V(free_cards);
        process card and generate line;
        P(free_lines); P(out_mutex);
          deposit line in output_buffer;
        V(out_mutex); V(num_lines)
      end
    end;

    process printer;
      var line : lineimage;
      loop
        P(num_lines); P(out_mutex);
          fetch line from output_buffer;
        V(out_mutex); V(free_lines);
        print line on lineprinter
      end
    end

end.
```

Figure 3. Batch operating system with semaphores.

---

[12] In this solution, careful implementation of the operations on the buffers obviates the need for semaphores *in_mutex* and *out_mutex*. The semaphores that implement condition synchronization are sufficient to ensure mutually exclusive access to individual buffer slots.

1974]. At all times, each process is either *ready* to execute on the processor or is *blocked*, waiting to complete a **P** operation. The kernel maintains a *ready list*—a queue of descriptors for ready processes—and multiplexes the processor among these processes, running each process for some period of time. Descriptors for processes that are blocked on a semaphore are stored on a queue associated with that semaphore; they are not stored on the ready list, and hence the processes will not be executed. Execution of a **P** or **V** operation causes a trap to a kernel routine. For a **P** operation, if the semaphore is positive, it is decremented; otherwise the descriptor for the executing process is moved to the semaphore's queue. For a **V** operation, if the semaphore's queue is not empty, one descriptor is moved from that queue to the ready list; otherwise the semaphore is incremented.

This approach to implementing synchronization mechanisms is quite general and is applicable to the other mechanisms that we shall discuss. Since the kernel is responsible for allocating processor cycles to processes, it can implement a synchronization mechanism without using busy-waiting. It does this by not running processes that are blocked. Of course, the names and details of the kernel calls will differ for each synchronization mechanism, but the net effects of these calls will be similar: to move processes on and off a ready list.

Things are somewhat more complex when writing a kernel for a multiprocessor or distributed system. In a multiprocessor, either a single processor is responsible for maintaining the ready list and assigning processes to the other processors, or the ready list is shared [Jones and Schwarz, 1980]. If the ready list is shared, it is subject to concurrent access, which requires that mutual exclusion be ensured. Usually, busy-waiting is used to ensure this mutual exclusion because operations on the ready list are fast and a processor cannot execute any process until it is able to access the ready list. In a distributed system, although one processor could maintain the ready list, it is more common for each processor to have its own kernel and hence its own ready list. Each kernel manages those processes residing at one processor; if a process migrates from one processor to another, it comes under the control of the other's kernel.

3.3 Conditional Critical Regions

Although semaphores can be used to program almost any kind of synchronization, **P**

and **V** are rather unstructured primitives, and so it is easy to err when using them. Execution of each critical section must begin with a **P** and end with a **V** (on the same semaphore). Omitting a **P** or **V**, or accidentally coding a **P** on one semaphore and a **V** on another can have disastrous effects. since mutually exclusive execution would no longer be ensured. Also, when using semaphores, a programmer can forget to include in critical sections all statements that reference shared objects. This, too, could destroy the mutual exclusion required within critical sections. A second difficulty with using semaphores is that both condition synchronization and mutual exclusion are programmed using the same pair of primitives. This makes it difficult to identify the purpose of a given **P** or **V** operation without looking at the other operations on the corresponding semaphore. Since mutual exclusion and condition synchronization are distinct concepts, they should have distinct notations.

The *conditional critical region* proposal [Hoare, 1972; Brinch Hansen 1972, 1973b] overcomes these difficulties by providing a structured notation for specifying synchronization. Shared variables are explicitly placed into groups, called *resources*. Each shared variable may be in at most one resource and may be accessed only in conditional critical region (CCR) statements that name the resource. Mutual exclusion is provided by guaranteeing that execution of different CCR statements, each naming the same resource, is not overlapped. Condition synchronization is provided by explicit Boolean conditions in CCR statements.

A resource r containing variables $v1$, $v2, \ldots, vN$ is declared as[13]

resource $r : v1, v2, \ldots, vN$

The variables in r may only be accessed within CCR statements that name r. Such statements have the form

region r **when** B **do** S

where B is a Boolean expression and S is a statement list. (Variables local to the executing process may also appear in the CCR statement.) A CCR statement delays the executing process until B is true; S is then executed. The evaluation of B and execution of S are uninterruptible by other CCR statements that name the same resource.

---

[13] Our notation combines aspects of those proposed by Hoare [1972] and by Brinch Hansen [1972, 1973b].

Thus *B* is guaranteed to be true when execution of *S* begins. The delay mechanism is usually assumed to be fair: a process awaiting a condition *B* that is repeatedly true will eventually be allowed to continue.

One use of conditional critical regions is shown in Figure 4, which contains another implementation of our batch operating system example. Note how condition synchronization has been separated from mutual exclusion. The Boolean expressions in those CCR statements that access the buffers explicitly specify the conditions required for access; thus mutual exclusion of different CCR statements that access the same buffer is implicit.

Programs written in terms of conditional critical regions can be understood quite simply by using the axiomatic approach. Each CCR statement implements an operation on the resource that it names. Associated with each resource *r* is an *invariant relation* I_r: a predicate that is true of the resource's state after the resource is initialized and after execution of any operation on the resource. For example, in *OPSYS* of Figure 4, the operations insert and remove items from bounded buffers and the buffers *inp_buff* and *out_buff* both satisfy the invariant

IB:

$0 \leq head, tail \leq N - 1$ **and**
$0 \leq size \leq N$ **and**
$tail = (head + size)$ **mod** N **and**
$slots[head]$ through $slots[(tail - 1)$ **mod** $N]$
  in the circular buffer contain
  the most recently inserted items
  in chronological order

The Boolean expression *B* in each CCR statement is chosen so that execution of the statement list, when started in any state that satisfies I_r and *B*, will terminate in a state that satisfies I_r. Therefore the invariant is true as long as no process is in the midst of executing an operation (i.e., executing in a conditional critical region associated with the resource). Recall that execution of conditional critical regions associated with a given shared data object does not overlap. Hence the proofs of processes are interference free as long as (1) variables local to a process appear only in the proof of that process and (2) variables of a resource appear only in assertions within conditional critical regions for that resource. Thus, once appropriate resource invariants

```
program OPSYS;

  type buffer(T) = record
                slots : array [0..N-1] of T;
                head, tail : 0..N-1 initial (0, 0);
                size : 0..N initial (0)
                end;
  var inp_buff : buffer(cardimage);
      out_buff : buffer(lineimage);

  resource ib : inp_buff;  ob : out_buff;

  process reader;
    var card : cardimage;
    loop
      read card from cardreader;
      region ib when inp_buff.size < N do
        inp_buff.slots[inp_buff.tail] := card;
        inp_buff.size := inp_buff.size + 1;
        inp_buff.tail := (inp_buff.tail + 1) mod N
        end
      end
    end;

  process executer;
    var card : cardimage;
        line : lineimage;
    loop
      region ib when inp_buff.size > 0 do
        card := inp_buff.slots[inp_buff.head]
        inp_buff.size := inp_buff.size - 1;
        inp_buff.head := (inp_buff.head + 1) mod N
        end;
      process card and generate line;
      region ob when out_buff.size < N do
        out_buff.slots[out_buff.tail] := line;
        out_buff.size := out_buff.size + 1;
        out_buff.tail := (out_buff.tail + 1) mod N
        end
      end
    end;

  process printer;
    var line : lineimage;
    loop
      region ob when out_buff.size > 0 do
        line := out_buff.slots[out_buff.head];
        out_buff.size := out_buff.size - 1;
        out_buff.head := (out_buff.head + 1) mod N
        end;
      print line on lineprinter
      end
    end

end.
```

Figure 4. Batch operating system with CCR statements.

have been defined, a concurrent program can be understood in terms of its component sequential processes.

Although conditional critical regions have many virtues, they can be expensive to implement. Because conditions in CCR statements can contain references to local variables, each process must evaluate its own conditions.[14] On a multiprogrammed processor, this evaluation results in numerous context switches (frequent saving and restoring of process states), many of which may be unproductive because the activated process may still find the condition false. If each process is executed on its own processor and memory is shared, however, CCR statements can be implemented quite cheaply by using busy-waiting.

CCR statements provide the synchronization mechanism in the Edison language [Brinch Hansen, 1981], which is designed specifically for multiprocessor systems. Variants have also been used in Distributed Processes [Brinch Hansen, 1978] and Argus [Liskov and Scheifler, 1982].

3.4 Monitors

Conditional critical regions are costly to implement on single processors. Also, CCR statements performing operations on resource variables are dispersed throughout the processes. This means that one has to study an entire concurrent program to see all the ways in which a resource is used. Monitors alleviate both these deficiencies. A *monitor* is formed by encapsulating both a resource definition and operations that manipulate it [Dijkstra, 1968b; Brinch Hansen, 1973a; Hoare, 1974]. This allows a resource subject to concurrent access to be viewed as a module [Parnas, 1972]. Consequently, a programmer can ignore the implementation details of the resource when using it, and can ignore how it is used when programming the monitor that implements it.

3.4.1 Definition

A monitor consists of a collection of *permanent variables*, used to store the resource's state, and some procedures, which implement operations on the resource. A monitor also has permanent-variable initialization code, which is executed once before any procedure body is executed. The values of the permanent variables are retained between activations of monitor procedures and may be accessed only from within the monitor. Monitor procedures can have parameters and local variables, each of which takes on new values for each procedure activation. The structure of a

monitor with name *mname* and procedures *op1, . . . , opN* is shown in Figure 5.

Procedure *opJ* within monitor *mname* is invoked by executing

call *mname.opJ*(arguments).

The invocation has the usual semantics associated with a procedure call. In addition, execution of the procedures in a given monitor is guaranteed to be mutually exclusive. This ensures that the permanent variables are never accessed concurrently.

A variety of constructs have been proposed for realizing condition synchronization in monitors. We first describe the proposal made by Hoare [1974] and then consider other proposals. A *condition variable* is used to delay processes executing in a monitor; it may be declared only within a monitor. Two operations are defined on condition variables: **signal** and **wait**. If *cond* is a condition variable, then execution of

cond.**wait**

causes the invoker to be blocked on *cond* and to relinquish its mutually exclusive control of the monitor. Execution of

cond.**signal**

works as follows: if no process is blocked on *cond*, the invoker continues; otherwise, the invoker is temporarily suspended and one process blocked on *cond* is reactivated. A process suspended due to a **signal** operation continues when there is no other process executing in the monitor. Moreover, signalers are given priority over processes trying to commence execution of a monitor procedure. Condition variables are assumed

```
mname : monitor;
    var declarations of permanent variables;
    procedure op1(parameters);
        var declarations of variables local to op1;
        begin
            code to implement op1
        end;
    ...
    procedure opN(parameters);
        var declarations of variables local to opN;
        begin
            code to implement opN
        end;
    begin
        code to initialize permanent variables
    end
```

Figure 5.   Monitor structure.

---

[14] When delayed, a process could instead place condition evaluating code in an area of memory accessible to other processes, but this too is costly.

```
type buffer(T) = monitor;

  var { the variables satisfy invariant IB — see Sec. 4.3 }
    slots : array [0..N−1] of T;
    head, tail : 0..N−1;
    size : 0..N;
    notfull, notempty : condition;

  procedure deposit(p : T);
    begin
      if size = N then notfull.wait;
      slots[tail] := p;
      size := size + 1;
      tail := (tail + 1) mod N;
      notempty.signal
    end;

  procedure fetch(var it : T);
    begin
      if size = 0 then notempty.wait;
      it := slots[head];
      size := size − 1;
      head := (head + 1) mod N;
      notfull.signal
    end;

  begin
    size := 0; head := 0; tail := 0
  end
```

Figure 6. Bounded buffer monitor.

to be fair in the sense that a process will not forever remain suspended on a condition variable that is signaled infinitely often. Note that the introduction of condition variables allows more than one process to be in the same monitor, although all but one will be delayed at **wait** or **signal** operations.

An example of a monitor that defines a bounded buffer type is given in Figure 6. Our batch operating system can be programmed using two instances of the bounded buffer in Figure 6; these are shared by three processes, as shown in Figure 7.

At times, a programmer requires more control over the order in which delayed processes are awakened. To implement such *medium-term scheduling*,[15] the *priority* **wait** statement can be used. This statement

cond.**wait**(p)

has the same semantics as cond.**wait**, except that in the former processes blocked on condition variable cond are awakened in ascending order of p. (Consequently, condition variables used in this way are not necessarily fair.)

---

[15] This is in contrast to *short-term scheduling*, which is concerned with how processors are assigned to ready processes, and *long-term scheduling*, which refers to how jobs are selected to be processed.

```
program OPSYS;

  type buffer(T) = ...; { see Figure 5 }

  var inp_buff : buffer(cardimage);
      out_buff : buffer(lineimage);

  process reader;
    var card : cardimage;
    loop
      read card from cardreader;
      call inp_buff.deposit(card)
    end
  end;

  process executer;
    var card : cardimage;
        line : lineimage;
    loop
      call inp_buff.fetch(card);
      process card and generate line;
      call out_buff.deposit(line)
    end
  end;

  process printer;
    var line : lineimage;
    loop
      call out_buff.fetch(line);
      print line on lineprinter
    end
  end

end.
```

Figure 7. Batch operating system with monitors.

A common problem involving medium-term scheduling is "shortest-job-next" resource allocation. A resource is to be allocated to at most one user at a time; if more than one user is waiting for the resource when it is released, it is allocated to the user who will use it for the shortest amount of time. A monitor to implement such an allocator is shown below. The monitor has two procedures: (1) *request*(*time* : *integer*), which is called by users to request access to the resource for *time* units; and (2) *release*, which is called by users to relinquish access to the resource:

```
shortest_next_allocator : monitor;

  var free : Boolean;
      turn : condition;

  procedure request(time : integer);
    begin
      if not free then turn.wait(time);
      free := false
    end;

  procedure release;
    begin
      free := true;
      turn.signal
    end;

  begin
    free := true
  end
```

3.4.2 Other Approaches to Condition Synchronization

3.4.2.1 Queues and Delay/Continue.
In Concurrent PASCAL [Brinch Hansen, 1975], a slightly simpler mechanism is provided for implementing condition synchronization and medium-term scheduling. Variables of type *queue* can be defined and manipulated with the operations **delay** (analogous to **wait**) and **continue** (analogous to **signal**). In contrast to condition variables, at most one process can be suspended on a given *queue* at any time. This allows medium-term scheduling to be implemented by (1) defining an array of queues and (2) performing a **continue** operation on that queue on which the next-process-to-be-awakened has been delayed. The semantics of **continue** are also slightly different from **signal**. Executing **continue** causes the invoker to return from its monitor call, whereas **signal** does not. As before, a process blocked on the selected queue resumes execution of the monitor procedure within which it was delayed.

It is both cheaper and easier to implement **continue** than **signal** because **signal** requires code to ensure that processes suspended by **signal** operations reacquire control of the monitor before other, newer processes attempting to begin execution in that monitor. With both **signal** and **continue**, the objective is to ensure that a condition is not invalidated between the time it is signaled and the time that the awakened process actually resumes execution. Although **continue** has speed and cost advantages, it is less powerful than **signal**. A monitor written using condition variables cannot always be translated directly into one that uses queues without also adding monitor procedures [Howard, 1976b]. Clearly, these additional procedures complicate the interface provided by the monitor. Fortunately, most synchronization problems that arise in practice can be coded using either discipline.

3.4.2.2 Conditional Wait and Automatic Signal.
In contrast to semaphores, **signals** on condition variables are not saved: a process always delays after executing **wait**, even if a previous **signal** did not awaken any process.[16] This can make **signal** and **wait** difficult to use correctly, because other variables must be used to record that a **signal**

---
[16] The limitations of condition variables discussed in this section also apply to queue variables.

was executed. These variables must also be tested by a process, before executing **wait**, to guard against waiting if the event corresponding to a **signal** has already occurred.

Another difficulty is that, in contrast to conditional critical regions, a Boolean expression is not syntactically associated with **signal** and **wait**, or with the condition variable itself. Thus, it is not easy to determine why a process was delayed on a condition variable, unless **signal** and **wait** are used in a very disciplined manner. It helps if (1) each **wait** on a condition variable is contained in an **if** statement in which the Boolean expression is the negation of the desired condition synchronization, and (2) each **signal** statement on the same condition variable is contained in an **if** statement in which the Boolean expression gives the desired condition synchronization. Even so, syntactically identical Boolean expressions may have different values if they contain references to local variables, which they often do. Thus there is no guarantee that an awakened process will actually see the condition for which it was waiting. A final difficulty with **wait** and **signal** is that, because **signal** is preemptive, the state of permanent variables seen by a signaler can change between the time a **signal** is executed and the time that the signaling process resumes execution.

To mitigate these difficulties, Hoare [1974] proposed the *conditional wait* statement

wait (B)

where B is a Boolean expression involving the permanent or local variables of the monitor. Execution of **wait**(B) delays the invoker until B becomes true; no **signal** is required to reactivate processes delayed by a conditional wait statement. This synchronization facility is expensive because it is necessary to evaluate B every time any process exits the monitor or becomes blocked at a conditional wait and because a context switch could be required for each evaluation (due to the presence of local variables in the condition). However, the construct is unquestionably a very clean one with which to program.

An efficient variant of the conditional wait was proposed by Kessels [1977] for use when only permanent variables appear in B. The buffer monitor in Figure 6 satisfies this requirement. In Kessels' proposal, one declares *conditions* of the form

cname : **condition** B

Executing the statement *cname*.**wait** causes B, a Boolean expression, to be evaluated. If B is true, the process continues; otherwise the process relinquishes control of the monitor and is delayed on *cname*. Whenever a process relinquishes control of the monitor, the system evaluates those Boolean expressions associated with all conditions for which there are waiting processes. If one of these Boolean expressions is found to be true, one of the waiting processes is granted control of the monitor. If none is found to be true, a new invocation of one of the monitor's procedures is permitted.

Using Kessels' proposal, the buffer monitor in Figure 6 could be recoded as follows. First, the declarations of *not_full* and *not_empty* are changed to

not_full : **condition** *size* $< N$;
not_empty : **condition** *size* > 0

Second, the first statement in *deposit* is replaced by

not_full.**wait**

and the first statement in *fetch* is replaced by

not_empty.**wait**

Finally, the **signal** statements are deleted.

The absence of a **signal** primitive is noteworthy. The implementation provides an *automatic signal*, which, though somewhat more costly, is less error prone than explicitly programmed **signal** operations. The **signal** operation cannot be accidentally omitted and never signals the wrong condition. Furthermore, the programmer explicitly specifies the conditions being awaited. The primary limitation of the proposal is that it cannot be used to solve most scheduling problems, because operation parameters, which are not permanent variables, may not appear in conditions.

3.4.2.3 Signals as Hints. Mesa [Mitchell et al., 1979; Lampson and Redell, 1980] employs yet another approach to condition synchronization. Condition variables are provided, but only as a way for a process to relinquish control of a monitor. In Mesa, execution of

cond.**notify**

causes a process waiting on condition variable *cond* to resume at some time in the future. This is called *signal and continue* because the process performing the **notify** immediately continues execution rather than being suspended. Performing a **notify**

merely gives a *hint* to a waiting process that it might be able to proceed.[17] Therefore, in Mesa one writes

while not B **do wait** *cond* **endloop**

instead of

if not B **then** *cond*.**wait**

as would be done using Hoare's condition variables. Boolean condition B is guaranteed to be true upon termination of the loop, as it was in the two conditional-wait/automatic-signal proposals. Moreover, the (possible) repeated evaluation of the Boolean expression appears in the actual monitor code—there are no hidden implementation costs.

The **notify** primitive is especially useful if the executing process has higher priority than the waiting processes. It also allows the following extensions to condition variables, which are often useful when doing systems programming:

(i) A time-out interval t can be associated with each condition variable. If a process is ever suspended on this condition variable for longer than t time units, a **notify** is automatically performed by the system. The awakened process can then decide whether to perform another **wait** or to take other action.

(ii) A **broadcast** primitive can be defined. Its execution causes all processes waiting on a condition variable to resume at some time in the future (subject to the mutual exclusion constraints associated with execution in a monitor). This primitive is useful if more than one process could proceed when a condition becomes true. The broadcast primitive is also useful when a condition involves local variables because in this case the signaler cannot evaluate the condition (B above) for which a process is waiting. Such a primitive is, in fact, used in UNIX [Ritchie and Thompson, 1974].

3.4.3 An Axiomatic View

The valid states of a resource protected by a monitor can be characterized by an assertion called the *monitor invariant*. This predicate should be true of the monitor's permanent variables whenever no process

---

[17] Of course, it is prudent to perform **notify** operations only when there is reason to believe that the awakened process will actually be able to proceed; but the burden of checking the condition is on the waiting process.

is executing in the monitor. Thus a process must reestablish the monitor invariant before the process exits the monitor or performs a **wait(delay)** or **signal(continue)**. The monitor invariant can be assumed to be true of the permanent variables whenever a process acquires control of the monitor, regardless of whether it acquires control by calling a monitor procedure or by being reactivated following a **wait** or **signal**.

The fact that monitor procedures are mutually exclusive simplifies noninterference proofs. One need not consider interleaved execution of monitor procedures. However, interference can arise when programming condition synchronization. Recall that a process will delay its progress in order to implement medium-term scheduling, or to await some condition. Mechanisms that delay a process cause its execution to be suspended and control of the monitor to be relinquished; the process resumes execution with the understanding that both some condition B and the monitor invariant will be true. The truth of B when the process awakens can be ensured by checking for it automatically or by requiring that the programmer build these tests into the program. If programmed checks are used, they can appear either in the process that establishes the condition (for condition variables and queues) or in the process that performed the **wait** (the Mesa model).

If the signaler checks for the condition, we must ensure that the condition is not invalidated between the time that the **signal** occurs and the time that the blocked process actually executes. That is, we must ensure that other execution in the monitor does not interfere with the condition. If the signaler does not immediately relinquish control of the monitor (e.g., if **notify** is used), interference might be caused by the process that established the condition in the first place. Also, if the signaled process does not get reactivated before new calls of monitor procedures are allowed, interference might be caused by some process that executes after the condition has been signaled (this can happen in Modula [Wirth, 1977a]). Proof rules for monitors and the various signaling disciplines are discussed by Howard [1976a, 1976b].

3.4.4 Nested Monitor Calls

When structuring a system as a hierarchical collection of monitors, it is likely that monitor procedures will be called from within other monitors. Such nested monitor calls have caused much discussion [Haddon, 1977; Lister, 1977; Parnas, 1978; Wettstein, 1978]. The controversy is over what (if anything) should be done if a process having made a nested monitor call is suspended in another monitor. The mutual exclusion in the last monitor called will be relinquished by the process, due to the semantics of **wait** and equivalent operations. However, mutual exclusion will not be relinquished by processes in monitors from which nested calls have been made. Processes that attempt to invoke procedures in these monitors will become blocked. This has performance implications, since blockage will decrease the amount of concurrency exhibited by the system.

The nested monitor call problem can be approached in a number of ways. One approach is to prohibit nested monitor calls, as was done in SIMONE [Kaubisch et al., 1976], or or to prohibit nested calls to monitors that are not lexically nested, as was done in Modula [Wirth, 1977a]. A second approach is to release the mutual exclusion on all monitors along the call chain when a nested call is made and that process becomes blocked.[18] This release-and-reacquire approach would require that the monitor invariant be established before any monitor call that will block the process. Since the designer cannot know a priori whether a call will block a process, the monitor invariant would have to be established before every call. A third approach is the definition of special-purpose constructs that can be used for particular situations in which nested calls often arise. The *manager* construct [Silberschatz et al., 1977] for handling dynamic resource allocation problems and the *scheduler monitor* [Schneider and Bernstein, 1978] for scheduling access to shared resources are both based on this line of thought.

The last approach to the nested monitor call problem, and probably the most reasonable, is one that appreciates that monitors are only a structuring tool for resources that are subject to concurrent access [Andrews and McGraw, 1977; Parnas, 1978]. Mutual exclusion of monitor procedures is only one way to preserve the integrity of

[18] Once signaled, the process will need to reacquire exclusive access to all monitors along the call chain before resuming execution. However, if permanent monitor variables were not passed as reference parameters in any of the calls, the process could reacquire exclusive access incrementally, as it returns to each monitor.

the permanent variables that make up a resource. There are cases in which the operations provided by a given monitor can be executed concurrently without adverse effects, and even cases in which more than one instance of the same monitor procedure can be executed in parallel (e.g., several activations of a read procedure, in a monitor that encapsulates a database). Monitor procedures can be executed concurrently, provided that they do not interfere with each other. Also, there are cases in which the monitor invariant can be easily established before a nested monitor call is made, and so mutual exclusion for the monitor can be released. Based on such reasoning, Andrews and McGraw [1977] defines a monitorlike construct that allows the programmer to specify that certain monitor procedures be executed concurrently and that mutual exclusion be released for certain calls. The Mesa language [Mitchell et al., 1979] also provides mechanisms that give the programmer control over the granularity of exclusion.

3.4.5 Programming Notations Based on Monitors

Numerous programming languages have been proposed and implemented that use monitors for synchronizing access to shared variables. Below, we very briefly discuss two of the most important: Concurrent PASCAL and Modula. These languages have received widespread use, introduced novel constructs to handle machine-dependent systems-programming issues, and inspired other language designs, such as Mesa [Mitchell et al., 1979] and PASCAL-Plus [Welsh and Bustard, 1979].

3.4.5.1 Concurrent PASCAL. Concurrent PASCAL [Brinch Hansen, 1975, 1977] was the first programming language to support monitors. Consequently, it provided a vehicle for evaluating monitors as a system-structuring device. The language has been used to write several operating systems, including Solo, a single-user operating system [Brinch Hansen, 1976a, 1976b], Job Stream, a batch operating system for processing PASCAL programs, and a real-time process control system [Brinch Hansen, 1977].

One of the major goals of Concurrent PASCAL was to ensure that programs exhibited reproducible behavior [Brinch Hansen, 1977]. Monitors ensured that pathological interleavings of concurrently executed routines that shared data were no longer possible (the compiler generates code to provide the necessary mutual exclusion). Concurrent execution in other modules (called *classes*) was not possible, due to compile-time restrictions on the dissemination of class names and scope rules for class declarations.

Concurrent PASCAL also succeeded in providing the programmer with a clean abstract machine, thereby eliminating the need for coding at the assembly language level. A systems programming language must have facilities to allow access to I/O devices and other hardware resources. In Concurrent PASCAL, I/O devices and the like are viewed as monitors implemented directly in hardware. To perform an I/O operation, the corresponding "monitor" is called; the call returns when the I/O has completed. Thus the Concurrent PASCAL run-time system implements synchronous I/O and "abstracts out" the notion of an interrupt.

Various aspects of Concurrent PASCAL, including its approach to I/O, have been analyzed by Loehr [1977], Silberschatz [1977], and Keedy [1979].

3.4.5.2 Modula. Modula was developed for programming small, dedicated computer systems, including process control applications [Wirth, 1977a, 1977b, 1977c, 1977d]. The language is largely based on PASCAL and includes processes, *interface modules*, which are like monitors, and *device modules*, which are special interface modules for programming device drivers.

The run-time support system for Modula is small and efficient. The kernel for a PDP-11/45 requires only 98 words of storage and is extremely fast [Wirth, 1977c]. It does not time slice the processor among processes, as Concurrent PASCAL does. Rather, certain kernel-supported operations—**wait**, for example—always cause the processor to be switched. (The programmer must be aware of this and design programs accordingly.) This turns out to be both a strength and weakness of Modula. A small and efficient kernel, where the programmer has some control over processor switching, allows Modula to be used for process control applications, as intended. Unfortunately, in order to be able to construct such a kernel, some of the constructs in the language—notably those concerning multiprogramming—have associated restrictions that can only be understood in terms of the kernel's implementation. A variety of subtle interactions between the various synchronization constructs must be understood in order to program in Modula without experiencing unpleasant surprises. Some of these pathological interactions are described by Bernstein and Ensor [1981].

Modula implements an abstract machine that is well suited for dealing with interrupts and I/O devices on PDP-11 processors. Unlike Concurrent PASCAL, in which the run-time kernel handles interrupts and I/O, Modula leaves support for devices in the programmer's domain. Thus new devices can be added without modifying the kernel. An I/O device is considered to be a process that is implemented in hardware. A software process can start an I/O operation and then execute a **doio** statement (which is like a **wait** except that it delays the invoker until the kernel receives an interrupt from the corresponding device). Thus interrupts are viewed as **signal** (**send** in Modula) operations generated by the hardware. Device modules are interface modules that control I/O devices. Each contains, in addition to some procedures, a *device process*, which starts I/O operations and executes **doio** statements to relinquish control of the processor (pending receipt of the corresponding I/O interrupt). The address of the interrupt vector for the device is declared in the heading of the device module, so that the compiler can do the necessary binding. Modula also has provisions for controlling the processor priority register, thus allowing a programmer to exploit the priority interrupt architecture of the processor when structuring programs.

A third novel aspect of Modula is that variables declared in interface modules can be exported. Exported variables can be referenced (but not modified) from outside the scope of their defining interface module. This allows concurrent access to these variables, which, of course, can lead to difficulty unless the programmer ensures that interference cannot occur. However, when used selectively, this feature increases the efficiency of programs that access such variables.

In summary, Modula is less constraining than Concurrent PASCAL, but requires the programmer to be more careful. Its specific strengths and weaknesses have been evaluated by Andrews [1979], Holden and Wand [1980], and Bernstein and Ensor [1981]. Wirth, Modula's designer, has gone on to develop Modula-2 [Wirth, 1982]. Modula-2 retains the basic modular structure of Modula, but provides more flexible facilities for concurrent programming and these facilities have less subtle semantics. In particular, Modula-2 provides coroutines and hence explicit transfer of control between processes. Using these, the programmer builds support for exclusion and condition synchronization, as required. In particular, the programmer can construct monitorlike modules.

3.5 Path Expressions

Operations defined by a monitor are executed with mutual exclusion. Other synchronization of monitor procedures is realized by explicitly performing **wait** and **signal** operations on condition variables (or by some similar mechanism). Consequently, synchronization of monitor operations is realized by code scattered throughout the monitor. Some of this code, such as **wait** and **signal**, is visible to the programmer. Other code, such as the code ensuring mutual exclusion of monitor procedures, is not.

Another approach to defining a module subject to concurrent access is to provide a mechanism with which a programmer specifies, in *one* place in each module, all constraints on the execution of operations defined by that module. Implementation of the operations is separated from the specification of the constraints. Moreover, code to enforce the constraints is generated by a compiler. This is the approach taken in a class of synchronization mechanisms called *path expressions*.

Path expressions were first defined by Campbell and Habermann [1974]. Subsequent extensions and variations have also been proposed [Habermann, 1975; Lauer and Campbell, 1975; Campbell, 1976; Flon and Habermann, 1976; Lauer and Shields, 1978; Andler, 1979]. Below, we describe one specific proposal [Campbell, 1976] that has been incorporated into Path PASCAL, an implemented systems programming language [Campbell and Kolstad, 1979].

When path expressions are used, a module that implements a resource has a structure like that of a monitor. It contains permanent variables, which store the state of the resource, and procedures, which realize operations on the resource. Path expressions in the header of each resource define constraints on the order in which operations are executed. No synchronization code is programmed in the procedures.

The syntax of a path expression is

path *path_list* **end**

A *path_list* contains operation names and *path operators*. Path operators include "," for concurrency, ";" for sequencing, "$n : (path\_list)$" to specify up to n concurrent activations of *path_list*, and "[*path_list*]" to specify an unbounded number of concurrent activations of *path_list*.

For example, the path expression

path *deposit, fetch* **end**

places no constraints on the order of execution of *deposit* and *fetch* and no constraints on the number of activations of either operation. This absence of synchronization constraints is equivalent to that specified by the path expressions

path [*deposit*], [*fetch*] **end**

or

path [*deposit, fetch*] **end**

(A useful application of the "[···]" operator will be shown later.) In contrast,

path *deposit; fetch* **end**

specifies that each *fetch* be preceded by a *deposit*; multiple activations of each operation can execute concurrently as long as the number of active or completed *fetch* operations never exceeds the number of completed *deposit* operations. A module implementing a bounded buffer of size one might well contain the path

path 1 : (*deposit; fetch*) **end**

to specify that the first invoked operation be a *deposit*, that each *deposit* be followed by a *fetch*, and that at most one instance of the path "*deposit; fetch*" be active—in short, that *deposit* and *fetch* alternate and are mutually exclusive. Synchronization constraints for a bounded buffer of size N are specified by

path N : (1 : (*deposit*); 1 : (*fetch*)) **end**

This ensures that (i) activations of *deposit* are mutually exclusive, (ii) activations of *fetch* are mutually exclusive, (iii) each activation of *fetch* is preceded by a completed *deposit*, and (iv) the number of completed *deposit* operations is never more than N greater than the number of completed *fetch* operations. The bounded buffers we have been using for *OPSYS*, our batch operating system, would be defined by

```
module buffer(T):
    path N:( 1:(deposit); 1:(fetch) ) end;
    var { the variables satisfy the invariant IB (see Sec. 4.3)
          with size equal to the number of executions of
          deposit minus the number of executions of fetch }
        slots : array [0..N−1] of T;
        head, tail : 0..N−1;
```

```
procedure deposit(p : T);
    begin
        slots[tail] := p;
        tail := (tail + 1) mod N
    end;

procedure fetch(var it : T);
    begin
        it := slots[head];
        head := (head + 1) mod N
    end;

begin
    head := 0; tail := 0
end.
```

Note that one *deposit* and one *fetch* can proceed concurrently, which was not possible in the *buffer* monitor given in Figure 6. For this reason, there is no variable *size* because it would have been subject to concurrent access.

As a last example, consider the readers/writers problem [Courtois et al., 1971]. In this problem, processes read or write records in a shared data base. To ensure that processes read consistent data, either an unbounded number of concurrent *reads* or a single *write* may be executed at any time. The path expression

path 1 : ([*read*], *write*) **end**

specifies this constraint. (Actually, this specifies the "weak reader's preference" solution to the readers/writers problem: readers can prevent writers from accessing the database.)

Path expressions are strongly motivated by, and based on, the operational approach to program semantics. A path expression defines all legal sequences of the operation executions for a resource. This set of sequences can be viewed as a formal language, in which each sentence is a sequence of operation names. In light of this, the resemblance between path expressions and regular expressions should not be surprising.

While path expressions provide an elegant notation for expressing synchronization constraints described operationally, they are poorly suited for specifying condition synchronization [Bloom, 1979]. Whether an operation can be executed might depend on the state of a resource in a way not directly related to the history of operations already performed. Certain variants of the readers/writers problem (e.g., writers preference, fair access for readers and writers) require access to the state of the resource—in this case, the number of waiting readers and waiting writers—in order to implement the desired synchronization. The *shortest_next_allocator* monitor of Section 3.4.1 is an example of a resource in which a parameter's value determines whether execution of an operation (*request*) should be permitted to continue. In fact, most resources that involve scheduling require access to parameters and/or to state information when making synchronization decisions. In order to use path expressions to specify solutions to such problems, additional mechanisms must be introduced. In some cases, definition of additional operations on the resource is sufficient; in other cases "queue" resources, which allow a process to suspend itself and be reactivated by a "scheduler," must be added. The desire to realize condition synchronization using path expressions has motivated many of the proposed extensions. Regrettably, none of these extensions have solved the entire problem in a way consistent with the elegance and simplicity of the original proposal. However, path expressions have proved useful for specifying the semantics of concurrent computations [Shields, 1979; Shaw, 1980, Best, 1982].

4. SYNCHRONIZATION PRIMITIVES BASED ON MESSAGE PASSING

Critical regions, monitors, and path expressions are one outgrowth of semaphores; they all provide structured ways to control access to shared variables. A different outgrowth is *message passing*, which can be viewed as extending semaphores to convey data as well as to implement synchronization. When message passing is used for communication and synchronization, processes send and receive messages instead of reading and writing shared variables. Communication is accomplished because a process, upon receiving a message, obtains values from some sender process. Synchronization is accomplished because a message can be received only after it has been sent, which constrains the order in which these two events can occur.

A message is sent by executing

send *expression_list*
    to *destination_designator*.

The message contains the values of the expressions in *expression_list* at the time **send** is executed. The *destination_designator* gives the programmer control over where the message goes, and hence over which statements can receive it. A message is received by executing

receive *variable_list*
    from *source_designator*

where *variable_list* is a list of variables. The *source_designator* gives the programmer control over where the message came from, and hence over which statements could have sent it. Receipt of a message causes, first, assignment of the values in the message to the variables in *variable_list* and, second, subsequent destruction of the message.[19]

Designing message-passing primitives involves making choices about the form and semantics of these general commands. Two main issues must be addressed: How are source and destination designators specified? How is communication synchronized? Common alternative solutions for these issues are described in the next two sections. Then higher level message-passing constructs, semantic issues, and languages based on message passing are discussed.

4.1 Specifying Channels of Communication

Taken together, the destination and source designators define a *communications channel*. Various schemes have been proposed for naming channels. The simplest channel-naming scheme is for process names to serve as source and destination designators. We refer to this as *direct naming*. Thus

send *card* **to** *executer*

sends a message that can be received only by the *executer* process. Similarly,

receive *line* **from** *executer*

permits receipt only of a message sent by the executer process.

Direct naming is easy to implement and to use. It makes it possible for a process to control the times at which it receives messages from each other process. Our simple batch operating system might be programmed using direct naming as shown in Figure 8.

The batch operating system also illustrates an important paradigm for process interaction—a pipeline. A *pipeline* is a collection of concurrent processes in which the output of each process is used as the input to another. Information flows analogously to the way liquid flows in a pipeline. Here, information flows from the *reader* process to the *executer* process and then from the *executer* process to the *printer* process. Di-

---

[19] A broadcast can be modeled by the concurrent execution of a collection of **sends**, each sending the message to a different destination. A nondestructive **receive** can be modeled by a **receive**, immediately followed by a **send**.

rect naming is particularly well suited for programming pipelines.

Another important paradigm for process interaction is the *client/server relationship*. Some *server* processes render a service to some *client* processes. A client can request that a service be performed by sending a message to one of these servers. A server repeatedly receives a request for service from a client, performs that service, and (if necessary) returns a completion message to that client.

The interaction between an I/O driver process and processes that use it—for example, the lineprinter driver and the *printer* process in our operating system example—illustrates this paradigm. The lineprinter driver is a server; it repeatedly receives requests to print a line on the printer, starts that I/O operation, and then awaits the interrupt signifying completion of the I/O operation. Depending on the application, it might also send a completion message to the client after the line has been printed.

Unfortunately, direct naming is not always well suited for client/server interaction. Ideally, the **receive** in a server should allow receipt of a message from any client. If there is only one client, then direct naming will work well; difficulties arise if there is more than one client because, at the very least, a **receive** would be required for each. Similarly, if there is more than one server

```
program OPSYS;

    process reader;
       var card : cardimage;
       loop
          read card from cardreader;
          send card to executer
          end
       end;

    process executer;
       var card : cardimage; line : lineimage;
       loop
          receive card from reader;
          process card and generate line;
          send line to printer
          end
       end;

    process printer;
       var line : lineimage;
       loop
          receive line from executer;
          print line on lineprinter
          end
       end
    end.
```

Figure 8. Batch operating system with message passing.

(and all servers are identical), then the **send** in a client should produce a message that can be received by *any* server. Again, this cannot be accomplished easily with direct naming. Therefore, a more sophisticated scheme for defining communications channels is required.

One such scheme is based on the use of *global names*, sometimes called *mailboxes*. A mailbox can appear as the destination designator in any process' **send** statements and as the source designator in any process' **receive** statements. Thus messages sent to a given mailbox can be received by any process that executes a **receive** naming that mailbox.

This scheme is particularly well suited for programming client/server interactions. Clients send their service requests to a single mailbox; servers receive service requests from that mailbox. Unfortunately, implementing mailboxes can be quite costly without a specialized communications network [Gelernter and Bernstein, 1982]. When a message is sent, it must be relayed to all sites where a **receive** could be performed on the destination mailbox; then, after a message has been received, all these sites must be notified that the message is no longer available for receipt.

The special case of mailboxes, in which a mailbox name can appear as the source designator in **receive** statements in one process only, does not suffer these implementation difficulties. Such mailboxes are often called *ports* [Balzer, 1971]. Ports are simple to implement, since all **receives** that designate a port occur in the same process. Moreover, ports allow a straightforward solution to the multiple-clients/single-server problem. (The multiple-clients/multiple-server problem, however, is not easily solved with ports.)

To summarize, when direct naming is used, communication is one to one since each communicating process names the other. When port naming is used, communication can be many to one since each port has one receiver but may have many senders. The most general scheme is global naming, which can be many to many. Direct naming and port naming are special cases of global naming; they limit the kinds of interactions that can be programmed directly, but are more efficient to implement.

Source and destination designators can be fixed at compile time, called *static channel naming*, or they can be computed at run time, called *dynamic channel naming*. Although widely used, static naming presents two problems. First, it precludes a program from communicating along channels not known at compile time, and thus limits the program's ability to exist in a changing environment. For example, this would preclude implementing the I/O redirection or pipelines provided by UNIX [Ritchie and Thompson, 1974].[20] The second problem is this: if a program might *ever* need access to a channel, it must permanently have the access. In many applications, such as file systems, it is more desirable to allocate communications channels to resources (such as files) dynamically.

To support dynamic channel naming, an underlying, static channel-naming scheme could be augmented by variables that contain source or destination designators. These variables can be viewed as containing *capabilities* for the communications channel [Baskett et al., 1977; Solomon and Finkel, 1979; Andrews, 1982].

4.2 Synchronization

Another important property of message-passing statements concerns whether their execution could cause a delay. A statement is *nonblocking* if its execution never delays its invoker; otherwise the statement is said to be *blocking*. In some message-passing schemes, messages are buffered between the time they are sent and received. Then, if the buffer is full when a **send** is executed, there are two options: the **send** might delay until there is space in the buffer for the message, or the **send** might return a code to the invoker, indicating that, because the buffer was full, the message could not be sent. Similarly, execution of a **receive**, when no message that satisfies the source designator is available for receipt, might either cause a delay or terminate with a code, signifying that no message was available.

If the system has an effectively unbounded buffer capacity, then a process is never delayed when executing a **send**. This is variously called *asynchronous message passing* and *send no-wait*. Asynchronous message passing allows a sender to get arbitrarily far ahead of a receiver. Consequently, when a message is received, it contains information about the sender's state

that is not necessarily still its current state. At the other extreme, with no buffering, execution of a **send** is always delayed until a corresponding[21] **receive** is executed; then the message is transferred and both proceed. This is called *synchronous message passing*. When synchronous message passing is used, a message exchange represents a synchronization point in the execution of both the sender and receiver. Therefore, the message received will always correspond to the sender's current state. Moreover, when the **send** terminates, the sender can make assertions about the state of the receiver. Between these two extremes is *buffered message passing*, in which the buffer has finite bounds. Buffered message passing allows the sender to get ahead of the receiver, but not arbitrarily far ahead.

The blocking form of the **receive** statement is the most common, because a receiving process often has nothing else to do while awaiting receipt of a message. However, most languages and operating systems also provide a nonblocking **receive** or a means to test whether execution of a **receive** would block. This enables a process to receive all available messages and then select one to process (effectively, to schedule them).

Sometimes, further control over which messages can be received is provided. The statement

receive *variable_list*
    from *source_designator* **when** B

permits receipt of only those messages that make B true. This allows a process to "peek" at the contents of a delivered message before receiving it. Although this facility. is not necessary—a process can always receive and store copies of messages until appropriate to act on them, as shown in the shortest-next-allocator example at the end of this section—the conditional receive makes possible concise solutions to many synchronization problems. Two languages that provide such a facility, PLITS and SR, are described in Section 4.5.

A blocking **receive** implicitly implements synchronization between sender and receiver because the receiver is delayed until after the message is sent. To implement such synchronization with nonblocking **receive**, busy-waiting is required. However, blocking message-passing statements can achieve the same semantic effects as non-

---

[20] Although in UNIX most commands read from and write to the user's terminal, one can specify that a command read its input from a file or write its output to a file. Also, one can specify that commands be connected in a pipeline. These options are provided by a dynamic channel-naming scheme that is transparent to the implementation of each command.

---

[21] Correspondence is determined by the source and destination designators.

blocking ones by using what we shall call *selective communications*, which is based on Dijkstra's guarded commands [Dijkstra, 1975].

In a selective-communications statement, a *guarded command* has the form

guard → *statement*

The guard consists of a Boolean expression, optionally followed by a message-passing statement. The guard *succeeds* if the Boolean expression is true and executing the message-passing statement would not cause a delay; the guard *fails* if the Boolean expression is false; the guard (temporarily) neither succeeds nor fails if the Boolean expression is true but the message-passing statement cannot yet be executed without causing delay. The alternative statement

if $G1$ → $S1$
[] $G2$ → $S2$
   ...
[] Gn → Sn
fi

is executed as follows. If at least one guard succeeds, one of them, Gi, is selected nondeterministically; the message-passing statement in Gi is executed (if present); then Si, the statement following the guard, is executed. If all guards fail, the command aborts. If all guards neither succeed nor fail, execution is delayed until some guard succeeds. (Obviously, deadlock could result.) Execution of the iterative statement is the same as for the alternative statement, except selection and execution of a guarded command is repeated until all guards fail, at which time the iterative statement terminates rather than aborts.

To illustrate the use of selective communications, we implement a *buffer* process, which stores data produced by a *producer* process and allows these data to be retrieved by a *consumer* process:[22]

process *buffer*;

```
var slots : array [0..N−1] of T;
    head, tail : 0..N−1;
    size : 0..N;

head := 0;  tail := 0;  size := 0;
do size<N;  receive slots[tail] from producer →
       size := size + 1;
       tail := (tail + 1) mod N
[] size>0;  send slots[head] to consumer →
       size := size − 1;
       head := (head + 1) mod N

od

end
```

The producer and consumer are as follows:

process *producer*;
```
  var stuff : T;
  loop
     generate stuff;
     send stuff to buffer
     end
  end;
```
process *consumer*;
```
  var stuff : T;
  loop
     receive stuff from buffer;
     use stuff
     end
  end
```

If **send** statements cannot appear in guards, selective communication is straightforward to implement. A delayed process determines which Boolean expressions in guards are true, and then awaits arrival of a message that allows execution of the **receive** in one of these guards. (If the guard did not contain a **receive**, the process would not be delayed.) If both **send** and **receive** statements can appear in guards,[23] implementation is much more costly because a process needs to negotiate with other processes to determine if they can communicate, and these processes could also be in the middle of such a negotiation. For example, three processes could be executing selective-communications statements in which any pair could communicate; the problem is to decide which pair communicates and which one remains delayed. Development of protocols that solve this problem in an efficient and deadlock-free way remains an active research area [Schwartz, 1978; Silberschatz, 1979; Bernstein, 1980; Van de Snepscheut, 1981; Schneider, 1982; Reif and Spirakis, 1982].

Unfortunately, if **send** statements are not permitted to appear in guards, programming with blocking **send** and blocking **receive** becomes somewhat more complex. In the example above, the *buffer* process above would be changed to first wait for a message from the *consumer* requesting data (a **receive** would appear in the second guard instead of the **send**) and then to send the data. The difference in the protocol used by this new *buffer* process when interacting with the *consumer* and that used when interacting with the *producer* process is misleading; a producer/consumer relationship is inherently symmetric, and the program should mirror this fact.

---

[22] Even if message passing is asynchronous, such a buffer may still be required if there are multiple pro-

---

[23] Also note that allowing only **send** statements in

Some process relationships are inherently asymmetric. In client/server interactions, the server often takes different actions in response to different kinds of client requests. For example, a shortest-job-next allocator (see Section 3.4.1) that receives "allocation" requests on a *request_port* and "release" requests on a *release_port* can be programmed using message passing as follows:

```
process shortest_next_allocator;

  var free : Boolean;
      time : integer;
      client_id : process_id;
      declarations of a priority queue and other local variables;

  free := true;
  do true; receive (time, client_id) from request_port →
       if free →
            free := false;
            send allocation to client_id
       [] not free →
            save client_id on priority queue ordered by time
       fi
  [] not free; receive release from release_port →
       if not priority queue empty →
            remove client_id with smallest time from queue;
            send allocation to client_id
       [] priority queue empty →
            free := true
       fi
  od
end
```

A client makes a request by executing

send (*time*, *my_id*) to *request_port*;
receive *allocation*
    from *shortest_next_allocator*

and indicates that it has finished using the resource by executing

send *release* to *release_port*

4.3 Higher Level Message-Passing Constructs

4.3.1 Remote Procedure Call

The primitives of the previous section are sufficient to program any type of process interaction using message passing. To program client/server interactions, however, both the client and server execute two message-passing statements: the client a **send** followed by a **receive**, and the server a **receive** followed by a **send**. Because this type of interaction is very common, higher level statements that directly support it have been proposed. These are termed *remote procedure call* statements because of the interface that they present: a client "calls" a procedure that is executed on a potentially remote machine by a server.

When remote procedure calls are used, a client interacts with a server by means of a **call** statement. This statement has a form similar to that used for a procedure call in a sequential language:

call *service*(*value_args*; *result_args*)

The *service* is really the name of a channel. If direct naming is used, *service* designates the server process; if port or mailbox naming is used, *service* might designate the kind of service requested. Remote **call** is executed as follows: the value arguments are sent to the appropriate server, and the calling process delays until both the service has been performed and the results have been returned and assigned to the result arguments. Thus such a **call** could be translated into a **send**, immediately followed by a **receive**. Note that the client cannot forget to wait for the results of a requested service.

There are two basic approaches to specifying the server side of a remote procedure call. In the first, the remote procedure is a declaration, like a procedure in a sequential language:[24]

remote procedure *service*
    (**in** *value_parameters*;
     out *result_parameters*)
  body
  end

However, such a procedure declaration is implemented as a process. This process, the server, awaits receipt of a message containing value arguments from some calling process, assigns them to the value parameters, executes its body, and then returns a *reply message* containing the values of the result parameters. Note that even if there are no value or result parameters, the synchronization resulting from the implicit **send** and **receive** occurs. A remote procedure declaration can be implemented as a single process that repeatedly loops [Andrews, 1982], in which case **calls** to the same remote procedure would execute sequentially. Alternatively, a new process can be created for each execution of **call** [Brinch Hansen, 1978; Cook, 1980; Liskov and Scheifler, 1982]; these could execute concurrently, meaning that the different instances of the server might need to synchronize if they share variables.

In the second approach to specifying the server side, the remote procedure is a statement, which can be placed anywhere any other statement can be placed. Such a statement has the general form

accept *service*(**in** *value_parameters*;
    out *result_parameters*) → *body*

---

[24] This is another reason this kind of interaction is termed "remote procedure call."

Execution of this statement delays the server until a message resulting from a **call** to the *service* has arrived. Then the body is executed, using the values of the value parameters and any other variables accessible in the scope of the statement. Upon termination, a reply message, containing the values of the result parameters, is sent to the calling process. The server then continues execution.[25]

When **accept** or similar statements are used to specify the server side, remote procedure call is called a *rendezvous* [Department of Defense, 1981] because the client and server "meet" for the duration of the execution of the body of the **accept** statement and then go their separate ways. One advantage of the rendezvous approach is that client **calls** may be serviced at times of the server's choosing; **accept** statements, for example, can be interleaved or nested. A second advantage is that the server can achieve different effects for **calls** to the same service by using more than one **accept** statement, each with a different body. (For example, the first **accept** of a service might perform initialization.) The final, and most important, advantage is that the server can provide more than one kind of service. In particular, **accept** is often combined with selective communications to enable a server to wait for and select one of several requests to service [U. S. Department of Defense, 1981; Andrews, 1981]. This is illustrated in the following implementation of the bounded buffer:

```
process buffer;

    var slots : array [0..N−1] of T;
        head, tail : 0..N−1;
        size : 0..N;

    head := 0;  tail := 0;  size := 0;
    do size<N;  accept deposit(in value : T) →
        slots[tail] := value;
        size := size + 1;
        tail := (tail + 1) mod N
    [] size>0;  accept fetch(out value : T) →
        value := slots[head];
        size := size − 1;
        head := (head + 1) mod N
    od

    end.
```

The *buffer* process implements two operations: *deposit* and *fetch*. The first is invoked by a producer by executing

call *deposit (stuff)*

The second is invoked by a consumer by executing

call *fetch (stuff)*

Note that *deposit* and *fetch* are handled by the *buffer* process in a symmetric manner, even though **send** statements do not appear in guards, because remote procedure calls always involve two messages, one in each direction. Note also that *buffer* can be used by multiple producers and multiple consumers.

Although remote procedure call is a useful, high-level mechanism for client/server interactions, not all such interactions can be directly programmed by using it. For example, the *shortest__next__allocator* of the previous section still requires two client/server exchanges to service allocation requests because the allocator must look at the parameters of a request in order to decide if the request should be delayed. Thus the client must use one operation to transmit the request arguments and another to wait for an allocation. If there are a small number of different scheduling priorities, this can be overcome by associating a different server operation with each priority level. Ada [U. S. Department of Defense, 1981] supports this nicely by means of arrays of operations. In general, however, a mechanism is required to enable a server to accept a **call** that minimizes some function of the parameters of the called operation. SR [Andrews, 1981] includes such a mechanism (see Section 4.5.4).

4.3.2 Atomic Transactions

An often-cited advantage of multiple-processor systems is that they can be made resilient to failures. Designing programs that exhibit this fault tolerance is not a simple matter. While a discussion of how to design fault-tolerant programs is beyond the scope of this survey, we comment briefly on how fault-tolerance issues have affected the design of higher level message-passing statements.[26]

Remote procedure call provides a clean way to program client/server interactions. Ideally, we would like a remote **call**, like a

---

[25] Different semantics result depending on whether the reply message is sent by a synchronous or by an asynchronous **send**. A synchronous **send** delays the server until the results have been received by the caller. Therefore, when the server continues, it can assert that the reply message has been received and that the result parameters have been assigned to the result arguments. Use of asynchronous **send** does not allow this, but does not delay the server, either.

---

[26] For a general discussion, the interested reader is referred to Kohler 1981.

procedure call in a sequential programming notation, to have *exactly once* semantics: each remote **call** should terminate only after the named remote procedure has been executed exactly once by the server [Nelson, 1981; Spector, 1982]. Unfortunately, a failure may mean that a client is forever delayed awaiting the response to a remote **call**. This might occur if

(i) the message signifying the remote procedure invocation is lost by the network, or
(ii) the reply message is lost, or
(iii) the server crashes during execution of the remote procedure (but before the reply message is sent).

This difficulty can be overcome by attaching a time-out interval to the remote **call**; if no response is received by the client before the time-out interval expires, the client presumes that the server has failed and takes some action.

Deciding what action to take after a detected failure can be difficult. In Case (i) above, the correct action would be to retransmit the message. In Case (ii), however, retransmittal would cause a second execution of the remote procedure body. This is undesirable unless the procedure is *idempotent*, meaning that the repeated execution has the same effect as a single execution. Finally, the correct action in Case (iii) would depend on exactly how much of the remote procedure body was executed, what parts of the computation were lost, what parts must be undone, etc. In some cases, this could be handled by saving state information, called *checkpoints*, and programming special recovery actions. A more general solution would be to view execution of a remote procedure in terms of atomic transactions.

An *atomic transaction* [Lomet, 1977; Reed, 1979; Lampson, 1981] is an all-or-nothing computation—either it installs a complete collection of changes to some variables or it installs no changes, even if interrupted by a failure. Moreover, atomic transactions are assumed to be indivisible in the sense that partial execution of an atomic transaction is not visible to any concurrently executing atomic transaction. The first attribute is called *failure atomicity*, and the second *synchronization atomicity*.

Given atomic transactions, it is possible to construct a remote procedure call mechanism with *at most once* semantics—receipt of a reply message means that the remote procedure was executed exactly once, and failure to receive a reply message means the remote procedure invocation had no (permanent) effect [Liskov and Scheifler, 1982; Spector, 1982]. This is done by making execution of a remote procedure an atomic transaction that is allowed to "commit" only after the reply has ben received by the client. In some circumstances, even more complex mechanisms are useful. For example, when nested remote **calls** occur, failure while executing a higher level call should cause the effects of lower level (i.e., nested) calls to be undone, even if those calls have already completed [Liskov and Scheifler, 1982].

The main consideration in the design of these mechanisms is that may it not be possible for a process to see system data in an inconsistent state following partial execution of a remote procedure. The use of atomic transactions is one way to do this, but it is quite expensive [Lampson and Sturgis, 1979; Liskov, 1981]. Other techniques to ensure the invisibility of inconsistent states have been proposed [Lynch, 1981; Schlichting and Schneider, 1981], and this remains an active area of research.

4.4 An Axiomatic View of Message Passing

When message passing is used for communication and synchronization, processes usually do not share variables. Nonetheless, interference can still arise. In order to prove that a collection of processes achieves a common goal, it is usually necessary to make assertions in one process about the state of others. Processes learn about each other's state by exchanging messages. In particular, receipt of a message not only causes the transfer of values from sender to receiver but also facilitates the "transfer" of a predicate. This allows the receiver to make assertions about the state of the sender, such as about how far the sender has progressed in its computation. Clearly, subsequent execution by the sender might invalidate such an assertion. Thus it is possible for the sender to interfere with an assertion in the receiver.

It turns out that two distinct kinds of interference must be considered when message passing is used [Schlichting and Schneider, 1982a]. The first is similar to that occurring when shared variables are used: assertions made in one process about the state of another must not be invalidated by concurrent execution. The second form of interference arises only when asynchronous or buffered message passing is used. If a sender "transfers" a predicate with a message, the "transferred" predicate must be true when the message is received: receipt of a message reveals information about the state of the sender at the time that the message was sent, which is not necessarily the sender's current state.

The second type of interference is not possible when synchronous message passing is used, because, after sending a message, the sender does not progress until the message has been received. This is a good reason to prefer the use of synchronous **send** over asynchronous **send** (and to prefer synchronous **send** for sending the reply message in a remote procedure body). One often hears the argument that asynchronous **send** does not restrict parallelism as much as synchronous **send** and so it is preferable. However, the amount of parallelism that can be exhibited by a program is determined by program structure and not by choice of communications primitives. For example, addition of an intervening buffer process allows the sender to be executed concurrently with the receiving process. Choosing a communications primitive merely establishes whether the programmer will have to do the additional work (of defining more processes) to allow a high degree of parallel activity or will have to do additional work (of using the primitives in a highly disciplined way) to control the amount of parallelism. Nevertheless, a variety of "safe" uses of asynchronous message passing have been identified: the "transfer" of monotonic predicates and the use of "acknowledgment" protocols, for example. These schemes are studied in Schlichting and Schneider [1982b], where they are shown to follow directly from simple techniques to avoid the second kind of interference.

Formal proof techniques for various types of message-passing primitives have been developed. Axioms for buffered, asynchronous message passing were first proposed in connection with Gypsy [Good et al., 1979]. Several people have developed proof systems for synchronous message-passing statements—in particular the input and output commands in CSP [Apt et al., 1980; Cousot and Cousot, 1980; Levin and Gries, 1981; Misra and Chandy, 1981; Soundararajan, 1981; Lamport and Schneider, 1982; Schlichting and Schneider, 1982a]. Also, several people have developed proof rules for asynchronous message passing [Misra et al., 1982; Schlichting and Schneider, 1982b], and proof rules for remote procedures and rendezvous [Barringer and Mearns, 1982; Gerth, 1982; Gerth et al., 1982; Schlichting and Schneider, 1982a].

4.5 Programming Notations Based on Message Passing

A large number of concurrent programming languages have been proposed that use message passing for communication and synchronization. This should not be too surprising; because the two major message-passing design issues—channel naming and synchronization—are orthogonal, the various alternatives for each can be combined in many ways. In the following, we summarize the important characteristics of four languages: CSP, PLITS, Ada, and SR. Each is well documented in the literature and was innovative in some regard. Also, each reflects a different combination of the two design alternatives. Some other languages that have been influential—Gypsy, Distributed Processes, StarMod and Argus—are then briefly discussed.

4.5.1 Communicating Sequential Processes

Communicating Sequential Processes (CSP) [Hoare, 1978] is a programming notation based on synchronous message passing and selective communications. The concepts embodied in CSP have greatly influenced subsequent work in concurrent programming language design and the design of distributed programs.

In CSP, processes are denoted by a variant of the **cobegin** statement. Processes may share read-only variables, but use input/output commands for synchronization and communication. Direct (and static) channel naming is used and message passing is synchronous.

An *output command* in CSP has the form

destination!expression

where *destination* is a process name and *expression* is a simple or structured value. An *input command* has the form

source?target

where *source* is a process name and *target* is a simple or structured variable local to the process containing the input command. The commands

Pr!expression

in process *Ps* and

Ps?target

in process *Pr match* if *target* and *expression* have the same type. Two processes communicate if they execute a matching pair of input/output commands. The result of communication is that the expression's value is assigned to the target variable; both processes then proceed independently and concurrently.

A restricted form of selective communications statement is supported by CSP. Input commands can appear in guards of alternative and iterative statements, but output commands may not. This allows an efficient implementation, but makes certain kinds of process interaction awkward to express, as was discussed in Section 4.2.

By combining communication commands with alternative and iterative statements, CSP provides a powerful mechanism for programming process interaction. Its strength is that it is based on a simple idea—input/output commands—that is carefully integrated with a few other mechanisms. CSP is not a complete concurrent programming language, nor was it intended to be. For example, static direct naming is often awkward to use. Fortunately, this deficiency is easily overcome by using ports; how to do so was discussed briefly by Hoare [Hoare, 1978] and is described in detail by Kieburtz and Silberschatz [1979]. Recently, two languages based on CSP have also been described [Jazayeri et al., 1980; Roper and Barter, 1981].

4.5.2 PLITS

PLITS, an acronym for "Programming Language In The Sky," was developed at the University of Rochester [Feldman, 1979]. The design of PLITS is based on the premise that it is inherently difficult to combine a high degree of parallelism with data sharing and therefore message passing is the appropriate means for process interaction in a distributed system. Part of an ongoing research project in programming language design and distributed computation, PLITS is being used to program applications that are executed on Rochester's Intelligent Gateway (RIG) computer network [Ball et al., 1976].

A PLITS program consists of a number of modules; *active modules* are processes. Message passing is the sole means for intermodule interaction. So as not to restrict parallelism, message passing is asynchronous. A module sends a message containing the values of some expressions to a module *modname* by executing

send *expressions* **to** *modname* [**about** *key*]

The "**about** *key*" phrase is optional. If included, it attaches an identifying *transac-*

tion key to the message. This key can then be used to identify the message uniquely, or the same key can be attached to several different messages to allow messages to be grouped.

A module receives messages by executing

receive *variables* [**from** *modname*]
    [**about** *key*]

If the last two phrases are omitted, execution of **receive** delays the executing module until the arrival of any message. If the phrase "**from** *modname*" is included, execution is delayed until a message from the named module arrives. Finally, if the phrase "**about** *key*" is included, the module is delayed until a message with the indicated transaction key has arrived.

By combining the options in **send** and **receive** in different ways, a programmer can exert a variety of controls over communication. When both the sending and receiving modules name each other, communication is direct. The effect of port naming is realized by having a receiving module not name the source module. Finally, the use of transaction keys allows the receiver to select a particular kind of message; this provides a facility almost as powerful as attaching "**when** *B*" to a **receive** statement.

In PLITS, execution of **receive** can cause blocking. PLITS also provides primitives to test whether messages with certain field values or transaction keys are available for receipt; this enables a process to avoid blocking when there is no message available.

PLITS programs interface to the operating systems of the processors that make up RIG. Each host system provides device access, a file system, and job control. A communications kernel on each machine provides the required support for interprocessor communication.

4.5.3 Ada[27]

Ada [U. S. Department of Defense, 1981] is a language intended for programming embedded real-time, process-control systems. Because of this, Ada includes facilities for multiprocessing and device control. With respect to concurrent programming, Ada's main innovation is the rendezvous form of remote procedure call.

Processes in Ada are called *tasks*. A task

---

[27]Ada is a trademark of the U. S. Department of Defense.

is activated when the block containing its declaration is entered. Tasks may be nested and may interact by using shared variables declared in enclosing blocks. (No special mechanisms for synchronizing access to shared variables are provided.)

The primary mechanism for process interaction is the remote procedure call. Remote procedures in Ada are called *entries*; they are ports into a server process specified by means of an **accept** statement, which is similar in syntax and semantics to the **accept** statement described in Section 4.3.1. Entries are invoked by execution of a remote **call**. Selective communications is supported using the **select** statement, which is like an alternative statement.

Both **call** and **accept** statements are blocking. Since Ada programs might have to meet real-time response constraints, the language includes mechanisms to prevent or control the length of time that a process is delayed when it becomes blocked. Blocking on **call** can be avoided by using the *conditional entry call*, which performs a **call** only if a rendezvous is possible immediately. Blocking on **accept** can be avoided by using a mechanism that enables a server to determine the number of waiting **call**s. Blocking on **select** can be avoided by means of the **else** guard, which is true if none of the other guards are. Finally, a task can suspend execution for a time interval by means of the **delay** statement. This statement can be used within a guard of **select** to ensure that a process is eventually awakened.

In order to allow the programmer to control I/O devices, Ada allows entries to be bound to interrupt vector locations. Interrupts become **call**s to those entries and can therefore be serviced by a task that receives the interrupt by means of an **accept** statement.

Since its inception, Ada has generated controversy [Hoare, 1981], much of which is not related to concurrency. However, few applications using the concurrent programming features have been programmed, and at the time of this writing no compiler for full Ada has been validated. Implementation of some of the concurrent programming aspects of Ada is likely to be hard. A paper by Welsh and Lister [1981] compares the concurrency aspects of Ada to CSP and Distributed Processes [Brinch Hansen, 1978]; Wegner and Smolka [1983] compare Ada, CSP, and monitors.

4.5.4 SR

SR (Synchronizing Resources) [Andrews, 1981, 1982], like Ada, uses the rendezvous form of remote procedure call and port naming. However, there are notable differences between the languages, as described below. A compiler for SR has been implemented on PDP-11 processors and the language is being used in the construction of a UNIX-like network operating system.

An SR program consists of one or more *resources*.[28] The resource construct supports both control of process interaction and data abstraction. (In contrast, Ada has two distinct constructs for this—the task and the package.) Resources contain one or more processes. Processes interact by using *operations*, which are similar to Ada entries. Also, processes in the same resource may interact by means of shared variables.

Unlike Ada, operations may be invoked by either **send**, which is nonblocking, or **call**, which is blocking. (The server that implements an operation can require a particular form of invocation, if necessary.) Thus both asynchronous message passing and remote **call** are supported. Operations may be named either statically in the program text or dynamically by means of capability variables, which are variables having fields whose values are the names of operations. A process can therefore have a changing set of communication channels.

In SR, operations are specified by the **in** statement, which also supports selective communications. Each guard in an **in** statement has the form

op_name(parameters) [**and** *B*] [**by** *A*]

where *B* is an optional Boolean expression and *A* is an optional arithmetic expression. The phrase "**and** *B*" allows selection of the operation to be dependent on the value of *B*, which may contain references to parameters. The phrase "**by** *A*" controls which invocation of *op_name* is selected if more than one invocation is pending that satisfies *B*. This can be used to express scheduling constraints succinctly. For example, it permits a compact solution to the shortest-job-next allocation problem discussed earlier. Although somewhat expensive to implement because it requires reevaluation of *A* whenever a selection is made, this facility

---

[28] SR's resources are not to be confused with resources in conditional critical regions.

turns out to be less costly to use than explicitly programmed scheduling queues, if the expected number of pending invocations is small (which is usually the case).

Operations may also be declared to be *procedures*. In SR, a procedure is shorthand for a process that repeatedly executes an **in** statement. Thus such operations are executed sequentially.

To support device control, SR provides a variant of the resource called a *real resource*. A real resource is similar to a Modula device module: it can contain device-driver processes and it allows variables to be bound to device-register addresses. Operations in real resources can be bound to interrupt vector locations. A hardware interrupt is treated as a **send** to such an operation; interrupts are processed by means of **in** statements.

4.5.5 Some Other Language Notations Based on Message Passing

Gypsy [Good et al., 1979], one of the first high-level languages based on message passing, uses mailbox naming and buffered message passing. A major focus of Gypsy was the development of a programming language well suited for constructing verifiable systems. It has been used to implement special-purpose systems for single- and multiprocessor architectures.

Distributed Processes (DP) [Brinch Hansen, 1978] was the first language to be based on remote procedure calls. It can be viewed as a language that implements monitors by means of active processes rather than collections of passive procedures. In DP, remote procedures are specified as externally callable procedures declared along with a host process and shared variables. When a remote procedure is called, a server process is created to execute the body of the procedure. The server processes created for different calls and the host process execute with mutual exclusion. The servers and host synchronize by means of a variant of conditional critical regions. An extension of DP that employs the rendezvous form of remote procedure call and thus has a more efficient implementation is described by Mao and Yeh [1980].

StarMod [Cook, 1980] synthesizes aspects of Modula and Distributed Processes: it borrows modularization ideas from Modula and communication ideas from Distributed Processes. A module contains one or more processes and, optionally, variables shared by those processes. Synchronization within a module is provided by semaphores. Processes in different modules interact by

means of remote procedure call; StarMod provides both remote procedures and rendezvous for implementing the server side. In StarMod, as in SR, both **send** and **call** can be used to initiate communication, the choice being dictated by whether the invoked operation returns values.

Argus [Liskov and Scheifler, 1982] also borrows ideas from Distributed Processes—remote procedures implemented by dynamically created processes, which synchronize using critical regions—but goes much further. It has extensive support for programming atomic transactions. The language also includes exception handling and recovery mechanisms, which are invoked if failures occur during execution of atomic transactions. Argus is higher level than the other languages surveyed here in the sense that it attaches more semantics to remote **call**. A prototype implementation of Argus is nearing completion.

5. MODELS OF CONCURRENT PROGRAMMING LANGUAGES

Most of this survey has been devoted to mechanisms for process interaction and programming languages that use them. Despite the resulting large variety of languages, each can be viewed as belonging to one of three classes: procedure oriented, message oriented, or operation oriented. Languages in the same class provide the same basic kinds of mechanisms for process interaction and have similar attributes.

In *procedure-oriented* languages, process interaction is based on shared variables. (Because monitor-based languages are the most widely known languages in this class, this is often called the *monitor model*.) These languages contain both active objects (processes) and shared, passive objects (modules, monitors, etc.). Passive objects are represented by shared variables, usually with some procedures that implement the operations on the objects. Processes access the objects they require directly and thus interact by accessing shared objects. Because passive objects are shared, they are subject to concurrent access. Therefore, procedure-oriented languages provide means for ensuring mutual exclusion. Concurrent PASCAL, Modula, Mesa, and Edison are examples of such languages.

Message- and operation-oriented languages are both based on message passing, but reflect different views of process interaction. *Message-oriented* languages provide **send** and **receive** as the primary means for process interaction. In contrast to procedure-oriented languages, there are no shared, passive objects, and so processes cannot directly access all objects. Instead, each object is managed by a single process, its *caretaker*, which performs all operations on it. When an operation is to be performed on an object, a message is sent to its caretaker, which performs the operation and then (possibly) responds with a completion message. Thus, objects are never subject to concurrent access. CSP, Gypsy, and PLITS are examples of message-oriented languages.

Operation-oriented languages provide remote procedure call as the primary means for process interaction. These languages combine aspects of the other two classes. As in a message-oriented language, each object has a caretaker process associated with it; as in a procedure-oriented language, operations are performed on an object by calling a procedure. The difference is that the caller of an operation and the caretaker that implements it synchronize while the operation is executed. Both then proceed asynchronously. Distributed Processes, StarMod, Ada, and SR are examples of operation-oriented languages.

Languages in each of these classes are roughly equivalent in expressive power. Each can be used to implement various types of cooperation between concurrently executing processes, including client/server interactions and pipelines. Operation-oriented languages are well suited for programming client/server systems, and message-oriented languages are well suited for programming pipelined computations.

Languages in each class can be used to write concurrent programs for uniprocessors, multiprocessors, and distributed systems. Not all three classes are equally suited for all three architectures, however. Procedure-oriented languages are the most efficient to implement on contemporary single processors. Since it is expensive to simulate shared memory if none is present, implementing procedure-oriented languages on a distributed system can be costly. Nevertheless, procedure-oriented languages can be used to program a distributed system—an individual program is written for each processor and the communications network is viewed as a shared object. Message-oriented languages can be implemented with or without shared memory. In the latter case, the existence of a communications network is made completely transparent, which frees the programmer from concerns about how the network is accessed and where processes are located. This is an advantage of message-oriented languages over procedure-oriented languages when programming a distributed system. Operation-oriented languages enjoy the advantages of both procedure-oriented and message-oriented languages. When shared memory is available, an operation-oriented language can, in many cases, be implemented like a procedure-oriented language [Habermann and Nassi, 1980]; otherwise it can be implemented using message passing. Recent research has shown that both message- and operation-oriented languages can be implemented quite efficiently on distributed systems if special software/firmware is used in the implementation of the language's mechanisms [Nelson, 1981; Spector, 1982].

In a recent paper, Lauer and Needham argued that procedure-oriented and message-oriented languages are equals in terms of expressive power, logical equivalence, and performance [Lauer and Needham, 1979]. (They did not consider operation-oriented languages, which have only recently come into existence.) Their thesis was examined in depth by Reid [1980], who reached many conclusions that we share. At an abstract level, the three types of languages are interchangeable. One *can* transform any program written using the mechanisms found in languages of one class into a program using the mechanisms of another class without affecting performance. However, the classes emphasize different styles of programming—the same program written in languages of different classes is often best structured in entirely different ways. Also, each class provides a type of flexibility not present in the others. Program fragments that are easy to describe using the mechanisms of one can be awkward to describe using the mechanisms of another. One might argue (as do Lauer and Needham) that such use of these mechanisms is a bad idea. We, however, favor programming in the style appropriate to the language.

6. CONCLUSION

This paper has discussed two aspects of concurrent programming: the key concepts—specification of processes and control of their interaction—and important language notations. Early work on operating systems led to the discovery of two types of synchronization: mutual exclusion and condition synchronization. This stimulated development of synchronization primitives, a number of which are described

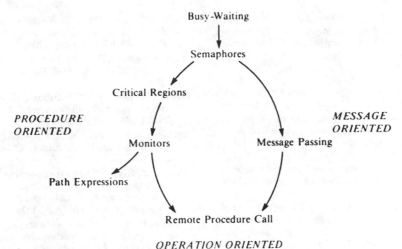

Figure 9. Synchronization techniques and language classes.

in this paper. The historical and conceptual relationships among these primitives are illustrated in Figure 9.

The difficulty of designing concurrent programs that use busy-waiting and their inefficiency led to the definition of semaphores. Semaphores were then extended in two ways: (1) constructs were defined that enforced their structured use, resulting in critical regions, monitors, and path expressions; (2) "data" were added to the synchronization associated with semaphores, resulting in message-passing primitives. Finally, the procedural interface of monitors was combined with message passing, resulting in remote procedure call.

Since the first concurrent programming languages were defined only a decade ago, practical experience has increased our understanding of how to engineer such programs, and the development of formal techniques has greatly increased our understanding of the basic concepts. Although there are a variety of different programming languages, there are only three essentially different kinds: procedure oriented, message oriented, and operation oriented. This, too, is illustrated in Figure 9.

At present, many of the basic problems that arise when constructing concurrent programs have been identified, solutions to these problems are by and large understood, and substantial progress has been made toward the design of notations to express those solutions. Much remains to be done, however. The utility of various languages—really, combinations of constructs—remains to be investigated. This requires using the languages to develop systems and then analyzing how they helped or hindered the development. In addition, the interaction of fault tolerance and concurrent programming is not well understood. Little is known about the design of distributed (decentralized) concurrent programs. Last, devising formal techniques to aid the programmer in constructing correct programs remains an important open problem.

ACKNOWLEDGMENTS

Numerous people have been kind enough to provide very helpful comments on earlier drafts of this survey: David Gries, Phil Kaslo, Lynn Kivell, Gary Levin, Ron Olsson, Rick Schlichting, and David Wright. Three referees, and also Eike Best and Michael Scott, provided valuable comments on the penultimate draft. Tony Wasserman has also provided helpful advice; it has been a joy to have him as the editor for this paper. Rachel Rutherford critiqued the ultimate draft and made numerous useful, joyfully picturesque comments.

This work was supported in part by NSF Grants MCS 80-01668 and MCS 82-02869 at Arizona and MCS 81-03605 at Cornell.

REFERENCES

AKKOYUNLU, E. A., BERNSTEIN, A. J., SCHNEIDER, F. B., AND SILBERSCHATZ, A. "Conditions for the equivalence of synchronous and asynchronous systems." *IEEE Trans. Softw. Eng.* **SE-4,** 6 (Nov. 1978), 507–516.

ANDLER, S. "Predicate path expressions." In *Proc. 6th ACM Symp. Principles of Programming Languages* (San Antonio, Tex., Jan. 1979). ACM, New York, 1979, pp. 226–236.

ANDREWS, G. R. "The design of a message switching system: An application and evaluation of Modula." *IEEE Trans. Softw. Eng.* **SE-5,** 2 (March 1979), 138–147.

ANDREWS, G. R. "Synchronizing resources." *ACM Trans. Prog. Lang. Syst.* **3,** 4 (Oct. 1981), 405–430.

ANDREWS, G. R. "The distributed programming language SR—Mechanisms, design, and implementation." *Softw. Pract. Exper.* **12**, 8 (Aug. 1982), 719–754.

ANDREWS, G. R., AND McGRAW, J. R. "Language features for process interaction." In *Proc. ACM Conf. Language Design for Reliable Software, SIGPLAN Not.* **12**, 3 (March 1977), 114–127.

APT, K. R., FRANCEZ, N., AND DE ROEVER, W. P. "A proof system for communicating sequential processes." *ACM Trans. Prog. Lang. Syst.* **2**, 3 (July 1980), 359–385.

ASCHCROFT, E. A. "Proving assertions about parallel programs." *J. Comput. Syst.* **10** (Jan. 1975), 110–135.

BALL, E., FELDMAN, J., LOW, J., RASHID, R., AND ROVNER, P. "RIG, Rochester's intelligent gateway: System overview." *IEEE Trans. Softw. Eng.* **SE-2**, 4 (Dec. 1976), 321–328.

BALZER, R. M. "PORTS—A method for dynamic interprogram communication and job control." In *Proc. AFIPS Spring Jt. Computer Conf.* (Atlantic City, N. J., May 18–20, 1971), vol. 38. AFIPS Press, Arlington, Va., 1971, pp. 485–489.

BARRINGER, H., AND MEARNS, I. "Axioms and proof rules for Ada tasks." *IEE Proc.* **129**, Pt. E, 2 (March 1982), 38–48.

BASKETT, F., HOWARD, J. H., AND MONTAGUE, J. T. "Task communication in DEMOS." In *Proc. 6th Symp. Operating Systems Principles* (West Lafayette, Indiana, Nov. 16–18, 1977). ACM, New York, 1977, pp. 23–31.

BEN-ARI, M. *Principles of Concurrent Programming.* Prentice-Hall, Englewood Cliffs, N. J., 1982.

BERNSTEIN, A. J. "Output guards and nondeterminism in communicating sequential processes." *ACM Trans. Prog. Lang. Syst.* **2**, 2 (Apr. 1980), 234–238.

BERNSTEIN, A. J., AND ENSOR, J. R. "A modification of Modula." *Softw. Pract. Exper.* **11** (1981), 237–255.

BERNSTEIN, A. J., AND SCHNEIDER, F. B. "On language restrictions to ensure deterministic behavior in concurrent systems." In J. Moneta (Ed.), *Proc. 3rd Jerusalem Conf. Information Technology JCIT3.* North-Holland Publ., Amsterdam, 1978, pp. 537–541.

BERNSTEIN, P. A., AND GOODMAN, N. "Concurrency control in distributed database systems." *ACM Comput. Surv.* **13**, 2 (June 1981), 185–221.

BEST, E. "Relational semantics of concurrent programs (with some applications)." In *Proc. IFIP WG2.2 Conf.* North-Holland Publ., Amsterdam, 1982.

BLOOM, T. "Evaluating synchronization mechanisms." In *Proc. 7th Symp. Operating Systems Principles* (Pacific Grove, Calif., Dec. 10–12, 1979). ACM, New York, 1979, pp. 24–32.

BRINCH HANSEN, P. "Structured multiprogramming." *Commun. ACM* **15**, 7 (July 1972), 574–578.

BRINCH HANSEN, P. *Operating System Principles.* Prentice-Hall, Englewood Cliffs, N. J., 1973. (a)

BRINCH HANSEN, P. "Concurrent programming concepts." *ACM Comput. Surv.* **5**, 4 (Dec. 1973), 223–245. (b)

BRINCH HANSEN, P. "The programming language Concurrent Pascal." *IEEE Trans Softw. Eng.* **SE-1**, 2 (June 1975), 199–206.

BRINCH HANSEN, P. "The Solo operating system: Job interface." *Softw. Pract. Exper.* **6** (1976), 151–164. (a)

BRINCH HANSEN, P. "The Solo operating system: Processes, monitors, and classes." *Softw. Pract. Exper.* **6** (1976), 165–200. (b)

BRINCH HANSEN, P. *The Architecture of Concurrent Programs.* Prentice-Hall, Englewood Cliffs, N. J., 1977.

BRINCH HANSEN, P. "Distributed processes: A concurrent programming concept." *Commun. ACM* **21**, 11 (Nov. 1978), 934–941.

BRINCH HANSEN, P. "Edison: A multiprocessor language." *Softw. Pract. Exper.* **11**, 4 (Apr. 1981), 325–361.

CAMPBELL, R. H. "Path expressions: A technique for specifying process synchronization." Ph.D. dissertation, Computing Laboratory, University of Newcastle upon Tyne, Aug. 1976.

CAMPBELL, R. H., AND HABERMANN, A. N. "The specification of process synchronization by path expressions." *Lecture Notes in Computer Science,* vol. 16. Springer-Verlag, New York, 1974, pp. 89–102.

CAMPBELL, R. H., AND KOLSTAD, R. B. "Path expressions in Pascal." In *Proc. 4th Int. Conf. on Software Eng.* (Munich, Sept. 17–19, 1979). IEEE, New York, 1979, pp. 212–219.

CONWAY, M. E. "Design of a separable transition-diagram compiler." *Commun. ACM* **6**, 7 (July 1963), 396–408. (a)

CONWAY, M. E. "A multiprocessor system design." In *Proc. AFIPS Fall Jt. Computer Conf.* (Las Vegas, Nev., Nov., 1963), vol. 24. Spartan Books, Baltimore, Maryland, pp. 139–146. (b)

COOK, R. P. "*MOD—A language for distributed programming." *IEEE Trans. Softw. Eng.* **SE-6**, 6 (Nov. 1980), 563–571.

COURTOIS, P. J., HEYMANS, F., AND PARNAS, D. L. "Concurrent control with 'readers' and 'writers'." *Commun. ACM* **14**, 10 (Oct. 1971), 667–668.

COUSOT, P., AND COUSOT, R. "Semantic analysis of communicating sequential processes." In *Proc. 7th Int. Colloquium Automata, Languages and Programming (ICALP80), Lecture Notes in Computer Science,* vol. 85. Springer-Verlag, New York, 1980, pp. 119–133.

DENNIS, J. B., AND VAN HORN, E. C. "Programming semantics for multiprogrammed computations." *Commun. ACM* **9**, 3 (March 1966), 143–155.

DIJKSTRA, E. W. "The structure of the 'THE' multiprogramming system." *Commun. ACM* **11**, 5 (May 1968), 341–346. (a)

DIJKSTRA, E. W. "Cooperating sequential processes." In F. Genuys (Ed.), *Programming Languages.* Academic Press, New York, 1968. (b)

DIJKSTRA, E. W. "Guarded commands, nondeterminacy, and formal derivation of programs." *Commun. ACM* **18**, 8 (Aug. 1975), 453–457.

DIJKSTRA, E. W. *A Discipline of Programming.* Prentice-Hall, Englewood Cliffs, N. J., 1976.

DIJKSTRA, E. W. "An assertional proof of a program by G. L. Peterson." EWD 779 (Feb. 1979), Nuenen, The Netherlands. (a)

DIJKSTRA, E. W. Personal communication, Oct. 1981. (b)

FELDMAN, J. A.. "High level programming for distributed computing." *Commun. ACM* **22**, 6 (June 1979), 353–368.

FLON, L., AND HABERMANN, A. N. "Towards the construction of verifiable software systems." In *Proc. ACM Conf. Data, SIGPLAN Not.* **8**, 2 (March 1976), 141–148.

FLOYD, R. W. "Assigning meanings to programs." In *Proc. Am. Math. Soc. Symp. Applied Mathematics*, vol. 19, pp. 19-31, 1967.

GELERNTER, D., AND BERNSTEIN, A. J. "Distributed communication via global buffer." In *Proc. Symp. Principles of Distributed Computing* (Ottawa, Canada, Aug. 18-20, 1982). ACM, New York, 1982, pp. 10-18.

GERTH, R. "A sound and complete Hoare axiomatization of the Ada-rendezvous." In *Proc. 9th Int. Colloquium Automata, Languages and Programming (ICALP82), Lecture Notes in Computer Science*, vol. 140. Springer-Verlag, New York, 1982, pp. 252-264.

GERTH, R., DE ROEVER, W. P., AND RONCKEN, M. "Procedures and concurrency: A study in proof." In *5th Int. Symp. Programming, Lecture Notes in Computer Science*, vol. 137. Springer-Verlag, New York, 1982, pp. 132-163.

GOOD, D. I., COHEN, R. M., AND KEETON-WILLIAMS, J. "Principles of proving concurrent programs in Gypsy." In *Proc. 6th ACM Symp. Principles of Programming Languages* (San Antonio, Texas, Jan. 29-31, 1979). ACM, New York, 1979, pp. 42-52.

HABERMANN, A. N. "Path expressions." Dep. of Computer Science, Carnegie-Mellon Univ., Pittsburgh, Pennsylvania, June, 1975.

HABERMANN, A. N., AND NASSI, I. R. "Efficient implementation of Ada tasks." Tech. Rep. CMU-CS-80-103, Carnegie-Mellon Univ., Jan. 1980.

HADDON, B. K. "Nested monitor calls." *Oper. Syst. Rev.* **11**, 4 (Oct. 1977), 18-23.

HANSON, D. R., AND GRISWOLD, R. E. "The SL5 procedure mechanism." *Commun. ACM* **21**, 5 (May 1978), 392-400.

HOARE, C. A. R. "An axiomatic basis for computer programming." *Commun. ACM.* **12**, 10 (Oct. 1969), 576-580, 583.

HOARE, C. A. R. "Towards a theory of parallel programming." In C. A. R. Hoare and R. H. Perrott (Eds.), *Operating Systems Techniques*. Academic Press, New York, 1972, pp. 61-71.

HOARE, C. A. R. "Monitors: An operating system structuring concept." *Commun. ACM* **17**, 10 (Oct. 1974), 549-557.

HOARE, C. A. R. "Communicating sequential processes." *Commun. ACM* **21**, 8 (Aug. 1978), 666-677.

HOARE, C. A. R. "The emperor's old clothes." *Commun. ACM* **24**, 2 (Feb. 1981), 75-83.

HOLDEN, J., AND WAND, I. C. "An assessment of Modula." *Softw. Pract. Exper.* **10** (1980), 593-621.

HOLT, R. C., GRAHAM, G. S., LAZOWSKA, E. D., AND SCOTT, M. A. *Structured Concurrent Programming with Operating Systems Applications.* Addison-Wesley, Reading, Mass., 1978.

HOWARD, J. H. "Proving monitors." *Commun. ACM* **19**, 5 (May 1976), 273-279. (a)

HOWARD, J. H. "Signaling in monitors." In *Proc. 2nd Int. Conf. Software Engineering* (San Francisco, Oct. 13-15, 1976). IEEE, New York, 1976, pp. 47-52. (b)

JAZAYERI, M., et al. "CSP/80: A language for communicating processes." In *Proc. Fall IEEE COMPCON80* (Sept. 1980). IEEE, New York, 1980, pp. 736-740.

JONES, A. K., AND SCHWARZ, P. "Experience using multiprocessor systems—A status report." *ACM Comput. Surv.* **12**, 2 (June 1980), 121-165.

KAUBISCH, W. H., PERROTT, R. H., AND HOARE, C. A. R. "Quasiparallel programming." *Softw. Pract. Exper.* **6** (1976), 341-356.

KEEDY, J. L. "On structuring operating systems with monitors." *Aust. Comput. J.* **10**, 1 (Feb. 1978), 23-27. Reprinted in *Oper. Syst. Rev.* **13**, 1 (Jan. 1979), 5-9.

KELLER, R. M. "Formal verification of parallel programs." *Commun. ACM* **19**, 7 (July 1976), 371-384.

KESSELS, J. L. W. "An alternative to event queues for synchronization in monitors." *Commun. ACM* **20**, 7 (July 1977), 500-503.

KIEBURTZ, R. B., AND SILBERSCHATZ, A. "Comments on 'communicating sequential processes.'" *ACM Trans. Program. Lang. Syst.* **1**, 2 (Oct. 1979), 218-225.

KOHLER, W. H. "A survey of techniques for synchronization and recovery in decentralized computer systems." *ACM Comput. Surv.* **13**, 2 (June 1981), 149-183.

LAMPORT, L. "Proving the correctness of multiprocess programs." *IEEE Trans. Softw. Eng.* SE-3, 2 (March 1977), 125-143.

LAMPORT, L. "The 'Hoare logic' of concurrent programs." *Acta Inform.* **14**, 21-37. (a)

LAMPORT, L. "The mutual exclusion problem." Op. 56, SRI International, Menlo Park, Calif., Oct. 1980. (b)

LAMPORT, L., AND SCHNEIDER, F. B. "The 'Hoare logic' of CSP, and all that." Tech. Rep. TR 82-490, Dep. Computer Sci., Cornell Univ., May, 1982.

LAMPSON, B. W. "Atomic transactions." In *Distributed Systems—Architecture and Implementation, Lecture Notes in Computer Science*, vol. 105. Springer-Verlag, New York, 1981.

LAMPSON, B. W., AND REDELL, D. D. "Experience with processes and monitors in Mesa." *Commun. ACM* **23**, 2 (Feb. 1980), 105-117.

LAMPSON, B. W., AND STURGIS, H. E. "Crash recovery in a distributed data storage system." Xerox Palo Alto Research Center, Apr. 1979.

LAUER, H. C., AND NEEDHAM, R. M. "On the duality of operating system structures." In *Proc. 2nd Int. Symp. Operating Systems* (IRIA, Paris, Oct. 1978); reprinted in *Oper. Syst. Rev.* **13**, 2 (Apr. 1979), 3-19.

LAUER, P. E., AND CAMPBELL, R. H. "Formal semantics of a class of high level primitives for coordinating concurrent processes." *Acta Inform.* **5** (1975), 297-332.

LAUER, P. E., AND SHIELDS, M. W. "Abstract specification of resource accessing disciplines: Adequacy, starvation, priority and interrupts." *SIGPLAN Not.* **13**, 12 (Dec. 1978), 41-59.

LEHMANN, D., PNUELI, A., AND STAVI, J. "Impartiality, justice and fairness: The ethics of concurrent termination." *Automata, Languages and Programming, Lecture Notes in Computer Science*, vol. 115. Springer-Verlag, New York, 1981, pp. 264-277.

LEVIN, G. M., AND GRIES, D. "A proof technique for communicating sequential processes." *Acta Inform.* **15** (1981), 281-302.

LISKOV, B. L. "On linguistic support for distributed programs." In *Proc. IEEE Symp. Reliability in Distributed Software and Database Systems* (Pittsburgh, July 21-22, 1981). IEEE, New York, 1981, pp. 53-60.

LISKOV, B. L., AND SCHEIFLER, R. "Guardians and actions: Linguistic support for robust, distributed programs." In *Proc. 9th ACM Symp. Principles of Programming Languages* (Albuquerque, New Mexico, Jan. 25–27, 1982). ACM, New York, 1982, pp. 7–19.

LISTER, A. "The problem of nested monitor calls." *Oper. Syst. Rev.* 11, 3 (July 1977), 5–7.

LOEHR, K.-P. "Beyond Concurrent Pascal." In *Proc. 6th ACM Symp. Operating Systems Principles* (West Lafayette, Ind., Nov. 16–18, 1977). ACM, New York, 1977, pp. 173–180.

LOMET, D. B. "Process structuring, synchronization, and recovery using atomic transactions." In *Proc. ACM Conf. Language Design for Reliable Software, SIGPLAN Not.* 12, 3 (March 1977), 128–137.

LYNCH, N. A. "Multilevel atomicity—A new correctness criterion for distributed databases." Tech. Rep. GIT-ICS-81/05, School of Information and Computer Sciences, Georgia Tech., May 1981.

MAO, T. W., AND YEH, R. T. "Communication port: A language concept for concurrent programming." *IEEE Trans. Softw. Eng.* SE-6, 2 (March 1980), 194–204.

MISRA, J., AND CHANDY, K. "Proofs of networks of processes." *IEEE Trans. Softw. Eng.* SE-7, 4 (July 1981), 417–426.

MISRA, J., CHANDY, K. M., AND SMITH, T. "Proving safety and liveness of communicating processes with examples." In *Proc. Symp. Principles of Distributed Computing* (Ottawa, Canada, Aug. 18–20, 1982). ACM, New York, 1982, pp. 201–208.

MITCHELL, J. G., MAYBURY, W., AND SWEET, R. "Mesa language manual, version 5.0." Rep. CSL-79-3, Xerox Palo Alto Research Center, Apr. 1979.

NELSON, B. J. "Remote procedure call." Ph.D. thesis. Rep. CMU-CS-81-119, Dep. of Computer Science, Carnegie–Mellon Univ., May 1981.

NYGAARD, K., AND DAHL, O. J. "The development of the SIMULA languages." *Preprints ACM SIGPLAN History of Programming Languages Conference, SIGPLAN Not.* 13, 8 (Aug. 1978), 245–272.

OWICKI, S. S., AND GRIES, D. "An axiomatic proof technique for parallel programs." *Acta Inform.* 6 (1976), 319–340. (a)

OWICKI, S. S., AND GRIES, D. "Verifying properties of parallel programs: an axiomatic approach." *Commun. ACM* 19, 5 (May 1976), 279–285. (b)

PARNAS, D. L. "On the criteria to be used in decomposing systems into modules." *Commun. ACM* 15, 12 (Dec. 1972), 1053–1058.

PARNAS, D. L. "The non-problem of nested monitor calls." *Oper. Syst. Rev.* 12, 1 (Jan. 1978), 12–14.

PETERSON, G. L. "Myths about the mutual exclusion problem." *Inform. Process. Lett.* 12, 3 (June 1981), 115–116.

REED, D. P. "Implementing atomic actions on decentralized data." *ACM Trans. Comput. Syst.* 1, 1 (Feb. 1983), 3–23.

REID, L. G. "Control and communication in programmed systems." Ph.D. thesis, Rep. CMU-CS-80-142, Dep. of Computer Science, Carnegie–Mellon Univ., Sept. 1980.

REIF, J. H., AND SPIRAKIS, P. G. "Unbounded speed variability in distributed communications systems." In *Proc. 9th ACM Conf. Principles of Programming Languages* (Albuquerque, N. M., Jan. 25–27, 1982). ACM, New York, 1982, pp. 46–56.

RITCHIE, D. M., AND THOMPSON, K. "The UNIX timesharing system. *Commun. ACM* 17, 7 (July 1974), 365–375.

ROPER, T. J., AND BARTER, C. J. "A communicating sequential process language and implementation." *Softw. Pract. Exper.* 11 (1981), 1215–1234.

SCHLICHTING, R. D., AND SCHNEIDER, F. B. "An approach to designing fault-tolerant computing systems." Tech. Rep. TR 81–479, Dep. of Computer Sci., Cornell Univ., Nov. 1981.

SCHLICHTING, R. D., AND SCHNEIDER, F. B. "Using message passing for distributed programming: Proof rules and disciplines." Tech. Rep. TR 82-491, Dep. of Computer Science, Cornell Univ., May 1982. (a)

SCHLICHTING, R. D., AND SCHNEIDER, F. B. "Understanding and using asynchronous message passing primitives." In *Proc. Symp. Principles of Distributed Computing* (Ottawa, Canada, Aug. 18–20, 1982). ACM, New York, 1982, pp. 141–147. (b)

SCHNEIDER, F. B. "Synchronization in distributed programs." *ACM Trans. Program. Lang. Syst.* 4, 2 (Apr. 1982), 125–148.

SCHNEIDER, F. B., AND BERNSTEIN, A. J. "Scheduling in Concurrent Pascal." *Oper. Syst. Rev.* 12, 2 (Apr. 1978), 15–20.

SCHWARTZ, J. S. "Distributed synchronization of communicating sequential processes." Tech. Rep., Dep. of Artificial Intelligence, Univ. of Edinburgh, July 1978.

SHAW, A. C. *The Logical Design of Operating Systems.* Prentice-Hall, Englewood Cliffs, N. J., 1974.

SHAW, A. C. "Software specification languages based on regular expressions." In W. E. Riddle and R. E. Fairley (Eds.), *Software Development Tools.* Springer-Verlag, New York, 1980, pp. 148–175.

SHIELDS, M. W. "Adequate path expressions." In *Proc. Int. Symp. Semantics of Concurrent Computation, Lecture Notes in Computer Science*, vol. 70. Springer-Verlag, New York, pp. 249–265.

SILBERSCHATZ, A. "On the input/output mechanism in Concurrent Pascal." In *Proc. COMPSAC '77—IEEE Computer Society Computer Software and Applications Conference* (Chicago, Ill., Nov. 1977). IEEE, New York, 1977, pp. 514–518.

SILBERSCHATZ, A. "Communication and synchronization in distributed programs." *IEEE Trans. Softw. Eng.* SE-5, 6 (Nov. 1979), 542–546.

SILBERSCHATZ, A., KIEBURTZ, R. B., AND BERNSTEIN, A. J. "Extending Concurrent Pascal to allow dynamic resource management." *IEEE Trans. Softw. Eng.* SE-3, 3 (May 1977), 210–217.

SOLOMON, M. H., AND FINKEL, R. A. "The Roscoe distributed operating system." In *Proc. 7th Symp. Operating System Principles* (Pacific Grove, Calif., Dec. 10–12, 1979). ACM, New York, 1979, pp. 108–114.

SOUNDARARAJAN, N. "Axiomatic semantics of communicating sequential processes." Tech. Rep., Dep. of Computer and Information Science, Ohio State Univ., 1981.

SPECTOR, A. Z. "Performing remote operations efficiently on a local computer network." *Commun. ACM* 25, 4 (Apr. 1982), 246–260.

U.S. DEPARTMENT OF DEFENSE. *Programming Language Ada: Reference Manual*, vol. 106, *Lec-*

ture Notes in Computer Science. Springer-Verlag, New York, 1981.

VAN DE SNEPSCHEUT, J. L. A. "Synchronous communication between synchronization components." *Inform. Process. Lett.* **13**, 3 (Dec. 1981), 127–130.

VAN WIJNGAARDEN, A., MAILLOUX, B. J., PECK, J. L., KOSTER, C. H. A., SINTZOFF, M., LINDSEY, C. H., MEERTENS, L. G. L. T., AND FISKER, R. G. "Revised report on the algorithm language ALGOL68." *Acta Inform.* **5**, 1–3 (1975), 1–236.

WEGNER, P., AND SMOLKA, S. A. "Processes, tasks and monitors: A comparative study of concurrent programming primitives." *IEEE Trans. Softw. Eng.*, to appear, 1983.

WELSH, J., AND BUSTARD, D. W. "Pascal-Plus—Another language for modular multiprogramming." *Softw. Pract. Exper.* **9** (1979), 947–957.

WELSH, J., AND LISTER, A. "A comparative study of task communication in Ada." *Softw. Pract. Exper.* **11** (1981), 257–290.

WETTSTEIN, H. "The problem of nested monitor cells revisited." *Oper. Syst. Rev.* **12**, 1 (Jan. 1978), 19–23.

WIRTH, N. "Modula: A language for modular multiprogramming." *Softw. Pract. Exper.* **7** (1977), 3–35. (a)

WIRTH, N. "The use of Modula." *Softw. Pract. Exper.* **7** (1977), 37–65. (b)

WIRTH, N. "Design and implementation of Modula." *Softw. Pract. Exper.* **7** (1977), 67–84. (c)

WIRTH, N. "Toward a discipline of real-time programming." *Commun. ACM* **20**, 8 (Aug. 1977), 577–583. (d)

WIRTH, N. *Programming in Modula-2.* Springer-Verlag, New York, 1982.

WULF, W. A., RUSSELL, D. B., AND HABERMANN, A. N. BLISS: A language for systems programming. *Commun. ACM* **14**, 12 (Dec. 1971), 780–790.

PROCESSES, TASKS, AND MONITORS: A COMPARATIVE STUDY OF CONCURRENT PROGRAMMING PRIMITIVES*

PETER WEGNER AND SCOTT A. SMOLKA

Abstract–Three notations for concurrent programming are compared, namely CSP, Ada, and monitors. CSP is an experimental language for exploring structuring concepts in concurrent programming. Ada is a general-purpose language with concurrent programming facilities. Monitors are a construct for managing access by concurrent processes to shared resources. We start by comparing "lower-level" communication, synchronization, and nondeterminism in CSP and Ada and then examine "higher-level" module interface properties of Ada tasks and monitors.

Similarities between CSP and Ada include use of the "cobegin" construct for nested process initiation and the "rendezvous" mechanism for synchronization. Differences include the mechanisms for task naming and nondeterminism. One-way (procedure-style) naming of called tasks by calling tasks in Ada is more flexible than the two-way naming in CSP. The general-purpose nondeterminism of guarded commands in CSP is cleaner than the special-purpose nondeterminism of the **select** statement in Ada.

Monitors and tasks are two different mechanisms for achieving serial access to shared resources by concurrently callable procedures. Both rely on queues to achieve serialization, but calls on monitor procedures are scheduled on a single monitor queue while task entry calls are scheduled on separate queues associated with each entry name. Monitors are passive modules which are activated by being called, while tasks are active modules that execute independently of their callers. Monitor procedures represent multiple threads of control each of which may be suspended and later resumed, while tasks have just a single thread of control. The attempt to map a monitor version of a shortest job scheduler into Ada yields interesting insights into the limitations of Ada mechanisms for synchronization, and suggests that Ada packages may be more appropriate than tasks as a user interface for concurrent computation.

Index Terms–Ada, concurrent programming, CSP, distributed processes, monitors, processes, tasks.

I. INITIATION AND TERMINATION OF CONCURRENT PROCESSES

THE unit of concurrency is called a *process* in CSP [11] and a *task* in Ada [5]. The CSP command below declares and initiates two processes p1, p2 with associated command lists that may contain declarations and statements.

Example 1 – Concurrent Execution Command in CSP:

[p1 :: *command-list* || p2 :: *command-list*]

Manuscript received January 12, 1982; revised January 14, 1983. This work was supported in part by the Office of Naval Research under Contract N00014-78-C-0656 and in part by the NASA Graduate Student Researchers Fellowship under Grant NGT-40-002-800.

P. Wegner is with the Department of Computer Science, Brown University, Providence, RI 02912.

S. A. Smolka is with the Department of Computer Science, Brown University, Providence, RI 02912 and with the Department of Computer Science, State University of New York at Stony Brook, Stony Brook, NY 11794.

This command imposes a nested (one-in, one-out) structure on task initiation and termination. Execution causes p1 and p2 to be concurrently initiated and requires both to terminate before the next command can be executed.

The Ada procedure WOMAN_WINE_AND_SONG below declares two tasks WOMAN and WINE with separately specified bodies and has a call to a procedure SONG in its statement part.[1] Execution of the procedure WOMAN_WINE_AND_SONG causes the tasks WOMAN and WINE to be initiated on entry to the statement part of the procedure and executed concurrently with the procedure SONG. Exit from WOMAN_WINE_AND_SONG requires execution of the two tasks as well as execution of procedure SONG to be completed.

Example 2 – Declaration and Initiation of Tasks in Ada:

```
procedure WOMAN_WINE_AND_SONG is
    task WOMAN;
    task WINE;
    task body WOMAN is separate;
    task body WINE is separate;
begin          --initiate WOMAN and WINE
    SONG;      --call the parameterless procedure SONG
    --WOMAN, WINE, and SONG are concurrently executed
    --all three activities must terminate before exit from the
    --procedure
end;
```

The keyword begin causes the single thread of control in the declarative part of WOMAN_WINE_AND_SONG to branch into three threads associated with the tasks WOMAN, WINE, and the parent procedure. The keyword end requires the three threads to rejoin into a single thread before it can be executed. Associating initiation and termination of tasks with begin and end keywords ties the lifetimes of task execution to the nested block structure of the program.

Execution of the two tasks WOMAN and WINE concurrently with SONG may be expressed in CSP notation as

[WOMAN :: task body || WINE :: task body || SONG :: procedure]

Nested task initiation and termination may be syntactically indicated by cobegin commands. We can write **cobegin** (T1,

[1] The phrase "woman, wine, and song" is attributed to Martin Luther in the *Oxford Book of Quotations*, 1972 edition, p. 321: "Who knows not woman, wine and song, remains a fool his whole life long."

T2) to represent nested initiation and termination of two tasks T1 and T2. The statement **cobegin**(T1, **cobegin**(T2, T3), T4) illustrates use of the cobegin statement for concurrent execution of three tasks, the second of which in turn involves nested concurrent execution of two tasks. The keyword **cobegin** is not part of CSP or Ada but is introduced here to bring out the common structure of nested task initiation adopted in both languages.

Early concurrent programming languages modeled task initiation by a **fork**(T) command to initiate a new thread of control for a task T, and modeled task termination by a join command to rejoin the thread of control of the executing task to its parent. fork commands in concurrent programming are like go to statements in sequential programming. Their undisciplined use may give rise to an unstructured tangle of threads of control just as the go to statement may give rise to an unstructured tangle of paths of control. A tangle of threads of control is potentially worse than a tangle of paths of control since threads of control eat up time and memory resources while paths of control in a sequential process can be exercised only one at a time.

Cobegin-style task initiation and termination are appropriate for applications whose patterns of concurrent execution are known at compile time, such as concurrent operations on non-overlapping components of a predefined array or database. However, dynamically evolving systems such as airline reservation systems and command and control applications have patterns of concurrency that cannot be predicted at compile time. When the number of tasks and their time of creation cannot be predicted, dynamic task-creation mechanisms not tied to the program structure are required.

Both CSP and Ada support nested task initiation and termination, but Ada also permits dynamic task initiation through access types (pointers). The procedure AIRPLANES below declares a task type AIRPLANE and an array SQUADRON of task pointers to tasks of the type AIRPLANE. SQUADRON is uninitialized and no tasks are therefore created on entry to the statement part of the AIRPLANES procedure. However, new AIRPLANE creates and initiates a new task every time it is executed in the for loop. It behaves like a fork command in the sense that it launches a new thread of control for each AIRPLANE while continuing execution of the AIRPLANES procedure. But all AIRPLANE tasks must terminate before exit from the AIRPLANES procedure, thus preserving a one-in, one-out flow of control.

Example 3—Dynamic Task Initiation:

```
procedure AIRPLANES is
    task type AIRPLANE;
    type AIRPLANE_PTR is access AIRPLANE;
    SQUADRON: array (1..100) of AIRPLANE_PTR;
    task body AIRPLANE is separate;
begin
    for 1 in 1..100 loop
        SQUADRON(I) := new AIRPLANE;
    end loop;
    --exit when all tasks are terminated
end AIRPLANES;
```

In the previous example the maximum number of tasks that can be dynamically accessed is fixed by the size of the array SQUADRON. Even greater flexibility can be obtained by associating dynamically created tasks with a list structure. Thus if each airplane in an airline reservation system (or air traffic control simulation) is associated with a task, the set of airplanes can be represented by an array which imposes a maximum on the number of permitted airplanes, or by a list of records with task components whose elements can be dynamically created and deleted during execution. The list-structure approach to dynamic task creation is illustrated in the next example for a fleet of ships.

Example 4—List Structures of Tasks:

```
procedure SHIPS is
    task type SHIP;
    type SHIP_PTR is access SHIP;

    type ELEMENT;              --incomplete type declaration
    type FLEET is access ELEMENT;

    type ELEMENT is
        record
            INDEX: INTEGER;    --name of ship
            S: SHIP_PTR;       --pointer to ship task
            NEXT: FLEET;       --next ship in the list
        end record;
    HEAD, C: FLEET := null;
    task body SHIP is separate;
begin
    for K in 1..100 loop
        --insert new ship at head of list
        C := new ELEMENT' (K, new SHIP, C);
        HEAD := C;
    end loop;
    --exit when all tasks are terminated
end SHIPS;
```

Examples 2, 3, and 4 represent three successively more dynamic mechanisms for task initiation. The cobegin mechanism is the most structured but its use is restricted to the case when patterns of concurrent execution can be specified in the source program. The array and list mechanisms provide greater power but must be used carefully if undisciplined proliferation of tasks is to be avoided.

Use of **begin ... end** for task initiation and termination imposes a one-in–one-out structure on task execution comparable to that imposed by **while ... end** on control paths of a sequential program. begin and end are specialized forms of fork and join commands in much the same sense that while is a specialized form of the go to command. The **begin ... end** (cobegin) construct may be referred to as a "closed" language construct in contrast to fork and join which may be referred to as "open" constructs. Dynamic initiation using access types may be referred to as semi-open (semi-closed) since it allows dynamic (open) task initiation, but imposes static (closed) termination at the end of the unit in which the task is initiated.

Ada permits task bodies to be defined and compiled separately from the task specification. The separation of specifications and bodies of program units facilitates the modular construction of large systems from their components. Task bodies, like procedure bodies, may contain a sequence of declarations followed by a sequence of statements.

Example 5 – Task Bodies:

```
task body T is
    sequence of declarations
begin
    sequence of statements
end;
```

Initiation of a task causes the task body to begin execution, starting with its sequence of declarations. Normal termination occurs when control reaches the end of the task body.

Both CSP and Ada view a task as a sequentially executable sequence of statements. Ada differs from CSP in defining the specification, body description, and initiation of a task by independent language constructs occurring at textually separate points of the program. CSP requires the name, body, and point of initiation of a task to be specified as a single textual unit.

Concurrent programming widens the gap between static and dynamic (execution-time) program structure. It introduces a new dimension of complexity into program structure which requires a new set of language primitives to manage this complexity. In the present section we have indicated some of the tradeoffs between static structuring and execution-time flexibility for task initiation and termination. In the sections that follow, structuring mechanisms for synchronization and communication among interacting tasks will be considered.

II. COMMUNICATION, SYNCHRONIZATION, AND RENDEZVOUS

Tasks may communicate with each other by message passing or by access to shared data. Both require synchronization to ensure orderly communication. Task initiation increases the logical concurrency in a computation while synchronized communication reduces concurrency by imposing temporal constraints on task execution.

The communication primitives of both CSP and Ada are message-based in the sense that communication among processes is by synchronization followed by message passing. Communication in CSP is accomplished by input and output commands. Passing of a value x by an output command $q!x$ in a process p to an input command $p?y$ in a process q is illustrated in the next example.

Example 6 – Message Passing by Input and Output Commands:

```
[p :: [...q ! x...] || q :: [...p ? y...]]
```

```
--The output command q!x in the process p outputs the
--value of x to process q that is waiting to execute an
--input command from p.
--The input command p?y in the process q inputs a value
--from a process p and stores the result in y.
```

Communication must be preceded by synchronization between the input and output commands of the processes p and q. If p reaches its output command first it must wait until q reaches its input command and conversely. Synchronization occurs when both p and q have reached their matching communication commands. The two processes can then communicate. When communication has been completed then separate concurrent execution may be continued. The process of synchronization followed by communication is called "rendezvous," reflecting the fact that input and output commands must "meet" at a common point in time for communication to take place. See Fig. 1.

CSP requires the sending process p to identify the process q to which the message is being sent, and requires q to identify the process p from which it is receiving the message. There is no distinction in CSP between calling and called processes. The sending process p and receiving process q are equally active in establishing the communication link. As noted in [1], such two-way naming between communicating processes is well-suited for programming "pipelines": a sequence of concurrent processes in which the output of one process is the input of another.

Ada tasks require a "specification" that contains the information used by other tasks to communicate with it. Communication is accomplished through task entries whose role in task communication is similar to that of input and output commands in CSP. The following task specification for a queueing task Q has two entries named APPEND and REMOVE with parameters that specify the mode of communication.

Example 7 – A Task Specification:

```
task Q is
    entry APPEND (M: in MESSAGE);
    entry REMOVE (M: out MESSAGE);
end Q;
```

Entries are indicated in the task body by accept statements that repeat the entry specification and have an accept body that specifies the communication to be performed when synchronization has occurred. Calling of a task entry is accomplished by entry calls that are syntactically indistinguishable from procedure calls, and is realized by a rendezvous similar to that of CSP. The example below illustrates calling of an APPEND entry in a queueing task Q from a producer task P.

Example 8 – Rendezvous with One-Way Naming:

```
task body P is                  task body Q is
    ...                             ...
    ...                             accept APPEND(M : in
                                        MESSAGE) do
    Q.APPEND(X);                        BUFFER := M;
    ...                             end;
                                    ...
end P;                          end Q;

--Calling Task P                --Called Task Q
--must name the called task     --does not know the
                                --names of its callers
```

Execution of Q.APPEND(X) requires rendezvous-style synchronization between the call and the accept statement. Synchronization is followed by communication (determined by

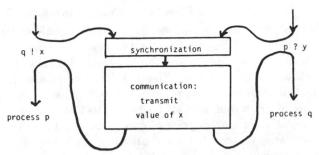

Fig. 1. Rendezvous: Synchronization followed by communication.

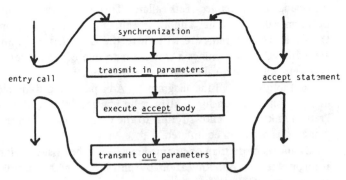

Fig. 2. Ada rendezvous: Remote procedure calls.

task entry parameters) and execution of the body of the **accept** statement (between the do and end keywords). When this has been completed, the calling and called tasks may resume concurrent execution. The body of the **accept** statement could in principle specify an arbitrary computation but should in practice include only computations involving data that are shared between the calling and called tasks, in order to maximize potential concurrency.

Each task entry has an associated entry queue for waiting calls that have not yet been serviced. Tasks impose a serial order of execution on concurrent entry calls that wish to use the computational services it provides. Calls for each entry name are executed in order of arrival, but can be handled only when control in the called task reaches an accept statement for the entry name. We shall see later that scheduling of entry calls may involve nondeterministic choice among alternative entries specified in a select statement, and that the scheduling rules are quite complex. Scheduling of entry calls for a given task cannot be modified by the programmer.

CSP specifies messages by identifiers in input and output commands while Ada specifies messages as parameters of entry calls. The direction of message passing is specified in CSP by the ! and ? symbols occurring in pairs of sending and receiving processes. It is specified in Ada by the binding modes in, out, and in out. The notion of sending and receiving is separated in Ada from the notion of calling and accepting. Thus, in the following example the calling task is a receiving task.

Example 9–A Calling Task which Receives a Message:

```
                    accept REMOVE(M):out MESSAGE);
Q.REMOVE(X);        M := BUFFER;
                    end;
```

```
--Calling task: Does not specify whether message is to be
--sent or received.
--Called task:Specifies message M is to be sent to the calling
--task upon completion of the body of the accept statement.
```

Rendezvous in Ada includes synchronization, communication, and execution of the accept body. in parameters are transmitted before execution of the body, while out parameters are transmitted after execution of the body. Thus the semantics of rendezvous is as shown in Fig. 2.

The calling and called tasks may reside on remote computers with no shared memory that communicate only by message passing. An Ada rendezvous may be viewed as a remote procedure call which is invoked by a message that transmits values of in parameters from the calling to the called task and is terminated by a message that returns values of out parameters to the caller. When there are no in or out parameters the messages become signals that perform synchronization without communication.

In an Ada rendezvous the caller is constrained to wait until execution of the called **accept** statement has been completed. This constraint is stronger than necessary since the caller could resume execution after synchronization and communication of the input parameters to the called procedure. However, delaying the resumption of the caller has the advantage that the caller can rely on the service promised by the accept statement as having been performed. Another advantage is that synchronization for the purpose of returning a result becomes unnecessary because it is part of the original rendezvous.

Server tasks for managing access by concurrent processes to shared resources represent an important use of concurrency. The role of accept statements in a server task is to allow sharing of the procedures that manage the shared resource by its concurrently executing users. For example, a queueing task allows sharing of the APPEND and REMOVE procedures among producers and consumers of queue elements.

An alternative to the sharing of APPEND and REMOVE procedures is to allow each producing and consuming task to directly append and remove queue elements instead of calling the entry in the server task. This would eliminate the overhead of synchronizing with a server task, which may involve a complete context switch, but would still require mutual exclusion when appending or removing elements to the shared queue data structure. There is thus a tradeoff between the convenience and simplicity of centralized resource management and the potentially greater efficiency of distributed resource management. The circumstances under which this optimization can be performed automatically by distributing the responsibility for executing server tasks to their users have been investigated by Haberman and Nassi and are further examined in [15].

Entry calls such as Q.APPEND(X) and Q.REMOVE(X) must specify the task name Q of the called task. The accept statement in the called task need not and cannot name the calling task. This asymmetry of naming between calling and called tasks is similar to that for subprograms. It enables the called module to be written as a library module (server task) without knowledge of the names of its callers. This enables the binding between called modules and their callers to be delayed from the time that programs are written to the time that programs are used. CSP determines a static one-to-one correspondence between calling and called programs that may be modelled by a fixed physical "wiring diagram." Ada permits a dynamic many-to-one relationship that may be realized by providing a "return link" which allows return to the point of call when the rendezvous has been completed.

Ada allows more than one named message to be passed during a single act of communication by entry calls with multiple parameters. CSP also permits more than one named message to be passed in a single input or output command, as in p ? (x,y,z). But all messages in CSP must be either input messages or output messages, since the ? or ! symbol is associated with the complete parameter list rather than with individual parameters.

Both Ada and CSP can perform "pure" synchronization without message passing. Pure synchronization is accomplished in Ada by parameterless entry calls and in CSP by signals such as request ( ), which are syntactically written as nullary functions. Pure synchronization in CSP requires matching signal names in input and output commands. For example, p ? request ( ) in process q can synchronize with q ! request ( ) in process p.

Ada, unlike CSP, also permits communication through shared nonlocal variables. When shared variables are used in Ada it is the programmer's responsibility to ensure that two tasks do not modify the same shared variable simultaneously. Shared variables allow concurrent processes to communicate efficiently provided the architecture supports shared memory, and accessing conflicts are properly handled.

Access variables provide a mechanism in Ada for implicit sharing between a calling task and a called task. If an access variable is passed as a parameter, the calling and called task share the associated value. As in the case of nonlocal variables, it is the programmer's responsibility to ensure that there are no accessing conflicts. Passing of access variables between tasks can cause serious efficiency and security problems, especially in distributed systems, and could be forbidden by language-level restrictions that prevent access from a given process to the address space of another process.

Message passing may be viewed as a restricted form of sharing where only the communication channel is shared. Sharing of channels by processes raises issues relating to communication protocols that parallel those relating to sharing of variables and are beyond the scope of this paper.

While there are a number of important differences between the communication primitives of CSP and Ada, the underlying synchronization mechanisms are similar. In both languages control must reach synchronization points in both tasks before communication can take place. The first of the two tasks to reach its point of synchronization must wait for the second. When both tasks are ready to communicate we say that a *rendezvous* occurs. During the rendezvous the two threads of control temporarily merge while information between the tasks is communicated. Then both tasks resume independent execution.

III. Coroutines, Concurrency, and Interrupts

It is instructive to examine the similarities and differences between coroutines and concurrent processes. Coroutines, like concurrent processes, have a thread of control that can be suspended and later resumed. Transfer of control between coroutines is realized by resume commands which save the current state of the coroutine in a "stateword" so that it can later be resumed at its current point of execution. The use of resume commands in coroutine communication is illustrated in the next example.

Example 10—Coroutine Resume Calls:

```
coroutine P is                 coroutine Q is
  --body of coroutine P          --body of coroutine Q
  ...                            ...
  resume Q;                      resume P;
  ...                            ...
end;                           end;
```

Coroutine control structures in sequential programming permit multiple threads of control but allow only one thread to execute at a time. Coroutines are sometimes referred to as "quasi-parallel processes." Concurrent programs that are constrained to execute on a single processor are like coroutines in that resumption of a given process requires suspension of the currently active process. There are also important differences.

1) Coroutines explicitly name the process to be resumed, while resumption of concurrent processes constrained to run on a single processor is generally determined by a scheduler.

2) Processes may be asynchronously interrupted while coroutines are generally assumed to operate in a synchronous environment. In the absence of asynchronous events, switching among processes could be accomplished entirely by **resume** calls between user processes and the scheduler, and optimizations such as the elimination of critical regions for shared variables could be performed. But the possibility of asynchronous interrupts appears to preclude such optimization. Interrupt messages from remote computers can be just as disruptive as interference from processes that share memory on a given computer.

Concurrent programs are likely to be executed primarily on uniprocessing computers for the near future. Logical concurrency may be realized on such computers in an interleaved serial fashion. The degree to which logical concurrency can be realized by coroutines on a uniprocessor depends on the extent to which serial computations can be shielded from asynchronous interrupts. Further work is required to understand the circumstances under which logical concurrency can be modeled by coroutines.

A rendezvous may be modeled by fork, join, and resume commands between calling and called tasks and an operating system. Calling of a task entry as well as arrival at an accept statement may be modelled by resume commands to the operating system. Rendezvous may be viewed as a concurrent form of coroutine control that requires the operating system to receive resume calls from both a calling and a called task, results in temporary merging (join) of the calling and called tasks for purposes of executing the body of the accept statement, and requires a fork with a resume call in each branch to resume separate concurrent execution of the calling and the called task when the rendezvous has been completed.

The above discussion indicates that rendezvous is a high-level control structure whose modeling in terms of lower-level primitives such as fork, join, and resume is quite complex. Since rendezvous is the basic communication mechanism of both Ada and CSP, we must think of both languages as "high-level" with regard to their communication primitives.

Concurrent programs permit far more complex control structures than sequential programs and require strong structuring mechanisms to manage this complexity. The **cobegin** construct for task initiation and termination and the rendezvous construct for synchronization and communication are examples of such mechanisms. In the next section control structures for nondeterministic selection among alternative courses of action will be considered.

IV. Nondeterminism in CSP and Ada

Nondeterministic control primitives are useful in sequential programming when we do not care about the order in which certain subcomputations are performed. They are useful in concurrent programming when the programmer does not know the order in which concurrent processes will be ready to execute. The examples below introduce the nondeterministic control primitives of both CSP and Ada, and illustrate their differences.

CSP adopts Dijkstra's guarded (nondeterministic) commands as the basic control structure. The two basic commands are alternative commands and repetitive commands.

Example 11 Alternative Command:

[G1 → A1 [] G2 → A2 [] ... [] GN → AN]

--G1,G2,...,GN are called *guards.*
--A guard may contain a Boolean condition followed by an
--input command, and is said to be true if the Boolean con-
--dition is true and the input command is ready.
--The set of true guards Gi determines the set of actions Ai
--eligible for execution.
--This alternative command nondeterministically selects
--one of the eligible actions Ai corresponding to a true
--guard Gi for execution.
--If none of the guards Gi is true then an error occurs and
--the computation is aborted.

The alternative command does not itself introduce concurrency into a computation. But it may be used to map a conceptually concurrent computation onto a single processor by nondeterministic sequential scheduling of its concurrent processes. The conceptually concurrent command [V1: INTEGER; X ? V1 || V2: INTEGER; Y ? V2], which concurrently inputs the values V1 and V2 from the process X and the process Y, can be simulated by a nondeterministic sequential process Z containing an alternative command.

Example 12 – Sequential Simulation of Concurrent Execution:

Z :: [V1,V2: INTEGER; X ? V1 → Y ? V2 [] Y ? V2 →
    X ? V1]

--If both X and Y are ready to communicate, choose either
--alternative arbitrarily.
--If one is ready to communicate choose that alternative.
--If neither X nor Y is ready wait for one to become ready.
--If one or both processes are terminated abort the com-
--putation.

As pointed out by Hoare, the semantics of the above command differs from that of the following command.

Example 13 – Simulation that may Result in Deadlock:

Z :: [V1,V2: INTEGER; true → X ? V1; Y ? V2 [] true →
    Y ? V2; X ? V1]

--Z commits itself to an alternative before testing whether
--processes are ready.
--If it commits itself to the first alternative and the pro-
--cesses Y and X are synchronized with each other so that
--Y must communicate with Z before X does, then a dead-
--lock will occur.

CSP does not permit output commands to appear in guards in order to avoid two-way nondeterminism during rendezvous. Thus, sequential simulation of the process Z :: [X ! 2 || Y ! 3], which outputs the values 2 and 3 to X and Y, cannot be accomplished using the method of Example 12.

The nondeterministic repetitive command is introduced by the symbol *.

Example 14 – Repetitive Command:

*[G1 → A1 [] G2 → A2 [] ... [] GN → AN]

--The * symbol specifies repetitive execution of this state-
--ment until none of the guards Gi are true.
--Behaves like an alternative command at each iteration in
--that an action Ai corresponding to one of the true guards
--is nondeterministically selected for execution.
--When there are no true guards, the repetitive command is
--a no-op, whereas the alternative command causes the com-
--putation to be aborted.

Repetitive commands in CSP can be illustrated by the following process X which copies characters from a process PRODUCE into a local buffer C and then copies the characters out to the process CONSUME.

Example 15 – Copying Characters via One-Element Buffer:

X :: *[C: CHARACTER; PRODUCE ? C → CONSUME ! C]

--PRODUCE ? C inputs a character from PRODUCE into
--the buffer C.
--CONSUME ! C outputs a character from the buffer C to
--CONSUME.

In order to execute this program, PRODUCE and CONSUME must already have been initiated. Input to X and output from

X are handled asymmetrically. The input command PRO-DUCE ? C is a guard which is triggered when PRODUCE executes a command of the form X ! MESSAGE. The output command CONSUME ! C is executed only when the buffer C has been filled by a PRODUCE command and CONSUME is waiting to execute a command of the form X ? MESSAGE. The input guard PRODUCE ? C causes a delay when the process PRODUCE is executing but has not reached the command X ! MESSAGE, and induces termination of the repetitive command when PRODUCE has terminated.

Note that the program *[C: CHARACTER; PRODUCE ? C; CONSUME ! C] is not equivalent to that of Example 15 because termination of PRODUCE causes this program to abort but causes the program of Example 15 to terminate normally.

Ada has conventional control structures for conditional branching and looping, with a special-purpose construct (the select statement) for nondeterministic scheduling of concurrent processes. The statement *[G1 → A1 [] G2 → A2 [] ... [] GN → AN] of CSP is simulated in Ada by a select statement with N guarded accept statements and a terminate alternative.

Example 16—Select Statement with Guarded Accept Statements:

```
loop
  select
    when guard 1 =>
      accept entry 1 do
        critical section 1
      end;
      concurrently executable code for entry 1
  or
    when guard 2 =>
      accept entry 2 do
        critical section 2
      end;
      concurrently executable code for entry 2
  or
  ...
  or
    when guard N
      accept entry N do
        critical section N
      end;
      concurrently executable code for entry N
  or
    terminate;
  end select;
end loop;
```

--First evaluate the N guards determining the true (open)
--alternatives.
--Then evaluate the subset which are both open and ready
--to accept.
--If there are more than one, select among them arbitrarily.
--If there is exactly one open and ready alternative execute
--it.
--Otherwise wait for the first open alternative that becomes
--ready.

--A select statement must have at least one branch that is
--an accept statement; complete syntax is given in Example
--19.

The CSP repetitive command does not require an explicit termination statement since it terminates automatically when all guards are false. Ada requires an explicit terminate alternative with a complex semantics. It is taken only if all tasks dependent on the program unit on which the task containing the terminate alternative depends have either terminated or are waiting at terminate alternatives. The set of dependent tasks of a program unit, which effectively corresponds to the set of potential callers of the given task, is not known at the time the task body is written. But it must be known to the system at execution time. Thus callers of a given task are anonymous only at the user level and not at the system level. However, the set of potential callers is determined at runtime and is known only to the system and not to the user, while the callers of a CSP process must be specified at the time the program is written.

Guards in Ada may contain only Boolean conditions, while CSP guards may also contain input commands. The Ada semantics for a guard followed by an accept statement is similar to the CSP semantics for a Boolean condition followed by an input command, in the sense that both the truth of the Boolean condition and readiness of the accept statement are needed as a precondition for choosing and executing the alternative. However, in CSP an attempt by an input guard to communicate with a terminated process X causes failure of the input guard, while in Ada an accept statement cannot know who will communicate with it and waits hopefully, forever. A wait on an accept can be avoided by embedding the accept in a select having an else clause. In this case, the else clause is chosen for execution whenever rendezvous is not immediately possible.

When more than one alternative is executable then both CSP and Ada may select among these alternatives in an arbitrary manner about which the user cannot make any assumptions. There is no requirement for fairness (a guarantee that each waiting alternative will be selected within a finite time). For example, if the first alternative is always open and ready the selection algorithm could always select it without looking any further, thereby perpetually excluding later alternatives. Issues relating to fairness in Ada are treated formally in [14].

CSP conceptually requires continuous evaluation of both Boolean conditions and input commands appearing in guards until both are ready. However, since the variables in Boolean guards must be local and cannot be changed except by execution of the process itself, Boolean guards need be evaluated just once and input guards corresponding to true Boolean conditions can be polled as in Ada. Ada permits nonlocal variables as well as sharing of local variables by other processes, so that Boolean guards could change their value while a task is waiting for a select alternative. Ada therefore provides a precise specification of when in the execution of a select statement Boolean guards are to be evaluated.

The CSP program of Example 15 may be realized in Ada by the following program unit.

Example 17–Replacing Input Guards By Accept Statements:

```
task body X is
    C: CHARACTER;
begin
    loop
        select
            accept (M: in CHARACTER);
                C := M;
            end;
        or
            terminate;
        end select;
        accept REMOVE(M: out CHARACTER) do
            M := C;
        end;
    end loop;
end X;
```

The CSP program Z :: [V1,V2: INTEGER; X ? V1 → Y ? V2 []
Y ? V2 → X ? V1] of Example 12 may likewise be written in
Ada without guards. In the task body below, the first accept
statement of each alternative acts like a CSP input guard,
while the second acts like a CSP input command in a nonguard
position.

Example 18–Sequential Simulation of Concurrent Execution:

```
task body Z is
    V1,V2: INTEGER;
begin
    select
        accept GETX(X: in INTEGER) do
            V1 := X;
        end;
        accept GETY(Y: in INTEGER) do
            V2 := Y;
        end;
    or
        accept GETY(Y: in INTEGER) do
            V2 := Y;
        end;
        accept GETX(X: in INTEGER) do
            V1 := X;
        end;
    end select;
end Z;
```

The communicating processes X and Y of the CSP example
cannot be directly named in Ada. However, local entry names
GETX and GETY are used to distinguish between tasks whose
value is to be stored in V1 and tasks whose value is to be stored
in V2. The select statement will make an arbitrary choice if
both GETX and GETY are ready to execute, and will choose the
first entry that is ready otherwise. Unlike process Z in Example 13, it does not commit itself to an alternative prematurely.

The concurrent programming primitives of Ada include real-
time primitives not available in CSP. The select statement may
include a delay alternative which is taken if none of the other
alternatives is executed within the specified delay.

Ada has conditional entry calls executed only if the entry
can be immediately handled. It has timed entry calls executed
only if the entry can be handled within a specified delay.

Entry calls are stored in an entry queue associated with each
entry name of the called process and are handled by accept
statements in the order of their occurrence in the entry queue.
Tasks which have a priority are handled so that all tasks with
a higher priority are scheduled before any task of a lower
priority.

The select statement is a specialized notation in Ada permitting nondeterminism in the called task. There is no provision
in Ada for nondeterminism at the point of call. Another restriction is that Boolean guards (when conditions) can precede
only concurrent select alternatives (accept, delay or terminate
statements). Guards are not permitted for alternatives consisting of just sequential code. Alternatives consisting only of
sequential code can be introduced only in an else clause, as
illustrated by the following syntax for select statements:

Example 19–Syntax for Select Statements:

```
selective_wait ::=
    select
        [when condition =>]
            select_alternative
        {or[when condition =>]
            select_alternative}
        [else
            sequence_of_statements]
    end select;

select_alternative ::=
        accept_statement [sequence_of_statements]
    | delay_statement [sequence_of_statements]
    | terminate;
```

The selective wait statement (select statement) has a complex
syntax and an even more complex semantics, with special rules
governing the evaluation and selection of open alternatives,
and the execution of delay, terminate, and else alternatives.

In contrast, the CSP mechanism for nondeterminism is orthogonal to its mechanism for concurrency. The statements
which follow guards can be either sequential or concurrent.
The primary exception to orthogonality is that output guards
are not permitted, thereby ruling out rendezvous between two
nondeterministic commands. Since output guards are not permitted, every rendezvous is guaranteed to be between a process
that is blocked on an output command and a second process
that may have several nondeterministic input command alternatives. Such a rendezvous can be realized by a mechanism
similar to that used by the Ada select statement. Two-way
nondeterminism would require a more complex mechanism to
guarantee rendezvous.

Nondeterminism at the point of call is useful when a set of
tasks must be called and it is not known which of these tasks is
ready for execution. Ada can model nondeterminism at the
point of call by conditional entry calls, which have the following syntax.

Example 20–Syntax of Conditional Entry Calls:

```
conditional_entry_call ::=
    select
        entry_call [sequence_of_statements]
```

```
        else
            sequence_of_statements
        end select;

    --Select entry call if it is ready to execute.
    --Otherwise execute sequence of statements following the
    --else.
```

Conditional entry calls do not directly allow nondeterministic selection among entry calls for alternative tasks. But the effect of nondeterministic selection among alternative tasks may be realized by embedding a conditional entry call in a for statement. For example, notification of all tasks in a task array T that an exception has occurred may be accomplished as follows.

Example 21 – Modeling Nondeterministic Entry Calls:

```
    while not_all_tasks_notified loop
        for I in 1..N loop
            if not_notified (I) then
                select
                    T(I).ENTRY_NAME;
                else
                    null;
                end select;
            end if;
        end loop;
        --delay a while
    end loop;
```

Nondeterminism is achieved by a for loop which selects between an entry call and null while not all tasks are notified. The conditional entry call allows us to skip tasks which have not been notified and are not ready to rendezvous in favor of those which are ready. In this way, blocking on entry calls to tasks which are not ready to rendezvous can be avoided. However, this solution does suffer from busy waiting; the for loop may be traversed an indefinite number of times before a task which is ready to rendezvous may be found. Thus Ada allows two-way nondeterminism to be achieved by two different notations in the calling program and the called program.

As pointed out by Francez and Yemini [7], the asymmetry of the nondeterminism between the calling and called tasks is as important an issue as the asymmetry of naming. Situations where nondeterminism of the caller would be useful include the case when a task wishes to broadcast information to a number of other tasks and there is no information about their readiness to receive the information (conjunctive transmission), such as in Example 21; and the case when a task wishes to call just one of a set of service tasks (say printing tasks) depending on which is first available (disjunctive transmission). In some applications it is natural to include both task calls and accept alternatives in a single select statement. These include pipeline applications where a given task may wish to choose between sending information to its successor or receiving information from its predecessor, depending on which of these tasks is ready.

Francez and Yemini propose a generalized "symmetric" select statement in which both entry calls and accept statements can appear as alternatives.

Example 22 – Symmetric Select Statement:

```
    select
        entry calls
            or
        accept statements
            or
        other alternatives
    end select;
```

The Ada select statement is modeled on server tasks. It does not directly support other "tasking idioms" such as broadcasting and pipelining which require the more flexible form of nondeterminism provided by the above generalized select statement. However, rendezvous between generalized select statements may involve many-to-many matching of alternatives. Rendezvous can no longer be handled by considering the unique called task associated with an entry call. A rule for breaking ties is needed when there is more than one pair of matching statements in a given pair of select statements, or more than one pair of select statements in which there is a match. In the latter case the "transitive closure" of all potentially matching select statements must be considered. These issues are similar to those which arise when output guards are added to CSP and have been addressed, for instance, by Bernstein [2].

V. Bounded Buffer in CSP and Ada

The nondeterminism of guarded commands in CSP and select statements in Ada will be compared using the familiar bounded buffer program as an example. The CSP program includes a declaration of a BUFFER array with a capacity of ten items and of variables IN, OUT. The main loop is a repetitive guarded command to model nondeterministic input of items from an APPEND task and output of items to a REMOVE task.

Example 23 – Bounded Buffer Example in CSP:

```
    X ::
    BUFFER: (0..9) CHARACTER;
    IN, OUT: INTEGER; IN := 0; OUT := 0;
    *[IN < OUT + 10; APPEND?BUFFER(IN mod 10) →
        IN := IN + 1;
    [] OUT < IN; REMOVE ? MORE( ) → REMOVE !
        BUFFER(OUT mod 10); OUT := OUT + 1]
```

OUT = IN corresponds to an empty buffer and inhibits the consuming process. IN = OUT + 10 corresponds to a full buffer and inhibits the producing process. When OUT < IN < OUT + 10 the buffer is neither empty nor full and selection of the alternative in the repetitive command will depend on whether the producer produces before the consumer is ready to consume.

Note that MORE( ) is a signal sent to the buffer process by the consumer to indicate that it is ready to receive further output from the buffer; it is needed due to the absence of output guards in CSP.

The CSP bounded buffer example may be implemented in Ada by a select statement to realize nondeterministic selection of producer or consumer processes, and a loop control structure to implement repetitive execution.

Example 24 – Bounded Buffer Example in Ada:

```
task body X is
    BUFFER: array(0..9) of CHARACTER;
    I,O: INTEGER := 0;
begin
 loop
  select
     when I < O + 10 =>
        accept APPEND (E: in CHARACTER) do
           BUFFER(IN mod 10) := E;
        end;
        I := I + 1;
  or
     when O < I =>
        accept REMOVE(E: out CHARACTER);
           E := BUFFER(OUT mod 10);
        end;
        O := O + 1;
  or
        terminate;
  end select;
 end loop;
end X;
```

This select statement contains two accept alternatives whose guards correspond to the Boolean conditions in the CSP repetitive command. Input and output guards with explicit references to external APPEND and REMOVE processes are replaced in Ada by accept statements for APPEND and REMOVE entries defined as part of the specification of the called task. The APPEND and REMOVE entries of the Ada task are declared in the task specification so that they are known both to the callers of the task and inside the task body.

VI. TASK IDENTIFICATION AND SERIAL BOTTLENECKS

CSP permits the definition of indexed families of processes, while Ada permits the definition of indexed families of entries. Scheduling of a resource among the family of n processes user(1), ..., user(n) can be accomplished by the following CSP program:

Example 25 – Mutual Exclusion with Task Identification:

resource :: *[(i:1..n) user(i) ? request ( ) → user(i) ? release ( )]

This process schedules mutually exclusive execution of code segments between request and release commands of user processes. It accepts a release signal only from the user who executed the immediately preceding request signal.

Since called tasks in Ada cannot name their users, this program cannot easily be simulated in Ada. The following Ada program accepts alternate calls of request and release entries without naming the tasks that request and release the resource.

Example 26 – Anonymous Request and Release:

```
task RESOURCE is
    entry REQUEST;
    entry RELEASE;
end;

task body RESOURCE is
begin
    loop
        accept REQUEST;
        accept RELEASE;
    end loop;
end RESOURCE;
```

This task has the same effect as the previous CSP process provided all its callers always perform request commands before release commands. However, a task that has a release before a request (either inadvertantly or maliciously) could completely disrupt mutually exclusive access to the shared resource.

As pointed out by Welsh and Lister [17], user identities can be reintroduced by the use of families of entries.

Example 27 – Identification by Families of Entries:

```
type ID is new INTEGER range 1..n;

task RESOURCE is
    entry REQUEST(I: in ID);
    entry RELEASE(ID'FIRST..ID'LAST);
        --declaration of family of entries
end;

task body RESOURCE is
    USER: ID;
begin
    loop
        accept REQUEST(I: in ID) do
           USER := I;
        end;
        accept RELEASE(USER);  --USER indexes
           --RELEASE family of entries
    end loop;
end RESOURCE;
```

A user task must supply a task identification when requesting the resource and can release the resource only by calling the RELEASE entry with the same task identifier. This mechanism will detect inadvertent misuse of the resource but not deliberate misuse such as one user usurping the identity of the other. The use of unforgeable identity keys to make malicious disruption of the scheduler harder is further discussed in Welsh and Lister [17].

Yemini [19] has identified another problem with task identification in Ada. Suppose an application requires an array of ten thousand concurrently executing tasks each of which requires independent initializing information. In CSP, a constituent process of an array of processes can access its index into the array, allowing the process to distinguish itself from the other processes in the array and to access initializing information through its array index. This is not possible for an array of Ada tasks. The only way to pass initializing information to individual tasks of a task array is by initializing entry calls to each task, as illustrated by the following example:

Example 28–Serial Bottleneck in Task Initialization:

```
procedure TEN_THOUSAND_TASKS is
    task type PROTOTYPE is
        entry INITIALIZE (I: in INTEGER range 1..10000);
    end;
    task body PROTOTYPE is
        PARAMETER: INTEGER;
    begin
        accept INITIALIZE (I: in INTEGER range 1..10000)
            do
            PARAMETER := I;
        end;
        --concurrent computation using PARAMETER
    end PROTOTYPE;

    T: array (1..10000) of PROTOTYPE;
begin                        --main procedure, create 10000 tasks
    for I in 1..10000 loop
        T(I).INITIALIZE (I);   --serially initialize each task
    end loop;
    --concurrent computation by 10000 initialized tasks
    --exit when all have completed their computation
end TEN_THOUSAND_TASKS;
```

The ten thousand tasks are concurrently created on entry to the main procedure and are immediately suspended at their initialization accept statements. The initializing for loop is a serial bottleneck to concurrent computation that could easily dominate computation time if the context-switching time for rendezvous is large compared with the time to execute the task body. Yemini has shown that there is no way around this serial bottleneck in current Ada and suggests that this makes Ada unsuitable for expressing certain classes of parallel algorithms.

In highly parallel computer architectures with thousands of processors the elimination of serial bottlenecks such as the above may be a critical factor in making computations economic. Yemini proposes an extension of Ada that allows tasks to have parameters and introduces a parloop construct for parallel creation of multiple instances of a task with different parameter values [19]. More research needs to be done on language constructs for highly parallel computer architectures.

VIII. Modules and Interfaces

CSP processes and Ada tasks are modules that export information to their users and are in turn dependent on imported information from other modules for their execution. A CSP process exports its name to processes desiring to communicate with it and must import the names of all processes with which it desires to communicate. Processes are global to the **"cobegin"** command in which they occur. Input and output commands use these names for interprocess communication. CSP variables have types that could be used by a CSP compiler for purposes of type checking. Type declarations for input and output variables could be regarded as part of the process interface.

Processes in CSP cannot share variables and must communicate with each other strictly by message passing. This facilitates the implementation of CSP in a distributed processing environment. However, processes must "share" the names of processes with which they communicate.

Ada has scope rules to determine the textual scope in which a variable is accessed. A given task may export its name, its entry points, and the types of its formal parameters to any task within the scope of its declaration. It need not be aware of the tasks that wish to use it but must be aware of the entry points of other tasks that it wishes to use. The mode and type of formal and actual parameters involved in task communication may be checked at compile time.

Task modules of Ada have the following interface properties.

1) Ada tasks may reference nonlocal variables and thus may communicate both through a shared memory and through message passing. However, the mechanisms for shared variables are orthogonal to those for message passing. By forbidding shared variables we get a set of concurrent processing primitives suitable for distributed processing that is comparable to CSP.

2) The rendezvous mechanism, which is a central feature of the communication interface in both CSP and Ada, has a complex semantics. Its complexity in Ada is further compounded by the many special-purpose features of the Ada select statement.

3) The direction of message passing is determined by the mode of the formal parameter in the entry declaration. It must be compatible with the type of the actual parameter, but need not be explicitly specified at the point of call.

4) Entries have queues associated with them. Requests for rendezvous with the entry are serviced one element at a time in a first-come-first-served order.

5) Ada permits task specifications and task bodies to be separately declared and compiled.

The separation between specifications and bodies of program units is one of the fundamental innovations of Ada. It allows interfaces to be viewed as separate tangible entities that can be separately compiled and manipulated. In order to realize this separation, language designers have carefully partitioned the information in a module into that required by users and that required to implement the resources promised to the user. Study of the partitioning process for tasks provides insight into mechanisms for task communication. For example, the fact that task interfaces consist of entry points with typed parameters indicates that communication by rendezvous is the only mechanism for task communication (global variables aside), and that compatibility of the type and mode of parameters is required during task communication.

The Ada designers used CSP as an important source of ideas in developing the multitasking primitives of Ada, and it is not therefore surprising that Ada has so many features that are similar to CSP. It *is* surprising that there are so many differences. One-way naming is more flexible than two-way naming, as it more readily permits the realization of server and library tasks. The existence of a well-defined task specification separate from the task body encourages an abstract view of tasks whose behavior may be specified separately from its implementation. Replacing the general nondeterministic control primitives of CSP by a special-purpose select statement seems to be a step backwards but was dictated by the fact that general nondeterministic primitives were considered to be beyond the state of the art when Ada was designed.

VIII. PORTS AND ENTRIES

The term "port" is derived from the Latin word "porta" which means "door." It is used in words such as "airport" to designate points at which goods and people can enter a country or a region. Ports in a concurrent processing module are points at which messages can enter and exit the module. Typically ports are typed—only messages of a specified type may be received from or sent to a given port—and they generally provide temporary storage for messages of communicating input and output processes, and queueing facilities for processes which must wait because port facilities become overloaded. Furthermore, since ports can be accessed by more than one process, they provide an extra level of indirection in the naming scheme for communicating processes. Thus, ports allow communication in which processes do not know each other's names.

We show how ports may be used to model concurrent communication in both CSP and Ada. Communication by two-way naming in CSP corresponds to ports which are associated with precisely one sending and one receiving process. Task entries in Ada can be modeled by ports which are owned by the task in which the entry is declared, can be accessed by anonymous calling processes, and require potentially unbounded queues since the number of waiting calling processes in the environment of use cannot be predicted when the task module is specified.

Silberschatz [16] has suggested a modification of CSP that allows port declarations accessible from other processes (like entries of an Ada task). The modified CSP buffer example below has a port B that is used both for input into the buffer and for output from the buffer. (In order to simplify the presentation, we allow output guards in the following examples.)

Example 29—Bounded Buffer Example with Ports:

```
X ::
B: PORT;
BUFFER: (0..9) CHARACTER;
IN, OUT: INTEGER; IN := 0; OUT := 0;
*[IN < OUT + 10; B ? BUFFER(IN mod 10) → IN := IN + 1;
[] OUT < IN; B ! BUFFER(OUT mod 10) →
    OUT := OUT + 1]
```

This example differs from Example 23 in that input and output commands of X refer to the internally declared port B rather than externally declared processes. The port B, like Ada entries, is accessible from other processes.

The example below introduces two port names APPEND and REMOVE for appending and removing items from the buffer.

Example 30—Bounded Buffer Example with APPEND and REMOVE Ports:

```
X ::
APPEND, REMOVE: PORT;
BUFFER: (0..9) CHARACTER;
IN, OUT: INTEGER; IN := 0; OUT := 0;
```

```
*[IN < OUT + 10; APPEND ? BUFFER(IN mod 10) →
    IN := IN + 1;
[] OUT < IN; REMOVE ! BUFFER(OUT mod 10) →
    OUT := OUT + 1]
```

This example has a user interface that is more like Ada than like CSP, but retains CSP guarded commands as its internal control structure. It differs from the Ada bounded buffer task in the following respects.

1) Its interface does not specify the parameter types explicitly in the PORT declaration, but only implicitly in input and output commands in the body of X.

2) It has a repetitive command, while the Ada example has a select statement enclosed in a loop statement.

3) Ada needs an explicit terminate command, while CSP handles termination automatically as part of the nondeterministic control structure.

As a further step in the transition from a CSP-like interface to an Ada-like interface, we can explicitly specify the mode of message passing and the message type in PORT declarations.

Example 31—Explicit Mode and Parameter Type Declarations:

```
APPEND in CHARACTER: PORT;
REMOVE out CHARACTER: PORT;
```

These PORT specifications differ from Ada entry specifications in not specifying a formal parameter name. In Ada one must redundantly specify formal parameter names in both entry specifications and accept statements. In designing a PORT interface for CSP we can choose the level of required specification redundancy. There are advantages to the Ada decision to have PORT interfaces that are syntactically indistinguishable from procedure interfaces, but it should be recognized that this introduces specification redundancy.

This section has illustrated the relation between CSP and Ada interface specification by showing how they can both be modeled in terms of ports. The step-by-step modification of CSP-like ports into Ada-like ports provides some insights into design alternatives for ports in concurrent programming languages. Ada believes in explicit specification of the mode and type of parameters for all ports (entries) of its concurrent processing modules, and in handling such specifications as entities which can be separately compiled. CSP does not separate the interface specification from the body of a concurrent processing module, which is clearly less modular.

IX. MONITORS, TASKS, AND PACKAGES

Monitors were conceived by Brinch Hansen [8] and further developed by Hoare [10] as modules for managing mutually exclusive access to shared concurrently accessible resources. A monitor has a user interface that provides a set of procedures callable by users, a mechanism for sequential scheduling of calls by concurrently executing users, and an internal mechanism for suspending and subsequently reawakening processes initiated by user calls. Our notation is close to that of Brinch Hansen's Distributed Processes (DP) [9], but contains syntactic sugaring designed to increase readability and bring out analogies with Ada. We assume that a monitor is a distributed process with no direct access to nonlocal variables, and that it can communicate with other monitors only by calling procedures declared in those monitors.

A monitor contains declarations of local data, a set of procedures callable by users of the monitor, and some initializing statements.

Example 32—Structure of Monitors:

```
monitor NAME is
    declarations of local data shared by monitor procedures
    declarations of monitor procedures callable by users
    code that implements monitor procedures
begin
    initializing statements
end monitor;
```

At most one procedure of the monitor may be executing at any given time. When a user calls a procedure of the monitor, and there is no other currently executing procedure, the call can be executed immediately. If the monitor is already executing, the calling procedure is placed on a monitor queue from which called procedures are executed in the order of call.

Both monitors and Ada tasks provide the user with a set of callable resources (monitor procedures, task entries) that are serially reusable in the sense that only one procedure or task entry may be executing at a given time. However, the control mechanisms for scheduling monitor calls and task entries are very different. Completion of the monitor call returns the monitor to an "initial state" in which it may execute the next monitor procedure on its input queue. In contrast, completion of an accept statement in a called task is followed by execution of the statements following the accept statement until the task terminates or until another accept statement is encountered. Thus, an entry call can execute only if the task reaches a control point where the entry call is expected. One consequence of this difference is that waiting entry calls for a task are placed on different queues for each entry name while waiting procedure calls on a monitor are all placed on the same queue. Other consequences of this difference will become clear later.

Following Brinch Hansen [9], we permit guarded regions with nondeterministic commands within monitor procedures. Guarded regions are introduced by the keyword when and have a body consisting of a set of guarded statements. They cause a process to be suspended when all guards are false and to be resumed when a guard within the guarded region becomes true.

Example 33—Syntax of Guarded Regions:

```
when B1: S1 [] B2: S2 [] ... [] Bn: Sn end;

--Execute an arbitrary statement Si corresponding to a true
--Bi.
--If no Bi is true suspend and wait until one becomes true.
--Suspended process is placed in a queue associated with
--the guarded region.
```

Monitors containing procedures with guarded regions may be illustrated by a resource scheduler with REQUEST and RELEASE procedures.

Example 34—Monitor for Scheduling Resources:

```
monitor RESOURCE is
    FREE: BOOL;
    procedure REQUEST: when FREE: FREE := FALSE;
        end; end;
    procedure RELEASE: if not FREE: FREE := TRUE;
        end;
begin
    FREE := TRUE;
end;
```

If a REQUEST call occurs while FREE is false then the REQUEST procedure will be suspended until FREE becomes true. Further REQUEST calls (along with the original call) will be placed in a queue associated with the guarded region. Internal queues associated with guarded regions receive priority over the monitor queue containing calls by users. Thus when FREE becomes true following execution of a RELEASE call, suspended REQUEST calls have priority over execution of waiting calls from external procedures on the monitor queue.

The if statement in the RELEASE procedure is a guarded (alternative) command which aborts when RELEASE is executed with FREE = TRUE. Thus an attempt to release a resource before it has been requested leads to a program error.

This monitor, like the Ada task of Example 26, executes REQUEST and RELEASE calls in alternate order and can be used to schedule mutually exclusive access to a shared resource by a group of distributed processes provided that they always execute REQUEST calls before RELEASE calls. The difference in program structure reflects the fact that Ada tasks consist of sequentially executable statements while monitor procedures have no inherent sequential order. Sequential execution of monitor procedures must be realized by explicit scheduling using a nonlocal variable or semaphore, while sequential execution in Ada is inherent in the control structure.

Sequential execution of entry calls is specified more naturally by Ada tasks than within monitors. However, choice among a set of procedures on the basis of which is called first is specified more naturally by monitors. The monitor call mechanism is effectively a select statement with a common queue for all procedures.

It is instructive to compare the effect of nondeterminism in a when statement within a monitor procedure and in a select statement within an Ada task. Both use a similar mechanism for selecting among viable alternatives when they are immediately executable. Both suspend themselves when no alternative can be executed. But monitors can activate a waiting procedure on an external or internal monitor queue when the current thread of control is suspended, while tasks must wait until an external event allows an alternative to be executed.

The ability to suspend and subsequently reactivate monitor procedures cannot be easily simulated in Ada. Tasks have no internal mechanism for initiating a secondary activity when a primary activity has been interrupted. We shall see below that this causes difficulty in implementing a job scheduler which places jobs on a queue when they arrive and reawakens them when it is their turn to execute.

Monitors have no mechanism for associating guards with callable procedures (like the guarded accept statements of Ada). But guarded regions occurring as the first statement of a callable procedure achieve the same effect, as illustrated by the following monitor version of the bounded buffer problem.

Example 35–Monitor Version of Bounded Buffer:

```
monitor X is
    BUFFER: array(0..9) of CHAR;
    IN,OUT: INTEGER;
    procedure APPEND(E: in CHAR);
        when IN < OUT + 10: BUFFER(IN mod 10) := E;
        IN := IN + 1; end;
    end APPEND;
    procedure REMOVE(E: out CHAR);
        when OUT < IN: E := BUFFER(OUT mod 10);
        OUT := OUT + 1; end;
    end REMOVE;
begin
    IN := 0; OUT := 0;
end X;
```

This monitor differs from the Ada bounded buffer program in that the queues for APPEND and REMOVE are associated with internal guarded regions of the monitor rather than with external entry points. If the buffer becomes full (IN = OUT + 10) then calls of APPEND will wait to enter the guarded region of APPEND and will be placed on an internal queue. An incoming REMOVE call frees a place in the buffer and will cause the next APPEND call on the internal APPEND queue to be executed with higher priority than calls on the external queue. Thus entry queues of Ada tasks may be modeled by internal monitor queues associated with guarded regions.

A monitor may be viewed as a concurrently executable Ada package. Whereas tasks consist of a sequence of instructions whose execution determines a thread of control and which terminate when execution is completed, monitors consist of a set of operations (procedures) on a private data structure. Operations of a monitor, like operations of a package, cause the monitor to "wake up," to perform the required operation, and to go back to sleep. Monitor calls must be initiated by a synchronization mechanism such as a rendezvous, and are placed on a queue if the monitor is busy at the time of call. There is a single queue for all operations of the monitor rather than a separate queue for each entry. If an executing operation is suspended because it must synchronize with another process, it is returned to the monitor queue when it is ready to resume execution.

Ada has chosen the procedure model for tasks both in not requiring a called task to know the names of its callers and in requiring a task to consist of a sequence of statements rather than a set of callable operations. Neither the coroutine model nor the package model were chosen although there were concurrent programming languages in which these models were being used. Modeling tasks as a concurrent extension of procedures provides a pleasing consistency. However, there is not enough experience with concurrent programming languages to evaluate the tradeoffs between the procedure model, coroutine

model and package model as a starting point for the design of concurrent processes. It is generally acknowledged that the concurrent programming primitives of Ada are the least well understood and highest risk parts of the language.

Monitors, like Ada packages, may have initializing statements that perform arbitrarily long computations. The shortest-job-next scheduler of Brinch Hansen [9] has initializing statements that form an infinite loop. This loop is executed as a coroutine with REQUEST and RELEASE procedures called by the processes being scheduled.

Example 36–Shortest-Job-Next Scheduler:

```
monitor SCHEDULER is
    --local declarations for scheduler
    procedure REQUEST(WHO,TIME: INTEGER);
        --place process in queue noting value of WHO and
        --TIME
        --suspend and call initializing statements as a coroutine
        --to recompute job with shortest time
        --wake up when job has been scheduled by initializing
        --code
    end REQUEST;
    procedure RELEASE;
        --RELEASE resource
        --so that it can be reallocated by initializing code
    end RELEASE;
begin  --initializing statements
    --Infinite loop activated by REQUEST and RELEASE
    --calls
    --when REQUEST occurs recompute job with shortest
    --TIME
    --when RELEASE occurs schedule job with shortest
    --TIME
end SCHEDULER;
```

The initializing statements are effectively an internal anonymous procedure that is executed as a coroutine with other monitor procedures. However, the mechanism used for transfer of control and synchronization between coroutines within a monitor are guarded regions rather than resume calls. Whereas resume calls name the coroutine to which control is to be transferred, guarded regions rely on system-defined scheduling rather than explicit naming to determine the next executable coroutine when a given coroutine gives up control, and the processes are executed in quasi-parallel mode.

Now that we have seen a monitor with an active initializing computation, let's return to the analogy between packages and monitors. Ada packages are structured like monitors with a local data structure, a set of callable procedures, and initializing statements. Initializing statements in packages may call procedures of the package and may determine an infinite computation. But it would not make sense in a sequential context to perform an infinite computation at the time of package initialization because this would forever prevent execution of other program units.

Concurrency fundamentally alters strategies for specifying flow of control in sequential components of a concurrent computation. Because monitors are executed concurrently with other components, they may have control structures fundamentally different from those appropriate for a sequential package. In particular, the role of initializing statements within a monitor may be much greater than in packages. In our example the initializing statements consist of an infinite loop and provide the glue for cooperative execution of monitor procedures. They provide a common local program unit that may be thought of as dual to the common local data.

The monitor implementation of the shortest job scheduler cannot be directly mapped into Ada because Ada tasks do not support coroutine-like scheduling within a concurrent programming module. The Ada rendezvous provides no way of suspending a task and subsequently resuming it except by synchronization with another task.

Let us try to implement a shortest job scheduler in Ada by a task with the following specification.

Example 37—Task Interface with Request and Release Entries:

```
task SCHEDULER is
   entry REQUEST(WHO,TIME: INTEGER);
   entry RELEASE;
end;
```

The task body corresponding to this specification must contain accept statements for accepting REQUEST and RELEASE calls. A REQUEST call should record its name and time of execution in the REQUEST queue, put itself to sleep, and return control to the calling task when it is reawakened by the scheduler.

Example 38—Desired Body for REQUEST Entry:

```
accept REQUEST(WHO,TIME: INTEGER) do
   --record identity and time of requesting process
   --suspend request call until scheduled
   --return control to calling task when scheduled
end;
```

In deciding when to exit from the accept statement we must choose between two unsatisfactory alternatives.

1) Exit from the accept statement after recording the time and identity of the user. This causes premature resumption of the requesting task before it is scheduled.

2) Remain in the critical section until the request is scheduled. This does not permit RELEASE entry calls or additional REQUEST entry calls to be properly handled.

It appears that there is no way to define a shortest job scheduler in Ada with the above task interface. The task mechanism cannot properly handle entry calls which require synchronization after some initial computation.

The scheduler may be realized by an alternative task specification which replaces the REQUEST entry by the two entries SAVE and ACQUIRE.

Example 39—Alternative Task Specification:

```
type TASK_ID is new INTEGER range 1..n;

task MODIFIED_SCHEDULER is
```

```
   entry SAVE(WHO,TIME: INTEGER);
                          --record identity and time
   entry ACQUIRE(TASK_ID'FIRST..TASK_ID'LAST);
                          --family of entries
   entry RELEASE;
end;
```

It is unreasonable to require a user to call both a SAVE and an ACQUIRE entry. However, we can hide the task in a package with the following specification.

Example 40—Package Specification for Scheduler:

```
package SCHEDULER is
   procedure REQUEST(WHO,TIME: INTEGER);
                          --obtain access to resource
   procedure RELEASE;    --free resource
end;
```

where the procedure REQUEST, hidden in the package body, contains calls to SAVE and ACQUIRE entries of a local scheduler task, say T:

```
procedure REQUEST(WHO,TIME: INTEGER) is
   T.SAVE(WHO,TIME);
                          --call task entry local to package
   T.ACQUIRE(WHO);    --call entry in entry family
end;
```

The package specification allows users to call REQUEST and RELEASE procedures in a manner that is indistinguishable from that required by task entry calls. A call of the REQUEST procedure gives rise to a SAVE entry call followed by an ACQUIRE entry call of a task local to the package body. Control is returned to the caller of REQUEST only after the resource has been acquired. But these details of implementation of REQUEST calls are hidden from the user.

The structure of the body of the task local to the SCHEDULER package is now given.

Example 41—Body of Shortest-Job-Next Scheduler:

```
task body MODIFIED_SCHEDULER is
   FREE: BOOLEAN := TRUE;  --initially resource is free
   NEXT: INTEGER;  --id of task next in line to use
                          --resource
   --declarations for a priority queue and
   --other local declarations
begin
   loop
      select
         accept SAVE(WHO, TIME: INTEGER) do
            --save WHO on priority queue ordered by TIME
            --let NEXT be the id at the head of the queue
         end;
      or
         when FREE => --grant resource to user NEXT
         accept ACQUIRE(NEXT) do
            FREE := FALSE;
         end;
```

```
    or
        when not FREE = >
            accept RELEASE do
                FREE := TRUE;  --free resource
            end;
        end select;
    end loop;
end;
```

This example illustrates that direct simulation of monitors by tasks is not always possible because tasks cannot simulate the coroutine-like protocols of monitors. However, monitor-like behavior can be realized by providing a package interface for monitor procedures and implementing synchronization within procedures by entry calls of a task local to the package body. It is no accident that simulation of package-like behavior of monitors is facilitated by the use of packages. However, the task synchronization mechanism of Ada is not, without the use of package interfaces, flexible enough to allow accept statements to simulate calls of procedures which may suspend themselves during execution.

The package SCHEDULER provides a monitor-like user interface. The package body contains a task that may be executed by package procedures either as a coroutine or concurrently. The mechanisms for synchronization within a package differ from those within a monitor but the user need never know about them.

The synchronization mechanisms for tasks in Ada are at a higher level than semaphores but at a lower level than guarded regions. Task interfaces may be too low-level to be appropriate as user interfaces for server tasks. The present example suggests that packages may be an appropriate user interface for server tasks, and that language mechanisms such as entry calls and accept statements should be hidden from users and encapsulated in the package body.

X. Discussion

The paper by Andrews and Schneider [1] is a worthwhile recent review of concepts and notations for concurrent programming. Our comparative study of concurrent programming primitives is most closely related to the study of Welsch and Lister [17]. They have performed a qualitative and quantitative comparison of CSP, DP, and Ada, concentrating on the issues of task identification, synchronization, and nondeterminism. Roberts *et al.* [15] evaluate Ada in the context of real-time multiprocessor systems and conclude that Ada is somewhat lacking in this regard. Van den Bos [4] provides a critical review of the concurrent programming facilities of Ada. Williamson and Horowitz [18] evaluate several concurrent programming primitives from the perspective of their implementability.

Our review of concurrent programming primitives suggests the following conclusions.

1) The one-way naming mechanism of Ada is more flexible than the two-way naming requirement of CSP because of its support of server tasks with anonymous callers, in spite of the fact that one-way naming complicates task identification and termination.

2) The simplicity and uniformity of CSP guarded commands appears to be preferable to the special-purpose nondeterministic facilities of Ada, but the tradeoffs between the generality of guarded commands and the potentially greater efficiency of select statements are not well understood. An alternative which stops short of general-purpose nondeterminism is the symmetric select statement that accommodates both task calls and accept statements and allows tasking idioms such as broadcasting and pipelining to be realized.

3) The entry call interface of Ada tasks cannot support coroutine-like suspension and resumption of subprocesses within a task. However, packages provide a monitor-like interface to procedures which can simulate suspension and resumption of multiple subprocesses by internal concurrency.

As we gain experience in the development of hardware and software for concurrent programming a number of broad application areas are emerging, each with their own tasking idioms. These include numerical applications, embedded applications, distributed processing applications, and computer networks. Ada was designed primarily for numerical applications and embedded applications for tasks that share memory. Numerical applications generally have static patterns of processes whose initiation and termination may be modeled by cobegin statements, and are concerned with concurrency primarily to achieve faster computation in repetitive structures. Embedded computations model the evolution of systems and organizations, and must allow dynamic task creation and termination.

Distributed and network applications have special requirements that are sufficiently common to be included in general-purpose languages. Primitives for distributed programming languages such as Argus [12] and Plits [6] and for network languages such as Nil [13] have not been considered in this paper. However, a successor to Ada should probably include constructs such as Argus guardians that model nodes of a distributed system and restrict communication to message passing. It should also include more finely grained access control such as selective access to some but not all entries of a task, and dynamic control of access rights by capabilities that may be passed from one module to another, independently of the block structure mechanism for static inheritance of access rights. The development of a comprehensive set of concurrent programming primitives based on a better understanding of tasking idioms is an important topic for further research.

Another class of concurrent applications not mentioned in this paper are those associated with distributed databases. The reader is referred to [3] for a discussion of issues in this area. Message passing with no shared memory and applications involving multiple activities on a shared database should both be supported in concurrent programming languages of the future. Ada allows both message passing and sharing among concurrent processes but does not provide language-level support for database concurrency control.

We hope that this paper will help readers gain a better appreciation of design issues for concurrent programming languages, offer perspectives concerning design decisions in Ada, and provide input to future designs of concurrent programming languages.

ACKNOWLEDGMENT

The authors would like to express their appreciation to D. Taffs and S. Yemini for critical reading of the manuscript.

REFERENCES

[1] G. R. Andrews and F. B. Schneider, "Concepts and notations for concurrent programming," *ACM Comput. Surveys*, June 1983.

[2] A. J. Bernstein, "Output guards and nondeterminism in 'communicating sequential processes,'" *ACM Trans. Programming Languages Syst.*, vol. 2, pp. 234–238, Apr. 1980.

[3] P. A. Bernstein and N. Goodman, "Concurrency control in distributed database systems," *ACM Comput. Surveys*, vol. 13, pp. 185–221, June 1981.

[4] J. van den Bos, "Comments on Ada process communication," *SIGPLAN Notices*, vol. 15, pp. 77–81, June 1980.

[5] U.S. Dep. Defense, "Reference manual for the Ada programming language," MIL-STD 1815A, Feb. 1983.

[6] J. A. Feldman, "High level programming for distributed computing," *Commun. Ass. Comput. Mach.*, vol. 22, pp. 353–368, 1979.

[7] N. Francez and S. Yemini, "A fully abstract and composable inter-task communication construct," IBM T. J. Watson Research Center, Yorktown Heights, NY, Nov. 1982.

[8] P. Brinch Hansen, *Operating System Principles.* Englewood Cliffs, NJ: Prentice-Hall, 1973.

[9] —, "Distributed processes: A concurrent programming concept," *Commun. Ass. Comput. Mach.*, vol. 21, pp. 934–941, 1978.

[10] C.A.R. Hoare, "Monitors: An operating system structuring concept," *Commun. Ass. Comput. Mach.*, vol. 17, pp. 549–557, Oct. 1974.

[11] —, "Communicating sequential processes," *Commun. Ass. Comput. Mach.*, vol. 21, pp. 666–677, Aug. 1978.

[12] B. Liskov, "Guardians and actions: Linguistic support for robust, distributed programs," in *Proc. 9th Ann. ACM Symp. on Principles of Programming Languages*, Albuquerque, NM, Jan. 1982, pp. 7–19.

[13] F. N. Parr and R. E. Strom, "Nil: A high level language for distributed systems programming," IBM T. J. Watson Research Center, Yorktown Heights, NY, Dec. 1982; to be published in the *IBM Syst. J.*

[14] A. Pnueli and W. P. DeRoever, "Rendezvous with Ada—A proof theoretical view," in *Proc. AdaTEC Conf. on Ada*, Arlington, VA, Oct. 1982, pp. 129–137.

[15] E. S. Roberts, A. Evans, R. Morgan, and E. M. Clarke, "Task management in Ada—A critical evaluation for real-time multiprocessors," *Software—Practice and Experience*, vol. 11, pp. 1019–1051, 1981.

[16] A. Silberschatz, "Port directed communication," *Comput. J.*, vol. 24, pp. 78–82, 1981.

[17] J. Welsh and A. Lister, "A comparative study of task communication in Ada," *Software—Practice and Experience*, vol. 11, pp. 257–290, 1981.

[18] R. Williamson and E. Horowitz, "Concurrent communication and synchronization mechanisms," Dep. Comput. Sci., Univ. Southern California, Los Angeles, CA, Tech. Rep., 1982.

[19] S. Yemini, "On the suitability of Ada multitasking for expressing parallel algorithms," in *Proc. AdaTEC Conf. on Ada*, Arlington, VA, Oct. 1982, pp. 91–97.

Peter Wegner was educated in England and taught at the London School of Economics, Penn State, and Cornell prior to his present position at Brown University, Providence, RI. He is the author of six books, including the first book on Ada (Prentice-Hall, 1980) and an edited book *Research Directions in Software Technology* (MIT Press, 1980). His current interests include programming language design, programming methodology, and the use of graphics-based personal computers for education, technology transfer, and knowledge engineering.

Scott A. Smolka received the B.A. and M.A. degrees in mathematics from Boston University, Boston, MA in 1975 and 1977, respectively.

He is currently completing his Ph.D. in computer science at Brown University, Providence, RI. His research interests include the formal semantics of communicating processes and related complexity issues, and the design of concurrent programming languages. In January 1983, he joined the faculty of the Department of Computer Science at the State University of New York at Stony Brook.

SECTION 6

OLD LANGUAGES WITH NEW FACES

FORTRAN77 BY W. BRAINERD

TRUE BASIC BY G. STEWART

BETTERBASIC BY G. M. VOSE

MACINTOSH BASIC BY S. KAMINS

THE RELATIONSHIP BETWEEN COBOL AND
COMPUTER SCIENCE BY B. SHNEIDERMAN

INTRODUCTION

OLD LANGUAGES WITH NEW FACES

One of the features of the programming language community that is often bemoaned is the fact that we cannot move away from our older languages. Despite the development of new and "improved" languages, many computer professionals still continue to use languages developed decades ago. Some people believe this is a very unfortunate thing, as the older languages have meager facilities. They are characterized by poor control structures, weak data structuring facilities, syntactic sloppiness, and semantic ambiguities. So we might ask ourselves, if there are so many negative reasons against using these older languages, why is it that they continue to be used?

One answer is that the labor force knows these languages. It was oberved by Hoare in Section 1 that once a person learns a language he is apt to stay with it as long as he can, getting around its deficiencies as best he can. Another answer is the large base of existing programs written in these languages. Many people must maintain and enhance these programs, and hence don't have the freedom to use another language. Another reason is the fact that these languages have been standardized. This gives a degree of confidence to the development of a programming system that is lacking with the use of newer languages. A further reason is that often the use of a language is mandated by the customer. Thus there are important reasons in the marketplace that favor the continued use of these languages.

In this section we address the issue of whether these older languages can be modernized. Surely we have learned a great deal about the proper design of programming languages. But can a language that was developed twenty or thirty years ago be brought up to date?

The first article is on FORTRAN77. FORTRAN was first standardized in 1966. This was done by the American National Standards Institute, ANSI for short. Then in 1977 a new revised standard was released. The paper by Brainerd describes many of the features of the new standard and provides motivation concerning why these features were added. I would pay special attention to the section on character strings, arrays, and control structures. All of these areas were well understood by the time this new standard was undertaken. Thus the compromises the committee felt it had to make to be compatible with older versions is informative. The goal of the committee's effort was to preserve the positive features of the language, such as efficient compilation and code execution.

The second paper is actually a *set* of papers on BASIC. Originally developed by Kemeny and Kurtz at Dartmouth, this language received a major impetus with the development of microcomputers. BASIC was the first non-assembly language implemented on a personal computer. In fact the implementation was done by Paul Allen and Bill Gates, the founders of Microsoft Corp. With the explosive growth of microcomputers, BASIC became the language of introduction for many thousands of people. The articles presented here are chosen to show the reader how far BASIC has come. Though it has a negative reputation, it has many recommendable features. In particular when the task is relatively simple, BASIC offers simplicity combined with immediate execution and a built-in editor.

True BASIC is a new version of BASIC contrived by the original developers. Their thesis is that BASIC for microcomputers was mistakenly stunted. Their own version contains better control structures and improved ability to generate graphics. Even recursive procedures are included. The second article describes the product BetterBASIC by Summit Technology. Features such as separate compilation are included. As BASIC is typically interpreted, BetterBASIC is designed for people who want to build larger applications. Explicit declaration of variables is required. Records and pointers have been added to the language. Is this still BASIC? The third BASIC article is Macintosh BASIC. The interesting elements here are the facilities provided for interfacing to the Macintosh windowing system. A new set of control constructs have been added plus a set of functions that permit a program to control the mouse. The traditional BASIC environment has been extended with a significant debugger.

The final article in this section is on COBOL. Personally, I have always felt a little queasy about the fact that computer science departments around the country neglect COBOL, a language extensively used. Certainly anyone believing himself to be a programming language expert cannot be ignorant of COBOL. The article contained here by Shneiderman surveys the contributions of COBOL. Major contributions include: the record structure, explicit file structure definition, separation of data definition and procedures, a general if-then-else statement, and the environment division for specifying machine or compiler dependencies.

FORTRAN 77

WALT BRAINERD

There is a new standard Fortran. The official title is "American National Standard Programming Language Fortran, X3.9-1978," but it is more commonly referred to as "Fortran 77," since its development was completed in 1977. It replaces the Fortran standard designated X3.9-1966. This paper describes many of the features of Fortran 77 and also provides some information about how and why the standard was developed.

Preface

This article was written by the following individuals:

Lloyd Campbell	U. S. Army — BRL
Frank Engel Jr.	Consultant
Thomas Gibson	Bell Telephone Laboratories
Martin Greenfield	Honeywell Information Systems
John Harkins	Texas Instruments Incorporated
Betty Holberton	National Bureau of Standards
Bruce Martin	Brookhaven National Laboratory
James Matheny	Computer Sciences Corporation
J. C. Noll	Bell Telephone Laboratories
Richard Ragan	Control Data Corporation
Charles Sampson	Computer Sciences Corporation
Brian Swain	Shawinigan Engineering Company

The editor was responsible for unifying and coordinating the efforts of the authors and for incorporating the many improvements suggested by the referees.

The authors would like to acknowledge the work of their ANSI X3J3 colleagues, who produced the standard described in this article. Many of them also made suggestions that improved the content or form of this article.

Introduction

A new standard Fortran was approved in April 1978. The official title is "American National Standard Programming Language FORTRAN, X3.9-1978," but it is more commonly referred to as "Fortran 77" because the technical work on the standard was completed in 1977. It replaces the Fortran standard designated X3.9-1966, which will be referred to in this article as 1966 Fortran or "the old standard." Members of the American National Standards Institute (ANSI) technical committee X3J3 that developed the new standard believe the new Fortran language to be a more effective, yet still very efficient, tool for specifying numerical computations.

This paper describes many of the features of Fortran 77 and also provides some information about how and why the standard was developed. Not every feature of Fortran 77 is discussed. Instead, the important features are illustrated with examples so that knowledgeable Fortran programmers can gain an understanding of the general content of the standard.

1. History

For most of its life, Fortran has been the blue collar worker of the programming languages. What Fortran may have lacked in savoire faire and style, it has returned in cost effectiveness. Fortran pioneered the way for the acceptance of higher level languages and for their standardization. Those who have influenced its development have been constantly aware of the underlying theme that the language must remain an efficient tool for producing results.

Fortran standardization dates back to early 1960, when the language had just been selected by industry over Algol as the de facto standard for scientific and engineering work. The major vendors recognized the requirement to provide Fortran compilers in order to compete with IBM. The general strategy was to provide a compiler with the functionality of the 704/709 Fortran but with additional features as a competitive inducement. The effect of added features was two edged: While new features contributed to the development of the language, at the same time they threatened to splinter the language into a myriad of uncontrolled and incompatible dialects. Adding to the problem was the fact that a rigorous definition of the language did not exist, even within IBM.

Fortunately at that time ASA (subsequently to become ANSI, the American National Standards Institute) and BEMA (subsequently to become CBEMA, the Computer and Business Equipment Manufacturing Association) undertook a massive standardization effort in a broad variety of data processing areas. Someone had the daring idea of including languages, and Fortran, Cobol, and Algol were selected as candidates. The ASA X3.4.3 subcommittee (to become the ANSI X3J3 Technical Committee) was formed in May 1962. Two subcommittees were established: One, under the chairmanship of Jack Palmer of IBM, was to provide a draft standard based on Fortran II; the other subcommittee, chaired by Martin Greenfield, was directed to provide a draft based on the then-emerging Fortran IV. Subsequently, the work of the group of Fortran II was set aside in favor of a subset extracted from the work of the Fortran IV group.

In October 1964, the proposed draft standards were published in the *Communications of the ACM* [1]. As the first standards were proposed for a programming language, they severely taxed the editing and approval mechanisms of ASA and BEMA. Until then, draft standards rarely contained more than a page of text, usually including diagrams, such as one for a screw thread. By contrast, the Fortran standard contained 26 pages, not counting appendices, including many tables, lists, and examples. Furthermore, the inability to rigorously check a processor for conformance to the standard was a shattering blow to the approval process. It is little wonder that almost a year and a half elapsed before final approval was obtained in March 1966.

Early in the standardization effort, the European Computer Manufacturers Association (ECMA) submitted a proposed draft of what they felt the full language should contain. Partly because they were separated from the developments in the United States, their proposal fell between the Basic Fortran and the full language. X3.4.3 voted to standardize on only two levels. When Fortran standardization was undertaken by the International Standards Organization (ISO), however, the ASA form and content were chosen as the basis, but the ECMA subset was added as an intermediate level.

Early in 1967, the then-disbanded X3.4.3 was revived to provide authoritative answers to the many questions of clarification which had arisen. One of the many sources of these questions was Betty Holberton of the National Bureau of Standards, who was attempting to produce a Federal standard for Fortran. The clarification process turned out to be more tedious and demanding than the standardization effort itself. Because the standard had been approved, not a single comma could be altered without repeating the same long approval cycle. Interpretations had to be based on a rationale developed from the actual wording that appeared in the standard, regardless of the intent of the original authors. More than three years of meetings were required to produce the two interpretation reports, which were published in *Communications of the ACM* in 1969 [2] and 1971 [3]. The difficulties experienced during this clarification effort have had an impact on the form of the current standard: Those who participated in both efforts took pains to examine every phrase carefully to reduce the possibility of misinterpretation.

By 1968, sufficient extensions had appeared in actual implementations for the Fortran group to appoint someone to study how these extensions could be standardized. Frank Engel was selected to conduct this study. Following his report in January 1969, the committee voted not to reaffirm X3.9-1966 when its review period came up, but to replace it with a revised standard. They further voted that the new standard should be an evolutionary development that would not invalidate programs written in the language of the original standard.

By 1970, it had been decided that, since the standard was supposed to be reviewed and either replaced or reaffirmed by 1971, it would be more productive to abandon further clarification work and devote energy to a revision. It is interesting that the most pessimistic schedule at that time projected that a draft would be available by the end of 1971.

The seven years of effort that culminated in the current standard represented work on several hundred technical proposals from all over the world. The cost of this effort has been estimated to be in excess of two million dollars.

2. The Document

The text of X3.9-1978 is almost six times the size of X3.9-1966. While some very significant language additions are present, the expansion is largely attributable to the effort to make the document more understandable.

The standard Fortran language is described in English, often utilizing technical terms whose definitions apply only to the document X3.9-1978. In the standard, the syntax is described using a simplified BNF-like notation. An appendix contains a formal description of the syntax in the form of "railroad" syntax charts. This formalism is more powerful than BNF in the sense that recursion is not required to express iterative constructs. It is also easier to read and understand than a full, formal description using BNF.

3. Criteria for Development of the Standard

When the standardization effort began, there was the basic question of whether there should be a standard Fortran. There are some disadvantages in having a standard. The presence of a standard implies the pressure of conformance to a static constraint over a long period of time. In a rapidly changing field, such as computer science, this could limit the natural growth and development of the language. An implementor constrained to conform might be prohibited from adding worthwhile extensions, even if motivated to do so. Programs would not be allowed that would require nonstandardized functionality, such as bit manipulation. More seriously, unanticipated requirements could not be satisfied until the many years needed for a new revision had elapsed. The difficulties of specification of a standard could artificially limit the functionality because it might be too difficult or unwieldy to describe the true restrictions. Once a feature is standardized, its life becomes semieternal, even if inclusion of the feature was a mistake. The result is that generally a very conservative posture must be taken in deciding what is to be included. Potentially useful but untested functionality usually is not included in the standard. These penalties must be weighed against the advantages of portability that standardization could provide.

A partial answer to these objections to standardization was worked into the interpretation section of X3.9-1966 and carried forward into X3.9-1978. The standard must be interpreted as "permissive." That is, the standard serves only to specify minimum requirements of the language. For example, a processor may have an extension for nonstandard array processing provided it interprets standard subscripts in the standard-conforming manner. Thus experimental extensions can be available in a standard processor. The processor must be able to interpret standard programs properly, but may also provide interpretation of a nonconforming program. The choice is then available to the programmer to conform or not as the economics dictate. Thus some useful but nonconforming extensions are not precluded.

The main criteria followed by the committee while developing the new standard were:
1. Inclusion of new features whose utility has been proven by actual usage.
2. Inclusion of new features that make programs easier to transport from one processor to another.
3. Minimal increase in the complexity of the language or of processors for the language.

4. Avoidance of features that conflict with X3.9-1966.
5. Elimination of features in the 1966 standard only if there is a clearly demonstrated reason for doing so.
6. Production of a more precise description of the language.

4. Interpretation of the Standard

It was not clear whether the document (X3.9-1966) described a standard-conforming processor or a standard-conforming program. It is made clear in the new standard that it describes programs. The standard is written from the viewpoint of a programmer using the language, and not from that of the implementor of a processor for the language.

A standard-conforming processor is one that accepts all standard-conforming programs and processes them according to the rules of the standard. Thus the specification of a standard-conforming processor must be inferred from the document.

A Permissive Standard

There is no statement in the standard that specifies what a standard-conforming processor must do with a program that does not conform to the standard.

For example, in Section 3.3 of the standard the assertion is made:

"... a statement must not contain more than 1320 characters."

This means that if a programmer writes a longer statement, then the program is not standard conforming. Therefore it may get different treatment on different processors. Some processors may accept the program and some may not. Some may even seem to accept the program, but process it incorrectly. The assertion means only that all standard-conforming processors must accept and process correctly statements up to 1320 characters long. No other inference about a standard-conforming processor should be made from the assertion.

The assertion does not mean that a standard-conforming processor is prohibited from accepting longer statements. Accepting longer statements would be an extension permitted by the standard. The assertion does not mean that a standard-conforming processor must diagnose statements longer than 1320 characters, although it may do so. In summary, the standard is regarded as "permissive" because a standard-conforming processor may allow extensions, even though a standard-conforming program must not use them.

In some places, explicit prohibitions or restrictions are stated, such as the above statement length restriction. Such prohibitions are limitations on what programmers may write in standard-conforming programs. As such they have no more weight in the standard than omitted features. For example, there is no mention anywhere in the standard of double precision integers. Because it is omitted, programmers may not use this feature in standard-conforming programs. A standard-conforming processor may or may not provide the feature or diagnose its use. Thus an explicit prohibition, such as statements longer than 1320 characters, and an omission, such as double precision integers, are equivalent in the standard.

Constraints on Subsets

A major issue of interpretation, not well handled by X3.9-1966, is that of the constraints on subsets. It is self-defeating to standardization to have a "subset" language that is not properly a subset of the full language. It would specify conformance that would not provide portability. However, all of the arguments for extension for the full language also hold for its subset. What would happen if a subset extension were to have the same syntax but a different interpretation from that of the full language? This did occur between X3.9-1966 and X3.10-1966 (Basic Fortran). Because the intrinsic functions for the double precision and complex types of the full language had no such significance in the subset, they were interpreted as external functions when appearing in a subset program. Thus the same program had different meanings in the full and subset languages.

The problem is handled in the new standard by properly constraining the extensions that appear in a subset. If a processor's extension to the subset has the same syntax as the full language, then the interpretation must be the same as that of the full language. A name that is an intrinsic function only in the full language must appear in an EXTERNAL statement if it is used as an external function in a subset program. A somewhat objectionable consequence is that the intrinsics have to some extent a reserved word status in the subset, but the penalty seems small and justified.

5. The Character Data Type

One of the most significant changes in standard Fortran is the addition of a character data type. The character data type replaces the Hollerith data type, one of the most nonportable features of 1966 Fortran. The features included for the manipulation of character data are illustrated with simple examples.

Character constants consist of character strings enclosed in apostrophes; for example,

```
'JOE'
'* :/'
'DON''T'
```

In a character constant, double apostrophes represent a single apostrophe. A character constant may contain any characters capable of being represented in a particular processor; thus the use of characters not in the Fortran character set is standard, but not portable.

Each character variable and array element has a fixed length, given by a specification statement. The following statements specify LINE to be a character

variable of length 80, COL to be a one-dimensional array of elements of default length 1, NAME to be a variable of length 6, INITLS to be a variable of length 2, and B to be a 2 × 4 array of length 6.

```
CHARACTER *80 LINE
CHARACTER COL (80)
CHARACTER *6 NAME, INITLS *2, B (2, 4)
```

Character variables and array elements may be given a value by the execution of an assignment statement.

```
NAME = 'JOAN'
B (2, 2) = LINE
```

Strings that are too long are truncated on the right before assignment and strings that are too short are padded on the right with blanks.

The concatenation operator is two slashes.

```
INITLS = 'JC'
NAME = INITLS // 'NOLL'
```

A substring of a string is indicated by specifying the beginning and ending character positions within the string, separated by a colon and enclosed in parentheses. Substring indicators may be used on either side of the equals sign in an assignment statement.

```
NAME = LINE (11 : 16)
LINE (6 : 6) = '*'
B (2, 3) (N : N + 1) = B (1, 2) (K : K) // 'Q'
```

In the second example, a single character of LINE is replaced without changing the remaining characters. In the last example, only two characters are replaced within the string comprising one array element.

Character strings may be compared using the relational operators. However, the collating sequence is specified only to the extent that the digits must be in order, the letters of the alphabet must be in order, and the character blank must precede both letters and digits. By these rules

'FOUR' .LT. 'FOURTEEN'	is true,
'FOURTEEN' .LT. 'THREE'	is true,
' 9' .GT. '8 '	is false.

Although character relationals may be evaluated using the processor's collating sequence, there are also intrinsic functions for making character comparisons in the ASCII collating sequence.

Character strings may be passed as arguments to functions and subroutines or returned as the value of a function.

```
FUNCTION LST FST (A, B)
CHARACTER LST FST *2, A *(*), B *(*)
LST FST = A (LEN (A) : LEN (A)) // B(1 : 1)
END
```

The intrinsic function LEN has as its value the length of its character string argument. The value of LST FST (A, B) will be the two-character string consisting of the last character in A followed by the first character of B. Dummy arguments must be declared to have either a constant length or a passed length indicated by "*".

Fortran 77 383

There are some restrictions on the use of character data. Character entities may be equivalenced only with other character entities. If a common block contains a character entity, it must contain only character entities. To prevent the requirement of dynamic storage allocation, expressions involving the concatenation of one or more character entities with a "passed" length (*) are prohibited in output lists and as actual arguments. No part of a character string that is being assigned a value by an assignment statement may be a part of the expression on the right side of the equals sign. For example,

```
CHARACTER *2, A, B
EQUIVALENCE (A, B (2 : 2))
A = B
```

is prohibited because the first character of A is also the second character of B. However,

```
B (1 : 1) = B (2 : 2)
```

is allowed.

The intrinsic functions ICHAR and CHAR convert a single character to an integer and vice versa. The intrinsic function INDEX determines if one character string is a substring of another and returns either zero or the starting position of the substring as in the following examples.

```
INDEX ('MONKEY', 'ON') = 2
INDEX ('MONKEY', 'OFF') = 0
INDEX ('BANANA', 'NA') = 3
```

Character strings provide important additional input/output capabilities that will be discussed in Section 9.

6. Arrays

Arrays may have up to seven dimensions. The lower bound for any dimension may be specified to be any integer; if the lower bound is omitted, the default is one.

```
DIMENSION A (2, 3, 3, 2)
REAL B (−5 : 5, 6, 0 : 9)
CHARACTER C (0 : 9, 6) *5
```

In a dummy array declaration, the subscript bounds may be specified by expressions containing integer variables that are in common or are dummy arguments. Also, the last upper bound of the last subscript of a dummy array may be omitted and an asterisk used in its place.

```
SUBROUTINE X (A, M)
COMMON N
REAL A (−M : 0, 2 * M − N), B (N : M, 0 : *)
```

In any array element reference, each subscript must be an integer expression. The expression may contain array elements and function references. Its value must be within the bounds specified for the corresponding dimension in the array declaration.

7. Expressions

Those who have been using a modern Fortran system probably will not be surprised by the descriptions of expressions in the new standard, even though things are quite different than the way they were in the 1966 standard. An example is the inclusion of mixed mode arithmetic.

Expressions may now appear in many places where only a constant, or perhaps a simple form of an expression, could appear formerly. For example, expressions may appear as dimension bounds, as subscripts, as the parameters in a DO statement, and many places in input/output statements, as illustrated in Section 9. For example,

```
REAL N (9)
DO 22 I = 1 + 4 * INT (X ** 2),
+ N (2 + MOD (MAX (N (1), 0), 10))
```

When reading about expressions in the standard, it is important to distinguish between formation (syntax) rules, interpretation (semantic) rules, and evaluation (execution) rules. Formation rules are given in a way that also indicates the interpretation of an expression. For example, the rule that says that the forms of a factor are

(1) primary
(2) primary ** factor

means that a factor is a sequence of one or more primaries separated by the exponentiation operator (**), but also indicates that exponentiations are to be combined from right to left, so that

```
2 ** 3 ** 2
```

has the same meaning as

```
2 ** (3 ** 2)
```

Integer, real, double precision, and complex operands may be mixed in arithmetic expressions, except that double precision and complex operands must not appear in the same expression. The type of the result of each operation is determined only by the type of its two operands. For example,

```
5 / 2 * 4.6
```

is computed by performing first the integer division 5 / 2, then converting the integer result, 2, to type real, and finally multiplying by 4.6 to yield a value of 9.2. On the other hand, since multiplications and divisions are interpreted from left to right, 11.5 is the value of the expression

```
4.6 * 5 / 2
```

Evaluation of Expressions

Although each expression has a unique interpretation, a processor may evaluate an expression by any means that produces a mathematically equivalent result, except where parentheses indicate a required order of evaluation. Thus, if R is real and I is integer, the expression

R * I / 2

may be evaluated as any of the following:

(I * R) / 2
(0.5 * I) * R
(R * I) * 0.5
(R / 2) * I

but must not be evaluated as R * (I / 2) because the mathematical value is different whenever the value of I is an odd number, due to the truncation of integer division.

It is recognized that evaluation of two mathematically equivalent expressions may produce quite different computational results due to rounding error. In a program where this is likely to be a problem, the programmer may control the order of evaluation with the use of parentheses.

Due to the presence of parentheses,

(A + B) + C

could be evaluated as

C + (A + B)

or

(B + A) + C

but not as

A + (B + C)

The processor is given this freedom in the choice of method to evaluate an expression in order to allow sophisticated optimization techniques to be applied. For the same reason, there are several additional rules and restrictions concerning the use and evaluation of expressions. As in 1966 Fortan, a processor need only evaluate a portion of an expression if that is sufficient to determine its value. For example, if, in the evaluation of the logical expression

X .GT. Y .OR. L (Z)

it is determined that X .GT. Y is true, then the logical function L (Z) need not be called. An even stronger statement is made concerning character expressions. Only as much of the character string as is needed in context must be evaluated. For example, for the statements

CHARACTER *2, C1, C2, C3, CF
C1 = C2 // CF (C3)

the function CF does not need to be evaluated because only the first two characters of the expression (the value of C2) will be assigned to C1.

If more than one function reference occurs in a statement, the functions may be evaluated in any order, with two exceptions. These two exceptions are illustrated by the statement

IF (G (F (X))) Y = H (X)

The function F must be evaluated first, because F is an argument of G. The function H is evaluated only after

G is evaluated, because the logical expression in a logical IF statement is evaluated before any portion of the statement that is to be executed conditionally.

Side Effects

Evaluation of a function must not affect the value of any other quantity in a statement. For example, if it is possible for the evaluation of F (I) to affect the value of I, each of the following statements is prohibited.

X = F (I) + I
A (I) = F (I)
WRITE (6, I) F (I)

This prohibition also extends to the value of other functions in the same statement. For example, two references to a random number function within a single statement would be prohibited if, as in most random number functions, the value returned is based on the value generated by the previous reference to the function.

In light of all of these rules and restrictions, a programmer is well advised to follow a very simple suggestion: Do not use functions that have side effects. If side effects are desired, use a subroutine, not a function.

8. Control Statements

The most significant changes in control statements are the addition of the IF-THEN-ELSE construct and the extensions to the DO statement.

The IF-THEN-ELSE Construct

The new block IF, ELSE IF, ELSE, and END IF statements allow a Fortran 77 programmer to specify conditional execution of a block of statements. This will greatly increase the ability of a programmer to write understandable programs. These statements are illustrated by the logical function subprogram PRIME that determines whether its argument is a prime number. In order to keep the example brief, comments are omitted.

```
      LOGICAL FUNCTION PRIME (N)
      IMPLICIT INTEGER (A – Z)
      IF (N .LE. 1) THEN
         PRIME = .FALSE.
      ELSE IF (N .EQ. 2) THEN
         PRIME = .TRUE.
      ELSE IF (MOD (N, 2) .EQ. 0) THEN
         PRIME = .FALSE.
      ELSE
         DO 18 DIVISR = 3, INT (SQRT (REAL (N))), 2
            IF (MOD (N, DIVISR) .EQ. 0) THEN
               PRIME = .FALSE.
               RETURN
            END IF
18       CONTINUE
         PRIME = .TRUE.
      END IF
      END
```

The DO Statement

Many significant changes have been made in the DO

statement and the execution of DO loops. Except for the deletion of extended range, none of these changes conflict with the old standard. However, some implementations of Fortran have extended the DO loop in ways that conflict with the new standard. Thus there are some existing programs that will produce different results if processed according to the new standard. It should be emphasized that these programs do not conform to the 1966 standard.

The new standard permits an optional comma after the statement label in the DO statement; allows an integer, real, or double precision DO variable; and permits the initial, terminal, and incremental values to be any integer, real, or double precision expression, including one which has a negative or zero value. For example,

```
DO 9 J = 10, −10, −2
DO 18, X = K + 1, −7 * ABS (Y + 6.7), −2.2
```

The number of times a DO loop is executed is called the *trip count*. The trip count specified by the statement

```
DO 55 v = e1, e2, e3
```

is

$$\text{MAX (INT ((m2 − m1 + m3) / m3), 0)}$$

where m1, m2, and m3 are the values of expressions e1, e2, and e3, respectively, converted to the type of the DO variable v.

A loop may be executed zero times. For example, the loop

```
    N = 9
    DO 33 I = 5, 1
33      N = N + 1
```

is executed zero times, terminating with N = 2. In 1966 Fortran, a DO statement in which the terminal parameter was less than the initial parameter was not permitted. Many processors extended the standard by permitting this situation and executing the loop once. Some processors executed such a loop zero times. Other processors aborted after diagnosing the condition as a violation.

Programs that were written in expectation of all loops being executed at least once may be converted quite easily to produce the same result on a processor that conforms to the new standard. All DO statements of the form

```
DO label v = e1, e2, e3
```

should be changed to

```
DO label v = e1, MAX (e2, e1), e3
```

The number of times a DO loop is to be executed (the trip count) is determined at the time the DO statement is executed. Although the standard does not specify how DO loops must be implemented, the effect must be as if the incrementation value and terminal value are calculated and saved for use during execution of the DO loop. Entities that appear in the expressions used to calculate these two values may be changed during execution of the loop without affecting the number of times the loop is executed. For example, the loop

```
    N = 3
    INC = 1
    DO 44 I = 1, N, INC + 1
        INC = INC − 1
4       N = N + 1
```

is executed twice terminating with INC = 0 and N = 5.

Upon completion of execution of a DO loop, the DO variable retains a value which is the value it would have had on the next execution of the loop. After the statements

```
    DO 66 J = 1, 8, 2
66      K = J
```

are executed, the values of K and J are 7 and 9, respectively, because J has the value 7 the last time through the loop.

A flowchart describing the execution of a DO loop is shown in Figure 1. Two final examples illustrate the execution of nested DO loops with the same terminal statement. They are the same except for the second DO statement.

```
    L = 99
    N = 0
    DO 10 I = 1, 10
        J = I
        DO 10 K = 1, 5
            L = K
10          N = N + 1
```

After execution of these statements, I = 11, J = 10, K = 6, L = 5, and N = 50.

```
    L = 99
    N = 0
    DO 10 I = 1, 10
        J = I
        DO 10 K = 5, 1
            L = K
10          N = N + 1
```

After execution of these statements, I = 11, J = 10, K = 5, L = 99, and N = 0, because statement 10 is part of the inner loop that is never executed.

9. Input/Output

Input/output features are probably the most difficult to standardize, because they are inherently more difficult to understand and describe than other operations. Also, the implementation of input/output features usually involves interfacing with an operating system, whose nature cannot be specified by a language standard.

The input/output facilities in 1966 Fortran can be illustrated by the following two statements:

```
READ (19, 66) I, A, J
WRITE (11), W, B
```

Fig. 1. DO loop flowchart.

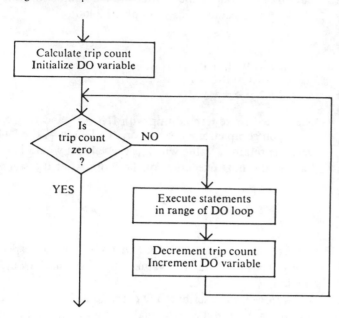

Omission of the format specifier in the WRITE statement indicates unformatted (binary) output.

The new standard allows the programmer to have direct (random) access to a file, to specify a default format, to specify a default unit, to open and close files, to inquire about the status of a file, to treat character strings as files, and to specify actions to be taken in the event of an end-of-file or error condition.

Specifiers

A READ or WRITE statement may contain *specifiers* determine a unit number or internal file, a format number, a record number for direct access, a variable to indicate end-of-file or error conditions, and labels for a branch on an end-of-file or error condition. Because these specifiers begin with a keyword, they may appear in any order within the parenthesized control list of a READ or WRITE statement. For compatibility with the old standard, the keywords UNIT and FMT may be omitted if those specifiers are the first and second ones in the statement, respectively. The following statements have identical interpretations.

```
      READ (10, 66, REC=I+2, IOSTAT=K,
   +     ERR=98, END=99) A
      READ (10, REC=I+2, FMT=66, IOSTAT=K,
   +     END=99, ERR=98) A
      READ (REC=I+2, ERR=98, END=99,
   +     FMT=66, IOSTAT=K, UNIT=10) A
```

List-Directed Input and Output

If an asterisk is used as a format specifier, the format is determined by the data and the processor. This eliminates the requirement for putting input data in certain columns, since the data generally can be written in the form of Fortran constants, separated by commas, blanks, or slashes. List-directed output provides a facility that does not require the programmer to specify the exact form of the output. Examples of list-directed input and output statements are

```
      READ *, A, B
      WRITE (FMT = *, UNIT = 6) (I, A, (I), I = 1, 9)
```

Formats

The format to be used by a READ, WRITE, or PRINT statement may be specified by the label of a FORMAT statement, an integer variable that has been assigned the label of a FORMAT statement, a character expression (including a character constant), or an asterisk. The asterisk specifies list-directed formatting, determined by the input/output list, the processor, and the form of the input data. Some examples follow.

```
      PRINT *, ' AVERAGE:      ', (X + Y) / 2

      WRITE (10, *) ' AVERAGE:      ', (X + Y) / 2

      WRITE (10, 7) ' AVERAGE:      ', (X + Y) /2
    7 FORMAT (A, F7.2)

      CHARACTER FORM *8
      FORM = '(A, F7.2)'
      WRITE (10, FORM) ' AVERAGE:      ', (X + Y) / 2

      WRITE (10, '(A, F7.2)') ' AVERAGE:      ', (X + Y) / 2
```

Internal Files

A character string or an array of character strings may serve as an internal file. This implements the ENCODE and DECODE facilities of some systems, but the programmer will not have to remember which of these is like READ and which one is like WRITE because the one like READ is the READ statement and the one like WRITE is the WRITE statement. A character string or array is used in place of a unit number in a formatted input or output statement.

An interesting example is the use of this feature to read data from a record using a format that depends upon data in the record itself. For example, if the data in the records to be read are

```
I349
I89
F6.7
I217
```

they can be read with the appropriate format using the statements

```
      CHARACTER BUFFER *80
      READ (UNIT = *, '(A80)') BUFFER
      IF (BUFFER (1 : 1) .EQ. 'I') THEN
         READ (UNIT = BUFFER, FMT = '(T2, I3)') I
      ELSE IF (BUFFER (1 : 1) .EQ. 'F') THEN
         READ (UNIT = BUFFER, FMT = '(T2, F3.1)') X
      ELSE
         CALL INP ERR
      END IF
```

In this case, the IF statement checks the first character of the input and selects the statement with the appropriate format and input list variable to read the data from the internal file called BUFFER.

Internal files also can be used to convert character strings to other data types and vice versa.

```
      INTEGER I, J
      CHARACTER A *3, B *7, C
1     READ (A, '(I3)') I
      J = I ** 2
2     WRITE (B, '(I7)') J
3     WRITE (C, '(L1)') X .GT. Y
```

The statement with label 1 converts the character string A to an integer. The statement with label 2 converts the integer J to a seven-character string. The statement with label 3 converts the value of the logical expression X .GT. Y to one of the character strings 'T' or 'F'.

The OPEN Statement

An OPEN statement establishes a connection between a unit number and a file; it also may be used to establish or verify properties of a file. For example,

```
      OPEN (10, NAME = 'JOAN', ACCESS = 'DIRECT')
```

connects a file named 'JOAN' to unit 10 and specifies that the file is to be accessed directly. The statement

```
      OPEN (NAME = 'JOAN', STATUS = 'OLD',
     +     UNIT = 10, ERR = 99)
```

has the same effect, plus a check to determine if JOAN is an old (existing) file. If it is not, a branch to label 99 will be made.

The OPEN specifiers are

UNIT=	unit
FILE=	file name
STATUS=	'OLD'
	'NEW'
	'SCRATCH'
	'UNKNOWN'
ACCESS=	'SEQUENTIAL'
	'DIRECT'
FORM=	'FORMATTED'
	'UNFORMATTED'
RECL=	length of records in a direct access file
BLANK=	'NULL' ignore blanks in input data
	'ZERO' treat blanks as zeros
ERR=	label
IOSTAT=	integer variable whose value indicates end-of-file or error

It is anticipated that many systems will enlarge the number of OPEN specifiers; by example, the standard has indicated the general form for these specifiers.

A sample CLOSE statement is

```
      CLOSE (10, STATUS = 'KEEP', ERR = 99)
```

The specifier STATUS = 'DELETE' may also be given to instruct the processor not to keep the file.

The INQUIRE Statement

The INQUIRE statement permits determination of properties of a file during program execution.

```
      LOGICAL JO XIST
      CHARACTER JO DRCT *10
      INQUIRE (NAME = 'JO', EXIST = JO XIST,
     +     DIRECT = JO DRCT)
C     JO XIST IS SET TO .TRUE. IF 'JO' EXISTS
C     JO DRCT IS SET TO 'YES' IF 'JO' MAY BE ACCESSED
C        DIRECTLY
      IF (JO XIST .AND. JO DRCT .EQ. 'YES') THEN
C        GOOD JO
         ...
      ELSE
C        NO JO, OR DIRECT ACCESS NOT PERMITTED ON JO
         ...
      END IF
```

The file being inquired about is determined by either a UNIT= or a FILE= specifier. The remaining specifiers may be given to indicate the disposition of the results of the inquiry.

EXIST=	logical	indicates whether file exists
OPENED=	logical	indicates whether file is open
NUMBER=	integer	gives unit number, if open
NAMED=	logical	indicates whether file is named
NAME=	character	gives name, if named
ACCESS=	character	gives type of access, if open
SEQUENTIAL=	character	can file be accessed directly
DIRECT=	character	can file be accessed sequentially
FORM=	character	is 'FORMATTED' or 'UNFORMATTED'
FORMATTED=	character	can file be formatted
UNFORMATTED=	character	can file be unformatted
BLANK=	character	indicates interpretation of zeros
ERR=	label	branch is taken on error
RECL=	integer	gives record length
NEXTREC=	integer	gives number of next record
IOSTAT=	integer	indicates type of error, if any

Edit Descriptors

For formatted input/output, several new *edit descriptors* have been added.

Iw.m	at least m digits produced
Ew.dEe	exactly e digits in exponent
Aw	character data
A	character data using length of entity for w
Tc	tab to column c
TLc	tab left c columns
TRc	tab right c columns
:	terminate I/O if no more items in I/O list
S, SP, SS	plus sign is optional, printed, suppressed
BN, BZ	ignore blanks, treat blanks as zeros

10. The Parameter Statement

The PARAMETER statement provides the means of giving a name to a constant. Once a parameter name has been given a value, it may be used in expressions in any way that a variable name may be used. It also may be used in specification and DATA statements. Some uses of parameters are illustrated by the following statements. The new optional PROGRAM statement is shown also.

```
      PROGRAM XAMPL P
      CHARACTER BLANK
      PARAMETER (
+        LENGTH = 80,
+        N = 9,
+        N ROWS = 4 * N + 1,
+        N COLS = N * N - 2 * N,
+        N ENTRY = N ROWS * N COLS,
+        BLANK = ' ')
      IMPLICIT CHARACTER * (LENGTH) (C)
      DIMENSION C ARRAY (N ROWS, N COLS)
      COMPLEX I, ONE I
      LOGICAL TRUE, FALSE
      CHARACTER MSG *(*)
      PARAMETER (
+        I = (0.0, 1.0),
+        ONE I = I + I,
+        ERR LIM = 1.0E-5,
+        TRUE = .TRUE.,
+        FALSE = .FALSE.,
+        MSG = 'INPUT ERROR')
      LOGICAL CNVRGD
      DATA C ARRAY / N ENTRY * BLANK /
      ...
      IF (X .LT. 0) PRINT *, MSG
      IF (REL DIF (X, OLD X) .LT. ERR LIM)
+        CNVRGD = TRUE
```

11. Subprograms

In the area of subprograms, the major changes involve generic functions, the alternate return, and the ENTRY, INTRINSIC, and SAVE statements.

The ENTRY Statement

The ENTRY statement allows any executable statement in a function or subroutine subprogram to be the first statement executed when the subprogram is called. An ENTRY name in a function subprogram is associated with the function name as if the two were equivalenced. Thus, assuming the names are the same type, assigning one a value also assigns the other the same value.

The SAVE Statement

The SAVE statement is a specification statement that provides the means for saving the values of local variables, local arrays, and named common blocks between calls to a subroutine or function. This facility is illustrated in the following portion of a random number generating function with an entry to initialize the integer seed used to generate the real random number.

```
      SUBROUTINE RANDOM (X)
      INTEGER SEED
      SAVE SEED
      X = ... SEED ...
      SEED = ... SEED ...
      RETURN
C
      ENTRY SET (N)
      SEED = N
      END
```

Under the 1966 standard, a processor was not re-quired to save the value of the local variable SEED between successive calls to the subroutine. This is discussed in more detail in Section 12.

Intrinsic Functions

All functions that were classified as either basic external or intrinsic in 1966 Fortran are classified as intrinsic in Fortran 77. Many of the intrinsic functions have generic names and allow more than one argument type. For example, the argument of the generic functions SIN and SQRT may be type real, double precision, or complex, and the argument of the generic function ABS may be type integer, real, double precision, or complex; the value of the function will be the same as the type of the argument. There are four type conversion generic functions, INT, REAL, DBLE, and CMPLX, whose arguments may be integer, real, double precision, or complex. The argument will be converted, if necessary, to the type indicated by the name of the function.

The new INTRINSIC statement must be used to name intrinsic functions that are passed as arguments. If a processor extends the standard by allowing additional intrinsic functions, programmers may list the names of those intrinsic functions in an INTRINSIC statement. Then, if the program is moved to a processor that does not provide the same intrinsic functions, a helpful diagnostic message may be given.

The EXTERNAL statement is used to name user-defined functions and subroutines that will be passed as arguments. It also may be used to indicate that user-defined functions are to be used rather than intrinsic functions having the same name. Putting all external procedures used by a program unit in an EXTERNAL statement provides insurance against having those procedures interpreted as intrinsic functions by a system that implements other intrinsic functions in addition to those specified in the standard.

Alternate Returns

The syntax and semantics of the ALTERNATE RETURN are illustrated by the following example.

```
      CALL SR (I, *427, J, *639)
305   CONTINUE
      ...
      END
      SUBROUTINE SR (ID, *, JD, *)
      READ *, K
      L = K + ID + JD
      RETURN L
      END
```

If L = 1, control is returned to the statement with label 427 in the calling program; if L = 2, control is returned to the statement with label 639 in the calling program; otherwise, control is returned to the CONTINUE statement with label 305 after the CALL statement in the calling program.

12. Features that Enhance Portability

As stated in Section 1.1 of the standard, its purpose is "to promote portability of Fortran programs for use on a variety of data processing systems." Several of the new features in Fortran 77 were added primarily to make it less difficult to adapt a carefully written standard-conforming program for use on many computer systems of different architecture. The replacement of the Hollerith data type with the character data type is perhaps the most noticeable example of such a change.

Some features added primarily for other reasons will also aid in the problem of transporting programs. A continual effort was made to avoid putting into the standard any features that would not be portable.

The effects of some of these features on portability are illustrated by contrasting examples of programs written to conform to the old and to the new standards.

Precision

Because Fortran is implemented on a wide variety of computers with different word lengths, it is often necessary to alter the program to perform the computation in double precision in order to obtain the desired precision. Even when the program has been written in a stylistic fashion to minimize the alteration effort, many areas of the program can be affected. Data statements are often greatly affected.

Suppose the following 1966 standard program segment is to be converted so that all real variables become double precision.

```
C-----1966 FORTRAN
      REAL
     +    PI, X (3)
      DATA PI, X (1), X (2), X (3)
     +    / 3.14159, 3 * 0.0 /
```

This is done by changing the declaration and the constants in the data statement.

```
      DOUBLE PRECISION
     +    PI, X (3)
      DATA PI, X (1), X (2), X (3)
     +    / 3.14159265359D0, 3 * 0.0D0 /
```

Under the new standard, the original program can be written as

```
C-----FORTRAN 77
      REAL
     +    PI, X (3)
      DATA PI, X
     +    / 3.14159265359, 3 * 0.0 /
```

because an array name may appear in a data statement and a constant may have more digits than the processor will retain as a real value. This program may be converted to double precision by simply replacing the word REAL with DOUBLE PRECISION. The constants in the data statement will be converted to the type of the variable PI and the array X.

When converting precision, functions are even more troublesome than variables. For example, under the 1966 standard, SQRT (X) is an illegal expression when X is double precision, because SQRT required a real argument. Consider the following 1966 standard program.

```
C-----1966 FORTRAN
      REAL
     +    FUNCTION F (X)
      REAL
     +    X, SIN, COS, SQRT
      F = SIN (X) − SQRT (1.0 − COS (X) ** 2)
      RETURN
      END
```

The type statements simply confirm the type to be real and do not affect the meaning of the intrinsic functions.

Perhaps the easiest way to convert this function to double precision under the old standard was to introduce additional statements that cause the intrinsic function names to become the names of statement functions.

```
C-----1966 FORTRAN
      DOUBLE PRECISION
     +    FUNCTION F (X)
      DOUBLE PRECISION
     +    X, SIN, COS, SQRT
C-----STATEMENT FUNCTIONS
      SIN (X) = DSIN (X)
      COS (X) = DCOS (X)
      SQRT (X) − DSQRT (X)
      F = SIN (X) − SQRT (1.0D0 − COS (X) ** 2)
      RETURN
      END
```

A program that conforms to the new standard is:

```
C-----FORTRAN 77
      FUNCTION F (X)
      REAL
     +    F, X
C-----GENERIC FUNCTIONS SIN, COS, SQRT
      F = SIN (X) − SQRT (1.0 − COS (X) **2)
      END
```

In the new standard, the function may be typed in a type statement, generic functions may accept arguments of more than one type, and there is no need for a RETURN statement. This function subprogram can be converted to double precision by replacing REAL with DOUBLE PRECISION in the type statement. This changes the type of the function name F, as well as the dummy argument X. The intrinsic functions SIN, COS, and SQRT, are generic functions, whose types are determined by their arguments. The function subprogram could be converted easily to complex type in similar manner.

Additions to the formatting capability also make it easier to change precision when transporting a program. In the 1966 standard, the F format edit descriptor was available only for real values and not double precision values. If the edit descriptor were changed to the D edit descriptor for printing, the field width and line length might not accommodate the number of characters and the exponential notation might be inappropriate for the user of the output data. If the double precision values were assigned to real variables by assignment statements, the printed values might be affected by the truncation from double to real assignment and the roundoff for printing might occur beyond the precision of the internal value.

In Fortran 77, the F, E, D, and G edit descriptors are available for use with either real or double precision values, eliminating the necessity to change the format when changing the precision.

Unit Numbers

Input/output unit numbers are not the same on all Fortran processors. In the 1966 standard, to ease the process of changing these numbers, assignment statements could be included in the main program as the first executable statements. However, the first executable statement may not appear until well into the program, after the specification statements, DATA statements, and statement functions.

```
C-----1966 FORTRAN
      INTEGER INPUT, OUTPUT, SCRTCH
C-----FIRST EXECUTABLE STATEMENTS
      INPUT = 5
      OUTPUT = 6
      SCRTCH = 9
      READ (INPUT, 1) A, B
1     FORMAT (2 F6.2)
      WRITE (OUTPUT, 2) A, B
2     FORMAT (1X, 2 (F6.2, 3X))
      WRITE (SCRTCH) A, B
```

In the new standard, the PARAMETER statement may be used to assign constant unit numbers and READ and PRINT statements may be used without unit numbers. Also, the program can be made briefer by including the format within the READ and PRINT statements.

```
C-----FORTRAN 77
      INTEGER SCRTCH
      PARAMETER (SCRTCH = 9)
      READ '(2 F6.2)', A, B
      PRINT '(T2, 2 (F6.2, 3X))', A, B
      WRITE (SCRTCH) A, B
```

Changing Formats

It may be necessary to change input/output formats when transporting programs. For example, it may be necessary to adapt a program to a different printer line length. This can be done in several ways that were not available in the 1966 standard.

1. A number of FORMAT statements covering the necessary edit changes to accommodate the various lengths can be written in the same program unit and one selected at execution time with the use of an ASSIGN statement that designates the FORMAT statement number.
2. The format specification may be in a DATA statement as a character constant.
3. The format specification may be created in a character expression and modified during the execution of the program.

4. The PARAMETER statement may be used to supply a character value to a DATA statement or a character expression.

In the following example, the number of F formats per line is calculated based on the line length LIN LEN and the field width WIDTH. The correct format is assigned as the value of the character variable FORM after the character variables C WIDTH and C FELDS have been set by means of WRITE statements using internal files.

```
      INTEGER FIELDS, WIDTH
      PARAMETER ( LIN LEN = 132, WIDTH = 10,
     +      FIELDS = (LIN LEN - 1) / WIDTH )
      CHARACTER C WIDTH *2, C FELDS *2, FORM *12
C-----CONVERT WIDTH AND FIELDS TO CHARACTERS
C     USING INTERNAL FILES
      WRITE (C WIDTH, '(I2)') WIDTH
      WRITE (C FELDS, '(I2)') FIELDS
      FORM = '(T2,' // C FELDS // 'F' // C WIDTH // '.1)'
C-----IN THIS CASE, FORM = '(T2,13F10.1)'
C-----IF LIN LEN WERE 120, FORM = '(T2,11F10.1)'
```

Interchange of Data

Several formatting facilities in the new standard were added to give the programmer greater control over the form of the output and the interpretation of input data. In many cases, this will permit the Fortran programmer to produce output that can be used by other programs, written in Fortran or other languages. The following facilities are available in Fortran 77.

1. The SS edit descriptor may be used to suppress optional plus signs in output.
2. The F, E, D, and G edit descriptors may be used for real and double precision values.
3. The number of digits in the exponent field of real and double precision values may be controlled by the use of the Ew.dEe edit descriptor.
4. The form of the output and the interpretation of input may be controlled by the use of the T, TL, and TR tabbing edit descriptors.
5. Blanks in input data may be ignored by using the BLANK = 'NULL' specifier in the OPEN statement or the BN edit descriptor.
6. Data may be edited in an internal file (character string) prior to output or following input.

The following example illustrates two ways to print real numbers without a decimal point.

```
      CHARACTER LINE *15, BLANK *1
      PARAMETER ( BLANK = ' ' )
      A = .0023
      B = .0421
      C = .0008
      PRINT '(T2, 3 F5.4)', A, B, C
C-----   .0023.0421.0008
      PRINT '(T2, 3 (F5.4, TL5, ' ', TR4))', A, B, C
C-----   0023 0421 0008
      WRITE (LINE, '(T2, 3 F5.4)') A, B, C
      DO 5 I = 2, 12, 5
5        LINE (I : I) = BLANK
      PRINT '(A)', LINE
C-----   0023 0421 0008
```

Saving Values Between Subroutine Calls

Contrary to what many Fortran programmers have learned to expect from their processors, there is no requirement in either the old standard or the new standard to retain values of local variables in subprograms between executions of the subprogram. Also, values in common blocks will not be saved in some cases. Nonstandard programs that were written relying on local variables being saved would not execute correctly on some processors.

A program that conformed to the 1966 standard and saved local variables was quite complicated. Suppose, for example, a variable KOUNT in subroutine S is to be 0 initially and increased by 1 each time the subroutine is executed. In order to conform to the 1966 standard, a common block had to be created. But entities in common blocks had to be initialized in a block data subprogram or an assignment statement in the main program. This is illustrated in the following program statements.

```
C-----1966 FORTRAN
      BLOCK DATA
      COMMON / SK / KOUNT
      DATA KOUNT / 0 /
      END

C ------------------------------------------------------
C-----MAIN PROGRAM
      COMMON / SK / KOUNT
      ...
      CALL S
      ...
      END
C ------------------------------------------------------
      SUBROUTINE S
      COMMON / SK / KOUNT
      KOUNT = KOUNT + 1
      ...
      END
```

The SAVE statement allows a much simpler Fortran 77 program. Note also that it would be very simple to change the type of the variable KOUNT if necessary.

```
C-----FORTRAN 77
      PROGRAM XAMPL S
      ...
      CALL S
      ...
      END
C ------------------------------------------------------
      SUBROUTINE S
C     THE NEXT STATEMENT CAUSES KOUNT TO BE SAVED
C        BETWEEN CALLS
      SAVE KOUNT
      DATA KOUNT / 0 /
      KOUNT = KOUNT + 1
      ...
      END
```

Intrinsic and External Functions

In the new standard it is recognized that a Fortran processor may extend the language both in statement constructs and intrinsic functions and subroutines. Because most programs are written and used on a single Fortran processor these extensions become, to the user, part of the Fortran language. However, if a Fortran program is prepared for use on another system, a name selected for an external procedure may conflict with the same name assigned by that processor as an extension to the intrinsic function table. To guard against this occurrence, each function used as an intrinsic function in a program unit can be placed in an INTRINSIC statement in that program unit and each external procedure can be placed in an EXTERNAL statement.

```
      INTRINSIC CDSIN, CDCOS
      EXTERNAL QSIN
```

If a program containing these statements is run on a processor that has a QSIN intrinsic, then the external QSIN will be used, not the intrinsic. If intrinsic functions CDSIN and CDCOS are not available, a diagnostic message may be provided.

These features that have been discussed assist in the writing of transportable programs. There has been no attempt to enumerate all the things that a programmer should not do, but rather to discuss some of the facilities that have been incorporated into Fortran 77 in order to make the task easier.

13. The Subset Language

The new standard Fortran contains, as a part of the standard, a description of a Fortran subset language. Therefore Basic Fortran (ANS X3.10-1966) has been withdrawn.

The Fortran committee realized quite early that the full language would contain many features not needed by a large portion of the user population, including some that might be very difficult to implement on minicomputers. At the same time, it was recognized that compiler technology had advanced quite a bit since 1966. Therefore criteria for the subset were developed which have resulted in a fairly rich Fortran—one which even exceeds the full Fortran language of the 1966 standard in many respects.

The committee originally developed specifications for a full language and two subsets. In 1975, the committee voted to standardize only the smaller subset and the full language. One of the primary reasons for this decision was that the intermediate level language had become very close to the full language.

Criteria for Development of the Subset

In the following paragraphs, the criteria for determining the content of the subset are listed and some examples are given showing how the criteria were applied. The criteria are not all consistent with one another, nor were they intended to be. Most of the work of the committee in defining the subset language involved the resolution of conflicts in the criteria.

Criterion 1. The subset will, in fact, be a subset of the full language.

This criterion can be restated as a desire that programs be "upward compatible." Thus we have the requirement that a subset language program is standard conforming only if its interpretation in the subset language is identical to its interpretation in the full language. This requirement has several effects, including an obligation on any implementor who supplies an extended subset compiler to be certain that the extensions do not conflict with the full language features.

Some of the implications of this criterion are fairly subtle. For example, the function CMPLX is not an intrinsic function in the subset. Any program unit that uses a function named CMPLX and is to conform to the subset standard must have the name CMPLX in an EXTERNAL statement; otherwise, if the same program were run on a processor that implements the full language, CMPLX would be interpreted as the intrinsic function. In short, the interpretation of the program would be different at the subset and at the full level unless the EXTERNAL statement were included.

Criterion 2. The subset will contain the ISO Recommendation R1539 Intermediate Level Fortran.

Based on this requirement, the logical data type is included and up to nine continuation lines must be accepted.

Criterion 3. The subset will include some aspects of those features of the full language which significantly increase the scope of the language.

The outstanding examples of Criterion 3 are the inclusion of a limited character data type and a limited direct access I/O. The character data type facilities include the capabilities of the old Hollerith data type, yet are limited so that a subset implementation may pack character data into words and at the same time begin all character data on a word boundary.

Criterion 4. The elements of the subset will make a minimum demand on primary storage requirements, particularly at execution time.

The restrictions on the character data type are a result of this criterion. Another example is the restriction of arrays to a maximum of three dimensions, rather than seven as in the full language.

Criterion 5. The subset will require a minimum of effort for the development and maintenance of a viable Fortran processor.

Criterion 5 is illustrated by the exclusion of the ENTRY statement, which is expected to be relatively complicated to implement. This is also an example of the conflict between the criteria; many people would argue that the ENTRY statement should be included under Criterion 3. In this case, the committee decided that the needs of Criterion 5 outweighed the benefits of Criterion 3.

Main Features of the Subset

The main features of the subset language are summarized briefly in the following list.

Up to nine continuation lines
Integer, real, logical, and character data types
Arrays up to three dimensions
Arrays with adjustable dimensions and assumed size
Mixed-mode arithmetic expressions
Relational and logical expressions
DIMENSION, EQUIVALENCE, COMMON, Type, IMPLICIT, EXTERNAL, INTRINSIC, and SAVE statements
Named COMMON
DATA statement
Arithmetic, logical, and character assignment statements
ASSIGN statement (including assignment of a FORMAT label)
Unconditional, computed, and assigned GO TO statements
Arithmetic IF, logical IF, block IF, ELSE IF, and ELSE statements
Do statement, including negative incrementation
CONTINUE statement
Sequential and direct access I/O
External and limited internal files
Character constants as formats
End-of-file specifier
READ, WRITE, OPEN, BACKSPACE, REWIND, and ENDFILE statements
FORMAT statement
Apostrophe, H, X, slash, P, BN, BZ, I, F, E, L, and A edit descriptors
STOP, PAUSE, and END statements
PROGRAM, FUNCTION, and SUBROUTINE statements
CALL and RETURN statements
Statement functions
Dummy procedures
SAVE statement

The main features in the full language, but not in the subset, are:

Complex and double precision data types
Substring and concatenation of character data
Nonunity lower bounds for arrays
Real and double precision DO variables
Implied-DO in a DATA statement
Parameter expressions in a DO statement
List-directed formatting
Error, format, and unit specifiers
Run-time formats
Colon, S, T, TL, TR, and G edit descriptors
Generic functions
Character functions
BLOCK DATA subprograms
PARAMETER, CLOSE, INQUIRE, and ENTRY statements

14. Implementation

One of the outstanding characteristics of Fortran is that the language can be compiled easily and efficiently. Fortran is also a language that permits the creation of efficiently executing code. In developing the new standard, the X3J3 committee has been successful in preserving these characteristics.

Many implementations of Fortran now exist. Almost all of them provide many extensions to the language of the 1966 standard. In fact, most current implementations on large computers are closer to the new standard than they are to the old standard.

It is probably true that most implementations include an extension that conflicts with the new standard. An outstanding example of this is the large number of systems that extended the 1966 standard by allowing the terminal parameter to be less than the initial parameter in a DO statement, but executed the DO loop one time, rather than zero times as specified by Fortran 77.

Only a few features in the new standard are not implemented in some form in most Fortran systems. Thus it is possible that the major effort required of implementors will be to modify current systems, rather than to create new ones.

All Fortran systems exist in some processor environment; the range of these environments is extremely great. In developing the new standard, the committee has been very careful not to impact operating systems adversely. However, the standard does impose certain requirements on the operating system of a processor. This is particularly true in the area of input/output, intrinsic functions, and the management of subprograms. Because the standard does not address directly the internal workings of an operating system, the implementor must read the standard very carefully in those areas that relate to the Fortran environment. For example, the description of the OPEN statement does not necessarily bear any relationship to what an OPEN operation means to any particular operating system. The concepts described in the standard, such as connection, preconnection, records, files, and so on, are meant to be general enough to apply to all environments.

In developing the standard, the committee expended considerable effort to eliminate any requirement for dynamic storage allocation or memory management of any kind during execution. One result is the somewhat artificial restriction that a character argument in a subprogram may not be an expression involving concatenation of an operand whose length is not given as a constant in the subprogram. The following subroutine is NOT permitted because it would be impossible to determine at compilation time how long a temporary storage area is needed to hold the value of C // 'X'.

```
SUBROUTINE S (C)
CHARACTER C *(*)
CALL T (C // 'X')
END
```

This type of restriction may be removed as an extension to the standard in an environment where dynamic storage allocation is feasible.

15. Summary

In summary, a compiler for Fortran 77 may be larger than one for the 1966 standard Fortran, but not much larger than most current compilers. The compilation should be almost as efficient as before and the code produced should be almost as efficient, except possibly for some of the new features such as the character data type and some of the new types of input/output. In several cases, such as DO loops (due to deletion of extended range) and IF blocks, it should be possible to generate even more efficient code than before. Furthermore the modest but powerful language extensions should serve to reduce greatly the costs of developing, maintaining, and transporting Fortran software. It is fortunate that these improvements could be made without any significant reduction in the simplicity and efficiency which has made Fortran such a cost-effective workhorse among programming languages.

Received July 1977; revised May 1978

References
1. A programming language for information processing on automatic data processing systems. *Comm. ACM 7*, 10 (Oct. 1964), 591–625.
2. Clarification of Fortran standards—initial progress. *Comm. ACM 12*, 5 (May 1969), 289 294.
3. ANSI Subcommittee X3J3, Clarification of Fortran standards—second report. *Comm. ACM 14*, 10 (Oct. 1971), 628–642.

TRUE BASIC*

GEORGE STEWART

AS FAST as things change in the world at large, things change faster in the world of microcomputers. Computers that cause a hoopla one year are passé the next. New software takes the industry by storm overnight. Companies make and lose fortunes at an unprecedented pace.

BASIC is a rarity amidst all this tumult. Written 20 years ago by John Kemeny and Thomas Kurtz, BASIC has weathered the changes. It's easy to learn, can be used for hundreds of applications, and runs on almost every microcomputer that comes along. It's probably the most popular programming language in the world today.

But over the years, BASIC has undergone changes of its own. As microcomputers developed increasingly greater capabilities, new versions of BASIC were designed to take advantage of them. Often, enhancements were added in such a way that the simplicity of the original language was lost. Moreover, these dialects differ so greatly from one another that once-standard features now vary from one dialect to the next. Such a babble of BASICs exists today that translating a program from one dialect to another is often a frustrating if not impossible task.

LAST YEAR, the original coauthors of BASIC teamed up again to give the language a major overhaul. This time joined by several partners, Kemeny and Kurtz have formed True BASIC Inc. to produce a revamped version of BASIC. Called True BASIC, it retains all the strengths of the original language. At the same time, True BASIC is faster and more powerful, making the most of the capabilities of 16- and 32-bit computers. It contains scores of new features (see "A Closer Look at True BASIC,") that allow structured programming as well as sophisticated graphics, mathematics, and text processing. And most important, the new version promises to be truly portable: any program written in True BASIC will run without modification on any computer equipped with the True BASIC language.

True BASIC is not the first or the only souped-up version of the language, nor will it be the last. Still, it will almost certainly find the same widespread acceptance within the educational community that its precursor did and find a similar response in the general consumer

market as well. To see why, let's look more closely at the strengths that catapulted the original BASIC to such widespread use, the problems that subsequently arose, and the solutions that True BASIC proposes. We'll also visit the offices of True BASIC Inc., housed in a red-brick building just a short walk from the Dartmouth College campus in Hanover, New Hampshire, to talk with BASIC's original coauthors about their latest creation.

BASIC's Start

Kemeny and Kurtz designed BASIC, which stands for Beginner's All-purpose Symbolic Instruction Code, in the mid-1960s as a way to make mainframe computer power accessible to students in the humanities and science and engineering departments at Dartmouth. The two colleagues derived their new language from two high-level languages, FORTRAN and ALGOL. Though sharing some characteristics of these languages, BASIC also had several significant differences from the start that made it easy to learn and use.

First, by using straightforward commands and simple punctuation, BASIC eliminated the need to memorize the complex syntax and vocabulary that other languages required. It also limited the number of statements to a dozen or so and enabled programmers to write compact, concise programs. Moreover, BASIC was interactive, providing beginning programmers with an instant response to lines they typed into the computer. This feature made it simple to debug and modify programs. For instance, in response to a simple error message, programmers could immediately check a faulty line, correct the error, and rerun the program with little trouble.

However, while ease of use is BASIC's chief advantage, it also directly contributes to what has long been a major drawback to the language: the tendency to encourage confusing, inadequately planned, and poorly organized programs. A programmer can start out with a clear concept, then readily expand and modify a program by adding new lines and variables as necessary. As a result, the final program often ends up a hodgepodge that's difficult to follow and debug.

Still, because the language is so easy to learn, BASIC was soon on its way to becoming firmly entrenched in the educational world. John Kemeny cites the reasons for BASIC's predominance in education. "You can grasp the rudiments very quickly," he explains. "Hardly any computer theory is required to get going." His own teaching experience is a case in point: he uses two 45-minute videotapes to introduce his students to the language, after which they're off and running. Thomas Kurtz, now chairman of Dartmouth's graduate program in computer and information science, says, "BASIC is a language in which a small problem can be solved with a small solution, which is certainly not true of Pascal and PL/I." Even a trivial two-line program in BASIC requires quite a few extra lines in most other languages.

In conjunction with designing BASIC, Kemeny and Kurtz set up a timesharing system that allowed dozens of individuals to use the Dartmouth mainframe computer simultaneously, almost as if each had his own desktop computer. In retrospect, the Dartmouth BASIC system clearly previewed the personal computer revolution that was still more than a decade away.

Street BASIC

During the mid-1970s, microcomputers appeared on the scene. Initially of interest to computer hobbyists and data-processing professionals, micros quickly spread to a whole new group of people. Because many buyers of the early microcomputers lacked the technical background or the desire to learn the complex languages that professional programmers used, manufacturers of the early machines needed a language that people without prior training could learn easily.

Thus with the explosion of microcomputers, BASIC took on a life of its own. People could handle almost any application they chose with BASIC, and its compactness lent itself to the smaller memories of microcomputers. Above all, BASIC made it easy for anyone to write the kind of short, interactive programs for which the early machines were so well suited.

But as microcomputers grew more sophisticated, they began to outgrow BASIC. Enhanced graphics, for example, demanded extensions to the language that enabled programmers to display the graphics the newer computers were able to produce. In addition, differences arose in how machines handled strings and variables, keyboard input, and random numbers, as well as in their character-coding systems, the types of arrays they allowed, the degree of precision in numeric calculations, and their memory capacity. As each new machine added more or different capabilities and as BASIC spread from one machine to another, it quickly evolved into scores of dialects. MITS BASIC, Tiny BASIC, SWTP BASIC, Applesoft BASIC, RM BASIC, BAZIC, BASIC-09, Better BASIC, Professional BASIC, Macintosh BASIC, and, of course, Microsoft BASIC are just a few of the names to come along.

What do the originators of BASIC think about the microcomputer descendants of their language? They are nonplussed. Kurtz cites numerous examples of sloppy implementation in the dialects, which he refers to collectively as "street BASIC." Kemeny laments that "features have been added in a screwy way." He points to the graphics-handling features of IBM BASIC as being particularly frustrating and inconsistent.

All these inconsistencies make it very inconvenient to "transport" a BASIC program from one machine to another. In particular, translating graphics often requires that a programmer totally rewrite entire sections of a BASIC program. And anyone who has tinkered with

microcomputer graphics knows the tedious process of counting pixels to determine where a picture or point will appear on the screen.

During the 1970s the American National Standards Institute (ANSI) began work on developing standards for BASIC and published the first standard in 1978. However, the BASIC described in that document was so minimal compared to the expanding capabilities of microcomputers that the industry largely ignored it.

A second, vastly expanded standard is now undergoing final review and is scheduled for publication this year. Thomas Kurtz has been the chairman of the technical draft committee since the beginning. Representatives from almost every major computer manufacturer and many software houses have also served on the committee.

The new standard describes an extremely powerful language consisting of a core plus several optional, special-purpose modules. Rather than being too modest for today's personal computers, the specified language exceeds the capabilities of 8-bit computers and challenges those of 16-bit computers.

The significance of the ANSI standard is potentially far-reaching. State and federal government agencies, public schools, and military branches might eventually require software vendors to certify that their BASIC programs are ANSI-BASIC compatible to one degree or another. Just as important, the standard sets up a common meeting ground for software design, so that duplicate BASIC functions from different vendors might not differ in arbitrary ways, as is so frequently the case now among popular microcomputer BASICs.

Enter True BASIC

While BASIC was mutating wildly in the microcomputer world, Dartmouth BASIC had itself undergone quite a few transformations. Kemeny and Kurtz took no part or profit in the commercial development of BASIC. Instead, they remained at Dartmouth, quietly overseeing a controlled evolution of BASIC in the Dartmouth mainframe computer and developing it into a rich, general-purpose language that in many ways is the prototype of True BASIC.

Probably the most significant improvement to Dartmouth BASIC was the addition of structured programming tools that facilitate programming in a logical, comprehensible manner. A finished program is more readable and thus easier to debug and modify than unstructured programs. In contrast, unstructured versions of BASIC make it awkward to represent logical structures and difficult to recognize them when reading a program. The hallmark of unstructured programs is a liberal use of GOTO statements, which cause program execution to skip backward and forward with no apparent rhyme or reason. Referring to Dartmouth BASIC, Kemeny says, "We haven't allowed students to use GOTOs in their programs for quite a few years now."

A uniform approach to graphics was also added to Dartmouth BASIC. BASIC programmers can plan pictures and graphs without having to know the physical

How True BASIC Works

Unlike most popular dialects of BASIC, True BASIC is a compiled language with special features that give it the convenience of an interpreter along with the performance of a compiler.

In simplified terms, interpreters use your original or source program as the actual operating instructions. But the text of a BASIC program is far removed from what the computer's microprocessor can understand. As a result, an interpreter spends quite a bit of time just figuring out what a command says before it can even begin carrying out the command.

Compilers translate your original program into a "predigested" form, called the compiled program or the object program, that is closer to the language the microprocessor can understand. The object program is fed to the microprocessor by a run-time interpreter (in reality, a reduced-size interpreter), so the computer spends much less time figuring out what each instruction says to do. As a result, compilers execute programs much more efficiently than interpreters do.

However, compilers have traditionally been awkward to work with, requiring numerous steps just to get a program ready to run. First, you must create the source program using a text editor. After compiling it and saving the object file on disk, you run the object program. If the program has errors, you must restart the editor, reload the original source program, recompile it, and so forth.

Interpreters have the advantage of being easy to use. You enter the program, run it, edit it, and run it again, all from the same command level or environment. However, in the usual interpreter BASIC, syntax errors are not caught until the program actually tries to execute the offending line. Quite often a program runs for a long time before finally hitting a syntax error, which voids the entire series of computations.

Because of True BASIC's structure, programmers reap the advantages of both interpreters and compilers: ease of use and speed. After typing in a source program or loading it from disk, you simply type RUN. The compiler takes over, storing the object program in memory rather than on disk. (True BASIC also has commands to save the object program on disk; these saved programs can be executed directly by the True BASIC run-time interpreter.)

The compiler scans through an entire program for syntax errors before converting any of it to object code. If it finds an error, the compiler points it out to you; using True BASIC's text-editing window, you can quickly correct the error and continue the compilation.

After compilation, the True BASIC run-time interpreter takes over automatically and executes the program. Afterward, your original source program is immediately available for further editing. You don't have to reload the editor to make changes in the program; you simply move the cursor into the listing window and start editing.

parameters of the output device. As Kemeny says, "No one counts pixels at Dartmouth anymore."

In contrast to languages in which features have been tacked on indiscriminately, Kemeny says that features have been added carefully and conservatively to Dartmouth BASIC. For instance, the language has one command, PLOT, to handle both points and lines. Its syntax is modeled after that of the versatile PRINT command. If you were drawing a series of points, PLOT X1,Y1 would plot single points, and PLOT X1,Y1; would draw lines connecting the points. If we think of a video display with its electron light beam, the semicolon means "leave the beam on while moving to the next point." Without the semicolon, the command means "turn the beam off while moving to the next point."

Along with his work on developing BASIC, Kemeny served as president of Dartmouth College from 1970 to 1981 and as chairman of the department of mathematics and computer science prior to that. Kurtz directed the Dartmouth Kiewit Computation Center from 1966 to 1975. But neither had the time or desire to personally design and implement a new language.

True BASIC Inc. was formed in August 1983 to do expressly that. Kemeny and Kurtz brought to the company much of the philosophy and technology they had developed during the past 20 years. Kemeny is chairman of the new company, and Kurtz is vice chairman. The pair teamed up with four other computer professionals, three of whom learned programming as student systems programmers in the Kiewit Computation Center.

Chris Walker, True BASIC Inc.'s president, was a project leader specializing in language development and programming prior to the company's founding. He was also closely involved in the development of an ANSI BASIC compiler. David Pearson, vice president of research and development of True BASIC Inc., was chief systems programmer for Dartmouth College and had been involved with efforts to keep Dartmouth BASIC ANSI compatible. Brig Elliott, True BASIC Inc.'s vice president of product development, had been active in software development as a programmer and manager for the past decade. Stewart Chapin, vice president of marketing, brought to the company his experience in applications programming and in developing marketing strategies for clients of a major consulting firm.

Highlights of True BASIC

Economy and simplicity have always been an asset of BASIC. True BASIC maintains that economy and adds a tremendous amount of power to the language. Programmers Pearson and Elliott claim that their product, in addition to its extensive capabilities, will be faster than other microcomputer BASICs, and several demonstration programs that combined graphics with mathematical problem solving seemed to bear this out.

In addition to its speed, True BASIC offers an exceptionally convenient programming environment that features a screen-oriented program editor, an easy-to-use compiler (see "How True BASIC Works" on page 99), and two windows. You can examine a program listing in one window while the program is outputting results to the other window, a very helpful facility for developing programs.

The screen-oriented text editor is specifically designed for use with True BASIC programs. As such, it recognizes many of the functional units of a program—keywords, punctuation, and so forth—and enables you to manipulate them with ease. You can define special key sequences, or macros, that let you quickly enter the structure of commonly used program blocks and perform other functions. For example, pressing CTRL D might produce

```
DO WHILE
. . .
LOOP
```

and position the cursor after WHILE so you can type in the condition.

True BASIC follows the core specifications of the soon-to-be-released ANSI standard with only a few exceptions (deletions, incompatibilities, and extensions). True BASIC programs can also be written for full compliance with the standard. None of the major microcomputer software vendors has attempted to follow the standard as closely as True BASIC does. In particular, Apple's Macintosh BASIC and Microsoft's latest BASIC (GWBASIC) are both largely incompatible with the ANSI standard.

But True BASIC's most noteworthy feature is its portability. Programs written in True BASIC will run on any computer for which True BASIC is available. Even programs that make extensive use of graphics and disk files, usually the downfall of supposedly portable programs written in other versions of BASIC, will run as is on any computer equipped with True BASIC. True BASIC achieves total portability by using the identical compiler for every host machine. Only the run-time interpreter must be customized to each host machine. To get the optimum performance, the run-time interpreter is written in the machine's assembly language, rather than being developed in a high-level language such as C or Pascal.

For programmers, portability means that a program need be written only once—all True BASIC machines will be able to use it automatically. All manufacturers of machines that run True BASIC will benefit equally from software development because every True BASIC program will run on every machine. Publishers will need only a single version of a program or book instead of requiring different versions for each model. (Software publishers will still need to supply programs on different media, however, depending on the storage system used by each machine.)

Bringing True BASIC to Market

Predictably, True BASIC Inc. will focus on the high school and college educational markets. The company has teamed up with Addison-Wesley, an educational publisher specializing in microcomputer textbooks and software, to put the finishing touches on True BASIC and market the language. True BASIC will be available for the IBM PC in December and for the Apple Macintosh early in 1985. Versions for other 16-bit machines are scheduled for release at intervals of about three months; possible target machines include the IBM PCjr, computers from Digital Equipment Corporation, and other computers with at least 128K bytes of random-access memory. True BASIC will sell for $150, certainly a bargain for a 64K-byte program development system. The language will come with a user's guide and a reference manual. At the time of this writing, neither was available, but a preliminary draft of the reference manual is concise and quite readable.

True BASIC Inc. will also produce educational software in conjunction with Addison-Wesley and other publishers. In some instances, the software will consist of a book covering an academic subject, packaged with a floppy disk containing True BASIC programs that demonstrate the subject. For example, an economics package might include programs that demonstrate economics equations; as the student changes the equations, the graph changes on the screen. Such packages, of course, are already available for use with other versions of BASIC. The difference with True BASIC is that one version of the software will work on all computers equipped with True BASIC.

The initial financing of True BASIC Inc. came from a group of private investors. "We explored the idea of going with a venture capital firm, but we found that the firm simply wanted too much control," says Kemeny. The founders insisted on maintaining enough control to develop the language as they envisioned it. "Sure, we want the company to be profitable," says Kemeny, "but we're going to be patient about that."

Apart from anticipating True BASIC's widespread acceptance in the educational market, True BASIC Inc. expects that the language will meet with equal success in the general consumer market as well. Its ease of use, structured programming tools, and standardized graphics should particularly appeal to novice programmers. In addition, experienced programmers who are already proficient with other versions of BASIC will welcome True BASIC's improved capabilities.

Renewed BASIC

Now a professor of mathematics and computer science at Dartmouth, Kemeny will focus on educational applications. Kurtz will monitor developments with respect to the ANSI standard and other areas of language development. The two friends and colleagues are also coauthoring a book exploring the evolution and philosophy of BASIC, entitled *Back to BASIC* (Addison-Wesley, 1984).

Certainly, no one can predict what will come down the pike in the world of microcomputers. The most we can say is that the machines and the programming languages that run them will continue to change. BASIC may not be around forever. But True BASIC should prove to be more than just another quick-fix version of BASIC. An exciting, high-performance addition to personal computing, True BASIC will give the language years of renewed life.

A Closer Look at True BASIC

True BASIC incorporates many new features as well as updating existing features of BASIC. A complete catalog of all these features is beyond the scope of this article, so we'll present highlights of the language in this section. We'll also see how True BASIC's features differ from those in other BASICs.

True BASIC essentially conforms to the ANSI standard. However, it offers options and extensions that the designers feel are improvements over the standard. The examples in this section use these options. Throughout the examples, we capitalize BASIC keywords and leave variables in lowercase letters. The exclamation point used in several examples is True BASIC (and ANSI BASIC) shorthand for REM (remark).

General Features

Line numbers are optional in True BASIC (ANSI BASIC requires them). However, if one line is numbered, all lines must be numbered. Line numbers are the plague of past versions of BASIC: when programs are modified, they must often be renumbered, and the process of referencing line numbers within a program is tedious and error-prone. Furthermore, line number references convey no information; for instance, what does GOSUB 1000 mean?

In True BASIC, variable names can be up to 31 characters long and can include an underscore, permitting the use of phrases such as rate_of_pay. In contrast, most microcomputer versions of BASIC limit variables to two characters. (Longer names can be used, but the extra characters do not make the name unique; rate and rank, for example, count as the same name.)

In most versions of BASIC, programmers are restricted from using keywords as variables. In some versions, scores of words cannot be used as variable names. In True BASIC, only 21 variable names are restricted, thanks to a smarter compiler and the requirement that all assignment statements begin with LET, as in:

```
LET c = 5.5
```

True BASIC also allows multiple assignments, giving one value to a list of variables:

```
LET a,b,c, = 100
```

In True BASIC, strings can be any length up to 32,000 characters. In Microsoft and most other versions of BASIC, strings are limited to 255 characters.

True BASIC's method of representing substrings (portions of strings) is also significantly improved. For instance, given a string name$, the notation name$[a:b] indicates the substring of name$ starting at position a and ending at position b. In Microsoft BASIC, you must use the function MID$(A$,a,b) to represent the substring.

Furthermore, True BASIC uses the same notation to assign data to substrings. The statement

```
LET name$[1:5] = "Jack "
```

stores "Jack" in the first five positions of name$ but leaves the rest of the string unchanged. Many versions of BASIC lack an easy way to perform this operation; some versions require a function call, as in:

LET MID$(name$,1,5) = "Jack "

True BASIC stores numbers with at least 10 digits of precision and performs all mathematical operations with at least that much precision as well. The exact precision depends on the particular computer. A True BASIC program can determine how much precision and range the host machine can handle with two built-in functions: MAXNUM and EPS (short for epsilon). MAXNUM returns the largest value representable by the computer. EPS(n) returns the smallest number that can be added to or subtracted from n to produce a number that is distinct from n. EPS(0) returns the smallest number representable by the computer.

In True BASIC, arrays can have any number of dimensions, and each dimension can have arbitrarily chosen upper and lower bounds. For example,

DIM year(1900 to 1999)

sets up an array of years with a lower bound of 1900 and an upper bound of 1999. Other versions of BASIC require that the lower bound be 0 or 1.

True BASIC includes a full arsenal of array-handling statements. The following statements can be used to load an entire array:

MAT READ	Read data into an array
MAT INPUT	Input data into an array from the keyboard
MAT LINE INPUT	Input a line of data from the keyboard

For printing an array, True BASIC uses these statements:

MAT PRINT	Standard printing
MAT PRINT USING	Formatted printing

True BASIC also includes all standard matrix-transformation functions (determinant, dot product, inverse, transposition, and so forth).

Structured Programming Mechanisms

Do loops. A loop is a block of instructions that a program executes repeatedly. True BASIC's DO loops are new features for BASIC. The number of times a program repeats a DO loop is not necessarily determined until you run the program.

True BASIC offers three variations of DO loops: infinite loops, WHILE loops, and UNTIL loops. An infinite loop takes this form:

```
DO
    . . .
LOOP
```

The statements inside the loop (represented by " . . . ") are executed repeatedly unless an EXIT DO statement ends the loop.

A WHILE loop is conditional:

```
DO WHILE x > 0
    . . .
LOOP
```

Before repeating the loop, the program checks whether x > 0. If the condition is true, the statements inside the loop are executed. Otherwise, execution continues at the statement that follows LOOP.

An UNTIL loop works similarly:

```
DO UNTIL x < = 0
    . . .
LOOP
```

Before each repetition of the loop, the program checks whether x < =0. If the condition is true, the loop ends. Otherwise, the program executes the statements inside the loop.

If you attach UNTIL and WHILE to the bottom of a loop, the condition is checked after the program executes the statements inside the loop:

```
DO
    . . .
LOOP UNTIL x < =0
```

FOR loops. Although FOR loops are not new features in BASIC, unstructured versions of BASIC do not provide any clean way of exiting from a FOR loop. True BASIC has added an EXIT FOR statement that lets the program exit from the middle of a loop. The following program, which gives you 10 chances to guess a number from 1 to 20, illustrates the use of EXIT FOR:

```
! Play Guess My Number
!
LET secret = int (rnd * 20 + 1)
PRINT "I have a secret number."
!
FOR try = 1 TO 10
    PRINT
    PRINT "Guess my number (1-20)";
    INPUT guess
    IF guess = secret THEN EXIT FOR
    PRINT "That's not it."
    PRINT 10-try;"tries left."
NEXT try
!
IF guess = secret THEN PRINT "That's it!"
END
```

If you guess the number correctly, the loop ends immediately (IF guess = secret THEN EXIT FOR).

Conditional Branches

Conditional branches alter the normal sequence in which a program executes statements. True BASIC allows you to set up whole blocks that are executed conditionally.

IF blocks. Single IF statements are common to all versions of BASIC:

IF a = 3 THEN LET d = 0

Many versions of BASIC allow this variation:

IF a = 3 THEN LET d = 0 ELSE PRINT "Ok"

True BASIC, however, allows the much more powerful IF block. To illustrate, let's take the problem of finding the real roots of the quadratic equation $ax^2 + bx + c = 0$. Here's the True BASIC solution, adapted with permission from the forthcoming book *Back to BASIC*:

```
! Quadratic equation
!
PRINT "Coefficients";
INPUT a,b,c
LET d = b*b − 4*a*c
!
IF d>0 THEN
     LET s = sqr(d)
     PRINT "The roots are:"
     PRINT (−b+s)/(2*a)
     PRINT (−b−s)/(2*a)
ELSEIF d = 0 THEN
     PRINT "The root is:"
     PRINT −b/(2*a)
ELSE
     PRINT "No real roots."
END IF
!
END
```

The solution depends on the value of d, which is called the discriminant, and three cases must be considered: $d>0$, $d=0$, and $d<0$. The three cases stand out clearly in the program.

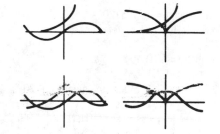

As these sine waves illustrate, you can define multiple windows on screen and assign X and Y coordinates to each

Compare the True BASIC program with this unstructured BASIC program solving the same problem:

```
100  ! Quadratic equation
110  !
200  PRINT "Coefficients";
210  INPUT a,b,c
220  LET d = b*b − 4*a*c
230  IF d < =0 THEN 290
240  LET s = sqr(d)
250  PRINT "The roots are:"
260  PRINT (−b+s)/(2*a)
270  PRINT (−b−s)/(2*a)
280  GOTO 360
290  IF d<0 THEN 330
300  PRINT "The root is:"
310  PRINT −b/(2*a)
320  GOTO 360
330  PRINT "No real roots."
360  END
```

In the unstructured version, it's difficult to see that we are treating three cases or to ascertain exactly what these cases are.

```
rem Finds primes by sieving.

dim slot (100)

let uppper = 100                   !primes to 100
for n = 2 to upper                 !run through numbers
   if slot(n) + 0 then             !0 means it's prime
      print n,
      if n*n <= upper then         !bother to remove multiples
         for i = n to upper step n !run through all multiples
            let slot(i) = 1         !mark as nonprime
         next i
      end if
   end if
next n
end


Ok. run
2              3              5              7              11
13             17             19             23             29
31             37             41             43             47
53             59             61             67             71
73             79             83             89             97
Ok.
```

Viewing a listing while the program runs makes editing easier.

SELECT CASE blocks. True BASIC's SELECT CASE structure allows a programmer to represent several optional sections of the program in a form that is easy to understand. ON...GOTO and ON...GOSUB are its closest counterparts in unstructured versions of BASIC.

To illustrate, here's a program from Kemeny and Kurtz's book that plays 10 games of the dice game craps:

```
! Simulate 10 plays of a dice game
!
FOR game = 1 TO 10
     LET die1 = int(6*rnd + 1)
     LET die2 = int(6*rnd + 1)
     LET dice = die1 + die2
     PRINT dice;
     SELECT CASE dice
     CASE 2,3,12
          PRINT "You lose"
     CASE 7,11
          PRINT "You win"
     CASE ELSE
          LET point = dice
          DO
               LET die1 = int(6*rnd + 1)
               LET die2 = int(6*rnd + 1)
               LET dice = die1 + die2
               PRINT dice;
          LOOP UNTIL dice = 7 OR dice = point
          IF dice = point THEN
               PRINT "You win"
          ELSE
               PRINT "You lose"
          END IF
     END SELECT
NEXT game
END
```

In unstructured BASIC, we would have to replace SELECT CASE with the ON...GOSUB mechanism, losing a great deal in clarity.

Functions and Subroutines

In most versions of BASIC, sections of a program that are used repeatedly can be incorporated into functions or subroutines. Calling a function or subroutine is simpler and clearer than repeating the corresponding lines of the program each time they are needed.

In True BASIC, functions and subroutines can be internal or external. An internal function or subroutine shares variables with the main program; an external function or subroutine has its own set of variables that are unaffected by and do not affect the main program's variables (except for explicitly defined parameters).

True BASIC allows multistatement functions, unlike most versions of BASIC that limit functions to a single statement. The arguments of functions (that is, the input values) can be strings, numbers, or arrays. The result returned by a function can also be a string or number.

Here's an example of a function definition, excerpted from the True BASIC reference manual:

```
! Function to reverse a string
DEF reverse$ (s$)
    LET result$ = ""
    FOR i = len(s$) TO 1 STEP -1
        LET result$ = result$ & s$[i:i]
    NEXT i
    LET reverse$ = result$
END DEF
```

The ampersand (&) in the fifth line indicates string concatenation (joining of two strings); it corresponds to the plus symbol (+) in Microsoft BASIC string expressions.

After this function definition is made, you can reverse a string by calling the function as shown in line 4 below:

```
DO
    LINE INPUT PROMPT "Another string? "; a$
    IF a$ = "" THEN EXIT DO
    PRINT reverse$(a$)
LOOP
END
```

Subroutines differ from functions in that they do not return a single value; instead they operate on the same variables that are used within the main program and on variables included in a parameter list. (External subroutines change only the variables in the parameter list.) Unlike other versions of BASIC, True BASIC lets you reference subroutines with meaningful names rather than by line number:

```
CALL distance(point_a,point_b)
```

Graphics

True BASIC's graphics features include most of the ANSI BASIC graphics module with several additions. We'll mention just a few of these features here.

To plot a point or draw a design, you don't need to know how many points your computer's screen contains. You need only know the range of points you want to plot.

Suppose you want to plot the sine function for angle X ranging from 0 to 360 degrees. High school trigonometry tells you that SIN(X) ranges from -1 to 1. Without further ado, here's all you need:

```
OPTION ANGLE DEGREES
SET WINDOW 0,360, -1,1
FOR angle = 0 TO 360 STEP 10
    PLOT LINES: angle, SIN(angle);
NEXT angle
END
```

The first line tells True BASIC you want to measure angles in degrees rather than in radians. The second line specifies the ranges for the horizontal and vertical axes in terms of the data you want to plot—you needn't be concerned with the resolution or row-column dimensions of your display. The FOR loop plots a continuous line of the sine of angles 0, 10, 20, . . ., 360.

In contrast, in most versions of BASIC you must consider the range of points available on your screen and then scale the calculated value's angle and SIN(angle) to fit on your screen.

True BASIC's primary graphics commands are PLOT POINTS, PLOT LINES, PLOT AREA (multisided figures), and PLOT TEXT (add labels to graphics).

Another command, OPEN SCREEN, lets you define any rectangular section of the screen to be used in place of the entire screen. This makes it relatively easy to design a program that uses the newest wrinkle in user-friendly software design: windows. True BASIC allows you to define multiple windows on the screen and assign a different set of X and Y coordinates to each window.

True BASIC also allows you to define pictures that function in a similar way to subroutines. Here's a picture definition for a square (taken from the True BASIC reference manual):

```
PICTURE Square(size)
    PLOT -size,size;      ! upper left corner
    PLOT size,size;       ! to upper rt corner
    PLOT size, -size;     ! to lower rt corner
    PLOT -size, -size;    ! to lower lf corner
    PLOT -size,size       ! back to upper left
END PICTURE
```

Once you've defined the square, you can call it with the statement:

```
DRAW Square(side)
```

The value of side determines the size of the box.

The DRAW statement also lets you perform various transformations on a picture before it is drawn. Commands include SHIFT, ROTATE, SCALE, and SHEAR (lean the vertical lines by a specified number of degrees or radians). Transformations can be combined as well. For example, we can turn the box just defined into a diamond with these commands.

```
OPTION ANGLE DEGREES
DRAW Square(1) WITH ROTATE(45)*SCALE(1,1.5)
END
```

Finally, keep in mind that these commands will work regardless of what host computer you are using. □

BetterBASIC*

G. MICHAEL VOSE

BetterBASIC is a product of Summit Software Technology Inc. (40 Grove St., Wellesley, MA 02181). It is a version of BASIC designed to run initially on the IBM PC and PCjr computers and their compatibles. The language will be available for other MS-DOS machines within a year.

BetterBASIC is incrementally compiled, provides separate user-defined procedures and functions, and is extensible through the use of modules. Modules can be created by programmers from within the language. Special-function modules for graphics, windows, and future capabilities will be available from the company in coming months.

BetterBASIC's design emphasizes the benefits of structured programming by offering strict data typing, readability enhancements, and a variety of control structures, particularly procedures and functions. Procedures and functions are scoped so that variables within them are local; they can be made accessible to outside structures with programmer intervention.

The Modular Structure of BetterBASIC

One of the unique features of BetterBASIC is its modularity. BetterBASIC consists of a number of different modules that you can configure to produce a version of BetterBASIC with exactly the capabilities of a particular hardware configuration and/or application. Furthermore, you can create your own new language statements and "package" these new statements into modules that can be made a permanent part of BetterBASIC.

In its most basic form, BetterBASIC consists of two separate modules that must always be present on the program disk:

B.COM — This is the primary executing portion of BetterBASIC, loaded into memory by the command "B." Once loaded, this program begins executing and will load B.DEF, the second portion of BetterBASIC, into memory.

B.DEF — This file contains the actual language definitions for BetterBASIC and will always be loaded immediately after B.COM. Both B.COM and B.DEF must be contained as files on the program disk.

Together, B.COM and B.DEF produce a limited but complete plain-vanilla version of BetterBASIC that executes in the standard MS-DOS operating-system environment. Because BetterBASIC is an extensible language, this form of BetterBASIC can now be used to extend the language through the creation of BetterBASIC modules.

A BetterBASIC module is a separately compiled, relocatable software unit containing BetterBASIC procedures and/or functions, as well as any static data shared by the procedures/ functions contained in the module. Once a module has been loaded into memory, those procedures and functions that have been declared public will be available as extensions to the vanilla version of BetterBASIC.

The BetterBASIC Programming System comprises these basic modules plus a number of sophisticated language-extension modules that together result in the BetterBASIC programming environment.

The BetterBASIC Configuration File

The loading/creation of a custom version of BetterBASIC is controlled by an optional configuration file, B.CNF, that contains the names of modules to be used in a programming session, as well as other information controlling the various operating modes of BetterBASIC. If B.CNF does not exist on the program disk, the plain-vanilla version of BetterBASIC results.

If B.CNF exists, it will be a simple ASCII file containing load-time information in the form of one or more lines of text. Each line of text generally specifies either the name of a module to be loaded or a BetterBASIC language parameter to be set (see Specifying BetterBASIC Parameters).

Specifying Modules

To specify that a particular module be included in the loaded version of BetterBASIC, simply add a line, as follows, to B.CNF:

MODULE=*filename*

More than one module may be specified in a single line, as follows:

MODULE=*filename1*+*filename2* +....+*filenameN*

Specifying BetterBASIC Parameters

B.CNF may also contain directives to set several BetterBASIC parameters to specified values, as follows:

STACK = hexnum — This directive allows you to specify the size of BetterBASIC's internal stack. This stack holds dynamic (recursive) variables. A larger stack allows more local dynamic variables. The default size is currently hexadecimal 2800. If the number given is less than hexadecimal 2800, the default size is used.

PREC = num — Allows you to specify the real math precision. The number must be in the range of 6 to 24 decimal.

AUTODEF = ON/OFF — Sets BetterBASIC's Autodef mode to on or off. The default is on.

INTERRUPT = ON/OFF — Sets BetterBASIC's Interrupt mode to on or off. The default is off.

USERMEM = hexnum — Reserves a given number of paragraphs for user memory, i.e., memory that will not be allocated to BetterBASIC and can be requested by an assembly-language procedure in a user module.

STATUS = ON/OFF — Enables/disables the status-line display at the bottom of the console display.

Available Modules

The full BetterBASIC system includes the following modules:

B.EXT — This module provides a number of useful procedures and functions in addition to the standard built-in procedures and functions provided by B.COM and B.DEF, such as RND, RANDOMIZE, HEX$, and others.

FILEIO.DOS — Provides a flexible interface to the MS-DOS disk-file system. It allows BetterBASIC to inter-

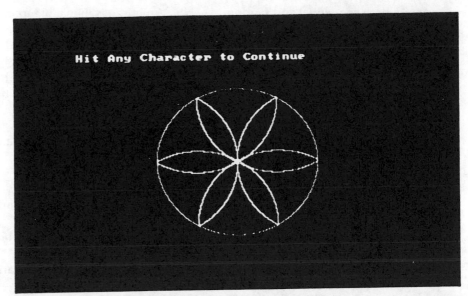
Photo 1: *A sample of BetterBASIC graphic output.*

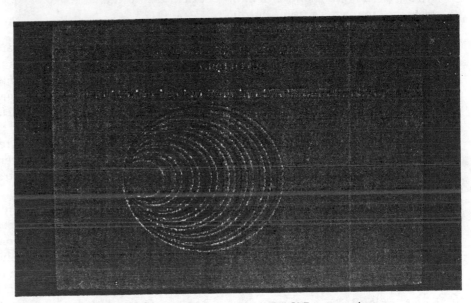
Photo 2: *A BetterBASIC graphic drawn using the CIRCLE command.*

Photo 3: *Windows, with standard BASIC on the left and BetterBASIC source code on the right.*

act with both sequential and random record disk files. For sequential disk-file access, the FILEIO procedures offer Microsoft BASIC-compatible syntax, while for record-oriented I/O, BetterBASIC's record variables provide a higher-level syntax.

CONSOLE.IBM# — Provides access to the IBM PC's special-function keys, and implements a screen editor that allows flexible editing of a Better-BASIC program. This module also provides compile-time and run-time support of the IBM PC's function keys (F1–F10).

GRAPHICS.IBM — Supports the IBM PC's color-graphics adapter and provides high-level graphics statements, such as CIRCLE, PAINT, DRAW, etc. Photos 1 and 2 demonstrate the language's graphic output.

WINDOWS.IBM — Allows the IBM PC's display screen (monochrome or color) to be divided into separate, independent display windows. Each window can display data independently in scrolling or nonscrolling modes. Data can be read from and written to any window. While the BetterBASIC windows will generally be nonoverlapping, provision has been made for "pop-up" windows that can temporarily overlay other windows. Photos 3 through 5 show sample BetterBASIC windows.

HELP — Provides on-line help functions using a pop-up window to display help information about a particular topic. Being a module, this allows the help feature to be removed once a user becomes proficient in BetterBASIC.

Industry Standards

BetterBASIC is syntax compatible with Microsoft GW (Gee Whiz) BASIC and IBM PC BASIC. Many of the Microsoft BASIC (MBASIC) keywords are duplicated within the language. In all, BetterBASIC has 140 keywords.

BetterBASIC implements approximately 80 percent of the keywords in the BASIC standard proposed by ANSI (American National Standards Institute). Its math conventions are the same as the proposed standard's, but its graphics keywords, added by a separate module, differ from the standard's, closely emulating the MBASIC graphic keywords.

The language differs from both standards in the following significant ways:

• It encourages strict data typing.
• It provides global and local variables.
• It provides procedures and functions.
• It offers the Pascal-like record-variable data structure.
• It provides the module for adding extensions to the language.

Compiled—Not Interpreted

The ultimate programming language must be easy to learn, easy to use, and easy to transport from computer to computer. These qualities inspired the authors of BetterBASIC to create a language that is compiled to offer speed and efficiency but that retains the interactive nature of interpreted languages like standard BASIC.

Incremental compiling provides both the speed *and* the interaction of BetterBASIC. Each line of source code compiles as it is entered into the computer's memory. As each line is entered, existing program fragments can be run and tested.

This is in contrast to traditional compilation techniques where the entire source-code program is compiled, run, and tested only *after* it is written.

Incremental compilation is fast but its primary advantage may be its error-handling capability. As source-code lines are entered, the compiler finds and reports syntax errors—often pointing out the exact error, like a missing parenthesis—allowing the correction of errors on the spot. Therefore, when a complete program is in memory, it is guaranteed to be syntactically error free.

Standard compilers report errors only during the compilation of the entire source-code program. This makes the correction of syntax and lexical errors time-consuming and tedious, as the source code must be changed and the entire program recompiled.

The code generated by the Better-BASIC compiler is not microprocessor machine code. Instead, the compiler generates pseudo-code (p-code) for the virtual machine, a software construct that interprets p-code for the IBM PC's microprocessor.

This virtual-machine architecture of BetterBASIC makes the language easily transportable among Intel 8086-based, and eventually Motorola MC68000-based, machines.

Readability

Because one of generic BASIC's strengths is its readable, English-like command structure, BetterBASIC strives to make the language even friendlier with a variety of enhancements.

First, the language permits variable names of unlimited length. Because all characters in a name are significant, names like TEMPERATURE1 and TEMPERATURE2 are possible. Several words can be strung together using the underscore character, as in NET_PROFIT_QUARTER.

These descriptive variable names are a blessing when you decide to make changes to the program. Making a modification in line 400 of your program will be easier if you're looking for the variable NET_PROFIT instead of X or NP.

A second enhancement to program readability is the indentation of code within loops. A BetterBASIC loop looks like this:

```
10 For I = 1 to 10
20    Print I
30    Count = I
40 Next
```

BetterBASIC indents multiple nested-code structures an additional two spaces. For example:

```
10 For I = 1 to 10
20   Print I;
30     For J = 1 to 4
40       Print J
50     Next
60 Next
```

There can be no confusion when reading this code that one FOR... NEXT loop executes *within* the other.

BetterBASIC's most significant contribution to readability, however, is its procedures/functions capability. Discussed in detail later, procedures and functions can replace subroutines, providing a way to write routines with meaningful names that are used in a program just like language keywords.

In addition to long variable names, named procedures and functions, and indentation of code within loops, BetterBASIC provides:

•a way to list all existing procedures and functions with their nesting status and argument types displayed
•a function to display current system status—parameters such as the current precision of floating-point math, and the status of switches such as automatic declaration of variables (see Variable Declaration)
•a function to query the type of variables
•another to determine the number of dimensions in an array

All of these features simplify the maintenance of your program environment and make BetterBASIC programs easier to understand.

Text Manipulators

Text-variable (also called string-variable or character-variable) manipulation in BetterBASIC is enhanced by a variety of functions unavailable in previous versions of BASIC. These functions include the traditional

```
Better BASIC {tm}

Highly Structured Programming Language with Basic-like Syntax

Supports The 'Standard' BASIC Syntax          BetterBASIC's Advanced Features Include:
    With Statements Such As:

ABS          ASC                    INCREMENTALLY COMPILED
CALL         CHRS                   INTERACTIVE LANGUAGE
CLEAR        CLOSE
CLS          DIM                    WIDE RANGE OF DATA TYPES SUCH AS
END          FOR NEXT
GOSUB        GOTO                     BYTE         INTEGER
INPUT        INSTR                    REAL         STRING
INT          LEFTS                    RECORD       POINTER
MIDS         RIGHTS
LET          LINE INPUT
LIST         NEW                    ARRAYS OF ALL THE ABOVE
ON...GOSUB   ON...GOTO              Hit Any Character to Continue

Etc.
```

Photo 4: *Another set of windows; note the available data types listed in the right window.*

```
BetterBASIC {tm}

Highly Structured Programming Language with Basic-like Syntax

Supports The 'Standard' BASIC Syntax          BetterBASIC's Advanced Features Include:
    With Statements Such As:

ABS          ASC                    STRUCTURED PROGRAMMING FACILITIES
CALL         CHRS
CLEAR        CLOSE                  DO...REPEAT
CLS          DIM                    DO{IF}...REPEAT
END          FOR NEXT               DO...REPEAT{IF}
GOSUB        GOTO                   WHILE...DO...REPEAT
INPUT        INSTR
INT          LEFTS
MIDS         RIGHTS                 Hit Any Character to Continue
LET          LINE INPUT
LIST         NEW
ON...GOSUB   ON...GOTO

Etc.
```

Photo 5: *A partial list of control structures (right window.)*

INSTR, LEFT$, RIGHT$, and MID$ operators and add new operators to convert between uppercase and lowercase, to insert and delete characters from strings, and to append text to a string.

The text operators in BetterBASIC not only perform standard string-search functions but also double as assignment statements. This permits operations such as

200 RIGHT$(Name$,6) = "Client"

Strings in BetterBASIC default to 16 characters but can be declared to any length up to 32,767 characters. The practical limit to string length is much lower, of course, but this limit is the only kind that BetterBASIC is subject to.

Variable Declaration

As highlighted earlier, BetterBASIC variables are easy to track because they use descriptive names. Of equal importance is the capability to type all variables—to specify a variable as an integer, string, or other type (see the A Closer Look at Data Types section that comes next).

Strict data typing gives you the flexibility to use the kind of variable types that will guarantee that your programs are as fast, and use as little memory, as possible. This facility also aids program maintenance. BetterBASIC lists all variables by type at the beginning of the source-code listing of all program structures.

There are two kinds of variable declaration in BetterBASIC: explicit declaration, a "structured-programming" technique useful primarily to aid maintenance and debugging; and first-use declaration, sometimes called automatic declaration.

Standard BASICs use both techniques, but BetterBASIC has a switch that lets you turn off the automatic declaration of variables, forcing you to use explicit declarations. In this way, BetterBASIC can help you acquire better programming technique.

A Closer Look at Data Types

BetterBASIC offers seven data types—integer plus a subset, byte, real-number, string or character, record, a pseudo-data type called a pointer, and arrays of all the other types.

A byte data type and an integer data type are both whole numbers. Bytes are in the range 0 to 255, while the range for integers is $-32,767$ to $+32,767$. Bytes require a single byte for storage in memory while integers consume up to 2 bytes.

Real numbers in BetterBASIC have a range of 9.99×10^{-255} to 9.99×10^{253}. Real numbers require up to 16 bytes for storage in memory, depending on the chosen precision for floating-point math operations.

String data types store the ASCII (American National Standard Code for Information Interchange) representation of the intended data and require 1 byte of storage for each character plus 2 bytes for overhead.

A record data type is a complex variable comprised of fields that can be any of the other BetterBASIC data types (see Record Variables).

A pointer is a pseudo-data type used to "point" to another data structure. Changing the value of a pointer changes the value of the variable it points to. Pointers are useful in linking record variable fields.

Arrays of all data types constitute another data type. BetterBASIC even supports arrays of arrays.

Arrays and record variables are structures that are built using the BetterBASIC command (*type* ARRAY) (RECORD) STRUC. This command lets you build and name shapes, or templates, of complex data structures without consuming any memory. You can then declare a structure of a given shape when you need it for data manipulation.

There are declaration statements for each data type in BetterBASIC. For example, the declaration

    INTEGER Counter, Flag, Number
    STRING Password
    REAL Net__Profit, Gross__Profit

creates three integer variables named Counter, Flag, and Number; a text variable called Password; and two real variables called Net__Profit and Gross__Profit.

These variables will always appear in a table at the top of any listing made of the source code of the program structure in which these variables appear.

BetterBASIC variables are local to the program structure in which they are created. You can declare an integer variable called Counter in your main program, and it will be unknown inside any procedures or functions you write. In fact, you can subsequently declare a variable called Counter within a procedure, and that variable will be different from the main program variable Counter and unknown to the main program. In

this way, BetterBASIC provides unparalleled data integrity.

Record Variables

Of all its data types, BetterBASIC's record variable is the most flexible. Similar to Pascal's record variable, this data type is an amalgam of separate fields, each of which can be any other data type—even arrays or other record variables. A record variable is thus similar to an array except that the elements can be of any type or size. The elements of a record are addressed using the notation

recordname.fieldname

For example, to extract the entry in a record variable named Payfile1 for the information for a Name field storing the value Jones, you would write

    PRINT PAYFILE1.NAME

and would receive the following display:

    JONES

The record, Payfile2, would contain another name (presumably with a variety of facts associated with the name).

Pointers

Pointers are pseudo-variables in BetterBASIC. Their primary purpose is to permit the linking of record variable fields. To establish a pointer, it must be SET—that is, it must be assigned to a variable to point to that variable.

An example will clarify this process. Assume the existence of a record variable, Payfile1, with a field, Name, containing the data, Jones. The assignment operation

    SET P = PAYFILE1.NAME

will establish P as a pointer, pointing at the variable, Payfile1.Name. A subsequent

PRINT P

yields

Jones

Similarly, the following steps alter the contents of Payfile1.Name:

P ="Smith"
PRINT PAYFILE1.NAME

Smith

Stand-alone procedures and functions are made possible by a division of the computer's memory resources into segmented work spaces. Initially, there is only a single BetterBASIC work space, the main program work space denoted by the prompt ".". But each time a procedure or function is declared, a new work space is created. A procedure/function work space is denoted by the prompt ":". The on-screen status line also indicates the current work space, in addition to other items such as real-number precision, auto-declaration on or off, and whether interrupts are on or off.

Procedures and functions are scoped so that they can be called at the level of their creation. If a procedure is declared at the main program level, it can be called from that level only. It cannot be called by another procedure or function (unless it is made external, see below). Similarly, a procedure created from within a procedure can be called by that procedure only—it cannot be called from the main program or from any other procedure outside the one that created it.

Procedures

Procedures are declared by entering the keyword, PROCEDURE, followed by a name. The name can be a simple word or a complex label containing several words linked by an underline character (_), as in SWAP_NUMBER_ROUTINE. On

Listing 1: *The function, Age, followed by a program to call it with the argument, Birthyear, and print the result. Note that Birthyear is a separate variable in the main program and the function.*

```
.INTEGER FUNCTION Age
Integer Function: Age
234567 Bytes Left
:10 INTEGER ARG Birthyear
:20 RESULT = 1984 - Birthyear
:main
INTEGER Birthyear
.10 INPUT "Enter the year of your birth: ";Birthyear
.20 PRINT "You are ";Age(Birthyear);" years old."
```

entry of the statement and name, the screen displays

```
.PROCEDURE CLS
Procedure:CLS
256712 Bytes Left
:
```

To write the code for the procedure, the programmer proceeds as in the main work space, using line numbers and any and all BetterBASIC keywords. Because line numbers and variables are local to the procedure, you can use the same line numbers and variable names used elsewhere without conflict (although possibly not without confusion with variable names). For example, to complete a clear-the-screen procedure, you could enter

```
:10 PRINT CHR$(12)
```

REM ASCII character 12 is the IBM PC clear-screen character

```
:20 PRINT "Ok"
```

REM just a fancy prompt

```
:main
```

The keyword MAIN prompts an exit from the procedure work space back to the main work space. At this point, the procedure is called by entering its name:

```
. CLS
```

or by using the name in a program line:

```
.100 CLS
```

This invokes the procedure and clears the screen, printing an "Ok" at the top.

The scope of procedures and functions can be altered with the keyword EXTERNAL. The scope of variables can also be changed using this keyword. EXTERNAL can make a variable or an entire procedure or function visible to other program levels.

Functions

Functions are created and called in the same way as procedures. In this way, they are substantially different from the functions in standard BASIC. They can be as long and complex as you care to make them. Functions are subject to the same scope rules as procedures.

Functions require at least one argument (it may be a dummy argument) and return a result. Listing 1 is an example function to compute a person's age—it requires the year of birth as an argument.

A RESULT statement forces an exit from the function with the returned value as the result. A function may have multiple RESULT statements but will exit on initial execution of one.

Arguments

Functions require at least one argument but either functions or procedures can receive arguments of any data type, including arrays and records. In the latter case, a special argument class, the ANY ARG, is used to permit the passage of an unknown data type (required because record variables can contain mixed data types). ANY argument declarations can be used at any time in a procedure or function, but specific data-type declarations are preferable and constitute good programming practice.

Error Handling

Procedures and functions can in-clude error-handling routines to handle the typical errors to which the construct might be vulnerable. If no error routine is included, the scoping rules of the language call the error-handling routines at the program level that called the procedure or function. If no routines exist at this level, all the way back to the main program level, BetterBASIC then issues a system error message and halts execution as in standard BASIC.

Extending the Language

BetterBASIC's most significant feature is its use of modules. A module can be created by any BetterBASIC programmer and linked to the existing language system at configuration (see The BetterBASIC Configuration File on page 302). A module is usually desirable as a permanent addition to the language. They are not limited to code written in BetterBASIC. Modules can also contain assembly-language code. In this way, it becomes simple to adapt the language to specific hardware or even to make application programs part of the language.

It is the module that makes the language extensible. For example, to make the earlier example procedure CLS part of BetterBASIC, it can be made into a module with the command

.MAKE MODULE

Execution of this command eliminates the procedure's source code and retains the virtual-machine object code. The module is assigned a module number that is displayed on the screen. At this point, CLS becomes a new keyword in the language, callable at any level.

Conclusion

BetterBASIC is a substantial improvement to previous versions of the language, but a major concern is whether there is a need for yet another version of BASIC. All BASIC designers hope their version will become standard, and a standard language would seem to allow no room for competitors. It could be that the public perception of Microsoft BASIC as a standard may make it impossible for other versions of BASIC, regardless of worth, to gain a toehold in the marketplace.

The problem, then, for purveyors of upgraded language products becomes one of educating the potential market about the advantages of their products. A modicum of luck may be required, as well. The history of successful microcomputer software to date has shown that the surest way to the top is often on the coattails of a significant new piece of hardware.■

MACINTOSH BASIC*

SCOT KAMINS

Since so many things about Apple's new Macintosh computer are different from other computers, it should come as no surprise that Donn Denman's Macintosh BASIC is also different. Briefly stated, Macintosh BASIC is a semicompiled, multitasking, structured language system (without line numbers), complete with a full-screen text editor and a highly sophisticated debugger, that takes advantage of many of the Macintosh's unique features. This article describes what is unique about the language.

Macintosh BASIC is semicompiled. When you type in a new program line, the line is immediately passed to a part of the system called the B-

code generator. This generator compiles the program line and updates the program data structures. The system checks the syntax of the line as the line is compiled and provides immediate feedback as to the line's general lexical correctness. Later, when the program is executed, the compiler makes another quick pass through the program (about 2 seconds for a 50K-byte program) to check the integrity of its control structures. Assuming there are no final compilation errors, program execution continues. The compact B-code is then interpreted, making for a very fast BASIC.

Macintosh BASIC is quite large (48K bytes), and it can grow. It is

segmented; about 32K bytes live in memory at any time, leaving about 50K bytes for program and variable table space. (Actually, because of the CALL command, programs can be virtually any length.) If a program needs a part of BASIC that isn't in RAM (random-access read/write memory), such as formatted output, the editor, the debugger, or some other large code segment, it loads in from the disk.

Macintosh BASIC lets you execute any number of programs simultaneously and develop one or more additional programs at the same time (see figure 1). Each time a line of code is interpreted, the system checks for other events that might need attention and handles them accordingly. Each program is granted a fixed amount of execution time in 1/60-second increments or any interval set by the programmer. When a program's time slice is up, the system moves to the next program for interpretation.

No line numbers are required in Macintosh BASIC. You get around the program by branching to sections of code identified by *labels*. You can use numbers, but labels tend to be a lot more meaningful and make tracing program flow much easier.

Environment

In most BASICs, the entire display area is ordinarily occupied by the program listing or by the output. In Macintosh BASIC, the display area, called the *desktop*, is typically oc-

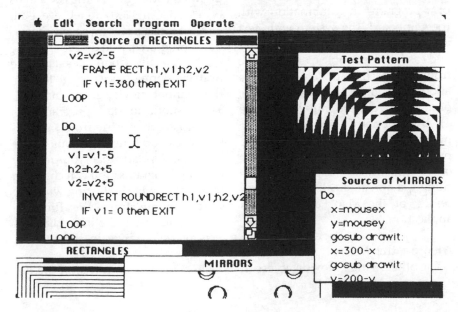

Figure 1: *Multitasking in Macintosh BASIC.*

cupied by a variety of graphics and text material. Most material appears in *windows*, sections of the desktop that can grow, shrink, or move at the discretion of the programmer. Figure 2a shows the BASIC desktop with three copies of the same program in windows of different sizes. Listing 1 shows what the whole program looks like; you can't see all of it because all of it won't fit in the viewing area of the Listing window. Figure 2b shows what running the program produces. Note that none of these windows shows an entire program; there are more lines in the program than will fit in any of the visible areas. To see the rest of the program listing, you press the mouse button with the pointer on the down arrow in the *scroll bar* (located at the right of the window), revealing the rest of the code.

When a Macintosh BASIC program is executed, the Listing window is overlaid by an Output window that displays any text or graphics produced by the executing program. Both the Listing window and the Output window can be (and often are) displayed at the same time, making program development and debugging easier than in traditional environments.

Macintosh BASIC's tools and command words (verbs that affect programs as a whole, like RUN, LOAD, and SAVE) appear in menus whose titles are listed in the *menu bar* running across the top of the desktop. To choose a menu item, use the mouse to move the pointer to the mouse you want, press and hold the menu button, and drag the pointer down to the specific tool or command you want.

The Macintosh BASIC interactive programming environment makes writing code a lot easier than do most other BASICs because of the huge variety of tools. The tools include those available to every Macintosh application (specifically, the *desk accessories*, the screen-oriented editor, and the Clipboard) and a set of special development and debugging aids designed for the language, including flexible search and replace capabilities, several printing options, and a very sophisticated debugger.

Desk Accessories

Among the desk accessories, accessible from the desktop menu, programmers will find the Calculator, the Note Pad, and the Clock most useful (see figure 3). The Calculator is a simple four-function calculator useful for doing quick operations; you can use the system editor to transfer calculation results into your program code. The Note Pad lets you write memos to yourself about special sections of code that need attention, or anything else you need to remember but don't want to scribble on a piece of paper that will quickly get lost. The Clock is extremely useful, either to time program execution or to remind a hacker when to eat lunch. You can have all these tools (and any others, for that matter) operating while you develop and run programs.

Using the mouse and the screen-oriented editor, you can cut, copy, paste, or entirely remove all or part of a program. In combination with the Clipboard, the system-wide text and graphics buffer, you can quickly and easily move whole blocks of code from one section of a program to another section of the same program or to a different program (see figure 4). Additionally, you can move material into (or out of) the BASIC programming environment from any other Macintosh application including a spreadsheet, a word processor, or the Mac Paint graphics application.

Also on the Menu

The other menus provide access to tools specific to Macintosh BASIC. Among the tools seldom seen in other systems are Search and Replace, in the Search menu; Debug, in the Program menu; and Directory, in the Operate menu.

The search tools help you to locate and/or change any group of characters, either once or repeatedly, matching or ignoring the case of the alphabetic characters. These search tools can be extremely useful for changing a nondescriptive variable to one that makes more sense—say, changing all occurrences of the variable E7 to EMPLOYEE.7—or to replace improper spellings in variable names, labels, or prompting phrases.

The Program menu (see figure 5) lists the command verbs, or menu selections, programmers tend to use most during code development, including certain commands not available or meaningful in other BASIC systems. Most notable here are the two Save commands, the Update command, and the Debug command.

Selecting Save Source sends an ASCII (American National Standard Code for Information Interchange) text copy of the program to the disk, just as it appears in the Listing window. Save Object stores only the program's B-code—that is, the code in its compiled form. You can retrieve, edit, and execute a program saved as text, but a program saved as code can be executed only. Code files are safe from tampering; once they go to disk, they cannot be viewed or changed. Thus, profit-minded programmers can protect their code from the prying eyes of unscrupulous code pilferers. Update lets you modify running programs. You can change a program line in the Listing window, select Update from the Program menu, and watch the immediate effects of the change in the Output window.

Choosing Debug turns on the de-

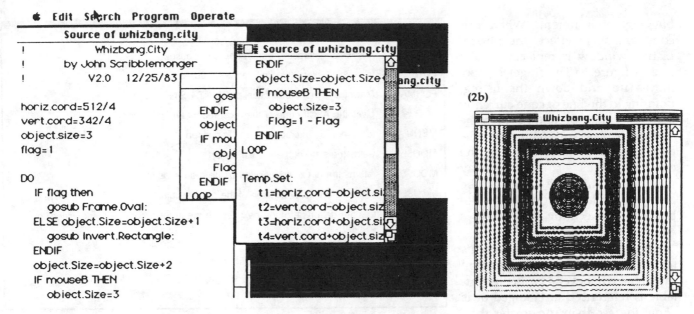

```
         Whizbang.City
     by John Scribblemonger
         V2.0    12/25/83

horiz.cord=512/4
vert.cord=342/4
object.size=3
flag=1

DO
    IF flag then
        gosub Frame.Oval:
    ELSE object.Size=object.Size+1
        gosub Invert.Rectangle:
    ENDIF
    object.Size=object.Size+2
    IF mouseB THEN
        object.Size=3
```

Figure 2: *Three "views" of the same program in windows of different sizes (2a). None of these windows shows an entire listing (see listing 1 below). Figure 2b shows the Output window for the program Whizbang.city (listing 1).*

Listing 1: *The Whizbang.city program.*

```
                 Whizbang.City
          by John Scribblemonger
             V2.0     12/25/83

horiz.cord=512/4
vert.cord=342/4
object.size=3
flag=1

DO
    IF flag then
        gosub Frame.Oval:
    ELSE object.Size=object.Size+1
        gosub Invert.Rectangle:
    ENDIF
    object.Size=object.Size+2
    IF mouseB THEN
        object.Size=3
        Flag=1 - Flag
    ENDIF
LOOP

Temp.Set:
    t1=horiz.cord-object.size
    t2=vert.cord-object.size
    t3=horiz.cord+object.size
    t4=vert.cord+object.size
Return

Frame.Oval:
    Gosub Temp.Set:
    Frame Oval t1,t2; t3,t4
Return

Invert.Rectangle:
    Gosub Temp.Set:
    Invert Rect t1,t2; t3,t4
Return
```

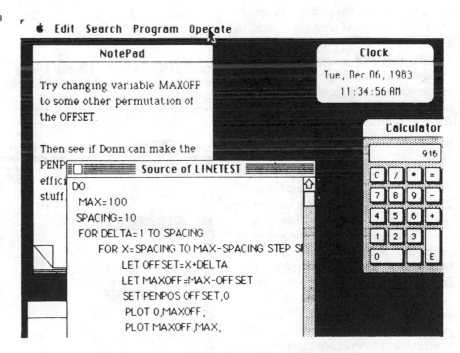

Figure 3: *Macintosh desk accessories run concurrently with program development. The Note Pad (in the background) has eight pages and holds 256 bytes per page.*

bugging environment. When this command is in effect, the normal Listing window is replaced by the one in figure 6. The finger symbol moves up and down the listing, pointing to the line of code currently being executed. Simultaneously, the system displays a dynamic variable and breakpoint table showing the current values of all non-array variables; all of these values can be changed while the code being debugged is executing (updating is automatic).

You can set and clear breakpoints for any or all variables. The program can break whenever a particular variable is referenced or changed or is equal to, less than, or greater than some value or other variable. When the program hits a breakpoint, execution halts and it waits for the programmer to determine what happens next. By using the mouse to press a button displayed on the desktop beneath the Listing window, you can make execution resume at full speed until the next breakpoint, full speed through the next control block (a DO/LOOP, FOR/NEXT, SELECT CASE, subroutine, etc.), or go immediately into a single-step mode. In single-step mode, only one line of code is executed; the programmer tells BASIC to execute each subsequent line of code by pressing the space bar.

Additionally, there's an alphabetical list of all the labels in the program. This feature makes it easy for you to see why you got that "undefined label" error when your program is trying to branch to CALL.YOUR. MOTHER: instead of to CALL. YOUR.MOM:.

The Operate menu holds commands you might typically use to test programs. RUN is the usual BASIC command to execute a program (something in this language has to be usual). In Macintosh BASIC, Halt and Continue are useful for checking the program's Output window and variable table from time to time. The Directory selection produces a menu of all BASIC programs on the disk; drag the pointer to one of the program names and BASIC loads the

Function	Description
BTN	tells which interactive button has been pushed
DIAL	tells which interactive dial has been activated
FORMAT$	Macintosh BASIC equivalent of PRINT USING
KBD	gives the ASCII code of the most recent key pressed
MENU	tells when an interactive menu is chosen
MOUSEB	yields the state of the mouse button
MOUSEX	returns the horizontal position of the mouse pointer
MOUSEY	returns the vertical position of the mouse pointer
TYP	tells the data type of the next item in the input stream (numeric, string, or picture)

Table 1: *Macintosh BASIC numeric data types.*

Storage Form	Symbol	Accuracy	Range
Double-precision real	none	15	1E +− 1022
Single-precision real	|	7	1E +− 126
Extended-precision real	\	18 +	1E +− 4000
Short integer	%	4 +	+− 32767
Long integer	#	18 +	+− 9E18
Boolean	`	1	0 or 1

Table 2: *Some Macintosh BASIC functions not available in most other BASICs. "Interactive" refers to graphics objects (menus, buttons, dials) that appear on the screen and can be manipulated with the mouse.*

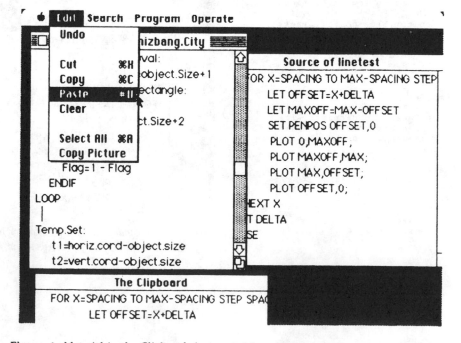

Figure 4: *Material in the Clipboard, just copied from the Linetest program on the right, is about to be pasted into a second program. The source lines in Linetest remain undisturbed.*

program for you. The Quit command is your way out of BASIC, returning you to the main Macintosh system (called the Finder).

With Macintosh BASIC, you can obtain four kinds of hard-copy printouts: everything on the screen, everything in the Listing window including material you can't see, all text and graphics in the Output window, and material sent to the printer by the running program itself. The listings in this article were all printed directly from the Macintosh.

The Language

Variable names in Macintosh BASIC can be of any length, and all characters in the name are significant. The first character must be alphabetic; the rest can be nearly anything you can type from the keyboard, which includes the entire ASCII code set plus nonroman and other special characters. The only exceptions are arithmetic symbols and other delimiters (comma, semicolon, colon, and space).

Macintosh BASIC supports array variables for all eight data types and subtypes discussed later. Arrays can have any number of dimensions, and each dimension can have 32,767 elements. All arrays must be dimensioned before use. When you DIM an array, you can specify ranges for element numbers. Thus, you can say DIM YEAR%(1900 TO 1986) to specify an 87-element integer (the % denotes integer) array whose first number is 1900 and whose last number is 1986. You can also stipulate ranges for separate dimensions, as in DIM NAME$(10 TO 75, 165 TO 300).

There are three main data types in the language: strings, pictures, and numerics. Strings are pretty standard; they are enclosed in quotes, either single or double, and their variable names end in the usual BASIC symbol, $.

You create a picture data type by either creating a shape or a whole picture in a graphics application (like Mac Paint) and transferring it to

BASIC through the Clipboard or by drawing a shape in BASIC using various graphics commands. You can then assign the shape to a picture variable; the variable name ends in the symbol @.

The numeric data type is further divided into six subtypes: Booleans, two types of integers, and three types of reals. Table 1 shows the storage form, symbol, range, and digits of accuracy for each subtype.

In addition to the five standard arithmetic operators $(+, -, *, /, \char94)$, Macintosh BASIC includes DIV for integer division and MOD for modulo, defined as the arithmetic remainder of integer division. The relational operators $(<, =, >, <>, ><)$ and logical operators (AND, OR, and NOT) are standard; the string concatenation symbol is &.

Macintosh BASIC has the usual range of arithmetic, trigonometric, and string functions, including DEF FN (user-defined functions) for both numbers and strings. Table 2 describes many of the functions that don't appear in most other BASICs or are unique to Macintosh BASIC in some major way. The term "interactive," appearing in several of the descriptions, refers to graphics objects (entire menus, buttons, dials) you can make appear on the screen and can manipulate with the mouse.

Control Structures

Most flow of control statements in Macintosh BASIC take the form of control structures. The language has a GOTO statement, but you never have to use it. In fact, the only place the GOTO statement appears in the language manual as part of a code example is in the section describing GOTO itself.

Besides the familiar FOR/NEXT structure and the DO/EXIT/LOOP structure, in which all statements between the keywords DO and LOOP are repeated infinitely (EXIT lets you escape the loop), this BASIC includes some variations on new structures proposed in the 1982 ANSI (Ameri-

can National Standards Institute) BASIC proposal. A multiline IF/THEN/ELSE/ENDIF lets you execute

Listing 2: *A multiple-line IF control block.*

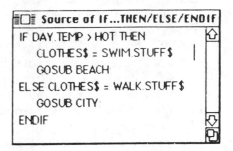

as many statements as you want if a condition is either true or false (see listing 2). An extremely flexible SELECT CASE/ENDCASE construct takes the place of the restrictive ON...GOSUB statement. It enables the program to transfer execution to sets of statements based on the value of some expression. There can be multiple statements for each case or range of cases (see listing 3). The language has several interrupt control structures, all of which are based on a structure bounded by the keywords WHEN and ENDWHEN; these interrupts let you determine which code is executed if any one of a number of events occurs anytime during program execution. You can plan interrupts to occur whenever a key is pressed, when the mouse is moved or its button pushed, when an error occurs, or at other times (see listing 4).

Subroutines are handled in the usual way (except that the language uses GOSUB labels); additionally there's a CALL statement that enables entire programs to act as subroutines. CALL lets you pass parameters back and forth with the summoned program; when the called program ends, control returns to the statement following CALL in the source program.

Graphics

Macintosh BASIC provides commands for both static and animated graphics on a bit-mapped 512- by 342-point screen. You can plot points with the PLOT command (controlling the size of the pixels with PENSIZE) or create shapes with the keywords RECT (for rectangle), ROUNDRECT (a rectangle with rounded corners), or OVAL. Shapes can be outlined (FRAME), filled in (PAINT) with a preestablished shade or pattern (SET PATTERN), complemented from the last appearance (INVERT), or erased altogether (ERASE). The various shapes can then be combined into a single picture and stored in a picture variable (RECORD PICTURE) and recalled (DRAW PICTURE). For animated sequences, you can ROTATE, SCALE, and ANIMATE a picture, moving it across the display. All graphics appear within the Output window, so your Listing and Debugging windows can coexist with a running graphics program.

Disk File Structures

Disk file structures have many options. I will cover only the major highlights; many of the available statements and options are not examined here.

There are three types of file organization: sequential (serial access for text data), stream (serial access for binary data), and relative (random access, usually for text data). Length of a record in a relative file must be set in advance, but it can be any length

Listing 3: *A SELECT CASE construct using strings (3a) and a SELECT CASE construct using numerics (3b).*

(3a)

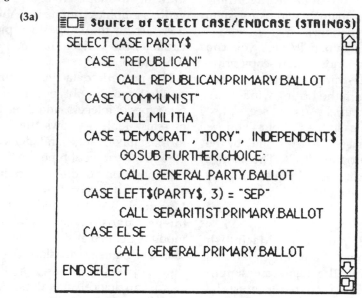

```
SELECT CASE PARTY$
    CASE "REPUBLICAN"
        CALL REPUBLICAN.PRIMARY.BALLOT
    CASE "COMMUNIST"
        CALL MILITIA
    CASE "DEMOCRAT", "TORY", INDEPENDENT$
        GOSUB FURTHER.CHOICE:
        CALL GENERAL.PARTY.BALLOT
    CASE LEFT$(PARTY$, 3) = "SEP"
        CALL SEPARITIST.PRIMARY.BALLOT
    CASE ELSE
        CALL GENERAL.PRIMARY.BALLOT
ENDSELECT
```

(3b)

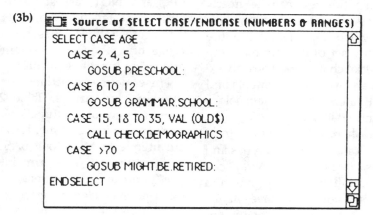

```
SELECT CASE AGE
    CASE 2, 4, 5
        GOSUB PRESCHOOL:
    CASE 6 TO 12
        GOSUB GRAMMAR.SCHOOL:
    CASE 15, 18 TO 35, VAL (OLD$)
        CALL CHECK.DEMOGRAPHICS
    CASE >70
        GOSUB MIGHT.BE.RETIRED:
ENDSELECT
```

Listing 4: *The interrupt construct for errors and keypress.*

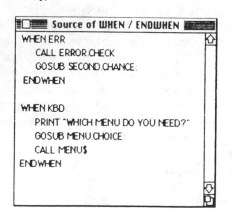

```
WHEN ERR
    CALL ERROR.CHECK
    GOSUB SECOND.CHANCE:
ENDWHEN

WHEN KBD
    PRINT "WHICH MENU DO YOU NEED?"
    GOSUB MENU.CHOICE:
    CALL MENU$
ENDWHEN
```

you choose; there is no limit (beyond memory) to the number of records in a file.

The keyword RECTYPE determines how data is stored: display files are standard ASCII and can be shown in a window or be printed; internal files are binary and are for storage only. You can designate any file, no matter what type, to be an input file (a file which can only be read), an output file (to which data is sent but not retrieved), or OUTIN (accessible for both input and output). You can later change a file's access designation.

You create a file, and later make it accessible for use, with the OPEN statement. OPEN sets the channel number (1 through 99) that links the file to the system and the name of the file associated with the channel:

OPEN #3: NAME "Macmumble"

The preceding statement opens a file named Macmumble and assigns it to channel #3. Since no further parameters are given, the file uses the default parameters, which makes it a sequential display file enabling OUTIN access. The following statement opens a relative file with a record length of 250 characters for the storage of ASCII text data.

Listing 5: *Five programs used for benchmark tests (5a). Listing 5b is the Sieve benchtest program using Print Quick from the Program menu.*

(5a)

```
Source of gosubs
print time$;' at start'
for x= 1 to 5000
    gosub foo:
next x
print time$;' when done'
end

foo: return
```

```
Source of loops
!Loops
Print "Start at ";time$
FOR I= 1 TO 5000
NEXT I
PRINT "Done at ";time$
```

```
Source of divs
print time$;' at start'
for x= 1 to 5000
    y=x div 3
next x
print time$;' when done'
```

```
Source of divides
print time$;' at start'
for x= 1 to 5000
    y=x/3
next x
print time$;' when done'
```

```
Source of mid$
print time$;' at start'
b$='Apple Computer Inc'
for x= 1 to 5000
    a$=mid$(b$,6,7)
next x
print time$;' when done'
print a$
end
```

(5b)

```
' Sieve
s%=8190
dim flags%(s%+1)
print "start ";time$
count%=0
for i%=0 to s%
    flags%(i%)=1
next i%
for i%=0 to s%
    if flags%(i%)=0 then goto 250
    prime%=i%+i%+3
    k%=i%+prime%
200     if k%>s% then goto 240
    flags%(k%)=0
    k%=k%+prime%
    goto 200
240 count%=count%+1
250 next i%
    print 'done ';time$
    print count% ;' primes'
```

Test	Time (seconds)
Empty GOSUBs	3.0
Empty FOR/NEXT loop	1.5
Midstring search	9.0
Real divide (by 3)	18.0
Integer divide (by 3)	3.0
Eratosthenes Sieve (1899 primes)	31.5

Table 3: *Benchmark results.*

OPEN #54: NAME "Foobar", ACCESS OUTPUT, ORGANIZATION RELATIVE, RECSIZE 250

The OPEN statement is intelligent: after you've opened a file, you don't have to restate the organization, record size, or RECTYPE each time you use it. Assuming you've issued the CLOSE statement for the file "Foobar" described above, you can later access it again by just saying OPEN #54: NAME "Foobar". Up to 10 channels can be open at the same time.

All devices (like the serial port, the printer, windows on the desktop) can be accessed in the same manner as files. Device names are specified in the same way as any filename except that the first character in the name is a period.

OPEN #1: NAME ".PRINTER"
OPEN #35: NAME ".SERIAL",
    ACCESS INPUT
OPEN #17: NAME ".WINDOW:
    FOOBAR"

The first of the three lines above assigns channel 1 to the printer. Because printers by their nature are write-only devices, you don't need to specify the file as access output. The second line provides the serial port channel #35; its access mode is specified because serial ports are two-way. The third line addresses the Output window created by the program FOOBAR. This enables some other file either to add to the Output window or to read the window's contents.

To send and retrieve data, use the keywords PRINT and INPUT for ASCII text (display files) and WRITE and READ for binary data (internal files). Potential overwriting or "out of data" problems are handled with the key phrases IF THERE and IF MISSING.

PRINT #7, RECORD 53, IF THERE THEN GOSUB DONT.WRITE. OVER:: A$

The preceding statement sends a field of text data (A$) to record 53 of the relative file on channel #7. If that record already exists, then program control branches to the subroutine called DONT.WRITE.OVER:. The first colon after the subroutine name is required by label syntax, the second by file syntax.

The following example retrieves two fields of binary data from an internal file hooked to channel 67 and stores them in real variable NUMBER and string variable NAME$; if there's no data there, control branches to a program named PROTECTIT.

READ #67, IF MISSING THEN CALL PROTECTIT: NUMBER, NAME$

The Macintosh provides some fairly sophisticated sound stuff, and BASIC takes advantage of it. You can control the volume, pitch, timbre, and amplitude of each of four individual tones. You can also play any note over a four-octave range. (You can play over a greater range, but really low notes sound too soft and really high ones sound too shrill for my ears.)

Set-options are system parameters that you can control. You can ASK or SET the current value of any set-option. There are set-options for nearly all parts of the language, but the most important ones have to do with graphics, windows, and text. Graphics options include the height and width of the penstroke and the pattern the penstroke produces. Window options control how much of a program's output is displayed on the desktop in pixels, how large the entire graphics area is, and what logical boundaries to associate with physical ones. Text set-options include the current position of the insertion point (the mouse's footprint), margins within which text is to appear, and the number of characters between tab stops.

Table 3 shows the results of some standard benchmark tests I ran on my Macintosh; the programs are shown in listing 5. I used the Macintosh's internal clock to do the timing; the smallest increment it reports is in full seconds. I ran each test five times; all but the Sieve were run for 5000 iterations. The results of two similar trials were sometimes different because the timing started in midsecond. ∎

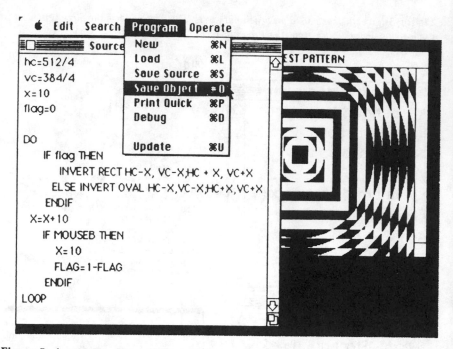

Figure 5: *A program menu with Save Object selected by the mouse. This command is used to save a binary version of a program.*

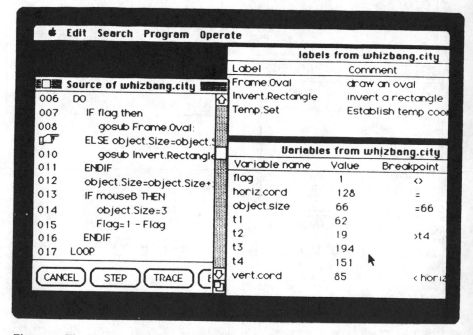

Figure 6: *The Macintosh BASIC Dynamic Debugger. The windows have been "shrunk" so that the major parts of all three would show. The Debugger adds line numbers for easy reference.*

THE RELATIONSHIP BETWEEN COBOL AND COMPUTER SCIENCE*

BEN SHNEIDERMAN

Based on interviews, reviews of the literature, and personal impressions, the author offers historical, technical, and social/psychological perspectives on the fragile relationship between COBOL and computer science. The technical contributions of COBOL to programming language design are evaluated. Five proposals for computer science research on COBOL and fourth-generation languages are described.

*Categories and Subject Descriptors: D.3.0 [**General**]—standards; D.3.2 [**Language Classifications**]—COBOL; K.2 [**History of Computing**]—COBOL, software; K.3.2 [**Computers and Education**] Computer and Information Science Education—computer science education*
General Terms: Design, Languages, Standardization

For a computer scientist to write sympathetically about COBOL is an act bordering on heresy. It requires courage because academic colleagues and data processing professionals are both likely to be suspicious of my motives. Therefore, I feel my first obligation is to make clear my intention and orientation.

I believe that COBOL has had a strong and largely positive influence on the emergence of computer usage. The development of COBOL was a pioneering effort that advanced the state of the art in practical data processing and language design. COBOL clearly had many flaws, some of which have been overcome by revisions to the original language. Designers of other languages have learned from the mistakes and overcome the problems with novel constructs. This paper offers three perspectives on the rise of COBOL (historical, technical, and social/psychological) and suggests directions for future cooperation.

My orientation is as a computer scientist whose early work was in database systems and programming.

More recently I have turned my attention to psychological or human-factors issues of programming, database query facilities, and human-computer interaction (Shneiderman 1980). I have taught introductory programming courses in FORTRAN, BASIC, Pascal, COBOL, APL, and PL/1 and have written or coauthored textbooks using the first three of these languages.

Historical Perspective

Five aspects of the historical development of COBOL can be traced as important influences in the alienation of COBOL from the computer science community. First, academic computer scientists did not participate in the design team. The developers of COBOL were from the commercial community: the manufacturers and users of large data processing systems in industry and government (see the minutes in this issue for lists of the participants).

In 1959–1960 very few academics could have been classified as computer scientists, of course, and few of them could have made useful contributions, but engaging them might have been beneficial.

The developers of the Ada language realized this possibility and made ambitious and successful efforts to elicit the participation of academic and industrial researchers. Computer scientists can do more than contribute ideas; they are often effective in disseminating new concepts through their publishing, teaching, and lecturing efforts.

Author's Address: Department of Computer Science, University of Maryland, College Park, MD 20742.

© 1985 AFIPS 0164-1239/85/040348–352$01.00/00

*Reprinted with the author's permission from the October 1985, Vol. 7, No. 4 issue of *Annals of the History of Computing*, AFIPS, Reston, VA.

The second historical aspect is that the COBOL developers apparently had little interest in the academic or scientific aspects of their work. The May 1962 issue of the *Communications of the ACM* was devoted to 13 papers describing COBOL and related issues. Every article was written by an industry or government person. These people did not have the academic frame of mind that involves referencing previous and related work; only four of the papers had any references. Sociologists of science who use citations to trace the flow of ideas would recognize this pattern as an indicator of intellectual separatism.

The third aspect is the decision of the COBOL developers not to use the Backus-Naur Form (sometimes called Backus Normal Form) notation as the metalanguage to describe COBOL. The COBOL developers were unaware of this work, which appeared in a conference report in June 1959. I don't see the failure to use BNF as central, but apparently the criticism at the time was severe (Sammet 1981, p. 233). The COBOL style of metalanguage has become widely used and might be considered as an important contribution.

A fourth concern is the process of describing COBOL to the academic and industrial community. Professionals could learn the language from programmer reference manuals, but a well-written book emphasizing the conceptual foundations of COBOL would have been an asset. It took a few years before successful introductions were available (McCracken 1963; Saxon 1963) to teach COBOL to novices. Note the contrast with the dissemination of Pascal. Niklaus Wirth published a precise description of the language in *Acta Informatica* (1971), an interesting book titled *Systematic Programming: An Introduction* (1973), the widely read *Pascal User Manual and Report* (1975), and a forward-looking textbook *Algorithms + Data Structures = Programs* (1976).

A search of the Library of Congress SCORPIO system revealed 252 books indexed under COBOL, 529 under FORTRAN, and 1054 under BASIC, demonstrating the relatively lower rate of publication on COBOL. Pascal is more recent, but already 208 books are indexed under that programming language.

The fifth historical aspect is that the people who might have accepted the title of computer scientist in 1960 were not interested in the problem domain of COBOL programs. The commercial file-processing problems were remote from the concerns of computer scientists, who generally dealt with numerical analysis, physics, engineering problems, and systems programming.

In summary, the people and the problems in the COBOL world were very different from the people and problems who were laying the basis for computer science. It is not surprising that they worked separately and in parallel. The development of computer science and data processing might have been substantially altered if these communities had taken the time to meet and work together.

Technical Perspective

Getting convergence on the technical successes and failures of COBOL was a difficult task. I spoke to 30–40 computer scientists and data processing professionals in trying to sort out the issues. The following analysis is my own view guided by the interviews.

First the successes. The strongest point of agreement was that COBOL contributed the record structure, explicit file structure definition, and the separation of data definition from procedural aspects. The COBOL record and file structure certainly influenced the design of PL/1 and Pascal. The notion of an aggregation of dissimilar items is a major advance over the FORTRAN array. The Pascal notion of variant records can be traced to the COBOL REDEFINES clause.

Explicit file structure definitions that included a hierarchy of names for fields and the separate DATA Division were the predecessors of the database management system (DBMS) concept. DBMSs are a vital part of computer science and are the source of a rich theory that is still developing rapidly.

Another contribution was the diverse set of control structures, which were quite sophisticated for the time. The COBOL IF-THEN-ELSE, in spite of its awkward scope delimiter rules, reduced the need for GOTOs and permitted the creation of more comprehensible code. The variety of PERFORM statements allowed convenient and powerful looping and some degree of modular design. The ease with which paragraphs could be created, named, and used facilitated hierarchical design.

A popular feature of COBOL that has appeared in other languages is the COPY statement. By including groups of statements from a library, organizational standards were easily enforced, programmers were encouraged to cooperate, and reuse of code became convenient.

Another interesting COBOL concept is the ENVIRONMENT Division, which allowed users to specify machine or compiler dependencies. It permitted definition of separate host and target computers, thus foreshadowing the idea of cross-compilers.

Finally, the COBOL community demonstrated the power of portability and standardization. In spite of some local variations, COBOL is largely machine independent. Programmers could successfully transfer their knowledge and often their programs from one organization to another. Standardization also encouraged the development of software tools and reuse of code.

Some of the perceived technical failures of COBOL might have been avoided by early consultation with computer scientists, but other problems would not have been recognized until the early 1970s. The most serious omission is a function or procedure definition facility with parameters and local scope of variables. The original version of COBOL has only global variables; therefore a generic subroutine to sum the elements of an array, search a string, or print a bar chart was not easy to write. Two programmers working together had to coordinate carefully to ensure that they did not inadvertently both use the same variable name for different values. The lack of protected module boundaries also allowed complex and sometimes dangerous programming techniques. A DEFINE macro feature was in the original language description and appears to be the first such facility in a high-level language. Unfortunately, it was never implemented and was eventually dropped from the language. The 1974 revision to COBOL included the now-popular CALL USING feature, which permitted parameters and run-time creation of procedure names.

Computer scientists often complained about the wordiness of COBOL statements and the clutter of the optional noise words. The designers of COBOL apparently believed that the English-like statements would make programs readable by managers or other nonprogrammers, but the semantics of programming are at least as challenging as the syntax. Computer scientists whose background emphasized mathematical notation, which is precise and concise, felt that COBOL was too wordy and somehow unscientific.

I found and was sympathetic to several complaints about COBOL control structures. The scope of an IF-THEN-ELSE is delimited by a period, which is often missed by programmers when reading and even when writing programs. It might have been better to have used a keyword such as ENDIF. The PERFORM statement cannot contain a list of statements, only the name of a paragraph. Studying a program is tricky because the reader must hunt for the body of the PERFORM statement. With short loops, the overhead is annoying, and confusion can increase.

Poor string-handling facilities were cited by several people as a major weakness of early COBOL. Moving and copying of strings was convenient, but insertion and deletion of characters inside a string was difficult. The EXAMINE verb and the TALLYING and REPLACING options were included in the early COBOL specifications to facilitate plans to write a COBOL compiler in COBOL. The 1974 version of COBOL contained the somewhat more powerful INSPECT command, plus STRING and UNSTRING.

Several computer scientists complained about the lack of recursion in COBOL, but I think that it hardly would have made a difference in the use of the language.

Knowledgeable COBOL programmers in my survey had other small complaints, but I did not judge them to be vital.

Social/Psychological Perspective

Now we move on to some more speculative areas that reflect on the fundamental differences between the computer science and business data processing communities. The rejection of COBOL by most computer scientists is a product of their desire to avoid the business data processing domain, their pursuit of mathematically oriented theory, and often their lack of knowledge about COBOL.

When asked for his comments, one computer scientist who is a widely respected expert in programming languages boldly replied, "What's COBOL?" His world did not have a place for COBOL. In fact, several programming language texts (e.g., MacLennan 1983) do not include COBOL in the index. Another responded, "It's terrible . . . ugly," but had difficulty explaining why. I suspect this prejudice emerges from the bias of many computer scientists against the problem domain and the wordy, nonmathematical style of COBOL, rather than from any serious consideration of the technical weaknesses. Dijkstra (1982) wrote, "COBOL cripples the mind," but he was equally harsh on FORTRAN ("infantile disorder"), PL/1 ("fatal disease"), BASIC, and APL. Tompkins (1983) sought to defend COBOL, and Reid (1983) responded with many legitimate criticisms.

The bias against the problem domain is stated explicitly in Pratt's programming language textbook (1975; 1984), which says that COBOL has "an orientation toward business data processing . . . in which the problems are . . . relatively simple algorithms coupled with high-volume input-output (e.g. computing the payroll for a large organization)." Anyone who has written a serious payroll program would hardly characterize it as "relatively simple." I believe that computer scientists have simply not been exposed to the complexity of many business data processing tasks. Computer scientists may also find it difficult to provide elegant theories for the annoying and pervasive complexities of many realistic data processing applications and therefore reject them.

Tucker's programming language textbook (1977) has this evaluation: "We judge COBOL's programming features as fair and its implementation dependent features as poor ... its overall writing as fair to poor, its overall reading as fair and its data processing support as good. ... [It has] tortuously poor compactness and poor uniformity." Not much to warm the heart of a COBOL programmer.

Several computer scientists remarked about the "trade school" nature of COBOL and that university professors did not like dealing with current practice, but sought to distinguish themselves with novel languages, theory, and an abstract, more mathematical orientation. One professor commented that he was "hostile to teaching what is used commercially," while a researcher sneered at the "folly of an English-looking language."

The desire to be aloof from current practice was a common theme and leads me to the

Theory Conjecture: Computer scientists like programming language theory, but find fault with any widely used language.

The Theory Conjecture should be comforting to COBOL supporters because it means that computer scientists will express displeasure for almost any programming language that is widely used. Since computer scientists desire to be with the state of the art, anything that is widely used must also be outdated. Commercial usage lowers academic prestige.

A related principle might be expressed as the

Egocentricity Conjecture: Computer scientists appreciate no programming language except the one that they design.

The role of a scientist is to innovate, so comments on other people's work are often in the form of criticism that lays the basis for a proposed improvement.

Summary

Jean Sammet's book on programming languages (1969) and her review of the history of COBOL (1981) offer lists of contributions of COBOL that are close to my own impressions:

- Readable language.
- Separate data declaration section with rich record structure.
- Decent control structures.
- Machine-independent, portable, standardized language.
- A useful alternative metalanguage.
- Creation of a successful and large community of data processing programmers.

In her review, Sammet (1981, p. 239) writes: "I personally do not see much language development ...

significantly influenced by COBOL," and goes on to say, "Most computer scientists are simply not interested in COBOL."

I do feel that COBOL was a major influence on PL/1, which was designed explicitly to include the popular features of COBOL, FORTRAN, and ALGOL. COBOL also had an impact on the use of record structures in languages such as Pascal and on the creation of database management systems.

Most important, COBOL greatly facilitated the enormous expansion of computer usage in data processing. The demand for programmers and computers benefited the entire industry and stimulated further scientific advances because there was such a large market for new ideas.

The Future: A Challenge to Computer Scientists

The story of COBOL is not over. The continuing changes to COBOL, refinements in design guidelines, and improvements in teaching strategies mean that the COBOL of today looks very different from the COBOL of 1960. COBOL and the so-called fourth-generation languages will still be around in 25 more years, and maybe computer scientists still have an opportunity to influence their evolution.

Let me propose five areas of beneficial COBOL and fourth-generation language research that might be of interest to computer scientists.

Code Optimization: There is a grand opportunity to apply traditional compiler optimization techniques to COBOL. Even more provocative would be to explore optimizations that are specific to the COBOL domain. Instead of eliminating redundant mathematical subexpressions, the COBOL compiler writers could concentrate on eliminating redundant MOVE or file operations. Global dataflow analysis would be a challenge in the COBOL context.

Formal Semantics: Precise descriptions of COBOL syntax are available, but there are variations in the semantics of some operations across implementations. Creating a formal semantic description of COBOL would be useful to implementors and might require novel techniques that could be applied in many programming language situations.

Maintenance Tools: The enormous and valuable libraries of COBOL programs are underutilized because tools are not adequate for indexing, searching, interpreting, and modifying this code. Library-science and expert-system concepts might be applied to making the voluminous "literature" of COBOL more readily available for reuse.

Programming-Style Research: Because COBOL is so widely used, we would see a substantial benefit if empirically tested style guidelines were available. Questions abound about the choice of mnemonic variable names, nesting of control structures, use of indentation, page formatting, modular design, commenting techniques, data structure design, etc. Empirical studies of program composition, comprehension, debugging, and modification by professional programmers would be valuable in resolving some of these issues and formulating a cognitive model of programmer behavior.

Software Engineering: In some ways COBOL is a convenient language as the target for a compiler or preprocessor. Indeed, numerous preprocessors attempt to offer higher-level control structures or data structures. How might procedural or data abstraction concepts be molded to fit the COBOL context? Can computer scientists offer an interesting theory of preprocessors to parallel the theory of compilers? Does large-system design in COBOL have features that are distinct from FORTRAN or Ada?

This list is only a starting point. COBOL and fourth-generation languages present many provocative challenges to computer scientists. Also, electronic spreadsheets such as VisiCalc and Lotus 1-2-3 are exciting innovations that have yet to be properly acknowledged in the computer science community.

Acknowledgments

In addition to the people I interviewed, I was greatly helped by knowledgeable reviews of early drafts by Robert Dewar, John Gannon, Rick Linger, Daniel McCracken, Terrence Pratt, Edward Reid, and Jean Sammet. My first consideration of this topic was stimulated by Hank Tropp and Jean Sammet's invitation to give a talk at the 1979 National Computer Conference's Pioneer Day celebration of the 20th anniversary of COBOL.

REFERENCES

Dijkstra, Edsger W. May 1982. How do we tell truths that might hurt? *ACM SIGPLAN Notices 17,* 5, pp. 13–15.

Jensen, Kathleen, and Niklaus Wirth. 1975. *Pascal User Manual and Report.* Second Edition, New York, Springer-Verlag.

MacLennan, Bruce J. 1983. *Principles of Programming Languages: Evaluation and Implementation.* New York, Holt, Rinehart and Winston.

McCracken, Daniel D. 1963. *A Guide to COBOL Programming.* New York, Wiley.

Pratt, Terrence W. 1984. *Programming Languages: Design and Implementation.* Second Edition, Englewood Cliffs, N.J., Prentice-Hall.

Reid, E. October 1983. Fighting the disease: More comments after Dijkstra and Tompkins. *ACM SIGPLAN Notices 18,* 10, pp. 16–21.

Sammet, Jean E. 1969. *Programming Languages: History and Fundamentals.* Englewood Cliffs, N.J., Prentice-Hall.

Sammet, Jean E. 1981. "The Early History of COBOL." In Wexelblat, R. (ed.), *History of Programming Languages,* New York, Academic Press, pp. 199–243.

Saxon, James A. 1963. *COBOL.* Englewood Cliffs, N.J., Prentice-Hall.

Shneiderman, Ben. 1980. *Software Psychology: Human Factors in Computer and Information Systems.* Boston, Little, Brown.

Tompkins, H. E. April 1983. In defense of teaching structured COBOL as computer science (or, Notes on being sage struck). *ACM SIGPLAN Notices 18,* 4, pp. 86–94.

Tucker, Allen B. 1977. *Programming Languages.* Reading, Mass, Addison-Wesley.

Wirth, Niklaus. 1971. The programming language Pascal. *Acta Informatica 1,* 1, pp. 35–63.

Wirth, Niklaus. 1973. *Systematic Programming: An Introduction.* Englewood Cliffs, N.J., Prentice-Hall.

Wirth, Niklaus. 1976. *Algorithms + Data Structures = Programs.* Englewood Cliffs, N.J., Prentice-Hall.

SECTION 7

MORE LANGUAGES FOR THE 1980s

AN OVERVIEW OF ADA BY J. G. P. BARNES

THE C PROGRAMMING LANGUAGE BY
D. M. RITCHIE, S. C. JOHNSON,
M. E. LESK, AND B. W. KERNIGHAN

ALGORITHM = LOGIC + CONTROL
BY R. KOWALSKI

LOGIC PROGRAMMING AND PROLOG: A
TUTORIAL BY R. E. DAVIS

INTRODUCTION

MORE LANGUAGES FOR THE 1980s

By the time this anthology appears, it is hard for me to believe that a reader may not have heard of Ada, the new programming language sponsored by the U.S. Department of Defense. The Ada design effort was initiated several years ago and culminated in a competition between the Yellow, Green, Red and Blue teams. The winning group was from Honeywell Bull, a French firm, with the team leader being Jean Ichbiah. The resultant language was renamed to Ada, after the collaborator of Charles Babbage, Ada Augusta, Countess of Lovelace.

The first paper in this section presents an overview of the Ada language. Ada is especially interesting as it has tried to incorporate all that is known about good programming language features. This paper by Barnes gives one a solid introduction to almost all of these features and thus covers the very broad scope of the language.

Ada was designed for so-called embedded computer systems, systems which must reside in aircraft or ships. Thus it must fit into a machine which usually has severe constraints on size and speed. Nevertheless the language which was developed is very broad in scope and will likely find itself most suited for large-scale software development on a large computer. It will be a while until the complete language can be fitted onto a microprocessor. At the time of this writing no production compiler for the complete language has appeared.

Ada is so vast that it is impossible to succinctly summarize its most interesting features in the limited space here. The reader is advised to peruse the Barnes paper first. Nevertheless, some of the essential traits to look for are:

- [ ] Pascal is a subset, but truly a small subset of Ada. However, all of the data typing facilities of Pascal are contained therein.
- [ ] Character strings are a predefined type.
- [ ] The priority of operators has been altered to have six levels.
- [ ] Boolean expressions allow short-circuit as well as complete evaluation.
- [ ] Comments are started by double hyphens and terminated at end-of-line.
- [ ] Statements for selection and looping are mostly traditional.
- [ ] The go-to statement is included.

- [ ] Besides the usual typing convention there exist two additional facilities called subtypes and derived types. Type equivalence is determined by the name rule.
- [ ] A feature called a package exists and permits the definition and use of an abstract data type. A package defines a type which can be used to instantiate variables, protect the representation, and to simply collect together related objects. Tasks are packages which can be executed concurrently. The mechanism used to communicate between processes is in the form of the remote procedure call. Nondeterministic statements are used as in CSP.
- [ ] Separate compilation is provided for including the testing of interfaces at load time via a library which was created during compilation.
- [ ] Exception handling is an included feature and follows closely the lines laid down by Liskov in CLU.
- [ ] Procedures and packages may be made generic, thus providing an additional means of abstraction.
- [ ] Overloading of operators and functions is permitted.
- [ ] Various forms of input and output are predefined parts of the language.

The next paper presents a language which has become very popular with the success of the operating system called UNIX.[2] C is the main programming language which was used to develop systems on the PDP-11 running under UNIX. Its history traces back to the systems programming language BCPL developed by Martin Richards at Cambridge University in England. Some people do not like C because of its reliance on special symbols and the tendency to use one or two letter identifiers. But C is truly a systems programming language designed for experienced programmers and for this group it seems most suitable.

Though C includes typing, coercions are easily done. Another feature that encourages efficiency is register variables. These are variables that should be placed in high-speed registers during program execution. Although C has been used for more than ten years, its use has increased with the microcomputer revolution.

The final pair of papers are devoted to Prolog. With the growing interest in artificial intelligence has come a desire for more powerful languages. Although LISP is generally the language of choice, Prolog has come into prominence. In part this is due to its choice by the Japanese for their fifth generation machine.

The first article, by Kowalski, is a seminal paper introducing the concept of logic programming. The important notion of *Horn Clause* is presented and it is shown how this can be used to define recursive relations. The second article, by Davis, provides an overview of logic programming as implemented in Prolog. Notions such as backward chaining, nondeterminism, and unification are carefully explained with examples.

---

[2]UNIX is a trademark of Bell Laboratories.

AN OVERVIEW OF ADA*

J. G. P. BARNES

SPL International Research Centre, The Charter, Abingdon, Oxfordshire OX14 3UE, U.K.

SUMMARY

This paper commences with an outline description of the development of the Ada programming language and its position in the overall language scene. The body of the paper is an informal description of the main features of the final language as revised after the Test and Evaluation phase of the DoD project. Comparison with the preliminary version is made where appropriate.

KEY WORDS   Ada   Languages

INTRODUCTION

The final form of the Ada programming language procured by the U.S. Department of Defense has just been made publicly available.[1] This paper contains an informal description of the main features of Ada with some notes on the parts of the language which have changed since the preliminary version.[2]

Before describing Ada we will first outline its historical development and its place in the overall language scene.

HISTORICAL BACKGROUND

In the early 1970s the United States Department of Defense perceived that it needed to take action to stem the tide of rising software costs. In 1973 for instance it is reputed that software cost the DoD some $3000M of which 56 per cent was incurred by the embedded systems sector. By comparison, data processing took 19 per cent and scientific programming 5 per cent with indirect costs accounting for the remainder.

Big savings were clearly possible by concentrating on the embedded systems sector which embraces applications such as tactical weapon systems, communications, command and control and so on. A survey of programming languages in use revealed that whereas data processing and scientific programming were catered for by the standard languages COBOL and FORTRAN respectively, the scene for embedded systems was confused. Languages in use included several variants of JOVIAL, CMS-2, TACPOL, SPL/1 plus many many more.

It was therefore concluded that it would be of major benefit if some degree of standardization could be brought into the embedded systems area. This led to the setting up of the U.S. DoD High Order Language project with two goals. The first, short term, goal was to introduce a list of approved interim languages. The second, long term, goal was to identify or procure a single language for embedded systems.

The short term goal was quickly achieved and resulted in a list of five approved languages: TACPOL, CMS-2, SPL/1, JOVIAL J3 AND JOVIAL J73.

*Reprinted from *Software Practice and Experience* vol. 10, 851–887, 1980, copyright 1980.

The first step in proceeding to the long term goal was to develop a set of requirements and to evaluate existing languages against the requirements to see if an existing language was suitable. The requirements were developed in progressively more refined documents entitled STRAWMAN, WOODENMAN, TINMAN, IRONMAN and finally STEELMAN.[3] These documents were refined as a result of wide and public consultation.

The evaluation of existing languages occurred in 1976 against TINMAN. Evaulation of FORTRAN, COBOL, PL/I, HAL/S, TACPOL, CMS-2, CS-4, SPL/1, J3B, J73, Algol 60, Algol 68, CORAL 66, Pascal, SIMULA 67, LIS, LTR, RTL/2, Euclid, PDL2, PEARL, MORAL and EL-1 have been made public. These evaluations resulted in four major conclusions:

1. No language was suitable as it was.
2. A single language was a desirable goal.
3. The state-of-the-art can meet the requirements.
4. Development should start from a suitable base.

The languages evaluated fell into three classes:

'not appropriate'. These were languages which were obsolete or addressed the wrong problem area. Little could be learnt from these. This category included FORTRAN and CORAL 66.

'appropriate'. These were languages which although not directly suitable neverthe-less contained interesting features which should be drawn upon. This category included RTL/2 and LIS.

'recommended bases'. These were the three languages Pascal, PL/I and Algol 68 which were perceived as starting points for design of a final language.

At this point in time TINMAN was revised to give IRONMAN and proposals were invited from potential contractors to design a new language starting from one of the recommended bases. Seventeen proposals were received and of these four were chosen to go ahead and design languages in parallel and in competition. The four contractors with their colour codings were:

CII Honeywell Bull	—	Green
Intermetrics	—	Red
Softech	—	Blue
SRI International	—	Yellow

(The colour codings were introduced to allow comparisons on an unbiased basis.) All four chose Pascal as the base.

At the end of the first phase, the Blue and Yellow designs were eliminated leaving Green and Red to fight on. The final choice was made in May 1979 and the Green design was the winner.

The choice between Green and Red was probably not an easy one for the DoD. It has been said that the Red language contained the embryo of a better language. However the Red language had changed dramatically during the second phase and there had not been time for the full development of all the consequences. The Green language had changed much less and the definition was essentially complete. Clearly Green was the choice with the lower risk. Green could and would work whereas there was significant doubt about the implementability of some basic concepts in Red.

At this time the DoD announced that the new language would be known as Ada. Ada was the Countess of Lovelace, daughter of Lord Byron and the assistant of Babbage. She was the world's first programmer.

The HOL project then entered its third and final phase. The objective of this was to refine the definition of Ada and a large component was the Test and Evaluation exercise. This exercise consisted of various groups writing programs in Ada in order to probe its applicability. Some 82 reports were written and conclusions presented at a conference in Boston in October 1979. The general conclusion was that Ada was good but a few areas needed correcting.

The Test and Evaluation exercise was not without its problems. The time available had not really been long enough to design programs in the Ada style—it had usually been necessary to more or less take an existing program in another language and rewrite it at the procedural level. Some of the newer, 'programming in the large', features of Ada were therefore not always used as intended. Another problem was the difficulty of using the interpretive Test Translator on sizeable programs. The Test Translator had been developed as part of the phase 2 effort in order to show the feasibility of executing the language. A third problem was the terse nature of the Ada manual. Although the manual attempted to fully define the language, it had not been designed as a tutorial document. The need for thorough and extensive training was therefore underlined by the Test and Evaluation exercise.

Using material from the evaluation exercise the language was then refined and the result is the language outlined in this paper.

TECHNICAL BACKGROUND

We will now briefly describe the position of Ada in the overall language scene. We first note the emergence of two programming language cultures which we can refer to as the professional culture and the amateur culture although these terms are not completely satisfactory.

The professional culture is concerned with writing programs of a fairly permanent nature. These programs are usually fairly large and written by teams of programmers whose profession is primarily the design and writing of programs. The programs will or should be adequately documented and will need maintenance throughout a lifetime which may be several years long. Such maintenance will often arise as the environment in which they work changes throughout their lifetime. Because of this maintenance need it is essential that the language used is standard and stable. Any language changes should occur in a controlled way at infrequent intervals. Important characteristics of such a language are the need for separate compilation, readability and compile time error detection. Interactive use is not required. Examples of existing languages aimed at this culture are COBOL, PL/I, CORAL 66, RTL/2 and CHILL.

The amateur culture is concerned with writing programs of a less permanent nature. These programs are usually small and often written by individuals who are amateur programmers; that is to say that their profession is in a different field such as accountancy, medicine or chemical engineering and they use the computer merely as a tool in the furtherance of their main goals. The programs are often very short lived—perhaps used only once—and consequently need little or no maintenance and hence do not deserve or get significant documentation. Because of the short-lived nature of the program it is not vital that the language used is standard or stable. Indeed, languages in this area are under rapid development and standardization could be counter productive. Important characteristics of such languages are the need for ease of writing and general 'user friendliness'; interactive use is inevitable. Examples of such languages are BASIC and APL.

Ada is a language for the professional culture.

A great milestone in the development of programming languages was the publication of the Algol report in 1960. The step forward taken by Algol 60 was truly remarkable; no language since then has made such an impact on later developments. In fact, 1960 can be taken as the beginning of the awakening out of the dark ages. At that time there were just three languages FORTRAN, COBOL and Algol 60. Since then all new languages can be traced back to Algol 60. FORTRAN and COBOL have developed and COBOL in particular has borne dialects but these developments are not of the same degree as those emanating from Algol 60.

An early and ambitious development from Algol 60 was PL/I. Of course, it included much from FORTRAN and COBOL but it could not have existed without the Algol framework. PL/I has, of course, been an expensive failure. It contains too much of the same sort of thing and not enough in real power to justify its size.

Algol 60 itself never really caught on. It was a little academic and unfortunately neglected the need for separate compilation and input–output. (Pascal made similar mistakes a decade later).

A practical early language was JOVIAL, in fact derived from Algol 58, a little known prototype of Algol 60. Descendents of JOVIAL are currently widely used in USAF systems. CORAL 64 and then CORAL 66 sprang from JOVIAL and Algol 60.

CORAL 66 is well-known as a language for embedded systems. It was designed as a permissive language framework to woo programmers away from assembly languages. Unfortunately it was too permissive and the variation between the different implementations of CORAL 66 means that program portability is rarely achieved.

A big step (although with hindsight not wholly in the right direction) was the development of Algol 68. Algol 68 developed the concepts of reference and expression to an extreme degree. Unfortunately Algol 68 took an academic approach towards publicity; the definition was couched in terms quite inaccessible to the normal programmer and this was one reason for the very slow take up of the language. Another reason was the sheer complexity of the language and the large compilers needed. The task of writing an Algol 68 compiler was really too large for an academic group and too obscure for a commercial group.

A very practical language derived from Algol 68 is RTL/2. RTL/2 is small, contains the best of Algol 68 and does not neglect the important concepts of separate compilation and input–output.

An underlying common feature that makes the Algol 60-based languages successful is the ability to write programs with a clearly discernible flow of control. This 'control abstraction' is a key feature of the so called 'structured programming' revolution. It distinguishes these languages from FORTRAN which despite attempts at cosmetic improvement does not encourage the writing of legible programs.

However, it remains a fact that these languages take a very simple view of data types. In all cases the data is directly described in numerical terms. Thus if the data to be manipulated is not really numerical (it could be traffic light colours) then some mapping of the abstract type must be made by the programmer into a numerical type (usually integer). This mapping is purely in the mind of the programmer and does not appear in the written program except perhaps as a comment. It is probably a consequence of this fact that software libraries have not emerged except in numerical analysis. Numerical algorithms, such as those for finding eigenvalues of a matrix, are directly concerned with manipulating numbers and so these languages, whose data items are numbers have proved appropriate. The point is that the languages provide the correct abstract values in this case only. In other cases, libraries are not successful because there is unlikely to be agreement on the required mappings. Indeed different situations may best be served by different mappings and these mappings pervade the whole program. A change in mapping usually requires a complete rewrite of the program.

Pascal took the first significant step towards providing data abstraction in programming languages. A good example is the enumeration type. Enumeration types allow us to talk about the traffic light colours in their own terms without our having to know how they are represented in the computer. Moreover, they prevent us from making an important class of programming errors—accidently mixing traffic lights with some other abstract type such as the names of fish. When all such types are described in the program as numerical types such errors can occur.

But the success of Pascal cannot be attributed to the introduction of enumeration types alone since they are but a small step along the road to data abstraction. Pascal was designed as a reaction against the enormity of Algol 68. It derives from Algol 60 and Algol W. Unfortunately the good ideas of Algol 68 were thrown away with the bad ones and Pascal inherits many of the poor syntactic features of Algol 60. Other problems with Pascal are its stringent view of types which leads to its inability to handle arrays in as flexible a manner as Algol 60 and the absence of a facility for separate compilation. Input–output, although included in Pascal is handled in an *ad hoc* and inextensible manner. Pascal has found favour in the academic environment. Its small size makes it a useful teaching tool and easy to implement. It is also finding increasing favour among users of small machines although most implementations contain extensions to overcome the difficulties mentioned above. Unfortunately these extensions are rarely compatible and as a consequence investment in Pascal needs care.

Another later language from the same source as Pascal is MODULA. This puts right some of the syntactic errors of Pascal but more importantly introduces the concept of a module as a scope wall. It has long been recognized that the traditional block structure of Algol 60 does not allow enough control of visibility. For example it is not possible in Algol 60 to write two procedures to operate on some common data and make the procedures accessible without also making the data directly accessible. Many languages have provided such control through the medium of separate compilation. Examples are PL/I and RTL/2. This technique is adequate for medium sized systems but since the separate compilation facility usually leans on some external system, total control of visibility is not gained. The module of MODULA separates scope control from separate compilation. Indeed, MODULA ignores the separate compilation issue.

The concept of type introduced by Pascal and module introduced by MODULA sowed the seed for the second great software revolution which one can see on the horizon. Other experimental languages too numerous to mention have also made detailed contributions.

Data abstraction is the message of the second revolution whereas control abstraction was the message of the first.

Data abstraction means separating the details of the representation of the data from the abstract operations defined upon it. Data abstraction offers the possibility of writing significant reusable software libraries for areas other than numerical analysis. It should therefore greatly increase the possibilities for the sale of software packages.

Ada is the first practical language of the second revolution and embodies the fruits of research of the last decade. It could not have been brought about without the tenacity of purpose and funding available from a large user organization such as the U.S. DoD.

KEY TECHNICAL FEATURES

The remainder of this paper is a technical overview of Ada. Key modern features which the reader should note are:

- Strong typing—how this makes more errors detectable at compilation.
- Programming in the large—the mechanisms for encapsulation and separate compilation.
- Exception handling—giving the user appropriate control of error recovery.
- Tasking—Ada is the first language likely to be widely used which has contained embedded facilities for tasking.
- Data abstraction—private data types and representation specifications which separate the abstract properties of data from its physical realization.
- Generic units—the ability to parameterize units over appropriate data types; of particular value for libraries.

OVERALL STYLE

Ada identifiers are a sequence of letters, digits and medial underscores of which the first is a letter. The case of letters is not significant but underscores are. Ada follows modern practice of reserving those words which introduce syntactic forms thereby avoiding the necessity for a special notation. Sixty-two such words are reserved (e.g. **array**, **case**, **with** etc.) and cannot be redefined. Words associated with built in types are merely predefined (INTEGER, TRUE, STRING etc.) and can be redefined. In this paper we follow the usual Ada style of using lower case bold face for the reserved words and uppercase for all others.

Ada has the same number of reserved words as the preliminary version (**rem**, **with** and **terminate** have been added; **assert**, **initiate** and **packing** deleted; **restricted** has been replaced by **limited**).

Comments start with a double minus (hyphen) and are terminted by the end of line. (There is no facility for embedded comments such as in RTL/2).

    -- this is a comment.

Character strings are enclosed in double quotes, must be on one line and treat spaces as significant. The concatenation operator & caters for control characters and strings which will not fit on one line.

    "THIS IS A STRING"

Ada distinguishes a string of length one (an array of one item) from a single literal character (a scalar).

    "A"   -- string of length one
    'A'   -- the literal A

Numeric literals take two forms, those denoting integers and those denoting approximate numbers used for both fixed point and floating point. In both cases the notation allows for any base from 2 to 16 as well as conventional decimal notation. Medial underscores are allowed in order to break up long numbers but are, of course, not significant.

    123_456_789   -- decimal integer
    1E6   -- exponent form of integer
    2#1011#   -- binary integer
    5#1234#   -- base 5 integer
    3.14159   -- decimal approximate
    16#FF.FF#   -- hexadecimal approximate
    16#FF.FF#e1   -- with exponent

TYPES

A type introduces a set of values and a set of operations on those values. In addition a subtype introduces a shorthand for a base type with possible constraints. Type equivalence in Ada is by name. Two type definitions always introduce two distinct types. Structural equivalence as in Algol 68 introduces both complexity and risk.

Ada contains a limited form of type parameterization for use with records, especially variant records and private types.

ENUMERATION TYPES

As a simple example of the benefits of strong typing consider the following fragment:

```
declare
    type COLOUR is (RED, AMBER, GREEN);
    type FISH is (COD, HAKE, PLAICE);
    X, Y: COLOUR;
    A, B: FISH:= COD;
begin
    X:= Y;         -- ok
    A:= HAKE;      -- ok
    X:= COD;       -- no
end;
```

First note the general style. This fragment is a block which introduces declarations in a declarative part between **declare** and **begin** and a sequence of statements between

begin and **end.** All declarations and statements are terminated by a semicolon ; it is a terminator and not a separator as in Pascal.

> **type** COLOUR **is** (RED, AMBER, GREEN);

declares COLOUR as an enumeration type with literal values RED, AMBER and GREEN.

> X, Y: COLOUR;

declares X and Y as variables which can take values of the type COLOUR.

> A, B: FISH := COD;

similarly declares A and B as variables which can take values of the type FISH but also gives them both the initial value COD.

> X := Y;   and   A := HAKE;

are legal assignment statements which place values of the respective types in X and A.

> X := COD;

is however not legal since it attempts to assign a fish to a colour. This is a consequence of the rules of strong typing which protect the user by preventing him from accidentally mixing objects of different types.

It T is an enumeration type and V a value of the type then

> T'SUCC(V) and T'PRED(V)

give the successor and predecessor while T'FIRST and T'LAST are the first and last values of the type.

Observe that the BOOLEAN type is predefined as

> **type** BOOLEAN **is** (FALSE, TRUE);

NUMERIC TYPES

Although Ada was not designed specifically for numerical analysis nevertheless it solves the numerical accuracy problems far better than FORTRAN. It will be interesting to see whether Ada can overcome the inertia behind FORTRAN and replace it for numerical analysis.

The basic objective is to be able to write a program in as portable a way as possible despite differing word lengths on target computers.

Ada contains predefined types INTEGER and FLOAT and a given implementation may have additional types LONG_INTEGER, LONG_FLOAT etc. as appropriate. It is not intended that the programmer use these predefined types directly if he wishes to write portable programs. Instead we use the concept of a derived type.

A derived type is introduced by a definition of the form

> **type** T **is new** S;

In such a case T inherits the literals and predefined operations of S but is nevertheless a distinct type. Thus if we write

> **type** LIGHT **is new** COLOUR;

then LIGHT is an enumeration type with literals RED, AMBER and GREEN. However values of the two types cannot be arbitrarily mixed since they are different although they can be converted using the type name.

```
declare
   C : COLOUR;
   L : LIGHT;
begin
   C := L;          -- no
```

```
    C := COLOUR(L);   -- ok
  end;
```

(It should be noted that derived types are simpler than those of preliminary Ada and in the case of a user defined type, the only operations inherited are those defined in the same package specification as the type. This simplification has been necessary because of the inconsistencies which seemed inherent in the previous formulation).

Returning now to our numeric types, consider

type REAL **is new** FLOAT;

REAL will have all the literals (0.0 etc.) and operations ($+$, $-$ etc.) of FLOAT and in general can be considered as equivalent. Now suppose we transfer our program to a different computer on which the built in FLOAT type is not so accurate and that LONG_FLOAT is necessary. The only change needed is to replace our definition by

type REAL **is new** LONG_FLOAT;

However Ada enables the choice of FLOAT or LONG_FLOAT to be made automatically.

type REAL **is digits** 10;

indicates the REAL is to be derived from a built in type with at least 10 digits of accuracy. The implementation will choose FLOAT or LONG_FLOAT as required without any change to the program. Thus provided all the variable declarations are in terms of the derived type REAL rather than the built in types then the desired portability will be achieved.

Additionally there is the so-called mathematical library problem. We assume that there exist functions SQRT etc. for each of the built in types FLOAT, LONG_FLOAT. The problem is to ensure that one can write SQRT(X) where X is of type REAL and for the compiler to then call the appropriate version of SQRT according to the predefined type from which REAL is derived. This is solved by the use of the generic facility and writing

package REAL_MATHLIB **is new** MATHLIB(REAL);
use REAL_MATHLIB;

It should be observed that in preliminary Ada there was no need for action on behalf of the user—but unfortunately the mechanism did not work!

We now see that the source text is entirely portable; Ada therefore has more power than FORTRAN since there is no need to systematically change E to D in literals or change SQRT to DSQRT for the mathematical functions.

Observe of course that the user can define several types such as

type REAL **is digits** 10;
type LONG_REAL **is digits** 14;

and then use the more accurate type in the sensitive part of the program; conversion between types again uses the type name

```
  declare
    X : REAL;
    XX : LONG_REAL;
  begin
    X := REAL(XX);
  end;
```

In some implementations both types will map onto the same predefined type and the conversion will be null. In other cases a genuine conversion will be necessary but this need not concern the user.

A similar approach is taken with integers. A declaration

type INT **is range** −10000 .. +10000;

will result in the introduction of an integer type equivalent to

type INT **is new** integer_type **range** −10000 .. +10000;

where integer_type will be INTEGER, SHORT_INTEGER etc as appropriate. Note that the expressed range constraint still applies.

The above discussion has been simplified somewhat but the general principles should be clear. Ada also contains fixed point types but the author has a personal aversion to fixed point arithmetic and so does not intend to discuss them.

The attributes FIRST and LAST also apply to all numeric types while SUCC and PRED also apply to integer types.

The following subtype will be useful for a later discussion on strings

subtype NATURAL **is** INTEGER **range** 1 .. INTEGER'LAST;

Note that NATURAL'FIRST is 1.

ARRAY TYPES

Ada overcomes one of the major problems with Pascal. It allows formal array parameters to have arbitrary bounds.

Array types take two forms

type TABLE **is array** (INTEGER **range** 1 .. 6) **of** INTEGER;
type MATRIX **is array** (INTEGER **range** < >, INTEGER **range** < >) **of** REAL;

In the case TABLE the bounds are explicitly given. In the case MATRIX they are not. The type MATRIX may be used as a formal parameter in which case the bounds will be obtained from the actual parameter. Otherwise the bounds must be given when an object (or subtype) is declared for type MATRIX either by an index constraint or by deduction from the initial value if the object is a constant. Possible declarations are

A : TABLE;
M : MATRIX(1 .. 2, 1 .. 3);
z2 : **constant** MATRIX : = ((0.0, 0.0), (0.0, 0.0));

or we could introduce

subtype MATRIX_2 **is** MATRIX(1 .. 2, 1 .. 2);
V : MATRIX_2;

Of course index ranges do not have to be of type INTEGER, they can be any discrete type, for example

type COLOURS **is array** (COLOUR) **of** BOOLEAN;

This is an array of 3 elements indexed by RED, AMBER and GREEN. In this case we give no range qualification and so the range is that of the whole type. There is a difference here

A : TABLE : = (2,4,4,4,0,0);

gives initial values for the 6 elements of A in order. This is the positional form. The following named forms are equivalent.

(1 => 2, 2 | 3 | 4 => 4, **others** = > 0);
(1 => 2, 2 .. 4 => 4, **others** = > 0);
(1 => 2, 5 .. 6 => 0, **others** = > 4);

In the named form the order is immaterial but **others**, if used, must be last. Moreover, **others** may not be used if the aggregate is expected to provide bounds information. Named and positional notation may not be mixed in array aggregates although **others** may be used with either form; this restriction eliminates some problems of preliminary Ada.

Note the form for multidimensional arrays. Mixed forms such as

$$(1 => (0.0, 0.0), 2 => (0.0, 0.0));$$
$$((0.0, 0.0), (1 => 0.0, 2 => 0.0));$$

are allowed since there is no mixing within one level. Note also possibilities such as

$$(1 .. 2 => (1 .. 2 => 0.0));$$

Access to array elements uses the conventional parentheses as in M(I,J).

CHARACTERS AND STRINGS

A character type is an enumeration type that contains character literals and possibly identifiers. A special case is the predefined type CHARACTER denoting the full ASCII set of 128 characters. It is rather as if the declaration took the form

```
type CHARACTER is
    (NUL, SOH, .. 'A', 'B', .., DEL);
```

The printable characters are denoted by literals in single quotes and control characters such as CR and LF by identifiers.

There is also the predefined type STRING

```
type STRING is array (NATURAL range < >) of CHARACTER;
```

Note that the bounds of STRING are not explicit and any string object must therefore derive its bounds from a constraint or initial value. In the case of arrays of character types the lexical string is an alternative form of aggregate for those elements denoted by character literals. Thus we may write

```
S : constant STRING := "GIN";
```

and S is then an array whose bounds are 1 and 3. The lower bound is NATURAL'FIRST since the index is of subtype NATURAL.

Alternatively we could write

```
S : constant STRING := ('G', 'I', 'N');
```

If we wished to use control characters then we would write

```
CRLF : constant STRING := (CR, LF);
```

It should be noted that the lexical string can be used for an aggregate of any character type and not just the built in type. The following is permissible

```
type ROMAN_DIGIT is ('I','V','X','L','C','D','M');
type ROMAN_NUMBER is array (NATURAL range < >) of ROMAN_DIGIT;
NINETY_SIX : constant ROMAN_NUMBER := "XCVI";
```

RECORD TYPES

Record types without discriminants are illustrated by the following.

```
declare
    type MONTH_NAME is (JAN, FEB, ..., DEC);
    type DATE is
      record
        DAY : INTEGER range 1 .. 31;
        MONTH : MONTH_NAME;
        YEAR : INTEGER;
      end record;
    type COMPLEX is
      record
        RE, IM : FLOAT := 0.0;
      end record;
```

D : DATE := (4, JUL, 1776);
c1 : COMPLEX;
c2 : COMPLEX := (1.0, 2.0);

If initial values are given for components (as in COMPLEX) then any variable declared of that type without an explicit initial value (such as c1) takes the values by default.

Again there is the possibility of named aggregates

D : DATE : = (MONTH =>JUL, DAY =>4, YEAR =>1776);

This is perhaps of particular relevance in this example because of lack of international agreement on the ordering of components of dates.

Access to record components uses the conventional dot notation as in D.YEAR.

DISCRIMINATED TYPES

Discriminated record types provide a limited form of type parameterization. This gives more power to private types as discussed later. Variant record types are a form of discriminated type.

Consider

JOHN: PERSON :=(M, (19, AUG, 1937), FALSE);
BARBARA : PERSON := (F, (13, MAY, 1943), 2);

A person is a record containing a variant part discriminated by SEX which is a component. Thus one can write JOHN . SEX giving M. The discriminant can only be changed by a whole record assignment. The usual subtype and object constraints can be applied.

subtype MALE **is** PERSON(M);
JOHN : MALE := (M, (19, AUG, 1937), FALSE);

Note that the discriminants must occur first in an aggregate and the aggregate must be complete even when the discriminant has already been constrained as in the above example.

A discriminant can be given a default initial value; thus

type PERSON(SEX : GENDER := F) **is** ...

All declarations must ensure that the discriminant is set either from an initial value or from the default value. Thus

P : PERSON;

is only allowed if the discriminant has a default value.

A discriminant can also be used as the bound of an array component of the record as in

type TEXT(MAX : NATURAL) **is**
record
    LENGTH : INTEGER := 0;
    VALUE : STRING(1 .. MAX);
end record;

An object of type TEXT can be thought of as a varying string whose maximum is MAX and current size is LENGTH. One could then write

DAY : TEXT(9);

with the intention of storing strings such as "MONDAY" in DAY. Direct manipulation is tedious

DAY := (9, 6, "MONDAY   ");

but one can introduce functions which provide a more convenient notation.

ACCESS TYPES

Ada introduces the concept of an access type for manipulating references or pointers. The term reference has been brought into disrepute because of dangling references in Algol 68 and pointer has been brought into disrepute because of anonymous pointers in PL/I. Thus the new term access should therefore be thought of as a polite term for reference. However, as we shall see there are no dangling reference problems in Ada.

Consider

```
type LINK;
type CELL is
  record
     VALUE : INTEGER
     PRED, SUCC : LINK;
  end record;
type LINK is access CELL;
HEAD : LINE : = null;
```

These declarations introduce type LINK which accesses CELL. The object HEAD can be thought of as a reference variable which can point at objects of type CELL containing three components, a VALUE of type INTEGER and SUCC and PRED which are also references to objects of type CELL. The records can therefore be formed into a doubly linked list. Initially there are no record objects, only the single pointer HEAD which is initialized to **null** which points nowhere.

The accessed objects are created by calls of an allocator thus

```
HEAD := new CELL(0, null, null);
```

The keyword **new** is followed by the type of the object and an aggregate giving values for the components of the new object. The new object has zero as its VALUE component and the two other components are **null**. The access variable HEAD now points to this new object.

Suppose we introduce a further variable

```
NEXT : LINK;
```

and then consider the sequence of statements

```
NEXT := new CELL(0, null, HEAD);
HEAD . PRED := NEXT;
HEAD := NEXT;
```

This sequence acquires a further object and links it onto the front of the chain accessed by HEAD. Note how HEAD . PRED gives access to the component of the object. Unlike Pascal, dereferencing is automatic. The notation

```
HEAD . all
```

is used to refer to the whole object accessed by HEAD. Thus

```
HEAD := NEXT;            -- copies the pointer
HEAD . all := NEXT . all;   -- copies the object
```

Access types need not only refer to records although they often will. Thus one could have

```
type REF_INT is access INTEGER;
R : REF_INT := new INTEGER(46);
```

However the objects to which R refers must all be acquired through the allocator and not be directly declared as in

```
I : INTEGER;
R : REF_INT := I;    -- is illegal
```

The accessed objects are conceptually all at the scope level of the declaration of the access type. In general they will cease to exist only when that scope is left but of course by then all the access variables will also have ceased to exist. Thus no dangling reference problems can arise.

An inconvenience with Ada access types is that all the objects have to be created using the allocator. One cannot as say in RTL/2 declare some records and cross linkages between them in the form of initial values.

EXPRESSIONS

The predefined operators in Ada are shown in the following tables

Table I. Unary operators

OPERATOR	OPERAND	RESULT
+	numeric	same
−	numeric	same
not	boolean [array]	same

Table II. Binary operators

OPERATOR	OPERANDS		RESULT
and or xor **and then** **or else**	boolean [array] boolean		same same
= / =	any		boolean
< <= > >=	scalar, discrete array		boolean
in not in	value	range, subtype, constraint	boolean
+ −	numeric		same
&	one dim array		same
*	integer fixed integer fixed floating	integer integer fixed fixed floating	same same fixed same fixed univ fixed same
/	integer fixed fixed floating	integer integer fixed floating	same same fixed univ fixed same
mod rem	integer	integer	same
**	integer floating	nonneg integer integer	same integer same floating

These operators are grouped into classes given in the following order of increasing precedence

> **and or xor and then or else**
> = /= < <= > >= **in not in**
> + − & (binary +, −)
> + − **not** (unary +, −)
> * / **mod rem**
> **

Curiously the unary operators are not the most binding but have intermediate precedence. the precedence rules are otherwise as expected and far preferable to those of Pascal.

Some additional rules protect the user from himself. For example **and**, **or** and **xor** cannot be mixed without using parentheses.

In general the operators are much as expected but the following points are notable.

Not equals is represented by / = rather than the unpronouncable < > of Pascal which in Ada does good service in array ranges and generic formals. The real objection to < > is that < and > areot defined for all types and therefore the conceptual pun of combining them misfires.

Ada contains **rem** as well as **mod**. Division truncates towards zero and **rem** is the remainder of division whereas **mod** is the mathematical modulus operator.

A **rem** B has the sign of A whereas A **mod** B has the sign of B.

Note also that Ada has upgraded the short circuit forms **and then** and **or else** as operators. These forms indicate that the second operand is only to be evaluated if the result of the opration cannot be determined from the value of the first operand.

It will be noticed that some operators apply to many different types. The operators may be thought of as being defined by several functions distinguished by different formal parameters. This multiple definition is known as overloading. The particular definition to be used is decided by, for example, the types of the actual parameters.

CONTROL STATEMENTS

Ada contains the normal conditional, case and loop statements of modern languages. In all cases bracketed syntactic forms are used (as in Algol 68) rather than the archaic notation which Pascal inherited from Algol 60.

The closing bracket is consistently **end** followed by the main opening keyword thus

> **if** HEAD /= **null then**
>   HEAD . PRED := NEXT;
> **end if**;

The normal **else** alternative is provided and the contracted form **elsif** saves an **end if.** Thus

> **if** I = 1 **then**
>   s1;
> **else**
>   **if** I = 2 **then**
>   s2;
>   **end if**;
> **end if**;

and

> **if** I = 1 **then**
>   s1;
> **elsif** I = 2 **then**
>   s2;
> **end if**;

are equivalent.

The case statement allows a sequence of statements after each choice and as in aggregates a choice may be composed of several individual values or ranges thus

```
case TODAY is
  when MON => INITIAL_BALANCE;
  when FRI => CLOSING BALANCE;
  when TUE .. THU => REPORT(TODAY);
  when SAT | SUN => null;
end case;
```

Note the explicit null statement which emphasises the fact that no action is to be performed. The null statement is mandatory in this context although it was not in preliminary Ada. Note also **is** rather than **of**.

Three forms of loop statement are provided. The traditional iteration in which a control variable takes successive values in a range; thus

```
for I in A'RANGE loop
  A(I) := 0;
end loop;
```

sets all elements of A to zero.

Unlike Pascal the control variable is implicitly declared. The iteration proceeds backwards if **in** is followed by **reverse**. Of course the range can also take a form such as 1 .. N.

There is also a while loop; thus

```
while NEXT /= null loop;
  SUM := SUM + NEXT . VALUE;
  NEXT := NEXT . SUCC;
end loop;
```

adds together the value components of our chain of access objects.

The third form is the infinite loop

```
loop
    :
end loop;
```

The statement **exit**; transfers control out of the immediately embracing loop. There are also forms for conditional exit and exit from a named outer loop.

There is also the maligned label and goto statement:

```
<<L>>
goto L;
```

Note the interesting notation for a label. The goto statement is necessary for the easy creation of automatically generated programs.

SUBPROGRAMS

Subprograms in Ada are classified into procedures and functions. Procedures are called as separate statements whereas functions are components of expressions and return values. (The value returning procedures of preliminary Ada have been eliminated; a satisfactory distinction between them and functions in the face of aliasing and side effects seemed unattainable.)

Consider

```
type VECTOR is array (INTEGER range < >) of REAL
function INNER(A, B : VECTOR) return REAL is
  SUM : REAL := 0.0;
begin
```

```
    for I in A'RANGE loop
        SUM := SUM + A(I)*B(I);
    end loop;
    return SUM;
end INNER;
```

The function INNER computes the element by element inner product of the two vectors A and B. It is assumed that A and B have similar bounds—a better formulation would check this. The local variable SUM is declared in the declarative part between **is** and **begin** and the statements of the body are between **begin** and **end**. Note the occurrence of INNER after **end**—this is optional but if present must match the designator of the function. Return from a function occurs via a return statement which contains an expression of the appropriate mode and is the result of calling the function. There could be several return statements.

The function INNER could be used in a sequence such as

```
declare
    P, Q : VECTOR(1 .. 100);
    R : REAL;
begin
    .
    .
    R : = INNER(P, Q);
    .
    .
end;
```

A function can be designated by an identifier such as INNER or by a character string denoting a language operator such as ''*''. A function so designated provides an additional overloading of the language operator and is called with the same syntax. So if we write

```
function ''*''(A, B : VECTOR) return REAL is
    .
    .
end ''*'';
```

then we could write

```
R : = P*Q;
```

The compiler determines that it is the newly declared function that is to be called rather than one of the predefined multiplication operations because of the types of P and Q. In cases of ambiguity, an expression can always be qualified by a type mark thus

```
R : = VECTOR'(P)*VECTOR'(Q);
```

The parameters of a subprogram may be of three modes.

in The formal parameter acts as a local constant whose value is provided by the corresponding actual parameter.

out the formal parameter acts as a local variable whose value is assigned to the corresponding actual parameter as a result of the execution of the subprogram.

in out the formal parameter acts as a local variable and permits access and assignment to the corresponding actual parameter.

In the case of a function only **in** parameters are permitted. If no mode is given (as in the example of INNER) then it is **in** by default.

Ada specifies that scaler and access types are passed by copy but that composite types may be passed by copy or reference.

As an example of a procedure we consider the following which performs the action of linking an extra record onto the chain referenced by HEAD in an earlier example and takes account of the possibility of the chain initially being empty.

```
procedure ADD_TO_LIST (L : in out LINK; V : INTEGER) is
```

```
        NEXT : LINK;
begin
    NEXT := new CELL(V, null, L);
    if L /= null then
        L . PRED := NEXT;
    end if;
    L := NEXT;
end ADD_TO_LIST;
```

This can be called by a statement such as

```
ADD_TO_LIST(HEAD, 3);
```

As well as the conventional calling notation in which the parameters are given in order, there is also a named form similar to aggregates

```
ADD_TO_LIST(L => HEAD, V => 3);
```

Like record aggregates, named and positional forms can be mixed and the order of named parameters is immaterial. (The notation for named parameters is different from the preliminary version.)

In some cases it may be necessary to specify a subprogram without giving its body. This will occur with mutually recursive procedures since in Ada one cannot use something until after its declaration. It also occurs with packages. In such cases we write for example

```
function INNER(A, B : VECTOR) return REAL;
```

and give the body later but when the body is given the specification is repeated in full.

An interesting facility in Ada is the ability to provide default parameters—this applies only to those of mode **in**. The subprogram heading contains initial values which are used if no corresponding actual parameters are provided.

Consider the problem of ordering a dry martini in the USA. One is faced with choices described by the following enumeration types

```
type SPIRIT is (GIN, VODKA);
type STYLE is (ON_THE_ROCKS, STRAIGHT_UP);
type TRIMMING is (OLIVE, TWIST);
```

Standard default values are indicated by the following specification of a suitable procedure

```
procedure DRY MARTINI
    (BASE : SPIRIT : = GIN;
     HOW : STYLE : = ON_THE_ROCKS;
     WITH : TRIMMING : = OLIVE);
```

Typical calls might be

```
DRY_MARTINI(VODKA, WITH => TWIST);
DRY_MARTINI(HOW => STRAIGHT_UP);
DRY_MARTINI;
```

The first call shows mixed positional and named parameters. The last call produces the standard gin-based drink on the rocks with an olive.

PACKAGES

The package is the main structuring unit of Ada. It typically encapsulates data and subprograms providing access to that data. Normally a package occurs in two parts, a specification describing the facilities it provides and a body which is the implementation of the facilities.

As an example consider the following

```
package STACK is                -- specification
  procedure PUSH(X : REAL);
  function POP return REAL;
end;

package body STACK is           -- body
  MAX : constant := 100;
  S : array (1 .. MAX) of REAL;
  PTR : INTEGER range 0 .. MAX;

  procedure PUSH(X : REAL) is
  begin
    PTR := PTR + 1;
    S(PTR) := X;
  end PUSH;

  function POP return REAL is
  begin
    PTR := PTR - 1;
    return S(PTR + 1);
  end POP;
begin
  PTR := 0;
end STACK;
```

This declares a package STACK which provides access to subprograms PUSH and POP which manipulate a stack of up to 100 REAL values. The stack is implemented as the array S and PTR indexes the top element. MAX is a constant giving the size of the stack. The statements between the begin and end of the body are obeyed when the package is declared and may be used to initialize the package. The items MAX, S and PTR are not accessible outside the package.

The items in the specification may be accessed from outside the package by dotted notation.

```
begin
  STACK . PUSH(X);
  ...
  X : = STACK . POP( );
end;
```

or alternatively by a use clause

```
declare
  use STACK;
begin
  PUSH(X);
  ...
  X := POP( );
end;
```

The use clause indicates that the identifiers in the specification may be used without naming the package explicitiy; in cases of ambiguity the dotted notation can still be used.

A further possibility is to use renames

```
declare
  procedure SPUSH(X : REAL) renames STACK . PUSH;
  function SPOP return REAL renames STACK . POP;
begin
```

```
        SPUSH(X);
        ...
        X := SPOP( );
    end;
```

Note that the signatures of SPUSH and SPOP are given in full.

A parameterless function call takes mandatory empty parentheses whereas they are not required or allowed for a parameterless procedure call.

Renaming is both a shorthand and a partial evaluation; one can write

```
    AI : REAL renames A(I);
```

and then

```
    AI := AI + 1;
```

in order to avoid repeated evaluation of the subscript I. If I changes subsequently then AI continues to refer to the previous location. Renaming does not hide the old name.

Note that a package need not have a body in the degenerate case where the specification merely acts as a common pool of items such as variables. If, on the other hand, the specification contains the specification of a subprogram then the subprogram body must occur in the corresponding package body. Similarly a specification may contain the specification of an internal package and again the internal body must be in the main body.

PRIVATE TYPES

An important form of package is one with a private part. This enables a type to be made visible without revealing its internal structure.

As an example suppose we wish to provide a package for the manipulation of complex numbers but do not wish the user to know how they are represented. We wish to retain the freedom to change their representation from say cartesian form to perhaps polar form and to know that the user's program will not need altering (although it will need recompiling).

The specification of such a package might be

```
    package COMPLEX_NUMBERS is
        type COMPLEX is private;
        function "+"(X, Y : COMPLEX) return COMPLEX;
        function "−"(X, Y : COMPLEX) return COMPLEX;
        function "*"(X, Y : COMPLEX) return COMPLEX;
        function "/"(X, Y : COMPLEX) return COMPLEX;
        function CONS(R, I : REAL) return COMPLEX;
        function RL_PART(X : COMPLEX) return REAL;
        function IM_PART(X : COMPLEX) return REAL;
    private
        type COMPLEX is
            record
                RL : REAL;
                IM : REAL;
            end record;
    end;
```

In this the specification has a private part after the normal visible part. The private part gives in full the definition of any types declared as private in the visible part.

It is also possible to have a private constant in the visible part

```
    I : constant COMPLEX;
```

and then in the private part

I : **constant** COMPLEX := (0.0, 1.0);

The package body might be

package body COMPLEX_NUMBERS **is**

    function " + "(X, Y : COMPLEX) **return** COMPLEX **is**
    begin
      return (X . RL + Y . RL, X . IM + Y . IM);
    end;
    ⋮

    function " − "(X, Y : COMPLEX) **return** COMPLEX **is**
    begin
      return (X . RL*Y . RL − X . IM*Y . IM, X . RL*Y . IM + X . IM*Y . RL);
    end;
    ⋮

    function CONS(R, I : REAL) **return** COMPLEX **is**
    begin
      return (R, I);
    end;
    ⋮

    function RL PART(X : COMPLEX) **return** REAL **is**
    begin
      return X . RL;
    end;
    ⋮

end COMPLEX_NUMBERS;

The package can then be used in a fragment such as

declare
  use COMPLEX_NUMBERS;
  I : **constant** COMPLEX := CONS(0.0, 1.0);
  C, D COMPLEX;
  R, S : REAL;
begin
  C := CONS(1.5, − 6.0);
  D := C + I;   -- complex +
  R := RL_PART(D) + 6.0;   -- real +
end;

In practise further overloadings of the operators could be introduced in order to allow convenient mixed operations between types REAL and COMPLEX.

Now if we change the definition of COMPLEX to

type COMPLEX **is**
  record
    R : REAL;   --polars
    THETA : REAL;
  end record;

then the package body will need rewriting but the user program will not. The functions CONS, RL_PART and IM_PART must still present a cartesian appearance of course. The constant I (if in the package) would now be

I : **constant** COMPLEX := (1.0, 0.5*PI);

Thus the private type enables the abstract properties to be separated from their implementation.

A private type may have discriminants. Our earlier example of TEXT could be made private thus

type TEXT(MAX : NATURAL) **is private**;

The implementing type in the private part must have the same discriminants.

Assignment and the operators = and / = are normally available to private types but if the definition is prefixed **limited** then this is not so. Furthermore, = and / = may not be redefined, although they may be explicitly defined for limited private types.

TASKS

A task declaration introduces a separate 'thread of control' which executes conceptually in parallel with other tasks. A single task may be declared with a similar lexical form to a package

declare

    task T **is**   -- specification

    .

    end;

    task body T **is**   -- body

    .

    end T;

begin   -- active here

The task automatically becomes active (i.e. its body is executed) when the task elaborating its declaration reaches the following **begin**. (The initiate statement of preliminary Ada has been deleted.)

Consider the following example which illustrates the problem of a family arriving at an airport and faced with three tasks, booking a hotel, claiming their baggage and renting a car.

    procedure ARRIVE_AT_AIRPORT **is**

        task CLAIM_BAGGAGE **is**

         :

        end;

        task body CLAIM_BAGGAGE **is**

         :

        end;

        task RENT_A_CAR **is**

         :

        end;

        task body RENT_A_CAR **is**

         :

        end;

```
begin
   BOOK_HOTEL;
end ARRIVE_AT_AIRPORT;
```

On reaching the **begin** of the **procedure** ARRIVE_AT_AIRPORT, the subtasks CLAIM_BAGGAGE and RENT_A_CAR are automatically set active (we can imagine the children and mother being dispatched to do these tasks) while the main task (the father) calls the procedure BOOK_HOTEL. The three tasks meet again at the **end** of the procedure ARRIVE_AT_AIRPORT. A task terminates normally by reaching its final end. The main procedure cannot be left until both the subtasks have terminated and will wait at its end until they have done so. Thus the family is reunited.

An alternative formulation would be to treat the three activities as equal and to have three subtasks and a null body.

The primary means of communication between tasks is through entries. An entry declaration is similar to a procedure specification and can only appear in a task specification. The only declarations allowed in a task specification are entries—this restriction solves several problems with tasking in preliminary Ada and emphasizes the concept that the package is the main structuring tool.

One or more bodies for the entry are provided by accept statements; these must appear in the corresponding task body. An entry is called by another task in the same way as a procedure call. The mechanism is that of the extended rendezvous.

Consider a task T containing

```
entry PUT(X : INTEGER);
```

in its specification and

```
accept PUT(X : INTEGER) do
   .
   .
   .
end;
```

in its body and another task with a call

```
T . PUT(V);
```

Whichever task reaches its statement (call or accept) first waits for the other. When they rendezvous the parameters are transferred in the usual manner and the body of the accept statement executed. The calling task is held up while this happens and is only allowed to continue when the accept statement is completed. The two tasks then continue on their separate ways.

As an example consider the following task which represents a box which can contain a single integer value. A value can only be placed into the box when it is empty and taken out when it is full.

```
task BOX is
   entry PUT(X : in INTEGER);
begin
   loop
      accept PUT(X : in INTEGER) do
         V := X;
      end;
      accept GET(X : out INTEGER) do
         X := V;
      end;
   end loop;
end BOX;
```

Calls of PUT and GET take the form

```
BOX . PUT(57);
BOX . GET(Y);
```

A use clause cannot refer to a task and so entry calls from outside a task always refer to the task explicitly. But an entry could be renamed as a procedure thus

```
procedure PUT(X : INTEGER) renames BOX . PUT;
```

The rendezvous mechanism in Ada is asymmetric. The called task is named by the caller but not vice versa. Associated with each entry there is a (possibly empty) queue of waiting tasks—these are processed on a first in first out basis. Note that a task can only be on one queue since it can only call one entry at a time.

In some cases the purpose of a rendezvous is only to synchronize the tasks and not to transfer data. In such cases a degenerate form applies. The entry declaration and accept statement become

```
entry SIGNAL;
accept SIGNAL;
```

and the call is then

```
T . SIGNAL;
```

Non-determinism is introduced by the select statement as illustrated by the following task which provides access to the variable v of the previous example in a slightly different manner. In this case the ordering requirement that calls of GET and PUT must alternate is deleted and the only intent is that multiple access is prevented.

```
task PROTECTED_VARIABLE is
  entry READ(X : out ELEM);
  entry WRITE(X : in ELEM);
end;

task body PROTECTED_VARIABLE is
  V : ELEM := ...;
begin
  loop
    select
      accept READ(X : out ELEM) do
        X := V;
      end;
    or
      accept WRITE(X : in ELEM) do
        V := X;
      end;
    end select;
  end loop;
end PROTECTED_VARIABLE;
```

This shows a simple form of select statement. It contains branches separated by **or** and each branch commences with an accept statement. When the select statement is obeyed various possibilities arise. If neither READ nor WRITE has been called then the task waits until one is called; if one of READ or WRITE has been called then the appropriate branch is taken; if both have been called then one branch is selected in an unspecified but fair manner. Of course on each execution of the select statement only one branch is obeyed.

The next example introduces guards. It shows the classical bounded buffer example. The task BUFFERING contains an internal buffer which is used cyclicly and can hold N values. The problem is to ensure that the buffer cannot be over filled or under emptied.

```
task BUFFERING is
  entry READ(X : out ELEM);
  entry WRITE(X : in ELEM);
end;

task body BUFFERING is
  BUFFER : array (1 . . N) of ELEM;
  I, J : INTEGER range 1 . . N := 1;
  COUNT : INTEGER range 0 . . N := 0;
```

```
    begin
      loop
        select
          when COUNT > 0 =>
          accept READ(X : out ELEM) do
            X := BUFFER(J);
          end;
          J := J mod N + 1; COUNT := COUNT − 1;
        or
          when COUNT < N =>
          accept WRITE(X : in ELEM) do
            BUFFER(I) := X;
          end;
          I := I mod N + 1; COUNT := COUNT + 1;
        end select;
      end loop;
    end BUFFERING;
```

The integers I and J index the next free and last used elements of BUFFER. The integer COUNT indicates how many elements of the buffer are in use.

In this case the branches of the select statement commence with

when condition =>

Each time the select statement is obeyed these guarding conditions are evaluated and only those branches for which the guard is TRUE are eligible for consideration on that execution. In the example, COUNT is initialized to zero since the buffer is initially empty and so on the first execution of the select statement the guard on the READ branch is FALSE. Hence the first time round only the WRITE branch can be taken. When the rendezvous occurs the value is copied into the buffer. Note how the subsequent updating of I and COUNT take place outside the rendezvous but within the select statement. The select statement is then repeated and the guards reevaluated. This time both are TRUE (assuming N > 1) and so either another item can be added to the buffer or the first one removed.

The final classical example considered is that of the readers and writers. The intent is to allow several readers at a time but only one writer. A solution is as follows

```
    package READER_WRITER is
      procedure READ(X : out ELEM);
      procedure WRITE(X : in ELEM);
    end;
    package body READER_WRITER is
      V : ELEM := ...;
      task CONTROL is
        entry START;
        entry STOP;
        entry WRITE(X : in ELEM);
      end;
      task body CONTROL is
        RDRS : INTEGER := 0;
      begin
        loop
          select
            accept START; RDRS := RDRS + 1;
          or
            accept STOP; RDRS := RDRS − 1;
          or
            when RDRS = 0 =>
            accept WRITE(X : in ELEM) do
              V := X;
            end;
          end select;
        end loop;
      end CONTROL;

      procedure READ(X : out ELEM) is
      begin
```

```
        CONTROL . START; X := V; CONTROL . STOP;
    end READ;
    procedure WRITE(X : in ELEM) is
    begin
        CONTROL . WRITE(X);
    end WRITE;
  end READER_WRITER;
```

The solution above involves a package containing an internal task whereas in preliminary Ada it was a task containing a procedure in its visible part but as observed above the only declarations now allowed in the visible part of a task are entries.

The task CONTROL is automatically made active when the package body is elaborated—a notional **begin** and null initialization part to the package are assumed.

The procedure READ imposes a protocol on internal rendezvous with the control task. The current number of readers is RDRS and calls of START and STOP act as logging on and off signals. Writing is only allowed when there are no readers by the guarding condition RDRS = 0.

A problem with this simple solution is that a steady stream of readers will block out any writers. The following alternative formulation of the body of the task CONTROL overcomes this by only allowing a new reader if there are no writers waiting. This change alone could swing the balance too far in favour of the writers and so additionally after a writer any waiting readers are immediately dealt with.

```
    task body CONTROL is
      RDRS : INTEGER := 0;
    begin
      loop
        select
          when WRITE'COUNT = 0 =>
          accept START; RDRS := RDRS + 1;
        or
          accept STOP; RDRS := RDRS - 1;
        or
          when RDRS = 0 =>
          accept WRITE(X : in ELEM) do
            V := X;
          end;
          loop
            select
          end loop;
        end select;
      end loop;
    end CONTROL;
```

This formulation uses the COUNT attribute of an entry and a form of select statement with an else part.

WRITE COUNT is the number of tasks on the queue of the entry WRITE and so the guard prevents new readers from being accepted if writers are waiting.

If a select statement has an else part and if no rendezvous is immediately possible then the else part is obeyed. Thus after the rendezvous with a writer we loop accepting calls of START so long as there are calls to be processed. When the queue is exhausted the else part is taken and this causes the loop to be terminated. The reader will note that this revised formulation is not perfect since it allows readers to block out further activity provided they arrive more rapidly than they can be dealt with. But in such a case the system is grossly overloaded anyway.

TIMING

The delay statement allows a task to suspend itself for a given interval. The statement takes an argument of a predefined fixed point type DURATION given in seconds. Thus

delay 3.5;   -- delay 3.5 seconds

The user may provide constants such as

```
SECONDS : constant DURATION := 1.0;
MINUTES : constant DURATION := 60.0;
HOURS : constant DURATION := 3600.0;
```

and then write

delay 2.0*HOURS + 45.0*MINUTES;

There is also a library package CALENDAR with specification

```
package CALENDAR is
  type TIME is
    record
      YEAR : INTEGER range 1901 .. 2099;
      MONTH : INTEGER range 1 .. 12;
      DAY : INTEGER range 1 .. 31;
      SECOND : DURATION;
    end record;
  function CLOCK return TIME;
  function "+"(A : TIME; B : DURATION) return TIME;
  function "+"(A : DURATION; B : TIME) return TIME;
  function "-"(A : TIME; B : DURATION) return TIME;
  function "-"(A,B : TIME) return DURATION;
end;
```

The range of YEAR in the type TIME simplifies the leap year calculation. The function CLOCK returns the current TIME.

Repetitive action without cumulative drift can be achieved as in the following

```
declare
  use CALENDAR;
  INTERVAL : DURATION := ...;
  NEXT_TIME : TIME := ...;          -- first time
begin
  loop
    delay NEXT_TIME - CLOCK( );
    ACTION;
    NEXT_TIME := NEXT_TIME + INTERVAL;
  end loop;
end;
```

The operators − and + in the above are overloadings from the package CALENDAR.

A delay statement may occur as a branch in a select statement in order to give a time out facility. Thus

```
select
  accept READ ...
or
  delay 1.0;
                              - - time out action
end select;
```

If a call of READ has not been accepted within one second, the time out action is taken instead.

Ada also allows timed out and conditional entry calls, thus

```
select              select
  T . READ(...);      T . READ(...);
or                  else
  delay 1.0;
  ...                 ...
end select;         end select;
```

TASK TYPES

A task type is specified by the form

```
task type T is
  entry E;
  ...
end;
```

The body is as before. A task type acts as a template and individual tasks are declared using the task name in the usual way. Thus

```
A : T;
```

introduces a new task referred to as A. All task types act as limited types. The entry E can then be called as A . E;. The simple tasks introduced earlier can be considered as single instances of anonymous task types.

Task types are useful for creating synchronization objects. Consider

```
task type SEMAPHORE is
  entry P;
  entry V;
end;

task body SEMAPHORE is
  ACQUIRED : BOOLEAN := FALSE;
begin
  loop
    select
      when not ACQUIRED =>
      accept P;
      ACQUIRED := TRUE;
    or
      accept V;
      ACQUIRED := FALSE;
    end select;
  end loop;
end SEMAPHORE;
```

It would then be possible to declare semaphores as if they were normal data objects. Indeed one could declare records containing a semaphore and the data it is to protect.

```
type R is
  record
    S : SEMAPHORE;
```

```
    D : DATA;
  end record;
```

One problem with synchronization objects is leaving the scope in which they are declared. There is a general rule that one cannot leave a scope unless all locally declared tasks have terminated. To have to explicitly terminate such tasks would be tedious and so Ada contains a feature whereby a task can indicate that it is willing to be terminated when its declaring scope is left. This is done through a further alternative in a select statement. In the above case we would write

```
    select
      when not ACQUIRED =>
      accept P;
      ACQUIRED := TRUE;
    or
      accept V;
      ACQUIRED := FALSE;
    or
      terminate;
    end select;
```

Each time around the loop the task is then willing to accept a call of P or a call of V or to be terminated if the scope declaring it is left.

EXCEPTIONS

Ada provides a means for dealing with errors or other exceptional situations. The language contains several predefined exceptions such as NUMERIC ERROR. The user can provide a handler on units such as blocks and subprograms thus

```
    begin
      -- sequence of statements
    exception
      when NUMERIC_ERROR =>
      -- emergency action
    end;
```

If the NUMERIC_ERROR exception is raised during the sequence of statements, control is immediately transferred to the handler which in a similar form to a case statement specifies the emergency action to be performed. It is important to notice that the block is then left and control is not returned to where the exception was raised.

Exception handling is a dynamic mechanism. If a handler is not provided for a particular exception at one level then the level is terminated and the exception propagated to the dynamically calling level. It is possible to provide an **others** alternative to catch all exceptions.

It is also possible to declare user exceptions. Our earlier example of the package STACK did not check for stack overflow or underflow. This could conveniently be done by introducing an exception thus

```
    package STACK is
      ERROR : exception;
      procedure PUSH(X : REAL);
      function POP return REAL;
    end;

    package body STACK is
      MAX : constant := 100;
      S : array (1 .. MAX) of REAL;
      PTR : INTEGER range 0 .. MAX;

      procedure PUSH(X : REAL) is
      begin
        if PTR = MAX then
```

```
            raise ERROR;
         end if;
         PTR := PTR + 1;
         S(PTR) := X;
      end PUSH;
      function POP return REAL is
      begin
         if PTR = 0 then
            raise ERROR;
         end if;
         PTR := PTR - 1;
         return S(PTR + 1);
      end POP;
   begin
      PTR := 0;
   end STACK;
```

The user could then write

```
   begin
      STACK . PUSH(X);
      ...
      X := STACK . POP( );
   exception
      when STACK . ERROR =>
         ...
   end;
```

The statement

```
      raise;
```

within a handler reraises the current exception at the next level. This is convenient for recovery on a layered basis.

A minor change from preliminary Ada is that a handler applies only to the statements in a block. An exception occurring in the declarations is raised at the next higher level. This overcomes a problem in preliminary Ada whereby a handler could attempt to access objects whose declaration had not been elaborated.

The interaction between exceptions and tasking is somewhat complex and will not be described here. However one of the more irritating interactions of preliminary Ada has been removed: if a caller is aborted during a rendezvous the called task is no longer disrupted the caller is essentially 'propped up' until the rendezvous is complete and only then allowed to die.

The number of exceptions has been reduced: NO_VALUE_ERROR, OVERLAP_ERROR, INITIATE_ERROR and UNDERFLOW are removed and some other exceptions have been grouped on the grounds that their distinction is rarely helpful for recovery purposes: thus OVERFLOW and DIVIDE_ERROR have both become NUMERIC_ERROR.

GENERICS

The generic mechanism allows a subprogram or package to be parameterized by types and subprograms as well as normal **in** parameters. The generic mechanism allows a more precise categorization of type parameters than in preliminary Ada; this reduces the need for additional parameters.

As a simple example consider the package STACK introduced earlier. This only declared a single stack of length 100 and operating on elements of type REAL. The following formulation gives a generic package with the length and type of element as parameters.

```
   generic
      MAX : INTEGER;
      type ELEM is private;
   package STACK is
```

```
      ERROR : exception;
      procedure PUSH(X : ELEM);
      function POP return ELEM;
   end;

   package body STACK is
      S : array (1 .. MAX) of ELEM;
         .
         .
         .
   end STACK;
```

A particular stack is then declared by a generic instantiation which includes appropriate actual parameters.

```
   declare
      package MY_STACK is new STACK(100, REAL);
      use MY_STACK;
   begin
      PUSH(X);
      ...
      X := POP( );
   exception
      when ERROR =>
      ...
   end;
```

Note that a use clause can now appear anywhere in a declarative part thereby avoiding the necessity for two blocks for this example as in preliminary Ada.

The next example illustrates dependencies between generic formal parameters.

```
   generic
      type ITEM is private;
      type VECTOR is array (INTEGER range < >) of ITEM;
      with function SUM(X, Y : ITEM) return ITEM;
   package ON_VECTORS is
      function SIGMA(A : VECTOR) return ITEM;
   end;

   package body ON_VECTORS is

      function SIGMA(A : VECTOR) return ITEM is
         TOTAL : ITEM : = A(A'FIRST);
      begin
         for I in A'FIRST + 1 .. A'LAST loop
            TOTAL := SUM(TOTAL, A(I));
         end loop;
         return TOTAL;
      end;

   end ON_VECTORS;
```

Since we know that VECTOR is an array we are assured of the existence of attributes such as A'FIRST. In preliminary Ada such attributes would have been passed as separate parameters. Note however that no constraint is placed on the type ITEM and therefore no attributes can be assumed.

Other forms of formal generic parameters enable distinctions to be made between enumeration types, integer, fixed and floating types and access types.

SEPARATE COMPILATION

Ada recognizes the need to be able to compile a program in distinct pieces and provides facilities for both bottom up and top down approaches.

In the bottom up approach, packages and subprograms may be separately compiled and placed in a program library. Another unit may then be compiled later and refer to the units in the library. The dependency is indicated by a with clause.

Thus the package COMPLEX NUMBERS could be separately compiled and placed in the library. A procedure to solve quadratic equations could then take the form

```
with (COMPLEX_NUMBERS, REAL_MATHLIB)
procedure SOLVE(A, B, C : REAL; R1, R2 : out COMPLEX) is
    use COMPLEX_NUMBERS, REAL_MATHLIB;
begin
    ...
end;
```

The with clause allows the packages and subprograms mentioned to be used in the unit in the usual way.

The library system ensures that separately compiled units have conforming interfaces. If a unit is recompiled then all dependent units must be recompiled.

It should be noted that a package specification and package body are treated as distinct units for library purposes and that the body must be compiled after the specification. Moreover any unit using the package is dependent only on the specification and not the body. Therefore if the body is changed in a manner consistent with not changing the specification then any unit using the package will not need recompiling. It is because of the desire to obtain this independence that the private part is in the specification and not the body.

The top down approach introduces the notion of a subunit. In this case a unit body nested inside a parent unit is replaced by a stub in the parent and the body is compiled separately.

As an example the body of the package STACK could be written as

```
package body STACK is
    MAX : constant := 100;
    s : array (1 .. MAX) of REAL;
    PTR : INTEGER range 0 .. MAX;
    procedure PUSH(X : REAL) is separate;
    function POP return REAL is separate;
begin
    PTR : = 0;
end STACK;
```

The two subunits are then separately compiled and take the form

```
separate (STACK)
procedure PUSH(X : REAL) is
begin
    PTR := PTR + 1;
    S(PTR) := X;
end PUSH;
```

and similarly for POP.

The general philosophy is similar to preliminary Ada although there are minor changes. Perhaps the most significant change is the replacement of the restricted clause by the with clause. Note that the with clause is only used at the outermost level. The complexity of the internal restricted clause has been abandoned.

INPUT–OUTPUT

Input–output is provided by a generic package INPUT OUTPUT for the manipulation of files of a single type and a standard package TEXT_IO for handling text. These packages are not part of the language but notionally written in it. Ada contains adequate functionality (overloading, default parameters etc.) to enable convenient facilities to be provided for the user without having to embed them in the language as in Pascal. The problem with embedding such things into a language is that extension and functional composition are not possible. On the other hand the risk with leaving them out is that different implementations will produce different standards as occurred with Algol 60. In the case of Ada this latter risk should be overcome by the adoption of the currently defined packages.

A full description is not possible here but as an example consider calls of PUT for the output of text. This is an overloaded procedure with different versions for different types. Moreover, default parameters allow a standard field to be used if none is given.

```
PUT(I);              - - integer in standard field
PUT(I,6);            - - integer in field of width 6
PUT("MESSAGE");      - - string
```

CONCLUSION

It is hoped that this paper will have given the reader some idea of the power of Ada. The discussion has not been complete and no doubt contains some inaccuracies for which the author is solely to blame; this paper is no substitute for the language reference manual which should be consulted for a full and accurate description. Indeed, important aspects such as representation specifications and the name identification rules have not been discussed.

However, Ada should not be looked upon as just another programming language. A very important complementary activity has been the development of a parallel series of documents intitled SANDMAN, PEBBLEMAN and finally STONEMAN[4] relating to the concept of an Ada Programming Support Environment (APSE). It is recognized that for program and programmer portability it is not enough to have a portable language. The environment must also be portable. The development of one or more APSE's will be an important factor in the acceptance and success of Ada.

Another important factor is the recognition that strictly enforced standards are important. The U.S. DoD is developing a validation suite which will be a key factor in ensuring that compilers conform to the standard. It should be noted that this suite will be available before the first compilers.

Whether Ada will be successful or not remains to be seen. However, it is clearly a significant step forward both technically and politically. If the willingness and needs of large organizations such as the U.S. DoD cannot produce the climate for the introduction of a good general purpose modern language then we will have to continue to use out-of-date and/or non-standard languages such as FORTRAN and Pascal for ever.

ACKNOWLEDGEMENTS

The author would like to acknowledge all those engaged in the design of Ada with whom he has had the privilege to be associated but especially Jean Ichbiah who as the team leader is the prime designer of Ada.

REFERENCES

1. *Reference Manual for the Ada Programming Language,* United States Department of Defense, July 1980.
2. 'Preliminary Ada reference manual', *SIGPLAN Notices*, **14**, 6, Part A, (June 1979).
3. *STEELMAN*, Defense Advanced Research Projects Agency, Arlington, Virginia, 1978.
4. *STONEMAN*, Defense Advanced Research Projects Agency, Arlington, Virginia, 1980.

THE C PROGRAMMING LANGUAGE*

D. M. RITCHIE, S. C. JOHNSON, M. E. LESK AND B. W. KERNIGHAN

C is a general-purpose programming language that has proven useful for a wide variety of applications. It is the primary language of the UNIX* system, and is also available in several other environments. This paper provides an overview of the syntax and semantics of C and a discussion of its strengths and weaknesses.

C is a general-purpose programming language featuring economy of expression, modern control flow and data structure capabilities, and a rich set of operators and data types.

C is not a "very high-level" language nor a big one and is not specialized to any particular area of application. Its generality and an absence of restrictions make it more convenient and effective for many tasks than supposedly more powerful languages. C has been used for a wide variety of programs, including the UNIX operating system, the C compiler itself, and essentially all UNIX applications software. The language is sufficiently expressive and efficient to have completely displaced assembly language programming on UNIX.

C was originally written for the PDP-11 under UNIX, but the language is not tied to any particular hardware or operating system. C compilers run on a wide variety of machines, including the Honeywell 6000, the IBM System/370, and the Interdata 8/32.

I. THE LINGUISTIC HISTORY OF C

The C language in use today[1] is the product of several years of evolution. Many of its most important ideas stem from the considerably older, but still quite vital, language BCPL[2] developed by Martin Richards. The influence of BCPL on C proceeded indirectly through the language B,[3] which was written by Ken Thompson in 1970 for the first UNIX system on the PDP-11.

Although neither B nor C could really be considered dialects of BCPL, both share several characteristic features with it:

(*i*)   All are able to express the fundamental flow-control constructions required for well-structured programs: statement grouping, decision-making (if), looping (while) with the termination test either at the top or the bottom of the loop, and branching out to a sequence of possible cases (switch). It is interesting that BCPL provided these constructions in 1967, well before the current vogue for "structured programming."

(*ii*)   All three languages include the concept of "pointer" and provide the ability to do address arithmetic.

(*iii*)   In all three languages, the arguments to functions are passed by copying the value of the argument, and it is impossible for

---

* UNIX is a trademark of Bell Laboratories.

the function to change the actual argument. When it is desired to achieve "call by reference," a pointer may be passed explicitly, and the function may change the object to which the pointer points. Any function is allowed to be recursive, and its local variables are typically "automatic" or specific to each invocation.

(*iv*)   All three languages are rather low-level, in that they deal with the same sorts of objects that most computers do. BCPL and B restrict their attention almost completely to machine words, while C widens its horizons somewhat to characters and (possibly multi-word) integers and floating-point numbers. None deals directly with composite objects such as character strings, sets, lists, or arrays considered as a whole. The languages themselves do not define any storage allocation facility beside static definition and the stack discipline provided by the local variables of functions; likewise, I/O is not part of any of these languages. All these higher mechanisms must be provided by explicitly called routines from libraries.

B and BCPL differ mainly in their syntax, and many differences stemmed from the very small size of the first B compiler (fewer than 4K 18-bit words on the PDP-7). Several constructions in BCPL encourage a compiler to maintain a representation of the entire program in memory. In BCPL, for example,

```
valof $(
        . . .
    resultis expression
        . . .
$)
```

is syntactically an expression. It provides a way of packaging a block of many statements into a sort of unnamed internal procedure yielding a single result (delivered by the **resultis** statement). The **valof** construction can occur in the middle of any expression, and can be arbitrarily large. The B language avoided the difficulties caused by this and some other constructions by rigorously simplifying (and in some cases adjusting to personal taste) the syntax of BCPL.

In spite of many syntactic changes, B remained very close to BCPL semantically. The most characteristic feature of both languages is their nearly identical treatment of addresses (pointers). They support a model of the storage of the machine consisting of a sequence of equal-sized cells, into which values can be placed; in typical implementations, these cells will be machine words. Each identifier in a program corresponds to a cell, and a cell may contain a variety of values. Most often the value is an integer, or perhaps a representation of a character. All the cells, however, are numbered; the address of a cell is just the integer giving its ordinal position. BCPL has a unary operator **lv** (in some versions, and also in B and C, shortened to **&**) that, when applied to a name, yields the address of the cell corresponding to the name. The inverse operator **rv** (later *****) yields the value in the cell pointed to its argument. Thus the statement

```
px = &x;
```

of B assigns to px the number that can be interpreted as the address of x; the statements

$$y = *px + 2;$$
$$*px = 5;$$

first use the value in the cell pointed to by px (which is the same cell as x) and then assign 5 to this cell.

Arrays in BCPL and B are intimately tied up with pointers. An array declaration, which might in BCPL be written

$$\text{let Array } = \text{ vec 10}$$

and in B

$$\text{auto Array[10];}$$

creates a single cell named Array and initializes it with the address of the first of a sequence of 10 unnamed cells containing the array itself. Since the quantity stored in Array is just the address of the cell of the first element of the array, the expression

$$\text{Array } + \text{ i}$$

is the address of the ith element, counting from zero. Likewise, applying the indirection operator,

$$* \text{ (Array } + \text{ i)}$$

refers to the value of the ith member of the array. This operation is so frequent that special syntax was invented to express it:

$$\text{Array[i]}$$

Thus, despite its asymmetric appearance, subscripting is a commutative operation; the above example could equally well be written

$$\text{i[Array]}$$

In BCPL and B there is only one type of object, the machine word, so when the same language operator is applied to two operands, the calculation actually carried out must always be the same. Thus, for example, if one wishes to provide the ability to do floating-point arithmetic, the "+" operator notation cannot be used, since it implies an integer addition. Instead (in a version of BCPL for the GE 635), a "." was placed in front of each operator that had floating-point operands. As may be appreciated, this was a frequent source of errors.

The machine model implied by the definitions of BCPL and B is simple and self-consistent. It is, however, inadequate for many purposes, and on many machines it causes inefficiencies when implemented. The problems became evident to us after B began to be used heavily on the first PDP-11 version of UNIX. The first followed from the fact that the PDP-11, like a number of machines (including, for example, the IBM System/370), is byte addressed; a machine address refers to any of several bytes (characters) in a word, not the word alone. Most obviously, the word orientation of B cut us off from any convenient ability to access individual bytes. Equally important was the fact that before any address could be used, it had to be shifted left by one place. The reason for this is simple: there are two bytes per PDP-11 word. On the one hand, the language guaranteed that if 1 was added to an address quantity, it would point to the next word; on the other, the machine architecture required that word addresses be even and equal to the byte number of the first byte in the word. Since, finally, there was no way to distinguish cells containing ordinary integers from those containing pointers, the only solution visible was to represent pointers as word numbers and then, at the point of use, convert to the byte representation by multiplication by 2.

Yet another problem was introduced by the desire to provide for floating-point arithmetic. The PDP-11 supports two floating-point formats, one of which requires two words, the other four. In neither case was it satisfactory to use the trick used on the GE 635 (operators like ".+") because there was no way to represent the requirement for a single data item occupying four or eight bytes. This problem did not arise on the 635 because integers and single-precision floating-point both require only one word.

Thus the problems evidenced by B led us to design a new language that (after a brief period under the name NB) was dubbed C. The major advance provided by C is its typing structure, which completely solved the difficulties mentioned above. Each declaration in a C program specifies (sometimes implicitly) a *type*, which determines how much storage the object requires and how it is to be interpreted. The original fundamental types provided were single character (byte), integer, single-precision floating-point, and double-precision floating-point. (Others discussed below were added later.) Thus in the program

$$double\ a,\ b;$$

$$. . .$$

$$a = b + 3;$$

the compiler is able to determine from the declarations of a and b the fact that they require four words of storage each, that the "+" means a double-precision floating add, and that "3" must be converted to floating.

Of course, the idea of typing variables is in no way original with C; in fact, it was the general rule among the most widely used and influential languages, including Algol, Fortran, and PL/I. Nevertheless, the introduction of types marked an important change in our own thinking. The typeless nature of BCPL and B had seemed to promise a great simplification in the implementation, understanding, and use of these languages. By the time that C was created (circa 1972), advocates of languages like Algol 68 and Pascal recommended a strongly enforced type structure on psychological grounds; but even disregarding their arguments, the typeless nature of BCPL and B seemed inappropriate, for purely technological reasons, to the available hardware.

II. THE TYPE STRUCTURE OF C

The introduction of types in C, although a major departure from the tradition of BCPL and B, was done in such a way that many of the characteristic usages of the earlier languages survived. To some extent, this continuity was an attempt to preserve as much as possible of the considerable corpus of existing software written in B, but even more important, especially in retrospect, was the desire to minimize the intellectual distance between the past and the future ways of expression.

2.1 Pointers, arrays and address arithmetic

One clear example of the similarity of C to the earlier languages is its treatment of pointers and arrays. In C an array of 10 integers might be declared

int Array[10];

which is identical to the corresponding declaration in B. (Arrays begin at zero; the elements of Array are Array[0], ..., Array[9].) As discussed above, the B implementation caused a cell named Array to be allocated and initialized with a pointer to 10 otherwise unnamed cells to hold the array. In C, the effect is a bit different; 10 integers are allocated, and the first is associated with the name Array. But C also includes a general rule that, whenever the name of an array appears in an expression, it is converted to a pointer to the first member of the array. Strictly speaking, we should say, for this example, it is converted to an *integer pointer* since all C pointers are associated with a particular type to which they point. In most usages, the actual effects of the slightly different meanings of Array are indistinguishable. Thus in the C expression

Array + i

the identifier Array is converted to a pointer to the first element of the array; i is scaled (if required) before it is added to the pointer. For a byte-addressed machine, the scale factor is the number of bytes in an integer; for a word-addressed machine the scale factor is unity. In any event, the result is a pointer to the ith member of the array. Likewise identical in effect to the interpretation of B,

* (Array + i)

is the ith member itself, and

Array[i]

is another notation for the same thing. In all these cases, of course, should **Array** be an array of, or pointer to, some objects other than integers, the scale factor is adjusted appropriately. The pointer arithmetic, as written, is independent of the type of object to which the pointer points and indeed of the internal representation of the pointer.

2.2 Derived types

As mentioned above, the basic types in C were originally int, which represents an integer in the basic size provided by the machine architecture; char, which represents a single byte; float, a single-precision floating-point number; and double, double-precision floating-point. Over the years, long, short, and unsigned integers have been added. In current C implementations, long is at least 32 bits; short is usually 16 bits; and int remains the "natural" size for the machine at hand. Unsigned integers exist mainly to squeeze an extra bit out of the machine, since the sign bit need not be represented.

In addition to these basic types, C provides a conceptually infinite hierarchy of derived types, which are formed by composition of the basic types with pointers, arrays, structures, unions, and functions. Examples of pointer and array declarations have already been exhibited; another is

```
double *vecp, vector[100];
```

which declares a pointer **vecp** to double-precision floating numbers, and an array **vector** of the same kind of objects. The size of an array, when specified, must always be a constant.

A *structure* is an aggregate of one or more objects, usually of various types, which can be treated as a unit. C structures are essentially the same as records in languages like Pascal, and semantically, though not syntactically, like PL/I and Cobol structures. Thus,

```
struct tag {
        int    i;
        float  f;
        char   c[3];
};
```

defines a template, called **tag**, for a structure containing three *members*: an integer i, a floating point number f, and a three-character array c. The declaration

```
struct tag x, y[10], *p;
```

declares a structure x of this type, an array y of 10 such structures, and a pointer p to this kind of structure. The hierarchical nature of derived types is clearly evident here: y is an array of structures whose members include an array of characters. References to individual members of structures use the . operator:

```
x.i
x.f
y[i].c[0]
(*p).c[1]
```

Parentheses in the last line are necessary because the . binds more tightly than *. It turns out that pointers to structures are so common that special syntax is called for to express structure access through a pointer.

```
p->c[1]
p->i
```

This soon becomes more natural than the equivalent

```
(*p).c[1]
(*p).i
```

A union is capable of holding, at different times, objects of different types, with the compiler keeping track of size and alignment requirements. Unions provide a way to manipulate different kinds of data in a single part of storage, without embedding machine-dependent information (like the relative sizes of int and float) in a program. For example, the union u, declared

```
union {
        int    i;
        float  f;
} u;
```

can hold either an int (written u.i) or a float (written u.f). Regardless of the machine it is compiled on, it will be large enough to hold
either one of these quantities. A union is syntactically identical to a
structure; it may be considered as a structure in which all the
members begin at the same offset. Unions in C are more analogous
to PL/I's CELL than to the unions of Algol 68 or the variant records
of Pascal, because it is the responsibility of the programmer to avoid
referring to a union that does not currently contain an object of the
implied type.

A *function* is a subprogram that returns an object of a given type:

unsigned unsf();

declares a function that returns **unsigned**. The type of a function
ignores the number and types of its arguments, although in general
the call and the definition must agree.

2.3 Type composition

The syntax of declarations borrows from that of expressions. The
key idea is that a declaration, say

int   ... ;

contains a part "..." that, if it appeared in an expression, would be
of type int. The constructions seen so far, for example,

int   *iptr;
int   ifunc();
int   iarr[10];

exhibit this approach, but more complicated declarations are common. For example,

int   *funcptr();
int   (*ptrfunc)();

declare respectively a function that returns a pointer to an integer,
and a pointer to a function that returns an integer. The extra
parentheses in the second are needed to make the * apply directly to
ptrfunc, since the implicit function-call operator () binds more
tightly than *. Functions are not variables, so arrays or structures of
functions are not permitted. However, a pointer to a function, like
ptrfunc, may be stored, copied, passed as an argument, returned by
a function, and so on, just as any other pointer.

Arrays of pointers are frequently used instead of multidimensional arrays. The usage of a and b when declared

int a[10][10];
int *b[10];

may be similar, in that a[5][5] and b[5][5] are both legal references
to a single int, but a is a true array: all 100 storage cells have been
allocated, and the conventional rectangular subscript calculation is
done. For b, however, the declaration has only allocated 10
pointers; each must be set to point to an array of integers. Assuming each does point to a 10-element array, then there will be 100
storage cells set aside, plus the 10 cells for the pointers. Thus the
array of pointers uses slightly more space and may require an extra
initialization step, but has two advantages: it trades an indirection

for a subscript multiplication, and it permits the rows of the array to be of different lengths. (That is, each element of b need not point to a 10-element vector; some may point to 2 elements, some to 20). Particularly with strings whose length is not known in advance, an array of pointers is often used instead of a multidimensional array. Every C main program gets access to its invoking command line in this form, for example.

The idea of specifying types by appropriating some of the syntax of expressions seems to be original with C, and for the simpler cases, it works well. Occasionally some rather ornate types are needed, and the declaration may be a bit hard to interpret. For example, a pointer to an array of pointers to functions, each returning an int, would be written

```
int (*(*funnyarray)[])();
```

which is certainly opaque, although understandable enough if read from the inside out. In an expression, funnyarray might appear as

```
i = (*(*funnyarray)[j])(k);
```

The corresponding Algol 68 declaration is

ref [] ref proc int *funnyarray*

which reads from left to right in correspondence with the informal description of the type if ref is taken to be the equivalent of C's "pointer to." The Algol may be clearer, but both are hard to grasp.

III. STATEMENTS AND CONTROL FLOW

Control flow in C differs from other languages primarily in details of syntax. As in PL/I, semicolons are used to terminate statements, not to separate them. Most statements are just expressions followed by a semicolon; since assignments are expressions, there is no need for a special assignment statement.

Statements are grouped with braces { and }, rather than with words like begin-end or do-od, because the more concise form seems much easier to read and is certainly easier to type. A sequence of statements enclosed in { } is syntactically a single statement.

The if-else statement has the form

if (*expression*)
statement
else
statement

The *expression* is evaluated; if it is "true" (that is, if *expression* has a non-zero value), the first statement is done. If it is "false" (*expression* is zero) and if there is an else part, the second *statement* is executed instead. The else part is optional; if it is omitted in a sequence of nested if's, the resulting ambiguity is resolved in the usual way by associating the else with the nearest previous else-less if.

The switch statement provides a multi-way branch depending on the value of an integer expression:

```
switch (expression) {
    case const:
        code
    case const:
        code
    ...
    default:
        code
}
```

The *expression* is evaluated and compared against the various **cases**, which are labeled with distinct integer constant values. If any case matches, execution begins at that point. If no case matches but there is a **default** statement, execution begins there; otherwise, no part of the **switch** is executed.

The **cases** are just labels, and so control may flow through one case to the next. Although this permits multiple labels on cases, it also means that in general most cases must be terminated with an explicit exit from the **switch** (the **break** statement below).

The **switch** construction is part of C's legacy from BCPL; it is so useful and so easy to provide that the lack of a corresponding facility of acceptable generality in languages ranging from Fortran through Algol 68, and even to Pascal (which does not provide for a **default**), must be considered a real failure of imagination in language designers.

C provides three kinds of loops. The **while** is simply

```
while (expression)
    statement
```

The *expression* is evaluated; if it is true (non-zero), the *statement* is executed, and then the process repeats. When *expression* becomes false (zero), execution terminates.

The **do** statement is a test-at-the-bottom loop:

```
do
    statement
while (expression);
```

statement is performed once, then *expression* is evaluated. If it is true, the loop is repeated; otherwise it is terminated.

The **for** loop is reminiscent of similarly named loops in other languages, but rather more general. The **for** statement

```
for (expr1; expr2; expr3)
    statement
```

is equivalent to

```
expr1;
while (expr2) {
    statement
    expr3;
}
```

Grammatically, the three components of a **for** loop are expressions. Any of the three parts can be omitted, although the semicolons must remain. If *expr1* or *expr3* is left out, it is simply dropped from the expansion. If the test, *expr2*, is not present, it is taken as permanently true, so

```
for (;;) {
        ...
}
```

is an "infinite" loop, to be broken by other means, for example by **break**, below.

The **for** statement keeps the loop control components together and visible at the top of the loop, as in the idiomatic

```
for (i = 0; i < N; i = i+1)
```

which processes the first N elements of an array, the analogue of the Fortran or PL/I DO loop. The **for** is more general, however. The test is re-evaluated on each pass through the loop, and there is no restriction on changing the variables involved in any of the expressions in the **for** statement. The controlling variable i retains its value regardless of how the loop terminates. And since the components of a **for** are arbitrary expressions, **for** loops are not restricted to arithmetic progressions. For example, the classic walk along a linked list is

```
for (p = top; p != NULL; p = p->next)
        ...
```

There are two statements for controlling loops. The **break** statement, as mentioned, causes an immediate exit from the immediately enclosing **while**, **for**, **do** or **switch**. The **continue** statement causes the next iteration of the immediately enclosing loop to begin. **break** and **continue** are asymmetric, since **continue** does not apply to **switch**.

Finally, C provides the oft-maligned **goto** statement. Empirically, **goto**'s are not much used, at least on our system. The operating system itself, for example, contains 98 in some 8300 lines. The PDP-11 C compiler, in 9660 lines, has 147. Essentially all of these implement some form of branch to the top or bottom of a loop, or to error recovery code.

IV. OPERATORS AND EXPRESSIONS

C has been characterized as having a relatively rich set of operators. Some of these are quite conventional. For example, the basic binary arithmetic operators are +, −, * and /. To these, C adds the modulus operator %; m%n is the remainder when m is divided by n.

Besides the basic logical or bitwise operators & (bitwise AND), and | (bitwise OR), there are also the binary operators ^ (bitwise exclusive OR), >> (right shift), and << (left shift), and the unary operator ~ (ones complement). These operators apply to all integers; C provides no special bit-string type.

The relational operators are the usual >, >=, <, <=, == (equality test), and != (inequality test). They have the value 1 if the stated relation is true, 0 if not.

The unary pointer operators * (for indirection) and & (for taking the address) were described in Section I. When y is such as to make the expressions &*y or &*y legal, either is just equal to y.

Note that & and * are used as both binary and unary operators (with different meanings).

The simplest assignment is written =, and is used conventionally: the value of the expression on the right is stored in the object whose address is on the left. In addition, most binary operators can be combined with assignment by writing

$$a \ op= \ b$$

which has the effect of

$$a \ = \ a \ op \ b$$

except that a is only evaluated once. For example,

$$x \ += \ 3$$

is the same as

$$x \ = \ x \ + \ 3$$

if x is just a variable, but

$$p[i+j+1] \ += \ 3$$

adds 3 to the element selected from the array p, calculating the subscript only once, and, more importantly, requiring it to be written out only once. Compound assignment operators also seem to correspond well to the way we think; "add 3 to x" is said, if not written, much more commonly than "assign x+3 to x."

Assignment expressions have a value, just like other expressions, and may be used in larger expressions. For example, the multiple assignment

$$i \ = \ j \ = \ k \ = \ 0;$$

is a byproduct of this fact, not a special case. Another very common instance is the nesting of an assignment in the condition part of an if or a loop, as in

$$while \ ((c \ = \ getchar()) \ != \ EOF) \ ...$$

which fetches a character with the function getchar, assigns it to c, then tests whether the result is an end of file marker. (Parentheses are needed because the precedence of the assignment = is lower than that of the relational !=.)

C provides two novel operators for incrementing and decrementing variables. The increment operator ++ adds 1 to its operand; the decrement operator −− subtracts 1. Thus the statement

$$++i;$$

increments i. The unusual aspect is that ++ and −− may be used either as prefix operators (before the variable, as in ++i), or postfix (after the variable: i++). In both cases, the effect is to increment i. But the expression ++i increments i *before* using its value, while i++ increments i *after* its value has been used. If i is 5, then

$$x \ = \ i++;$$

sets x to 5, but

$$x = ++i;$$

sets x to 6. In both cases, i becomes 6.

For example,

$$stack[i++] = ... ;$$

pushes a value on a stack stored in an array **stack** indexed by i, while

$$... = stack[--i];$$

retrieves the value and pops the stack. Of course, when the quantity incremented or decremented is a pointer, appropriate scaling is done, just as if the "1" were added explicitly:

$$*stackp++ = ... ;$$
$$... = *--stackp;$$

are analogous to the previous example, this time using a stack pointer instead of an index.

Tests may be combined with the logical connectives **&&** (AND), **||** (OR), and **!** (truth value negation). The **&&** and **||** operators guarantee left-to-right evaluation, with termination as soon as the truth value is known. For example, in the test

$$if (i <= N \&\& array[i] > 0) ...$$

if i is greater than N, then **array[i]** (presumably at that point an out-of-bounds reference) will not be accessed. This predictable behavior is especially convenient, and much preferable to the explicitly random order of evaluation promised by most other languages. Most C programs rely heavily on the properties of **&&** and **||**.

Finally, the *conditional expression,* written with the ternary operator **? :**, provides an analogue of if-else in expressions. In the expression

$$e1 ? e2 : e3$$

the expression *e1* is evaluated first. If it is non-zero (true), then the expression *e2* is evaluated, and that is the value of the conditional expression. Otherwise, *e3* is evaluated, and that is the value. Only one of *e2* and *e3* is evaluated. Thus to set z to the maximum of a and b,

$$z = (a > b) ? a : b;   /* z = max(a, b) */$$

We have already discussed how integers are scaled appropriately in pointer arithmetic. C does a number of other automatic conversions between data types, more freely than Pascal, for example, but without the wild abandon of PL/I. In all contexts, **char** variables and constants are promoted to int. This is particularly handy in code like

$$n = c - '0';$$

which assigns to n the integer value of the character stored in c, by subtracting the value of the character '0'. Generally, in fact, the basic types fall into only two classes, integral and floating-point; **char** variables, and the various lengths of int's, are taken to be representations of the same kind of thing. They occupy different amounts of storage but are essentially compatible. Boolean values as such do not exist; relational or truth-value expressions have value 1 if true, and 0 if false.

Variables of type int are converted to floating-point when combined with floats or doubles and in fact all floating arithmetic is carried out in double precision, so floats are widened to double in expressions.

Conversions that involve "narrowing" an expression (for example, when a longer value is assigned to a shorter) are also well behaved. Floating point values are converted to integer by truncation; integers convert to shorter integers or characters by dropping high-order bits.

When a conversion is desired, but is not implicit in the context, it is possible to force a conversion by an explicit operator called a *cast*. The expression

$$(type) \ expression$$

is a new expression whose type is that specified in *type*. For example, the sin routine expects an argument of type double; in the statement

$$x = sin((double) \ n);$$

the value of n is converted to double before being passed to sin.

V. THE STRUCTURE OF C PROGRAMS

Complete programs consist of one or more files containing function and data declarations. Thus, syntactically, a program is made up of a sequence of declarations; executable code appears only inside functions. Conventionally, the run-time system arranges to call a function named main to start execution.

The language distinguishes the notions of *declaration* and *definition*. A declaration merely announces the properties of a variable (like its type); a definition declares a variable and also allocates storage for it or, in the case of a function, supplies the code.

5.1 Functions

The notion of *function* in C includes the subroutines and functions of Fortran and the procedures of most other languages. A function call is written

$$name (arglist)$$

where the parentheses are required even if the argument list is empty. All functions may be used recursively.

Arguments are passed by value, so the called function cannot in any way affect the actual argument with which it was called. This permits the called program to use its formal arguments as conveniently initialized local variables. Call by value also eliminates the class of errors, familiar to Fortran programmers, in which a constant is passed to a subroutine that tries to alter the corresponding argument. An array name as an actual argument, however, is converted to a pointer to the first array element (as it always is), so the effect is as if arrays were called by reference; given the pointer, the called function can work its will on the individual elements of the array.

When a function must return a value through its argument list, an explicit pointer may be passed, and the function references the ultimate target through this pointer. For example, the function swap(pa, pb) interchanges two integers pointed to by its arguments:

```
swap(px, py)          /* flip int's pointed to by px and py */
int *px, *py;
{
      int temp;

      temp = *px;
      *px = *py;
      *py = temp;
}
```

This also demonstrates the form of a function definition: the name is followed by an argument list; the arguments are declared, and the body of the function is a block, or compound statement, enclosed in braces. Declarations of local variables may follow the opening brace.

A function returns a value by

```
                    return expression;
```

The *expression* is automatically coerced to the type that the function returns. By default, functions are assumed to return int; if this is not the case, the function must be declared both in the calling routine and when it is defined. For example, a function definition is

```
double sqrt(x)          /* returns square root of x */
double x;
{
        ...
}
```

In the caller, the declaration is

```
                    double y, sqrt();

                    y = sqrt(y);
```

A function argument may be any of the basic types or a pointer, but not an array, structure, union, or function. The same is true of the value returned by a function. (The most recent versions of the language, still not standard everywhere, permit structures and unions as arguments and values of functions and allow them to be assigned.)

5.2 Data

Data declared at the top level (that is, outside the body of any function definition) are static in lifetime, and exist throughout the execution of the program. Variables declared within a function body are by default *automatic*: they come into existence when the function is entered and vanish when it is exited. Automatic variables may be declared to be **register** variables; when possible they will be placed in machine registers, which may result in smaller, faster code. The **register** declaration is only considered a hint to the compiler; no hardware register names are mentioned, and the hint may be ignored if the compiler wishes.

Static variables exist throughout the execution of a program, and retain their values across function calls. Static variables may be local to a function or (if defined at the top level) common to several functions.

External variables have the same lifetime as static, but they are also accessible to programs from other source files. That is, all references to an identically named external variable are references to the same thing.

The "storage class" of a variable can be explicitly announced in its declaration:

```
static int x;
extern double y[10];
```

More often the defaults for the context are sufficient. Inside a function, the default is **auto** (for automatic). Outside a function, at the top level, the default is **extern**. Since automatic and register variables are specific to a particular call of a particular function, they cannot be declared at the top level. Neither top-level variables nor functions explicitly declared **static** are visible to functions outside the file in which they appear.

5.3 Scope

Declarations may appear either at the top level or at the head of a block (compound statement). Declarations in an inner block temporarily override those of identically named variables outside. The scope of a declaration persists until the end of its block, or until the end of the file, if it was at the top level.

Since function definitions may be given only at the top level (that is, they may not be nested), there are no internal procedures. They have been forbidden not for any philosophical reason, but only to simplify the implementation. It has turned out that the ability to make certain functions and data invisible to programs in other files (by explicitly declaring them **static**) is sufficient to provide one of their most important uses, namely hiding their names from other functions. (However, it is not possible for one function to access the internal variables of another, as internal procedures could do.) Similarly, the ability to conceal functions and data in one file from access by another satisfies some of the most crucial requirements of modular programming (as in languages like Alphard, CLU, and Euclid), even though it does not satisfy them all.

VI. C PREPROCESSOR

It is well recognized that "magic numbers" in a program are a sign of bad programming. Most languages, therefore, provide a way to define symbolic names for constants, so that the value of a magic number need be specified in only one place, and the rest of the code can refer to the value by some mnemonic name. In C such a mechanism is available, but it is not part of the syntax of the language; instead, symbolic naming is provided by a macro preprocessor automatically invoked as part of every C compilation. For example, given the definitions

```
#define    PI    3.14159
#define    E     2.71284
```

the preprocessor replaces all occurrences of a defined name by the corresponding defining string. (Upper-case names are normally chosen to emphasize that these are not variables.) Thus, when the programmer recognizes that he has written an incorrect value for *e*, only the definition line has to be changed to

```
#define    E    2.71828
```

instead of each instance of the constant in the program.

Providing this service by a macro processor instead of by syntax has some significant advantages. The replacement text is not restricted to being numbers; any string of characters is permitted. Furthermore, the token being replaced need not be a variable, although it must have the form of a name. For example, one can define

```
#define    forever        for (;;)
```

and then write infinite loops as

```
forever {
    ...
}
```

The macro processor also permits macros to have arguments; this capability is heavily used by some I/O packages.

A second service of the C preprocessor is library file inclusion: a source line of the form

```
#include    "name"
```

causes the contents of the file **name** to be interpolated into the source at that point. (**include**s may be nested.) This feature is much used, especially in larger programs, for making sure that all the source files of the program are supplied with identical **#define**s, global data declarations, and the like.

VII. ENVIRONMENTAL CONSIDERATIONS

By intent, the C language confines itself to facilities that can be mapped relatively efficiently and directly into machine instructions. For example, writing matrix operations that look exactly like scalar operations is possible in some programming languages and occasionally misleads programmers into believing that matrix operations are as cheap as scalar operations. More important, restricting the domain of the C compiler to those areas where it knows how to do a relatively effective job provides the freedom to design subroutine libraries for the remaining tasks without constraining them to fit into some language specification. When the compiler cannot implement some facility without heavy costs in nonportability, complexity, or efficiency, there are many benefits to leaving out such a facility: it simplifies the language and the compiler, frequently without inconveniencing the user (who often rejects a high-cost built-in operation and does it himself anyway).

At present, C is restricted to simple operations on simple data types. As a result, although the C area of operation is comparatively clean and pleasant, the user must know something about the polluting effects of the environment to get most jobs done. A program can always access the raw system calls on each system if very close interaction with the operating system is needed, but standard library routines have been implemented in each C environment that try to encourage portability while retaining speed and flexibility. The basic areas covered by the standard library at present are storage allocation, string handling, and I/O. Additional libraries and utilities are available for such areas as graphics, coroutine sequencing, execution time monitoring, and parsing.

The only automatic storage management service provided by C itself is the stack discipline for automatic variables. Two subroutines exist for more flexible storage handling. The function calloc (n, s) returns a pointer to a properly aligned storage block that will hold n items each of which is s bytes long. Normally s is obtained from the sizeof pseudo-function, a compile-time function that yields the size in bytes of a variable or data type. To return a block obtained from calloc to the free storage pool, cfree (p) may be called, where p is a value returned by a previous call to calloc.

Another set of routines deals with string handling. There is no "string" data type, but an array of characters, with a convention that the end of a string is indicated by a null byte, can be used for the same purpose. The most commonly used string routines perform the functions of copying one string to another, comparing two strings, and computing a string length. More sophisticated string operations can often be performed using the I/O routines, which are described next.

Most of the routines in the standard library deal with input and output. Most C programmers use stream I/O, although there is no reason why record I/O could not be used with the language. There are three default streams: the standard input, the standard output, and the error output. The most elementary routines for dealing with these streams are getchar( ) which reads a character from the standard input, and putchar(c), which writes the character c on the standard output. In the environments in which C programs run, it is generally possibly to redirect these streams to files or other programs; the program itself does not change and is unaware of the redirection.

The most common output function is printf (format, data1, data2, ...), which performs data conversion for formatted output. The string format is copied to the standard output, except that when a conversion specification introduced by a % character is found in format it is replaced by the value of the next data argument, converted according to the specification. For example,

$$\text{printf("n = \%d, x = \%f", n, x);}$$

prints n as a decimal integer and x as a floating point number, as in

$$\text{n = 17, x = 12.34}$$

A similar function scanf performs formatted input conversion.

All the routines mentioned have versions that operate on streams other than the standard input or output, and printf and scanf variants may also process a string, to allow for in-memory format conversion. Other routines in the I/O library transmit whole lines between memory and files, and check for error or end-of-file status.

Many other routines and utilities are used with C, somewhat more on UNIX than on other systems. As an example, it is possible to compile and load a C program so that when the program is run, data are collected on the number of times each function is called and how long it executes. This profile pinpoints the parts of a program that dominate the run-time.

VIII. EXPERIENCE WITH C

C compilers exist for the most widely used machines at Bell Laboratories (the IBM S/370, Honeywell 6000, PDP-11) and perhaps 10 others. Several hundred programmers within Bell Laboratories and many outside use C as their primary programming language.

8.1 Favorable experiences

C has completely displaced assembly language in UNIX programs. All applications code, the C compiler itself, and the operating system (except for about 1000 lines of initial bootstrap, etc.) are written in C. Although compilers or interpreters are available under UNIX for Fortran, Pascal, Algol 68, Snobol, APL, and other languages, most programmers make little use of them. Since C is a relatively low-level language, it is adequately efficient to prevent people from resorting to assembler, and yet sufficienctly terse and expressive that its users prefer it to PL/I or other very large languages.

A language that doesn't have everything is actually easier to program in than some that do. The limitations of C often imply shorter manuals and easier training and adaptation. Language design, especially when done by a committee, often tends toward including all doubtful features, since there is no quick answer to the advocate who insists that the new feature will be useful to some and can be ignored by others. But this results in long manuals and hierarchies of "experts" who know progressively larger subsets of the language. In practice, if a feature is not used often enough to be familiar and does not complete some structure of syntax or semantics, it should probably be left out. Otherwise, the manual and compiler get bulky, the users get surprises, and it becomes harder and harder to maintain and use the language. It is also desirable to avoid language features that cannot be compiled efficiently; programmers like to feel that the cost of a statement is comparable to the difficulty in writing it. C has thus avoided implementing operations in the language that would have to be performed by subroutine call. As compiler technology improves, some extensions (e.g., structure assignment) are being made to C, but always with the same principles in mind.

One direction for possible expansion of the language has been explicitly avoided. Although C is much used for writing operating systems and associated software, there are no facilities for multiprogramming, parallel operations, synchronization, or process control. We believe that making these operations primitives of the language is inappropriate, mostly because language design is hard enough in itself without incorporating into it the design of operating systems. Language facilities of this sort tend to make strong assumptions about the underlying operating system that may match very poorly what it actually does.

8.2 Unfavorable experiences

The design and implementation of C can (or could) be criticized on a number of points. Here we discuss some of the more vulnerable aspects of the language.

8.2.1 Language level

Some users complain that C is an insufficiently high-level language; for example, they want string data types and operations, or variable-size multi-dimensional arrays, or generic functions. Sometimes a suggested extension merely involves lifting some restriction. For example, allowing variable-size arrays would actually simplify the language specification, since it would only involve allowing general expressions in place of constants in certain contexts.

Many other extensions are plausible; since the low level of C was praised in the previous section as an advantage of the language, most will not be further discussed. One is worthy of mention, however. The C language provides no facility for I/O, leaving this job to library routines. The following fragment illustrates one difficulty with this approach:

```
printf("%d\n", x);
```

The problem arises because on machines on which int is not the same as long, x may not be long; if it were, the program must be written

```
printf("%D\n", x);
```

so as to tell printf the length of x. Thus, changing the type of x involves changing not only its declaration, but also other parts of the program. If I/O were built into the language, the association between the type of an expression and the format in which it is printed could be reconciled by the compiler.

8.2.2 Type safety

C has traditionally been permissive in checking whether an expression is used in a context appropriate to its type. A complete list of examples would be long, but two of the most important should illustrate sufficiently. The types of formal arguments of functions are in general not known, and in any case are not checked by the compiler against the actual arguments at each call. Thus in the statement

```
s = sin(1);
```

the fact that the sin routine takes a floating-point argument is not noticed until the erroneous result is detected by the programmer.

In the structure reference

```
p->memb
```

p is simply assumed to point to a structure of which memb is a member; p might even be an integer and not a pointer at all.

Much of the explanation, if not justification, for such laxity is the typeless nature of C's predecessor languages. Fortunately, a justification need no longer be attempted, since a program is now available that detects all common type mismatches. This utility, called lint because it picks bits of fluff from programs, examines a set of files and complains about a great many dubious constructions, ranging from unused or uninitialized variables through the type errors mentioned. Programs that pass unscathed through lint enjoy about as complete freedom from type errors as do Algol 68 programs, with a few exceptions: unions are not checked dynamically, and explicit escapes are available that in effect turn off checking.

Some languages, such as Pascal and Euclid, allow the writer to specify that the value of a given variable may assume only a given subrange of the integers. This facility is often connected with the usage of arrays, in that any array index must be a variable or expression whose type specifies a subset of the set given by the bounds of the array. This approach is not without theoretical difficulties, as suggested by Habermann.[4] In itself it does not solve the problems of variables assuming unexpected values or of accessing outside array bounds; such things must (in general) be detected dynamically. Still, the extra information provided by specifying the permissible range for each variable provides valuable information for the compiler and any verifier program. C has no corresponding facility.

One of the characteristic features of C is its rather complete integration of the notion of pointer and of address arithmetic. Some writers, notably Hoare,[5] have argued against the very notion of pointer. We feel, however, that the facilities offered by pointers are too valuable to give up lightly.

8.2.3 Syntax peculiarities

Some people are annoyed by the terseness of expression that is one of the characteristics of the language. We view C's short operators and general lack of noise as a benefit. For example, the use of braces { } for grouping instead of begin and end seems appropriate in view of the frequency of the operation. The use of braces even fits well into ordinary mathematical notation.

Terseness can lead to code that is hard to read, however. For example,

$$*++*argv$$

where argv has been declared char **argv (pointer into an array of character pointers) means: select the character pointer pointed at by argv (*argv), increment it by one (++*argv), then fetch the character that *that* pointer points at (*++*argv). This is concise and efficient but reminiscent of APL.

An example of a minor problem is the comment convention, which is PL/I's /* ... */. Comments do not nest, so an effort to "comment out" a section of code will fail if that section contains a comment. And a number of us can testify that it is surprisingly hard to recognize when an "end comment" delimiter has been botched, so that the comment silently continues until the next comment is reached, deleting a line or two of code. It would be more convenient if a single unique character were reserved to introduce a comment, and if comments always terminated at an end of line.

8.2.4 Semantic peculiarities

There are some occasionally surprising operator precedences. For example,

$$a >> 4 + 5$$

shifts right by 9. Perhaps worse,

$$(x \text{ \& } MASK) == 0$$

must be parenthesized to associate the proper way. Users learn quickly to parenthesize such doubtful cases; and when feasible lint warns of suspicious expressions (including both of these).

We have already mentioned the fact that the **case** actions in a switch flow through unless explicitly broken. In practice, users write so many **switch** statements that they become familiar with this behavior and some even prefer it.

Some problems arise from machine differences that are reflected, perhaps unnecessarily, into the semantics of C. For example, the PDP-11 does sign extension on byte fetches, so that a character (viewed arithmetically) can have a value ranging from -128 to $+127$, rather than 0 to $+255$. Although the reference manual makes it quite clear that the precise range of a **char** variable is machine dependent, programmers occasionally succumb to the temptation of using the full range that their local machine can represent, forgetting that their programs may not work on another machine. The fundamental problem, of course, is that C permits small numbers, as well as genuine characters, to be stored in **char** variables. This might not be necessary if, for example, the notion of subranges (mentioned above) were introduced into the language.

8.2.5 Miscellaneous

C was developed and is generally used in a highly responsive interactive environment, and accordingly the compiler provides few of the services usually associated with batch compilers. For example, it prepares no listing of the source program, no cross reference table, and no indication of the nature of the generated code. Such facilities are available, but they are separate programs, not parts of the compiler. Programmers used to batch environments may find it hard to live without giant listings; we would find it hard to use them.

IX. CONCLUSIONS AND FUTURE DIRECTIONS

C has continued to develop in recent years, mostly by upwardly compatible extensions, occasionally by restrictions against manifestly nonportable or illegal programs that happened to be compiled into something useful. The most recent major changes were motivated by the extension of C to other machines, and the resulting emphasis on portability. The advent of **union** and of casts reflects a desire to be more precise about types when moving to other machines is in prospect. These changes have had relatively little effect on programmers who remained entirely on the UNIX system. Of more importance was a new library, which changed the use of a "portable" library from an option into an effective standard, while simultaneously increasing the efficiency of the library so that users would not object.

It is more difficult, of course, to speculate about the future. C is now encountering more and more foreign environments, and this is producing many demands for C to adapt itself to the hardware, and particularly to the operating systems, of other machines. Bit fields, for example, are a response to a request to describe externally imposed data layouts. Similarly, the procedures for external storage allocation and referencing have been made tighter to conform to requirements on other systems. Portability of the basic language seems well handled, but interactions with operating systems grow ever more complex. These lead to requests for more sophisticated data descriptions and initializations, and even for assembler windows. Further changes of this sort are likely.

What is not likely is a fundamental change in the level of the language. Realistically, the very acceptance of C has compelled changes to be made only most cautiously and compatibly. Should the pressure for improvements become too strong for the language to accommodate, C would probably have to be left as is, and a totally new language developed. We leave it to the reader to speculate on whether it should be called D or P.

REFERENCES

1. B. W. Kernighan and D. M. Ritchie, *The C Programming Language,* Englewood Cliffs, N.J.: Prentice-Hall, 1978.
2. M. Richards, "BCPL: A Tool for Compiler Writing and Systems Programming," Proc. AFIPS SJCC, *34* (1969), pp. 557-566.
3. S. C. Johnson and B. W. Kernighan, "The Programming Language B," Comp. Sci. Tech. Rep No. 8, Bell Laboratories (January 1973).
4. A. N. Habermann, "Critical Comments on the Programming Language PASCAL," Acta Informatica, *3* (1973), pp. 47-58.
5. C. A. R. Hoare, "Data Reliability," ACM SIGPLAN Notices, *10* (June 1975), pp. 528-533.

ALGORITHM = LOGIC + CONTROL*

ROBERT KOWALSKI

An algorithm can be regarded as consisting of a logic component, which specifies the knowledge to be used in solving problems, and a control component, which determines the problem-solving strategies by means of which that knowledge is used. The logic component determines the meaning of the algorithm whereas the control component only affects its efficiency. The efficiency of an algorithm can often be improved by improving the control component without changing the logic of the algorithm. We argue that computer programs would be more often correct and more easily improved and modified if their logic and control aspects were identified and separated in the program text.

Key Words and Phrases: control language, logic programming, nonprocedural language, programming methodology, program specification, relational data structures

CR Categories: 3.64, 4.20, 4.30, 5.21, 5.24

Introduction

Predicate logic is a high level, human-oriented language for describing problems and problem-solving methods to computers. In this paper, we are concerned not with the use of predicate logic as a programming language in its own right, but with its use as a tool for the analysis of algorithms. Our main aim will be to study ways in which logical analysis can contribute to improving the structure and efficiency of algorithms.

This research was supported by a grant from the Science Research Council.

Author's address: R.A. Kowalski, Dept. of Computing and Control, Imperial College of Science and Technology, 180 Queens Gate, London SW7 2BZ, England.

The notion that computation = controlled deduction was first proposed by Pay Hayes [19] and more recently by Bibel [2] and Vaughn–Pratt [31]. A similar thesis that database systems should be regarded as consisting of a relational component, which defines the logic of the data, and a control component, which stores and retrieves it, has been successfully argued by Codd [10]. Hewitt's argument [20] for the programming language PLANNER, though generally regarded as an argument against logic, can also be regarded as an argument for the thesis that algorithms be regarded as consisting of both logic and control components. In this paper we shall explore some of the useful consequences of that thesis.

We represent the analysis of an algorithm A into a *logic component* L, which defines the logic of the algorithm, and a *control component* C, which specifies the manner in which the definitions are used, symbolically by the equation

$$A = L + C.$$

Algorithms for computing factorials are a simple example. The definition of factorial constitutes the logic component of the algorithms:

1 is the factorial of 0;
u is the factorial of $x + 1$ *if* v is the factorial of x *and* u is v times $x + 1$.

The definition can be used *bottom-up* to derive a sequence of assertions about factorial or it can be used *top-down* to reduce the problem of computing the factorial of $x + 1$ to the subproblems of computing the factorial of x and multiplying the result by $x + 1$. Different ways of using the same definition give rise to different algorithms. Bottom-up use of the definition behaves like iteration. Top-down use behaves like recursive evaluation.

The manner in which the logic component is used to solve problems constitutes the control component. As a first approximation, we restrict the control component C to general-purpose problem-solving strategies which do not affect the meaning of the algorithm as it is determined by the logic component L. Thus different algorithms A_1 and A_2, obtained by applying different methods of control C_1 and C_2 to the same logic definitions L, are equivalent in the sense that they solve the same problems with the same results. Symbolically, if $A_1 = L + C_1$ and $A_2 = L + C_2$, then A_1 and A_2 are equivalent. The relationship of equivalence between algorithms, because they have the same logic, is the basis for using logical analysis to improve the efficiency of an algorithm by retaining its logic but improving the way it is used. In particular, replacing bottom-up by top-down control often (but not always) improves efficiency, whereas replacing top-down sequential solution of subproblems by top-down parallel solution seems never to decrease efficiency.

Both the logic and the control components of an algorithm affect efficiency. The logic component expresses the knowledge which can be used in solving problems and the control component determines the way in which that knowledge can be used. The distinction between logic and control is not wholly unambiguous. The same algorithm A can often be analyzed in different ways.

$$A = L_1 + C_1.$$
$$A = L_2 + C_2.$$

One analysis might include in the logic component what another analysis includes in the control component. In general, we prefer an analysis which places the greatest burden for achieving efficiency on the control component. Such an analysis has two advantages: (1) the logic component can afford to be a clearer and more obviously correct statement of the problem and the knowledge which can be used in its solution and (2) the control component assumes greater responsibility for the efficiency of the algorithm, which consequently can be more readily improved by upgrading the efficiency of the control.

It is the intention that this paper should be self-contained. The first part, accordingly, introduces the clausal form of predicate logic and defines the top-down and bottom-up interpretations of Horn clauses. The body of the paper investigates the following decomposition of algorithms into their various components.

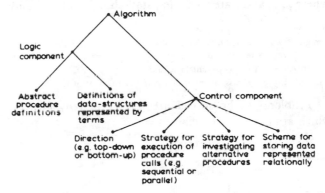

We study the affect of altering each of the above components of an algorithm. The final section of the paper introduces a graphical notation for expressing, more formally than in the rest of the paper, certain kinds of control information. Much of the material in this paper has been abstracted from lecture notes [23] prepared for the advanced summer school on foundations of computing held at the Mathematical Centre in Amsterdam in May 1974.

Notation

We use the clausal form of predicate logic. Simple assertions are expressed by clauses:

Father (Zeus, Ares) ←
Mother (Hera, Ares) ←
Father (Ares, Harmonia) ←
Mother (Semele, Dionisius) ←
Father (Zeus, Dionisius) ←
etc.

Here Father (x, y) states that x is the father of y and Mother (x, y) states that x is the mother of y.

Clauses can also express general conditional propositions:

Female (x) ← Mother (x, y)
Male (x) ← Father (x, y)
Parent (x, y) ← Mother (x, y)
Parent (x, y) ← Father (x, y).

These state that

x is female *if* x is mother of y,
x is male *if* x is father of y,
x is parent of y *if* x is mother of y, and
x is parent of y *if* x is father of y.

The arrow ← is the *logical connective* "if"; "x" and "y" are *variables* representing any individuals; "Zeus," "Ares," etc. are *constant symbols* representing particular individuals; "Father," "Mother," "Female," etc. are *predicate symbols* representing relations among individuals. Variables in different clauses are distinct even if they have the same names.

A clause can have several joint conditions or several alternative conclusions. Thus

Grandparent (x, y) ← Parent (x, z), Parent (z, y)
Male (x), Female (x) ← Parent (x, y)
Ancestor (x, y) ← Parent (x, y)
Ancestor (x, y) ← Ancestor (x, z), Ancestor (z, y)

where x, y, and z are variables, state that for all x, y, and z

x is grandparent of y *if* x is parent of z *and* z is parent of y;
x is male *or* x is female *if* x is parent of y;
x is ancestor of y *if* x is parent of y; and
x is ancestor of y *if* x is ancestor of z *and* z is ancestor of y.

Problems to be solved are represented by clauses which are denials. The clauses

← Grandparent (Zeus, Harmonia)
← Ancestor (Zeus, x)
← Male (x), Ancestor $(x,$ Dionisius)

where x is a variable state that

Zeus is not grandparent of Harmonia,
for no x is Zeus ancestor of x, and
for no x is x male *and* is x an ancestor of Dionisius.

A typical problem-solver (or theorem-prover) reacts to a denial by using other clauses to try to refute the denial. If the denial contains variables, then it is possible to extract from the refutation the values of the variables which account for the refutation and represent a solution of the problem to be solved. In this example, different refutations of the second denial find different x of which Zeus is the ancestor:

$x =$ Ares, $x =$ Harmonia, $x =$ Dionisius.

More generally, we define clauses and their interpretation as follows. A *clause* is an expression of the form

$B_1, ..., B_m$ ← $A_1, ..., A_n$ $m, n \geq 0$,

where $B_1, ..., B_m, A_1, ..., A_n$ are atoms. The atoms A_1,

..., A_n are *conditions* of the clause and the atoms $B_1, ...,$ B_m are alternative *conclusions* of the clause. If the clause contains the variables $x_1, ..., x_k$ then interpret it as stating that

for all $x_1, ..., x_k$
B_1 or ... or B_m if A_1 and ... and A_n.

If $n = 0$, then interpret it as stating unconditionally that
for all $x_1, ..., x_k$
B_1 or ... or B_m.

If $m = 0$, then interpret it as stating that
for no $x_1, ..., x_k$
A_1 and ... and A_n.

If $m = n = 0$, then interpret the clause as a sentence which is always false.

An *atom* (or *atomic formula*) is an expression of the form

$P(t_1, ..., t_n)$

where P is an n-place predicate symbol and $t_1, ..., t_n$ are terms. Interpret the atom as asserting that the relation called P holds among the individuals called $t_1, ..., t_n$.

A *term* is a variable, a constant symbol, or an expression of the form

$f(t_1, ..., t_n)$

where f is an n-place function symbol and $t_1, ..., t_n$ are terms.

The sets of *predicate symbols*, *function symbols*, *constant symbols*, and *variables* are any mutually disjoint sets. (By convention, we reserve the lower case letters u, v, w, x, y, z, with or without adornments, for variables. The type of other kinds of symbols is identified by the position they occupy in clauses.)

Clausal form has the same expressive power as the standard formulation of predicate logic. All variables x_1, ..., x_k which occur in a clause C are implicitly governed by universal quantifiers $\forall x_1, ..., \forall x_k$ (for all x_1 and ... and for all x_k). Thus C is an abbreviation for

$\forall x_1 ... \forall x_k\, C.$

The existential quantifier $\exists x$ (there exists an x) is avoided by using constant symbols or function symbols to name individuals. For example, the clauses

Father (dad (x), x) ← Human (x)
Mother (mum (x), x) ← Human (x)

state that for all humans x, there exists an individual, called dad (x), who is father of x, and there exists an individual, called mum (x), who is mother of x.

Although the clausal form has the same power as the standard form, it is not always as natural or as easy to use. The definition of subset is an example: "x is a subset of y if for all z, z belongs to y if z belongs to x." The definition in the standard form of logic

$x \subseteq y$ ← $\forall z\, [z \in y$ ← $z \in x]$

is a direct translation of the English. The clausal form of

the definition can be systematically derived from the standard form. It can take considerable effort, however, to recognize the notion of subset in the resulting pair of clauses:

$$x \subseteq y, \ arb \ (x, y) \ \epsilon \ x \leftarrow$$
$$x \subseteq y \leftarrow arb \ (x, y) \ \epsilon \ y.$$

(Here we have used infix notation for predicate symbols, writing xPy instead of $P(x, y)$.)

In this paper, we shall avoid the awkwardness of the clausal definition of subset by concentrating attention on clauses which contain at the most one conclusion. Such clauses, called *Horn clauses*, can be further classified into four kinds:

assertions (of the form)	$B \leftarrow$
procedure declarations (of the form)	$B \leftarrow A_1, \dots, A_n$
denials	$\leftarrow A_1, \dots, A_n$
and *contradiction*	$\leftarrow$

Assertions can be regarded as the special case of procedure declarations where $n = 0$.

The Horn clause subset of logic resembles conventional programming languages more closely than either the full clausal or standard forms of logic. For example, the notion of subset can be defined recursively by means of Horn clauses:

$$x \subseteq y \leftarrow \text{Empty } (x)$$
$$x \subseteq y \leftarrow \text{Split } (x, z, x') \ z \ \epsilon \ y, \ x' \subseteq y.$$

Here it is intended that the relationship Empty (x) holds when x is empty, and Split (x, z, x') holds when x consists of element z and subset x'. Horn clauses used in this way, to define relations recursively, are related to Herbrand-Gödel recursion equations as described by Kleene [22], elaborated by McCarthy [28], employed for program transformation by Burstall and Darlington [13], and augmented with control annotations by Schwarz [34].

Top-Down and Bottom-Up Interpretations of Horn Clauses

A typical Horn clause problem has the form of

(1) a set of clauses which defines a problem domain and

(2) a theorem which consists of (a) hypotheses represented by assertions $A_1 \leftarrow, \dots, A_n \leftarrow$ and (b) a conclusion which is negated and represented by a denial $\leftarrow B_1, \dots, B_m$.

In top-down problem-solving, we reason backwards from the conclusion, repeatedly reducing goals to subgoals until eventually all subgoals are solved directly by the original assertions. In bottom-up problem-solving, we reason forwards from the hypotheses, repeatedly deriving new assertions from old ones until eventually the original goal is solved directly by derived assertions.

The problem of showing that Zeus is a grandparent of Harmonia can be solved either top-down or bottom-up. Reasoning bottom-up, we start with the assertions

Father (Zeus, Ares) ←
Father (Ares, Harmonia) ←

and use the clause Parent $(x, y) \leftarrow$ Father (x, y) to derive new assertions

Parent (Zeus, Ares) ←
Parent (Ares, Harmonia) ←

Continuing bottom-up we derive, from the definition of grandparent, the new assertion

Grandparent (Zeus, Harmonia) ←

which matches the original goal.

Reasoning top-down, we start with the original goal of showing that Zeus is a grandparent of Harmonia

← Grandparent (Zeus, Harmonia)

and use the definition of grandparent to derive two new subgoals

← Parent (Zeus, z), Parent (z, Harmonia)

by denying that any z is both a child of Zeus and a parent of Harmonia. Continuing top-down and considering both subgoals (either one at a time or both simultaneously), we use the clause Parent $(x, y) \leftarrow$ Father (x, y) to replace the subproblem Parent (Zeus, z) by Father (Zeus, z) and the subproblem Parent (z, Harmonia) by Father (z, Harmonia). The newly derived subproblems are solved compatibly by assertions which determine "Ares" as the desired value of z.

In both the top-down and bottom-up solutions of the grandparent problem, we have mentioned the derivation of only those clauses which directly contribute to the eventual solution. In addition to the derivation of relevant clauses, it is often unavoidable, during the course of searching for a solution, to derive assertions or subgoals which do not contribute to the solution. For example, in the bottom-up search for a solution to the grandparent problem, it is possible to derive the irrelevant assertions

Parent (Hera, Ares) ←
Male (Zeus) ←

In the top-down search it is possible to replace the subproblem Parent (Zeus, z) by the irrelevant and unsolvable subproblem Mother (Zeus, z).

There are both proof procedures which understand logic top-down (e.g. model elimination [17], SL-resolution [20], and interconnectivity graphs [35]) as well as ones which understand logic bottom-up (notably hyper-resolution [35]). These proof procedures operate with the clausal form of predicate logic and deal with both Horn clauses and non-Horn clauses. Among clausal proof procedures, the connection graph procedure [25] is able to mix top-down and bottom-up reasoning. Among non-clausal proof procedures, Gentzen systems [1] and Bledsoe's related natural deduction systems [5] provide facilities for mixing top-down and bottom-up reasoning.

The terminology "top-down" and "bottom-up" applied to proof procedures derives from our investigation of the parsing problem formulated in predicate logic [23, 25]. Given a grammar formulated in clausal form, top-down reasoning behaves as a top-down parsing algorithm and bottom-up reasoning behaves as a bottom-up algorithm. David Warren (unpublished) has shown how to define a general proof procedure for Horn clauses, which when applied to the parsing problem, behaves like the Earley parsing algorithm [16].

The Procedural Interpretation of Horn Clauses

The procedural interpretation is the top-down interpretation. A clause of the form

$$B \leftarrow A_1, \dots, A_n \qquad n \geq 0$$

is interpreted as a *procedure*. The *name* of the procedure is the conclusion B which identifies the form of the problems which the procedure can solve. The *body* of the procedure is the set of *procedure calls A_i*. A clause of the form

$$\leftarrow B_1, \dots, B_m \qquad m \geq 0$$

consisting entirely of procedure calls (or problems to be solved) behaves as a *goal statement*. A procedure

$$B \leftarrow A_1, \dots, A_n$$

is *invoked* by a procedure call B_i in the goal statement:

(1) By matching the call B_i with the name B of the procedure;
(2) By replacing the call B_i with the body of the procedure obtaining the new goal statement
$$\leftarrow B_1, \dots, B_{i-1}, A_1, \dots, A_n, B_{i+1}, \dots, B_m$$
and;
(3) By applying the matching substitution θ
$$\leftarrow (B_1, \dots, B_{i-1}, A_1, \dots, A_n, B_{i+1}, \dots, B_m) \theta.$$

(The *matching substitution* θ replaces variables by terms in a manner which makes B and B_i identical: $B\theta = B_i\theta$.) The part of the substitution θ which affects variables in the original procedure calls $B_1, \dots, B_m$ transmits *output*. The part which affects variables in the new procedure calls $A_1, \dots, A_n$ transmits *input*.

For example, invoking the grandparent procedure by the procedure call in

$$\leftarrow \text{Grandparent (Zeus, Harmonia)}$$

derives the new goal statement

$$\leftarrow \text{Parent (Zeus, } z), \text{Parent (} z, \text{Harmonia)}.$$

The matching substitution

$x = \text{Zeus}$
$y = \text{Harmonia}$

transmits input only. Invoking the assertional procedure

Father (Zeus, Ares) ◂

by the first procedure call in the goal statement

$$\leftarrow \text{Father (Zeus, } z), \text{Parent (} z, \text{Harmonia)}$$

derives the new goal statement

$$\leftarrow \text{Parent (Ares, Harmonia)}.$$

The matching substitution

$z = \text{Ares}$

transmits output only. In general, however, a single procedure invocation may transmit both input and output.

The top-down interpretation of Horn clauses differs in several important respects from procedure invocation in conventional programming languages:

(1) The body of a procedure is a *set* rather than a *sequence* of procedure calls. This means that procedure calls can be executed in any sequence or in parallel.
(2) More than one procedure can have a name which matches a given procedure call. Finding the "right" procedure is a search problem which can be solved by trying the different procedures in sequence, in parallel, or in other more sophisticated ways.
(3) The input-output arguments of a procedure are not fixed but depend upon the procedure call. A procedure which *tests* that a relationship holds among given individuals can also be used to *find* individuals for which the relationship holds.

The Relationship Between Logic and Control

In the preceding sections we considered alternative top-down and bottom-up control strategies for a fixed predicate logic representation of a problem-domain. Different control strategies for the same logical representation generate different behaviors. However, information about a problem-domain can be represented in logic in different ways. Alternative representations can have a more significant effect on the efficiency of an algorithm than alternative control strategies for the same representation.

Consider the problem of sorting a list. In one representation, we have the definition

sorting x gives $y \leftarrow y$ is a permutation of x, y is ordered.

(Here we have used distributed infix notation for predicate symbols, writing $P_1 x_1 P_2 x_2 \dots P_n x_n P_{n+1}$ instead of $P(x_1, \dots, x_n)$ where the P_i (possibly empty) are *parts* of P.) As described in [24], different control strategies applied to the definition generate different behaviors. None of these behaviors, however, is efficient enough to qualify as a reasonable sorting algorithm. By contrast, even the simplest top-down, sequential control behaves efficiently with the logic of quicksort [17]:

sorting x gives y ← x is empty, y is empty
sorting x gives y ← first element of x is x_1, rest of x is x_2,
                partitioning x_2 by x_1 gives u and v,
                sorting u gives u',
                sorting v gives v',
                appending w to u' gives y,
                first element of w is x_1,
                rest of w is v'.

Like the predicates "permutation" and "ordered" before, the predicates "empty," "first," "rest," "partitioning," and "appending" can be defined independently from the definition of "sorting." (Partitioning x_2 by x_1 is intended to give the list u of the elements of x_2 which are smaller than or equal to x_1 and the list v of the elements of x_2 which are greater than x_1.)

Our thesis is that, in the systematic development of well-structured programs by successive refinement, the logic component needs to be specified before the control component. The logic component defines the problem-domain-specific part of an algorithm. It not only determines the meaning of the algorithm but also influences the way the algorithm behaves. The control component specifies the problem-solving strategy. It affects the behavior of the algorithm without affecting its meaning. Thus the efficiency of an algorithm can be improved by two very different approaches, either by improving the logic component or by leaving the logic component unchanged and improving the control over its use.

Bibel [3, 4], Clark, Darlington, Sickel [7, 8, 9], and Hogger [21] have developed strategies for improving algorithms by ignoring the control component and using deduction to derive a new logic component. Their methods are similar to the ones used for transforming formal grammars and programs expressed as recursion equations [13].

In a logic programming system, specification of the control component is subordinate to specification of the logic component. The control component can either be expressed by the programmer in a separate control-specifying language, or it can be determined by the system itself. When logic is used, as in the relational calculus, for example [11], to specify queries for a database, the control component is determined entirely by the system. In general, the higher the level of the programming language and the less advanced the level of the programmer, the more the system needs to assume responsibility for efficiency and to exercise control over the use of the information which it is given.

The provision of a separate control-specifying language is more likely to appeal to the more advanced programmer. Greater efficiency can often be achieved when the programmer is able to communicate control information to the computer. Such information might be, for example, that in the relation $F(x, y)$ the value of y is a function of the argument x. This could be used by a backtracking interpreter to avoid looking for another solution to the first goal in the goal statement

← $F(A, y), G(y)$

when the second goal fails. Another example of such information might be that one procedure

$P ← Q$

is more likely to solve P than another procedure

$P ← R$.

This kind of information is common in fault diagnosis where, on the basis of past experience, it might be known that symptom P is more likely to have been caused by Q than R.

Notice, in both of these examples, that the control information is problem-specific. However, if the control information is correct and the interpreter is correctly implemented, then the control information should not affect the meaning of the algorithm as determined by its logic component.

Data Structures

In a well-structured program it is desirable to separate data structures from the procedures which interrogate and manipulate them. Such separation means that the representation of data structures can be altered without altering the higher level procedures. Alteration of data structures is a way of improving algorithms by replacing an inefficient data structure by a more effective one. In a large, complex program, the demands for information made on the data structures are often fully determined only in the final stages of the program design. By separating data structures from procedures, the higher levels of the program can be written before the data structures have been finally decided.

The data structures of a program are already included in the logic component. Lists for example can be represented by terms, where

nil   names for the empty list and
cons (x, y) names the list with first element x and rest which is another list y.

Thus the term

cons $(2, cons\ (1, cons\ (3, nil)))$

names the three-element list consisting of the individuals 2, 1, 3 in that order.

The data-structure-free definition of quicksort in the preceding section interacts with the data structure for lists via the definitions

nil is empty ←
first element of *cons* (x, y) is x ←
rest of *cons* (x, y) is y ←

If the predicates "empty," "first," and "rest" are eliminated from the definition of quicksort by a preliminary bottom-up deduction, then the original data-structure-free definition can be replaced by a definition which mixes the data structures with the procedures

sorting *nil* gives *nil* ←
sorting *cons* (x_1, x_2) gives y ← partitioning x_2 by x_1 gives u and v,
  sorting u gives u',
  sorting v gives v',
  appending to u' the list *cons* (x_1, v') gives
  y.

Clark and Tarnlund [6] show how to obtain a more efficient version of quicksort from the same abstract definition with a different data structure for lists.

Comparing the original data-structure-free definition with the new data-structure-dependent one, we notice another advantage of data-structure-independence: the fact that, with well-chosen names for the interfacing procedures, data-structure-independent programs are virtually self-documenting. For the conventional program which mixes procedures and data structures, the programmer has to provide documentation, external to the program, which explains the data structures. For the well-structured, data-independent program, such documentation is provided by the interfacing procedures and is part of the program.

Despite the arguments for separating data structures and procedures, programmers mix them for the sake of run-time efficiency. One way of reconciling efficiency with good program structure is to use the macroexpansion facilities provided in some programming languages. Macroexpansion flattens the hierarchy of procedure calls before run-time and is the computational analog of the bottom-up and middle-out reasoning provided by some theorem-proving systems. Macro-expansion is also a feature of the program improving transformations developed by Burstall and Darlington.

Notice how our terminology conflicts with Wirth's [39]: program = algorithm + data structure. In our terminology the definition of data structures belongs to the logic component of algorithms. Even more confusingly, we would like to call the logic component of algorithms "logic programs." This is because, given a fixed Horn clause interpreter, the programmer need only specify the logic component. The interpreter can exercise its own control over the way in which the information in the logic component is used. Of course, if the programmer knows how the interpreter behaves, then he can express himself in a manner which is designed to elicit the behavior he desires.

Top-Down Execution of Procedure Calls

In the simplest top-down execution strategy, procedure calls are executed one at a time in the sequence in which they are written. Typically an algorithm can be improved by executing the same procedure calls either as coroutines or as communicating parallel processes. The new algorithm

$$A_2 = L + C_2$$

is obtained from the original algorithm

$$A_1 = L + C_1$$

by replacing one control strategy by another leaving the logic of the algorithm unchanged.

For example, executing procedure calls in sequence, the procedure

sorting x gives y ← y is a permutation of x, y is ordered

first generates permutations of x and then tests whether they are ordered. Executing procedure calls as coroutines, the procedure generates permutations, one element at a time. Whenever a new element is generated, the generation of other elements is suspended while it is determined whether the new element preserves the orderedness of the existing partial permutation. This example is discussed in more detail elsewhere [24].

Similarly the procedure calls in the body of the quicksort definition can be executed either in sequence or as coroutines or parallel processes. Executed in parallel, partitioning the rest of x can be initiated as soon as the first elements of the rest are generated. Sorting the output, u and v, of the partitioning procedure can begin and proceed in parallel as soon as the first elements of u and v are generated. Appending can begin as soon as the first elements of u', the sorted version of u, are known.

Philippe Roussel [33] has investigated the problem of showing that two trees have the same lists of leaves:

x and y have the same leaves ← the leaves of x are z,
  the leaves of y are z',
  z and z' are the same

x and x are the same ←

Executing procedure calls in the sequence in which they are written, the procedure first constructs the list z of leaves of x, then constructs the list z' of leaves of y, and finally tests that z and z' are the same. Roussel has argued that a more sophisticated algorithm is obtained, without changing the logic of the algorithm, by executing the same procedure calls as communicating parallel processes. When one process finds a leaf, it suspends activity and waits until the other process finds a leaf. A third process then tests whether the two leaves are identical. If the leaves are identical, then the first two processes resume. If the leaves are different, then the entire procedure fails and terminates.

The parallel algorithm is significantly more efficient than the simple sequential one when the two trees have different lists of leaves. In this case the sequential algorithm recognizes failure only after both lists have been completely generated. The parallel algorithm recognizes failure as soon as the two lists begin to differ.

The sequential algorithm, whether it eventually succeeds or fails, constructs the intermediate lists z and z' which are no longer needed when the procedure terminates. In contrast, the parallel algorithm can be implemented in such a way that it compares the two lists z and z', one element at a time, without constructing and saving the initial lists of those elements already compared and found to be identical.

In a high level programming language like SIMULA it is possible to write both the usual sequential algorithms and also coroutining ones in which the programmer controls when coroutines are suspended and resumed. But, as in other conventional programming languages, logic and control are inextricably intertwined in the program text. It is not possible to change the control strategy of an algorithm without rewriting the program entirely.

The arguments for separating logic and control are like the ones for separating procedures and data structures. When procedures are separated from data structures, it is possible to distinguish (in the procedures) what functions the data structures fulfill from the manner in which the data structures fulfill them. When logic is separated from control, it is possible to distinguish (in the logic) what the program does from how the program does it (in the control). In both cases it is more obvious what the program does, and therefore it is easier to determine whether it correctly does what it is intended to do.

The work of Clark and Tarnlund [6] (on the correctness of sorting algorithms) and the unpublished work of Warren and Kowalski (on the correctness of plan-formation algorithms) supports the thesis that correctness proofs are simplified when they deal only with the logic component and ignore the control component of algorithms. Similarly, ignoring control simplifies the derivation of programs from specifications [3, 4, 7, 8, 9, 21].

Top-Down vs. Bottom-Up Execution

Recursive definitions are common in mathematics where they are more likely to be understood bottom-up rather than top-down. Consider, for example, the definition of factorial

The factorial of 0 is 1 ←
The factorial of x is u ← y plus 1 is x,
                     the factorial of y is v,
                     x times v is u.

The mathematician is likely to understand such a definition bottom-up, generating the sequence of assertions

The factorial of 0 is 1 ←
The factorial of 1 is 1 ←
The factorial of 2 is 2 ←
The factorial of 3 is 6 ←
etc.

Conventional programming language implementations understand recursions top-down. Programmers, accordingly, tend to identify recursive definitions with top-down execution.

An interesting exception to the rule that recursive definitions are more efficiently executed top-down than bottom-up is the definition of a Fibonacci number, which is both more intelligible and efficient when interpreted bottom-up:

the 0-th Fibonacci number is 1 ←
the 1-th Fibonacci number is 1 ←
the u + 2-th Fibonacci number is x ←
                     the u + 1-th Fibonacci number is y,
                     the u-th Fibonacci number is z,
                     y plus z is x.

(Here the terms $u + 2$ and $u + 1$ are expressions to be evaluated rather than terms representing data structures. This notation is an *abbreviation* for the one which has explicit procedure calls in the body to evaluate $u + 2$ and $u + 1$.)

Interpreted top-down, finding the $u + 1$-th Fibonacci number reintroduces the subproblem of finding the u-th Fibonacci number. The top-down computation is a tree whose nodes are procedure calls, the number of which is an exponential function of u. Interpreting the same definition bottom-up generates the sequence of assertions

the 0-th Fibonacci number is 1 ←
the 1-th Fibonacci number is 1 ←
the 2-th Fibonacci number is 2 ←
the 3-th Fibonacci number is 3 ←
etc.

The number of computation steps is a linear function of u.

In this example, bottom-up execution is also less space-consuming than top-down execution. Top-down execution uses space which is proportional to u, whereas bottom-up execution needs to store only two assertions and can use a small constant amount of storage. That only two assertions need to be stored during bottom-up execution is a consequence of the deletion rules for the connection graph proof procedure [25]. As Bibel observes, the greater efficiency of bottom-up execution disappears if similar procedure calls are executed top-down only once. This strategy is, in fact, an application of Warren's generalization of the Earley parsing algorithm.

Strategies for Investigating Alternative Procedures

When more than one procedure has a conclusion which matches a given procedure call, the logic component does not determine the manner in which the alternative procedures are investigated. Sequential exploration of alternatives gives rise to iterative algorithms.

Although in theory all iterations can be replaced by top-down execution of recursive definitions, in practice some iterations might better be thought of as bottom-up execution of recursive definitions (as in the definition of factorial). Other iterations can better be regarded as controlling a sequential search among alternatives.

Assume, for example, that we are given data about individuals in the parenthood relationship:

Parent (Zeus, Ares) ←
Parent (Hera, Ares) ←
Parent (Ares, Harmonia) ←
Parent (Semele, Dionisius) ←
Parent (Zeus, Dionisius) ←
etc.

Suppose that the problem is to find a grandchild of Zeus

← Grandparent (Zeus, u)

using the definition of grandparent. In a conventional programming language, the parenthood relationship might be stored in a two-dimensional array. A general procedure for finding grandchildren (given grandparents) might involve two iterative loops, one nested inside the other, with a jump out when a solution has been found. Similar behavior is obtained by interpreting the grandparent procedure top-down, executing procedure calls one at a time, in the sequence in which they are written, trying alternative procedures (assertions in this case) one at a time in the order in which they are written. The logical analysis of the conventional iterative algorithm does not concern recursion but involves sequential search through a space of alternatives. The sequential search strategy is identical to the backtracking strategy for executing nondeterministic programs [18].

Representation of data by means of clauses, as in the family relationships example, rather than by means of terms, is similar to the relational model of databases [10]. In both cases data is regarded as relationships among individuals. When data is represented by conventional data structures (terms), the programmer needs to specify in the logic component of programs and queries both how data is stored and how it is retrieved. When data is represented relationally (by clauses), the programmer needs only to specify data in the logic component; the control component manages both storage and retrieval.

The desirability of separating logic and control is now generally accepted in the field of databases. An important advantage is that storage and retrieval schemes can be changed and improved in the control component without affecting the user's view of the data as defined by the logic component.

The suitability of a search strategy for retrieving data depends upon the structure in which the data is stored. Iteration, regarded as sequential search, is suitable for data stored sequentially in arrays or linked lists. Other search strategies are more appropriate for other data structures, such as hash tables, binary trees, or semantic networks. McSkimin and Minker [29], for example, store clauses in a manner which facilitates both parallel search and finding all answers to a database query. Deliyanni and Kowalski [15], on the other hand, propose a path-finding strategy for retrieving data stored in semantic networks.

Representation of data by means of terms is a common feature of Horn clause programs written in PROLOG [12, 33, 38]. Tärnlund [36], in particular, has investigated the use of terms as data structures in Horn

clause programs. Several PROLOG programs employ a relational representation of data. Notable among these are Warren's [37] for plan-formation and those for drug analysis written in the Ministry of Heavy Industry in Budapest [14].

Two Analyses of Path-Finding Algorithms

The same algorithm A can often be analyzed in different ways:

$$A = L_1 + C_1 = L_2 + C_2.$$

Some of the behavior determined by the control component C_1 in one analysis might be determined by the logic component L_2 in another analysis. This has significance for understanding the relationship between programming style and execution facilities. In the short term sophisticated behavior can be obtained by employing simple execution strategies and by writing complicated programs. In the longer term the same behavior may be obtained from simpler programs by using more sophisticated execution strategies.

The path-finding problem illustrates a situation in which the same algorithm can be analyzed in different ways. Consider the problem of finding a path from A to Z in the following directed graph.

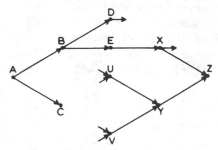

In one analysis, we employ a predicate $Go(x)$ which states that it is possible to go to x. The problem of going from A to Z is then represented by two clauses. One asserts that it is possible to go to A. The other denies that it is possible to go to Z. The arc directed from A to B is represented by a clause which states that it is possible to go to B if it is possible to go to A:

$Go(A) ←$	$← Go(Z)$
$Go(B) ← Go(A)$	$Go(Z) ← Go(X)$
$Go(C) ← Go(A)$	$Go(Z) ← Go(Y)$
$Go(D) ← Go(B)$	$Go(Y) ← Go(U)$
$Go(E) ← Go(B)$	$Go(Y) ← Go(V)$
$Go(X) ← Go(E)$	etc.

Different control strategies determine different path-finding algorithms. Forward search from the initial node A is bottom-up reasoning from the initial assertion $Go(A) ←$. Backward search from the goal node Z is top-down reasoning from the initial goal statement $← Go(Z)$. Bidirectional search from both the initial node and the goal node is the combination of top-down and bottom-up reasoning. Whether the path-finding algorithm investigates one path at a time (depth-first) or develops all paths simultaneously (breadth-first) is a matter of the search strategy used to investigate alternatives.

In the second analysis, we employ a predicate $Go^*(x, y)$ which states that it is possible to go from x to y. In addition to the assertions which describe the graph and the goal statement which describes the problem, there is a single clause which defines the logic of the path-finding algorithms:

$$\leftarrow Go^*(A, Z)$$

$Go^*(A, B) \leftarrow$	$Go^*(X, Z) \leftarrow$
$Go^*(A, C) \leftarrow$	$Go^*(Y, Z) \leftarrow$
$Go^*(B, D) \leftarrow$	$Go^*(U, Y) \leftarrow$
$Go^*(B, E) \leftarrow$	$Go^*(V, Y) \leftarrow$
$Go^*(E, X) \leftarrow$	etc.

$$Go^*(x, y) \leftarrow Go^*(x, z), G0^*(z, y)$$

Here both forward search from the initial node A and backward search from the goal node Z are top-down reasoning from the initial goal statement $\leftarrow Go^*(A, Z)$. The difference between forward and backward search is the difference in the choice of subproblems in the body of the path-finding procedure. Solving $Go^*(x, z)$ before $Go^*(z, y)$ is forward search, and solving $Go^*(z, y)$ before $Go^*(x, z)$ is backward search. Coroutining between the two subproblems is bidirectional search. Bottom-up reasoning from the assertions which define the graph generates the transitive closure, effectively adding a new arc to the graph directed from node x to node y, whenever there is a path from x to y.

Many problem domains have in common with path-finding that an initial state is given and the goal is to achieve some final state. The two representations of the path-finding problem exemplify alternative representations which apply more generally in other problem domains. Warren's plan-formation program [37], for example, is of the type which contains both the given and the goal state as different arguments of a single predicate. It runs efficiently with the sequential execution facilities provided by PROLOG. The alternative formulation, which employs a predicate having one state as argument, is easier to understand but more difficult to execute efficiently.

Even the definition of factorial can be represented in two ways. The formulation discussed earlier corresponds to the one-place predicate representation of path-finding. The formulation here corresponds to the two-place predicate representation. Read

$$F(x, y, u, v)$$

as stating that

the factorial of x is y
given that the factorial of u is v.
$$F(x, y, x, y) \leftarrow$$
$$F(x, y, u, v) \leftarrow u \text{ plus } 1 \text{ is } u', u' \text{ times } v \text{ is } v', F(x, y, u', v').$$

To find the factorial of an integer represented by a term t, a single goal statement incorporates both the goal and the basis of the recursion

$$\leftarrow F(t, y, 0, 1).$$

The new formulation of factorial executed in a simple

top-down sequential manner behaves in the same way as the original formulation executed in a mixed top-down, bottom-up fashion.

A Notation for Expressing Control Information

The distinction between top-down and bottom-up execution can be expressed in a graphical notation which uses arrows to indicate the flow of control. The same notation can be used to represent different combinations of top-down and bottom-up execution. The notation *does not*, however, aim to provide a complete language for expressing useful control information.

Arrows are attached to atoms in clauses to indicate the direction of transmission of processing activity from clause to clause. For every pair of matching atoms in the initial set of clauses (one atom in the conclusion of a clause and the other among the conditions of a clause), there is an arrow directed from one atom to the other.

For top-down execution, arrows are directed from conditions to conclusions. For the grandparent problem, we have the graph:

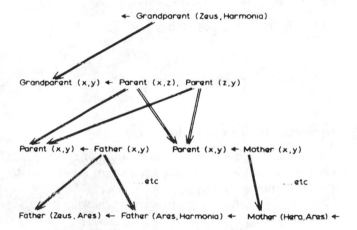

Processing activity starts with the initial goal statement. It transmits activity to the body of the grandparent procedure, whose procedure calls, in turn, activate the parenthood definitions. The database of assertions passively accepts processing activity without transmitting it to other clauses.

For bottom-up execution, arrows are directed from conclusions to conditions:

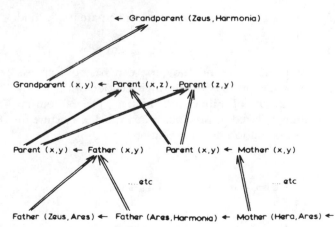

Processing activity originates with the database of initial assertions. They transmit activity to the parenthood definitions, which, in turn, activate the grandparent definition. Processing terminates when it reaches all the conditions in the passive initial goal statement.

The grandparent definition can be used in a combination of top-down and bottom-up methods. Using numbers to indicate sequencing, we can represent different combinations of top-down and bottom-up execution. For simplicity we only show the control notation associated with the grandparent definition. The combination of logic and control indicated by

$$
\begin{array}{c}
3 \\ \Uparrow
\end{array}
$$
Grandparent $(x, y) \leftarrow$ Parent (x, z), Parent (z, y)
$$
\quad\quad\quad\quad\quad\quad\quad\quad \Uparrow \quad\quad\quad\quad \Downarrow \\
\quad\quad\quad\quad\quad\quad\quad\quad 1 \quad\quad\quad\quad 2
$$

represents the algorithm which

(1) waits until x is asserted to be parent of z, then
(2) finds a child y of z, and finally
(3) asserts that x is grandparent of y.

The combination indicated by

$$
\begin{array}{c}
2 \\ \Downarrow
\end{array}
$$
Grandparent $(x, y) \leftarrow$ Parent (x, z), Parent (z, y)
$$
\quad\quad\quad\quad\quad\quad\quad\quad \Uparrow \quad\quad\quad\quad \Downarrow \\
\quad\quad\quad\quad\quad\quad\quad\quad 1 \quad\quad\quad\quad 3
$$

represents the algorithm which

(1) waits until x is asserted to be parent of z, then
(2) waits until it is given the problem of showing that x is grandparent of y,
(3) which it then attempts to solve by showing that z is parent of y.

The algorithm represented by

$$
\begin{array}{c}
1 \\ \Downarrow
\end{array}
$$
Grandparent $(x, y) \leftarrow$ Parent (x, z), Parent (z, y)
$$
\quad\quad\quad\quad\quad\quad\quad\quad \Uparrow \quad\quad\quad\quad \Downarrow \\
\quad\quad\quad\quad\quad\quad\quad\quad 2 \quad\quad\quad\quad 3
$$

(1) responds to the problem of showing that x is grandparent of y,
(2) by waiting until x is asserted to be parent of z, and then
(3) attempting to show that z is parent of y.

Using the arrow notation, we can be more precise than before about the bottom-up execution of the recursive definition of Fibonacci number. The bottom-up execution referred to previously is, in fact, a mixture of bottom-up and top-down execution:

$$
\begin{array}{c}
4 \\ \Uparrow
\end{array}
$$
the $u + 2$ Fib is $x \leftarrow$ the $u + 1$ Fib is y, the u Fib is z, y plus z is x.
$$
\quad\quad\quad\quad\quad\quad \Uparrow \quad\quad\quad \Uparrow \quad\quad\quad\quad \Downarrow \\
\quad\quad\quad\quad\quad\quad 2 \quad\quad\quad 1 \quad\quad\quad\quad 3
$$

Arrow notation can also be used to give a procedural interpretation of non-Horn clauses. The definition of subset, for example, "x is a subset of y if, for all z, if z belongs to x, then z belongs to y," gives rise to a procedure which shows that x is a subset of y by showing that every member of x is a member of y. It does this by asserting that some individual belongs to x and by attempting to show that the same individual belongs to y. The name of the individual must be different from the name of any individual mentioned elsewhere, and it must depend upon x and y (being different for different x and y). In clausal notation with arrows to indicate control, the definition of subset becomes

$$
\quad\quad 1 \quad\quad\quad\quad\quad\quad\quad\quad 2 \\
\quad\quad \Downarrow \quad\quad\quad\quad\quad\quad\quad\quad \Uparrow
$$
x is a subset of y, arb (x, y) belongs to $x \leftarrow$
x is a subset of $y \leftarrow arb$ (x, y) belongs to y
$$
\quad \Uparrow \quad\quad\quad\quad\quad\quad\quad\quad \Downarrow \\
\quad 1 \quad\quad\quad\quad\quad\quad\quad\quad 2
$$

Given the goal of showing that x is a subset of y, the first clause asserts that the individual named arb (x, y) belongs to x and the second clause generates the goal of showing that arb (x, y) belongs to y.

The grandparent definition illustrates the inadequacy of the arrow notation for expressing certain kinds of control information. Suppose that the grandparent definition is to be used entirely top-down.

$$
\Downarrow
$$
Grandparent $(x, y) \leftarrow$ Parent (x, z), Parent (z, y).
$$
\quad\quad\quad\quad\quad\quad\quad\quad \Downarrow \quad\quad\quad\quad \Downarrow
$$

The effective sequencing of procedure calls in the body of the procedure depends upon the parameters of the activating procedure call:

(1) If the problem is to find a grandchild y of a given x, then it is more effective (i) first to find a child z of x; (ii) and then to find a child y of z.
(2) If the problem is to find a grandparent x of a given y, then it is better (i) first to find a parent z of y; (ii) and then to find a parent x of z.

Such sequencing of procedure calls depending on the pattern of input and output cannot be expressed in the arrow notation.

In relational database query languages, input-sensitive sequencing of procedure calls needs to be determined by the data retrieval system rather than by the user. Consider, for example, a database which defines the following relations:

Supplier (x, y, z) supplier number x has name y and status z,
Part (x, y, z) part number x has name y and unit cost z,
Supply (x, y, z) supplier number x supplies part number y in quantity z.

Given the query

What is the name of suppliers of pens?
$\leftarrow$ Answer (y)
Answer $(y) \leftarrow$ Supplier (x, y, z), Supply (x, u, v), Part $(u,$ pen, $w)$

the system needs to determine that, for the sake of efficiency, the last procedure call should be executed first; whereas given the query

What is the name of parts supplied by Jones?
← Answer (y)
Answer (y) ← Supplier (x, Jones, z), Supply (x, u, v), Part (u, y, w)

the first procedure call should be executed before the others.

The arrow notation can be used to control the behavior of a connection graph theorem-prover [12]. The links of a connection graph are turned into arrows by giving them a direction. A link may be activated (giving rise to a resolvent) only if the link is connected to a clause all of whose links are outgoing. The links of the derived resolvent inherit the direction of the links from which they descend in the parent clauses. Connection graphs controlled in such a manner are similar to Petri nets [16].

Conclusion

We have argued that conventional algorithms can usefully be regarded as consisting of two components:

(1) a logic component which specifies what is to be done and
(2) a control component which determines how it is to be done.

The efficiency of an algorithm can often be improved by improving the efficiency of the control component without changing the logic and therefore without changing the meaning of the algorithm.

The same algorithm can often be formulated in different ways. One formulation might incorporate a clear statement, in the logic component, of the knowledge to be used in solving the problem and achieve efficiency by employing sophisticated problem-solving strategies in the control component. Another formulation might produce the same behavior by complicating the logic component and employing a simple problem-solving strategy.

Although the trend in databases is towards the separation of logic and control, programming languages today do not distinguish between them. The programmer specifies both logic and control in a single language while the execution mechanism exercises only the most rudimentary problem-solving capabilities. Computer programs will be more often correct, more easily improved, and more readily adapted to new problems when programming languages separate logic and control, and when execution mechanisms provide more powerful problem-solving facilities of the kind provided by intelligent theorem-proving systems.

Acknowledgments. The author has benefited from valuable discussions with K. Clark, A. Colmerauer, M. van Emden, P. Hayes, P. Roussel, S. Tärnlund, and D. Warren. Special thanks are due to W. Bibel, K. Clark, M. van Emden, P. Hayes, and D. Warren for their helpful comments on earlier drafts of this paper. This research was supported by a grant from the Science Research Council. The final draft of this paper was completed during a visiting professorship held in the School of Computer and Information Science at the University of Syracuse.

Received December 1976; revised February 1978

References

1. Bibel, W., and Schreiber, J. Proof procedures in a Gentzen-like system of first-order logic. Proc. Int. Comptng. Symp., North-Holland Pub. Co., Amsterdam, 1975, pp. 205–212.
2. Bibel, W. Programmieren in der Sprache der Prädikatenlogik. Eingereicht als Habibitationsarbeit. Fachbereich Mathematik, Techn. München, Jan. 1975. Shorter versions published as: Prädikatives Programmieren. Lecture Notes in Computer Science, *33*, GI-2. Fachtagung über Automatentheorie und formale Sprachen, Springer-Verlag, Berlin, Heidelberg, New York, 1975, pp. 274–283. And as: Predicative Programming. Séminaires IRIA, théorie des algorithmes, des languages et de la programmation 1975–1976, IRIA, Roquencourt, France, 1977.
3. Bibel, W. Syntheses of strategic definitions and their control. Bericht Nr. 7610, *Abt. Mathem.*, Techn. Munchen, 1976.
4. Bibel, W. A uniform approach to programming. Bericht Nr. 7633, *Abtl. Mathem.*, Techn. München, 1976.
5. Bledsoe, W.W., and Bruell, P. A man-machine theorem-proving system. *Artif. Intell.* 5 (Spring 1974), 51–72.
6. Clark, K.L., and Tärnlund, S.A. A first order theory of data and programs. *Information Processing 77*, North-Holland Pub. Co., Amsterdam, 1977, pp. 939–944.
7. Clark, K., and Sickel, S. Predicate logic: A calculus for the formal derivation of programs. Proc. Int. Joint Conf. Artif. Intell., 1977.
8. Clark, K. The synthesis and verification of logic programs. Res. Rep., Dept. Comptng. and Control, Imperial College, London, 1977.
9. Clark, K., and Darlington, J. Algorithm analysis through synthesis. Res. Rep., Dept. Comptng. and Control, Imperial College, London, Oct. 1977
10. Codd, E.F. A relational model for large shared databases. *Comm. ACM 13*, 6 (June 1970), 377–387.
11. Codd, E.F. Relational completeness of data base sublanguages. In *Data Base Systems*, R. Rustin, Ed., Prentice-Hall, Englewood Cliffs, N.J., 1972.
12. Colmerauer, A., Kanoui, H., Pasero, R., and Roussel, P. Un systeme de communication homme-machine en francais. *Rapport preliminaire, Groupe de Res. en Intell. Artif.*, U. d'Aix-Marseille, Luminy, 1972.
13. Darlington, J., and Burstall, R.M. A system which automatically improves programs. Proc. of Third Int. Joint Conf. Artif. Intell., S.R.I., Menlo Park, Calif., 1973, pp. 437–542.
14. Darvas, F., Futo, I., and Szeredi, P. Logic based program for predicting drug interactions. To appear in *Int. J. Biomedical Computing*.
15. Deliyanni, A., and Kowalski, R.A. Logic and semantic networks. *Comm. ACM 22*, 3 (March 1979), 184–192.
16. Earley, J. An efficient context-free parsing algorithm. *Comm. ACM 13*, 2 (Feb. 1970), 94–102.
17. van Emden, M.H. Programming in resolution logic. To appear in *Machine Representations of Knowledge* published as *Machine Intelligence 8*, E.W. Elcock and D. Michie, Eds., Ellis Horwood and John Wylie.
18. Floyd, R.W. Non-deterministic algorithms. *J. ACM 14*, 4 (Oct. 1967), 636–644.
19. Hayes, P.J. Computation and deduction. Proc. 2nd MFCS Symp., Czechoslovak Acad. of Sciences, 1973, pp. 105–118.
20. Hewitt, C. Planner: A language for proving theorems in robots. Proc. of Int. Joint Conf. Artif. Intell., Washington, D.C., 1969, pp. 295–301.
21. Hogger, C. Deductive synthesis of logic programs. Res. Rep., Dept. Comptng. and Control, Imperial College, London, 1977.
22. Kleene, S.C. *Introduction to Metamathematics*. Van Nostrand, New York, 1952.

23. Kowalski, R.A. Logic for problem-solving. Memo No. 75, Dept. Comput. Logic, U. of Edinburgh, 1974.

24. Kowalski, R.A. Predicate logic as programming language. *Information Processing 74*, North–Holland Pub. Co., Amsterdam, 1974, pp. 569–574.

25. Kowalski, R.A. A proof procedure using connection graphs. *J. ACM 22*, 4 (Oct. 1974), 572–95.

26. Kowalski, R.A., and Kuehner, D. Linear resolution with selection function. *Artif. Intell. 2* (1971), 227–260.

27. Loveland, D.W. A simplified format for the model-elimination theorem-proving procedure. *J. ACM 16*, 3 (July 1969), 349–363.

28. Mac Carthy, J. A basis for a mathematical theory of computation. In *Computer Programming and Formal Systems*, P. Bratfort and D. Hirschberg, Eds., North–Holland Pub. Co., Amsterdam, 1967.

29. McSkimin, J.R., and Minker, J. The use of a semantic network in a deductive question-answering system. Proc. Int. Joint Conf. Artif. Intell., 1977, pp. 50–58.

30. Petri, C.A. Grundsatzliches zur Beschreibung diskreter Prozesse. 3. Colloq. uber Automathentheorie, Birkhauser Verlag, Basel, Switzerland, 1967.

31. Pratt, V.R. The competence/performance dichotomy in programming. Proc. Fourth ACM SIGACT/SIGPLAN Symp. on Principles of Programming Languages, Santa Monica, Calif., Jan. 1977, pp. 194–200.

32. Robinson, J.A. Automatic deduction with hyper-resolution. *Int. J. Comput. Math. 1* (1965), 227–34.

33. Roussel, P. Manual de reference et d'Utilisation. Groupe d'Intell. Artif., UER, Marseille-Luminy, France, 1975.

34. Schwarz, J. Using annotations to make recursion equations behave. Res. Memo, Dept. Artif. Intell., U. of Edinburgh, 1977.

35. Sickel, S. A search technique for clause interconnectivity graphs. *IEEE Trans. Comptrs.* (Special Issue on Automatic Theorem Proving), Aug. 1976.

36. Tärnlund, S.A. An interpreter for the programming language predicate logic. Proc. Int. Joint Conf. Artif. Intell., Tiblisi, 1975, pp. 601–608.

37. Warren, D. A system for generating plans. Memo No. 76, Dept. Comput. Logic, U. of Edinburgh, 1974.

38. Warren, D., Pereira, L.M., and Pereira, F. PROLOG—The language and its implementation compared with LISP. Proc. Symp. on Artif. Intell. and Programming Languages; SIGPLAN Notices (ACM) *12*, 8; SIGART Newsletters (ACM) *64* (Aug. 1977), pp. 109–115.

39. Wirth, N. *Algorithms + Data Structures = Programs*. Prentice-Hall, Englewood Cliffs, N.J., 1976.

LOGIC PROGRAMMING
AND PROLOG: A TUTORIAL*

RUTH E. DAVIS

Logic programming offers significant advantages for the massively parallel computer systems of tomorrow. This tutorial examines the potential of Prolog to implement those advantages.

Interest in logic programming is growing as the fifth generation of computers is being discussed more widely. The Japanese Fifth Generation Computer Project has selected Prolog as the basis for development of a language for the artificial intelligence machines of the 1990s. However, one should not assume that logic programming is programming in Prolog. As the first practical relational language, Prolog represents a first step in a promising direction, but several compromises on the advantages of logic languages had to be made to implement Prolog efficiently on third and fourth generation computers. It is important that one understands what logic programming is before discovering how it is attempted in Prolog.

Concept of logic programming

There are at least three styles of programming languages: procedural, functional, and relational. Each embodies a unique approach to computation; thus, there are fundamental differences in the way one designs algorithms among the three styles of languages, and the style one chooses can affect the way one thinks about algorithms in general.

In a procedural language, one specifies a sequence of steps that will eventually produce a desired effect. The result is a side effect of some computational process. The atomic unit of a procedural program is the statement. We understand a procedural program by tracing through an execution of the statements making up the program.

In a functional language, one defines values. The atomic unit from which functional programs are built is the expression. We can understand a functional program operationally, evaluating expressions until we deter-

mine the final value; or we can understand it declaratively, as a definition of the desired value.

In a relational language—that is, a logic programming language—one specifies a relationship among values. This relationship is defined in terms of conditions or constraints that, when met, imply that the relationship holds. For example, an algebraic equation expresses a relationship among the values of its variables. One can solve it for any variable, given the values of the others. Similarly, a logic program describing a relationship can often be used to find the unknown values in terms of the known. The logic program is understood as a definition of a relationship; each clause of the definition specifies that the relationship holds under certain conditions.

The true logic programmer is less concerned with how a definition will be executed by a machine than with ensuring that the definition given is accurate. The beauty of logic programming is this separation of concerns: the logic and control components (the what and the how) of a program can be specified separately, perhaps by different individuals, or, with the advent of "intelligent" machines and interpreters, control can be left entirely to the system. Changes in the control component of a program can affect only efficiency; one need not worry about a change in control affecting the correctness of results computed by the program.

Procedural programming languages were developed as notations for describing operations that can be performed by a machine. On the other hand, logic was developed to formalize the methods by which humans make correct deductions or convincing arguments. When programming in logic, one need only specify the facts on

The author is with the University of Santa Clara.

which an algorithm would be based, rather than figure out a sequence of steps to be performed. It can be argued that this separation of concerns makes programming in logic easier. For example, in a procedural language, one might use a subtractive algorithm to find the greatest common divisor of two positive integers, m and n:

```
while m ≠ n
  do begin
    temp := minimum(m, n);
    n := |m − n|;
    m := temp
  end
```

We know that this algorithm will work because we know that for all positive integers m and n:

$$gcd(m,n) = gcd(minimum(m,n), |m − n|)$$

However, many people with programming experience make the jump from problem to sequence of steps producing a solution without clearly formulating the facts on which their solution is based. For someone adept at this form of programming, it may seem difficult to ignore process and focus on specification. But the logic programmer must suspend the process-oriented mode of thought and think of the logic program as a description of a solution rather than a prescription of a process that results in the computation of a solution.

Horn clauses

There is more than one style of executable logic language, but we are concerned here only with Horn clause logic programming. First we will present a simple example, then we will describe Horn clauses—their syntax, declarative semantics, and procedural interpretation. We will consider several advantages of Horn clauses as a nondeterministic programming language before investigating the extent to which these advantages are inherited by Prolog. Finally, we mention some extensions and variations of Prolog for logic programming.

An example. As mentioned earlier, programming in logic is the process of defining relationships. Since most people do not have preconceived notions

of processes that compute family relationships, we'll use this domain as a source of examples.

We program in logic by asserting some facts and rules about individuals and their relationships. We call these programs by asking questions about individuals and their relationships. If we wish to build a database of family relationships, we will need to assert certain facts. We'll represent the relationships

X is the father of Y.
X is the mother of Y.

by the atomic formulae

father (X, Y)
mother (X, Y)

We can then supply facts about a family tree by giving the clauses listed in Figure 1. (The :- to the right of a relationship can be read "if," indicating that the relationship holds if the conditions following it are met. If there are no conditions, then the relationship is asserted to hold unconditionally.) The clauses provide a linear representation of the partial family tree, also shown in Figure 1.

We do not want to assert every possible family relationship; there are too many, and such an approach would result in a database with a lot of redundant information in it. We have a choice of either storing assertions of specific relationships or computing relationships from general definitions. For example, if we know that two people have the same parents, then we can conclude that they are siblings. Similarly, we can define the grandparent relationship in terms of parent by the following clauses:

```
grandparent(X,Y) :- parent (X, Z),
                    parent (Z, Y)
parent(X, Y) :- mother (X, Y)
parent(X, Y) :- father (X, Y)
```

These clauses are examples of rules with conditions. X is the grandparent of Y *if* X is the parent of someone who is a parent of Y. We let Z stand for the required parent of Y. The last two rules define the parent relationship in terms of mother and father.

We can build a database of facts and rules that describe all sorts of family relationships (aunt, uncle, cousin, ancestor, etc.). We can then ask questions of the database. Using Horn clauses, queries take the form of conditions to be satisfied that yield no conclusion. Thus, they are written with the :- to the left. Some require simple yes or no answers:

Is Bev a sibling of Theresa?
:- sibling(bev, theresa)

Some queries require that a name be supplied as an answer; that is, they compute a value of X:

Who is a grandparent of Aaron?
:- grandparent(X, aaron)

Some queries, requiring two or more names, compute two or more values:

Who are the parents of Rob?
:- mother(X, rob), father(Y, rob)

Before we consider how these questions get answered, we present a precise definition of the syntax and semantics of Horn clauses.

Syntax. A Horn clause is an implication in which the conjunction of zero or more conditions implies at most one conclusion. We emphasize the conclu-

```
father(paul, rob) :-
mother(mary, rob) :-
father(rob, bev) :-
mother(dorothy, bev) :-
father(rob, theresa) :-
mother(dorothy, theresa) :-
father(jeff, aaron) :-
mother(theresa, aaron) :-
```

Figure 1. Unconditional assertions and their tree representation.

sion by writing it first; the conditions, to the right of :−, are separated by commas (read as "and"). The conditions and conclusions are atomic formulae of predicate logic. The conclusion of a clause is also referred to as the head of the clause. The empty clause (with no conditions or conclusions) is written □ and read as "box."

An atomic formula is an *n*-ary predicate applied to *n* terms as arguments. A term is a constant, a variable, or an *n*-ary function applied to *n* terms. We follow the Prolog convention that variables begin with uppercase letters and that words beginning with lowercase letters signify constants, predicates, and functions. Numbers are built-in constants. A grammar for Horn clauses is shown in the box at right.

An atomic formula is always the expression of a relationship (named by the predicate of the formula) among the terms that are the arguments of the atomic formula. It will be true or false, depending on the values of the terms. The terms represent objects; they can be constants, variables, or complex terms constructed by function application. The value represented by a function application is an object; the value represented by a predicate application is a statement that is true or false.

Semantics. As mentioned above, a Horn clause is an implication. It states that for all possible values of the variables appearing in the clause, if all the conditions to the right of the :− hold, then the conclusion (left of :−) is true. In other words, every variable is assumed to be universally quantified over the clause in which it appears. Each clause thus stands alone. It is either an accurate representation of a fact, or it is not—regardless of what other clauses may appear in the program.

To determine that a program will compute only correct results, one need only consider each clause individually and determine that each clause produces a valid conclusion if the conditions are met.

To determine that the definition is complete—that is, that *all* correct

---

Grammar for Horn clauses

Horn_clause:: = atmf ":−" | atmf ":−" atmfs
                | ":−" atmfs | "□"
atmfs :: = atmf ("," atmf)*
atmf :: = pred "(" terms ")"
terms :: = term ("," term)*
term :: = variable | constant | function "(" terms ")" | list
variable :: = (uppercase_letter | "_") word
word :: = (letter | digit)*
constant :: = number | lowerword
function :: = lowerword
predicate :: = lowerword
lowerword :: = lowercase_letter word
list :: = "[ ]" | "[" head "|" tail "]"
head :: = term
tail :: = list

In Prolog the :− following an unconditional assertion is dropped, and each clause must be terminated by a period. A list can also be indicated explicitly by enclosing the elements of the list (separated by commas) in square brackets, or it may have some of the elements explicitly listed and the tail of the list given in the notation above. For example, [a | [b | [c | [ ]]]] may be written in a number of ways, including [a, b, c,], or [a, b | [c]], or [a | [b, c]].

---

results are attainable—one must see that a clause is included to cover every possible case.

Whether or not one chooses to use logic as an implementation language, one can benefit from the Horn clause definition as a specification of the problem at hand. If a formal verification is to be attempted, one must have a formal specification against which to verify the implementation, regardless of the implementation language. Horn clauses provide a specification language that is both formal and executable.[1,2]

Procedural interpretation. We can view Horn clauses as a programming language if we interpret each clause as a procedure definition. The conclusion of a clause is the procedure name, and the conditions of the clause represent the procedure body. A main program is then a procedure body with no name—that is, a set of conditions to be satisfied with no conclusion. One attempts to satisfy conditions by invoking them as procedures. To execute the body of a procedure, one calls each procedure listed.

Procedures are invoked by unification, a generalized pattern match. Given a procedure call, one looks for a clause whose head (conclusion) matches (or unifies with) the call. After renaming the variables in the clause so that it shares no variables with the current set of calls, one finds the most general unifier of the selected call and the head of the selected clause. A unifier is a substitution that, when applied to both the call and the clause head, makes them syntactically identical. It is most general if it makes as few and as general bindings as possible.

This substitution is made throughout the current list of procedure calls and throughout the body of the selected procedure. Then, as in the familiar substitution and simplification model of computation, the original procedure call is replaced by the body of the selected clause. (This replacement of a goal by the subgoals that allow us to conclude it is also known as backward chaining.) See the box on page 56 for a summary of the unification algorithm.

Execution terminates when all procedures have successfully terminated.

A procedure with no body terminates as soon as the unifying substitution is made (the call is replaced by the empty body).

For example, suppose we want to know whether Aaron has a grandparent. Our goal (or main program) is

: – grandparent(G, aaron)

We look for all clauses that have grandparent in their conclusions (there is only one):

grandparent(X, Y) : – parent(X, Z),
                          parent (Z, Y)

We make the substitution {X = G, Y = aaron} and replace the call by the

body of the grandparent procedure with the substitution made, yielding

: – parent(G, Z), parent (Z, aaron)

Now we are left with two calls on parent. We can choose to work first on either one. We'll work on the second one (applying a heuristic that it is often more efficient to select a call in which more arguments are supplied values). We now need a clause defining parent. There are two:

parent(X, Y) : – mother(X, Y)
parent(X, Y) : – father(X, Y)

We can use either clause; suppose we choose the first one. We make the substitution {X = Z, Y = aaron} throughout and replace the call by the body, leaving

: – parent(G, Z), mother(Z, aaron)

Again choosing to work on the second call, we must find a definition of mother that will match this call. There is only one candidate; the substitution we need is {Z = theresa}. Since the body of the chosen procedure definition is empty, we are left with

: – parent(G, theresa)

(Recall that the unifying substitution is made throughout both the procedure body and the current list of procedure calls, also referred to as subgoals, before the body is substituted for the selected call.) Using the first definition of parent, this reduces to

: – mother(G, theresa)

Finally, with the substitution {G = dorothy}, we are through. Successful

---

Robinson's unification procedure

We wish to find a most general substitution that when applied to the atomic formulae in a given set renders them syntactically identical.

If E is a set of atomic formulae, then the result of applying the substitution $\sigma = \{X_1 = t_1, ..., X_n = t_n\}$ to E is a new set, denoted $E\sigma$, that is identical to E except that for every component $X_i = t_i$ of σ where E contains an occurrence of X_i, $E\sigma$ contains an occurrence of t_i. We construct the unifying substitution in a piecemeal fashion.

We add a new component, $X_k = t_k$, to a substitution $\sigma = \{X_1 = t_1, ..., X_n = t_n\}$, where $X_k \neq X_i$ for any i in σ, by applying the substitution to each t_i in σ, and adding the new component to σ. We denote this by $\sigma[X_k = t_k]$.

Let $L = \{L_1, ..., L_n\}$ be a set of atomic formulae. (In practice we will be unifying only two atomic formulae at a time.) The disagreement set of L is the set of all well-formed subexpressions of the atomic formulae in L that begin at the first symbol position at which not all the atomic formulae have the same symbol. For example, $\{p(X, f(X, g(Y)), V), p(X, f(X, Z), W)\}$ has the disagreement set $\{g(Y), Z\}$.

Now we are prepared to present the algorithm. Let L be a set of atomic formulae to be unified:

1. Set $\sigma_1 = \phi$ (the empty substitution). Set $k = 0$.
2. Set $k = k + 1$. If the elements of $L\sigma_k$ are all equal, σ_k is the desired most general unifier.
3. Let s_k and t_k be the two earliest expressions in a lexical ordering (variables come first in the ordering) of the disagreement set of $L\sigma_k$; if s_k is a variable and does not occur in t_k, set $\sigma_{k+1} = \sigma_k[s_k = t_k]$ and go to step 2. Otherwise, there is no unifier of the given set.

Source: J. A. Robinson, "A Machine-Oriented Logic Based on the Resolution Principle," *J. ACM*, Vol. 12, No. 1, Jan. 1965, pp. 23-41.

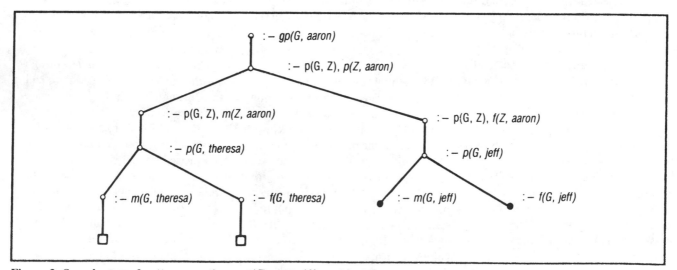

Figure 2. Search space for ": – grandparent(G, aaron)" problem.

termination simply means we have nothing left to do. The answer to our original query is found in the substitutions made along the way. In this example we found that Dorothy, the binding made to G of the original call (or goal), is a grandparent of Aaron. A summary of our computation scheme is given in the box below right.

Nondeterminism. A logic programming language based on Horn clauses is nondeterministic in two different ways: We are free to choose any order in which to execute several procedure calls (or satisfy several subgoals) in the body of a procedure (subgoal selection); and, when executing a selected procedure call (subgoal), we are free to choose any procedure definition whose name can be made to match the selected call (clause selection).

The original goal and the selection of subgoals at each step along the way determine a search space containing several possible computations. A search space containing all possible answers for the problem just described is shown in Figure 2. In the figure, we have abbreviated all predicate names to save space and have underlined the selection of subgoal to be attempted next in each clause. The box, □, indicates successful termination. Darkened nodes represent dead ends (computationally speaking); they indicate that there is no clause whose head matches the selected subgoal. Any path in the search space from the original goal to a box represents a successful computation. Different paths may result in different bindings (answers) to the variables of the original goal. Along the path we took, we found that Dorothy is a grandparent of Aaron; we might have chosen a different path and discovered that Rob is a grandparent of Aaron.

If we had chosen to satisfy the subgoals in a different order, we would have generated a different search space. For example, Figure 3 illustrates the search space we obtain by choosing to work on the subgoal p(G, Z) before p(Z, aaron). Beyond that point, all names are abbreviated by their first characters.

Invertibility. There is nothing about the definition of grandparent that implies we must always be supplied a grandchild and asked to find a grandparent. We could use the same definitions given above and ask for a grandchild of Mary:

: − grandparent(mary, Gchild)

Or we might supply both names and ask, for example, whether Paul is a grandparent of Bev:

: − grandparent(paul, bev)

We might even supply no values, asking whether any grandparent relationships can be derived in our database:

Backward-chaining Horn clause computation

Computation is initiated by a main program (or query) consisting of a set of procedure calls:

1. Select a call to execute.
2. Select a procedure to use in executing the chosen call.
3. Standardize apart—rename variables as necessary to ensure that there are no variables that occur both in the current set of calls and in the selected procedure.
4. Find a most general unifier (MGU) of the selected call and the name (left-hand side) of the selected procedure.
5. Replace the selected call by the body of the procedure.
6. Apply the MGU to the new set of calls resulting from step 5.
7. (a) If no calls remain, you have terminated successfully. (b) If you found no procedure name to match the selected call, back up and redo the previous call, using a different procedure than the one you already used. (c) If all options under (b) have been exhausted, terminate with failure.

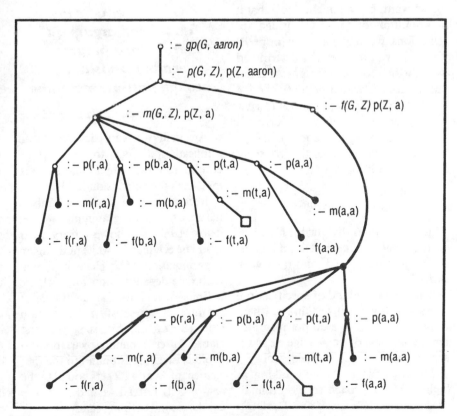

Figure 3. Search space obtained by changing order of subgoals.

: – grandparent(Gpar, Gchild)

We refer to this flexibility of calling styles as the invertibility of logic programs. The terminology stems from the special case that the same definition may be used to compute a function and its inverse.

Invertibility is not restricted to database applications. An appropriate definition of multiplication can also be used for division or even square root. (Of course, it is more efficient to make use of the arithmetic capabilities supplied as primitives.) A program that translates English words into their French equivalents can do just as well translating French to English. Not all relationships are invertible in all directions. For discussions of invertibility, see Shoham and McDermott[3] and Sickel.[4]

Partial computations. Since program evaluation is done by means of pattern matching (unification), one never gets an "undefined argument" error message. If a value is undetermined, it is represented by a variable. It might also be partially determined. We may not know completely the value we want, but we might know that it is a multiple of three. Or, in list applications, we may not know (or need) the entire list, but we have determined what its first four elements are. Partial information is always better than none at all, and we often prefer not to generate an entire answer before performing some other computation on it.

For example, consider the following top-level specification of a sort routine:

sort(Old, New) : –   perm(Old, New),
ord(New)

This clause states that the list New is a sorted version of the list Old, if New is a permutation of Old, and if New is ordered.

This is not the kind of specification of a sort routine that we think of when in process mode. We do not mean to ignore the mass of knowledge we have accumulated about efficient sorting techniques. We are simply taking a higher level approach to the original specification. See Clark and Darlington[5] for a discussion of the logic

specification of several standard sorting algorithms, all derived from the ordered permutation description.

It is easy to see that an ordered permutation is an accurate definition of sort if perm and ord are properly defined. We can also agree that ord should check the order of the proposed permutation as it is being generated rather than wait until the list is completely determined, only to discover that it fails to be ordered in the first two elements. We can define perm and ord as follows:

perm([ ], [ ]) : –
perm(L, [X|Y]) : – delete(X, L, L2),
perm(L2, Y)

delete(X, [X|L], L) : –
delete(X, [Y|L], [Y|Z]) : –
delete(X, L,Z)

ord([ ]) : –
ord([X|[ ]]) : –
ord([X|[Y|L]]) : – X < Y, ord([Y|L])

We indicate the empty list by the empty brackets [], and [X|Y] represents the list whose first element is X and tail is Y.

One never gets an "undefined argument" error since program evaluation is done through pattern matching.

Again, if we read each line as an implication, it is easy to see that if the conditions on the right-hand side are met, then the conclusion holds.

Because of the nondeterministic nature of logic programming, we can delete elements in any arbitrary order from the original list while building up a permutation. The element chosen each time depends upon which clause defining delete is used at that time. For example, if we satisfy the condition delete(X, L, L2) by using the first clause (after renaming variables to avoid clashes), X is bound to the first element of L, and L2 gets bound to the rest of L. If instead we had chosen to use the second defining clause of delete and then the first clause on the new

condition, our original X would be bound to the second element of L, and L2 would get everything but the second element of L.

As an example, in Figure 4 we generate the entire search space for the problem of deleting an element from the list [a, b, c]. We ensure that our clauses are standardized apart before unification by generating a new instance of each definitional clause (generating new variables by attaching a number to each variable in the clause) each time we need to use it. In this example, we show the substitution made at each step of the computation.

The element chosen to be deleted from L becomes the first element of the permutation being generated. We generate the next element of the permutation by deleting an element from what was left of the list after the first deletion. Once two elements have been generated, it makes sense to check that they are in order. This means that when we have the following set of conditions:

: – perm(Old, [X|[Y|L]]),
ord([X|[Y|L]])

in which X and Y have been bound to specific values, we should use the partial results to check whether the permutation generated thus far is ordered, rather than continue generating a permutation of Old. If the partial permutation is ordered, then we continue with more of the permutation; if not, we back up and make a new choice for the first pair of elements. This swapping of control back and forth between goals is known as coroutining.

This example shows how partial results (a permutation in which only the first two elements are known) might be used to guide the efficient execution of a program that will eventually compute the entire result. The same mechanism also allows computation with infinite objects. Although an infinite object is never fully realizable, one can compute as much of it as one desires. Thus, one might write a program involving a term that represents a list of all the positive integers. (Of course, one should never attempt to print such a term.)

Another advantage of pattern matching is the elimination of the need for selector functions on complex data structures. Consider the definition of ord given above. We have no need for functions to select the head or tail of a list; nor do we need functions to test whether a list is empty, has only one element, or at least two elements. We simply rely on the pattern matching to succeed if possible, and if it has, we refer to the pieces of the structure by the names we gave them in the pattern.

Prolog

Prolog (for *pro*gramming in *log*ic) is a deterministic language based on Horn clauses. Existing in many forms on many different machines, Prolog varies somewhat in syntax and features supported. Some of the better known variations include DEC10 Prolog, Micro-Prolog, Waterloo Prolog, and IC-Prolog. The following discussion is based largely on DEC10 Prolog, developed at the University of Edinburgh.

The syntax of Prolog programs is the same as that of Horn clauses except that each clause must be terminated by a period and the : − is dropped on the right-hand side of an assertion of fact.

The semantics of a Prolog program is affected by the deterministic order of execution imposed by the language. Clauses and subgoals within clauses are always attempted in the order given. Any (partially) correct Horn clause program is a (partially) correct Prolog program; the reverse is not true. The imposition of a fixed order of execution does not render a correct logic program incorrect (*any* order should suffice); however, to improve efficiency, most Prolog programmers depend on the given order, and their programs may yield incorrect results if the control scheme is changed.

For example, the following Prolog program, defining insert(X, L, NewL), is intended to describe the relationship that exists when NewL is the sorted list consisting of the sorted list L with the element X inserted in its proper place:

insert(X, [], [X]).
insert(X, [Y|L], [X, Y|L]) : − X ≤ Y.

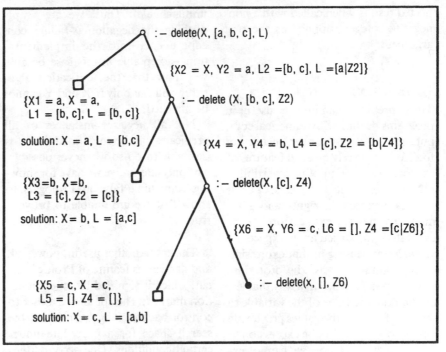

Figure 4. Search space for "delete(X, [a, b, c], L)."

insert(X, [Y | L], [Y | NewL])
 : − insert(X, L, NewL).

The first clause describes the fact that inserting any element into the empty list results in a list consisting of that single element. The second clause states that the result of inserting X into a list whose first element is Y and whose tail is L is the list whose first element is X, second element is Y, and tail is L, if X is less than or equal to Y. The third clause states that the result of inserting X into a list whose first element is Y and whose tail is L is the list whose first element is Y and whose tail is the result of inserting X into L.

The correctness of this program relies on the attempt to use the second clause before the third clause; the third clause is attempted only if X > Y. If we assume that the clauses can be attempted in any order (as the semantics of a logic program dictate), then the third argument to insert can be the second argument in which X is inserted anywhere. To correct the logic, we can include a test, X > Y, as an additional condition in the body of the third clause; on a sequential machine, however, such a test would be redundant and is usually omitted.

Extralogical features. Prolog has several extralogical constructs that facilitate the writing of efficient programs dealing with a variety of problems. Input and output are accomplished by predefined predicates for reading and writing terms and characters. In most Prolog implementations, these predicates can be satisfied only once (it is not possible to backtrack over input or output, whatever that might mean). Other predicates enable one to construct and then assert new facts and rules and call new procedures programmatically. One can also retract facts and rules from the database.

As described earlier, execution is the unification-driven replacement of goals by subgoals until all are satisfied. The values output at the top level by the Prolog interpreter are the bindings of the variables in the original call. The unification process does not evaluate expressions; it merely matches them. Thus, if X is bound to +(Y,1), and Y is bound to +(Z,2), and Z is bound to 3, the binding given for X at the top level would be +(+(3,2),1), not 6. Prolog provides a predicate, is, to force evaluation of expressions.

The following definition of factorial, for example, will yield the expected results when called with a non-negative integer supplied as the first argument:

```
fact(0,1).
fact(N, X) : − N1 is N − 1,
    fact(N1, X1), X is N * X1.
```

The is predicate can be very useful in programs dealing with numerical computations, but this convenience is not free. When we rely on such features of Prolog, we give up the invertibility property of logic programs. The is predicate expects its right-hand argument to be an expression to be evaluated; in particular, it expects all variables appearing in that expression to be bound. That is, the procedure must always be called in a way that lets us compute the value of the variable to the left of is using the values previously bound to variables in the expression to the right of is. Hence, we cannot expect the above definition of factorial to succeed on a call such as fact(N, 6).

Negation by failure. We have seen how to derive the fact that a relationship exists and how to supply values for which the relationship holds. But we often define relationships in terms of negative constraints, as well as conditions that must hold. How do we show that a relationship does not hold? In Prolog, we show not-P by attempting and failing to show P—a method known as negation by failure.[6] Although the method is acceptable in some situations (such as database applications in which we can assert that our knowledge about the data is complete), it is semantically disturbing.

One need not always rely on failure to establish negation. It is possible to define relations that include an argument indicating whether the relation holds on the other arguments.[7] For example, one can state "the assertion that X is a member of the empty list is false" by defining the predicate member with three arguments:

```
member(X, [ ], false).
member(X, X.Y, true).
member(X, Y.L, ANS) : − X ≠ Y,
    member(X, L, ANS).
```

This example relies upon the failure to show that X and Y are equal to establish that they are unequal (that is,

unmatchable). Thus, we are simply pushing the negation-as-failure concept deeper into the implementation—acceptable in this case because we know that the unification algorithm will fail only if X and Y cannot be matched.

Not all negative instances of all predicates can be so defined, but it is desirable to do so whenever possible. The only alternative we have for showing something false in Prolog is to show that we are unable to prove it true.

The cut. Another useful, powerful, and dangerous feature of Prolog is the cut, which is signified by an exclamation mark, !. The cut allows a user to control backtracking by pruning the search space for a procedure under certain conditions. One accomplishes this by using the cut as one of the goals in a procedure definition. A cut succeeds the first time it is encountered, but it cannot be resatisfied. It also has the side effect of freezing all choices made after the parent goal (the one that matched the left-hand side of the clause containing the cut) is invoked. Thus, if it becomes necessary to backtrack over a cut, not only is the current clause abandoned as a means of satisfying the parent goal, but the parent goal is failed.

Some of the common uses of the cut are

(1) to indicate that the current clause is the only one applicable to the given problem;

(2) to indicate that the parent goal is unsatisfiable (the cut-fail combination); and

(3) to indicate that the relationship being computed is in fact functional—that is, there is only one answer, and one should not bother backtracking to find an alternative answer.

In the first use, one can consider the calls that appear before the cut in a clause to be guards—preconditions that determine a class of situations that must all be handled the same way. Thus, the user has the ability to implement a program flow similar to an if-then-else in other languages. Because

of the dependence upon ordering of clauses in Prolog programs, one knows that a second clause will never be attempted if the first will succeed. The cut allows one to indicate that a second clause should not be attempted if some subset of the calls in the first clause has succeeded, even though the clause may have failed in later calls.

In combination with the fail goal (which always fails), the cut indicates that a relationship is unsatisfiable. Under certain conditions we may be able to state that something is definitely not true. For example, X is not a model student if X has been convicted of cheating on exams. The cut-fail combination can also be used to define negation as failure:

```
not(P) : − call(P), !, fail.
not(P).
```

(The call routine takes an atomic formula as argument and executes it as a query. Therefore, : − call(P) and : − P are equivalent in effect.) Thus, not(P) will fail if P succeeds (since the cut will prevent selection of an alternative clause after P succeeds and fail will fail the current clause), and succeed (due to the second clause) if P fails.

The cut is often used to terminate generate-and-test situations. We might have a predicate capable of generating an infinite number of values, but we are interested only in a specific value determined by conditions that must be met. If we prevent backtracking over those conditions once they are met, we can avoid an infinite search for alternatives. Also, there may be many ways of generating one answer, and we simply want to improve efficiency by eliminating different paths to the same answer.

For example, suppose we are interested in the least natural number, X, satisfying some condition P(X). We could use the following defining clause:

```
least(X) : − number(X), P(X), !.
number(0).
number(Z) : − number(Y), Z is Y + 1.
```

By calling number(X) in the body of least, we bind X to 0. If P(0) fails, we backtrack to get a different value for X. The next value for X generated by

Prolog will be 1—then 2, then 3, until the condition P(X) is satisfied. After executing the cut, we will not be able to look for another number satisfying P.

Possible improvements. Prolog can be improved in several ways. Notational conveniences, such as an if-then-else predicate or a more general conditional construct, could be included to eliminate redundancy, thereby improving the readability of logic programs without compromising their semantics.[7] Many uses of the cut operator could be isolated to define constructs that better preserve the semantics of logic programs. This improvement would be similar to the invention of if-then-else, while, and for constructs for procedural languages to avoid the indiscriminate use of the goto operator.

Parlog and Concurrent Prolog take advantage of Horn clauses as a natural way of expressing parallel computations. Both languages add constructs that aid in the specification of parallel computations. However, they relinquish much of the flexibility of logic programs by enforcing commitment to computational choices that cannot be reversed later.

It is useful to be able to evaluate and match terms on the basis of equality rather than syntactic identity. In Prolog, computation is driven by unification, which is strictly a syntactic matching process. For example, we can match the terms $+(2,X)$ and $+(2,4)$ but not the terms $+(2,X)$ and $+(3,4)$, even though we know that if X were bound to 5, the two expressions would have the same value.[8]

There are more difficult language problems to be solved. Any system expected to behave intelligently must be capable of some degree of introspection. That is, it must be able to represent and reason about its own problem-solving techniques. If it is to learn, it must be able to modify those techniques on the basis of its experience. It should be able to answer questions about its behavior (how did it arrive at a certain conclusion?). At a more mundane level, a compiler operates on programs as objects, transforming them into other programs that preserve their semantics and can be run more efficiently. Thus, we must be able to consider functions and predicates as objects among which relationships can be established. In other words, functions and predicates should be first class in that they can be created and manipulated as freely as any other kind of object. Several people are investigating ways of combining functional programming with relational programming to synthesize a powerful and semantically satisfying language.[9-13]

Efficiency. In this article, we have not dealt in detail with the issue of specification of efficient logic programs. We have been more concerned with the efficient use of the designer's time than with the machine's. This is not to imply that the issue need not be addressed. In fact, it may be desirable

---

Any system expected to behave intelligently must be capable of some degree of introspection.

(on sequential machines it is usually necessary) for a logic programmer to specify how a program should be run. The important point is that the specification of the logic component of an algorithm and the specification of the control component can be, and should be, separate tasks so as not to compromise the correctness of the logic program.

There are several advantages to maintaining separate logic and control specifications. Since the correctness of the algorithm is determined by the logic component, one need not worry that changes in control will cause incorrect results. This implies that control need not be specified by the same individual who specified the logic. More important, it means that the logic program can be ported from system to system without ever changing the logic specification. As more sophisticated systems become available, the control component will change, either explicitly taking advantage of new capabilities or leaving more and more of the control to the system itself.

An intelligent logic programming system of the future will be implemented on a truly parallel machine. It will have heuristics for choosing among alternative computation paths and the ability to follow several in parallel if the situation calls for it. We will be able to specify certain control strategies for individual programs and to specify conditions under which one strategy should be used over another. It has been shown that the backward-chaining (top-down) interpretation scheme is not always the most reasonable.[14] Undoubtedly, backtracking will always be with us in some form. We have not been able to eliminate it in human problem solving, but we have been able to backtrack intelligently. Similarly, our logic programming system should be able to analyze what led it to a dead end and backtrack intelligently to undo the cause of the problem.

Logic programming has much to recommend it, whether it is used as an executable specification language or an implementation language. Separation of the logic and control aspects of a program allow a very-high-level description of the desired relationships without the overspecification that results from prescribing how they are to be computed. The declarative semantics of logical implication, the locality of reference, and the unification-driven computation scheme ensure that there can be no side effects and that each clause can be understood without reference to its position in a set of clauses. The specification of relationships rather than computations allows the same definition to be used in different ways, depending on what is supplied as input and what is expected as result. Unification, as the procedure-calling mechanism, obviates the need for selector functions and allows computation with partially defined objects.

Some, but not all, of these advantages are compromised in Prolog programs. Usually, in a Prolog program, one must consider together all the clauses defining a given predicate, since the correctness of a clause may depend on its position with respect to the others. It is also possible, and in some applications necessary, to "side-effect" the database within a Prolog program. The extent to which Prolog programs are invertible depends largely on one's programming style and the avoidance of the extralogical features of Prolog. Prolog inherits all the advantages of unification-driven computation and the easy-to-read, high-level specification afforded by Horn clauses.

The nondeterminism inherent in logic programs is a natural application area for systems with massive parallelism built in. As mentioned, several aspects of Prolog need improvement, and many hard problems are still to be solved. Most researchers believe that the efficiency issue must be attacked at a lower level than language design. If we keep our high-level logic programming language free of the concerns of efficient control, we stand to gain more in the long run. We can expect more from computers as problem-solving assistants than as computational slaves. □

References

1. R.E. Davis, "Runnable Specifications as a Design Tool," in *Logic Programming*, K.L. Clark and S.-A. Tarnlund, eds., Academic Press, New York, 1982.
2. R.E. Davis, "Executable Specifications as Basis of Program Life Cycle," *Proc. 18th Hawaii Conf. System Sciences*, Vol. II, Jan. 1985.
3. Y. Shoham and D.V. McDermott, "Directed Relations and Inversion of Prolog Programs," in *Fifth Generation Computer Systems 1984*, Institute of New Generation Computer Technology (ICOT), ed., North-Holland, Amsterdam, 1984, pp. 307-316.
4. S. Sickel, "Invertibility of Logic Programs," *Proc. Fourth Workshop Automated Deduction*, Austin, Texas, Feb. 1979, pp. 103-109.
5. K.L. Clark and J. Darlington, "Algorithm Classification Through Synthesis," *Computer J.*, Vol. 23, No. 1, 1980.
6. K. Clark, "Negation as Failure," in *Logic in Data Bases*, H. Gallaire and J. Minker, eds., Plenum Press, New York, 1978, pp. 293-322.
7. R.E. Davis, "Keeping the Logic in Logic Programming," technical report, University of Santa Clara, Santa Clara, Calif.
8. M. Fay, "First-Order Unification in an Equational Theory," *Proc. Fourth Workshop Automated Deduction*, Austin, Texas, Feb. 1979, pp. 161-167.
9. J.A. Goquen and J. Meseguer, "Equality, Types, Modules, and (Why Not?) Generics for Logic Programming," *J. Logic Programming*, Vol. 1, No. 2, 1984, pp. 179-210.
10. J.A. Robinson and E.E. Sibert, "LogLisp: an Alternative to Prolog," *Machine Intelligence*, Vol. 10, 1982, pp. 339-419.
11. *Proc. 1984 Int'l Symp. Logic Programming*, Atlantic City, N.J., Feb. 1984.
12. *Proc. Second Int'l Logic Programming Conf.*, Uppsala, Sweden, July 1984.
13. *Proc. Int'l Conf. Fifth Generation Computer Systems 1984*, published as *Fifth Generation Computer Systems 1984*, Institute of New Generation Computer Technology (ICOT), ed., North-Holland, Amsterdam, 1984.
14. D.R. Brough and A. Walker, "Some Practical Properties of Logic Programming Interpreters," in *Fifth Generation Computer Systems 1984*, North-Holland, Amsterdam, 1984.
15. L.M. Pereira and A. Porto, "Selective Backtracking," in *Logic Programming*, K.L. Clark, and S.-A. Tarnlund, eds., Academic Press, New York, 1982, pp. 107-116.

Additional reading

K.L. Clark and S. Gregory, "Notes on Systems Programming in Parlog," in *Fifth Generation Computer Systems 1984*, North Holland, Amsterdam, 1984.

Logic Programming, K.L. Clark and S.-A. Tarnlund, eds., Academic Press, New York, 1982.

W.F. Clocksin and C.S. Mellish, *Programming in Prolog*, Springer-Verlag, New York, 1981.

J.R. Ennals, *Beginning Micro-Prolog*, Harper & Row, New York, 1984.

R. Kowalski, "Algorithm = Logic + Control," *Comm. ACM*, Vol. 22, No. 7, July 1979, pp. 424-431.

R. Kowalski, *Logic for Problem Solving*, North-Holland, New York, 1979.

Proc. First Int'l Logic Programming Conf., Marseilles, France, Sept. 1982.

Proc. Logic Programming Workshop, 1980. (This is difficult to come by, but much of it is reproduced in the book *Logic Programming*, K. L. Clark and S.-A. Tarnlund, eds., Academic Press, New York, 1982.)

J.A. Robinson, "A Machine-Oriented Logic Based on the Resolution Principle," *J. ACM*, Vol. 12, No. 1, 1965, pp. 23-41.

E.Y. Shapiro, *A Subset of Concurrent Prolog and Its Interpreter*, technical report, Weizmann Institute of Science, Jan. 1983.

M. Van Emden and R. Kowalski, "The Semantics of Predicate Logic as a Programming Language," *J. ACM*, Vol. 23, No. 4, 1976, pp. 733-743.

Ruth E. Davis is on the faculty of the Electrical Engineering and Computer Science Department at Santa Clara University in California. She is also vice president of the Lisp Company (TLC), which provides microcomputer implementations of Lisp and Logo. Davis is coauthor with John R. Allen of an introductory computer science book, *Thinking About TLC-Logo*.

Davis's research interests include declarative logic programming and intelligent environments for logic program development and execution.

She received a PhD in information sciences from the University of California at Santa Cruz in 1979. Her dissertation, *Generating Correct Programs for Logic Specifications*, won an award from the 1979 ACM Doctoral Forum.

Davis's address is EECS Dept., Santa Clara University, Santa Clara, CA 95053.

BIBLIOGRAPHY

FURTHER READINGS

The following bibliography contains a list of references on the general subject of programming languages. No attempt has been made to be complete. I wish merely to supply to the reader a wide set of references on a variety of programming language topics. The section is divided into the following subject areas: Programming Languages (Ada, ALGOL60, COBOL, FORTRAN, LISP, Pascal, SNOBAL, Other Languages), Semantics, Programming Language Comparisons, Concurrency, and other Topics of Interest. By following these references, the reader can determine where to look for any particular article or subject they desire to read about. However, as these lists invariably go out of date, the reader should be aware that more recent topics subsequent to this printing are likely to be covered less adequately than I would have hoped, or not at all.

PROGRAMMING LANGUAGES

Ada

Barnes, J.G.P. *Programming in Ada*, Addison Wesley, Reading, Ma., 2nd edition, 1984.

Barringer, H., and Mearns, I. "Axioms and Proof Rules for Ada Tasks" *IEEE Proc. 129*, March 1982, 38–48.

Gehani, N. *Ada: Concurrent Programming*, Prentice-Hall, Englewood Cliffs, N.J., 1984.

Habermann, N., Perry, D. *Ada for Experienced Programmers*, Addison Wesley, Reading, Ma., 1983.

Proc. Ada International Conf., eds. Barnes & Fisher, Cambridge Univ. Press, Paris, 1985.

"Rationale for the Design of the Ada Programming Language" *ACM Sigplan Notices*, 14, 6, June 1979.

Reference Manual for the Ada Programming Language, U.S. Dept. of Defense, MIL-Standard-1815, ANSI Standard, 1982.

"Requirements for High Order Computer Programming Languages—STEELMAN," U.S. Dept. of Defense, A.R.P.A., reprinted in Wasserman, 1986.

Wegner, P. *Ada: A Graduated Introduction*, Prentice-Hall, revised edition, Englewood Cliffs, N.J., 1981.

Welsh, J., Lister, A. "A Comparative Study of Task Communication in Ada" *Software Practice and Experience*, vol. 11, 1981, 257–290.

ALGOL60

Extended ALGOL Reference Manual, Burroughs Corp., Detroit, Mich., Form no. 5000128, 1971.

"Suggestions on ALGOL 60 (Rome) Issues" *Comm ACM*, 6, 1, 20–23.

Knuth, D.E. et al. "A Proposal for Input/Output Conventions in ALGOL60" *Comm. ACM*, 7, 5, 1964, 173–283.

de Morgan, R.M.; Hill I.D.; and Wichmann, B.A. "A Supplement to the ALGOL60 Revised Report" *Computer Journal*, 19, 3, 1976, 276–288.

de Morgan, R.M.; Hill, I.D.; and Wichmann, B.A. "Modified Report on the Algorithmic Language ALGOL60" *Computer Journal*, 19, 4, 1976, 364–379.

Randell, B., and Russell, L. *ALGOL 60 Implementation*, Academic Press, New York, 1964.

COBOL

American National Standard COBOL (ANS X3.23-1968) American National Standards Institute, New York, 1968.

American National Standard Programming Language—COBOL X3.23, American National Standards Institute, New York, 1974.

Jackson, M. "COBOL," in Perrott (ed.) *Software Engineering*, Academic Press, New York, 1977.

Sammet, J. "The Early History of COBOL," in Wexelblat (ed., *History of Programming Languages*, Academic Press, New York, 1981, 199–224.

FORTRAN

American National Standard FORTRAN (ANS X3.9-1966) American National Standards Institute, New York, 1966.

American National Standard FORTRAN (ANS X3.9-1977) American National Standards Institute, N.Y., 1977.

American National Standard Programming Language—FORTRAN, X3.9, American National Standards Institute, New York, 1978.

504   Bibliography

Backus, J.W.; Beeber, R.J.; Best, S.; Goldberg, R.; Haibt, L.M.; Herrick, H.L.; Nelson, R.A.; Sayre, D.; Sheridan, P.B.; Stern, H.; Ziller, I.; Hughes, R.A.; and Nutt, R. "The FORTRAN Automatic Coding System" *Proc. Western Jt. Comp. Conf.*, AIEE (now IEEE), Los Angeles, 188–198.

Backus, J. "The history of FORTRAN I, II, and III" *ACM Sigplan Notices*, 13, 8, August, 1978, 165–180. Also in *History of Programming Languages*, Wexelblat (ed.), 1981.

Boillot, M. *Understanding FORTRAN 77*, West Publishing, St. Paul, Minn., 1984.

"Draft Standard, Industrial Real-Time FORTRAN, *ACM Sigplan Notices*, 16, 7, 1981, 45–60.

Dyck, V.A., Lawson, J., Smith, J. *FORTRAN 77*, Reston Pub. Co., Reston, Va., 1984.

LISP

Allen, J. *the Anatomy of LISP*, McGraw-Hill, New York, 1979.

Berk, A.A. *LISP, The Language of Artificial Intelligence*, Van Nostrand, N.Y., 1985.

Bobrow, D. and Murphy, D. "Structure of a LISP System Using Two-Level Storage" *C.ACM*, 10, 3, 1967, 155–159.

Friedman, D. *The Little Lisper*, Science Research Associates, Chicago, 1974.

McCarthy, J. "History of LISP" in Wexelblat (ed.), *History of Programming Languages*, Academic Press, New York, 1981, 173–184.

McCarthy, J. "Towards a Mathematical Theory of Computation" *Proc. IFIP Congress 62*. 21–28, North-Holland, Amsterdam, 1962.

Moses, J. "The Function of FUNCTION in LISP" *SIGSAM Bull*. July, 1970, 13–27.

Sandewall, E. "Programming in an Interactive Environment: The LISP Experience" *ACM Computing Surveys*, 10, 1, 1978, 35–72.

Sansonnet, J. et al. "Direct Execution of LISP on a List-Directed Architecture" *ACM Sigplan Notices*, 17, 4, 1982, 132–139.

Siklossy, L. *Let's Talk LISP*, Prentice-Hall, Englewood Cliffs, N.J., 1976.

Steele Jr., G. *Common LISP*, Digital Press, Maynard, Mass., 1984.

Sussman, G. et al. "SCHEME 79-LISP on a Chip" *IEEE Computer*, July 1981.

Teitelman, W. *INTERLISP Reference Manual*, Xerox Palo Alto Research Center, Palo Alto, Calif., 1974.

Weissman, C. *LISP 1.5 Primer*, Dickenson Publishing Company, Inc., Encino, Calif.

Winston, P. and Horn, B. *LISP*, Addison-Wesley, Reading, Mass., 1981. 2nd edition 1984.

MODULA-2

Wirth, N. *MODULA-2* Eidgenossische Technische Hochschule Zurich, Institut for Informatili, Bericht Nr.27, Dec. 1978 and Bericht Nr. 36, March 1980.

Wirth, N. *Programming in MODULA-2*, Springer-Verlag, New York, Heidelberg, Berlin, 1982.

See the articles in this book.

Pascal

American National Standard Pascal Computer Programming Language, IEEE Computer Society, Los Alamitos, Calif., 1983.

Brinch-Hansen, P. "The Programming Language Concurrent-Pascal" *IEEE Trans. on Soft. Eng.*, 1, 2, June 1975, 199–207.

Conradi, R. "Further Critical Comments on Pascal, Particularly as a Systems Programming Language" *ACM Sigplan Notices*, 11, 11, (1976) 8–25.

Feuer, A.R., and Gehani, N.H. "A Comparison of the Programming Languages C and Pascal" *ACM Computing Surveys*, 14, 1, 1982, 73–92.

Fischer, Charles N., and LeBlanc, R.J., "Efficient Implementation and Optimization of Run-Time Checking in Pascal" *ACM Sigplan Notices* 12, 3, March 1977, 19–24.

Habermann, A.N. "Critical Comments on the Programming Language Pascal" *Acta Informatica* 3, 1973, 47–57.

Hoare, C.A.R. and Wirth, N. "An Axiomatic Definition of the Programming Language Pascal" *Acta Informatica*, 2, 1973, 335–355.

Jensen, K. and Wirth, N. *Pascal Users Manual and Report*, Springer-Verlag Berlin, 1974. 3rd edition, 1985.

LeBlanc, R.J., and Fischer, C.N. "A Case Study of Run-Time Errors in Pascal Programs" *Software-Practice and Experience*, 12, 9 (1982), 825–834.

ISO-International Organization for Standardization Programming Languages-Pascal, ISO/DIS 7185, 1982-08-12.

Moffat, D. "1981 Pascal Bibliography" *ACM Sigplan Notices*, 16, 11, 1981, 7–21.

Sale, A.H.J. "Implementing Strings in Pascal—Again" *Software Practice and Experience*, 9, 1979, 839–841.

Sale, A.H.J. "Strings and the Sequence Abstraction in Pascal" *Software Practice and Experience* 9, 8, 1979, 671–683.

Strait, J.P.; Mickel, A.B.; and Easton, J.T. "Pascal 6000 Release 3 Manual" University of Minnesota, January 1979.

Tennent, R.D. "Another Look at Type Compatibility in Pascal" *Software-Practice and Experience*, 8, 1978, 429–437.

Wirth, N. "The Design of a Pascal Compiler" *Software-Practice and Experience*, 1, 4, 1971, 309–333.

Wirth, N. "The Programming Language Pascal" *Acta Informatica*, 1, 1, 1971, 35–63.

SNOBOL

Dewar, R., and McCann, A. "Macro SPITBOL—A SNOBOL4 Compiler" *Software—Practice and Experience*, 7, 1, 1977, 95–114.

Gimpel, J. "A Theory of Discrete Patterns and Their Implementation in SNOBOL4." *Comm. ACM*, 16, 2, 1973, 91–100.

Farber, D.J.; Griswold, R.E.; Polonsky, F.P. "SNOBOL, A String Manipulation Language" *JACM*, 11, 1, 1964, 21–30.

Griswold, R. "A History of the SNOBOL Programming Language," in Wexelblat (ed.) *History of Programming Languages*, Academic Press, New York, 1981.

Griswold, R., *The Macro Implementation of SNOBOL4* W.H. Freeman, San Francisco, 1971.

Griswold, R., and Griswold, M. *A SNOBOL4 Primer*, Prentice-Hall, Englewood Cliffs, N.J., 1973.

Griswold, R.; Poage, J.; and Polonsky, I. *The SNOBOL4 Programming Language* 2nd ed., Prentice-Hall, Englewood Cliffs, N.J., 1971.

Tennent, R. "Mathematical Semantics of SNOBOL4" *Acm Symp. Principles Prog. Langs.*, ACM, Boston, 1973, 95–108.

Other Languages

Abrahams, P. "The CIMS PL/I Compiler" *Proc. Sigplan Symp. on Compiler Construction, ACM Sigplan Notices*, 14, 8, 1979.

American National Standard Programming Language PL/I, X3.53, American National Standards Institute, New York, 1976.

American National Standard Programming Language PL/I General Purpose Subset, X3.74, American National Standards Institute, New York, 1981.

Backus, J. "Can Programming be Liberated—from the von Neumann Style? A Functional Style and its Algebra of Programs" *Comm. ACM*, 21, 8, August 1978, 613–641.

Beech, D. "A Structural View of PL/I" *ACM Computing Surveys*, 2, 1, 1970, 33–64.

Birtwistle, G.M.; Dahl, O-J.; Myhrhaug, B.; Nygaard, K. *SIMULA Begin* Petrocelli/Charter, New York, 1973.

Breed, L., and Lathwell, R. "The Implementation of APL/360" in Klerer & Reinfelds (eds.), *Interactive Systems for Experimental Applied Mathematics*, Academic Press, New York, 1968.

Brinch-Hansen, P. "Edison" *Software Practice and Experience*, 11, 4, April 1981.

Campbell, J.A. *Implementations of Prolog*, Halstead Press-John Wiley, N.Y., 1984.

Clocksin, W.F., and Mellish, C.S. *Programming in Prolog*, Springer-Verlag, New York, 1981. 2nd ed., 1984.

Dahl, O. "Discrete Event Simulation Languages," in Genuys (ed.), *Programming Languages*, Academic Press, New York, 1968, 349–395.

Dahl, O., and Hoare, C.A.R. "Hierarchical Program Structures" in Dahl-Dijkstra-Hoare, *Structured Programming*, Academic Press, New York 1972.

Dahl, O., and Nygaard, K. "SIMULA—An ALGOL-Based Simulation Language" *Comm. ACM* 9, 9, 1966, 671–678.

Dennis, J.B. and Ackermann, W.B. "VAL—A Value Oriented Algorithmic Language: Preliminary Reference Manual" Laboratory for Computer Science, MIT, Cambridge, Mass. 1979.

Falkoff, A., and Iverson, K. "The Evolution of APL" in Wexelblat (ed.), *History of Programming Languages*, Academic Press, New York, 1981, 661–673.

Feuer, A. *The C Puzzle Book*, Prentice Hall, Englewood Cliffs, N.J., 1982.

Freiburghouse, R. "The Multics PL/I Compiler" *Proc. AFIPS Fall Jt. Computer Conf.*, 35, 1969, 187–199.

Geschke, C.M., Morris Jr., J.H., and Satterthwaite, E.H. "Early Experience with MESA" *Comm. ACM*, 20, 8, 1977.

Glaser, H., Hankin, C., Till, D., *Principles of Functional Programming*, Prentice-Hall, Englewood Cliffs, N.J., 1984.

Goldberg, A., Robsom S. *Smalltalk80*, Addison Wesley, Reading, Ma., 1983.

Harbison, S., Steele, Jr., G. *A C Reference Manual*, Prentice-Hall, Englewood Cliffs, N.J., 1984.

Horning, J.J. "A Case Study in Language Design: Euclid" *Lecture notes in computer science (compiler construction)* Springer-Verlag, 1979.

Hughes, J.K. PL/I *Structured Programming*, 2nd ed. J. Wiley, N.Y., 1979.

Iverson, K. *A Programming Language*, Wiley, New York, 1962.

"JOVIAL J73/1 Specifications" Rome Air Development Center, Air Force Systems Command, Griffis Air Force Base, New York, 13441, 1976.

Kernighan, B.W., Ritchie, D.M. *The C Programming Language*, Prentice Hall, Englewood Cliffs, N.J., 1978.

Kiviat, P.; Villanueva, R.; and Markowitz, H. *The SIMSCRIPT II Programming Language*, Prentice-Hall, Englewood Cliffs, N.J., 1969.

Lampson, B.W., Horning, J.J.; London, R.L.; Mitchell, J.G.; and Popek, G.J., "Report on the Programming Language Euclid" *ACM Sigplan Notices*, 12, 2, 1977.

Lawson, H. "PL/1 List Processing" *Comm. ACM*, 10, 6, 1967, 358–367.

Liskov, B. et al. "CLU Reference Manual" Laboratory for Computer Science, MIT, TR-225, October, 1979.

Lucas, P. and Walk, K. "On The Formal Description of PL/I" *Ann. Rev. Automatic Prog.* 6, 3, 1969, 105–182.

Marcotty, M., and Sayward, F. "The Definition Mechanism for Standard PL/I" *IEEE Trans. Soft. Engineering*, SE-3, 6, 1977, 416–430.

McCracken, D. "Whether APL" *Datamation*, Sept. 15, 1970, 53–57.

Mitchell, James G., Maybury, William; and Sweet, Richard, "Mesa Language Manual" Technical Report CSL-78-1, Xerox Palo Alto Research Center, 1979.

Newell, A. et al. *Information Processing Languages V. Manual*, Prentice-Hall, Englewood Cliffs, N.J., 1964.

Nygaard, K., and Dahl, O.J. "The Development of the SIMULA Languages" Preprints ACM Sigplan History of Programming Languages Conf., *SigPlan Notices*, 13, 8 (Aug. 1978) 245–272.

Pakin, S. *APL/360 Reference Manual* 2nd ed., Science Research Associates, Chicago, 1972.

Radin, G. "The Early History and Characteristics of PL/I" in Wexelblat (ed.), *History of Programming Languages*, Academic Press, New York, 1981, 551–574.

Richards, M., Whitby-Strevens, C. *BCPL - The Language and its Compiler*, Cambridge University Press, 1980.

Schneider, F.B. "Synchronization in Distributed Programs" *ACM Trans. Prog. Lang. Syst.*, 4, 2 (April 1982), 125–148.

Shaw, Mary "Abstraction and Verification in ALPHARD: Design and Verification of a Tree Handler" *Proc. Fifth Texas Conf. Computing Systems.*, 1976, 86–94.

Shaw, M.; Wulf, W.; and London, R., "Abstraction and Verification in ALPHARD: Defining and Specifying Iteration and Generators" *Comm. ACM*, 20, 1977, 553.

Spence, J.W. *COBOL for the 80's*, West Publishing Co., St. Paul, Minn., 1985.

Teitelman, W. *INTERLISP Reference Manual*, Xerox Palo Alto Res. Center, Palo Alto, Ca. 1975.

Van Wijngaarden, A., ed.; Mailloux, B.; Peck, J.; and Koster C., "Report on the Algorithmic Language ALGOL 68" *Numerische Mathematik*, 14, 2, 1969, 79–218.

Van Wijngaarden et al., "Revised Report on the Algorithmic Language ALGOL68" *Acta Informatica* 5, 1975, 1–236.

Wegbreit, B. "The ECL Programming System" *Proc. Fall Joint Computer Conference*, vol. 39, 1971.

Wirth, N. "Design and Implementation of MODULA" *Software Practice and Experience* 7, 1977, 67–84.

Wirth, N. "The Use of MODULA" *Software Practice and Experience* 7, 1977, 37–65.

Wulf, W.; Russell, D.B.; and Habermann, A.N. "BLISS: A Language for Systems Programming" *Comm. ACM*, 14, 12, December 1971, 780–790.

SEMANTICS

Dennis, J.B., and van Horn, E.C. "Programming Semantics for Multiprogram Computations" *Comm. ACM* 9, 3 (March 1966), 143–155.

Floyd, R.W. "Assigning Meanings to Programs" In *Mathematical Aspects of Computers Science*, ed. J.T. Schwartz, American Mathematical Society, Providence, 1967.

Gordon, M. "The Denotational Description of Programming Languages" Springer-Verlag, 1979.

Hoare, C.A.R. "An Axiomatic Basis for Computer Programming" *Comm. ACM*, 12, 10, 1969, 576–583.

Hoare, C.A.R. "Proofs of Correctness of Data Representation." *Acta Informatica* 1, 1972, 271–281.

Hoare, C.A.R., Lauer, P. "Consistent and Complimentary Formal Theory of the Semantics of Programming Languages," *Acta Informatica*, 3, 1974, 135–155.

Johnston, J. "The Contour Model of Block Structured Processes." *ACM Sigplan Notices*, 6, 2, 1971, 55–82.

Lee, J. *Computer Semantics*, Van Nostrand Reinhold, New York, 1972.

Scott D. "Outline of a Mathematical Theory of Computation" *Proc. 4th Princeton Conf. on Info. Sci. and Sys.* 1970.

Scott, D. and Strachey, C., "Towards a Mathematical Semantics for Computer Languages" *Proc. Symp. on Computers and Automata*, Polytechnic Inst. of Brooklyn, 1971.

Scott D. "Mathematical Concepts in Programming Language Semantics" *AFIPS conf. proc. SJCC*, vol. 40, 1972, 255–234.

Scott, D. "Data Types as Lattices" *SIAM J. on Computing*, 5, September, 1976, 522–587.

Stoy, J.E. *Denotational Semantics - The Scott-Strachey Approach to Programming Language Theory*, M.I.T. Press, 1977.

Wegner, P. "The Vienna Definition Language" *ACM Computing Surveys*, 4, 1, March 1972, 5–63.

PROGRAMMING LANGUAGE COMPARISONS

Boom, H.J., DeJong, E. "A Critical Comparison of Several Programming Language Implementations" *Software Practice and Experience*, 10, 1980, 435–473.

Cheatham, T. "The Recent Evolution of Programming Languages" *Proc. IFIP Cong. 1971*, C.V. Freiman, (ed.), North-Holland, Amsterdam, 118–134.

Feuer, A., and Gehani, N. "A Comparison of the Programming Language C and Pascal" *ACM Computing Surveys*, 14, 1, 1982, 73–92.

Horning, J.J. "Programming Languages" *Computing Systems Reliability*, T. Anderson and B. Randell eds., Cambridge University Press, 1979.

Leavenworth, B. (ed.) "Control Structures in Programming Languages" *ACM Sigplan Notices* 7, 11, 1972.

Ledgard, H. "Ten Mini-Languages: A Study of Topical Issues in Programming Languages" *Computing Surveys*, 3, 3, 1971, 115–146.

Sammet, J. *Programming Languages: History and Fundamentals*, Prentice-Hall, Englewood Cliffs, N.J., 1969.

Shaw, M.; Almes, G.T.; Newcomer, J.M.; Reid, B.K.;

Wulf, W.A. "A Comparison of Programming Languages for Software Engineering" *Software Practice and Experience*, 11, 1–52, 1981.

Valentine, S.H. "Comparative Notes on Algol68 and PL/I" *Computer Journal*, 17, 1974, 325–331.

Wegner, P. "Programming Languages - Concepts and Research Directions" *Research Directions in Software Technology*, MIT Press, Cambridge, 1979, 425–489.

CONCURRENCY

Apt, K.R., Francez, N., and DeRoever, W.P. "A Proof System for Communicating Sequential Processes" *ACM Trans. Prog. Lang. Syst.* 2, 3, July 1980, 359–385.

Ben-Ari, M. *Principles of Concurrent Programming*, Prentice-Hall, Englewood Cliffs, N.J. 1982.

Bernstein, A.J. "Output Guards and Nondeterminism in Communicating Sequential Processes" *ACM Trnas. Prog. Lang. Syst.* 2, April, 1980, 234–238.

Brinch-Hansen, P. "Structured Multiporgramming" *Comm. ACM*, 15, 7, July 1972, 574–578.

Brinch-Hansen, P. "Distributed Processes: A Concurrent Programming Concept" *Comm. ACM*, 21, 11, November, 1978, 934–941.

Dijkstra, E. "Cooperating Sequential Processes" In *Programming Languages*, ed. Genuys, Academic Press, 1968.

Dijkstra, E. *A Discipline of Programming*. Prentice-Hall, Englewood Cliffs, N.J., 1977.

Dijkstra, E. "Guarded Commands, Nondeterminacy and Formal Derivation of Programs" *Comm. ACM*, 18, 8, August 1975, 453–457.

Floyd, R. "Nondeterministic Algorithms" *J. ACM*, 14, 4, 1967, 636–644.

Hoare, C.A.R., "The Emperor's Old Clothes" *Comm. ACM*, 24, 2, February 1981, 75–83.

Hoare, C.A.R. "Monitors: An Operating System Structuring Concept" *Comm. ACM*, 17, 10, October 1974, 549–557.

Holt, R.C.; Lazowska, E.D.; Graham, G.S.; Scott, M.A. *Structured Concurrent Programming with Operating Systems Applications*, Addison-Wesley, 1978.

Lamport, L. "The 'Hoare logic' of Concurrent Programs" *Acta Informatica*, 14, 21–37.

Levin, G.M., and Gries, D. "A Proof Technique for Communicating Sequential Processes" *Acta Informatica*, 15 1981, 257–290.

Marlin, C. *Coroutines*, Lecture Notes in Computer Science, No. 95, Springer-Verlag, New York, 1980.

Welsh, J., and Lister, A. "A Comparative Study of Task Communication in Ada" *Software-Practice & Experience*, 11 1981, 257–290.

Wirth, N. "Toward a Discipline of Real-Time Programming" *Comm. ACM*, 20, 8, August 1977.

OTHER SUBJECTS OF INTEREST

Aho, A., and Ullman, J., *The Theory of Parsing, Translation and Compiling* Prentice-Hall, Englewood Cliffs, N.J.

Bobrow, D., and Raphall, B. "New Programming Languages for Artificial Intelligence" *ACM Computing Surveys*, 6, 3, 1974, 153–174.

Bobrow, D., and Wegbreit, B. "A Model and Stack Implementation of Multiple Environments" *Comm. ACM*, 16, 10, 1973, 591–602.

Burge, W.H. *Recursive Programming Techniques*, Addison-Wesley, Reading, Mass. 1975.

Dahl, O.J.; Dijkstra, E.W.; and Hoare, C.A.R., *Structured Programming* Academic Press, London and New York, 1972.

Dijkstra, E. "GoTo Statement Considered Harmful" *Comm. ACM*, 11, 3, 1968, 147–148.

Dijkstra, E. "The Humble Programmer" *Comm. ACM*, 15, 10, 1972, 859–866.

Dunlap, D., and Basili, V. "A Comparative Analysis of Functional Correctness" *ACM Computing Surveys*, 14, 2, 1982, 229–244.

Freiburghouse, R. "The Multics PL/1 Compiler" *Proc. AFIPS Fall Jt. Comp. Conf.* 35, 1969, 179–199.

Friedman, D.P. and Wise, D.S., "CONS Should not Evaluate its Arguments" *Automata, Languages and Programming*, S. Michaelson and R. Milner eds., Edinburgh Univ. Press, Edinburgh, England, 1976.

Friedman, D.P. and Wise, D.S., "The Impact of Applicative Programming on Multiprocessing" *Proc. 1976 Intl. Conf. on Parallel Processing*, August 1976, 263–272.

Friedman, D.P. and Wise, D.S., "A Note on Conditional Expressions" *Comm. ACM*, 21, 11, November 1978.

Gannon, J.D., and Horning, J.J., "Language Design for Programming Reliability." *IEEE Trans. Software Engineering SE-1* 2, 179–191, 1975.

Gannon, J. "An Experimental Evaluation of Data Type Conventions." *Comm. ACM*, 20, 8, 1977, 584–595.

Goodenough, J.B. "Exception Handling: Issues and a Proposed Notation." *Comm. ACM*, 18, 12, December 1975, 683–696.

Guttag, J. "Abstract Data Types and the Development of Data Structures" *Comm. ACM*, 20, 6, June 1977, 396–404.

Guttag, J.; Horowitz, E.; and Musser, D., "Abstract Data Types and Software Validation" *Comm. ACM*, 21, 12, December 1978, 1048-1064.

Guttag, J.; Horowitz, E.; and Musser, D., "The Design of Data Type Specifications" *Current Trends in Programming Methodology*, ed. R. Yeh, vol. IV, Prentice Hall, 1978.

Henderson, P. *Functional Programming: Application and Implementation*, Prentice-Hall, Englewood Cliffs, N.J., 1980.

Hoare, C.A.R. "A Note on the FOR Statement" *BIT*, 12, 1972, 334–341.

Hoare, C.A.R. "Recursive Data Structures." *Int. J. Comp. Inf. Sci.* 4, 1975.

Horning, J.J. and Wortman, D.B. "Software Hut: a Computer Program Engineering Program in the Form of a Game." *IEEE Trans. Software Engineering* SE-3, 4, 325–330, 1978.

Knuth, D. "Structured Programming with GoTo Statements" *Comp. Surveys*, 6, 4, 1974, 261–301.

Knuth, D. and Floyd, R. "Notes on Avoiding GoTo Statements" *Info. Proc. Letters*, 1, 1, 1971, 23–32.

Landin, P.J. "The Mechanical Evaluation of Expressions" *Computer Journal*, 6, 1965, 308–320.

Landin, P.J. "The Next 700 Programming Languages" *Comm. ACM*, 9, 3, March 1966, 157–164.

Lewis, P., Rosenkrantz, D., and Stearns, R. *Compiler Design Theory*, Addison-Wesley, Reading, Mass., 1976.

McKeeman, W.M. "On Preventing Programming Languages from Interfering with Programming" *IEEE Trans. Software Engineering*, SE-1, 1, 1975. 19–26.

Morgan, H.L. "Spelling Correction in System Programs." *Comm. ACM*, 13, 2, 90–94.

Morris, J.H. Jr. "Protection in Programming Languages" *Comm. ACM*, 16, 1, January 1973.

Morris, J.H. Jr. "Types are not Sets" *ACM Symposium on the Principles of Programming Languages*, October 1973.

Parnas, D.L. "Information Distribution Aspects of Design Methodology." *Proc. IFIP Congress 71*, 339–344, North-Holland, Amsterdam.

Parnas, D.L. "On The Criteria to Be Used in Decomposing Systems into Modules" *Comm. ACM*, 15, 12, 1972, 1053–1058.

Prenner, C., et al. "An Implementation of Backtracking for Programming Languages" in Leavenworth (ed.), *Control Structures in Programming Languages, ACM Sigplan Notices*, 7, 11, 1972.

Ripley, G.D. and Druseikis, F.C. "A Statistical Analysis of Syntax Errors" *Computer Languages*, vol. 3, 1978, 227–240.

Sammet, J. "Programming Languages: History and Future" *Comm. ACM*, 15, 7, 1972, 601–610.

Satterthwaite, E. "Debugging Tools for High-Level Languages" *Software-Practice and Experience* 2, 1972, 197–217.

Teitelman, W. "Toward a Programming Laboratory" *Proc. Inter. Jt. Conf. Artif. Intel.*, Washington, D.C., 1969.

Wegbreit, B., "The Treatment of Data Types in EL1" *Comm. ACM*, 17, 5, May 1974, 251–264.

Winograd, T. "Beyond Programming Languages" *Comm. ACM*, 22, 7, July 1979, 391–401.

Wirth, N. "Program Development by Stepwise Refinement" *Comm. ACM*, 14, 4, 1971, 221–227.

INDEX